ESSENTIALS
OF SPORTS LAW

ESSENTIALS
OF SPORTS LAW

Third Edition

GLENN M. WONG

PRAEGER

Westport, Connecticut
London

Library of Congress Cataloging-in-Publication Data

Wong, Glenn M.
  Essentials of sports law / Glenn M. Wong.—3rd ed.
    p. cm.
  Rev. ed. of: Essentials of amateur sports law / Glenn M. Wong. 2nd ed. 1994.
  Includes index.
    ISBN 0–275–97121–X (alk. paper)
  1. Sports—Law and legislation—United States. I. Wong, Glenn M. Essentials of
amateur sports law. II. Title.
KF3989.W66 2002
344.73'099—dc21   2001058043

British Library Cataloguing in Publication Data is available.

Library of Congress Catalog Card Number: 2001058043
ISBN: 0–275–97121–X

First published in 2002

Praeger Publishers, 88 Post Road West, Westport, CT 06881
An imprint of Greenwood Publishing Group, Inc.
www.praeger.com

Printed in the United States of America

The paper used in this book complies with the
Permanent Paper Standard issued by the National
Information Standards Organization (Z39.48–1984).

10 9 8 7 6 5 4 3 2 1

CONTENTS

CHAPTER 11
Labor Law   491

PREFACE TO THE
FIRST EDITION

In my several professional roles as attorney, teacher, and consultant, I meet frequently with individuals and groups active in amateur sports. Athletic administrators and others around the country have repeatedly expressed a need for a "practitioner's" book because sports law has become such an integral part of their day-to-day operation. They want to have a background on sports law before they deal with attorneys on legal issues. Even more important, they want to attempt to avoid litigation. The interest and concerns of these people motivated the writing of this book.

I started with the concept that the book should be written for those affected by sport law issues who are not necessarily lawyers, including college or high school athletic administrators or coaches, student-athletes, school board members, institutional representatives, and those involved in amateur sports organizations. There is, for example, a chapter on the court system, a glossary, and an appendix of sample forms that can be used by practitioners as starting points for developing their own forms. The major intercollegiate and interscholastic amateur sports organizations, such as the U.S. Olympic Committee and the National Collegiate Athletic Association, are described in detail. All new legal concepts and issues are discussed, as are basic tort law, contract law, trademark law, and constitutional law. Each of the chapters has been designed as a self-contained unit that can be used as a quick reference. Case citations and brief summaries of cases (rather than lengthy discussions) have been included in the notes. The notes also include law review articles, names and addresses of relevant organizations, and other information which can lead the reader to additional sources of information.

I would like to thank some of the many people who have been instrumental in assisting me with *Essentials of Amateur Sports Law*. First, Margaret M. Kearney, the editor, helped express the thoughts and principles in this book. In addition, she kept the project moving and made sure that legalese was eliminated. As for research and writing, I would like to thank and acknowledge the work of Professor Richard J. Ensor of the University of Massachusetts, Amherst. He co-authored Chapter 9 (sports broadcasting) and Chapter 10 (trademark law). His numerous reviews of the manuscript and comments were invaluable in that he provided the perspectives of a sports lawyer and of an experienced athletic administrator. I also acknowledge the contributions of several research assistants: David Knopp, William Hubbard, Scott Proefrock, and Scott Zuffelato. The many drafts of the manuscript were typed by Susan McBride, to whom I am grateful. Several others, too numerous to mention individually, also contributed in various ways to this project. And, finally, I would like to thank Professor Robert Berry of Boston College Law School for getting me started in sports law.

PREFACE TO THE SECOND EDITION

How much has changed since 1988, when the first edition of *Essentials of Amateur Sports Law* was published? The Knight Commission has been formed, disbanded, and reinstated; Dick Shultz has resigned as Executive Director of the NCAA; and the impact of the passage of the Civil Rights Restoration Act is being felt and has even spawned a new term—*gender equity*. The first edition of this book does not mention idiopathic cardiomyopathy (Hank Gathers' heart disease); Jerry Tarkanian was still Head Basketball Coach at the University of Nevada, Las Vegas; and there is another new term—*ambush marketing*. The first Proposition 48 (now Propositions 48/42/26) student-athletes have graduated, but it has not stopped the debate over academic requirements for NCAA initial eligibility. Butch Reynolds has a judgment in hand for $27.3 million dollars and a new law is coming into place—Americans with Disabilities Act.

These are only some of the significant changes in the constantly changing area of sports law. Many of the changes since 1988 have further clouded the line between professional and amateur athletics: a case-decision ruling that a college football player was an employee of the university, the 1992 Men's Olympic basketball team dominated by professional basketball players from the NBA, and a proposal to pay Olympic athletes for performance in the 1994 Olympics.

As you can see from this brief overview, there have been significant changes and important litigation that continue to shape athletics. Some will be discussed in a global manner in Chapter 1 and then discussed in more detail throughout the book. In all, there are approximately 165 new cases in this edition. The title of the book, however, remains the same. The reason for this is analogous to baseball's antitrust exemption, it is done for precedent reasons and not because it is the most appropriate title in 1994. The number of chapters and major topical areas covered in the book have not changed, but they have been updated.

For me, a major reason for putting together a second edition was the positive, strong, and encouraging responses I received from the audience. I would like to thank them. Many of these people have provided comments which have been incorporated into the second edition.

The second edition has been a challenge. While trying to finish the revision, I served for several months in 1992–93 as Director of Athletics and Dean of the School of Physical Education at the University of Massachusetts. Also, I was appointed as Faculty Athletics Representative to the NCAA. While these positions made completion of the second edition more difficult, it also served to provide me with different insights and to confirm on a first-hand basis some of my thoughts and ideas. In addition, a second son, Gary, arrived. I dedicate the second edition to him, to my first son, Glenn, and to my wife, Paula.

There were many people who assisted in seeing this project through. Carol Barr, my research assistant, kept this project going and my colleague, Lisa Pike, Assistant Professor, provided invaluable assistance with the manuscript, including feedback from the use of the book in her Sports Law course.

Other students and research assistants who assisted in the production of this second edition include Jack Woodbury, Jesse Wilde, Peter Carton, Leslie Keast, Margaret Driscoll, Steve Hilliard, Jeff Craig, and Burke Magnus. All of these students and research assistants have already moved on to their careers in the sports industry.

For those of you who know publishing, you are well aware that there are several months' lag time between submission of the final manuscript and the published book. By the time you read this, my files will already include cases for the third edition. I anticipate many new cases involving discrimination issues (and also reverse discrimination), litigation or arbitration regarding eligibility for the Olympics, changes in NCAA enforcement procedures, drug testing and contractual rights, conference contract issues, additional litigation relative to medical issues, and a host of new issues which no one can predict. These new issues will continue to make sports law a constantly changing, interesting, and varied discipline, and will certainly provide cause for a third edition of *Essentials of Amateur Sports Law*.

PREFACE TO THE
THIRD EDITION

This is the third edition of *Essentials of Sports Law*. It has been eight years since the second edition, *Essentials of Amateur Sports Law*, was published. Over the course of these eight years, there have been significant changes in sports law.

The preface to the second edition mentions the passage of the Americans with Disabilities Act, and the third edition contains the court decision in *Casey Martin v. PGA Tour*, in which the United States Supreme Court ruled in favor of Martin and allowed him to participate on the PGA Tour while using a golf cart. There have been significant developments in the Gender Equity area, including the important cases of *Cohen v. Brown University*, which dealt with participation opportunities for women student-athletes. Other important gender equity decisions involved *Pederson v. Louisiana State University* and *Boucher v. Syracuse University*. A recently filed court case should be followed. The National Wrestling Coaches Association (NWCA) filed a lawsuit in 2002 challenging the U.S. Department of Education's Title IX regulations interpreting proportionality. If the NWCA is successful in its case, it will have significant ramifications for Title IX. In the tort liability area, the litigation continues, and more supervision cases and waiver cases were litigated. Courts have had to deal with injuries from higher risk activities such as the "adventure sports" and injuries caused by team or school mascots. The NCAA has again faced the antitrust challenge and was on the losing end of the coach's restricted earnings case *Law v. National Collegiate Athletic Association*. This resulted in a significant damages settlement by the NCAA, and led to further litigation against the NCAA based on the antitrust theory. In the area of Agents, there are continued abuses by some player agents. The Uniform Athlete Agents Act, which is model state legislation, was passed and has been adopted by several states. If this is done, it will create some uniformity in state legislation. The National Football League Players Association has adopted regulations regulating financial advisors of players. In the constitutional law area, the freedom of expression reached the United States Supreme Court in *Sante Fe Independent School District v. Doe* and drug testing cases continued to be litigated. The Olympic movement made significant changes in its drug testing procedures and its dispute resolution system. There have been several important court cases including *Slaney v. The International Amateur Athletic Federation and the United States Olympic Committee* and many arbitration decisions. There was also a significant amendment to the 1978 Amateur Sports Act, the "Ted Stevens Olympic and Amateur Sports Act," which was passed in 1998.

In addition to including the aforementioned developments, the third edition of *Essentials of Sports Law* incorporates professional sports law issues; hence, the reason why "Amateur" has been removed from the title. This reflects the feedback from sport lawyers; sport managers, and students who suggested that professional sports law issues be included. Furthermore, the line between professional and amateur sport has become blurred over the years. There is no better example than the Olympic movement. When the first edition of *Essentials of Amateur Sports Law* was written in 1988, the Olympics were only for amateurs. Now professional athletes are commonplace and (mostly) accepted as part of the Olympic Games. There are many who believe that college athletics can no longer be properly characterized as amateur athletics, and point primarily to Division I football and basketball. While certainly the NCAA clings to its notion that the student-athlete should not be paid, the commercialism of the games, the broadcasts, the price of tickets, the salaries of coaches, and many other aspects closely parallel professional sports. There are some in college sports who no longer talk about amateurism, but refer to a different and unique model from professional sports. The changes and additions to this third edition reflect both the interests of the audience and the changing landscape of sports.

These are these new chapters in *Essentials of Sports Law*:

Chapter 10, Antitrust Law

Chapter 11, Labor Law

Chapter 13, Intellectual Property Law (Copyright Law and Patent Law have been added to Trademark Law)

Chapter 15, Business Law: Business Structures, Tax Laws, and Employment Law

Chapter 16, Additional Legal Concerns (Disabilities Laws have been added)

In these chapters some of the recent developments include the continued contentious labor situation in Major League Baseball, which led to the cancellation of the 1994 World Series. Management and labor are currently involved in another bitter round of labor negotiations, in which management has tried the new approach of contraction of two teams. Whether contraction is successful remains to be seen, but this attempt has led to much new litigation. Two interesting discipline cases were decided in arbitration involving Latrell Sprewell and the National Basketball Association and John Rocker and Major League Baseball. In new professional sports leagues, the "single entity" form of league ownership and operation has been implemented. In *Fraser v. Major League Soccer*, the players were unsuccessful in challenging this form of ownership based on an antitrust theory. In the Intellectual Property area, the Internet and other forms of new technology have led to new revenue streams and new terminology such as the Web, domain names, and cybersquatting. But this has also led to disputes concerning ownership of the properties. There have also been numerous employment law cases in sports, mostly involving gender discrimination claims, but also racial and age discrimination cases.

Sport and the Law have changed significantly in the last eight years. There was also a significant amount of change in the six years between the first and second editions. Since I expect the litigation and legislation to continue, there is a need to keep the reader of *Essentials of Sports Law* current on new litigation, legislation, and agreements. Therefore, the third edition of *Essentials of Sports Law* will be supported by supplements. For those who teach a course using *Essentials of Sports Law*, an instructor's manual will be available. A case book, with edited court and arbitration decisions is planned for 2003. And finally, a web site will be available to provide information on the book, updates, and information for instructors.

I would like to thank all of the people who have read previous editions of *Essentials of Amateur Sports Law*. Sports lawyers and sports managers have made numerous suggestions. The students in my sport law classes at the University of Massachusetts have also provided significant feedback. I have also received suggestions from people in the sports industry who have attended the seminars I have presented on various sport law issues. I have tried to incorporate my work experiences, both as a lawyer and sport administrator, into the book. I have considered all of these experiences and comments and have tried to address many of them in the third edition of *Essentials of Sports Law*.

Law students, law school professors, and lawyers will see that this is not a typical law school case book. The book is written in a narrative style. The accompanying case book will be important and helpful to law students, professors, and lawyers. *Essentials of Sports Law: Third Edition* will hopefully be the starting point, with the case references in the book, and the casebook providing the resources you need. The note sections in the text contain brief case summaries of leading cases and important and different fact situations, but do not have every case decision on the particular topic. *Essentials of Sports Law* is not designed to provide legal advice, but to provide a starting point for sports lawyers and students.

For sport management students and professors, the book can be used as a textbook for sport law courses. It has been used in both undergraduate and graduate level courses. At the University of Massachusetts, it is used in "Introduction to Sport Law," a required course in the sport management program. For graduate level programs, *Essentials of Sports Law* can be used in conjunction with edited court and arbitration decisions.

There are many people who have contributed to this book. Four sport management graduate students who helped bring the manuscript to the finish line are John Shukie, Dominic Rivers, Stephanie Tryce, and Tim Cohane. And since this has been a work in progress for many years, there are many other students who contributed, including Mario Garcia, Steve Condrin, Karen Skinner, Karen Duncan, Doron Azrialy, Matthew Clark, John Clark, Vincent Dolan, and Luke Flockerzi.

Two colleagues made significant contributions, John T. Wolohan, attorney and faculty member at Ithaca College and Lisa Pike Masteralexis, attorney and faculty member at the University of Massachusetts. I would like to thank Robert C. Berry and Harold J. Vanderzwaag, for their continued guidance and support. Other people have supported this project with information, ideas, and support, and include Richard J. Ensor, Herb Rudoy, Mike Gibbons, Gene Bailey and Steve Abbott, Barbara Morgan, Burke Magnes, Elsa Cole, Diane Morse, Kevin Kelly, Ethan Orlinsky, and Selin Dixon-Wheeler.

I would also like to thank three deans at the University of Massachusetts who have supported my research efforts and particularly this book, Cleve Willis, Robert Helgeson, and David Bischoff.

I would like to thank John Harney of Book Consultants of Boston, who started me on my journey into the publishing world almost twenty years ago, and has always provided me good and sensible counsel along the way.

I would like to thank Dr. James T. Sabin, Director, Academic Research and Development, Greenwood Publishing, who has supported and guided this project from the beginning. Beth Wilson did an excellent job with the copyediting. And a thank you also to these Greenwood Publishing people who worked on this project: Liz Leiba, Nicole Cournoyer, Michelle Scott, Margaret Maybury and Paulette Chase.

Finally, I would like to thank my wife, Paula Nassif, and our two sons, Glenn and Gary, for their support.

Chapter 1

INTRODUCTION

INTRODUCTION

Athletic organizations have grown tremendously since the 1970s in terms of their scope, power, and financial status. In the United States alone, athletic organizations envelop the lives and athletic experiences of people from their early school years (e.g., Pop Warner football and Little League), through high school years (e.g., the National Federation of State High School Associations), through college (e.g., the National Collegiate Athletic Association), and beyond (e.g., the U.S. Olympic Committee and professional sports leagues). Sports law has shaped the operations of those organizations, and continues to have a pervasive impact on everyone involved, from ticket managers, to public relations directors, to team doctors, to the athletes themselves.

Sports law helps to explain why sport businesses are structured the way they are. Oftentimes, court decisions have had a significant impact on sports leagues, associations, and entities. Thus, the purpose of this chapter is to give the reader an overview of the structure and involvement of these organizations, an understanding of those who are involved in rule making, and examples of the types of litigation involving these athletic organizations. The chapter begins with an introduction to the sports industry. Next, it presents information on the various segments of the sports industry, and finally shows how the rules and regulations of the organizations affect their constituencies.

1.1. THE SPORTS INDUSTRY

This chapter will first explore the segments or organizations of the sports industry. It will discuss various organizations' structure, rules and procedures, internal power and authority, and relationships with other organizations. The sports industry segments have been broken down into six groups. Below is an outline of the six groups, in order of appearance.

1. Professional leagues in the United States
    a. "Big Four" leagues, the National Basketball Association (NBA), the National Football League (NFL), the National Hockey League (NHL), and Major League Baseball (MLB)
    b. Single entity leagues, which include Major League Soccer (MLS), the Women's National Basketball Association (WNBA), and the Women's United Soccer Association (WUSA)
2. Intercollegiate athletics (which will primarily cover the National Collegiate Athletic Association)
3. The Olympics (which will investigate the U.S. Olympic Committee, the International Olympic Committee, the International Federations for sports, and the National Governing Bodies for sports)
4. Interscholastic athletics (such as the umbrella organization, the National Federation of State High School Associations, and state organizations such as the Massachusetts Interscholastic Athletic Association). This designation also includes leagues for youths that are not "interscholastic" per se, such as Little League, Knothole, and Pop Warner.
5. Public/private associations for professional and recreational sports, including
    a. Professional Golf Association (PGA), Ladies Professional Golf Association (LPGA), and Association of Tennis Professionals (ATP)
    b. Country clubs, fitness clubs, recreation centers, and other places of leisure athletic participation
6. Facilities, agency firms, & media

These six groups have become increasingly interconnected as sports has evolved as a business. This is especially true as it relates to the law. Exhibit 1.1 illustrates how common legal concerns unite the six groups by minimal degrees of separation. Consequently, it may be beneficial for participants in one area (e.g., college athletics) to possess a working knowledge of the legal and business aspects of another area (e.g., high school athletics).

NOTES

1. Information on the sports business industry can be found in *Street and Smith's Sports Business Journal*, a weekly publication dedicated to the business issues of sport. *SBJ* provides the critical news and information that sports industry leaders need to stay competitive and successful. Every issue features in-depth information on the deals, contracts, and power plays that shape the industry. Regular columns cover every aspect of the industry from media and marketing to finance and facilities. Subscription information can be found at www.sportsbusinessjournal.com.

2. For more information on the sports business industry, see Lisa Pike Masteralexis, Carol Barr, and Mary Hums, *Principles and Practice of Sport Management* (Gaithersburg, MD: Aspen Publishers, Inc., 1998).

1.2. PROFESSIONAL SPORTS LEAGUES

Professional sports leagues make up a large share of the more than $150 billion sports industry in the United States, transforming sports into an increasingly businesslike field since the 1970s. Because of the large amounts of money involved in professional sports leagues, industry professionals must understand a wide range of legal issues, including but not limited to: labor and antitrust, merchandising, television, drug testing, contracts, and employment law.

This section will focus on legal issues indigenous (but not exclusive) to the professional sports segment of the sports industry. It will include a brief economic overview of professional leagues and team operations, move to an overview of league office structure, and finish with a closer look at specific problems facing individuals who practice in the professional sports setting. Since the "Big Four" are the best-known and lucrative leagues, many other professional and amateur sports entities try to mimic their operations. Likewise, newer leagues such as the WNBA and MLS, have learned from the legal histories of the "Big Four," and have structured themselves accordingly. Thus, persons involved in the sports industry may find issues covered in this chapter that pertain to topics outside their field of specialization. Each professional league, team, or association has unique legal issues surrounding its operation. While this chapter cannot possibly cover each specific problem, it will provide a foundation for a better understanding of the professional sports industry.

1.2.1. A Brief Economic Overview

The basic agreements of the "Big Four" leagues allow for all types of *private* franchise ownership, including sole proprietorships, partnerships, and corporations (see Chapter 15.1, "Business Structures"). Sole proprietorships are decreasing due to the dramatic increase in franchise costs. Therefore, ownership groups must generally choose between the lower tax rates of a partnership and the decreased financial risk of a corporation (see note 1). The NFL prohibits public

Exhibit 1.1
Legal Issues Connecting the Sports Industries

Interscholastic & Little League

Intercollegiate Athletics

The Olympics

Professional Sports Leagues

Associations, Country Clubs, Recreational

Facilities, Agency Firms, & Media

Constitutional law cases at the collegiate level, such as due process and discrimination cases, may also apply at the high school level, and vice versa.

In his dissent against the decision *PGA Tour v. Casey Martin*, U.S. Supreme Court Justice Antonin Scalia worried that Little League hitters with attention deficit disorder might obtain court orders forcing umpires to grant them four strikes instead of three.

College eligibility, student-athlete compensation, and the regulation of agents all affect the inflow of talent to professional sports. Likewise, collective bargaining and litigation concerning amateur drafts may accelerate the exodus of high school and college players into the pros.

Olympic athletes must undergo drug testing. However, collective bargaining agreements in professional sports leagues often shield players from drug testing.

With the trend toward vertical integration, it is now possible for a corporation to own a sports team, the team's arena, the agents who represent the players, and the radio stations that broadcast the games. This creates potential antitrust issues and conflicts of interest for sport managers.

Legal decisions and legislation affecting major arenas may pertain to smaller organizations. Even private clubs may be considered public when certain criteria are met.

and corporate ownership of teams, requiring one person to hold at least a 30% ownership share. The one NFL exception is the founding member Green Bay Packers, who own a grandfather-clause exemption. However, public ownership has occurred increasingly in the other leagues, such as the Boston Celtics (NBA), Mighty Ducks of Anaheim (NHL), and Los Angeles Dodgers (MLB) (see note 2). Aside from certain regulations to ensure competitive balance (e.g., the draft, salary caps), teams may compete against one another as rival companies, just as they would in any other business.

As stated previously, the finances of professional sports have grown exponentially in recent years. Expenses such as player salaries have increased considerably in all Big Four Leagues. While the million-dollar salary was once the benchmark for the highest-paid athlete, it is common today for the top professional athletes to earn over $10 million annually (see exhibit 1.2). In fact, Alex Rodriguez's contract (2001–2010) with MLB's Texas Rangers pays him an astronomical average annual salary of $25.2 million (see exhibit 1.3).

Franchise owners also benefit from the increased demand for professional sports. Teams generate millions of dollars per year from ticket sales, sponsorships agreements, the leasing of luxury suites, merchandise sales, and national and local broadcast agreements. Teams that own their stadium, or teams that have a beneficial lease agreement, also earn revenue from concession sales, parking, signage, and non-franchise-related events held in their arena, such as concerts and skating revues. The high price of player salaries notwithstanding, these potential streams of revenue have resulted in an exponential increase of franchise values and expansion fees for franchise owners.

Despite these gains, a league's governing documents (collective bargaining agreement, league constitution, and bylaws) may not prevent franchises in a larger market from earning a disproportionate amount of revenue compared to franchises in smaller markets. For example, in 2001, the New York Yankees (2000 World Series champions) had MLB's highest-ever opening day payroll of $109.8 million, but also earned a total operating revenue of $242 million (see note 3). Meanwhile, the Montreal Expos maintained one of the league's lowest payrolls at $34.7 million. Nevertheless, the Expos suffered an operating loss, with a total operating revenue of only $34.1 million (see note 4). Newer leagues such as MLS and the WNBA have largely shielded themselves from large market/small market competitive imbalance by constructing "single-entity" models. However, much more disparate revenue earnings occur in the more established leagues, especially MLB. That great disparity in revenue earning comes primarily from differing local broadcast contracts.

NOTES _____

1. For increased information about the pros and cons of corporate vs. partnership structures in professional sports, consult Martin J. Greenberg and James T. Gray, *Sports Law Practice* (Charlottesville, VA: Lexis Law Publication, 1998).

2. Public ownership of sports teams has some inherent disadvantages for investors. Unlike other public stocks that increase in value when the company either buys other companies or expands, it is difficult for a single sports team to grow or expand. Likewise, when a sports team is part of a larger public company (e.g., Anaheim Angels and Mighty Ducks of Anaheim are a part of Disney Sports), it is difficult for these teams to contribute to the growth of that stock. Investors will typically exert pressure on the board of directors to dump or streamline their sports holdings. This largely explains the NFL's stance against

Exhibit 1.2
The "Big Four" Salaries, 1990–2001

MLB		1990	1995	1998	2001
	Minimum Salary	$100,000	$109,000	$200,000	$200,000
	Average Salary	$597,537	$1.07 million	$1.40 million	$2.26 million
	Highest Paid Player	Robin Yount	Cecil Fielder	Gary Sheffield	Alex Rodriguez
	His Salary	$3.2 million	$9.2 million	$14.9 million	$22.0 million

NBA		1990 - 1991	1994 - 1995	1998 - 1999	2001 - 2002
	Minimum Salary	$120,000	$150,000	$242,000	$316,969
	Average Salary	$825,000	$1.47 million	$2.16 million	$3.20 million
	Highest Paid Player	Patrick Ewing	David Robinson	Michael Jordan	Kevin Garnett
	His Salary	$4.25 million	$7.3 million	$33.1 million	$19.6 million

NFL		1990 - 1991	1994 - 1995	1998 - 1999	2001 - 2002
	Minimum Salary	$50,000	$110,000	$144,000	$209,000
	Average Salary	$350,000	$716,000	$990,000	$1.17 million
	Highest Paid Player	Joe Montana	John Elway	Deion Sanders	Drew Bledsoe
	His Salary	$3.2 million*	$4.6 million	$7.6 million	$8.5 million

NFL "highest paid" and "average" numbers include performance bonuses. *Montana's salary represents the average annual salary from his then four-year contract.

NHL		1990 - 1991	1994 - 1995	1998 - 1999	2001 - 2002
	Minimum Salary	$100,000 Canadian	$125,000 U.S.	$150,000 U.S.	$150,000* U.S.
	Average Salary	$271,000	$733,000	$1.15 million	$1.6 million
	Highest Paid Player	Wayne Gretzky	Wayne Gretzky	Joe Sakic	Jaromir Jagr
	His Salary	$3.0 million	$6.5 million	$17 million	$11.0 million

While $150,000 is the CBA's minimum salary, only three opening day players had salaries below $300,000.

public ownership. The NFL's Constitution and Bylaws from 1960 states in Article V, Section 4(a): "New members must pledge that their organization is primarily for the purpose of operating a football team." For further information on increasing public ownership, consult James Quirk and Rodney Fort, *Pay Dirt: The Business of Professional Team Sports* (Princeton: Princeton University Press, 1997).

3. For 2001 team-by-team MLB revenues and expenses forecast see www.usatoday.com/sports/baseball/stories/2001-12-05-focus~expenses.html

1.2.2. Impact of Broadcast Contracts

All of the "Big Four" professional leagues have national television contracts, which are divided equally among member teams. For example, the NFL signed a contract covering 1998 through the 2006 Super Bowl with FOX Sports ($4.4

Exhibit 1.3
Top "Big Four" Salaries by Position

League	Player	Position	Team	2001 Salary
MLB	Alex Rodriguez	Shortstop	Texas Rangers	$22.0
MLB	Kevin Brown	Starting Pitcher	Los Angeles Dodgers	$15.7
MLB	Mike Piazza	Catcher	New York Mets	$13.6
MLB	Mo Vaughn	First Base	Anaheim Angels	$13.2
MLB	Manny Ramirez	Right Field	Boston Red Sox	$13.0
MLB	Bernie Williams	Center Field	New York Yankees	$12.4
MLB	Albert Belle	Left Field	Baltimore Orioles	$12.0
MLB	Chipper Jones	Third Base	Atlanta Braves	$10.3
MLB	Mariano Rivera	Relief Pitcher	New York Yankees	$9.1
MLB	Craig Biggio	Second Base	Houston Astros	$7.8

League	Player	Position	Team	2001 - 2002 Salary
NBA	Kevin Garnett	Small Forward	Minnesota Timberwolves	$22.4
NBA	Shaquille O'Neal	Center	Los Angeles Lakers	$21.5
NBA	Juwan Howard	Power Forward	Dallas Mavericks	$18.8
NBA	Gary Payton	Point Guard	Seattle Supersonics	$12.9
NBA	Allan Houston	Shooting Guard	New York Knicks	$12.8

League	Player	Position	Team	2001 - 2002 Salary
NHL	Jaromir Jagr	Right Wing	Washington Capitals	$11.0
NHL	Paul Kariya	Left Wing	Anaheim Mighty Ducks	$10.0
NHL	Joe Sakic	Center	Colorado Avalanche	$9.8
NHL	Chris Pronger	Defense	St. Louis Blues	$9.5
NHL	Patrick Roy	Goalie	Colorado Avalanche	$8.5

League	Player	Position	Team	2000 - 2001 Salary
NFL	Drew Bledsoe	Quarterback	New England Patriots	$8.5
NFL	John Randle	Defensive Line	Minnesota Vikings	$7.6
NFL	Edgerrin James	Running Back	Indianapolis Colts	$6.7
NFL	Jason Sehorn	Defensive Back	New York Giants	$5.6
NFL	Levon Kirkland	Linebacker	Pittsburgh Steelers	$5.5
NFL	Brad Hopkins	Offensive Line	Tennessee Titans	$4.7
NFL	Jerry Rice	Wide Receiver	San Francisco 49ers	$4.5
NFL	Frank Wycheck	Tight End	Tennessee Titans	$2.4
NFL	Tom Tupa	Punter	New York Jets	$1.1
NFL	Morten Andersen	Kicker	Atlanta Falcons	$1.1

Amounts are in millions
NFL numbers include pro-rated signing bonuses
and performance bonuses.

billion), CBS Sports ($4 billion), and ABC/ESPN ($9.2 billion). The contract, signed in 1998, makes those networks the exclusive broadcasters of regular season and post-season league games. The total received ($17.6 billion) is divided equally among league teams (see note 1) over the length of the contract. Individual teams are allowed to negotiate their own local television contracts for pre-season contests (not part of the national package) and local radio broadcasts for all games.

It is the absence of an equitable sharing of these *local* broadcast contracts in MLB that creates a wide gap between the large market and small market franchises. For example, the New York Yankees, like all other MLB teams, receive a ⅓₀ share of MLB's national television contract with FOX Sports and ESPN. However, in 2001 the Yankees earned over $55 million in local television money, whereas the Montreal Expos earned less than $600,000. Furthermore, the $55 million plus Yankees figure is expected to more than double in the 2002 season, due to YankeeNets'™ successful creation of a regional television network and buy back of the rights to 150 Yankee games per year starting in 2002 (see note 2). This local revenue gulf between large market teams such as the Yankees, Baltimore Orioles, Los Angeles Dodgers, and Chicago Cubs and small market teams (Expos, Minnesota Twins, etc.) leads directly to the ability to spend more money on player salaries. Hence, disparity and competitive imbalance, as argued by Major League Baseball. The more money a franchise earns, the more it will be able to spend on retaining its talented free agents as well as acquiring free agents from other teams. The wealthier franchises in Major League Baseball earn a disproportionate amount of their revenue from local broadcasting contracts. This topic is discussed further in Chapter 14, "Television and Broadcasting."

NOTES

1. In some cases, new franchises entering a league, or franchises willing to relocate, will cede their portion of the television revenue for a set period of time. This issue can be a source of contention between owners because there is no set criterion for imposing this forfeiture of broadcasting revenue.

2. The packaging of local broadcasting contracts was challenged in the New York State courts in 2000. YankeeNets™, the parent company of the New York Yankees, New Jersey Nets, and New Jersey Devils, threatened to create its own television network. Cablevision's MSG™, which was in the final year of a contract to televise Yankee games, brought suit against YankeeNets™, arguing that the proposed YankeeNets network was merely a sham to subvert MSG's rights to last refusal. The two sides settled out of court for an undisclosed amount of money in April 2001. In June 2001, YankeeNets™ finalized a plan to create its own regional television network that began televising Yankees and Nets games in 2002 and New Jersey Devils NHL games beginning in 2007.

1.2.3. Attendance

Another major stream of revenue is generated through ticket sales. Ticket revenue depends on the amount of available seating, cost per ticket, local population size and demographics, presence of "superstar" or celebrity players, and the team's performance. Many franchises in the "Big Four" leagues are building or lobbying to build new stadiums in hopes of improving the seating inventory they have to sell. New stadiums are being built with additional amenities such as luxury suites, expanded club seating, children's areas, restaurants, and merchandise stores with the hope that the franchise will be able to generate more revenue. Franchises owning their own facility or franchises that receive concession, merchandise, and parking revenue may reduce ticket prices to fill their stadium to capacity in hopes of recuperating lost ticket revenue through concession sales, merchandise sales, and parking. Yet, as players' salaries continue to increase, franchises adjust ticket, concession, parking, and merchandise prices upward. For example, prior to the 2001 season, the Boston Red Sox raised ticket prices 27.4% to an average of $36.08. The ticket price increase equates to approximately $20 million in additional ticket revenue each year, assuming that attendance averages near capacity. Coincidentally (or not) $20 million is equivalent to the average annual salary of Manny Ramirez, who was the Red Sox's high-profile free agent signee during the 2000–2001 off-season.

The distribution of ticket revenue between franchises differs between leagues. In the NFL, 60% of non-luxury-box gate receipts are retained by the home team, and the remainder is channeled into a general fund. In the NHL, NBA, and MLB gate receipts are not divided among the competing franchises. Teams with more seating than the market demands have shifted more focus to marketing efforts to fill empty seats. But teams that consistently sell out their stadium must seek alternative revenue streams to keep up with the continuously rising cost of franchise operation.

NOTES

1. For detailed information about the price of tickets, concessions, parking, and other related game-day fan expenses, see Team Marketing Report's "Fan Cost Index™" survey, which can be sampled and ordered at www.teammarketing.com

2. For reasons likely related to the increase in the price of MLB tickets, attendance has increased at minor league baseball games. According to a *Business Week* article titled "For the Love of the Game—and the Cheap Seats" (May 28, 2001, p. 46), minor league baseball regular season attendance increased from approximately 20 million in 1986 to nearly 40 million in 2000.

3. The nineteen-team Arena Football League attracted more than 1 million fans in each of the six seasons prior to 2001. In the three years prior to 2001, AFL franchises increased in value by 250%. In the fall of 2001, the NFL had a contractual option to purchase 49.99% of the AFL. Due to the AFL's financial success, it is expected that the NFL will pick up the option, and then expand the AFL by placing teams around the world. For more information see Richard Weiner, "Success of League Has NFL's Attention," *USA Today*, July 11, 2001, p. 1C.

1.2.4. Luxury Suites

One attempt to find alternative revenue streams is the leasing of luxury suites. Luxury suites are often sold by franchises to corporate clients, who lease the suites for the course of the season. Franchises that have this type of seating in their inventory realize far greater revenues from luxury suites than they earn from regular seating sales. Franchises that do not control the sale of suites, or that play in stadiums without luxury suites, are at a marked disadvantage in generating revenue. Luxury suites are viewed by some leagues and teams as a more important revenue stream than that of regular seating.

1.2.5. Personal Seat Licenses

Several professional franchises have resorted to charging a fee for a spectator to have the right to purchase tickets to the home contests over the course of a season. These personal seat licenses (PSLs) are sold to fans who pay a predetermined amount to reserve the preferred seat location before they actually buy tickets to the event. The individual is then considered the owner of the seat and usually (see note 1) is able to resell that particular seat. This concept is similar to owning a condominium. A person can purchase a condominium and, when he or she decides to move, has the right to sell the unit to the highest bidder. The individual taking out a PSL then must buy season tickets for the team's home games. Failure to do so results in a forfeiture of the seats and the money paid to reserve the seats. PSLs are another attempt by franchises to inject revenue into their operation from an otherwise stagnant or sold-out marketplace. Personal seat licenses can range from around $1000 per seat for seats farther from the field to several thousand dollars for the best seats in the facility. In 1993, the Carolina Panthers NFL expansion franchise began selling personal seat licenses (PSLs) to help fund the building of Ericsson Stadium. By the time the stadium opened in 1996, the Panthers had sold 61,000 PSLs, which cost between $750 and $5,400. These sales helped raise more than $150 million for the franchise, which helped finance the stadium, player contracts, and other general improvements. The case of the Panthers is an excellent example of how PSL revenue can help a new franchise.

NOTE _____

1. Personal seat licenses also affect Division I-A college sports. Demand for PSLs is so high at certain institutions that they no longer allow patrons to resell their seats. For example, at Ohio State University's Jerome Schottenstein Center™ and Value City Arena, patrons must purchase PSLs for a forty-year term. During that term, they may not resell their seats to other patrons but may sell their seats back to the university, which in turn sells the PSL to someone on a waiting list. Ohio State raised over $15 million, almost 10% of the total cost of construction, from the sale of PSLs, which cost fans anywhere from $1,000 to $15,000. Given the high demand at certain professional sporting events, it is likely that pro teams will adopt this policy in the future in order to finance new stadiums.

2. For more information on stadiums, see Martin J. Greenberg and James T. Gray, *The Stadium Game* (Milwaukee, WI: National Sports Law Institute of Marquette University Law School, 1996).

1.2.6. Sponsorships/Licensing/Merchandising

After the escalating value of television contracts and luxury suite revenues, licensing and merchandising have been the areas in professional sports that have seen the most revenue growth. Professional sport franchises receive revenue from team and leaguewide sponsorship agreements. These agreements allow an organization to license the team and/or league logo for commercial use in marketing efforts. Legal issues often revolve around or include a facet of these economic influences. For example, some owners have entered into agreements on an individual franchise level that are incongruous with leaguewide deals negotiated by the Properties arms. Such was the case in *NFL Properties Inc.* v. *Dallas Cowboys Football Club, Ltd.* (see note 1).

Licensed products such as hats, jerseys, shorts, and T-shirts are prevalent throughout the world, but licensed apparel is not the only category from which the "Big Four" have reaped profits. They have put their league and team logos on items such as trading cards, publications, backpacks, pencils, sporting goods, and even food! Manufacturers of these items believe that their company and products will benefit from the association with a particular sport and its league through increased awareness and brand equity, and thereby contribute to their bottom line. The companies pay an up-front fee plus a percentage of each unit sale to be an official licensee of a particular league. Another way that "Big Four" properties departments generate income is by the licensing of teams and/or franchises for use in the marketing of logoed merchandise, or in advertising, or promotional programs on the part of the licensee. For example, Sprite™ is the 2002 official non-cola soft drink of the NBA, and Wilson™ makes the official ball for the NFL. The revenue from these agreements is distributed among the league and its member franchises.

Corporations will enter into licensing agreements with sport entities for the right to associate with a particular event, better known as sport sponsorships. Corporate sponsors pay a fee to the controlling entity in exchange for having their company or product name prominently associated with an event. A distinct example of this practice can be seen in the names of the Bowl Coalition Series. The Nokia™ Sugar Bowl, the Federal Express™ Orange Bowl, and the Tostitos™ Fiesta Bowl are three such examples of a corporation's becoming the title sponsor for a sporting event. The "Big Four" professional leagues have thus far restricted the sponsoring of major events like the Super Bowl and World Series to protect the integrity of the event. However, top-flight sponsors of these events are given prominent presenting sponsorships. The "Big Four" leagues will allow title sponsors for lesser events like Major League Baseball's Radio Shack™ All-Star Game.

A final prominent form of sponsorship that has developed and grown in recent years is the practice of selling naming rights to a team facility or arena. Sponsors pay large sums of money to have their name on the stadium or arena of a franchise for the duration of the sponsorship agreement. As a result, we have witnessed the Hoosier Dome in Indianapolis change its name to the RCA® Dome; Oakland-Alameda County Coliseum in Oakland, to Network Associates® Park; and Anaheim Stadium in Anaheim, to Edison® Field. Many franchises have taken naming rights one step further. Before ground is even broken, many franchises enter into agreement with a sponsor to name the facility. The benefit of this practice is that it gains capital which can help finance construction of the facility. The benefit to the sponsor is that it may capitalize on the publicity associated with construction of the facility before the team even plays a game (see exhibit 1.4).

Lawsuits stemming from the area of licensed merchandising often involve the reproduction of league or team logos by manufacturers without proper consent from the governing organization. This unlicensed or "pirated" merchandise is a billion-dollar industry throughout the world. To combat the production of these types of goods, leagues warn customers to look for the official logo that indicates that the product is an endorsed product of the league. While the "Big Four" attempt to curtail the flow of this pirated merchandise, they are somewhat limited in their effectiveness by the wide scope of such illegal activity. The benefit to the merchandise pirates is that they can confuse the consumers into thinking

Exhibit 1.4
Top Stadium Naming Rights Deals

Venue	Major Tenant(s)	City	Years	Price
Reliant Stadium (& Astrodome complex)	Texans (NFL)	Houston	32	$300 million
FedEx Field	Redskins (NFL)	Washington, DC.	27	$205 million
American·Airlines Center	Mavericks (NBA) Stars (NHL)	Dallas	30	$195 million
Philips Arena	Thrashers (NHL) Hawks (NBA)	Atlanta	20	$185 million
CMGI Field	Patriots (NFL)	Foxboro, MA	15	$120 million
Invesco Field	Broncos (NFL)	Denver	20	$120 million*
PSINet Stadium	Ravens (NFL)	Baltimore	20	$105 million
Staples Center	Lakers (NBA) Clippers (NBA) Kings (NHL)	Los Angeles	20	$100 million
Conseco Fieldhouse	Pacers (NBA)	Indianapolis	20	$90 million
Gaylord Entertainment Center	Predators (NHL)	Nashville	20	$80 million
Xcel Energy Center	Wild (NHL)	St. Paul	25	$75 million
Great American Ballpark	Reds (MLB)	Cincinnati	30	$75 million

*includes $60 Million in naming rights &
$60 Million for in-stadium advertising

that their product is endorsed or associated with a particular player, team, or league. This "likelihood of confusion" argument is often at the core of the trademark violation lawsuits. For a more complete description of trademark violation issues and cases, see Chapter 13, section 13.1., "Trademark Law."

The area of licensing also extends to individual professional athletes. For example, NBA players, in addition to being obligated per the collective bargaining agreement to make appearances on behalf of the teams they play for, are also obligated to make appearances for the league's Properties division. These appearances require the player to wear the official NBA licensed apparel of the team they represent. The NBA Uniform Player Contract states that a player has fulfilled this duty if "during each year of the period covered by such Contract, the Player makes five individual personal appearances and five group appearances for or on behalf of or at the request of the Team by which he is employed and/or the NBA" (see Chapter 12, exhibit 12.2, "NBA Uniform Player Contract," and section 12.11, "Endorsement Contracts").

Players can use their own likeness for promotions and receive all the funds they are paid. In this case, the player may not appear wearing any items that would associate him with his team or the league. A player who is well known (such as Shaquille O'Neal) is not hampered by this limitation. But a lesser-known player may not be recognized without his uniform on.

NOTES _____

1. Various theories are asserted by the NFL in the *Cowboys* case: violation of joint contract, violation of Lanham Act, breach of good faith, tortious interference, misappropriation of funds (nine counts in all). (See Chapter 9, "Contract Law.")

2. For a case involving individual team broadcasting agreements incongruous with

league limitations, see *Chicago Professional Sports Limited Partnership* v. *NBA*, 95 F.3d 593 (7th Cir. 1996). (See Chapter 14, "Television and Broadcasting.")

3. For more information on professional sports sponsorships and merchandising see Stephen Hardy, Bernard J. Mullin, and William A. Sutton, *Sport Marketing* (Champaign, IL: Human Kinetics, 2000).

1.2.7. Commissioners

Perhaps the most visible individual in these leagues is the commissioner. In many ways, the commissioner is an *employee* of the owners. For example, the owners hire the commissioner, and possess mechanisms to terminate him when his decisions are adverse to their interests (see note 1). In other ways, the commissioner is a *boss* of the owners. He may stringently discipline owners if their behavior is detrimental to the integrity of the sport. For example, NBA Commissioner David Stern fined Dallas Mavericks owner Mark Cuban a total of $505,000 during the 2000–2001 season for derogatory gestures, berating officials, and courtside misbehavior. In January 2002, Stern again fined Cuban over $500,000 for his continuous derogatory public comments regarding NBA officials. Also, in 2000–2001, Stern fined Minnesota Timberwolves owner Glen Taylor $3.5 million for signing a secret contract with Joe Smith, in violation of league salary cap rules. In MLB, New York Yankees owner George Steinbrenner endured two unrelated yearlong suspensions for illegal political contributions in the 1970s and involvement with gambler Howard Spira in the 1980s.

However, commissioners may not arbitrarily utilize this power of discipline over the owners. Due to the diversity of owners' interests, an effective commissioner must politic in order to have a successful and lengthy tenure in office. Owners' interests are often split along big market and small market lines, especially in relation to issues of revenue sharing. Sometimes owners differ over whether to take a hard line in collective bargaining negotiations. Depending on the team's financial position, an owner may or may not be prepared for a long work stoppage (i.e., strike or lockout). A commissioner must weigh all such interests while simultaneously representing his sport as a chief ambassador and guarding the sport's long-term interests.

The commissioner's office also deals with issues involving players. The commissioner or his representatives may discipline or expel players. However, the commissioner's power (and the owners' power, for that matter) over the players is regulated by a sport's three main governing documents: the league's Basic Agreement, the Uniform Player Contract, and the Collective Bargaining Agreement (CBA). When there is a conflict between the documents, arbitrators and judges normally yield to the CBA because the CBA is negotiated by both employees (via the union) and management. As a hypothetical example, a commissioner might suspend a player for life for beating up a referee during a game, citing a code of conduct in the Basic Agreement and Uniform Player Contract. However, the player might bring legal action against the commissioner, citing a clause in the CBA that all discipline cases must go to arbitration. In such a case, the courts are likely to favor the player because the CBA trumps the other governing documents.

Clearly, then, the existence and content of the CBA (whether it is promanagement or pro-player) is pivotal in determining a commissioner's, owner's, or player's likelihood of success in a legal dispute. For more details on this issue, see Chapter 11, section 11.3., "Collective Bargaining in Professional Sports." A CBA (even after expiration) also can shield a league from most antitrust litigation brought by individual players or the union. For more details on this issue, see Chapter 10, section 10.3.5, "Exemption After Decertification: *McNeil*."

NOTES ─────────────────────────────────

1. MLB owners forced commissioner Fay Vincent from office after Vincent made certain decisions that were contrary to many owners' interests. For a detailed account of this and other MLB commissioners' tenures, see John Helyar, *Lords of the Realm* (New York: Ballantine Books, 1994).

2. For real-life examples of legal challenges leading to the clarification or reduction of the commissioner's powers, see *Atlanta National League Baseball Club Inc.* v. *Kuhn*, 432 F.Supp. 1213 (N.D. Ga 1977) and *Chicago National League Ball Club Inc.* v. *Vincent*, No. 92C 4398, 1992 U.S. Dist. LEXIS 11033 (N.D. Ill. July 23, 1992).

1.2.8. Single Entity Leagues

While the "Big Four" leagues have shown an ability to generate significant revenues, they have also generated their share of problems. One of these problems has been competitive imbalance between large and small market teams (see section 1.2.1., "A Brief Economic Overview") in certain sports like baseball and hockey. A second problem has been spiraling operating costs brought about by competitive bidding for players. Were it legal, owners of the "Big Four" teams would gladly work cooperatively in order to keep player salaries, and thus expenses, artificially low (see note 1). However, Section 1 of the Sherman Antitrust Act forbids such conspiracy as do Collective Bargaining Agreements such as Major League Baseball's, which prevents collusion (see note 1).

Beginning as a single entity league is an apparently legal way for new leagues to avoid some of the problems faced by the established "Big Four" leagues. Logically, one cannot conspire with oneself. Therefore, players who sue their single entity league on the basis of conspiracy are unlikely to succeed.

The two preeminent single entity leagues in the United States are Major League Soccer (MLS) and the Womens' National Basketball Association (WNBA). MLS was established in 1996 as a limited liability corporation organized under Delaware law. Instead of team owners, the league has "operator-investors." Some of these operator-investors, such as Lamar Hunt, run more than one of the league's twelve teams. Players are hired by MLS, sign a contract with the league, and then are assigned to the various teams rather than being direct employees of a team. Furthermore, MLS distributes profits and losses to the operator-investors in a way similar to distribution of dividends to shareholders of a corporation. Players have challenged this structure as a "sham" to subvert Section 1 of the Sherman Act. However, the courts have so far held that the MLS structure is legally viable in *Fraser v. Major League Soccer* (see note 2). Therefore, while owners and commissioners of leagues like the NBA and NFL must bargain for salary restraints like a "cap," single entity leagues like MLS can impose such restraints unilaterally.

The WNBA's structure is similar to that of MLS, the main difference being that the "operator-investors" are owners of *NBA* franchises or agents of the NBA itself. In fact, the WNBA offices are housed within the NBA building in New York City. Instead of a commissioner, the league has a president, much as one would see in a standard corporation. Furthermore, the marketing goals of the NBA and WNBA are closely aligned. The leagues attempt to attract common sponsors, and have showcased events featuring both NBA and WNBA players. All sixteen WNBA teams play in the same arenas as their NBA counterparts.

Finally, the short lived XFL structured itself similarly to the WNBA, an eight-team single entity league owned by World Wrestling Entertainment, Inc. (WWE). The league folded in April 2001 due to disappointing television ratings and pressure from investors (WWE is a public company). Nevertheless, the XFL's decision for a single entity structure, like the MLS and WNBA, suggests that American start-up leagues will continue to adopt single entity structure unless the courts prevent them from doing so.

NOTES

1. Arbitrators George Nicolau and Tom Roberts found baseball executives guilty of player salary collusion during the years 1985–1987. Cash awards totaling in the hundreds of millions of dollars were paid to affected free-agent players of this era (see Chapter 11, section 11.4.4., "Baseball Collusion Cases").

2. The legal test of the viability of single entity leagues is *Fraser* v. *Major League Soccer*, 97 F. Supp. 2d 130 (D. Mass. 2000). In addition to the Section 1 conspiracy complaints, the plaintiffs alleged Section 2 monopolization. Section 2 antitrust complaints do not require existence of conspiracy (see Chapter 10, section 10.1., "Overview of Antitrust Law").

3. Major League Lacrosse (MLL) and arenafootball2 (af2) are additional examples of single entity leagues. MLL began play in 2001 with a six-team, fourteen-game regular season schedule and procured television coverage on regional networks such as FOX Sports New England and MSG. Additional information is available at www.majorleaguelacrosse.com. The af2 began play in 1999 to serve as a minor league feeder system for the Arena Football League. By 2001, the league consisted of twenty-eight teams. More information is available at www.arenafootball.com/af2/

1.3. INTERCOLLEGIATE ATHLETICS

The governance of intercollegiate athletics consists primarily of five national organizations: (1) the National Collegiate Athletic Association (NCAA); (2) the National Association of Intercollegiate Athletics (NAIA), which governs four-year institutions; (3) the National Small College Athletic Association (NSCAA), which governs four-year colleges with enrollment of fewer than 500 male and/or female undergraduates; (4) the National Christian College Athletic Association (NCCAA), which is comprised of over 100 members and is open only to four-year Christian institutions that are willing to subscribe to a "Statement of Faith"; and (5) the National Junior College Athletic Association (NJCAA), which encompasses men's and women's junior college athletic programs. The NCAA is the largest organization and it is the primary governing body for more than 1,000 institutions of higher education in the United States. It serves a diverse constituency encompassing all sizes of athletic programs. Because of this diverse membership base, the NCAA faces unique challenges in the administration of collegiate athletics. This section will focus primarily on the NCAA.

This section will examine three areas of the NCAA that persons involved in the sports industry need to be familiar with in order to better understand legal issues involving the NCAA and its member institutions. This section will begin by discussing the organizational structure of the NCAA and how legislation is enacted. Next, a brief economic analysis of the NCAA, including revenues and expenses, will be covered. Finally, we will examine one member institution's finances. This section will focus primarily on Division I-A athletics with brief mentions of Division I-AA, Division II, and Division III. A more detailed description of the four intercollegiate associations other than the NCAA can be found in Chapter 5, section 5.1.4., "Other Athletic Associations."

1.3.1. Organizational Structure

The NCAA is a not-for-profit educational entity that was founded in 1906 to provide institutions of higher education an opportunity to administer athletic issues on the national level. Each member institution joins the NCAA voluntarily, and theoretically can withdraw at any time (see note 1). Since 1906, its membership has grown from sixty-two institutions to comprise colleges and universities, conferences, organizations, and individuals totaling over 1,200 members.

The NCAA is headquartered in Indianapolis, Indiana, and houses ten membership groups staffed by full-time employees. These groups are the following:

• Executive Team
• Governance Structure Team
• Executive Affairs
• Championship Group
• Education Services Group
• Enforcement and Student-Athlete Reinstatement Group
• Finance and Information Services Group
• Marketing, Licensing, and Promotions Group
• Membership Services Group
• Public Affairs Group

These central office employees carry out the day-to-day duties necessary to execute strategies and programs decided upon by the governance structure of the NCAA.

On August 1, 1997, the NCAA altered its governing structure to allow for more self-determination by individual divisions on specific division-level matters. Issues facing Division I member institutions are not necessarily the same issues facing Division II and Division III institutions. The new structure implemented by the NCAA gives divisional presidents and athletic administrators the ability to make decisions on certain issues separate from other divisions. In the past, Division II and III administrators had the ability to veto decisions that affected the NCAA membership as a whole. However, the balance of power has now shifted to the major Division I conferences, and with the new governance structure, Division II and III schools no longer have this impact. As exhibit 1.5 illustrates, the new governance structure is headed by the Executive Committee. This committee is the leading decision-making entity of the NCAA and is com-

Exhibit 1.5
NCAA Governance Structure

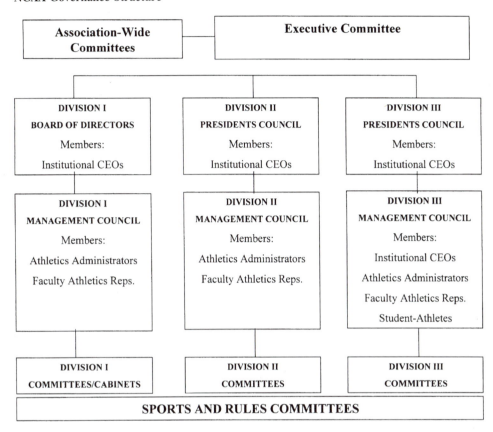

prised of eight members from the Division I Board of Directors, two Division I-AA and I-AAA members each from the Division I Board of Directors, and two members from both the Division II and Division III Presidents Council. These members are the chief executive officers of member institutions (usually college or university presidents). In addition, the executive director of the NCAA and the chairs of the Division I, II, and III Management Councils serve on this committee in a non-voting capacity. The Executive Committee rules on and enacts legislation that is brought to it by the lower councils and committees from the respective divisions.

The next tier of the governance structure is the Division I Board of Directors, the Division II Presidents Council, and the Division III Presidents Council. These bodies are also manned by CEOs of member institutions who review proposed legislation from the respective division's Management Council and related subcommittees. Division specific legislation can be approved and enacted at this level.

The next level of this structure is the Division I, II, and III Management Councils, made up of athletic administrators and faculty athletics representatives from the respective division's member institutions. In the Management Councils, athletic issues relating to the particular division are researched and discussed, and potential legislation is forwarded to the next higher level in the governance structure for approval. Often subcommittees are formed and assigned particular issues to research in order for them to return to the Management Council with a recommendation for action. It is important to understand that all legislation enacted by the NCAA governance structure is designed and approved by administrators from member institutions. Particularly sensitive issues, such as Proposition 48 and the revocation of freshman eligibility rules, are often discussed at the annual NCAA convention in an attempt to gauge membership support for the legislation. Ideally, all legislation passed by the NCAA is in the best interest of the student-athletes and member institutions; however, due to the large constituency of the NCAA, an ever-increasing amount of litigation faces the association (see Chapters 5 and 6).

NOTE _____

1. In *Tarkanian* v. *NCAA*, 511 U.S. 1033 (1994), the plaintiff alleged that the NCAA was not a voluntary association, and that its member institutions had no viable alternatives in intercollegiate athletics. The court eventually ruled for the NCAA, holding that the association was not a state actor, but a private organization.

2. More information on NCAA rules, regulations and bylaws can be found in the *2001–02 NCAA Division I Manual* (www.ncaa.org).

1.3.2. Economic Overview

Despite its not-for-profit designation, the NCAA does generate substantial revenues and incur considerable expenses throughout the course of its operations. Most of the NCAA's operating revenue is generated from a few revenue-producing sports. The Division I men's basketball championship, in particular, is essential to the financing of NCAA operations, and is ultimately responsible for the NCAA's financing of the majority of intercollegiate championships. This section will briefly examine such sources of revenues and expenses within the NCAA.

1.3.2.1. Revenues

The major source of revenue for the NCAA is the money it receives from its television contracts. For example, in fiscal year 2000–2001, television revenue accounted for 78.7% of the NCAA's total revenue. Exhibit 1.6 lists seven-year revenues for the NCAA and the corresponding year's revenues earned from the television contract.

It is easy to see how dependent the NCAA is on its television contract for revenues, much the way the "Big Four" professional sports leagues are dependent upon their broadcasting contracts. As long as networks are willing to pay large rights fees for premier events, the NCAA will be able to continue growing this particular revenue stream.

The premier revenue-generating event for the NCAA is the NCAA Division I men's basketball championship, which in 2001 brought in an estimated $276.1 million from television and ticket sales alone—nearly 85% of the association's total revenue. Due to an eleven-year broadcast rights agreement with CBS, this amount will grow to more than $764 million per year by the 2012–2013 season. This will virtually assure that this single three-week championship will account

Exhibit 1.6
NCAA Total Revenues and Television Revenues, 1994–2001

Year	Total Revenue	T.V. Revenue
1994-95	$212,033,960	$168,227,085
1995 - 1996	$232,244,833	$180,970,362
1996 - 1997	$247,701,483	$191,277,515
1997 - 1998	$275,915,104	$213,628,467
1998 - 1999	370,804,049	228,512,998
1999 - 2000	364,546,859	282,692,985
2000 - 2001*	$325,560,000	256,200,000

* Figures for 2000 - 2001 are budgeted figures, not actual dollars received.

for more than 90% of the NCAA's total revenue by 2013. Recognizing its dependence on one main revenue stream, the NCAA had undertaken efforts to generate new sources of revenue. The association entered into an agreement with a private company that gave radio broadcast rights, television show, and publication rights to the company in exchange for a royalty fee. In 1998, the NCAA received $11.5 million from this agreement, and expects that figure to grow annually. This corporate partnership program allows the sponsoring partner to develop promotions to help its business in conjunction with NCAA-sponsored events.

Another source of revenue for the NCAA is the championship events themselves. Admission fees from championship events such as the College World Series (baseball) and the women's Division I basketball championship accounted for an estimated $36.2 million of the NCAA's total revenue in 2000–2001.

Although football is one of the largest revenue generators for its member schools, the NCAA does not benefit financially from the enormous popularity of college football. As of 2002, there is no post-season NCAA tournament for football; instead qualified teams play in individually sponsored bowl games, with the top eight teams playing in four bowls run by the BCS (Bowl Coalition Series). The BCS is not affiliated with the NCAA, but essentially equates to determining a national champion, and is run by the major Division 1-A football conferences. The champions of the Atlantic Coast, Big East, Southeastern, Pac 10, Big Ten, and Big 12 Conferences are given automatic berths in one of the four bowls while the other slots are filled by the two teams with the highest ranking according to the "BCS Formula." The BCS computer formula takes into account the polls of the writers and coaches, computer rankings, strength of schedule rankings and team record. The number one and two ranked teams play for the National Championship in one of the four bowls (each bowl gets to host this game once every four years), while the other three bowls select the teams they want from the remaining pool of six. The two highest-ranking teams have played to determine the National Champion since 1998.

1.3.2.2. Expenses

The expenses of the NCAA are concentrated in two major areas, one being the expenses the organization needs in order to operate, pay its staff, and manage championships. However, due to the NCAA's non-profit status, the majority of the remaining money is distributed to member institutions. Since Division I institutions provide the majority of the contests from which the NCAA generates revenue, they receive the majority of the revenue distributed. For instance, the total dollars of revenue distributed to Division I institutions in 2000 was $171,170,000. Division II institutions received $13,746,000 in revenue distribution, and Division III institutions received $10,003,000. The bulk of the money distributed to Division I institutions is based on team and/or conference participation in the men's Division I basketball championship. The distribution of the revenue to Division I conferences is based upon their performance in the tournament over a six-year period. For example, the money distributed in 2000–2001 is based upon a conference's performance over the period 1995–2000. The total dollars distributed by the NCAA in 2000 for this fund was $69,999,996. It also distributes funds to Division I institutions for academic enhancement, special assistance for student-athletes, conference grants, and a broad-based distribution based on the number of varsity sports a Division I institution sponsors and the number of athletic scholarships the institution offers.

The NCAA also must pay the lease for its offices and the salaries of its employees from the revenue it generates. In addition, it incurs the normal expenses for its full-time employees such as a pension plan and other benefits.

Another significant expense for the NCAA is litigation. For example, in 1995 a certain class of Division I coaches brought suit against the NCAA alleging their compensation limitation rules were a violation of federal antitrust laws. A decision in favor of the plaintiffs, which was upheld by a Circuit Court of Appeals, resulted in a settlement costing the NCAA over $54 million. This, and other cases, could be a large expense to the NCAA and upset the distribution of its revenues to member institutions. NCAA antitrust issues are further investigated in Chapter 10.

NOTE _____

1. More information on NCAA finances can be found in the following resources:

   (a) www.ncaa.org

   (b) Nand Hart-Nibbrig and Clement Cottingham, *The Political Economy of College Sports* (Lexington, MA: Lexington Books 1986).

   (c) Murray Sperber and Henry Holt, *College Sports Inc.: The Athletic Department vs. The University* (New York: Henry Holt, 1990).

1.3.3. The Institutions

As mentioned above, the NCAA serves member institutions belonging to Divisions I, II and III. Shortly, we will examine the athletic operation of a single Division I institution. But first, we will examine the differences among the three divisions.

Division I member institutions are required by NCAA guidelines to sponsor at least seven varsity sports for men and women (or six for men and eight for women), with two sports being sponsored for both men and women (i.e., basketball and track and field). Every playing season must have a sport sponsored for each gender. Each Division I school has contest minimums and participant minimums that must be met in each sport. In addition, each member institution must be within the guidelines for granting athletic scholarships. The biggest difference in Division I is that Division I-A football institutions must meet minimum attendance requirements, while Division I-AA institutions need not (see note 1).

Division II institutions also have sport sponsorship requirements to meet. For an institution to be classified as Division II, it must sponsor at least four sports for men and women, with two of those sports being the same for men and women, and each sex being represented for each season. Division III institutions also must meet contest and participant requirements, as well as stay within approved guidelines for offering financial aid.

Division III institutions also must sponsor four sports for men and women with two of those sports being the same, and each gender must be represented in every season. Minimum contest and participant requirements also apply to Division III institutions. The biggest difference between the other two divisions is that Division III institutions do not offer athletic scholarships—only financial aid based upon need.

NOTE _____

1. In 2002, the NCAA voted to implement a new standard that would drop football programs that do not meet a minimum attendance requirement from Division I-A to 1-AA.

1.3.4. Institution Case Study: University of Michigan Athletic Department

The athletic programs of many Division I-A colleges and universities have emerged as big businesses. Budgeting pressures have forced athletic administrators at these institutions to make some difficult decisions. Here is one example demonstrating the big-business, tight-budget environment of Division I-A athletics. This atmosphere at the micro level (at *one* NCAA institution) is both an outgrowth and an explanation of the complex compliance regulations imposed by the NCAA.

The University of Michigan Athletic Department was chosen to illustrate the budgetary concerns of all Division I programs. Michigan is a high-profile Division I-A athletic program, and a member of a major conference, the Big Ten. In addition, since it is a public institution, financial information is made available to the public. Despite large inflows of revenue, the department runs a deficit. This is the norm, rather than the exception. According to a report published by the University of Virginia, only 46% of Division I-A athletic departments reported budgetary surpluses in 1999, while 54% reported a deficit. All told, Michigan projected a $2.05 million deficit for the year ending June 30, 2001, after a $2.6 million deficit in the previous fiscal year.

Michigan's revenues exceed $40 million annually, about one-third of which comes from the sale of football tickets. This is an unusually high percentage for a school, attributable to Michigan's 107,501-seat stadium that is sold out for every game. Also unusual is that the Athletic Department does not receive state funding or funding from student fees. Instead, additional revenues are gained from booster donations, sponsorships, licensing (such as merchandise bearing Michigan logos), shared earnings from the NCAA and Big Ten, and local broadcast deals.

Athletic Department sources cite several main reasons for the unexpected deficit: a sudden decrease in the sale of items bearing Michigan logos (accounting for $1.35 million in lost revenue alone), decreasing ticket sales to men's basketball games, a terminated radio contract and less than anticipated donations. However, the problem may also stem from the school's generous offering of sports options. The school maintains twenty-five varsity sports and claims to offer the most scholarship dollars in the Big Ten ($9 million). In particular, Michigan added women's soccer and crew in the 1990s in order to comply with Title IX (for more information see Chapter 8).

Athletic directors at Michigan have several options for dealing with their deficit problems. They may cut some men's teams, they may continue to raise ticket prices for demand-friendly football, and they may dip into the reserves of the department's $36 million endowment. The first two options may endanger the school's goodwill with alumni donors, and the last cannot be sustained forever.

While not every NCAA athletic program enjoys the prestige and on-field success of the Michigan Wolverines, many programs are feeling a similar financial squeeze. The University of Nebraska, another football powerhouse, responded to comparable budgetary crunch in 2001 by cutting men's swimming and diving. So far, Michigan has not taken such a step.

NOTES _____

1. For differing perspectives on the issues at the University of Michigan, see the following articles: Jane R. Elgass, "Report Released on Athletic Department Financial Management," *The University Record* (University of Michigan), July 6, 1999; M. Gunderson and J. Jiang, "U.S. Universities Find Funds Short to Meet Title IX," *Daily Illini* (University of Illinois), October 21, 1998; and "Michigan Athletics Projects Deficit for 2000–01 Academic Year," Press release on university Web site (2000), www.mgoblue.com/00–01/release-07–13.html

2. In 2001, the University of Kansas cut men's tennis and swimming, and Big 12 rival Iowa State cut men's baseball and swimming. Michigan State cut men's gymnastics. For articles on similar problems faced by other major Division I programs, consult Jennifer Lee, "Small Sports Die as School Deficits Grow," *Street & Smith's Sports Business Journal*, June 11–17, 2001; G. Gaul and F. Fitzpatrick, "At Penn State, Others, Corporate Sponsors, Boosters Fund Athletic Juggernaut," *Philadelphia Inquirer*, September 10, 2000; and "Nebraska Cuts Men's Swimming and Diving," *Topeka Capital-Journal Online* (2001), www.hawkzone.com/stories/032601/cov_nebraska.shtml. For detailed financial information on men's and women's athletics at all of the Big 12 Conference schools, see Welch Suggs, "The Struggle to Stay Competitive is a Big-Time Conference," *Chronicle of Higher Education*, June 22, 2001.

3. For more information on the effects of increased dollars entering intercollegiate sports, consult Andrew Zimbalist, *Unpaid Professionals* (Princeton: Princeton University Press, 1999), and Don Yaeger and Douglas Looney, *Under the Tarnished Dome: How*

Notre Dame Tarnished It's Ideals for Football Glory (New York, NY: Simon and Schuster 1993).

4. For a more detailed understanding of the accounting of NCAA athletic programs, see Mitchell H. Raiborn, *Revenues and Expenses of Intercollegiate Athletics Programs* (Overland Park, KS: National Collegiate Athletic Association, 1994).

5. For information on the financial and athletic turnaround of a university athletic department, see Rick Telander, *From Red Ink to Roses: The Turbulent Transformation of a Big Ten Program* (New York, NY: Simon and Schuster 1994).

6. For new perspectives on the place of athletics in an educational setting, see James L. Shulman and William G. Bowan, *The Game of Life: College Sports and Educational Values* (Princeton, NJ: Princeton University Press, 2001), and James J. Duderstadt, *Intercollegiate Athletics and the American University: A University President's Perspective* (Ann Arbor: University of Michigan Press, 2000).

1.3.5. Knight Foundation Commission on Intercollegiate Athletics

Concerns about abuses in college sports inspired the reconvening of the John and James L. Knight Foundation on Intercollegiate Athletics in 2000 and 2001. The meeting culminated in a report offering the following fifteen recommendations for the NCAA and its member institutions:

1. Athletes should be filtered through "the same academic processes as other students" including admission standards and degree requirements.

2. By 2007, teams that do not graduate at least 50 percent of their players should be banned from post-season play (180 of the 321 colleges with Division I basketball teams failed to meet that standard in 2000).

3. "Scholarships should be tied to specific athletes until they (or their entering class) graduate."

4. The length of playing seasons, practice seasons, and post-seasons must be reduced.

5. The NBA and the NFL should be encouraged to develop minor leagues. (This would present an alternative for athletes who are not interested in or are unqualified for higher education.)

6. Football and basketball expenditures should be reduced, including the total number of scholarships that are awarded in Division I-A football.

7. Compliance with Title IX and support of women's athletics should be ensured.

8. Coaches' salaries should be reduced and "brought into line with prevailing norms across the institution."

9. Agreements for coaches' outside income should be negotiated with institutions, not individual coaches, because "[a]dvertisers are buying the institution's reputation no less than the coaches'."

10. The NCAA plan for distribution of revenue from the CBS contract should be revised so that it is based on academic performance and gender equity compliance rather than on winning and losing.

11. Institutions alone should determine when games are played, how they are broadcast, and which companies are permitted to advertise.

12. Institutions should be discouraged from signing commercial contracts that violate "traditional academic values."

13. In-arena and in-stadium advertising should be minimized.

14. The NCAA should ban corporate logos on uniforms. (This presumably would include bowl game sponsors.)

15. Federal legislation to ban legal gambling on college sports in Nevada should be supported, and college presidents should address illegal gambling on their campuses.

If some of the Knight Commission's 2001 recommendations are adopted, the business of Division I-A basketball and football will be significantly altered. Many top high school athletes might no longer be recruited, and top coaches might consider leaving the college ranks for professional leagues. However, the NCAA's adoption of the Knight recommendations is uncertain. While the commission has no formal authority over the NCAA, the NCAA has adopted most of its recommendations in the past (see note 2).

For detail on the history and composition of the Knight commission, as well as its recommendations, see Chapter 5, section 5.3.2.1., "The Knight Commission."

NOTES _____

1. The report of the 2001 Knight Foundation Commission on Intercollegiate Athletics, *A Call to Action: Reconnecting College Sports and Higher Education*, can be downloaded from the Knight Foundation's web site: www.knightfdn.org

2. The 2001 Knight Commission was a follow up to the first edition of the commission that met in 1993, and whose recommendations led to the 1996 restructuring of the NCAA, which placed presidents and chancellors of member schools in control of their athletic programs.

1.4. THE OLYMPICS

The Olympic Games have been a part of sports history since ancient Greece; however, while the underlying concept to the games may still be intact, the organizational structure of the games is greatly different today compared to the early games. The Olympic Games have become a business, much like other sporting events. For individuals working in or with Olympic contests, a thorough understanding of the modern Olympic movement is imperative in order to effectively manage Olympic-related entities. Issues such as drug testing (see Chapter 7, section 7.2.3., "Olympic and International Sports"), eligibility of athletes, and boycotts of Olympic games by countries have been sources of litigation for the International Olympic Committee (IOC). This section will review the structure and briefly examine the economics of the Olympic Games.

1.4.1. Organizational Structure

Created in 1894 to revive the ancient Greek games, the International Olympic Committee is an international, non-governmental, not-for-profit organization located in Switzerland. Its main duty is to oversee all aspects of the Olympic movement, but its most visible role is that of supervisor for the summer and winter Olympic Games. As the highest governing body of the Olympics, the IOC owns all of the rights to the Olympic symbol, anthem, flag, and motto.

The international nature of the Olympics complicates its study from a legal perspective since the countries in the Olympic movement have different laws, judicial systems and decisions, and different individual rights. The International Olympic Committee (IOC), International Federations (IFs), National Olympic Committees (NOCs), and National Governing Bodies (NGBs) all have their own

Exhibit 1.7
Olympic Structure

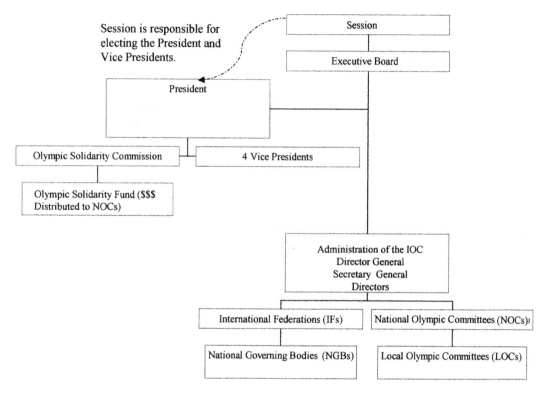

by-laws or charters. However, the IOC Charter is the ultimate governing document for all such organizations. Likewise, the IOC is the "supreme authority" on all matters pertaining to the Olympic Games. Exhibit 1.7 shows the organizational structure of the IOC.

The highest-ranking body in the IOC hierarchy is the Executive Board. The Executive Board is elected by delegates of each organizational member in an annual meeting. This group of delegates who serve a one-year term is called a session. The session elects a president of the IOC (current president Jacques Rogge was elected in 2001), who serves an initial eight-year term and thereafter is elected to four-year terms. The session also elects four vice presidents and six other members of the Executive Board who all serve four-year terms. The vice presidents and six other members can be re-elected, but not in the same year that their original term expires, unless they are elected by the president. The Executive Board meets either when the president orders a meeting or when a majority of its members request a meeting.

The Executive Board's main functions are the following:

• To attend to the observance of the Olympic Charter
• To assume responsibility for the administration of the IOC
• To approve the IOC's internal organization and all internal regulations relating to the organization
• To be responsible for the management of the IOC's finances

- To report to the session on any proposed rule changes
- To submit to the session the names of persons it recommends for election to the IOC
- To establish the agenda for the sessions
- To appoint the director general and secretary general (on recommendation from the president)
- To keep records of the IOC
- To pass legislation and policy to ensure proper adherence to the Olympic Charter and the proper organization of the Olympic Games
- To perform any other duties assigned to it by the session (see www.olympic.org)

Beneath the Executive Board is the administration of the IOC. The administration is led by the director general, secretary-general and directors. The director general is similar to a chief operating officer of a corporation in that under the direction of the president of the IOC, he/she directs the day-to-day operations of the organization. The secretary general is like an executive vice president in a corporation, overseeing daily operations. The individual directors in the administration control specific areas of the IOC, such as international cooperation, Olympic Games coordination, finance, marketing, legal affairs, technology, operations, communications, medical, and relations with the International Federations, National Olympic Committees, and Organizing Committees of Olympic Games (OCOG). The main duties of the administration are as follows:

- Implementing decisions made by the session, the Executive Board, and the president
- Implementation and follow-up of work from all commissions
- Serve as a liaison with all IFs, NOCs, and OCOGs
- Coordinate the preparation of all Olympic Games and other Olympic events
- Disseminate information within the Olympic movement
- Consult candidate cities on their bids to host the Olympic Games
- Promote sport, education, and culture with international government and non-government agencies
- Execute tasks assigned by the president and the Executive Board (see www.olympic.org)

Beneath the IOC administration are the individual International Federations. The IFs are non-governmental bodies given the authority by the IOC to administer specific sports on the international level. IFs must adhere to the Olympic movement rules and regulations regarding fair play, humanitarian efforts, environmental concerns, and elevating the status of women in sport, but they maintain their independence as far as establishing and enforcing rules governing their respective sports. They set their definitions of "amateur" and decide whether or not professional athletes will be allowed to compete in the Olympic Games in their particular sports. IFs are also responsible for the organization and execution of their sport at all Olympic Games and any other games affiliated with the IOC, such as the PanAm Games. For example, the International Federation for the sport of basketball is known by the acronym, FIBA (Fédération Internationale de Basketball). Since the IFs are responsible for individual sports on an international level, they are directly above the National Governing Bodies of each sport. As an example, the NGB of basketball in the United States is called USA Basketball. As such, USA Basketball works with FIBA and must adhere to

FIBA's rules and regulations. To be eligible to participate in the Olympic Games, an individual must be deemed eligible by the particular IF and NGB presiding over the sport. Rule 45 of the Olympic Charter explains how Olympic athletes become eligible for competition:

> To be eligible for participation in the Olympic Games, a competitor must comply with the Olympic Charter as well as with the rules of the IF concerned as approved by the IOC, and must be entered by his NOC. He must notably:
>
> • Respect the spirit of fair play and non-violence, and behave accordingly on the sports field
>
> • Refrain form using substances and procedures prohibited by the rules of the IOC, the IFs, or the NOCs
>
> • Respect and comply in all aspects with the Olympic Movement Anti-Doping Code (see www.olympic.org)

In addition, the bylaw to Rule 45 describes the role of the IFs and obligations of athletes when participating in the Olympic Games.

> • Each IF establishes its sport's own eligibility criteria in accordance with the Olympic Charter. Such criteria must be submitted to the IOC Executive Board for approval.
>
> • The application of the eligibility criteria lies with the IFs, their affiliated national federations, and the NOCs in the fields of their respective responsibilities.
>
> • Except as permitted by the IOC Executive Board, no competitor who participates in the Olympic Games may allow his person, name, picture or sports performance to be used for advertising purposes during the Olympic Games.
>
> • The entry or participation of a competitor in the Olympic Games shall not be conditional on any financial consideration. (see www.olympic.org)

Therefore, the eligibility rules for each sport are determined by the IF of that sport—an issue that came under international scrutiny when more professional athletes were allowed to participate in the Olympic Games. Furthermore, the bylaw to Rule 45 prohibits Olympic athletes from entering into sponsorship agreements on their own behalf but does not prohibit NGBs from promoting the Olympics using these same athletes.

The National Olympic Committees administer Olympic programs for a particular nation. For example, the United States Olympic Committee (USOC) is the NOC for all activities related to the Olympics in the United States. Despite the non-political ideals of the Olympics, most governments exert a high level of influence over their countries' NOCs. The United States is no different, as witnessed by the political 1980 boycott of the Moscow games, and various legislation devoted to the Olympics. In particular, Congress passed the Amateur Sports Act in 1978 and amended it in 1998, establishing the USOC's authority over international amateur sports competition (as opposed to the Amateur Athletic Union [AAU] or NCAA).

A responsibility of the National Olympic Committees is to establish training programs and funds so athletes have a competitive opportunity to earn a spot on the Olympic roster. The NOCs also supervise any attempt by a city in their country to host an Olympic Games. If there is more than one city from a country vying to host the games, then that country's NOC must decide which city will represent the country in the selection process in front of the IOC. In addition, the NOCs implement any rule changes passed by the IOC in their national

Olympic programs. It is this structure that theoretically maintains a uniform playing field from country to country.

When a city is chosen to host an Olympic Games by the IOC, a managing body from that city is formed to coordinate all the operations undertaken to stage the games. These bodies are known as Local Organizing Committees (LOCs). For example, the Salt Lake Organizing Committee (SLOC) was the organizing body for Salt Lake City, Utah, when it hosted the 2002 winter Olympics. The LOCs are responsible for developing infrastructure, facilities, transportation, athlete housing, and any other elements deemed necessary by the IOC to ensure a successful Olympiad. Most countries' LOCs receive some funding from their national government to stage the games; the United States is the only country that *does not* grant any federal government subsidies to a city hosting the Olympic Games. Thus, the host city is burdened with providing additional revenue from the games in order to offset the expenditures undertaken in hosting the games. This topic will be covered in more depth below.

NOTE _____

1. For more information on the structure of the International Olympic Committee, see www.olympic.org and Christopher R. Hill, *Olympic Politics: Athens to Atlanta, 1896–1996* (1997).

1.4.2. International Federations and National Governing Bodies

As mentioned above, the International Federations are the governing bodies for a specific Olympic sport worldwide. They determine eligibility rules, game rules, and other procedures related to a particular sport. Let us return to our example of the Fédération Internationale de Basketball (FIBA), the IF for the sport of basketball. FIBA is responsible for the overall management of all Olympic-related basketball activities, contests, and regulations. Operating from its statutes and laws, FIBA governs the NGBs to safeguard the game against corruption, to grow the game worldwide, and to foster competition between member nations.

Since FIBA is an International Federation, the rules of play differ from collegiate or professional rules to which most Americans are accustomed. For example, the size of the lane in FIBA rules is 19', 8.2" × 19', 0.3"; in the NBA the lane is 16' × 19'; and in NCAA competition the lane is 12' × 19'. FIBA also passes rules on eligibility of players. For instance, for the first time in 1988, FIBA allowed professional basketball players to participate in Olympic competition. Until that time, all the teams including those from the U.S. were comprised of amateur players. As a result of FIBA's rule change, the United States sent to the 1992 Olympics a team largely comprised of NBA players who routed all of their opponents. This "Dream Team" was met with great anticipation from around the world as the United States showcased its best athletes. However, these players were selected instead of amateur collegiate players who had represented the United States until then.

USA Basketball is the National Governing Body (NGB) for international basketball in the United States. As an NGB, USA Basketball is subject to the rules and regulations set forth by FIBA. However, within this framework, USA Basketball governs all basketball-related activities undertaken by the United States as it pertains to FIBA-sanctioned international competition and to national competition that falls under the Olympic umbrella. USA Basketball is comprised of thirty-one members of differing levels—active, associate, and affiliate. Active members are national sport organizations such as the NCAA, AAU, and NBA that operate a nationally active basketball program. Associate members, such as Athletes in Action and YWCA of the USA, also conduct active basketball operations, but do not qualify for active membership. Affiliate members like Basketball Travelers, Inc. and Sports Tours International, Inc. are basically for commercial groups that are involved in basketball in their businesses.

USA Basketball operations are derived from the Constitution of USA Basketball which sets forth the organizational hierarchy, jurisdiction, grievance procedures, membership criteria, selection processes, and all other functions of the entity (see note 1). Of particular interest is the authority of USA Basketball as indicated in Article 4 of the Constitution. This article reads as follows:

> Authority. This Association shall exercise the following powers:
>
> 4.1 Represent the United States in FIBA.
>
> 4.2 Establish national goals and encourage the attainment of those goals in the sport of basketball.
>
> 4.3 Serve as the coordinating body for amateur athletic activity in the sport of basketball in the United States.
>
> 4.4 Exercise jurisdiction over international amateur athletic activities and sanction international amateur athletic competition held in the United States and sanction the sponsorship of international amateur athletic competition held in the United States in the sport of Basketball, in accordance with the provisions of the Constitution.
>
> 4.5 Conduct amateur athletic competition in the sport of basketball, including national championships, and international amateur athletic competition in the United States, and establish procedures for the determination of eligibility standards for participation in such competitions, except for restricted competition referred to in the provision here below.
>
> 4.6 Recommend to the USOC individuals and teams to represent the United States in the Olympic Games and the Pan American Games in the sport of basketball.
>
> 4.7 Designate individuals and teams to represent the United States in international amateur athletic competition (other than the Olympics and Pan American Games) in the sport of basketball and certify, in accordance with the rules of FIBA, the amateur eligibility of such individuals and teams; provided that any amateur sports organization which conducts amateur athletic competition, participation in which is restricted to a specific class of amateur athletes (such as high school students, college students, members of the Armed Forces, or similar groups or categories) shall have exclusive jurisdiction over such competition.

As stated in the USA Basketball Constitution, USA Basketball has the authority to choose the players who represent the United States and the coaches who lead these teams. It also gives USA Basketball the authority to promote, coordinate, and regulate amateur athletic participation in basketball by many U.S. organizations. Due to this broad field of responsibility, the Board of Directors for USA Basketball boasts a constituency from a diverse group of basketball-related organizations. The organizations represented on the board are Amateur Athletic Union (one member); National Association of Intercollegiate Athletics (one member); National Basketball Association (four members); National Collegiate Athletic

Association (four members); National Federation of State High School Associations (one member); National Junior College Athletic Association (one member); and the U.S. armed forces (one member).

USA Basketball uses internal mechanisms to determine membership and eligibility issues as well as sanctioning of competition. In the case of declaring a participant ineligible, the association must inform the individual in writing and offer a hearing before the Board of Directors. The board's decision is not subject to appeal. However, if the internal mechanisms fail to satisfy either party, they may petition for a binding arbitration process following the rules and regulations of the American Arbitration Association.

NOTE

1. Information about the NGB for basketball in the United States, USA Basketball, can be found at www.usabasketball.com.

1.4.3. Economic Overview of Olympic Bodies

While the Olympic movement was originally designed to promote goodwill and international competition, it has since become a multimillion-dollar enterprise. Funding must be procured to finance the staging of the Olympic Games. Athletes need funding for equipment, training, travel, and competition. Full-time employees in the IOC, IFs, NOCs, and NGBs are all usually paid salaries and benefits, and offices for the organization and employees must be provided. Therefore, the modern Olympic Games have needed to rely on fundraising, donations, and commercialism in order to sustain their existence for the past one hundred years. However, it wasn't until the 1984 summer games, when the IOC developed a comprehensive plan for marketing the Olympic Games called "controlled commercialism," that Olympic revenues began to grow substantially. The IOC designed this plan to stabilize the finances of the Olympic organizations; to build an ongoing marketing program for all LOCs, instead of starting over with every Olympic Games; to distribute revenues earned equally throughout the Olympic organizational hierarchy; to control broadcasts of the Olympics enabling the world to view the games; and to control commercialism and promote the Olympic ideals throughout the world.

The IOC marketing efforts fall under the control of the IOC Marketing Department, which works with sponsors, broadcasters, National Organizing Committees, and Local Organizing Committees to develop new and creative ways to develop revenue in each organization's respective territory. One program, The Olympic Partners (TOP) program, began in 1985 in an effort to secure more sponsorship dollars and provide sponsors with greater return on their investment, is organized in four-year increments (called quadrenniums) surrounding an Olympic Game. Sponsors pay a sum of money to associate their brand name with the Olympics and be able to conduct promotions and run advertising utilizing the Olympic logo. This revenue has decreased the dependence the IOC had in previous years on the revenue received from selling broadcast rights. For example, in the 1997–2000 quadrennium, TOP revenue was approximately 36% of the total revenue received by the IOC, while television revenue was only 50%, down substantially from the 90% share television revenue accounted for fifteen years earlier.

1.4.4. IOC Responses to Prevailing Legal Issues

In 1995, the IOC awarded the 2002 Winter Olympics to Salt Lake City. In subsequent years, the IOC faced the largest corruption scandal in its history. Ten IOC members resigned or were expelled in cases allegedly involving fraud, conspiracy, and bribery (see note 1). Investigators determined that IOC members accepted more than $1 million in cash, improper gifts, and favors from backers of Salt Lake City's LOC in order to influence their votes. In an attempt to prevent such corruption in the future, the 109th IOC session adopted the following amendment in 1999:

> Decisions to expel an IOC member or honorary member are taken by a majority of two-thirds of the members present at the Session on the proposal of the Executive Board. . . . A member or honorary member expelled from the IOC may not be a member of an NOC, an association of NOCs or an OCOG. Under no circumstances may he again become a member or honorary member of the IOC. (Rule 20, Paragraph 3.5)

"Doping" has been another point of controversy for the IOC. The term "doping" refers to the use of performance-enhancing drugs in athletic competition. (The topic is covered in more detail in Chapter 7.) Sometimes an athlete is disqualified for a positive drug test immediately prior to his or her Olympic event. When this occurs, it does not afford much time for the athlete to obtain due process. In order to handle disputes over matters such as a positive drug test, the Court of Arbitration for Sport (CAS) was created in 1983 (see note 3). It also allows disputes that arise during (or right before) the Olympic Games to be settled quickly and relatively inexpensively (see note 2).

It is important to point out that CAS arbitration can be used to settle disputes over matters other than doping. For example, it can be used to settle conflicts between IFs and NGBs, and disputes involving sponsorship or television rights contracts. Athletes, sports federations, clubs, sponsors, suppliers, and television companies all have access to CAS.

NOTES ─────────────────────────────────

1. For further information on Olympic dispute resolution, see Mary Fitzgerald, "The Court of Arbitration for Sport: Doping and Due Process During the Olympics," *Sports Lawyer's Journal* 7 (spring 2000): 213.

2. The Romanian gymnast Andrea Raducan, sixteen, received a gold medal in the 2000 Sydney games. She was stripped of her medal after testing positive for a drug contained in a cold remedy. She appealed her case to CAS, but her appeal was rejected within days.

3. For additional information on CAS, see Chapter 5, section 5.3.5., "Court of Arbitration for Sport (CAS)."

1.5. INTERSCHOLASTIC ATHLETICS

High school athletics is governed at the national level by the National Federation of State High School Associations (NFSHSA) and at the state level, in all fifty states, by bodies such as the Massachusetts Interscholastic Athletic Association (MIAA). The legal issues involving high school athletic administrators are covered throughout the text, including injury liability (Chapter 4), constitutional law rights of high school athletes (Chapter 6), drug testing (Chapter 7), employment discrimination (Chapter 15), hiring issues (Chapter 8), and contracts (Chapter 9).

Considerable tort litigation has been been directed toward employees and volunteers of non-scholastic youth sports organizations (such as Little League and Pop Warner). The Youth Sports Volunteer Coalition (YSVC) was established to protect volunteers from what the YSVC calls "frivolous" lawsuits (see Chapter 4, section 4.4.3., "Civil Liability Immunity Legislation"). However, this protection varies by region, and thus a thorough knowledge of state laws is important for volunteers of youth sports. Finally, such volunteers should be aware of lawsuits involving gender discrimination that have occurred in non-scholastic sports. Even private organizations can be held liable for discrimination claims when certain criteria are met (see notes 1 and 2).

NOTES

1. In *Sternberg v. U.S.A. National Karate-Do Federation, Inc.*, 123 F. Supp. 2d 659 (E.D.N.Y. 2000), a member of a women's karate team brought suit against the sport's governing body after the body withdrew its women's team—though not its men's team—from the 1998 World Championships in Brazil. The judge ruled that the federation receives indirect financial assistance from the federal government, and that its activities are educational in nature, thus making Title IX's ban on gender discrimination applicable to its activities.

2. In *Fortin v. Darlington Little League, Inc.*, 376 F.Supp. 473 (D.R.I. 1974), rv'd, 514 F.2d 344 (1st Cir. 1975), an action was brought by a ten-year-old girl who was denied the opportunity to try out for Little League baseball solely because of her sex. Because the baseball park where the team played was public property, the appeals court found sufficient proof for state action, ruling in favor of the plaintiff.

1.6. INDIVIDUAL SPORT ISSUES

The courts in the United States have sometimes faced the question of whether to respect the autonomy of private organizations or to accommodate the public good. The sports world has increasingly emerged as an epicenter of this debate. Even private recreational organizations, such as country clubs, can be susceptible to significant financial damages by engaging in discrimination (see note 2). Furthermore, the PGA's lost legal battle with Casey Martin demonstrates how even the highest-profile sport organizations can be compelled to alter their established regulations (see note 1). Industry professionals working in these or similar associations can better understand laws of equal protection and the Americans with Disabilities Act after reading Chapters 8 and 16, respectively.

Professional athletes in sports governed by associations such as the PGA, LPGA, and ATP may not find the level of advocacy in their organizations that occurs in the unionized sports. As a result, athletes in these individual sports are on their own. One reason for this is because of the broad scope and goals of these organizations. For example, the PGA claims 26,000 members and a dedication to the promotion of the *game* of golf. By contrast, the National Basketball Players Association (a union) represents fewer than 500 active NBA players and states goals that are solely geared toward the promotion of *player* interests (see Chapters 11 and 12 for more information on players' unions). Furthermore, athletes in sports such as tennis and golf are not guaranteed income merely by participating in professional athletic competitions. Generally, such athletes earn income in two ways, tournament prize money and product endorsements. Due to the latter, the player agent becomes especially vital for athletes in these sports (see Chapter 12, section 12.2., "Player Agents").

NOTES ───

1. In the majority decision of *PGA Tour Inc. v. Casey Martin*, 532 U.S. 661 (2001), the U.S. Supreme Court determined that granting a disabled plaintiff a golf cart would not fundamentally alter the character of competition. Title III of the Americans with Disabilities Act (ADA) requires that a private business which accommodates the public must make "reasonable modifications . . . to individuals with disabilities, unless the entity can demonstrate that making such modifications would fundamentally alter the nature of such . . . accommodations." For more on the ADA and its potential impact on sports, see Chapter 16, Section 16.3.2., "Application to Athletic Organizations."

2. In *Borne v. The Haverhill Golf and Country Club, Inc.*, No. 96-6511-C, 1999 Mass. Super. LEXIS 523 (Mass. Super. Nov. 19, 1999) a jury in Massachusetts awarded $1.9 million to female plaintiffs who accused the private club of not extending full benefits of membership to women.

1.7. FACILITIES, AGENCY FIRMS, & MEDIA

Corporate mergers at the turn of the 21st century began to unite the three formerly distinct industry segments of facilities, agency firms, and media. In particular, strategic acquisitions by Clear Channel Inc. and International Management Group (IMG) have joined these three aspects of sport business. This vertical integration raises potential legal and conflict-of-interest issues.

For example, Tom Hicks holds a controlling interest in MLB's Texas Rangers, but is also vice chairman of Clear Channel Inc. Clear Channel also owns small shares of MLB's Colorado Rockies and Tampa Bay Devil Rays. However, Clear Channel's subsidiary SFX represented 15% of MLB players in 2001, as well as various athletes in other sports. In 2001, the Major League Baseball Players Association warned their members about this possible conflict of interest. In response, SFX created an autonomous company to represent baseball players. SFX hopes that this will quell concerns that their player agents answer to a boss with a vested interest in driving down player salaries.

In a separate matter, IMG was forced to end a sponsorship sales agreement with the NHL in 2001 after the NHL Players Association noted a league rule forbidding agents to represent both players and management. IMG sold sponsorships for the NHL in Europe, but also handled contract negotiations and endorsements for several NHL players, including Jaromir Jagr, Brett Hull and Sergei Federov. Although ultimately unsuccessful, TWI (IMG's baseball division) pursued talks to become producer and part owner of a New York Yankees cable television station.

Consequently, practitioners in these sectors should become cognizant of the antitrust issues in professional sports (see Chapter 11, "Labor Law"). At the same time, there are legal issues pertaining directly to facility owners (Chapter 4), agency firms (Chapter 12), and media (Chapter 14). Chapter 9 is directly relevant to all three sectors.

SUMMARY

This chapter has provided background on the organizations involved in the sports industry. The discussion included information on the structure, rules and procedures, power and authority, and types of litigation that can involve these organizations. The rest of the chapters provide further detail on areas of the law and types of litigation that occur. Case decisions will be discussed in more detail with additional description of the constituency group involved and the type of complaint, the legal arguments, and the court decisions. The reader should refer to this chapter if questions arise about the organizations and constituencies involved in the litigation discussions presented in the rest of the chapters.

THE COURT AND LEGAL SYSTEM IN THE UNITED STATES

INTRODUCTION

Directors of athletic organizations need a fundamental understanding of the legal system of the United States to deal effectively with the wide variety of legal matters they face today. While the overview given in this chapter is brief and general in nature, the reader can consult the notes for source materials that provide greater detail.

The purpose of the judiciary is to decide cases and controversies between parties by functioning as the neutral finder of fact (judge or jury). The judicial system in the United States is an adversarial one; that is, the parties, usually represented by lawyers, takes opposing sides when they appear before the judge or jury. It is thought that the adversarial approach to resolving legal disputes is the most effective way for the finder of fact to arrive at the truth and reach a fair decision.

The American legal system is based primarily on the common law traditions established in England. The law in every state has its roots in common law, except Louisiana, whose law is based on the French Civil Code. *Common law* is established when judges apply previous decisions (precedent) to present cases with similar facts or issues. It is to be distinguished from statutory law. The written decisions, called opinions, are binding on future decisions of lower courts within the same jurisdiction (*binding authority*). In addition, opinions may serve to function as *persuasive authority*, that is, advice for consideration to courts outside the deciding court's jurisdiction that are adjudicating a case with similar facts or issues.

Predictability and stability in the law are major objectives of the legal system. Parties should be able to regulate their behavior and enter into relationships with reasonable assurance of the governing rules of law. The principles of *stare decisis* (to abide by or adhere to decided cases) and precedent (an adjudged case which serves as the authority for identical or similar cases or questions of law that subsequently arise) serve to provide this continuity. In addition, each court (except the U.S. Supreme Court) is bound by the decisions of courts of higher authority. The ruling of a court sets precedent that may be altered only by a court of higher authority.

The court system in the United States is generally viewed as having three functions: (1) administering state and national laws, (2) resolving disputes among parties, and (3) interpreting the legislative intent of a law in deciding a case. These functions are generally related to providing remedy to a party that has been unlawfully affected. Two forms by which remedy can be provided are civil and criminal legal proceedings. Civil law is between private parties only, and provides individuals with a cause of action by which they may be compensated through the recovery of damages. Criminal law is between private parties and society. It is designed to protect the public from harm through the punishment of conduct likely to cause harm. The state is a party to criminal action whereby the state attempts to protect society.

There are two basic legal systems in the United States: the federal system and the state system. Chapter 2 begins with a description of the federal court system, which includes the U.S. Supreme Court, U.S. courts of appeals, U.S. district courts, and several administrative agencies. The chapter next discusses the state legal system, which consists of the primary sources of law in each state's constitution and court decisions in each state. Naturally, there is variation among state legal systems.

As important as understanding the legal system in the United States is knowing how to find legal information. The next section identifies and describes numerous legal sources that coaches and administrators may find useful. Chapter 2, section 2.3., "Civil Legal Process" describes the steps in a civil lawsuit. This information will assist the athletic administrator in understanding the trial process.

2.1. THE FEDERAL COURT SYSTEM

The federal court system in the United States consists of the Supreme Court, thirteen courts of appeals, ninety-four district courts, certain specialized courts, and administrative agencies (exhibit 2.1). Federal cases usually are first heard in a district court, although certain cases are initiated in the courts of appeals or in the Supreme Court. Cases that are appealed after being heard in the district courts usually go to a court of appeals or, in rare cases, directly to the Supreme Court. The thirteen courts of appeals (representing eleven judicial circuits, the District of Columbia, and the Federal Circuit) also review orders issued by administrative agencies such as the Securities and Exchange Commission, the Federal Trade Commission, the Internal Revenue Service, and the National Labor Relations Board.

The special federal courts include the U.S. Claims Court, the U.S. Court of International Trade, the U.S. Court of Military Appeals, the U.S. Tax Court, the U.S. Bankruptcy Court, and the Temporary Emergency Court of Appeals. The jurisdiction of these courts is rather narrow. For example, the U.S. Claims Court hears only cases in which individuals have a claim against the federal government, and the Court of International Trade hears civil actions against the United States arising from federal laws governing import and trade transactions. These courts generally are not of concern to athletic administrators.

2.1.1. U.S. Supreme Court

The U.S. Supreme Court is the highest court in the nation and the ultimate dispute arbitrator. Once the Supreme Court decides an issue, all other federal courts must interpret the law by its lead. The Supreme Court has two types of jurisdiction: original and appellate.

Original jurisdiction covers two types of cases: those involving ambassadors, ministers, and consuls, and those involving a state as one of the parties to a lawsuit. The Supreme Court hears very few cases under original jurisdiction. An example of a case heard under original jurisdiction is *Kansas* v. *Colorado*, 533 U.S. 1 (2001), which deals with a violation of the Arkansas River Compact relating to development of the River basin.

Appellate jurisdiction covers cases tried or reviewed by the individual states' highest court involving federal questions, including those bearing on the U.S. Constitution, congressional acts, or foreign treaties. It also covers cases tried or reviewed by the federal courts of appeals or the district courts. *Federal Baseball Club of Baltimore, Inc.* v. *National League of Professional Baseball Clubs*, 259 U.S. 200 (1922) is an example of a case heard under appellate jurisdiction; this case deals with the applicability of the antitrust laws to professional baseball.

A chief justice and eight associate justices sit on the U.S. Supreme Court. The

Exhibit 2.1
The United States Court System

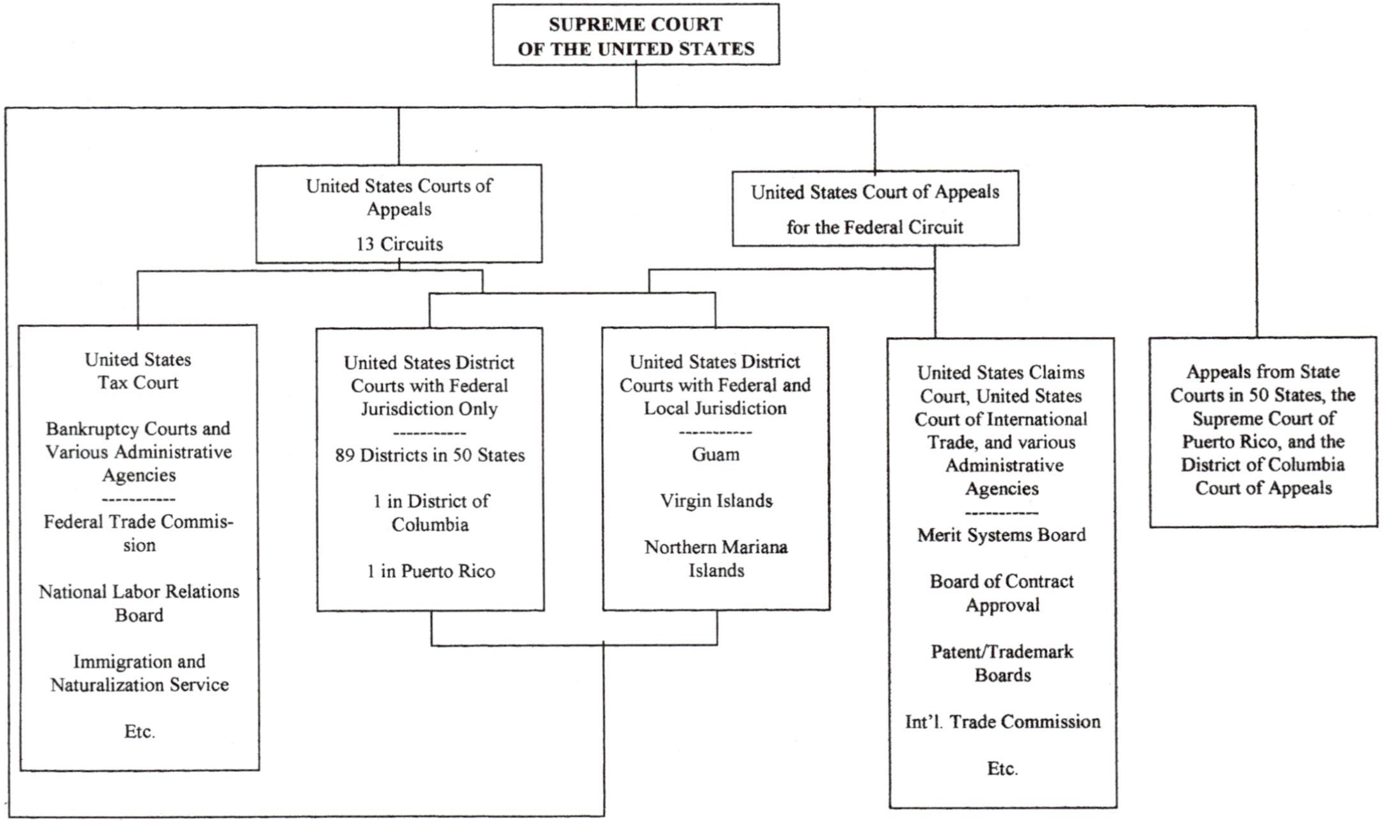

SUPREME COURT
OF THE UNITED STATES

United States Courts of
Appeals
13 Circuits

United States Court of Appeals
for the Federal Circuit

Appeals from State
Courts in 50 States, the
Supreme Court of
Puerto Rico, and the
District of Columbia
Court of Appeals

United States
Tax Court

Bankruptcy Courts and
Various Administrative
Agencies
- - - - - - - - -
Federal Trade Commis-
sion

National Labor Relations
Board

Immigration and
Naturalization Service

Etc.

United States District
Courts with Federal
Jurisdiction Only
- - - - - - - - -
89 Districts in 50 States

1 in District of
Columbia

1 in Puerto Rico

United States District
Courts with Federal and
Local Jurisdiction
- - - - - - - - -
Guam

Virgin Islands

Northern Mariana
Islands

United States Claims
Court, United States
Court of International
Trade, and various
Administrative
Agencies
- - - - - - - - -
Merit Systems Board

Board of Contract
Approval

Patent/Trademark
Boards

Int'l. Trade Commission

Etc.

nine justices are appointed by the President of the United States and confirmed by the U.S. Senate. They serve lifetime tenures. The chief justice receives a salary of $181,400, and the associate justices receive $173,600 each (2000).

The U.S. Supreme Court has broad discretion in determining whether to hear an appeal, with few exceptions. A person or party that wants a case to be heard by the Supreme Court must ask in an application for a *writ of appeal* where jurisdiction is mandatory, or a *writ of certiorari* where jurisdiction is discretionary. When the Supreme Court grants a writ, that case comes before the Court. A *writ of appeal* applies only to decisions made by three-judge federal district court panels that grant or deny injunctive relief. A *writ of certiorari* allows the Court to hear cases not covered by the writ of appeal. It is a written order to call up for review a case from a lower court. Four of the nine justices have to vote to review a case under a *writ of certiorari*. Certiorari gives the Supreme Court broad discretion in deciding which cases to review. It can be employed by the Court to review the following:

1. Any civil or criminal case from the federal court of appeals
2. Any state supreme court decision where the constitutionality of a federal or state statute or a treaty is questioned
3. Any state supreme court decision that rules a state statute violates federal law

The Supreme Court hears oral arguments from the attorneys for the parties when it decides to hear a case. Prior to oral arguments, the parties submit *briefs*, or written arguments, to the Court. Sometimes the Court allows a brief termed *amicus curiae*, or "friend of the court," to be submitted by third parties who believe that they (or the organization they represent) may be affected by the Court's decision in a case. For instance, in a 2001 Supreme Court case, *Casey Martin v. PGA Tour*, 532 U.S. 661 (2001), World Team Sports, an organization that creates and operates events which integrate athletes with disabilities with non-disabled athletes, was one of nine disabled sport organizations allowed to file an amicus brief.

Supreme Court decisions are made after the justices have heard the oral presentations and reviewed the briefs from both parties. Each justice renders an opinion on why a certain decision should be made, and then the justices vote in order of seniority. After a decision has been reached by majority vote, a justice is chosen to write the *opinion of the Court*. A justice who disagrees with the opinion and who did not vote with the majority may write a *dissenting opinion*. A justice who agrees with the majority opinion but not with the reasoning by which it was reached may write a *concurring opinion*. Other justices may join a dissenting or concurring opinion.

Some of the reasons that the overwhelming majority of cases filed at the trial level never reach the U.S. Supreme Court or the courts of appeals are the following: cases are settled; parties do not believe they will be successful on appeal; costs can be prohibitive; and appellate courts have discretion to refuse to hear an appeal. Cases that the appellate courts do review are those in which there may have been an error at the trial court level, those which involve novel legal issues, and those where the lower courts have been inconsistent in their decisions.

2.1.2. U.S. Courts of Appeals

There are thirteen U.S. Courts of Appeals. In addition to the eleven judicial districts, there are the District of Columbia and the United States Court of Appeals for the Federal Circuit (exhibit 2.2). The appeals courts have one type of jurisdiction, *appellate*. That means they review cases tried in the federal district courts and cases heard and decided by the federal regulatory commissions mentioned earlier.

2.1.3. U.S. District Courts

The district courts are the trial courts of the federal court system. Each state has at least one district court, and some of the larger states have as many as four. A total of ninety-four district courts cover the fifty states, the District of Columbia, the Commonwealth of Puerto Rico, Guam, the Virgin Islands, and the Northern Mariana Islands (see exhibit 2.3). Each district court has at least one federal district judge, and some have as many as twenty-seven.

2.1.4. Administrative Agencies

Rulings made by federal agencies such as the Federal Trade Commission, the Internal Revenue Service, and the National Labor Relations Board fall into the category of administrative law. For a number of reasons, notably specialization, efficiency, and flexibility, Congress and the state legislatures decided to grant certain judicial powers to administrative agencies such as those named in exhibit 2.1. These agencies are authorized to formulate rules for the administrative area they regulate, enforce the rules, hold hearings on any violations, and issue decisions, including penalties. This delegation of power to adjudicate controversies has been generally held to be constitutional, although the agencies must follow specific guidelines in their administration of these delegated powers. On the federal level, Congress has enacted the Administrative Procedure Act, which sets guidelines for the agencies to follow. Many states have similar state statutes. A party to an administrative law decision can appeal such decisions and sometimes obtain judicial review, depending on the nature of the dispute and whether all administrative remedies have been exhausted. It should be noted that absent abuse of discretion, courts give great deference to the decisions of administrative agencies.

2.2. THE STATE COURT SYSTEM

In general, state courts are similar in structure to the federal courts; the more important the court, the fewer they are in number. State courts, however, vary widely in nomenclature. In most states there is a three-tiered court system: a trial court level, an appellate level, and a supreme court level of review (see exhibit 2.4).

The lowest level of state courts, often referred to as inferior courts, may include the following: magistrate court, municipal court, justice of the peace, traffic court, and county court. Such tribunals handle only minor civil and criminal cases.

The superior courts are general jurisdiction trial courts, which hear the more serious offenses. Most jury trials occur here. Typically, these courts are organized

Exhibit 2.2
U.S. Courts of Appeals Locations

Circuit	Location	States
District of Columbia	Washington D.C.	
First	Boston, San Juan	Maine, Massachusetts, New Hampshire, Puerto Rico
Second	New York	Connecticut, New York, Rhode Island, Vermont
Third	Philadelphia, Virgin Islands	Delaware, New Jersey, Pennsylvania, U.S. Virgin Islands
Fourth	Richmond	Maryland, North Carolina, South Carolina, Virginia, West Virginia
Fifth	New Orleans, Fort Worth, Houston, Jackson	Louisiana, Mississippi, Texas
Sixth	Cincinnati	Kentucky, Michigan, Ohio, Tennessee
Seventh	Chicago	Illinois, Indiana, Wisconsin
Eighth	St. Louis, Kansas City, Omaha, St. Paul	Arkansas, Iowa, Minnesota, Missouri, Nebraska, North Dakota, South Dakota
Ninth	San Francisco, Honolulu, Los Angeles, Portland, Seattle	Arizona, California, Hawaii, Idaho, Montana, Nevada, Oregon, Washington
Tenth	Denver, Wichita, Oklahoma City	Colorado, Kansas, New Mexico, Oklahoma, Utah, Wyoming
Eleventh	Atlanta, Jacksonville, Miami, Montgomery, West Palm Beach	Alabama, Florida, Georgia
Federal	Washington D.C.	

Exhibit 2.3
U.S. District Court Locations

Alabama	3 districts (Northern, Middle, and Southern)
Alaska	1 district
Arizona	1 district
Arkansas	2 districts (Eastern and Western)
California	4 districts (Northern, Eastern, Central, and Southern)
Colorado	1 district
Connecticut	1 district
Delaware	1 district
District of Columbia	1 district
Florida	3 districts (Northern, Middle, and Southern)
Georgia	3 districts (Northern, Middle, and Southern)
Guam	1 district
Hawaii	1 district
Idaho	1 district
Illinois	3 districts (Northern, Central, and Southern)
Indiana	2 districts (Northern and Southern)
Iowa	2 districts (Northern and Southern)
Kansas	1 district
Kentucky	2 districts (Eastern and Western)
Louisiana	3 districts (Eastern, Middle, and Western)
Maine	1 district
Maryland	1 district
Massachusetts	1 district
Michigan	2 districts (Eastern and Western)
Minnnesota	1 district
Mississippi	2 districts (Northern and Southern)
Missouri	2 districts (Eastern and Western)
Montana	1 district
Nebraska	1 district
Nevada	1 district
New Hampshire	1 district
New Jersey	1 district
New Mexico	1 district
New York	4 districts (Northern, Southern, Eastern, and Western)
North Carolina	3 districts (Eastern, Middle, and Western)
North Dakota	1 district
Northern Mariana Islands	1 district
Ohio	2 districts (Northern and Southern)
Oklahoma	3 districts (Northern, Eastern, and Western)
Oregon	1 district
Pennsylvania	3 districts (Eastern, Middle, and Western)
Puerto Rico	1 district
Rhode Island	1 district
South Carolina	1 district
South Dakota	1 district
Tennessee	3 districts (Eastern, Middle, and Western)
Texas	4 districts (Northern, Southern, Eastern, and Western)
Utah	1 district
Vermont	1 district
Virgin Islands	1 district
Virginia	2 districts (Eastern and Western)
Washington	2 districts (Eastern and Western)
West Virginia	2 districts (Northern and Southern)
Wisconsin	2 districts (Eastern and Western)
Wyoming	1 district

Exhibit 2.4
A Typical State Court System

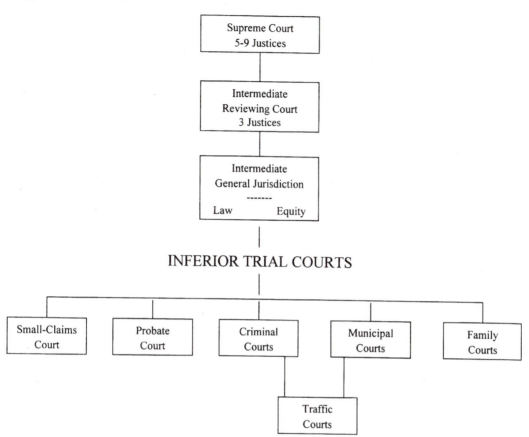

by counties. They hear appeals from the inferior courts and have original jurisdiction over major civil suits and serious crimes.

The highest state court, called either the appellate court, state court of appeals,
or state supreme court hears appeals from the state superior courts and in some
instances has original jurisdiction over particularly important cases. Some of the
larger states, such as New York and Pennsylvania, also have intermediate appellate courts.

Each state judicial system hears cases and reviews the law on the basis of its
state constitution, state statutes, and court decisions. In addition, a state court
often must interpret the federal constitution and/or federal statutes in terms of
how they impact state criminal or civil laws that are reviewed under its jurisdiction.

2.3. CIVIL LEGAL PROCESS

For many non-lawyers, a group that includes most athletic administrators, the
threat of litigation is a very upsetting proposition, with the potential of great
expense. However, with some basic information about how the trial system
works, the athletic administrator will be better able to assist counsel.

An athletic administrator should follow these basic guidelines when there is a possibility of a lawsuit:

1. Know your organization's attorney and insurance carrier. If some event occurs that may lead to litigation, inform them immediately so that they can take steps to protect your organization's interests.
2. In preparing for litigation, it is imperative to be completely honest and open about the facts of the case. Be prepared to supply any information or records that are needed for trial.
3. Do not talk to outsiders, especially the media, about the pending litigation.
4. If possible, review any alternatives for possible settlement of the case before it goes to trial.

 The civil legal process can be broken down into three major components: pre-trial, trial, and post-trial.

Pre-Trial
> The Complaint
> The Parties
> Court Jurisdiction
> The Summons
> The Answer
> Discovery
> Pre-Trial Motions

Trial
> Type of Court
> The Trial
> Judgment

Post-Trial
> Appeals Process

2.3.1. The Complaint

The plaintiff files the *complaint*, the initial pleading in a trial, in a civil case, as does the prosecutor (e.g., attorney general, district attorney) in a criminal case, *NFL* v. *Prime Time 24 Joint Venture*, 211 F.3d 10 (2d Cir. 2000) is an example of a civil case. The plaintiff, NFL, filed a civil complaint against Prime Time 24 Joint Venture for violating U.S. copyright law by retransmitting NFL game broadcasts to satellite subscribers in Canada.

To illustrate an example of a criminal case, in 2000, the Vancouver district attorney's office issued a criminal complaint against Marty McSorley, a professional hockey player, for assault with a weapon. McSorley delivered a blow to Donald Brashear's head with his stick in the closing moments of a hockey game.

2.3.2. The Parties

The *plaintiff* is a person or party that initiates a legal action by bringing a lawsuit against another person or party. The *defendant* is the person or party against whom relief or recovery is sought in a legal action or lawsuit. The defendant does the defending or denying of the charges brought by the plaintiff. Sometimes another party will be joined in litigation as a *third-party defendant* when its involvement is such as to make its presence at trial imperative. Athletic associations such as the National Collegiate Athletic Association (NCAA) are often named as third-party defendants. For instance, a student-athlete who is suing the school over an eligibility matter often names the NCAA (or athletic governing organization) as a third-party defendant, because the NCAA implements or oversees the regulations being enforced by the school against the student-athlete.

2.3.3. Court Jurisdiction

Two types of jurisdiction must be satisfied before a court can hear a case: personal and subject matter. *Personal jurisdiction* means that a court must have sufficient contact with the defendant to bring the defendant into its jurisdiction. Simply stated, the defendant must have some contact within the boundaries of that court's jurisdiction to be eligible to be brought into it for a trial. Some criteria that would be considered by a court to establish personal jurisdiction would be residency, voter registration, driver's license, or business activity. *Subject matter jurisdiction* means that the court must have authority to hear the subject matter that is being tried. For instance, a state court would not be the correct jurisdiction in which to bring a suit involving a federal law, which is within the subject matter jurisdiction of the federal courts.

2.3.4. The Summons

When filing a complaint, the plaintiff must make sure that notice of the legal action being instituted against the defendant is served. The *summons* is the actual serving of notice. The plaintiff (or prosecutor) serves a summons on the defendant ordering the defendant to "answer" the charge by a certain date. Often the summons is served by a process server or officer of the court, such as a sheriff. Until a complaint is lawfully served to the defendant, a court has no jurisdiction to review the dispute.

2.3.5. The Answer

The *answer* is the defendant's initial pleading on the alleged violation of criminal or civil law. The defendant may deny or admit to the allegations made by the plaintiff, and state his or her own facts about the matter in dispute. In some instances, a defendant may file a *counterclaim* against the plaintiff, which essentially means the defendant admits no guilt and, in fact, has been injured by the plaintiff.

2.3.6. Discovery

Discovery is a pre-trial procedure by which each party to a lawsuit obtains facts and information about the case from the other parties in order to assist the party's preparation for trial. Discovery is designed to do the following:

1. Discover facts and evidence concerning the case. It apprises the parties to the lawsuit of the nature of the claim to be litigated.

2. Bind the other party to a legal position. It is advantageous for the litigant to have the other party's legal position clearly stated in advance, so as to anticipate what legal arguments are likely to be argued and what witnesses and evidence will be introduced at the trial.

3. Seek out weaknesses in the other party's legal position.

4. Preserve testimony that may become unavailable at trial.

5. Narrow the issues in contention.

A party can ascertain information about the case being litigated from the other party to the lawsuit by using a number of methods. The three most common discovery techniques are depositions, interrogatories, and requests for production of documents. A *deposition* is an out-of-court examination of a witness to a lawsuit, under oath, during which questions and answers are recorded by a notary public or court official. An *interrogatory* is a set of written questions sent by one party involved in a lawsuit to another party involved in the litigation. The questions must be answered under oath and must be returned within a specific period. A *request for production of documents* is a request by one party involved in a lawsuit to the other to produce and allow for the inspection of any designated documents. The documents produced must be returned within a specific period.

2.3.7. Pre-Trial Motions

Pre-trial motions are proposed by either side concerning any number of legalities—for example, a motion to dismiss. In a motion, one of the parties to the suit is attempting to gain a better strategic position for the upcoming trial, or trying to have certain procedural matters settled prior to trial. For instance, a defendant may try to make a motion to dismiss because of a lack of sufficient grounds for the suit. Often, a judge will hold a pretrial conference in the judge's chambers in an effort to resolve the dispute or elements of the dispute before trial.

2.3.8. The Type of Court

The *trial court* is the court of original jurisdiction where all issues are brought forth, argued, and decided on by either a judge or a jury. The *appeals court* is the court of review where issues decided at trial are reviewed for error. No new evidence or issues may be entered. Generally, in order to be reviewed, an issue must have been objected to and put on the record at trial.

In the federal court system, original jurisdiction is limited to all criminal cases involving a federal law and civil cases that fall into the following categories:

Federal Question
(a) All civil actions arising under the Constitution, laws, or treaties of the United States
Diversity of Citizenship; Amount in Controversy; Costs
(a) All civil actions where the amount in controversy exceeds the sum or value of $75,000, exclusive of interest and costs, and is between
    1. Citizens of different states
    2. Citizens of a state and citizens or subjects of a foreign state

3. Citizens of different states, and citizens or subjects of a foreign state are additional parties
4. A foreign state as plaintiff and citizens of a state or of different states

In the state court system, original jurisdiction exists for all state law matters, including disputes among the state's citizens and disputes between one of its citizens and a citizen of another state when the out-of-state party has made itself amendable to the jurisdiction of the suing party's state courts. For example, the NCAA, which is located in Indiana, is often a party in state court actions because it is a national organization with members in all the states and therefore has the requisite contact with each state to make it amenable to each state's jurisdiction.

2.3.9. The Trial

Trials can involve a jury or they can take place without a jury present. Whether a trial will be a jury or a non-jury trial depends on the nature of the trial. Federal criminal cases require a trial by a jury of twelve persons. State criminal cases generally require a jury of no fewer than six persons. If a defendant pleads guilty or waives the right to a jury trial, a jury is not required. In civil cases a trial by jury is not always required, and may be waived. Jury size in civil cases may vary.

The state prosecutor in a criminal case or the plaintiff in a civil suit gives the *opening statement* to the court; then the defendant may do the same. The opening statement is designed to alert the triers of fact (either the judge or the jury, depending on the type of trial) to the nature of the case and to the types of evidence that will be presented during trial. Such statements set expectations and, when delivered correctly, can serve as the basis for a persuasive argument that will be presented during the trial.

After the opening statements have been made, the plaintiff (or the prosecutor) presents the case first. The plaintiff calls witnesses and examines them; the witnesses are cross-examined by the defendant (or the defense attorney), redirected by the plaintiff, and recrossed by the defendant. The defendant then presents its case and repeats the whole process—that is, the defense calls and examines its witnesses, and these witnesses are cross-examined by the plaintiff. After the witnesses are redirected by the defendant and recrossed by the plaintiff, both parties are allowed to call rebuttal witnesses.

At the conclusion of the trial, the defendant (or defense attorney) gives a closing statement first. Then the plaintiff (or prosecutor) gives a closing statement.

2.3.10. The Judgment

After the closing statements when a trial is being argued before a jury, the judge instructs the members of the jury on their options in reaching a decision based on the applicable state and/or federal law or laws. These instructions can be quite involved and are often a subject of appeal by the losing party. Case law and precedent are noted in the instructions. If any statutes are involved, they are read to the jury. After deliberation, the jury renders a decision.

In a trial without a jury, the judge can either recess the court while reaching a decision or render a decision immediately on completion of closing statements. Some decisions are given orally; others are written.

2.3.11. The Appeals Process

Many judgements by trial courts are *appealed*—that is, the party who lost the case requests that the trial proceedings be reviewed by a higher court in the hope that the decision will be reversed. Among the reasons allowed for an appeal are the following:

1. The plaintiff did not have an opportunity to state his or her case at trial.
2. Evidence was incorrectly allowed into or disallowed at the trial.
3. The judge interpreted the law incorrectly.

The party who takes an appeal from one court to another is called the *appellant*. The party in a case against whom an appeal is taken—the winning party at trial—is called the *appellee*.

In an appeals procedure, no new jury, no new witnesses, and no new facts are allowed to be introduced. The basis for appeal is the record, which may include copies of the testimony, exhibits, and any other evidence introduced at trial. Attorneys for the appellant and the appellee may appear before the court, argue their cases, and submit briefs.

An appeals court may *reverse* (disagree with) a lower court's ruling totally or in part. It may *remand* (return) the case back to the lower court for further proceeding, or it may *affirm* (agree with) the lower court's decision. After a decision has been rendered, the case may be appealed again, to either a state supreme court or the U.S. Supreme Court, depending on what court system is involved. (State supreme court cases involving a federal question—for example, a constitutional law claim—may in some circumstances be appealed to the U.S. Supreme Court.)

NOTES _____

1. Exhibit 2.5 contains a list of some of the legal and sports-related abbreviations used frequently in this text and in reported case decisions.

2. In any research involving a legal issue, or in preparation for litigation, an athletic administrator should attempt to answer some basic questions, including the following:

- Who are the plaintiffs in the case?
- Who are the defendants in the case?
- What are the legal theories of the plaintiffs?
- What are the defenses raised by the defendants?
- Is it state or federal court?
- Is it an administrative agency?
- Is it a decision on a pretrial motion?
- Is it a trial or appellate-level decision?
- What issue or issues did the judge have to decide in the case?
- For whom did the judge rule?
- What was the rationale for the judge's ruling?
- What is the impact of the case?
- Does the decision set any case precedent?

Exhibit 2.5
Glossary of Legal and Sports-Related Abbreviations

AAU	Amateur Athletic Union	n/a	not applicable
ABA	American Bar Association	NAIA	National Association of Intercollegiate
ABA	American Basketball Association		Athletics
AE	assignee	NASL	North American Soccer League
aff'd	affirm(ed)	NBA	National Basketball Association
AFL	American Football League	NBPA	National Basketball Players Assn.
agt	agent	NCAA	National Collegiate Athletic Assn.
AIAW	Association of Intercollegiate	neg	negligence
	Athletics for Women	NFHSAA	National Federation of High
ans	answer		School Athletic Associations
AR	assignor	NFL	National Football League
a/r	assumption of risk	NFLPA	NFL Players Association
b/c	because	NGB	National Governing Bodies
b/p	burden of proof	NHL	National Hockey League
br/K	breach of contract	NHLPA	NHL Players Association
c/a	cause of action	NJCAA	National Junior College Athletic
CBA	Continental Basketball Association		Association
c/c	counterclaim	OE	offeree
c/d	corpus delicti	OR	offeror
c/l	common law	P	plaintiff
c/n	contributory negligence	PE	promisee
Con	constitutional(ity)	p/f	prima facie or partner(ship)
corp	corporation	PGA	Professional Golf Association
c/p	condition precedent	PR	promisor
c/s	condition subsequent	Q	question (or issue)
ct	court	R	rule (or holding)
c/x	cross examination	rd/x	redirect examination
D	defendant	rem	remanded
d>	distinguish (compare)	rev'd	reversed
dem	demurrer	RIL	res ipsa loquitur
d/x	direct examination	RS	restatement
eq	equity	S	statute
ev	evidence	S/F	statute of frauds
g/r	general rule	TC	trial court
int	interest	TP	third party
IOC	International Olympic Committee	TPB	third party beneficiary
J	judgment	UCC	Uniform Commercial Code
J/aff'd	judgment affirmed	USBL	United States Basketball League
J/D	judgment for defendant	USFL	United States Football League
J/P	judgment for plaintiff	USOC	United States Olympic Committee
J/rev'd	judgment reversed	v	versus
K	contract	w	with
lcc	last clear chance	w/a	weight of authority
LPGA	Ladies Professional Golf Association	WFL	World Football League
maj	majority view	WLAF	World League of American Football
min	minority view	w/i	within
MISL	Major Indoor Soccer League	w/o	without
MLB	Major League Baseball	xn	action
MLBPA	MLB Players Association		

Note: Please see Glossary for specific term definitions.

2.4. SOURCES OF LEGAL INFORMATION

The athletic administrator should know how to locate legal information. Sources include legal dictionaries, directories, encyclopedias, indexes, treatises, guides, law reviews, state and federal constitutions and legislation, federal administrative rules and regulations, and case law.

2.4.1. Legal Reference Materials

2.4.1.1. Legal Dictionaries

Legal dictionaries contain definitions of words and functions that are commonly used in the legal system in the United States and other common law jurisdictions, such as Great Britain, Canada, and Australia. The following are three of the best and most popular legal dictionaries:

1. *Black's Law Dictionary*, 7th ed. (St. Paul, MN: West Group, 1999)
2. *Ballentine's Legal Dictionary and Thesaurus* (Albany, NY: Delmar Thomson Learning; 1995)
3. *Oran's Dictionary of the Law*, 3rd ed. (Albany, NY: West Legal Studies, 2000).

2.4.1.2. Legal Research Guides

Legal research guides are texts that explain how to conduct legal research. They include instruction on different sources of law and how best to utilize the sources. The athletic administrator will find the following guides most helpful:

1. Miles O. Price and Harry Bitner, *Effective Legal Research* (Buffalo, NY: William S. Hein, 1999). This guide is considered to be the most comprehensive, basic manual on legal research methods. It is clear and concise while providing in-depth descriptions of legal research sources.
2. J. Myron Jacobstein and Roy M. Mersky, *Fundamentals of Legal Research*, 8th ed. (Mineola, NY: Foundation Press, 2000).
3. Morris C. Cohen and Kent C. Olson, *Legal Research in a Nutshell* (Nutshell Series), 7th ed. (St. Paul, MN: West/Wadsworth, 2000) A condensed guide that briefs the reader on how to perform legal research. This book may be most appropriate for the athletic administrator's introduction to legal research material.
4. Stephen Elias, *Legal Research: How to Find and Understand the Law*, 10th ed. (Berkeley, CA: Nolo Press, 2002).

2.4.1.3. Annotated Law Reports

The American Law Reports (ALR) gives comprehensive annotations on legal subject matters. It consists of five series. An *annotation* is a commentary on how a particular legal subject developed and the current status of the law on that subject. The annotations in the *ALR* often include a list of cases that have discussed the point of law that the annotation explains. For a good example of an *ALR* annotation, see "Tort Liability of Public Schools and Institutions for Accidents Occurring During School Athletic Events," 35 *ALR* 3d 725.

2.4.1.4. Legal Encyclopedias

Legal encyclopedias are texts designed to give the reader a broad view of the law on any given legal subject. The following are two of the best:

1. *Corpus Juris Secundum (C.J.S.)* (St. Paul, MN: West Publishing Company, 1936–current date). *C.J.S.* was initially intended to be a compilation of the entire body of American law, however its new subtitle, "A Contemporary Statement of American Law as Derived from Reported Cases and Legislation," indicates it no longer references every case. There are over 150 actual volumes of this text.
2. *West's Encyclopedia of American Law* (St. Paul, MN: West Publishing Company, 1998).

2.4.1.5. Restatements of the Law

The *Restatements of the Law* are produced by communities of distinguished judges, law professors, and lawyers and provide the reader with a "black letter" rule in specific legal areas, such as torts, agency, contract, trusts, and property. In addition, the *Restatements* provide case authority and cross-reference to *ALR* annotations.

2.4.1.6. Treatises

Treatises are texts designed to give the user legal information on one particular legal subject. Some treatises are: Raymond Yasser, James McCurdy, C. Peter Gopeland, and M. Arellano Weston, *Sports Law Cases and Materials*, 4th ed. (Cincinnati, OH: Anderson, 1999); Robert C. Berry and Glenn M. Wong, *Law and Business of Sports Industries*, vols. 1 and 2 (Westport, CT: Praeger, 1993); and Michael J. Cozzillio and Mark S. Levinstein, *Sports Law: Cases and Materials* (Carolina Academic Press, 1997). Textbooks are narratives on a particular area of law (see, e.g., Michael E. Jones, *Sports Law* [Upper Saddle River, NJ: Prentice-Hall, 1999]; John C. Weinstart and Cym H. Lowell, *The Law of Sports* [Indianapolis: Bobbs, 1978]). Hornbooks are texts designed to produce rudimentary knowledge on a particular subject of law (see, e.g., *Understanding Business and Legal Aspects of the Sports Industry* [New York: Practicing Law Institute, 2000]).

2.4.1.7. Legal Indexes

Legal indexes are lists of articles that contain information on legal subjects, case decisions, and general legal information that has been published in law reviews and other legal periodicals. The following are legal indexes:

1. *Index to Legal Periodicals* (Bronx, NY: H. W. Wilson, 1908–current date). Includes periodicals published in the United States, Canada, Great Britain, Ireland, Australia, and New Zealand, and is therefore comprehensive in nature. The index is available in print, on Wilson Web, and on CD-Rom.
2. *Index to Periodical Articles Related to Law* (Dobbs Ferry, NY: Glanville, 1958–current date). Contains articles that appear to be of value and are not covered by the *Index to Legal Periodicals*. This index is useful in locating newly developing areas of law.
3. *Current Law Index* (CLI) (Foster City, CA: Information Access, 1980–current date). This index is issued monthly and provides access to over 900 legal and law related periodicals.
4. *Legaltrac* (Farmington Hills, MI: Gale Group, 1980–current date) is a CD-ROM database that indexes approximately 875 legal periodicals published in the United States,

Canada, the United Kingdom, Australia, and other major English-speaking countries, and is updated monthly.

2.4.1.8. Law Review Articles

Law reviews, published by law schools and administered by a student editorial board, contain current or historical articles that relate to the study of law and lawmaking (e.g., legal, legislative, entertainment, and sport law). A school usually publishes a general law review (e.g., *Boston College Law Review*), and many opt to publish additional reviews of specific areas of the law (e.g., *Seton Hall Journal of Sport Law*).

Law reviews are designed to add to the process of developing a better understanding of law and the legal process. This is accomplished by reviewing cases and the impact of decisions, analyzing the legal reasoning behind court decisions, reviewing legislative enactments, proposing reforms, and reviewing legal writings through book reviews (see notes 1–4).

NOTES _____

1. S. W. Miller, "What Do You Mean My Facility Is Obsolete?" *How 21st Century Technology Could Change Sports Facility Development.*" 10 *Marquette Sports Law Journal* (2000): 335.

2. Adam S. Taylor and M. Darren Traub, "Cureton v. NCAA: Scrutinizing Proposition 16 and the Consequences of Its Disparate Impact on Prospective Minority Student-Athletes." 7 *The Sports Lawyers Journal* (2000): 59.

3. Rob Remis and Diane Sudia, "Escaping Athlete Agent Statutory Regulation: Loopholes and Constitutional Defectiveness Based on Tri-Parte Classification of Athletes." 9 *The Journal of Sports Law* (1999): 1.

4. W. Kent Davis, "Why Is the PGA Teed Off at Casey Martin? An Example of How the Americans with Disabilities Act (ADA) Has Changed Sports Law." 9 *Marquette Sports Law Journal* (1998): 1.

2.4.1.9. Shepard's Citations

Citators are used to research reported case decisions to determine whether the case being researched has been cited as authority by another court or whether a reported case has been overruled, modified, or questioned in a later decision. They provide a complete history of any case since it was first reported. *Shepard's Citations* are available in print or online via *Lexis-Nexis*, a legal computer service (see below). *KeyCite* is the other major citator service. It is only available online through *Westlaw*, another legal computer service (see below).

2.4.1.10. Legal Computer Services

Legal computer services offer subscribers access through remote terminals to federal and state court decisions, annotated reports, statutes, law reviews, and so forth. They generally are the most up-to-date source for legal information. While students, professors, and administrators may have access to *LEXIS* through the school library, unfortunately the services are not readily available to the layperson. Further, they are expensive and require some training to use.

The two major legal computer services are *LEXIS* (New York: Mead Data Central) and *Westlaw* (St. Paul, MN: West Publishing Company).

The use of the Internet has emerged as a powerful tool for conducting legal research. The following are some resources that may be useful to access federal- and state-related information:

1. The Federal Judicial Center: http://www.fjc.gov/
2. U.S. Federal Court Finder, Emory Law Library: http://www.law.emory.edu/FEDCTS
3. The Federal Web Locator, Lycos: http://www.infoctr.edu/fwl/fedweb.exec.html
4. The State Court Locator: http://vls.law.vill.edu/locator/statecourt
5. State, local, and territorial: http://www.ll.georgetown.edu:80/lr/lg/state.html

2.4.2. Constitutions

A constitution is the written instrument that serves as the ultimate source of legal authority by which a government and the courts derive their power to govern and adjudicate. The courts in the United States use the federal Constitution or a state constitution as the source for interpreting whether enacted laws are constitutional and whether individual rights granted to citizens are legal. The laws and actions of a government must be consistent with the constitution of that government to be considered legal. A constitution may not always contain language that specifically covers every governmental action, and in such instances the courts must interpret the constitution broadly to include certain governmental actions that are not specifically covered in the constitution. Constitutions can be amended.

2.4.3. Legislation

Legislation is the process by which laws are enacted. Laws created by this process are also referred to as *statutes*. Federal legislation is enacted by the U.S. Congress. Very little federal legislation is geared specifically to amateur athletics. One notable exception is the Ted Stevens Olympic and Amateur Sports Act (36 U.S.C. §§ 220501–220529 Supp. IV 1998), which governs some of the operation of amateur athletics, especially the U.S. Olympic efforts, in the United States. It should be noted that non-sport-specific legislation may be applied to athletics. An example is Title IX, which governs education and applies to athletics because athletics pertains to the educational mission of an institution. Bills can be introduced by individual representatives or senators or groups of commissioned representatives or senators. Copies of pending legislation can be obtained by writing to the following addresses (enclose a self-addressed, gummed return label):

Senate Document Room	House Document Room
B04, Hart Senate Office Bldg.	B18 Ford House Office Building
Washington, DC 20510	Washington, DC 20515
(202) 228–2815	(202) 226–5200
www.senate.gov	www.hdocs@hr.house.gov

The public may receive up to six different items per request, but only one request will be filled per day. Also, only one copy of an individual item will be distributed at a time.

When legislation is enacted and first issued, it is called a *slip law*. Once a session of Congress ends, all the slip laws are published as a group and called *U.S. Statutes at Large*. This is a chronological list of legislation that has been enacted. Every six years, the *U.S. Statutes at Large* is codified—that is, arranged by subject—and published as the *United States Code* (U.S.C.). The *United States*

Code includes the public and permanent laws in effect, arranged alphabetically under fifty different titles. The annotated codes are also published by private firms; for example, the *United States Code Annotated* (U.S.C.A.) is published by West Group, and the *United States Code Service* (U.S.C.S.), is published by Lexis Law Publishing.

State legislation is enacted by the legislature in each state. As with federal legislation, very little state legislation is geared specifically to athletics. However, one example is Utah's Uniform Athlete Agents Act (15-9-101), which regulates athletes or sports agents. On the state level, bills are also introduced by individual legislators or groups of legislators. Copies of legislation can usually be obtained from the legislators or from the state office that handles legislative services. Each state publishes all the laws that it has passed in a given year. These are called *session laws*. Session laws are compiled into statutes, which may be single or multivolume editions. Annotated editions are usually available from private publishing companies.

2.4.4. Federal Administrative Rules and Regulations

Federal administrative rules and regulations attempt to translate enacted laws into practices that must be followed in order to comply with the law. For instance, when Congress enacted Title IX of the Education Amendments of 1972—a federal statute that prohibited gender discrimination in education (see Chapter 8)—the Department of Health, Education and Welfare had to develop rules and regulations to be followed in order to comply with the new law.

2.4.5. Case Law

Although this book is not written as a case law text, case law is often cited to give the athletic administrator a better understanding of a legal point in sports law by providing an actual set of circumstances tried before a court. In the Notes sections, case law is provided to give the athletic administrator a source for further information on a sports law subject.

A case law citation consists of a case title and a case citation. The case title explicitly identifies the persons or parties involved. The case citation includes the publication in which the decision can be found, the volume and the page number in the corresponding reporter, the court that made the decision, and the year the case was decided.

The best reference for checking the correct form for legal decisions or writings is *The "Blue Book," A Uniform System of Citation*, 17th ed. (Cambridge, MA: Harvard Law Review Association, 2000). Case decisions and opinions are reported in different legal sources depending on the jurisdiction of the court that decided the case, as is illustrated below.

2.4.5.1. U.S. Supreme Court

All opinions that result from a Supreme Court case are reported in the following publications:

1. *United States Reports* (official reporter), Washington, USGPO; cited U.S.
2. *Supreme Court Reporter* (St. Paul, MN: West, 1939–1957), cited S.Ct. Replaced by *United States Supreme Court Reports*.

3. *United States Supreme Court Reports*. Lawyers' edition (Rochester, NY: Lawyers Co-operative Publishing, 1956–1997), cited L.Ed. or L.Ed.2d. Replaced by *United States Reports: Supreme Court Reporter* and *United States Supreme Court Reports* are unofficial reporters. Most lawyers and researchers use the unofficial sets because they include editorial features known as annotations, which are explanatory comments about the issues and holding of the opinion.
4. *United States Law Week* (Washington, DC: Bureau of National Affairs), cited U.S.L.W. The publication is composed of two looseleaf volumes; one contains the current opinions of the U.S. Supreme Court, and the other volume deals with matters that do not relate to the U.S. Supreme Court.

Only a small percentage of cases that are filed on the trial level ever reach the Supreme Court for the following reasons: cases are settled; parties do not believe they will be successful on appeal; costs can be prohibitive; and appellate courts can refuse to hear an appeal. Cases that the appellate courts do review are those in which there may have been an error at the trial court level or ones that may involve important questions of law. Even so, former chief justice Warren Berger often complained that the U.S. court system does not filter out enough cases and that the Supreme Court is overburdened. Some critics of the judicial system believe an additional level of judicial review between the courts of appeals and the Supreme Court is needed.

Exhibit 2.6
Regional Reporters

Pacific Reporter (P. or P.2d)	Alaska, Arizona, California, Colorado Hawaii, Idaho, Kansas, Montana, Nevada, New Mexico, Oklahoma, Oregon, Utah, Washington, and Wyoming
North Western Reporter (N.W. or N.W. 2d)	Iowa, Michigan, Minnesota, Nebraska, North Dakota, South Dakota, and Wisconsin
South Western Reporter (S.W. or S.W. 2d)	Arkansas, Kentucky, Missouri, Tennessee, and Texas
North Eastern Reporter (N.E. or N.E. 2d)	Illinois, Indiana, Massachusetts, New York, and Ohio
Atlantic Reporter (A. or A. 2d)	Connecticut, Delaware, Maine, Maryland, New Hampshire, New Jersey, Pennsylvania, Rhode Island, Vermont, and District of Columbia Municipal Court of Appeals
South Eastern Reporter (S.E. or S.E. 2d)	Georgia, North Carolina, South Carolina, Virginia, and West Virginia
Southern Reporter (So. or So. 2d)	Alabama, Florida, Louisiana, and Mississippi

Exhibit 2.7
Case Citation

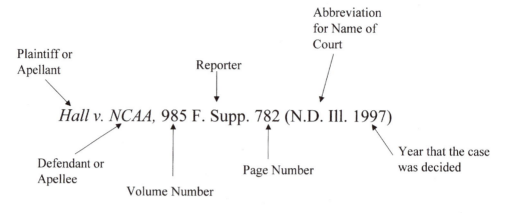

2.4.5.2. U.S. Courts of Appeals

Decisions of the appeals courts (also called appellate courts) are reported in the *Federal Reporter* (Minneapolis, MN: West Publishing Company) and are cited F., F. 2d, or F. 3d, depending on the date of the court decision. The *Federal Reporter* has now limited the number of published opinions because of the caseload.

2.4.5.3. U.S. District Courts

Select decisions of the district courts are reported in the *Federal Supplement* (Minneapolis, MN: West Publishing Company) and are cited F. Supp. or F. Supp. 2d. In a district court opinion, the district involved is always included as a part of the citation. For example, D.N.J. 2001 is the citation for District of New Jersey, 2001. When there is more than one federal district court in a state, the particular district involved in the decision is cited. For example, S.D.N.Y. 2001, is the citation for Southern District of New York, 2001, which differentiates it from the Northern District of New York, 2001, or N.D.N.Y. 2001.

On the trial level of review, a case citation usually notes the plaintiff first and the defendant second. For example, in *Rodriquez v. Topps Co.*, 104 F. Supp. 2d 1224 (S.D.Cal. 2000), Rodriquez is the plaintiff and Topps Co. is the defendant.

2.4.5.4. State Courts

State court decisions can be reported (although only a small percentage are) in a state or regional collection of reports called a *reporter*. A regional reporter groups decisions from a number of states in one publication. The regional reporters as a group are termed the *National Reporter System*, which is published by the West Publishing Company and includes West's federal law reports and some additional special court reporters. The *National Reporter System* provides a quick method of making the opinions of the state courts known to the public. The seven regional reporters are listed in exhibit 2.6.

The main components of a case citation are illustrated in exhibit 2.7.

Chapter 3

LEGAL PRINCIPLES IN TORT LAW

INTRODUCTION

Tort law is an important area of sports law. There has been an increase in the number of cases filed based on intentional or unintentional tort theories over the past several decades. There are many reasons for this increase, including the astronomical rise in medical costs that injured athletes or other plaintiffs are unable to meet, along with a prevailing notion that one who injures deliberately or negligently should pay for such actions when they create serious harm.

Civil law provides injured individuals with a cause of action by which they may be compensated or "made whole" through the recovery of damages. This cause of action comes under the general heading of torts. A *tort* is a private (or civil) wrong or injury, suffered by an individual as the result of another person's conduct. Tort law deals with the allocation of losses via monetary compensation of the individual for injuries sustained as a result of another's conduct.

Civil law and criminal law share the common end of inducing people to act for the benefit of society by preventing behavior that negatively affects society and by encouraging behavior that has a positive effect. Civil law and criminal law differ, however, in their means of achieving this common end. Criminal law is designed to protect the public from harm through the punishment of conduct likely to cause harm. Civil law, on the other hand, aims to compensate (to make whole) an injured party for the harm suffered as a result of another person's conduct.

Criminal actions emphasize the immorality or bad intentions of the defendants. Tort actions, on the other hand, seek to achieve desirable social results by resolving the conflicting interests of individuals. Society tends to distinguish criminal wrongs by condemning or judging the morality of the criminal more severely than that of the tortious wrongdoer. Once a crime has been discovered, the state or a subdivision of the state (e.g., county), in its capacity as protector of the public interest, brings an action against the accused. In a tort action, however, the injured party institutes the action as an individual in an effort to recover damages as compensation for the injury received. It is important to distinguish between intentional and unintentional torts. The responsibility of distinguishing between intentional and unintentional torts lies with the court because the court determines the manner in which it will assess the case. The degree of the defendant's intent toward the plaintiff (intent of harm) can be differentiated on the following three levels:

1. Intentional tort (e.g., assault and battery): intent to commit the act and intent to harm the plaintiff

2. Reckless misconduct or gross negligence: intent to commit the act, but no intent to harm the plaintiff

3. Unintentional tort or negligence: no intent to commit the act and no intent to harm the plaintiff, but a failure to exercise reasonable care.

Reckless misconduct (also called gross negligence) falls somewhere between intentional torts and ordinary negligence. It differs from negligence in degree rather than in substance. The court may view a single act either as negligent or as grossly negligent, depending on the state of mind of the actor.

Unintentional and intentional torts are the most common tort actions in the sports setting. *Negligence, an unintentional tort; reckless misconduct,* somewhere between intentional and unintentional torts; and *assault and battery*, intentional torts, are therefore emphasized in the first part of the chapter. The section on intentional torts includes a discussion of *tortious interference with contractual relations*, a tort that recognizes a cause of action against one who intentionally induces another to breach a contract. The less common torts of *invasion of privacy* and *intentional infliction of emotional distress* are followed by a discussion of defamation law and the issues of libel and slander. The chapter then discusses *products liability law*, a growth area in sports because it allows a party who has been injured by a product (e.g., sports equipment) that is defectively designed, manufactured, or distributed to recover damages. The doctrine of *vicarious liability*, often used in tort cases to sue an employer for the negligence of employees, is presented next. Finally, the chapter concludes with an examination of *workers' compensation* issues present in amateur athletics.

3.1. THE TORT OF NEGLIGENCE

Negligence is an unintentional tort that focuses on an individual's conduct or actions. Accordingly, negligence is distinguished from intentional torts, which focus on the individual's state of mind or intent.

Negligent conduct is defined as the failure to use ordinary care and caution, as would be expected by a prudent person, for the protection of others against an unreasonably great risk of harm.

The ability of the injured party to sue and to recover damages for negligence is based on the idea that one who acts should anticipate the consequences of those actions that might involve unreasonable danger to others.

A person must take precautions only against unreasonable risks of harm. Unreasonable risks are those whose danger is apparent or should be apparent to one in the position of the actor. The law, however, does not seek to burden the freedom of human action with excessive or unreasonable demands and restraints. Therefore, one is not expected to guard against situations or occurrences that are unlikely to happen. The reasonable person standard measures the standard of care required. The reasonable person is one who selects a course of action that would be selected by an ordinary, prudent person residing in the affected community under the same conditions. The law excuses all persons from liability for accidents that are either unavoidable or unforeseeable.

The following four elements must be proven by the plaintiff in order to sustain a negligence claim:

1. Duty of care owed by the defendant
2. Breach of that duty by the defendant
3. Actual and proximate causation
4. Damages

3.1.1. Duty of Care Owed

The plaintiff in a negligence case must initially establish the duty of care owed to him or her by the defendant. Duty is divided into two categories: a duty to act and a duty not to act in an unreasonable manner. A *duty of care* is an obligation, recognized by law, that requires an individual or a group to conform to a particular standard of conduct toward another. A general duty of care governs all activities. A person engaged in an activity has a legal duty to act as an ordinary, prudent, reasonable person, and thereby take precautions against creating unreasonable risks of injury to other persons. A person need only take precautions against foreseeable risks of injury. Other factors, such as statutes or status of the parties (e.g., doctor or coach), may limit or extend this general duty.

The duty of care required of an individual is established by reference to any special qualifications. In the case of a professional (e.g., doctor or trainer), a duty of care is determined by uniform requirements that establish minimum standards of behavior. All professionals are judged not as individuals in society at large but as members of a specified class. When acting in a professional capacity, the professional person will be judged by the standards of the profession in the same or similar communities in existence at the time.

The concept of *legal duty* is based on the relationship that exists between the parties involved. Certain relationships, such as employer-employee, principal-agent, teacher-student, and coach-athlete, establish a legal duty to act. An employer, for example, has the duty to render aid and assistance to an employee who is injured during the course of employment. However, absent a duty-imposing relationship, an individual is not liable for an omission to act.

A moral obligation to act does not create a legal duty to act, and hence the individual who failed to act cannot be held liable for negligence. If one without a duty to act does undertake to act, however, that person may be held liable if he or she acts negligently. By acting, one can create a duty between oneself and another that may not have previously existed. For example, a person who undertakes to rescue another may not abandon the rescue attempt if it becomes inconvenient. By acting, the would-be rescuer has created a duty to continue to aid the person in trouble.

In sports cases the duty is often described as the "reasonable care" necessary to avoid creating risks that may result in injuries to players or spectators. For example, Peter Perry suffered a serious neck injury in a high school football practice. Coach Foot attempted to provide medical assistance. In doing so, he became responsible for causing further damage that left Peter paralyzed. Peter may prevail in a negligence suit against the coach if the court finds that Coach Foot had a duty to act, and breached that duty by not acting as a "reasonable football coach" would have acted in this situation, causing actual damage.

The determination of a legal duty will rest on whether the court designates the act or non-act as misfeasance, nonfeasance, or malfeasance. *Misfeasance* is the term applied to lawful conduct that is improperly done. *Nonfeasance* is an omission of an action that ought to be taken. *Malfeasance* is the doing of an act that is wholly wrongful and unlawful.

NOTES

1. In *Howell v. Calvert*, 1 P.3d 310 (Kan. 2000), the Supreme Court of Kansas ruled that the district court did not err in instructing a jury that a private college owed a duty of care to two student athletes who were killed by a truck during a mandatory conditioning run.

2. In *Sammis v. Nassau Suffolk Football League*, 693 N.Y.S.2d 237 (N.Y. App. Div. 1999), the Supreme Court of New York upheld a summary judgment ruling that the defendant had no duty to warn the plaintiff of an obvious danger. The plaintiff was injured while helping move a cardboard box out of an elevated shaft in an equipment

shed. The defendant had been in the shed approximately 30 times before the instance of injury.

3. In *Boyd v. Texas Christian University, Inc.*, 8 S.W.3d 758 (Tex. App. 1999), a student at a private university and his parents sued the university after the student was seriously injured in a fight at an off-campus bar with four football scholarship athletes attending the same university. The plaintiffs alleged that the university was negligent in failing to properly supervise and discipline athletes, and failing to provide a safe environment for the student. The university was granted summary judgment, and the student appealed. As a matter of first impression, the Court of Appeals held that the university owed the student no duty to control student-athletes during an off-campus event that was not organized or sponsored by the university, and the university did not have a duty to protect students at an off-campus bar.

4. In *May v. Mitchell Brothers*, 712 So. 2d 622 (La. Ct. App., 1st Cir., 1998), a senior citizen passerby sued the operator of a milk-bottle-toss game after he was hit in the face by a softball that deflected out of an enclosed booth; the court held that the danger was not unreasonable and that the passerby should have been aware of the dangers of traveling close to the booth.

5. In *Jordan v. Maple Ski Ridge, Inc.*, 645 N.Y.S.2d 598 (N.Y. App. Div. 1996), plaintiff, a novice skier, was injured when one of her ski bindings released during a ski lesson at a resort. The court ruled that the defendant, who was "not involved in the rental, inspection, maintenance or adjustment of [plaintiff's] ski equipment," had no duty to the plaintiff relative to this injury.

6. In *Kleinknecht v. Gettysburg College*, 989 F.2d 1360 (3rd Cir. 1993), the litigants confront the issue of a college's duty of care to recruited college athletes who become injured during participation in their sports. The issue of reasonable care is relevant because an institution has a greater duty of care for recruited athletes, who are engaging in their recruited activity, than it has to students under normal circumstances. The appellate court reversed the district court's holding that the college acted reasonably and also dismissed the district court's holding that the college was entitled to immunity under the Good Samaritan law.

3.1.1.1. Reasonable Person Standard

Even if a particular relationship does not exist between parties, a person owes to others the duty of exercising reasonable care in his or her activities. The courts "measure" the conduct in each negligence case against the "reasonable person" standard—that is, how a person of ordinary sense, using ordinary care and skill, would react under similar circumstances. It is important to note that the conduct of the "reasonable person" is not necessarily "perfect" conduct but is that of a prudent and careful individual. As employed by the courts, the standard of reasonableness takes into account the risk apparent to an actor, the capacity of the actor to meet the risk, and the circumstances under which the person must act.

The "reasonable person" possesses a minimum level of knowledge common to the community in which the injury occurs. A negligent defendant who possesses superior knowledge, skill, or intelligence will be held to a greater degree of care—that is, conduct which conforms to that of others with similar knowledge and/or skill. For example, a team doctor performing a procedure on an athlete on the playing field would be held to the same standard of skill and conduct exhibited by other team doctors in the same specialty performing a similar procedure. When the reasonable person standard entails a degree of skill or knowledge higher than that of a judge or layperson sitting on a jury, qualified expert testimony is utilized to establish the proper standard of care for the defendant.

Again, using the case of a team doctor sued for negligence, both parties would probably call as witnesses other qualified team doctors to testify as to how the procedure is usually performed and what precautions or steps are taken under normal circumstances. This expert testimony would help establish the appropriate standard of care. The jury would then determine whether the defendant doctor met that standard of care.

The reasonable person is deemed to possess physical characteristics identical to those of the defendant. If the actor is exceptionally strong, for example, the standard of care demands that the person exhibit conduct which parallels that of a reasonably prudent person of like strength under similar circumstances. The reasonable person standard does not take into account the temperament or emotions of the individual actor. The law seeks an objective standard, not a subjective one based on a person's mental attributes. There are several reasons for this. First, it would be extremely difficult, if not impossible, to prove what was in an individual's mind at the time of the particular conduct. Second, the harm caused by a negligent act is not changed by the actor's particular thoughts or feelings. Finally, the courts have determined that a person must learn to conform to the standards of the community and to pay for violating those standards.

It is argued that in extreme cases of mental deficiency, the actor cannot comprehend the danger inherent in certain conduct. In the past, the courts applied the reasonable person standard when dealing with insane defendants. This was based on the public policy consideration of promoting the responsibility of guardians for those in their care. Recently, courts have held that insane persons are not negligent if their mental state prevented them from understanding or avoiding the danger. A "greater degree of care" may be required when dealing with an inherently dangerous object or an activity in which it is reasonably foreseeable that an accident or injury may occur.

NOTES

1. In addition to the notes below, the standard of care for persons working in the sports industry, such as that for sports facility owners, is described in greater detail in Chapter 4.

2. In *Moulas v. PBC Productions, Inc.*, 570 N.W.2d 739 (Wis. Ct. App. 1997), a spectator at a hockey game who was struck by a puck sued the owners of the team and the arena. The court of appeals ruled that the arena had exercised reasonable care in installing high plastic protective barriers. The court adhered to the precedent set in baseball cases, which absolves facility owners from liability for injuries sustained by patrons who are hit with flying objects (balls and bats).

3. In *Mozier v. Parsons*, 852 F. Supp. 925 (D. Kan. 1994), defendants requested summary judgment after plaintiffs sued them for the wrongful drowning death of their 3½ year old daughter. Plaintiff's daughter had drowned in a backyard swimming pool, while plaintiff was a social guest (licensee) of the defendants. The swimming pool was not protected by a gate or locked door. The defendants requested summary judgment based on the fact that, under Kansas law, a possessor only owes a licensee the duty to refrain from "willfully, wantonly, or recklessly injuring him or her." However, the plaintiffs defeated the defendants' motion for summary judgment by citing the "attractive nuisance doctrine." The attractive nuisance doctrine raises a possessor's standard of care vis-à-vis children— even children who trespass. According to the case, the Kansas Supreme Court has described the attractive nuisance doctrine as follows: A possessor of land is subject to liability for bodily harm to children intruding thereon caused by some condition that he maintains on the premises if:

(1) the possessor knows, or in the exercise of ordinary care should know, that young children are likely to trespass upon the premises, and

(2) the possessor knows, or in the exercise of ordinary care should know, that the condition exists and that it involves an unreasonable risk of bodily harm to young children, and

(3) the children because of their youth either do not discover the condition or understand the danger involved in coming into the dangerous area, and

(4) one using ordinary care would not have maintained the condition when taking into consideration the usefulness of the condition and whether or not the expense or inconvenience to the defendant in remedying the condition would be slight in comparison to the risk of harm to children.

3.1.1.2. Standard of Care for Children

Children as defendants in a negligence case present an important exception to the reasonable person standard. Children are not held to the same objective standard of duty that is applied to adults. The courts recognize that at young age levels there exists a wide range of mental capabilities and experiences. The law attempts to accommodate for this range by viewing the reasonable child as one who exercises in his or her actions a degree of care that is to be expected of children of like age, intelligence, and experience. For example, in a baseball game, an eleven-year-old boy swung at a pitched ball and missed it; the bat slipped from his hands, struck his teammate in the head, and caused serious injuries. The court held that there was no negligence because the batter exercised a reasonable degree of care for a person of his age, intelligence, and experience. However, under this more subjective standard, it follows that if a six-year-old boy has intelligence vastly superior to that of his peers, the child will be held to the standard of care encompassing his superior knowledge.

Several states have established age brackets that purport to distinguish childhood from adulthood. This method has been criticized, however, because of the problems inherent in setting an accurate age level guideline regarding mental capabilities. An exception to the application of this subjective standard for children occurs when a child engages in an activity normally reserved for adults, such as driving an automobile or hunting with a gun. In cases such as these, the courts in many jurisdictions will apply the reasonable standard for adults without any special consideration of the fact that the individual is a child.

3.1.2. Breach of Duty Owed

Once a plaintiff has demonstrated that the defendant owed the plaintiff a duty of care, the plaintiff must prove the defendant violated this duty by establishing that the defendant's conduct imposed an unreasonable risk of harm on the plaintiff. There are three methods by which the plaintiff may sustain this burden of proof:

1. Direct evidence of negligence
2. Violation of a statute
3. Res ipsa loquitur.

Direct evidence of negligence is evidence tending to establish negligence through firsthand proof of actual factual occurrences. A prime example of direct evidence is eyewitness testimony. For instance, Larry Lacrois suffered an injury to his back in a high school lacrosse game. The athletic trainer told Coach Winatallcosts not to allow Larry to play and later served as a eyewitness against the coach at the trial. Coach Winatallcosts, ignoring the trainer's warning, coerced Larry to play the last ten minutes because the state championship was on the line. As a result of further play, Larry was more severely injured. Coach Winatallcosts breached the duty of care he owed Larry. The trainer's testimony and the injury constituted the direct evidence.

When direct evidence is not available, certain procedural devices are used to enable a plaintiff to prove his or her case. One such device is a presumption. A *presumption* is a legal fiction that requires the judge or jury to assume the existence of one fact on the basis of the existence of another fact or group of facts. It is used in the absence of sufficient direct evidence to prove the fact itself. The classic example is the common legal presumption that a person who has been gone seven years without explanation is dead. Another type of presumption involves an individual who violates a valid statute.

NOTE

1. In *Rose v. Diocese of Bridgeport*, No. CV92-0293727, 1993 Conn. Super. LEXIS 880 (Apr. 16, 1993), plaintiff was injured during a long jump event at a track meet. Plaintiff alleged that the high school athletic conference and its president were negligent in that they "(a) failed to inspect the landing pit to insure that it did not contain foreign objects; (b) failed to adequately supervise the track meet; (c) failed to adequately train its employees and staff in the care and maintenance of the track facilities; (d) used large rocks around the landing pit and allowed these rocks to be in the pit; (e) failed to provide adequate regulations to provide for the care, maintenance, and supervision of the athletic facilities." The court denied defendants' motion to strike the complaint against them.

3.1.2.1. *Violation of a Statute, Negligence* Per Se

Violation of a statute is sometimes referred to as *negligence per se*. Negligence per se means that upon finding a violation of an applicable statute, there is a conclusive presumption of negligence. This conclusive presumption requires that a jury find for the plaintiff, although the plaintiff still has to prove the amount of damages. It does not allow the jury to weigh all the evidence and independently determine the relative liabilities of the parties. Although in some states, the violation of a valid statute may be considered negligence per se, in other states, the violation of a statute, ordinance, or administrative regulation is deemed only evidence of negligence.

Presumptions, however, are rebuttable. Once a court uses a presumption, the opposing party may rebut that presumption with factual information. The current trend is away from viewing violations of statutes as negligence per se. When a violation of a statute is treated as evidence of negligence and not negligence per se, it is accorded a different weight. A jury will not be required to conclude negligence; instead, a violation merely establishes an inference of negligence that may or may not be accepted by the jury.

In order for a statutory violation to provide evidence of negligence, the complaining party must establish two points. First, the statutory violation must be causally related to the plaintiff's harm. If an individual's taillights are out in violation of a statute, that violation may be used to establish negligence only when the failure of the taillights causes an accident. The second factor to be considered is that if the driver of one car pushes another car into a wall, the fact that the pusher's car taillights do not work in violation of a motor vehicle safety statute is of little or no significance.

3.1.2.2. Res Ipsa Loquitur

The last method of establishing the negligence of the defendant is through the use of the legal doctrine of *res ipsa loquitur* ("The thing speaks for itself"). Res ipsa loquitur permits the fact finder to infer both negligence and causation from circumstantial evidence. It is, in effect, another type of presumption. The plaintiff must establish that more likely than not, the harm to the plaintiff was a result of the defendant's negligence. In order to defeat the application of this doctrine, the defendant must establish that there is another, equally believable explanation of the injury to the plaintiff.

The most common types of cases utilizing res ipsa loquitur involves airplanes and elevators. When those machines fail, it is almost always because of the operator or supervisor's negligence. The possibility that the operator or supervisor can rebut this presumption by demonstrating "another, equally believable explanation" of plaintiff's injuries is obviously minimal.

Res ipsa loquitur is strictly a procedural device designed to allow a plaintiff to establish an otherwise unprovable case. In negligence cases, direct evidence of the defendant's negligence may not be available. This doctrine allows a plaintiff to recover on the basis of what probably happened. The following three requirements must be met before the doctrine will be applied:

1. The event ordinarily does not occur except through the negligence of someone.
2. The plaintiff must show that the instrument which caused plaintiff's injury was in the exclusive control of the defendant at the relevant time.
3. The plaintiff must show that his or her injury was not due to plaintiff's own action.

NOTES _____

1. In *Hale v. City of Jefferson*, 6 S.W. 3d 187 (Mo. Ct. App. 1999), a child suffered severe jaw injuries after he caught his tooth on an allegedly defective waterslide at a public pool. The court barred the use of res ipsa loquitur to determine whether a ¼" raised lip on the waterslide was the proximate cause of the plaintiff's injuries, as other reasonable explanations for the injury existed.

2. In *Grauer v. State of New York*, 181 N.Y.S.2d 994 (N.Y. App. Div. 1959), the plaintiff successfully raised the doctrine of res ipsa loquitur, when the ski lift chair that he attempted to sit on swung or was tipped such that it struck the back of his leg, fracturing it. The court held for the plaintiff as the defense presented no other reasonable causes for the plaintiff's injury.

3.1.3. Actual and Proximate Causation

The primary issue in the area of causation is that of proximate cause, that is, whether the defendant's negligent act is sufficiently closely related to the defendant's action that liability should attach, which means that the injury is reasonably foreseeable. Before the defendant's actions will be deemed the proximate cause of plaintiff's injury, the defendant's conduct must be shown to be the actual "cause in fact" of the plaintiff's harm. If the same harm would have resulted if the negligent act had never occurred, then the act is not the actual cause of the harm. This is sometimes referred to as the "but for" test: the particular harm in question would not have been suffered "but for" the defendant's negligent act.

Two other tests are sometimes used to determine actual cause in cases where more than one act or event may have caused an injury. The first test is called the *"substantial factor test."* It is used in cases where two individual acts contributed to the injury. This "substantial factor test" precludes liability for inadvertent or minor causation factors. The second test is known as the *"alternative causes approach."* This test applies when there are two acts, only one of which causes the injury, and it is not known which one caused the injury. The burden of proof shifts from the plaintiff to the defendant to prove that he or she did not cause the injury.

After establishing the existence of actual causation between the plaintiff's harm and the defendant's act, recovery requires proving that the defendant's act also *proximately* caused the plaintiff's injury. Proximate cause is determined by establishing whether or not the harm to the plaintiff was a reasonable, foreseeable consequence of the defendant's act. To demonstrate proximate cause, it is sufficient to show that the probable consequence of the defendant's act was harm of the same general character as that which befell the plaintiff. It is not necessary to show that the defendant should have foreseen the harm to the plaintiff in its precise form or particular manner. For example, Jerry Janitor, in cleaning a spot off the basketball court, used a cleaning substance that left the floor extremely slippery. During the game later that day, Ralph Rocket slipped on the spot and seriously injured his knee. Jerry's use of the improper cleaning substance was the proximate cause of Ralph's injury because it was foreseeable that someone would slip on the slick surface of a basketball court.

One last problem of determining causation occurs when there is more than one cause of injury. When a combination of causes leads to the damage, a defendant can defeat liability claims by demonstrating that an unforeseeable intervening act caused the injury. An *intervening cause* is one that comes into existence after the defendant's negligent action and contributes to that negligence in bringing about the plaintiff's injury. The intervening cause will relieve the defendant of liability if the defendant could not have foreseen either that the intervening cause might occur or that the plaintiff would suffer such great harm.

NOTES ———————————————————————————

1. In *Ascher v. Scarsdale School District*, 700 N.Y.S.2d 210 (N.Y. App. Div. 1999), the court determined that a teacher's failed supervision was not the proximate cause of injuries suffered by a child, after the child attempted a "back flip" dismount from a moving playground swing.

2. In *Alexander v. Sportslife, Inc.*, 502 S.E.2d 280 (Ga. App. 1998), after suffering injuries in a fight in an informal basketball game, the injured party sued the other player for battery and the facility owner under the theories of vicarious liability and breach of contract. The defendant player filed a counterclaim against plaintiff and also a claim against the facility owner. The court of appeals ruled that neither the facility owner nor its employees proximately caused injuries.

3. In *Reagan v. State of New York*, 654 N.Y.S. 2d 488 (N.Y. App. Div. 1997), the court determined that the field's abnormal slope was not the proximate cause of the paralysis of an experienced rugby player.

4. In *Thomas v. United States Soccer Federation, Inc.*, 653 N.Y.S.2d 958 (N.Y. App. Div. 1997), the court determined that a soccer referee's inexperience was not the proximate cause of one participant biting off another participant's ear during a match.

5. In *Singerman v. Municipal Serv. Bureau, Inc.*, 455 Mich. 135, 565 N.W.2d 383, (Mich. 1997), a hockey coach, acting as goalie without protective gear, claimed that poor lighting in the arena caused him to not see the puck that injured him. The Supreme Court of Michigan granted summary judgment to the defendant arena owners, overturning the appellate court decision, which had refused to do so. The Supreme Court reasoned, "Plaintiff was an adult and an experienced hockey player. The lighting in the rink is alleged to have been consistently inadequate, not subject to unexpected fluctuations or other changes. There was nothing to prevent plaintiff from realizing that the rink was inadequately lighted. Nor was there any chance that he would forget the potentially hazardous condition, because the condition was constantly before him. Finally, plaintiff was not compelled to use the rink for work, or profit, or any other overriding or substantial motivation. He chose to participate in a dangerous sport under conditions that he knew to be dangerous."

6. In *Shorten v. City of White Plains*, 637 N.Y.S.2d 791 (N.Y. App. Div. 1996), the court refused summary judgment to a city-owned skating rink. A teenage boy, after skating recklessly for about an hour, injured the plaintiff. According to the court, the defendant could have prevented the injury with adequate supervision.

7. In *Weller v. Colleges of the Senecas*, 635 N.Y.S. 2d 990 (N.Y. App. Div. 1995), the court ruled that the plaintiff's venturing off a college campus's bike path was not the sole proximate cause of an accident in which the plaintiff struck a tree root and crashed. The case against the college was dismissed.

8. In *Wertheim v. U.S. Tennis Ass'n.*, 540 N.Y.S.2d 443 (N.Y. App. Div. 1989), the New York Supreme Court Appellate Division reversed the lower court finding for the plaintiff who sought recovery for the wrongful death of a tennis umpire who died after being hit in the groin by a served tennis ball. The court ruled that even if the tennis tournament operator breached a duty of care owed to the umpire, it was unlikely that this breach of duty was the proximate cause of the umpire's death. The umpire had chronic cardiovascular disease and eyewitness testimony was consistent with the opinion of appellant's expert that the umpire suffered a stroke upon being hit by the ball.

9. In *Gehling v. St. George University School of Medicine*, 705 F. Supp. 761 (E.D.N.Y. 1989), plaintiff's family sued the medical school for his death, which resulted from his running in a student-sponsored road race. The school was found not to be the proximate cause of the plaintiff's death, because the participant, a medical student, was aware of the dangers of running the race in tropical weather, being seventy-five pounds overweight, suffering from high blood pressure, and having ingested an amphetamine-like drug prior to the race.

10. In *Locilento v. Coleman Catholic High School*, 523 N.Y.S.2d 198 (N.Y. App. 1987), the court found in favor of a student injured in an intramural football game in a suit against the school. The court held that the evidence sustained a finding that the school's failure to provide the student with proper equipment during an intramural tackle football game was a proximate cause of the shoulder injury and that the student's voluntary participation was merely an implied assumption of risk which did not preclude all recovery.

11. In *Burkart v. Health and Tennis Corporation of America*, 730 S.W.2d 367 (Tex. Ct. App. 1987), plaintiff brought suit against a health club for injuries received when he fell from a machine (Gravity Gym) which allows its user to hang upside down. Plaintiff alleged that the club failed to supervise his activities properly, that the club failed to inspect the Gravity Gym properly, and that the club's negligent failure to instruct its employees in the correct manner of using the Gravity Gym was the proximate cause of his injuries. The Texas Court of Appeals affirmed the lower court's decision in favor of the defendant, stating that the club's actions were not the proximate cause of the plaintiff's injuries.

12. In *Allen v. Rutgers State University*, 523 A.2d 262 (N.J. Super. Ct. 1987), a student patron at a football game at the university brought negligence action against the university

after suffering injuries at the game. The plaintiff was injured when he vaulted over a four-foot wall and fell approximately thirty feet. The plaintiff had been drinking although the university had a no alcohol policy in its stadium. The superior court entered judgment on a jury verdict in favor of the defendant, and the plaintiff appealed. The appellate court affirmed the lower court's decision and held that the lower court jury could properly find that the plaintiff had failed to establish that his injuries were proximately related to negligence of the university.

3.1.4. Damages

Damages are monetary compensation given to any person who suffers an injury through the unlawful act, omission, or negligence of another. Damage is an essential element of a negligence claim; therefore actual injury or harm must be proven. Unlike intentional tort claims, harm will not be presumed; thus nominal damages are not available in a negligence claim.

Damages may be either compensatory or punitive. *Compensatory damages* consist of money given to the injured party that is measured by the amount of actual injury incurred: past, present, and prospective. A plaintiff may be compensated for medical expenses, lost earnings, pain and suffering (including mental distress), and impaired future earning capacity. For example, Suzie Slowpitch suffered an injury as a result of the negligence of the school district in not properly maintaining the softball field. She was hospitalized and missed work at her part-time job for three weeks. The court instructed the school district to compensate her for hospital costs and lost wages.

Punitive damages are awarded to an injured party to punish the defendant for outrageous, reckless, willful, or wanton conduct. In addition, punitive damages also serve to punish the defendant and to set an example for other wrongdoers. They are awarded to a plaintiff in an amount over and above the amount given to compensate for the actual loss, where the wrong done was aggravated by violence, oppression, malice, fraud, or excessively wicked conduct. They are based on entirely different policy considerations than are compensatory damages, which merely reimburse a plaintiff for any actual loss suffered. For example, Kenny Kicker, after failing to successfully complete a football drill in practice, was forced by Coach Haze to push a football back and forth in front of the school fifty times with his nose during school hours. Kenney sued Coach Haze and the school, and was awarded punitive damages for suffering mental anguish, shame, and degradation.

In a negligence action, the plaintiff may seek recovery of damages, past, present, and prospective, in any or all of the following three areas:

1. Economic loss—medical expenses, lost or diminished earning capacity.
2. Physical pain—pain and suffering
3. Mental distress—fright, anxiety, humiliation, depression caused by the inability to lead one's previous life.

In addition, the spouse of an injured plaintiff may bring a separate cause of action for loss of consortium, which is the right to a spouse's companionship. Similarly, some courts allow children of an injured plaintiff have a cause of action against a negligent defendant for loss of companionship and guidance.

3.1.5. Defenses for Negligence

The defendants in such lawsuits can employ a number of defenses once the plaintiff has proven the elements essential to a negligence action. The following are the most common defenses employed by defendants in tort actions for negligence:

1. No negligence
2. Contributory negligence
3. Comparative negligence
4. Assumption of risk
5. Statute of limitations
6. Immunity and Good Samaritan statutes

3.1.5.1. No Negligence

The defendant usually attempts to prove first that his or her behavior did not constitute negligence. This can be approached in two ways. The defendant can dispute the negligence claim either by attacking one or more of the four previously discussed requirements for negligence or by proving that he or she exercised reasonable care in his or her actions. Thus, a defendant may defend against a claim of negligence by asserting that he or she had no duty toward the plaintiff. Or, if the defendant had a duty toward the plaintiff, he or she did not breach that duty. Therefore, any harm to the plaintiff would not be actionable negligence on the part of the defendant.

NOTE _____

1. In *Gray v. Girous*, 730 N.E.2d 338 (Mass. App. 2000), after a golfer struck another golfer in the head with a misplaced shot, the injured party sued for negligence. The appeals court ruled against the plaintiff, stating that golfers cannot be held liable for injuries to other participants unless their actions are willful, wanton, or reckless. The defendant's actions did not constitute any of these.

3.1.5.2. Contributory Negligence

The doctrine of contributory negligence provides that a plaintiff who is negligent and whose negligence contributes to the proximate cause of his or her injury is totally barred from recovery. Contributory negligence is, in essence, a departure from the standard of reasonableness required of all people, including plaintiffs. There does not have to be an actual appreciation of the risk involved. There need only be a risk that is known or would be known, and would be avoided by a reasonable person. A plaintiff also has a duty to exercise ordinary care. Without such care, the plaintiff is at least to some degree contributorily negligent. Only four states—Alabama, Maryland, North Carolina, and Virginia— still adhere to the common law doctrine of contributory negligence. The success of the defense of contributory negligence rests on the defendant's ability to prove that the plaintiff failed to exercise due care for his or her own safety and that the lack of due care was the proximate cause of the plaintiff's injury. In contributory negligence theory, as in negligence theory, the standard of care for children is reasonableness. The child's age, intelligence, and experience, however, are relevant to the issue of whether reasonable care was exercised. With respect to both negligence and contributory negligence, there are situations in which the negligent conduct of one party may be imputed to a second party under the doctrine of *respondeat superior*, which means "let the superior reply" (see section 3.6., "Vicarious Liability").

3.1.5.3. Comparative Negligence

The remaining forty-six states and the District of Columbia have adopted some version of the comparative negligence doctrine to alleviate the harshness of the contributory negligence doctrine. Comparative negligence provides a basis for recovery to an injured plaintiff while still apportioning fault to each side for the determination of damages.

Where both the plaintiff and the defendant are negligent, comparative negligence statutes seek to divide the responsibility between the two negligent parties. Under a comparative negligence statute, the jury or fact finder determines the proportionate degree of negligence that will be attributed to all parties involved. The damages are then assessed pro rata.

In states that have adopted the doctrine of comparative negligence, contributory negligence on the part of the plaintiff is not necessarily a complete bar to recovery. In some states, the rule that is applied under the theory of comparative negligence is:

> If the plaintiff's negligence, as compared with total negligence of all defendants, is greater than 50 percent, plaintiff is totally barred from recovery. For example, a plaintiff who is determined to be 60 percent at fault will not be able to recover against the defendant. If the plaintiff's negligence, as compared with the total negligence of all defendants, is 50 percent or less, plaintiff's damages are reduced in proportion to his or her negligence. For example, a plaintiff who suffers $100,000 in damages and whose negligence is determined to be 40 percent recovers $60,000 ($100,000 total damages less 40 percent of $100,000, plaintiff's proportion of negligence).

NOTES ——————————————————————————————————————

1. In *Nunez v. Recreation Rooms and Settlement, Inc.*, 645 N.Y.S.2d 789 (N.Y. App. Div. 1996), the court denied summary judgment to an ice skating rink after a 9-year-old first-time skater fell and broke her arm. The 9-year-old plaintiff testified that she had fallen while trying to skate away from a group of children who were pushing and playing in a rowdy fashion. No other child actually touched the plaintiff. Therefore, the defendants argued that the plaintiff's inexperience, not their failure to supervise, was the proximate cause of the plaintiff's injury. However, the court stated: "New York's comparative negligence statute allows for consideration of plaintiff's culpability in determining liability and apportioning damages . . . [P]laintiff's admission that she did not know how to skate does not preclude a finding that Midtown is also liable for her injuries."

2. In *Bazazi v. Michaud*, 856 F. Supp. 33 (D.N.H. 1994), a karate instructor was sued after injuring the plaintiff while sparring. The court dismissed the assumption of risk defense because the instructor knew of the dangers involved with karate, and therefore, should be expected to spar with caution. However, the court did not rule out comparative negligence as a defense.

3. In *Ford v. Gouin*, 266 Cal. Rptr. 870 (Cal. Ct. App. 1990), the relationship between the defenses of assumption of risk and comparative negligence is discussed.

4. For more information, also see the following law review article: Kirtan K. Khalsa,

"A Cause of Action for Negligent Horseplay: *Yount v. Johnson*," 27 *New Mexico Law Review* 661 (1997).

3.1.5.4. Assumption of Risk

Assumption of risk means that the plaintiff has voluntarily consented to take chances that harm will occur. The plaintiff must know of the risk and voluntarily assume it. This consent effectively relieves a defendant's obligation to a certain standard of conduct toward the plaintiff. There is no longer any legal duty existing between the two. When there is no duty, there is no negligence.

The general rule in athletics is that participants assume the normal and reasonable events of activities in which they participate, where those activities do not rise to the level of recklessness. There are two major exceptions to the general rule. First, there is no assumption of risk when something occurs that is not normal or reasonable for the activity. Second, the assumption of the risk defense will be unsuccessful when the participant is unaware of the risk. In addition to knowing and appreciating the risk, the plaintiff must also carefully and reasonably agree to assume whatever risk is involved.

In addition to knowing and appreciating the risk, the plaintiff must also carefully and reasonably agree to assume whatever risk is involved. There are two types of assumption of risk. The first is an *express assumption of risk*, which arises when a plaintiff gives advance consent to relieve a defendant of a legal duty and to take his or her chances from a known risk. The second is *implied assumption of risk*, which arises when a plaintiff's reasonable conduct in encountering a known risk creates an inference that he or she has agreed to relieve the defendant's duty of care.

The defense of assumption of risk may be utilized in those states which have not passed a comparative negligence statute to supplement the contributory negligence statute. In such states, the defendant may claim that the plaintiff, by assuming the risk of injury, is barred from any recovery. Under the comparative negligence statute, however, partial recovery is allowed in many situations in which the plaintiff's contributory negligence proximately contributed to his or her injury. This does not reconcile with the legal interpretation under which no recovery is allowed to a plaintiff who is found to have assumed the risk, even when such assumption of risk was considered reasonable under the circumstances. In states in which assumption of risk has been abolished as a defense in negligence actions, a plaintiff is entitled to full recovery if his or her assumption of risk was reasonable. In sports cases, assumption of risk is an important defense because it may negate a plaintiff's case.

NOTES

The following represent cases where the defendant raised a successful assumption of the risk defense.

1. In *Lee* v. *Maloney*, 704 N.Y.S. 2d 729 (3 N.Y. App. Div. 2000), the court ruled that an experienced weightlifter assumes the risk that he may lose control of a 565-pound object, even with the help of spotters.

2. In *Bouchard* v. *Smile Bros.*, 685 N.Y.S. 2d 289 (2 N.Y. App. Div. 1999), the court ruled against the estate of a deceased hiker, saying that the hiker had assumed the risk that she might lose her footing and fall off a cliff to her death.

3. In *Balthazor* v. *Little League Baseball Inc.*, 72, Cal. Rptr. 2d 337 (Cal. Ct. App.,

1998), the appellate court held that a Little League baseball player assumes the risk of being hit by a pitched ball.

4. In *Shelly* v. *Stepp*, 73 Cal. Rptr. 2d 323 (Cal. Ct. App., 1998), the court ruled that assumption of risk applies to those who exercise race horses.

5. In *Lilley* v. *Elk Grove Unified School District*, 68 Cal. App. 4th 939, 80 Cal. Rptr. 2d 638 (Cal. App. 1998), junior high wrestlers, by participating in a dangerous sport, assume the risk of serious injury.

6. In *Sandler* v. *Half Hollow Hills West High School*, 672 N.Y.S. 2d 120 (N.Y. App. Div. 1998), a high school field hockey player assumed risks of injury that were clearly foreseeable consequences of her voluntary participation in athletic competition, despite her relative inexperience in the sport.

7. In *Davis* v. *Sayona Central School District*, 675 N.Y.S.2d 269 (N.Y. App. Div. 1998), a high school student was injured after striking an unpadded portion of school gymnasium wall during an interscholastic basketball game. The student sued the school district, architects, contractor, and athletic equipment company. The Supreme Court, Appellate Division, held that the student assumed the obvious risks inherent in playing basketball in the school gymnasium.

8. In *Morgan* v. *State*, 685 N.E.2d 202 (N.Y. 1997), bobsledders assumed the risk of injuries that occurred when their bobsled crashed into a wall and continued through an opening.

9. In *Capello* v. *Village of Suffern*, 648 N.Y.S.2d 699 (N.Y. App. Div. 1996), a basketball player assumed the risk of playing on a slippery court. The court was covered with a dusty substance, but the player continued to play even though he was aware of the substance.

10. In *Swan* v. *Town of Grand Island*, 652 N.Y.S.2d 166 (N.Y. App. Div. 1996), a softball player assumed the risk of playing on a wet field. Although the condition of the field was poor, the player continued to play despite the fact that it was obvious the conditions were hazardous.

11. In *Fortier* v. *Los Rios Community College District*, 52 Cal. Rptr. 2d 812 (Cal. Ct. App. 1996), plaintiff brought suit against a community college as a result of a "no tackling" football class. The plaintiff suffered severe facial injuries during a collision with another participant. The court reasoned, "Plaintiff's injuries were the result of his voluntary participation in a sport in which the risk of injury due to accidental collision is known, acknowledged and accepted. Plaintiff's injuries could have occurred in the most benign forms of football, i.e., touch or flag . . . or even in other sports considered to be non-contact e.g., baseball (collision of two defensive players trying to catch a fly ball) or basketball (collision between offensive and defensive rebounders or between offensive player driving for the basket and defender)." The appellate court affirmed the judgment for the defendant community college.

12. In *Ford* v. *Gouin*, 266 Cal. Rptr. 870 (Cal. Ct. App. 1990), plaintiff was injured when, while waterskiing on a narrow river channel, he collided with a tree limb overhanging the waterway. As a result, plaintiff suffered severe head injuries. At the time of the accident plaintiff was skiing backward and barefoot and the boat towing the plaintiff was driven by the defendant. Evidence showed the plaintiff had skied in this area over fifty times before and was well aware of the channel and branches hanging over the waterway. Thus, the court held that the plaintiff reasonably assumed the risks inherent in the activity because of his extensive experience as a water skier in the area where his injuries occurred.

13. In *Wertheim* v. *U.S. Tennis Ass'n.*, 540 N.Y.S.2d 443 (N.Y. App. Div. 1989), plaintiff executrix sought recovery for the wrongful death of a tennis umpire who died after being hit in the groin by a served tennis ball. In reversing the lower court finding for the plaintiff, the New York Supreme Court held that the umpire had assumed the risk of being struck by a served tennis ball.

14. In *Benitez* v. *New York City Board of Education*, 541 N.E.2d 29 (N.Y. 1989), plaintiff high school football player brought personal injury action against the board of education

and the city public school athletic league. The plaintiff alleged negligence of the coach and principal in permitting him to play in a mismatched game in a fatigued condition. In reversing the lower court's decision, the appeals court ruled in favor of the defendants and held that the board of education and its organized athletic counsels must exercise ordinary reasonable care to protect student-athletes voluntarily involved in extracurricular sports from unassumed, concealed, or unreasonably increased risks. In this case, the school district was not liable to the player because player assumed the risks of injury in competition and was not under inherent compulsion to play.

15. In *Ordway v. Superior Court*, 243 Cal. Rptr. 536 (Cal. Ct. App. 1988), a professional jockey's claim for damages for injuries sustained when thrown from his horse in a race as a result of another jockey's rule violation. The court found that when the plaintiff raced, he voluntarily and reasonably assumed the risk of injury, thereby reducing the defendant's duty of care.

16. In *Novak v. Lamar Insurance Co.*, 488 So. 2d 739 (La. Cir. Ct. App. 1986), plaintiff softball player brought action against a second softball player, the homeowner's insurer of that player's father, and the insurer of the church which sponsored the defendant softball player's team. Plaintiff sought recovery for injuries sustained when the two collided as defendant softball player ran to first base. The court held that the defendant softball player was not acting in a reckless or unsportsmanlike manner. The court reasoned that the risk of collision was a foreseeable risk which the plaintiff had assumed.

17. In *Richmond v. Employers' Fire Insurance Co.*, 298 So. 2d 118 (La. Ct. App. 1974), plaintiff, a college baseball player, sought recovery from the defendant college coach and insurance company for injuries sustained during practice in which the coach was allegedly negligent in allowing a bat to fly from his hands. In ruling for the defendants, the court of appeals held that the coach was not negligent and that the player had assumed the risk of injury inherent in a baseball practice session.

18. In *Schentzel v. Philadelphia Nat'l League Club*, 96 A.2d 181 (Sup. Ct. Pa. 1953), plaintiff, a spectator viewing a baseball game for the first time, sought recovery for injuries sustained when she was struck by a foul ball while seated in the upper deck near first base. The court held that the plaintiff knew or should have known that foul balls sometimes go astray, and that the defendant was not negligent in failing to provide screens for the upper deck.

The following are cases where the defense of assumption of the risk failed.

19. In *Kane v. North Colonie Central School District*, 708 N.Y.S.2d 203 (N.Y. App. Div. 2000), plaintiff was injured during an indoor track practice, which took place in the hallway of the high school building. The plaintiff argued, "the risk of contact and falling is unreasonably increased where the runners do not maintain a safe and appropriate distance, typically a stride, from one another." The appellate court held that the testimony of Kane and her expert witness was sufficient to "raise a question of fact as to whether the defendant's supervision was inadequate and resulted in the failure to exercise reasonable care to protect Kane from an unreasonably increased risk."

20. In *Kevan v. Manesiotis*, 728 A.2d 1006 (Pa. Commw. 1999), a defendant school district's poorly lit gym prevented its successful use of the assumption of risk defense. The plaintiff had been struck by a batted ball, hit at a high velocity.

21. In *Sauray v. City of New York*, 690 N.Y.S.2d 716 (N.Y. App. Div. 1999), a mountain biker, injured when he struck a chain over a path in a city park, did not assume risk of injury from such collision.

22. In *Solano v. Abrenica*, 81 Cal. Rptr. 2d 881 (Cal. Ct. App. 1999), a tennis player did not assume the risk of being hit in the eye with a served ball after the conclusion of tennis practice.

23. In *Calhanas v. South Amboy Roller Rink*, 679 A.2d 185 (N.J. Super. Ct. App. Div. 1996), the Superior Court of New Jersey had ruled that the plaintiff was precluded from recovering damages from a skating rink, after an unidentified rowdy skater caused the plaintiff to fall and break a bone. According to New Jersey Law [N.J.S.A. 5:14–6], "The

assumption of risk . . . shall serve as a complete defense to a suit against an operator by a roller skater." However, the appellate court ruled that this law did not supercede the rink's duty to supervise, and therefore, remanded to a jury the question of whether the rink took reasonable care to thwart rowdy skaters.

24. In *Codd v. Stevens Pass, Inc.*, 725 P.2d 1008 (Wash. Ct. App. 1986), a skier chose to ski an "ungroomed area" between two "groomed" trails and fell, struck his head, and was killed. The decedent's wife brought suit against the ski area, claiming that it had not met the duty of care owed the decedent. The court found that as an invitee, the decedent was owed by the ski operator an affirmative duty of care for the "area of invitation." The defendant claimed that an ungroomed trail was an unimproved area and that under Washington statute, the decedent assumed the risk of such injury. The court disagreed and extended the area of invitation to encompass the entire area serviced by the chair lifts.

25. In *Rutter v. Northeastern Beaver County School District*, 437 A.2d 1198 (Pa. 1981), the plaintiff lost an eye as a result of an injury which occurred during a summer football practice supervised by the high school coaches. The plaintiff was playing a type of touch football known as "jungle football" when he was injured. The court abolished the doctrine of assumption of risk because of the extreme difficulty in applying the doctrine and because the doctrine is duplicative of two other concepts—the scope of the defendant's duty and the plaintiff's contributory negligence.

26. In *Stevens v. Central School District*, 270 N.Y.S.2d 23 (N.Y. App. Div. 1966), plaintiff sought recovery for injuries sustained when, while playing basketball in defendant's school building, his momentum carried him through a glass window in a door just behind the basket. In ruling for the plaintiff, the court held the plaintiff had not assumed the risk of the dangerous condition caused by use of ordinary window glass in the door. The court ruled that the defendant was negligent in not using safety glass in the doors.

Also see the following law review articles.

27. John Bianco, "The Dawn of a New Standard? Assumption of Risk Doctrine in a Post-Knight California," 15 *Whittier Law Review* 1155 (1994).

28. Jason R. Jenkins, "Not Necessarily the Best Seat in the House: A Comment on the Assumption of Risk by Spectators at Major Auto Racing Events," 35 (1) *Tulsa Law Journal* 163 (1999).

3.1.5.5. Statute of Limitations

Statute of limitations prescribes the periods within which certain causes of action may be brought or certain rights enforced. Statute of limitations may begin at the time of the negligent act or at the time of its discovery. Today, statutes and case law apply the "time of discovery" rule. If a plaintiff does not institute a lawsuit within the time period prescribed by the statute of limitations, he or she will lose the right to sue.

3.1.5.6. Immunity and Good Samaritan Statutes

Immunity is a condition that protects a possible defendant against a tort action. It exists because of a position of the defendant, not because of any action taken by the defendant. This defense may exist either because of a relationship between the plaintiff and the defendant, or because of the capacity of the defendant. Examples of the relationships that in some states permit a defense of immunity in intentional torts include those between husband and wife or between parent and child.

Other immunity defenses that may be raised when appropriate are those of sovereign immunity, charitable immunity, and Good Samaritan statutes. The same type of immunity that can be raised in assault and battery cases—that stemming from relationships between the parties or the capacity of the parties—can also be applied to negligence actions. The trend, however, is to move away from an immunity defense based solely on the relationship of the parties.

Sovereign immunity developed in English common law. It was otherwise known as immunity of the king, which was expressed as "the king can do no wrong." This English rule was applied by early American courts to mean that the United States could not be sued without consent. Today, by statute and judicial decision, this immunity is considerably limited.

By virtue of the Federal Tort Claims Act, Title 28 U.S.C., the United States has waived immunity for tortious acts and can be held liable to the same extent as a private individual when its employees are negligent within the scope of their employment. There are still circumstances where the immunity will apply: intentional torts; discretionary acts at the planning or decision-making level; and independent contractors, who may assert the immunity where the government had authority and control, and exercised substantial supervision of the activities.

Like the U.S. government, most states have substantially waived their immunity from tort claims. Again, the immunity still attaches for discretionary acts and for legislative and judicial decisions. This applies to the government and governmental agencies. At least half of the states have abolished municipal tort immunity by statute or judicial decision to the same extent that they have waived their own state immunity.

Charitable immunity emerged from common law and provides charitable organizations with immunity from lawsuits. The rationale for such protection is (1) the donors have not given funds to the charitable organization for use to pay tort claims and (2) the beneficiary of the charity has waived his or her right to raise a tort claim, simply by virtue of having accepted the benevolence. More than a third of states have abolished charitable immunity on the following bases: the availability of liability insurance, the view that liability should not be determined based on whether or not a charity can satisfy a judgment, and the existence of a category of people for whom it is not possible to waive their right to sue (i.e., baby or unconscious victim).

Another statutory defense involves the Good Samaritan doctrine. Good Samaritan statutes, as a matter of law, preclude negligence liability for one who sees and attempts to aid another person who has been placed in imminent and serious peril due to the negligence of a third person. States that have adopted Good Samaritan statutes will impose a lesser standard of care for doctors and other individuals trained in first aid who gratuitously render medical assistance to a sick or injured person. Good Samaritan statutes generally protect medical personnel rendering aid from liability, unless the treatment provided is grossly negligent or actually worsens the condition of the person in need of treatment.

NOTES

The following are cases where defendants raised a successful immunity defense.

1. In *Eneman v. Richter*, 577 N.W.2d 386 (Wisc. Ct. App. 1998), employees of the University of Wisconsin were sued for negligence after fans charged the football field to celebrate a victory and knocked over the goal posts, injuring more than seventy spectators. The appellate court dismissed charges of negligence against officers of the state, because plaintiffs could not refute the fact that such officers were entitled to immunity. A lower court had already dismissed a claim against the university itself, which had been named as a co-defendant in the suit under the theory of vicarious liability.

2. In *Evans* v. *Oaks Mission Public School*, 945 P.2d 492 (Okla. 1997), defendant school board was found to be statutorily immune from liability for injuries occurring as a result of a physical education wrestling match.

The following are cases where the defense of immunity failed.

3. In *Home v. North Kitsap School District*, 965 P.2d 1112 (Wash. Ct. App. 1998), a junior high football coach who was injured when he attempted to protect player from a raised curb that separated the field from a surrounding running track, and was then struck by a second player, sued the school district, which owned the field. The court of Appeals held that (1) the district was not protected by immunity under recreational land use statute, because the field was not open for public use at the time of the scheduled school football game during which coach was injured, and (2) the fact issue as to whether the coach had no reasonable alternative but to stand in front of curb in order to protect his players, and thus could not be said to have voluntarily assumed the risk created by the curb, precluded summary judgment.

4. In *Bilides* v. *Town of New Haven*, No. 365636, 1996 Conn. Super. Ct. LEXIS 1383 (May 24, 1996), a minor on school premises for educational purposes suffered injuries in playground. Immunity statutes were deemed inapplicable since plaintiff was among a class of foreseeable victims whom a duty of protection is owed regarding the maintenance and safety of school grounds.

Also see the following law review articles.

5. Joan M. O'Brien, "The Connecticut Recreational Use Statue: Should a Municipality Be Immune from Tort Liability?" 15 *Pace Law Review* 963 (1995).

6. Bradley Colwell, "Recreational Property and Injuries: 'Playing with Governmental Tort Immunity,'" 87 *Illinois Bar Journal* 654 (December 1999).

3.1.6. Wrongful Death Statutes

Wrongful death statutes exist in all states. They provide a statutory cause of action in favor of certain of the decedent's personal beneficiaries (e.g., a spouse, parent, or child) against the person who negligently caused the death. The provision changes the common law rule that the tort action was extinguished with the death of the person who was negligently injured by the defendant. The cause of action is for the wrong to the beneficiaries and for their loss of companionship and suffering—not for the harm done to the decedent.

The majority of the statutes award compensatory damages. The award of these money damages is based on an evaluation of the monetary worth of the decedent to each. In a minority of jurisdictions, the statutes measure damages by the level of culpability shown by the negligent party. The damages awarded are greater for injuries inflicted intentionally as opposed to those negligently inflicted. A few states employ a combination of the two methods to determine damages.

3.2. THE TORT OF RECKLESS MISCONDUCT (GROSS NEGLIGENCE)

Reckless misconduct, or gross negligence, falls between the intentional torts of assault and battery and the unintentional tort of negligence. Behavior constituting reckless misconduct is characterized by defendant's *intent to commit the act*, but not the *intent to harm the plaintiff*. Reckless misconduct occurs when the actor intentionally performs an act while disregarding a risk known to him, and that risk is so great as to make the harm highly probable. It must usually be accompanied by a conscious disregard of the circumstances. For example, Frankie Fieldevent, after a high school track practice, was throwing the javelin at some of his teammates who were running around the track. He had no intention of hitting any of his friends, but Mikey Marathon fell while running, and the javelin pierced him in the shoulder. Mikey successfully brought suit against Frankie for reckless misconduct.

Reckless misconduct is particularly important in the area of participant-against-participant tort cases. Only since the 1970s have courts found a duty of sports participants to refrain from reckless misconduct toward another player. To find reckless misconduct, an action must be more than ordinary inadvertence or inattention but less than conscious indifference to the consequences. It is defined as an action that is willful, wanton, or reckless; while reckless misconduct is not an intentional action, the degree of the care exercised is so far below the usual standard that in effect, it is treated as an intentional action. Reckless misconduct encompasses action that evidences an extreme departure from the ordinary degree of care required from the actor in the particular circumstances. However, the damages awarded, especially in the area of punitive damages, may be greater if the defendant's action is deemed reckless.

Several common problems are involved in the majority of sports-related tort cases. The first is the difficulty of determining exactly what a tort is in an athletic context. The second is that a public policy consideration is also involved, since it has been suggested in several court decisions that court interference with sports will destroy athletics and unreasonably restrict the free play of sports. The third common problem is that litigation may discourage participation in the more dangerous sports. For these reasons, athletic administrators must be aware of the legal principles involved in tort liability relating to sports so that they can be better prepared to take preventive measures that will minimize the adverse effects of such litigation.

NOTES

1. Courts in most states will follow the general rule that a sport participant may not recover damages from a negligent co-participant, unless co-participant acts willfully, wantonly, or recklessly (see case of *Nabozny* in note 3). However, courts will sometimes make exceptions to this rule when the negligence occurs during breaks in the action, immediately after competition, or at other periods where the court believes that injured party did not assume the risk of injury. For example, in *Hoke v. Cullinan*, 914 S.W.2d 335 (Ky. 1995), plaintiff brought action against defendant for injuries that occurred during a doubles tennis match. Plaintiff alleged that, "at a time when tennis play had stopped," defendant carelessly drove a ball into plaintiff's eye. The county circuit court dismissed the case, stating, "the law required proof of reckless or intentional conduct." The court of appeals overruled the circuit court, remanding the question of negligence to a jury. However, the Kentucky Supreme Court reinstated the ruling of the circuit court, despite the dissent of two of its justices.

2. An exception to the general rule described in note 1 is the Wisconsin Supreme Court's decision in *Lestina v. West Bend Mutual Insurance*, 501 N.W.2d 28 (Wis. 1993). In this case, defendant was sued for violating a "no slide tackling rule" during an "Old Timers Soccer League Game" and injuring the plaintiff. The court ruled that defendant's actions constituted ordinary negligence, but still allowed for the plaintiff's recovery of damages.

3. In *Nabozny v. Barnhill*, 334 N.E.2d 258 (Ill. App. Ct. 1975), plaintiff soccer player filed suit for injuries received when he was kicked in the head by an opponent during an amateur soccer game involving two teams composed of high school age players. The defendant, David Barnhill, was playing a forward position for one team, and the plaintiff,

Julian Nabozny, was the goaltender for the other team. Barnhill kicked Nabozny in the head while Nabozny was in possession of the ball. Contact with the goaltender while he is in possession of the ball is a violation of FIFA (soccer's international governing body) rules which governed the contest. The resultant injury left the plaintiff with permanent skull and brain damage. Nabozny brought suit, and the trial court directed a verdict in favor of the defendant. On appeal, the court noted that it did not wish to "place unreasonable burdens on the free and vigorous participation in sports by our youth," but also stated that "athletic competition does not exist in a vacuum." Therefore, in reversing the trial court decision, the court held that a player is charged with a legal duty to every other player on the field to refrain from conduct proscribed by a safety rule. The court held that when athletes are engaged in athletic competition, all teams involved are trained and coached by knowledgeable personnel; a recognized set of rules governs the conduct of the competition; and a safety rule is contained therein which is primarily designed to protect players from serious injury. Thus, a reckless disregard for the safety of other players cannot be excused.

4. For more information, see the following law review article: Brandon D. Miller, "Note: *Hoke v. Cullinan* as the Standard for Recreational Sports Injuries," 23 *Northern Kentucky Law Review* 409 (Spring 1996).

3.3. INTENTIONAL TORTS

Assault and battery can be both a criminal and a civil offense. Most people associate assault and battery with criminal law because most state statutes broadly define criminal assault to include both attempted and actual battery. This differs from civil law, where assault and battery constitute two separate and distinct torts. Further elaboration clarifies the distinction between the criminal and civil law definitions of assault and battery.

A *civil law assault* is any intentional act that creates reasonable apprehension of immediate harmful or offensive contact, while a *civil law battery* is an intentional harmful or offensive contact with another person. For civil assault and battery, as for all intentional torts, there does not have to be harm to the plaintiff to establish a claim of assault and/or battery. The mere fact that a person has done and intended to do a proscribed action will suffice to provide at least nominal damages, but the degree of harm will be important in assessing monetary damages.

3.3.1. The Tort of Assault

For an action to constitute civil assault, each of the following three elements must be proven:

1. Any act that creates a reasonable apprehension in plaintiff of immediate harmful or offensive contact with plaintiff
2. Intent by defendant to cause plaintiff's apprehension
3. Causation, defendant's act brought about the apprehension.

Words alone are not enough to create an apprehension of immediate harm. Some sort of action on the part of the defendant must accompany the words. Courts rely upon the apparent ability to carry out a threat rather than the actual ability in determining assault. The defendant who claims he or she had no actual ability to carry out a threat will not be successful if he or she had the apparent ability to do so. For example, a defendant's claim that the gun pointed in the direction of the plaintiff was not loaded is not a successful defense against a reasonable person's being placed in apprehension of immediate harm by the defendant. The plaintiff had no way of knowing whether or not the gun was loaded. The apprehension of immediate harm by the plaintiff must be reasonable. In determining whether the apprehension is reasonable, the courts will apply the *reasonable person standard*. An unusually timid plaintiff may not recover for an assault where a normal person would not have been in apprehension of the harmful or offensive contact. However, the defendant will be held responsible if the defendant knows of the plaintiff's timidness.

Actual contact between the defendant and the plaintiff need not have occurred for assault to be committed; however, the plaintiff must be aware of the possibility of contact. The distinction between actual physical contact and its mere apprehension marks the dividing line between assault and battery. For example, in a high school baseball game, the pitcher threw a pitch that unintentionally got away from him and passed dangerously close to an opponent's head. The opponent took offense at the closeness of the pitch, charged the mound, and intentionally threw his bat in the direction of the pitcher. The pitcher saw the opponent throw the bat toward him. The bat missed the pitcher. Nevertheless, the pitcher could bring suit against the batter for assault.

Regarding the intent element, the plaintiff does not have to prove that the defendant intended to inflict bodily harm, only that the defendant intended to bring about plaintiff's apprehension of an immediate harmful or offensive contact.

· Causation exists where the plaintiff's apprehension was brought about by a direct or indirect act by the defendant. An indirect act includes that which the defendant sets in motion.

3.3.2. The Tort of Battery

For an action to constitute civil battery, three elements must be proven:

1. A harmful or offensive act by the defendant toward the plaintiff
2. Intent by defendant to bring about the harmful or offensive contact to plaintiff
3. Causation; defendant's action brought about the harmful or offensive contact.

With regard to the first element, the plaintiff must prove that a *harmful* or *offensive contact occurred*. Mere apprehension of contact is not sufficient. An act is construed as harmful or offensive by the reasonable person's standard—that is, a person of ordinary sensibilities. The plaintiff's awareness of the contact at the time of the battery is not essential. For example, plaintiffs have made successful battery claims in cases in which the contact occurred when they were asleep or under anesthesia.

Contact does not necessarily have to be "harmful"; it may instead be "offensive," such as spitting at another person. Contact is considered "offensive" if the plaintiff did not consent to it. For the purposes of determining whether a battery has been committed, anything connected to the plaintiff is considered a part of the plaintiff's person (e.g., clothing or an object held by the plaintiff). Similarly, the contact by the defendant need not be direct (with the plaintiff's body); it may be indirect, such as making contact with an object such as a bat or ordering a dog to attack the plaintiff.

The second element of *intent* requires that the plaintiff prove that the defendant intended to bring about a harmful or offensive contact with the plaintiff. The plaintiff does not have to prove that the defendant intended the specific harm incurred by the victim. The rationale is that the defendant is presumed to have intended the natural and probable consequences of the act. A touching that results from a reflex action is not considered intentional.

The third element required is causation. The defendant is liable for direct and indirect contact. The plaintiff need only prove that the defendant set in motion a force that brought about the harmful or offensive contact with the plaintiff.

In contact sports, participants are expected to use force because it is one of the necessary terms and conditions of the game. The contact is justified if it is reasonable under the circumstances. Many contacts that occur in the sports setting would be considered battery in a non-sports setting. However, the key distinction in sports battery is whether the participant has consented to a particular contact. If the court concludes that consent was given and the contact was reasonable, a plaintiff will not be successful in a claim of battery. For example, during a basketball game, Bully Smith was guarding Tommy Timid as Tommy was about to receive a pass. Without provocation, Bully intentionally pushed Tommy from behind and punched him in the back of the head. As Tommy fell, Bully hit him again, knocking Tommy unconscious. The acts of Bully are not of the type to which Tommy would consent in a game of basketball. Thus, Tommy can bring suit against Bully for battery, because there was an intended harmful contact caused by Bully. However, Tommy cannot bring an action for assault; there was no apprehension of harm because Tommy did not see the punch coming.

3.3.3. Defenses for Assault and Battery

The defenses that a defendant may raise against a plaintiff's claim of an intentional tort fall into two broad categories: (1) consent and (2) privilege, imposed as a matter of law, not the result of the investigation of facts. Under privilege, the defendant's actions that would otherwise constitute a tort, are excused because the action furthers an interest of social importance deserving of protection.

3.3.3.1. Consent

Consent is a voluntary yielding to an invasion of one's interests by another. It is an act of reason, accompanied by deliberation, that is made by an individual possessing sufficient mental capacity to make an intelligent choice. To be effective, consent must be made without fraud or duress. Consent may be expressed or it may be reasonably implied by the circumstances surrounding the situation.

The defense of consent presents a special problem in the realm of sports in general and for athletic participants in particular. The traditional interpretation in many assault and battery cases in the sports setting has been that the athlete, by participating in a given event, consents to the degree of contact commonly found within the rules of the sport. A special problem arises in sports because it is often difficult to determine the extent or scope of the implied consent given. Consent implied by participation in athletic events is not a blanket consent protecting athletes from the consequences of their actions under all circumstances.

Instead, many plaintiffs argue that the scope of consent is limited to acts that occur in the ordinary and normal conduct of the game.

The difficulty arises from the determination of what is "ordinary and normal conduct" in a particular game. For example, the consent defense may be raised in a sports-related assault and battery action. The defendant could claim that no tort was committed, given the nature of the relationship with the plaintiff. The defendant could further argue that the plaintiff, by his or her participation in the sport contest, consents to a certain degree of contact. Problems arise with a tort action in a sports case given the difficulty of ascertaining exactly when or how a tort occurs in a game allowing physical contact.

3.3.3.2. *Privilege*

A privilege is a particular, limited benefit enjoyed by an individual or class of individuals that extends beyond the common advantages of other citizens. In certain situations a privilege is more appropriately classified as an exemption from a burden rather than as a benefit to be enjoyed. A privilege is commonly enjoyed in situations in which the defendant has acted in defense of his or her person or property. The defendant bears the burden of proof to establish that a privilege existed and that the force used pursuant to the privilege was reasonable under the circumstances.

The defense will be denied and the defendant will be held liable if the force used is found to be excessive or unreasonable. The defendant must argue and bear the burden of proving the privilege. Privilege includes the following:

1. Self-defense
2. Defense of others
3. Defense of property
4. Recapture of chattels (personal property)
5. Necessity
6. Arrest
7. Discipline.

Self-defense is the most commonly used privilege in sports cases. To argue self-defense successfully, the defendant must prove that he or she used no more force than reasonably necessary to repel an attack.

The self-defense privilege rests upon the public policy that allows a person being attacked to come to his or her own defense. The privilege arises when danger exists or there is a reasonable belief that danger is imminent. It is limited to the use of force that is necessary or appears to be necessary for adequate protection. There is never any privilege to use force when immediate danger is past.

Another viable legal defense against an intentional tort such as assault or battery is the *defense of others*. In order for the defense to be effective, certain requirements must be met. First, the privilege extends only to the reasonable force necessary to defend another from imminent harm. Second, the defense must occur in reaction to events as they exist at the time of the threat. There is no privilege for physical reactions to future threats or past attacks.

This privilege is available to anyone who reasonably defends another. No special relationship between the defender and the victim need exist. The view of the majority of courts is that the defender "steps into the shoes" of the victim.

If the victim would not have been privileged to use force in self-defense, neither does the defender. Accordingly, the defender would be liable even if he or she acted upon a reasonable mistake as to the victim's right to self-defense. There is a substantial modern trend that permits the defender to use force whenever he or she reasonably believes the victim would have the privilege of self-defense.

3.3.4. Tortious Interference with Contractual Relations

Tortious interference with contractual relations occurs where a third party, without justification, intentionally induces one person not to perform a contract with another person. The third party is liable to the person with whom the original contract was going to be signed. This type of tort liability protects the rights of a party to a contract from third-party interference. The plaintiff in such a suit bears the burden of proving that the defendant intentionally interfered with the plaintiff's contractual relationship such that the performance of the contract was either prevented or made difficult. The defendant must have actual knowledge of the contract and have the intent to interfere with it. The defendant can rebut or justify the interference by showing that the conduct was not "improper." The *Restatement (Second) of Torts* sets forth the following seven factors to be considered in determining whether the conduct was improper:

1. The nature of the actor's conduct
2. The actor's motive
3. The interests of the other with which the actor's conduct interferes
4. The interests sought to be advanced by the actor
5. The social interests in protecting the freedom of the action of the actor and the contractual interests of others
6. The proximity or remoteness of the actor's conduct to the interference
7. The relations between the parties.

This theory has been used when a player or coach signs a contract with a rival team while already under contract with his or her present team. Often, the temptation to obtain a player or a coach already obligated to another team is too difficult to resist, and a player or coach will be induced to breach a current contract to sign with a new employer. In such a situation, the party injured by the breach of the contract may sue the new party for intentionally interfering with the previous contract. Recently, universities have used the doctrine of tortious interference with contractual relations against agents who have interferred with their players' eligibility.

NOTE _____

1. In *Cardtoons, L.C. v. Major League Baseball Players Association*, 208 F.3d 885 (10th Cir. 2000), *cert denied*, 531 U.S. 873 (2000), plaintiff company had contracted with a manufacturing company to produce humorous trading cards featuring satirical caricatures of active baseball players. When the MLBPA heard about this plan, it sent a "cease and desist" letter threatening to sue both Cardtoons and the manufacturing company for copyright infringement. As a result of this threat, the manufacturing company backed out of the deal to produce the cards. Cardtoons then sued the MLBPA for tortious interference. The MLBPA defended itself by claiming that "threatening to sue" does not constitute

tortious interference. The U.S. Court of Appeals disagreed, remanding the case to a federal trial judge after the U.S. Supreme Court denied certiorari.

3.3.5. The Tort of Intentional Infliction of Emotional Distress

The tort of intentional infliction of emotional distress protects a person's emotional tranquillity. Simple minor disturbances and infringements are not actionable. The provoking conduct must be outrageous for the plaintiff to have a viable action for intentional infliction of emotional distress. An increasing number of states are recognizing intentional infliction of emotional distress as an independent tort. To establish a claim for intentional infliction of emotional distress, the following elements must be proven by plaintiff:

1. There must be extreme and outrageous conduct by the defendant.
2. The intention by the defendant was to cause plaintiff to suffer severe emotional distress or recklessly disregarded the high probability that emotional distress would occur.
3. The defendant's conduct must be the cause of emotional distress.
4. Damages; the distress must be severe.

The necessary mental state of the defendant is broader than that of other intentional torts. For other intentional torts, the required intent includes the defendants' desire to cause a certain result and the defendant's knowledge to "substantial certainty" that a particular result will occur. In an intentional infliction of emotional distress claim, the mental state of the defendant can be either the intent to cause the emotional distress, knowledge with a substantial certainty that emotional distress would occur, or reckless action in disregard of the high probability that emotional distress would occur.

For example, if the defendant is joking and informs the plaintiff that her son has been killed and the plaintiff suffers emotional distress, the defendant will be liable. Or if a doctor falsely or recklessly makes it known to a person that he or she is suffering from a fatal disease, then the doctor will be liable.

The conduct required is outrageous and extreme. The plaintiff has an initial burden of showing enough evidence for reasonable persons to find extreme and outrageous conduct. The plaintiff is required to show that he or she actually suffered severe emotional distress.

A leading case in the area of intentional infliction of emotional distress is *Chuy v. Philadelphia Eagles Football Club*, 431 F.Supp. 254 (E.D. Pa. 1977), *aff'd*, 595 F.2d 1265 (3d Cir. 1979). Chuy, a professional football player, brought suit against the Eagles and the National Football League seeking to recover the balance of his salary allegedly due on his contract and for damages for defamation and intentional infliction of emotional distress.

Chuy had suffered a serious injury while playing football. Chuy's claims for emotional distress were based on a statement made by a team physician who was being interviewed by the press. The doctor reported that Chuy had contracted a rare blood disease that would prevent him from ever playing football again. Chuy, having no prior knowledge of the existence of such a condition, claimed that upon hearing the report, he was put under incredible emotional anguish and he anticipated death.

The court held that the doctor's conduct was sufficiently outrageous. The court found that the doctor intentionally told reporters that Chuy was suffering from a blood disease, knowing that this was in fact not true. Chuy recovered $10,000 in compensatory damages for this infliction of emotional distress. He also recovered $60,000 in punitive damages, which was affirmed on appeal as not being excessive.

Athletic administrators must also be on their guard about statements made by members of an organization's staff that could lead to litigation such as that in *Chuy*. The following are examples of instances in which such statements to the media could lead to similar litigation:

- A coach's statement about the playing ability of a student-athlete, including professional career aspirations
- An administrator's statement about the employment tenure of a coach
- A trainer's announcement about the playing ability or injury of a student-athlete
- A sports information director's comments about student-athletes and coaches.

In any of these situations, if the statement was "extremely outrageous" and injured the individual about whom it was made, an athletic administrator might anticipate that litigation will be filed.

3.3.6. Damages for Intentional Torts

In a case involving intentional torts, the plaintiff may recover for lost earning capacity, medical expenses, pain and suffering, and for the loss of consortium (i.e., affection, assistance, and marital fellowship). These damages are termed *actual damages*. In an intentional tort case it is not necessary to prove actual damages in order to recover. The plaintiff may recover substantial damages without proving specific bodily injuries. Furthermore, torts involving intentional harm allow for recovery of damages for emotional suffering (i.e., humiliation, indignity, injury to feelings), as long as this suffering was proximately caused by the defendant's conduct.

Certain conduct by the plaintiff that is not sufficient to constitute a defense to the action may be considered in mitigation of damages. For example, although provocative words by the plaintiff do not justify the defendant's use of force, these words may be considered to mitigate the amount of damages awarded to the plaintiff.

In addition to actual damages, a plaintiff may recover *punitive damages*. Punitive damages are awarded to penalize a defendant who has acted willfully or has exhibited outrageous conduct. These damages are awarded on the theory that they may help to deter future wrongful conduct.

3.4. HARM TO ECONOMIC AND DIGNITARY INTERESTS

3.4.1. Defamation Law

Defamation law protects a person's reputation. The focus of a defamation action is on the alleged defamatory statement and its impact on third persons. The elements that must be proven to establish liability for defamation are the following:

1. A false statement concerning the plaintiff
2. The publication (communication) of the false statement by the defendant to a person(s) other than plaintiff
3. Fault, amounting to at least negligence, on the part of the defendant
4. Damage or injury to the reputation of the plaintiff.

A defamatory statement exposes the plaintiff to public hatred, shame, contempt, or ridicule. A statement may be oral or written, a photograph, a cartoon, or any other form of communication. The reputation protected by the law of defamation is the opinion of others. The plaintiff must show that his or her reputation was injured in the eyes of a respectable group of the community.

Defamation is divided into two categories, libel and slander. *Libel* is the publication of a defamatory statement in writing. There are three classes of libel: (1) libel per se, which includes materials that are obviously defamatory; (2) materials that could be taken as defamatory; and (3) materials that are not by themselves defamatory but when combined with other facts become libelous. *Slander* is the publication of defamatory matter through spoken words.

3.4.1.1. Libel

The basic elements of libel are a defamatory statement, its publication, and damages. Truth is a defense to a libel action, but it is only a qualified defense— not an absolute defense. The defendant has the burden of proving the truth of the communication if his or her defense is truth. If the statement is false, the plaintiff has the burden of proving that it was published with malice. To prove malice, the plaintiff must prove that the statement was made with hatred, ill will, or malevolent intent. The plaintiff must also prove that a third person was exposed to the publication. Finally, the plaintiff must prove actual damages.

There are two basic forms of damages in this context, general and special damages. *General damages* include humiliation and mental and physical suffering. *Special damages* are damages that are the natural, but not the necessary, result of the alleged wrong. The defendant may be able to mitigate damages by making a retraction or taking some other measure. General damages are presumed if the publication is libelous per se; special damages must still be proven.

3.4.1.2. Slander

Slander is publication of defamatory matter by spoken words. There must be a publication, and the plaintiff must be held up to scorn and ridicule as a result of the defamatory statement.

Truth is an absolute defense to a slander action. Again, however, the plaintiff must show that the statement was heard and understood by a third person. Unlike libel, the injury to reputation is not presumed. Therefore, the plaintiff must prove special damages, usually required to be of a pecuniary nature, unless it is slander per se.

In *slander per se* an injury to the reputation is presumed without proof of special damages if it falls into one of the following categories:

1. It accuses the plaintiff of a crime involving moral turpitude.
2. It adversely affects plaintiff's abilities in his or her profession, business, or trade.

3. It accuses the plaintiff of having a loathsome disease.

4. It accuses the plaintiff of sexual misconduct.

The U.S. Supreme Court has established standards that apply in libel and slander situations. In its decisions, the Court has balanced the competing interests of protecting the reputation of an individual against freedom of the press. In the first of its decisions in 1964, the Court held that the constitutional guarantee of a free press requires a public official to prove actual malice in the publication of a defamatory falsehood in order to recover for defamation (*New York Times Company* v. *Sullivan*, 376 U.S. 254 (1964)).

In 1967 the Court extended the constitutional privilege to public figures as well as public officials. Finally, in *Gertz* v. *United States*, 418 U.S. 323 (1974), the Court extended the "actual malice" standard. A public official or public figure who has been defamed must prove that the defendant published the statement with actual malice—that is, knowing that the material was false or in reckless disregard as to whether it was false or not.

Defamation should be distinguished from both intentional infliction of emotional distress and invasion of privacy. *Intentional infliction of emotional distress* is classified as an intentional tort and is concerned with the impact on the individual plaintiff without regard to third persons. *Defamation* involves the element of publication to third persons, as well as the requirement that the material be taken by these third persons as damaging. Defamation must also be distinguished from the tort of invasion of privacy. An action for *invasion of privacy* concerns one's right to peace of mind and comfort, while an action for defamation involves the plaintiff's character or reputation. Invasion of privacy can also be distinguished from defamation in that truth is an absolute defense to the defamation action, but truth is not a defense to an invasion of privacy action.

A leading sports case in the area of defamation law is *Curtis Publishing Co.* v. *Butts*, 388 U.S. 130 (1967). Curtis Publishing Company had printed an article alleging that Wallace Butts, while the athletic director at the University of Georgia, had supplied to Paul Bryant, the head football coach at Alabama, information concerning Georgia's game plan for an upcoming game against Alabama. The article was based on a phone conversation between Butts and Bryant, supposedly overheard by an insurance salesman.

Butts filed a libel suit against Curtis in federal court and the court awarded compensatory and punitive damages. Curtis appealed the decision to the Supreme Court, arguing that Butts was a public figure, and thus needed to prove that a public figure who is not a public official may recover damages for a defamatory falsehood which is obviously damaging to his reputation, through showing that the conduct of the publisher was highly unreasonable and constituted an extreme departure from the standards of investigation and reporting ordinarily adhered to by responsible publishers. The Supreme Court affirmed the trial court's decision.

Sports are played in public settings and are coached and administered in what often seems like "the heat of battle." Thus, athletic administrators have to be extremely cautious that what began as a sporting event does not erupt into litigation involving defamation—either libel or slander. The passions of the contest should not be allowed to evolve into inappropriate statements about an individual to the media or the general public.

Athletic administrators always have to be on guard for such possibilities and must instruct their staff about the potential litigation any such statement could cause for the organization or individuals involved.

NOTES

1. In *Riggs v. Clark County School District*, 19 F.Supp. 2d 1177 (D. Nev. 1998), a former high school volleyball coach sued the district and a district official for defamation for remarks allegedly made to parents of students following coach's termination. On defendants' motion to dismiss, the District Court held that under Nevada law, the statement that coach "was being replaced for the betterment of the program" constituted pure opinion.

2. In *Van Horne v. Muller*, 705 N.E. 2d 898 (Ill. 1998), a former professional football player, Van Horne, sued two radio broadcasters and their employers, alleging that statements made regarding an encounter between the one of the broadcasters and the athlete were defamatory. The statements claimed that Van Horne had physically threatened one of the two broadcasters. The complaint also asserted that the radio station had engaged in negligent and reckless hiring, supervision and retention of the broadcasters. The circuit court dismissed the defamation claim, reckless hiring, supervision and retention claims. However, the appellate court reversed the circuit court's dismissal of all counts. The Illinois Supreme Court agreed in part with the appellate court, ruling that there was sufficient evidence to state a cause of action for defamation against the broadcasters, writing, "A statement is considered defamatory if it tends to cause such harm to the reputation of another that it lowers that person in the eyes of the community or deters third persons from associating with them." However, the Illinois Supreme Court dismissed the claims against the radio station, because while the broadcasters had a history of "outrageous" behavior, they did not have a history of defaming persons. Therefore, the station took reasonable care in hiring and supervising the broadcasters.

3. In *Moore v. University of Notre Dame*, 968 F. Supp. 1330 (N.D. Ind. 1997), a former football coach alleged that he was defamed by his head coach who stated that the plaintiff only could coach for one or two more years, and that he was no longer physically capable of putting in long hours, like his coaching colleagues. Under Indiana law, this was deemed to be not defamatory per se. Furthermore, the plaintiff coach failed to demonstrate actual damages or establish actual malice as required for claim of defamation. The defendant's motion to dismiss was therefore granted.

Also see the following law review articles:

4. "College Administrator Loses Defamation Suit," 13 *The Sports Lawyer* 14 (January/February 1995).

5. Stephen G. Strauss, "Defamation and the Collegiate Athlete: The Case of Failed Reporting and an NFL Drug Test," 3 *Sports Lawyers Journal* 51 (Spring 1996).

3.4.2. The Tort of Invasion of Privacy

An action for invasion of privacy is designed to protect against unreasonable interferences with a person's solitude or "right to be let alone." Although some intrusions into a person's life are expected and must be tolerated in society, when the intrusions become excessive or unjustified, then a cause of action will exist for invasion of privacy.

One can invade the privacy of another in four distinct ways:

1. Intrusion by the defendant upon plaintiff's affairs or solitude
2. Publicly disclosing private facts about the plaintiff by the defendant
3. Publication by defendant of facts that put plaintiff in a false light in the public eye

4. Appropriation by defendant of plaintiff's picture or name for defendant's commercial gain.

In an action for invasion of privacy, the intrusion must be substantial and must be into an area for which there is an expectation of privacy. For example, simply staring at a person would not generally amount to an intrusion; wiretapping, on the other hand, would amount to an intrusion.

The plaintiff must also show that the publication of private matters involved a matter that in fact was truly private. Newsworthy public interest matters or public facts are not considered to be of a purely private nature. Court records, for example, are open to the public and are therefore not viewed as private facts.

The U.S. Supreme Court in *Time, Inc. v. Hill*, 385 U.S. 374 (1967) held that the First Amendment to the U.S. Constitution protects reports of newsworthy matters. These matters can be publicized unless, as was discussed in the previous section, actual malice is shown. The actual malice standard may be applied even though a plaintiff was a private person who did not want the publicity.

In *Bilney* v. *Evening Star Newspaper Co.*, 406 A.2d 652 (Md. Ct. App. 1979), a leading case in the area, members of the University of Maryland basketball team brought suit against two newspapers. The newspapers published an article concerning certain players whose academic standing was threatening their eligibility. The players based their action, in part, on the theory of invasion of privacy. The court, basing its decision on the *Restatement (Second) of Torts*, §652, held that the players were public figures. The court found that there was widespread public interest in Maryland basketball. When the players' academic standing threatened their eligibility, then the privacy of those facts lessened. The court stated that "the publication of their eligibility-threatening status was not unreasonable and did not trample community mores" of what is legitimate public interest.

The court relied primarily on the reasoning of the *Restatement (Second) of Torts*, §652D. Under this section, a public figure cannot complain when given publicity that was sought, even though it may be unfavorable. The *Restatement (Second) of Torts* also states that the publicity of public figures "is not limited to the particular events that arouse the interests of the public" (§652D, comment). The legitimate public interests of these figures extends into some of their private matters. The court also held that the right to make public the private facts of a public figure is not an unlimited right, and that what is allowable is determined by community mores: "The line is to be drawn when the publicity ceases to be the giving of information to which the public is entitled and becomes a morbid and sensational prying into private lives" (§652D, comment).

The *Bilney* case typifies the difficult burden an athlete has in winning an invasion of privacy action. The Maryland players were unsuccessful because the news article did not invade a "private" area. The opinion reflects how difficult it is for a person classified as a public figure to recover for invasion of privacy. Public figures must put up with more publicity concerning their private lives than those who are not public figures. Since most pro athletes and the majority of big-time college student-athletes would probably be classified as public figures, it would be difficult for them to recover under the theory of invasion of privacy.

3.5. PRODUCTS LIABILITY LAW

Products liability is an expansive area of tort law that allows a party who has been injured by a product defectively designed, manufactured, or distributed to recover under several possible causes of action. The causes of action in products liability cases are intent, negligence, strict liability, and breach of implied warranty of merchantability and fitness and representation theories (express warranty and misrepresentation).

The class of possible defendants in a products liability action is broad. Everyone in the chain of distribution of a product is potentially liable, from the manufacturer to the seller or lessor of the product to those who service or install the product. A product is any item of personal property, most commonly consumer goods, including the container in which it is sold. Even vacant land that has been altered by earth-moving equipment to be made into a baseball diamond can be a "product," so that the manufacturer (earth mover) could be liable for injuries caused by holes or bumps in the surface.

The plaintiff in a products liability case must show that a defect existed at the time the product left the control of the defendant and that the injury was caused by the defect. Courts have most frequently applied a definition of defect from the *Restatement (Second) of Torts*, §402A, which states that a product is in a defective condition if it is "unreasonably dangerous to the user." Comment (i) of section §401A further defines a defect:

> The article sold must be dangerous to the extent beyond that which would be contemplated by the ordinary consumer who purchases it, with the knowledge common to the community as to its characteristics.

In the amateur sports setting, an athletic administrator has to be particularly aware of potential product liability problems. Sports involve the participation of individuals and the use of equipment by those individuals, and both factors are the basis for any product liability lawsuit. Ultimately, such litigation leads to increases in a sports organization's insurance premiums, a subject discussed in Chapter 4, section 4.9., "Liability Insurance."

3.5.1. Products Liability Based on Intent

A defendant is liable to a plaintiff injured by an unsafe product if the defendant intended the consequences or knew with substantial certainty that they would occur. Liability based on an intentional tort is uncommon in products liability cases. It is more likely that such a case would be brought to court as a battery claim.

3.5.2. Products Liability Based on Negligence

In products liability law, a manufacturer of a product has the duty to meet legal standards of safety and care in the product's design, manufacture, and use. The product supplier and seller may additionally be liable for negligence if they have not exercised reasonable care.

The courts generally balance the probability and gravity of the potential harm against the social value of the product and the inconvenience of taking precautions in determining whether or not a duty of care has been breached. The standard of care involved in manufacturing is one of reasonable care in both the manufacture and the design of the product to ensure that it will be reasonably safe when used in the manner intended.

Where a product may be dangerous even when properly used, the manufacturer may have an additional *duty to warn* the product's users of the hazard. However, the manufacturer is not required to make the safest or best possible product, although the product will be compared to similar products. The similar products will be used to help determine what is a "reasonably" safe product.

Suppliers, the wholesalers of a product, must also exercise reasonable care. First, a supplier has a duty to use reasonable care to make a product safe. If the supplier knows or has reason to know that the product is dangerous and that the user is not likely to realize the danger, the supplier must additionally exercise reasonable care to *notify* the user of the potential dangers. For example, the Flybynight Company was contracted to replace a drainage system at a high school soccer field. After completion of the job, the ground around one of the drainpipes settled, leaving the pipe exposed. Kenny Keeper dived to make a save; he fell on the pipe and suffered severe injuries. The Flybynight Company was negligent for its failure to ensure the safety of the field. The school would also be a potential defendant for negligently hiring an incompetent contractor to install the new drainage system.

Sellers of a product are also subject to liability for negligence in some circumstances. A seller who knows a product is dangerous has a duty to warn a purchaser, who has no knowledge of the dangerous nature of the product. A seller may also have a duty to inspect a product manufactured by another if the seller knows or has reason to know that it is likely to be hazardous.

Advertisers and marketers of a product also have a duty to exercise reasonable care. When a product appears on the market, a warning about the dangers associated with the product must accompany it. This warning must be adequate and disclose the dangers from an improper use as well as dangers that are possible even when the product is properly used. The warning must also be sufficient to protect third parties who might reasonably be expected to come into contact with the product.

NOTE _____

1. In *Ford* v. *Nairn*, 717 N.E. 2d 525 (Ill. App. Ct. 1999), a minor trampoline user who injured her knee when jumping on the trampoline sued the trampoline's owners and manufacturer on theories of negligence and products liability. The manufacturer asserted a third-party claim against the owners. The Circuit Court of Jersey County granted summary judgment for defendants. Plaintiffs appealed, and the owners also appealed, seeking dismissal of the third-party complaint. The appellate court held that (1) a reasonable fourteen-year-old would appreciate the open and obvious danger of jumping on a recreational trampoline, and thus, there was no duty to warn, and (2) warnings issued by the manufacturer were adequate in any event.

3.5.3. Products Liability Based on Strict Tort Liability

The theory behind strict liability is that when the seller markets its product for use and consumption by the public, it assumes a special responsibility to any member of the public for any injury caused by the product. The public has the right to expect that the seller will provide a reasonably safe product. There is a strong public policy supporting the demand that the burden of accidental injuries caused by a seller's products be placed on those who marketed them. The theory is that the cost inherent in the assumption of responsibility can be insured; it will be treated as a cost of production and added to the cost of the item.

Therefore, the consumer is given the maximum possible protection from unreasonably dangerous products in that the people in the best position to provide this protection are those who market and profit from the products.

The strict tort liability definition states that one who sells a product which is unreasonably dangerous to the user or consumer because of a defect—whether in design or in manufacture—is held liable for any physical harm to the ultimate user or consumer, or that person's property, proximately caused by use of the product.

The following elements must be proved to establish a strict tort liability claim:

1. Strict duty owed by a commercial supplier
2. Breach of that duty by the defendant
3. Actual and proximate causation
4. Damages.

The seller must be engaged in the business of selling such a product and not merely a causal seller. This would include manufacturers, retailers, assemblers, or wholesalers. The plaintiff need not prove that the defendant was at fault or negligent in selling or producing a defective product—only that the product, in fact, is defective, causing it to be "unreasonably dangerous." This strict liability standard applies even if a seller exercised all necessary and appropriate care in the preparation and sale of the product.

The seller will be liable if the defective product was the actual cause of plaintiff's harm, provided that the product has not been changed from its initial state or condition upon leaving defendant's control. The same concepts of proximate causation governing general negligence claims are applicable to strict tort liability for defective products. Damages under a product liability claim are the same as those recoverable in negligence, i.e. personal injury and property damage.

Regarding defenses to a strict tort liability claim, ordinary contributory negligence is *not* a defense in a strict product liability action. Assumption of the risk for voluntarily and knowingly risky behavior on the part of the plaintiff, however, is a valid defense. Note that liability can be found only if the product has been used in the manner and for the purposes intended by the seller. Accordingly, a seller will not be liable for harm resulting from unforeseeable, abnormal use of the product.

3.5.4. Products Liability Based on Implied and Express Warranties

A cause of action for product liability may be based on a breach of warranty claim against a manufacturer. This is basically an adaptation of contract law to tort problems. First, the plaintiff must establish that there was an express or implied warranty. The plaintiff must then prove that the defendant breached the warranty. The advantage to a claim based on warranty principles is that the plaintiff does not have to prove that the product was defective in its design.

An *express warranty* is an affirmation of material fact concerning the nature and fitness of a particular product upon which the buyer might reasonably rely. An *implied warranty* does not arise from any words of the seller, either oral or in writing, but is a rule of law in every state. The rule is embodied in §2–314 of the Uniform Commercial Code, which states: "A warranty that the goods shall be merchantable is implied in a contract for their sale if the seller is a merchant with respect to goods of that kind." Merchantable goods are fit for the ordinary purposes for which such goods are ordinarily used.

3.6. VICARIOUS LIABILITY

The doctrine of vicarious liability imposes liability for a tortious act upon a person who is not personally negligent but is held liable because of the relationship between the parties. The most typical relationships that give rise to vicarious liability are master-servant (employer-employee) and principal-agent.

Vicarious liability is also known as the doctrine of *respondeat superior*. The most frequent situation in which vicarious liability exists is within the relationship of employer-employee. If A, an employee of C, negligently causes an injury to B, vicarious liability imposes liability for the negligent act by A upon C if the negligence occurs within the scope of that employment relationship. Under the doctrine of vicarious liability, C is liable to B, the party injured by A, even though C was not himself negligent, did not aid or encourage the negligence of A, and did everything he could to prevent harm to B. For example, if a player was injured due to the negligence of the groundskeeper, the employer of the groundskeeper (jointly with the groundskeeper) may be held vicariously liable to the injured player, if the tortious act occurs within the scope of his employment.

The rationale behind the doctrine is based on public policy considerations. Since the servant is furthering the master's enterprise, any accident that arises directly or indirectly from the enterprise should be paid for by the enterprise (owner). Such costs are considered as a cost of doing business. This places an increased burden on the master, but the master is in a better position to bear the risks of injuries to others by obtaining insurance against work-related accidents. This doctrine allows an innocent plaintiff to recover from the master, who is said to have "deep pockets," while the employee may be judgment-proof.

Vicarious liability causes the employer to be held responsible when the employer exercises control and direction over the employee, and the employee is negligent while acting within the scope of his employment. Vicarious liability is usually not imposed on the employer for intentional torts committed by the employee. An intentional tort is usually considered beyond the scope of authority and control of the employer, and not in the furtherance of the employer's business. For example, if a coach assaults a bartender after work, the school district will not be held liable under a vicarious liability theory. However, an employer may be held responsible for an intentional tort committed by an employee if the employee was under the authority and control of the employer and the employee is in a position where such torts may be encouraged or expected in furtherance of the employer's business. These same general rules apply to principal-agent vicarious liability situations in sports-related cases.

The doctrine of vicarious liability is widely applicable to tort actions for negligence in the sports setting. For example, a coach may be held liable for the actions of his players, a school district may be held liable for the actions of a coach or a teacher, or an athletic administrator may be held liable for the actions of a coach. In order for an employer to be held liable in these situations, the employee must first be found negligent under the primary standard of reasonable care, and then the action must be determined to have been within the scope of the defendant's employment.

In a case (sport or non-sport) involving a monetary award for damages, it is common practice to sue in the alternative—that is to sue each party involved in the alleged incident of negligence. This practice serves three primary purposes:

1. It allows the plaintiff to determine exactly who is liable for the particular injury.
2. It allows the plaintiff to determine which party involved in the suit has money sufficient to pay the damages award ("deep pockets").
3. It allows judicial efficiency by preventing multiple suits on the same cause of action against various defendants.

NOTES

1. In *Daniels v. Reel*, 515 S.E.2d 22 (N.C. Ct. App., 1999), the American Legion Department of North Carolina was named as a defendant under the theory of vicarious liability. Coaches for an American Legion baseball team had solicited members of the team to provide rides to an away game. One of the team members, a sixteen-year-old, was involved in an accident on the way to the game, killing another team member. While the lower court awarded summary judgment in the vicarious liability aspect of the suit, the appellate court reversed that decision, claiming that there was enough evidence of vicarious liability to pose the question to a jury.

2. In *Aboubakr v. Metropolitan Park District of Tacoma*, No. 25343-9-II, 1999 Wash. Ct. App. LEXIS 3440 (Wash. Mar. 19, 1999), plaintiff sustained a serious eye injury in an altercation with an opposing player following a baseball game, and brought suit against the park district which owned, operated, and maintained the field. By summary judgment, the trial court dismissed claims against the park district, the umpires, and coach, finding that they owed no legal duty to plaintiff. The court of appeals held that lack of foreseeability precluded the park district, umpires and coach from being held vicariously liable for the players' actions.

3. Chapter 4, "Application of Tort Law to Sports," discusses the ways that the doctrine of vicarious liability is applied to various persons in the sports industry, such as facility owners, university presidents, directors of athletic organizations, and owners of professional sports franchises.

3.6.1. Exception: Independent Contractors

The existence of independent contractors raises an important issue in understanding the scope of the doctrine of vicarious liability. An independent contractor is a person who, although in some way is connected to the employer, is not under the employer's control, and thus vicarious liability may not be imposed. To determine the status of any person, the law examines the degree of control that the employer has over the employee's actions. A person hired for a specific, limited purpose, with no direct supervision, who works without allowing the employer to have control over his or her actions, is most likely an independent contractor. If the person is an independent contractor, the employer may not be liable for negligence committed by that independent contractor.

As a general rule, a doctor who is provided by a school that is hosting a football game is considered to be an independent contractor. Here, although paid by the school district, the doctor is not in any way under its control when making medical decisions. Thus, the doctrine of vicarious liability would not be applicable, and the school would not be liable for the doctor's medical negligence.

Another group classified as independent contractors is officials and referees. In most cases the referee has been determined by the courts to be an independent contractor. (See Chapter 4, section 4.7., "Liability of Officials, Referees, and Umpires").

NOTES ──────────────────────────────────────

In the following case, the court did not adhere to the general principle that referees and officials are independent contractors.

1. In *Brighton School District v. Lyons*, 873 P.2d 26 (Colo. Ct. App. 1993), the court held that the official was an employee of the school district because the district exercised the right of control over the official.

In the following cases, the courts did adhere to the general principle that referees and officials are independent contractors.

2. In *Harvey v. Ouachita Parish School Board*, 545 So. 2d 1241 (La. Ct. App. 1989), an injured football player sued the state high school athletic association for negligence for injuries suffered as a result of excessively rough behavior. The court held for the defendant on the basis that the association was not responsible for the referees' failure to remove football players who were displaying excessively rough behavior. The court reasoned that though the association had registered the referees, the referees were neither agents nor servants of the association.

3. In *Classen v. Izquierdo*, 520 N.Y.S.2d 999 (N.Y. County Sup. Ct. 1987), plaintiff widow brought action against ringside physicians and the proprietor of the sports facility to recover damages for the death of her husband, a boxer. The proprietor did not participate in the selection of the referee or ringside physicians and did not provide them with training, instruction, or supervision. Consequently, the court held that the proprietor was not vicariously liable for any negligence of the referee in the boxing match for allowing the contest to continue since the referee was an independent contractor.

4. In *Wilson, et al. v. Vancouver Hockey Club*, 5 D.L.R. (4th) 282 (B.C. Sup. Ct. 1983), a doctor employed by the hockey club to treat players for hockey injuries failed to refer plaintiff hockey player to a specialist for a biopsy on a mole on plaintiff's arm. The plaintiff claimed that the doctor negligently failed to tell the player that he suspected cancer. Evidence indicated that the doctor made the final decision as to what treatment an injured player would have and whether an injured player would play, without advice from the management of the club; therefore, the doctor acted as an independent contractor and not as a servant of the hockey club. The court held that the club was not vicariously liable for the negligence of the doctor because he was an independent contractor.

5. In *Cramer v. Hoffman*, 390 F.2d 19 (2d Cir. 1968), the court found, on the basis of New York law, that an institution was not liable for the negligence of a physician who was an independent contractor exercising his own discretion. The court concluded that there was not an automatic agency relationship established between the university and its physician.

Also see the following law review articles:

6. Darryll M. Halcomb Lewis, "After Further Review, Are Sports Officials Independent Contractors?" 35 *American Business Law Journal* 249 (Winter 1998).

7. Mel Narol, "The Legal Status of Sports Officials," 11 *Sports Lawyers Journal* 1 (Mar./Apr. 1994).

3.7. WORKERS' COMPENSATION

Workers' compensation is a statutorily created method for providing cash benefits and medical care to employees and their dependents when employees suffer personal injuries or death in the course of employment. The purpose of the benefits is to provide employees and their dependents with greater protection than afforded by the common law remedy of a suit for damages. Each state has its own workers' compensation act that provides a system of monetary payments for the loss of earning capacity to an employee, according to a scale established by the state. The act may also have provisions for paying burial, medical, or other expenses incurred by the employee.

Workers' compensation acts differ as to where the funds are derived and the method of payment used in compensating claims. Some acts require the employer to make payment directly to the employee. Other acts provide payment out of a fund to which many different employers contribute. In other acts, the employer's private insurer makes payments.

The primary reason for passage of workers' compensation statutes was to eliminate the inadequacies of the common law remedies that resulted from the injured party having to show that the employer was negligent. Proving negligence was often difficult for the employee because of defenses available to the employer, such as contributory negligence, assumption of the risk, and co-worker negligence. Under a worker's compensation act the injured employee need only show that the employer was subject to the act, that he or she was an employee under the act's definition, and that the injury occurred during the course of employment. Fault or employer negligence is not a prerequisite to receiving worker's compensation benefits. Payments are made at intervals, when the injured party and his or her dependents need money most, instead of waiting until the completion of costly litigation. To claim a right to compensation, an employee need only fall within the terms of the statute.

This theory of compensation shifts the burden of economic loss from the employee and the employee's dependents under common law to the employer under the act. While the employer considers workers' compensation benefits part of the production cost, it is the consumer who will most likely bear the economic burden of the cost of the benefits, since the employer adds the costs to his products or services.

Every state's worker's compensation act has the same fundamental principle—the worker's right to benefit payments for injuries arising out of the worker's employment. Although each jurisdiction varies in the details of its act, the various acts have some general similarities.

For example, in all jurisdictions there is a short waiting period during which the employee must be either totally or partially incapacitated. This is to avoid small and insignificant claims. When the period ends, the worker is eligible for compensation beginning from the date of the injury. Every jurisdiction sets its own rate schedule prescribing minimum and maximum compensation amounts for total disability, partial disability, or permanent and total disability. These amounts are determined by each state's legislature and may be revised yearly. An additional benefit, separate from weekly compensation, is added for every person wholly dependent on the injured provider. An additional sum may be awarded for certain specific injuries, such as the loss of eyesight. Each state may have its own procedure for arriving at dollar amounts depending on the state's average wage or its economy.

Workers' compensation eligibility issues are of particular significance to college athletic administrators for three reasons: (1) a determination that scholarship athletes are employees of their institutions will allow injured student-athletes to collect workers' compensation benefits in some circumstances, increasing insurance costs for institutions and their athletic departments; (2) injured student-athletes, if found to be employees, may bring more workers' compensation claims or costly tort actions against institutions and their personnel in order to collect workers' compensation benefits; and (3) an athletic department or institution employee injured in an employer-sponsored athletic event may be found to be acting within the scope of employment and thus be eligible for workers' compensation benefits.

Workers' compensation claims filed by injured student-athletes against their institutions increased during the early 1980s. In response to this trend the NCAA in 1985 instituted a catastrophic injury protection insurance plan that could be purchased by member institutions. The NCAA's insurance policy provides benefits to catastrophically injured student-athletes regardless of fault. In many cases, the NCAA program may be more attractive than a successful workers' compensation claim because the student-athlete may obtain benefits immediately and avoid the time delays, costs, and uncertainties of litigation involved in filing for workers' compensation benefits. Yet, because the scholarship athlete/employee issue had not been firmly resolved, injured student-athletes may still bring worker's compensation cases.

However, the NCAA program has met its objectives. The NCAA would rather have the costs of the benefits to the injured student-athlete covered by an insurance policy than paid for through the more costly and more tenuous method of worker's compensation. The catastrophic injury protection plan is paid for by the NCAA and its member institutions, and benefits the institutions by protecting them against the sudden and substantial costs of injury benefits. The student-athlete also benefits from the plan, because it provides immediate benefits without depending on a worker's compensation board or judge's opinion on the issue.

Student-athletes receiving some form of compensation for athletic activities, including athletic scholarships, have at times been considered employees by the courts and thus entitled to workers' compensation benefits for sports injuries. This view is, however, the minority position.

This issue was raised in *Rensing* v. *Indiana State University Board of Trustees* (see note 10) and in *University of Denver* v. *Nemeth* (see note 6). In these cases the courts were divided as to whether the student-athlete was eligible to receive workers' compensation benefits.

In finding that the student-athlete was an employee of the institution, and thus eligible for benefits, one court ruled that the continued receipt of a job, free meals, or scholarship money was conditioned on the student-athlete's participation in football, thereby creating a contract for employment. With the employment contract established, workers' compensation benefits were then paid to the employee-athletes injured or killed during the course of their employment.

In other cases, however, courts did not find that the proper employment contract existed, and benefits were denied. In two such cases it was found that football was not an integral moneymaking part of the university's educational function. Therefore, while the student-athlete was employed because of the receipt of an athletic scholarship, that employment was not in the institution's usual trade or business.

When considering the issue of whether an athletic department or institution's employee who was injured while participating in employer-sponsored athletic activities is entitled to workers' compensation benefits, the courts attempt to determine whether the injury occurred in the course of employment. Factors the courts will consider include whether the event occurred on the employer's property and during working hours; whether the employer provided financial support, awards, and/or equipment; the level of encouragement to participate expressed by the employer; and any benefits derived by the employer as a result of the employee's participation in the event. For instance, if the employer required employees to participate in athletic activities with prospective clients as a means of increasing business and income, an employee injured in such activities may prove that the injury occurred while he or she was acting in the course of his or her employment. In addition, injuries sustained while participating in a local school system's basketball league to promote better public relations have been found compensable under worker's compensation statutes (see note 2).

NOTES

The following are cases where the court granted worker's compensation:

1. In *Bowen v. Worker's Compensation Appeals Board*, 86 Cal. Rptr. 2d 95 (Cal. Ct. App. 1999), a California Court of Appeals ruled that a promising young minor league pitcher should not be denied benefits under California's workers' compensation law simply because the player's contract was subsequently signed by his team outside of the state and because the contract was approved by the Major League Baseball Office of the Commissioner, also located outside of the jurisdiction.

2. In *Dozier v. Mid-Del School System*, 959 P.2d 604 (Okla. App. Div. 1998), a teacher sought award of workers' compensation benefits for injury he sustained while playing in a charity basketball game to raise funds for a school athletic program. The Court of Civil Appeals held that the school district derived substantial direct benefit from the teacher's participation in basketball game, and thus teacher was entitled to award of benefits.

3. In *Connery v. Liberty Northwest Insurance Corp.*, 929 P.2d 222 (Mont. 1996), the Supreme Court of Montana posed the question of whether an injury that occurred in a warm-up run for an employee-ski instructor immediately prior to her class is compensable. The court held that a "warm-up run" was a prescribed duty of her employment as a ski instructor, so that her injury occurred during the course and within the scope of her employment.

4. In *McCarthy v. Quest International Co.*, 667 A.2d 379 (NJ Super. Ct. App. Div. 1995), plaintiff was injured while participating in a tug-of-war during company picnic. Compensation was allowed, because her attendance was mandatory; she was urged to enter the tug-of-war by her company's president against her own desires; and the employer so involved the plaintiff in the activities of the picnic as to make the activity an incident of her employment.

5. In *Van Horn v. Industrial Accident Comm*, 33 Cal. Rptr. 169 (Cal. Ct. App. 1963), a student-athlete was killed in a plane crash while returning from a game in a plane provided by the school. The court held that his family's worker's compensation claim did fall under the state's act.

6. In *University of Denver v. Nemeth*, 257 P.2d 423 (Colo. 1953), Nemeth, a student-athlete injured during football practice, was found eligible for worker's compensation. Since Nemeth was given meal money and a job on campus only if he performed well on the football field, he fulfilled the worker's compensation act's requirement that the injury arise out of an act in the course of employment.

The following are cases where the court denied worker's compensation:

7. In *Waldrep v. Texas Employers Insurance Association*, No. 03-98-00053, 2000 Tex. Ct. App. LEXIS 4023 (Tex. Nov. 16, 2000), the Texas Court of Appeals let stand a lower court ruling that an injured college football player was not an employee of the school at the time of his paralyzing injury 26 years earlier, and therefore, he could not claim worker's compensation benefits.

8. In *Dandenault v. Workers' Comp Appeals Bd*, 728 A. 2d 1001 (Pa. Commw. 1999), a professional hockey player sought benefits for injury he sustained while playing summer

hockey in order to remain in shape during off-season. The court held that the player's injury did not arise in the course of his employment so as to be compensable.

9. In *Farren v. Baltimore Ravens, Inc.*, 720 N.E. 2d 590 (Ohio Ct. App. 1998), the court found that a professional football team could not deny player worker's compensation benefits merely because he was between contracts.

10. In *Rensing v. Indiana State University Board of Trustees*, 444 N.E. 2d 1170 (Ind. 1983), the court noted a number of factors that suggested that the scholarship did not constitute an employment contract: (1) Rensing had not reported his benefits on his income tax returns; (2) NCAA regulations are incorporated by reference into the scholarship agreement, and since these regulations prohibit payment for athletic participation, the scholarship cannot be a job contract; and (3) the employer's right to dismiss Rensing on the basis of poor performance was conspicuously absent. Finally, the court also found that neither of the parties had the intent to enter into an employment contract.

11. In *Coleman v. Western Michigan University*, 336 N.W.2d 224 (Mich. Ct. App. 1983), the Michigan State Court of Appeals found that an injured college football player was not entitled to worker's compensation benefits. According to the court, the plaintiff was not an "employee" under the meaning of the Michigan worker's compensation act. The Michigan act, unlike that of some other states (the Court named California's as an example) places the burden of proof in establishing employment on the plaintiff. In other states, the burden of proof is placed on the *employer* to disprove an employer-employee relationship. The court was also persuaded by the language of a dissenting Indiana Court of Appeals judge in *Rensing* (see note 10). Quoting Judge Young of Indiana: "[Plaintiff's] participation in football may well have benefited the university in a very general way. That does not mean that [plaintiff] was in the service of the Trustees. If a student wins a Rhodes scholarship or if the debate team wins a national award that undoubtedly benefits the school, but does not mean that the student and the team are in the service of the school. [Plaintiff] performed no duties that would place him in the service of the university."

Also see the following law review articles:

12. Eric D. LeBeau and Thomas H. Sawyer, "Worker's Compensation and Scholarship Athletes: Are They Protected?" 10 *Journal of Legal Aspects of Sports* 18 (2000).

13. Sean Alan Roberts, "College Athletes, Universities, and Workers' Compensation: Placing the Relationship in the Proper Context by Recognizing Scholarship Athletes as Employees," 37 *South Texas Law Review* 1315 (October 1996).

14. David W. Woodburn, "College Athletes Should be Entitled to Workers' Compensation for Sports-Related Injuries: A Request to Broaden the Definition of Employee Under Ohio Revised Code sec. 4123.01," 28 *Akron Law Review* 611 (Spring 1995).

Chapter 4

APPLICATION OF TORT LAW TO SPORTS

INTRODUCTION

Chapter 4 is organized according to possible defendants in sports tort cases. The chapter begins with a discussion of the potential liabilities of a *participant* in a sporting event. It then focuses on the potential liabilities of *coaches and teachers* in the areas of supervision, instruction and training, medical assistance, and vicarious liability for actions of fans and players. The legal theory most commonly used in this area is negligence. The chapter next covers the potential liabilities of *administrators, schools, and universities*. Administrators may be found negligent in hiring personnel (an employee such as a coach or teacher) or in supervising personnel. Administrators may also be found vicariously liable for the negligence of an employee in rendering medical assistance. Finally, administrators may be found negligent for not providing equipment, or vicariously liable if an employee did not furnish equipment or furnished ill-fitting or defective equipment. Schools and universities may also be sued under a vicarious liability theory for the negligence of any of their employees in the areas of supervision and personnel, medical assistance, and equipment. A defense for the administrator, school or university may be the doctrine of sovereign immunity.

The next topics presented in Chapter 4 are that of charitable immunity and civil liability immunity legislation, followed by the liability of *facility owners and possessors*, which may include defects in a building or negligent supervision of a crowd, and the liability of *medical personnel* for negligent treatment of an injured athlete or fan.

The chapter continues with a discussion of the potential liabilities of *officials, referees*, and *umpires*. Some officials have been sued for injuries to athletes that have allegedly resulted from a failure to take corrective action to remedy the injury-causing situation. Examples include failing to stop a game during inclement weather or allowing objects or spectators to be too close to the playing area. Officials, referees, and umpires have also been sued for the incorrect application of game rules and making incorrect judgment calls.

The next section sets forth cases involving defects in equipment. It is followed by a discussion of liability insurance, waivers and releases of liability. High school athletic associations and high schools are purchasing insurance to combat the rising number of tort claims being made by those associated with sports activities. (The National Collegiate Athletic Association has maintained a disability insurance program since the 1985–1986 academic year.)

4.1. LIABILITY OF PARTICIPANTS

The liability stemming most directly from sports activity is that for injuries to participants. At one time, most sport-related injuries were viewed as a natural outgrowth of the competitive and physical nature of sports. This attitude was supported by the traditional belief that a participant assumes the dangers inherent in the sport and is therefore precluded from recovery for an injury caused by another participant. Although this theory has some merit, it fails to address injuries that occur during a game that are not necessarily an outgrowth of competitive spirit.

This traditional attitude has been strictly scrutinized in decisions beginning with *Nabozny v. Barnhill*, 334 N.E.2d 258 (Ill. App. Ct. 1975), which clearly establish that a player does not necessarily assume the risk of all injuries resulting from the gross recklessness of another player (see note 1(j)). Nor does the player necessarily consent to intentional attacks falling outside the recognized rules of the sport. Thus, the defenses of assumption of the risk or of consent must be reviewed on a case-by-case basis to determine whether or not they are applicable in a particular instance (see chapter 3, section 3.1.5., "Defenses for Negligence").

This change in attitude has occurred in part because of the increasing number of serious injuries to sports participants. The increased volume of sports participation resulting from the involvement of boys and girls, and men and women, in unprecedented numbers has produced a corresponding increase in the number of sports-related injuries. The NCAA estimates that in football, basketball, and wrestling seasons alone there are approximately 1.3 million injuries at 32,650 high schools and 70,000 injuries at 900 colleges and universities (78 per institution). On the average, there is one injury per player per year in the National Football League.

A second reason for the change in attitude is that professional sports, and to some extent intercollegiate and Olympic athletics, are now viewed as businesses. Because of this, people are more inclined to see the situation as one in which a lawsuit is a viable option. Athletic organizations have greater revenues and may have "deep pockets" to pay large awards. A third reason is that legal precedents have been established which allow injured athletes to recover. Finally, the rise in sport-related lawsuits is a result of society becoming increasingly reliant on the judicial system for the resolution of disputes.

An increase in claims of negligence and other tortious conduct has paralleled the rising number of sports injuries in recent years. One factor behind the rise in participant-versus-participant lawsuits is the steady erosion of the athlete's traditional reluctance to sue fellow participants. The increasing recognition of the dangers involved in playing a game against an opponent who does not follow an accepted safety rule has increased the likelihood of a lawsuit. Players are refusing to accept injury-provoking actions of opponents when the actions are not sanctioned by the rules of the game. There are legal precedents which recognize that each player has a legal duty to refrain from unreasonably dangerous acts (see Chapter 3, section 3.2., "The Tort of Reckless Misconduct (Gross Negligence)").

Courts have found that many sports, including soccer, softball, and football, have created safety rules to help define the often unclear line between legal and illegal behavior on the field. A safety rule is one that is initiated to protect players and to prevent injuries. The existence of safety rules mandates that in many situations a player be charged with a legal duty to every other player involved in the activity. In cases involving the alleged violation of a safety rule, the courts have held that a player is liable for tort action only if his or her conduct displays deliberate, willful, or reckless disregard for the safety of other participants and results in injury to another participant. Thus, a participant may recover either for an intentional tort or for gross negligence. Actions based on ordinary negligence are still difficult to establish in athletic participant cases, though case law indicates that there are situations in sports for which the commonly accepted defenses of assumption of risk and contributory negligence are not adequate to bar recovery by the plaintiff.

NOTES _____

1. The courts discussed the liability of participants in sports in the following cases.

(a) In *Kiley* v. *Patterson*, 763 A.2d 583 (R.I. 2000), a second baseman filed a lawsuit seeking damages for injuries she suffered as a result of a collision with a base runner during a recreational game of softball. The Supreme Court of Rhode Island held that the duty of care owed by participants in team athletic events to each other is not measured by ordinary negligence. Instead, in order for a participant plaintiff to prevail, he or she must prove willfulness or recklessness on the part of the other participant.

(b) In *Monk* v. *Phillips*, 983 S.W.2d 323 (Tex. App. Ct. 1998), a golfer's partner hit the golf ball off the toe of his golf club and injured the golfer. However, the courts held that this did not rise to the level of recklessness or intentional conduct that would make the golf partner liable for injuries.

(c) In *Jaworski* v. *Kiernan*, 241 Conn. 399, 696 A. 2d. 332 (1997), the Supreme Court of Connecticut concluded that the defendant owed the plaintiff a duty of care to refrain from reckless or intentional conduct during a co-ed soccer game.

(d) In *Dotzler* v. *Tuttle*, 449 N.W.2d 774 (Neb. Sup. Ct. 1990), plaintiff sued defendant for injuries arising out of a collision between them during a "pick-up" basketball game. The trial court found for the defendant and the plaintiff appealed. The supreme court held that a participant in a contact sport is liable for tortious conduct only if he acts willfully or with reckless disregard for the safety of the plaintiff, but is not liable for ordinary negligence. The case, however, was reversed and remanded on the issue of the plaintiff's contributory negligence, which was improperly submitted to the jury.

(e) In *Picou v. Hartford Insurance Co.*, 558 So. 2d 787 (La. Ct. App. 1990), the court of appeals held that a softball base runner could not be held liable for negligence toward the second base player who suffered an ankle injury in a collision. The court held that the defendant did not act in an unreasonable or unsportsmanlike manner and thus could not be held liable in negligence.

(f) In *Gauvin v. Clark*, 537 N.E.2d 94 (Mass. 1989), plaintiff hockey player sued the defendant for injuries sustained when the defendant "butt-ended" the plaintiff in the abdomen with his stick. The supreme judicial court held that the defendant was not liable for injuries caused by his violation of a safety rule where he did not act in reckless disregard of the plaintiff's safety.

(g) In *Novak v. Lamar Insurance Co.*, 488 So. 2d 739 (La. Ct. App. 1986), plaintiff softball player brought action against a second softball player, the homeowner's insurer of that player's father, and the insurer of the church which sponsored the defendant softball player's team. Plaintiff sought recovery for injuries sustained when the two collided as defendant softball player ran to first base. The court held that the defendant softball player was not acting in a reckless or unsportsmanlike manner. The court reasoned that the risk of collision was a foreseeable risk which the plaintiff had assumed.

(h) In *Osborne v. Sprowls*, 419 N.E.2d 913 (Ill. 1981), a bystander sued a participant for injuries incurred during a "tackle-the-football" game. This game is a combination of football, keep-away, and soccer in which all players chase the person with the football until he or she is tackled or kicks or throws the ball away. The Supreme Court of Illinois determined that an ordinary negligence standard would apply because Osborne was neither a participant nor was he located in an area where the game was or could be in progress. The court determined the defendant owed the plaintiff the duty to select an area free from the presence of nonparticipating individuals.

(i) In *Barrett v. Phillips*, 223 S.E.2d 918 (N.C. Ct. App. 1976), a wrongful death suit against a high school and an athletic association was brought when Barrett's son was killed in a collision during a high school football game with a player over twenty years old. The defendants were in violation of a rule prohibiting players over age nineteen from playing. The court reasoned that the purpose of the rule was not for the safety of the players, and there was no actionable negligence because there was no causal connection between the death and the violation of the rule.

(j) In *Nabozny v. Barnhill*, 334 N.E.2d 258 (Ill. App. Ct. 1975), plaintiff soccer player filed suit for injuries received when he was kicked in the head by an opponent during an amateur soccer game involving two teams composed of high school age players. The defendant, David Barnhill, was playing a forward position for one team, and the plaintiff, Julian Nabozny, was the goaltender for the other team. Barnhill kicked Nabozny in the head while Nabozny was in possession of the ball. Contact with the goaltender while he is in possession of the ball is a violation of FIFA (International Association Football Federation—soccer's international governing body) rules which governed the contest. The resultant injury left the plaintiff with permanent skull and brain damage. Nabozny brought suit, and the trial court directed a verdict in favor of the defendant.

On appeal, the court noted that it did not wish to "place unreasonable burdens on the free and vigorous participation in sports by our youth," but also stated that "athletic competition does not exist in a vacuum." Therefore, in reversing the trial court decision, the court held that a player is charged with a legal duty to every other player on the field to refrain from conduct proscribed by a safety rule. The court held that when athletes are engaged in athletic competition, all teams involved are trained and coached by knowledgeable personnel; a recognized set of rules governs the conduct of the competition; and a safety rule is contained therein which is primarily designed to protect players from serious injury. Thus, a reckless disregard for the safety of other players cannot be excused.

(k) In *Gaspard v. Grain Dealers Mutual Insurance Co.*, 131 So. 2d. 831 (La. Ct. App. 1961), Andrus Gaspard brought suit for damages for personal injuries on behalf of his son, Ronnie, after an injury to the boy in a playground baseball game. Defendant, Grain Dealers Mutual Insurance Company, had issued a comprehensive liability policy to Alfred Viator, the father of the boy responsible for the plaintiff's injury. At the trial court level, the defendant denied any negligence on the part of Ronald Viator and pleaded assumption of risk as a bar to plaintiff's recovery. In the alternative, the defendant alleged contributory negligence of Ronnie Gaspard. After a decision in the defendant's favor, the plaintiff filed this appeal. The appeals court found that young Viator's action did not constitute negligence because he exercised a reasonable degree of care. Gaspard assumed the risk as he "knew of the danger and clearly acquiesced or proceeded in the face of danger by voluntarily playing the game." Accordingly, the court denied Gaspard's appeal.

(l) In *Griggas v. Clauson*, 128 N.E.2d 363 (Ill. App. Ct. 1955), Griggas, a nineteen-year-old member of an amateur basketball team, brought suit for injuries received during a game. During that game he was guarded by La Verne Clauson. While Griggas had his back to Clauson and was about to receive a pass from a teammate, Clauson pushed him and then struck him in the face with his fist. As Griggas fell, Clauson struck him again and knocked him unconscious. Clauson began to swear profusely and made statements to the effect that he was going to teach Griggas a lesson and that one of the two was going to play in the city and the other was not. Griggas was hospitalized for about three weeks. The Appellate Court of Illinois supported a trial court decision for Griggas. It held that the evidence in the record supported the finding that Griggas was subjected to a wanton and unprovoked battery.

2. The liability of participants has also been a subject of much judicial scrutiny on the professional sports level. The following cases examine this area of sports law.

(a) In *McKichan v. St. Louis Hockey Club*, 967 S.W. 2d. 209 (Mo. Ct. App. 1998), plaintiff, a professional hockey goaltender for a minor league affiliate of the NHL's Vancouver Canucks, was injured during a game. Plaintiff sued the opposing player who charged into him, as well as the offending player's team owners. About three weeks before trial, the plaintiff and defendant players settled their claims and counterclaims against each other. However, the case proceeded against the team under vicarious liability theory, and a jury awarded the plaintiff $175,000. The state appellate court overturned the jury award, however, stating, "we find that the specific conduct at issue in this case, a severe body check, is a part of professional hockey. This body check, even several seconds after the whistle and in violation of several rules of the game, was not outside the realm of reasonable anticipation. For better or for worse, it is 'part of the game' of professional hockey. As such, we hold as a matter of law that the specific conduct which occurred here is not actionable."

(b) In *Hackbart v. Cincinnati Bengals*, 435 F. Supp. 352 (D. Colo. 1977), *rev'd*, 601 F.2d 516 (10th Cir. 1979), Charles Clark, a running back with the Cincinnati Bengals, was sued for reckless misconduct by Dale Hackbart, a defensive back for the Denver Broncos. Clark had struck Hackbart in the head, an action outside the rules of the game of football. The trial court had ruled that there was no duty between the players. However, the appeals court found enough justification for a retrial on a reckless misconduct theory before a jury to determine the liability of defendant Charles Clark. The case was settled before trial for a reported $200,000.

3. In 2002 Chicago Cubs pitcher Ben Christensen settled his portion of a battery claim filed against him and several other defendants by former University of Evansville player, Anthony Molina. An incident occurred in 1999 while Christensen was a student at Wichita State University. Molina was standing about 24 feet from home plate when he was hit in the left eye by a Christensen fastball. Molina said Christensen deliberately hit him after being warned about "timing" Christensen's pitches. The case against the university and members of the coaching staff is pending in Sedgwick County (Kansas) District Court.

4. For further information on participant liability in sports, see the following law review articles.

   (a) Robert Carroll, "Determining Duty of Care Between Sports Co-Participants in Light of the Indiana Comparative Fault Statute," 11 *DePaul University Journal of Sports and Entertainment Law* 425 (Fall 2001).

   (b) Terrence J. Centner, "Tort Liability for Sports and Recreational Activities: Expanding Statutory Immunity for Protected Classes and Activities," 26 *Journal of Legislation* 1 (2000).

   (c) Ray Yasser, "In the Heat of Competition: Tort Liability of One Participant to Another: Why Can't Participants Be Required to Be Reasonable?" 5 *Seton Hall Journal of Sports Law* 253 (1995).

4.2. LIABILITY OF COACHES AND TEACHERS

Coaches and teachers, as individuals, are always responsible for any intentional torts they commit in their capacity as coaches or physical education teachers. They are generally not shielded (see Chapter 3, section 3.3.3., "Defenses for Assault and Battery") from liability by virtue of their positions through the defenses of consent, privilege, and immunity.

The coach is judged by the standard of a "reasonable coach," and the teacher by the standard of a "reasonable teacher." There are some limited exceptions in which coaches and teachers are held to a lower standard of care and will not be held liable unless they are deemed to be grossly negligent. One situation involves coaches or teachers who are given the status "in loco parentis"—that is, the coach or teacher is placed in the position of the parents of the student-athlete. A coach or teacher may, however, have a number of defenses available (see Chapter 3, section 3.1.5., "Defenses for Negligence").

Since a minor is often involved in this area, note should be taken that certain defenses, such as contributory negligence, comparative negligence, and assumption of the risk, may be affected by the different standard of care for children (see Chapter 3, section 3.1.1.2., "Standard of Care for Children"). The defense of sovereign immunity is a particularly important one for coaches and teachers. Generally, the coach or teacher cannot be sued individually when the school district is protected under sovereign immunity as discussed in section 4.4.1. of this chapter. However, this protection is limited, and may not cover the coach who is acting outside the scope of employment or who has performed his or her job in a clearly improper manner (acted with misfeasance). The sovereign immunity protection is also limited to coaches at public institutions, as opposed to coaches at private institutions.

Until recently, very little litigation was brought against coaches and teachers as a result of the sovereign immunity protection and the reluctance of potential plaintiffs to bring lawsuits. This was especially true in the case of coaches and teachers, who were often members of the community and highly respected for their work. However, the coach and teacher are increasingly likely to be sued due to the greater likelihood of injured student athletes filing lawsuits and the erosion of the sovereign immunity doctrine.

In many cases, the institution is sued under the doctrine of respondeat superior (also called the doctrine of vicarious liability) for the individual coach's or teacher's negligence, although the individual is also named as a defendant. In future cases the coach and teacher may be sued individually. Areas of responsibility for which a coach or teacher may be successfully sued include supervision, instruction and training, and medical assistance. Coaches and teachers have also been sued under the theory of vicarious liability for the actions of fans and players. However, vicarious liability lawsuits for the actions of fans and players usually have not been successful.

Prior to addressing those areas individually, certain important points are beneficial for institutional administrators to remember regarding the liability of coaches and teachers. Those include the following:

1. Coaches and teachers must be aware of safety issues when coaching and instructing.
2. Coaches and teachers must be careful with punishment-type drills.
3. In terms of risk management, administrators need to know the activities of the coaches and teachers.
4. Also in terms of risk management, coaches and teachers need to be aware of liability issues.

Adherence to these key points may prove tremendously valuable in eliminating potential liability of coaches and teachers, as well as subsequent institutional liability under vicarious liability theories, by minimizing potentially injurious situations.

4.2.1. Failure to Provide Adequate Supervision

Coaches and teachers are responsible for providing reasonable supervision to the student-athletes under their direction. However, they are not insurers of everyone under their supervision. Examples of failure to provide adequate supervision include negligent supervision at a football game and failure to provide the proper equipment for the game. Examples may also include improperly supervising an off-season weight training program or encouraging an injured student-athlete to play. An additional responsibility for the coach or teacher is to check the playing area to make sure it is in proper condition and that nothing is on or near the playing area that could cause injury; such obstructions include benches, other participants, and spectators.

Finally, the coach or teacher also may be sued for non-playing field activities, such as supervising student-athletes who are going to or from the playing field. The coach or teacher is responsible for providing reasonable supervision. Any supervisory capacity carries with it the responsibility to exercise due care—that is, the care of a "reasonable supervisor" (see Chapter 3, section 3.1.1., "Duty of Care Owed"). This due care must be provided for the safety of anyone who is likely to or actually does come into contact with the area under supervision. The duty entails using reasonable care in either rectifying dangerous situations or warning those who may encounter them of the possible hazards. A supervisor generally is not liable for any *intentional* acts of his employees unless it can be proved that he or she was negligent in choosing or supervising the employee(s) involved. A school district or supervisor is liable in such instances only if the institution, or one to which the district or supervisor is legally responsible, breaches the requisite standard of reasonable care. The school district and/or supervisor will only be liable if the employee and the action taken satisfy the requirements of vicarious liability (see Chapter 3, section 3.6., "Vicarious Liability"). Also, the doctrine of sovereign immunity (see section 4.4.1.) may bar the action depending on the state where the action took place.

A supervisor is not, however, an insurer of everyone's safety; rather, the supervisor needs only to exercise reasonable care. Unless there is information or notice to the contrary, the supervisor is entitled to assume that all under his or her supervision will be exercising due care. Thus, a spectator who is injured by another spectator may not enforce a claim against a school district or its administrators unless the school district or administrator, having had notice that the other spectator was likely to cause an unreasonably dangerous condition, failed to take steps to prevent the injury. Past experience, moreover, will be considered when assessing liability. For example, if the same spectator appeared at a later contest and injured a fellow spectator, the school district might be held liable because the first situation provided warning of the person's potentially dangerous nature. The duty of care required may depend on the type of event. Hockey games, for instance, may require more security and precautions than track and field events.

The general rule is that the coach has no duty regarding the matching up of participants. Yet the prudent athletics administrator would ensure reasonable matchups in order to minimize risk of litigation in this area, as well as decrease the potential for injury to the participant.

NOTES _____

1. In *Gruenke v. Seip*, 225 F.3d 290 (3rd Cir. 2000), a female high school swimmer filed suit against her swim coach, alleging he invaded her privacy by pressuring her to take a pregnancy test. In December 1996 Emmaus High School Coach Michael Seip noticed that the then 17-year-old Gruenke appeared to be heavier in the water and suspected she might be pregnant. In talks with her coach, Gruenke denied that she was pregnant or even sexually active. Over the next month, Seip had a female coach, teammates, a nurse, a guidance counselor and even teammates' mothers talk to Gruenke about the issue, and allegedly pressured her to take a pregnancy test. By the time a private doctor confirmed the pregnancy in early March, Gruenke was nearly six months pregnant. She gave birth on July 3, 1997. In 2002, Gruenke and her mother, Joan, settled a federal civil suit they had filed against Seip alleging that he violated the swimmer's privacy.

2. In *Prejean vs. East Baton Rouge Parish School Board*, 729 So.2d 686 (La. Ct. App. 1999), a fifth grade student was injured on an outdoor basketball court while practicing basketball with other fourth and fifth graders. A volunteer basketball coach was actively playing on one of the teams when the plaintiff lost the ball out of bounds. The coach pushed a student, who fell on the plaintiff's leg, causing his injury. The coach immediately called for paramedics, who promptly transported the plaintiff to the hospital. The appeals court, in reversing the decision of the trial court, held that the volunteer basketball coach did not breach the duty he owed students by participating in a basketball scrimmage. The

court reasoned that all team sports involve a risk of injury as a result of physical contact, and that the other students could have provided a risk just as great as that of the coach.

3. In *Sciotto v. Marple Newtown School District*, No. 98-2768, 1999 U.S. Dist. LEXIS 16386 (E.D. Pa. Oct. 22, 1999), a high school wrestler was seriously injured when he was thrown to the floor by a visiting college wrestler. The student's parents filed suit alleging constitutional violations, contending that the coach knew or should have known of the likely risk of injury inherent in allowing a high school student to wrestle with an older, stronger, and heavier college wrestler. This case was settled for an undisclosed amount.

4. In *City of Miami v. Cisneros*, 662 So. 2d 1272 (Fla. Dist. Ct. App. 1997), during a city-sponsored football game, a 70–75 pound participant broke his leg in his attempt to tackle a 128-pound opponent. The appellate court disallowed the assumption of the risk defense because the coach had promised the participant's parents he would not wrestle the boy against anyone over 90 pounds.

5. In *Searles v. Trustees of St. Joseph's College*, 695 A. 2d. 1206 (Me. 1997), plaintiff college basketball player sued his coach for repeatedly playing him in games despite the fact that the coach knew he had a serious knee injury. The player sought damages for his injuries and reimbursement for related medical expenses, and also alleged intentional infliction of emotional distress and sought punitive damages. While the superior court granted summary judgment to the coach, the Supreme Judicial Court of Maine remanded the question to a jury, stating that the coach was charged with a duty to exercise reasonable care for his players and that questions of material fact existed as to whether the coach had exercised such care.

6. In *Edelson v. Uniondale Union Free School District*, 631 N.Y.S.2d 391 (N.Y. App. Div. 1995), a high school wrestler received injuries during a match against an opponent in a higher weight classification than plaintiff's normal category. The appellate court granted summary judgment, finding the school district's duty of care "limited to exercising ordinary reasonable care in protecting the plaintiff from unassumed, concealed or unreasonably increased risks." The plaintiff was an experienced wrestler who could properly calculate the risks involved in the match, and the court deemed the ultimate cause of his injury was the way he received a wrestling move, not the size of his opponent.

7. *Vargo v. Svitchan*, 301 N.W.2d I (Mich. Ct. App. 1980), was a suit brought by a high school athlete who, while participating in a summer weight training program at the high school gymnasium, attempted to lift a 250- to 300-pound weight, fell, and received injuries resulting in paraplegia. The plaintiff's lawsuit charged the school's athletic director, principal and superintendent with negligent supervision of the football coach. The court of appeals held that the school's principal and athletic director were sued for "personal neglect" in maintaining inadequate school facilities, in allowing an illegal summer weight-lifting program and providing insufficient supervision. Therefore, they were not entitled to the protection of the governmental immunity statute. The school superintendent was entitled to protection under the government immunity standard because there was no "personal neglect" on his part.

8. In *Lynch v. Board of Education of Collingsville Community School District*, 390 N.E.2d 526 (Ill. App. Ct. 1979), parents of a junior in high school brought a negligence suit on her behalf against the school district for damages she received as a result of an injury suffered in a "powderpuff" intramural football game. Plaintiffs alleged ordinary negligence on the part of the defendant in failing to provide adequate equipment and willful and wanton misconduct in failing to adequately supervise the game. An appeals court, in affirming the trial court's decision for the parents, held that since the teams' coaches were teachers and the field on which the contest was played was fenced and could have been locked to keep students out, there was sufficient evidence for the jury to conclude that the game was authorized by the school. The court also held that the presence of the plaintiff's parents at the game site did not obviate the school's duty to provide adequate equipment.

9. *Morris v. Union High School District A*, 294 P. 998 (Wash. 1931), was a suit brought

by a high school athlete who injured his back during football practice. The coach, who was well aware of the injury, or should have become aware of it in the exercise of reasonable care, "permitted, persuaded and coerced" the athlete to play in a game. As a result of the athlete's participation, he suffered more serious injuries to his back and spine. The athlete brought suit against the school district alleging that the school district was liable for the negligence of its coach, who negligently coerced him to play. The court ruled in favor of the plaintiff and held that the school district was liable.

    10. For more information, also see the following law review articles:

      a. Anthony S. McCaskey, "A Guide to the Legal Liability of Coaches for a Sports Participant's Injuries," 6 *Seton Hall Journal of Sports Law* 7 (1996).

      b. Gerard T. Noce, "Individual and Institutional Liability for Injuries Arising from Sports and Athletics," 63 *Defense Counsel Journal* 517 (Oct. 1996).

4.2.2. Failure to Provide Proper Instruction and Training

Coaches and teachers are responsible for providing proper instruction and training to the student-athletes, and they should be qualified to teach the particular activity involved. The coach additionally must properly instruct the student-athletes on the activity, the safety rules, and the proper method of playing. In a number of cases, the injured player alleged that the coach or teacher did not provide proper instruction and training. A proper preseason conditioning program should also be provided, although such programs become an issue where football practice begins in August and some players experience fatal injuries related to heat exhaustion.

Coaches and teachers should keep detailed records of their instruction and training sessions. They should also be aware of any new developments in their sport. Some companies have started producing instruction and training films to assist coaches and teachers in preparing their student-athletes. Another area of potential liability for the coach or teacher is a claim by a student-athlete of assault and battery. Several issues are raised in this area. Is there a defense of privilege? Is the standard of care "reasonable care" or "gross negligence"? Does sovereign immunity protect the coach and teacher? Can force be used to bring about compliance with commands and to punish prohibited conduct? Can force be used when the player has not performed adequately? There has not been a great deal of litigation in this area, but coaches and teachers should be aware that cases may be brought.

NOTES _____

    1. In *Schultz v. Foster-Glocester Reg'l School Dist.*, 755 A.2d 153 (R.I. 2000), the plaintiff, a cheerleader, was injured at cheerleading practice while practicing a basket toss. The basket toss required two cheerleaders to toss the plaintiff into the air and catch her in their interlocking arms; however, they failed to catch her and she missed the safety mat. The plaintiff badly injured her elbow and suffered a displaced radia head fracture. The plaintiff filed a negligence suit against the school, alleging that it failed to properly train, supervise, and instruct. She further alleged that they failed to provide proper equipment and proper post-injury treatment. The Supreme Court remanded the case to a Superior Court trial on the question of whether the minor assumed the risk of this injury.

    2. In *Taylor v. Massapequa International Little League*, 689 N.Y.S.2d 523 (N.Y. App. Div. 1999), a ten-year-old participant in a youth baseball league brought personal injury action against the league for injuries he sustained upon sliding into a base at the coach's direction. There were factual questions as to whether the plaintiff was aware of, appre-

ciated, and voluntarily assumed the risks of sliding into a base. The court therefore denied the defendant's motion to dismiss the complaint.

3. In 1996, fourteen-year-old Chris Ondras was rendered a quadriplegic as a result of participating in a football drill near Seattle. Ondras alleged that his coach was negligent and the school district was vicariously liable in instructing him to tackle another player and allowing the tackle to take place. Ondras' family received a $6.25 million settlement from the Snohomish School District in 1999.

4. In *Trustees of Trinity College v. Ferris*, 491 S.E.2d 909 (Ga. Ct. App. 1997), while practicing for a regatta, a member of the men's rowing team was injured in a collision with a boat rowed by the college's women's team. Plaintiff sued the college and coaches of the men's and women's teams for gross negligence. The court ruled that a jury had a right to conclude that the program's supervision and instruction was poor enough to warrant gross negligence.

5. In *Hammond v. Board of Educ.*, 639 A.2d 223 (Md. Ct. Spec. App. 1994), Tawana Hammond, the first female high school football player in Carroll County, Maryland's history, was injured in her team's initial scrimmage. Her family filed suit in the Circuit Court for Carroll County against the Board of Education of Carroll County seeking $1.25 million in compensatory damages. The Hammonds claimed that the high school authorities negligently failed to warn them of the potential risk of injury inherent in playing football and that if they had been so warned Tawana would not have chosen to play football and her mother would not have permitted her to do so. After the parties conducted discovery, the Board moved for summary judgment, which the circuit court granted and the appellate court subsequently affirmed. The appellate court reasoned that the danger of football was "ordinary and obvious," and that the school board, therefore had no duty to warn the Hammonds of the danger.

6. In *Rutledge v. Arizona Board of Regents*, 660 F.2d 1345 (9th Cir. 1981), *aff'd. sub norm. Kush v. Rutledge*, 460 U.S. 719 (1983), plaintiff student-athlete sued his college football coach for assault and battery, demotion, harassment, embarrassment, defamation, and deprivation of his scholarship. Plaintiff claimed that in October 1978, the coach took his helmeted head between his hands, shook it from side to side, yelled obscenities, and then struck his mouth with his fist. Plaintiff filed suit in Arizona state court but was denied relief. He then filed suit in federal district court. The court dismissed the complaint, and Rutledge appealed. On appeal, the 9th Circuit Court of Appeals held that the university, the board of regents, and the athletic director were entitled to at least partial immunity. The coaches were not entitled to immunity, and the athletic director was not immune on the claim he failed to supervise the coach properly. However, the court dismissed Rutledge's assault and battery complaint because it had been previously litigated in state court.

7. In *Pirkle v. Oakdale Union Grammer School Dist.*, 253 P.2d 1 (Cal. Sup. Ct. 1953), an eighth grade student brought an action against the school district for injuries received from being blocked during a touch football game that was played without supervision. The court held for the defendant on appeal, ruling that the players had been properly selected and instructed. The court also held that plaintiff's injuries could not have been readily apparent to a lay person and that no further damage resulted from a delay in receiving medical treatment.

8. In *Hogenson v. Williams*, 542 S.W.2d 456 (Tex. 1976), an action for assault was brought when the coach, displeased with the blocking of a seventh grade player, grabbed him by the face mask and knocked him to the ground. The player received a severe cervical sprain. The jury found for the defendant, but the appeals court held the trial judge had improperly interpreted the rule of "privileged force" granted a teacher when he instructed the jury that "intent to injure is the gist of an assault." Rather, a teacher or coach can use force necessary to invoke compliance with his commands or to punish the child for prohibited conduct. A coach cannot use force merely because the student's performance is inadequate, even though the coach may consider such violence to be constructive. The jury verdict was reversed and remanded.

9. In *Kluka v. Livingston Parish School District*, 433 So. 2d 302 (La. 1983), a basketball coach was held not liable for injuries to a student who caught his foot between two mats while wrestling the coach in a friendly match. The court held that the student initiated the match and knew that wrestling could lead to injury.

10. In *Thompson v. Seattle Public School District* (unpublished decision 1985), plaintiff high school football player sought to recover damages for injuries sustained during a high school football game. The plaintiff was injured after lowering his head to ward off tacklers. The court decided in favor of the plaintiff on the basis that the player was not properly warned of the dangers of lowering his head while carrying the football.

11. In *Vendrell v. School District No. 26C, Malheur County*, P.2d 406 (Or. 1961), plaintiff, a freshman football player who had played two years of junior high football, brought suit against the school district for damages for the neck injury he sustained while playing in a high school game. The plaintiff suffered a fractured neck when he lowered his head and collided with two opposing players. The plaintiff contended that he was an inexperienced player and had been improperly trained. The court of appeals ruled against the plaintiff, holding that the plaintiff was not inexperienced in that he had played for two years in junior high school and during those years had received substantial football training from competent coaches. The court held that the game of football is an inherently rough sport in which body contact and some degree of injury are inevitable and that no player should need to have this explained.

4.2.3. Failure to Provide Prompt and Capable Medical Assistance

A common risk encountered in the area of sports is that of serious injury. There are two important points for the coach's attention regarding medical assistance. First, the coach should know what medical personnel are present. Second, if medical personnel are not present, their accessibility should be determined in advance. When an injury to an athlete or spectator appears to be serious, those in charge of the activity are under a duty to use reasonable efforts to obtain reasonably prompt and capable medical assistance. At the same time, there is a duty to refrain from actions that might aggravate an injury, when a reasonable person would know of the risk. The coach and teacher are held to a standard of "reasonable care" when rendering medical assistance to an injured student-athlete. They are not expected to provide the assistance of a doctor or one with medical training. In fact, some of the obligations of the coach and teacher have been shifted to others. For example, many states have passed statutes requiring that medical personnel be in attendance at games. Such laws may reduce the liability exposure for the coach and teacher.

The institution may be the responsible party if medical personnel have not been provided. In addition, the institution may be responsible for having medical personnel "reasonably" available, even when it is not statutorily mandated. With medical personnel available, the care of the injured student-athlete may not be undertaken by the coach or teacher. Therefore, in most situations, the main responsibilities of the coach and teacher are twofold. First, they may have to render assistance before the medical personnel arrive. First-aid training may be helpful to prevent a situation in which, for example, the coach improperly moves an injured student-athlete. The second responsibility is to exercise reasonable care in sending an injured athlete for medical treatment.

NOTES ⎯⎯⎯⎯⎯⎯⎯⎯⎯⎯⎯⎯⎯⎯⎯⎯⎯⎯⎯⎯⎯⎯⎯⎯⎯⎯⎯⎯⎯⎯⎯⎯⎯

1. In the summer of 2001, two highly publicized legal cases resulted following football players' deaths during pre-season training camp. Both cases are pending.

(a) Minnesota Vikings' offensive lineman Korey Stringer died of heat stroke after collapsing in practice on a hot day. In 2002, the Stringer family announced a $100 million wrongful death lawsuit in Minnesota's Hennepin County state court, naming as defendants the Vikings; then-head coach Dennis Green; offensive line coach Mike Tice; trainer Fred Zamberletti; head trainer Chuck Barta; Dr. W. David Knowles of the Mankato Clinic, who was in charge of medical care on the field at the time; and the Mankato Clinic. The complaint alleges that Coach Tice had called Stringer a "big baby" as he was struggling for breath on the hot day. The complaint can be viewed online at http://news.findlaw.com/hdocs/docs/sports/strngrvkngs011502cmp.pdf.

(b) Northwestern University football player Rashidi Wheeler died after collapsing during a wind sprint conditioning drill. The Cook County medical examiner ruled that the cause of death was exercise-induced bronchial asthma, and Wheeler's family alleges that the university did not provide reasonable and prompt medical care for an asthma attack. However, university President Henry Bienen has publicly maintained that Wheeler did not die of an asthma attack, suggesting instead that performance-enhancing dietary supplements played a role in the death. Wheeler's family filed a wrongful death complaint in the Cook County Circuit Court against the university, Head Coach Randy Walker, and several members of the training and coaching staff. For more information, see Lance Pugmire, "Wheeler Attorney Doesn't Expect a Settlement," *Los Angeles Times*, Sports; Part 4; Page 6, November 30, 2001.

2. In *Gahan* v. *Mineola Union Free School District*, 241 A.D.2d 439, 660 N.Y.S.2d 144 (N.Y. App. Div. 1997), coaches may have exacerbated a high school softball player's injury by moving her before medical personnel arrived, creating an additional risk. The question was remanded to a jury for consideration.

3. In *Kleinknecht* v. *Gettysburg College*, 989 F.2d 1360 (3rd Cir. 1993), the court held that when a college or university recruits an athlete to play a particular sport, a special relationship arises which imposes a duty of reasonable care. In this instance, the college has a duty to provide prompt medical care for an athlete injured while engaged in a school-sponsored athletic activity.

4. In *Stineman* v. *Fontbonne College*, 664 F.2d 1082 (8th Cir. 1981), plaintiff was a deaf student-athlete whose softball coaches were aware of her handicap. Plaintiff had signed an authorization for emergency medical treatment in the event of an injury. During the course of practice plaintiff was struck in the eye with a ball. A coach applied ice and advised her, despite the great amount of pain she was experiencing, to go to her room and rest and she would be all right. Neither coach who was present suggested that she seek medical attention. No immediate professional medical attention was given, even though the school infirmary was across the street. Permanent eye damage resulted from the injury. The trial court found negligence of the college in failing to provide the proper medical assistance. The appeals court affirmed the decision; however, it reduced the damages from $800,000 to $600,000.

5. In *Mogabgab* v. *Orleans Parish School Board*, 239 So. 2d 456 (La. Ct. App. 1970), an action brought by parents for the wrongful death of their son, a high school football player who died as a result of heatstroke and exhaustion following a practice. The plaintiffs sued the coach, the school principal, and the school district on the theory that the school was negligent in not making sure the coach was properly trained. They argued also that the school was negligent in making arrangements for the proper care of sick and injured players. The court held that the coach who actively denied the student-athlete access to medical treatment for two hours after symptoms of heatstroke and shock appeared was guilty of negligence. However, the court did not find negligence attributable to the principal, school district, physical education supervisor, or school superintendent because they were unaware of the events.

6. In *Welch* v. *Dunsmuir Joint Union High School District*. 326 P.2d 633 (Cal. Ct. App. 1958), plaintiff high school football player was injured during a scrimmage between two high school teams and brought suit against the school district. The player was lying on the ground unable to get to his feet. One coach suspected the player might have a serious

neck injury and had him take hold of his hands to see whether they could grip. The evidence was conflicting as to whether or not the team physician, who was present at the scrimmage, examined the player before he was moved to the sidelines. Evidence indicated, however, that plaintiff was carried from the field without the aid of a stretcher or board or any other solid structure beneath him. Medical testimony established that the plaintiff became a permanent quadriplegic as a result of damage to the spinal cord. The jury ruled for the plaintiff and the appeals court held that from the evidence presented the jury could have reasonably inferred that both the doctor and the coach were negligent in the removal of the plaintiff from the field—the coach for failing to wait for the doctor and allowing the plaintiff to be moved, and the doctor for failing to act promptly after the injury.

4.3. LIABILITY OF ADMINISTRATORS, SCHOOLS, AND ATHLETIC ORGANIZATIONS

Sports-related injuries that occur within the confines of an educational institution raise the issue of legal accountability of the institution itself. From the perspective of the seriously injured plaintiff, it may be more desirable to obtain a judgment against an institution rather than an individual coach or instructor, because the institution is much more likely to have a "deep pocket" from which the plaintiff bringing suit can receive monetary damage awards.

If an administrator or institution is subject to liability, the standards to which it will be held are the same as in similar areas of tort law. The administrator and institution are required to exercise reasonable care to prevent reasonably foreseeable risks and to make foreseeably dangerous conditions safe by repairing or warning. If the institution fails to maintain a reasonable standard of care, it may be sued for negligence. For example, the administrator or institution should establish rules for the safe use of facilities, provide supervision of athletic activities, hire qualified personnel, provide proper medical assistance, and provide proper equipment. Institutions cannot guarantee the safety of students, but they are subject to liability when the institution or someone for whom the institution is legally responsible does not meet the standard of care required by the law.

The administrator, school, or university may also be sued under the theory of vicarious liability for the alleged negligence of an employee. An administrator may be sued in his or her role as the supervisor of a coach or teacher. The institution may also be sued in its role as the employer of the administrator, coach, teacher, referee, or doctor, or as the owner or processor of a facility.

One roadblock in the path of the potential plaintiff, however, is the sovereign immunity doctrine (see section 4.4.1., "Sovereign Immunity"). This doctrine is a rule of law, which in many states exempts public schools and universities from private suit. Sovereign immunity has been around for centuries, but more recently the doctrine has eroded out of concern for injured plaintiffs, who previously could not collect when injured. In states where sovereign immunity has been partially eliminated, there are usually special rules of procedure that the plaintiff must carefully follow.

Vicarious liability and sovereign immunity issues may substantially overlap with the liability of facilities, where administrators, schools, and universities are often the facility owners and possessors. In these cases, the administration needs to be careful about the duty to control crowds at athletic events, such as when fans rush to tear down goalposts. In 1993, more than seventy spectators were injured at a University of Wisconsin football game when fans rushed onto the field after an upset victory over Michigan, forcing those at the front of the crowd against a chain-link fence. A state appeals court dismissed a suit filed by eight injured students in 1998, finding they could not sue school officials due to Sovereign Immunity.

4.3.1. Failure to Provide Supervision of Athletic Activities and to Hire Qualified Personnel

The administrator is the supervisor of the coach or teacher, and as such may be held liable in negligence for failing to exercise reasonable care in fulfilling this responsibility. Many of the administrator's duties and responsibilities are similar to the supervisory duties of the coach or teacher in dealing with student-athletes. In dealing with personnel, administrators may be held liable if they have not exercised reasonable care in hiring coaches and teachers with proper skills and qualifications, and in ensuring that properly qualified personnel are supervising.

Schools and universities are generally sued on a vicarious liability theory, meaning that the negligence of their employee is imputed to the employer. The negligent individual may be an administrator, a teacher, a coach, a substitute teacher, a student teacher, or a referee. Any of these individuals, and the school or university, may be immune from lawsuit based on sovereign immunity (see section 4.4.1., "Sovereign Immunity").

NOTES

1. In *Kane v. North Colonie Central School District*, 708 N.Y.S.2d 203 (N.Y. App. Div. 2000), a high school student sued the school district, alleging inadequate supervision by the school stemming from injuries sustained by the plaintiff during an indoor track practice. The coach directed the plaintiff and her teammates to run up and down the hallway of the high school for thirty minutes. The plaintiff tripped and sustained injuries. She sued the school district, alleging inadequate supervision. On appeal, the plaintiff offered evidence that "the risk of contact and falling is unreasonably increased where the runners do not maintain a safe and appropriate distance, typically a stride, from one another." The appellate court held that there was sufficient evidence "to raise a question of fact as to whether the defendant's supervision was inadequate and resulted in the failure to exercise reasonable care."

2. In *Phillipe v. City of New York Board of Education*, 678 N.Y.S.2d 662 (N.Y. App. Div. 1998), a student was killed in a pickup football game that took place in a school yard. The survivors of the decedent filed suit against the city board of education. The Supreme Court, Appellate Division reasoned that since the game occurred prior to the start of the school day, the defendant school board had no duty of supervision.

3. In *Moose v. Massachusetts Institute of Technology*, 683 N.E. 2d 706 (Mass. App. Ct. 1997), a university was held liable for injuries a pole-vaulter sustained when he fell off of the back edge of a landing pit and hit his head. Evidence was provided indicating that the length of the landing pit and its closeness to the hard track surface did not provide a safe environment. This was exacerbated by the fact that the pole-vaulter was using a pole that was too light for his weight and he was running too fast on his approach. The court determined that this sort of accident was reasonably foreseeable, and therefore held the defendant liable.

4. In *Scott v. Rapides Sch. Bd.*, 732 So. 2d 749 (La. Ct. App. 1999), the court held that the school district breached its duty to a student who was injured while attempting a long jump in physical education class. The coach did not provide adequate and proper instructions regarding the method to successfully and safely complete a long jump under maximum effort and conditions.

5. In *Giovinazzo v. Mohawk Valley Community College*, 617 N.Y.S.2d 90 (N.Y. App. Div. 1994), a softball player injured her foot while playing in muddy conditions on the softball field, and filed suit against her college for negligence, specifically in the maintenance of the playing conditions but also for failure to provide adequate supervision. The defendant institution was found not liable under a successful assumption of the risk defense. The plaintiff's awareness of the poor field conditions, and voluntary participation nevertheless, sufficiently established her assumption of the risk. Therefore, the court found no failure in the duty of care by the defendants.

6. In *Schiffman v. Spring*, 609 N.Y.S.2d 482 (N.Y. App. Div. 1994), a college varsity soccer player brought suit against the athletic director and coach after being injured on a wet, mud-soaked playing field. Although the plaintiff and several teammates had complained about the field to the coach and suggested that the game should not have been played, the appellate court ruled that the experienced soccer player consented to the risk of playing on the muddy field and dismissed the complaint.

7. In *Benitez v. New York City Bd. of Educ.*, 541 N.E.2d 29 (N.Y. App. Ct. 1989), plaintiff high school football player brought personal injury action against the board of education and the city public school athletic league. The plaintiff alleged negligence of the coach and principal in permitting him to play in a fatigued condition in a mismatched game. In reversing the lower court's decision, the appeals court ruled in favor of the defendants and held that the player assumed the risks of injury in competition and was not under inherent compulsion to play.

8. In *Hemphill v. Sayers*, 552 F. Supp. 685 (S.D. Ill. 1982), a university football player, who sustained an injury to his cervical spine as a result of an allegedly defective football helmet, brought an action against the university's athletic director, football coach, athletic trainer, and helmet manufacturer. The court denied the motion by the defendants to dismiss. The court held, *inter alia*, that the university athletic director, football coach, and athletic trainer were not immune under the Eleventh Amendment from liability for negligence in failing to warn of dangers of a football helmet because they were being sued in their individual capacities.

9. In *Montgomery v. City of Detroit*, 448 N.W.2d 822 (Mich. Ct. App. 1989), the mother of a student who died of a heart attack after collapsing on a school's athletic field sued the principal, the teacher, and the operator of the emergency medical service telephone. The court found for the defendants, holding that (1) the principal was immune from liability; (2) the alleged failure of the teacher to learn to make emergency calls was immune as a discretionary decision; (3) the telephone operator was not negligent; (4) the statute which provided that school officials could be sued for discretionary acts constituting gross negligence did not apply; (5) the student's civil rights were not violated by schoolteacher's acts, which allegedly delayed student's arrival at hospital.

10. In *DeMauro v. Tusculum College, Inc.*, 603 S.W.2d 115 (Tenn. 1980), plaintiff brought suit for injuries he received in a golf class. Plaintiff was injured when a teaching assistant, an inexperienced golfer who was assigned to supervise plaintiff's class, was attempting to demonstrate how to hit a golf ball. The teaching assistant "shanked" the shot, which struck the plaintiff in the face. The court allowed the plaintiff to sue the college under the doctrine of vicarious liability.

11. In *Cook v. Bennett*, 288 N.W.2d 609 (Mich. Ct. App. 1979), plaintiff elementary school student brought suit after being seriously injured while playing "kill" during recess. In the game of "kill" all participants attempt to obtain the ball by tackling the lone participant who has it. In regards to the school's principal, the appeals court reversed the trial court's decision and held that "the extent to which a school principal is protected by immunity is dependent on whether the act complained of falls within the principal's discretionary or ministerial powers." The court held that inadequate supervision is not a discretionary function and is not protected by governmental immunity.

12. *Brahatcek v. Millard School District*, 273 N.W.2d 680 (Neb. 1979), was a suit involving an action for the death of a ninth-grade student who was accidentally struck by a

golf club during physical education class. The court held that the school district and instructors were negligent in not providing supervision and that the lack of supervision was the proximate cause of the student's death. It held that the instructors should have foreseen the intervening negligent act of the student who fatally struck the other student. If there had been proper supervision, the death would not have occurred, and therefore, intervening negligence of the classmate did not preclude the district from liability for the death.

13. In *Carabba v. Anacortes School District*, 435 P.2d 936 (Wash. 1967), the plaintiff, a high school wrestler, brought suit against the defendant school district to recover injuries sustained in a match. The plaintiff was injured when the referee's attention was diverted and his opponent applied an illegal "full nelson" hold. The plaintiff was paralyzed below the neck due to substantial severance of his spinal cord. The court held that because the referee was an agent for the school district the school could be held vicariously liable for the referee's negligence.

14. Multiple tort cases have arisen from the actions of mascots at professional sporting events.

(a) A spectator at a Miami Heat game brought claims for physical and emotional damages after 'Burnie,' the Heat mascot, pulled her to the ground. The spectator had fallen to the ground while resisting Burnie's insistent tugging, as he urged her to come onto the floor and dance with him. In *Gil-De-Rebollo v. Miami Heat Ass'n*, 137 F.3d 56 (1st Cir. 1998), the U.S. Court of Appeals for the First Circuit affirmed a jury's $50,000 damage award to the plaintiff.

(b) In 1998, a jury in Philadelphia awarded a man $2.5 million in compensatory damages from the Philadelphia Phillies. The team's mascot, the Phillie Phanatic, allegedly permanently disabled the plaintiff by rupturing a disc in his back during a bear hug. This was at least the second successful jury verdict against the Phillies for actions of the Phanatic. In 1995, a 72-year-old man won a $128,000 verdict against the team, after he was knocked down by the mascot at a church fair. For more information, see Elizabeth Raymer, "Baseball Mascot Runs Afoul of Law," 18 *The Lawyers Weekly* 14 (August 21, 1998).

(c) In 2001, a man sued the Florida Marlins for an undisclosed amount after he was allegedly hit in the eye by a rolled up t-shirt fired into the stands from Billy Marlin's makeshift cannon. The case is pending.

15. For more information, see the following law review article: Howard P. Benard, "Little League Fun, Big League Liability," 8 *Marquette Sports Law Journal* 93 (Fall 1997).

4.3.2. Failure to Provide Proper Medical Assistance

Administrators, schools, and universities are generally not responsible for providing direct medical treatment to an injured student, student-athlete, or spectator. However, the administrator, school, or university may be sued on the doctrine of vicarious liability if the coach improperly provided medical treatment. The administrator, school, or university generally will not be held responsible for the medical malpractice of a doctor, since in most cases the doctor is held to be an independent contractor and not an employee. However, the administrator, school, or university may be held responsible for the negligent selection, supervision, or hiring of medical personnel. Potential liability also exists if the administrator, school, or university was negligent by not providing medical personnel at a game or practice. Many schools and universities have rules that require medical personnel at certain events, such as football or basketball games. Many states, including Massachusetts, require a physician or person trained in emergency medical care to be assigned to all interscholastic football games. See Mass. Gen. Law Ann. Ch. 71, § 54A (see note 1). And, finally, the school or university may be held responsible on the theory of vicarious liability if the administrator is found to be negligent.

NOTES ⎯⎯⎯⎯⎯⎯⎯⎯⎯⎯⎯⎯⎯⎯⎯⎯⎯⎯⎯⎯⎯⎯⎯⎯⎯⎯

1. Mass. Gen. Law Ann. Ch. 71, § 54A, reads: "A physician employed by a school committee or a person who has completed a full course in emergency medical care as provided in section six of chapter one hundred and eleven C shall be assigned to every interscholastic football game played by any team representing a public secondary school in the commonwealth, and the expenses of such physician or person shall be paid by the school committee of the city, town or district wherein such football game is played."

2. In *Kennedy v. Syracuse*, No. 94-CV-269 1995 U.S. Dist. LEXIS 13539 (N.D. N.Y. Sept. 12, 1995), the court reasoned that a university was not negligent in failing to provide a trainer at a gymnastics practice simply because it had traditionally provided a trainer at all basketball and football practices. The plaintiff, an injured scholarship gymnast, had argued that the university had failed to take reasonable care.

3. In *Kleinknecht v. Gettysburg College*, 989 F.2d 1360 (3rd Cir. 1993), a twenty-year-old student-athlete died of cardiac arrest while participating in a practice session of the intercollegiate lacrosse team at Gettysburg College. His parents brought a wrongful death suit against Gettysburg College, claiming that the school breached the duty of care it owed their son by failing to provide proper medical services at the time of his death.

The student-athlete was participating in a drill when suddenly he stepped away from the play and dropped to the ground. There was no trainer on the field during the practice because the practice session was held during the nontraditional fall practice season and the school did not require trainers to be at these practices. The practices were being held on the softball fields outside the football stadium. The nearest telephone was in the football stadium's training room, which required scaling an eight-foot fence in order to get inside the stadium. The head trainer was the first to administer CPR, but five to twelve minutes passed before he was summoned and arrived on the field. It was also estimated that another ten minutes elapsed before the first ambulance arrived at the scene.

The district court ruled for the defendant, stating that even though the parents had presented evidence showing that severe and life-threatening injuries can occur and are not out of the question during contact sports, the college still had no duty to the student-athlete because it could not foresee that a young athlete who had no previous history of medical trouble was likely to suffer cardiac arrest during a practice or game. The court of appeals, however, ruled that the district court's definition of foreseeability was too narrow and felt that the parents had produced ample evidence that a life-threatening injury occurring during participation in an athletic event such as lacrosse was reasonably foreseeable. The college, therefore, owed the student-athlete a duty, which required the college to have measures in place at the lacrosse team's practice in order to provide prompt treatment in the event that any member of the lacrosse team suffered a life-threatening injury.

4. In *Cramer v. Hoffman*, 390 F.2d 19 (2nd Cir. 1968), plaintiff brought suit after being seriously injured while making a tackle during football practice. Plaintiff alleged that the cervical injuries and paralysis which he received were a consequence of negligence in moving him and in treatment. The action was brought against the university, the coach, and the treating physician. The plaintiff in his suit sought to hold the university liable for any negligence of the doctor under an agency theory. The trial judge ruled as a matter of law that the alleged negligence of the doctor could not be imputed to the university. The court held that the plaintiff failed to set forth any substantial facts to prove an agency relationship between the doctor and the university. The Circuit Court of Appeals agreed and noted that under New York law an institution is not responsible for the negligence of physicians who are independent contractors exercising their own discretion.

4.3.3. Failure to Provide Safe Equipment

The failure to provide equipment or the failure to provide satisfactory equipment has been the basis for a number of lawsuits brought against administrators, schools, and universities. The individuals who are involved with equipment vary from institution to institution. They include the coach, teacher, and equipment manager; business managers who purchase the equipment; the athletic director; and/or other administrators. All of these individuals are employees of the institution, and the institution may be responsible for their negligent acts under the theory of vicarious liability.

Although many lawsuits filed against institutions regarding equipment have been unsuccessful, they indicate potential liability areas. The first consideration is the purchase of appropriate equipment for the athletic activities offered. The second consideration is the purchase of equipment that is of satisfactory quality. For example, with respect to football helmets, the institution should adhere to guidelines established by the National Operating Committee on Standards for Athletic Equipment (NOCSAE). Its web site is www.NOCSAE.org. The third consideration is the provision of equipment for the athletic activities in which equipment is necessary. For example, a plaintiff may allege that a defendant school or school district was negligent in not providing equipment for a tackle football game. The fourth consideration is the provision of properly fitting equipment. For example, a plaintiff may allege that football equipment did not fit properly and that it was the proximate cause of the resulting injuries. The fifth and last consideration is the periodic inspection of the equipment and reconditioning when necessary. The NOCSAE guidelines will again be useful.

NOTES

1. In *Palmer* v. *Mount Vernon Township High School District 201*, 169 Ill.2d 55, 662 N.E.2d 1260 (Ill. 1996), the plaintiff, a star high school basketball player who had previously injured his cheekbone under his left eye, was told by his coach not to use his protective eye goggles because someone else might get hurt. The plaintiff lost the vision in his left eye after he was hit in the eye by another player's finger. The Illinois Supreme Court held that the school district has a duty of ordinary care to provide adequate safety equipment for students' use during athletic activities, but did not impose a separate duty to warn students to wear safety equipment and the duty to allow students to provide their own safety equipment.

2. In *Vance* v. *Jefferson Area Local Sch. Dist.*, No. 94-A-0041 1995 Ohio Ct. App. LEXIS 5041 (Ohio Ct. App. Nov. 9, 1995), the family of a nine-year-old brought suit against the school board alleging that Vance's injuries were the result of a poorly maintained playground and a lack of padding on the steel pole holding up a basketball hoop. The family also alleged failure to properly supervise children. The appellate court granted summary judgment to the school board claiming that the family had failed to show adequate evidence that a "hole" existed in the court. Consequently, the family did not present any evidence that the surface or equipment was a contributing factor to the Vance's falling on the playground.

3. In *Baker* v. *Briarcliff School Dist.*, 613 N.Y.S. 2d. 660 (N.Y. App. Div. 1994), a 16-year-old student was injured during a field hockey game while not wearing a mouth guard. The appellate court denied the defendant's request for summary judgment stating, "There exists, on this record, questions of fact regarding whether the coach adequately warned

the players about the risks involved in not wearing a mouthpiece, and whether reasonable care was exercised in the supervision of the practice, and whether the coach's conduct constituted a breach of sound coaching practices, thereby exposing Ms. Baker to unreasonably increased risks of injury."

4. In *Gerrity v. Beatty*, 373 N.E.2d 1323 (Ill. Sup. Ct. 1978), plaintiff alleged that the school district provided unsatisfactory equipment, which resulted in a severe injury. The plaintiff had complained about the ill-fitting equipment but no replacement equipment was provided. The court held the school district negligent for failing to ensure that equipment provided for student-athletes was fit for the purpose intended.

4.3.4. Vicarious Liability for Actions of Fans and Players

The coach and teacher may be sued under a vicarious liability theory for either the unintentional or the intentional tort of a fan or player. However, plaintiffs generally have difficulty in winning cases based on a vicarious liability theory. For instance, in *Toone* v. *Adams*, an umpire was injured by a fan, and the umpire sued, among others, the manager for inciting the fan to act. The court held for the manager and found that the manager's actions were not the proximate cause of the umpire's injuries (see note 1).

The nexus between the coach and the injury may be more easily established in other fact situations which have occurred but have not resulted in litigation. For example, a coach who orders a player to fight or attempt to injure an opposing player may be liable under the vicarious liability theory if injuries occur.

NOTES ───

1. For a case involving coaches' vicarious liability for the actions of fans and players, see *Toone* v. *Adams*, 137 S.E.2d 132 (N.C. 1964). A baseball umpire brought suit against the manager and the owner of the team after being assaulted by a fan after a game. The umpire contended that the conduct of the manager, who had been ejected from the game, and the lack of adequate protection were the proximate causes of his injury. The court found that umpires are used to having their calls disputed and that disagreements, as such, are not a major problem. The plaintiff was well escorted on his way to the dressing room, and though the guards themselves could have been more diligent, lack of protection was not the proximate cause of the plaintiff's injury. The court asserted that the club and its manager did not actually intend, and could not have reasonably anticipated, that one or more persons would assault the plaintiff as a result of the manager's conduct.

2. For more information, see the following law review article: Steven I. Rubin, "The Vicarious Liability of Professional Sports Teams for On-The-Field Assaults Committed by Their Players," 1 *Virginia Journal of Sports and the Law* 266 (Fall 1999).

3. For more information specifically for the athletic administrators, see the following book: Gil Fried, *Safe at First: A Guide to Help Sports Administrators Reduce Their Liability* (Durham, NC: Carolina Academic Press, 1999).

4.4. THE DEFENSE OF IMMUNITY

Immunity is a condition that protects against tort liability regardless of the circumstances. Immunity is to be distinguished from a *privilege*, which operates to excuse the commission of an intentional tort under specific conditions (see Chapter 3, section 3.1.5.6., "Immunity and Good Samaritan Statutes").

4.4.1. Sovereign Immunity

Sovereign immunity is the type of immunity most often encountered in a sports setting, although charitable immunity may, in some instances, be a consideration. Historically, all states had sovereign immunity laws. Recently, however, some state courts and state legislatures have determined that the state can be sued in certain situations for certain activities. To determine if an entity is immune from legal recourse, one must first determine whether it is a governmental entity. Governmental entities may be federal, state, or local governments, municipalities, or any activity that is under the control of any of the aforementioned.

Certain public policy considerations underlie the establishment of sovereign immunity. One rationale is that public agencies have limited funds and should expend them only for public purposes. To allow an individual to sue a public entity unfairly restricts the amount of funds that should be devoted to the public welfare. Another rationale for sovereign immunity is the idea that the state can do no wrong. This is a vestige of the historical policy that a king could do no wrong and was the original basis for the establishment of sovereign immunity. Other reasons include the idea that the public cannot be held responsible for the torts of their government employees and that public bodies themselves have no authority to commit torts. Many believe that the aforementioned policy considerations are not compelling, and the trend in several jurisdictions is to repeal or limit the immunity granted to governments.

Sovereign immunity rests on the concept that a state must give consent to be sued. Most states have given such consent, either in the form of a statute, which authorizes an individual to sue or by providing special courts (e.g. court of claims) and procedures to be followed when an instrumentality of the state is responsible for an injury. In addition, these statutes generally limit the amount a tort claimant may recover in an action against the government. These statutes generally are narrowly interpreted, but they have been extended to agencies related to, but not part of, the actual state government. Public high schools and high school athletic associations are usually included on the list of agencies whose traditional sovereign immunity may be eliminated by statutes of this kind.

In those states governed by a sovereign immunity statute, the distinction between governmental and proprietary activities presents an important legal issue. A *governmental activity* is one that can be performed only by the state and as such is commonly protected from lawsuits on the grounds of sovereign immunity. Education is a governmental activity. A *proprietary activity* is one that is done by the state but that could be undertaken by the private sector, and is therefore not given the protection of sovereign immunity. An example is when a town leases a facility for a professional sporting event.

In any lawsuit brought against a government entity, it must first be determined whether the activity on which the plaintiff's case against the state entity is based is a governmental or a proprietary activity. If the activity is found to be a governmental one, the action brought by the plaintiff is automatically dismissed on the basis of the sovereign immunity statute that protects the governmental body. A determination that the activity is proprietary in nature, however, permits continuation of the case and possible recovery of damages by the plaintiff. Naturally, then, in the initial stages of a case involving the state, the defendant commonly argues that the activity in question was governmental and the plaintiff claims it was proprietary.

The distinction between governmental and proprietary functions is very difficult to make. A sports facility may be conducting either a proprietary or a governmental function. In the case of a public school using its own sports facility, the courts have usually found that the holding of athletic contests is part of the educational function of the state, and is therefore a governmental function protected by the sovereign immunity doctrine. If the facility is leased for use by the private sector, the courts have concluded that the school will be conducting a proprietary activity (by leasing), and will therefore be liable for injuries sustained as a result of the negligent maintenance or construction of the facility.

NOTES

1. In *Ilott* v. *University of Utah*, 12 P.3d 1011 (Utah Ct. App. 2000), a spectator was allegedly injured when a plank broke beneath her foot as she walked down bleachers during a university football game. She brought a negligence claim against the university. The district court entered summary judgment in favor of the university. However, the plaintiff appealed, and the court of appeals held that the university was not immune from liability for the spectator's injury because, among other things, genuine issues of material fact existed.

2. In *Caldwell* v. *Griffin Spalding County Bd. Of Ed.*, 503 S.E.2d 43 (Ga. Ct. App. 1998), a freshman on a varsity football team was beaten by members of the team in an apparent "initiation ritual" at the team's summer football camp. The victim's father, who alleged that the defendants should have known of the "initiations" and should have prevented the attack, filed a lawsuit against the Board of Education, head football coach, and principal. The trial court granted summary judgment to the defendants based on the board's sovereign immunity and the official immunity of the head football coach and the principal.

3. In *Quinn* v. *Mississippi State University*, 720 So. 2d 843 (Miss. 1998), the parents of an injured baseball camp attendee sued the state university, its president, its head football coach, and an assistant baseball coach. The Supreme Court of Mississippi held that the university was protected by sovereign immunity, and the president, head football coach, and assistant baseball coach were entitled to qualified immunity.

4. In *Singerman* v. *Municipal Service Bureau, Inc.*, 565 N.W.2d 383 (Mich. 1997), an experienced hockey player was hit in the face by a hockey puck then sued the city, the company created by the city to run the hockey arena, the arena manager, and the arena assistant manager. The plaintiff alleged that poor lighting in the arena was the cause of his injury. The trial court barred the city as a defendant based on governmental immunity. The state Supreme Court dismissed the case against the other defendants, reasoning that the danger of playing hockey in poor light was open and obvious to the plaintiff.

5. In *Carter* v. *New Trier High School*, 650 N.E.2d 657 (Ill. App. Ct. 1995), a tennis player, who had injured his ankle on a poorly maintained high school court, named the high school as a co-defendant under the theory of vicarious liability. The immunity statute absolved state agencies from liability except in cases of "willful or wanton" conduct on the part of its employees. The high school was therefore dismissed as a defendant. On appeal, the plaintiff claimed that the trial judge erred in referring to the culpability attached to *willful and wanton* conduct as being similar to the culpability associated with *criminal* conduct. In fact, the immunity law in question defined willful and wanton conduct as "a course of action which shows an actual or deliberate intention to cause harm or which, if not intentional, shows utter indifference to or conscious disregard for the safety of others or their property." The appellate court agreed that willful and wanton conduct is different from criminal conduct and remanded the immunity question to a jury.

6. In *Acosta v. Unified School District*, 37 Cal Rptr. 2d. 171 (Cal. Ct. App. 1995), a high school gymnast was rendered quadriplegic and eventually died after being injured in the school gymnasium under the supervision of his coach. The school district argued that it should not be held vicariously liable for the negligence of the coach because Section 831.7 of the Government Code immunizes a public entity from liability for injuries resulting from participation in a "hazardous recreational activity." The appellate court ruled that the immunity did not apply "under these circumstances," charging the school board with a reasonable duty of care. The question of the school board's liability was remanded to a jury.

7. In *Lennon v. Peterson*, 624 So. 2d 171 (Ala. 1993), a coach and athletic trainer from the University of Alabama at Huntsville were absolved from liability in applying negligent medical care because both were state employees, and were therefore protected by the state's "discretionary function" immunity statute.

8. In *Brown v. Wichita State University*, 547 P.2d 1015 (Kan. 1967), plaintiffs sought to recover as third-party beneficiaries after a charter airplane carrying the school football team crashed. The Kansas Supreme Court made the distinction between a governmental function and proprietary function. The court found the carrying of the football team to be a proprietary function and held the action could be maintained. See also, *Shriver v. Athletic Commission of Kansas State University*, 222 Kan. 216 (1977).

9. The availability of insurance will not eliminate immunity as a defense. See, for example, the following cases.

  (a) In *Weinstein v. Evanston Township Community*, 351 N.E.2d 236 (Ill. App. Ct. 1976), the court held that the purchase of liability insurance did not waive general immunity of the school district, and no damages were awarded to a junior high school student who was injured while exercising on the parallel bars.

  (b) In *Merrill v. Birhanzel*, 310 N.W.2d 522 (S.D. 1981), plaintiff sued the teacher who was in charge of a required wrestling class at the time of plaintiff's injury. During the match, the plaintiff was thrown to the ground and his left ankle was broken. The court failed to find any grounds for the district to be sued given its sovereign immunity. It noted that the "authority to purchase, and the purchase of liability insurance does not provide that permission. . . . We have consistently held that if there is to be a departure from the immunity rule, the policy must be declared and the extent of liability fixed by the legislature."

4.4.2. Charitable Immunity

Charitable immunity was developed to limit the liabilities of charitable organizations. The justifications for applying the charitable immunity laws are based on the following reasons:

1. Donations to charitable organizations constitute a trust fund which may not be used for an unintended purpose.

2. No profits have been accumulated, so the doctrine of vicarious liability cannot apply.

3. Charities perform governmental or public duties, and therefore should be immune.

4. The overall good of a charity is protected by not diverting its money to pay damage claims.

The doctrine of charitable immunity, similar to sovereign immunity, has been eliminated in many jurisdictions.

NOTES _____

1. In *Pomeroy v. Little League Baseball of Collingswood*, 362 A.2d. 39 (N.J. Super. Ct. App. Div. 1976), plaintiff spectator at a Little League game sought to recover for injuries sustained when a bleacher collapsed. In affirming judgment for the defendant, the court held that the league had been established for purely educational purposes—that is, to build character and sportsmanship—and that the charitable immunity statute prevented the plaintiff from recovery from the defendant.

2. In *Southern Methodist University v. Clayton*, 176 S.W.2d 749 (Tex. 1943), plaintiff spectator sought recovery from Southern Methodist University (SMU) for injuries sustained when a temporary bleacher collapsed during the SMU-Texas A&M football game in 1940. The court held that SMU, a charitable institution, was immune from liability for torts of its agents unless the injured party was an employee of the charity. The Supreme Court of Texas reasoned, in affirming a trial court decision: "It is better for the individual to suffer injury without compensation than for the public to be deprived of the benefit of the charity."

4.4.3. Civil Liability Immunity Legislation

Increasingly, and for a number of reasons, governmental bodies have seen a need to institute regulations that govern certain aspects of sports. An area that has undergone particular legislative scrutiny is liability for sports coaches, administrators, and officials, especially in regard to youth sports organizations. Legislation has been proposed on both the federal and state levels of government and has been enacted in several states.

Proponents of civil liability immunity legislation that is directed to youth sport organizations contend that it is needed because of a proliferation of civil lawsuits that threaten to force many of those involved in sports, especially volunteers, from participating in sport organizations. It is reasoned that coaches and managers of youth sport organizations and other like groups cannot carry out their roles without fear of being sued for damages. For instance, during consideration of legislation in New Jersey, the most frequently cited case involving Little League lawsuits was a complaint filed by a Camden County mother against the Runnemede Youth Athletic Association seeking $750,000 in damages after her son misjudged a fly ball and was struck in the eye.

NOTES _____

1. On June 18, 1997, the "Volunteer Protection Act of 1997" was enacted into law by the United States Congress (111 Stat, 218). The act states, with some noted exceptions, that "no volunteer of a nonprofit organization or governmental entity shall be liable for harm caused by an act or omission . . . on behalf of the organization . . ." One stated purpose of the act was to encourage citizens to volunteer their services, and to make people feel less deterred by the potential liability of doing so.

2. Two 1997 Ohio laws, R.C. 1533.18 and 1533.181 provide that private entities that hold land open for recreational use without charge are immune from tort liability for any injury sustained by a recreational user.

3. Also, see section 4.7., "Liability of Officials, Referees, and Umpires," for legislation directly related to such persons.

4.5. LIABILITY OF FACILITY OWNERS AND POSSESSORS

The duty that the owner or possessor of a facility owes varies, depending on the characterization of the party who was injured while on the premises. To establish a duty for owners, operators, supervisors, or possessors of land, the status of the person injured must be determined. Generally, there are two classes of persons: licensees and invitees. A *licensee* is one who enters the property of another, with the owner's consent, for the licensee's own purposes. The occupier of the property owes only a duty of ordinary care. There is no obligation to inspect the area to discover dangers currently unknown, or to warn of conditions that should be obvious to the licensee. The occupier of the property owes a licensee a duty to warn only when a risk is known or should have been known under the reasonable person standard, which the licensee is unaware of.

An *invitee* is owed a greater degree of care by the owner, operator, supervisor, or occupier of the property. There is an affirmative duty to be free from known defects as well as from defects that should have been discovered by the exercise of reasonable care. The basis of liability is the implied representation at the time of the invitation that the premises are safe to enter. The invitation does not have to be extended personally for an individual to be classified as an invitee. The invitation implies that reasonable care has been exercised for the safety of the invitee. The owner or possessor of the property is not, however, an insurer of the safety of the invitee. That is, the owner does not guarantee safety under all possible circumstances. Instead, the owner or possessor must exercise only reasonable care for the invitee's protection.

The distinction between licensee and invitee is important because the different standards of care that may be applied can be decisive in determining the outcome of a lawsuit. An athlete or a spectator at a sports event is characterized as a business invitee. A *business invitee* is a visitor who brings a monetary benefit to the person in possession of the property. The business invitee is also a person whom the possessor encourages to enter onto the property. By such encouragement the possessor implicitly represents that the premises are safe to enter.

The distinction between patent and latent defects is also important in any discussion of the liability of owners and possessors of sports facilities. Both types of defects are potentially injury-causing, but an owner or operator cannot be held liable for undiscovered and undiscoverable defects.

A *patent defect* is one that is plainly visible or that could easily be discovered upon inspection. A facility owner or a lessee is liable for obvious defects, such as debris on steps that creates a hazard, if they cause an injury. A *latent defect* is a hidden or concealed defect that could not be discovered by reasonable inspection. It is a defect of which the owner has no knowledge, or of which, in the exercise of reasonable care, the owner should not have knowledge. Owners and lessees are generally not liable for injuries caused by latent defects.

In the eyes of the law, when a facility is leased, it is, in effect, sold for a period of time. Thus, the lessee—the person taking control of the property—assumes the responsibilities of the lessor—the person giving up control of the property—toward those who enter the property. The lessor still has a duty, however, to disclose any concealed or dangerous conditions—any latent defects—to lessees, their guests, and others reasonably expected to be on the premises. For this duty to attach, the lessor does not have to believe that the condition is dangerous or to have definite knowledge of the defect. Instead, it is sufficient that the lessor be informed of facts from which a reasonable person would conclude that there is a possible danger. The lessor has no duty to warn about patent defects, which are defined as known, open, or obvious conditions. When a property is leased for a purpose that includes admission to the public, the lessor has an affirmative duty to exercise reasonable care to inspect and repair the leased property. This duty is imposed to prevent an unreasonable risk to the public. Liability will extend only to parts of the premises open to the public and to invitees who enter for the purpose for which the place was leased.

Facility owners and possessors have a duty to exercise reasonable care in maintaining the premises and in supervising the conduct of others at the facility. They are, however, entitled to assume that participants will obey the rules and that employees will not be negligent, absent notice to the contrary. Thus, their duty does not include protecting consumers from unreasonable risks. An unreasonable risk is one such that the probability of injury outweighs the burden of taking adequate precautions.

The general rule is that facility owners and possessors are liable for conditions on their premises which cause physical harm if they know or should reasonably have known about the existence of the dangerous condition when such a condition poses an unreasonable risk to an invitee. The requirement of reasonable care is supported by the assumption that a spectator or a participant assumes all the ordinary and inherent risks of the particular sport. These inherent risks are those commonly associated with the sport. The application of this common knowledge rule will depend on the circumstances. No invitee, whether a player or a spectator, assumes the risk that an owner will fail to meet his or her duty of reasonable care.

A facility owner and possessor's duty of reasonable care can be divided into three areas. First is the duty to protect invitees from injurious or defective products. An owner and possessor must exercise reasonable care in the selection of equipment necessary for the operation of the facility. Second, owners and possessors must exercise reasonable care in the maintenance of the facility itself and any equipment in the facility. Standards of safety, suitability, and sanitation must be maintained. In addition, if an invitee uses any of the equipment and the facility owner or possessor supervises, then the facility owner or possessor is held to a standard of reasonable care. Third, an owner and possessor must guard against foreseeable harmful risks caused by other invitees. A breach of any of these duties may subject a facility owner or operator to liability for negligence.

Promoters and other sports event organizers often use the facility for only a day or a few days. They do not own the facility, and they are not in a long-term lease situation; therefore, they cannot be considered a permanent tenant. Some examples are a boxing match, the Harlem Globetrotters, and the ice shows. The promoter owes a duty of reasonable care in the maintenance and supervision of the facility. With respect to maintenance, the owner is more likely to be responsible for patent defects that are uncorrected. With respect to supervision, the promoter is responsible for reasonable care in the running of the event, although the determination of reasonable care may differ depending on the type of event. For example, the amount and type of security may differ for a family event as opposed to a rock concert. The promoter, however, is not responsible for unique or unforeseeable events causing injury in the absence of notice that an injury is apt to occur. Therefore, courts have often refused to find liability for patrons' injuries caused by other spectators. Promoters are required only to exercise reasonable precautions. However, to protect themselves in the event that an invitee is successful in a claim against a promoter, facility owners or possessors may require a promoter to execute a lease agreement. (See Chapter 9, Section 9.2.9., "Facilities Contracts.") An agreement will usually require the promoter to obtain general liability insurance and agree to indemnify and hold harmless the facility owner or possessor.

Owners of facilities that allow alcoholic drinks to be consumed at athletic events have instituted some of the following procedures:

- To purchase beer, customers must go to the concession stand. Beer vendors no longer are allowed to sell beer to customers in their seats. In addition, low-alcohol (3.2 beer) and no-alcohol beer are offered for sale.
- At football games, the sale of beer is discontinued at the beginning of the third quarter.
- The largest container of beer sold is twenty ounces, instead of the thirty-two ounce "big beers."
- Season ticket holders can lose their ticket rights for subsequent seasons if they become involved in fights or other such rowdy behavior.
- No-alcohol seating sections are designated.

Generally, a facility operator is not responsible for all injuries that occur at its stadium or arena; it only needs to take reasonable precautions. Control of alcohol beverage sales in the facility, limiting or supervising the practice of tailgating in pre-game and post-game situations, and ensuring that security is present inside and outside the facility would seem to address these concerns. At a minimum, sponsored activities require some type of increased safety measures, especially if there have been incidents of rowdiness or other disruptive behavior in the past. If such measures are undertaken, liability should be greatly reduced.

Another potential problem area for facility owners is tailgating, which has become a standard component of the traditional college football weekend. In fact, many colleges and universities have actively promoted the concept, seeking to capitalize on its popularity to market their intercollegiate athletic programs. In most cases, tailgating is a harmless afternoon's pleasure for fans, but on occasion it can lead to excessive drinking and rowdy behavior. It is this aspect of tailgating that must concern facility administrators.

In general, there has been an increasing concern by society about excessive drinking and its impact on public safety. Some states have acted on these concerns by raising the drinking age and eliminating "happy hours," and in addition there have been toughening attitudes about alcohol-related crimes among the judiciary.

Sports administrators have also been concerned about drinking at intercollegiate events. The National Collegiate Athletic Association has long banned the sale of alcoholic beverages at NCAA tournaments and post-season championship events, and many campuses have policies that limit consumption of alcoholic beverages at on-campus athletic events.

As a general summary, the following checklist will help facility owners protect themselves against possible litigation:

1. Anticipate any potentially injurious situations in the facility (stadium, arena, pool, etc.) or event site (baseball field, soccer field, etc.).
2. Ensure that the facility is adequately maintained, and perform regular inspections (with written reports) on the condition of the facility.
3. In designing a facility, make safety a top concern of the architects and planning committee. Ensure that safe materials are used throughout the facility (glass, padding, mats, etc.).

4. Designate an individual on the staff to serve as the safety expert.

5. Develop a clear, written policy concerning safety in the facility, institute a reporting procedure for potential problems, and document any mishaps in detail.

6. Develop policies for alcohol consumption at the facility.

NOTES

1. The following cases were brought against facility owners or possessors by spectators hit with flying objects:

(a) In *Benejam v. Detroit Tigers Inc.*, 635 N.W.2d 219 (Mich. Ct. App. 2001), a young girl was injured by a flying bat particle along the third base line. Although plaintiff was behind a protective net, a fragment of the bat curved around it. Plaintiffs sued the Tigers claiming that the net was insufficiently long and that warnings about the possibility of projectiles leaving the field were inadequate. Plaintiff suffered crushed fingers as a result of the accident and a jury awarded plaintiffs non-economic damages (past and future) totaling $917,000, lost earning capacity of $56,700 and $35,000 for past and future medical expenses. The appellate court overturned the verdict reasoning that the Tigers had no duty to warn of an open and obvious danger, and because protected seating was available to patrons who wished to purchase it.

(b) In *City of Coral Springs v. Rippe*, 743 So. 2d 61 (Fla. Dist. Ct. App. 1999), plaintiff was watching her son play in a Little League game from park bleachers. For a better view of the game, she moved in front of the players' bench, where the fence was only four feet high. She was struck by a foul ball, knocked unconscious, and suffered injuries. She then sued and alleged vicarious liability against the city. A jury concluded that the plaintiff was 60% at fault and the city was 40% at fault and awarded the plaintiff a judgment of $130,000. The jury concluded that the city either negligently failed to warn of or correct a known dangerous condition. The appellate court affirmed the verdict based on the city's demonstrated failure to correct a known dangerous condition.

(c) In *Jasper v. Chicago Nat'l League Ball Club*, 722 N.E.2d 731 (Ill. App. Ct. 1999), plaintiff sued the owner of Wrigley Field (the Chicago Cubs) after he was struck by a foul ball during a baseball game. The plaintiff alleged that before 1992 a net hung between the upper deck and a backstop behind home plate at Wrigley Field. However, in 1992, the club removed the net when it built "skyboxes" behind home plate just below the upper deck. Hence, the plaintiff alleged that the club had "willfully and wantonly, or negligently, removed the netting, failed to warn patrons of the increased risk, failed to offer safer seating, and allowed the sale of food and beverages in an area where vendors would distract patrons from approaching foul balls." The defendant sought protection for its conduct under the Illinois "Baseball Act." That act provides: "The owner or operator of a baseball facility shall not be liable for any injury to the person or property of any person as a result of that person being hit by a ball or bat unless: (1) the person is situated behind a screen, backstop, or similar device at a baseball facility and the screen, backstop, or similar device is defective (in a manner other than in width or height) because of the negligence of the owner or operator of the baseball facility; or (2) the injury is caused by willful and wanton conduct, in connection with the game of baseball, of the owner or operator or any baseball player, coach or manager employed by the owner or operator." 745 ILCS 38/1 (West 1996). The plaintiff argued that the Baseball Act was unconstitutional special legislation and that it therefore violated the equal protection guarantees of the Illinois and United States Constitutions (see Chapter 5, section 5.4.3., "Equal Protection"). The plaintiff reasoned that the act violated the principle of equal protection by conferring a special benefit or exclusive privilege on a person or class to the exclusion of others, and specifically that "no legitimate state interest is reasonably served by providing special tort protection to owners who host baseball games solely to make a profit." The court disagreed, stating, "We believe the sport of baseball does have unique characteristics that would reasonably prompt a legislature to enact limited liability legislation." The court also stated that the act encourages the building and use of parks for recreational activity, and that, therefore, professional teams were not the sole beneficiaries of the limited liability protection. Because the court found the act to be constitutional and the defendant's conduct to be neither wanton nor reckless, it affirmed the lower court's finding in favor of the Cubs.

(d) In *Hawley* v. *Binghamton Mets Baseball Club Inc.* 691 N.Y.S.2d 626 (N.Y. App. Div. 1999), plaintiff, a spectator at a minor league baseball game, was hit in the eye during a fly ball catching contest held during the game. The plaintiff sued the team and sponsor of the contest. The Supreme Court, Appellate Division, of New York held that the fan assumed the risk inherent in attempting to catch fly balls, and that neither the team nor the sponsor of the contest had a duty to provide protective eyewear or warn the fan.

(e) In *Moulas* v. *PBC Productions Inc.*, 570 N.W.2d 739 (Wis. Ct. App. 1997), spectator at a minor league hockey game was barred from recovery when struck by a puck that flew into the stands, past the protective glass surrounding the rink. The plaintiff failed to establish a breach of duty on the part of the owners of the team and arena.

(f) *Benjamin* v. *State*, 453 N.Y.S.2d 329 (N.Y. Ct. Cl. 1982), was an action brought by an eleven-year-old spectator, who in November 1979 was injured in a college hockey doubleheader at Romney Arena, a state facility on the campus of the State University of New York at Oswego. Plaintiff was seated behind the protective fence, ten to fifteen feet north of the nearest players' bench. While there, an errant puck found its way through the open area in front of the players' bench, passed behind the protective fence, and struck plaintiff on the left side of the forehead. Plaintiff brought action against the state alleging that the state failed to provide adequate protection for the safety of spectators seated in the arena. At the trial an expert testified that in similar facilities it was the usual and customary practice to protect the area around the players' bench. Absent such protection, it was the usual and customary practice to restrict seating in an arena without protection from the zone of danger. Since neither course of action was chosen, the court held that the state failed to provide plaintiff with adequate protection that evening. The court found that the failure of the state to provide for the safety of its patrons in the protected seating area constituted negligence and that such negligence was a substantial factor in bringing about the injuries.

(g) In *Duffy* v. *Midlothian Country Club*, 481 N.E.2d 1037 (Ill. App. Ct. 1985), plaintiff spectator sought recovery after being struck by a golf ball at the 1972 Western Open and losing an eye. She was standing in the rough between the first and 18th holes, watching play on the first hole. She was hit by a golfer playing the 18th hole, 200 to 250 yards away. Duffy was found 10 percent at fault when her negligence was compared to the tournament sponsors', but was awarded compensation. The court barred the assumption-of-risk defense.

(h) In *Williams* v. *Strickland*, 112 S.E.2d 533 (N.C. 1960), plaintiff race track patron sued defendant race track owner in negligence for injuries sustained when a wheel came off a race car and struck her. The North Carolina Supreme Court held that the operators of the race track could be held liable for failure to exercise care commensurate with known or reasonably foreseeable dangers incident to motor vehicles racing at high speed, because no seats were provided and no ropes strung to indicate where patrons could stand to view the races safely.

(i) In *Rich* v. *Madison Square Garden*, 266 N.Y.S. 283 (N.Y. Sup. Ct. 1933) *aff'd* 270 N.Y.S. 915 (N.Y. App. Div. 1934), plaintiff spectator sought recovery for injuries sustained when struck by a hockey stick during a game at defendant's rink. The trial court held that the defendant was not required to foresee that a hockey stick would fly into the stands and was therefore not liable for failure to have constructed protective screens.

2. In the following cases, spectators brought suit against facility owners or possessors for reasons other than flying objects:

(a) In *Rogers* v. *Professional Golfers Association of America*, 28 S.W.3d 869 (Ky. Ct. App. 2000), the plaintiff of this negligence claim was a spectator who suffered a leg injury when she slipped and fell on a golf course while watching a PGA championship tournament. The court of appeals found in favor of the PGA, holding that the condition of the hillside on the golf course was open and obvious to the spectator-invitee, had she exercised ordinary prudence.

(b) In *Hayden v. University of Notre Dame*, 71b N.E.2d 603 (Ind. Ct. App. 1999), a landowner should reasonably have foreseen injury to fans which resulted from a third party's action when a football landed in the seating area.

(c) In *Daniels v. Atlanta National League Baseball Club, Inc.*, 524 S.E.2d 801 (Ga. Ct. App. 1999), the plaintiff sustained injuries when she slipped on either a cup or the liquid from the cup upon exiting the stadium. She filed suit against the Braves organization, alleging that they failed to exercise ordinary care. The court rejected the plaintiff's claim, holding that the "risk of a cup left on the aisle steps is not an 'unreasonable risk of harm' for one exiting a baseball stadium at the end of a game." To expect the defendant to inspect every aisle and walkway for debris before tens of thousands of people exit would be "unduly burdensome."

(d) In *Bearman v. University of Notre Dame*, 453 N.E.2d 1196 (Ind. Ct. App. 1983), plaintiff sued the University of Notre Dame for injuries she suffered as she left a Notre Dame home football game. The injury occurred in the stadium's parking lot when a third party, who was tailgating and became involved in a fight, fell onto the plaintiff and broke her leg. Plaintiff claimed that the school had "a duty to protect her from injury caused by the acts of other persons on the premises" since she was a business invitee. The university argued that it could not be held liable for the act of a third person since it had no knowledge or notice of any danger to the woman. The Court of Appeals of Indiana, Third District, noted that the issue involved two different factors: An operator of a place of public entertainment generally "owes a duty to keep the premises safe for its invitees"; on the other hand, "an invitor is not the insurer of invitee's safety and before liability may be imposed on invitor, it must have actual or constructive knowledge of the danger." The court reasoned that Notre Dame was aware of the tailgate parties in the parking areas around the stadium and the fact that drinking occurs. It recognized that while Notre Dame did not have particular knowledge of any danger for the plaintiff, it was aware that intoxicated people pose a threat to the safety of patrons at the games. The appeals court therefore reversed the lower court's decision and held that Notre Dame had a duty to do all it could reasonably do to protect those people who attend the games from injury inflicted by the acts of third parties.

(e) In *Guttenplan v. Boston Professional Hockey Ass'n*, No. 80–415, 1981 U.S. Dist. LEXIS 10434 (S.D. N.Y. 1981), four hockey fans sued nine individual Boston Bruin hockey players, the Bruins, the New York Rangers, Madison Square Garden, Inc., the National Hockey League, and the city of New York for $7 million in damages for injuries suffered when a players' brawl on the ice spilled over into the stands in December 1979. The suit charged that the plaintiffs were "stomped" by the Bruins players while league and arena security personnel "merely observed and made no attempt to prevent or stop" the altercation. Criminal charges against individual Bruin players were dropped due to conflicting evidence and testimony that indicated fans had provoked the players. A federal judge dismissed the civil damage suit on jurisdictional grounds.

(f) In *Woodring v. Board of Education of Manhasset*, 435 N.Y.S.2d 52 (N.Y. App. Div. 1981), plaintiff brought a wrongful death suit against the school district after a platform railing in the gymnasium gave way, throwing decedent to his death. In affirming the $1,400,000 award to plaintiff, the appeals court found evidence that the school district (1) lacked a preventive maintenance program, (2) improperly constructed the platforms, (3) failed to inspect its gymnasium facilities regularly, and (4) should have known—given the extensive use of the platforms by students—that injury was foreseeable if the railings were not properly maintained or constructed. The appeals court thus sustained the jury's determination of the defendant's negligence.

(g) In *Turner v. Caddo Parish School Board*, 214 So. 2d 153 (La. 1968), plaintiff spectator grandmother sued defendant school authorities for negligence when she was run down on a football play that was intended to carry the ball out of bounds. The Louisiana Supreme Court held that defendant was not negligent in failing to anticipate spectators who did not know that plays are often carried out of bounds or for failing to have a barricade.

(h) In *Townsley v. Cincinnati Gardens, Inc.*, 314 N.E.2d 409 (Ohio Ct. App. 1974), plaintiff, a minor, brought suit after being assaulted in a washroom by a group of boys while he was attending a Harlem Globetrotters exhibition at Cincinnati Gardens. The plaintiff, as a business invitee of the facility owner, sought damages for negligence on the part of the facility. The trial court held for the plaintiff, stating that "the defendant either knew, or, in the exercise of ordinary care, should have known of the danger which victimized the plaintiff." On appeal, the decision of the trial court was reversed. The appeals court ruled that there was no evidence to indicate that the defendant could have anticipated, or reasonably have known of, the danger to the plaintiff.

(i) In *Philpot v. Brooklyn Nat'l League Baseball Club*, 100 N.E.2d 164 (N.Y. 1951), plaintiff spectator sought recovery for injuries sustained when she was struck by a broken bottle in defendant's ballpark. In reversing judgment for defendants, the court of appeals held that whether defendant provided a sufficient means of protecting plaintiff from reasonably fore-seeable risk of harm from a bottle where no waste receptacles were provided and where the park seats were slanted so as to allow bottles to spill, was a question for the jury to decide.

(j) In *Wiersma v. Long Beach*, 106 P.2d 45 (Cal. Ct. App. 1940), plaintiff, who purchased a ticket to watch a wrestling match held in defendant's municipal auditorium, sought recovery for injuries sustained when one of the wrestlers deliberately hit him with a chair. The district court of appeals held that, since the city had leased the auditorium to a promoter, it was not responsible to the plaintiff for the misconduct of its tenant.

3. In the following cases, participants brought suit against facility owners or possessors:

(a) In *Plotsker v. Whitey Ford's Grand Slam, Inc.*, 693 N.Y.S.2d 219 (N.Y. App. Div. 1999), the appellate court granted summary judgment to the defendant possessor of a basketball court after plaintiff blamed his injury on the "worn and uneven" court. Even if the plaintiff could have demonstrated that the court was the proximate cause of his injuries, he was precluded from recovery because the danger was "open and obvious."

(b) In *Rigano v. Coram Bus Serv.*, 641 N.Y.S.2d 285 (N.Y. App. Div. 1996), the appellate court denied summary judgment to a ski resort after a skier was killed while skiing at the resort. The court ruled that a jury must decide "whether the decedent was skiing out of control and beyond his ability; whether defendants created additional risks that are not generally associated with the sport of skiing; whether defendants negligently permitted the relevant ski trail to become hazardous to skiers; and, whether the barrier fence in question was adequate under the circumstances." As for the assumption of risk defense, the court stated "While decedent may have assumed a risk involved in partaking in the sport of skiing . . . it cannot be said, as a matter of law, that decedent assumed all the risks under the instant circumstances."

(c) In *Maddox v. City of New York*, 455 N.Y.S.2d 102 (N.Y. App. Div. 1982), 487 N.Y.S.2d 354 (N.Y. App. Div. 1985), a former New York Yankee center fielder brought suit against the owner, maintenance company, and designer of the Shea Stadium for an injury that occurred when he slipped on the wet field in Shea Stadium. In ruling for the plaintiff on defendant's motion for a summary judgment, the court found that Maddox did not assume the risk of playing on a dangerous field in that, as an employee, he was under the orders of his superiors. The appeals court reversed the lower court decision and held (1) that the doctrine of assumption of risk completely barred recovery; (2) that a professional baseball player did not fall within protected individuals under the statute governing general duty of the employer to protect health and safety of employees; (3) that even if eligible under the statute, the ballplayer failed to allege any fault by employer which resulted in the wet condition of the playing field; and (4) that player was not acting within the confines of the superior's instructions when he was injured.

(d) In *Wilkinson v. Hartford Accident and Indemnity Co.*, 411 So. 2d 22 (La. 1982), plaintiff sued athletic coach, school board, and school's liability insurer to recover for injuries son sustained when he crashed through a glass panel of the gymnasium foyer while engaging in an unsupervised race during physical education class. The Louisiana Supreme Court reversed a lower court's decision and held for the plaintiff, reasoning that the school board was negligent because several years previous a visiting coach had broken the glass panel when he walked into it. The glass panel was so close to spectator traffic that school authorities should have known of the hazard it created.

(e) In *Eddy v. Syracuse University*, 433 N.Y.S.2d 923 (N.Y. App. Div. 1980), plaintiff sought recovery for injuries he received during a frisbee game. Plaintiff was an "ultimate frisbee" player for a team of college students. In March 1977, the team traveled to Syracuse University to play against a group of Syracuse students, although the latter team was neither officially recognized nor sponsored by the defendant. During the course of an "ultimate frisbee" game played in the basketball gymnasium, the plaintiff crashed through a glass window in one door, severely lacerating his arm. The plaintiff sued the university for negligence in a personal injury action. The defendant argued that since it did not authorize use of the gym, had no foreknowledge of plaintiff's use, could not have foreseen that students would use the basketball courts for an "ultimate frisbee" game, and that the gym was not defective in design or construction for its ordinary purposes, there was lack of evidence to even submit the issue of negligence. The trial court ruled for the plaintiff. In affirming the trial court verdict, the appeals court held: "Surely the jury could have concluded that . . . on the campus of a large university . . . some of its students, and their guests, might use the facility without express permission . . . (in novel games)." Also properly left to the jury were the questions of whether the glass doors, located as they were in a building intended to be used for strenuous physical activity, constituted a dangerous condition and whether the risk presented by the glass doors could have been alleviated without imposing an undue burden on the university.

(f) In *Clary v. Alexander County Board of Education*, 199 S.E.2d 738 (N.C. 1974), *aff d*, 203 S.E.2d 820 (N.C. Sup. Ct. 1974), plaintiff senior student on a high school basketball team brought suit after suffering severe lacerations when he collided with some glass panels along one wall of the gymnasium while running wind sprints. Plaintiff alleged negligence on the part of the school board for permitting breakable glass to be used in the gym and in permitting the coaches to direct the players to run wind sprints toward the glass panels. An appeals court affirmed a trial court decision and held that the evidence indicated the plaintiff was contributorily negligent. The court reasoned that the plaintiff had run similar wind sprints in the gym during his three previous years in the basketball program. "Yet he chose to run at the panel at full speed without slowing down until he was within three feet of the glass. Anyone [doing such] . . . would be compelled by his momentum to crash into the wall and suffer injury." Plaintiff contended he was excused from contributory negligence because he was acting under the instructions of his coach. The court disagreed and held that a reasonable person disregards orders when compliance with such orders could result in injury.

(g) In *Ragni v. Lincoln-Devon Bounceland, Inc.*, 234 N.E.2d 168 (Ill. App. Ct. 1968), plaintiff trampoline user sought recovery for injuries sustained in landing on the frame of defendant's trampoline. In affirming a lower court verdict, the appellate court held that owner had no duty to warn plaintiff, who had received instruction on indoor trampolines in college, that the mat in the middle of the trampoline was the only safe place to land.

(h) In *Praetorius v. Shell Oil Co.*, 207 So. 2d 872 (La. Ct. App. 1968), plaintiff baseball player sought recovery from a defendant baseball field owner for injuries sustained when he stepped into a hole while running from home to first. In reversing the trial court's judgment for the plaintiff, the court of appeals held that the defendants were not negligent in failing to properly maintain the area in the batter's box where small holes and depressions were dug by batters' cleats during the course of a softball game. Defendants cannot be held negligent for lack of reasonable care because of holes made inadvertently by participants during the course of a game.

(i) In *Kaiser v. State*, 285 N.Y.S.2d 874 (N.Y. Ct. Cl. 1967), plaintiff bobsledders sought recovery for injuries sustained when their bobsled crashed on the state's bobsled run. In granting summary judgment for the plaintiffs, the court of claims held that evidence established that the state was negligent in failing to close the run, when it had actual notice of a gash in the wall in sufficient time to suspend operation before bobsledders were injured.

4. For more information, also see the following law review article: E.G Hochuli, "Liability to Spectators at Sporting Events," 47 *Federation of Insurance & Corporate Counsel Quarterly* 209 (Winter 1997).

4.6. LIABILITY OF MEDICAL PERSONNEL

A person or an organization in charge of a sports activity has a duty to provide reasonable medical assistance to participants as well as to spectators. To determine if this duty has been met, both the quality of care and the speed of the treatment must be considered. The quality of the treatment will be assessed by looking at the qualifications of the provider and the type of treatment offered. The speed of the treatment may be determined by the response time and availability of medical personnel.

There are many different levels of health care providers within the American medical system. With respect to athletic events, these providers may be doctors or nurses; more often they are trainers or emergency medical technicians (EMTs). The standard of care required of each medical provider is based on the person's training and qualifications (see Chapter 3, section 3.1.1., "Duty of Care Owed"). A higher standard of care is established if the class of medical personnel can perform skills and training beyond what is expected of the reasonable lay person. For example, the standard of care imposed on the medical profession is that the doctor must have met the level of skill and knowledge common to the profession in adherence to a uniform standard of conduct.

In the case of a specialist, however, the duty has increasingly become more stringent. A specialist must act with the skill and knowledge reasonable within his or her specialty. Thus, while in the past, little has distinguished medical malpractice cases involving athletes from other cases, the growing ranks of doctors practicing sports medicine will certainly lead to a higher standard of care for doctors specializing in sports injuries in negligence lawsuits brought by injured athletes.

The standard of care is usually established by expert testimony. For example, a doctor may be negligent while others of lesser skill and expertise would not be. The standard for any other member of the medical system would be applied in a similar fashion.

Generally, medical personnel are considered independent contractors rather than employees (see Chapter 3, section 3.6.1., "Exception: Independent Contractors"), even though they may be paid by a school district, facility owner, or other supervisory body. As independent contractors, even if they are found to have been negligent, their employers cannot be held liable under the doctrine of vicarious liability (see Chapter 3, section 3.6., "Vicarious Liability"). To determine if a doctor or other medical person is an independent contractor, the court considers the degree of control exercised by the employee's supervisor over actual medical decisions. Although the general rule is that medical personnel are independent contractors, there have been cases in which the employer has been held liable under the doctrine of vicarious liability. In these cases, courts have found that the employer exercised control and direction over the medical personnel.

There are some special considerations for a doctor involved in the area of athletics. The first concerns the relationship between doctor and patient. Typically, the doctor is paid by the patient. However, in sports, the doctor is hired and paid by the athletic organization. Usually, there is a confidential relationship between doctor and patient. When the doctor is employed by a third party, however, the normal relationship is not established. In effect, then, team doctors have two masters to serve: the athletic organization for which they work and the players they treat. In addition, while both the organization and the player are concerned with restoring the player to full health, there are potential situations in which the team may seek a shorter rehabilitation program while the player may favor a more cautious time frame for recovery. The team doctor is placed in the middle. The doctor's dilemma is highlighted by suits involving the team doctor if the player believes the doctor has not placed his or her long-term recovery before the program's wishes.

In one case, a team doctor and athletic trainer allowed a college football player to play with a sprained neck. The doctor altered the player's equipment to restrict movement. The player was injured during the game and rendered a quadriplegic. Such a case also raises the issue of the duty of a player to refuse to play with an injury after a team doctor has declared him or her healthy enough to participate.

In addition to this potential conflict, the normal confidential relationship between a doctor and patient (the athlete) changes when a third party, the athletic organization, pays the doctor. The athletic organization typically has full access to the athlete's medical records and often discusses the appropriate treatment for the injured athlete with the doctor and patient.

The potential for abuse in this situation was demonstrated in *Kreuger v. San Francisco Forty-Niners*, 234 Cal. Rptr. 579 (Cal. App. 1st Dist. 1987). Kreuger, a player with the Forty-Niners, sued the team personnel for fraudulent concealment of medical information. The court found that due to the team's interest in keeping Kreuger on the field, he never received a full disclosure of the extent of his knee injury, and thus continued to play when he should have retired from the game. In some situations, the athletic organization has access to the medical records and the athlete does not. As an example, Rafael Septien, a placekicker formerly with the Dallas Cowboys, sued the Cowboys for full access to his medical records. The confidential relationship between a doctor and a patient may also preclude a doctor's release of information to the athletic organization or anyone else without permission from the patient.

Another consideration concerns the prescribing of painkilling drugs to enable the athlete to continue playing for the benefit of the team but to the potential detriment of the player's career. There have been situations on the professional level in which athletes—for example, Bill Walton and Dick Butkus—have brought lawsuits against their employers and team physicians for prescribing painkilling drugs that allowed them to play without informing them of the potential harm to their long-term careers. These cases could be applicable at the collegiate level given similar circumstances. Furthermore, they raise the issue of the responsibility a doctor has to his patient—the injured player—and the responsibility the doctor has to his or her employer—the team.

One final consideration is that even though doctors may be negligent in their handling of an injured player, they may not be legally liable under normal tort analysis. When a player is injured through intentional or negligent actions on the part of a coach, referee, player, spectator, or anyone else, subsequent negligent action will not usually relieve the original negligent party from liability created by the original action. Doctors may, however, be liable as an additional defendant if their conduct is found to be a substantial factor in the injury or if additional injuries occurred because of their negligence. Subsequent medical negligence is generally not an unforeseeable and unreasonable cause that would relieve the original party from liability.

NOTES

The duty to provide prompt medical services for recruited athletes injured on the playing field figures in the cases listed below.

1. In *Campbell* v. *Shelton*, 727 N.E.2d 495 (Ind. Ct. App. 2000), a high school football

player hit his head on a concrete track. A jury found for the plaintiff in a misdiagnosis claim that cleared him to play.

2. In *Pinson* v. *Tennessee*, No. 02A01-9409-BC-00210 1995 Tenn. Ct. App. LEXIS 807 (Tenn. Ct. App. Dec. 12, 1995), the court ruled that trainers have an obligation to relay pertinent medical information to the attending physician.

3. In *State of Oregon* v. *Superior Court*, 29 Cal Rptr 2d 909 (Cal. Ct. App. 1994), a basketball prep star, who had previously suffered a stroke, was instructed by the college medical staff to reduce his anti-coagulation medication so that he could be eligible to compete. One month after his medication was reduced, the basketball player suffered a fatal stroke. The California appellate court denied the defendant's request to quash the case on jurisdictional grounds, finding that personal jurisdiction was warranted (see Chapter 2, section 2.3.3., "Court Jurisdiction").

4. Boston Celtics' star, Reggie Lewis, died suddenly on July 27, 1993 while practicing at Brandeis University. He had previously collapsed during a Celtics playoff game less than two months prior to his death. Following the playoff incident, Lewis received treatment by a team of New England Baptist Hospital doctors who told him he had a life-threatening heart condition that could end his career. Lewis was warned to restrict physical activity. However, Lewis sought a second opinion from Dr. Gilbert Mudge and two consulting physicians at Brigham and Women's Hospital. At a news conference on May 10, 1993, Mudge announced that Lewis had a neurological condition that caused fainting spells and that Lewis could likely return to professional basketball. After Lewis' death, his widow sued the insurance company of the Brigham and Women's doctors, Controlled Risk Insurance Company, claiming negligence. The hospitals were not named in the suit because Massachusetts law limits their liability under a charitable immunity law (see section 4.4.2., "Charitable Immunity"). After an initial 15-week trial, two of the physicians were found not negligent, while the jury was hung on the fate of the third physician, Dr. Gilbert Mudge. Lewis' widow then filed a second lawsuit against Dr. Mudge, which the insurance company defended and won. In his defense, Mudge testified that Lewis had confessed to him that he was a drug user. Allegedly, while the two were sitting in Mudge's car parked at Brandeis University just days before his death, Lewis said that he used cocaine. Mudge either testified or implied that Lewis' drug use, rather than his misdiagnosis was the proximate cause of Lewis' death. For more information on this case see the following law journal articles.

(a) "CRICO of Vermont RRG Wins Celebrity Lawsuit After Two Trials" 14 *The Risk Retention Reporter* 9 (September 2000).

(b) "Cardiologist Says Lewis Confessed" 13 *Workplace Substance Abuse Advisor* 15 (July 1, 1999).

5. In *Kleinknecht* v. *Gettysburg College*, 989 F.2d 1360 (3rd Cir. 1993), a twenty-year-old student-athlete died of cardiac arrest while participating in a practice session of the intercollegiate lacrosse team at Gettysburg College. There was no trainer on the field during the practice because the session was held during the nontraditional fall practice season and the school did not require trainers to be at these practices. When the student-athlete collapsed during the practice, a trainer had to be summoned from one of the on-campus training facilities. The head trainer was the first to administer CPR, but five to twelve minutes passed before he arrived at the field. It was also estimated that another ten minutes elapsed before the first ambulance arrived at the scene.

This decision is based on the appeal after the trial court had ruled that the college had no duty to the student-athlete because the school could not foresee that a young athlete who had no previous history of medical trouble was likely to suffer a cardiac arrest during a practice or game. The court of appeals ruled that the parents of the student-athlete had provided ample evidence showing that a life-threatening injury occurring during participation in an athletic event such as lacrosse was reasonably foreseeable. The college, therefore, owed the student-athlete a duty which required the college to have measures in place at the lacrosse team's practice in order to provide prompt treatment in the event that any member of the lacrosse team suffered a life-threatening injury. The court of appeals ruled only on the duty issue and sent the case back to trial court to determine whether there was a breach of this duty.

6. On March 4, 1990, during an intercollegiate basketball game between Loyola Marymount University and the University of Portland, Hank Gathers, star of the Loyola Marymount team, collapsed and died as a result of a heart disorder known as cardiomyopathy. Shortly after his death, several members of Gathers's family filed suit claiming that Gathers's death was a result of negligence of Gathers's physicians, the Loyola Marymount trainer, the head basketball coach, the athletic director, and the university itself.

The lawsuit revolved around allegations made by the family about the treatment and information Gathers was given prior to his death. After passing out during a game earlier in the season, Gathers was examined by a number of doctors and underwent tests to discover the nature of his illness. Gathers was diagnosed with a syncope, a temporary suspension of respiration and circulation due to an obstructed flow of blood to the brain, and cardiac arrhythmia, an alteration in the normal rhythm of the heartbeat.

Gathers was started on medication to help regulate his heartbeat and cleared to rejoin the basketball team. The lawsuit claims, however, that doctors decreased the dosage of the medication because of its effect on Gather's on-court performance. In addition, the school purchased a defibrillator, a machine used to help restore the rhythm of the heart, and kept it courtside during practices and games. The family alleged, however, that the defibrillator was not used within the required timeframe after Gathers had collapsed.

In settlements reached with Loyola Marymount and Dr. Vernon Hattori, a cardiologist who treated Gathers, Lucille Gathers, Hank's mother, received $545,000 from the university and $350,000 from Hattori, while Aaron Crump, Gathers's eight-year-old son, received $855,000 from the school and $650,000 from Hattori. These settlements were a result of the wrongful death claims made against the involved parties. Earlier in the proceedings, Loyola Marymount athletic director Brian Quinn, head basketball coach Paul Westhead, former trainer Chip Schaefer, and four of the five named physicians were dismissed from the suit.

The final lawsuit, a civil action brought by the family against two doctors who attended to Gathers on the night he collapsed, was dismissed September 9, 1992, after the plaintiffs did not appear in court to testify. The family members had contended that the doctors were negligent and caused the family emotional distress in the way they treated Gathers at courtside and outside the gym.

7. In *Krueger v. San Francisco Forty-Niners*, 234 Cal. Rptr. 579 (Cal. Ct. App. 1987), the court ruled in favor of a retired professional football player and held that he might be entitled to damages for fraudulent concealment of medical information by team personnel.

8. Former Citadel football player Marc Buoniconti sued Citadel team doctor E. K. Wallace, Jr., Citadel athletic trainer, Andy Clawson, and Citadel, as employer, for injuries which rendered him a quadriplegic after he tackled an opponent in a 1985 football game. Buoniconti alleged that the doctor should not have allowed him to play in the game with a sprained neck. A major issue in the trial was the doctor's addition of a ten-inch fitted strap to Buoniconti's uniform, running from the face mask and hooked to the shoulder pads. Plaintiff's experts testified that the strap restricted movement and contributed to the injury, whereas the defense experts stated that the strap prevented hyperextension of the neck and did not cause the injury. The jury raised a question: If helmet manufacturers are held liable for faulty design or construction, should not the team doctor also be liable for a fault in the design or construction of his alteration of that equipment? The jury found no liability for the doctor. The athletic trainer and Citadel settled out of court for $800,000.

9. In *Wilson v. Vancouver Hockey Club* (1983), 5 D.L.R. (4th) 282, a doctor employed by the hockey club to treat players for hockey injuries failed to refer plaintiff hockey

player to a specialist for a biopsy on a mole on plaintiff's arm. The plaintiff claimed that the doctor negligently failed to tell the player that he suspected cancer. Evidence indicated that the doctor made the final decision as to what treatment an injured player would have and whether an injured player would play, without advice from the management of the club, and, therefore, the doctor acted as an independent contractor and not as a servant of the hockey club. The court held that the club was not vicariously liable for the negligence of the doctor because he was an independent contractor.

10. In *Robitaille v. Vancouver Hockey Club*, 3 W.W.R. 481 (Ct. App. B.C. 1981), plaintiff professional hockey player brought suit against his club for injuries incurred while playing. A shoulder injury caused the plaintiff recurring problems, which the club's management and physicians attributed to mental rather than physical causes. The plaintiff was ordered to play while injured and sustained a minor spinal cord injury during a game. He requested medical attention but was ignored, because he was perceived as having mental problems. Further play aggravated the minor injury, and the plaintiff suffered a spinal cord injury which left him permanently disabled. The appeals court upheld the award of damages to the plaintiff and held that the club had breached its duty to ensure the fitness, health, and safety of its player. The club was also found to have exercised sufficient control over the doctors to make the doctors employees of the club. Therefore, the club was liable for the acts of the doctors.

11. In *Walton v. Cook*, Civil Case No. A8003-0165 (Or. 1981), professional basketball player Bill Walton filed suit against Robert Cook, the team doctor of the Portland Trail Blazers, and twenty other unnamed physicians of the Oregon City Orthopedic Clinic for $632,000 in lost income and medical expenses and $5 million in general damages. The complaint alleged negligence in the examination, diagnosis, and treatment of his left foot, along with failure to provide him with accurate information concerning the true nature of the injury. Drugs were prescribed and shots of steroids were given Walton and he was advised to play in games. Three months later, Walton consulted other physicians and discovered that he had actually fractured a bone in his foot, which caused damage to the nerves, muscles, and tissues of the left foot, as well as a permanent weakness in that foot and an increased chance of subsequent fractures. Further, Walton could not continue to play basketball. The case was settled for an undisclosed amount prior to the trial.

12. In *Bayless v. Philadelphia National League Club*, 472 F. Supp. 625 (E.D. Pa. 1979), plaintiff baseball player argued that he had been given pain-killing drugs without knowledge of their potential side effects. The court determined that the plaintiff's exclusive remedy for the action lay under the state workers' compensation act, not under legal jurisdiction.

13. In *Fish v. L.A. Dodgers Baseball Club*, 128 Cal. Rptr. 807 (Cal. Ct. App. 1976), plaintiffs sought recovery from defendant club and defendant physician for the death of their son, who died as a result of an allegedly negligent diagnosis after being struck by a foul ball. In reversing judgment, the court of appeals held for the plaintiffs, finding that negligence of the ballpark doctor in failing to ascertain decedent's symptoms necessitated the emergency surgery which resulted in death. This converted decedent from a patient who probably would have survived without emergency surgery to a patient who had little hope of recovery. The trial court's verdict in favor of the club was also reversed for consideration of the issue of the agency relationship between the parties.

14. For further information on the liability of medical personnel, see the following law review articles:

(a) Sigmund J. Solares, "Preventing Medical Malpractice of Team Physicians in Professional Sports: A Call for the Players Union to Hire the Team Physicians in Professional Sports," 4 *Sports Lawyers Journal* 235 (Spring 1997).

(b) Matthew J. Mitten, "Team Physicians and Competitive Athletes: Allocating Legal Responsibility for Athletic Injuries," 55 *University of Pittsburgh Law Review* 129 (Fall 1993).

4.7. LIABILITY OF OFFICIALS, REFEREES, AND UMPIRES

Officials, referees, and umpires have sought recovery in civil litigation for injuries suffered in the course of employment. They may also be protected against violence, in certain states, by criminal statutes.

Officials, referees, and umpires of athletic contests may incur tort liability as a result of their actions or inactions on the playing field. There have been two distinct areas in which suits against officials, referees, and umpires have been filed: the personal injury area, in which the official, referee, or umpire is sued for negligence, and the judicial review of an official's, referee's, or umpire's decision. There have been a few reported cases in both of these areas, since few cases have been filed and many of those have been settled. However, this area has the potential for increased litigation.

In the personal injury area, the official, referee, or umpire may be sued for negligence in a number of different situations. The first is when there has been a failure to inspect the premises. For instance, a plaintiff may contend that a referee should have inspected the field for holes or other dangerous conditions that could cause injury to players. In the second situation the official, referee, or umpire fails to keep the playing area free of equipment and/or spectators. For example, a ball or bat may be left on the playing field, and a player trips, falls, and is injured by the equipment. With respect to spectators, an injured spectator might contend that the official, umpire, or referee should have stopped play on the field and warned the spectators to move from the playing area. A player who is injured by running into a spectator might contend that the official, referee, or umpire should have moved the spectator away from the playing area. The third situation involves weather conditions; an injured player may contend that the official, referee, or umpire should not have started the game or that the game should have been stopped. The fourth situation involves equipment that causes injury to a player. It could be argued that the official, referee, or umpire has the responsibility to prevent a player from participating if the player's equipment is obviously ill-fitting. A situation that may be more likely to result in successful litigation is when a referee does not enforce a rule, especially a safety rule such as the "no jewelry" rule in basketball. The fifth and final situation involves a potential claim that the official, referee, or umpire did not properly enforce the rules of the games. For example, the plaintiff may allege that the basketball referees failed to control the game by not calling fouls or technical fouls, and that this resulted in a much rougher game, which was the proximate cause of the injuries suffered by the plaintiff.

The area of judicial review of an official's, referee's, or umpire's decision is one that has been infrequently litigated. Generally, courts are reluctant to review playing field decisions, whether they have been judgmental errors or a misapplication of a rule. Plaintiffs have not been successful in this area, and the courts will continue to show their reluctance to become involved in decisions on the playing field unless fraud or corruption can be found.

A problem not related to the liability of referees, officials, and umpires but one that an athletic administrator and the official should be aware of is the type of relationship created by the association of referees, officials, and umpires. The official may be classified as an independent contractor or an employee. This distinction becomes important if an official is injured in the course of performing his or her duties. If acting as an independent contractor, the official will not be eligible for workers' compensation. If classified as an employee, the official would be entitled to receive those benefits. In addition, the athletic administrator could be held liable for the actions of the referee under the legal theory of vicarious liability if the referee is deemed to be an employee. The athletic administrator will generally not be held responsible for the actions of the official if he or she is an independent contractor (see Chapter 3, section 3.6.1., "Exception: Independent Contractors"). The interpretation of a referee's status differs from state to state, on the basis of state laws and the legal relationship between the referees and the hiring institution. An examination of legal cases involving the question to determine a particular state's interpretation of the relationship is advised (see note 5).

The following liability checklist will help officials, referees, and umpires protect themselves against possible litigation.

1. Inspect playing surface, including sidelines and end lines, for visible and potential hazards.

2. Determine if weather conditions are appropriate for competition, and do not allow coaches or other athletic officials to influence the decision.

3. Inspect game equipment, such as bases and goalposts.

4. Inspect players' equipment for safety and make sure that players are not wearing any potentially dangerous jewelry or accessories.

NOTES

1. In 2001, former Cleveland Brown's offensive tackle, Orlando Brown, filed a $200 million lawsuit in Bronx, New York state court against the National Football League. Brown suffered career-ending impaired vision as a result of a penalty flag thrown by referee Jeff Triplette, which accidentally struck Brown in his right eye. Brown's complaint alleges that the league failed "to properly supervise and enforce rules that flags be properly weighted and thrown in a proper fashion." The case is pending. NFL referees are likely to be considered employees by the courts, rather than independent contractors, because they are members of a union sanctioned by the National Labor Relations Board (NLRB). Section 11 of the National Labor Relations Act (NLRA) specifically states that independent contractors are not covered under the act. See Chapter 11, "Labor Law" for more information.

2. In 1999, Neal Goss, a 15-year-old captain of a Chicago-area high school hockey team was paralyzed from the chest down after being slammed into the boards by an opposing player. Goss contended that the paralyzing hit occurred after the final buzzer of the game, thus making the hit an act of battery rather than an act that one assumes the risk of during the course of a hockey game. Criminal battery charges were filed against the opposing player, whose identity was kept anonymous under state law, since he was a minor. The defendant subsequently plea-bargained to a lesser battery charge that carried a maximum penalty of one year in prison. Goss also filed a civil suit in December 2000 against the Illinois Hockey Officials Association, claiming that the officials failed "to adequately and ably control the game." Defendants in the civil suit also included the player who injured Goss, the opposing team's coach, the hockey league, the sponsors of the opposing hockey team, and the Amateur Hockey Association of Illinois. For more information, see Jason R. Schuette, "Adolescent Sports—Violence When Prosecutors Play Referee. Making Criminals Out of Child Athletes, but Are They the Real Culprits?" 21 *Northern Illinois University Law Review* 515 (2001).

3. In *Rolison* v. *City of Meridian*, 691 So. 2d 440 (Miss. 1997), during a softball game, which was supervised by the officials chosen and compensated by the city, a player neg-

ligently threw a baseball bat, causing plaintiff, who was running the bases, to be knocked unconscious and suffer the loss of 5% of his brain function. The plaintiff sued the city, alleging that the officials were negligently selected and inadequately trained, and that the city allowed the game to be conducted in an unreasonably unsafe manner. The city responded by asserting an assumption of the risk defense. Furthermore, the city stated that the officials were independent contractors who were immune from liability by statute, and such immunity flowed to the city. The court granted summary judgment for the defendants. On appeal, the court held that a referee does not have the duty to protect a participant or a spectator from a thrown bat.

4. In *Santopietro* v. *City of New Haven*, 682 A.2d 106 (Conn. 1996), the court stated that umpires have a duty "to exercise reasonable judgment as umpires in order to maintain control of the baseball game so as to prevent an unreasonable risk of injury to others. . . . The breach of this duty, however, must be proved, in the absence of exceptional circumstances, by expert testimony establishing that the allegedly negligent action or failure to act by the umpire constituted an abuse of the umpire's discretion to evaluate the particular circumstances and to take only such disciplinary action as the umpire deems appropriate. Moreover, the expert testimony must establish an abuse of that discretion sufficient to permit a jury to infer that the umpire's action or failure to act constituted such a loss of control of the game as to give rise to an unreasonable risk of injury to the plaintiff." The Supreme Court of Connecticut found that the umpires' actions did not lead to an unreasonable risk of injury and, therefore, affirmed the lower courts judgment in favor of the umpires.

5. In *Harvey* v. *Ouachita Parish School Board*, 545 So. 2d 1241 (La. Ct. App. 1989), an injured football player sued the state high school athletic association under negligence for injuries suffered as a result of excessively rough behavior. The court held for the defendant on the basis that the association was not responsible for the referees' failure to remove football players who were displaying excessively rough behavior. The court reasoned that though the association had registered the referees, the referees were neither agents or servants of the association.

6. In *Bain* v. *Gillespie*, 357 N.W.2d 47 (Iowa Ct. App. 1984), plaintiff, a Big-10 basketball referee, filed suit for injunctive relief and damages against defendants who produced T-shirts with his likeness in a noose imprinted on them. Defendants had produced the T-shirts after a controversial call by the referee at an intercollegiate basketball game. Injunctive relief was granted to the referee.

7. In *McHugh* v. *Hackensack Public Schools*, 483 A.2d 148 (N.J. 1984), plaintiff high school basketball referee was attacked by an unknown fan after a state tournament game and sought damages from the public school system because it did not provide a safe place to work, safe entry and exit before and at the conclusion of the game, or proper supervision of the crowd. The trial court granted summary judgment in favor of the school since the school was immune under the New Jersey Tort Claims Act. For another case involving intentional and negligent injury of officials, see *Toone* v. *Adams* in Chapter 4, section 4.3.4., "Vicarious Liability for Actions of Fans and Players," earlier in this chapter.

8. In *Georgia High School Ass'n* v. *Waddell*, 285 S.E.2d 7 (Ga. 1981), the Georgia Supreme Court ruled that it does not possess authority to review the decision of a high school football referee. The high school referee admitted that he made the error—not awarding an automatic first down on a roughing-the-kicker penalty—which might have been determinative of the final outcome for the game. The trial court had overturned the referee's ruling based on a school's property right in the game of football being played according to the rules. The court ordered the game to be replayed from the point of the referee's error. The Georgia Supreme Court reversed, stating: "We now go further and hold that courts for equality in this state are without authority to review decisions of football referees because those decisions do not present judicial controversies."

9. In *Ford* v. *Bonner County School District*, 612 P.2d 557 (Idaho 1980), the Idaho Supreme Court found that a high school football official injured while officiating is

an employee of the school district and entitled to workers' compensation under Idaho law.

10. In *Carroll v. State of Oklahoma*, 620 P.2d 416 (Okla. Crim. App. 1980), appellant challenged an Arizona statute under which he was convicted for assault. Appellant was an assistant coach for the losing team at a baseball tournament. After the game, the home plate umpire was at the trunk of his car in the parking lot changing uniforms in preparation for the next game. He was surrounded by a group of players from the losing team who were criticizing his calls. The assistant coach approached the group, exchanged words with the umpire, and struck the umpire on the jaw with his fist. The assistant coach was convicted of "assault upon a sports officiary" under Oklahoma law.

The appellant challenged the statute on the grounds that it was unconstitutionally vague. The court of criminal appeals, however, held that the statute clearly indicated which persons were covered and also apprised the public of what particular conduct was deemed punishable, for which reasons the court found the statute neither unconstitutionally vague and indefinite, nor void for uncertainty.

11. In *Dillard v. Little League Baseball Inc.*, 390 N.Y.S.2d 735 (N.Y. App. Div. 1977), plaintiff umpire sued Little League for negligence in failing to provide him with a cup which provides groin protection after he was seriously injured when struck by a pitched ball in the groin area during a game. The court dismissed the case on the grounds that plaintiff had assumed the risks of such injury when he volunteered to umpire the game. The court based its decision on the fact that it was not customary for Little League to provide such equipment, as it is personal to the wearer. Additionally, the plaintiff could have provided it himself at little expense.

12. In *Pantalone v. Lenape Valley Regional High School*, Docket No. L-40828-26, Sussex Co. (N.J. Sup. Ct. 1976), a New Jersey high school wrestling referee was sued for allegedly allowing a wrestler to continue an illegal hold on his opponent, which resulted in a paralyzing injury. The case was settled by monetary damages.

13. In *Gale v. Greater Washington, D.C. Softball Umpires Ass'n*, 311 A.2d 817 (Md. Ct. Spec. App. 1973), the court ruled that an umpire is not an employee of an umpire association, but an "independent contractor," thereby precluding the umpire from receiving workers' compensation under Maryland law.

14. The National Association of Sports Officials (NASO) has drafted model legislation to encourage individual states to adopt some statutory protections limiting or preventing liability in regard to sports officials (see below). For more information see NASO's website at www.naso.org. According to NASO, sixteen states have currently adopted limited liability legislation for sports officials. Those states are Arkansas, Delaware, Georgia, Illinois, Louisiana, Maryland, Massachusetts, Mississippi, Nevada, New Jersey, North Dakota, Ohio, Pennsylvania, Rhode Island, and Tennessee. Here is the model legislation that was used to craft many of these state statutes:

Section 1: Sports officials who officiate athletic contests at any level of competition in this State shall not be liable to any person or entity in any civil action for injuries or damages claimed to have arisen by virtue of actions or inactions related in any manner to officiating duties within the confines of the athletic facility at which the athletic contest is played.

Section 2: Sports officials are defined as those individuals who serve as referees, umpires, linesmen, and those who serve in similar capacities but may be known by other titles and are duly registered or members of a local, state, regional or national organization which is engaged in part in providing education and training to sports officials.

Section 3: Nothing in this law shall be deemed to grant the protection set forth to sports officials who cause injury or damage to a person or entity by actions or inactions which are intentional, willful, wanton, reckless, malicious or grossly negligent.

Section 4: This law shall take effect immediately, and shall apply to all lawsuits filed after the effective date of this law, including those which allege actions or inactions of sports officials which occurred prior to the effective date of this law.

15. For more information, also see the following law review articles:

(a) Mark A. Grober, "Law and Sports Officiating: A Misunderstood and Justly Neglected Relationship," 16 *Constitutional Commentary* 293 (Summer 1999).

(b) Shlomi Feiner, "The Personal Liability of Sports Officials: Don't Take the Game into Your Own Hands, Take Them to Court," 4 *Sports Lawyers Journal* 213 (Spring 1997).

(c) Carole J. Wallace, "The Men in Black and Blue: A Comment on Violence Against Sports Officials and State Legislative Reaction," 6 *Seton Hall Journal of Sport Law* 341 (1996).

(d) Kenneth Biedzynski, "Comment: Sports Officials Should Only Be Liable for Acts of Gross Negligence: Is That the Right Call?" 11 *University of Miami Entertainment & Sports Law Review* 375 (1994).

4.8. APPLICATION OF LEGAL PRINCIPLES TO DEFECTS IN EQUIPMENT

The "failure to warn" theory is established upon the finding of a manufacturer's duty to warn of known latent and potential injury-causing defects in the design of equipment. The extent of the duty is based on the age and experience of the reasonably foreseeable users of the product.

In order to maintain a suit based on a theory of a "failure to warn," the plaintiff must prove that the product is defective in design. The test used by courts has two distinct prongs. The first prong involves looking at the product to see if it has failed to perform as safely as an ordinary consumer would expect. Whether it was used as intended, or was misused or tampered with, will be considered in making the determination of safety. If the plaintiff cannot directly establish that the product failed to perform adequately, this part of the test may be satisfied by the second prong, which involves proving that the product's defective design proximately caused the injury and that the benefits of the challenged design do not outweigh the inherent risk of danger created by the design. To aid in its determination as to both defectiveness and resultant liability, the court will also consider factors such as the nature of the sport, the type of injury, the amount of use or foreseeable misuse, the degree to which the particular risk is greater due to the defect, and the current state of the art in designing an absolutely safe product (see Chapter 3, section 3.5., "Products Liability Law").

NOTES ————————————————————————————————————

1. The following cases involve the application of legal principles to defects in equipment.

(a) In *Everett v. Bucky Warren, Inc.*, 380 N.E.2d 653 (Mass. 1978), plaintiff hockey player claimed that his serious head injury resulted from the defective design of the helmet he wore. The team's hockey coach distributed to the team helmets which were of a three-piece design, consisting of three plastic pieces. One piece covered the back of the head, one the forehead, and one the top of the head. The pieces were attached to each other by elastic straps. The straps expanded, depending on the size of the wearer's head, leaving gaps as large as three-fourths of an inch. This design was somewhat unique; however, there were also available on the market helmets which were of a one-piece design with no gaps.

During a game with the Brown University freshman team, plaintiff threw himself in front of a Brown player's shot in an attempt to block it. The puck struck Everett above the right ear, penetrating a gap in the helmet and causing a skull fracture. The injury required that a steel plate be inserted in his skull and caused recurring headaches. Everett then brought suit against the school, the manufacturer, and the retailer on the grounds of strict liability.

The appeals court held that the manufacturer could be found strictly liable for producing a helmet with an "unreasonably dangerous design." Factors that the court weighed when determining whether a particular design is reasonably safe included "the gravity of the danger posed by the challenged design, the likelihood that such danger would occur, the mechanical feasibility of a safer alternative design, the . . . cost of an improved design, and the adverse consequences to the product and the consumer that would result from an alternative design." The court held that the gravity of the danger was demonstrated by the injuries, that helmets of the one-piece design were safer than the model used and were in manufacture prior to the injury, and that, while more expensive than the helmets used, the one-piece helmets were not economically unfeasible.

(b) In *Heldman v. Uniroyal, Inc.*, 371 N.E.2d 557 (Ohio Ct. App. 1977), a professional tennis player injured her knee during a tennis championship and brought suit for damages against Uniroyal, Inc., which supplied the tennis court surface for the matches. Plaintiff claimed that the defendant made certain representations and warranties, both expressed and implied, concerning its court surface. An appeals court ruled that there was sufficient evidence to raise a jury question as to whether plaintiff assumed the risk by playing in the match. The court reached its conclusion based on the reasons that the plaintiff told all the members of her team that the court was in a dangerous condition, that she was a professional tennis player and is presumed to know the various risks attendant with playing on different types of surfaces, and that a higher degree of knowledge and awareness is imputed to professional tennis players than to average nonprofessional tennis players as to the dangers of playing on a synthetic tennis court having obvious bubbles on the playing surface.

(c) In *Byrns v. Riddell, Inc.*, 550 P.2d 1065 (Ariz. 1976), plaintiff student-athlete brought a products liability action against Riddell, Inc., a manufacturer of football helmets, after he had sustained a head injury in an interscholastic football contest in October 1970. Plaintiff was injured in a play in which he received an "on-side" kick. The supreme court examined evidence relating to proof of strict liability in tort to determine whether the trial court properly found for Riddell. The Arizona Supreme Court reversed on the basis of doubts raised as to the possibility of a defect in the design of the helmet, the place of impact, and the presence of the defect at the time the helmet left the seller's hands. The case was remanded to the trial court to make these determinations.

(d) In *Dudley Sports Co. v. Schmitt*, 279 N.E.2d 266 (Ind. Ct. App. 1972), a sixteen-year-old high school boy sought recovery for injuries received when he was struck in the face by the throwing arm of an automatic baseball pitching machine, which was purchased in March 1965 by Danville High School. Designed and manufactured by Dudley, the machine consisted of a frame and an open extended metal throwing arm. No protective shield guarded the throwing arm. When the arm reached a ten o'clock energized position and it received a ball, energy was released from the coiled spring and transmitted to the arm; the arm passed through a clockwise pitching cycle at a high rate of speed and came to rest in a four o'clock position. The machine was capable of delivering a powerful blow in the ten o'clock position, even if it was unplugged.

When the machine was uncrated, it came with a parts list, assembly instructions, and a tool to deactivate the spring. The only warning instruction contained in the crate was a general warning tag which said: "Warning! *Safety First* STAY CLEAR OF THROWING ARM AT ALL TIMES." No operating instructions were included in the crate. The machine was stored, unplugged, behind locked doors in locker room no. 2. However, the two adjoining locker rooms, with inside entrances to locker room no. 2, were not locked from the outside hallway entrance. On the day he was injured, plaintiff student was sweeping in locker room no. 2, as he had done in the past at the request of the coaching staff. He said that as he approached the front of the machine he heard a whistling noise and a pop. He was hit in the face by the throwing arm and received extensive facial injuries.

Plaintiff brought this action alleging negligence against the high school, the sporting goods company, and Dudley. The appeals court held that Dudley was negligent in the design, manufacture, and sale of the machine. The ability of the machine to operate while unplugged as a result of even a slight vibration was considered a latent danger, which could only be discovered through an examination of the machine combined with knowledge of the engineering principles which produce the action of the machine. Such knowledge is not ordinarily possessed by a sixteen-year-old high school boy who had never seen the machine before.

(e) *Halbrook v. Oregon State University*, Case No. 16-83-04631, Circuit Court of the State of Oregon for Lane County (1983) (pending), was an action brought by the family of a boy who died from injuries received during baseball practice. In March 1982, the student-athlete was participating in an Oregon State University baseball practice on an Astroturf field when he collided with another player, fell to the ground, and struck his head. As a result of the injuries, Halbrook died. Plaintiff-estate alleges that the university and the Oregon State Board of Higher Education were responsible for the proper selection, installation, maintenance, and repair of the athletic field surface. More specifically, the university and state board of higher education failed to hire a competent and qualified installer for the Astroturf, they failed to adequately supervise the activities of the installer they had hired, and they failed to perform adequate shock absorbency tests upon the Astroturf when they knew or should have known that continued use would diminish its shock absorbency characteristics. Plaintiff alleged that the Astroturf sold by defendant Monsanto was in a defective condition, was unreasonably dangerous, and created an unreasonable risk of harm because it was too hard and without adequate cushioning. In addition, plaintiff claims that Monsanto marketed the Astroturf without adequate warnings to the average user. Plaintiff also sued Matrecon, the company which sold the asphalt that was placed under the Astroturf, under many of the same theories that were alleged against Monsanto.

(f) In *Breeden v. Valencia, Inc.*, 557 So. 2d 302 (La. Ct. App. 1990), a twelve-year-old injured while riding a jet ski at camp claimed that the jet ski was unreasonably dangerous and contained inadequate warnings. The court found no evidence that a defect existed in the design or manufacture of the steering mechanism. It further found that warnings contained in the instruction manual were adequate to inform riders about the turning ability of the jet ski.

(g) In *King v. Kayak Manufacturing Corp.*, 387 S.E.2d 511 (W. Va. 1989), the plaintiff sued a manufacturer of an aboveground swimming pool under a product liability claim when he was rendered quadriplegic after diving into four feet of water. The trial court held the manufacturer strictly liable and directed the verdict for the plaintiff. The appellate court reversed and remanded the case to resolve the issues of whether the plaintiff was contributorily negligent and assumed the risk of injury on the dive. The court recognized that the defense of assumption of risk is available in a strict product liability case where there is evidence that the plaintiff had actual knowledge of the risk and accepted the chance of injury.

2. For a case in which liability for failure to warn was based on constructive knowledge, see *Filler v. Rayex Corp.*, 435 F.2d 336 (7th Cir. 1970). Plaintiff baseball player sued defendant sunglass manufacturer for negligence, strict liability, and breach of implied warranty of fitness for a particular purpose when the glasses shattered into his eye. The court of appeals, in affirming the district court in favor of the plaintiff, held that defendant, which advertised the glasses as providing protection against baseballs, had constructive knowledge of the danger and was liable for failure to warn and liable for breach of warranty of fitness for a particular purpose.

3. For a case in which the court held there is no duty to warn of known dangers, see *Garrett v. Nissen Corp.*, 498 P.2d 1359 (N.M. 1972). Plaintiff, an experienced trampoline user, sued defendant trampoline manufacturer for negligence for failure to warn of the danger involved in landing incorrectly. The New Mexico Supreme Court held there is no duty to warn of dangers known to user of the product, either under strict liability or negligence theories.

4. The National Operating Committee on Standards for Athletic Equipment (NOCSAE) was organized to research and test equipment, develop new standards, and improve existing ones. NOCSAE was founded in 1969 in an effort to reduce death and injuries through the adoption of standards and certification for athletic equipment. According to its Web site, www.nocsae.org, "Comparing the incidences of head injury fatalities for pre and post-NOCSAE periods ranging from 1959 through 1990 seasons, from the National Federation of State High School records, a 74 percent reduction has occurred. Of even more fundamental importance, the incidence of serious head injuries, the leading cause of disability and death in football, estimated to average 4.25/100,000 players in the 1964–68 era, immediately prior to the formation of NOCSAE, has averaged only 0.68/100,000 players during the 1987–90 season, an 84 percent drop."

5. For further information on the application of legal principles to defects in equipment, see the following law review articles:

(a) Gil B. Fried, "Punitive Damages and Corporate Liability Analysis in Sports Litigation," 9 *Marquette Sports Law Journal* 45 (Fall 1998).

(b) Laura J. Perkins, "Comment: A Practical Guide to Recovery for Injured Air Sport Participants," 62 *Southern Methodist University School of Law Journal of Air Law and Commerce* 559 (November/December 1996).

4.9. LIABILITY INSURANCE

Liability insurance is a form of indemnity whereby the insurer undertakes to indemnify or pay the insured for a loss resulting from legal liability to a third person. It is based on contract law principles. Liability insurance protects an insured against financial loss resulting from lawsuits brought against him or her for negligent behavior. Common subjects for liability insurance in athletics are risks from use of the premises, from faulty products, from use of vehicles, and from the practice of professions.

Insurance is effective even if the insured has committed a minor violation of the criminal law. A minor violation will not invalidate the insurance or deprive the defendant of protection. An insurance policy may be invalidated, however, if the insured's conduct was so outrageous that it would be against public policy to indemnify it. The policy may also be invalidated if the insured misrepresented a material fact at the time of the application for the policy.

One of the standard provisions in any insurance policy requires the insured to cooperate fully with the insurance company by providing full and accurate information about the accident. It may also require the insured to attend the trial, to take part in it if required, and to do nothing for the injured party that would harm the insurance company. A violation of any of the above requirements would relieve the insurance company of liability to the injured third party.

The term "subrogation" is often found in tort cases involving insurance claims. *Subrogation* is the right of the insurance company that has paid the legal obligation of the insured party to recover payment from the third party who was negligent. For example, a fan is injured at a baseball stadium by a foul ball that passed through a hole in the netting behind home plate, and the hole was there because of the negligence of a third-party contractor who damaged the screen during installation. If the liability insurer for the stadium pays the injured fan, it has a right, under subrogation, to sue the installer for negligence, just as its insured, the stadium owner, had.

Typically, insurance policies contain a clause that entitles the insurer to be subrogated to his insured cause of action against any party who caused a loss that the insurer paid. The insurer can also be entitled to subrogation in the absence of an express contractual provision. This is called *equitable subrogation*. In some states, however, an insurance company must prove it was not a gratuitous payment in order to recover under equitable subrogation.

One response by institutions and sports associations to the increasing number of lawsuits brought under a tort liability theory is to use insurance. The National Federation of High School Associations and many state high school athletic associations and their member schools have adopted a liability/lifetime catastrophe medical plan. The plan covers the National Federation of State High School

Associations, the state high school athletic/activity associations, their member schools and school districts, and member school administrators, athletic directors, coaches, and trainers. This type of insurance allows the student-athlete who suffers a catastrophic injury to waive suit and opt for medical, rehabilitation, and work-loss benefits for the rest of his or her life. The philosophy behind the insurance plan is to provide needed benefits to the injured student-athlete without the time, costs, and risks involved in litigation. If the injured student-athlete opts for the benefits provided by the insurance policy, the institution saves time, expense, and a possible award in favor of the plaintiff.

The NCAA instituted a similar catastrophic injury protection plan. The NCAA's plan accomplished two important objectives. First, by having this type of plan, it reduced—if not eliminated—the number of workers' compensation cases filed against NCAA member institutions. The NCAA policy is similar to workers' compensation in that it provides benefits to catastrophically injured student-athletes regardless of fault. And the benefits offered by the NCAA program may be more attractive than a successful workers' compensation claim. For instance, a student-athlete's claim for workers' compensation benefits may have to be litigated. Second, the NCAA insurance policy assists the catastrophically injured student-athlete by providing benefits immediately, without time delays, without the costs of litigation, and without the uncertainties involved in litigation. The benefits are provided for the lifetime of the student-athlete, and the plan is extremely helpful to the student-athlete who is injured without fault.

The student-athlete who is catastrophically injured as a result of negligence of an institution or one of its employees still has the alternative of litigating the case and not collecting the benefits provided by the NCAA policy.

4.10. WAIVER AND RELEASE OF LIABILITY

In the law, there are often competing legal theories in a given situation. The resolution of this type of situation is usually based on the pre-eminent public policies existing at the time the conflict arises. In the area of waivers and releases of liability, the underlying principles of tort law and contract law conflict. *Waivers* or *exculpatory agreements* are contracts that alter the ordinary negligence principles of tort law. *Contract law* is based on the idea that any competent party should have the absolute right to make a binding agreement with any other competent party. The only limit to this right to make such agreements is that a contract is invalid if it violates public policy. For example, a contract in which the parties agree to commit a crime would violate an important public policy of preventing crime.

Tort law, on the other hand, is based on the idea that a party should be responsible for negligent or intentional actions that cause injury to another person. Waivers, then, create a conflict between the right to enter into contracts and the policy that one should be held responsible for injury-causing negligent actions. The conflict between contract and tort law principles has been resolved in favor of the general rule that waivers and releases of liability will be enforceable unless they frustrate an important public policy or unless the party getting the waiver is unfairly dominant in the bargaining process. This resolution is based on the general contract law principle that a party is bound by the signing of a contract unless there is evidence of fraud, misrepresentation, or duress.

In order to determine if fraud, misrepresentation, or duress exists, a court will consider whether the party waiving its rights knew or had an opportunity to know the terms. This does not mean that merely failing to read or to understand a waiver and release of liability will invalidate it. It must be conspicuous and not be hidden in fine print so that a careful reader is unlikely to see it. The waiver and release of liability must also result from a free and open bargaining process. If one party forces the other to agree to a waiver, it may not be enforceable. The last consideration is whether the express terms of the waiver and release of liability are applicable to the particular conduct of the party whose potential liability is being waived. In other words, the language of the waiver must be clear, detailed, and specific. A waiver and release of liability will not be enforceable if it attempts to insulate one party from wanton, intentional, or reckless misconduct. Therefore, only liability for negligent actions can be waived.

If the person signing the waiver and release of liability is a minor, other issues are raised. Under basic contract principles, a minor may repudiate an otherwise valid contract. A problem may also arise when parents sign waivers for their children. Courts are struggling with the issue of the rights of minors that may be waived by their parents.

For competent adult participants in sports activities, waivers and releases of liability are generally upheld unless the waiver or release of liability violates public policy. However, questions are frequently litigated in the area of auto racing. Courts have reasoned that a driver is under no compulsion to race; therefore, a driver has the ability to make a decision whether to race and to assume all the risks inherent in auto racing. This may include risks that arise as a result of negligence on the part of the event's promoters. Courts are generally more reluctant to enforce a waiver and release of liability signed by spectators, based on the theory that they may not be as familiar with the risks of auto racing or that they are entitled to assume that the premises are reasonably safe.

NOTES

1. In *Holzer v. Dakota Speedway, Inc.*, 610 N.W.2d 787 (S.D. 2000), a pit crew member was struck and severely injured by a detached car wheel during a stock car race. The co-guardians of the injured pit crew member brought suit against the racetrack owner (and the liability insurer), alleging negligence, reckless disregard for life, safety, and health, negligent inspection, and breach of duty to third parties. The Supreme Court of South Dakota held, among other things, that the release signed by the crew member was enforceable.

2. In *Lund v. Bally's Aerobic Plus, Inc.*, 93 Cal.Rptr.2d 169 (Cal. App.Ct. 2000), a member of a health club alleged that the personal trainer was negligent in his instruction on how to use an inclined bench press. The club member sued the club for her personal injuries. The Court of Appeals of California held that the waiver and release of liability served a written assumption of the risk, effectively barring recovery.

3. In *Covert v. South Florida Stadium Corp.*, 762 So.2d 938 (Fla. App.Ct. 2000), a holder of a "club level" seat sued the stadium owner for personal injuries sustained as a spectator of a professional football game. The plaintiff sustained injuries as a result of allegedly intoxicated fans beating him up. The district court overruled the circuit court's decision to enter judgment on the pleadings for stadium owners. The district court held that the contract signed by club level season ticket holders, which relieved the stadium of liability for negligence, was ambiguous and therefore did not support judgment on the pleadings.

4. In *Hiett v. Lake Bancroft Community Ass'n*, 418 S.E.2d 894 (Va. 1992), the plaintiff was competing in a triathlon when he dove into the water during the swim portion and

struck his head on the bottom or some unseen object beneath the surface. The injury left Hiett a quadriplegic. Prior to competing in the triathlon, each participant had been required to sign an entry form which included a waiver releasing the event's organizers and sponsors from liability "for any and all injuries" suffered in the event. Hiett cited a Virginia Supreme Court decision from 1890, *Johnson's Adm'x v. Rich Danville R.R. Co.*, 11 S.E. 829 (Va. 1890), in which the court found that an agreement with the railroad company excusing them from liability for any injuries or death resulting from any cause whatsoever was in violation of public policy and therefore invalid. Hiett argued that this precedent still stands and Virginia law has voided any preinjury agreement releasing a party from liability for negligence. The Supreme Court agreed with this argument and found that the release of liability on the entry form for the triathlon violated public policy and was therefore invalid.

5. In *Childress by Childress v. Madison County*, 777 S.W.2d 1 (Tenn. Ct. App. 1989), a severely retarded student and his parents sued a county and its board of education, alleging negligence in supervision of the student, who was taken to a public pool for training for the Special Olympics. The court found the county negligent in failing to supervise the student adequately and also found that the release signed by the student's mother relieved the county of liability to the mother, but in no way waived the rights of the student or the father to sue the county for negligence.

6. In *Wagenblast v. Odessa School District*, 758 P.2d 968 (Wash. 1988), the court did not decide the question presented as to whether the standardized release of liability forms used for athletics could stand as an express assumption of the risk. The court said that in order to determine that question an actual lawsuit with facts on which to base the conclusion was required.

7. In *Brown v. Racquetball Centers, Inc.*, 534 A.2d 842 (Pa. Super. Ct. 1987), a fitness club member sued his club to recover injuries caused when he slipped on a wet tile floor. The court held that the release he signed stating that fitness club member assumed all risks of injury sustained in connection with activities in and about the premises did not absolve the fitness center of liability for its negligence.

8. In *Doyle v. Bowdoin College v. Cooper International, Inc.*, 403 A.2d 1206 (Me. 1979), an action was brought by plaintiffs on behalf of their son Brian, who was injured while playing floor hockey at a clinic sponsored by defendant college and directed by the school's agents. Plaintiffs alleged that the defendant's negligence resulted in their son's injury when a plastic hockey blade flew off the end of another boy's stick, hitting Brian in the eye, shattering his glasses, and damaging his retina so as to leave him partially blind.

The case was tried before a jury which concluded that the negligent conduct of defendants Bowdoin College and its agents proximately caused plaintiffs' son's injuries. The defendants appealed this judgment, contending that the trial court erred in holding (1) that certain documents were *not* releases relieving defendants of all liability for future injuries Brian might suffer as a result of defendants' negligent conduct and (2) that another document was not a contract of indemnification obligating the injured child's mother to reimburse defendants for any liability they might incur regarding injuries sustained by him at the clinic.

The appeals court denied the defendants' appeal. It noted that courts have traditionally disfavored contractual exclusions of negligence liability. The court found that the documents executed by the child's parents contained no express reference to defendants' liability for their own negligence: "Though the documents state that Bowdoin College will not 'assume' or 'accept' any 'responsibility' for injuries sustained by participants unless the waiver violates public policy." The court held that the contract signed by the plaintiff was valid.

9. Releases are not valid if they are not clearly stated. For example, in *Hertzog v. Harrison Island Shores Inc.*, 251 N.Y.S.2d 164 (N.Y. App. Div. 1964), plaintiff beach and yacht club member sought recovery for injuries received in a fall from the gangplank

leading to the dock on club premises. The court held for the plaintiff, despite the fact that the plaintiff signed a release of liability. The court reasoned that a provision of the membership application, providing that, if accepted as a member, plaintiff would waive his claim for any loss to personality or for personal injury while a member of club, was not sufficiently clear or explicit to absolve club of its own negligence in regard to the plaintiff's fall.

10. For more detailed analysis of the viability of waivers in sports, see Doyice J. Cotten and Mary B. Cotten, *Legal Aspects of Waivers in Sport, Recreation and Fitness Activities* (Canton, OH: PRC Publishing Inc., 1997). This book identifies particular U.S. states as "lenient," "moderate," or "rigorous" with respect to allowing waivers to stand up in court. Furthermore, the book provides specific examples of waivers that were upheld or disregarded by the courts.

11. The following are examples of waivers and releases of liability:

(a) The following is an NCAA Ticket Release of Liability Statement:

Dear College Basketball Season Ticket Holder:

Enclosed are your NCAA tickets. Please safeguard your tickets; lost tickets will not be replaced.

**Please note there will be no drop-off of tickets at the Reservations Window for the rest of the season or NCAA games. Tickets *Will Not Be Accepted* under any circumstances. Please distribute any tickets prior to day of game.

THIS TICKET IS A REVOCABLE LICENSE
USER ACCEPTS RISK OF INJURY

The holder of this ticket voluntarily assumes all risks of property loss and personal injury arising during its use. Management may revoke the license and eject or refuse entry to the holder by refunding the stated purchase price. Tickets reported as lost or stolen may not be honored. If lost or stolen, this ticket will not be replaced nor the price refunded. Holder may not solicit contributions or distribute literature on the premises. Every person, regardless of age, must have a ticket to enter the facility. Holder may not bring alcoholic beverages, bottles, cans or containers, irritants (e.g., noise makers), videotape cameras, cups, shakers or strobe lights onto the premises without the written permission of the NCAA. Large signs, flags or banners are not permitted. It is the tournament manager's responsibility to confiscate all prohibited articles. No signs, flags or banners of any size may be affixed to the facility. Items that reflect good sportsmanship that can be held by one individual and do not block the view of other ticket patrons may be permitted. Unless specifically authorized in advance by the NCAA, this ticket may not be offered as a prize in a sweepstakes or contest. No readmittance.

(b) The following waiver was considered by the court in the case of *Brown v. Racquetball Centers Inc.* (see note 7).

I, LeRoy F. Brown, voluntarily enter the Westend Racquet Club, . . . to participate in the athletic, physical and social activities therein. I have inspected the premises and know of the risks and dangers involved in such activities as are conducted therein and that unanticipated and unexpected dangers may arise during such activities. I hereby and do assume all risks of injury to my person and property that may be sustained in connection with the stated and associated activities in and about those premises.

In consideration of the permission granted to me to enter the premises and participate in the stated activities, I hereby, for myself, my heirs, administrators and assigns, release, remise and discharge the owners, operators and sponsors of the premises and its activities and equipment and their respective servants, agents, officers, and all other participants in those activities of and from all claims, demands, actions and causes of action of any sort for injury sustained to my person and/or property during my presence on the premises and my participation in those activities due to negligence or any other fault.

Chapter 5

ATHLETIC ASSOCIATIONS

INTRODUCTION

The organizations that govern athletics are collectively referred to in this chapter as athletic associations. These athletic associations include (1) high school and college athletic associations such as the National Federation of State High School Associations (NFSHSA), the National Collegiate Athletic Association (NCAA), the National Association of Intercollegiate Athletics (NAIA), and the National Junior College Athletic Association (NJCAA); (2) high school and college athletic conferences such as the California Interscholastic Federation (CIF), and the Pacific-10 Conference (Pac-10); and (3) national and international governing bodies such as the International Olympic Committee (IOC), U.S. Olympic Committee (USOC), the International Amateur Athletic Federation (IAAF), and USA Track and Field.

The organizations mentioned above are usually set up as non-profit associations, with a constitution and bylaws. The constitution and bylaws are generally drafted by the members of the organization, and can be modified only by a vote of the association members and/or their representatives. In general, associations are comprised of a board of directors, chief operating officer (i.e., president, executive director), various other association officers (depending upon the size of the association), and representatives from the association members (i.e., athletic directors, athletes, faculty representatives, etc.). While this organizational model is a typical one, each association may vary its structure, depending upon its member's needs. Larger organizations, such as the NCAA, for example, elect the officers and/or board of directors. Often, however, organizations hire people from outside their membership to run the day-to-day activities of the association. These officials, whether elected or hired, comprise the association office.

The association office is charged with many duties. Among its various obligations, association offices are generally responsible for decisions concerning the eligibility of athletes, the implementation and administration of drug testing programs, and the imposing of disciplinary sanctions upon association members and athletes. They generally are not responsible for formulating the rules that govern their particular association. The creation of rules is generally controlled by the governing body of the particular association.

The validity of association rules, under the U.S. Constitution, in intercollegiate and high school athletics has historically come under frequent scrutiny. A key component in deciding such cases is whether or not the defendant association is considered a public or a private institution in the eyes of the court. For an association to be found guilty of violating the Constitution, the association must be deemed a "state actor" or public corporation (see section 5.4.1., "State Action Requirement"). Historically, court decisions concerning state action in athletics have varied. However, since the mid-1980s the Supreme Court has issued two decisions on this topic that have clarified the previously inconsistent position of the courts, relative to the state action issue.

First, on the collegiate level, in the case of *NCAA v. Tarkanian*, 488 U.S. 179 (1988), the U.S. Supreme Court, in a 5–4 decision, decided that the NCAA cannot be construed as a state actor for purposes of constitutional law. Tarkanian brought a case against the NCAA stating that the association had violated his due process rights under the U.S. Constitution in its sanctioning of his program due to NCAA violations. The Superior Court disagreed, stating:

The Nevada state university's actions with respect to the coach, in compliance with the rules and recommendations of the association of which the university was a member, did not turn the association's conduct into such state action, or action under color of state law, because it would be more appropriate to conclude that the university conducted its athletic program under the color of the policies adopted by the association, rather than that those policies were developed and enforced under color of the law of Nevada.

However, in the case of *Brentwood Academy v. Tennessee Secondary School Athletic Association*, 531 U.S. 288 (2001), the U.S. Supreme Court decided that the *high school athletic association* for the state of Tennessee was a state actor, and therefore subject to litigation for violations of the First and Fourteenth Amendments. The court believed that members of the state government were so involved in the association that the association must be considered a state actor: "The Association's regulatory activity is state action owing to the pervasive entwinement of state school officials in the Association's structure, there being no offsetting reason to see the Association's acts in any other way." These influential cases will be discussed further later in the chapter, because the debate over whether or not athletic associations are private or public entities has been a pervasive issue in athletics.

Associations can be challenged legally by both their members and outside groups. For example, the NCAA has found itself involved in litigation over antitrust issues with member schools (*NCAA v. Board of Regents, Univ. of Oklahoma*, 468 U.S. 85 (1984); see Section 14.2.5.1, "Antitrust Issues in Broadcasting for Colleges"), as well as with coaches (*Law v. NCAA*, 134 F.3d 1010 10th Cir. (1998), see Section 10.1.3., "Clayton Act"). Also, the sportswear manufacturer Adidas challenged the association because NCAA rules limited the size of the logos allowed on member institution's uniforms (*Adidas v. NCAA*, 40 F. Supp. 2d. 1275 (D. Kan. 1999), see Chapter 14, Section 14.3.1, "Restrictions on the Use of Advertising"). Historically, the NCAA and other associations were not frequently challenged in terms of legal accountability, though their pervasive influence in the world of athletics has led to increasing legal scrutiny. Some argue that this scrutiny has resulted in better protection of individual rights from arbitrary or unfair actions of governing organizations, institutions, schools, or coaches and teachers. Others argue that this increased judicial presence is an unwarranted intrusion into athletics.

In addition to association committees and association offices, three other groups are involved in the governance of interscholastic and intercollegiate athletics in the United States: the educational institutions (represented by presidents, chancellors, and principals), athletic directors, and coaches. These groups, together with the athletic associations, operate in a pyramid-like fashion: athletic associations set certain minimum standards and requirements for eligibility and participation; conferences and educational institutions may impose stricter obligations on their student-athletes; and athletic directors and coaches may demand further stringent requirements that they judge to be necessary for successful performance in their individual sport or for proper functioning of the educational department as a whole. Since educational institutions and coaches must act within the scope of the association and conference regulations, our focus within this chapter will be primarily on the activities, rules, and governance of athletic associations and conferences.

Chapter 5 analyzes the impact of the law on athletics and notes the growing power of the organizations that govern athletics. The chapter begins with a description of influential athletic associations. It next discusses significant legal principles that must be understood within the context of athletics. The third segment of the chapter involves the authority that is vested in these associations, and how they enforce their rules and regulations. The next section deals with the effect that constitutional law has had upon athletic associations, and how athletes have been able to argue for their constitutional rights through the court system. The final portion of the chapter deals with the responsibility that athletic associations have to the public.

NOTES

1. For further information on the emergence of intercollegiate athletics as big business, see the following:

a. Matthew J. Mitten, "Essay: Applying Antitrust Law to NCAA Regulation of 'Big Time' College Athletics: The Need to Shift from Nostalgic 19th and 20th Century Ideals of Amateurism to the Economic Realities of the 21st Century," 11 *Marquette Sports Law Journal* (Fall 2000).

b. James Duderstadt, *Intercollegiate Athletics and the American University: A University President's Perspective* (Ann Arbor: University of Michigan Press, 2000); Andrew Zimbalist, *Unpaid Professionals* (Princeton: Princeton University Press, 1999).

c. Alan Sack and Ellen Staurowsky, *College Athletes for Hire: The Evolution and Legacy of the NCAA's Amateur Myth* (Westport, Conn.: Praeger, 1998).

d. Murray Sperber, *Onward to Victory: The Crises That Shaped College Sports* (New York: Henry Holt, 1998).

2. For further information on the politics and history of the modern Olympic Games, see the following:

a. Andrew Jennings and Clare Sambrook, *The Great Olympic Swindle: When the World Wanted Its Games Back* (New York: Simon and Schuster, 2000).

b. Helen Jefferson Lensky and Varda Burstyn, *Inside the Olympic Industry: Power, Politics and Activism* (Albany, N.Y.: State University of New York Press, 2000).

c. Kay Schaffer and Sidonie Smith, eds., *The Olympics at the Millennium: Power Politics and the Games* (New Brunswick, N.J.: Rutgers University Press, 2000).

d. Christopher R. Hill, *Olympic Politics: Athens to Atlanta, 1896–1996* (Manchester, U.K.: Manchester University Press, 1997).

5.1. VOLUNTARY ATHLETIC ASSOCIATIONS

5.1.1. Introduction

All athletic associations are subject to fundamental legal principles. Athletic associations and conferences, such as the National Federation of State High Schools Association, the NCAA, and the Big Ten, although private and voluntary organizations, are nevertheless scrutinized within the legal system. The courts are questioning these supposedly "private" athletic associations and conferences for two reasons: (1) large numbers of public institutions form the membership of these organizations, and (2) the opinion that these organizations are performing a traditional governmental or public function.

In this vein of serving the public, over the past century many organizations have been created to serve different groups of individuals in a variety of athletic activities. The Amateur Athletic Union (AAU) has, for almost 100 years, dedicated itself to the development of amateur sports and physical fitness for amateur athletes of all ages. Similarly, the NCAA has taken upon itself the role of coordinator and overseer of college athletics, in the interest of individuals and their educational institutions. As these organizations increasingly become a part of the public domain in the eyes of the judicial system, it becomes imperative to understand the nature and composition of these "private" associations.

As mentioned in the introduction, a major issue surrounding athletic associations has been the categorizing of associations as either private or public entities for purposes of litigation involving constitutional law. For the purposes of discussion within this chapter, the focus will be upon traditionally "amateur" associations. Professional sport leagues and associations are inapplicable to this chapter for two reasons.

First, professional sports franchises and associations are generally private entities. While some professional sports franchises are considered public, this simply signifies that the public can buy stock in the franchise, and *not* that they are public in the sense that they are funded by the state or any state entity. Second, through their collective bargaining agreements, professional athletes waive many of their constitutional rights relative to litigation (see Chapter 11, "Labor Law"). There are a few rare instances, however, where professional athletes may litigate on constitutional law grounds, which will be discussed in Chapter 6.

Athletic organizations are often distinguished on the basis of sport (e.g., USA Track and Field, the national governing body for track and field in the United States), educational level (e.g., National Junior College Athletic Association), or geographic location (e.g., the California Interscholastic Federation). Some amateur sports organizations govern institutions (e.g., the NCAA governs colleges and universities), and some govern individual athletes (e.g., National Governing Bodies, such as USA Track and Field). Belonging to one such organization does not preclude membership in another. In fact, most educational institutions belong to an allied conference (e.g., Big East Conference) in addition to being a member of a national association with a broader constituency (e.g., NCAA). Allied conferences, a subset of the larger amateur sports associations, usually consist of a number of schools that have similar institutional goals and interests. These schools compete against each other in a number of sports and often vie for conference championships in each of the sports.

5.1.2. The U.S. Olympic Committee

The Amateur Sports Act of 1978 (36 U.S.C. 371-396) was passed by the U.S. Congress to recognize and coordinate amateur athletics in the United States and to encourage and strengthen participation of U.S. amateurs in international competition. It focuses on two primary areas: (1) the relationship between athletes eligible for international amateur competition and the ruling bodies that govern these competitions and (2) the relationship between the ruling bodies themselves. This act establishes the U.S. Olympic Committee (USOC) as the principal mechanism for attaining these goals. One of its major objectives was to allow the USOC to make its own decisions concerning matters of eligibility without the outside interference of the court system.

The Amateur Sports Act creates a governing structure for the USOC by empowering it to select one National Governing Body (NGB) for each Olympic or Pan-American sport (see exhibits 5.1 and 5.2). The act enumerates specific responsibilities for an NGB, including the determination of eligibility rules for

Exhibit 5.1
Organizational Chart Showing Regulatory Power of Amateur Sport Governing Bodies

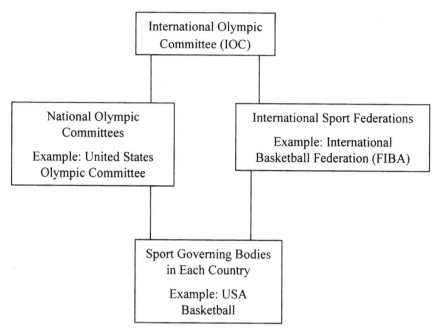

Exhibit 5.2
U.S. Olympic Committee Organizational Structure

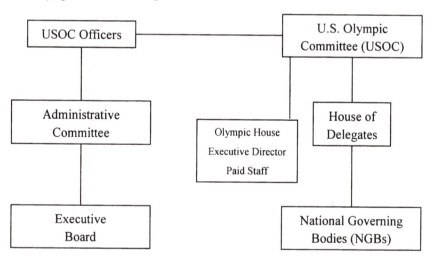

participation. In addition, NGBs make decisions that pertain to team selection, drug testing, and eligibility status. They also do the actual organizational work of developing athletes, organizing teams, instructing coaches and officials, and scheduling events. The act details explicit requirements for sports organizations to become NGBs and provides a mechanism for the resolution of disputes between two organizations wishing to be recognized as the sole NGB. One important requirement of NGBs is that they have the backing of the sport's participants in the United States. International governing bodies must also recognize these associations as official bodies for the particular sport.

Although the USOC has chosen to concentrate on Olympic and Pan-American sports, its control in this area is not exclusive. Not only must an international governing body approve the NGBs, but the USOC itself must also contend with and conform to the policies and regulations of the International Olympic Committee (IOC). Furthermore, the Amateur Sports Act specifies that "any amateur sports organization which conducts amateur athletic competition, participation in which is restricted to a specific class of amateur athletes (such as high school students, college students, members of the Armed Forces or similar groups or categories), shall have exclusive jurisdiction over such competition." It is only when that group wishes to become involved in international competition that the USOC may play a role through the granting of a sanction or "certificate of approval issued by an NGB," which is required for such international competition. Even here, the USOC does not have exclusive control. For instance, when the United States hosts the Olympic or Pan-American Games, the USOC must work in concert with local and state governments and in conjunction with the organizing committee of the host city.

The Amateur Sports Act underwent a series of amendments in 1998 when the Ted Stevens Olympic and Amateur Sports Act Amendments were passed into law (36 U.S.C. §§220501-220529 Supp. IV 1998). The changes include (1) the USOC incorporates athletes with disabilities into the governance structure by requiring the USOC to serve as the national Paralympic representative to the International Paralympic Committee; (2) requirement that athletic representatives, elected by fellow athletes, make up at least 20 percent of the membership and voting power of all USOC legislative bodies; (3) requirement of a USOC report, issued every four years, that shall contain data on the participation of women, racial and ethnic minorities, and disabled athletes; (4) new language that prevents the issuance of injunctive relief against the USOC in any suit concerning the "right to participate" by an athlete within twenty-one days of the beginning of the respective Olympic Games; and (5) the creation of an "athlete ombudsman" to provide free, independent advice to athletes about the Amateur Sports Act, the USOC bylaws and regulations, and rules of the NGBs with respect to the resolution of any right to compete dispute.

Most courts have upheld both the act and its legislative history. However, in *Reynolds v. International Amateur Athletic Federation*, 505 U.S. 1301 (1992) (see note 5) the court defied premise of the act and judged arbitration to be only one of many available administrative remedies available to an amateur athlete. The decision in *Reynolds*, however, seems to be an exception among cases involving the Amateur Sports Act. Courts have been reluctant to interfere with the decisions of the USOC because the act gives the USOC discretion in applying its rules, and does not create a private right of action (see notes 1, 2, and 6). However, courts have intervened in questions involving the act when the court believes that the USOC, or other NGBs, have incorrectly applied their rules (see notes 3 and 4).

NOTES ⎯⎯

1. In *Slaney v. USOC*, 244 F.3d 580 (7th Cir. 2001), Olympic runner Mary Decker Slaney brought suit against the USOC after she tested positive for drug use after Olympic trials in 1996. She was found to have a high enough ratio of testosterone to epitestosterone

in her body to be consistent with blood doping (for more information on Drug Testing of Olympic athletes, see Chapter 7, section 7.2.3., "Olympic and International Sports"). In her complaint against the USOC, Slaney alleged that the testing discriminated against women, and was not scientifically valid. The Seventh Circuit concluded that the Amateur Sports Act provides the USOC with complete jurisdiction over decisions concerning an athlete's eligibility. The court reasoned that the USOC was the most qualified body for determining questions of eligibility. The court went on to state that the USOC could be held liable in questions of eligibility if they do not follow their own stated rules.

2. In *Floyd v. USOC*, 965 S.W.2d 35 (Tex. Ct. App. 1998), a runner tested positive for amphetamines after using a carbohydrate supplement named Sydnocarb. She believed that she could use the supplement without worrying about testing positive because when her husband had called the USOC to see if Sydnocarb was a banned substance, the USOC operator had responded that it was not. The operator did not say, however, that the supplement was safe to use or provide any other assurances. After Floyd tested positive she brought a claim of negligence against the USOC, alleging that it had provided her with false information regarding the supplement. The court ruled that, under the Amateur Sports Act, no athlete has a right to a private cause of action against the USOC, and dismissed Floyd's claim.

3. In *Foschi v. United States Swimming Inc.*, 916 F.Supp. 232 (E.D. N.Y. 1996), the court concluded that while the USOC has jurisdiction concerning eligibility determinations, courts have the ability to intervene to make sure that the USOC is following its own rules for determining eligibility. The federal district court granted the plaintiff's motion to remand back to New York state court the question of whether she was wrongfully suspended from United States Swimming. However the court stopped short of granting the plaintiff injunctive relief, due to its lack of jurisdiction.

4. In *Harding v. United States Figure Skating Association*, 851 F.Supp. 1476 (D. Or. 1994), the court enjoined the defendant Association from proceeding with a disciplinary hearing because the association had violated its own by-laws by scheduling a disciplinary hearing too early for Harding to prepare her defense. The ruling in this case, allowing a court to intervene with an amateur athletic association, was limited by the judge's opinion, which stated, "Intervention is appropriate only in the most extraordinary circumstances, where the association has clearly breached its own rules, that breach will imminently result in serious and irreparable harm to the plaintiff, and the plaintiff has exhausted all internal remedies. Even then, injunctive relief is limited to correcting the breach of the rules. The court should not intervene in the merits of the underlying dispute."

5. Butch Reynolds, the reigning world record holder in the 400 meters, had not been allowed entry into the Olympic trials of 1992 because he had tested positive for steroids, and had been suspended for two years from track and field competition. Reynolds appealed this decision within the court system seeking a preliminary injunction allowing him to compete, instead of following the administrative remedies available to him under the Amateur Sports Act, such as arbitration. The district court heard his case and ruled in his favor, allowing Reynolds to compete. However, the appeals court overturned the decision, stating that Reynolds did not exhaust his administrative remedies, as outlined in the act. The Supreme Court stated, "Of course . . . this ruling may not establish applicant's right to compete in the Olympics at Barcelona, but that opportunity will presumably be foreclosed if he is not allowed to participate in the Olympic Trials. On the other hand, the harm, if any, to the IAAF can be fully cured by a fair and objective determination of the merits of the controversy. Indeed, applicant may fail to qualify, thus mooting the entire matter, if he does qualify, his eligibility can be reviewed before the final event in Barcelona."

6. In *Dolan v. United States Equestrian Team, Inc.*, 608 A.2d 434 (N.J. Super. Ct. App. Div. 1992), a horse rider brought a claim against the U.S. Equestrian Team, claiming that the Team had violated the Amateur Sports Act with its procedure and criteria for selecting team members. The court held that Dolan had not exhausted her administrative

remedies under the Amateur Sports Act, and until she had met that condition she was not able to bring a private right of action. The court also held that requiring Dolan to exhaust her administrative remedies was fair and also consistent with the purpose of the Amateur Sports Act, to have jurisdiction over resolution of disputes in Olympic sports.

7. For further information on the USOC and its powers, see *DeFrantz v. United States Olympic Committee*, 492 F. Supp. 1181 (D.D.C. 1980), *aff'd* without opinion, 701 F.2d 221 (D.C. Cir. 1980). The federal district court held that the Amateur Sports Act of 1978 did not establish a cause of action for twenty-five designated Olympic athletes who sought to prohibit the USOC from barring them from participating in the 1980 Olympic Games in Moscow. The court noted:

> We . . . conclude that the USOC not only had the authority to decide not to send an American team to the summer Olympics, but also that it could do so for reasons not directly related to sports considerations.
> We . . . find that the decision of the USOC not to send an American team to the summer Olympics was not state action, and therefore does not give rise to an actionable claim for the infringements of the constitutional rights alleged.

8. In *Michels v. United States Olympic Committee*, 741 F.2d 155 (7th Cir. 1984), a weightlifter was suspended by the International Weightlifting Federation for two years after showing an impermissible testosterone level during a drug test. The weightlifter brought suit against the USOC, claiming a violation of the Amateur Sports Act in not conducting a hearing on his behalf. The court of appeals held that the weight lifter had no private cause of action under the Amateur Sports Act, and thus the USOC was not required to fulfill his demand of providing a hearing on the validity of the test results.

9. Additional cases involving the interpretation of the Amateur Sports Act include the following:

(a) In *Oldfield v. The Athletic Congress*, 779 F.2d 505 (9th Cir. 1985), the plaintiff was disallowed by TAC from competing in the 1980 Olympic trials on the grounds that he signed a professional performance contract with the International Track Association in 1972 and was therefore, according to an IOC rule, not an amateur anymore. The court of appeals concluded that TAC and the USOC, under the Amateur Sports Act of 1978, had acted appropriately, and therefore affirmed the summary judgment granted by the district court for the defendants.

(b) In *Martinez v. United States Olympic Committee*, 802 F.2d 1275 (10th Cir. 1986), the plaintiff filed a wrongful death action as representative of the estate of a boxer killed during an amateur match. The court of appeals agreed with the district court ruling that the plaintiff showed no cause of action under the Amateur Sports Act.

10. For information on how the federal courts interpret IOC decisions, see *Martin v. International Olympic Committee*, 740 F.2d 670 (9th Cir. 1984). The U.S. Court of Appeals for the Ninth Circuit turned down a request by eighty-two women athletes from twenty-seven countries for an injunction that would order the IOC to let women compete in the 5,000-meter and 10,000-meter races at the 1984 Los Angeles Olympics. The court held that California civil rights law does not authorize the establishment of "separate but equal" events for men and women, and that the IOC rule which governed the addition of new events to the games was applied equally to men and women, and thus was not discriminatory.

5.1.3. National Collegiate Athletic Association

As discussed in Chapter 1, section 1.3., "Intercollegiate Athletics," the NCAA is a voluntary association that is comprised of colleges and universities, conferences, organizations, and individuals totaling over 1,200 total members.

Member schools agree to be bound by NCAA rules and regulations, and are obligated to administer their athletic programs in accordance with the NCAA rules. Over half of the NCAA's members are state universities, and most receive some form of federal financial assistance. The NCAA does not offer membership to individual student-athletes. Instead, it operates under the principle of institutional control. In essence, this means that the NCAA deals only with a school administration, and the school is responsible for individual student-athletes. When a violation that concerns a student-athlete is discovered, the NCAA informs the school of its findings and requests that the school declare the student-athlete ineligible. If the school does not comply with the request, the NCAA may invoke sanctions against all or any part of the institution's athletic program.

The purposes of the NCAA are stated in its constitution:

(a) To initiate, stimulate and improve intercollegiate athletic programs for student-athletes and to promote and develop educational leadership, physical fitness, athletics excellence and athletics participation as a recreational pursuit;

(b) To uphold the principle of institutional control of, and responsibility for, all intercollegiate sports in conformity with the constitution and bylaws of this Association;

(c) To encourage its members to adopt eligibility rules to comply with satisfactory standards of scholarship, sportsmanship and amateurism;

(d) To formulate, copyright and publish rules of play governing intercollegiate athletics;

(e) To preserve intercollegiate athletics records;

(f) To supervise the conduct of, and to establish eligibility standards for, regional and national athletic events under the auspices of this Association;

(g) To cooperate with other amateur athletics organizations in promoting and conducting national and international athletics events;

(h) To legislate, through bylaws or by resolutions of a Convention, upon any subject of general concern to the members related to the administration of intercollegiate athletics; and,

(i) To study in general all phases of competitive intercollegiate athletics and establish standards whereby the colleges and universities of the United States can maintain their athletic programs on a high level. (2001–2002 NCAA Manual, Bylaw 1.2)

In addition, the fundamental policy upon which the NCAA is based is as follows:

The competitive athletics programs of member institutions are designed to be a vital part of the educational system. A basic purpose of this Association is to maintain intercollegiate athletics as an integral part of the educational program and the athlete as an integral part of the student body and, by so doing, retain a clear line of demarcation between intercollegiate athletics and professional sport. (2001–2002 NCAA Manual, Bylaw 1.3.1)

The NCAA is structured in such a way that the entire regulatory responsibility does not lie within the Association office. Instead, the NCAA is divided into conferences, based primarily on geographic location. Each conference is responsible for regulating its member institutions and ensuring that the minimum standards, as outlined in the NCAA Manual, are not violated. Each conference has a detailed set of rules and regulations, and a mechanism to enforce those rules. Most NCAA member institutions are part of one conference or another, and some institutions belong to more than one conference. Not all institutions must be part of a conference to participate in college athletics. For example, Notre Dame is part of the Big East Conference for all of its athletic programs except football. In Division I-A football, Notre Dame is considered an "independent." Because most institutions belong to a conference, it is important to briefly analyze the structure and organization of these conferences.

Conferences are an extension of the NCAA structure. Originally formed to foster regional rivalries among universities, conferences bring the governance of institutions to a more local level. However, the trend in conference expansion since 1990 has not necessarily been dictated by geography. While regional rivalries still exist, especially in older and well-established conferences, the priority in conference expansion has changed drastically in the past ten years. For example, the University of Miami was added to the Big East Conference, which was predominantly comprised of universities located in the northeast. Despite its geographic distance from other schools in the conference, Miami provided the conference with national exposure, and a national championship caliber team in the revenue-producing sport of football. The conference decided to dismiss Temple University, in Philadelphia, from its membership in football effective June 30, 2002, while adding Connecticut in football. The date of Temple's dismissal was subsequently pushed back to 2005.

The development of Conference USA, headquartered in Chicago, is another example of the diverse geographic trend in conference expansion. Despite major geographical distances, the conference includes universities such as Marquette University (Wisconsin), the University of South Florida, and the University of Memphis for basketball. The conference, which was formed in 1995, was developed in order to provide each university with strong athletic competition and the power of a league office. The conference has gradually grown from the eleven inaugural members to fifteen universities effective in 2003.

Each conference, which is commonly made up of ten to twelve institutions, has its own constitution and bylaws, which contain the rules by which all members must abide. These regulations cover eligibility standards, dispute resolution mechanisms, sportsmanship rules, championship guidelines, and player/coach conduct. It is important to remember that each conference is still governed by the NCAA; therefore, no conference rule may be contradictory to an NCAA rule.

The conferences that make up the NCAA were historically split into geographic or regional units. For example, the Pac-10 is made up of the University of Arizona, Arizona State University, the University of California at Berkeley, UCLA, the University of Oregon, Oregon State University, the University of Southern California, Stanford University, the University of Washington, and Washington State University. As can be seen, each of these universities is within a specific geographical area. In addition, the level of competition is comparable. This fosters regional rivalries that encourage fans to travel from one city to another to view a basketball or football game, and to reduce travel expenses for the institutions. In addition, some conferences are made up of teams with similar philosophies and comparable academic ideals, such as the Ivy League, which includes Harvard, Princeton, and Brown.

The role of the conference is similar to that of the NCAA, except on a more local level. The purposes section of the Southeastern Conference (SEC) Constitution reads:

Constitution, Article 1

*1.2 PURPOSES

The purpose of the Southeastern Conference shall be to assist its member institutions in the maintenance of programs of intercollegiate athletics which are compatible with the highest standards of education and competitive sports. To this end, through the orderly establishment and enforcement of legislation, the Conference aims:

(a) to encourage sound academic practices for student-athletes;

(b) to foster strong competition among the teams of its member institutions in a broad spectrum of amateur sports and championships;

(c) to assure proper emphasis on the funding of athletic activities;

(d) to stimulate good sportsmanship;

(e) to provide leadership and a voice in the development of public attitudes toward intercollegiate sports generally; and

(f) to address the future needs of athletics in a spirit of cooperation and mutual benefit of the member institutions.

Each conference has an institutional framework that allows it to enforce league and conference rules, plan championships, and publicize conference games. Each conference has a commissioner who is the chief administrative officer of the conference and is responsible for its day-to-day operation. For example, the responsibilities of the commissioner in the Colonial Athletic Association include, but are not limited to, the following:

1. To act as the principal enforcement officer of the association rules

2. To present an annual operational budget to the Executive Committee for approval

3. To develop a continuous educational program aimed at the development of scholarship, sportsmanship, and understanding of the values of competitive athletics

4. To have jurisdiction over all questions of student eligibility.

A commissioner also is generally responsible for maintaining the fiscal health of the conference. This objective is accomplished by marketing the conference, using methods such as selling sponsorships to local and national corporations and negotiating television contracts with broadcast networks. The conference office has various other employees. For example, a conference office will typically employ an assistant commissioner for championships or an assistant commissioner for NCAA compliance. Employees of a conference office may also include a marketing staff, media relations specialists, and employees to coordinate the operations of conference tournaments.

For all conferences, a formal governance structure has been established to act as the official governing body. For example, the Pac-10 Conference Constitution reads, "The management of the conference shall be vested in the Council. The powers of the Council in relationship to the Chief Executive Officer are set forth in Bylaw 1-1" (Bylaw 4-1). Bylaw 1-1 reads: "The Council shall be the operating body for the administration of the Pacific-10 Conference, under the direction of the Chief Executive Officers as provided herein. The CEO's may propose actions by the Conference, and such proposals shall immediately be referred to the Council for appropriate recommendations unless eight Chief Executive Officers vote to take action without referral to the Council." Each institution in the conference is entitled to three representatives on the Council; they are also part of Council committees, including structural committees (Championship, Officiating, Revenue-Sharing, Television) and standing committees (Budget and Finance, Executive, Legislative, and Selection).

Each conference in the NCAA has a set of rules and regulations that cannot be contradictory to what is established in the *NCAA Manual*. Conference regulations may be stricter than the NCAA's, but they may not be more relaxed. For example, each conference must have eligibility requirements that meet the minimum standards set forth by the NCAA. The Pac-10 handbook reads:

> Student eligibility and participation rules for Pacific-10 teams and individuals are the NCAA rules of eligibility, except where the Pacific-10 has a more strict rule or where special exceptions are made and recorded in the Pacific-10 Handbook. (Article 7(1)(a), *2001–2002 Pac-10 Conference Handbook*)

One of the more rigid eligibility rules concerns intra-conference transferring. The Pac-10 Conference maintains strict guidelines concerning student-athletes who transfer from one Pac-10 institution to another Pac-10 institution. (See note 1 for discussion of a case involving the Pac-10 intra-conference transfer rule.)

> Each institution, before it permits a student who has transferred directly, or indirectly from, or practiced at, another Pacific-10 member institution to compete in intercollegiate athletics, shall require the student to fulfill a residence requirement of two full academic years (four full semesters or six full quarters), and shall charge the student with two years of eligibility in all Pacific-10 sports, and during the period of ineligibility shall not offer, provide, or arrange directly or indirectly any earned or unearned athletically related financial aid. (Article 7(3)(b)(1), *2001–2002 Pac-10 Conference Handbook*)

Conferences also have the ability to make legislative amendments to conference rules and regulations. Each conference has a procedure that governs conference rules, regulations, and decisions. For example, in the PAC-10 Conference eight of the ten members must vote in favor of a constitutional amendment. In terms of amendments to the bylaws, seven affirmative votes are required; in the area of enlarging the membership of the conference, a unanimous vote of all the members is necessary. The annual budget of the conference and selection and employment of the commissioner are based on a majority vote of the member institutions (*2001–2002 PAC-10 Handbook*, Bylaw 2).

NOTE _____

1. In the case of *Tanaka v. University of Southern California*, 252 F.3d 1059 (9th Cir. 2001), a former female soccer player for the University of Southern California brought an antitrust claim against USC and the Pac-10 Conference, charging that the conference rule on intra-conference transfers was a violation of the Sherman Antitrust Act because the rule was an unreasonable restraint on her ability to transfer to her school of choice, UCLA. Tanaka charged that this rule was applied to her only because, before leaving the university, she had charged the university and athletic department with academic fraud. She believed that the rule was employed in her case as retaliation for her allegations against the athletic department. The court decided in favor of the university and the Pac-10,

stating, "Tanaka has failed to identify a relevant market for antitrust purposes. If the relevant market is national in scope, the Pac-10 transfer rule could not have a significant anticompetitive effect, because by its own terms the rule does not apply to interconference transfers. Moreover, even if the relevant market is limited to the Pac-10 itself, Tanaka characterizes the Pac-10's imposition of sanctions against her for her intraconference transfer as an isolated act of retaliation. Tanaka simply has no antitrust cause of action." (See Chapter 10, "Antitrust Law.")

5.1.4. Other Athletic Associations

In addition to the NCAA, several other athletic organizations govern collegiate sports participation. One of these is the National Association of Intercollegiate Athletics (NAIA), an intercollegiate athletic governing organization composed of four-year institutions. The NAIA was formed in 1940 as the National Association of Intercollegiate Basketball. The association changed its name to the NAIA in 1952 as it expanded into sports other than basketball. The NAIA quickly grew from a small organization and had 510 member institutions as of July 2001.

A good description of the NAIA is contained in *Williams v. Hamilton*, 497 F.Supp. 641 (D.N.H. 1980):

> [The] NAIA is a voluntary association of 512 four-year colleges ranging in size from small (500) to moderate (1100), whose primary purpose as set forth in its constitution is "to promote the development of athletics as a sound part of the educational offerings of member institutions." The member institutions of NAIA pay dues to the Association, which are scaled by enrollment. Among other things, NAIA sets standards for recruiting and eligibility, and it sponsors post-season national championships in various collegiate sports, including soccer.
>
> NAIA is divided into several districts, each of which is governed by a "District Executive Committee." Each district has voting representation at NAIA's Annual National Convention, at which time policy decisions are made. Also at the National Convention delegates vote for new members of the National Executive Committee, the overall governing body of NAIA.

The NAIA is open to any four-year, degree-granting college or university in the United States or Canada that is fully accredited by accrediting agencies or commissions of the Council on Postsecondary Accreditation. Those institutions belonging to the NAIA must operate their intercollegiate athletic programs according to the association's regulations and rules. Of course, member institutions can establish even stricter standards than those of the association. The NAIA's eligibility regulations are very similar to those of the NCAA, except that the NAIA's eligibility rules govern all play in sports recognized by the association, whereas the NCAA has special rules for post-season tournaments.

Another athletic organization that governs amateur sports participation is the National Small College Athletic Association (NSCAA). Four-year colleges with enrollments of less than 500 male and/or female undergraduate students qualify for membership. The National Christian College Athletic Association (NCCAA) offers championships to both sexes and governs athletics in four-year institutions. The NCCAA, which is composed of 104 members, is open only to four-year Christian institutions that are willing to subscribe to a "Statement of Faith."

The National Junior College Athletic Association (NJCAA), which has approximately 530 members as of 2002, is another intercollegiate organization that performs functions similar to those of the NSCAA and NCCAA, except that it encompasses men's and women's junior college athletic programs. It was described in *State ex rel. National Junior College Athletic Ass'n. v. Luten*, 492 S.W.2d 404 (Mo. Ct. App. 1973) as a

> not-for-profit corporation which coordinates the scheduling and playing of inter-collegiate athletics among its member schools. . . . who agree to "supervise and to control athletics sponsored by this corporation so that they will be administered in accordance with the eligibility rules . . . set forth in the . . . Bylaws." Among its functions it issues and enforces rules relating to the eligibility of students at its member schools participating in intercollegiate athletics.

Like the NCAA, the NAIA and other smaller intercollegiate athletic associations must be evaluated as to whether or not they are state actors. With the exception of the National Christian College Athletic Association, these associations are comprised of both private and public institutions. Therefore, the leading case involving state action and the NCAA, *Tarkanian v. NCAA* (see "Introduction," this chapter), also should apply to these other associations, determining that associations of this type cannot be construed as state actors.

NOTES

1. For further information on how the NAIA's governing authority is viewed by the courts, see the following cases:

   a. In *Manuel v. NAIA*, 833 P.2d 288 (Okla. Ct. App. 1992), Manuel was able to obtain an injunction that disallowed the NAIA from interfering with his scholarship to participate on the Oklahoma City University basketball team. The NAIA appealed this decision even though Manuel had already graduated, to make OCU and Manuel subject to retroactive penalties. Manuel had been declared ineligible under NCAA rules at the University of Kentucky, and the NAIA immediately declared Manuel ineligible upon his entrance at an NAIA member school, although this rule had not been applied in other cases with similar fact patterns. The court upheld the injunction against the NAIA, stating. "The manner in which the NAIA chose to interpret its own rules with regard to Manuel appears, from the evidence, to be contrary to the way it has interpreted them in the past as to other student athletes . . . The hard reality is that a college education is outside the reach of many students without the assistance of athletic scholarships. Once a student is fortunate enough to receive one, it should not be revoked through an arbitrary exercise of authority vested in a voluntary association such as the NAIA."

   b. In the case of *Williams v. Hamilton*, 497 F.Supp. 641 (D.N.H. 1980), a college student-athlete challenged the NAIA transfer rule requiring him to be in residence at his new college for sixteen weeks before becoming eligible for intercollegiate athletics. The rule was imposed, in part, to prevent "tramp athletes" from transferring from school to school for the sole purpose of participating in sports. The court held that the transfer rule was valid and did not deny due process or equal protection guarantees.

2. The National Junior College Athletic Association is a nonprofit corporation with over 500 junior colleges (two-year programs of study) as member institutions. For further information on the NJCAA's governing authority as viewed by the courts, see *State ex rel. National Junior College Athletic Ass'n. v. Luten*, 492 S.W.2d 404 (Mo. Ct. App. 1973). For more information on the NJCAA, visit their Web site at www.njcaa.org

3. For more information on the NAIA, visit the organization's Web site at www.naia.org

4. For more information on the NSCAA, visit the organization's Web site at www.thenscaa.com

5. For more information on the NCCAA, visit the organization's Web site at www.bright.net/~nccaa/

5.1.5. High School Athletic Associations

High school athletic associations are voluntary associations consisting of all high schools within a state that wish to participate in association events, agree to abide by the rules of the association, and meet membership requirements. High school associations are often given authority to organize through state legislation, which in effect creates a private corporation to perform a quasi-public function. Each of the fifty states has its own high school athletic association to govern interscholastic athletics, and several states have more than one association. Generally, the need for multiple associations has arisen in two situations. First, the geography or population of the state makes it infeasible for one central state association to conduct all tournaments and other administrative duties. In these cases, states will form regional associations to administer the association rules. The second situation is when separate athletic associations are set up for schools in urban environments and schools in non-urban settings. Nevertheless, most state associations are set up so that all schools which wish to abide by association rules will be allowed entry into the association. One example of a state with multiple sub-associations is California (California Interscholastic Federation; CIF), which is comprised of the following regions:

1. Central
2. Central Coast
3. Los Angeles
4. North Coast
5. Northern
6. Oakland
7. San Joaquin
8. San Diego
9. San Francisco
10. Southern

In most cases, membership in the association is open to all high schools in the state that are approved by the appropriate state department of education, secondary education, or public instruction. Generally, the association's purpose is to promote, develop, direct, protect, and regulate amateur interscholastic athletic relationships among member schools and to stimulate fair play, friendly rivalry, and good sportsmanship among contestants, schools, and communities throughout the state.

State interscholastic athletic associations have had litigation brought against them claiming that association rules are unconstitutional, or that the sanctions imposed on schools or athletes are discriminatory or unjust. Historically, athletic association rules have been vulnerable to litigation because they have been written in an unclear, vague, or ambiguous manner, or have been applied in an arbitrary and capricious manner. In the majority of these cases, the courts have found that the state athletic association has the responsibility to enforce its rules, and that the student-athlete's participation in interscholastic athletics is a privilege, not a right. However, the courts have found that the association's rules cannot be arbitrary or irrational; if found so, these rules will be declared unconstitutional.

The National Federation of High School State Associations (NFSHSA) is the governing body for high school athletics. Founded in 1920, the federation was based on the belief that strong state and national high school organizations are necessary to protect the integrity of interscholastic programs and to promote healthy growth of these programs (see exhibit 5.3). The NFSHSA as a federation has much less power the NCAA (which has national authority). The high school athletic associations, which are funded by membership dues and which control rule making and enforcement procedures, are established on a state basis, largely unaffected by the NFSHSA.

NFSHSA services include a press service subscribed to by editors of local, state, and national publications; a national film library; national federation publications for thirteen sports; national records for more than 40,000 performances, listed in the National Interscholastic Records Book; sanctioning of applications for interstate and international events among schools; athletic directors conferences; printed proceedings; and a quarterly magazine. The NFSHSA membership serves over 200,000 high schools, 500,000 coaches and sponsors, and 500,000 officials and judges.

The California Interscholastic Federation (CIF) is a typical example of a high school association. Its members include public and private secondary schools, as well as technical and vocational schools. Prior to membership, an applicant school must be approved by the Federated Council, which is a governing body within the CIF that has representatives from each of the ten regions within the federation, a representative from the California Department of Education, and officials within the federation. Among the responsibilities of the Federated Council are the following:

1. Determine the credentials of its own membership.

2. Exercise jurisdiction over all interscholastic athletic games, events, and meets involving CIF schools. The Federated Council delegates jurisdiction to each CIF section for all interscholastic athletic games, events, and meets in which only CIF member schools of that particular section participate.

3. Be responsible for state and regional CIF playoff contests.

4. Act as a final court of appeals in protests.

5. Establish and enforce penalties for any violation of the constitution, bylaws, or other rules of the CIF. Schools, leagues, and sections may establish and enforce penalties, provided that such penalties are not in conflict with penalties that have been established by higher authority.

6. Determine which athletic activities shall be conducted by the federation.

7. Prescribe ways and means by which standards of eligibility shall be met.

8. Elect its own officers.

9. Institute and conduct impeachment of officers of the federation and sanctions thereof.

10. For any matter of appeal not covered in the constitution and bylaws, an appeal to the Federated Council will be heard by its Appeals Committee.

11. Award life passes to its members after three years of service.

It is important to reiterate that state associations are the administrative bodies that have the final decision in all matters of eligibility, discipline, and rules. The

Exhibit 5.3
Organizational Structure of the NFSHSA

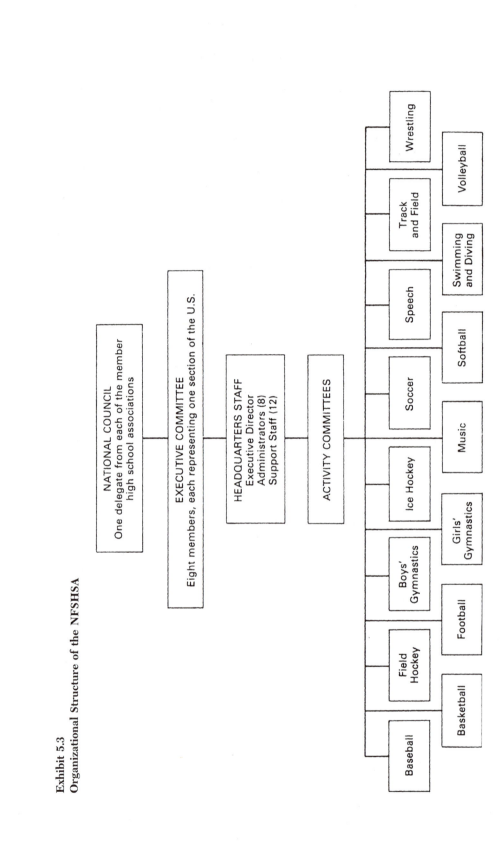

CIF has set up a system where one official within each sport is designated as the rules interpreter for that sport. For matters of eligibility and discipline, the sectional bodies are in charge of managing disputes in light of the CIF regulations. Only when these disputes cannot be resolved will the CIF Federated Council become involved in the dispute process (see section 5.3.3., "Interscholastic Enforcement Procedures").

State high school associations are usually non-profit corporations per the guidelines of the Internal Revenue Service. Most associations generate revenue through gate receipts and membership dues. For example, the CIF generates much of its revenues via gate receipts from championship competitions, preseason games and tournaments, and sanctioned invitational tournaments and meets. The other areas of revenue for associations come from membership dues, officials' registration fees, media contracts, corporate sponsorship, licensing, and royalties. As non-profit organizations, state associations have the advantage of tax-exempt status. For example, CIF declares its tax-exempt status within its bylaws (Bylaw 12):

> The property of this organization is irrevocably dedicated to charitable and educational purposes, meeting the requirements for exemption provided by Section 214 of the Revenue and Taxation Code. No part of the net income or assets of this organization shall ever inure to the benefit of any director, officer, or member thereof nor to the benefit of any private persons. Upon the dissolution or winding up of the organization, which is dedicated to charitable and educational purposes meeting the requirements for exemption provided by Section 214 of the Revenue and Taxation Code, its assets remaining after payment, or provision for payment, of all debts and liabilities of this organization, shall be distributed to a non-profit fund, foundation, or corporation which is organized and operated exclusively for educational purposes and which has established its tax exempt status under Section 501C(3) of the Internal Revenue Code.

As mentioned in the beginning of the section, the majority of states have one high school association that is open to public, private, and parochial schools. However, some states have three or four different governing associations defined by geographic boundaries. For example, the cities of New York and Philadelphia have separate associations that govern the city schools, which do not compete for state titles.

Whether or not private and public schools are mixed varies from state to state. For example, in the state of Connecticut, the Connecticut Interscholastic Athletic Conference (CIAC) is open to "any public or parochial school in Connecticut which is accredited by the State Department of Education, any private school or academy which serves the community as a public school, and any private school holding associate institutional membership in the Connecticut Association of Schools." Conversely, in the state of Texas, membership in the state association, the University Interscholastic League (UIL), is open only to open enrollment charter schools and public schools that have paid their dues.

The question of whether to allow private schools to compete against public schools is one that has seen some litigation. The leading case in this area of high school association governance is *In the Matter of Kellenberg Memorial High School et al., Appellants, v. Section VIII of the New York State Public High School Athletic Association*, 679 N.Y.S.2d 660 (N.Y. App. Div. 1998). Two high schools, Kellenberg Memorial High School and Chaminade High School, were refused enrollment into the New York State Public High School Athletic Association by a vote of the members of the association, in part due to the fear that these private, not-for-profit schools would be able to recruit players to enhance their athletic teams. The New York Supreme Court decided that the schools failed to demonstrate a constitutionally protected interest in membership in the association, and denied their petition for membership. (See Note 3 for a discussion of another case involving participation in high school associations.)

While cases involving a school's membership in an association have increased, much of the litigation that has involved high school associations has generally pertained to associations' eligibility rules. The courts have commonly allowed associations to maintain restrictive rules and regulations so long as they follow their own rules and apply the rules in a reasonable and consistent manner. For example, in the case of *Marshall v. Alabama High School Athletic Association*, 717 So.2d 404 (Ala. Civ. App. 1998), the plaintiff's son had been suspended from playing high school football after it was found that he had struck a referee after a football game in which he participated. The association decided that the school would have to forfeit any remaining games that Marshall played in for the rest of the year. In his case against the association, Marshall was denied injunctive relief at both the district court and the appellate level, and therefore was not allowed to play for the high school team. In deciding for the AHSAA, the court stated, "the law in the State of Alabama is clear that courts should not interfere with the internal operations of the [AHSAA] unless its actions are the result of fraud, lack of jurisdiction, collusion or arbitrariness."

The courts will, however, rule against high school athletic associations if the rules they maintain are unreasonable. For example, in *Davis v. Massachusetts Interscholastic Athletic Association*, No. 94-2887, 1995 Mass. Super. LEXIS (Mass. Jan. 18, 1995), the MIAA was attempting to block a young girl who was home-schooled from participating in interscholastic athletics for her local high school. The plaintiffs received an injunction allowing her to play on the high school softball team, and the court ruled that the MIAA regulation distinguishing between home-schooled students and others "creates varying treatment of students based on in-school and home-school status and the classification and varying treatment are not rationally related to a legitimate State purpose." Therefore, the MIAA was not able to provide a rational basis for its rule (see section 5.4.3., "Equal Protection"). It is also important to note that an association's rules and regulations can be challenged if they violate constitutional law protections of individual athletes. Much litigation has been initiated in the areas of drug testing and freedom of expression. Litigation concerning student-athlete freedoms and other eligibility rules are discussed in greater detail in Chapter 6.

NOTES ───

1. For further information on the high school athletic associations mentioned in this chapter visit the following Web sites:

   (a) www.nfsh.org (National Federation of State High School Associations)

   (b) www.cifstate.org (California Interscholastic Federation)

   (c) www.casciac.org (Connecticut Interscholastic Athletic Conference)

   (d) www.uil.utexas.edu (University Interscholastic League)

2. The California Interscholastic Federation can be contacted at 664 Las Gallinas Avenue, San Rafael, CA 94903.

3. In *Archbishop Walsh High School v. Section VI of the New York State Public High School Athletic Association, Inc.*, 660 N.E.2d. 521 (N.Y. 1996), a New York court held that it was not unconstitutional for a high school athletic association to restrict its membership to non-public high schools. The Association could provide a rational basis for its restrictive rule: that they wanted to make sure that competition between schools within its membership was even. The Association feared that allowing entry to non-public schools increased the possibility of uneven competition.

4. In *Denis J. O'Connell High School v. The Virginia High School League*, 581 F.2d 81 (4th Cir. 1978), *cert denied*, 440 U.S. 936 (1979), the case involved a league's denial of membership to a private high school. The court of appeals ruled for the Virginia High School League and reasoned that a state is justified in taking any reasonable steps to prevent actual or potential abuse of student-athletes. The league had defended its policy of exclusion of private schools because it was rationally related to the league's interest in enforcing its eligibility rules concerning transfer student-athletes. The league presented evidence that because public schools draw students from strictly defined areas, while private schools are not so limited, it would be difficult to enforce transfer rules with respect to private schools.

5.2. LEGAL PRINCIPLES PERTAINING TO AMATEUR ATHLETIC ASSOCIATIONS

5.2.1. Introduction

This section explores the mechanisms and principles of law as they pertain to amateur athletic associations, examines the structures of these organizations, and reviews litigation involving these organizations. In order to understand litigation involving these associations, three legal concepts that are particularly important in the application of law to the areas of amateur athletics will be discussed within this section. Limited judicial review, standing, and injunctive relief are important legal concepts that are recurring themes in cases involving athletics.

The concept of *limited judicial review* derives from the theory that courts should not review every legislative judgment of an organization but, rather, defer to the organization's decisions. As a general rule the legal system intervenes through judicial review only when legislative actions violate rights guaranteed by the Constitution, rights granted by the institution concerned, or basic notions of fairness. It should be noted that federal courts possess a more limited power of review than do state courts. This means that only cases involving certain constitutional issues will be heard at the federal level, while most others are deferred to the state level. The federal courts may thus be prevented from reviewing cases that might be subject to review at the state court level. A case in which an action by the state violates a federal constitutional right is, however, usually subject to judicial review at the federal level.

Standing is a procedural device that must be demonstrated prior to the initiation of any lawsuit. The requirement of standing is based on the theory that all cases brought before the legal system must be part of an ongoing controversy. Academic curiosity or contrived situations are not sufficient requisites for a plaintiff to demonstrate standing.

The type of relief granted is the third important legal concept. Two types of relief are commonly sought: monetary damages and injunctive relief. Since monetary damages do not always give the plaintiff appropriate or adequate relief, the equitable remedy of injunctive relief is available. *Injunctive relief* is a fair, nondiscriminatory form of judgment to redress a wrong or an injury. This type of relief is particularly important in sports during the period in which legal action involving participation is being tried in the courts. Time is often of the essence, and injunctive relief may be critical to the student-athlete, since it allows him or her to continue competing.

5.2.2. Judicial Review

College and high school administrators make decisions and take actions regarding rules and regulations every day, and it is important to stress that the courts can review some of these decisions. Prior to the 1960s, courts had refused to intervene in the internal affairs of organizations that govern any aspect of a school's athletic program. However, beginning in the early 1960s, student-athletes began to challenge the authority that was delegated to directors of athletic programs because, in some instances, these administrators were regulating personal behavior, including marriage and physical appearance. Courts accepted jurisdiction over these cases and invalidated rules that interfered with constitutional rights of individual participants. Since the 1980s, however, rules concerning physical appearance and marriage have not been frequently challenged, and consequently cases in these areas have not frequently reached the court system. However, there have been numerous challenges involving athletic eligibility and team eligibility.

As a general rule, the courts will review a voluntary association's rules only if one of the following conditions are present:

1. The rules violate public policy because they are fraudulent or unreasonable.
2. The rules exceed the scope of the association's authority.
3. The organization violates one of its own rules.
4. The rules are applied unreasonably or arbitrarily.
5. The rules violate an individual's constitutional rights.

Even if a rule is subject to review, the role of the court is very limited. A court will not review the merits of the rule involved. It will only determine whether the rule or the enforcement of the rule is invalid by virtue of the five standards listed above. If a violation is found, the case is remanded or referred back to the athletic administration for further consideration based on directions from the court. Constitutional violations that require judicial intervention are based on either due process or equal protection considerations. Due process involves infringements on life, liberty, or property; equal protection involves the fair application of laws to individuals. Both of these constitutional standards require that state action be present prior to judicial review. (See Sections 5.4.1–5.4.3, "State Action Requirement," "Due Process," and "Equal Protection.")

Athletic associations can guard against judicial scrutiny by reviewing and updating rules and regulations so that they (1) protect the health and welfare of athletes and serve to protect a justifiable public interest, and (2) are consistent with court decisions in the state, region, or nation regarding similar rules. If a case is brought, the court is then more likely to show great deference to the judgment of the athletic administrators who created these rules and are best equipped to decide controversies concerning them. Only evidence of fraud, collusion, or unreasonable, arbitrary, or capricious action will cause a court to intervene on behalf of an athlete concerning the interpretation of a rule.

NOTES

1. In the following cases, courts used judicial review to examine cases involving voluntary athletic associations:

a. In *Indiana High School Athletic Association v. Durham*, 748 N.E.2d 404 (Ind. Ct. App. 2001), the Indiana High School Athletic Association (IHSAA) argued that the trial court should not have been able to issue a permanent injunction to the athlete, Durham, because the court "failed to apply the deferential standard of review afforded to its administrative rulings in granting Durham's request for a permanent injunction." The appellate court agreed with the trial court's issuance of the injunction and use of judicial review, stating, "Given the evidence in this case, the trial court did not abuse its discretion in overturning the IHSAA's denial of full eligibility and refusal to grant a hardship exception. While it may be true that in other cases we have recognized the IHSAA's broad discretion in refusing to grant a student a hardship exception, this discretion is not unreviewable and is subject to the arbitrary and capricious standard upon review."

b. In the case of *Scott v. Ohio High School Athletic Association*, No. 1999CA00269 2000 Ohio Ct. App. LEXIS 3193 (Ohio Ct. App. July 10, 2000), the court decided that a ruling made by the association, choosing to suspend an athlete under allegations of illegal recruiting, was arbitrary because the association did not have enough solid evidence of wrongdoing. The trial court found that there was no independent evidence to establish that the recruiting contacts alleged did, in fact, occur and that, therefore, the commissioner's decision was not supported by reliable evidence. Because the court believed the commissioner's decision to be without any substantive reason, it overturned the association's decision.

c. In the case of *Washington v. Indiana High School Athletic Association* 181 F.3d 840 (7th Cir. 1999), the court decided to affirm the granting of a preliminary injunction by the trial court to allow the plaintiff, Washington, to participate in interscholastic athletics even though he had used eight semesters of athletic eligibility. The court decided that IHSAA did not have any legitimate reason why it should not grant a waiver to Washington, stating, "Nor will the record support the argument that a waiver of the rule in Mr. Washington's case would place an undue administrative or financial burden on the IHSAA. The record indicates that Mr. Washington is the only student-athlete to seek a waiver because of a learning disability in more than a decade. The few case-by-case analyses that the IHSAA would need to conduct hardly can be described as an excessive burden."

2. In the following cases, the court decided not to implement judicial review, letting decisions by voluntary associations stand:

a. In the case of *Missouri State High School Activities Association v. The Honorable Kenneth Romines, Circuit Judge of the Circuit Court of the County of St. Louis*, 37 S.W.3d 421 (Mo. Ct. App. 2001), the Missouri State High School Activities Association appealed a decision of the circuit judge to issue an injunction to allow a student-athlete to remain eligible despite breaking the association's transfer rule, which made him ineligible in the eyes of the association. The court ruled for the association, deciding that the judicial review of the court was not necessary in this case, stating, "We are unable to find any basis upon which the Circuit Court could exercise its jurisdiction to enjoin the Association's decision. There was no allegation in the petition of lack of procedural due process, and no indication of malice, fraud or collusion."

b. In the case of *Hart v. NCAA*, 550 S.E.2d 79 (W. Va. 2001), the NCAA appealed a preliminary injunction that was awarded to Hart, a wrestler at Appalachian State University, which allowed him to participate in a fifth season of eligibility under NCAA rules. The appellate court overturned the injunction, deciding that the circuit court had abused its discretion in ordering the injunction for Hart. The district court made an erroneous decision in granting the preliminary injunction because Hart did not possess a right to participate in intercollegiate wrestling that merited protection by an issuance of an injunction.

c. In *Phillip v. Fairfield University*, 118 F. 3d 131 (2nd Cir. 1997), Fairfield University and the NCAA appealed the decision of a trial court to issue a preliminary injunction allowing a student-athlete to compete although he had not satisfied NCAA initial eligibility requirements. The appellate court overturned the decision of the trial court, concluding that the trial court had erred in assessing that the NCAA had arbitrarily not granted Phillip a waiver. The appellate court stated, "The district court purported to find without adequate explanation that some sort of a contractual duty was owed by the NCAA to Phillip as a result of the contracts between Fairfield and the NCAA and Phillip and the NCAA. We express no view of whether such a duty did exist. However, we think it clear that the district court erred in finding that the NCAA evidenced bad faith simply by acting arbitrarily."

d. In the case of *McPherson v. Michigan High School Athletic Association*, 119 F.3d 453 (6th Cir. 1997), the court decided that a rule allowing players to be eligible for only eight semesters of athletic competition was not crafted in order to discriminate against disabled students. The court stated, "The plaintiff has no evidence, and has not even suggested, that the formulation or implementation of the MHSAA's eight-semester rule has in any way been motivated by considerations of barring students with learning disabilities from play." The court dubbed the rule a "neutral" rule, meaning that it was non-discriminatory in its intent. The court did not believe that the MHSAA had an obligation to waive the eight-semester rule in each case that it was faced with, stating, "To do so would amount to an improper delegation to the MHSAA of this court's responsibility to independently determine whether the rule is, in fact, necessary."

e. In a case nearly identical to *McPherson*, the court in *Frye v. Michigan High School Athletic Association*, No. 95–1266, 1997 U.S. App. LEXIS (6th Cir. Aug. 5, 1997), decided in the same fashion as *McPherson* to allow an association rule prohibiting athletes to compete after eight semesters of eligibility is exhausted.

f. In *Jones v. NCAA*, 679 So.2d 1337 (La. 1996), the student-athlete, Jones, was originally granted an injunction to allow him to play intercollegiate football despite running out of NCAA eligibility after his fourth year. The appellate court, in a short decision, overturned the lower court, stating, "Courts should not interfere with the internal affairs of a private association except in cases when the affairs and proceedings have not been conducted fairly and honestly, or in the cases of fraud, lack of jurisdiction, the invasion of property or pecuniary rights, or when the action complained of is capricious, arbitrary, or unjustly discriminatory."

g. In the case of *NCAA v. Brinkworth*, 680 So.2d 1081 (Fla. Dist. Ct. App. 1996), Brinkworth, a football player for the University of Miami, was awarded a temporary injunction from the trial court, allowing him to play football. The NCAA appealed the decision, and was successful, with the court stating, "It is up to the NCAA to interpret its own rules, not the judiciary. The NCAA followed fair procedures in allowing the university the opportunity to state its case on behalf of the student-athlete, including an appeal within the NCAA when dissatisfied with the initial ruling. As the procedures were adequate and fair, there was no basis on which to intervene in the internal affairs of the NCAA."

3. For the proposition that harshness by itself is not grounds for judicial review, see the following cases:

a. In *Indiana High School Athletic Association v. Vasario*, 726 N.E.2d 325 (Ind. Ct. App. 2000), a student in a foreign exchange program of study in the state was denied participation in interscholastic athletics. The ISHAA rule stated that all exchange programs must be approved programs if a student wished to participate in athletics. The plaintiff's program had lost its official approval, and therefore he was not able to participate. The court, reversing a trial court ruling, held that the rule was not arbitrary or capricious, and did not violate any of the plaintiff's rights.

b. In *Indiana High School Athletic Association v. Carlsberg*, 694 N.E.2d 222 (Ind. 1997), a student transferred from one high school to another for academic reasons. He was deemed ineligible for athletic participation even though his reasons for transferring were for academic reasons. The court upheld the association's transfer rule because it was not arbitrary or capricious and was rationally related to a legitimate interest.

c. In *Shelton v. National Collegiate Athletic Ass'n*, 539 F.2d 1197 (9th Cir. 1976), the court found no violation of equal protection of an NCAA eligibility rule as applied to a college basketball player. The court did admit that "the application of such [eligibility] rules may produce unreasonable results in certain situations." Although the court recognized that the eligibility rule and its means of enforcement may not be the best way to achieve the objective of ensuring amateurism, it stated: "It is not judicial business to tell a voluntary athletic association how best to formulate or enforce its rules."

d. In *Marino v. Waters*, 220 So. 2d 802 (La. Ct. App. 1969), a high school student-athlete who had transferred to another school because of his marriage, violated a policy of the private school he had originally attended. The court held that the rule was not arbitrary because it was promulgated for a legitimate purpose and was not applied in a discriminatory manner. Again, the mere harshness of a rule in its application to an individual does not make it subject to proper judicial review.

e. In *State v. Judges of Court of Common Pleas*, 181 N.E.2d 261 (Ohio 1962), the state high school athletic association suspended a member high school from participating in athletics for one year and declared two boys from the high school ineligible for interscholastic athletics for failure to abide by association rules. The court held that this action should not be prohibited when, although harsh, determination was not the result of mistake, fraud, collusion, or arbitrariness.

4. Certain federal statutes are commonly cited in an effort to obtain federal court jurisdiction in athletic cases. Among them are the following:

(a) 28 U.S.C. section 1343—Civil Rights and Elective Franchise.

The district courts shall have original jurisdiction of any civil action authorized by law to be commenced by any person:

(1) To recover damages for injury to his person or property, or because of the deprivation of any right or privilege of a citizen of the United States, by any act done in furtherance of any conspiracy mentioned in section 1985 of Title 42;

(2) To recover damages from any person who fails to prevent or to aid in preventing any wrongs mentioned in section 1985 of Title 42 which he had knowledge were about to occur and power to prevent;

(3) To redress the deprivation, under color of any State law, statute, ordinance, regulation, custom or usage, of any right, privilege or immunity secured by the Constitution of the United States or by any Act of Congress providing for equal rights of citizens or of all persons within the jurisdiction of the United States;

(4) To recover damages or to secure equitable or other relief under any Act of Congress providing for the protection of civil rights, including the right to vote.

For purposes of this section—

(1) the District of Columbia shall be considered to be a State; and

(2) any Act of Congress applicable exclusively to the District of Columbia shall be considered to be a statute of the District of Columbia.

(b) 42 U.S.C. section 1983—Civil Action for Deprivation of Rights.
"Every person who, under color of any statute, ordinance, regulation, custom, or usage, of any State, Territory, or the District of Columbia, subjects, or causes to be subjected, any citizen of the United States or other person within the jurisdiction thereof to the deprivation of any rights, privileges, or immunities secured by the Constitution and laws, shall be liable to the party injured in an action at law, suit in equity, or other proper proceeding for redress, except that in any action brought against a judicial officer for an act or omission taken in such officer's judicial capacity, injunctive relief shall not be granted unless a declaratory decree was violated or declaratory relief was unavailable. For the purposes of this section, any Act of Congress applicable exclusively to the District of Columbia shall be considered to be a statute of the District of Columbia."

5.2.3. Standing

In order to establish standing in court, the plaintiff must meet three criteria. First, the plaintiff must demonstrate that the action in question did in fact cause an injury. Second, the plaintiff must establish that the interest to be protected is at least arguably within the zone of interests protected by the Constitution, legislative enactments, or judicial principles. This criterion is often labeled "substantiality of federal question." Finally, the plaintiff must be the party whose interest was infringed upon. That is, the plaintiff must be an interested party or be otherwise directly involved. If the plaintiff has only a peripheral interest, there may be no standing. This often applies in the case of an amateur association and one of its member institutions. An individual student-athlete is not directly involved in the controversy because the individual is not a member of the amateur association. Consequently, the student-athlete who brings suits may be deemed to lack the necessary standing. An example is the NCAA, whose membership consists of colleges and universities, and not of individual student-athletes.

NOTES

1. In *Hairston v. National Collegiate Athletic Association*, 101 F.3d 1315 (9th Cir. 1997), former and current University of Washington football players brought action against the Pac-10 Conference and the NCAA for sanctions that the football program received after findings of recruiting violations. The majority opinion does not touch upon the issue of standing because it does not see it as relevant; however, in a concurring opinion, the concurring judge states, "The practical consequences of allowing the players to bring this lawsuit after their university—which has suffered enormous economic losses—has agreed to the sanctions, demonstrates that the players are not the proper antitrust plaintiffs. If we were to hold that these four players had antitrust standing to alter the sanctions against the UW, we would invite numerous groups of indirectly injured parties to bring antitrust lawsuits and argue that the Pac-10 should have imposed different sanctions or remedies."

2. In *National Collegiate Athletic Ass'n v. Califano*, 444 F.Supp. 425 (D. Kan. 1978), *rev'd*, 622 F.2d 1382 (10th Cir. 1980), the NCAA challenged the Department of Health, Education and Welfare's jurisdiction with regard to Title IX. On appeal, the Tenth Circuit ruled that the NCAA had standing to challenge the application of Title IX legislation to intercollegiate athletic programs. The court based its decision on the fact that individual NCAA member institutions have the necessary standing to test the validity of Title IX regulations. The court stated that the NCAA could bring suit on behalf of its member institutions if it could show that it had their support. (See Chapter 8.)

3. In *Fluitt v. University of Nebraska*, 489 F.Supp. 1194 (D. Neb. 1980), the court found that there was a substantial federal question for two reasons: (1) the Supreme Court had not, in prior decisions, spoken clearly enough on the issues raised by the college student-athlete—in this case to render the claims frivolous or the subject foreclosed—and (2) the student-athlete's claim alleged that two people in the identical situation are treated differently solely on the basis of their sex, and sex discrimination is one of the categories the Tenth Circuit Court has heard as presenting a substantial federal question.

5.2.4. Injunctive Relief

Provided the plaintiff has been successful on the issues of limited judicial review and standing, the next step is to request relief. Because enforcement of the rules and regulations of athletic associations frequently prohibits athletes from competing, student-athletes and their schools often bring lawsuits to obtain relief in the form of an injunction that forces associations to allow the student-athlete to participate. These attempts to keep the student-athlete eligible are critical to the high school athlete hoping to obtain a college scholarship, to the collegiate athletic program striving for a profitable and prestigious winning team and possibly to the student-athlete's eventual professional career. Injunctive relief is critical to a student-athlete because it allows the athlete to compete for his or her institution pending the trial by the court. In many cases, by the time a trial on the merits of a case and an appeal take place, the situation becomes moot because the player has completed his season(s) of play.

An injunction is a court order for one of the parties to a lawsuit to behave in a certain manner. Injunctive relief is designed to prevent future wrongs—not to punish acts. Injunctive relief is also applied to prevent current wrongs from being perpetuated. It is used only to prevent irreparable injury, which is suffered when monetary damages cannot be calculated or when money will not adequately compensate the injured party. An injury is considered irreparable when it involves the risk of physical harm or death, the loss of some special opportunity, or the deprivation of unique, irreplaceable property. For example, a high school football star who may have violated a school rule, may request an injunction to compete in the All-Star game because an inability to do so would cause irreparable harm, such as jeopardizing his chances of obtaining a college scholarship.

The injunction is a form of equitable relief that can be used to force an athletic association to engage in or refrain from an action that affects an institution, an individual student-athlete, or a staff member. There are three types of injunctive relief: a *temporary restraining order*, a *preliminary injunction*, and a *permanent injunction*.

A *temporary restraining order* is issued to the defendant without notice and is usually effective for a maximum of ten days. The defendant is not bound by the injunction until actual notice is received. After receiving notice, the defendant can immediately ask the court for a review. A *preliminary injunction* is granted prior to a full hearing and disposition of a case. The plaintiff is obligated to give the defendant notice and also to post a bond. The defendant is usually present at the preliminary injunction hearing. A hearing on the issuance of a preliminary injunction is granted only in an apparent emergency and only if the plaintiff shows a likelihood of winning the case on the merits. Temporary restraining orders or preliminary injunctions may also be granted during the course of a trial to preserve the status quo until the rights of the litigants can be determined. A *permanent injunction* may be issued after a full hearing, and if it is issued, it remains in force until the completion of the lawsuit.

The issuance of any injunctive relief requires the exercise of sound judicial discretion. A judge generally considers three factors before granting or denying any form of judicial relief: the nature of the controversy, the objective of the injunction, and the comparative hardship or inconvenience to both parties. The judge then weighs these factors on a sliding scale before making a determination; e.g., the more likely a plaintiff is to succeed on the merits at trial, the less harm the plaintiff needs to show to obtain relief. However, if the prospects of success on the merits of the case are not as strong, a plaintiff would have to show a far greater degree of potential harm before relief would be granted.

An example of the use of the preliminary injunction by a student-athlete is the case of *Pagnotta v. Pennsylvania Interscholastic Athletic Association*, 681 A.2d 235 (Pa. Commw. Ct. 1996). Pagnotta, a high school wrestler in the Methacton School District, was disqualified from continuing to participate in the state wrestling tournament as a result of being suspended for striking an opponent with his open hand after the opponent allegedly bit his finger during the match. Pagnotta was awarded a preliminary injunction from the trial court, and was allowed to participate in the remainder of the state tournament. By the time the PIAA was able to have its appeal heard, the tournament had been completed, and the case before the court was dismissed as moot, thus dismissing the claims that association's rulings should not be subject to judicial review.

NOTES

1. In the case of *Cruz v. Pennsylvania Interscholastic Athletic Association*, 157 F.Supp.2d 485 (E.D. Pa 2001), the court granted a permanent injunction to allow the plaintiff, Luiz Cruz, to participate in interscholastic athletics after the age of eighteen due to learning disabilities. The association rule did not allow Cruz to participate. The court, taking a very active stance in this case, ordered not only that Cruz receive the permanent injunction, but ruled that the association should adopt a waiver procedure to deal with Cruz and other students in similar situations.

2. In the case of *Johnson v. Florida High School Activities Association*, 102 F.3d 1172 (11th Cir. 1997), a lawsuit was brought by an interscholastic athlete, Dennis Johnson, who was ruled ineligible to play for his high school football team because he had reached the age of nineteen in August of his senior year in school. Johnson alleged that the association was discriminating against him because he had learning disabilities, which required him to take extra time in school, and consequently was the reason that he remained in high school at his age. Johnson was issued a temporary injunction by the trial court, and was allowed to play during the football season. The association appealed the decision, but the appellate court dismissed the case as moot because Johnson had finished his senior season of football, and therefore whether or not he was ineligible to play was no longer an arguable point.

3. In *Hall v. NCAA*, 985 F.Supp. 782 (N.D. Ill. 1997), the court did not grant a preliminary injunction to plaintiff, Hall, who was seeking to be eligible for participation in intercollegiate athletics. The NCAA had ruled that four classes that Hall took during high school should be not considered as core courses counting toward his initial eligibility. The court did not believe that the plaintiff had "more than a negligible chance at success" upon the merits, and therefore did not satisfy one of the requirements to receive a preliminary injunction. The court also found that the balance of harms in the case would negatively affect the NCAA more than Hall.

4. In *Kite v. Marshall*, 454 F.Supp. 1347 (S.D. Tex. 1978), Greg Kite was a high school basketball player who was declared ineligible for his senior year for participating in a summer basketball camp, attendance at which was against state interscholastic association rules. Kite sued and was granted a preliminary injunction to prevent the high school athletic association from enforcing its training camp rule against him. The court maintained that Kite had a strong likelihood of success in winning the case, that he would suffer irreparable harm if he lost his senior year of competition, that it served the public interest to have Kite eligible, and that when the hardships were balanced, he would suffer more material harm if the injunction were denied than the association would suffer in having Kite compete until the matter went to trial.

Two years after Kite graduated, the trial concluded with the Houston District Court ruling for Kite. The court found that the parents' decision to send their child to summer basketball camp was important enough to warrant constitutional protection under the family's right of personal privacy, and that the interscholastic rule forbidding such summer camp participation was a violation of this privacy, and therefore unconstitutional. On appeal, *Kite v. Marshall*, 661 F.2d 1027 (5th Cir. 1981), the interscholastic association was successful in reversing the lower court's decision. The court of appeals found that the interscholastic league's summer camp rule did not violate either the due process or equal protection clause of the Fourteenth Amendment because the rule was rationally related to the legitimate business purpose of ensuring that interscholastic sports were fair and competitive.

5.3. ASSOCIATION ENFORCEMENT AUTHORITY

5.3.1. Introduction

The authority of athletic associations to regulate their membership originates from two sources. First, as corporate bodies, athletic associations must be recognized as entities of the state. Associations, once created, must create rules to govern their members. After those rules are created, the association takes on the role of enforcing those rules, similar to the functions of the state government. Second, in order for the association to govern effectively, a condition of membership is to agree to be so regulated. When, for example, a school chooses to enter an association it voluntarily agrees to abide by the rules that the association sets forth. At the collegiate level, the stakes of revenue-producing sports such as football and basketball have made it necessary to more stringently police a university's athletic programs for rules violations. At the interscholastic level, often there is pressure to produce high-quality athletes and win, and this pressure can lead to violations of academic eligibility as well as recruiting violations.

5.3.2. NCAA Enforcement Procedure

The NCAA is a voluntary association whose members agree to honor certain conditions and obligations of membership, including the obligation to conduct their individual institutional athletic programs in a manner consistent with NCAA legislation. The enforcement procedure rules, as well as the NCAA rules, are published annually in the *NCAA Manual*, which is available to every member of the association. It is important to note that schools are the members of the NCAA, and not the individual athletes and coaches. Athletic directors, faculty athletic representatives, and college/university presidents represent the institutions in the NCAA.

The first NCAA enforcement program was enacted by the association in 1948, and was designed to correct recruiting abuses. In addition, the NCAA created a Constitutional Compliance Committee, which was designed to interpret the new code and investigate violations. The Constitutional Compliance Committee was replaced in 1951 by the Committee on Infractions, which was given broader investigative powers. In 1973, the NCAA membership voted to divide the responsibilities between the Enforcement Staff (investigations) and the Committee on Infractions (hearings).

As a result of an integrity crisis in the early 1980s, the NCAA called a special summer convention (only the fifth in its history) and enacted stronger enforcement and penalty procedures for member schools that violate NCAA regulations. The "death penalty" was created whereby an institution that is guilty of violating a major NCAA rule infraction twice in five years can be suspended from play for up to two years.

Southern Methodist University (SMU) is the only institution that has received the NCAA's death penalty through 2002. SMU received the suspension due to a multitude of serious recruiting violations, culminating in a finding that alumni boosters had paid athletes more than $60,000 during the 1986 season. SMU was forced to suspend play in football for the 1987 season, and voluntarily chose to opt out of the 1988 season. The penalty so weakened the program that it has enjoyed only one winning season since the lifting of the suspension. Stiff penalties against programs such as the UNLV men's basketball program (see Chapter 5, "Introduction"), were attempts by the NCAA to send a message of intolerance for lack of control over athletic programs.

Notwithstanding the two-year bowl ban and five-year probation handed to the University of Alabama's football program in 2002, the NCAA has been more lenient in its penalty enforcement since giving the death penalty to SMU. The NCAA has not applied the death penalty, although some institutions' actions have arguably rivaled those of SMU. As will be seen in the following sections, the NCAA now asks athletic programs to conduct institutional reviews of their own athletic programs, and penalties have gradually become less harsh for academic, recruiting, and institutional control violations.

The general mission of the NCAA enforcement program is stated as follows:

> To eliminate violations of NCAA rules and impose appropriate penalties should violations occur. The program is committed to fairness of procedures and the timely and equitable resolution of infractions cases. The achievement of these objectives is essential to the conduct of a viable and effective enforcement program. Further, an important consideration in imposing penalties is to provide fairness to uninvolved student-athletes, coaches, administrators, competitors, and other institutions. (*2001–2002 NCAA Manual*, Bylaw 19.01.1)

Along with the implementation of enforcement procedures, the NCAA instituted a procedure for appeals of its rulings. The NCAA Appeals Committee was formed so universities would have an opportunity to appeal the findings of the NCAA's Committee on Infractions.

The enforcement procedure of the NCAA was developed to involve the accused institution in the investigative process, so as to ensure that all necessary information is uncovered and that a degree of collegiality is maintained (see note 2). The enforcement policies were developed with due process considerations in mind, which has resulted in a process that allows the NCAA and the charged institution to work together, and also allows the accused institution ample opportunity to present its case and defend itself in an appropriate manner. The NCAA enforcement procedure consists of the following seven steps (see Exhibits 5.4 and 5.5, illustrating the procedure for violations and resulting appeals):

1. *Reporting*: Information concerning a possible violation is sent to the NCAA by the college's athletic department, and is evaluated by the NCAA enforcement staff. While many investigations are consummated by institutions, the NCAA enforcement staff maintains the right to initiate an investigation as well (see *2001–02 NCAA Division I Manual*, Bylaw 32.2.1.1). When considering punishments, the NCAA will take into account whether or not an institution was the body that began investigations (see *2001–02 NCAA Division I Manual*, Bylaw 32.2.1.2).

2. *Preliminary Inquiries*: Once the NCAA enforcement staff evaluates all of the information from the institution it must decide what party will conduct further investigation, the university or the NCAA. If the enforcement staff believes that a violation may have occurred, the matter will be assigned to an enforcement representative (see *2001–02*

NCAA Division I Manual, Bylaw 32.2.2.1.3). After defining whether the violations are major or secondary in nature (see *2001–02 NCAA Division I Manual*, Bylaw 32.2.2.2) the enforcement staff, or its representative, shall make a thorough preliminary inquiry concerning all of the charges and decide whether there is adequate evidence to warrant an official inquiry. If the violation is secondary in nature, the staff will recommend an appropriate penalty. If the preliminary inquiry indicates a major infraction, an institution may choose to deal with the issue using a summary procedure before the Committee on Infractions instead of undertaking an official inquiry (see *2001–02 NCAA Division I Manual*, Bylaw 32.6).

3. *Official Inquiry*: An official inquiry is authorized by the NCAA's Committee on Infractions on the basis of the results of the enforcement staff's preliminary inquiry. To begin the official inquiry the enforcement staff will send a letter to the chief executive officer of the institution informing him/her of the matter under inquiry and requesting cooperation (see *2001–02 NCAA Division I Manual*, Bylaw 32.5.1). The NCAA staff asks for disclosure of all relevant information, identifies all of the allegations involved, and the persons that the staff will rely upon in presenting its case (see *2001–02 NCAA Division I Manual*, Bylaw 32.5.1.1–32.5.1.3).

   The NCAA has a gag rule in effect on its involvement in an investigation. It remains in effect throughout the entire procedure (see *2001–02 NCAA Division I Manual*, Bylaw 32.1.1). The NCAA will not comment on the existence of an investigation unless it is in response to information released by the institution (see *2001–02 NCAA Division I Manual*, Bylaw 32.1.2).

   The enforcement procedures also provide that the NCAA's primary investigator will be available to meet with the institution to discuss the development of its response and to assist in the case (see *2001–02 NCAA Division I Manual*, Bylaw 32.1.2). The two parties attempt to reach agreement on certain facts of the case in order to streamline the hearing process.

4. *Committee on Infractions Hearing*: Attendance at committee hearings is limited to officials of the NCAA, the officials of the institution, legal counsel, any affected student-athletes, and other affected individuals (see *2001–02 NCAA Division I Manual*, Bylaw 32.7.4.2). The exact procedure to be followed during the hearing is determined by the Infractions Committee and consists of the following steps:

   (a) *Case Summary*: A summary of the case is presented to all in attendance as an aid in following the discussion (see *2001–02 NCAA Division I Manual*, Bylaw 32.7.5.1).

   (b) *Opening and Closing Statements*: The procedure then continues with opening statements from the institution, often by an attorney, who is then followed by a spokesperson for the enforcement staff. These opening statements express the overall position of the university and of the enforcement staff (see *2001–02 NCAA Division I Manual*, Bylaw 32.7.5.2).

   (c) *Presentation of Evidence*: The heart of the hearing is a detailed review of the allegations. The enforcement staff presents all evidence that it has, regardless of whether it supports or refutes the allegations. The institution's spokesperson then responds and may wish to refer to or add to the school's written response. This is an informal procedure, with frequent verbal exchanges between committee members and the university. Rigid rules of evidence are not enforced at these hearings, which may proceed for several days until all allegations have been covered (see *2001–02 NCAA Division I Manual*, Bylaw 32.7.5.3–32.7.5.4).

5. *Basis of Finding*: Findings are made after the members of the Committee have deliberated over the case on an individual basis and have reviewed each allegation. Sometimes additional information is needed (see *2001–02 NCAA Division I Manual*, Bylaw 32.7.6.1). The NCAA has charged the committee to base its findings on information it determines to be "credible, persuasive and of a kind which reasonably prudent persons

Exhibit 5.4
Processing of a Typical NCAA Infractions Case

Information indicating possible violation received and evaluated by NCAA enforcement staff.

Information is not substantiated. No further review is warranted. (END)

Information determined to be reasonably substantial. Institution is notified that preliminary investigation will be conducted by enforcement staff.

Staff determines that case should be closed for lack of evidence. Decision is reviewed and approved by Committee on Infractions. Institution is notified that case is closed. (END)

Violation is confirmed, and it is believed by staff to be major in nature. The institution and enforcement staff discuss the summary-disposition process.

Violation is confirmed, and it is determined to be secondary in nature. An appropriate penalty is determined by the enforcement staff and approved by a designated Committee on Infractions member. Institution is notified of the penalty, if any, and may appeal to Committee on Infractions. (END)

Institution, in consultation with enforcement staff and other involved parties, determines its position on possible violations.

An official inquiry with statements of allegations is forwarded to institution and involved parties.

Institution and involved parties conduct investigation (if necessary) and prepare written responses to official inquiry or elect summary-disposition process.

A summary-disposition report is written and accepted by all involved parties and forwarded to Committee on Infractions for its review in private.

Committee does not accept findings.

Committee accepts findings but not proposed penalties.

Committee accepts findings and proposed penalties. Infractions report is released. (END)

Expedited hearing is held concerning penalties only, or full hearing concerning findings and penalties is held.

180

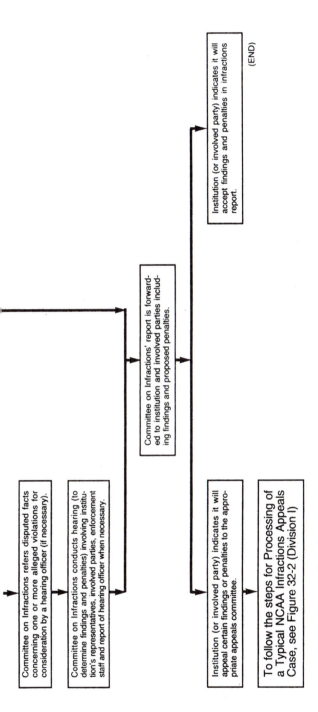

Committee on Infractions refers disputed facts concerning one or more alleged violations for consideration by a hearing officer (if necessary).

Committee on Infractions conducts hearing (to determine findings and penalties) involving institution's representatives, involved parties, enforcement staff and report of hearing officer when necessary.

Committee on Infractions' report is forwarded to institution and involved parties including findings and proposed penalties.

Institution (or involved party) indicates it will accept findings and penalties in infractions report.

(END)

Institution (or involved party) indicates it will appeal certain findings or penalties to the appropriate appeals committee.

To follow the steps for Processing of a Typical NCAA Infractions Appeals Case, see Figure 32-2 (Division I).

Source: 2001–2002 NCAA Manual.

Exhibit 5.5
Processing of a Typical NCAA Infractions Appeals Case

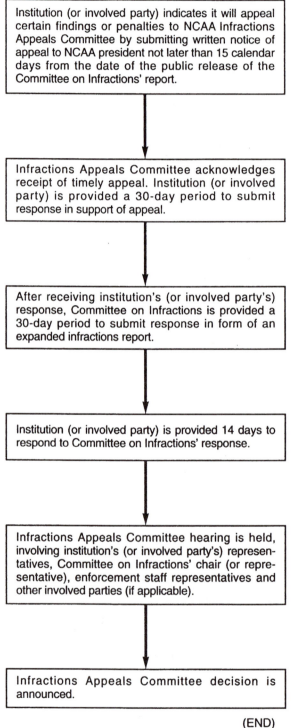

Institution (or involved party) indicates it will appeal certain findings or penalties to NCAA Infractions Appeals Committee by submitting written notice of appeal to NCAA president not later than 15 calendar days from the date of the public release of the Committee on Infractions' report.

Infractions Appeals Committee acknowledges receipt of timely appeal. Institution (or involved party) is provided a 30-day period to submit response in support of appeal.

After receiving institution's (or involved party's) response, Committee on Infractions is provided a 30-day period to submit response in form of an expanded infractions report.

Institution (or involved party) is provided 14 days to respond to Committee on Infractions' response.

Infractions Appeals Committee hearing is held, involving institution's (or involved party's) representatives, Committee on Infractions' chair (or representative), enforcement staff representatives and other involved parties (if applicable).

Infractions Appeals Committee decision is announced.

(END)

Source: 2001–2002 NCAA Manual.

rely in the conduct of serious affairs" (see *2001–02 NCAA Division I Manual*, Bylaw 32.7.6.2). Once the members of the committee reach a consensus, all findings are compiled into a confidential report. The report is then sent to the institution's chief executive officer.

6. *Infractions Report/Penalties*: If warranted, penalties are included in the Committee's final report. These may include prohibiting an institution's team or teams from television appearances, taking away athletic scholarships, and barring teams from postseason play. Such actions are often referred to as being "put on probation."

   In some cases when violations are deemed to be less severe, the penalty imposed by the NCAA may take the form of a private reproach. Once the Infractions Report has been received by the institution, the report is made available to the press, along with an official announcement by the Committee (see *2001–02 NCAA Division I Manual*, Bylaw 32.9.2).

7. *Appeal (Optional)*: If an institution wishes to have its appeal considered, it must provide written notice within 15 days of the public release of the Committee of Infractions' report. The Appeal is then heard by a five-member Infractions Appeals Committee (see *2001–02 NCAA Division I Manual*, Bylaw 32.10.1). The appealing institution may elect to represent itself in person or in writing only. Infractions Appeals Committee Members may question either members of the member institution or the Committee on Infractions. The Infraction Appeals Committee may then act upon the matter by majority vote, and its decision shall be final and binding (see *2001–02 NCAA Division I Manual*, Bylaw 32.11.5).

An important facet of the NCAA is that conferences and institutions have control over their own affairs. Therefore, each conference has a procedure to enforce the regulations of the conference and the NCAA. For example, the Pac-10 Conference has its own enforcement policy established to enforce the regulations in the Pac-10 Conference. The general policy reads as follows:

It shall be the policy of the Pacific-10 Conference to maintain an active compliance and enforcement program. Its goal shall be the conduct of high quality of intercollegiate athletic programs in observance of Conference and NCAA rules.

The Conference believes that by conducting its own compliance program it can best serve its members through timely investigation and resolution of potential enforcement matters. Such a conference program recognizes the unique personality of each Conference member and its athletic program.

The Commissioner, assisted by the compliance and enforcement staff members, shall serve as the principal enforcement officer regarding adherence to Conference and NCAA rules and regulations. In the conduct of its compliance program, the Pacific-10 shall work closely with the NCAA and shall at all times seek through this cooperative relationship to maintain the highest possible level of compliance by its members and to assure the NCAA that it is the goal of the Conference and each member to sustain compliance.

The guiding principle of this relationship shall be the enhancement of the intercollegiate athletic programs of the members of the Pacific-10 Conference. (*2001–2002 Pac-10 Conference Handbook*)

The Pac-10 has established a Compliance and Enforcement Committee to determine whether alleged violations have occurred, and to recommend penalties and corrective actions. Individual institutions have the option, upon discovering potential violations of the NCAA regulations, to conduct a self-investigation or to ask the conference to investigate. An institution that conducts a self-investigation must do so in accordance with the conference's standards for thoroughness and due process. The commissioner of the conference is technically in charge of the investigation until such time as the commissioner can determine whether the issue should go before the Compliance and Enforcement Committee. Once a matter goes before the committee, a hearing is set up at which the information is presented by the conference and by the affected institution or individual. The committee, after hearing the testimony, will recommend appropriate disciplinary and/or corrective actions, generally from the list of penalties used by the NCAA.

NOTES

1. For more information on the NCAA, its enforcement procedures, and cases involving rules violations, visit the NCAA's Web site at www.ncaa.org/enforcefrontF.html. Also see Tom Farrey, "NCAA's Once-Rabid Watchdog Loses Its Bite," www.espn.go.com/ref/s/2001/1126/1284940.html

2. In 1999, the NCAA found widespread examples of academic fraud, unethical conduct, and lack of institutional control within the University of Minnesota men's basketball program. Information concerning this academic fraud was not discovered by the athletic department, but was uncovered by a newspaper reporter in Minneapolis. Once the allegations were brought to light, the university took it upon itself to conduct a review of its program. After the review, the university imposed the following sentence upon itself as a demonstration of institutional cooperation with the NCAA:

1. The university sought and obtained the resignation of the head coach and did not renew the contracts of his assistants.

2. The university imposed a post-season ban following the 1999–2000 season for the men's basketball team.

3. For the 2000 academic year, the total number of athletic scholarships were reduced from thirteen to ten. Further, over the course of the next three academic years (2001–2004) the university proposed to reduce the total number of athletics scholarships by a total of four, with a reduction of at least one in each academic year so that at the end of the four-year period there would be a total reduction of seven scholarships.

4. For each of the next three academic years (2000–2001 to 2002–2003), the university proposed to reduce the number of official visits from twelve to eight.

5. For each of the next three academic years (2000–2001 to 2002–2003), the university proposed to reduce the number of evaluation days from fifty to forty.

6. For each of the next three academic years (2000–2001 to 2002–2003), the university proposed to reduce the number of in-person recruiting contacts for each prospect from five to four.

7. For each of the next three summers (2000–2002), the university proposed to reduce the number of coaches permitted to evaluate off-campus during the summer evaluation period from three to two.

8. For each of the next three summers (2000–2002), the university proposed to reduce the number of July evaluation days from twenty-three to eighteen.

9. Pursuant to Bylaw 31.2.2.5, the university decided to return to the NCAA an amount equal to 90 percent of the monies it has received or is scheduled to receive from the Big Ten Conference for participation in the 1994, 1995, and 1997 NCAA Division I men's basketball championships. In each of these tournaments the university competed with ineligible student-athletes as identified by institutional and NCAA investigation.

Despite the institutional cooperation of the University of Minnesota, the basketball program was found to be in violation of numerous NCAA regulations, and received the following penalties from the NCAA:

1. Public reprimand and censure.

2. Four years of probation from October 24, 2000 (the date of the report release).

3. The number of grants-in-aid for men's basketball will be reduced by a total of five for the 2001–2002, 2002–2003, and 2003–2004 academic years with a reduction of at least one (from thirteen to twelve) scholarship in each of the three academic years. (Note: The university proposed a reduction of four scholarships over the three academic years, with a reduction of at least one scholarship each year.)

4. Official paid visits in men's basketball shall be reduced by six for the 2001–2002 and 2002–2003 academic years, limiting the university to six official visits under current rules. (Note: The university proposed to limit itself to eight visits for each of the next three academic years (2000–2001 to 2002–2003). However, the committee noted that over the past four academic years, the university had averaged only eight official paid visits in men's basketball.)

5. For each of the next three academic years (2000–2001 to 2002–2003) the number of evaluation days will be reduced by 25 percent from the maximum number allowed (rounded to the nearest whole number). (Note: The university had proposed that for each of the next three academic years (2000–2001 to 2002–2003) the number of evaluation days be reduced from fifty to forty, with the number adjusted to reflect future changes in NCAA legislation governing evaluation days.)

6. Regarding the 1994, 1995, and 1997 NCAA Division I men's basketball tournaments, and the 1996 and 1998 National Invitational Tournaments (NIT), and pursuant to NCAA Bylaw 19.6.2.2-(e)-(2), the university will vacate its team record as well as the individual records of any student-athlete who engaged in academic fraud as set forth in this report. Further, the university's records regarding men's basketball as well as the record of the former head coach will be reconfigured to reflect the vacated records and so recorded in all publications in which men's basketball records for the 1993–1994 through the 1998–1999 seasons are reported, including, but not limited to, university media guides and recruiting material and university and NCAA archives. Further, any public reference to tournament performances won during this time shall be removed, including, but not limited to, athletics department stationery and banners displayed in public areas such as the arena in which the men's basketball team competes.

7. The former head coach and the former academic adviser will be informed in writing by the NCAA that, due to their involvement in certain violations of NCAA legislation found in this case, if they seek employment or affiliation in an athletically related position at an NCAA member institution during a seven-year period (October 24, 2000, to October 23, 2007), they and any involved institution shall be requested to appear before the Committee on Infractions to consider whether the member institution(s) should be subject to the show-cause procedures of Bylaw 19.6.2.2-(1), which could limit athletically related duties of the head coach and academic adviser at any such institution for a designated period.

8. The former secretary will be informed in writing by the NCAA that, due to her involvement in certain violations of NCAA legislation found in this case, if she seeks employment or affiliation in an athletically related position at an NCAA member institution during a five-year period (October 24, 2000, to October 23, 2005), she and any involved institution shall be requested to appear before the Committee on Infractions to consider whether the member institution should be subject to the show-cause procedures of Bylaw 19.6.2.2-(1), which could limit her athletically related duties at any such institution for a designated period.

9. The university shall show cause why it should not be penalized further if it fails to disassociate from its athletics program the owner of a local automobile dealership, who is also a representative of the university's athletics interests, based upon his refusal to cooperate with the investigation as set forth in finding II-P. The length of the disassociation shall be for at least the university's probationary period and shall include the following:

   a. Refraining from accepting any assistance from him, including aid in the recruitment of prospective student-athletes, the support of enrolled student-athletes, or providing benefits for athletics department personnel

     b. Refusing his financial assistance or contributions (in cash or in kind) to the university's athletics program

     c. Ensuring that no athletics benefits or privilege, including preferential tickets, are provided to him, either directly or indirectly, that are unavailable to the public at large

     d. Implementing other actions that the university determines to be within its authority to eliminate his involvement in the university's athletics program.

10. During this period of probation, the university shall do the following:

     a. Continue to develop and implement a comprehensive educational program on NCAA legislation, including seminars and testing, to instruct the coaches, the faculty athletics representative, all athletics department personnel, and all university staff members with responsibility for the certification of student-athletes for admission, retention, financial aid, or competition

     b. Submit a preliminary report to the director for the NCAA Infractions Committee by December 15, 2000, setting forth a schedule for establishing this compliance and educational program

     c. File with the committee's director annual compliance reports indicating the progress made with this program by September 1 of each year during the probationary period. Particular emphasis should be placed on monitoring programs and educational measures designed to enhance academic integrity within the institution's athletics programs. The reports must also include documentation of the university's compliance with the penalties (adopted and) imposed by the committee as well as copies of current men's basketball media guides and other published material.

11. At the conclusion of the probationary period, the university's president shall provide a letter to the committee affirming that the university's current athletics policies and practices conform to all requirements of NCAA regulations.

12. As required by NCAA legislation for any institution involved in a major infractions case, the University of Minnesota, Twin Cities, shall be subject to the provisions of NCAA Bylaw 19.6.2.3, concerning repeat violators, for a five-year period beginning on the effective date of the penalties in this case.

3. For further information, see the following law review article: Rodney K. Smith, "A Brief History of the National Collegiate Athletic Association's Role in Regulating Intercollegiate Athletics," 11 *Marquette Sports Law Review* 9 (Fall 2000).

4. For a case that examines the NCAA enforcement procedures, see *Trustees of the State Colleges and Universities v. National Collegiate Athletic Ass'n*, 147 Cal. Rptr. 187 (Cal. Ct. App. 1978). Although a university's NCAA appeal involved only the penalty imposed and not the findings for an alleged failure to comply with a decision regarding the eligibility of two student-athletes, this did not bar relief on the grounds of failure to exhaust administrative remedies.

5.3.2.1. The Knight Commission

In 1989, trustees of the John and James L. Knight Foundation (a philanthropic organization established by newspaper moguls in the 1950s) created a commission in order to reform college sports. The Knight Foundation was concerned that abuses in college athletics were threatening the integrity of higher education. The Commission on Intercollegiate Athletics began as an independent panel of twenty-two leaders from the fields of education, business, and sports. While this commission had no formal authority over intercollegiate athletics, the NCAA would adopt approximately two-thirds of its recommendations by 1996 (see note 1). The most significant recommendation adopted by the NCAA in the 1990s was to alter the governance structure of college athletic departments so that college presidents, not athletic departments, were placed in charge of all policy and budgeting decisions.

The Knight Commission reconvened in 2000 and 2001 in order to assess the impact of the NCAA's adopted changes in the 1990s. The 2000–2001 meeting included "NCAA representatives, university presidents, a trustee board chair, faculty, conference commissioners, athletics directors, coaches, athletes, authors, professional sports executives, television officials, a sports apparel representative, a gambling lobbyist, leaders of national higher education associations, and a U.S. senator," and in June 2001 produced a report entitled *A Call to Action: Reconnecting Sports to Higher Education*. The language of the 2001 report is largely conciliatory, citing NCAA and university sincerity in adopting the commission's recommendations of the 1990s. However, the report makes it clear that the institutional *effort* in the 1990s failed to reduce corruption.

[In the 1980s] 57 out of 106 Division I-A institutions (54 percent) had to be censured, sanctioned or put on probation for major violations of NCAA rules. . . . In the 1990's, 58 out of 114 Division I-A colleges and universities (52 percent) were similarly penalized. In other words, more than half the institutions competing at the top levels continue to break the rules. Wrongdoing as a way of life seems to represent the status quo.

In addition to "wrongdoing," the report also noted a "financial arms race," poor graduation rates, problems of increased commercialism, and the decaying of amateur ideals: "There is no question about who is winning this open, ever-escalating war between the academic and athletic cultures. In too many places, the tail already wags the dog." The report therefore crafted the following 15 recommendations for the NCAA and its member institutions:

1. Athletes should be filtered through "the same academic processes as other students," including admission standards and degree requirements.
2. By 2007, teams that do not graduate at least 50 percent of their players should be banned from post-season play (180 of the 321 colleges with Division I basketball teams failed to meet that standard in 2000—see note 2).
3. Scholarships should be tied to specific athletes until they (or their entering class) graduate.
4. The length of playing season, practice season, and post-season must be reduced.
5. The NBA and the NFL should be encouraged to develop minor leagues. (This would present an alternative for athletes who are not interested in or are unqualified for higher education.)
6. Football and basketball expenditures should be reduced, including the total number of scholarships that are awarded in Division I-A football.
7. Compliance with Title IX and support of women's athletics should be ensured.
8. Coaches salaries should be reduced and "brought into line with prevailing norms across the institution."
9. Agreements for coaches' outside income should be negotiated with institutions, not individual coaches, because "[a]dvertisers are buying the institution's reputation no less than the coaches'."
10. The NCAA plan for distribution of revenue from the CBS contract should be revised so that it is based on academic performance and gender equity compliance rather than on winning and losing.
11. Institutions alone should determine when games are played, how they are broadcast, and which companies are permitted to advertise.

12. Institutions should be discouraged from signing commercial contracts that violate "traditional academic values."

13. In-arena and in-stadium advertising should be minimized.

14. The NCAA should ban corporate logos on uniforms. (This presumably would include bowl game sponsors.)

15. Federal legislation to ban legal gambling on college sports in Nevada should be supported, and college presidents should address illegal gambling on their campuses.

If the Knight Commission's 2001 recommendations are adopted, the business of Division I-A football and basketball would be significantly altered. Many top high school athletes would no longer be recruited, and top coaches might consider leaving the college ranks for professional leagues. However, some of the Knight recommendations would be subject to legal scrutiny. For example, it would be difficult for the NCAA to mandate a reduction of head coaches' salaries, considering that the NCAA was penalized $55 million by the courts for limiting assistant coaches' salaries in *Law v. National Collegiate Athletic Association* (see Chapter 10). An additional logistical concern was expressed by James Delany, commissioner of the Big Ten Conference (see note 2). The commission recommended support for women's sports, yet called for limits on commercialism. However, the revenues from corporate sponsorship deals often help fund women's sports and lower-profile men's sports.

While two-thirds of the Knight Commission's recommendations were adopted in the 1990s, the NCAA must reconcile a greater number of interests before implementing its recommendations in 2001.

NOTES

1. The report of the Knight Foundation Commission on Intercollegiate Athletics, *A Call to Action: Reconnecting College Sports and Higher Education*, can be found at the Knight Foundation's Web site: www.knightfdn.org

2. Welch Suggs covered institutional reaction for *The Chronicle for Higher Education* in the days following the release of the Knight Commission 2001 report. His articles include "Knight Panel Urges Presidents to Join Forces and Take Control of College Sports" (June 27) and "College Presidents Urged to Take Control of College Sports" (July 6).

5.3.3. Interscholastic Enforcement Procedures

The National Federation of State High School Associations does not have regulatory power in the same way that the National Collegiate Athletic Association or the International Olympic Committee does. It does set standards for competition and writes high school contest rules for the majority of sports in its jurisdiction, but it does not have enforcement procedures like those of the NCAA and IOC. Instead, the regulatory responsibilities fall to the state associations described earlier in the chapter. Each state association has a dispute resolution procedure which handles all conflicts that may arise between student-athletes, coaches, officials, and institutions. Each institution also has its own internal mechanisms, but if the disputes are not resolved at the local level, they are referred to the state associations.

The California Interscholastic Federation (CIF) is the state association for the state of California. Concerning the issue of dispute resolution, the CIF's constitution states that "the CIF is limited to facilitating the establishment of these regulations and minimum standards and to the application of appropriate sanctions when failure to meet these standards, rules, and regulations comes to the attention of the CIF." The CIF has two separate procedures: one for eligibility appeals and one for all other matters.

The student eligibility appeals and review procedure at the CIF state level reads as follows:

1100. CIF Section Student Eligibility Appeals Procedures

Each CIF section shall establish appellate procedures which incorporate the following requirements in final Section determination of student eligibility questions.

Upon written appeal, the Section shall cause the appointment of either:

A. A hearing panel, or

B. A single hearing officer.

Said panel or hearing officer shall be empowered to hear the matter under consideration and rule on the eligibility status of the appellant under Section and State CIF eligibility requirements. Neither members of the hearing panel, nor a single hearing officer can have been directly associated with the matter under consideration or directly associated with the schools involved in the matter or have any other interest, personal or professional, that would preclude a fair and impartial hearing. If it is apparent from the facts that the panel or the hearing officer have no authority to adjudicate the matter under the rules, the section may find the appeal to be without merit and deny a hearing. All business and deliberations of the appeal process must be conducted in public, except for those deliberations by a single hearing officer or when matters declared by law to be confidential are being reviewed. The section hearing need not be conducted according to the rules of evidence and those related to witnesses. Any relevant evidence including hearsay evidence shall be admitted. All testimony shall be given under oath or affirmation administered by hearing officer (a member of the panel or a single hearing officer). (Revised February 2000, Federated Council.)

1101. State CIF Student Eligibility Appeals and Review Procedure

Appeals of final decisions determined through the CIF section appeals procedure concerning student eligibility may be presented to the State CIF Executive Director's office after the CIF section decision has been made in accordance with the following, if the appellant believes that the Section violated one or more of the following procedural guidelines:

A. Was the section's decision or action lawful; i.e., did the decision or action violate Title V, the Education Code, etc. and did it extend appropriate due process to the parties?

B. Was the section's decision or action fraudulent?

C. Did the section act arbitrarily?

(1) Did the section have rules and criteria by which it reached its decision?

(2) Were the section's rules and criteria reasonable, i.e., do the section's rules reasonably relate to a legitimate objective?

(3) Did the section follow its own rules and criteria?

(4) Does the section's action or decision have a basis in reason, or in other words, a reasonable basis? The test to be employed in the application of this criterion is whether responsible people, acting in a thoughtful manner, could reasonably have

reached the same decision as the section and not whether others might personally believe the decision. The Executive Director, upon receiving such an appeal, may review the section's decision based on the above guidelines to determine whether their action was a violation of any of the above. If, in his or her judgment, this is the case, the Executive Director may return this matter to the section for further review or, if necessary, set aside the decision and take jurisdiction consistent with Bylaw 1108 A.

The California Interscholastic Federation also has a set of procedures that address matters other than student eligibility or section playoffs. Like the eligibility appeals process, there are separate section and state appeals processes. If a decision at the section level is appealed to the state level, the appeals procedure is similar to the eligibility appeals procedure at the state level in that the same questions are asked: Was the decision lawful? Did the section act arbitrarily? And so on. If a dispute concerning matters other than eligibility is not resolved at this level, the dispute will go to arbitration. The CIF constitution reads, "Each member school, by becoming or remaining a member of the CIF, and each CIF section agrees that in the event of a dispute with a fellow member school, or with a CIF section or CIF, such a dispute shall be submitted to binding arbitration."

NOTES ———————————————————————————————

1. In *Somerville School Committee v. Massachusetts Interscholastic Athletic Ass'n*, No. 00-01042B, 2000 Mass. Super LEXIS 109 (Mass. Mar. 15, 2000), the Somerville High School girl's basketball team was the victim of an incorrect call made by a referee during a tournament game. If the correct call had been made, the Somerville squad would have won the game. The committee was seeking an injunction to stop the finals of the tournament from occurring until this error could be resolved. The court issued a decision in favor of the MIAA, stating, "The court is not unmindful of the harm to plaintiff's team. Were it to be balanced only with the potential harm to the MIAA, the balance may be in the plaintiff's favor. However, the plaintiff's harm should also be balanced with the harm to innocent third parties, i.e. the Methuen and Brockton (the two teams scheduled to play in the championship game) team members. In light of the impact of the order sought on those third parties and questions concerning the appropriateness of the court's intervening in a matter such as this, the court declines to enter the order requested."

2. In *Ruiz v. Massachusetts Interscholastic Athletic Ass'n*, No. CV00-68, 2000 Mass. Super LEXIS 213 (Mass. Feb. 7, 2000), the plaintiff, Rafael Ruiz, was seeking an injunction that would allow him to compete on the varsity basketball team for the remainder of the season. Ruiz had transferred to his current school, Canton High School, from Thayer Academy (a private school where he had a scholarship), because he had lost his scholarship due to non-maintenance of a satisfactory grade point average. The court decided in favor of Ruiz, citing his particular circumstances as extraordinary, and not applicable under the MIAA transfer law. The court found that Ruiz met all requirements of obtaining an injunction. The court stated, "Ruiz is likely to prevail in establishing that the MIAA rule concerning ineligibility is not applicable as a matter of law to his involuntary transfer from a private school back into the public school system of his hometown."

3. In *Robbins v. Indiana High School Athletic Ass'n*, 941 F.Supp. 786 (S.D. Ind. 1996), the plaintiff, Robbins, was seeking to gain an injunction against the enforcement of the IHSAA transfer rule, which would prevent her from participating in interscholastic volleyball on the varsity level at her new school. The court ruled that Robbins failed to meet any of the criteria established to attain an injunction, and subsequently denied her

request. The rule was found to have legitimate purpose and was not arbitrary and capricious.

4. Interscholastic federations, since the 1990s, have seen an increase in the cases involving eligibility enforcement and the Americans with Disabilities Act. For more information see the following cases that have been heard in court:

    a. *Cruz v. Pennsylvania Interscholastic Athletic Ass'n*, 157 F.Supp. 2d 485 (E.D. Pa 2001)

    b. *Washington v. Indiana High School Athletic Ass'n*, 181 F.3d 840 (7th Cir. 1999)

    c. *Dixon v. Ohio High School Athletic Ass'n*, No. C-1-99-827, 1999 U.S. Dist. LEXIS 21388 (S.D. Ohio Nov. 4, 1999)

    d. *McPherson v. Michigan High School Athletic Ass'n*, 119 F.3d 453 (6th Cir. 1997)

    e. *Johnson v. Florida High School Activities Ass'n*, 102 F.3d 1172 (11th Cir. 1997)

    f. *Frye v. Michigan High School Athletic Ass'n*, Case No. 95-1266 (6th Cir. 1997)

    g. *Rhodes v. Ohio High School Athletic Ass'n*, 939 F.Supp. 584 (N.D. Ohio 1996)

5. The NCAA has recently been faced with many cases concerning enforcement of eligibility requirements in light of the Americans with Disabilities Act. For more information, see the following cases that have been heard in court:

    (a) *Bowers v. NCAA*, 130 F.Supp. 2d 610 (D. N.J. 2001)

    (b) *Matthews v. NCAA*, 79 F.Supp. 2d 1199 (E.D. Wash. 1999)

    (c) *Ganden v. NCAA*, No. 96 C 6953 1996 U.S. Dist. LEXIS 17368 (N.D. Ill. Nov. 21, 1996)

5.3.4. Olympic Enforcement Procedures

Chapter 1 discussed in some detail the relationship between the International Olympic Committee, the International Federations, the National Olympic Committees, and the National Governing Bodies. Each level of organization has a set of rules and regulations that cannot be violated by those it serves.

The highest authority is, of course, the IOC, which is a non-governmental institution that is the apex of international sport regulation. The IOC is guided by the Olympic Charter, the supreme document that gives the IOC sole authority over decision-making. In recent years, the IOC has given more authority to the International Federations to regulate their respective sports, but there is no doubt that the IOC remains the highest governing authority.

The IOC's Ethics Commission is charged with the responsibility for, among other things, investigating complaints raised in relation to the disregard for ethical procedures. In the context of the Olympic movement, the Ethics Commission can request sanctions against IOC members and honorary members, International Federations, National Olympic Committees, and host cities. For example, possible sanctions against National Olympic Committees include (1) withdrawal of the right to enter competitors into the Olympic Games; (2) suspension; (3) provisional or permanent withdrawal; (4) withdrawal of the right to organize a session or an Olympic Congress.

In the context of the Olympic Games, individual competitors and teams, officials, managers, referees, and any other accredited persons are all subject to discipline under the Ethics Commission. It is important to note that the charged party has important due process rights. To acknowledge these rights, the IOC must comply with the following:

The Ethics Commission will bear in mind the Olympic Charter as they build on the Olympic Movement to promote positive ethics and ensure transparency and accountability. The commission will also establish standards and rules that are understandable and applicable in the forthcoming IOC Code of Ethics, as well as verify that the response to ethical issues is active, comprehensive, and effective. (www.olympic.org)

It is important to review the role of the International Federations:

The International Sports Federations (ISF) are responsible for the integrity of their sport on the international level. These organizations establish the playing and eligibility rules, set the schedule of events and select the referees, judges and other officials to "run" their respective sports at the Olympic Games as well as other international competitions. (www.olympic.org)

Thus, the IFs have the power to establish and enforce rules and regulations that do not contradict those rules espoused by the Olympic Charter. Therefore, if there is a dispute in the area of figure skating concerning eligibility standards, the grievant would go through the procedure set forth by the International Federation responsible for figure skating, the International Skating Union.

Earlier in this chapter we looked at the U.S. Olympic Committee as an example of a National Olympic Committee. An NOC is responsible for representing the interest of its respective country with respect to the Olympic Games, and is also obligated to follow the rules and regulations as defined by the IOC.

National Olympic Committees have extensive arbitration procedures that are implemented when disputes arise. For example, the USOC has an "Arbitration of Challenge" section in its constitution that deals with all disputes between an athlete and a National Governing Body. It states:

(a) RIGHT TO REVIEW.—A party aggrieved by a determination of the corporation under section 220527 or 220528 of this title may obtain review by any regional office of the American Arbitration Association.

(b) PROCEDURE.—

(1) A demand for arbitration must be submitted within 30 days after the determination of the corporation.

(2) On receipt of a demand for arbitration, the Association shall serve notice on the parties to the arbitration and on the corporation, and shall immediately proceed with arbitration according to the commercial rules of the Association in effect at the time the demand is filed, except that—

(A) the arbitration panel shall consist of at least 3 arbitrators, unless the parties to the proceeding agree to a lesser number;

(B) the arbitration hearing shall take place at a site selected by the Association, unless the parties to the proceeding agree to the use of another site; and

(C) the arbitration hearing shall be open to the public.

(3) A decision by the arbitrators shall be by majority vote unless the concurrence of all arbitrators is expressly required by the contesting parties.

(4) Each party may be represented by counsel or by any other authorized representative at the arbitration proceeding.

(5) The parties may offer any evidence they desire and shall produce any additional evidence the arbitrators believe is necessary to an understanding and determination of the dispute. The arbitrators shall be the sole judges of the relevancy and materiality of the evidence offered. Conformity to legal rules of evidence is not necessary.

(c) SETTLEMENT.—The arbitrators may settle a dispute arising under this chapter before making a final award, if agreed to by the parties and achieved in a manner not inconsistent with the constitution and bylaws of the corporation.

(d) BINDING NATURE OF DECISION.—Final decision of the arbitrators is binding on the parties if the award is not inconsistent with the constitution and bylaws of the corporation.

(e) REOPENING HEARINGS.—

> (1) At any time before a final decision is made, the hearings may be reopened by the arbitrators on their own motion or on the motion of a party.
>
> (2) If the reopening is based on the motion of a party, and if the reopening would result in the arbitrators' decision being delayed beyond the specific period agreed to at the beginning of the arbitration proceedings, all parties to the decision must agree to reopen the hearings. (*USOC Constitution*, Article VIII, Section IV)

After the filing of a complaint, the USOC first needs to determine whether the complainant has exhausted its available remedies with the National Governing Body. If it is shown that the complainant did not exhaust all such remedies, the USOC will direct the parties to follow the applicable NGB procedures before the issue comes back to the USOC. If the USOC finds that the NGB in question is not in compliance with Article 4, Sec. [c] and Article 7, Sec. 1 and 2, the USOC shall have two options of punishment:

A. Place the National Governing Body on probation for a specified period of time, not to exceed 180 days, which the corporation considers necessary to enable the national governing body to comply with those sections.

B. Revoke the recognition of the National Governing Body.

Another conflict that Article 7 of the USOC Constitution addresses is when an organization seeks to replace an existing National Governing Body for a particular sport. When this arises, the applicant sports organization must establish by a preponderance of the evidence that it meets the criteria for recognition as a National Governing Body, and that the current NGB does not meet the criteria for recognition. After hearings, the USOC shall make one of four decisions:

1. Uphold the right of the National Governing Body to continue as the National Governing Body for its sport

2. Revoke the recognition of the National Governing Body and declare a vacancy in the National Governing Body for the sport

3. Revoke the recognition of the National Governing Body and recognize the applicant as the National Governing Body

4. Place the National Governing Body on probation for a period not exceeding 180 days, pending the compliance of the National Governing Body, if the National Governing Body would have retained recognition except for a minor deficiency in one of the requirements of section 220522, 220524, or 220525 of this title, and notify such National Governing Body of such probation and of the actions needed to comply with such requirements. (USOC Constitution, Article VII, Section 3(d))

If either of the parties are not satisfied with the decision of the USOC they may file an appeal within 30 days and the matter will go to binding arbitration with the American Arbitration Association. The arbitration panel will make a final and binding decision on the matter.

NOTE ————————————————————————————————

1. For more information, see the following law review articles:

    a. Melissa R. Bitting, "Mandatory, Binding Arbitration for Olympic Athletes: Is the Process Better or Worse for Job Security?" 25 *Florida State University Law Review* 655 (Spring 1998).

    b. Christine Ansley, "International Athletic Dispute Resolution: Tarnishing the Olympic Dream," 12 *Arizona Journal of International and Comparative Law* 277 (Spring 1995).

    c. Edward E. Hollis, III, "The United States Olympic Committee and the Suspension of Athletes: Reforming Grievance Procedures Under the Amateur Sports Act of 1978," 71 *Indiana Law Journal* 183 (Winter 1995).

5.3.5. Court of Arbitration for Sport

To deal with the increase in the number of international legal disputes in the sports industry, former IOC President Juan Antonio Samaranch began the process of creating an international court that would deal exclusively with international sports-related disputes. The Court of Arbitration for Sport (CAS), which began operation in 1984, was composed of sixty members appointed by the IOC, the International Federations, the National Olympic Committees, and the IOC president.

Between 1984 and 1991 the CAS was involved in cases pertaining to the nationality status of athletes, television rights, sponsorship, employment contracts, and licensing. To take advantage of the CAS, several International Federations inserted a clause into their statutes and regulations that read: "Any dispute arising from the present Statutes and Regulations of the ——— Federation which cannot be settled amicably shall be settled finally by a tribunal composed in accordance with the Statutes and Regulations of the Court of Arbitration for Sport to the exclusion of any recourse to the ordinary courts. The parties undertake to comply with the said Statutes and Regulations, and to accept in good faith the award rendered and in no way hinder its execution."

In 1992, a member of the International Equestrian Federation (FEI) appealed to the CAS to overturn an FEI judgment. The CAS decision partly overturned the FEI decision, but still levied a judgment against the rider. The rider appealed the decision to the Swiss Federal Tribunal, claiming that the arbitration panel did not meet the conditions of impartiality needed to be considered a proper arbitration court. The tribunal found in favor of the CAS. However, the tribunal did criticize the relationship between the IOC and the CAS, and noted that should the IOC ever come before the CAS, the court may not be able to perform independently or impartially. The result of the decision was three-fold:

1. The International Council of Arbitration for Sport (ICAS) was created to look after the running and financing of the CAS, thereby taking the place of the IOC.

2. Two arbitration divisions were created. The first deals with issues concerning decisions made by federations, commonly involving concerns over things such as television rights and sponsorships. The second division handles disputes characterized as last instance disputes, where the bylaws of certain athletic federations state that the ICAS will be

the court of final jurisdiction if a satisfactory decision can't be reached within their own proceedings.

3. The reforms were outlined in a Code of Sports-Related Arbitration, which details the procedures that must be followed during all arbitration proceedings conducted by the Council.

Due to its break with the IOC, the CAS is now structured in a more impartial fashion, as it does not have to report back to the IOC. Instead, it is truly the final arbitrator in international sporting disputes (see notes).

At the 1996 Olympic Games in Atlanta, the ICAS created an ad hoc division of the CAS in order to send a group of arbitrators to the Games to ensure that any disputes which arose would be settled within a twenty-four-hour period. The division dealt with six cases during the Games, the disputes ranging from disciplinary actions to a late entry. Due to the success of the ad hoc division, the precedent was duplicated in 1998 at the winter Olympic Games at Nagano, Japan, where the division handled four cases. At the 2000 summer Olympics in Sydney, Australia CAS decided a record number of cases. A total of fifteen cases were brought before the Court, with a range of issues including nationality, to doping cases and disputes over close finishes. (See notes for a discussion of cases from the 2000 Sydney Olympics.)

NOTES

1. In the arbitration case of *United States Olympic Committee (USOC) and USA Canoe/Kayak v. International Olympic Committee*, the USOC brought its case to the arbitration panel of the CAS at Sydney because the IOC was not going to allow Mr. Angel Perez to participate on the U.S. kayaking team in the Olympic Games. Mr. Perez had competed for Cuba in the 1992 Olympic Games in Barcelona, then had fled from his native country, and received full citizenship in the United States in 1999. Although he had competed for the United States in the world championships in 1997–1999, the IOC rules state that three years must pass before a newly nationalized citizen can compete in the Olympic Games for his/her new country. The USOC disagreed with the IOC, stating that Perez had achieved permanent residence status as a "resident alien" in 1995, and therefore should have been eligible for competition as a U.S. citizen. The CAS sided with the IOC, stating, "On the basis of a straightforward reading of Bylaw 2 of Rule 46 of the Olympic Charter, . . . Mr. Perez acquired his new nationality less than three years ago, and . . . the Cuban Olympic Committee did not agree to a reduction of this period."

2. In *Andrea Raducan v. International Olympic Committee (IOC)*, the CAS handled one of its most controversial cases to date. Andrea Raducan was a gold-medal-winning gymnast in both the team and the all-around competition for the Romanian national team. While competing for the all-around title, after winning the team gold medal, Raducan complained to the team doctor that she was not feeling well. The doctor gave her a Nurofen Cold and Flu tablet, which she took in his presence on two different occasions. After winning the all-around title she was sent to supply a urine sample in accordance with Olympic Doping Control. The tablets she received were found to be in violation of the doping rules, and the CAS ruled in favor of the IOC decision, stripping the medals that she received, testing positive for the banned substance. The court stated, "The Panel is aware of the impact its decision will have on a fine, young, elite athlete. It finds, in balancing the interests of Miss Raducan with the commitment of the Olympic Movement to drug-free sport, the Anti-Doping Code must be enforced without compromise."

3. In *Bernardo Segura v. International Amateur Athletic Federation*, Segura was a race-walker for the Mexican national team. He was disqualified, under sport rules, because

he had committed three infractions during the course of the race. There was a question as to whether Segura had seen the warnings and cautions that the judges of the event had issued to him. It is definite that he had seen the first warning, unclear whether he had seen the second warning, and most likely that he had not seen the third warning. Segura crossed the finish line believing he was the gold medalist, and was not informed of his disqualification until fifteen minutes after the end of the race. Segura did not question the infractions, but said that because he had not been made aware of the disqualification immediately, the IAAF should not be able to strip him of his gold medal. The CAS decided in favor of the IAAF, stating, "The IAAF Rules do not provide that disqualifications are invalid if they are not communicated 'immediately.' The Panel believes that it would be intolerable to disregard the unchallenged finding that on three occasions three separate judges found the Applicant to have infringed the rules."

4. For more information on the ICAS, visit its Web site at www.tas-cas.org. This site provides information concerning the history and purpose of the court, as well as addresses and published court opinions.

5.4. ASSOCIATIONS AND CONSTITUTIONAL ISSUES

Athletic administrators at the high school and college level oftentimes question the frequency of claims directed against them alleging that certain penalties stemming from violations of an association's rules are violations of a student-athlete's constitutional rights. Recent judicial decisions clearly illustrate that institutions or associations that impose severe penalties that impair or jeopardize an individual's career, could be found to have violated the athlete's constitutional law rights. The fact that an association can be held liable for its actions does not preclude it from imposing penalties for violations of its rules. When courts analyze cases involving private association rules or imposition of penalties, they will hesitate to intervene in the association's decision, unless the court finds that a rule has been applied unfairly or is unreasonable. In making such determinations, courts consider whether such rules are related to legitimate principles or business purposes of the association.

A student-athlete involved in a dispute with an athletic organization may decide to initiate a lawsuit based on the theory that a constitutional right has been violated. In light of the problems of limited judicial review and standing, the constitutionally based claims of due process and equal protection may be the only avenues available. In addition, the constitutional law approach has other advantages. Most important is that it allows the student-athlete to bring the case to a federal court, thereby utilizing the federal constitutional law claims of due process or equal protection. To succeed on a federal constitutional claim, three factors must be present: (1) state action exists; (2) the claim is not frivolous; and (3) the claim concerns a right of sufficient importance to be litigated in federal court. If these three points can be established, the student-athlete can then proceed on an equal protection and/or due process challenge. The student-athlete may also pursue state constitutional arguments.

5.4.1. State Action Requirement

The constitutional safeguards of the Fifth and Fourteenth Amendments of the U.S. Constitution apply only when state action is present. Any action taken directly or indirectly by a state, local, or federal government is *state action* for constitutional purposes. In addition, action by any public school, state college, or state university or any of its officials can be construed as state action. The issue of state action arises only when alleged wrongdoers argue that they are not acting directly on behalf of the government. In order to subject voluntary, private associations to constitutional limitations, some degree of state action must be present. Of course, actions by private organizations that are deemed to be performing a public function or are authorized under the laws of the state (quasi-public institutions) are also construed as state action.

If the actions taken by high school and college athletic associations are considered state action, it may be argued that private institutions acting in compliance with these organizations are also engaging in state action. However, action by strictly private individuals does not constitute state action. Three common methods of analysis used to determine whether or not state action exists in particular circumstances are the public function theory, the entanglement theory, and the balancing approach theory.

The *public function theory* is somewhat limited and is traditionally confined to essential governmental services that have no counterparts in the public sector. A good example is American Telephone and Telegraph Company, which is a private company performing an essentially public function. The NCAA has, in at least one case, been deemed a public functionary on the basis of its comprehensive regulation of an area that would otherwise have to be regulated by the states. The alternatives—having each state regulate college athletic programs without the existence of the NCAA—would be extremely inefficient and not viable. High school athletic association activities have also been found to be state action under the public function theory. In one case, the functions served by the high school athletic association were deemed to be so similar to the functions of the state in providing education that the association's rules were judged to be state action (see note 1c).

In the second method of analysis, commonly known as the *entanglement theory*, the usual focal point is the amount of state and/or federal aid directly or indirectly given to the private organization. Under this view, state action issues involve a conflict between rights, and the court must balance these rights in determining whether the Constitution mandates a preference for one right over another. The receipt of such aid may subject a recipient's action to constitutional review. For this theory to be used by the court, total state and/or federal control over the organization need not exist. Instead, the state or federal government must only have substantial influence over the association's activities. State and association actions must be intertwined to the extent that the organization's actions are supported or sanctioned by the government. State action is found on the basis of the relationship of the association to the government.

During the 1970s, case law had held the NCAA's actions to be the equivalent of state action under this theory. In these cases, the rationale typically had been that over half of the NCAA's members were state-supported schools. In addition, most NCAA member schools received federal aid, and their students received federal financial aid (work-study, National Defense loans). Therefore, albeit indirectly, the NCAA was supported by state and federal governments. The NCAA also provided a service that was beyond the competence or authority of any one state.

In the 1980s, court decisions began to change as the NCAA was seen as not a state actor. Courts began to take a narrower interpretation of what was a state actor, beginning with *Arlosoroff v. National Collegiate Athletic Ass'n.* (note 2c).

In 1988, the U.S. Supreme Court decision in *NCAA v. Tarkanian*, 109 S. Ct. 454 (1988), found that the NCAA was not a state actor. The NCAA's policies were determined by several hundred public and private member institutions independent of any particular state, and the NCAA enjoyed no governmental powers to facilitate its investigation of UNLV and Tarkanian; therefore, no state action existed.

High school associations similarly have had their actions scrutinized under the entanglement theory. Many high schools and high school associations receive financial assistance from the state, have public officials who make decisions concerning policies and procedures, and/or a portion of the membership consisting of public schools. These circumstances are sufficient to constitute state action. For example, in *Brentwood Academy v. Tennessee High Secondary School Athletic Ass'n*, 531 U.S. 288 (2001), the Supreme Court decided that the actions of the THSAA can be construed as state action under the entanglement theory. In this decision the court discussed exactly how the THSSA constituted a state actor:

> The Association's nominally private character is overborne by the pervasive entwinement of public institutions and public officials in its composition and workings, and there is no substantial reason to claim unfairness in applying constitutional standards to it. To the extent of 84% of its membership, the Association is an organization of public schools represented by their officials acting in their official capacity to provide an integral element of secondary public schooling, interscholastic athletics. There would be no recognizable Association without the public school officials, who overwhelmingly determine and perform all but the Association's purely ministerial acts. Only the 16% minority of private school memberships keeps the entwinement of the Association and public schools from being total and their identities totally indistinguishable. To complement the entwinement from the bottom up, the State has provided entwinement from the top down: State Board members sit ex officio on the Association's governing bodies and Association employees participate in the state retirement system. Entwinement to the degree shown here requires that the Association be charged with a public character and judged by constitutional standards.

The *balancing approach theory* is more general and not widely accepted. Here, if the merits of allowing the organizational practice are outweighed by the limitations on asserted/protected rights, courts have found state action, which allows judicial intervention for the protection of individual constitutional rights.

In cases involving the NCAA, the court has moved away from all three of these methods, finding that the decisions of the NCAA do not constitute state action. In *Tarkanian v. NCAA*, 488 U.S. 179 (1988), the Supreme Court found that even when the organization may have threatened a university with further sanctions if it did not suspend its basketball coach, neither the percentage of public members nor the organization's function was sufficient to find state action. In *Hawkins v. National Collegiate Athletic Ass'n*, 652 F.Supp. 602 (C.D. Ill. 1987), the court ruled that the NCAA was a voluntary association of public and private institutions, and although the NCAA may perform a public function in overseeing the nation's intercollegiate athletics, there was not state action.

As far as state action for high school level student-athletes, when an alleged state or federal statute violation involves a public high school, state action is obvious. The rights and liberties of the public high school students are therefore protected by the federal Constitution. However, when a private school is involved, the courts have looked for sufficient ties between the alleged wrongful activity and the state to justify intervention. If no state influence related to the wrongful activity is found, no state action will be present and the federal Constitution will not protect the rights and liberties of the students.

NOTES ─────────────────────────────────────

1. In the following cases, the NCAA's decisions were found to have constituted state action. Note that none of these court decisions have been decided since the decision in *Tarkanian* v. *NCAA*:

(a) In *Howard University v. NCAA*, 510 F.2d 213 (D.C. Cir. 1975), the court noted that state-supported educational institutions and their members and officers play a substantial role in the NCAA's program, and that such state participation is a basis for finding state action (entanglement theory).

(b) In *Parish v. NCAA*, 361 F.Supp. 1220 (W.D. La. 1973), *aff'd.*, 506 F.2d 1028 (5th Cir. 1975), the court found state action, since over half of the NCAA's members are state-supported schools and the NCAA performs a public function by regulating intercollegiate athletics (entanglement theory).

(c) *Buckton v. NCAA*, 366 F.Supp. 1152 (D. Mass. 1973), was the first case to declare the NCAA to be engaged in state action under the public function theory. The public function theory has since been supplanted by other theories.

(d) In *Regents of the University of Minnesota v. NCAA*, 422 F.Supp. 1158 (D. Minn. 1976), the court acknowledged that the action taken by the NCAA has generally been accepted as the equivalent of state action.

(e) In *Associated Students, Inc. v. NCAA*, 493 F.2d 1251 (9th Cir. 1974), the court determined that the actions of the NCAA did constitute state action since the NCAA regulates schools and universities, at least half of which are public.

2. In the following cases, the NCAA's decisions were found not to have constituted state action. All cases since *Tarkanian* have used the logic employed in that case in their decisions:

(a) In *Hall v. NCAA*, 985 F.Supp. 782 (N.D. Ill. 1997), the court found that the NCAA was not a state actor in a case dealing with Bradley University, a private university. The court concluded, "If the NCAA's relationship with UNLV, a public university, was insufficient to translate the NCAA's actions into state action, then the NCAA is clearly not a state actor by virtue of its relationship with Bradley, a private university. Since the NCAA is not a state actor, it is not subject to constitutional restraints and cannot be sued under §1983 for alleged equal protection violations."

(b) In *McDonald v. NCAA*, 370 F.Supp. 625 (C.D. Calif. 1974), the court concluded that the NCAA is not sufficiently state supported to be considered state action, and it has an existence separate and apart from the educational system of any state. In the court's words, "If an institution is unable to concur with a voluntary organization without contravening the constitutional rights of its students, it must withdraw from the organization."

(c) In *Arlosoroff v. NCAA*, 746 F.2d 1019 (4th Cir. 1984), the court stated that the "fact that NCAA's regulatory function may be of some public service lends no support to the finding of state action, for the function is not one traditionally reserved to the state."

3. In the following cases, state action was found in the actions of interscholastic athletic associations:

(a) In the case of *Indiana High School Athletic Association v. Carlsberg*, 694 N.E.2d 222 (Ind. Ct. App. 1997), the court found that the IHSAA was a state actor. However, it is also found that the right to participate in interscholastic athletics was not a protected right, and that the plaintiffs had to prove that they were being discriminated against because they were members of a suspect class.

(b) In *Indiana High School Athletic Association v. Reyes*, 694 N.E.2d 249 (Ind. 1997), the court made the same decision as in *Carlsberg*, reasoning that the ISHAA constituted a state actor for questions of constitutional law.

(c) In *Barnhorst v. Missouri State High School Athletic Ass'n.*, 504 F.Supp. 449 (W.D. Mo. 1980), the court found that the close identification of the functions served by the state high school athletic association with the state's provision of education (including extracurricular activities) to all children of school age is a sufficient link to transmute into state action the challenged association rule forbidding any student-athlete transferring from one member school to another member school to participate in interscholastic athletic competition for 365 days.

(d) In *Yellow Springs Exempted School District v. Ohio High School Athletic Ass'n.*, 443 F.Supp. 753 (S.D. Ohio 1978), *rev'd on other grounds*, 647 F.2d 651 (6th Cir. 1981), the court found that the OHSAA's conduct constituted state action because (1) the association depended on the state for operating revenue, (2) school officials were involved in the decision-making process, (3) public schools were predominant within the association membership, and (4) the association had the ability to impose sanctions upon state schools.

4. For a case in which the court ruled that an Olympic organization was not acting under color of state action, see *DeFrantz v. United States Olympic Committee*, 492 F.Supp. 1181 (D.D.C. 1980), *aff'd. without decision*, 701 F.2d 221 (D.C. Cir. 1980). Twenty-five athletes sought an injunction to bar the USOC from boycotting the 1980 Moscow Olympics. Emphasizing that the USOC receives no federal funding and that it operates and exists independently of the federal government, the court found that the state was not in a position of interdependence with the USOC. The court also stated that the plaintiffs failed to prove that some form of control, or governmental persuasion or pressure, was behind the challenged action. (See Chapter 1, "Introduction.")

5. For further information, see the following law review article: David W. Dulabon, "First (Amendment) & Goal: High School Recruiting and the State Actor Theory," 2 *Vanderbilt Journal of Entertainment Law & Practice* 219 (Spring 2000).

5.4.2. Due Process

Constitutional guarantees afforded citizens in general apply equally to educational institutions, administrators, coaches, and student-athletes. The courts are reviewing with less hesitancy cases claiming a violation of protected rights. In light of this legal development, a primary concern of athletic administrators when imposing penalties that jeopardize an individual's career should be minimum standards of "due process of law."

Due process is an elusive concept. One definition for the term *due process* is "a course of legal proceedings which have been established in our system of jurisprudence for the protection and enforcement of private rights" (*Pennoyer v. Neff*, 95 U.S. 714 [1877]). The concept may vary, depending on three basic considerations: (1) the seriousness of the infraction, (2) the possible consequences to the institution or individual in question, and (3) the degree of sanction or penalty imposed.

The constitutional guarantee of due process is found in both the Fifth and Fourteenth Amendments to the U.S. Constitution. The Fifth Amendment, enacted in 1791, is applicable to the federal government. It states that "no person . . . shall be deprived of life, liberty, or property without due process of law." In 1868, the Fourteenth Amendment was ratified, reading, "nor shall any state deprive any person of life, liberty, or property without due process of law. . . ." This amendment extended the applicability of the due process doctrine to the states. Both amendments apply only to federal or state governmental action, and not to the conduct of purely private entities. While the Constitution extends these liberties to all persons, it is also limiting in that a person must demonstrate deprivation of life, liberty, or property to claim a violation of due process guarantees.

Since athletic associations and conferences rarely deprive a person of life, the major interests that trigger application of the due process clause in the athletic context are deprivations of liberty and property. Unless an athlete or other party can establish that he or she has been deprived of liberty or property, he or she will not be able to establish a deprivation of due process.

The due process doctrine presses two inquiries. The first is *procedural due process*, which refers to the procedures required to ensure fairness. The second is *substantive due process*, which guarantees basic rights that cannot be denied by governmental action. Procedural due process has as its focal point the questioning of the decision-making process that is followed in determining whether the rule or regulation has been violated and the penalty, if any, that is imposed. Was the decision made in an arbitrary, capricious, or collusive manner? Was the accused given the opportunity to know what to defend against and to know reasonably well in advance what is thought to have been violated? Substantive due process involves the rule, regulation, or legislation being violated—namely, is it fair and reasonable? In other words, when measuring substantive due process, does the rule or legislation have a purpose and is it clearly related to the accomplishment of that purpose?

Claims to due process protection may be based not only on protections guaranteed by state constitutions and by federal and state statutes, but also on the regulations and constitutions of athletic institutions, conferences, and other athletic governing organizations.

5.4.2.1. Procedural Due Process

The two minimum requirements of procedural due process are the right to a hearing and notice of the hearing's time, date, and content. The requirements are flexible, and the degree of formality depends on the nature of the right involved as well as on the circumstances surrounding the situation. If the deprivation concerned is not that of a fundamental right or is a right marginally affected by the challenged rule, only the minimal due process requirements may be necessary (see exhibit 5.6).

On the other hand, when a fundamental right is involved or when an infringement on personal freedom is present, the hearing must be more formal, with additional safeguards. The full protections of due process include notice and the right to a hearing in front of a neutral decision maker, with an opportunity to make an oral presentation, to present favorable evidence, and to confront and cross-examine adverse witnesses. In addition, there may also be a right to have an attorney present during the proceedings, a right to receive a copy of the transcript of the hearing, and a right to a written decision based on the record (see exhibit 5.7).

Although an individual may enjoy the guarantee of due process, the actual process is rarely spelled out. The type of due process protections guaranteed in a given situation are determined by a consideration of the importance of the right involved, the degree of the infringement, and the potential harm of the violation. As a general rule, the more an individual has at stake, the more extensive and

Exhibit 5.6
Minimal Due Process Checklist

General Considerations

☐ Determine whether applicable state law imposes any special requirements or procedures regarding the suspension of students or the imposition of other minor disciplinary measures.

☐ Consistent with state law adopt, and when a matter arises requiring rudimentary due process follow, board policies or procedures regarding the suspension of students or the imposition of other minor disciplinary measures.

☐ If the student is disabled, comply with any special procedures applicable to the discipline of disabled students.

☐ Determine whether the matter requires rudimentary due process or formal due process.

☐ Determine the person or persons who have authority to suspend a student or impose other disciplinary measures.

Due Process Procedures

☐ Determine whether the alleged misconduct is a proper basis for the proposed disciplinary action.

☐ The person disciplining a student should promptly give the student oral or written notice of the specific misconduct of which he is accused and the proposed disciplinary measure.

☐ If the student denies the misconduct of which he is accused, provide the student an explanation of the evidence which the educational institution has against him.

☐ Allow the student an opportunity to present his side of the story.

☐ If the student's presence endangers persons or property or threatens disruption of the academic process, immediately remove the student from school even without rudimentary due process, but provide notice and a hearing as soon as practicable thereafter.

☐ Subject to any special procedures required by state law or board rule, impose the proposed disciplinary measure unless the student adequately refutes the misconduct of which he is accused.

☐ Notify the student's parents or guardian, if appropriate, of the disciplinary measure imposed.

formal are the due process requirements. Since a number of factors are involved, administrative agencies must examine the merits of each case to determine the required procedures on a case-by-case basis.

The Supreme Court has further applied a three-pronged inquiry to determine what is due process: the private interest that will be affected by the official action; the risk of an erroneous deprivation of such interest through the procedures used and the probable value, if any, of additional or substitute procedural safeguards; and the government's interest, including the function involved and the fiscal and administrative burdens that the additional or substitute procedural requirement would entail (*Mathews v. Eldridge*, 424 U.S. 319 [1976]). Some have suggested that athletic organizations fashion a set of notice and hearing procedures that will withstand constitutional scrutiny. The benefits to establishing a set of procedures include the following:

Exhibit 5.7
Full Due Process Checklist

General Considerations

☐ Determine whether applicable state law imposes any special requirements or procedures regarding student expulsion, long-term suspension or the imposition of other major disciplinary measures.

☐ Consistent with state law adopt, and when a matter arises requiring formal due process, follow board policies or procedures regarding expulsion, long-term suspension, or the imposition of other major disciplinary measures.

☐ If the student is disabled, comply with any special procedures applicable to the discipline of disabled students.

☐ Determine whether the matter requires rudimentary due process or formal due process.

☐ Determine the person or persons who have authority to expel a student or impose a long-term suspension or other major disciplinary measure.

Preliminary Due Process Procedures

☐ Determine whether the alleged misconduct is a proper basis for the proposed disciplinary action.

☐ If grounds exist for the proposed disciplinary action, initiate charges consistent with applicable procedures.

☐ Notify the student, and if a minor, his parents or guardian, in writing, of the misconduct of which he is accused, the factual basis for the charges, the specific provisions of any student disciplinary code allegedly violated, the right of the student to a hearing and the procedures to be followed at that hearing, the right of the student to be represented by an attorney or other counsel, whether a hearing must be requested or whether it has been or will be scheduled automatically, and provide the student or, if a minor, his parents or guardian, a copy of any applicable rules governing student conduct or disciplinary proceedings.

☐ If appropriate, precede or follow the written notice with a telephone or personal conference with the student or, if a minor, his parents or guardian.

☐ If circumstances warrant, as where the student's continued presence poses a continuing danger to persons or property or an ongoing threat of disrupting the academic process, suspend the student pending the hearing, but only after affording rudimentary due process if possible or as soon as practicable.

☐ Schedule a hearing if requested or required automatically under applicable disciplinary procedures.

☐ If requested, provide the student or the student's counsel the names of witnesses against him and an oral or written report on the facts to which each witness will testify unless, perhaps, such disclosures may result in reprisals against the witnesses.

☐ If requested and within the power of the educational institution, compel the attendance of any witnesses desired by the student.

☐ Arrange for a transcript or record of the hearing to be kept if required or desired.

☐ Review the interests of the members of the tribunal or hearer of the case to assure the tribunal or hearer is impartial.

☐ Clearly define the role of each person involved in the hearing, including the attorney for the tribunal or hearer and faculty and staff members to assure fairness.

Conduct of Hearing

☐ The presiding officer should begin by declaring the hearing convened and stating the matter to be considered.

☐ If a board or panel is hearing the case, the roll of its members must be taken and the existence of a quorum confirmed.

☐ All persons present at the hearing should be identified, as well as their interest in the matter.

Exhibit 5.7 (continued)

Conduct of Hearing
- ☐ If desired, the meeting may be closed to the public and those without a proper interest in the matter excluded.
- ☐ The presiding officer should summarize the procedures to be followed.
- ☐ The student or his counsel should be asked whether any objections exist with regard to the time, place or procedures of the hearing.
- ☐ The student or his counsel should be allowed the opportunity to raise any questions regarding the impartiality of any member of the tribunal or the hearer.
- ☐ The charges against the student should then be read and the student requested to confirm that he has received a copy of them.
- ☐ If the parties to the matter have stipulated or agreed upon any facts or exhibits in the case, they should be requested to present them.
- ☐ Each party should be provided an opportunity to make any opening statements.
- ☐ Subject to the applicable rules of evidence, the person bringing the charges and, thereafter, the student, should be allowed to present any relevant, material and reliable evidence, generally subject to a right of cross-examination by the other.
- ☐ Following the initial presentation of evidence, the parties should be allowed to present rebuttal and surrebuttal evidence.
- ☐ At the close of all the evidence, the parties should be invited to make closing statements or arguments.
- ☐ The hearing should then be closed with an explanation of the timetable and procedures to be used for rendering a decision.

Post-Hearing Procedures
- ☐ Commence deliberations of the case.
- ☐ Allow only the members of the tribunal or hearer and their attorney or advisor to participate in or attend the deliberations.
- ☐ When a decision is reached, reduce it to writing, setting forth findings of fact, the basis of the decision, and the disciplinary measure imposed.
- ☐ Notify the student and, if a minor, his parents or guardian of the decision.
- ☐ Consistent with applicable procedures, advise the student of any available administrative review and provide that review.
- ☐ Recognize that the student may always seek appropriate judicial relief.

1. Establishing procedures may be fairer to student-athletes, thereby building good-will.

2. Courts, which are already inclined to defer to athletic decision makers, will in most cases find the procedures adequate, particularly if the procedures are originally fashioned in light of the *Mathews* case.

3. Provided that the procedures are basically fair and balance the factors outlined in *Mathews*, they are less likely to be challenged by the student-athletes themselves because some due process will already have been afforded the aggrieved party.

4. Establishing procedures would contribute some certainty to an area otherwise fraught with ambiguity.

Having a set of notice and hearing procedures would benefit the organization as well as the athlete, thereby reducing the role of the courts in fashioning and implementing required procedures.

NOTES

1. In *Robbins v. Indiana High School Athletic Ass'n*, 941 F.Supp. 786 (S.D. Ind. 1996), the court decided that the hearing which the plaintiff had received was adequate, and therefore concluded, "Robbins, however, does not argue that the notice and hearing she received from the IHSAA are inadequate, and the court does not find that those procedures are inadequate. This court cannot conclude that plaintiff has been denied procedural due process."

2. For more information on due process rights and the NCAA, see the following law review articles:

   (a) Rodney K. Smith, "Essay: A Brief History of the National Collegiate Athletic Association's Role in Regulating Intercollegiate Athletics," 11 *Marquette Sports Law Review* 9 (Fall 2000).

   (b) W. Burlette Carter, "Student-Athlete Welfare in a Restructured NCAA," 2 *Virginia Journal of Sports Law* 1 (Spring 2000).

   (c) Lee J. Rosen, "Comment; Proposition 16 and the NCAA Initial Eligibility Standards: Putting the Student Back in Student-Athlete," 50 *Catholic University Law Review* 175 (Fall 2000).

3. In the following cases the courts ruled that there was no violation of due process rights:

   (a) In *L.P.M. and D.J.T. v. School Board*, 753 So. 2d 130 (Fla. Dist. Ct. App. 2000), two students were not allowed to participate in extracurricular athletics after it was found that they had violated a school rule by drinking alcohol off campus. The students were given a full administrative hearing where they were represented by counsel. The court held that the students had no protected right to participate in extracurricular athletics, and that they had been given full due process under the school board's system.

   (b) In *In Re University Interscholastic League*, 20 S.W.3d 690 (Tex. 2000), the Texas Supreme Court found that a constitutional right was not violated when a student-athlete is not allowed to participate in extracurricular activities. In this case an entire baseball team was ruled ineligible to compete in a high school playoff tournament because one of its players was declared ineligible. The court did not believe that because the players might suffer immediate and irreparable harm that they could show a constitutional violation.

   (c) In *Mazevski v. Horseheads Central School District*, 950 F.Supp. 69 (W.D. N.Y. 1997), the court held that a high school student did not have protected property interest in participating in extracurricular activities. In this case, a student was dismissed from his school's marching band because of an unexcused absence at an event. The parents of the student, the plaintiffs, brought a claim of procedural due process violations. The court did not rule on the merits of the plaintiff's case because the plaintiff was not able to establish that membership in an extracurricular activity is a protectable property right. The court reasoned that the only right that the plaintiff had was the right to an education, not to extracurricular activities.

   (d) In *James v. Tallahassee High School*, 907 F. Supp. 364 (M.D. Al. 1995), a high school cheerleader alleged that her due process rights had been violated because she had not been selected as a head cheerleader for the football season. The cheerleading coach, prior to tryouts, had given notice to the aspiring cheerleaders that she would be choosing the captains for the squad instead of the members of the squad choosing, which were the rules in the school handbook. The plaintiff alleged that she had been denied her property interest in being a captain of the squad. The court swiftly dismissed her claim of due process violations by stating that a property right in an activity must be based on more than a need or desire, stating, "Ms. James does not have a federally-protected property interest in having the opportunity to be selected as the head or co-head cheerleader of the football cheerleading squad."

   (e) In *McFarlin v. Newport Special School District*, 784 F.Supp. 589 (E.D. Ark. 1992), the Arkansas District Court denied an athlete's request for an immediate hearing, preliminary injunction, and temporary restraining order in order to reinstate her onto her high school's basketball team after the coach had dismissed her. The plaintiffs argued that the athlete's chances of athletic scholarship would be irreparably harmed if she were not allowed to play on the high school team, and that her dismissal violated her due process rights. The court upheld the autonomy of the high school coach, stating, "If individuals are going to participate in sports, a club, or in a corporation, they must be willing to submit themselves to the authority of another individual in the role of a coach, club president, or chairman of the board. It is a virtual certainty that they will be subjected, on occasion, to arbitrary and unjust treatment. . . . However, the mere fact that a coach may be wrong does not convert the matter into a federal case."

(f) In *Palmer v. Merluzzi*, 868 F.2d 90 (3rd Cir. 1989), the plaintiff argued that he should be given additional procedural due process rights following the imposition of additional penalties, after he was caught smoking marijuana and drinking beer. The court of appeals concluded that the single proceeding which resulted in two sanctions being imposed was enough to satisfy the due process rights of the plaintiff.

(g) In *Brands v. Sheldon Community School*, 671 F.Supp. 627 (N.D. Iowa 1987), the plaintiff, a high school athlete, brought an action challenging the school board's decision declaring him ineligible to compete on his high school wrestling team. On the plaintiff's motion for a temporary restraining order or preliminary injunction, the court held that the athlete was not deprived of a liberty or property right when the school declared him ineligible; therefore, procedural due process rights did not apply.

(h) In *Spring Branch I.S.D. v. Stamos*, 695 S.W.2d 556 (Tex. 1985), an action was brought on behalf of several students, seeking a permanent injunction to bar the enforcement of a rule requiring students to maintain a 70 average in all classes to be eligible for participation in extracurricular activities. The lower court held the rule unconstitutional and issued an order enjoining its enforcement. On appeal, the Supreme Court of Texas held that the rule was rationally related to a legitimate state interest in providing high-quality education to public school students, and thus was not violative of constitutional equal protection guarantees. Further, the court held that the students did not possess a constitutionally protected interest in their participation in extracurricular activities and, therefore, the rule was not violative of due process rights.

(i) In *Marcum v. Dahl*, 658 F.2d 731 (10th Cir. 1981), college basketball student-athletes claimed their right to due process had been violated when they were dropped from the team for disciplinary reasons without a hearing. The court held that the college had offered the opportunity for a hearing, but the student-athletes had failed to take advantage of it, thus freeing the college of any further due process responsibilities.

(j) In *Pegram v. Nelson*, 469 F.Supp. 1134 (M.D.N.C. 1979), the court held that a short suspension (less than ten days) from participation in after-school extracurricular activities required only an informal hearing.

(k) In *Hamilton v. Tennessee Secondary Athletic Ass'n.*, 552 F.2d 681 (6th Cir. 1976), the court of appeals ruled that the privilege of participating in interscholastic athletics is outside the protection of due process.

(l) In *Southern Methodist University v. Smith*, 515 S.W.2d 63 (Tex. Civ. App. 1974), the court held that no due process was required if the facts are not disputed, or if the issues have already been resolved (see *Graesen v. Pasquale*, 200 N.W.2d 842 [1978]).

(m) In *Mitchell v. Louisiana High School Athletic Ass'n.*, 430 F.2d 1155 (5th Cir. 1970), the court of appeals ruled that the association's eligibility rules did not violate students' rights under due process and equal protection clauses of the Fourteenth Amendment, since a substantial federal question was not raised.

4. In the following cases the courts ruled that there was a violation of due process rights:

(a) In *Butler v. Oak Creek-Franklin School District*, 172 F.Supp.2d 1102 (E.D. Wis. 2001), a student-athlete was cited for possessing fireworks, intoxicants, and committing disorderly conduct. These were the student's fourth and fifth violations of the athlete conduct code, and the player was suspended for 12 months from competition. Although it was held that the student did not have a protected interest to participate in athletics, the court reasoned that he was not given his full due process rights, because he was not given notice of the hearing regarding his misconduct and that the hearing was not impartial because it involved the school's athletic director. The court refused to dismiss the plaintiff's due process claims and ordered that a status conference be held within eleven days.

(b) In *Christ the King Regional High School v. Catholic High Schools Athletic Ass'n*, 624 N.Y.S.2d 755 (N.Y. Sup. Ct. 1995), the girl's basketball team at the plaintiff high school was suspended from post-season play for one season for violating a league rule concerning traveling to out-of-state games. Upon reviewing the penalty imposed by the association's Principals Committee, the court discovered that the penalty was arbitrary and capricious because it violated the rules of the association, which only allowed for the association's Infractions Committee to enact such penalties.

(c) In *Diaz v. Board of Education, City*, 618 N.Y.S.2d 948 (N.Y. Sup. Ct. 1994), the court found that the due process rights of an entire high school soccer team had been violated when it was not allowed to compete for an entire season due to the actions of one of its players. The director of the Public School Athletic League (PSAL), in a letter dated November 2, 1993, had warned the members of the Newtown High School soccer team that if they received one more red card during the season the entire team would be withdrawn from competition in the league. Nine days later, one player started a fight after spitting in the face of a referee and subsequently received a red card. After a disciplinary hearing was scheduled, the Newtown team was deemed ineligible to participate on the varsity level for the 1994–95 season. The court found that this decision was erroneous on two grounds. First, the court believed that the director of the PSAL was not in a position to promulgate such a penalty, because under the bylaws of the PSAL, all such policy decisions must be adopted by committee. Second, the court found that, even if the director had the authority to hand out the penalty, the ruling was arbitrary and capricious. The court argued that the entire soccer team should not be condemned for the actions of one of its players, and also pointed to evidence that such rules had never been handed out to other teams, leading the court to believe that the imposition of the penalty upon Newtown was discriminatory.

(d) In *Duffley v. New Hampshire Interscholastic Athletic Ass'n.*, 446 A.2d 462 (N.H. 1982), the New Hampshire Supreme Court ruled that plaintiff student-athlete had been denied procedural due process because the New Hampshire Interscholastic Athletic Association failed to state the reasons for denial of eligibility.

(e) In *Regents of University of Minnesota v. NCAA*, 560 F.2d 352 (8th Cir. 1977), the court held that due process required notice and a hearing.

(f) In *Wright v. Arkansas Activities Ass'n.*, 501 F.2d 25 (8th Cir. 1974), the court of appeals ruled that a rule prohibiting football practice prior to a certain date may provide fair notice that a school may be sanctioned. However, imposition of a sanction resulting in the loss of a coaching/teaching position denied the coach due process. The rule gave no notice of the fact that the coach could be subject to a sanction resulting in unemployment.

(g) In *Behagen v. Intercollegiate Conference of Faculty Representatives*, 346 F.Supp. 602 (D. Minn. 1972), two college basketball players who had been suspended for the season sought to prohibit the ICFR (also known as the Big Ten Conference) from enforcing their suspension until they were granted due process. The court found it consistent with the powers of the commissioner to suspend the players temporarily pending a hearing, if such action was not arbitrary or capricious and was done to protect the interest of the conference. However, due process could not be denied since the suspensions bordered on punitive actions, with a notable concern being that the players were prevented from displaying skills that could lead to future economic rewards as professionals.

(h) In *Taylor v. Alabama High School Athletic Ass'n.*, 336 F.Supp. 54 (M.D. Ala. 1972), plaintiff high school was prohibited from hosting or participating in invitational basketball tournaments for one year because of the "misconduct and unruliness" of spectators at one of its games. The Alabama High School Athletic Association violated the plaintiff's due process rights for the following reasons:

    (1) There were no preexisting standards.
    (2) No punishments were provided for violation of the rules.
    (3) No specific charge was made.
    (4) No notice was given.

(5) There was no opportunity for an adequate hearing.

(6) The hearing was not convened as required by the association's rules.

The court also found that the penalty imposed exceeded any other previously imposed penalty.

(i) In *O'Connor v. Board of Education*, 316 N.Y.S.2d 799 (N.Y. Sup. Ct. 1970), a high school student-athlete was deprived of his athletic award (letter) after his coach turned him in for allegedly violating a "no drinking" rule. The court held that the process required a hearing prior to revocation of a high school athlete's letter.

(j) In *Kelley v. Metropolitan County Board of Education*, 293 F.Supp. 485 (M.D. Tenn. 1968), plaintiff high school student-athlete was suspended from athletic competition by the board of education without being formally charged with a rule violation. The court held that due process involves the right to be heard before being condemned. Due process requires published standards, formal charges, notice, and a hearing. The court granted an injunction that prevented the enforcement of the suspension.

5.4.2.2. *Substantive Due Process*

If the court finds that the right deprived involves life, liberty, or property, then full due process rights may be granted to the individual (see exhibit 5.7). In sports cases, the interest most commonly cited is the property interest, although in some instances the personal liberty interest is involved (see hair length cases in Chapter 6). For the purposes of the due process clause, types of property are not distinguished. Therefore, the first problem encountered in many of these cases is a determination of whether the interest involved constitutes property.

Traditionally, *property* has been defined as all valuable interests that can be possessed outside oneself, which have an exchangeable value or which add to an individual's wealth or estate. Since 1972, in the Supreme Court's decision in *Board of Regents v. Roth*, 408 U.S. 564 (1972), property has been defined as all interests to which an individual could be deemed "entitled." Entitlements occur only if there is some form of current interest in or current use of the property. For example, a holder of a scholarship has a property right because he or she is currently entitled to benefits derived from it. Once this entitlement is established, there is a property right. Due process protections are triggered only when there is an actual deprivation of the entitled rights. This "entitlement" standard does not encompass wishes that do not come true or expectations that fail to materialize; an entitlement to property must be more than an abstract need or desire for it.

The property right involved in sports is the right to participate in athletic activities. The major controversy revolves around the question of whether participation is an individual protectable right or a privilege that is unprotected. This question is analyzed differently depending on whether the athletic activity is on the high school or the college level. On both levels defendants have argued that participation in athletics is a privilege and therefore falls outside the parameters of the due process clause.

In the collegiate area, however, plaintiffs have sometimes been successful in claiming a property interest based on the proximity of monetary benefits currently or potentially available to the student-athlete. A property interest has been found in athletic participation because there exists a potential economic benefit to the student-athlete in the form of either a scholarship or a future professional contract. A current holder of a scholarship who would be deprived of that scholarship has a well-defined property interest based on the present economic value of the award.

A college student-athlete may also have a protectable interest in a future professional contract, as in *Behagen v. Intercollegiate Conference of Faculty Representatives*, 346 F.Supp. 602 (D. Minn. 1972). Some courts, however, by looking at a statistical analysis of the percentage of people who successfully enter professional sports, have discounted a legitimate property interest in a future professional contract as being too speculative. Also, at least one court has indicated that it would find a protectable property interest only if there were a professional league in that particular sport.

In the interscholastic area, the right or privilege dichotomy is analyzed differently. A high school student-athlete with only the possibility of obtaining a scholarship generally has no present economic interest, and the possibility of obtaining a scholarship is too speculative an interest to receive protection. Similarly, a high school student-athlete is usually considered to have an entirely speculative interest in a future professional contract.

In high school cases, the right versus the privilege controversy involves the student-athlete's argument that he or she has a right to an education and that participation in interscholastic athletics is included in that right. The threshold issue is whether there is a right to an education. The Supreme Court has specifically denied a general constitutional right to education (see *San Antonio Independent School District v. Rodriguez*, 411 U.S. 1 [1973]). Even though the right to an education is not grounded in federal law, a state may grant a right to an education either explicitly or implicitly by requiring school attendance. Through this measure, the state effectively gives each child within its boundaries an interest in the education provided. This interest has been held to be a type of property interest protected by the due process clause. (See *Pegram v. Nelson*, 469 F. Supp. 1134 [M.D.N.C. 1979] and *Goss v. Lopez*, 419 U.S. 565 [1974].) Whether a right is stated explicitly or implicitly, once it has been established, it cannot be limited or removed without due process protections.

After finding a right to education based on statutory attendance requirements, a determination must then be made as to whether or not that right includes participation in extracurricular activities. If the right to education means a right to the "total" educational process provided by a school, the courts may find participation in athletic competition to be a right. The right to participate would then be protected by due process considerations. Many courts, however, interpret educational rights as encompassing only classroom learning and view all other activities as unprotected privileges.

NOTES

1. In the following case the court ruled that there was no violation of due process rights:

(a) In *Pearson v. Indiana High Sch. Athletic Ass'n*, No. IP99-1857-C-T/G, 2000 U.S. Dist. LEXIS 10501 (S.D. Ind. Feb. 22, 2000), the court decided that the plaintiffs, two interscholastic tennis players, were not being deprived of a liberty interest for not being allowed to participate in the interscholastic state tournament. The plaintiffs claimed that their rights of substantive or procedural due process were denied, and the court stated, "Pearson and Elder have not established a protectable liberty interest implicated by the IHSAA's actions in this case. Even if they had a protectable liberty interest which was impugned, the process which they received comports with the requirements of the Due Process Clause."

2. See the following law review articles concerning due process:

(a) Rodney K. Smith, "Essay: A Brief History of the National Collegiate Athletic Association's Role in Regulating Intercollegiate Athletics," 11 *Marquette Sports Law Review* 9 (Fall 2000).

(b) W. Burlette Carter, "Student-Athlete Welfare in a Restructured NCAA," 2 *Virginia Journal of Sports Law* 1 (Spring 2000).

(c) Travis L. Miller, "Home Court Advantage: Florida Joins States Mandating Due Process in NCAA Proceedings," 20 *Florida State University Law Review* 871 (Spring 1993).

(d) Robin J. Green, "Does the NCAA Play Fair: A Due Process Analysis of NCAA Enforcement Regulations," 42 *Duke Law Journal* 99 (October 1992).

3. In *Fluitt* v. *University of Nebraska*, 489 F.Supp. 1194 (D. Neb. 1980), a fifth-year college student-athlete requested one additional year of eligibility because an injury had terminated his freshman season, but was denied. The court reasoned that the Faculty Committee was solely responsible for all determinations of hardship, a procedure that had been followed for at least twenty-five years. Any denial of due process at a first hearing was remedied at the second hearing, and thus no violation of due process occurred.

4. In the following cases the court decided that there was not a property interest in intercollegiate athletics:

(a) In *Hall* v. *NCAA*, 985 F. Supp. 782 (N.D. Ill. 1997), the plaintiff, a prospective collegiate student-athlete, did not meet the minimum academic standards to qualify for participation in the NCAA. He did not take an adequate number of core courses in high school, and did not maintain a minimum G.P.A. The court held that the right to participate in athletics was not a protected property interest and that hopes for a career in basketball were also too speculative to be a constitutionally protected right.

(b) In *Knapp* v. *Northwestern University*, No. 95-C-6454 1996 U.S. Dist. LEXIS 12463 (N.D. Ill Aug. 23, 1996), a student that had received an athletic scholarship to play basketball at Northwestern University was not cleared to play by team doctors because of a heart condition. The player argued that he had a substantial interest in playing because of the hopes of a professional career. The court, however, found this theory to be speculative, stating, "While participation in intercollegiate basketball has been recognized as a training ground for a professional basketball career, the possibility of obtaining that professional basketball career is too speculative to even constitute a present economic interest."

(c) In *Karmanos* v. *Baker*, 816 F.2d 258 (6th Cir. 1987), a college hockey player was declared ineligible because he played in a professional league in Canada. The court denied the due process claim brought by him and his father on the grounds that his father's "right to direct the upbringing and education [of his son] does not extend so far as to give [him] the right to direct his child to play hockey on a professional team without losing his amateur status."

(d) In *McHale* v. *Cornell University*, 620 F.Supp. 67 (N.D.N.Y. 1985), a student-athlete transferred for "academic reasons alone" and opposed a loss of eligibility as it infringed upon his right to play football. The court found that the NCAA was not a state actor and thus there was no due process violation.

(e) In *Weiss* v. *Eastern College Athletic Conference*, 563 F.Supp. 192 (E.D. Pa. 1983), a student who challenged the transfer rule when it deprived him of a year of eligibility to play tennis at the University of Pennsylvania was unsuccessful in his due process claim, as the court did not find sufficient evidence of irreparable harm to grant an injunction.

(f) In *NCAA* v. *Gillard*, 352 So. 2d 1072 (Miss. 1977), the court ruled that a player's right to play intercollegiate football was not a property right to be protected by due process guarantees. The court ruled that the denial of a player's eligibility to compete for having accepted clothing at a discount did not infringe on the plaintiff's constitutional right to due process.

5. In the following cases the court decided that there was not a property interest in interscholastic athletics:

(a) In *Ryan* v. *California Interscholastic Federation*, 94 Cal. App. 4th 1048 (Cal. Ct. App. 2001), a student enrolled in a high school after completing the 12th grade in a high school in Australia. He was found to be ineligible for athletic participation in California under CIF bylaws. The court held that California law did not provide a protected property right to participate in interscholastic athletics, and that participation was only a privilege.

(b) In *Jordan* v. *O'Fallon Township High School*, 706 N.E.2d 137 (Ill. App. Ct. 1999), the plaintiff student was suspended from participating in interscholastic football because he was found by the police in an inebriated state, which was in violation of the school's conduct policy. The court found that athletic participation is not a protected right, stating, "Students can need, want, and expect to participate in interscholastic athletics, but students are not entitled to participate in them. Football is neither an integral part of a quality education nor a requirement under any rule or regulation governing education in this State . . . Simply put, playing high school football is a privilege rather than a right."

(c) In *Indiana High School Athletic Ass'n v. Carlsberg*, 694 N.E.2d 222 (Ind. 1997), the plaintiff, Carlsberg, transferred from one high school to another within the same state. The court found that the right to participate in interscholastic athletics was not a protected one, and that a transfer rule limiting students' participation was rationally related to a legitimate interest in interscholastic athletics, the avoidance of "school-hopping."

(d) In *Graham v. Tennessee Secondary School Athletic Ass'n*, No. 1:95-CV-044 1995 U.S. Dist. LEXIS 3211 (E.D. Tenn. Feb. 20, 1995), parents of students at a private high school brought due process and equal protection claims against the TSSAA, alleging that an association "quota" rule violated the rights of the students. A quota rule allowed private schools to supply financial aid to only a certain number of athletes. If a school chose to grant financial aid to more than the allotted number of students it would not be allowed to participate in post-season tournament play. The court held that the plaintiffs did not have a valid due process claim because extracurricular activities were not subject to constitutional protection.

(e) In *Mississippi High School Activities Ass'n v. Coleman*, 631 So. 2d 768 (Miss. 1994), the plaintiff attended a high school that was not in the same district as his parent's residence. Under the Mississippi association's anti-recruiting rule, he was not able to participate on his high school's athletic teams. He brought a claim alleging that his property interest had been violated because he was not allowed to participate in extracurricular activities. The court held that there is no property interest in interscholastic athletics, and therefore no likelihood of success on a due process claim.

(f) In *Palmer v. Merluzzi*, 868 F.2d 90 (3rd Cir. 1989), the court of appeals concluded that participation in extracurricular activities is not a fundamental right under the Constitution.

(g) In *Stock v. Texas Catholic Interscholastic League*, 364 F.Supp. 362 (N.D. Tex. 1973), the court held that the plaintiff high school student's interest in playing interscholastic football was too insignificant to justify federal court jurisdiction. The plaintiff failed to show that he had been deprived of a right under color of state law such that jurisdiction under 42 U.S.C. section 1983 should be granted. The court held, "Nowhere in the Constitution is there any guarantee of a right to play football. . . . Even if the participation was thwarted under color of state law, the interest at stake was still too insignificant to justify jurisdiction."

(h) In *Taylor v. Alabama High School Athletic Ass'n.*, 336 F.Supp. 54 (M.D. Ala. 1972), the district court held that participation in interscholastic athletics is a privilege. The mere chance of receiving a college scholarship based on display of athletic ability at tournaments was not a protectable property right.

(i) In *Robinson v. Illinois High School Ass'n.*, 195 N.E. 2d 38 (Ill. App. Ct. 1963), plaintiff high school student was denied eligibility because he was over the age limit set by the defendant association. The court held that no property interest was sufficient to justify judicial intervention when the association's determination of eligibility did not show fraud, collusion, or unreasonable or arbitrary acts.

6. In the following cases the court determined that there was a property interest in interscholastic or intercollegiate athletics:

(a) In *Boyle v. Pennsylvania Athletic Ass'n*, 676 A.2d 695 (Pa. Commw. Ct. 1996), the Athletic Association denied eligibility to a student that had transferred from a public school to a Catholic school within the same association. The Association was not swayed to change its decision even though the student transferred because of an altercation with his former coach at the public school. The student was seeking an injunction that would allow him to play on the Catholic school team. The court conceded that the plaintiff did not have a property interest in interscholastic athletics, and that its right to interfere with the decisions of the Association was limited. Nevertheless, the court held that the plaintiff was entitled to the injunction. The court analyzed the purpose of the Pennsylvania transfer rule, which was to prevent transfers and recruiting done for athletic purposes. The court held that ruling that the student should be ineligible for competition was arbitrary and capricious, and therefore that the Association violated his right to equal protection. There was no evidence to show that the student transferred because he was recruited or for any athletic purpose.

(b) In *Lesser* v. *Neosho County Community College*, 741 F. Supp. 854 (D. Kan. 1990), the plaintiff was cut from his college baseball team shortly after receiving a scholarship. During his tenure on the team he was subject to fines for violating a team appearance standard. The court analyzed claims of both property and liberty interest violations. The court held that he did not have a liberty interest to participate in intercollegiate athletics. Nevertheless, the court held that the plaintiff did have a property interest in the money that he was fined during his time with the team. It was clear that the athletes were not afforded their due process rights before punishment if they violated the team's grooming policies.

(c) In *Hall* v. *University of Minnesota*, 530 F.Supp. 104 (D. Minn. 1982), in granting an injunction for the plaintiff, the court found that a property interest existed in the plaintiff's ability to remain eligible for college basketball. The court recognized Hall's need to play college basketball his senior year and possibly to land an NBA contract. Although the court found it difficult to place a definite dollar value on the loss of eligibility, it looked to the value of a professional contract and stated that because the exceptionally talented student-athlete was led to perceive college athletic programs as farm systems for the professional ranks, Hall did deserve at least minimal due process protection.

(d) In *Gulf South Conference* v. *Boyd*, 369 So.2d 553 (Ala. 1979), "the Supreme Court of Alabama held that the right to participate in college athletics is a property right of present economic value. The case was distinguished from *Scott* v. *Kilpatrick* [at note 6(g)] as a college athlete receives a scholarship for his efforts and a high school athlete only receives an opportunity to try for a scholarship. Thus, the college athlete may place a dollar value on his efforts, whereas the high school athlete's interest is only speculative."

(e) In *Moran* v. *School District #7, Yellowstone County*, 350 F.Supp. 1180 (D. Mont. 1972), the court held that the right to attend school includes the right to participate in extracurricular activities. The court reasoned that sports are an integral part of the total educational process. This educational process is extremely important, and sport participation may not be denied when there is no reasonable basis upon which to distinguish among the various parts of the educational process.

(f) In *Behagen* v. *Intercollegiate Conference of Faculty Representatives*, 346 F.Supp. 602 (D. Minn. 1972), the court noted that although "big time" college athletics may not be a total part of the educational experience as athletics is in high schools, nonetheless the ability to participate is of substantial economic value to some students. Further, the court recognized that the opportunity to display one's talents may be of greater economic value than the opportunity to receive an education.

(g) In *Scott* v. *Kilpatrick*, 237 So.2d 652 (Ala. 1970), the Supreme Court of Alabama held that the "speculative possibility" of receiving a college football scholarship was not a sufficient basis for finding that a student was deprived of a property right when he was declared ineligible to participate for one year.

7. In *Behagen* v. *Amateur Basketball Ass'n of the United States*, 884 F.2d 524 (10th Cir. 1989), the court of appeals ruled that the district court erred when they allowed the due process claim of the plaintiff to go to jury and be decided in favor of the plaintiff. The court of appeals ruled that the plaintiff's claim that he had been denied a "property right" by being declared ineligible to play basketball in Italy after competing in professional basketball in the United States was inadmissible because the Amateur Basketball Association was a private rather than a governmental actor, and thus not subject to due process requirements.

8. In *Puchalski* v. *School District of Springfield*, 161 F.Supp. 2d 395 (E.D. Pa. 2001), a football coach that had been fired by a public school brought, among other allegations, a claim that he had been deprived of a property interest by being fired and not being evaluated before his termination. The court disagreed, holding that property interest in public employment did not exist, and that he had no right to evaluation unless made explicit by the employment contract.

14th

5.4.3. Equal Protection

Through the equal protection clause of the Fourteenth Amendment of the U.S. Constitution, student-athletes and coaches are provided with the means to challenge certain rules and regulations that are of a discriminatory nature. This source of law forbids discrimination of one form or another in various contexts, and thus serves to limit the regulatory power of athletic organizations controlling sports activities.

Equal protection is the constitutional method of checking on the fairness of the application of any law. This independent constitutional guarantee governs all federal, state, and local laws that classify individuals or impact on individual rights. The equal protection guarantee is found in the Fourteenth Amendment of the U.S. Constitution. It reads: "No state shall . . . deny to any person within its jurisdiction the equal protection of the laws." It is specifically applicable only to the states, but the federal government is held to similar standards under the due process clause of the Fifth Amendment. Equal protection requires that no person be singled out from similarly situated people, or have different benefits bestowed or burdens imposed, unless a constitutionally permissible reason for doing so exists.

Three standards of review are used under equal protection analysis. The highest standard of review is that of *strict scrutiny*. Application of the strict scrutiny standard by the court means that the rule challenged will be invalidated unless the defendant can demonstrate that the rule is supported by a compelling state interest. When a rule abridges a fundamental right or makes a distinction based on suspect criteria, the defendant has the burden of proof. This standard tests only whether a classification is properly drawn, not whether an individual is properly placed within that classification. This type of review is triggered by the use of either a suspect class or a fundamental interest.

The Supreme Court has found three suspect classes: alienage, race, and national origin. Any time a rule discriminates directly or indirectly on the basis of these suspect classifications, the strict scrutiny standard will be applied.

There are a number of fundamental interests, and the vast majority of these rights arise expressly from the U.S. Constitution. They include the First Amendment guarantees, such as the right to freedom of religion, speech, and press, as well as the right to assemble peaceably and to petition the government for redress of grievances. In addition to these specific rights, the Supreme Court has found three other fundamental rights: the right to travel, the right to vote, and the right to privacy (which involves decisions about marriage, abortion, and other family choices).

Some interests have been specifically found to be non-fundamental; these include subsistence and welfare payments, housing, government employment, and education. The fact that education has been deemed a non-fundamental interest is particularly important in cases involving high school or college athletic associations. This designation makes it difficult for the student-athlete plaintiff to establish athletic participation as a fundamental interest.

The second standard of review under the equal protection guarantee is that of *rational basis*. This standard requires only that the rule have some rational relationship to a legitimate organizational purpose. It is used in the absence of a classification defined as suspect or as a fundamental right. Rules reviewed under this standard are difficult for a plaintiff to challenge successfully because the defendant is generally able to present some rational relationship between the restriction and a legitimate governmental objective. The rational basis test is the most commonly applied constitutional standard.

The third standard of review or category of classes imposes an *intermediate test*, which falls between the strict scrutiny and rational basis tests. It requires that rules classifying certain groups satisfy an "important" but not necessarily a "compelling" interest. Two "quasi-suspect" classifications have been established: gender and legitimacy. Use of either gender- or legitimacy-based classifications will trigger this intermediate standard of review. To date, the difference between a "compelling" interest and an "important" interest has not been made explicit, and remains the subject of much examination and speculation when argued before the courts.

Equal protection does not bar states from creating classifications. Instead, it requires that classifications not be predicated on race, alienage, or national origin. It also requires that the criteria bear a reasonable relationship to the purpose of the law. Otherwise, the distinction is automatically suspect. Once a law is suspect, it will be held valid only if a compelling interest is established and there is no less intrusive means by which the same end may be achieved. The burden of proof is on the states to establish the compelling nature of the interest. The same analysis is used when a fundamental interest is infringed upon by a state law. In summary, the theory of equal protection is used to protect individuals by ensuring that they are fairly treated in the exercise of their fundamental rights and by assuring the elimination of distinctions based on constitutionally impermissible criteria.

The equal protection guarantee relates to classes and distinctions inevitably drawn whenever a legislative body makes rules relating to specific groups. One method typically employed to challenge a rule under the equal protection clause is that which claims either under- or overinclusiveness. Under- or over-inclusiveness can make a rule impermissibly discriminatory. *Overinclusiveness* means that the legislative class includes many people to whom the rule in question lacks a rational relationship. In other words, at least some of the class of affected individuals are not part of the problem addressed by the rule, and the rule as applied to these people has no relationship to its purpose. A rule's validity depends not on whether classes differ but on whether differences between the classes are pertinent to the subject with respect to which the classification is made. Whereas overinclusiveness exists when a rule creates a class more extensive than necessary to effectuate the purpose of the rule, *underinclusiveness* exists when a class does not contain all the members necessary to effectuate the rule's purpose.

It is possible for a rule to be both over- and underinclusive. For example, consider the following rule: "All transfer students from public high schools will not be eligible for interscholastic play for one year from date of entry." This rule is overinclusive with respect to public school transfers that were made for reasons unrelated to athletics. It would be underinclusive, however, if it permitted immediate eligibility for transfer students from private schools who might be transferring for solely athletic reasons.

To draw perfect classifications that are neither over- nor underinclusive is extremely difficult. In light of this, when no important constitutional rights are involved, the courts can and do uphold both over- and underinclusive categories as long as they can find a rational relationship between the rule and its purpose.

For example, only when an athletic association cannot demonstrate the connection between the rule and its purpose will the court find that an equal protection violation has occurred.

Another reason why the court will uphold rules that do not make perfect classifications is to allow athletic associations to deal with problems on an objective basis. Associations or legislatures do not have to create perfect solutions prior to attacking specific problems. In many cases, the court will not decide whether the rule itself is invalid, but may conclude that its application to a specific individual violates the person's constitutional rights. The court can therefore pay deference to the legislative judgment initiating the rule while upholding the rights of the individual.

Technically, there is a two-tiered system for equal protection analysis; however, the trend may be toward a sliding scale that would dissolve the absolute categories of fundamental rights and interests. The advantage of a sliding-scale approach is that it is much more flexible and would in effect create a flexible scale of rights and/or classes that would be directly compared with the governmental interest involved.

NOTES

1. In the following cases, violations of equal protection were found in the application of an athletic association's rules or decisions:

(a) In *Fusato v. Washington Interscholastic Activities Ass'n*, 970 P.2d 774 (Wash. Ct. App. 1999), the court found that the WIAA had violated Fusato's equal protection rights by not allowing her to play interscholastic athletics. Under their transfer rule, student-athletes who transfer to a high school are not allowed to compete immediately unless they move with the entire "family unit." In Fusato's case, she moved from Okinawa by herself to live with her aunt and uncle in Washington, and was not allowed to play immediately for her high school due to the transfer rule. The court decided for Fusato because it believed that she was being discriminated against due to her nation of origin, which is a suspect class in questions of equal protection. The court stated, "We hold the trial court did not err applying the strict scrutiny test when deciding the WIAA residence and transfer rules violated Ms. Fusato's equal protection rights under the Fourteenth Amendment. Although Ms. Fusato cannot prove a fundamental right is threatened, she established she was a member of a suspect class based upon national origin or alienage. Upon her showing of disparate impact, together with discriminatory purpose or intent, the WIAA was required to meet the burden of showing a compelling state interest was served by the challenged rules. The WIAA failed to meet its burden and made no effort to demonstrate that the least restrictive regulatory means were used to accomplish the stated purposes of their rules."

(b) In *Buckton v. NCAA*, 366 F.Supp. 1152 (D. Mass. 1973), Canadian ice hockey players were denied eligibility because they had received funding from junior league hockey teams in Canada rather than from high schools, as is the custom in the United States. The court prohibited the NCAA from enforcing ineligibility, because the rule in effect discriminated against plaintiffs on the basis of the suspect class of national origin.

(c) In *Indiana High School Athletics Ass'n v. Raike*, 329 N.E.2d 66 (Ind. Ct. App. 1975), a public high school rule that prohibited married students from participating in any extracurricular activities was held invalid, even though the court decided the right to marry was not a fundamental right. The court, in using a sliding-scale approach, held that the rule denied equal protection because there was no fair and substantial relationship between the classification (married students) and the objective sought (preventing dropouts).

(d) In *Rivas Tenorio v. Liga Atlética Interuniversitaria*, 554 F.2d 492 (1st Cir. 1977), the trial court, in dismissing the complaint that questioned the constitutionality of an athletic association's regulation banning non-Puerto Ricans from competing in intercollegiate athletics if they enrolled in member institutions after their twenty-first birthday, erred in failing to subject the regulation to strict constitutional scrutiny in view of the fact that it discriminated, on its face, against aliens. The case was reversed and sent back to the district court.

(e) In *Howard University v. NCAA*, 510 F.2d 213 (D.C. Cir. 1975), the court applied strict scrutiny in striking down the NCAA's "Foreign Student Rule" because the classification was based on alienage. Even though the court accepted the purpose of the rule, it held that the rule was not closely tailored to achieve its goal, since it penalized foreign student-athletes for activities that citizens participated in without penalty.

2. In the following cases, violations of equal protection were *not* found in the application of an athletic association's rules or decisions:

(a) In *Mitchell v. Louisiana High School Athletic Ass'n.*, 430 F.2d 1155 (5th Cir. 1970), the case litigated on the theory that there was discrimination against students who chose to repeat a junior high school grade for academic or personal reasons. The court held that allowing those who failed a year still to have four years of high school eligibility, while reducing eligibility to three years for those who chose to repeat a year, had a rational relationship with regard to the problem of redshirting (see Chapter 6). Therefore, it was not appropriate for the judiciary to intervene, even when the rule was unduly harsh on an individual.

(b) In *Moreland v. Western Pennsylvania Interscholastic Athletic League*, 572 F.2d 121 (3rd Cir. 1978), a high school basketball player claimed denial of equal protection when he was prohibited from competing in post-season play because he was absent from school for more than twenty days, a violation of a league rule. The court held that the rule was rationally related to the purpose of safeguarding educational values, cultivating high ideals of good sportsmanship, and promoting uniformity of standards in athletic competition.

(c) In *Graham v. NCAA*, 804 F.2d 953 (6th Cir. 1986), a football player challenged the NCAA transfer rules on an equal protection basis. The court, however, found that no state action was present, and thus it was unnecessary to address claims of due process or equal protection.

(d) In *McHale v. Cornell University*, 620 F.Supp. 67 (N.D.N.Y. 1985), a student who transferred for academic reasons unsuccessfully challenged the loss of athletic eligibility on equal protection grounds, because his was not the type of transfer the NCAA rules were intended to curtail.

5.5. PUBLIC RESPONSIBILITY OF ATHLETIC ASSOCIATIONS

As legal bodies, athletic associations have certain duties to fulfill to the public as a condition of their corporate existence. Public responsibilities can include broadcast rights (see Chapter 14), access to records, antitrust liabilities (see Chapter 10), and disclosure and funding of public facilities. Even a voluntary association that considers itself a private organization may have a responsibility to the general public. For example, the NCAA is responsible to the public for maintaining amateurism in college athletics, providing competition in intercollegiate sports for both male and female student-athletes, and allowing greater access to televised football.

Generally, any athletic organization that is public or quasi-public in nature is a potential defendant in a public responsibility case. A case that dealt with the public responsibilities of athletic associations was *Greene v. Athletic Council of Iowa State University*, 251 N.W.2d 559 (Iowa 1977). In *Greene*, the Iowa Superior Court ruled that an amateur college association, although private in name, is "quasi-public" in character. The Iowa court discussed the specific statute and decided that the controlling issue was whether the athletic council was a "council" as authorized by the laws of the state. The record showed that the Iowa State University (ISU) athletic council was an entity established by officials of ISU to manage and control its intercollegiate athletic program. After a discussion of specific powers, the court found that the athletic council exercised powers that clearly made it a governmental entity. The court went on to decide that the athletic council was granted authorization under the laws of the state, which allowed the board of regents of the university to delegate responsibility to it. In conclusion, the court held that since this body was a council as authorized by the laws of the state, it was subject to the Iowa open-meeting law.

The NCAA has argued that only through confidentiality can it investigate itself properly and thereby maintain its amateur integrity and fulfill this additional public responsibility. It argues that opening confidential investigation files compromises the NCAA's cooperative principles, to which all member institutions agree to adhere when they join the association. The NCAA, as previously discussed, is a voluntary association whose members, by joining the organization, agree to follow certain conditions and obligations of membership, including the obligation to conduct their individual institutional athletic programs in a manner consistent with NCAA legislation. In addition, member institutions agree to be policed in regard to the organization's rule by the NCAA's enforcement staff. The key to the NCAA investigative process is the cooperative principle—that is, the accused member institution and the NCAA's enforcement staff work together to ascertain the truth of alleged infractions.

5.5.1. Disclosure

Disclosure cases involve the argument that certain information possessed by associations or meetings held by organizations should be a matter of public record and, therefore, open to the public. Designation as a governmental or other public body may require an agency to be subject to the Freedom of Information Act (5 U.S.C. §552) or to state "sunshine laws." Thus, a quasi-public association may have to open its records for public inspection, while a private organization would not be held to this obligation. The degree of disclosure that a quasi-public institution may be required to give varies from state to state. For example, under the state of Florida's public record laws, interviews related to searches for new coaches or athletic directors are open to the media when state institutions are involved with such searches. For the media and the public, such laws provide factual accounts of who is actually running for the job, where the interviews are conducted, what is being asked, and how those being interviewed are responding. For athletic administrators and institutions, these laws put pressure on them to be unbiased, fair, evaluative, and accurate in selecting candidates for vacant positions.

Disclosure cases illustrate conflicts that arise concerning the right of the public to be accurately informed by athletic organizations against the need of an organization to protect the confidentiality of its files. In *Kneeland v. NCAA*, 850 F.2d 224 (5th Cir. 1988), a reporter sought to gain disclosure of information from the NCAA and the Southwest Conference about a recruiting scandal at Southern Methodist University. The U.S. Court of Appeals for the Fifth Circuit concluded that the NCAA and Southwest Conference were not governmental bodies, and thus were not subject to the Texas Open Records Act. However, in *Hansberry v. Massachusetts Interscholastic Athletic Ass'n*, No. 95-6807-B 1998 Mass. Super LEXIS 706 (Mass. Super. Ct. Oct. 21, 1998), the plaintiff Hansberry was not allowed under MIAA regulations to participate in interscholastic athletics because he had exhausted his semesters of eligibility. Upon appeal, his application for a waiver was denied. Hansberry brought a claim against the MIAA because he had not been informed of the meeting to review his case, claiming that the MIAA was a de facto governmental body, and therefore subject to open meeting laws. The court agreed with Hansberry, and decided that his disqualification from participation was moot because his case had been decided in violation of open meeting laws.

NOTES

1. In *State, ex rel. Cincinnati Enquirer v. Krings*, 758 N.E.2d 1135 (Ohio 2001), Hamilton County had agreed to fund the building of a stadium for the Cincinnati Bengals. The Supreme Court of Ohio ruled that all records concerning the funding and building were public information. Therefore, the County commissioners had no right to preclude the plaintiff newspaper from access to this information. The court held that the records of the construction were public records even if they were in the possession of the private construction companies.

2. In *M.G. v. Time Warner, Inc.*, 89 Cal. App. 4th 623 (Cal. Ct. App. 2001), the defendant magazine publisher and television producer used a team photograph including the plaintiffs in both print and television stories about the molestation of child athletes. The team manager had plead guilty to molesting five of the children, including the children in the photograph. The plaintiffs survived a motion to dismiss the claim brought by defendant because the court believed that the plaintiffs had a reasonable chance of success on an invasion of privacy claim. The court reasoned that it was important that the team or players had never been revealed in previous media coverage of the scandal. The journalistic importance clearly did not outweigh the importance of maintaining the anonymity of the victims.

3. In 2000, a group of plaintiffs brought a suit against Indiana University for violating public meetings laws because the meetings concerning the firing of the Indiana basketball coach were not open to the public. Under state law, the university must give the public forty-eight hours notice before any such meeting takes place. A special court, in an unpublished opinion, ruled that Indiana had the right to fire Coach Knight but that plaintiffs could still bring a claim of violating the State's Open Door Law.

4. In *Smith v. Plati*, 56 F. Supp. 2d 1195 (D. Co. 1999), the plaintiff was an independent Web site operator who maintained a Web site about the University of Colorado athletics. When he first began coverage of the athletic programs on his site, he received the same treatment as members of the press concerning access to sports information. However, the media relations department of the university reduced his access to only published material in order to limit his access to "publishable information." The court found that the university could claim sovereign immunity, and that the defendant media relations director did not have a duty to give the plaintiff press access because the plaintiff had not been deprived of a protected right and he had no right to be qualified as "press."

5. In *Kirwan v. The Diamondback*, 721 A.2d 196 (Md. Ct. App. 1998), the Court of Appeals of Maryland ruled that parking tickets received by persons affiliated with an institution are not personnel records, and therefore are open to the public. *The Diamondback*, a school newspaper, had alleged that basketball players on the University of Maryland campus were parking illegally, and coaches for the team were paying their parking tickets. The court rejected the school's argument that the parking tickets were financial records, and therefore should remain confidential.

6. In *Board of Regents of the Regency University System v. Reynard*, 686 N.E.2d 1222 (Ill. App. Ct. 1997), the University of Illinois was found to be in violation of the Open Meetings Act and the Freedom of Information Act. The athletic council had meetings concerning the elimination of men's sports teams in order to comply with Title IX. It was alleged that the council meetings fell under the parameters of the two acts, and that the meetings should have been open. The court ruled that because the council was a public

body, meetings should have been open to the public, notwithstanding any inconvenience this may have caused.

7. In *Re Subpoena to Testify Before Grand Jury*, 864 F.2d 1559 (11th Cir. 1989), four Florida newspapers sought to overturn a district court ruling that restrained counsel and parties from disclosing content of pleadings and memoranda in connection with a grand jury investigation into the University of Florida athletic program. The district court ordered it closed to stop the publication of sensitive information in regard to the investigation. The U.S. Court of Appeals affirmed the district court ruling, stating that the newspapers had no right of access to grand jury proceedings under the First Amendment.

8. In 1984, the Miami Herald Publishing Company, the *St. Petersburg Times*, and Campus Communications, publisher of the University of Florida student newspaper, *The Gator*, had a declaratory suit filed against them in Florida State District Court by the University of Florida. The university asked the court to decide what information the university could reveal to the newspapers in response to their request that files pertaining to an NCAA preliminary investigation into the school's football program be opened to the media. The University of Florida said that strict federal and state laws involving the confidentiality of student and employee records led to the decision to file the suit.

The University of Florida subsequently decided to release the requested information. The information released included the seventy-five-page official letter of inquiry from the NCAA that listed 107 violations by Florida's football program, as well as 1,700 pages of documents about the violations. These included transcripts of interviews with a number of witnesses.

9. In the following cases, the courts required athletic associations to open their records to the public under the individual states' Freedom of Information Acts:

(a) In *Arkansas Gazette Co.* v. *Southern State College*, 620 S.W.2d 258 (Ark. 1981), the newspaper brought suit against the Arkansas Intercollegiate Athletic Conference, seeking to compel it to disclose the amount of money member institutions dispensed to student-athletes during the school year. The court held that the records were not protected by the federal Family Education Rights Privacy Act of 1974, disclosure was allowed under the Arkansas Freedom of Information Act, and such disclosure did not violate student-athletes' reasonable expectation of privacy.

(b) In *Palladrium Publishing Co.* v. *River Valley School District*, 321 N.W.2d 705 (Mich. Ct. App. 1982), a newspaper sought declaration that the school district and board of education were required to disclose names of students suspended for alleged drug-related activities on school property. The court held that minutes of a school board must identify any student suspended by board action by name rather than student number, and that the Freedom of Information Act did not prevent disclosure of this information.

(c) In *Pooler* v. *Nyguist*, 392 N.Y.S.2d 948 (N.Y. Sup. Ct. 1976), the court ruled that according to the Freedom of Information Act, dropout rates are subject to disclosure after an investigation of a complaint.

10. See the following article for a discussion of disclosure in professional sports: Anthony Millican, "Watchdog Caught Council Violations: Open Meeting Law Broken a Dozen Times," *San Diego Union-Tribune*, Local; P.B-1, October 26, 2000.

5.5.2. Funding of Public Facilities

Another development with respect to public responsibilities of athletic associations is the challenge to the way public funds are spent. Challenges have been made to the building of sports facilities by faculty governing bodies that have been concerned that funds would be diverted from other educational areas. In *Lester v. Public Building Authority of County of Knox*, No. 78491 (1983), a case settled out of court, the issues raised shed light on potential problem areas in financing athletic facilities. This suit was brought by faculty members of the

University of Tennessee against the university in order to block its planned funding and construction of a $30 million assembly center and sports arena. The faculty was successful in placing pressure on school officials and, in return for not delaying the construction of the arena, won the right to be involved in the approval process when projects would affect faculty members.

NOTES

1. For more information on the funding of public facilities, see the following law review articles:

  a. Annoop K. Bhasin, "Tax-Exempt Bond Financing of Sports Stadiums: Is the Price Right?" 7 *Villanova Sports & Entertainment Law Journal Forum* 181 (2000).

  b. John R. Dorocak, "Tax Advantages of Sports Franchises: Part I—The Stadium," 1999 *L. Rev. Law Review of Michigan State University-Detroit College of Law* 579 (1999).

  c. Scott A. Jensen, "Financing Professional Sports Facilities with Federal Tax Subsidies: Is It Sound Tax Policy?" 10 *Marquette Sports Law Journal* 425 (Spring 2000).

  d. Mark D. Oram, "The Stadium Financing and Franchise Relocation Act of 1999," 2 *Virginia Journal of Sports Law* 184 (Spring 2000).

2. The courts will often be very protective of a perceived public interest. A key question is how much of the amateur athletic organization's power can be delegated. For an examination of this subject in regard to the Boston Marathon, see the following cases:

  (a) In *Boston Athletic Ass'n. v. International Marathons, Inc.*, 467 N.E.2d 58 (Mass. 1984), the board of directors of the Boston Athletic Association (BAA) brought a lawsuit against International Marathons, Inc. (IMI) to prevent it from representing itself to the public as the association's agent. The hearing examiner found that the contract which set up the agency relationship and was signed by the president of the BAA violated state law and that the president had exceeded his authority in entering into the agreement.

  (b) In *International Marathons, Inc. v. Attorney General*, 467 N.E.2d 55 (Mass. 1984), IMI appealed the hearing examiner's decision in *BAA* v. *IMI*, but the court refused to review the decision because it was a moot question. The hearing examiner had disapproved the contract between IMI and BAA because it was violative of state law.

3. Individuals involved with a public athletic organization (administrators, coaches, and others) should be aware that such involvement may come under a high degree of scrutiny by a court because of the "public trust" issue. For an examination of the strict standards of ethics the courts expect from an organization such as the NCAA, see *Tarkanian v. University of Nevada, Las Vegas*, Case No. A173498, 8th Judicial District Court of the State of Nevada (June 25, 1984). The University of Nevada, Las Vegas (UNLV), basketball coach successfully brought this suit to prohibit the enforcement of an NCAA-mandated sanction, which required UNLV to sever all ties with coach Tarkanian. The court held that the NCAA and UNLV acted arbitrarily and with prejudice in accepting investigative information and reaching their decisions. The injunction was affirmed by the Supreme Court of Nevada (*Tarkanian v. NCAA*, 741 P.2d 1345 [Nev. Sup. Ct. 1987]). However, the U.S. Supreme Court later reversed this decision, finding that the acts of the NCAA were not under color of state law, and thus not subject to the same standards as those set forth in the lower court's decision (*Tarkanian v. National Collegiate Athletic Ass'n.*, 488 U.S. 179 [1988]).

Chapter 6

THE ATHLETE AND CONSTITUTIONAL LAW

INTRODUCTION

The previous chapter, "Athletic Associations," studied the various athletic associations that govern amateur athletes in the United States. Previously it was titled "Amateur Athletic Associations," but the changing definition of "amateur" has necessitated the deleting of that word from the title. While some associations hold to the "traditional" sense of "amateur," other associations, such as the International Olympic Committee, have modified their designation of "amateur" since the mid-1980s. This chapter begins with a discussion on the interpretation of an eligible athlete, especially in the light of the official status of Olympic athletes, and then discusses individual eligibility requirements for student-athletes. Many of the requirements, such as academic requirements, participation rules, and amateur eligibility, will be viewed at both the interscholastic and the intercollegiate levels. Regardless of how an association defines an eligible athlete, the most important aspect of associations to focus upon is the rules of the association: initial eligibility rules, continuing eligibility rules, and scholarship restrictions.

Although this chapter primarily examines individual eligibility requirements for participation at the high school and collegiate level, a brief section is devoted to the eligibility requirements for Olympic competition. The significance of this topic is not confined to the Olympic arena, because participation in Olympic competition may affect a student-athlete's participation in interscholastic or intercollegiate competition.

The applicability of constitutional law to professional sports, however, is not discussed because constitutional law is generally not applicable to the professional sports arena for two primary reasons.

First, in professional sports, the athletes are parties to a collective bargaining agreement, which voluntarily restricts the constitutional rights that a professional athlete would otherwise possess (see Chapter 11, section 11.2., "Collective Bargaining"). For example, in 2000, Atlanta Braves pitcher John Rocker was involved in a controversy concerning rights of free expression and league authority. Rocker, in an interview with a *Sports Illustrated* reporter, made some disparaging and intolerant remarks about minority groups within the United States. The commissioner's office of Major League Baseball was able to suspend Rocker from Major League Baseball for five games because of his remarks. When the players' union agrees to the collective bargaining agreement in Major League Baseball, or any other professional sport, certain rights are given up, including the freedom of expression. In the case of Rocker, his right to freedom of expression was waived under the collective bargaining agreement, and the commissioner's office was able to punish him with any reasonable punishment that was deemed appropriate. The second reason why sports leagues will not be discussed within this chapter is that professional sports leagues are not state actors, but solely private entities. For a constitutional law violation to be found, state action must be present, which therefore leaves professional sports leagues immune.

A significant portion of this chapter will deal with what avenues are available for a student-athlete who is unhappy with the decision or regulation of a governing association. First, the affected student-athlete should review the legal documents of the entity, especially rules and regulations relating to athletes. The importance of the organizational rule book cannot be overstated, no matter which organization the athlete is dealing with. While the scope and detail of a rule book will vary depending upon the organization, the rule book lays out all rules and regulations, and outlines the procedures for athletes to appeal decisions. Second, the athlete should assess whether or not there is recourse within the organization for solving the problem, such as an arbitration or appeals process. If the affected athlete does not have recourse within the association, he or she may consider a court case against the organization. If the athlete does decide to bring litigation against the association, it is imperative to determine the legal status of the organization: is it a public or a private organization? If the association is a state organization, the door is opened for the athlete to bring a constitutional law case on both federal and constitutional law arguments. The athlete, if it is determined that the association is not a state actor, should establish whether or not the organization receives federal funds. If the organization receives federal funds, the athlete should examine whether any federal legislation may apply in the particular situation, such as Title IX. If the organization is a state actor, the next step for the athlete is to determine whether or not the use of constitutional law arguments, such as due process and equal protection, will be successful. The court will then have to balance, under constitutional law, the individual rights of the athlete against the authority of the coach or administrator to govern a sport. For example, courts have had to balance a coach's authority against the censoring of an individual's freedom of expression in cases involving everything from hair length to pre-game prayer (see section 6.3.3.1., "Freedom of Expression").

What follows in this chapter is a discussion of how constitutional law issues affect athletes on the interscholastic, intercollegiate, and Olympic levels. While this chapter does not cover all the various rules, regulations, and athlete challenges (see Chapter 7, "Drug Testing and Policies" or Chapter 5, "Athletic Associations"), it provides a general overview of the types of cases that can be brought by athletes. The chapter begins with a discussion of the ever-changing definitions of eligibility within different sports organizations. The next section deals with the many eligibility requirements for athletes on both the interscholastic and the intercollegiate levels, including initial academic eligibility rules and continuing eligibility regulations. The third section deals with the individual rights of the student-athlete guaranteed under the Constitution, and the conflicts that arise over these rights in athletics. The final segments of the chapter deal with requirements for participation in the Olympic Games and the Buckley Amendment's protections for students and their families.

6.1. DEFINITIONS OF ELIGIBILITY

Each athletic association has developed its own definition of an eligible athlete. Historically, most amateur organizations refused to allow athletes to receive any money at all in compensation for their time or expenses. In fact, this restriction was the basis for distinguishing the amateur athlete from the professional athlete. Increasingly, however, athletes are allowed to receive compensation for certain living, training, and competition expenses. The amount and type of reimbursement allowed are determined by the governing athletic association. Furthermore, in the Olympics, there are still organizations, such as U.S. Rowing, that allow only amateur athletes to compete.

The National Collegiate Athletic Association's Bylaw 14.01.3.2 addresses eligibility in the following fashion: "A student-athlete shall not be eligible for participation in an intercollegiate sport if the individual takes or has taken pay, or has accepted the promise of pay in any form, for participation in that sport. . . ."

NCAA Bylaw 12.1.1. stipulates that a student shall lose his/her eligibility

"if the individual:

a. Uses his or her athletics skill (directly or indirectly) for pay in any form in that sport;

b. Accepts a promise of pay even if such pay is to be received following completion of intercollegiate athletics participation;

c. Signs a contract or commitment of any kind to play professional athletics, regardless of its legal enforceability or any consideration received;

d. Receives, directly or indirectly, a salary, reimbursement of expenses or any other form of financial assistance from a professional sports organization based upon athletics skill or participation, except as permitted by NCAA rules and regulations;

e. Competes on any professional athletics team and knows (or had reason to know) that the team is a professional athletics team (per Bylaw 12.02.4), even if no pay or remuneration for expenses was received; or

f. Enters into a professional draft or an agreement with an agent. . . ."

The IOC allows its International Federations (IFs) to make decisions concerning the eligibility status of the athletes within their sports. The Olympic Charter specifies the following in Bylaw 45:

To be eligible for participation in the Olympic Games a competitor must comply with the Olympic Charter as well as with the rules of the IF concerned as approved by the IOC, and must be entered by his NOC.

• Each IF establishes its sport's own eligibility criteria in accordance with the Olympic Charter. Such criteria must be submitted to the IOC Executive Board for approval.

• The application of the eligibility criteria lies with the IFs, their affiliated National Federations and the NOCs in the fields of their respective responsibilities.

• Except as permitted by the IOC Executive Board, no competitor who participates in the Olympic Games may allow his person, name, picture, or sports performances to be used for advertising purposes during the Olympic Games.

• The entry or participation of a competitor in the Olympic Games shall not be conditional on any financial consideration.

Like the IOC, the U.S. Olympic Committee (USOC) allows decisions concerning eligibility status to be determined by the governing bodies of the individual sports. Within Article VII, Section III, of the USOC Constitution, the USOC authorizes its governing bodies in the following manner:

. . . conduct amateur athletic competitions, including national championships, and international amateur athletic competitions, in the United States, and establish procedures for the determination of eligibility standards for participation in such competitions.

The California Interscholastic Federation, discussed in detail within Chapter 5, outlines, within its Constitution, which athletes are eligible to compete in interscholastic competition, and how eligibility may be lost. In rules 200 and 603–605 these regulations are explained:

200. General provisions

F. PROFESSIONAL TRYOUT

A student shall become ineligible for CIF competition if he/she participates in any tryout for a professional team in any CIF approved sport from September 15 to June 15 unless:

(1) His/her principal has given written approval to a request for such participation from a professional team, and

(2) The tryout is limited to five students or less.

603. PAN-AMERICAN OR OLYMPIC COMPETITION

During the high school season of sport, a high school student who has been selected or qualified for participation on the United States team which will engage in Pan-American or Olympic competition, may participate on that team.

604. SPECIAL PROGRAMS/OLYMPIC DEVELOPMENT PROGRAMS

During the high school season of sport, a high school student who has been selected or qualified for an Olympic development program shall be permitted to participate in such a program without loss of interscholastic eligibility, if the following conditions are met:

A. The Olympic development program is:

(1) Certified as such by the National Federation, verified by the State CIF; and (2)

(a) Conducted or sponsored by the United States Olympic Committee; or

(b) Directly funded

(c) and conducted by the national governing body for the sport on a national level; or

(d) Authorized by a national governing body for athletes having potential for future national team participation; and

B. The student informs the high school principal at least thirty days prior to participating in the program; and

C. The principal verifies the authenticity of the program; and

D. The student makes prior arrangement to complete missed academic lessons, assignments, and tests before the last day of classes of the semester in which the student's absence occurs.

605. INTERNATIONAL COMPETITION

Each CIF section may grant approval, upon individual petition, for a gifted athlete to travel to a foreign country to participate in international competition sanctioned by the governing body for that sport in the United States.

U.S. Rowing is an example of a governing body that has maintained the traditional definition of an amateur for its competitors. The definition of amateur applied is found within Article IV of its constitution:

Article IV—Amateur Standing (U.S. Rowing)

Section 1—no oarsmen or oarswoman can be an amateur who practices rowing and derives any direct monetary gain therefrom.

Section 2—the decision as to whether individuals are amateurs or professionals shall be made only by the Board of Directors.

The U.S. Tennis Association (USTA) is an example of sports association that allows members to be professionals, and also allows professionals to compete in the Olympic Games. The Association does, nevertheless, maintain a definition of an amateur within its constitution, in order to conduct events involving solely amateur competitors:

1. An amateur shall not receive pecuniary advantage because of his skills as a tennis player. Any tennis player is an amateur if he does not receive and has not received, directly or indirectly, pecuniary advantage by the playing, teaching, demonstrating, or pursuit of the game except as expressly permitted by the USTA.

2. Definition of professional. All other tennis players who accept the authority of, and who are in good standing with, the USTA shall be designated as professionals.

3. An amateur remains an amateur throughout a tournament. A player starting play in a tournament as an amateur shall remain an amateur for the purposes of that tournament.

The changing definitions of an amateur have sparked a lively debate because of the serious consequences of defining an amateur athlete. At the international level, in 1986 the International Olympic Committee endorsed a proposed rule change to eliminate the distinction between amateur and professional athletes. Although the international federation retains control over deciding who can compete at the Olympic level, the federation has opened the games to professional athletes since 1986. In 1998, the National Hockey League decided to allow its players to play in the Olympic Games in Nagano, Japan, and even stopped play for two weeks to accommodate traveling athletes. In figure skating, a controversy erupted in 1998 when figure skaters who had been considered professional were allowed to compete at the Olympic level.

High school and collegiate athletic administrators should be familiar with these definitions because student-athletes who receive money or products related to a USA Track and Field-approved competition, or compete with professionals on a team in an annual world championship, may lose their eligibility under NCAA or high school regulations. Participation as an athlete in one sport may also impact eligibility under NCAA or high school regulations. For example, Renaldo Nehemiah, a former world-class hurdler who joined the San Francisco Forty-Niners of the National Football League, lost his amateur track status for several years as a result of his professional status in football. He was reinstated after he retired from the Forty-Niners, and returned to amateur track and field. Historically, if an association maintained a traditional definition of "amateur" for eligibility, it was generally true that a member athlete could not be a professional in any sport, including sports that he/she does not compete in on the amateur level. However, this rule has become increasingly more flexible. In the NCAA, for example, athletes that have participated in professional sports are allowed to play intercollegiate athletics as long as it is in a different sport than the one they played professionally. For example, 2000 Heisman Trophy winner Chris Weinke of Florida State University was allowed to participate in intercollegiate football after playing minor league baseball. Still, the NCAA maintains that an athlete cannot participate in collegiate athletics in the same sport that he/she played professionally (see note 1).

NOTE _____

1. In the case of *Lasege* v. *NCAA*, 53 S.W. 3d 77 (Ky. 2001), the NCAA appealed a decision to grant a preliminary injunction to a basketball player whom the association had deemed ineligible. Lasege was a basketball player at the University of Louisville, when it was discovered that he had received funds to play basketball professionally before he had arrived in the United States. Louisville requested a waiver of the eligibility rules because Lasege, a native of Nigeria, had been ignorant of the rules of the NCAA when accepting the money to play, and was not aware that his eligibility could be jeopardized by such

actions. Louisville was granted an injunction on the district court level, which was affirmed in the appellate court. The NCAA sought interlocutory relief in this action, which is granted only when the plaintiff can show "extraordinary" cause. The court, in a split decision, found that the NCAA was deserving of this interlocutory relief, and granted the NCAA's motion to disallow Lasege from playing basketball. The court stated, "In this case, we find that the trial court abused its discretion by: (1) substituting its judgment for that of the NCAA on the question of Lasege's intent to professionalize; (2) finding that the NCAA has no interest in this case which weighs against injunctive relief; and (3) declaring NCAA Bylaw 19.8 invalid. This combination of clearly erroneous conclusions constitutes extraordinary cause warranting [interlocutory] relief."

6.2. ELIGIBILITY REQUIREMENTS: COLLEGE AND HIGH SCHOOL

Individual eligibility requirements are a major area of legal concern because they impact both the student-athlete and the institution. For instance, intercollegiate athletics, primarily football and basketball, are potentially financially lucrative and lead to career advancement for the individual athlete or coach. Institutions also may reap tremendous monetary rewards from successful athletic programs. To capture these financial benefits, there are several ways an athletic department can be set up. Some departments operate under the university budget, with revenues going directly to the general fund and expenses covered as line items; others are operated like businesses; still others are separately incorporated and are responsible for covering the expenses of the department solely with revenues taken in by the department. As football and basketball have become more lucrative, the stakes in intercollegiate athletics have become higher and the pressure to be successful has become greater (see Chapter 1, section 1.3.2., "Economic Overview"). Consequently, athletic excellence has been pursued in some instances at the expense of academic performance. College and high school athletic associations have tried to address this problem by establishing academic, amateur, and participation requirements. Eligibility rules that are enacted by a college or a high school athletic association have been instituted to protect student-athletes and institutions.

Many standards must be maintained by individual student-athletes in order for them to be eligible for intercollegiate and interscholastic practice and/or competition. Each school, conference, or association such as the NCAA, has rules and regulations that extend its authority to various areas surrounding sports activities. For collegiate and high school student-athletes there are usually academic standards, rules governing personal conduct, and rules for each individual sport. Individual institutions on the collegiate and scholastic level may also establish eligibility requirements that are stricter than the minimum standards imposed by that institution's conference or association. In addition, a conference may impose a stricter rule than its association.

Under the NCAA's principle of *institutional control*, it is the institution's responsibility to determine which of its student-athletes meet, and do not meet, the eligibility standards. The process of determining eligibility for each student-athlete may be very time-consuming for an institution's athletic department, depending on the number of student-athletes participating, the number of sports offered by the institution, and the complexity of institutional, conference, and association rules, regulations, and interpretations.

In some cases, an institution's conference may assist member institutions in keeping track of the eligibility status of every student-athlete. The most a conference might do in this area is to recheck, confirm, and correct, when necessary, all institutional information. Conferences may aid in the complex process of eligibility determination because correct eligibility status may be the best, if not the first, preventive of rules violations.

An institution's athletic department is usually the primary governing body, and it is responsible for enforcing the rules and regulations relative to the eligibility of student-athletes. Penalties or sanctions may be levied against a student-athlete and the team and/or institution for knowingly or unknowingly competing despite the student-athlete's ineligible status. In addition to enforcement, college and high school athletic associations recommend changes in rules, make policy decisions, and interpret the eligibility rules and regulations.

Eligibility rules that are enacted by a college or high school athletic association are instituted to protect student-athletes and institutions and to promote amateur athletics. Consistent with these objectives, individual eligibility requirements are established with regard to grade point average, academic progress, transferring, age restrictions, years of athletic participation, professional pay, drug use, and full-time student status, among others.

6.2.1. Academic Eligibility: College and High School

The purpose of academic eligibility rules is to ensure that student-athletes are able to perform adequately in the classroom as well as on the field. With the financial stakes to both schools and athletes increasing, athletic associations want to prohibit institutions from recruiting athletes who have no desire to pursue an education. It is important to remember that high schools and colleges are educational institutions whose primary responsibility is to give a student an education. Academic eligibility rules are designed to encourage student-athletes to perform adequately in the classroom; a student who does not meet the academic eligibility requirements will be deemed ineligible. Thus, student-athletes, coaches, and athletic directors want to ensure that the academic requirements are met. A delicate balance must be struck between the educational institution and the governing athletic association concerning which entity will develop academic eligibility rules. There is often a conflict between allowing institutional self-control over academic standards and the need for governing associations to set uniform minimum standards for their member institutions. After many academic scandals, associations have increased the number of minimum rules that institutions must abide by.

6.2.1.1. Initial Eligibility: NCAA

The grade point average is one method the NCAA has employed to ensure that student-athletes are academically qualified to participate at the collegiate level. The grade point average is also used by the several conferences to determine the student-athletes' eligibility. The grade point average (GPA) has long been used and recognized as a measure of a student's academic achievement. To compute a student's GPA, the letter grade in each course is converted to the 4.000 scale (A = 4, B = 3, C = 2, D = 1, F = 0). Grade points are weighted according to the number of credits awarded for each class. The points are then totaled for the courses to be included in the computation, and that total is divided by the number of courses. A student's GPA is usually calculated for each academic term each year, and cumulatively for the student's entire high school or college career. The method and the subjects to be considered in the computation of a student's GPA vary from school to school. The GPA is used both as a measure of initial eligibility at the interscholastic level and as an indicator of progress to maintain the athlete's eligibility at the collegiate level. The use of GPA in determining eligibility will be discussed in this section.

The grade point average is a mechanism whereby the NCAA and/or the conferences and schools can measure a student-athlete's success in the classroom by comparing that student-athlete's grade with a selected marker (i.e., 2.0 GPA). A student-athlete who is not able to maintain a grade above that marker can be deemed ineligible for athletic participation. Rules regarding the grade point average have been subject to judicial review. One issue before the courts is which types of courses should be included in the computation of the grade point average. For example, should physical education courses involving athletic skills be included? The NCAA has attempted to address these issues.

In 1983, the NCAA passed Proposition 48 (hereinafter referred to as Prop 48), which required an incoming freshman student-athlete to achieve both a grade point average of 2.0 in a core curriculum of at least eleven academic courses, and a score of at least 700 on the SAT test or an 18 composite score on the ACT. Proponents of Prop 48 saw the core curriculum requirements as providing an athlete exposure to a solid base of academic work. It also eliminated the use of non-core curriculum courses, such as physical education classes, from being used to increase overall GPA. The test score requirement would also provide some uniformity in standards among institutions. Prop 48 was a signal to high school athletes that they needed to play close attention to their academic preparation if they planned to participate in college athletics. It was designed to give them a better chance of obtaining a college degree and to end the exploitation of talented athletes that had been commonplace at many Division I institutions.

In an attempt to ease the criticism of Prop 48, the concept of "partial qualifier" was introduced in 1991. A *partial qualifier* was a student-athlete who met some, but not all, of the requirements for first-year eligibility under Prop 48. A partial qualifier could still receive institutional financial aid, including an athletic scholarship, but could not play or practice with the team as a freshman. The student-athlete would have only three years of eligibility remaining.

In August 1994, the NCAA's Initial Eligibility Clearinghouse came into existence. This central clearinghouse determines the initial eligibility of all incoming freshman student-athletes. Under the new Proposition 16 (Prop 16), an "initial eligibility index" was established that uses a *sliding scale* to determine the eligibility status of incoming collegiate freshman. For example, a student who carries a 2.50 GPA in high school core courses (see exhibit 6.1), needs to score only 820 on the SAT or a total score of 68 on the ACT. However, a student with a core GPA of 2.0 must receive a 1010 SAT score or sum of 86 on the ACT. This provides some flexibility for students who do not score well on the test, yet are solid students in a classroom environment, and students who do not perform as well in the classroom can compensate for this deficiency with higher test scores.

The NCAA presently divides incoming freshman into three categories: qualifiers (as described above), partial qualifiers, and non-qualifiers (see exhibit 6.2). A qualifier is a student who has met all of the minimum academic eligibility standards set out by the association and institution. If a student-athlete does not

Exhibit 6.1
Minimum Core-Curriculum and Grade-Point Average Requirements for Initial Eligibility

Courses	Effective August 1, 1995 (for those student-ath-letes first entering a col-legiate institution on or after August 1, 1995)	Effective August 1, 1996 (for those student-ath-letes first entering a col-legiate institution on or after August 1, 1996)
English	3 years	4 years
Mathematics	2 years	2 years (at the level of Algebra I or above)
Natural/physical science	2 years	2 years
Social science	2 years	2 years
Additional academic courses in English, math or natural/ physical science	2 years	1 year
Additional academic courses in any of the above areas or foreign language, computer science, philosophy or nondoctrinal religion	2 years	2 years
Core curriculum grade-point average	2.000	See Bylaw 14.3.1.1.1 for initial-eligibility index

meet the qualifying standards under the sliding scale used by the NCAA, a similar scale is used to determine if the student-athlete can be considered a partial qualifier. Entering students must meet lower standards than total qualifiers for GPA and SAT/ACT to receive partial qualification status. The third group of incoming student-athletes is known as non-qualifiers. These are students who either have not graduated from high school or have not met the GPA or SAT/ACT requirements to become a partial qualifier. Non-qualifiers are not allowed to practice or compete with the institution's team, and are not allowed to receive any athletic scholarship monies.

Under Prop 16, while partial qualifiers and non-qualifiers are not allowed to compete during their first academic year, it is possible for these students to participate in four seasons of competition in college. If a partial qualifier or non-qualifier receives a baccalaureate degree before the beginning of his or her fifth year of academic eligibility, that student-athlete will receive an additional, fourth year of competitive eligibility.

NOTES

1. The following are cases where eligibility requirements concerning grade point average were challenged by student-athletes:

(a.) In *Bowers v. NCAA*, 130 F.Supp.2d 610 (D.N.J. 2001), a student-athlete who had been determined by the NCAA to be a non-qualifier brought a suit against the association, claiming that he had been discriminated against due to a learning disability under the Americans with Disabilities Act (see section 16.3.1.4., "Americans with Disabilities Act"), among other state claims. He also brought claims of discrimination against Temple

Exhibit 6.2

Relationships Between Academic Requirements, Recruitment, Financial Aid, and Eligibility (Bylaw 14.3) for High School Graduates First Entering During the 2001–2002 Academic Year

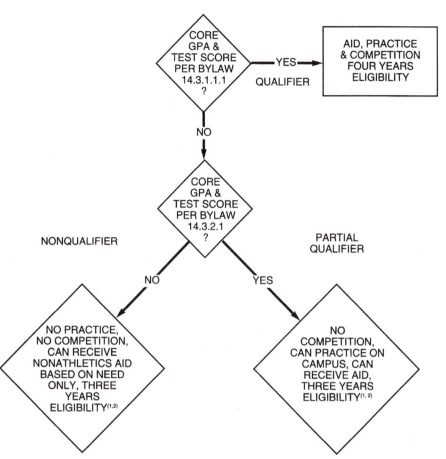

1. A fourth season of intercollegiate competition shall be granted to a partial qualifier (per Bylaw 14.02.9.2) or non-qualifier (per Bylaw 14.02.9.3) provided that at the beginning of the fifth academic year following the student-athlete's initial, full-time collegiate enrollment, the student-athlete has received a baccalaureate degree (see Bylaw 14.3.3.1).

2. A fourth season of intercollegiate competition shall be granted to a student-athlete with a diagnosed learning disability, provided that at the beginning of the fifth academic year following the student-athlete's initial, full-time collegiate enrollment, the student-athlete has completed at least 75 percent of his or her designated degree program and the specified conditions are met (see Bylaws 14.3.3.2 and 14.3.3.2.1).

University, the University of Iowa, and American International College because they stopped recruiting him after he was found to be ineligible for intercollegiate competition. The NCAA decided that Bowers did not qualify because he did not satisfy the core course requirements of the initial eligibility clearinghouse. The court decided for the NCAA, deciding that the NCAA was not subject to the ADA because it was not a public entity. In numerous appeals, Bowers was not successful in receiving any injunctive relief which would have allowed him to compete.

(b.) In *Cole v. NCAA*, 120 F.Supp.2d 1060 (N.D. Ga. 2000), a high school student who had been diagnosed with a learning disability was classified as a partial qualifier under NCAA rules after entering a waiver allowing him to qualify completely. Cole's high school grades did not qualify him as even a partial qualifier. He argued that the NCAA was violating the Americans with Disabilities Act by not allowing him to play in his freshman season of college. The court did not grant Cole an injunction to compete for two reasons. (See section 16.3.1.4., "Americans with Disabilities Act.") First, the case had been rendered moot because Cole's one year of ineligibility as a partial qualifier had passed. Second, the court stated, "Abandoning the eligibility requirements altogether for this or any athlete is unreasonable as a matter of law and is not required by the ADA. In addition, the NCAA's rules and decisions regarding the concerns and challenges of student-athletes are entitled to considerable deference and this court is reluctant to replace the NCAA sub-committee as the decision-maker on private waiver applications."

(c.) In *Cureton v. NCAA*, 37 F.Supp.2d 687 (E.D. Pa. 1999), *rev'd.* 198 F.3d 107 (3rd Cir. 1999), two potential college student-athletes brought a suit against the NCAA, claiming that the association's initial eligibility rules violated Title IV of the Civil Rights Act of 1964 because the SAT test unintentionally discriminated against African-Americans. (See Chapter 15, section 15.3.2.3., "Title VII of the Civil Rights Act of 1964.") The students had maintained A grade point averages on the high school level, yet both had not achieved the minimum SAT score to qualify for initial eligibility on the collegiate level. In fact, the students ranked fifth and twenty-seventh in a graduating class of 305 students. Although the students were able to achieve admission to college based on grades alone, they were not allowed to receive athletic financial aid or compete in athletics under NCAA rules. The federal appeals court ruled for the NCAA, deciding that although it did receive some federal financial assistance, the NCAA was not subject to this federal legislation as a private entity.

(d.) In *Adams v. Kansas State University*, 27 F.Supp.2d 469 (S.D.N.Y. 1998), a student-athlete brought a claim against Kansas State University because KSU withdrew a full athletic scholarship offer to Adams after it was realized that Adams was a non-qualifier under NCAA eligibility standards. The court decided in favor of Kansas State under the doctrine of sovereign immunity.

(e.) In *Tatum v. NCAA*, 992 F.Supp. 1114 (E.D. Mo. 1998), a student-athlete sought an injunction allowing him to play basketball although he had not qualified under initial eligibility standards adopted by the NCAA. The NCAA did not accept Tatum's ACT score that was received under non-standard conditions. The court refused to award Tatum a preliminary injunction, stating that he did not have a likelihood of winning the case on the merits, and it was uncertain whether or not he would suffer irreparable harm as a result of not playing basketball.

(f.) In *Hall v. NCAA*, 985 F.Supp. 782 (N.D. Ill. 1997), an aspiring student-athlete sought an injunction that would allow him to qualify under NCAA initial eligibility standards. The NCAA initial eligibility clearinghouse had decided that four courses that Hall, the lead plaintiff, took as a high school student, Microsoft Office, Microsoft Works, Scripture, and Ethics/Morality, did not qualify as "core courses" and therefore did not count toward the thirteen core courses needed for eligibility. The courts decided against granting a preliminary injunction for the students stating, among other items, that "Plaintiffs have no more than a negligible chance of success on the merits with regard to any of the nine counts in their Complaint. Thus, the preliminary injunction must be denied," and "the NCAA would suffer great harm if the preliminary injunction were granted improvidently because it would have allowed Reggie to make an end-run around the NCAA's well-established and consistently applied initial eligibility requirements."

(g.) In *Phillip v. NCAA*, 118 F.3d 131 (2nd Cir. 1997), the NCAA appealed the decision of a trial court which issued a preliminary injunction allowing a student-athlete to compete, although he had not satisfied NCAA initial eligibility requirements. The appellate court overturned the decision of the trial court, concluding that the trial court had erred in assessing that the NCAA had arbitrarily not granted Phillip a waiver. The appellate court stated, "The district court purported to find without adequate explanation that some sort of a contractual duty was owed by the NCAA to Phillip as a result of the contracts between Fairfield and the NCAA and Phillip and the NCAA. We express no view of whether such a duty did exist. However, we think it clear that the district court erred in finding that the NCAA evidenced bad faith simply by acting arbitrarily."

(h.) In *Ganden v. NCAA*, No. 96C6953 1996 U.S. Dist. LEXIS 17368 (N.D. Ill. Nov. 21, 1996), a district court did not grant a preliminary injunction for a student-athlete who alleged that he was discriminated against under Title III of the Americans with Disabilities Act. The court decided against granting the injunction because Ganden would not be able to prove that he was intentionally discriminated against due to his disability, and therefore did not have a likelihood of success on the merits of his case. Following the case, the NCAA eased its initial eligibility policy toward learning disabled students, adopting Division I Bylaw 13.3.1.2.1.1 in 1997. This rule allowed any student diagnosed with a learning disability to use all core courses completed prior to initial full-time enrollment at the collegiate institution. The determination as to whether courses taken at the high school would constitute core courses is now made on the basis of a statement issued to the high school where the student completed the classes.

(i.) In *Associated Students Inc. v. NCAA*, 493 F.2d 1251 (9th Cir. 1974), the court held that the purpose of the 1.6 GPA rule was to guarantee that only bona fide students would be eligible to participate in intercollegiate athletics in their first year, to help discourage recruiting violations, and to encourage weak students to concentrate on developing proper study skills prior to being involved in time-consuming intercollegiate athletics. The court found that the rule was reasonably related to its purposes, even as applied to students who had earned a 1.6 GPA after the first year, but had failed to predict a 1.6 GPA prior to being admitted to college.

(j.) A leading case in the area of academic requirements for intercollegiate participation is *Parrish v. NCAA*, 361 F.Supp. 1220 (W.D. La. 1973), *aff'd.*, 506 F.2d 1028 (5th Cir. 1975). Parish and some fellow basketball players sought injunctive relief in this litigation to prevent member institutions from enforcing an NCAA rule that declared players ineligible if they did not predict a grade point average of 1.6 when entering college (the 1.6 rule was the predecessor of the 2.0 rule, and it was stricter). The court held that the 1.6 rule limiting eligibility did not raise a federal question since there was no restriction of constitutional rights. The court ruled that judicial intervention was not required for a rule that was enacted and implemented by a private, voluntary organization. This case and several others indicate that courts will allow amateur athletic organizations to make reasonable rules related to academic requirements.

2. For more information on NCAA initial eligibility requirements, see the following law review articles:

(a.) Jay Cherwin, "Not-So-Great Expectations: The NCAA's Initial Eligibility Requirements," 9 *Kansas Journal of Law and Public Policy* 706 (Summer 2000).

(b.) "Title VI—Third Circuit Upholds Viability of Standardized Test Scores as a Component of Freshman Athletic Eligibility Requirements.—*Cureton v. NCAA*, 198 F.3d 107 (3d. Cir. 1999)," 114 *Harvard Law Review* 947 (January 2001).

(c.) Tyler J. Murray, "Illegalizing the NCAA's Eligibility Rules: Did *Cureton v. NCAA* Go Too Far, or Not Far Enough?" 26 *Journal of Legislation* 101 (2000).

(d.) Lee J. Rosen, "Proposition 16 and the NCAA Initial Eligibility Standards: Putting the Student Back in Student-Athlete," 50 *Catholic University Law Review* 175 (Fall 2000).

(e.) Adam S. Taylor, and Darren M. Traub, "*Cureton v. NCAA*: Scrutinizing Proposition 16 and the Consequences of Its Disparate Impact on Prospective Minority Student-Athletes," 7 *Sports Law Journal* 59 (Spring 2000).

(f.) Michael Thompson, "Educational Necessity or Simple Discrimination: The NCAA's Initial Eligibility Standards and Prop. 16," 9 *Seton Hall Journal of Sport Law* 521 (1999).

6.2.1.2. Grade Point Average: High School

In an attempt to guarantee academic achievement for their student-athletes, most high schools have adopted grade point average standards. These rules serve the dual purpose of assuring that their student-athletes make sufficient academic progress during high school and are eligible for participation in intercollegiate athletics as incoming freshman. A generally accepted rule concerning grade point average and eligibility on the high school level is the "no pass, no play rule."

For example, in 1985, legislators in Texas passed such a rule requiring all students involved in extracurricular activities to maintain a minimum grade of 70 in each class to retain eligibility. A score below 70 during a six-week grading period will result in ineligibility during the next six-week grading period. It is important to note that incoming college freshman eligibility is dependent upon both the grade point average standard, and the standardized test score. In most cases, courts have declined to review high school eligibility rules and, instead, to leave these matters in the hands of the schools and associations.

NOTES _____

1. In *Hoot v. Michigan High School Athletic Ass'n*, 853 F.Supp. 243 (E.D. Mich. 1994), a student who had not achieved a satisfactory grade point average to compete on the high school level (.981 out of 4.0) brought a case against the MHSAA alleging a violation of equal protection and the Americans with Disabilities Act because Hoot had been diagnosed with a learning disability. The MHSAA was denied a preliminary injunction dismissing the case, having not supplied sufficient information to the court. The court believed "that a genuine issue of material facts exists as to each count within the Complaint. While discovery and an answer may shed light on some of the factual issues, the MHSAA's Motion for Summary Judgment must be denied without prejudice."

2. In *Thompson v. Fayette County Public Schools*, 786 S.W.2d 879 (Ka. Ct. App. 1990), the plaintiff sued the school district, claiming a violation of his high school son's civil rights because he was excluded from the wrestling team for failure to maintain a satisfactory grade point average. The court of appeals affirmed the trial court ruling by stating that there was no violation of the student's rights since he had neither a property interest nor any fundamental right to participate in extracurricular activities.

3. In *Bartmess v. Board of Trustees*, 726 P.2d 801 (Mont. 1986), the plaintiff challenged the enforcement of a school district's eligibility rule that required a student to maintain a 2.0 GPA for the preceding nine-week period as a prerequisite to participate in any extracurricular activities in the following nine-week period. The interesting aspect of this case is that the school district's 2.0 rule was more stringent than the 1.0 GPA required by the Montana High School Association. The court held that the school district's no-pass rule had a rational relationship to the state's legitimate goal and therefore ruled in favor of the school district.

6.2.1.3. *Academic Progress: NCAA*

At the intercollegiate level, the general rule for continued academic eligibility under NCAA rules (Divisions I and II) is that a student-athlete, after the first academic year, must maintain satisfactory progress toward a degree based on the member institution's academic eligibility rules, the NCAA rules, and the member institution's conference affiliation. Regulations for continuing eligibility are different than initial eligibility rules for two reasons. First, academic progress rules are set by the academic institutions or conferences in addition to those of the NCAA, which allows institutions to create standards that relate to their own academic programs. Second, rules for continuing eligibility generally deal solely with grade point average while at the institution, and not standardized test scores, which are only used for initial eligibility. The purpose of this rule is to ensure that the student-athlete is meeting certain academic standards. Like the grade point average standard, academic progress was initiated to guarantee that student-athletes were receiving an education, and were not solely at the institution to participate in athletics.

Bylaw 14.4.1 of the *2001–02 NCAA Manual* explains the academic progress rule:

> **Satisfactory-Progress Requirements—All Divisions**. To be eligible to represent an institution in intercollegiate athletics competition, a student-athlete shall maintain satisfactory progress toward a baccalaureate or equivalent degree at that institution as determined by the regulations of that institution. As a general requirement, "satisfactory progress" is to be interpreted at each member institution by the academic authorities who determine the meaning of such phrases for all students, subject to controlling legislation of the conference(s) or similar association of which the institution is a member. (See Constitution 3.2.4.10 regarding the obligations of members to publish their satisfactory-progress requirements for student-athletes.) (Note: The restrictions, exceptions and waivers set forth in Bylaws 14.4.3.4.4, 14.4.3.4.5 and 14.4.3.7 also apply to the general requirements for good academic standing and satisfactory progress.

The NCAA requires that a student-athlete satisfactorily complete an average of at least twelve semester or quarter hours of coursework for all regular academic terms or satisfactorily complete twenty-four semester or thirty-six quarter hours since the beginning of the institution's preceding regular two semesters or three quarters (*2001–02 NCAA Division 1 Manual*, Bylaw 14.4.3.1). In addition, a student-athlete must have completed successfully at least 25 percent of the course requirements in the student's degree program when entering his or her third year of enrollment, 50 percent by the fourth year, and 75 percent by the fifth year (*2001–02 NCAA Division 1 Manual*, Bylaw 14.4.3.2). In addition, academic progress in college requires that a student-athlete be accepted into a degree-granting program by the beginning of the third year of enrollment and thereafter make satisfactory progress toward that specific degree (*2001–02 NCAA Division 1 Manual*, Bylaw 14.4.3.2.1). Schools, instead of the NCAA, are generally handed the administrative duties of monitoring the satisfactory academic progress of their student-athletes. Cases involving academic progress have rarely reached the level of the courts. It has been the policy of most courts to uphold the ideal of institutional control and limited judicial review in cases involving these matters.

NOTES

1. In *Matthews v. NCAA*, 79 F.Supp.2d 1199 (E.D. Wash. 1999), the plaintiff was not allowed to play in intercollegiate competition because he did not qualify under the "75/25" rule of the NCAA. This rule states, "A student-athlete shall earn at least 75 percent of the minimum number of semester . . . hours required for satisfactory progress during the academic year. The student-athlete shall earn no more than 25 percent of the minimum number of semester . . . hours required for satisfactory progress during the summer." The NCAA applied this rule to ensure that student-athletes undertake a course load similar to other college students. Matthews requested a preliminary injunction allowing him to play, but was denied by the court. Matthews brought his case on the Americans with Disabilities Act because he had a diagnosed learning disability, and on due process because he had not been notified directly of his status. (See Chapter 13, section 13.6.1.4., "Americans with Disabilities Act (ADA)".) The court decided that the NCAA had accommodated Matthews' disability by granting him two previous waivers in the past, and also found that, due to the fact that the NCAA is a private entity, it is not subject to federal claims of due process violations.

2. For a case in which the academic progress rule was challenged, see *Hall v. University*

of Minnesota, 530 F.Supp. 104 (D. Minn. 1982). Hall, a former basketball player, brought suit against the University of Minnesota for its failure to admit him to a degree-granting program, which resulted in his being declared ineligible to play basketball for his senior year. Big Ten Conference rules require a student-athlete to be enrolled in such a degree-granting program to maintain eligibility. The court found in favor of Hall, stating that a constitutionally protected property interest in a potential professional basketball contract was involved; therefore, Hall's due process rights had been violated.

3. See the following law review article for a discussion of academic eligibility in the NCAA: Alfred Dennis Mathewson, "The Eligibility Paradox," 7 *Villanova Sports & Entertainment Law Forum* 83 (2002).

6.2.1.4. *Academic Progress: High School*

Academic progress rules are designed to ensure that student-athletes enroll in the type of courses required to obtain a high school diploma or college degree. At the interscholastic level, most state high school athletic associations do not set minimum academic progress rules. Instead, most state associations allow the individual schools to set the minimum standards for academic progress. The most common standard academic progress rule is a "no pass, no play" standard. This standard signifies that a student-athlete must maintain a minimum "passing" grade point average in order to participate in interscholastic athletics. Depending on the preference of the institution, the passing standard can be set at a "C" level or "D" level. Unlike intercollegiate athletics, high schools are allowed a greater amount of latitude when drafting and administering academic progress regulations. The Massachusetts Interscholastic Athletic Association (MIAA), for example, has the following regulations:

58. Student Eligibility: Academic Requirements

58.1 A student must secure during the last marking period preceding the contest (e.g., second quarter marks and not semester grades determine third-quarter eligibility) a passing grade in the equivalent of four traditional English courses.

58.2 A student cannot any time represent a school unless that student is taking courses which would provide Carnegie Units equivalent to four traditional English courses.

58.3 To be eligible for the fall marking period, students are required to have passed for the previous academic year the equivalent of four traditional year-long major English courses.

58.4 Academic eligibility of all students shall be considered as official and determining only on the published date when the report cards for that ranking period are to be issued to the parents of all students within a particular class.

Note: The MIAA academic eligibility standards are designed to ensure that a student is fully enrolled in school and actively engaged in his/her academic life on a consistent basis throughout the school year. When utilizing a 4 × 4 block schedule, a student must pass at least two of the four required major courses (or equivalent) in each academic marking period.

The questions you must ask in determining eligibility are:

"How many minutes per day/week/semester does this course meet?"

"How many credits toward graduation as approved in advance by school committee policy will be offered for this course?"

"Is this equivalent to past academic requirements?"

58.5. Incomplete grades may not be counted toward eligibility.

58.6. A student who repeats work upon which she/he has once received credit cannot count that subject a second time for eligibility.

58.7 A student cannot count for eligibility any subject taken during the summer, unless that subject has been previously pursued and failed.

58.8 *KINDLY NOTE: Previous reference to special education students with 502.4 prototypes is rendered valueless given current special education law. Academically ineligible special education students may not participate unless a waiver has been requested and granted by the MIAA.* (*Source*: Part IV, Article 58, 2001–2003 Rules and Regulations Governing Athletics, Massachusetts Interscholastic Association.)

A case in which the academic progress rules of an interscholastic state association were addressed is *Jordan v. Indiana High School Athletic Ass'n*, 16 F.3d 785 (7th Cir. 1994). Jordan was a high school student who had serious academic problems during his first two years at Marshall Metro, in Chicago. In his third year, Jordan was absent so many times that he was forced to withdraw from school. He did not receive any academic credit for that school year, and he was not allowed to participate on any athletic teams due to his substandard academic performance. Jordan then transferred to a school in Fort Wayne, Indiana, where he began his junior year again, and played for the high school basketball team. Jordan turned around his academic performance in Fort Wayne. However, before his senior year, the IHSAA decided that Jordan could not compete because he had already been eligible for eight semesters of competition. On the district court level, Jordan was granted a preliminary injunction allowing him to play in his senior season. The IHSAA appealed the decision, and the appeals court decided that the case was moot because Jordan had completed his senior year of competition, and he would not be affected by the outcome of the trial. The judgment of the district court was vacated, and remanded with instructions to dismiss the case as moot.

NOTE _____

1. In *Stone v. Kansas State High School Activities Ass'n, Inc.*, 761 P.2d 1255 (Kan. Ct. App. 1988), the plaintiff, Stone, was declared ineligible for the 1987 fall semester because he had passed only four classes the previous semester, not the KHSAA requirement of five classes. During the summer of 1987, Stone was tutored by his teacher of English, the class he failed during the 1987 spring semester. During September 1987, Stone and his parents asked for his eligibility to be restored because he had made up the fifth class requirement over the summer. The KHSAA executive board denied his request because of a rule that prevents a student from making up work after the end of the semester for the purpose of regaining eligibility. Stone challenged this rule on due process and equal protection grounds. In October 1987, Stone sought and was granted a temporary restraining order prohibiting KHSAA and the school district from preventing his participation in interscholastic activity during the 1987 fall semester. The court ruled that the no makeup rule had a rational basis and its application to Stone did not violate his due process rights. Stone also argued the rule on equal protection grounds because of another student who had transferred from Iowa to Kansas. This student did not pass the required number of classes in Iowa but was allowed to make up the coursework during the summer. Upon transferring to Kansas for the fall semester, the student was declared eligible. Stone argued that if this student was allowed to make up work during the summer and then transfer to Kansas, and be eligible for participation, not allowing Stone the same opportunity to make up coursework during the summer was a violation of his equal protection rights. The court determined that Iowa allowed classes to be made up during the summer; therefore, when the student transferred to Kansas, he had already completed the necessary requirements to restore his eligibility in Iowa. Because he was eligible in Iowa, he was therefore eligible for participation in Kansas. The court ruled that the difference between these two students'

situations was not based on a suspect classification, and therefore Stone's equal protection rights were not violated. The appellate court reversed the district court's granting of a temporary restraining order to Stone.

6.2.2. Participation Rules

6.2.2.1. Redshirting: NCAA

The practice of redshirting is a means by which to extend the playing career of a student-athlete by postponing or passing over a year of intercollegiate athletic participation, while not affecting the student-athlete's maximum allowable time for participating. The *2001–02 NCAA Division I Manual* reads:

> A student-athlete shall complete his or her seasons of participation within five calendar years from the beginning of the semester or quarter in which the student-athlete first registered for a minimum program of studies in a collegiate institution, with time spent in the Armed Forces, on official church missions or with recognized foreign aid services of the U.S. government being excepted. For foreign students, service in the armed forces or on an official church mission of the student's home country is considered equivalent to such service in the United States.

Redshirting rules are designed to allow delaying a student-athlete's eligibility on the basis of legitimate factors such as injury or academic difficulty, while preventing abuse by coaches and student-athletes seeking to gain a competitive advantage through an extension of a student-athlete's career. High school athletic associations and conferences, which do not allow redshirting, employ a four-year eligibility rule. Under most high school association rules, a student-athlete has eight consecutive semesters in which to participate in interscholastic competition, beginning with the student-athlete's entry into the ninth grade.

The practice of redshirting may be initiated for a number of reasons, including the following:

1. *Medical reasons.* Includes a serious injury or illness occurring in the off-season or before the start of the season. The student-athlete might consider it advantageous to recover fully from such a problem by postponing for a year the resumption of athletic competition (*2001–02 NCAA Division I Manual*, Bylaw 14.4.3.6(a)).
2. *Academic reasons.* Includes a student-athlete's becoming ineligible for play because of low grades or wishing to study abroad for a year of college education (*2001–02 NCAA Division I Manual*, Bylaw 14.4.3).
3. *Transfers.* The five-year rule also protects the playing career of first-time transfer students, allowing them the opportunity to switch schools once without eliminating one of their four seasons of playing time. The student-athlete must complete one full year of academic residence at the institution before being eligible to compete (Division I) (*2001–02 NCAA Division I Manual*, Bylaw 14.6.1).
4. *Coaching strategy.* The coach might ask a student-athlete to redshirt a season because the coach wants to use and schedule the player's eligibility to fit the long-term needs and requirements of the team.

Colleges, competing under NCAA governance, are allowed to have their student-athlete's compete in four complete seasons of play within five calendar years (in Division I) from the beginning of the semester or quarter in which the student-athlete first registers in a minimum full-time program of studies in a collegiate institution. Any participation during a season in an intercollegiate sport, including a scrimmage with an outside opponent, counts as a season of competition toward the four-year total, as does any season of competition at the junior-college level.

A case involving this type of situation is *NCAA v. Brinkworth*, 680 So.2d 1081 (Fl. Dis. Ct. App. 1996). Brinkworth, a football player for the University of Miami, was redshirted his first year at Miami, and proceeded to participate in three full years of competition. During his fourth year at Miami, as the starting fullback, Brinkworth was injured during the first game of the season. He was unable to compete for the remainder of the season due to the injury. Miami applied for an eligibility waiver on behalf of Brinkworth from the NCAA, and his application was denied. Based on this decision, Miami did not allow Brinkworth to compete until a resolution was made with the NCAA, because Miami could have faced sanctions if they allowed him to play. Brinkworth initially received a preliminary injunction from a state court allowing him to play, and the NCAA appealed this decision. The appeals court sided with the NCAA, stating that the procedures for waivers and appeals were fair and not arbitrary; many student-athletes in Brinkworth's situation had been denied waivers in the past. The court found that it was not their place to interfere with how the NCAA interprets its own rules, concluding, "The issue Brinkworth seeks to raise is beyond our province to review. It is up to the NCAA to interpret its own rules, not the judiciary. The NCAA followed fair procedures in allowing the university the opportunity to state its case on behalf of the student-athlete, including an appeal within the NCAA when dissatisfied with the initial ruling. As the procedures were adequate and fair, there was no basis on which to intervene in the internal affairs of the NCAA." This decision demonstrates the reluctance that courts have in interfering with legitimate rules and regulations that the NCAA institutes. The court reasoned that it is up to the NCAA's policy of allowing five years to complete four years of athletic eligibility.

NOTES

1. In *Jones v. NCAA*, 679 So.2d 1337 (La. 1996), the student-athlete, Jones, was originally granted an injunction to allow him to play intercollegiate football despite running out of NCAA eligibility after his fourth year. The appellate court, in a short decision, overturned the lower court, stating, "Courts should not interfere with the internal affairs of a private association except in cases when the affairs and proceedings have not been conducted fairly and honestly, or in the cases of fraud, lack of jurisdiction, the invasion of property or pecuniary rights, or when the action complained of is capricious, arbitrary, or unjustly discriminatory."

2. A case involving redshirting is *Kupec v. Atlantic Coast Conference*, 399 F. Supp. 1377 (M.D. N.C. 1975), in which a football player sought an injunction from enforcement of the Atlantic Coast Conference (ACC) eligibility rule that allows a medical redshirt if a student-athlete incurs an injury or illness which prevents him or her from participating in more than one football game or more than three contests in other sports. Kupec played during the 1971, 1972, and 1974 seasons. During 1973, Kupec played in two games before being injured and missing the rest of the season. The court found that the ACC was not in error in ruling Kupec ineligible because he participated in two games during the 1973 season, and that participation constituted a loss of eligibility for that year.

3. The NCAA grants what it terms a "hardship waiver," which is often confused with redshirting. A student-athlete may be granted an additional year of competition by the Eligibility Committee for reasons of *hardship*, which is defined as an incapacity resulting from an injury or illness that has occurred under all of the following conditions:

    (a) The incapacitating injury or illness occurs in one of the four seasons of intercollegiate competition at any two-year or four-year collegiate institution;

    (b) The injury or illness occurs prior to the completion of the first half of the traditional playing season in that sport (measured by the number of contests or dates of competition rather than calendar days) and results in incapacity to compete for the remainder of the traditional playing season;

    (c) The injury or illness occurs when the student-athlete has not participated in more than two events or 20 percent (whichever number is greater) of the institution's completed events in his or her sport. (*2001–02 Division I NCAA Manual*, Bylaw 14.2.4.)

6.2.2.2. Redshirting: High School

At the interscholastic level, the practice of redshirting is not as commonplace as on the intercollegiate level, primarily because the rules do not allow the flexibility provided at the intercollegiate level. Therefore, the only alternative at the high school level in many states may be keeping back a student-athlete for an extra year before the student-athlete enters high school. This allows a student-athlete another year to develop his or her body and playing skills before entering high school competition. However, the student-athlete who does this must be careful about maximum age restrictions. For instance, the Massachusetts Interscholastic Athletic Association (MIAA) does not allow students aged nineteen and above to compete in high school athletics unless they turn nineteen after September 1 of the school year (*MIAA Rules and Regulations Governing Athletics 2001–2003*, Part IV). The MIAA also restricts competition to twelve consecutive athletic seasons (fall, winter, and spring grading semesters for four years) past the eighth grade. However, although it occurs infrequently, the MIAA Eligibility Review Board can authorize exceptions to the twelve-consecutive-season rule because of injury or illness.

High school regulations prohibiting the practice of redshirting have been justified on the basis of preventing competition between individuals with vast differences in strength, speed, and experience. Such rules are designed to promote equitable competition and player safety as well as to prevent schools from abusing athletes by holding them back a grade or "redshirting" them to allow them to mature and develop athletically. However, high school rules may make exceptions for students who academically fail a grade, enabling the student to maintain athletic eligibility, since the retention was not related to athletics. Therefore, the student-athlete is allowed to compete in the fifth year but cannot compete for more than four seasons. Notable, however, are the inroads that disabled athletes have made in interscholastic athletics after the passage of the Americans with Disabilities Act. Many state associations or individual institutions have made allowances for disabled athletes to compete athletically even if they are not able to finish their studies within the prescribed period allotted to non-disabled student-athletes (see Chapter 16, section 16.3.1.4, "Americans with Disabilities Act (ADA)").

NOTES ————————————————————————————————————

1. In the following cases, courts upheld association redshirt rules:

(a) In *Rhodes v. Ohio High School Athletic Ass'n*, 939. F. Supp. 584 (N.D. Ohio 1996), the court upheld the OHSAA's rule regarding eight semesters of play. The plaintiff, Rhodes, sought a preliminary injunction allowing him to play interscholastic athletics under the Americans with Disabilities Act. (See Chapter 16, section 16.3.1.4., "Americans with Disabilities Act [ADA].") Although the court found that there would be irreparable harm if the plaintiff was not allowed to compete, it found that the plaintiff did not have a likelihood of success on the merits, and therefore the injunction was denied.

(b) In *Mitchell v. Louisiana High School Athletic Ass'n.*, 430 F.2d 1155 (5th Cir. 1970), a redshirt rule that restricted all incoming high school students who voluntarily repeated eighth grade to six semesters of competition rather than the normal eight semesters was held valid because it was rationally related to a legitimate state interest.

(c) In *David v. Louisiana High School Athletic Ass'n.*, 244 So. 2d 292 (La. Ct. App. 1971), a student who repeated a grade for reasons unrelated to athletics may still be validly restricted to six semesters (three years) of athletic eligibility rather than the normal eight semesters (four years).

(d) In *Smith v. Crim*, 240 S.E.2d 884 (Ga. 1977), a student challenged the application of a rule that counted his absence against his four-year limit of eligibility after he dropped out of school for a year to care for his invalid mother. The court, however, upheld the rule because it was rationally related to the goals of assuring fair competition and preventing redshirting.

(e) In *Alabama High School Athletic Ass'n. v. Medders*, 456 So.2d 284 (Ala. Sup. Ct. 1984), a student who had successfully completed but voluntarily repeated eighth grade was declared ineligible to play football on the high school team during his senior year under the eight-semester rule. The court held that although the rule was susceptible to two interpretations, it had been interpreted in the same way as in the student's case for thirty-five years, and that interpretation fell short of fraud, collusion, or arbitrariness.

2. In the following cases, courts struck down association redshirt rules:

(a) In *Bingham v. Oregon School Activities Ass'n*, 37 F. Supp. 2d 1189 (D. Or. 1999), a student-athlete was granted an injunction allowing him to participate in interscholastic athletics although he had been eligible for participation in athletics in eight previous semesters, and therefore was not eligible under Oregon state rules. The student, Bingham, had not played in his freshman year of high school but did compete in his sophomore year. Bingham transferred to another school in Florida before the next school year, and due to academic/learning difficulties, he repeated his sophomore year while continuing in athletics. The family then moved to Oregon, where Bingham enrolled in high school, and competed in athletics as a junior. As a senior he was ruled ineligible under state association rules because he had completed eight semesters of high school. The court ruled for Bingham, deciding that because Bingham had repeated his sophomore year due to his disability, he was covered under the Americans with Disabilities Act, and the waiving of the eight-semester rule by the association would be a reasonable accommodation for Bingham considering his disability.

(b) In *Florida High School Activities Ass'n. v. Bryant*, 313 So.2d 57 (Fla. Dist. Ct. App. 1975), an association sought reversal of a final judgment that found a student eligible to play more than four years of interscholastic basketball. Affirming the judgment, the court of appeals held that for this student, basketball was vital because it provided the impetus for his general scholastic and social development and rehabilitation from prior problems of juvenile delinquency. The student had presented an adequate case of undue hardship, meriting a waiver of the four-year rule.

(c) In *Lee v. Florida High School Activities Ass'n.*, 291 So.2d 636 (Fla. Dist. Ct. App. 1974), the student stayed out of school for ten months to help alleviate his family's troubled financial situation. Upon returning to school, he sought a waiver of the four-year (successive) rule to participate in athletics. It was denied by the association. The court found his participation in athletics would have enhanced his chances of being admitted to college and of winning a scholarship. Except for the four-year rule, the student would have been eligible. Therefore, the court found that the denial of a waiver was a violation of due process because no justification had been given for denying eligibility in such extreme circumstances. The rule was held unconstitutional as it applied to the student.

(d) In *Duffley v. New Hampshire Interscholastic Athletic Ass'n.*, 446 A.2d 462 (N.H. Supp. Ct. 1982), the court held that a student-athlete must be given procedural due process when he or she is denied a waiver of the four-year eligibility rule.

6.2.2.3. *Longevity: NCAA*

The initiation of the NCAA's rule of longevity was to address concerns that some student-athletes, particularly in soccer and track, were gaining experience in amateur leagues in the United States and foreign countries before matriculating at an NCAA member institution. It was believed that these older, more experienced athletes would place younger and more inexperienced athletes at a disadvantage in competition and in competing for scholarship monies.

Bylaw 14.2.3.5 of the *2001–02 NCAA Division Manual* reads:

> Any participation as an individual or a team representative in organized sports competition by a student during each 12-month period after the student's 21st birthday and prior to initial full-time enrollment in a collegiate institution shall count as one year of varsity competition in that sport. Participation in organized competition during time spent in the U.S. armed services shall be excepted.

An important case dealing with longevity in the NCAA is *Butts v. NCAA*, 751 F.2d 609 (3rd Cir. 1984), where the NCAA was successful in upholding the longevity rule (see note 1). It should be noted that the NCAA's longevity rule at the time of the *Butts* case was the twentieth birthday. This was subsequently changed in the 1990s to the twenty-first birthday.

NOTES ───────────────────────────────────

1. The case of *Butts v. NCAA*, 751 F.2d 609 (3rd Cir. 1984), shows how the courts view the purpose of the NCAA longevity rule. Butts had played for the Frederick Military Academy basketball team after reaching the age of twenty. When Butts entered LaSalle, a private university, it was feared that under NCAA Bylaw 5-1-(d)-(3) his post-high school experience would be counted against his four years of college eligibility. Bylaw 5-1-(d)-(3) stated that "any participation by a student as an individual or as a representative of any team in organized competition in a sport during each 12-month period after his 20th birthday and prior to his matriculation at a member institution shall count as one year of varsity competition in that sport." When the NCAA indicated that Butts would be ineligible to play basketball during his senior year, he filed suit against the NCAA and LaSalle, seeking declaratory and injunctive relief. Butts claimed that the bylaw violated 42 U.S.C. §2000d (1982), which states, "No person in the United States shall, on the grounds of race, color, or national origin, be excluded from participation in, be denied the benefits of, or be subjected to discrimination under any program or activity receiving federal financial assistance."

The district court concluded that Butts had shown a strong likelihood that the bylaw had a racially disparate impact (affected some races more than others even though unintentionally); however, it also concluded that the NCAA had advanced a legitimate, nondiscriminatory reason for the bylaw:

> The bylaw is designed and intended to promote equality of competition among its members at each level so as to prevent college athletics and access to athletic scholarships from being dominated by more mature, older, more experienced players, and to discourage high school

students from delaying their entrance into college in order to develop and mature their athletic skills.

The district court held that Butts had the burden of showing that the bylaw was pretextual or that "some other, less intrusive, rule would accomplish the stated objects of the present rule." The district court found that Butts had not shown a reasonable likelihood of being able to meet this burden, and it upheld the rule and the NCAA's position and denied a preliminary injunction.

2. In *Spath v. National Collegiate Athletic Ass'n*, 728 F.2d 25 (1st. Cir. 1984), the plaintiff was a Canadian citizen who had played after his twentieth birthday for a team in Canada prior to entering college in the United States. The plaintiff filed suit after he was deemed ineligible for the fourth season after playing three years of intercollegiate hockey. The court found that the rule was reasonable and the plaintiff's due process rights had not been violated.

3. In *Howard University v. National Collegiate Athletic Ass'n*, 510 F.2d 213 (D.C. Cir. 1975), the court ruled invalid the NCAA's "Foreign Student Rule," NCAA Bylaw 4-(1)-(f)-(2), which provides that if an alien participated in organized athletics in a foreign country after his/her nineteenth birthday, the time spent doing so counts against the athlete's period of collegiate eligibility. Even though the court accepted the rule's purpose, it held that the rule was not closely tailored to achieving its goal because foreigner athletes were punished for activities that citizens participated in without penalty.

6.2.2.4. Longevity: High School

The longevity rule is also used at the high school level. High school athletic associations have been forced to adopt certain rules that limit the age of participants, usually 19 years of age, in interscholastic athletic competition.

NOTES

1. In the following cases, the court upheld the state association's longevity rule:

   a. In *McPherson v. Michigan High School Athletic Ass'n*, 119 F.3d 453 (6th Cir. 1997), the court decided that a rule allowing players to be eligible for only eight semesters of athletic competition was not crafted in order to discriminate against disabled students. The court stated, "The plaintiff has no evidence, and has not even suggested, that the formulation or implementation of the MHSAA's eight-semester rule has in any way been motivated by considerations of barring students with learning disabilities from play." The court dubbed the rule a "neutral" rule, meaning that it was non-discriminatory in its intent. The court did not believe that MHSAA had an obligation to force the MHSAA to waive the eight-semester rule in each case that it was faced with, stating, "To do so would amount to an improper delegation to the MHSAA of this court's responsibility to independently determine whether the rule is, in fact, necessary."

   b. In a case nearly identical to *McPherson, Frye v. Michigan High Sch. Athletic Ass'n*, No. 95-1266, 1997 U.S. App. LEXIS 21071 (6th Cir. Mich. Aug. 5, 1997), the court decided in the same fashion as *McPherson* to allow an association rule prohibiting athletes to compete after eight semesters of eligibility is exhausted.

   c. In *Reaves v. Mills*, 904 F.Supp. 120 (W.D.N.Y. 1995), a student-athlete sought a temporary restraining order allowing him to play in a November 11, 1995, football game and the rest of the interscholastic sport seasons for the academic year. Reaves had been diagnosed in the fourth grade with mild mental retardation, but had been rediagnosed in middle school and determined that he was not in fact mentally retarded. He had, while under the original diagnosis, repeated one grade. The court did not grant the order for Reaves, noting that he was not disabled, and stating, "The State's limitation for participation in interscholastic sports is based upon a student's age, not his or her mental abilities. Therefore, the rule is applied uniformly among the student population regardless of whether a student has a mental disability. It is undisputed that until he turned nineteen years of age, Kelvin fully participated in interscholastic sports at Edison, even while laboring under his alleged disability. Clearly, he was only barred from playing sports once he turned nineteen in August 1995."

2. In the following cases, the court struck down the state association's longevity rule:

a. In *Kling v. Mentor Public School District*, 136 F. Supp. 2d 744 (N.D. Ohio 2001), a student-athlete who suffers from cerebral palsy and a hearing impairment was granted a preliminary injunction allowing him to compete in the public high school district's athletic competitions. The court granted the injunction because it believed that the disabled student had a probability of success of proving at trial that he would suffer irreparable harm in his development by not being allowed to participate in athletics.

b. In *Cruz v. Pennsylvania Interscholastic Athletic Ass'n*, 157 F. Supp. 2d 485 (E.D. Pa. 2001), the court granted a permanent injunction to allow the plaintiff, Luiz Cruz, to participate in interscholastic athletics after the age of eighteen due to learning disabilities. The association rule did not allow Cruz to participate. The court, taking a very active stance in this case, ordered not only that Cruz receive the permanent injunction, but that the association should adopt a waiver procedure to deal with Cruz and other students in similar situations.

c. In *Washington v. Indiana High School Athletic Ass'n*, 181 F.3d 840 (7th Cir. 1999), the court decided to affirm the granting of a preliminary injunction by the trial court to allow the plaintiff, Washington, to participate in interscholastic athletics even though he had passed eight semesters of athletic eligibility. The court decided that IHSAA did not have any legitimate reason why it should not grant a waiver to Washington, stating, "Nor will the record support the argument that a waiver of the rule in Mr. Washington's case would place an undue administrative or financial burden on the IHSAA. The record indicates that Mr. Washington is the only student athlete to seek a waiver because of a learning disability in more than a decade. The few case-by-case analyses that the IHSAA would need to conduct hardly can be described as an excessive burden."

d. In *Johnson v. Florida High School Activities Ass'n*, 102 F.3d 1172 (11th Cir. 1997), a case was brought by an interscholastic athlete, Dennis Johnson, who was ruled ineligible to play for his high school football team because he had reached the age of nineteen during August of his senior year in school. Johnson alleged that the association was discriminating against him because he had learning disabilities, which required him to take extra time in school and caused the situation he was in. Johnson was issued a temporary injunction by the trial court, and was allowed to play during the football season. The association appealed the decision, but the appellate court dismissed the case as moot because Johnson had finished his senior season of football, and therefore whether or not he was ineligible to play was not an arguable point.

e. In *Sandison v. Michigan High School Athletic Ass'n*, 863 F.Supp. 483 (E.D. Mich. 1994), two high school students wished to continue competing on their high school cross-country and track and field teams despite the fact that they were nineteen years old, and had surpassed the MHSAA longevity standard. Both students had suffered from learning disabilities, and were held back a grade in middle school due to academic problems stemming from the disability, and brought their case using the Americans with Disabilities Act. At the time, the MHSAA did not have a waiver procedure for students who had surpassed the longevity standard in high school. The students were successful in receiving a temporary restraining order and meeting the standards necessary for a preliminary injunction allowing them to compete on the teams. The court stated, "Plaintiffs have shown a probability of success on the merits; that they will suffer irreparable harm if they are not permitted to participate on the cross-country and track teams at their respective high schools; that the harm to plaintiffs, if the injunction is not granted, would outweigh any injury that defendants would suffer by the imposition of the injunction; and that the public interest is best served by the issuance of the preliminary injunction."

f. In *Pottgen v. Missouri State High School Activities Ass'n*, 857 F.Supp. 654 (E.D. Mo. 1994), the court granted a preliminary injunction to a student-athlete who wished to compete despite surpassing the state association's longevity standard. Similar to the case in *Sandison*, the student-athlete had repeated a grade due to learning disabilities and was bringing a case using the Americans with Disabilities Act. The court decided that Pottgen had satisfied all four areas necessary for a preliminary injunction, and also asserted, "While there is also a legitimate public interest in regulating interscholastic activities in order to promote fairness and protect the safety and well-being of students, the Court concludes this interest must accommodate the more compelling public interest of prohibiting discrimination against those with disabilities."

6.2.2.5. Transfer Rules: NCAA

At the intercollegiate level of competition, the issue of student-athletes transferring from one institution to another is often a controversial issue. For the student-athlete, the issue centers on the individual's rights to attend school and compete in athletics wherever he or she wishes. For the institutions, conferences, and the NCAA, the rules are designed to prevent continuing recruitment of student-athletes, stability of programs, and to prevent student-athletes from moving from one program to another.

Transfer rules were created to deter: (1) the recruiting of student-athletes by colleges that the student-athlete does not attend; and (2) the shopping around by student-athletes for institutions that seem to offer them the best opportunities for advancing their athletic careers. The courts have generally upheld transfer rules, basing their decisions on the fact that a suspect class has not been involved nor has a fundamental right been violated. The transfer rule need only be rationally related to the legitimate state interest.

A recent case in the area of student-athlete transfer rules in the NCAA is *Tanaka v. University of Southern California*, 252 F.3d 1059 (9th Cir. 2001). A former female soccer player for the University of Southern California (USC) brought an antitrust claim against USC and the Pac-10 Conference, charging that the conference rule on intra-conference transfer was a violation of the Sherman Antitrust Act because it was an unreasonable restraint on her ability to transfer to her school of choice, UCLA. Tanaka charged that this rule was applied to her only because, before leaving the university, she had charged the university and athletic department with academic fraud.

She believed that the rule was enforced in her case as retaliation for her allegations against the athletic department. The court decided in favor of the university and the Pac-10, stating, "Tanaka had failed to identify a relevant market for antitrust purposes. If the relevant market is national in scope, the Pac-10 transfer rule could not have a significant anti-competitive effect, because by its own terms the rule does not apply to inter-conference transfers. Moreover, even if the relevant market is limited to the Pac-10 itself, Tanaka characterizes the Pac-10's imposition of sanctions against her for her intra-conference transfer as an isolated act of retaliation. Tanaka simply has no antitrust cause of action" (see Chapter 10, "Antitrust Law").

NOTE _____

1. In the following cases, the court upheld the NCAA's transfer rule:

 a. In *Tanaka v. University of Southern California*, 252 F.3d 1059 (9th Cir. 2001), a former female soccer player for the University of Southern California (USC) brought an antitrust claim against USC and the Pac-10 Conference, charging that the conference rule on intra-conference transfer was a violation of the Sherman Antitrust Act because the rule was an unreasonable restraint on her ability to transfer to her school of choice, namely UCLA. Tanaka charged that this rule was applied to her only because, before leaving the university, she had charged the university and athletic department with academic fraud. She believed that the rule was employed in her case as retaliation for her allegations against the athletic department. The court decided in favor of the university and the Pac-10, stating, "Tanaka has failed to identify a relevant market for antitrust purposes. If the relevant market is national in scope, the Pac-10 transfer rule could not have a significant anticompetitive effect, because by its own terms the rule does not apply to interconference transfers. Moreover, even if the relevant market is limited to the Pac-10 itself, Tanaka characterizes the Pac-10's imposition of sanctions against her for her intraconference transfer as an isolated act of retaliation. Tanaka simply has no antitrust cause of action." (See Chapter 10 for more discussion of antitrust principles.)

b. In *Williams v. Hamilton*, 497 F. Supp. 641 (D.N.H. 1980), a college student-athlete challenged the NAIA transfer rule requiring him to be in residence at his new college for sixteen weeks before becoming eligible for intercollegiate athletics. The rule was imposed, in part, to prevent "tramp athletes" from transferring from school to school for the sole purpose of participating in sports. The court held that the transfer rule was valid and did not deny due process or equal protection guarantees.

6.2.2.6. Transfer Rules: High School

High school athletic associations usually restrict eligibility for student-athlete transfers in two ways, through either blanket restrictions or complex transfer regulations. Some associations, in an effort to limit abuse, apply the blanket restriction approach on all students who change schools regardless of the reason. This approach is often overly restrictive and unduly harsh. Even so, such rules are often upheld by the courts, and those bringing suit have failed to gain monetary or equitable relief. The rules are said to be reasonably related to alleviating recruiting problems, and courts have been reluctant to get involved with private voluntary organizations.

Interscholastic transfer rules have come under scrutiny when the transfer is due to the movement of school boundaries or for religious reasons. Two noteworthy cases are *Indiana High School Athletic Association v. Durham* and *Beck v. Missouri State High School Activities Association* (see notes 1 and 7). In the *Durham* case, the court decided that Indiana's transfer rule was arbitrary and capricious because it did not take into account the fact that Durham's parents had separated, which had created his reason for transferring. In *Beck*, the court decided that a transfer rule was not a violation of freedom of religion even if the affected student-athlete transferred from a public school to a private parochial school for religious reasons.

Many court cases have challenged high school transfer rules on several different legal theories, including equal protection, freedom of religion, right to travel, and due process grounds (see notes 4 and 7). However, in most cases, the courts have upheld such rules, except in those cases where the student-athlete established a violation of a constitutionally protected right, or if fraud, collusion, or arbitrariness was found (see notes 1 and 3). For example, the court ruled in favor of the plaintiff when it found regulations presuming that all transfers were made for improper reasons, and also when a student-athlete moves from one state to another because of a change in a parent's employment.

States may also adopt a statute or rule preventing implementation of a transfer rule, as Oregon did in response to a suit in which it was determined that transfer rules did not violate any statutory constitutional restrictions. According to such a statute, the student who moved with his or her parents may not be declared ineligible to participate in athletics as a result of the transfer. On the other hand, the student who moved just to live with friends of the family could be declared ineligible as a result of the transfer. In addition, such a statute prohibits the declaration of ineligibility when the declaration is based solely on the fact that the student-athlete formerly participated in a given sport at another school.

NOTES

1. In the case of *Indiana High School Athletic Ass'n v. Durham*, 748 N.E.2d 404 (Ind. Ct. App. 2001), the Indiana High School Athletic Association (IHSAA) argued that the trial court should not have issued a permanent injunction to the athlete, Durham, because the court "failed to apply the deferential standard of review afforded to its administrative rulings in granting Durham's request for a permanent injunction." Durham's parents had separated, and his mother was not able to afford the tuition for the private school he had attended in the past, forcing Durham to attend the regional public school, at which point, under IHSAA transfer rules, he was deemed ineligible for competition. The appellate court agreed with the trial court's issuance of the injunction and use of judicial review, stating, "Given the evidence in this case, the trial court did not abuse its discretion in overturning the IHSAA's denial of full eligibility and refusal to grant a hardship exception. While it may be true that in other cases we have recognized the IHSAA's broad discretion in refusing to grant a student a hardship exception, this discretion is not unreviewable and is subject to the arbitrary and capricious standard upon review."

2. In the case of *Missouri State High School Activities Ass'n v. Romines*, 37 S.W.3d 421 (Mo. Ct. App. 2001), the Missouri State High School Activities Association (MSHSAA) appealed a decision of the circuit judge to issue an injunction to allow a student-athlete to remain eligible despite breaking the association's transfer rule, which made him ineligible in the eyes of the association. The court ruled for the association, deciding that the judicial review of the court was not necessary in this case, stating, "We are unable to find any basis upon which the Circuit Court could exercise its jurisdiction to enjoin the Association's decision. There was no allegation in the petition of lack of procedural due process, and no indication of malice, fraud or collusion."

3. In *Ruiz v. Massachusetts Interscholastic Athletic Association*, No. CV00–68, 2000 Mass. Super. LEXIS 213 (Mass. Super. Feb. 7, 2000), the plaintiff, Rafael Ruiz, was seeking an injunction which would allow him to compete on the varsity basketball team for the remainder of the season. Ruiz had transferred to Canton High School from Thayer Academy (a private school where he had a scholarship) because he had lost his scholarship due to non-maintenance of a satisfactory grade point average. The court decided in favor of Ruiz, citing his particular circumstances as extraordinary, and not applicable under the MIAA transfer law. The court found that Ruiz met all requirements of obtaining an injunction. The court stated, "Ruiz is likely to prevail in establishing that the MIAA rule concerning ineligibility is not applicable as a matter of law to his involuntary transfer from a private school back into the public school system of his hometown."

4. In *Fusato v. Washington Interscholastic Activities Ass'n*, 970 P.2d 774 (Wash. 1999), the court found that the WIAA had violated Fusato's equal protection rights by not allowing her to participate in interscholastic athletics. Under the WIAA's transfer rule, student-athletes who transfer to a high school are not allowed to compete immediately unless they move with the entire "family unit." In Fusato's case, she moved from Okinawa by herself to live with her aunt and uncle in Washington, and was not allowed to immediately play for her high school due to the transfer rule. The court decided for Fusato because it believed that she was being discriminated against due to her national origin, which is a suspect class in questions of equal protection. The court stated, "We hold the trial court did not err applying the strict scrutiny test when deciding the WIAA residence and transfer rules violated Ms. Fusato's equal protection rights under the Fourteenth Amendment. Although Ms. Fusato cannot prove a fundamental right is threatened, she established she was a member of a suspect class based upon national origin or alienage. Upon her showing of disparate impact, together with discriminatory purpose or intent, the WIAA was required to meet the burden of showing a compelling state interest was served by the

challenged rules. The WIAA failed to meet its burden and made no effort to demonstrate that the least restrictive regulatory means were used to accomplish the stated purposes of their rules."

5. In *Wajnowski v. The Connecticut Ass'n of Schools*, No. CV 000432727, 1999 Conn. Super. LEXIS 3448 (Conn. Super. Dec. 17, 1999), a student-athlete who had been attending a private institution for two years was not allowed to play automatically after transferring to a public school. The plaintiff had been able to attend a private school through the generosity of an uncle who supplied the necessary tuition, but after the first two years, the uncle was no longer able to supply this tuition money, and the plaintiff was forced to attend the public high school. He applied for a hardship waiver, and his application was denied by the state association, which applied the strict transfer rule, which allowed only students who moved to compete without waiting one year. The court upheld the decision of the state association, stating that although the circumstances surrounding the transfer were unfortunate, the plaintiff could not prove that any of his rights were violated.

6. In *Robbins v. Indiana High School Athletic Ass'n*, 941 F.Supp. 786 (S.D. Ind. 1996), the plaintiff, Robbins, was seeking to gain an injunction against the enforcement of the IHSAA transfer rule, which would prevent her from participating in interscholastic volleyball on the varsity level at her new school. The court ruled that Robbins failed to meet any of the criteria established to attain an injunction, and subsequently denied her request. The rule was found to have legitimate purpose, and was not arbitrary and capricious.

7. In *Beck v. Missouri State High School Activities Ass'n*, 837 F.Supp. 998 (E.D. Mo. 1993), a student-athlete who had transferred from a public school to a private school alleged that the transfer rule in place was an infringement upon his freedom of religion. The court decided for the high school association, determining that the transfer rule did not violate the student's freedom of religion or freedom of association rights guaranteed by the Constitution, and that the transfer bylaw was not overly inclusive, arbitrary, or capricious. The court also explicitly reprimanded the two parties for not being able to come to a compromise before reaching the court system, stating, "Both sides seem overly concerned with whether this particular young man plays in a basketball game during the next two months, without any regard to the more fundamental underlying concern, his education. Perhaps the resources of all those involved would have been better served by a non-judicial resolution."

8. In *Kentucky High School Athletic Ass'n. v. Hopkins County Board of Education*, 552 S.W.2d 685 (Ky. Ct. App. 1977), a high school student-athlete sought a permanent injunction to stop the Kentucky High School Athletic Association (KHSAA) from denying him eligibility to participate in interscholastic athletics. The student-athlete's parents were divorced, with legal custody awarded to the mother. After living with his mother and playing varsity sports at the high school where he was enrolled, the student-athlete decided to move to his father's home and enrolled in another school. The court of appeals found that the student-athlete was not compelled to change his residence, but did so because of his own wishes, and therefore the transfer was not involuntary. The appeals court also found that the association did not act arbitrarily in applying the transfer rule to the student-athlete. The district court's issuance of an injunction was therefore reversed.

After deciding the essential issue, the court discussed at length a particular problem illustrated by this appeal:

> In the court's mind, this case demonstrates why courts are a very poor place in which to settle interscholastic athletic disputes, especially since this type of litigation is most likely to arise at playoff or tournament time. If an injunction or restraining order is granted erroneously, it will be practically impossible to unscramble the tournament results to reflect the ultimate outcome of the case. In almost every instance, the possible benefits flowing from a temporary restraining order or injunction are far outweighed by the potential detriment to the Association, as well as to its member schools who are not before the court. Only in a rare instance should a temporary restraining order or preliminary injunction be granted.

6.2.2.7. *Scholarship and Financial Assistance: NCAA*

The amount of financial assistance that a student-athlete may receive from his/ her institution or from outside sources is strictly regulated under NCAA guidelines. Student-athletes may lose their eligibility if their financial assistance exceeds a certain amount. Under NCAA guidelines, scholarships for student-athletes may not exceed commonly accepted educational expenses. Scholarships in Divisions I and II are limited to tuition, fees, room and board, and books; a school is not allowed to pay expenses exceeding these (*2001–02 NCAA Division I Manual*, Bylaw 15.2).

In addition, a team is limited to a certain number of full scholarships or value of the financial aid awards (equivalents) that can be in effect at one time in a given sport. For example, an intercollegiate baseball team may be allowed to divide ten full scholarships among the members of its team. Therefore, the coach is left with options on how to divide the aid among his players. For example, he may choose to carry 10 players on full scholarship. However, the more likely, and common, scenario is that the scholarship money will be divided among the players on the team; for example 20 players on the team may receive half-scholarships. The maximum number of equivalent scholarships that can be granted per sport can be found in the *2001–02 NCAA Division I Manual*, Bylaw 15.5.3. A team may forfeit games or an entire season if the number of full scholarships or equivalents exceeds the limits established by the NCAA for that particular sport. Other sports, referred to as "head-count sports," have a limited total number of student-athletes who may be receiving any portion of a scholarship (*2001–02 NCAA Division I Manual*, Bylaw 15.5.2).

Under NCAA rules, a former professional athlete may receive institutional financial aid provided all of the following conditions are met:

1. The student-athlete is no longer involved in professional athletics;
2. The student-athlete is not receiving any remuneration from a professional sports organization; and
3. The student athlete has no active contractual relationship with any professional athletics team, although the student-athlete may remain bound by an option clause [i.e., a clause in the contract that requires assignment to a particular team if the student-athlete's professional athletics career is resumed].

Acceptance of either payment or the promise of money for participation, with few exceptions, in a sport at the collegiate level automatically categorizes the student-athlete as a professional and thus makes him or her ineligible. The student-athlete is also not entitled to be paid or in sponsored sporting events even though he or she may not be representing the collegiate institution. Also, the student-athlete may not receive special treatment because of his or her athletic prowess (e.g., loans on a deferred pay-back basis, automobiles, or special living quarters) (*2001–02 NCAA Division I Manual*, 12.1.1.1). For a more in-depth review of pay restrictions placed on amateur athletes, see section 6.2.2.8, "Pay and Expenses: NCAA."

The rule of thumb regarding payment/receipt of expenses provides that an individual, including a student-athlete, may not receive money for expenses that are in excess of the actual and necessary expenses involved in any activity authorized by the NCAA. Examples of prohibited expense payments include travel expenses to a special location for an article and/or photographs of a student-athlete (unless in conjunction with the receipt of an established/authorized award at that location) and expenses from an agent seeking to represent the student athlete in the marketing of his or her athletic skills (*2001–02 NCAA Division I Manual*, Bylaw 12.3.1.2). The courts have historically upheld the NCAA rules restricting excess financial assistance unless the regulations violate constitutionally protected rights (see notes 1 and 2).

A leading case in the area of excess financial assistance is *Wiley v. NCAA*, 612 F.2d 473 (10th Cir. 1979), *cert. denied*, 446 U.S. 943 (1980). An action was brought by Wiley, a student-athlete who was declared ineligible to compete because his financial aid exceeded the amount allowed by the NCAA. Wiley had been awarded a full Basic Educational Opportunity Grant in addition to an athletic scholarship. Taken together, these exceeded the financial limitations imposed by the institutions under NCAA regulations and made the student ineligible to compete. Wiley filed suit, and the court applied a rational basis analysis rejecting a strict scrutiny approach because poverty or wealth is not a suspect classification (see Chapter 5, Section 5.4.3., "Equal Protection"). The court refused to prohibit the NCAA from enforcing its regulations on the grounds that "unless clearly defined constitutional principles are at issue, suits by student-athletes against high school athletic associations or NCAA rules do not present a substantial federal question."

Under NCAA rules, a member school may allow a student-athlete a maximum of four complimentary admissions for each contest in his or her particular sport. However, in Division I the student-athlete's guest must sign for the admission and receive no hard tickets (*2001–02 NCAA Division I Manual*, Bylaw 16.2.1.2). Tickets are prohibited as a result of previous abuses by student-athletes who received money for selling their tickets for more than face value.

Athletic scholarships are technically renewable each year, but after being granted, they cannot be increased, reduced, or canceled during the period of the award on the basis of the student athlete's ability or contribution to the team. In addition, athletic scholarships cannot be withdrawn during the period of the award because of an injury to a student athlete or for any other athletically related reasons (*2001–02 NCAA Division I Manual*, Bylaw 15.3.4.3). NCAA rules do not, however, prohibit all types of scholarship revision or rescission. Scholarship aid may be canceled or reduced during the period of the award for any of the following reasons:

1. The student-athlete's rendering himself/herself ineligible for competition.

2. Fraudulent misrepresentation by the student-athlete on an application, letter of intent, or financial aid agreement.

3. Serious misconduct by the student-athlete warranting substantial disciplinary penalty.

4. Voluntary withdrawal by the student-athlete from a sport for personal reasons; however the recipient's financial aid may not be awarded to any other student-athlete in the academic term in which the aid was reduced or cancelled (*2001–02 NCAA Division I Manual*, Bylaw 15.3.4.1 [a–d]).

Any gradation or cancellation of aid per the reasons mentioned above is permissible only if such action is taken for proper cause by the regular disciplinary or financial aid authorities of the institution and the student-athlete has had an opportunity for a hearing (*2001–02 NCAA Division I Manual*, Bylaw 15.3.4.1.3).

As indicated by the preceding rules on cancellation and reduction of scholarships, the renewal or non-renewal of a scholarship award is the responsibility of the institution (usually the head coach of the sport). When a scholarship is not renewed, care should be taken to provide due process in the case the student-athlete chooses to request a hearing or file suit. The non-renewal letter sent to the student-athlete should include the reasons for the action and a statement informing the athlete that he or she is entitled to a hearing on the non-renewal of the scholarship. This letter should be kept on file in the athletic director's office and be available upon request to the student-athlete.

In the case of a scholarship revocation, the student-athlete must be given an opportunity for a hearing. Again, according to due process considerations, a written notice of the action, containing specific time and place, should be given to the student-athlete. The hearing, depending on the school's policy, may include a presentation of statements from both parties, cross-examination of witnesses, and the right to legal counsel.

The national letter of intent was developed to regulate the intense competition surrounding the recruitment of talented student-athletes to play college athletics. Letters of intent were developed on the conference level in the late 1940's, during a period when intercollegiate athletics first gained national prominence.

Another important issue in the area of scholarships is the national letter of intent. The Collegiate Commissioners Association (CCA), through the commissioners of athletic conferences, administers the letter of intent program. An institution must be an NCAA member to belong to the program, and the national letter of intent applies only to four-year member institutions in Divisions I and II. Independent institutions that belong to the letter of intent program file all necessary paperwork through an athletic conference of their choice. The program in its present form was started in 1964 with seven conferences and eight independent institutions joining for a total of sixty-eight schools. In 1982, a women's letter of intent was added. In 2002, 547 institutions in fifty conferences belong to the program.

The letter of intent is considered a pre-enrollment application by the CCA, although much of the language creates the possibility that it may be construed as a contract. The men's and women's letters of intent contain identical regulations and procedures; only the membership differs. Both have five signing dates based on sports categories of (1) midyear junior college transfer, (2) football, (3) basketball (basketball has two signing dates—an early signing period in November and the traditional period beginning in April), (4) field hockey, soccer and men's water polo, and (5) all other sports.

The guiding principle behind the letter of intent is that it provides certainty and closure to the recruiting process. Once the recruited athlete signs a national letter of intent, there are no further limits on contacting the student-athlete by the *signing* institution. On a specific date, high school student-athletes can sign a letter of intent, and after the signing no other member institution subscribing to the program will make any effort to recruit the student-athlete. With a membership of nearly 550 institutions, coaches can feel secure that their recruits will not be bombarded with contact from other schools after signing the letter.

NCAA regulations prohibit the colleges' use of press conferences, receptions, and dinners to announce the fact that a student-athlete has signed a letter of intent (*2001–02 NCAA Division I Manual*, Bylaw 13.11.8.2). A student who signs the letter, whether or not the athlete actually enrolls at the institution, is not eligible to compete at any other institution subscribing to the letter of intent program for two calendar years of intercollegiate competition with certain exceptions. However, the student-athlete is free to enroll at any member institution to pursue his or her academic interests. The letter of intent also contains some strict regulations; for example, an athlete will lose one year of eligibility if he/she transfers within the first year of attendance at the institution.

A letter of intent becomes invalid if any of the following circumstances exists:

1. The player does not meet minimum academic standards to play as a freshman.
2. The player attends and graduates from a junior college.
3. The player does not enroll and the institution withdraws its scholarship offer the next year.
4. The player serves in the armed forces or a church mission for at least eighteen months.
5. The institution discontinues the sport.

For more information on the National Letter of Intent Program, visit the Collegiate Commissioners Association Web site at www.national-letter.org

NOTES

1. A case in which a court *denied* a student-athlete's eligibility on the basis of his receipt of excess financial aid is *Jones v. NCAA*, 392 F.Supp. 295 (D. Mass. 1975). An American ice hockey player brought an action against the NCAA for a preliminary injunction to prohibit the NCAA from declaring him ineligible to compete and from imposing sanctions against his college if they allowed him to play because of excess financial aid he received. Prior to entering college, the student-athlete had been compensated while playing junior hockey in Canada. During one of those years, he was paid a weekly salary and received a signing bonus. The court denied Jones injunctive relief, finding that the NCAA's rules on financial aid were reasonable.

2. A court *granted* eligibility to a student-athlete in *Buckton v. NCAA*, 366 F.Supp. 1152 (D. Mass 1973), despite the NCAA's contention that the student-athlete received excess financial aid. Buckton and other Canadian ice hockey players were denied eligibility because they had received funding from Junior League Hockey teams in Canada rather than from high schools, as is the custom in the United States. The court prohibited the NCAA from enforcing ineligibility because the rule, in effect, discriminated against individuals on the basis of national origin.

6.2.2.8. Pay and Expenses: NCAA

Under NCAA regulations, student athletes may not receive pay without jeopardizing their eligibility. The prohibition on payment of student-athletes is predicated on the concept of amateurism, and should not be confused with employment, which is permitted in certain situations under NCAA regulations. The purpose of the regulations relative to pay is to maintain the level of amateurism at the intercollegiate level, while simultaneously discouraging institutions from recruiting players with the promise of pay. Student-athletes may not participate in any competition for cash or prizes, either for themselves or for a donation on their behalf, unless they are eligible to receive such monies under NCAA guidelines. For example, the NCAA does not approve of the granting of scholarship funds in a student-athlete's name if the person was selected as the most valuable player by a national advertiser or sponsor of an event. Further, the NCAA has not approved a student-athlete's participation in "Superstars" competitions or similar staged sporting events. A student-athlete would also jeopardize eligibility if he or she received, for example, a country club membership as a prize or compensation.

The NCAA will automatically consider an individual ineligible for competition if they have violated regulations concerning pay. The following situations are examples of forms of pay under NCAA regulations:

1. Any direct or indirect salary, gratuity or comparable compensation (*2001–02 NCAA Division I Manual*, Bylaw 12.1.1.1.1).

2. Educational expenses not permitted by the governing legislation of the NCAA (*2001–02, NCAA Division I Manual*, Bylaw 12.1.1.1.3). For examples of these types of expenses see section 6.2.2.7., "Scholarship and Financial Aid."

3. Any division or split of surpluses such as bonuses or game receipts (*2001–02 NCAA Division I Manual*, Bylaw 12.1.1.1.2).

4. Excessive or improper expenses, awards and benefits (*2001–02 NCAA Division I Manual*, Bylaw 12.1.1.1.4).

5. Expenses received from an outside amateur sports team or organization in excess of actual and necessary travel, room and board expenses, and apparel and equipment (*2001–02 NCAA Division I Manual*, Bylaw 12.1.1.1.4.3).

6. Actual and necessary expenses or any other form of compensation to participate in athletics competition (while not representing an educational institution) from a sponsor other than the individual upon whom the athlete is naturally or legally dependent or the non-professional organization that is sponsoring the competition (*2001–02 NCAA Division I Manual*, Bylaw 12.1.1.1.4.5).

7. Expenses received by the parents or legal guardians of a participant in athletics competition from a non-professional organization sponsoring the competition in excess of actual and necessary travel, room, and board expenses, or any entertainment expenses, provided such expenses are made available to the parents or legal guardians of all participants in the competition (*2001–02 NCAA Division I Manual*, Bylaw 12.1.1.1.4.6).

8. Payment to individual team members or individual competitors for unspecified or unitemized expenses beyond actual and necessary travel, room, and board expenses for practice and competition (*2001–02 NCAA Division I Manual*, Bylaw 12.1.1.1.4.4).

9. Expenses incurred or awards received by an individual that are prohibited by the rules governing an amateur, non-collegiate event in which the individual participates (*2001–02 NCAA Division I Manual*, Bylaw 12.1.1.1.4.2).

10. Any payment, including actual and necessary expenses, conditioned on the individual's or team's place of finish or performance or given on an incentive basis (*2001–02 NCAA Division I Manual*, Bylaw 12.1.1.1.5).

11. Educational expenses provided to an individual by an outside sports team or organization that are based in any degree upon the recipient's athletic ability (*2001–02 NCAA Division I Manual*, Bylaw 12.1.1.1.3.1).

12. Cash, or the equivalent thereof, as an award for participating in competition at any time, even if such award is permitted under the rules governing an amateur non-collegiate event in which the individual is participating (*2001–02 NCAA Division I Manual*, Bylaw 12.1.1.1.4.1).

13. Preferential treatment, benefits or services because of the individual's athletic reputation or skill or pay-back potential as a professional athlete, unless such treatment, benefits or services are specifically permitted under NCAA legislation (*2001–02 NCAA Division I Manual*, Bylaw 12.1.1.1.6).

14. Receipt of a prize for participation (involving the utilization of athletics ability) in a member institution's promotional activity (*2001–02 NCAA Division I Manual*, Bylaw 12.1.1.1.7).

The issue of expense can provide a unique source of trouble for the NCAA student-athlete. In general, an athlete is allowed to receive money for expenses, but prior to receiving such compensation, should distinguish between those that are permissible to receive under NCAA rules, and, more important, those that are not.

In the NCAA, expenses are limited to those that are actual and necessary. Actual and necessary expenses are defined by the NCAA as amounts received for reasonable travel and meals associated with practice and game competition. The NCAA considers any expenses in excess of "reasonable" to be compensation for athletic ability, and warns that receipt of same can lead to a loss of eligibility. Expenses are to be paid on a regular basis, and must not be determined by performance or any other incentive plan (see note 2).

NOTES ───

1. The NCAA rules concerning pay were challenged in *Shelton* v. *NCAA*, 539 F.2d 1197 (9th Cir. 1976). Lonnie Shelton, a student-athlete at the time, was allegedly persuaded to sign a professional contract by the use of fraud and undue influence by an agent. After being declared ineligible by the NCAA, Shelton sued the NCAA, claiming that the rule should not be enforced against him since the misconduct of the agent rendered the contract voidable.

The court, however, after examining the rule, upheld it because the NCAA goals of protecting and promoting amateurism, which were incorporated into the rule, were legitimate. Therefore, although the rule might, when applied in certain situations, produce unreasonable results, it did not violate the U.S. Constitution because the rule was rationally related to its goals.

2. The NCAA allows very minimal expenses, such as actual and necessary travel expenses while representing an institution in competition, a per diem for foreign-tour expenses, and other actual and necessary expenses associated with the student-athlete's participation (*2001–02 NCAA Division I Manual*, Bylaw 16.8).

3. Under NCAA regulations, a student-athlete remains eligible in a sport even though, prior to enrollment in a collegiate institution, he or she may have tried out with a professional team. However, the expenses paid by the team(s) are limited:

> A student-athlete remains eligible in a sport even though, prior to enrollment in a collegiate institution, the student-athlete may have tried out with a professional athletics team in a sport or received not more than one expense-paid visit from each professional team (or a combine including that team), provided such a visit did not exceed 48 hours and any payment or compensation in connection with the visit was not in excess of actual and necessary expenses. A self-financed tryout may be for any length of time (*2001–02 NCAA Division I Manual*, Bylaw 12.2.1.1).

6.2.2.9. Employment: NCAA

A student-athlete who is receiving a full athletic scholarship from an institution can, as of 1998, be employed during the academic year. However, the student-athlete's earnings cannot exceed the total value of their athletic scholarship grant plus $2,000. In addition, the student-athlete must have spent one academic year in residence at the university, and must be eligible academically to compete for the institution (*2001–02 NCAA Division I Manual*, Bylaw 15.2.6.1.).

A student-athlete who is receiving only partial financial assistance from an institution, including a partial athletic scholarship, is also allowed to receive employment compensation from work-study on campus or employment off campus, up to the limit established by the institution as the cost of attendance. This employment compensation also counts toward the value of the total financial aid awards in effect at one time for each sport (*2001–02 NCAA Division I Manual*, Bylaw 15.02.3.1).

Student-athletes can hold campus jobs or employment through alumni of the institution, but they must be paid only for the work actually done. Student-athletes who receive remuneration for work not performed are no longer eligible for participation in intercollegiate athletics. Furthermore, student-athletes must be paid at a rate commensurate with the going rate in the particular locality for services of a similar character (*2001–02 NCAA Division I Manual*, Bylaw 12.4.1).

With some exceptions, any compensation received over commonly accepted educational expenses as set by the individual institution must be deducted from the financial assistance package received by the student-athlete (including athletic scholarships), or else the student-athlete will be ineligible to compete for the institution (see note 1).

There are limits to the types of employment a student-athlete can consider to maintain amateur status and collegiate eligibility. For example, student-athletes are not permitted to be employed by their institutions as teachers or coaches in any sport for which they wish to remain eligible, and may be employed by other organizations as teachers or coaches in their particular sport only under certain circumstances.

Monitoring a student-athlete's employment activities during the academic year is an important endeavor for an athletic administrator. Weekend jobs, jobs with friends, or odd jobs on and off campus, while seemingly insignificant to the casual bystander or to the student-athlete, may in fact be a threat to retaining eligibility to compete in intercollegiate athletics.

NOTES _____

1. A student-athlete may not receive compensation for teaching sports skills or techniques in his or her sport on a fee-for-lesson basis. Student-athletes are permitted to perform these lessons, however, before they are enrolled in an NCAA institution (*2001–02 NCAA Division I Manual*, Bylaw 12.4.2.1).

2. Under NCAA regulations, a student-athlete who is preparing to compete or has competed in the Olympic Games is entitled to recover any financial loss occurring as a result of absence from employment to prepare for or participate in the Games only if authorized by the United States Olympic Committee. The period involved in recovering the losses must immediately precede and/or include actual Olympic competition (*2001–02 NCAA Division I Manual*, Bylaw 12.4.2.2).

6.2.2.10. Summer Camps: NCAA and High School Rules

Prospective student-athletes, with the exception of football players, are allowed to enroll in, participate in, or be employed at camps, schools, and clinics that are run by an NCAA member institution. However, this allowance comes with many regulations. In Division I, it is permissible to employ a prospective student-athlete, provided that the student-athlete is not a "senior prospect." The NCAA defines a "senior prospect" as a prospect who is eligible for admission to a member institution or who has started classes for the senior year of high school. A prep school or two-year college student is considered a senior prospect (*2001–02 NCAA Division I Manual*, Bylaw 13.13.1.2). While a senior prospect may attend a camp or clinic, he is not allowed to participate in any physical activities (*2001–02 NCAA Division I Manual*, Bylaw 13.13.1.2.1.2). These rules have been established to stop the use of summer camps as "tryouts" for prospective student-athletes.

In the case of *Kite v. Marshall*, 454 F. Supp. 1347 (Tex. Dist. Ct. 1978), parents of high school student-athletes brought an action that challenged the constitutionality of the "summer camp rule," which was adopted by the defendant University Interscholastic League (UIL), the high school athletic association in Texas. The rule stated that any person who attended a special athletic training camp would be ineligible for one year of competition. The rationale underlying the rule's adoption was that it ensured that high school athletes would compete on a relatively equal basis. The court decided that:

> the decision to send a child to summer basketball camp is important enough to warrant constitutional protection under the family's fundamental right of personal privacy. . . .
>
> Having found a fundamental constitutional right, the remaining inquiries are whether or not the UIL rule in question infringes the right and if so, whether the rule is motivated by compelling state interest and has been narrowly drawn to express only those interests.

In deciding the degree of infringement, the court stated:

> The summer camp rule is, however, directly and purposefully aimed at discouraging a specific parental decision made during the summer months when the school is not acting *in loco parentis*. The interference posed by the UIL rule . . . is neither indirect nor incidental.

The court reasoned, "As it presently reads, the summer camp rule constitutes an overbroad and unreasonable infringement on the right of a family to make decisions concerning the education of its children."

In *Kite v. Marshall*, 661 F.2d 1027 (5th Cir. 1981), UIL appealed the lower court ruling striking down its "summer camp rule." The court of appeals held that the "summer camp rule" did not violate either the due process or the equal protection clause of the Constitution. It reversed the opinion of the district court. The court of appeals found that, "this case implicates no fundamental constitutional right." The court subjected the rule to the rational basis analysis.

The court also upheld a similar high school rule in *Texas High School Gymnastics Coaches Ass'n. v. Andrews*, 532 S.W.2d 142 (Tex. Civ. App. 1975). This suit was brought by parents and coaches of gymnasts who sought to overturn a Texas High School Gymnastics Coaches Association rule that governed dual membership. The Association rule read as follows:

> A Texas high school gymnast must not work out with, practice with, take lessons with, or compete with a private club, and be eligible for dual regional or state competition during the school calendar year of their school district.

The complaint alleged that the rule was an "unfair, unlawful and unconstitutionally restriction upon the individual rights of high school students who . . . desire to compete in high school gymnastic competition." The trial court granted an injunction that temporarily prohibited the Association from enforcing the rule. The Association appealed.

The appeals court noted that there was not sufficient evidence to support the conclusion that the rule was unreasonable, capricious, or arbitrary. The court held that the rule must be upheld unless it could be shown that the rule bears no rational relationship to the achievement of a legitimate purpose. The court found that the purpose of the rule was valid because it prevented inequality and unfair advantage between students of different economic means and schools located in different areas of economic wealth.

These cases show the reluctance of the court to overturn association rules that are reasonably related to a legitimate purpose.

NOTES

1. At the 1983 NCAA convention, the membership enacted legislation that prohibited a member of a Division I basketball coaching staff from being employed by a basketball camp that has been established, sponsored, or conducted by an individual or organization that provides recruiting or scouting services. Since the 1983 convention, this legislation has been updated to restrict Division I football coaches in the same way, and has added the restriction that a coach is also not allowed to lecture at a non-institutional (i.e., privately owned) football or basketball camp or clinic in which prospective student-athletes of either gender participate (*2001–02 NCAA Division I Manual*, Bylaw 13.13.2.3.2).

2. In the initial district court decision of *Kite v. Marshall*, 454 F. Supp. 1347 (Tex. Dist. Ct. 1978), the court determined that the plaintiff was entitled to a preliminary injunction that prohibited the interscholastic league from enforcing a rule which stated that students who play in special basketball training camps are ineligible for one year for any athletic contest in the league. The court stated that the rule was overly broad and the player would suffer material harm if relief was denied.

3. The following cases also involve camp participation:

(a) In *Art Gaines Baseball Camp, Inc. v. Houston*, 500 S.W.2d 735 (Mo. Ct. App. 1973), a camp sought to restrain the Missouri High School Activities Association from enforcing a rule which stated that a student-athlete who attended a camp specializing in one sport for more than two weeks during a summer would lose eligibility to represent his or her school in that particular sport the following school year. In affirming judgment for the high school athletic association, the court of appeals held that the rule did not infringe on public policy or law and was not unreasonable or arbitrary.

(b) In *Brown v. Wells*, 181 N.W.2d 708 (Minn. 1970), a hockey player challenged rules excluding his participation on the high school hockey team if he participated in nonschool hockey, including hockey schools or camps. The court held that when rules are adopted for the purpose of deemphasizing extracurricular athletics that may detract from student interest in education, the court cannot deem such rules arbitrary or unreasonable. The court found that the school board had the discretion to deal with the issue as it thought best. The courts should not attempt to control the discretion of the school board.

4. The Florida High School Activities Association (FHSAA) has the following regulation regarding high school student-athletes who work at summer camps, clinics or recreational programs:

Policy 24: The following guidelines govern participation of students of FHSAA member schools in coaching schools, camps, clinics or workshops for an interscholastic sport.

1. Individuals
Students from FHSAA member schools may participate as individuals in coaching schools, camps, clinics or workshops at any time of the year without jeopardizing their interscholastic athletic eligibility, provided:
(a) Students participating in the event do not, in any way, represent their school.

(b) Fees for the students who participate in the event are not paid by the school, coach or school district. (*2001–2002 FHSSA Handbook*, Policy 24, www.fshaa.org)

6.2.2.11. Participation on Independent Teams

Many high school and college athletic associations establish rules that prohibit student-athletes from participating on independent teams (YMCA, private clubs, church leagues) while the student-athlete is participating in the same sport as a member of a high school or college team. The rules are intended to prevent players from obtaining unfair additional training and competition, and to keep overzealous coaches from involving student-athletes in excessive athletic participation. Not all sports are subject to these rules however. For example, under NCAA rules, athletes in archery, badminton, bowling, cross-country, fencing, golf, gymnastics, ice hockey, rifle, rowing, skiing, squash, swimming, tennis, track and field, water polo, and wrestling are allowed to compete on independent amateur teams during the summer (*2001–02 NCAA Division I Manual*, Bylaw 17). On the high school level, debates are growing over the validity of not allowing high school student-athletes to compete in such programs as the Olympic Development Program for soccer.

The courts have generally upheld independent team participation rules on the grounds that the restrictions do not violate any constitutionally protected rights. In one case, the court dismissed a student-athlete's complaint because the limitation on the student-athlete's participation created no circumstances violative of either state or federal constitutions.

There has been one successful challenge to an independent team rule in the case of *Buckton v. NCAA*, 366 F. Supp. 1152, 1155 (D. Mass. 1973). Two resident alien college hockey players brought suit against the Eastern College Athletic Conference (ECAC) and the NCAA to challenge an ECAC and NCAA regulation that declared them ineligible because they had competed as members of the Canadian Amateur Hockey Association's major junior A classification. The challenged independent team rule stated: "Any student-athlete who participated as a member of the Canadian Amateur Hockey Association's major junior A hockey classification shall not be eligible for intercollegiate athletics" (NCAA Constitution, Article 3, Section 1, 0.I.5. [1973–74]; ECAC Bylaws, Article 3, Section 1, 0.I.5. [1972]). The court struck down the rule after finding that it violated the equal protection clause of the Fourteenth Amendment because resident aliens are granted the same constitutional right of equal protection as American citizens. The court ruled that the university must declare the student-athletes eligible, and the NCAA was prohibited from bringing sanctions against the university.

NOTES

1. In *Burrows et al. v. Ohio High School Athletic Ass'n.*, 712 F.Supp. 620 (S.D. Ohio 1988), the plaintiffs brought action challenging the constitutionality of the defendant's bylaw which provided that no soccer squad member could participate in independent soccer and maintain eligibility for interscholastic soccer without approval of the commissioner of the association. The court held that high school students' association with others for the purpose of participating in independent spring soccer and out-of-season instruction was not private association or expressive association within the constitutional protection of freedom of association. Further, the bylaw did not violate the equal protection guarantee because it did not apply to students who had not played interscholastic soccer the previous

fall, or because it did not apply to certain sports involving primarily individual rather than team competition.

2. In *Zuments v. Colorado High School Activities Ass'n.*, 737 P.2d 1113 (Colo. Ct. App. 1987), student-athletes enrolled in various Colorado public high schools sued to enjoin the defendant from enforcing its "outside competition" rule, which prevented students from practicing with non-school teams while participating in interscholastic athletics. The lower court granted a preliminary injunction to the students. On appeal, the court of appeals held that the association's enforcement of the "outside competition" rule was not arbitrary, capricious, or haphazard, and that it rationally furthered legitimate state purposes, so as not to violate the students' right to equal protection. Further, the outside competition rule did not impermissibly burden the students' constitutional right of free association.

3. In *University Interscholastic League v. North Dallas Chamber of Commerce Soccer Ass'n*, 693 S.W.2d 513 (Tex. Ct. App. 1985), the lower court had granted a permanent injunction prohibiting enforcement of a rule restricting club soccer activities of varsity school athletes. The rule declared public high school contestants who had previously played on their high school varsity soccer team ineligible for participation on their high school soccer team, in the event that they had played or practiced with nonschool soccer teams between the first day of school and November 12. On appeal, the court reversed the decision, holding that the rule was reasonably related, for equal protection purposes, to its objectives, which were the prevention of competitive advantage and coaching pressure, and the encouragement of participation by student-athletes in activities other than competitive soccer. Further, the soccer association had failed to establish a fundamental right to participation in varsity school athletics, so as to invoke the protection of the due process clause.

4. In *Kubiszyn v. Alabama High School Athletic Ass'n.*, 374 So.2d 256 (Ala. 1979), members of a high school basketball team were declared ineligible after playing on YMCA and church basketball teams at the same time they were playing for their high school team. The high school athletic association rule provided that any member of a high school athletic team who participated in an athletic contest as a member of a similar team during the same season was ineligible to play for the high school team for the remainder of the season. The court found that the rule did not violate the state or federal constitution, in absence of some evidence that the student-athlete suffered some impairment of a property right, or that the acts of the athletic association were the result of fraud or collusion.

5. In *Dumez v. Louisiana High School Athletic Ass'n.*, 334 So.2d 494 (La. Ct. App. 1976), parents of high school student-athletes who were declared ineligible to participate in interscholastic baseball by an athletic association sought a permanent injunction to prohibit enforcement of the ruling. In reversing judgment for the parents, the court of appeals held that determination by the Association to declare the students ineligible because they violated the "independent team rule" by participating in practice sessions held by the Babe Ruth Baseball League was not subject to judicial rescission or modification on the grounds that it constituted a serious "inequity" to the students when similar action was not taken against coaches or schools.

6. In *Texas High School Gymnastics Coaches Ass'n. v. Andrews*, 532 S.W.2d 142 (Tex. Civ. App. 1975), the court considered the appeal of a temporary injunction forbidding the association from applying its dual membership rule. The rule prohibited gymnasts from competing on the high school team as well as for a private club during the school calendar year. The court reversed the judgment of the trial court and dissolved the temporary injunction, finding that there was no basis at all for finding the rule to be invalid.

6.3. ATHLETE'S CHALLENGE OF RULES

The authority of an athletic association and a coach to make rules regarding a student-athlete's private life is limited. As in the case of the rules of athletic associations and conferences, the rules of coaches and their institutions are held to the standards of reasonableness and rational relationship to a legitimate purpose. Generally, the purpose of the rules created and enforced must be reasonably related to the pursuit of the sport itself. Without this relationship, the rule may be deemed impermissible on constitutional grounds by the courts. Even when a rational relationship does exist, a rule may be impermissible if it infringes on the constitutional rights of life, liberty, and property, which are protected by due process guarantees (see Chapter 5, section 5.4.2., "Due Process"). In other words, rules have been struck down when they deal with areas that might be loosely termed "personal choice" or "preference." In these cases, the courts have to weigh the personal freedoms of the student-athlete against the institution's or the coach's regulation of athletics in the name of character building, fair play, and esprit de corps (see Chapter 5, section 5.4.3., "Equal Protection").

The authority of a coach is limited to his or her position within the institution. The first possible legal basis for a coach's authority is *in loco parentis*. This means that the relationship between the coach or institution and the student-athlete is analogous to that of parent and child. Although this principle would seem to give a coach virtually a free rein in disciplining players, its validity, particularly as it applies to college student-athletes, many of whom are adults in the eyes of the law, has not been absolute.

The sections that follow are broken down into three different areas. Section 6.3.1. will discuss freedom of expression and will look at how institutions are allowed or prohibited from infringing upon an athlete's rights to self-expression, including such issues as tattoos, prayer, hair-length, and right to marriage. Section 6.3.2. will look at the presence of discipline within athletics and what rights student-athletes, coaches, and institutions possess. The third and final section, 6.3.3., will deal with the effects of alcohol and drug rules in high school athletics.

6.3.1. Freedom of Expression

Freedom of expression is often raised in an amateur athletics context whenever the athlete's or coach's right to speak is impeded. Student-athletes, coaches, and others have brought claims alleging that they lost their scholarships or jobs for engaging in expressive activity or speech that was unacceptable to their superiors. If the superior who is limiting the right to free expression is found to be engaged in state action, the student-athlete or coach may have grounds to sue the superior, using a constitutional law argument.

Freedom of expression is the cornerstone of the Bill of Rights and individual liberty under the U.S. Constitution. Freedom of expression is a broad term describing the right to free "speech." The term *freedom of expression* is used rather than *free speech* because certain non-verbal types of communication are protected under the First Amendment—for example, carrying a sign with a written message. Therefore, while the First Amendment uses the words "Congress shall make no law . . . abridging the freedom of *speech*" (emphasis added), a broader range of expression is protected.

The question of a student-athlete's right to freedom of expression has recently reached the Supreme Court. In *Santa Fe Independent School District v. Doe*, 530 U.S. 290 (2000), the Court decided that the recitation of prayers before a public high school football game was a violation of the requirement of the separation of church and state under the First Amendment (see note 1). The players were therefore not allowed to read prayers before the games, in what they contended was a violation of their rights to freedom of expression. This decision shows that the conduct engaged in by student-athletes does not necessarily have to be malicious in order to be suppressed.

For purposes of analysis, expression must be broken down into two component parts. First is the element of conduct or physical action, which is a necessary part of communicating a message. For example, a demonstration requires conduct by the demonstrators that can be either peaceful or violent. Violence is a noncommunicative aspect of speech that may be regulated because there are compelling government interests in peace and order involved. Second is the component that is the actual message or content of speech. This communicative aspect of speech, consisting of the thoughts or informational content of the communication, may be regulated if there is a clear and present danger of imminent lawless action—for example, shouting "fire" in a crowded theater.

Some student-athletes, coaches, and athletic personnel have been successful in challenging the termination of scholarships or suspension from their jobs on freedom-of-expression grounds (see notes 1f and g). In analyzing these situations, the courts have examined whether or not the individual's communication involved a public or a private concern. Only if the matter is of public concern have the courts been inclined to protect the individual's right to express his or her views, but this protection is not absolute. The courts must balance the speaker's interest against the other party's interest. As a general rule, the courts have favored the speaker's interest over that of the other party. However, the courts also seem ready to allow restrictions on student-athletes' speech by deciding that players' comments (as opposed to those of students and coaches) are not matters of public concern. However, student-athletes have, on occasion, received some protection of First Amendment rights.

A leading case in the area of freedom of expression concerning athletics is *Stotts v. Community Unit School District*, 230 F.3d 989 (7th Cir. 2000). Stotts was a rising senior when his local school board enacted a rule, applied only to the boy's basketball team, that prohibited basketball players from having tattoos, body graffiti, and unnatural hair coloring, and addressed their uniforms and other appearance issues. Consequently, Stotts got a tattoo of a dragon on his back, which was visible only if someone tugged on his uniform shirt. Stotts was suspended from the first half of the season, and was told that if he did not have the tattoo removed, he would be suspended for the entire season. Stotts, after appealing unsuccessfully to the school board, sought a preliminary injunction allowing him to play for the team on the grounds of violations of his First Amendment right to free speech, and Fourteenth Amendment right to due process and equal protection. Stotts's request for a preliminary injunction was denied, and he was not allowed to play for the entire season. Upon appeal, the appeals court dismissed the case as moot because Stotts had already graduated from high school and therefore was not an affected party anymore. The court did, however, leave an opening for others who might want to challenge the constitutionality of the rule, stating, "While Stotts' case became moot before an appellate ruling on the merits could be made, a case challenging the appearance regulation will not necessarily evade review. A freshman who challenges the regulation, for example, would have a four-year window within which to litigate the issue."

While most litigation of athletic rules on constitutional grounds has been based on allegations of infringement upon a property interest, cases involving hair-length regulations have been attacked for being infringements of personal liberty interests. Some courts have recognized a student-athlete's right to govern his or her personal appearance while attending public school, while other circuit courts see this liberty interest as too insubstantial to create a protectable interest. Due to shifts in culture and grooming style, issues of hair length have not been hotly debated topics within the courts in recent years (See notes 2 and 3 for cases involving hair length).

Rules that relate to high school marriages have also resulted in much litigation. In the early cases, rules excluding married student-athletes from interscholastic competition were upheld under the rational relationship standard (i.e., they bore a rational relationship to a legitimate objective). These rules were considered reasonable because it was believed that exclusion of married students from athletics was necessary to (1) protect unmarried students from bad influences, (2) encourage students to finish high school before marriage, and (3) give married students the opportunity for more time together to develop their family life. Similar to the issue of hair length, rules regarding high school marriages have virtually disappeared due to changes in cultural norms (see notes 4 and 5 for cases involving marriage and interscholastic athletics).

More recently, however, such rules have been struck down as invalid and improper invasions of the right to marital property (i.e., the right to be married). Marriage rules have also been overturned on the basis of a property interest. In other words, the courts have reasoned that such rules deprive student-athletes of a chance for a college scholarship and therefore infringe upon their property interest of obtaining a free education (see note 5(f) for the *Moran* case). Most courts have refused to accept the property interest found by *Moran*, noting that such an interest is too speculative at the high school level to merit legal protection as a property interest. However, the courts now typically hold that marital classifications are unconstitutional on equal protection grounds.

NOTES

1. The following cases also involve freedom of expression:

(a) In *Santa Fe Independent School District v. Doe*, 530 U.S. 290 (2000), the Supreme Court decided in a 6–3 decision that saying prayers before a public high school football game was a violation of the First Amendment clause of the separation of church and state. The school board had allowed students to read overtly Christian prayers at graduation ceremonies and home football games. At the district court level, the court adopted a policy, the October policy, that allowed the school to deliver a non-denominational prayer, and allowed the students to vote on whether they wanted to have a prayer, and who would deliver the prayer. The appellate court found that this decision was erroneous because it still violated the establishment of religion clause in the First Amendment. On writ of certiorari, the Supreme Court found the following : "1) under the circumstances presented, a student invocation pursuant to the October policy violated the establishment of religion clause, as (a) such invocations were not private student speech, but rather public speech, (b) the student election did nothing to protect minority views, (c) the policy involved perceived and actual endorsement of religion, (d) the student election mechanisms did not insulate the school from the coercive element of the message, (e) the elections encouraged divisiveness along religious lines in a public school setting, and (f) even if every high school student's decision to attend a home football game were regarded as purely voluntary, the delivery of a pregame prayer had the improper effect of coercing those present to participate in an act of religious worship; and (2) the simple enactment of the policy was a facial constitutional violation, even if no student ever offered a religious message pursuant to the policy."

(b) In the case of *Chandler v. Siegelman*, 230 F.3d 1313 (11th Cir. 2000), a similar fact pattern existed as in *Santa Fe Independent School District v. Doe*. In this case, a message with religious content was broadcast over a public address system in a public high school. The case was appealed to the Supreme Court, but the Court, after making the decision in *Santa Fe*, remanded the case to the appeals court for a decision that was consistent with the *Santa Fe* case, determining in fact that a violation of the First Amendment separation of church and state had occurred.

(c) Although this case did not reach the trial court level, in 2001 a Cal-State Fullerton track runner was suspended from participating on the track and field team at the university because she maintained a part-time job as an exotic dancer. The coach of the team told her that her job as a stripper violated university athletic policies. Upon reconsideration of the decision, officials at the institution decided to reinstate the runner to the team if she was able to achieve the required academic eligibility standards. The university officials noted that stripping is a "constitutionally protected form of expression," and feared a lawsuit if the suspension were upheld.

(d) A leading case in the area of freedom of expression concerning athletics is *Williams v. Eaton*, 468 F.2d 1079 (10th Cir. 1972). The plaintiffs were a group of fourteen black football players for the University of Wyoming. In October 1969, prior to a game against Brigham Young University, the players had approached head football coach Lloyd Eaton wearing black armbands to protest the beliefs of the Mormon Church. Coach Eaton dismissed them from the team for violating team discipline rules, which did not allow protests or demonstrations by players.

The players brought suit in district court, but their action was dismissed. The players appealed, and the court of appeals affirmed the decision in part while sending the case back for further proceedings. Upon the second hearing, the lower court held that the players had been given a full and impartial hearing before their suspensions and that their procedural due process rights had not been violated. The court reasoned that Coach Eaton's rule had not been arbitrary or capricious, and up until their action, there had been no complaint concerning the rule by any of the players. In addition, Coach Eaton, acting as an agent of the University of Wyoming and the state of Wyoming, was compelled not to allow the players, under the guise of the First Amendment rights of freedom of speech, to undertake a planned protest demonstration against the religious beliefs of the Mormon Church and Brigham Young University. The demonstration would have taken place in a tax-supported facility, and had the officials of the university acceded to the demands of the players, such action would have been violative of Brigham Young University's First Amendment rights. The court held that the rights of the players to freedom of speech as guaranteed by the First Amendment could not be held paramount to the rights of others under the same amendment to practice their religion free from state-supported protest or demonstration.

(e) In *Menora v. Illinois High School Ass'n*, 527 F.Supp. 637 (N.D. Ill. 1981), *vacated*, 683 F.2d 1030 (7th Cir. 1982), *cert. denied*, 103 S. Ct. 801 (1983), a federal district court ruled that an Illinois High School Association (IHSA) rule that prohibited student-athletes from wearing soft barrettes or yarmulkes during basketball games violated their right to freedom of religion guaranteed by the First Amendment. Orthodox Jewish students are required by their religion to keep their head covered at all times except when unconscious, immersed in water, or in imminent danger of loss of life.

On appeal to the court of appeals, the decision was overturned. The court ruled that the students have no constitutional right to wear yarmulkes during the basketball games. It noted that Jewish religious law requires only that the head be covered, not specifically by yarmulkes.

(f) In *Marcum v. Dahl*, 658 F.2d 731 (10th Cir. 1981), two members of the University of Oklahoma women's basketball team had their scholarships terminated after publicly voicing opposition to the renewal of the head coach's contract. The student-athletes contended that such an action, in response to their comments, was a violation of their right to free speech under the First Amendment. The court disagreed and held that the termination of the scholarships was a result of months of dissension, and not solely a product of the players' comments.

(g) In *Pickering v. Board of Education of Township High School District 205, Will County, Illinois*, 205, 391, U.S. 563, 568, (1968), the Supreme Court held that the dismissal of a high school teacher for openly criticizing the school board's allocation of funds between athletics and education was unconstitutional on First Amendment grounds. The court reasoned that because Pickering's criticism was a matter of public concern necessary for the free and open debate which was vital to the decision-making process, it was constitutionally protected.

(h) In *Tinker v. Des Moines Independent School District*, 93 U.S. 503 (1969), student-athletes wearing politically motivated black armbands in a public high school were found to have a constitutionally protected right of expression. The court recognized that the student-athletes' First Amendment rights do not stop at the schoolhouse or gym door, and that constitutional protection extends to forms of expression other than speech or written communication.

(i) In *Hall v. Ford*, 856 F.2d 255 (D.C. Cir. 1988), the plaintiff, a former athletic director, brought action against the University of the District of Columbia officials, challenging his termination. The lower court dismissed the action, and the plaintiff appealed. The court of appeals held that the plaintiff occupied a position from which he could be discharged for the exercise of the right to free speech with respect to matters of university policy, and that he did not have a property interest in continued employment. Further, the plaintiff's discharge did not violate his liberty interest, and a memorandum written by another university officer was not libelous per se.

2. The following cases viewed issues involving hair length warranted constitutional review:

(a) In *Dostert v. Berthold Public School Dist. No. 594*, 391 F. Supp. 876 (D.N. Dak. 1975), a student-athlete sought relief from a rule regulating hair length. The court held that the school's interest in requiring uniformity was such a compelling part of its public educational mission as to outweigh the constitutionally protected interest of student-athletes in regard to personal appearance.

(b) In *Long v. Zopp*, 476 F.2d 180 (4th Cir. 1973), a high school football player challenged the denial of his football letter because of his hair length. The court held unlawful the coach's regulation of the hair length of his players after the end of the football season. The holding was based on the analysis that it was reasonable for a coach to require short hair during a playing season for health and safety reasons. However, it was not reasonable to deny an athletic award or an invitation to a sports banquet when a student-athlete allowed his hair to grow long after the season.

(c) In *Dunham v. Pulsifer*, 312 F. Supp. 411 (D. Vt. 1970), a high school student-athlete requested an injunction to stop Brattleboro (Vermont) High School from enforcing an athletic grooming code. Alleged violations of this code had resulted in dismissal of the student-athlete from the school tennis team. The court noted that although one of the asserted justifications for these rules was the promotion of closer teamwork and discipline, the tennis team had no such problems prior to the enactment of the dress code. "Outside of uniformity in appearance, no evidence was introduced as to advantages to be derived from the athletic code except the question of discipline for the sake of discipline." The court reasoned that, "there are few individual characteristics more basic to one's personality and image than the manner in which one wears his hair.... The cut of one's hair style is more fundamental to personal appearance than the type of clothing he wears.... Hair style has been shadowed with political, philosophical and ideological overtones."

3. In the following cases, the court found issues of hair length were too insubstantial to warrant constitutional review:

(a) In *Davenport v. Randolph County Bd. of Education*, 730 F.2d 1395 (11th Cir. 1984), high school football student-athletes sought an injunction from the school board's decision that refused them participation in athletics unless they complied with the coach's "clean-shaven" policy for football and basketball team members. The district court denied the injunction. The court of appeals affirmed the decision.

(b) In *Zeller v. Donegal School District*, 517 F.2d 600 (3rd Cir. 1975), a high school soccer player sought an injunction and monetary damages under the Civil Rights Act for his dismissal from the soccer team for noncompliance with the athletic grooming code, regulating length of hair. The district court dismissed the complaint, and the student-athlete appealed. The court of appeals held that the nature of the constitutional interpretation calls for the making of a value judgment in areas that were regulated by the state and in which the federal courts should not intrude, and it stated: "We hold that plaintiff's contention does not rise to the dignity of a protectable constitutional interest." The court based its decision on the concept that a student-athlete's liberties and freedoms are not absolute and stated: "We determine today that the Federal System is ill-equipped to make value judgments on hair-lengths in terms of the Constitution." The court concluded that the student-athlete hair-length case should be left to school regulation, "where the wisdom and experience of school authorities must be deemed superior and preferable to the federal judiciary's."

4. Rules barring married student-athletes from participation in extracurricular activities were held constitutionally *permissible* in the following cases.

(a) An early case in the area of interscholastic athletic eligibility and marriage is *Estay v. La Fourche Parish School Board*, 230 So.2d 443 (La. Ct. App. 1969). In *Estay*, a married high school student challenged his exclusion from all extracurricular participation based on a school board regulation. The court of appeals held that the school board had the authority to adopt the regulation. It found the regulation to be reasonable—not arbitrary or capricious—and concluded that enforcement of the rule did not deprive the student of any constitutional rights. The court reasoned that there was a rational relationship between the rule and its stated objective of promoting completion of high school education prior to marriage. The court held that the classification rested on a sound and reasonable basis and that the criteria were applied uniformly and impartially.

(b) In *Board of Directors v. Green*, 147 N.W.2d 854 (Iowa 1967), an action was brought to prohibit enforcement of a school board rule barring participation in extracurricular activities by married pupils. Upon appeal, the Iowa Supreme Court held that engaging in extracurricular activities, such as basketball, is a privilege that may be enjoyed only in accordance with standards set by the school district. The student did not have a "right" to participate; therefore, no violation of the equal protection clause occurred.

(c) In *State ex rel. Baker v. Stevenson*, 189 N.E.2d 181 (Ohio C.P. 1962), the Court of Common Pleas held that the rule precluding married high school students from participating in extracurricular activities was valid.

(d) In *Starkey v. Board of Education*, 381 P.2d 718 (Utah Sup. Ct. 1963), the Utah Supreme Court held that the "rule against participation in extracurricular activities by married students bore a reasonable relationship to the problem of 'dropouts' and did not constitute an abuse of school board's discretion."

(e) In *Cochrane v. Board of Education*, 103 N.W.2d 569 (Mich. 1960), proceedings were held to compel the board of education to allow married high school student-athletes to play football during the 1958 school year. On appeal, the Michigan Supreme Court affirmed the circuit court's decision and held that the "school district did not violate the statute guaranteeing to all students an equal right to public educational facilities by excluding married high school students from participation in co-curricular activities."

(f) In *Kissick v. Garland Independent School District*, 330 S.W.2d 708 (Tex. Civ. App. 1959), the court of appeals held that the "resolution of school district providing that married students or previously married students should be restricted wholly to classroom work and barring them from participation in athletics or other exhibitions and prohibiting them from holding class offices or other positions of honor other than academic honor—was not arbitrary, capricious, discriminatory, or unreasonable."

5. Rules barring married students from participation in extracurricular activities were held *impermissible* in the absence of a finding of a rational basis for the rules:

(a) In *Beeson v. Kiowa County School District*, 567 P.2d 801 (Colo. Ct. App. 1977), the court of appeals ruled for the plaintiff, stating that the student had a fundamental right to marry and reasons given by the school board regarding a policy that prohibited married students from participating in extracurricular activities did not establish compelling state interest to justify violation of the plaintiff's fundamental right.

(b) In *Indiana High School Athletic Ass'n v. Raike*, 164 Ind. App. 169, 329 N.E.2d 66 (Ind. Ct. App. 1975), a public high school rule that prohibited married students from participating in any extracurricular activities was held invalid. The court found the rule both overinclusive because it barred married students of good moral character and underinclusive because it did not bar unmarried students of questionable character. The court concluded, therefore, that the rule did not have a substantial relationship to its goal, and thus it violated the equal protection clause.

(c) In *Bell* v. *Lone Oak Independent School District*, 507 S.W.2d 636 (Tex. Ct. App. 1974), the court of appeals reversed a district court decision and held that a regulation prohibiting married high school students from participating in extracurricular activities was a violation of the equal protection clause of the Fourteenth Amendment.

(d) In *Hollon* v. *Mathis Independent School District*, 358 F. Supp. 1269 (S.D. Tex. 1973), the plaintiff sought a temporary injunction against the enforcement of a school district policy that prohibited married students from engaging in interscholastic league activities. The district court held that the policy was unconstitutional. The court decided "there was no justifiable relationship between the marriage of high school athletes and the overall dropout problem; nor does it appear that preventing a good athlete, although married, from continuing to play . . . would in any way deter marriages or otherwise enhance the dropout problem."

(e) In *Davis* v. *Meek*, 344 F. Supp. 298 (N.D. Ohio 1972), a married high school baseball player challenged his exclusion from the baseball team and all other extracurricular activities. The student-athlete was aware of the rule prior to his marriage and had been informed that it would be enforced against him.

The court held that extracurricular activities are an integral part of the total educational program. Therefore, the rule denied the student-athlete an opportunity that, under Ohio statutes, he had a right to receive. The issue therefore was whether the school board could enforce against the student-athlete "a rule which will in effect punish him by depriving him of a part of his education." The court held that the school board should be precluded from imposing this restriction because the deterrent effect the rule had was minimal.

(f) In *Moran* v. *School District, Yellowstone County*, 350 F. Supp. 1180 (D. Mont. 1972), a marriage rule was held invalid because it deprived a student-athlete of the chance for a college scholarship without showing any evidence that the presence of married students would result in a reasonable likelihood of imposing moral pollution on unmarried students. No rational basis on which to restrict participation existed.

(g) In *Romans* v. *Crenshaw*, 354 F.Supp. 868 (S.D. Tex. 1971), a student challenged a public high school regulation that prohibited any married or previously married student from participating in any extracurricular activity. The district court held that "absent factual support for considerations urged by the school district to sustain its regulation, the same denied equal protection"; the court granted judgment for the student.

6.3.2. Discipline

The topic of discipline of individual student-athletes is particularly important and sensitive, since the act of disciplining a student-athlete is usually the precipitating event in the decision-making process of an athlete contemplating litigation as a recourse to address a potential wrong. The high school or college that fails to carry out a disciplinary action against a student-athlete, as prescribed by an association or conference, risks forfeiting games and championships, returning television and championship money, and possibly losing its membership in the governing athletic organization. These unpleasant alternatives often place the high school or college athletic administrator in a precarious position between the student-athlete and the athletic association or conference.

Athletes who have been disciplined will often bring claims that their rights are violated because they are not allowed to participate in athletics. Other claims raise issues of due process violations when athletes are not provided adequate hearings or appeal proceedings when they are disciplined. Probably the best way to illustrate the issues involved in disciplining athletes is to examine a few situations that have been litigated in the courts. In the case of *Wooten v. Pleasant*

Hope School Dist., 139 F. Supp.2d 835 (W.D. Mo. 2000), a softball player was not allowed to participate on her high school team after she failed to appear for a game. The plaintiff alleged that she was denied her procedural due process rights because she was not given notice of her right or a hearing before her dismissal from the team.

It was true that Wooten had been dismissed from the team before she was able to plead her case to her coach. When she met with the coach, the coach told her that the players did not want her back on the team, and under this understanding, she told the coach that she did not want to be reinstated to the team. After a month away from the team, however, Wooten discovered that the coach was mistaken in his statement concerning the attitude of her teammates, and she applied to be reinstated to the team through an appeals board. The appeals board denied her a right to a hearing because they said that she had waived it by voluntarily asking not to be reinstated.

The court ruled against Wooten because it did not believe that she had a protected interest in playing softball. The court provided an eloquent discussion of the merits of allowing a coach to have discretion when disciplining its players by stating,

> That Pleasant Hope encourages its students to participate in extracurricular activities does not mean that students have an unqualified right to be a member of specific team, club or group. Notably, none of the Handbook passages discussing disciplinary action limits a coach's ability to train or punish the athletes for whom he/she is responsible. The Court recognizes that coaches must have discretionary decision-making authority to act in the best interests of the team, even if that has a negative effect on an individual team member. Accordingly, without explicit Handbook language stating that students have a protected right to participate in extracurricular activities, the Court declines to find that such a right exists.

The decision in Wooten demonstrates the power that a court grants to a coach to exercise his or her right to discipline athletes. As long as a coach can offer legitimate reasons for their disciplinary actions, and is not acting with malice or viciousness, courts will be unlikely to interfere with their decisions.

Another area where cases involving discipline are seen is disputes between individual institutions and governing athletic associations. The leading case for disputes over discipline involving institutions and associations is *Regents of University of Minnesota v. National Collegiate Athletic Association*, 422 F. Supp. 1158 (D. Minn. 1976). In this case the University of Minnesota challenged an NCAA sanction that placed all the university's athletic teams on indefinite probation when the university refused to declare three student-athletes ineligible for intercollegiate competition.

The student-athletes had admitted to the NCAA violations, which consisted of (1) selling complimentary season tickets; (2) accepting an invitation to stay at a cabin with all meals, lodging, and entertainment provided by a member of the booster club; and (3) using a private WATS line to place long-distance calls. After admitting to the violations, the student-athletes donated the proceeds from the sale of the tickets to charity to satisfy a university committee. However, the NCAA was not satisfied. The NCAA's proposed penalty for Minnesota's not declaring the student-athletes ineligible to compete was a three-year probation and a two-year ban on post-season play and televised games. Additionally, the NCAA imposed a two-year restriction on the granting of athletic scholarships for basketball.

Minnesota, as was its policy for all students, had afforded the three basketball players a hearing before the Campus Committee on Student Behaviors and the Assembly Committee on Intercollegiate Athletics. These committees voted not to declare the student-athletes ineligible, despite the findings of the NCAA's Committee on Infractions.

The court found that participation in intercollegiate athletics was a substantial property right entitled to due process guarantees. Thus, a student-athlete had to be afforded due process rights before the right to an education or any substantial element of it could be adversely affected. The court reasoned that the NCAA's action transgressed on the university's legal duty to afford due process hearings to student-athletes and to abide by the results of the hearing.

The court concluded that the plaintiffs had demonstrated a strong possibility of success on the merits and that Minnesota would be irreparably harmed if a preliminary injunction was not issued while the NCAA would not be harmed. The court directed the NCAA to lift the probation and temporarily prohibited the NCAA from imposing further sanctions pending a hearing on the merits of the case.

The NCAA appealed the district court's decision in *Regents of University of Minnesota v. National Collegiate Athletic Ass'n.*, 560 F.2d 352 (8th Cir. 1977). The appeals court dissolved the preliminary injunction. The court noted that, as a voluntary member of the NCAA, the university agreed to adhere to association rules, including Constitution 4-2-(a), which required Minnesota "[t]o administer their athletic programs in accordance with the Constitution, the Bylaws and other legislation of the Association."

In another discipline case, *Southern Methodist University v. Smith*, 515 S.W.2d 63 (Tex. Civ. App. 1974), Southern Methodist University (SMU) appealed an order which temporarily prohibited the university from declaring student-athlete Smith ineligible to play intercollegiate football. Smith admitted to receiving financial aid in excess of the amounts allowed under NCAA rules. The NCAA ordered SMU to declare Smith ineligible. Faced with the possibility of losing its membership in the NCAA, SMU notified Smith of his ineligibility after it protested the sanction and exhausted its appeals to the NCAA Council.

Smith filed suit, claiming that he was deprived of due process when he was denied notice and a hearing concerning his violations and penalty. The court held that Smith had no legal right to a hearing by SMU. In addition, he failed to establish a constitutional or contractual right to claim a benefit or privilege from playing football. The court reasoned that the NCAA had sole authority over the eligibility decision, and its rules did not provide for the type of hearing that Smith had requested. An SMU hearing on the issues could not have declared him eligible to compete in the NCAA. Moreover, a hearing could not have afforded any relief in light of Smith's admission that he had violated the rule.

In the case of *Carlton Walker v. NCAA*, No. El-C-916 (W.D. Wis. 1981), Walker, a starting guard for the University of Wisconsin football team, was declared ineligible to participate in a post-season football game (the Garden State Bowl) as a result of an investigation of recruiting violations. Previously, in July 1981, the NCAA had officially charged the university and its alumni with twenty violations of NCAA regulations and bylaws in connection with Walker's recruitment. Neither the NCAA nor the university charged Walker with any violation.

Walker immediately filed a motion for a preliminary injunction to gain eligibility for the post-season bowl game. Walker contended that he was not afforded due process in connection with the declaration of ineligibility, since athletic participation was a property right protected by the Constitution. The district court denied Walker's motion on the grounds that he failed to establish a reasonable likelihood of success on the merits and a degree of irreparable harm necessary to afford the requested relief.

Walker, who attended the University of Wisconsin from the fall of 1980 to the spring of 1982, then transferred to the University of Utah and enrolled as a full-time student. In August 1982, pursuant to NCAA Bylaw 5-3-(3), the University of Utah requested a waiver of Walker's one-year loss of eligibility due to his transfer (NCAA Bylaw 5-1-[j]-[7]).

The NCAA Committee on Infractions reviewed the waiver request by Utah. The committee determined from the available evidence that Walker's involvement in the Wisconsin recruiting violations was not inadvertent or innocent. The waiver was denied.

Walker amended his initial complaint in November 1982, and claimed that the NCAA had tortiously and arbitrarily interfered with the contractual relations between Walker and the Universities of Wisconsin and Utah, thereby depriving him of the opportunity to compete in collegiate athletics and damaging his ability to secure a professional contract.

The NCAA filed a brief in support of a motion to dismiss, or in the alternative for summary judgment. Regarding Walker's due process claims, the NCAA stated that it was well settled that a student possesses no liberty or property interest in intercollegiate athletics. Therefore, the NCAA argued, the privilege of participating in intercollegiate athletics falls outside the parameters of the due process clause.

Of course, the situations exhibited in these cases will not arise if the student-athlete can avoid being declared ineligible. This, obviously, can be accomplished if the athlete obeys the rules and regulations of the associations and conferences to which the institution belongs. This, however, is not as easy as it sounds. An athlete may unknowingly violate eligibility rules or be deceived or coerced into rules violations by a third party. Other athletes may be declared ineligible as part of a larger sanction against their high school or college, as when a football team is placed on probation and suspension of post-season competition for recruiting violations.

A student-athlete who is declared ineligible can follow a number of steps in response to such a disciplinary action. First, the athlete should exhaust all remedies available under the school's or association's policies. These remedies may include the opportunity to appeal the decision, ask for a reconsideration, or initiate other procedures for reevaluating the initial ruling of ineligibility.

Once these procedures are exhausted, the athlete may then resort to bringing a lawsuit against the governing body. Even though most claims against the NCAA or other amateur athletic association rules have ended in unsuccessful challenges by the student-athletes involved, it is still possible in some cases for student-athletes to obtain their objective—another season of competition. The student-athlete achieves this objective by asking the court for a preliminary injunction in response to a ruling that the particular rule violated by the student-athlete is unenforceable. To declare an eligibility rule unenforceable, the student-athlete must argue that the rule violates due process or equal protection clauses of the state and federal constitutions, or that it violates federal antitrust and other federal laws, or that it represents breach of contract. Together with this attack on the rule, the student-athlete asks for a court order to prohibit the enforcement of the rule as it is applied to his or her individual case until the case goes to trial. Since this may be months or years later, the student-athlete can compete in the interim. (These and other legal principles are discussed in Chapters 3, 4, and 13.)

NOTES

1. The discipline decisions of intercollegiate athlete associations were *upheld* in the following cases.

    (a) In *Samara v. NCAA*, 1973 Trade Cases (CCH) 74,536 (E.D. Va.), the court upheld an NCAA decision that participation by a student-athlete in a non-certified track and field event resulted in ineligibility for further NCAA competition. The court stated that the NCAA rule and its subsequent sanctions were not illegal. This was true even though the event would have been certified if the Amateur Athletic Union (AAU) had requested the NCAA to provide such authorization.

    (b) In *NCAA v. Gillard*, 352 So.2d 1072 (Miss. Sup. Ct. 1977), sanctions were imposed against a non-NCAA member player who accepted a 20 percent clothing discount. There was some evidence that this discount policy was not limited to student-athletes. The NCAA decided there was a rule transgression. The Mississippi Supreme Court held that the player's rights were adequately protected by the NCAA's procedures and that the player's right to play intercollegiate football was not a property right protected by due process guarantees.

    (c) In *McDonald v. NCAA*, 370 F. Supp. 625 (C.D. Cal. 1974), the court ruled that student-athletes had no due process rights infringed when the NCAA imposed sanctions against their school for bylaw violations that affected their opportunity to compete.

2. For a case in which discipline decisions of intercollegiate athletic associations have been *struck down*, see *Hall v. University of Minnesota*, 530 F.Supp. 104 (D. Minn. 1982). This case, also discussed in note 1 and in section 6.2.1.3., "Academic Progress: NCAA" of this chapter, concerned a conference academic progress rule. The court was quick to point out that the student-athlete had been recruited as "a basketball player and not a scholar," and that "his academic record reflects that he has lived up to those expectations as do the academic records of many of the athletes presented to this court." The court ruled that a constitutionally protected interest was involved and that Hall's due process rights had been violated. The court ordered the restoration of Hall's scholarship money and mandated his acceptance into a degree-granting program.

3. The following cases involve discipline issues relating to student-athletes in interscholastic athletics:

    (a) In *In Re University Interscholastic League*, 20 S.W.3d 690 (Tex. 2000), the Texas Supreme Court found that a constitutional right was not violated when a student-athlete was not allowed to participate in extracurricular activities due to disciplinary reasons. In this case an entire baseball team was ruled ineligible to compete in a high school playoff tournament because one of their players was declared ineligible. The court did not believe that because the players may suffer immediate and irreparable harm they could show a constitutional violation of their rights.

    (b) In *Mazevski v. Horseheads Central School District*, 950 F. Supp. 69 (W.D. N.Y. 1997), the court held that a high school student did not have protected property interest in participating in extracurricular activities. In this case, a student was dismissed from his school's marching band because of an unexcused absence at an event. The parents of the student, the plaintiffs, brought a claim of procedural due process violations. The court did not reach the merits of the plaintiff's case because the plaintiff was not able to establish that membership in an extracurricular activity was a protectable property right. The court reasoned that the the plaintiff's right to an education should be protected, not his right to extracurricular activities.

    (c) In *Florida High School Activities Ass'n. v. Bradshaw*, 369 So.2d 398 (Fla. Dist. Ct. App.

1979), a high school football player sought to prohibit the state high school activities association from imposing a forfeiture of two of his team's games in which an ineligible player competed. The court upheld the penalty, reasoning that there was an absence of actual harm to the player and that the coach and other team members lacked standing to assert a claim of denial of equal protection. The court also held that the opportunity to participate is a privilege, not a constitutionally protected right; therefore, the court would not intervene in an association's discipline of its members.

4. A case that involved discipline issues relating to the Amateur Athletic Union is *Santee v. Amateur Athletic Union*, 153 N.Y.S.2d 465 (N.Y. Sup. Ct. 1956). The court ruled that the Amateur Athletic Union (AAU) had the authority and the jurisdiction to determine the eligibility of athletes who wished to participate in its sanctioned events. This included selection of squads for the Olympic Games, which were held under the auspices of the International Amateur Athletic Federation, from which the AAU received its sanctioning authority.

5. The following cases overturned the disciplinary decisions of an interscholastic association:

(a) In *Christ the King Regional High School v. Catholic High School Athletic Ass'n*, 624 N.Y.S.2d 755 (N.Y. App. Div. 1995), the girl's basketball team at the plaintiff high school was suspended from post-season play for one season for violating a league rule concerning traveling to out-of-state games. Upon reviewing the penalty meted out by the Association's Principals Committee, the court discovered that the penalty was arbitrary and capricious because it violated the rules of the Association, which only allowed for the Association's Infractions Committee to dispense such penalties.

(b) In *Diaz v. Board of Education*, 618 N.Y.S.2d 948 (N.Y. Sup. Ct. 1994), the court found that the due process rights of an entire high school soccer team had been violated when they were not allowed to compete for an entire season due to the actions of one of their players. The director of the Public School Athletic League (PSAL), in a letter dated November 2, 1993, had warned the members of the Newton High School soccer team that if they received one more red card during the season the entire team would be withdrawn from competition in the league. Nine days later, one player started a fight after spitting in the face of a referee and subsequently received a red card. After a disciplinary hearing was scheduled, the Newton team was deemed ineligible to participate on the varsity level for the 1994–95 season. The court found that this decision was erroneous on two grounds. First, the court believed that the director of the PSAL was not in such a position to promulgate such a penalty because under the bylaws of the PSAL, all such policy decisions must be adopted by Committee. Second, the court found that even if the director had the authority to hand out the penalty, the ruling was arbitrary and capricious. The court argued that the entire soccer team should not be condemned for the actions of one of its players, and also pointed to evidence that such rules had never been handed out to other teams, leading the court to believe that the imposition of the penalty upon Newtown was discriminatory.

6.3.3. Alcohol and Drug Rules: High School

Another set of rules frequently contested in the courts are those regulating the use and abuse of alcohol and other drugs. While acknowledging that a school and its coaches have a strong interest in the prevention of drug abuse (see Chapter 7, "Drug Testing and Policies"), the courts have consistently required that any rule established in this area be closely related to the problem of drug abuse.

Many high schools and high school athletic associations also have "good conduct" rules. These rules can be general in nature, as opposed to specific alcohol and drug rules. These good conduct rules usually require the student-athlete to adhere to some standard of conduct. If these rules, like the alcohol and drug rules, extend to a legitimate sports-related purpose, they will most likely be upheld. If, on the other hand, the rule is too broad and attempts to overly regulate an athlete's conduct, it may be struck down by the courts.

A recent case in this area is the case of *Butler* v. *Oak Creek Franklin School District*, 116 F.Supp.2d 1038 (E.D. Wis. 2000). A student-athlete sought an emergency preliminary injunction allowing him to play interscholastic football despite his suspension from participation due to violations of the school's athletic code. The athletic code at Oak Creek High School required, "student athletes to refrain from consuming, selling, buying, distributing, or possessing" any amount of alcoholic beverages, controlled substances, and drug paraphernalia. Rule 2 required student athletes to refrain from using and possessing tobacco products. Rule 3 required students to refrain from violating any criminal law or local ordinance, and from being at any gathering where minors were partaking of alcohol or drugs. The code provided that a student who broke the Code three times would be suspended from a year of competition. Butler had broken the athletic code five times before August 31, 2000. Butler did not receive the injunction because the court decided that it was unlikely he would be able to prove that his suspension was a violation of his rights under the U.S. Constitution or Wisconsin state Constitution.

NOTES _____

1. In *L.P.M. and D.J.T* v. *School Board*, 753 So. 2d 130 (Fla. Dist. Ct. App. 2000), two students were not allowed to participate in extracurricular athletics after it was found that they had violated a school rule by drinking alcohol off-campus. The students were given a full administrative hearing where they were represented by counsel. The court held that the students had no protected right to participate in extracurricular athletics, and that they had been given full due process under the school board's system.

2. In *Zehner* v. *Central Berkshire Regional School District*, 921 F. Supp. 850 (D. Mass. 1996), the plaintiff was suspended from school and his school soccer team after arriving at a school-sponsored dance in an obviously inebriated state. He was told the morning after the dance that he was not permitted to play on the soccer team for the rest of the season. The plaintiffs claimed that his participation in athletics was a protectable property interest, and that he was denied his rights of due process before being suspended. The court agreed with the majority of federal courts when it decided that Zehner did not have a protected property interest in participating in athletics, only an expectation. Even though the plaintiff may have been an exceptional soccer player, this factor was irrelevant when determining whether a right had been violated.

3. In *Bonner* v. *Lincoln Parish School Board*, 685 So.2d 432 (La. Ct. App. 1996), a student was suspended from participating in basketball and also suspended from school after being caught in possession of alcohol during a school-sponsored field trip. Although he was afforded hearings on his suspension from school following the incident, the plaintiff was dismissed from the basketball team by the coach without the privilege of a hearing. While the court concluded that the plaintiff must receive the benefit of due process for his suspension from school he was not entitled to the same due process for his dismissal from the basketball team. The court stated, "We are not super referees over high school athletic programs. Questions about eligibility for competition may loom large in the eyes of youths, and even their parents. We do not disparage their interest in concluding, as here, that these issues are not of constitutional magnitude. Behind this observation rest important values of federalism and the reality that the mighty force of the constitutional commands ought not be so trivialized."

6.4. OLYMPIC ELIGIBILITY REQUIREMENTS

While many high schools or colleges are not fortunate enough to have a student-athlete of Olympic quality as a member of their athletic program, high school and college athletic administrators need to know how Olympic governing bodies view the student-athletes and their eligibility, as well as how the courts view the governing bodies and their rules and regulations. The consequences of not understanding these relationships may affect a student-athlete's eligibility for interscholastic, intercollegiate, and/or Olympic athletic participation. As was discussed in section 6.1., "Definitions of Eligibility," the definition of who can participate in the Olympic games will differ depending upon the decisions of the governing body of each sport. It is in the best interest of the administrator and student-athlete to conduct research in the bylaws of the national and international governing bodies of the sport in which they participate to understand what the requirements are of athletes in the sport.

The USOC has specific regulations that govern the eligibility of athletes who try out for a spot on the U.S. Olympic team. Any athlete who is a U.S. citizen at the time the team is selected and is eligible under the international rules of the IOC for selection for membership on the U.S. Olympic or Pan-American team is allowed to try out directly or indirectly under the authority of any National Governing Body. All members qualifying for the Olympic or Pan-American teams must pass the USOC medical examination before being accepted on the team, as well as sign an oath attesting to their eligibility (USOC Constitution. Chapters XL, XLI). Although the specific eligibility rules and regulations are determined by the IOC and the International Federations for each sport, the USOC does play an important role in serving to reconcile differences in eligibility requirements that exist among the various athletic organizations and Olympic governing bodies.

For more information on the Olympics see the following sections within the text: Chapter 5, section 5.1.2., "The United States Olympic Committee," and section 5.3.4., "Olympic Enforcement Procedure."

NOTES

1. The following cases deal with the relationship between the athlete and Olympic governing bodies.

(a) In *Slaney v. United States Olympic Committee*, 244 F.3d 580 (7th Cir. 2001), the strength of the Amateur Sports Act received a judicial boost. In this case, Olympic runner Mary Decker Slaney brought suit against the USOC after she tested positive for drug use after Olympic trials in 1996. She was found to have a high enough ratio of testosterone to epitestosterone in her body to be consistent with blood doping (for more information on Drug Testing of Olympic athletes, see Chapter 7, section 7.2.3., "Olympic and International Drug Testing"). In her complaint against the USOC, Slaney alleged that the testing discriminated against women, and was not scientifically valid. The Seventh Circuit upheld the strength of the Amateur Sports Act (see Chapter 5, section 5.1.2, "The United States Olympic Committee," for more information on the Amateur Sports Act) when it concluded that the Act provides the USOC with complete jurisdiction over decisions concerning an athlete's eligibility. The court reasoned that the USOC was the most qualified body for determining questions of eligibility. The court went on to state that the USOC could be held liable in questions of eligibility if they do not follow their own stated rules.

(b) In *Floyd v. United States Olympic Committee*, 965 S.W.2d 35 (Tex. Ct. App. 1998), a runner tested positive for amphetamines after using a carbohydrate supplement named Sydnocarb. She believed that she could use the supplement without worrying about testing positive because when her husband had called the USOC to see if Sydnocarb was a banned substance, the USOC operator had responded that it was not. The operator did not say, however, that the supplement was safe to use or provide any other assurances. After Floyd tested positive she brought a claim of negligence against the USOC, alleging that they had provided her with false information regarding the supplement. The court ruled that, under the Amateur Sports Act, no athlete has a right to a private cause of action against the USOC, and dismissed Floyd's claim.

(c) In *Foschi v. United States Swimming, Inc.*, 916 F. Supp. 232 (E.D. N.Y. 1996), the court concluded that while the USOC has jurisdiction concerning eligibility determinations, courts have the ability to intervene to make sure that the USOC is following its own rules for determining eligibility.

(d) In *Harding v. United States Figure Skating Association*, 851 F. Supp. 1476 (D. Or. 1994), the court enjoined the defendant Association from proceeding with a disciplinary hearing because they had violated their own by-laws by scheduling a disciplinary hearing too early for Harding to prepare her defense. The ruling in this case, allowing a court to intervene with an athletic association, was limited by the judge's opinion, which stated, "Intervention is appropriate only in the most extraordinary circumstances, where the association has clearly breached its own rules, that breach will imminently result in serious and irreparable harm to the plaintiff, and the plaintiff has exhausted all internal remedies. Even then, injunctive relief is limited to correcting the breach of the rules. The court should not intervene in the merits of the underlying dispute."

(e) In *Dolan v. United States Equestrian Team, Inc.*, 608 A.2d 434 (N.J. Super. Ct. App. Div. 1992), a horse rider brought a claim against the U.S. Equestrian Team, claiming that the Team had violated the Amateur Sports Act with their procedure and criteria for selecting team members. The court held that Dolan had not exhausted her administrative remedies under the Amateur Sports Act, and until she had met that condition she was not able to bring a private right of action. The court also held that requiring Dolan to exhaust her administrative remedies was fair and also consistent with the purpose of Amateur Sports Act to have jurisdiction over resolution of disputes in Olympic sports.

(f) In *Martin v. International Olympic Committee*, 740 F.2d 670 (9th Cir. 1984), women runners and runners' organizations filed suit against the IOC and sought to require the IOC to institute 5,000-meter and 10,000-meter track events for women at the 1984 summer Olympic games in Los Angeles. The U.S. District Court (C.D. Cal.) denied a request for a preliminary injunction, and the U.S. Court of Appeals affirmed this decision. The two courts reasoned that the IOC's Rule 32, which was the process for adding new events, was not arbitrary. In addition, it was reasoned that state law should not be applied to alter the structure of Olympic events.

(g) In *Michels v. United States Olympic Committee*, 741 F.2d 155 (7th Cir. 1984), a federal appeals court found that an individual athlete had no private cause of action (a reason or means by which to challenge the USOC's authority) against the USOC, under the Amateur Sports Act of 1978. In reversing a district court decision, the appeals court noted that the Supreme Court had emphasized congressional intent in ruling on cause of action suits and that "the legislative history of the Act clearly reveals that Congress intended not to create a private cause of action under the Act."

(h) In *DeFrantz v. United States Olympic Committee*, 492 F.Supp. 1181 (D.D.C. 1980), *aff'd. without opinion*, 701 F.2d 221 (D.C. Cir. 1980), the district court held that the Amateur Sports Act of 1978 did not establish a cause of action for twenty-five designated Olympic athletes who sought to prohibit the USOC from barring these American athletes from participating in the 1980 Olympic Games in Moscow because of an American boycott of the event. The court concluded "that the USOC not only had the authority to decide not to send an American team to the summer Olympics, but also . . . could do so for reasons not directly related to sports considerations."

(i) In *Oldfield v. The Athletics Congress*, 779 F.2d 505 (9th Cir. 1985), the plaintiff was a world-class athlete in the shot put competition. After the 1972 Olympics, Oldfield signed a professional performance contract with the International Track Association and competed for them for four years. He then wished to reestablish his standing as an amateur and participate in the 1980 Olympic trials. The Athletics Congress sought to exclude Oldfield from these trials on the grounds that he was ineligible to participate in the Olympics because he had been registered as a professional. The Court of Appeals affirmed the district court awarding of a summary judgment for the defendants based on the fact that the plaintiff had no private right of action under the Amateur Sports Act.

(j) In *Behagen v. Amateur Basketball Association*, 884 F.2d 524 (10th Cir. 1989), the plaintiff, after having played professional basketball in the NBA, wanted to return to Italy and play for an amateur team he had played for the year before. The Amateur Basketball Association had informed the International Basketball Association (FIBA) of Behagen's professional playing career; thus FIBA declared Behagen ineligible to compete for the Italian team. Behagen filed suit, claiming a violation of antitrust laws, through the formation of a boycott preventing him from competing in Italy, and a violation of his due process rights. The court of appeals held for the defendants, stating that the actions of the amateur basketball association, in refusing to reinstate plaintiff's amateur status, were exempt from the federal antitrust laws, and that the association was a private rather than a governmental actor, and thus not subject to due process requirements.

2. For a fuller discussion on the roles of the different governing bodies in the Olympic Games organization, see *United States v. Wrestling Division of the AAU*, 545 F.Supp. 1053 (N.D. Ohio 1982), in which the federal court prohibited one national sports organization (the Amateur Athletic Union) from exercising any of the National Governing Body (NGB) power and ordered it to sever all ties with the international governing body for that sport pursuant to the Amateur Sports Act of 1978, since the U.S. Olympic Committee had selected a competing national sports organization to be the NGB. The USOC was also ordered to terminate its recognition of the AAU group as the NGB and the U.S. representative to the international federation. See also the companion case *United States Wrestling Federation v. United States Olympic Committee*, Civil Action No. 13460-78, Superior Court, District of Columbia (1978), in which the USWF successfully filed suit against the USOC to compel it to recognize it as its NGB and Group A member for amateur Olympic wrestling.

3. Another major purpose of the Amateur Sports Act of 1978 was to protect the USOC's ability to raise financial revenues to field American Olympic teams, which receive no direct government funding. In *United States Olympic Committee v. Intelicense Corporation*, 737 F.2d 263 (2nd Cir. 1984), the U.S. court of appeals affirmed the judgment of the district court, which ruled that, pursuant to the Amateur Sports Act, the USOC's consent is a prerequisite to marketing the Olympic symbol (five interlocking rings) in the United States.

6.5. THE BUCKLEY AMENDMENT

An integral aspect of the NCAA's enforcement program is the compilation of information regarding the alleged infraction and also the operation of the institution's athletic department. Access to student-athletes' records concerning academic and financial aid information may be critical in the investigation. In order to protect against an invasion of a student's privacy and to prevent the likelihood that such information may be used in a way that hurts the student, Congress enacted the Family Educational Rights and Privacy Act, which regulates the release and review of such records. Consequently, the NCAA and other third parties can be restricted and sometimes prevented from access to or publication of certain types of student-athlete information. The Family Educational Rights and Privacy Act of 1974 is often referred to as the Buckley Amendment.

The Buckley Amendment was designed to enhance comprehensive civil rights protections with two objectives in mind: (1) to assure parents of students, and students themselves, if they are attending an institution of post-secondary education or are eighteen years old, access to their education records; and (2) to protect the students' right to privacy by restricting the transferability and disclosure of information in their records without prior consent. The procedures established by the Buckley Amendment for accomplishing these two objectives apply only to public or private educational agencies or institutions that receive funds, directly or indirectly, from a program that is administered by the secretary of education (e.g., Basic Educational Opportunity Grant, Guaranteed Student Loan, or National Direct Student Loans). The agency or institution is also obligated to establish a written policy and procedure for the access, disclosure, and challenge of education records. The secretary of education has the power to withdraw federal funding from any educational agency or institution that does not comply with the Buckley Amendment.

This amendment to the General Education Provisions Act primarily involves release of information concerning a student-athlete's education records, including academic rank, biographical material, and injury and health records. This type of information is often used in athletic department publications and media releases. Sports information directors, especially, should be aware of the provisions and limitations enacted by the Buckley Amendment.

Two basic rights created under the Buckley Amendment are particularly important to athletic administrators. First, students have the right to challenge any information in their education record that they or their parents believe to be inaccurate, misleading, or in violation of the student's rights. The student can bring the challenge in a hearing, or, if the institution still refuses the challenge, the student can note his or her concerns on the education record. Second, the Buckley Amendment also protects the right to prevent personally identifiable information from being disclosed, with some exceptions, in the absence of prior written consent of the parent or student. A school official with a "legitimate educational interest" may have access without consent.

As a general rule, information concerning student-athletes should not be disclosed unless the student has filled out and signed a consent-disclosure statement form. These consent-disclosure statements are intended to protect both the student-athlete and the institution. The NCAA has a student-athlete sign a Buckley Amendment consent disclosure statement as part of the student-athlete statement. Written consent-disclosure statements must include the following information:

1. A specification of the records to be disclosed
2. The purpose or purposes of the disclosure
3. The party or class of parties to whom the disclosure may be made.

In addition, the form should contain language that allows for the disclosure of unforeseen events, such as academic ineligibility, injury reports, and sudden illness affecting athletic involvement.

Another section of the Buckley Amendment deals with specific parties who do not have to receive a prior written authorization from the student to see the student's education files. Athletic department personnel fall into the school official exemption category and can review student-athlete files as needed to evaluate grade point average qualifiers, academic eligibility, and other matters that affect eligibility.

Athletic administrators should also be aware that some states impose additional and sometimes more restrictive requirements regarding the privacy of education records. However, these state statutes may not pre-empt the Buckley Amendment.

High school student-athletes' education records are also covered under the Buckley Amendment. A potential problem may arise when members of a community desire access to student records to determine the effectiveness of their educational system.

NOTES ———————————————————————————————————————

1. The Buckley Amendment, introduced by Senator James Buckley, appeared as an amendment to the Family Educational Rights and Privacy Act of 1974. The bill extended the Elementary and Secondary Education Act of 1965, Pub. L. No. 93–380, 20 U.S.C. §1232g(a)(4)(A).

2. In *Doe v. Woodford County Board of Education*, 213 F.3d 921 (6th Cir. 2000), the defendant high school was cleared of violating the Buckley Amendment. In this case, the plaintiff student-athlete suffered from hemophilia and Hepatitis-B. The principal of the school, who was privy to this information, saw that the student was practicing with the basketball team. He approached the coach of the team during practice and told him that he should check the student's medical record. It was possible, but not likely that this conversation was overheard by other students. The court believed that this did not violate the amendment for two reasons. First, the plaintiff, who was seeking summary judgment, did not show enough evidence that the other students heard the conversation of medical records, which might amount to a disclosure. Second, the court reasoned that the communication between the administrator and the coach was protected by the amendment because, "An educational institution also 'may disclose personally identifiable information from an educational record to appropriate parties' if it is necessary to protect the health or safety of the student or others."

3. In *Kirwan v. The Diamondback*, 721 A. 2d 196 (Md. 1998), the Court of Appeals of Maryland ruled that parking tickets received by an employee are not personnel records or educational records, and therefore, are open to the public. The Diamondback, a school newspaper, had alleged that basketball players on the University of Maryland campus were parking illegally, and subsequently coaches for the team were paying off their parking tickets. The court rejected the school's argument that the parking tickets were financial records, and therefore personnel records. Therefore, the court allowed the disclosure of the records.

4. In *Arkansas Gazette Co. v. Southern State College*, 620 S.W.2d 258 (Ark. 1981), a newspaper publisher brought suit against an intercollegiate athletic conference seeking to compel it to disclose the amount of money its member institutions disbursed to student-athletes during the school year. The court held that records of disbursements to student-athletes by member institutions were subject to public inspection. The court reasoned that no one has a reasonable expectation of privacy concerning the amount of public funds distributed to him unless that person clearly comes within a specific exception of law, which in this case does not, under the Arkansas Freedom of Information Act. The court also ruled that such records maintained by an intercollegiate athletic conference were "educational records" required to be closed under Family Education Rights Privacy Act of 1974. (See also Chapter 5, section 5.5.1., "Disclosure.")

Chapter 7

DRUG TESTING AND POLICIES

INTRODUCTION

In 1998, Mark McGwire of the St. Louis Cardinals hit seventy home runs to eclipse the thirty-seven-year-old Major League Baseball record of sixty-one home runs by Roger Maris. Instead of admiring McGwire's historic season, however, many athletes, coaches, administrators, and scientists debated whether Mc-Gwire's use of the performance-enhancing drug androstenedione ("andro") tainted his record. Andro is a controversial substance that boosts male testosterone levels by an average of 34 percent (see note 3). Some athletes believe that it increases muscle mass and aids their recovery from weight-lifting workouts. McGwire claimed that andro, which can be purchased without a prescription, and is *legal* in Major League Baseball, did not enhance his performance. Shortly thereafter, Major League Baseball and the Major League Baseball Players Association undertook a joint medical study to determine andro's impact on health. Most other athletic organizations including the Olympics, the NCAA, and the NFL prohibit the use of the drug.

In 2000, the sixteen-year-old Romanian gymnast Andreea Raducan delighted a worldwide television audience with her gold-medal performance in the Sydney Olympic Games. Many in that television audience were shocked by the subsequent decision to strip Raducan of her medal after she tested positive for a banned substance. The positive test result occurred as a result of Raducan's taking cold medication, not out of an effort to chemically enhance her performance. Despite the fact that all parties agreed it was from cold medication, the decision was upheld in an arbitration hearing.

The cases of McGwire and Raducan demonstrate how a substance policy, when perceived as excessively lenient or excessively strict, can create a variety of issues for sports governing bodies to address. Organizations might enact a particular substance abuse policy for several reasons, including (1) the concern for the health/safety of the participants, (2) the concern that a player's substance abuse might affect a team's chance of winning, and (3) to gain the confidence of the public. The second reason particularly applies to athletes who abuse street, as opposed to performance-enhancing, drugs. A player who abuses street drugs is presumed not to play at his or her best, thereby depriving a team of its investment in him or her.

It is crucial to understand that an athletic organization does not always possess unilateral power to implement the drug policy that it believes is optimal. Organizations are always limited by existing laws and court precedents, and are sometimes (in the case of professional sports leagues) limited by the terms of a collective bargaining agreement. For example, in 1992 an arbitrator overturned Major League Baseball's indefinite suspension of repeat cocaine user Steve Howe. In the hearing, which was mandated by MLB's collective bargaining agreement, the commissioner's office had argued that reducing Howe's penalty would cause Major League Baseball to lose "its credibility with all other players [and] its ability to deter abuse through firm sanctions." Nevertheless Howe's suspension was reduced from an indefinite lifetime ban to 119 days. The arbitrator in the case, George Nicolau, ruled that Howe suffered from a "psychiatric disorder," an attention deficit hyperactivity disorder, that "has been a contributing factor to his use of drugs." This medical ruling led to the reduction in sanctions. This ruling was widely criticized by Major League Baseball officials, including Commissioner Fay Vincent who said the ruling "made baseball look silly," and Deputy Commissioner Steve Greenburg who called for the development of a strict drug policy agreement through collective bargaining (see note 6).

While performance-enhancing drug use and recreational drug use by elite athletes is nothing new, what is alarming is the growth of the problem. According to reports in the year 2000, anabolic steroid abuse had increased among male and female high school students (see note 1). These young athletes will eventually feed into professional and Olympic sport organizations that are already facing substantial drug problems. MLB player Cliff Floyd speculated that 40 percent of Major League Baseball players have engaged in doping at one time or another (see note 4), and NBA player Charles Oakley estimated in 2001 that 60 percent of NBA players smoke marijuana (see note 2). Many dispute these estimates, since these figures have not been confirmed. There is no way to be sure. All that is sure is that there are many more reported problems.

To ensure that athletic competitions are fair and equitable, as well as to protect the health and safety of the athletes, many athletic organizations at the inter-scholastic, intercollegiate, Olympic, and professional levels have implemented drug testing programs. The first full-scale testing program was implemented at the 1976 summer Olympic Games in Montreal. The NCAA instituted drug testing in 1986. The NFL began testing for steroids in 1987, with the first suspensions levied in 1989 and random testing instituted in 1990. As illustrated by Mark McGwire's use of andro and Andrea Raducan's use of cold medication, the line between legal performance enhancement and rules violation is not always a clear one (see note 5). Some organizations such as the Olympics, have extensive lists of banned substances and random mandatory testing programs, while others, such as the National Hockey League, have shorter lists of banned substances and do not have a random mandatory drug testing program. This dichotomy must be resolved each time NHL players participate in the Olympics (see section 7.2.4.4., "National Hockey League").

Chapter 7 takes a look at the general considerations that should be considered by any athletic organization or institution with athletic teams, especially those which implement a drug testing program. The chapter begins by examining the legal principles in drug testing, and then moves on to address the issues that are relevant to interscholastic sports, intercollegiate sports, Olympic sports, and professional sports. In each section, prominent cases and legislation are discussed.

NOTES

1. Evidence shows that performance-enhancing drug use is increasing at the high school level and in Olympic-type sports, according to Daniel P. Fox, "Structural Barriers in Antidoping Measures," 8 *Sports Lawyers Journal* 271 (Spring 2001). One of the highest-profile scandals occurred in the 1998 Tour de France when French police raided hotel rooms, arresting trainers and athletes. Fox speculates that doping is not only rampant in Olympic-type sports like cycling, but also in the National Football League. However, full exposure of NFL use is unlikely due to the structural differences between the National Football League and the Union Cycliste Internationale (UCI). NFL players, unlike cyclists, are protected from exposure by their collective bargaining agreement (see section 7.2.4.1., "National Football League"). The point is explained further in section 7.2.4., "Professional Sports."

2. Oakley's "60 percent" comment was reported by several members of the media in

2001, including ESPN's David Aldridge at www.espn.go.com/nba/columns/aldridge/1116475.html

3. A Harvard University study commissioned by Major League Baseball in 2000 confirmed that andro raises testosterone levels. The study did not confirm that andro builds muscle mass. However, testosterone itself is an agent that often promotes muscle growth. See Tom Farrey, "Harvard Study Says Andro Gives 34 Percent Boost," (2000) www.espn.go.com/mlb/s/andro.html

4. In addition to Floyd's comment that 40 percent of major league players have used steroids, Bret Andress, strength coach for the Colorado Rockies, estimated the figure at 30 percent. When the San Diego Padres tested their non-unionized minor league players, 20 percent of the players tested positive. These figures were reported in James McKinley Jr., "Guessing the Score: Open Secret—A Special Report. Steroid Suspicions Abound In Major League Dugouts," *New York Times*, October 11, 2000, p. A1.

5. For more information on the controversy over deciding which drugs are performance-enhancing, see John Hoberman, "Listening to Steroids," 35 *Wilson Quarterly* (Winter 1995).

6. The *Howe* case citation is *In the Matter of the Arbitration Between Major League Baseball Players Association and the Commissioner of Major League Baseball*, Grievance No. 92–7, Suspension of Steven Howe, Nicolau, Chairman of Arbitration Panel, November 12, 1992.

7.1. LEGAL PRINCIPLES IN DRUG TESTING

The three main legal areas governing drug testing of athletes are constitutional law, contract law, and labor law. The legal principle that will govern a particular complaint depends on the individual's circumstances. For example, the drug testing of high school or college athletes raises a number of constitutional issues concerning the athlete's right to due process, equal protection, and privacy, as well as protection against illegal search and seizure and self-incrimination. Many of the same constitutional issues have applied to Olympic athletes, although the recent trend is to resolve disputes through the arbitration process. In professional sports, most of the issues and cases involving drug policy are governed by league rules and collective bargaining agreements, and are resolved through internal grievance and arbitration systems. The court system is likely to serve only as an appellate review of decisions made by an arbitrator or the *National Labor Relations Board* (NLRB), and the scope of judicial review will be limited (see Chapter 11, section 11.3.13., "Arbitration" and its notes). However, while labor law will control most disputes in professional team sports, contract law may also apply. For example, a team may negotiate a provision regarding drug testing into an individual player's contract if such clauses are allowed under the collective bargaining agreement. These clauses are usually inserted into the contracts of players who have already tested positive for drug use, or who have had a drug-related problem in the past.

7.1.1. Constitutional Law

The first legal principle to be examined is *state action*. The due process, equal protection, and other safeguards of the U.S. Constitution apply only when state action is present. State action is defined as any action taken directly or indirectly by a state, municipal, or federal government. Therefore, while public high schools and colleges and their officials are state actors, professional sports leagues and their teams, for the most part privately owned, are not subject to the same array of constitutional restrictions. For example, in *Long v. NFL*, 870 F.Supp. 101 (U.S. Dist. 1994), a former football player sued the NFL in connection with his suspension pursuant to the league's policy after he tested positive for presence of anabolic steroids. The district court dismissed Long's claim, holding that there was insufficient evidence to find state action and support a constitutional law claim. In most cases, private entities are not subject to constitutional challenges. For a more detailed discussion on state action and when the actions of private organizations can be found to be state action, see Chapter 5, section 5.4., "Associations and Constitutional Issues."

Another legal principle prevalent in drug testing cases is *due process*. Due process was reviewed in Chapter 5, section 5.4.2., "Due Process." Some of the potential claims a plaintiff may argue under the due process theory are: an objection to the consent forms for drug testing to be signed by the student-athlete as prerequisite to participation; an appropriate hearing to rebut a positive test result as inadequate or denied; or an argument that penalties assessed on the grounds of evidence brought forth by an unreliable test were unfair. Under the due process clause, the plaintiff needs to show the deprivation of a significant liberty or property interest. Legal precedent in this area has most often found that a student-athlete does not have a liberty or property interest in athletics.

A third legal principle is *equal protection*. Student-athletes may argue under this principle that they are being singled out, through a student-athlete versus non-student-athlete class distinction. An institution or organization cannot discriminate against a group, such as student-athletes, in a drug testing program unless they can establish a rational relationship for the existence of this classification in order to justify the drug testing program.

The fourth constitutional law principle affecting the legality of drug testing programs is the Fourth Amendment to the U.S. Constitution. The Fourth Amendment states:

> The right of the people to be secure in their persons, houses, papers, and effects, against unreasonable searches and seizures, shall not be violated, and no warrants shall issue, but upon probable cause, supported by Oath or affirmation, and particularly describing the place to be searched, and the persons or things to be seized.

The fifth legal principle is the Fourteenth Amendment, which is a guarantee against unreasonable searches and seizures by states.

In 1989, in the cases of *Skinner v. Railway Labor Executive Assn.* and *National Treasury Employees Union v. Von Raab*, the U.S. Supreme Court held that state-compelled collecting and testing of urine constitutes a "search" subject to the demands of the Fourth Amendment (see note 3). In the 1995 case of *Vernonia School District v. Acton*, the U.S. Supreme Court held that "The legality of a search of a student should depend simply on the reasonableness, under all the circumstances, of the search" (see note 1). In determining whether a drug test is reasonable, the court balances the intrusion of the test on an individual's Fourth Amendment interests against its promotion of legitimate governmental interests. For example, if the intrusion is minimal and the state benefit is substantial, the test would not violate an individual's Fourth Amendment rights. If, however, the intrusion is substantial, and the state benefit is minimal, then the test would violate an individual's Fourth Amendment rights. In conducting this balancing test, the court examines three factors.

The first factor to be considered is the *nature of the privacy interest* upon which the search intrudes. The Fourth Amendment protects only those expectations of privacy that society recognizes as "legitimate." What expectations are legitimate varies, of course, with context, depending upon whether the individual asserting the privacy interest is at home, at work, in a car, or in a public park. In addition, the legitimacy of certain privacy expectations vis-à-vis the state may depend upon the individual's legal relationship with the state. For example, in high school, athletes would have a lesser expectation of privacy than individuals in college or members of the general population. The reason that high school athletes would have lower privacy expectations is due to the fact that schools have a custodial and tutelary responsibility for the students. The Supreme Court also noted that high school athletes shower and change together before and after each practice or game. Therefore, their privacy expectations are small.

The second factor to be considered is the *character of the intrusion*. In determining the character of the intrusion in a drug testing case, the court examines both how the sample is produced and what type of information is being collected. In examining the intrusiveness of the drug test, the degree of intrusion will depend upon the manner in which the drug test is conducted. For example, the court will examine how the sample is collected and monitored. Is the individual required to give a blood or urine sample? The court may reject a drug test that called for blood samples, since the collection and testing of urine samples is far less invasive. As for the type of information obtained by the test, the test should look only for illegal drug use and not HIV/AIDS or pregnancy. Also, test results should be disclosed only to those individuals who have a need to know and have been specified.

The final factor to be considered is the *nature and immediacy of the governmental concern* and the efficacy of the drug test in meeting that concern. In other words, the court must determine whether the state's interest in conducting the drug test is important enough to justify intruding upon an individual's genuine expectation of privacy.

The second part of the Fourth Amendment requires that before any search can be conducted, there must be probable cause. The Supreme Court, however, has recognized that a search unsupported by probable cause can be constitutional when the state has special needs. However, a school or athletic team will have a difficult time establishing that it has a "special need" to test athletes. Therefore, in most situations, a school or athletic team must show probable cause.

Finally, it is important to note that nearly all state constitutions include sections quite similar to the Fourth Amendment. In fact, some state constitutions may afford more protections to citizens with respect to search and seizure than the U.S. Constitution. The plaintiffs in *Hill* v. *NCAA* successfully invoked the state constitution before losing their case on appeal (see note 2). Article I, section 1, of the California Constitution states:

> All people are by nature free and independent and have inalienable rights. Among these are enjoying and defending life and liberty, acquiring, possessing, and protecting property, and pursuing and obtaining safety, happiness, *and privacy*. [Italics added]

As a result, it is possible for a state court to find that drug testing violates the state's constitution even if the program does not violate the U.S. Constitution.

Athletic or school administrators should contact their state attorney general's office for an interpretation of their state's constitution or laws related to this matter.

A plaintiff who is unable to show state action on the part of the organization conducting the drug testing or that the test violated constitutional rights, may be forced to rely on contract and/or labor law for possible legal theories.

NOTES

1. In *Vernonia School District v. Acton*, 515 U.S. 646 (1995), a high school athlete sued the school district, challenging a requirement that student-athletes submit to random, mandatory drug testing. The U.S. Supreme Court, in upholding the constitutionality of the drug testing program, held that taking into account the decreased expectation of privacy, the relative unobtrusiveness of the search, and the severity of the need met by the search, the school district's policy was reasonable and constitutional.

2. In *Hill v. NCAA*, 7 Cal.4th 1, 865 P.2d 633 (Cal. S.Ct. 1994), two private university students brought an action challenging the NCAA's drug testing program. The students argued that the program violated the Privacy Initiative of the California State Constitution. The plaintiffs not only objected to the invasiveness of a urine test, but also resented a requirement to disclose medications, such as those which indicate sexual activity. The California Supreme Court, in overturning the lower courts, held that the benefits of the NCAA drug testing policy justified the invasion of privacy. In a 4–3 decision, the majority reasoned: "These kinds of disclosures are reasonably necessary to further the threshold purpose of the drug testing program—to protect the integrity of competition through the medium of accurate testing of athletes engaged in competition. The NCAA's interests in this regard adequately justify its inquiries about medications and other substances ingested by tested athletes." The majority also cited a diminished expectation of privacy on the part of the athletes in its rationale.

3. *National Treasury Employees Union v. Von Raab*, 489 U.S. 656 (1989) and *Skinner v. Railway Labor Executive Assn.*, 489 U.S. 602 (1989) were not sports-related cases. They pertained, respectively, to the testing of U.S. Customs officers in high security positions and to the drug testing of train crews following accidents. However, these cases expressed the high court's approval of testing of state workers without suspicion, so long as "special needs" can be demonstrated. In *Von Raab*, the "special need" was safety; in *Skinner*, it was security.

7.1.2. Contract and Labor Law

Other legal areas that impact the ability of a sports organization to conduct drug testing are contract and labor law. In professional sports, the players' conduct is governed by a contract that is negotiated between the league, representing the owners, and the players' association, representing the players. This contract or Collective Bargaining Agreement deals with any issue related to the players' hours of work, wages, and conditions of employment. Since a drug testing program effects athletes' conditions of employment, most of the issues and cases involving drug testing are resolved through internal grievance and arbitration systems set up within the league's Collective Bargaining Agreement. The court system is likely to serve only as an appellate review of decisions made by an arbitrator or the NLRB, and the scope of judicial review will be limited.

For example, in *Holmes v. NFL*, 939 F.Supp 517 (1996), a professional football player was involuntarily enrolled in the league's drug program and then suspended after testing positive for marijuana use. He sued the league, alleging that its actions constituted a breach of the Collective Bargaining Agreement. However, the court upheld the ruling of the league, reasoning that constitutional rights do not apply to procedures of arbitration between league and players pursuant to the Collective Bargaining Agreement. Collective bargaining and the sanctity of arbitration are discussed in greater detail in Chapter 11, sections 11.3.7. and 11.3.13., "Collective Bargaining Agreements in Professional Sports" and "Arbitration."

Normally, professional leagues cannot negotiate into the Standard Player Contract (see Chapter 9, section 9.2.1., "Standard Player Contract") of an individual player any provisions regarding drug use and testing, unless such clauses are agreed to as part of the collective bargaining agreement. An example of this occurred in 1986 when the owners' MLB Player Relations Committee attempted to add one of two clauses to individual players' contracts that would have required mandatory random drug testing. The Players Association filed a grievance, and arbitrator Thomas T. Roberts ruled that "the drug testing clauses . . . are in violation of the CBA [Collective Bargaining Agreement]" and that "any such clauses must be negotiated with the Players Association."

Exceptions to this general rule are allowed only for special covenants between the player and his club that provide benefits beyond those found in the Uniform Player Contract. For example, the NBA banned Roy Tarpley in 1991 for cocaine use. As a condition of his reinstatement in 1994, Tarpley signed a contract that contained a provision requiring him to participate in the league's aftercare program, which included frequent drug testing. The contract also stated that his contract could be voided if he was found to be using alcohol or drugs.

NOTES

1. In *Foschi v. United States Swimming, Inc.*, 916 F.Supp. 232 (E.D.N.Y. 1996), a competitive swimmer brought a state court action against the National Governing Body for the sport of swimming (United States Swimming) and the U.S. Olympic Committee, alleging breach of "contractual due process" arising from her two-year suspension due to her failing a drug test. Defendants removed action to federal court. On the plaintiff's motion for remand to state court, the court held that Foschi's claims did not arise under federal law. The USOC's constitution and bylaws and United States Swimming's rules and regulations entitled Foschi to certain "due process" rights. Therefore, even though the case might at some point involve the interpretation of a federal statute, namely the Amateur Sports Act of 1978, Foschi's claims were contractual in nature.

2. In *Dimeo v. Griffin*, 721 F.Supp. 958 (N.D. Ill. 1989), the Illinois Racing Board promulgated a substance abuse rule providing for random drug testing and individualized suspicion drug testing of licensees, including outriders, parade marshals, starters, assistant starters, drivers, and jockeys. A class action was brought against the Board, alleging that various provisions of the rule violated the Fourth Amendment prohibition against unreasonable searches and seizures. The court granted an injunction with respect to random drug testing, but held that individualized suspicion drug testing which granted limited discretion to stewards was justified by the Board's interest in preserving the integrity and safety of the sport.

3. In *Shoemaker v. Handel*, 795 F.2d 1136 (3rd Cir. 1986), horse racing jockeys brought an action challenging the New Jersey Racing Commission regulations, which permitted a state racing steward to direct any official, jockey, trainer, or groom to submit to Breathalyzer and urine testing to detect alcohol or drug consumption. The jockeys claimed that this constituted an illegal search and seizure, and was a violation of their Fourth Amend-

ment rights. The court of appeals, in upholding the regulations, held that the commission's concern for racing integrity warranted the tests, and that as long as the commission kept the results confidential, there was no violation of the jockeys' rights.

7.2. SPECIFIC POLICIES AND LEGAL CHALLENGES

Drug tests today are much more sophisticated and yield much more information than whether or not the athlete is on drugs. They can be used to identify the use of performance-enhancing drugs, street drugs, birth control pills, and any other medication an individual might be taking. This intrusion into the individual's privacy rights raises an issue for organizations wishing to test athletes. Should an organization's drug policy include random mandatory testing? If so, what type of drugs should it test for? For example, should it test for illegal drugs like marijuana or for alcohol (illegal for those under twenty-one), which are not considered performance-enhancing? How about legal drugs, such as androstenedione, which is banned by the NFL as performance-enhancing, but can be purchased by anyone?

The rest of this chapter examines the drug policies and testing programs of high schools, the NCAA, intercollegiate athletic conferences and individual colleges, the Olympics, and professional sports. The following sections will also examine the rationale for the policies, the legal barriers to policies that include testing, the types of drugs that are tested for, the penalties imposed for testing positive, and the results of any subsequent litigation.

7.2.1. Interscholastic Athletics

To deter the use of performance-enhancing or recreational drugs, schools may consider enacting a drug policy that includes testing. As the following case will demonstrate, the court in this case held that it is legal to test athletes for drugs, largely due to their diminished expectation of privacy. Both drug *education* and drug *testing* programs can be prohibitively expensive. While the former is unlikely to face legal scrutiny, a school implementing a drug testing program should first understand the legal issues involved. The leading case in drug testing of high school athletes is *Vernonia School District* v. *Acton*, 515 U.S. 646 (1995).

7.2.1.1. Vernonia School District v. Acton

In the mid-to-late 1980s, teachers and administrators in Vernonia, Oregon, began to observe a sharp increase in drug use and an increase in disciplinary problems. Not only were student-athletes among the drug users, they were the leaders of the drug culture. This caused administrators particular concern, since drug use increased the risk of sports-related injury. In an effort to combat this trend, the school board approved a drug testing policy. The policy's expressed purpose was to prevent student-athletes from using drugs, to protect their health and safety, and to provide drug users with assistance programs. The policy applied to all students participating in interscholastic athletics.

In the fall of 1991, James Acton, then a seventh grader, signed up to play football at one of the district's grade schools. He was denied participation after he and his parents refused to sign the testing consent forms. The Actons filed suit, "seeking declaratory and injunctive relief from enforcement of the policy on the grounds that it violated the Fourth and Fourteenth Amendments to the United States Constitution and Article I, § 9, of the Oregon Constitution."

The U.S. Supreme Court held that the ultimate measure of the constitutionality of a governmental search under the Fourth Amendment is "reasonableness." Whether a particular search meets the reasonableness standard, the Supreme Court held, "is judged by balancing its intrusion on the individual's Fourth Amendment interests against its promotion of legitimate governmental interests." Taking into account the decreased expectation of privacy, the relative unobtrusiveness of the search, and the severity of the need met by the search, the Court concluded Vernonia's policy was reasonable, and hence constitutional.

The first factor to be considered is the nature of the privacy interest upon which the search here at issue intrudes. The Fourth Amendment does not protect all subjective expectations of privacy, but only those which society recognizes as "legitimate," as outlined in section 7.1.1., "Constitutional Law."

In examining the nature of the privacy interest, the Supreme Court held that Fourth Amendment rights, no less than First and Fourteenth Amendment rights, are different in public schools than elsewhere; the "reasonableness" inquiry cannot disregard the schools' custodial and tutelary responsibility for children. For their own good and that of their classmates, public school children are routinely required to submit to various physical examinations and to be vaccinated against various diseases. Therefore, with regard to medical examinations and procedures, "students within the school environment have a lesser expectation of privacy than members of the population generally." The Supreme Court further stated:

> Legitimate privacy expectations are even less with regard to student athletes. School sports are not for the bashful. They require suiting up before each practice or event, and showering and changing afterwards. Public school locker rooms, the usual sites for these activities, are not notable for the privacy they afford. . . . There is an additional respect in which school athletes have a reduced expectation of privacy. By choosing to go out for the team they voluntarily subject themselves to a degree of regulation even higher than that imposed on students generally.

Finally, the Supreme Court examined the nature and immediacy of the governmental concern at issue and the efficacy of this means for meeting it. In determining whether drug testing in the absence of individualized suspicion "must demonstrate a 'compelling need' for the program," the court found that the phrase "compelling state interest" describes an interest that appears important enough to justify the particular search at hand, in light of other factors that show the search to be relatively intrusive upon a genuine expectation of privacy.

In *Vernonia*, the Supreme Court found that the school's interest in deterring drug use by schoolchildren was an important state interest. As to the efficacy of this means for addressing the problem, the Court concluded that a drug problem largely fueled by the "role model" effect of athletes' drug use, and of particular danger to athletes, is effectively addressed by the drug testing of athletes.

Since the Supreme Court's decision in *Vernonia*, a number of schools across the country have instituted similar drug testing policies for their interscholastic athletes in hopes of deterring drug use. Provided the drug testing program fulfills a compelling need and the "reasonableness" requirement, the objectives necessitating the implementation of a drug testing program will outweigh the potential invasion of privacy of the student-athletes. Institutions that implement testing programs should remain cognizant of the invasiveness of the test. The Court clearly stated that athletes can be compelled to produce a urine sample under the circumstances described. However, the Court did not give an opinion on the use of blood or hair as the testing medium. Are these procedures more invasive or less invasive than urinalysis? Furthermore, should technology produce a testing method that is clearly less invasive than urinalysis, it is uncertain whether the Supreme Court would continue to consider urinalysis drug testing to be a justifiable invasion of Fourth Amendment rights. While *Vernonia* currently stands as the definitive case on the issue of interscholastic drug testing, clearly there are several questions on the matter may arise.

7.2.1.2. Considerations in Enacting Drug Testing Programs

When an association, institution, or organization considers implementing a drug testing plan for its athletes, a number of serious questions have to be answered:

- Should the organization implement a drug education program? If so, what type of program?
- Should the organization implement a drug testing program? If so, what type of program?
- If the organization has a drug testing policy, is it clearly defined and in writing?
- Does the organization's drug testing policy conform to conference and association rules and regulations?
- Who will conduct the tests?
- Who will be tested?
- Who will pay for the tests?
- Will the tests be random and mandatory, or only for probable cause or reasonable suspicion?
- What constitutes probable cause or reasonable suspicion?
- How much notice should be given before testing begins?
- What types of drugs are to be tested for, and how frequently?
- Should testing include "street drugs" such as marijuana and cocaine, or just performance-enhancing drugs, such as steroids?
- What actions will be taken when an athlete tests positive?
- Will there be an appeal process for a positive test result?
- Is there a method for retesting when the initial results are positive?
- What confidentiality and constitutional law issues does drug testing raise?
- Do the sanctions to be imposed adhere to federal and/or state constitutional law and statutes?

The answers to these critical questions, and many others like them, should provide the basis for a carefully designed drug testing program. A meaningful program should, at the very least, consider the following components:

1. A *policy statement*—The purpose(s) behind the implementation of a drug testing program must be clearly stated from the outset.
2. *Notification of testing*—Before starting a drug testing program, it is imperative to give advance written notice to all who could be affected by its implementation. This information should include all policies and procedures utilized by the program, as well as

the voluntary consent form, to be signed by the amateur athlete, which allows for urinalysis testing and for the release of test result information.

3. *Identification of banned substances*—The organization needs to decide what types of drugs the athlete will be tested for and provide a comprehensive list of these banned substances to its athletes.

4. A *testing component*—The organization needs to decide whether the drug testing program will be random, in that all athletes are mandatorily required to submit to testing on a periodic basis, or based on reasonable suspicion, so that only athletes suspected of drug involvement are required to submit to testing.

5. *Accuracy of the tests*—No drug testing method is 100 percent accurate, so the organization needs to address the problem of "false positives" before implementing a testing program. One sound method of dealing with the problem of false positive results is to conduct a second, more sensitive test following any positive test result. Another possible concern relates to the actual collection process and "chain of custody" used in testing. Detailed security procedures regarding the sample need to be followed, and documented maintenance of the specimen needs to be assured.

6. *Sanctions*—Decisions must be made as to what action will be taken when an athlete tests positive.

7. *Due process considerations*—When implementing a program, consideration should be given to an athlete's right to have a hearing in response to a positive test result or to challenge penalties imposed as a result of a positive test.

8. *Confidentiality issues*—Steps should be taken to be sure that the procedures outlined in the program will not violate the privacy of the athlete.

NOTES

1. The direct and indirect costs of analytic laboratory testing procedures are expensive, ranging from $40 to $120 per sample, depending on the type and sensitivity level of the analysis. For example, for a school with 100 athletes who are all tested initially each season and then another 10% tested randomly each week for thirty-five weeks, the school can expect to pay from $13,500 to $54,000 annually. The cost of the test will depend on the type of drugs searched for in the sample. Tests that look for marijuana, cocaine, and amphetamines are about $40 per urine sample. Testing for steroids is more difficult, and could cost in excess of $100 per test.

2. According to the 2000 "Monitoring the Future" study conducted by the University of Michigan's Institute for Social Research, 54 percent of youths will experiment with illicit drugs before graduating high school. Four out of five students will consume alcohol before finishing high school. The rates for steroid use (not including legal supplements such as andro, or times when taken legally—e.g., prescribed by a doctor) were 2.2%, 3.6%, and 2.5% in grades 8, 10, and 12, respectively, for boys, and 1.0%, 0.8%, and 0.9% in grades 8, 10, and 12, respectively for girls.

3. In *Earls v. Board of Education*, 242 F.3d 1264 (10th Cir. 2001), students challenged the constitutionality of the school's random drug testing policy. A public high school implemented a policy requiring students' written consent to random drug testing prior to participation in any extracurricular activity, including non-competitive ones. The students claimed the policy was unconstitutional. The court held for the school stating that while the Fourth Amendment ordinarily requires some level of individualized suspicion before a search may constitutionally proceed, the ultimate measure of the constitutionality of a government search is reasonableness. The existence of a drug problem at the school constituted a special need, thus rendering the random drug testing reasonable.

4. In *Todd v. Rush County School*, 133 F.3d 984 (7th Cir. 1998), the court, in upholding the testing of all participants in any extracurricular activity or driving to school, citing

Vernonia, held that the tests applied only to those students wishing to participate in these activities. This type of participation was voluntary and a privilege; therefore, the court held it was the student's choice whether or not to participate in the program.

5. Not all extracurricular activities are protected under the *Vernonia* decision. In *Trinidad School District* v. *Lopez*, 963 P.2d 1095 (Colo. 1998), the Supreme Court of Colorado refused to extend *Vernonia* into all extracurricular activities. James Lopez was suspended from the high school marching band for refusing to submit to a random drug test. Lopez sued the school district, claiming that the testing policy violated the Fourth Amendment. The Colorado Supreme Court held that marching band members had a higher expectation of privacy than student-athletes, and that the testing program as applied to marching band members was not an effective approach to the problem of illicit drug use in schools. Another important element of *Lopez* was the fact that Lopez was enrolled in a two-credit band class, which was required of all band members.

6. In *Schail by Kross v. Tippecanoe County School Corp.*, 864 F.2d 1309 (7th Cir. 1988), two student-athletes alleged that the random urinalysis drug testing program instituted by the defendant violated their rights under the Fourth Amendment and the due process clause of the Fourteenth Amendment. The court determined that the urine collection was a "search," but that Tippecanoe County School Corporation had substantial interest in enforcement of its random urinalysis program because of the evidence that drug use among student-athletes is a problem with serious implications for their health and safety. The student-athletes claimed that the drug testing program violated their due process rights, because the program was insufficient in allowing a student to challenge a positive result. The court found that the Tippecanoe County School Corporation drug testing program provided sufficient due process to the student-athlete who tested positive. The constitutionality of this drug testing was therefore upheld.

7. For more information on interscholastic drug testing, see The National Federation of State High School Associations Web site www.nfsha.org/sportsmed.htm

7.2.2. Intercollegiate Athletics

This section examines drug testing at the intercollegiate level. Most of the section focuses on the NCAA's policy. It then considers the policies of specific institutions and conferences. Relevant litigation is also discussed.

7.2.2.1. NCAA Policy and Legal Challenges

In January 1986, the NCAA membership at its annual convention agreed to begin a drug testing program for NCAA-sanctioned championships and other events such as football bowl games.

The decision to implement a drug testing policy was not easily reached. Chief among the dissenting views of the policy was that it singles out the student-athlete, who may or may not be a scholarship athlete, to undergo urine testing that is not required of any other student who participates in student activities. In other words, why should an athlete be treated any differently from a member of the band, drama society, or glee club? However, with the passage of a random mandatory drug testing policy, the NCAA made the mandatory signing of a consent form to allow testing a condition of athletic participation.

From 1986 to 2001, the NCAA tested more than 110,000 athletes. Clearly, drug testing is an expensive proposition. When the policy first began in 1986–1987, the testing program cost $950,000 for approximately 3,000 tests. In 1998–1999, almost $3 million was budgeted by the NCAA for drug testing and education, 2.5 percent of its overall budget. In April 2001, the NCAA Committee on Competitive Safeguards and Medical Aspects of Sports considered an expansion of drug testing between 2001 and 2003, which would have cost an additional $1.7 million per year (see note 1). While the expansion of drug testing was not fully approved, Division II baseball schools underwent a pilot year-round drug testing program in 2000–2001.

Additional costs accrued to individual schools or conferences that chose to implement their own programs (see section 7.2.2.2., "College Conferences and Schools—Policies and Legal Challenges").

Critics of the NCAA's drug-testing program claim that it does not

1. Safeguard student-athletes' procedural rights, especially in regard to the appeal process for a positive test
2. Safeguard the student's privacy rights, especially when the media become aware of a test result
3. Give the student-athletes sufficient information before they sign the mandatory consent form
4. Ensure that the school will represent the student-athlete's interests and rights when an athlete tests positive.

In addition, many coaches have criticized the plan for the effect it has on a team when team members must participate in drug testing after an NCAA tournament or a championship victory. John Chaney, basketball coach at Temple University, noted that the NCAA drug testing program is "just another example of their [NCAA] imposing themselves into becoming Big Brother." Chaney noted further:

> What they're trying to do is overcome something that is already inherent in our society, and there's no way they can do that. They are applying a tourniquet to a wound that requires a much greater covering.
> You can't take the evils of society at large and solve them through sports. The education has to come at a much lower level, in the grade schools. Drug testing here just diverts attention from the areas where we should be concentrating. We're dibbling and dabbling here. And what are we going to find? The majority of players are clean livers.

The NCAA drug testing plan is constantly evolving and being modified, but as it is offered, it presents the athletic administrator with the basic materials needed to make an informed decision when dealing with coaches, medical staff, student-athletes, and the NCAA about the plan.

The NCAA provides a list of banned substances to its membership. More than seventy drugs in six different categories are included in this list. These are drugs that the NCAA considers to be "performance-enhancing and/or potentially harmful to the health and safety of the student-athlete." The NCAA refers to the use of any of the banned substances as "doping." Any student-athlete who tests positive will be subject to disciplinary action, including being declared ineligible for further participation in post-season and regular season competition during the period ending one calendar year after the student-athlete's positive drug test result and until the student-athlete retests negative, and until restored to eligibility by the NCAA Eligibility Committee (*2001–02 NCAA Manual*, Bylaw

18.4.1.5). A brief description of the six categories follows. Examples of specific drugs in each of these categories are listed in exhibit 7.1.

1. *Psychomotor and central nervous system stimulants*: Psychomotor stimulants prevent or delay fatigue, mask pain, and increase self-confidence and aggressiveness. The danger in masking pain is that serious injury can occur. Preventing or delaying fatigue can lead to heat exhaustion, heat stroke, and even death. Central nervous system stimulants increase endurance because they stimulate respiration and heart rate. The danger associated with their use in sports is that by increasing heart rate, they also increase blood pressure and can cause dehydration, cerebral hemorrhage, stroke, and cardiac irregularities that could lead to heart arrest or even death.

2. *Anabolic steroids*: It has long been believed that anabolic steroids increase muscle mass. They are a derivative of the male hormone testosterone. Some serious side effects can occur, including cardiac disorders and bone growth damage in children.

3. *Substances banned for specific sports*: Alcohol is sometimes used in rifle competitions to minimize tremor in the shooter's arms. Beta-blockers are sometimes used to decrease the heart rate and lower the blood pressure so that the shooter can get off a shot between heart contractions and pulsations in the arm. Both are banned by the NCAA. Beta-blockers are known to affect the functioning of the cardiovascular system adversely.

4. *Diuretics*: Diuretics remove body fluids quickly and thus lower body weight. They are used by athletes who need to make weight classifications. They are also used to flush out other drugs that an athlete might have been taking prior to competition. The problem with their use is that electrolytes are removed along with body fluids, and an upset electrolyte balance can lead to cardiac arrest.

5. *Street drugs*: Drugs such as cocaine, marijuana, heroin, and amphetamines are used mainly outside the sports setting. They bring about a sense of euphoria and relax inhibition. In the sports setting, they prevent or delay fatigue and mask pain. In or out of sports, the use of these substances can cause memory impairment, respiratory distress, convulsions, coma, and even death.

6. *Peptide hormones and analogues*: The NCAA added this category to be in agreement with banned drugs by the USOC. This group consists of chemically produced drugs that have effects similar to already existing substances in the body (i.e., growth hormone and other hormones that increase testosterone and other steroids) and increase the effects of these steroids in the body.

The NCAA bans these drugs for either of two reasons—because they illegally enhance performance or because they are potentially harmful to the student-athlete's health. The practice of blood doping—the intravenous injection of whole blood, packed red blood cells, or blood substitutes—and the use of growth hormone—human, animal, or synthetic—are also prohibited by the NCAA.

There are two general exceptions to the NCAA banned drug list. These exceptions involve the use of local anesthetics and asthma- or exercise-induced bronchospasm medications. As long as they are administered correctly and their use is medically justified, the NCAA approves them.

Almost since the inception of the NCAA drug testing program, student-athletes claiming that the test is a violation of their constitutional rights have challenged the program in the courts. Some lawsuits have been filed when a student refuses to sign a consent form and is therefore deemed ineligible to participate. Other times, a lawsuit occurs as the result of a positive test (see notes 2 and 3).

Exhibit 7.1
NCAA Banned Substances List

The following is the list of banned drug substances, Bylaw 31.2.3.1 (updated June 26, 2001)

(a) Stimulants

amiphenazole
amphetamine
bemigride
benzphetamine
bromantan
caffeine[1]
chlorphentermine
cocaine
cropropamide
crothetamide
diethylpropion
dimethylamphetamine
doxapram
ephedrine
ethamivan
ethylamphetamine

fencamfamine
meclofenoxate
methamphetamine
methylene-dioxymethamphetamine
(MDMA) (Ecstasy)
methylphenidate
nikethamide
pemoline
pentetrazol
phendimetrazine
phenmetrazine
phentermine
picrotoxin
pipradol
prolintane
strychnine
and related compounds*

(b) Anabolic Agents

anabolic steroids
androstenediol
androstenedione
boldenone
clostebol
dehydrochlormethyl-testosterone
dehydroepiandrosterone (DHEA)
dihydrotestosterone (DHT)
dromostanolone
fluoxymesterone
mesterolone
methandienone
methenolone

methyltestosterone
nandrolone
norandrostenediol
norandrostenedione
norethandrolone
oxandrolone
oxymesterone
oxymetholone
stanozolol
testosterone[2]
and related compounds*

Other anabolic agents
clenbuterol

(c) Substances Banned for Specific Sports
Rifle

alcohol
atenolol
metoprolol
nadolol

pindolol
propranolol
timolol
and related compounds*

(d) Diuretics

acetazolamide
bendroflumethiazide
benzthiazide
bumetanide
chlorothiazide
chlorthalidone
ethacrynic acid
flumethiazide
furosemide

hydrochlorothiazide
hydroflumethiazide
methyclothiazide
metolazone
polythiazide
quinethazone
spironolactone
triamterene
trichlormethiazide
and related compounds*

Exhibit 7.1 (continued)

(e) Street Drugs:
heroin
marijuana[3]

THC (tetrahydrocannabinol)[3]

(f) Peptide Hormones and Analogues
chorionic gonadotropin (HCG—human
   chorionic gonadotropin)

corticotropin (ACTH)
growth hormone (HGH, somatotropin)

All the respective releasing factors of the above-mentioned substances also are banned.

erythropoietin (EPO)

sermorelin

(g) Definitions of positive depend on the following
[1]For caffeine—if the concentration in urine exceeds 15 micrograms/ml.
[2]For testosterone—if the administration of testosterone or the use of any other manipulation has the result of increasing the ratio of the total concentration of testosterone to that of epitestosterone in the urine to greater than 6:1, unless there is evidence that this ratio is due to a physiological or pathological condition.
[3]For marijuana and THC—if the concentration in the urine of THC metabolite exceeds 15 nanograms/ml.
*The term "related compounds" comprises substances that are included in the class by their pharmacological action and/or chemical structure. No substance belonging to the prohibited class may be used, regardless of whether it is specifically listed as an example.

Supplements
Nutritional supplements are not strictly regulated and may contain substances banned by the NCAA. For questions regarding nutritional supplements, contact the National Center for Drug Free Sport Resource Exchange Center (REC) at 877/202–0769.

One of the most noteworthy cases is *Hill v. NCAA*, 865 P.2d 633 (Cal. 1994). Hill, a member of the swimming team at Stanford University, brought action challenging the NCAA's drug testing program. Hill argued that the program violated her privacy rights under the California State Constitution. In particular, Hill pointed to the NCAA's procedure for collecting urine samples and the consent form, which asked students to disclose medical and sexual information.

Although Hill was successful in the lower courts, the California Supreme Court, in overturning the lower courts, held that the NCAA's drug testing policy involving monitoring of urination, testing of urine samples, and inquiry concerning medication did not violate the students' constitutional right to privacy. In holding that the program was consistent with the privacy provisions of the state constitution, the California Supreme Court held that the NCAA's interest in protecting both the health and safety of the athletes and the integrity of the programs outweighed Hill's privacy interests.

In addition to claims that the NCAA's drug testing program is an invasion of the student-athlete's privacy rights, student-athletes have also challenged the sample collection and notification protocol in *Premock v. Montana*, Case 74947/40 (Mont. Dist. Ct. 1991), (see note 2(b)) and the legality of the consent form signed by all students in *Bally v. NCAA*, 707 F. Supp. 57 (D. Mass. 1988) (see note 3(b)).

Another criticism of the NCAA drug testing program is that it is ineffective

Exhibit 7.2
NCAA Drug Testing results

NCAA Drug-Testing Program
Year-Round Program
July 1999-December 1999

Sport	Number of Samples	Positive Ineligible	Positive Eligible	Total
Division I Football	2,473	8 Nandrolone 4 T/E > 6:1 1 Stanozolol 1 Methandienone 1 Boldenone	11 (12) T/E > 6:1*	26 (27)
Division II Football	1,183	5 Nandrolone 4 Boldenone 2 Fail to Show 1 Probenecid 1 Methandienone 1 T/E > 6:1	2 T/E > 6:1*	16
Division I Track and Field	692	1 Fail to Show	1 Hydrochlorothiazide 1 Fail to Show	3
Total	4,348	30	15 (16)	45 (46)

*() indicates the total number of positive tests, including follow-up tests on individual student-athletes.

NCAA Drug-Testing Program
Postseason Program
Year-Round — July 1999-December 1999

Championship	Specimens	Positive Ineligible	Positive Eligible	Total
I-AA Football	48	2 Ephedrine 2 Marijuana		4
I-A Bowls	121	7 Marijuana		7
II Football	24			0
III Football	26	1 Nandrolone (Pending)		1
I Men's Soccer	20			0
III Women's Volleyball	12		1 Ephedrine	1
Total	251	12	1	13

Source: *The NCAA News*, September 25, 2000
http://www.ncaa.org/news/2000/20000925/active/3720n11.html

and does not stop individuals from using performance-enhancing drugs. For example, between July 1999 and December 1999, the NCAA conducted a total of 4,599 drug tests, but only 59 samples (1.28 percent) tested positive (see exhibit 7.2). Approximately half of the positive tests were either for nandrolone (an anabolic agent) or for THC (marijuana). Since there are so few positive results each year, critics claim that the tests prove that there is no drug problem among college athletes. The NCAA, however, argues that the test is a success, because it discourages student-athletes from using drugs.

NOTES ——————————————————————————————

1. More information on the NCAA drug testing program can be found on the NCAA Web site www.ncaa.org/sports_sciences. Information on the April 2001 budgetary pro-

posal was obtained from www1.ncaa.org/membership/governance/division_II/docs/mgmt_
council/Supplements_April_2001_Meeting/S06_Attachment_A_CSMAS_Report.htm

2. The following are examples of cases stemming from a student's positive drug test:

(a) In *Brennan v. Board of Trustees for University of Louisiana Systems*, 691 So.2d 324 (La.
Ct. App. 1 Cir. 1997), a student-athlete who had been suspended from intercollegiate athletic competition after testing positive for the anabolic steroid testosterone sued the university's board of trustees, seeking to enjoin enforcement of suspension imposed by the
NCAA. The court of appeals, in rejecting the plaintiff's claim, held that the student-athlete
had a diminished expectation of privacy, and the small compromise of privacy from a urine
test was outweighed by the significant interest of the university and NCAA. The court also
held that the student-athlete has no liberty or property interest protected by due process
in participating in intercollegiate athletics.

(b) In *Premock v. Montana*, No. 74947/40 (Mont. Dist. Ct. 1991), a student-athlete brought a
complaint regarding the drug testing protocol that was used, which resulted in a positive
result. The judge found that although the NCAA's "goal of drug-free sports is commendable,
their methods of achieving that goal are deplorable." The judge found that the drug testing
area lacked the control required for a credible collection process (Premock had left the
collection area for several minutes, and his urine sample was left unattended during that
time); there were violations of the NCAA's chain-of-custody requirements (the NCAA could
not account for the specimens from the time they reached the campus of UCLA, where
they were to be tested, until they arrived at the drug-testing laboratory); the lab breached
the protocol in the testing and retesting process (the urine analysis test on both samples
was conducted by the same person and took more than twenty-four days to complete); and
the NCAA failed to notify the university of Premock's test results until thirty-three days
after the sample was collected. Premock won a restraining order from the district court
judge restoring his eligibility, but Premock had already completed his eligibility and the
case was settled out of court.

(c) In *Barbay v. NCAA*, No. 86–5697 1987 U.S. Dist. LEXIS 393 (E.D. La. Jan. 20, 1987),
the plaintiff, a football player at Louisiana State University, tested positive for steroids prior
to the January 1987 Sugar Bowl and was thus prohibited from competing in the bowl game
by the NCAA. The plaintiff sought a preliminary injunction preventing the NCAA from
enforcing this penalty based on a violation of his Fourteenth Amendment rights. The plaintiff stated that the NCAA penalty prohibiting student-athletes from competing in post-season
competition after testing positive for drugs was instituted after he had taken steroids to
help in his rehabilitation of a knee injury. He should not be punished, therefore, for taking
steroids prior to the establishment of this penalty. The district court first found that there
was no state action; thus the plaintiff had no claim against the NCAA. In addition, the
plaintiff could not demonstrate an irreparable harm if a ruling in his favor was not granted;
therefore, the court denied the plaintiff's petition for a preliminary injunction.

(d) In *Mira v. NCAA*, No. 87–55213 (Fla. Dist. Ct. 1988), the plaintiff sought a temporary and
permanent restraining order preventing the NCAA from enforcing its drug testing program.
The plaintiff argued that the drug testing program violated the plaintiff's constitutional
rights. The district court ruled that there was no state action, and therefore no claim upon
which it could base relief.

3. The following are examples of cases stemming from students' refusals to sign a consent form or unwillingness to submit to testing:

(a) In *Hill v. NCAA*, 865 P.2d 633 (Cal. 1994), the California Supreme Court held that the
NCAA's drug testing policy involving monitoring of urination, testing of urine samples, and
inquiry concerning medication did not violate the student's state constitutional right to
privacy.

(b) In *Bally v. NCAA*, 707 F.Supp. 52 (Mass. 1988), the Superior Court of Massachusetts ruled
that the NCAA consent form did not infringe on any rights secured by the Massachusetts
Civil Rights Act and that the consent form by itself does not subject the plaintiff to an
illegal search and seizure or violate his or her right to privacy.

7.2.2.2. College Conferences and Schools—Policies and Legal Challenges

Although the NCAA conducts over 10,000 drug tests of student-athletes each year, its program is limited, given that over 325,000 athletes participate in NCAA sponsored events each year. In most sports, the NCAA conducts drug tests only at NCAA championships or in conjunction with post-season bowl events. While the NCAA has considered expansion of year-round testing, the only student-athletes who are currently subject to year-round drug testing are those who participate in Division I-A, I-AA, or II football or Division I track and field.

To fill the gaps in the NCAA's program, many athletic conferences have taken a position on the drug testing issue, from providing statements regarding drug usage in their handbooks to implementing their own drug testing program. The Big 12 Conference has established a drug testing program whereby each year, drug testing of student-athletes will be conducted at four randomly selected championship events sponsored by the conference. In addition, the conference will conduct on-campus drug testing at each member institution once each semester. The conference also reserves the right to conduct a second drug test during a semester at a randomly selected institution. A total of thirty student-athletes from all intercollegiate sports sponsored by each member institution shall be selected at random to participate in each on-campus drug test. Member institutions are notified twenty-four hours in advance. The student-athletes, who are randomly selected to participate in the drug test, are notified two hours in advance.

In addition to NCAA testing and conference testing, some schools conduct their own drug testing programs. The University of North Carolina at Chapel Hill adopted random, unannounced testing of its athletes in 1999. Banned substances include steroids, diuretics, and a variety of street drugs. An athlete testing positive for the first time may receive probation and required counseling, and his or her parents will be informed. A second positive test will result in permanent suspension from athletics and a possible termination of his or her scholarship. Bowling Green State University requires its athletes to submit to "reasonable suspicion" testing for performance-enhancing and recreational drugs. A refusal to test, when confronted with reasonable suspicion, will result in a suspension of athletic participation and scholarship award for one year.

The NCAA has encouraged, but not mandated, that member institutions implement some type of drug testing program such as the ones described above. A 1999 NCAA Drug Education and Testing Survey, which was conducted by the NCAA Committee on Competitive Safeguards and Medical Aspects of Sports, showed that 56% of the schools surveyed, responded that they had a drug/alcohol education program. An additional 9% of the institutions responded that they were actively planning to begin a program. The percentage of institutions that have instituted a drug testing program increased dramatically, from 10% in 1984 to 42% in 1999 (see note 1).

NCAA member institutions have taken a varied approach to the issue of drug testing. These approaches can be categorized as follows:

1. No drug testing or drug education programs
2. An educational program on the drug issue but no drug testing
3. Random mandatory testing only for street drugs, such as marijuana and cocaine

4. Random mandatory testing only for performance-enhancing drugs, such as steroids

5. Random mandatory drug testing for both street drugs and performance-enhancing drugs

A characteristic of the majority of conference and institutional drug testing programs is that there is mandatory testing for student-athletes but not for coaches and staff. The programs provide a specific written policy on testing to student-athletes and require the student-athlete to sign an institutional waiver or consent form.

Institutional drug testing programs have come under scrutiny by student-athletes, much as the NCAA drug testing program has, for possible violations of the student-athlete's constitutional rights (see notes 2–4).

NOTES ⎯⎯⎯⎯⎯⎯⎯⎯⎯⎯⎯⎯⎯⎯⎯⎯⎯⎯⎯⎯⎯⎯⎯⎯⎯⎯⎯⎯⎯

1. The 1999 NCAA Drug Education and Testing Survey can be viewed online at www.ncaa.org/sports_sciences/education/1999drugsummary.html

2. In *University of Colorado v. Derdeyn*, 863 P.2d 929 (Colo. 1993), student-athletes challenged the state university's mandatory drug testing program. The Colorado Supreme Court found that the program failed to meet the warrant and probable cause requirements of the Fourth Amendment of the U.S. Constitution and Article II, Section 7, of the Colorado Constitution. In years prior to the case, the university had modified the testing procedures to be less invasive to the athletes (in the 1980s, trainers had to watch the athlete urinate into a receptacle). Despite the less invasive procedure, the court cited the absence of voluntary consent on the part of the student-athlete, and ruled the drug testing program to be an unconstitutional search.

3. In *Bally v. Northeastern University*, 532 N.E.2d 49 (Mass. 1989), a student-athlete challenged the university's drug testing program by claiming the policy of requiring student-athletes to consent to drug testing as a condition of participating in intercollegiate athletics was a violation of civil rights and the right to privacy, and also constituted a breach of contract. The court ruled for the university and upheld the constitutionality of the drug testing program.

4. In *O'Halloran v. University of Washington*, 679 F.Supp. 997 (W.D. Wash. 1988), a student-athlete claimed that the NCAA and the school's drug testing program violated her privacy, and constituted an unreasonable search and seizure. The district court found that the collection of a urine sample was a "search" for the purposes of the Fourth Amendment, but that the compelling interest of the university and the NCAA in implementing the drug testing program far outweighed the hardships on the student-athlete. The court ruled for the university.

7.2.3. Olympic and International Sports

Some argue that perhaps the greatest threat to the image, integrity, and even the continued existence of elite-level international competitions, from the World Cup to the Tour de France to the Olympic Games themselves, is the use of illicit performance-enhancing drugs. When a millisecond difference between gold and silver can amount to millions in endorsement contracts and appearance fees, some athletes are willing to risk using drugs to get that winning edge. With so much at stake, it is not surprising to see some athletes caught for testing positive for drug use.

A major doping scandal in international sports occurred during the 1998 Tour de France cycling race. During the competition, French police raided hotel rooms and arrested trainers and athletes. At least six teams pulled out of the race, and the leading team, Festina, was disqualified because of suspected doping. The negative legacy of the 1998 scandal extended into the event in subsequent years. When American cyclist Lance Armstrong won the championship in 1999 and 2000, after recovering from cancer, rumors began to circulate that he was engaging in doping. A full French judicial investigation into Armstrong's team, U.S. Postal, was opened in November 2000, following a preliminary probe resulting from an anonymous tip. The case is pending, although preliminary reexaminations of the team's urine samples and searches of its hotel garbage had yielded no incriminating evidence as of July 2002.

Drug use by Olympic athletes is nothing new. Ancient Greek athletes are reported to have used various substances to increase their strength and endurance. In the 1960 Olympic Games in Rome, two athletes died from overdosing on drugs they took before competing in their events. To protect the health of the athletes and to ensure fair and equable competition, the International Olympic Committee began to routinely perform drug tests at the 1968 summer Olympic Games in Mexico City, and began full-scale testing at the 1976 summer Olympic Games in Montreal.

To discourage drug use by athletes, any athlete caught doping faces the loss of medals and a suspension from competition. One of the more famous cases is that of Canadian sprinter Ben Johnson, who tested positive for steroids at the Olympic Games in Seoul in 1988, and was stripped of his gold medal and world record. The introduction to this chapter discussed the case of Andrea Raducan, and the notes of this subsection discuss Butch Reynolds, Mary Slaney, and others. The IOC, which has a $20 million annual drug testing budget (approximately five times that of the NCAA), uses state-of-the-art testing. The IOC's list of banned substances is extensive, filling a seven-page, single-spaced document (see note 4). The categories of banned substances are stimulants, narcotics, anabolic agents (steroids or beta-2 antagonists), diuretics, and peptide hormones. Athletes can even be suspended for excessive caffeine.

Despite all the actions of the IOC, athletes continue to use drugs to augment performance. In discussing the IOC's drug testing policy, Prince Alexandre de Merode, who has headed the IOC's Medical Commission for all of its thirty-one years, stated that it is ridiculously easy to dope and not get caught. Therefore, to protect the future of the Olympic Games, the IOC held the World Conference on Doping in Sport in February 1999 at Lausanne, Switzerland. The purpose of the conference was to establish uniform policies under which all athletes and sports federations would be tested. The conference, which was attended by approximately 600 representatives of National Olympic Committees, National Governing Bodies, government officials, and athletes, was held to establish an international anti-doping agency, develop penalties (including a proposed automatic two-year suspension for all doping offenses), and get the international governing bodies of sports such as swimming and track and field to agree to the same rules. While governing bodies of certain sports refused to recognize uniform penalties, the conference recommendations were sanctioned in the form of the Anti-doping Code on January 1, 2000 (see note 5).

While some believe that IOC drug sentences have been unduly harsh, many believe that the IOC has a conflict of interest in any drug testing program. The IOC, while wanting to ensure fair competition, also must be concerned with the impact a positive doping test could have on the Olympic image, resulting in the loss of corporate sponsorship and fans. "It's very simple," charges John Leonard, executive director of the American Swimming Coaches Association, "The IOC doesn't want sponsors to be unhappy, and sponsors are unhappy any time their brand name is tarnished." In fact, there is increasing evidence to suggest that the IOC and some sport federations, far from being the stalwart defenders of the purity of athleticism, are soft on drugs. At the 1998 winter Olympic Games, for example, the IOC discarded two positive test results, claiming that the games had already ended. At the 1996 Summer Olympic Games in Atlanta, several athletes tested positive for probenecid, a masking agent for steroids that is banned by the IOC. The IOC, however, took no action. Only two athletes tested positive for steroids. However, Donald Catlin, the clinical pharmacologist who oversaw the Atlanta Olympic drug testing, said that other positive samples went unreported.

A major point of interest concerns unannounced or short-term testing. Canada, England, Sweden, and a handful of other countries have instituted frequent, random, out-of-competition testing for anabolic steroids. The purpose of this type of testing is to combat the use of performance-enhancing drugs taken during training. In many cases, the evidence of drug use has left the body by the time of the competition. However, the drugs' impact will have already carried over and given the athlete a possible advantage. For example, steroids are training drugs, not something you take the day of the competition; therefore it is possible for athletes to avoid detection. An example of the success of random, out-of-competition testing is the case of the Olympic swimming champion Michelle Smith de Bruin of Ireland. Smith, who won three gold medals at the Atlanta Olympics in 1996, came under widespread suspicion after her Olympic performances. Smith de Bruin denied any drug use and tested negative during the Atlanta Games. In 1998, however, Smith de Bruin was banned by FINA, the international aquatic federation, for allegedly tampering with a urine sample. The sample was taken during an out-of-competition test at her home and was contaminated with whiskey (see note 6).

The U.S. Olympic Committee (USOC) employs its own drug education program for events involving national team tryouts and competitions. This program helps the USOC to instruct its athletes about the vast international drug regulations and to support its program to deter drug use. In October 2000, the USOC turned over responsibility for testing of Olympic and Pan American athletes to the U.S. Antidoping Agency (USADA). Any athlete eligible to compete in events sanctioned by his or her sports federation or by the USOC will be subject to unannounced out-of-competition testing. The USADA tests for steroids, masking agents, diuretics, and peptide hormones.

The testing process begins with the collection of two specimens (A and B). Specimen A is tested; if a positive result occurs, another sample from A will be tested. If this second test of specimen A results in another positive test, the athlete will be notified immediately by the USADA. This notification will also tell the athlete the time and date of the testing of specimen B. The athlete may witness this testing or a surrogate representative will be assigned to witness the testing of specimen B. If specimen B tests positive, the appropriate penalties will be imposed. The athlete has the right to request a hearing on the positive drug result. Penalties for positive tests vary, depending on the substance. A confirmed first positive test will result in a suspension ranging from three months to two years. A confirmed second positive test will result in a two-year suspension for some substances and a lifetime ban for other substances.

The USADA's strict policies were put into effect prior to the 2002 Winter Olympic games in Salt Lake City. Before the games, the USADA administered unannounced tests on most of the 2,500 athletes competing in the games. All athletes at the games carried a "doping passport" which showed when and how they were drug tested. During the games, the USADA administered post-event drug tests to athletes in the first four places of their respective events. A "doping escort" was assigned to each athlete and administered the test within an hour of the event's finish. If an athlete tested positive for any prohibited substance, a series of hearings decided if the athlete would be stripped of his or her medals and banned from future competition.

The USADA operates a twenty-four-hour, toll-free drug hotline that athletes, coaches, trainers, doctors, and administrators can call for more information on banned drugs, drug testing procedures, and the drug education program. The USADA has budgeted $2 million per year for support of research related to the deterrence of the use of performance-enhancing drugs in sports. The agency is funded by the federal government.

In some cases, National Governing Bodies (NGB) and International Federations (IF) will call for stricter penalties for positive tests than the USOC or IOC. For example, the NGB for the biathlon may recommend a four-year penalty for the use of a substance, whereas the USOC/IOC may recommend a two-year penalty. In that case, the governing body's sanction will take precedence over the USOC/IOC prescribed penalties.

Historically, due to several parties' being involved in international competition (IFs, NGBs, IOC, etc.), complications can arise over penalties after positive tests. For instance, when Butch Reynolds, a U.S. athlete, challenged a positive drug test result that occurred at an international track and field meet in Monte Carlo, the organizations that were involved in this dispute included the USOC, The Athletics Congress (the national governing body for track and field in the United States at the time), the IAAF (the IF for track and field), and the court system in the United States (see note 10). The problem arises as to which organization and/or country has the final authority in disputes involving a drug testing program.

Sometimes an athlete is disqualified for a positive drug test immediately prior to his or her Olympic event. When this occurs, it does not afford much time for the athlete to obtain due process. In order to handle disputes over matters such as a positive drug test, the Court of Arbitration for Sport (CAS) was created in 1983. The option of the CAS allows disputes that arise during (or right before) the Olympic Games to be settled quickly and inexpensively. The CAS sets up ad hoc (non-permanent) courts and sends representatives to the Olympic Games in the event that a situation arises where a hearing and ruling must be pronounced within twenty-four hours of the disputed claim. Athletes, NGBs, and IFs all have access to CAS (see note 3).

NOTES ─────────────

1. In 2001, an independent commission, created after doping controversies at the Sydney Olympics, criticized the USA Track and Field (USATF) for not following procedures or promptly identifying athletes who were using performance-enhancing steroids or other banned drugs. The USATF claimed that it was not covering up positive tests, or stalling,

but merely protecting the identity of athletes pending verification of positive tests. The commission concluded that USATF did not intentionally cover up athletes' positive drug tests, but did not follow procedures and was slow to inform authorities about violators.

2. German freestyle wrestler Alexander Leipold was stripped of his gold medal in the 2000 Sydney Olympics and banned from international competition for two years after testing positive for the anabolic steroid nandrolone. The Olympic medical commission reported that Leipold's sample showed 20 nanograms of nandrolone per milliliter of urine. The commission's limit is 2 nanograms per milliliter. However, critics contend that nandrolone is found naturally in the body, and nandrolone levels can rise when persons are dehydrated or under stress. Finally, some scientists believe that supposedly clean nutritional supplements may contain traces of the steroid. In July 2001 the Court of Arbitration for Sport (CAS) reduced the ban against Leipold from two years to one, but upheld his disqualification from the games and the stripping of his medal.

(a) In March 2001, USATF suspended 1999 world shot put champion C. J. Hunter for two years due to Hunter's positive test for nandrolone prior to the 2000 Sydney Olympic Games. Hunter, who announced his retirement around the time of the suspension, did not formally contest the charges. However, he claimed the test was the result of an otherwise legal supplement that had become contaminated.

(b) Others who have allegedly tested positive for nandrolone include British former 100-meter Olympic champion Linford Christie (1999), Jamaican sprinter Merlene Ottey (1999), Dutch soccer player Frank de Boer (2001), and German former 5,000-meter Olympic champion Dieter Baumann (1999).

3. For further information on Olympic dispute resolution, see Mary Fitzgerald, "The Court of Arbitration for Sport: Doping and Due Process During the Olympics," 7 *Sports Lawyer's Journal* (Spring 2000): 213. Also see the Court of Arbitration for Sport Web site, www.tas-cas.org/

4. A complete list of IOC banned substances can be found at www.nodoping. olympic.org/welcome_e.html; for information on the USOC program, see the USADA Web site at www.usantidoping.org/

5. In February 1999, the World Conference on Doping in Sport, sponsored by the IOC, tried to establish a working group of athletes, government representatives, sports governing body members, and IOC members to define the anti-doping agency's structure, mission, and funding. Those on the committee agreed that the anti-doping agency should be independent of the IOC in order to avoid conflict-of-interest issues such as concerns that positive doping tests could tarnish the image of the Olympics and hurt the IOC financially. Delegates agreed that the new organization should consider expanding out-of-competition drug testing, coordinating research, promoting preventive and educational programs, and harmonizing scientific and technical standards, procedures for testing, and equipment. The conference also proposed an automatic two-year suspension for all doping offenses. The two-year sanction for a first offense was adopted with compromise wording that the suspension could be modified in "specific, exceptional circumstances" to be evaluated by international sports federations. Representatives from soccer, cycling, and tennis who wanted to retain autonomy over athlete suspensions opposed the proposal for uniform penalties.

6. In 1999, Michelle Smith de Bruin appealed her case to the Court of Arbitration for Sport. A three-member arbitration panel upheld her four-year doping penalty, claiming that based on the facts of the case and the evidence before them, the arbitrators were of the opinion that FINA had convinced them that [Smith] was the only person who had the motive and opportunity to manipulate the sample. After the arbitrators announced their decision, Smith de Bruin announced that she was going to retire from competition.

7. In 1997, USA Track and Field, the NGB for track and field in the United States, suspended Mary Slaney after she allegedly tested positive for testosterone at the 1996 U.S. Olympic trials. Slaney had a testosterone-to-epitestosterone (T/E) ratio of 11.6:1, higher than the allowable 6:1. Slaney claimed that the reason her T/E ratio was high was

because she was at the end of her menstrual cycle at the time, she was taking birth-control pills for the first time, and she had had a glass or two of red wine the night before the test. All these are factors that can affect a woman's T/E ratio. After originally imposing its own suspension, the USATF submitted the case to a panel of the USATF doping hearing board, which, upon review, "concluded Mary Slaney committed no doping violation last year." The International Amateur Athletic Federation referred the case to arbitration in Monaco. In April 1999, an arbitration panel appointed by the IAAF concluded that Slaney had tested positive for excessive levels of the male sex hormone testosterone. Slaney failed to appear at the hearing and was tried in absentia. Slaney filed a lawsuit in Indianapolis against the International Amateur Athletic Federation, track and field's world governing body and the United States Olympic Committee. In *Slaney v. The International Amateur Athletic Federation*, 244 F 3d 580 (7th Cir., 2001), the court refused to overturn the decision of binding arbitration, stating, "Our judicial system is not meant to provide a second bite at the apple." The highest T/E ratio ever uncovered in an international sport drug test is the 42:1 that Britain's Diane Modahl registered when she tested positive in 1994. Modahl's lawyers were able to show that there must have been a mistake with the test, in particular how the sample was stored.

8. In the 1998 Winter Olympic Games in Nagano, Japan, gold medal snowboarder Ross Rebagliati made headlines when he tested positive for having 17.8 nanograms of marijuana in his system, exceeding the limit of 15. Although Rebagliati claimed that the finding was a result of secondhand smoke, the IOC stripped him of his medal. Rebagliati's medal was returned to him, however, when the Committee for the Arbitration for Sport ruled that the International Ski Federation, the organization that governs snowboarding, did not explicitly bar marijuana in its rules. Certain International Federations have their own lists of prohibited substances. The arbitration panel also felt that the purpose for testing should determine which drugs are to be tested for. If tests are done primarily to keep athletes from getting an unfair advantage over competitors, then the drugs tested should be those that have evidence of enhancing performance.

9. In *Walton-Floyd v. United States Olympic Committee*, 965 S.W.2d 35 (1998), an athlete banned from competition for failing a drug test brought an action against the USOC for breaching its duty of care. The athlete was issued a card that listed several banned substances and a phone number to call for a complete list of banned substances. The instructions on the card directed that it was the responsibility of the athlete to call the hotline and to be aware of all the banned substances included. The athlete called the number numerous times to check on a particular substance, Sydnocarb, and was told by the hotline operator that the substance was permitted. The drug test that disqualified the athlete indicated the presence of amphetamines that were produced by Sydnocarb. In the lawsuit, the athlete asserted that the USOC breached its duty by not keeping hotline officials up to date on the status of Sydnocarb. The USOC countered that the Amateur Sports Act, 36 U.S.C.A. 371–396, did not create any legal duty of care for the USOC to protect a governed athlete and that it was the athlete's responsibility to be aware of banned substances. The District Court, Harris County, granted summary judgment in favor of USOC. On appeal, the court held that (1) the Amateur Sports Act did not provide for implied private cause of action permitting athlete to recover monetary damages against USOC, and (2) the act pre-empted claims asserted by an athlete against the USOC under state tort law.

10. In August 1990, Butch Reynolds, world record holder in the 400 meters and a 1988 Olympic silver medalist, allegedly tested positive for the anabolic steroid nandrolone after an international track and field meet in Monte Carlo. Shortly thereafter, the International Amateur Athletic Federation (IAAF), the NGB for track and field, suspended Reynolds from competition for two years. Reynolds immediately filed suit in U.S. District Court in Ohio, claiming that the testing procedure was flawed and that he had not used steroids. The court ruled, however, that Reynolds must first exhaust all administrative remedies. Reynolds next took his case before the American Arbitration Association, a procedure

specified by the U.S. Amateur Sports Act and the USOC Constitution, and was exonerated. Both the IAAF and the Athletics Congress (TAC), however, refused to accept the decision because the USOC's administrative proceedings were inconsistent with the IAAF's adjudication process. In September 1991, however, TAC also exonerated Reynolds after finding clear and convincing evidence that the test results were tainted. Once again, the IAAF refused to accept the decision.

In the three weeks preceding the 1992 U.S. Olympic trials, Reynolds once again turned to the courts in order to gain the right to compete for the U.S. Olympic team. The district court, in *Reynolds v. International Amateur Athletic Federation*, 841 F.Supp. 1444 (S.D. Ohio 1992), found that Reynolds had established a likelihood of success on the merits of his case, ruling that a breach of contract appeared to have occurred when evidence showed inconsistencies in the testing and that the IAAF, ignoring its own policy of confidentiality, released information that Reynolds had tested positive before granting him a hearing. The court issued a preliminary injunction on June 19, 1992, which allowed Reynolds to participate in all track and field competitions, including the Olympic trials and Olympic Games. TAC appealed the decision to the U.S. Sixth Circuit Court of Appeals, which overturned the lower court's decision, ruling that no U.S. court had the jurisdiction to allow Reynolds to compete in Barcelona. In addition, the court ruled that granting Reynolds an injunction would harm other athletes through the IAAF's threat to invoke the "contamination rule," which would bar from the Olympic Games any athlete who competed against Reynolds. Reynolds appealed to the U.S. Supreme Court. In 1992, Justice John Paul Stevens reinstated the injunction, claiming that the IAAF's threatened harm to other athletes could not dictate the disposition of Reynolds's claim. The issue of whether or not Reynolds could compete in the 1992 Barcelona Olympiad was rendered moot when he failed to qualify.

On December 3, 1992, a U.S. District Court in Ohio awarded Reynolds $27.3 million ($6.8 million in compensatory damages and $20.5 in punitive damages) from the IAAF as a result of the lawsuit he filed against TAC and the IAAF, citing lost earnings and personal anguish. Judge Joseph P. Kinneary stated in his ruling that the IAAF had defamed Reynolds, had acted with "malice" and "a spirit of revenge," and had "purposefully avoided the truth" in the case. The IAAF maintained that no court in the United States had any legal jurisdiction over it. The IAAF even went so far as not to appear in court throughout the proceedings. The IAAF appealed, and in May 1994, the U.S. Sixth Circuit Court of Appeals reversed and remanded the district court's $27.3 million judgment. The Court of Appeals held that finding the IAAF amenable to suit in an Ohio court under the fact of the case comports with "traditional notions of fair play and substantial justice." Upon remand, the district court was ordered to dismiss the case for lack of personal jurisdiction over the IAAF. *Reynolds v. International Amateur Athletic Federation*, 23 F.3d 1110 (6th Cir. 1994).

7.2.4. Professional Sports

Due to the widespread media coverage of professional sports, the drug problems of many professional athletes are now exposed to anyone who reads the sports pages. This media attention has made drug abuse and the drug testing of players two of the most emotionally charged issues facing athletes, coaches, and fans of professional sports. Unlike interscholastic and intercollegiate sports organizations, professional sports organizations face a different set of legal concerns when trying to establish a drug policy.

The first distinction is state action. As mentioned in section 7.1.1., "Constitutional Law," professional sports teams are for the most part privately owned, and therefore not subject to the same array of constitutional law arguments that face many interscholastic and intercollegiate sports organizations. Even when the state is involved in the drug testing of professional athletes, the courts have afforded wide latitude to such programs.

Another major distinction between interscholastic and intercollegiate sports organizations and professional sports is the fact that professional athletes are considered employees. As discussed in Chapter 11, the National Labor Relations Act (NLRA) grants all employees the right to organize and bargain collectively with their employer with respect to their wages, hours, and conditions of employment. Since many professional athletes in the United States are unionized, the leagues and clubs have a duty under the NLRA to bargain in good faith with the players regarding conditions of employment. Drug testing is a condition of employment. Furthermore, fines or suspensions for drug use affect a player's wages. Therefore, a drug policy is a mandatory subject of bargaining between the leagues and the players. If a professional sports league wants to adopt a drug testing program, it must bargain for it. If a professional sports league wants to increase penalties for cocaine use, it must bargain for it.

In order to "bargain for" something, a side must give up something else. In other words, if a league asks a players' union if it may implement a drug testing program, the players' union may ask for an increased pension, an increased minimum salary, a reduction in free agency restrictions, or something else of benefit to the players. As the remainder of this chapter will illustrate, the strictness of a sport's drug policy is inversely proportional to the bargaining leverage of the league's players and the strength of the players' union.

This is not to suggest that players' unions will *always* fight for a more lenient drug policy. For example, an NFL player who has never used steroids might encourage his union to adopt a stronger policy against steroids. The job of the players' unions is to protect the players' (workers) right to work and their wages. However, unions also have a duty to ensure that the players (workers) are able to perform their jobs in a safe work environment. The union must therefore balance these two obligations before agreeing to any drug policy.

To combat drug use by players and protect their investments, professional sports leagues began drug testing athletes in the 1980s. Even professional sports organizations that do not test for drugs have some type of substance policy. The following sections briefly examine and compare the drug policies of five prominent sports leagues as well as the Professional Golf Association.

NOTE ⎯⎯⎯⎯⎯⎯⎯⎯⎯⎯⎯⎯⎯⎯⎯⎯⎯⎯⎯⎯⎯⎯⎯⎯⎯⎯

1. For more information regarding legal challenges to professional sport drug testing programs, see Howard Ganz, Kevin Gilmore, Jeffrey Kessler, and James Quinn, *Understanding Business & Legal Aspects of the Sports Industry*, Vol. 1 (New York: Practising Law Institute, 1999).

7.2.4.1. National Football League

The National Football League's drug testing program was first implemented in the 1982 Collective Bargaining Agreement. The NFL's policy prohibits steroids, cocaine, marijuana, opiates, phencyclidine (PCP), amphetamines, and excessive use of codeine and decongestants unless prescribed by a doctor. In 1994, in an addendum to the Collective Bargaining Agreement, the NFL reduced the penalties for drug use and expanded its treatment program. The stated cornerstone of the NFL's drug program is intervention. Under the program, which

Exhibit 7.3
NFL Substance Policy

Substance	1st Offense	2nd Offense	3rd Offense	4th Offense +
Recreational drugs, via drug test	No penalty	No penalty	Suspended 4 games w/out pay	Banished 1 year or more
DUI, alcohol offense	Maximum fine $20,000	NFL discretion	NFL discretion	NFL discretion
Steroids	Suspended 4 games w/out pay	Suspended 6 games w/out pay	Minimum one-season suspension	
Violation of law (guilty/no contest)	Suspended 4 games w/out pay	NFL discretion	NFL discretion	NFL discretion

prohibits the illegal use of drugs and the abuse of prescription and over-the-counter drugs, players are tested, evaluated, treated, and monitored for substance abuse.

In contrast to most other professional team sports, in the NFL every player is subject to both random and mandatory drug tests (exhibit 7.3 outlines the NFL's substance abuse policy and the various penalties associated with multiple offenses). Regarding illegal drugs *other* than steroids, *all* players must be tested once between May 1 and August 20, at a random time determined by the NFL's medical director. The medical director may choose to test an entire team at a time, or an entire position group at a time. In addition, draft-eligible players are tested prior to the draft. Also, a pre-employment test may be administered to a free agent player (rookie or veteran) not under contract at the end of the preceding year, prior to the execution of a new NFL player contract. Regarding steroids, the league may test at random times throughout the season, "with limits on the number of times any given player can be tested to be negotiated between the Commissioner and the NFLPA."

Players submit two urine specimens, A and B. If A tests positive, the player is notified and B is tested two days later. A player's refusal to produce a specimen constitutes a positive test. The first time a player is confirmed to test positive for illegal drugs other than steroids, he enters Stage 1 of drug treatment. This treatment will involve more frequent tests, but the player is neither fined nor suspended. When a player violates Stage 1 of treatment (usually via a second positive test for drugs other than steroids), he is assigned to Stage 2 of treatment. Again, the player is neither fined nor suspended. Players in Stage 2 are subject to testing two to ten times per month. The first violation of the terms of Stage 2 will result in a suspension of up to four regular season games without pay. A second violation of the terms of Stage 2 will result in a suspension of up to six regular season games without pay, and the player moves to Stage 3. Players who violate terms of Stage 3 will be banished from the NFL for no less than one year.

It will normally require four positive drug tests before a player is suspended from the NFL for at least one year. This policy may strike some as lenient, or at least one that focuses on rehabilitation rather than treatment. Nevertheless, as the rest of the chapter will demonstrate, the NFL drug policy is the strictest of the Big Four sports.

Interestingly, the penalties for illegal drug use are harsher if they are discovered via a violation of law rather than via a positive drug test. If a player is discovered to have violated the terms of the drug policy via a violation of law, he will "normally" be suspended without pay for four regular and/or post-season games (normally six games for a second violation of law). In addition, he will be admitted to the appropriate stage of treatment, depending on his history of positive tests. However, the commissioner reserves the right to impose more stringent penalties (suspensions and larger fines) for more egregious conduct, such as drug trafficking. The commissioner's decisions may be appealed. However, the commissioner has the power to unilaterally decide that appeal in this instance.

Penalties for performance-enhancing drug use are harsher than those for recreational drug use. The penalties for steroid abuse are a four-game suspension for the first positive test and a six-game suspension for the second positive test. A third positive test results in a minimum one-year suspension.

The NFL's program also covers alcohol. The program states that when consumed abusively, alcohol not only produces or contributes to conduct that is unlawful and threatens the health and safety of players and other persons, but is also detrimental to the integrity of and the public confidence in the NFL. If a player is convicted of or admits to an incident involving alcohol, such as DUI, typically there is a maximum $20,000 fine for the first offense. However, the commissioner reserves the right to impose more stringent penalties (suspensions and larger fines) for more egregious conduct, such as incidents that result in serious injury or death. The commissioner's decisions may be appealed, but the commissioner may unilaterally decide that appeal.

The NFL and the players' association did not always agree on how to handle drug testing. In 1986, NFL Commissioner Pete Rozelle unilaterally implemented a new drug testing policy when he was unable to convince the NFL Players' Association to agree to a stricter policy. The players' association filed for an arbitration hearing, and the arbitrator ruled that since the new policy unilaterally changed the terms and conditions of the players' employment, provided for in the Collective Bargaining Agreement, it was unenforceable (see note 4).

NOTES

1. The NFL's drug policy, steroid policy, and Collective Bargaining Agreement are viewable online at www.nflpa.org/media/main.asp.

2. In 1997, former Tampa Bay Buccaneer and Pittsburgh Steeler Steve Courson filed a damage suit against the NFL, claiming that the league had failed to enforce its steroid policy against him. Courson contended that his steroid use caused him to develop a weakened heart condition, and that he had become an alcoholic by drinking to mask pain. Courson claimed that chronic alcoholism should be considered similar to an injury suffered during a game. Winning the suit would have entitled Courson to as much as $224,000 in benefits annually, instead of the $21,000 he was receiving. In 2000, Courson's claim was rejected by a three-judge panel of the U.S. Court of Appeals for the 3rd Circuit. "'While all of Courson's assertions linking alcohol consumption with league play may be true, they fall short of establishing that NFL teams actually condoned or encouraged the consumption of alcohol,' Judge Carol Mansmann wrote. 'If anything, the evidence shows that the

league and member teams discouraged alcohol abuse.' " For more information, see Richard Willing, "Court: Courson's Alcoholism Not Football's Fault," *USA Today*, June 2, 2000, p. 18-C.

3. In *Long* v. *NFL*, 66 F.3d 311 (3rd Cir. 1994), Terry Long, a member of the Pittsburgh Steelers, failed a drug test when his urine tested positive for anabolic steroids. He was then suspended pursuant to the NFL's drug testing policy. Long sued the National Football League, the Pittsburgh Steelers, the city of Pittsburgh, and the Stadium Authority of Pittsburgh, claiming that the league's policy violated the Fourth and Fourteenth Amendments of the U.S. Constitution; Article I, section 8, of the Pennsylvania Constitution; and various state laws. The court held that Long failed to show a sufficiently close nexus between the actions of the city and city officials and the decision of the NFL to establish an actionable constitutional claim based on his suspension for use of anabolic steroids. The court concluded that Long was suspended based on independent medical conclusions and NFL policy objectives over which the state had no influence.

4. The important aspect of Arbitrator Sam Kogel's 1986 decision is that he ruled that Commissioner Pete Rozelle had the authority, under the auspices of the "integrity of the game" clause, to augment the existing drug policy as long as it did not contradict the terms of the existing policy. Areas the commissioner could address were the definition of prohibited substances, a player's entitlement to get paid for the time spent in the hospital for drug treatment, and the extent to which the commissioner can discipline players for improper drug involvement. These topics were not addressed in the existing policy; therefore, the commissioner could address them through his "augmented" program.

7.2.4.2. *National Basketball Association*

In the early 1980s, NBA Commissioner David Stern was facing a drug problem with his league. Some estimated that 70% of NBA players were using cocaine, and that such activity was contributing to the league's difficulty attracting top sponsors and broadcasting contracts. Consequently, the NBA sought mandatory testing of all players in 1982. The National Basketball Players Association (NBPA), however, resisted this type of testing. After negotiations, the NBPA agreed to allow testing only when there was reasonable cause, and later made another concession in 1988 when it allowed rookies to be tested. Though credited with cleaning up the image of a league, the drug testing policy lacked some key provisions, from the NBA's perspective. For example, players were not tested for marijuana; teams were not required to report drug abusers to the NBA office; and veterans were not subject to random testing. By the late 1990s, the NBA was again facing a reputation for excessive drug use, culminating in Toronto Raptor Charles Oakley's claim that 60% of NBA players were using marijuana.

Despite the residual labor strife from the preceding lockout, the NBA successfully negotiated a tougher drug policy into the Collective Bargaining Agreement in 1999. The terms of the program are as follows: Banned substances included amphetamine and its analogues, cocaine, LSD, opiates (heroin, codeine, and morphine), PCP, steroids—*and* marijuana. (Until the 1999 Collective Bargaining Agreement, the only prohibited drugs were cocaine and heroin.) The testing mechanism (urine sample, hair, etc.) may be determined by the medical director, who is chosen jointly by the NBA and NBPA. A player may come forward voluntarily regarding his use of a prohibited substance and seek treatment in the program. There is no penalty the first time a player comes forward voluntarily, unless he fails to cooperate with treatment. (See exhibit 7.4).

Players submit a specimen, which is divided into A and B samples. If sample A tests positive, players can request that sample B goes to a different lab for testing. The testing frequency is as follows:

Exhibit 7.4
NBA Substance Policy

Substance	1st Offense	2nd Offense	3rd Offense
Steroids	5 games without pay; enter program	10 games without pay; reenter program	25 games without pay; reenter program
Marijuana	No penalty; enter program	$15,000 fine; reenter program	5 games without pay; reenter program
Others (drugs of abuse)	Disqualification (see note 2)	Disqualification	Disqualification

- A *first-year player* can be tested once during training camp, and three times during the regular season. All such tests are at the discretion of the NBA and without prior notice to the player.
- *Veteran players* can be tested once during training camp, or, if a player reports during the season or with less than fifteen days remaining in training camp, once during the first fifteen days after he reports to his team. All such tests are at the discretion of the NBA, and without prior notice to the player.
- *Reasonable cause*: If the NBA or NBPA receives information that provides reasonable cause for a player's use, they may request a hearing with the other party and the independent expert (hired jointly by the NBA and NBPA). If the independent expert believes there is reasonable cause, the NBA will arrange for testing of a player four times during the next six-week period.

The penalties for drug use in the NBA vary substantially, depending on the substance abused and the circumstances under which the offense is discovered. Similar to the NFL policy, penalties are stiffer if the offense is discovered via a violation of law. However, there is a clear difference in emphasis between the two policies. The NFL policy is tougher on steroids, while the NBA policy is tougher on "street drugs" such as cocaine and opiates. Here are the particulars of the NBA's penalties for substance violations:

1. Via a positive test
    a. Steroids: First offense (five games without pay and player enters treatment program), second offense (ten games without pay and enter program), third and subsequent offense (twenty-five games without pay and enter program)
    b. Marijuana: First offense (enter program), second offense ($15,000 fine and enter program), third offense (5 games' suspension without pay and enter program)
    c. Other banned substances: Disqualification
2. If the grievance arbitrator determines that a player has used or possessed amphetamines and its analogues, cocaine, LSD, opiates, or PCP, *or has distributed any prohibited substance*, he will be dismissed and disqualified from the NBA.
3. A conviction or no-contest plea in criminal trial for either possession or distribution of banned substances (other than marijuana) will result in disqualification from the NBA.
4. Non-compliance with the drug program

a. Fines and suspensions, which will be imposed until that player fully complies with the requirements of the program

b. A player in the program for substances *other than steroids and marijuana* who fails to comply with his in-patient or aftercare treatment will automatically be suspended during his period of in-patient treatment and for at least six months of his aftercare.

(1) Second offense will result in disqualification from the NBA.

NOTES

1. The NBA Collective Bargaining Agreement, including the drug policy and grievance procedure, is viewable online at www.nbpa.com

2. To clarify, a player who is "disqualified" is not necessarily expelled from the NBA forever. Any veteran player who is disqualified will be disqualified for a period of not less than *two* years. Any first-year player who is disqualified will be disqualified for a period of not less than *one* year. A player may be reinstated only with the approval of both the NBA and the NBPA, and such approval may be conditioned on random testing and other terms.

7.2.4.3. *Major League Baseball*

Major League Baseball's program is unique in that it is not part of the Collective Bargaining Agreement. The reason for this is that the players' association (MLBPA) has not formally agreed to the policy. Rather, it has worked informally with MLB on drug-related issues involving players as they arise, such as the case of Steve Howe (see note 2).

Due to the marked increase of drug-related problems in MLB in 1982–1983 and the resulting media fallout, the MLBPA and MLB adopted the Joint Drug Agreement (see note 4). The agreement established a joint review council consisting of three experts in the field of drug abuse who were to make recommendations on treatment and other issues. Not everyone was happy with the agreement, however. Ken Moffett, executive director of the MLB Players Association, was dismissed in November 1983 by the MLBPA, in part because of his willingness to work with MLB executives to develop a drug testing plan for players.

In 1985, the new commissioner of baseball, Peter Ueberroth, announced a plan under which minor league players and non-playing personnel in the major leagues would be randomly tested. Ueberroth sought the voluntary participation of major league players in a similar program. However, unable to reach an agreement on random testing with the players' association, MLB terminated the Joint Drug Agreement in October 1985.

In 1986, in connection with the so-called Pittsburgh Drug Trial, Commissioner Ueberroth placed all drug testing under the control of the commissioner's office (see note 3). The drug testing program, which has been updated by later commissioners, has remained under the control of the commissioner's office.

In 1997, Commissioner Bud Selig distributed a memorandum to all clubs regarding the league's drug policy. The main points of the memorandum included no unannounced testing for major league players, random unannounced testing for minor league players, a program to help treat and rehabilitate individuals with a drug problem, as well as a new disciplinary code for positive test results and those engaging in the sale or distribution of illegal drugs or controlled substances (see note 5). As mentioned previously, these provisions were not achieved via collective bargaining. While the provisions pertaining to MLB employees and minor league players can be considered binding, any provisions pertaining to major league players are subject to the grievance procedure. This is because club fines exceeding $250 or commissioner suspensions or fines exceeding $500 are subject to the grievance procedure according to Article VII (Discipline) of the Collective Bargaining Agreement.

NOTES

1. Androstenedione (andro) is not banned by Major League Baseball. Though legal and available over the counter, it is banned by the Olympics, the NBA, the NFL, and other organizations. Such organizations punish the use of it in the same way as steroids. This issue is further addressed in the introduction of this chapter.

2. In *In the Matter of the Arbitration Between Major League Baseball Players Association and the Commissioner of Major League Baseball*, Grievance No. 92–7; Suspension of Steven Howe, Nicolau, Chairman of Arbitration Panel, November 12, 1992, Commissioner Fay Vincent banned New York Yankee pitcher Steve Howe from baseball for life for violating the terms of his reinstatement in 1990 after being suspended during the 1988 and 1989 seasons. Between 1982 and 1988 Howe was hospitalized for drug-related treatment six times and was reinstated in 1990 on the condition that he refrain from using or selling drugs. However, the arbitrator found that there was no "just cause" for the lifetime ban because Vincent did not do all that was contractually required for Howe (periodic drug tests) prior to the total ban.

3. The Pittsburgh drug trial was held during the 1985 playoffs and the World Series. The trial involved Curtis Strong, a Philadelphia resident accused of selling cocaine to MLB players. In the first week of Strong's trial, Lonnie Smith of the Kansas City Royals described, under a grant of immunity, his introduction to cocaine in the major leagues and how the drug was purchased and distributed in MLB. In following days some of MLB's best-known players, including Keith Hernandez, Dale Berra, Enos Cabell, Dave Parker, and John Milner, also testified under immunity about drug use in baseball. While no MLB player was charged in the Pittsburgh case, by the time the trial ended in late September and Curtis Strong had been convicted and sentenced to ten years in prison, it seemed to many fans that professional baseball had been judged guilty.

4. In 1983, MLB Commissioner Bowie Kuhn, in response to the arrest of and conviction of four Kansas City Royals players and the resulting media attention, the MLBPA and MLB adopted the Joint Drug Agreement. The agreement established a joint review council, consisting of three experts in the field of drug abuse, who were to make recommendations on treatment and other issues. Most owners considered the joint program too watered down, but Commissioner Kuhn felt otherwise. Kuhn stated that the program was a "dramatic breakthrough in labor relations and sports." The policy included the following provisions:

1. The program excluded marijuana, amphetamines, and alcohol. Players who were found to be abusing these substances would continue to be subject to action by the commissioner, and the union would continue to have the right to file grievances in such cases.

2. A cornerstone of the new agreement was a salary abatement procedure to penalize players who continued to use drugs. A player who asked for help with a drug program would receive full pay for the first thirty days of treatment and half pay for the next thirty days. Beyond sixty days, if kept on the roster by the club, the player would be paid at a rate of $60,000 a year, the minimum salary.

3. A club that suspected a player of drug involvement would ask the person to undergo examination. If the player refused, the evidence would be presented to a review council that included drug counselors. The members of this council were to be selected by a joint committee of owners and players. If the council recommended that the player undergo

testing or treatment and the player refused, he would be subject to disciplinary action by the commissioner.

5. Here are part of the contents of the May 15, 1997, memorandum from Commissioner Selig to all clubs regarding the league's substance policy:

- Prohibition applies to all illegal drugs and controlled substances, including steroids or prescription drugs for which the individual in possession of the drug does not have a prescription.

- Players who are taking a prescription drug must notify the team physician of this fact and of the drug(s) prescribed.

- Baseball will attempt to treat and rehabilitate individuals with a drug problem through a Club's Employee Assistance Program (EAP) or through resources identified by the Commissioner's Office.

- Any player or personnel may request treatment for drug use or alcohol abuse without penalty.

- *Major* League Players are *not* subject to unannounced testing for illegal drugs. However, Major League players who have admitted to illegal drug use, or who have been detected using illegal drugs, may be subject to mandatory testing for the remainder of the player's career.

- All *minor* league players may be subject to unannounced testing for illegal drugs, which shall be conducted in a manner consistent with the applicable law of the state where the Club is located. The list of players to be tested on each occasion will be selected at random by a computer.

- All amateur entry-level players, whether or not selected in the June draft, will be tested for illegal drug use.

- Samples will be tested for the following controlled substances: cocaine, marijuana, amphetamines, opiates and phencyclidine (PCP). Other drugs may be added to this list if necessary and with prior notice.

- Samples will be taken no more than four times per season (between March and October) for any individuals covered by the program. Individuals with prior dependency problems will be tested more frequently if their recovery program so requires.

- Each specimen will be divided into two containers, sealed against tampering, coded to protect anonymity.
  Penalties
- An initial positive test result, the admission of drug use, or the identification of drug use through other means will not immediately result in discipline for the player or Baseball personnel involved other than being required to participate in Baseball's testing program.

- A second and any subsequent violation of Baseball's policy on the use of illegal drugs and controlled substances will result in immediate discipline.

- Players engaging in the *sale or distribution* of any illegal drug or controlled substance will be disciplined immediately on the first offense.

- Baseball will not hesitate to permanently remove from the game those players and personnel who, despite efforts to treat and rehabilitate, refuse to accept responsibility for the problem and continue to use illegal drugs.

- In addition to any discipline that the league office may impose, a Club also may take action under applicable provisions of and special covenants to the Uniform Player's Contract.

- If any Club covers up or otherwise fails to disclose to this office any information concerning drug use by a player, that Club will be fined $250,000, the highest allowable amount under the Major League Agreement.

- Refusal to test = positive test

7.2.4.4. *National Hockey League*

The NHL does not have a mandatory or random drug testing program. The NHL does maintain and enforce a drug policy for its players, however this policy is not generally made available to the public due to privacy concerns. What is known is that it usually takes more than one offense to lead to a suspension without pay. U.S. hockey players who competed in the 2002 Olympics were subject to unannounced drug testing under an agreement reached between the USOC and the NHL. Player drug offenses are handled in the same way as other matters of discipline. The NHL's Collective Bargaining Agreement stipulates that the suspension and expulsion of players are subject to grievance arbitration. Nevertheless, arbitration has rarely been necessary for drug-related issues. For example, in 1999 when New Jersey Devil Kevin Stevens was arrested for, and later admitted to, smoking crack cocaine and soliciting a prostitute (the former being a felony), he was merely enrolled in the NHL's substance abuse program. By comparison, this activity would constitute an automatic one-year or two-year suspension under the NBA's policy, depending on the player's seniority.

With NHL players playing in the Olympics, they must submit to random drug tests in order to participate in the Olympics, starting with the 2002 games in Salt Lake City. During the 1998 games, NHL and NBA players were given an "exemption" from testing. However, due to a compromise between the USOC and NHL Players Association, players are tested only for steroids or masking agents, *not* street drugs.

NOTE _____

1. A mandatory drug testing program was proposed in 1986 by John Ziegler, the president of the National Hockey League, and Alan Eagleson, executive director of the NHL Players Association. The announcement was an apparent reaction to a published report in the May 12, 1986 issue of *Sports Illustrated* on cocaine problems among players in the NHL. Ziegler and Eagleson, in a joint news release, proposed the program as a means of cleaning up the league's image. The proposal, however, required the approval of a majority of the NHL Players Association members before it could be incorporated into the league's Collective Bargaining Agreement. The players decided against the program.

7.2.4.5. *Professional Golf Association*

"How do they keep getting away with it? . . . They get paid these huge sums of money . . . some are caught with marijuana; some are caught with cocaine; and they just go play. . . . That's not right. They should make an example of these guys, kick them out of the league and tear up their contracts. Maybe it would clean the sports up."—Payne Stewart, PGA golfer, in 1998

Golfers on the PGA tour are not unionized. They are not even employees. While widely considered to be independent contractors working on the PGA tour, the U.S. Supreme Court has suggested that their legal relationship may be more akin to *customers* of the PGA tour. In *PGA Tour Inc.* v. *Casey Martin*, 532 U.S. 661 (2001, U.S.), the court noted that golfers must pay a $3,000 fee to attend Qualifying School before qualifying for the tour, making them, essentially, paying customers.

Regardless of the precise legal status of PGA golfers, they are not unionized, and therefore the PGA tour is under no obligation to bargain with them over the terms of a drug policy. Just as the commissioner of Major League Baseball was free to institute random drug testing over non-unionized minor league baseball players (see section 7.2.4.3., "Major League Baseball"), the PGA commissioner *does* reserve the right to demand a urine sample from any suspected violator of the PGA substance abuse policy.

The PGA substance abuse policy is as follows:

1. Any member found to be using or selling illegal substances shall be considered to have engaged in conduct unbecoming a professional and shall be subject to a very significant penalty (minimum fine of $1,000 and multiyear suspension up to and including expulsion).

2. Any member found to have violated any of the following provisions relating to the use of alcohol shall be considered to have engaged in conduct unbecoming a professional and shall be subject to a significant penalty (a minimum fine of $1,000, suspension from play of no less than four weeks, and one year probation):

   A. Consuming an alcoholic beverage during any practice round or tournament round (whether a pro-am round or a tournament competition round), on the practice tee or putting green.

   B. Moderate, responsible consumption of alcoholic beverages after play or during social functions is permitted. But players should know that alcohol-related unprofessional incidents will carry the above minimum penalties.

3. A PGA tour member's responsibility to conduct himself in a professional manner and lend credit to himself and his organization extends beyond the time that the member is engaging in tournament play at a tournament site. Accordingly, the membership should be aware that, depending on the circumstances, being under the influence of alcohol at any time in a public place, whether at a tournament site or otherwise, may constitute conduct unbecoming a professional under the PGA tour alcohol and substance abuse policy, and may be subject to appropriate penalties.

4. The commissioner will conduct such inquiries and investigations as shall be appropriate (taking statements from witnesses, requiring urinalysis tests, etc.) to determine whether a member has violated the alcohol and substance abuse policy or any interpretations thereof (see note 1).

The policy of the PGA is strict in relation to the policies of the "Big Four" leagues, all of which had to be negotiated with players' unions. The contrast is particularly revealing when one considers the paucity of substance-related incidents in the sport of golf. While John Daly and Notah Begay have experienced bouts with alcohol abuse (see note 2), few others are known to the public. There have been no legal challenges to the PGA substance policy, nor have there been any publicized instances of the PGA commissioner requesting a drug test.

NOTES

1. For more information on PGA policy towards the use of drugs and alcohol on the PGA tour, see Mark Sotlau, "When It Comes to Drugs, Golfers Mostly Keep Lives in Bounds," July 22, 1998, www.cbs.sportsline.com/u/page/covers/others/jul98/golfdrug7229 8.htm

2. John Daly was suspended in 1997 after he "nearly drank himself to death" at the Players Championship. Notah Begay was not suspended in 2000, after serving seven days in jail for his second driving while intoxicated (DWI) offense. For more information, see Pete Herrera, "Begay Had Previous Drunken Driving Conviction in Arizona," *Associated Press*, January 21, 2000.

7.2.4.6. Women's National Basketball Association

WNBA players have managed to avoid the negative substance-abuse publicity that has plagued their male counterparts in the NBA. The WNBA players are represented by the same union as the NBA players—the NBPA.

While very similar to the NBA substance policy, the WNBA policy is slightly stricter in the area of penalties for marijuana use. WNBA players are suspended after their second positive marijuana test, while NBA players are suspended after their third marijuana test. Perhaps more important, veteran players can be tested *twice* per year in the WNBA (once in the pre-season and once in the regular season). NBA veterans, after passing their initial random drug test in the pre-season, are not tested for marijuana during the regular season.

It should be noted that drug-related fines in the NBA can be large, consistent with the NBA players' much higher salaries. Nevertheless, the fact that the NBA and WNBA policies are different demonstrates that the strictness or leniency of a league's drug policy is *not* always attributable to the scope of the league's drug problem, but instead is a product of the parties' bargaining leverage and other interests. When the WNBA players negotiated their first Collective Bargaining Agreement in 1999 (see Chapter 11, section 11.3.6.1., "WNBA Unionization"), their demands were much more modest than those of the Big Four leagues. In a league where players average five-figure salaries, instead of seven-figure salaries, the players were fighting for such basic things as dental insurance and a 401K plan—demands that employees fight for in more typical (non-sports) unions. Consequently, WNBA players were not willing to play "hardball" on the drug issue when (a) they lacked the leverage of their male counterparts (lower television ratings, etc.) and (b) due to the "drug problem" not being a significant one, there was little reason to risk a loss of benefits to fight for a less crucial issue.

NOTES ──

1. Other than the discrepancy in marijuana penalty, the NBA and WNBA policies are quite similar—especially in the testing mechanism and non-penalty aspects. Here are the particulars of the policy from the WNBA's April 1999–September 2001 Collective Bargaining Agreement:

    1. A medical director and independent expert are jointly chosen by WNBA and NBPA to administer and evaluate drug tests.

    2. Testing mechanism (urine sample, hair, etc.) is determined by the medical director.

    3. The WNBA assumes all expenses of the program not covered by insurance.

    4. Banned substances include amphetamines, cocaine, marijuana, opiates, phencyclidine (PCP), and steroids.

    5. Players submit two specimens, A and B. If A tests positive, the player can request that B go to a different lab for testing.

    6. "Reasonable suspicion" testing

        a. Any player can be tested for drugs at any time based on "reasonable suspicion." The independent expert acts as the final authority in determining "reasonable suspicion."

           (1) This testing occurs four unannounced times within a six-week period.

        b. *Rookies*, three months or less prior to entering the draft, or others who have not yet signed a standard contract, can be tested based on reasonable suspicion.

    7. Non-suspicion testing

        a. *First-year* players can be tested once in training camp, and twice during or immediately following the season. Suspicion is not necessary, and testing is done at the sole discretion of the WNBA.

   b. *Veteran* players can be tested once in training camp and once during the regular season.

8. First offense—marijuana and steroids:

   a. Rookies who test positive for marijuana/steroids enter the "program."

9. First offense—other banned substances ("drugs of abuse"):

   a. Potential rookies (prior to signing contract) are disqualified for two years.
   b. First-year players are disqualified for one year.
   c. Veteran players are disqualified for two years.

10. Reinstatement of disqualified players is not guaranteed. Players must be approved by both the WNBA and the NBPA before being readmitted into the league.

11. Players under contract may voluntarily enter the "program" for *any* banned substance without penalty.

12. Non-compliance with treatment:

    a. Marijuana/steroids: Reentry into the "program" and an escalating suspension.

       (1) Example: two games, five games, ten games, indefinite

    b. Drugs of abuse: If a player has already undergone Stage 2 of treatment, he receives a two-year disqualification. If a player is not yet in Stage 2 of treatment, he is moved there.

GENDER DISCRIMINATION IN ATHLETICS

INTRODUCTION

Since the 1970s, gender discrimination in sports has become a highly litigated topic. The initial development of athletic opportunities for women may be attributed, to a large extent, to Title IX of the Education Amendments of 1972, a federal statute that prohibits gender discrimination. Title IX gave women an important legal option to fight gender discrimination, and in turn the availability of legal options brought about an increased reliance on the legal system to redress gender discrimination. Women brought complaints about unequal treatment to court and were often successful in their litigation.

Throughout the mid-1980s, however, a series of setbacks besieged the women's athletic movement. The failure to enact the federal Equal Rights Amendment and limitations imposed on Title IX enforcement by the Supreme Court in *Grove City College v. Bell*, 465 U.S. 555 (1984), brought the opportunities for women to attack perceived gender discrimination through the court system and legislation at a virtual standstill throughout much of this period. With the passage of the Civil Rights Restoration Act by Congress in 1988 and, consequently, the resolution that athletic programs which did not directly receive federal funds were nevertheless bound by Title IX, the movement toward equality in athletics regained momentum. In 1992, the U.S. Supreme Court found, in *Franklin v. Gwinnett County Public Schools* 503 U.S. 60 (1992), that victims of discrimination under Title IX could be entitled to monetary damages. This decision to make funds available for winners of Title IX lawsuits gave plaintiffs additional strength in Title IX cases, caused a proliferation of lawsuits by student-athletes, and forced many athletic departments to comply with regulations or settle pending litigation in fear of paying large settlements to plaintiffs. Today, Title IX, along with other legal options, are effective legal theories for increasing opportunities for women in athletics in the courtroom.

Participation in women's athletics has increased for many reasons. A major factor is the drastic change in social attitudes about women, including a new perception among women of their own athletic capabilities and interest in participation. After the U.S. Women's National Soccer Team won the Women's World Cup in the summer of 1999, many credited Title IX for the victory. Title IX has enabled women to demand equality in sports, which in turn has given them the opportunity to compete. A generation later, U.S. women are seeing the results. In 2002, the United States is home to a professional women's basketball league (WBNA) and a professional women's soccer league (WUSA). Also, women have had great success in individual sports such as tennis and golf for many years.

Before the passage of Title IX, women composed only 7% of the total number of athletic participants in high school and 16% in college. By 1992, 37% of all interscholastic participants and 35% of all NCAA intercollegiate participants were women. In a report released in 2000, the NCAA found that during the 1998–1999 academic year, there were 145,832 female athletes competing at NCAA member schools; which is 41% of collegiate athletes, and the number of female participants in intercollegiate athletics increased 58% in the 1990s alone. (see notes 1 and 2)

The Miller Lite Report in 1985 and the Melpomene Institute in 1995 concluded that women who were active in sports at a young age feel greater confidence and self-esteem in their physical and social selves than women who were sedentary as youths. The Women's Sports Foundation notes that women who participate in sports are more likely to experience academic success than women who do not participate in sports. Also, girls who participate in sports are more likely to do well in science courses. The NCAA reports higher graduation rates for female athletes than for women students in general (68% versus 58% in 1999).

While participation in women's sports has increased dramatically since the passage of Title IX, other problems have emerged. According to the 1994 "Women in Intercollegiate Sport," report, by R. Vivian Acosta and Linda Carpenter of Brooklyn College, "The positive/negative pattern of the last 19 years can be summarized as: An increase in sports participation by girls and women and a decrease in women in leadership positions" (see note 7).

Most plaintiffs utilize Title IX as the primary legal theory in their gender discrimination lawsuits. However, some plaintiffs also use the constitutional law theory of equal protection and a state equal rights amendment if the state has enacted one. For employment discrimination cases involving gender, Title IX is often used, but plaintiffs also make use of Title VII, a federal anti-employment discrimination law, and the Equal Pay Act, a federal law that ensures equal pay for equal work and experience (see Chapter 16, "Additional Legal Concerns").

Title IX, however, has been the most important of the legal theories used in gender discrimination cases. The first type of Title IX cases involved participation rates of females in athletics. Plaintiffs were largely successful in these cases, and this type of litigation has consistently been decided in favor of increasing opportunities for women. The most important case on participation rates is *Cohen v. Brown University*, which is discussed in depth in section 8.2.2., "Post-Civil Rights Restoration Act Litigation." The second area being litigated under Title IX involves equitable financial assistance. In these cases, courts look at how men and women's teams are funded as well as the equivalent availability of athletic scholarships to men and women. The third area of potential litigation involves "other benefits" that schools provide to athletic teams. This topic is in the early stages of litigation, and the number of lawsuits involving "other benefits" will likely increase in the future. The area of "other benefits" involves topics such as equality of access to facilities; coaching staff and support staff; publicity for both men and women; and equal quality of facilities for both genders (see note 3).

Title IX, despite its generally favorable consequences for women, has not been without its many opponents. With the mandate to increase opportunities for women in athletics, athletic departments have taken varied approaches on how to address their particular situations and comply with the legislation. The most frequent downside to Title IX has been the elimination of men's athletic programs to compensate for the addition of women's programs. Many universities have not had the necessary funds to add women's programs while maintaining the same number of men's athletic programs. Athletic departments have been forced to cut men's sports such as wrestling, gymnastics, and baseball. In addition to cutting sports, departments have also reduced the number of scholarships available to men's athletic teams. The elimination of men's athletic programs has led to a number of lawsuits filed by male athletes, claiming reverse discrimination under Title IX. Generally, men have not been successful with their claims of reverse discrimination (see note 4).

Some athletic departments, albeit rarely, have been able to fully accommodate the interests of female athletes while not reducing participation opportunities for male athletes. These athletic programs generally are very well funded. The most common approach used to comply with Title IX in intercollegiate athletics has been to increase women's opportunities while reducing men's opportunities. Therefore, Title IX has many opponents who believe that Title IX has unfairly taken away opportunities for male athletes.

Chapter 8 is organized into three major sections. The first part of the chapter discusses the various legal theories and principles utilized in gender discrimination cases in high school and intercollegiate athletics, and the legality, scope, and applicability of Title IX. The second part of the chapter discusses early legal challenges to Title IX and the evolution of the policy from the 1970s through the early twenty-first century. The final part of the chapter discusses gender discrimination cases involving individual athletes. The cases have been grouped according to the presence or absence of teams available for either gender and according to whether the sport involved is a contact or non-contact sport.

NOTES

1. At NCAA member institutions, the number of female participants in intercollegiate athletics increased from 32,000 in 1971–1972 to 91,000 by 1988–1989, and then rose to 145,832 in 1998–1999. During that period, the number of NCAA member institutions that sponsored women's intercollegiate sports increased as follows:

	1971	1988	1991–1992	1998–1999
Basketball	307	764	810	1,001
Cross country	10	638	677	891
Softball	147	549	605	831
Swimming	140	397	394	458
Tennis	243	691	723	877
Track and field	78	540	561	671
Volleyball	208	719	762	960

2. On the high school level, prior to the enactment of Title IX in 1972, fewer than 300,000 girls took part in high school athletics. In 2000, this figure rose to 2,675,874 million (compared with 3,861,749 million boys participating).

3. In 1992, prompted by the immense impact of Title IX upon intercollegiate athletics, the NCAA established the NCAA Gender Equity Task Force to study how the NCAA could effectively accommodate female athletes under Title IX. Gender equity is defined as follows: "An athletics program is gender equitable when either the men's or women's sports program would be pleased to accept as its own the overall program of the other gender" (NCAA Gender-Equity Task Force, 2000 Manual). The task force was given the charge "to develop a definition of gender equity; to assure that no NCAA policy, practice or legislation could deter a member institution from compliance with Federal or state law relevant to gender equity; to examine the policies of the Association for gender bias; to attempt to correct any such policy; and to assist the member institutions in achieving gender equity" (NCAA Gender-Equity Task Force, 2000 Manual). In 1993, the task force released its findings/recommendations. Among these recommendations was the establishment of a manual that would serve as a guide to help member institutions to understand and implement Title IX. In addition, a yearly conference to discuss Title IX was proposed, and adopted. Also adopted at the 1993 convention was a certification program for institutions to comply with Title IX. By 2001, all of these recommendations had become part of the NCAA's comprehensive efforts to maintain Title IX compliance within its member institutions.

The first recommendation, the manual for complying with Title IX, has evolved since 1993. The manual, *A Basic Guide to Title IX and Gender Equity in Athletics for Colleges and Universities*, which was published in its third edition in 2000, involves six main areas to help understand and comply with Title IX. These six areas are:

1. Title IX Basics (provides historical background and legislative language)
2. Current Case Law (keeps members up to date on recent litigation involving Title IX)
3. Division I Athletics Certification (discusses the certification process for institutions)
4. Promotion Ideas (offers low-cost ideas on how to promote traditionally non-revenue-generating sports)
5. Emerging Sports (discusses what sports are up-and-coming for women athletes)
6. Resources (points the reader in the right direction for finding additional material on sports, and women in sports).

The manual can be downloaded or purchased at the NCAA's Web site, www.NCAA.org.

The NCAA sponsors an annual Title IX seminar for its members to assist institutions in complying with Title IX. Speakers such as athletic directors, representatives from the Office for Civil Rights, and attorneys with Title IX experience make presentations to the attendees at the seminar on varied aspects of Title IX.

The NCAA has maintained a program of certification of its member institutions under Title IX. A basic summary of the program areas to be reviewed is presented in the gender equity manual released by the NCAA. Each institution must go through two cycles of certification, and provide a plan of how gender equity is, or will be, achieved at the institution.

Other recommendations put forth by the NCAA Gender Equity Task Force in 1993 included additional NCAA-sponsored championships for women; the exploration of the addition of one graduate assistant or volunteer coach, who must be a female, to the numbers of allowable coaches in men's and women's sports, excepting football and basketball; and the recommendation that institutions conduct gender equity self-studies and formulate strategies to address their inequities in a timely manner.

4. The following cases have been brought by male athletes charging reverse discrimination under Title IX:

   (a) In *Neal v. Board of Trustees*, 198 F.3d 763 (9th Cir. 1999), a plaintiff wrestler at California State University-Bakersfield was unsuccessful in claiming reverse gender discrimination under Title IX after his sport was cut due to disproportionate participation rates between male and female athletes.

   (b) In *Boulahanis v. Board of Regents*, 198 F.3d 633 (7th Cir. 1999), plaintiff wrestlers and soccer players from Illinois State University claimed they were discriminated against based on gender because their teams were eliminated in order to comply with Title IX. Prior to their elimination, the ratio of male-to-female athletes was 65% male and 35% female, while the enrollment was 45% male and 55% female. After the changes, the rates were 52% female and 48% male, placing Illinois State in compliance. The plaintiffs were unsuccessful in their claim, the court stating, "The elimination of men's athletic programs is not a violation of Title IX as long as men's participation in athletics continues to be 'substantially proportionate' to their enrollment."

   (c) In *Kelley v. Board of Trustees, University of Illinois*, 35 F.3d 265 (7th Cir. 1995), the plaintiffs were members of the men's swimming team at the University of Illinois. Their program was cut from the athletic department, and they charged gender discrimination under Title IX as well as equal protection violations. The plaintiffs were unsuccessful in their claims, the court stated, "The University could, however, eliminate the men's swimming program without violating Title IX since even after eliminating the program, men's participation in athletics would continue to be more than substantially proportionate to their presence in the University's student body."

5. Many articles have been written criticizing Title IX for its negative consequences for male athletes. Refer to the following:

   (a) George Will, "Extortion Holds a Nation Hostage," *Chicago Sun-Times*, February 26, 2000.

(b) Curt A. Levey, "Title IX's Dark Side: Sports Gender Quotas," *USA Today*, July 12, 1999. (Employs claim that Title IX quotas are unfair because males are inherently more interested in sports than females.)

(c) Ira Berkow, "Baseball; The Other Side of Title IX," *New York Times*, May 19, 1999. (A criticism of Title IX, and how it led to the elimination of the baseball team at Providence College.)

6. Administrators and coaches will find the following organizations' resources useful:

(a) Women's Sports Foundation, located at Eisenhower Park in Nassau County, Long Island, New York. This organization publishes *Women's Sports and Fitness*, a monthly magazine. The foundation also created The Sporting Woman Exhibit, a traveling exhibit. The Women's Sports Foundation also has a Web site at www.womenssportsfoundation.org

(b) National Association for Girls and Women in Sport, 1900 Association Drive, Reston, VA 22091. The association regularly publishes official rulebooks for many women's sports. In addition, the National Association for Girls and Women in Sport has a Web site at www. aahperd.org/nagws/nagws-main.html

(c) National Women's Law Center, 11 Dupont Circle, Suite 800, Washington, DC 20036. The National Women's Law Center has a Web site at http://www.nwlc.org

(d) National Organization for Women Task Force on Women's Sports, National NOW Action Center, 733 Fifteenth Street, N.W., 2nd floor, Washington, DC 20005. NOW's Web site is at www.now.org

(e) Gender Equity in Sports, University of Iowa Gender Equity in Sport Project, 340 Carver-Hawkeye Arena, Iowa City, IA 52242. Doctors Christine H. B. Grant and Mary C. Curtis maintain a Web site www.bailiwick.lib.uiowa.edu/ge/ that provides current information on the status of Title IX and gender equity.

7. The Acosta-Carpenter study reveals that in 1972, 90% of women's athletic programs were run by female administrators, compared with only 17.8% in 2000. The report also states that women hold 34% of all administrative jobs in collegiate women's programs. However, in 23% of women's programs, no woman is involved in the administration. Among the intercollegiate coaching ranks, the percentage of women coaching women's teams has steadily dropped over the years. In 2000, 45.6% of women's teams are coached by women, while only 2% of men's teams are coached by women. While this problem may be, in part, a reflection of the limited experience of women in the coaching ranks, some claim it is also because women have a limited role in the governing procedures of the NCAA. The most startling of these statistics, however, is that the number of female administrators and coaches has been declining since 1995.

8.1. LEGAL THEORIES IN GENDER DISCRIMINATION CASES

Gender discrimination in high school and intercollegiate athletics has been challenged using a variety of legal arguments, including Title IX of the Education Amendments of 1972, state equal rights amendments, and equal protection laws under the U.S. Constitution.

Equal protection arguments are based on the Fifth and Fourteenth Amendments of the U.S. Constitution, which guarantee equal protection of the law to all persons within the United States. The law states, "No state shall . . . deny to any person within its jurisdiction the equal protection of the laws." (See Chapter 5, section 5.4.3., "Equal Protection.")

Title IX has had the greatest impact in attacking gender discrimination in athletics. Although the original legislation was passed in 1972, implementation was delayed for the promulgation of regulations and policy interpretations. Even with the delay, many have claimed that the rise in women's participation in athletics was directly related to the passage of Title IX. Title IX states, "No person in the United States shall, on the basis of sex, be excluded from participation in, be denied the benefits of, or be subjected to discrimination under any education program or activity receiving Federal financial assistance."

A state equal rights amendment can also be used to attack alleged gender discrimination. However, not all states have passed such legislation (see section 8.1.2., "The ERA and State Equal Rights Amendments" [note 6]). State Equal Rights Amendments, and the proposed and defeated federal Equal Rights Amendment, were formulated to provide more protection from sex-based discrimination than the federal Constitution provides under the equal protection clause of the Fourteenth Amendment. The goal of the legislation is to protect against all sex-based discrimination and to protect women's rights.

Most gender discrimination challenges have been based on either the equal protection laws or Title IX, or both. For example, in *Adams v. Baker*, 919 F.Supp. 1496 (D. Kan. 1996), a fifteen-year-old female plaintiff sought a preliminary injunction, alleging that the school district violated her equal protection rights *and* violated Title IX because it did not allow her on the school's all-male wrestling team. The court concluded that the school district's reasons in not allowing plaintiff on the wrestling team were either not "important governmental objectives" or "not substantially related" to its objectives, and granted the preliminary injunction for Adams on the grounds of equal protection. However, if the plaintiff had only filed a complaint under Title IX, she would not have been successful; the court stated, "[b]ecause wrestling is a contact sport, Title IX does not require that Valley Center High School allow a female to try out for the boys wrestling team." The court ruled that plaintiff was not likely to succeed on the merits of her Title IX claim and, therefore, an injunction was not warranted on those grounds. However, the plaintiff was still able to receive the injunction due to the violation of equal protection under the U.S. Constitution.

Regardless of whether plaintiffs employ a Title IX or an equal protection approach in a gender discrimination case, they generally will argue that they are being deprived of equality under the law. When a court deals with claims of equal protection or Title IX violations there are three important factors that courts commonly will consider when analyzing whether or not there is actual discrimination.

The first factor that a court will consider is whether or not a sport is a contact sport. Total exclusion from sports, and especially non-contact sports, is generally considered a prima facie violation of equal education opportunities. However, Title IX provides for a "contact sport exception" that allows athletic programs to bar women from engaging in contact sports with men.

The second factor that the court will consider is the quality or quantity of available opportunities for each gender. The OCR in the Department of Education (formerly part of the Department of Health, Education and Welfare) monitors compliance with the dictates of the law. Under the OCR interpretation of Title IX, courts must look to see if the institution in question is meeting the interests of the underrepresented gender and whether equal treatment is given. Under an equal protection analysis, courts will determine if the regulations in place unfairly discriminate against one gender.

The third factor that a court will consider is the age and level of competition involved in the dispute. The younger the athletes involved, the fewer actual physiological differences exist. Without demonstrable physiological differences, the justification of inherent biological differences as a rational basis for the exclusion of one sex from athletic participation is negated. Courts are reluctant to enforce discriminatory practices at a young age, when there are only negligible physiological differences between the two sexes.

8.1.1. Title IX

Title IX, since its inception in 1972, has undergone a series of changes and revisions while remaining true to its original mission of abolishing discrimination based on gender in federally funded activities. From the original policy interpretation by the Department of Health, Education and Welfare (HEW), through the decision in *Grove City College v. Bell*, the passage of the Civil Rights Restoration Act, and subsequent litigation, the history and effect of Title IX will be discussed within the following sections.

8.1.1.1. *Legislative History of Title IX*

Section 901 (a) of Title IX of the Education Amendments of 1972 contains the following language:

> No person in the United States shall, on the basis of sex, be excluded from participation in, be denied the benefits of, or be subjected to discrimination under any education program or activity receiving Federal financial assistance.

Title IX became law on July 1, 1972, as Public Law 92-318 (codified at 20 U.S.C. §§1681–1987). It specifically and clearly recognizes the problems of gender discrimination and forbids such discrimination in any program, organization, or agency that receives federal funds. Athletics and athletics programs, however, were *not* specifically mentioned in Title IX when it first became law in 1972. HEW, taking the position that sports and physical education were an integral part of education, specifically included athletics, despite strong lobbying efforts to exempt revenue-producing intercollegiate sports from the Title IX requirements. This specific inclusion of athletics into Title IX occurred in 1974, and extended from general athletic opportunities to athletic scholarships. The principles governing athletic scholarships included the idea that all recipients of federal aid must provide *"reasonable opportunities"* for both genders to receive scholarship aid. The existence of *"reasonable opportunities"* is determined by examining the ratio of male to female participants. Scholarship aid must then be distributed according to this participation ratio (see 45 C.F.R. §86.13 (c)).

A long process of citizen involvement preceded the first set of regulations. In July 1975, the Department of Health, Education and Welfare issued the regulations designed to implement Title IX. These regulations are found in Title 45, Code of Federal Regulations (C.F.R.), section 86 A–F. The regulations were criticized by many as being vague and inadequate. In December 1978, HEW attempted to alleviate the criticism by releasing a proposed policy interpretation that attempted to explain, but did not change, the 1975 requirements. However, not until December 1979, seven years after the original passage of Title IX, did the Office for Civil Rights (OCR), the successor to HEW, release the policy interpretation for Title IX. These final guidelines specifically included interscholastic and intercollegiate athletics. Developed after numerous meetings and countless revisions, they reflected comments from universities, legislative sources, and the public.

8.1.1.2. *OCR Policy Interpretation of Title IX*

The policy interpretation, finalized in 1979, focused on three areas that the OCR evaluates to determine whether an institution is in compliance with Title IX regulations with regard to athletics. In assessing compliance with Title IX, the OCR looks at several factors, including athletic expenditures and program components. Athletic expenditures need not be equal, but the pattern of expenditures must not result in a disparate effect on opportunity. Institutions may not discriminate in the provision of necessary equipment, supplies, facilities, and publicity for sports programs.

Another step that also was crucial to providing clear guidelines in the interpretation of Title IX legislation and what Title IX compliance involves was the publication of the *Title IX Athletics Investigator's Manual* in 1990 by the Office of Civil Rights. This manual superseded the *Interim Title IX Intercollegiate Athletics Manual 1980* and the memorandum "Guidance for Writing Title IX Intercollegiate Athletics Letters of Findings," issued in 1982. This manual set out three main areas that are involved in Title IX compliance and would be investigated by the OCR and the courts when ruling on whether an institution is complying with Title IX. The OCR also released a report in 1997, *Title IX: 25 Years of Progress*, which provides an overview of the impact of Title IX in improving educational opportunities for students (see note 1 for more information on the OCR).

The first area that is identified in the *Investigator's Manual*, and that OCR assesses, is the extent to which the institution has met the interests and abilities of male and female students. The policy interpretation requires that the school "equally and effectively" accommodate the athletic interests and abilities of both men and women. This determination requires an examination of the institution's assessment of the athletic interests and abilities of its students, its selection of offered sports, and its available competitive opportunities. The OCR evaluates the level of competitive opportunities in one of three ways:

1. Are intercollegiate competitive opportunities provided in numbers substantially proportionate to the respective enrollment of each gender?
2. Is the institution's current and historical practice of program expansion responsive to the athletic interests of the underrepresented gender?
3. Does the institution fully accommodate the abilities and the interests of the underrepresented gender in the current program?

In analyzing this area, the OCR and the courts must determine the extent to which the institution has met the interests and abilities of male and female students. In other words, a determination must be made as to whether there are equal opportunities to compete for both men and women, and whether the opportunities are at equivalent levels of competition. In analyzing this particular area, the OCR and the courts compare the ratio of male and female athletes to the ratio of undergraduate full-time students of each gender. The ratios should be equivalent. If the OCR determines that an institution complies with any one of these tests, the institution is judged to have effectively accommodated the interest and the abilities of its student-athletes.

Second, the OCR assesses the financial assistance that male and female athletes receive from the institution. This involves assessing whether an institution's athletic scholarships are awarded on a "substantially proportional" basis. In analyzing this area, the OCR and the courts determine the proportion of scholarship dollars that are spent on male and female athletes and compare this proportion to the proportion of athletes of each gender. However, if a disparity is explained by legitimate and nondiscriminatory factors, the OCR will find compliance. These proportions should be equivalent when an institution is complying with Title IX.

For example, compare schools A, B, and C. At school A, 50% of the athletes are female, but only 25% of the total financial assistance goes to females. At school B, 50% of athletes are female, and 45% of the financial assistance goes to females. At school C, 50% of the athletes are female and 50% of the financial assistance goes to females. School A would not be in compliance with Title IX because the 25% assistance to females is significantly below the 50% participation rate. School C is clearly in compliance because the proportion of financial assistance equals the proportion of participation to females. School B's situation requires further analysis. When the proportions are not exactly equal, but close, the OCR applies certain statistical tests to determine whether the proportions are substantially equal.

The policy manual also suggests certain nondiscriminatory factors that may explain disparities in financial assistance to men's and women's athletic programs. An example of a nondiscriminatory factor would be the difference between in-state and out-of-state tuition. Two students in a public institution may both have a scholarship for one year, but since one of the students is from out of state, his or her scholarship has a much higher price tag.

The third area of assessment under the policy interpretation is the degree to which the institution provides equal treatment, benefits, and opportunities in certain program areas. Some areas considered by the OCR in evaluating equivalent treatment include equipment, coaching, and facilities. The OCR may use additional factors in determining whether an institution is providing equivalent opportunity for members of both genders in its sports program. However, some of these factors (publicity, academic tutoring, housing, and dining services) are relevant in intercollegiate programs but are not generally relevant in assessing a sports program in a secondary school.

The OCR has distinguished eleven program component areas that have been targeted when investigating this area:

- Provision of equipment and supplies
- Scheduling of games and practice times
- Travel and per diem allowances
- Opportunity to receive academic tutoring, and assignment and compensation of tutors
- Opportunity to receive coaching, and assignment and compensation of coaches
- Provision of locker rooms, and practice and competitive facilities
- Provision of medical and training facilities and services
- Provision of housing and dining facilities and services
- Publicity
- Provision of support services
- Recruitment of student-athletes.

Title IX requires that both genders receive comparable or equivalent services in each of these program component areas. However, the *Investigator's Manual* identifies some potential differences that do not cause the institution to be out of compliance with Title IX. These differences are allowed if they are based on certain factors the OCR has identified as nondiscriminatory:

- Unique nature of the particular sport
- Special circumstances of a temporary nature
- The need for greater funding for crowd control at more popular athletic events
- Differences that have not yet been remedied but that an institution is voluntarily working to correct.

In the area of compensation for men's and women's coaches, HEW assessed rates of compensation, length of contracts, experience, and other factors, while taking into account mitigating conditions such as nature of duties, number of assistants to be supervised, number of participants, and level of competition. As long as these differences in the program component areas are based on one of the nondiscriminatory factors, the OCR and the courts have not found non-compliance with Title IX. (See note 2 in section 8.1.3., "Equal Protection Laws.")

The major issues raised regarding Title IX revolve around the scope of the legislation and the programs to which it is applicable. The July 1975 policy regulations issued by HEW covered three areas of activity within educational institutions: employment, treatment of students, and admissions. Several sections of the regulations concerned with the treatment of students included specific requirements for interscholastic, intercollegiate, intramural, and club athletic programs.

Another section of the HEW Title IX regulations specifies requirements for athletic programs (see 45 C.F.R. §86.41(c)). Contact sports are subject to regulations distinct from those governing non-contact sports. The regulations in this section state that separate teams are acceptable for contact sports and for teams in either contact or non-contact sports in which selection is based on competitive skill. There is one exception to the rule forbidding separate teams when a selection is based on competitive skill: if a school sponsors a team in a particular sport for one gender, but not for the other, and if athletic opportunities for the excluded gender have been historically more restricted than athletic opportunities for the other gender, members of the excluded gender must be allowed to try out for the team. The exception does not apply if the sport is a contact sport. For non-contact sports, if only one team exists, both sexes must be allowed to compete for positions on the team.

8.1.1.3. OCR Analysis and Method of Enforcement

The procedures for Title IX analysis are established in the regulations that list specific factors that should be examined in determining whether or not equality in athletics exists. The number of sports, the type of arrangements, and benefits offered to women competing in athletics are reviewed. When teams of one gender are favored in such areas as funding, coaching, and facilities, resulting in severely reduced opportunities for the other gender to compete, the courts will closely examine program expenditures, number of teams, and access to facilities to determine if the school is fulfilling the requirements of Title IX. Title IX does not require a sport-by-sport analysis, but an overall program assessment.

The final area of coverage within the regulations is the method of enforcement of Title IX. The procedure to be followed is initiated by the OCR, which makes random compliance reviews and also investigates complaints submitted by individuals. The first step in the process is to examine the records kept by the institution under investigation in order to review its attempt to comply with Title IX. Each institution must adopt and publish compliance procedures and designate one employee to carry out its Title IX responsibilities, including investigation of complaints. The institution must notify all students and employees of the designated employee's name, office address, and telephone number. After a preliminary review, the OCR has the option to conduct a full hearing or to drop the case.

If the OCR calls a full hearing, the institution has the right to have counsel present and to appeal an adverse decision; the complainant has neither of these rights. The affected individual is not a party involved in the hearing. Instead, the OCR becomes the complainant and pursues the claim. If the OCR finds that there has not been substantial compliance, it may turn its finding over to federal or local authorities for prosecution under the appropriate statutes (see note 5).

This section has provided the basic legislative history of Title IX legislation and the subsequent policy interpretation. For an in-depth discussion of the earliest cases involving Title IX, ensuing policy reinterpretations, review of recent cases involving Title IX, and the effect that Title IX has had upon intercollegiate athletics, refer to section 8.2.1., "Legality and Scope of Title IX."

NOTES

1. To view and order all of the information that has been released by the Office for Civil Rights, including *Equal Opportunity in Intercollegiate Athletics, Clarification of Intercollegiate Athletics Policy: The Three-Part Test, Title IX and Sex Discrimination, Title IX Grievance Procedures: An Introductory Manual*, and *25 Years of Title IX*, visit the following Web site: www.ed.gov/offices/OCR/publications.html#TitleIX

2. In *Daniels v. School Board*, 985 F.Supp. 1458 (M.D. Fla. 1997) and 985 F.Supp. 1394 (M.D. Fla. 1997), two members of the Merritt Island High School (MIHS) girls' varsity softball team sought an injunction against the school board for violations of Title IX and the Florida Educational Equity Act. The plaintiffs claimed that there were significant inequalities between MIHS' baseball and softball facilities. Some of the differences included the following: an electronic scoreboard for the baseball field while the softball field had no scoreboard at all, the baseball team had a batting cage while the softball team did not, there was a sign advertising "Merritt Island Baseball" and not one for the softball team, and the baseball field had lights, but the softball field did not. The court concluded that there was enough evidence that plaintiffs were likely to succeed on the merits of the Title IX claim, and therefore an injunction was proper. The court allowed MIHS an opportunity to submit a plan to rectify the Title IX violations. The court determined that the plan was not sufficient. In fact, the court stated that it "is inclined to agree with Plaintiffs that many of the Board's proposals seem more retaliatory than constructive." The court granted the injunction ordering the school board to eliminate the inequalities.

3. In *Gonyo v. Drake University*, 879 F.Supp. 1000 (S.D. Iowa 1995), plaintiffs, former members of the Drake wrestling team, brought action against the university alleging Title IX and equal protection violations after the university dropped the wrestling program due to lack of funding for athletic scholarships. Male athletes at Drake received only 47 percent of the university's athletic scholarships even though they made up 75.3 percent of the university's athletes. This appears to be a violation of Title IX if participation rates are

not considered. The court concluded that there was not a violation of Title IX and stated, "The court concludes that the participation test more comprehensively serves the remedial purposes of Title IX than does the scholarship test and therefore must prevail."

4. In *Alexander v. Yale University*, 631 F.2d 178 (2d Cir. 1978), the court held that a party seeking relief under Title IX must demonstrate a personal "distinct and palpable injury," and the relief requested must "redound to that party's personal benefit." Former students lacked standing to get any relief from sexual harassment charges.

5. The Office for Civil Rights is responsible for conducting compliance reviews of Title IX. The OCR selects schools randomly for Title IX compliance reviews and will also review schools based on complaints brought by individuals. Educational institutions are required to keep and submit to the Department of Education accurate compliance reports to enable it to determine whether Title IX requirements have been satisfied. The educational institution is also required to permit access by the Department of Education to its books, records, accounts, and other sources of information, and its facilities, that may be pertinent to ascertaining compliance. The OCR begins its investigation by notifying the school and then collecting data on the overall athletic program. The information may include the number of teams, scheduling of games and practice times, travel and per diem allowances, compensation of coaches, provision of facilities, and amount of publicity (press releases, media guides, etc.). Aggrieved individuals may also sue an institution directly, without being required to rely on the enforcement mechanism of the Department of Education. On the basis of a review of the data, the OCR will determine whether or not equivalent treatment, benefits, and opportunities, as mandated by Title IX, have been afforded to both genders.

OCR officials will meet with the administrators of an investigated institution and review the OCR's proposed findings before a letter of noncompliance is issued. If the institution voluntarily adopts a plan to rectify its violations within a reasonable period, the institution will be granted a letter of compliance. The Department of Education is then responsible for monitoring the progress of the plan. If the plan is not implemented within the time specified or proves to be an inadequate remedy, the institution will be found in noncompliance and further legal action against the school could be taken.

If there is a failure to comply with Title IX, or a voluntary compliance agreement cannot be reached, or the violations cannot be corrected by informal means, compliance may be effected by the suspension or termination of, or refusal to grant or to continue, federal financial assistance. In addition, the Department of Education may refer the matter to the Department of Justice, with a recommendation that appropriate proceedings be brought to enforce any rights of the United States.

Prior to suspending, terminating, or refusing to grant or continue federal financial assistance, an institution must be afforded the opportunity for a hearing before an administrative law judge. If the educational institution does not request a hearing within the time allowed, the right to the hearing is waived and a decision will be made on the basis of the information then on file.

After a hearing is held, the hearing judge will either make an initial decision on the institution's compliance or certify the entire record, including his or her recommended findings and proposed decision, to the appropriate reviewing authority for a final decision. Both the Department of Education and the institution may appeal that determination to the department's reviewing authority. If the reviewing authority affirms the administrative law judge's decision, the institution may request a review by the secretary of education.

If the Department of Education decides to withdraw funding, it must report that decision to the appropriate congressional committees thirty days prior to the termination of funds. Having exhausted its administrative remedies, the institution could then seek judicial review of the department's actions.

For more information on the Office for Civil Rights and its analysis and enforcement of Title IX, visit the OCR Web site at www.ed.gov/offices/OCR/.

8.1.2. The ERA and State Equal Rights Amendments

Although there are many legal alternatives to allegations of gender discrimination, there has been a recent push for a nationwide comprehensive prohibition of gender discrimination. Supporters of the Equal Rights Amendment (ERA) argued that passage of a constitutional amendment would remedy the lack of such a general prohibition. In order to amend the U.S. Constitution, the proposed amendment must first be passed by a three-fourths vote of both the U.S. Senate and the House of Representatives. Then it must be ratified by at least thirty-eight state legislatures. The ERA was passed in both houses of Congress in 1972, but it did not receive the necessary thirty-eight ratifications from state legislatures by the required deadline of July 1, 1982. (See note 1 for a discussion of the proposed federal ERA.)

While uniform prohibition of gender discrimination has not materialized, many states and the District of Columbia have enacted their own Equal Rights Amendments. Thus, Equal Rights Amendments have impacted athletics at the state level but not at the federal level. Several cases have been decided in favor of the complainant on the basis of a state ERA. It is important to note that many of these cases, however, could have been brought on other arguments in states without ERAs. As of 2001, eighteen states have included an Equal Rights Amendment within their constitution that provides more protection against sex-based discrimination (see notes 6 and 7).

Supporters of a constitutional amendment continue to argue that the effectiveness and importance of an Equal Rights Amendment can be demonstrated in *Commonwealth v. Pennsylvania Interscholastic Athletic Association* (see note 5). In *Commonwealth*, the court decided that the rule of the PIAA violated the Pennsylvania State Equal Rights Amendment, which states, "Equality of rights under the law shall not be denied or abridged in the Commonwealth of Pennsylvania because of the sex of the individual." Although the plaintiffs had also claimed a violation of the equal protection clause of the Constitution, the court did not have to consider this claim because it was found that the PIAA had violated the state ERA. Regardless of the precarious position in which protection against gender discrimination exists, the existence of an Equal Rights Amendment on the state level is often helpful, and may even be crucial to the success of gender discrimination cases.

NOTES ⎯⎯⎯⎯⎯⎯⎯⎯⎯⎯⎯⎯⎯⎯⎯⎯⎯⎯⎯⎯⎯⎯⎯⎯⎯⎯⎯⎯⎯⎯⎯

1. In general, the proposed federal ERA absolutely prohibited discrimination based on gender and required that any law using gender as a basis for classification be subject to a strict scrutiny analysis by the courts. Supporters of the ERA argued that without proper enforcement, neither Title IX nor Title VII could alleviate the basic problems of gender discrimination. The weakness of Title IX, in particular, is its dependence on federal funding, since reduction in funding can effectively diminish the OCR's enforcement capabilities. In addition to this financial vulnerability, gender discrimination statutes are also subject to congressional revisions, which may lessen or even negate much of the available protection. It has been argued that a constitutional amendment would be more sheltered from fluctuating political interests.

2. In *Blair v. Washington State University*, 740 P.2d 1379 (Wash. 1987), female athletes and coaches of female athletes brought a gender discrimination action under the state

Equal Rights Amendment. The trial court ruled for plaintiffs and awarded damages, injunctive relief, attorney fees, and costs. On appeal, the Washington Supreme Court affirmed the lower court's conclusion of gender discrimination but modified the lower court's calculations of comparative scholarships for male and female athletes and attorney fees.

3. In *MacLean v. First Northwest Industries of America*, 600 P.2d 1027 (Wash. Ct. App. 1979), a class action was brought against the city of Seattle and the corporation operating a professional basketball team that alleged "Ladies Night" price-ticketing policies were violations of the state's equal rights amendment that prohibited gender discrimination. The court of appeals reversed a lower court decision and found the ticket practice a violation of the amendment.

4. In *Darrin v. Gould*, 540 P.2d 882 (Wash. 1975), an action was brought by the parents of high school students Carol and Delores Darrin, who appealed a Washington Superior Court decision denying them relief in their class action claim of illegal discrimination against females in interscholastic football competition. The Washington Supreme Court found that the school board's denial of permission for the girls to compete on the boys' interscholastic contact football team constituted "a discrimination by state action based on ability to play." Under the due process clause of the Fourteenth Amendment, "performers are entitled to an individualized determination of their qualifications, not a determination based on the qualifications of a majority of the broader class of which the individual is a member." The Supreme Court decided that the Darrin girls could participate, based on the provision of Washington's Equal Rights Amendment, which stated: "Equality of rights and responsibility under the law shall not be denied or abridged on account of sex."

5. In *Commonwealth v. Pennsylvania Interscholastic Athletic Ass'n.*, 334 A.2d 839 (Pa. Commw. Ct. 1975), the state of Pennsylvania, acting through its attorney general, filed suit against the Pennsylvania Interscholastic Athletic Association (PIAA), charging that Article XIX, Section 38, of the PIAA bylaws, which states that "girls shall not compete or practice against boys in any athletic contest," was in violation of both the Fourteenth Amendment of the U.S. Constitution and Pennsylvania's Equal Rights Amendment. Plaintiff claimed that the association's rule denied to female athletes the same opportunities to practice and compete in interscholastic sports that were afforded male athletes. Pennsylvania's ERA provided that "equality of rights under law shall not be denied or abridged in the Commonwealth of Pennsylvania because of the sex of the individual." The court found the association's rule to be "unconstitutional on its face under the ERA" and proclaimed, "None of the justifications for it offered by the PIAA, even if proved, could sustain its legality." The court found it unnecessary to consider whether or not the rule also violated the Fourteenth Amendment.

6. As of 2001, the following eighteen states had enacted their own individual Equal Rights Amendments within their state constitutions: Alaska, California, Colorado, Connecticut, Hawaii, Illinois, Louisiana, Maryland, Massachusetts, Montana, New Hampshire, New Mexico, Pennsylvania, Texas, Utah, Virginia, Washington, and Wyoming.

7. An example of an Equal Rights Amendment is Massachusetts Constitution Pt. 1, Art. 1, Amend. Art. 106:

> Art. CVI, Article I of Part the First of the Constitution is hereby annulled and the following is adopted:
> All people are born free and equal and have certain natural, essential and unalienable rights; among which may be reckoned the right of enjoying and defending their lives and liberties; that of acquiring, possessing and protecting property; in fine, that of seeking and obtaining their safety and happiness. Equality under the law shall not be denied or abridged because of sex, race, color, creed or national origin.

8. Title IX and educational equity laws, which have been passed on the state level, parallel the intent and coverage of the federal Title IX legislation; thirteen states (Alaska, California, Florida, Illinois, Maine, Montana, Massachusetts, Nebraska, New Jersey,

Oregon, Rhode Island, Washington, and Wisconsin) have each enacted state laws that closely mirror the federal regulation. Another eighteen states (Arizona, Colorado, Connecticut, Hawaii, Idaho, Indiana, Iowa, Kansas, Maryland, Michigan, Minnesota, New Hampshire, New York, North Carolina, Pennsylvania, South Dakota, Vermont, and Wyoming) have enacted gender equity laws that incorporate various aspects of the federal regulation.

9. The State of Florida adopted legislation in 2001 (updating legislation from 1994) that consisted of a number of gender equity issues. Some of the topics covered in this legislation are the following:

(d) Students may be separated by sex for any portion of a class which deals with human reproduction or during participation in bodily contact sports. For the purpose of this section, bodily contact sports include wrestling, boxing, rugby, ice hockey, football, basketball, and other sports in which the purpose or major activity involves bodily contact.

(e) Guidance services, counseling services, and financial assistance services in the state system of public education shall be available to students equally. Guidance and counseling services, materials, and promotional events shall stress access to academic, career, and vocational opportunities for students without regard to race, national origin, sex, handicap, or marital status.

(3)(a) No person shall, on the basis of sex, be excluded from participating in, be denied the benefits of, or be treated differently from another person or otherwise be discriminated against in any interscholastic, intercollegiate, club, or intramural athletics offered by an educational institution; and no educational institution shall provide athletics separately on such basis.

(b) Notwithstanding the requirements of paragraph (a), an educational institution may operate or sponsor separate teams for members of each sex if the selection for such teams is based upon competitive skill or the activity involved is a bodily contact sport. However, when an educational institution operates or sponsors a team in a particular sport for members of one sex but does not operate or sponsor a team for members of the other sex, and athletic opportunities for that sex have previously been limited, members of the excluded sex must be allowed to try out for the team offered unless the sport involved is a bodily contact sport.

(c) This subsection does not prohibit the grouping of students in physical education classes and activities by ability as assessed by objective standards of individual performance developed and applied without regard to sex. However, when use of a single standard of measuring skill or progress in a physical education class has an adverse effect on members of one sex, the educational institution shall use appropriate standards which do not have such effect.

(d) An educational institution which operates or sponsors interscholastic, intercollegiate, club, or intramural athletics shall provide equal athletic opportunity for members of both sexes. In determining whether equal opportunities are available, the Commissioner of Education shall consider, among other factors:

  1. Whether the selection of sports and levels of competition effectively accommodate the interests and abilities of members of both sexes.
  2. The provision of equipment and supplies.
  3. Scheduling of games and practice times.
  4. Travel and per diem allowances.
  5. Opportunities to receive coaching and academic tutoring.
  6. Assignment and compensation of coaches and tutors.
  7. Provision of locker room, practice, and competitive facilities.
  8. Provision of medical and training facilities and services.
  9. Provision of housing and dining facilities and services.
  10. Publicity. Unequal aggregate expenditures for members of each sex or unequal expenditures for male and female teams if an educational institution operates or sponsors separate teams do not constitute nonimplementation of this subsection, but the Commissioner of Education shall consider the failure to provide necessary funds for teams for one sex in assessing equality of opportunity for members of each sex.

(e) An educational institution may provide separate toilet, locker room, and shower facilities on the basis of sex, but such facilities shall be comparable to such facilities provided for students of the other sex.

8.1.3. Equal Protection Laws

The basic analysis utilized for equal protection questions is discussed in Chapter 5, section 5.4.3., "Equal Protection." Within the U.S. Constitution, the equal protection guarantee is found in the Fourteenth Amendment. It states that "No state shall . . . deny to any person within its jurisdiction the equal protection of the laws." Under this clause, people are allowed to challenge laws, rules, and regulations that seem to unfairly classify and discriminate. Here we examine more closely the effects of using gender to classify persons for different athletic opportunities.

Historically, gender has been an acceptable category for classifying persons for different benefits and burdens under any given law. In 1873, the Supreme Court, in *Bradwell v. State*, 83 U.S. 130 (1873), opened with the statement that a woman's place was in the home. The Court went on to say that this was part of a "divinely ordained law of nature." In 1908, the Court stated in *Muller v. Oregon*, 208 U.S. 412 (1908), that a classification based on gender was a valid constitutional classification. Such a classification was not considered to be a violation of equal protection, regardless of whether it was based on actual or imagined physical differences between men and women. Modern equal protection theories have now gained preeminence, and the use of gender to classify persons is considered less acceptable.

A school's, conference's, or athletic association's rules prohibiting mixed-gender competition have typically been challenged on equal protection grounds. In a number of cases, women have been successful in asserting their right to participate on an equal basis with men, and one legal theory they have utilized on these occasions has been the equal protection clause.

Under traditional equal protection analysis, the legislative gender-based classification must be sustained unless it is found to be patently arbitrary and/or if it bears absolutely no rational relationship to a legitimate governmental interest. Under this traditional rational basis analysis, overturning discriminatory laws has been extremely difficult. The implication for gender discrimination sports litigation in high schools and colleges is that women may be excluded from athletic participation upon a showing of a rational basis for their exclusion. The rational reason must be factually supported and may not be based on mere presumptions about the relative physical athletic capabilities of women and men. It remains, however, a relatively easy standard for the defendant to meet, as it invokes only the lowest standard of scrutiny by the court.

The court will apply its highest standard, that of strict scrutiny, if it finds that the classification restricts a "fundamental right" or if the rule involves a "suspect" classification. Under the standard of strict scrutiny, the institution seeking to uphold the regulation must show that the rule's classification is necessary to promote a compelling governmental purpose or interest. To date, most courts have not found gender to be a suspect class, which would elevate it to the status held by race, national origin, and alienage. (See note 4 for a case that used strict scrutiny for gender classification.) However, gender and other classifications may, however, be deemed "suspect" under a state equal protection clause.

If the courts were, however, to decide that gender is a suspect class or athletic participation is a fundamental right, all rules that classify on the basis of gender would become subject to strict scrutiny analysis. If this were the standard, the rule makers would have to demonstrate that there are compelling reasons for the classification and that there is no less restrictive alternative. They would also have to prove that the classification was directly related to the constitutional purpose of the legislation and that this purpose could not have been achieved by any less objectionable means. Many rules and laws would fail to meet this high standard, and hence would be judged discriminatory.

The Supreme Court has moved away from the broad interpretation of the rational relationship test by increasing the burden on the defendant. This intermediate test, between the rational basis and strict scrutiny tests, was first established in *Reed v. Reed*, 404 U.S. 71 (1971). The Supreme Court established therein that gender-based classifications must be "reasonable, not arbitrary, and must rest upon some ground of difference having a fair and substantial relation to the object of the legislation, so that all persons similarly circumstanced shall be treated alike." The Supreme Court again addressed this issue in *Frontiero v. Richardson*, 411 U.S. 677 (1973); in a plurality opinion, Justice Brennan stated, "What differentiates sex from such non-suspect statuses as intelligence or physical disability . . . is that the sex characteristic frequently bears no relation to ability to perform or contribute to society." Finally, in *Craig v. Boren*, 429 U.S. 190 (1976), and again in *Mississippi University for Women v. Hogan*, 458 U.S. 718 (1982), the Supreme Court held that a gender classification will fail unless it is substantially related to a sufficiently important governmental interest. Thus, the Supreme Court has established the *intermediate* level of scrutiny to apply in gender-based discrimination cases.

A factual basis for any gender classification must exist. Mere preferences or assumptions concerning the ability of one gender to perform adequately are not acceptable bases for a discriminatory classification. The intermediate standard requires more than an easily achieved rational relationship but less than a strict scrutiny standard would demand. The class must bear a substantial relationship to an important but not compelling governmental interest. Also, the relationship between a classification and a law's purpose must be founded on fact, not on general legislative views of the relative strengths and/or abilities of the two genders.

Three key factors are commonly considered in an equal protection analysis of athletic discrimination cases. The first factor is state action. Before any claim can be successfully litigated, a sufficient amount of state action must be present. Without state action, an equal protection argument under the U.S. Constitution is not applicable. This factor has significant ramifications in cases in which the athletic activity is conducted outside the auspices of a state or municipal entity or a public educational institution. Examples include youth sport leagues such as Little League Baseball, Pop Warner Football, and the YMCA's youth basketball association.

The second factor is whether the sport involves physical contact. In contact sports the courts have allowed separate men's and women's teams. This "separate but equal" doctrine is based on considerations of the physical health and safety of the participants. For example, in the case of *Mercer v. Duke University*, the football team had no obligation under Title IX to allow Mercer to try out for the football team because football is classified as a contact sport. (See note 1 in section 8.3.1., "Men's Team, No Women's Team.") In non-Title IX cases, when separate teams do not exist, both genders may have to be given an opportunity to try out and to meet the necessary physical requirements on an individual basis. A complete ban on the participation of one gender will not be upheld if it is based on generalizations about characteristics of an entire gender rather than on a reasonable consideration of individual characteristics.

The third factor to be considered is whether both genders have equal opportunities to participate. This "equal opportunity" usually requires the existence of completely separate teams or an opportunity to try out for the one available team. If there are separate teams, however, it is permissible for the governing organization to prohibit coed participation. Unlike classifications based on race, when gender is a determining factor, "separate but equal" doctrines may be acceptable. The issue then often becomes whether the teams are indeed equal (see *O'Connor v. Board of Education of School District No. 23* in section 8.3.3., "Women's Teams and Men's Teams"). Other factors that have been taken into consideration are the age of the participant and the level of the competition. Physical differences between boys and girls below the age of twelve are minimal. Therefore, health and safety considerations that might be applicable to older athletes have not constituted legitimate reasons for restricting young athletes' access to participation.

The legal analysis of any particular case also depends on the philosophy of the court and the particular factual circumstances presented (see *Alston v. Virginia High School League, Inc.* in section 8.3.5., "Same Sport, Different Seasons"). Some courts are reluctant to intervene in discretionary decisions made by an association governing athletic events unless there are obvious abuses. (See Chapter 5, section 5.2.2, "Judicial Review.") Other courts have been reluctant to intervene in discretionary decisions because they do not believe they have the administrative knowledge or time necessary to oversee the administration of sports programs effectively.

Historically, challenging sex discrimination based on equal protection laws has been generally ineffective. Under the intermediate test used for gender classification, the defendant must show an important state interest for the rule in question. (See notes 1 and 4.) One disadvantage of the equal protection laws is that they constitute a private remedy. Therefore, the plaintiff must be in a position to absorb the costs of litigation. This reduces the number of complaints filed and encourages settlement before judicial resolution of a number of equal protection claims.

NOTES

1. In *Adams v. Baker*, 919 F.Supp. 1496 (D. Kan. 1996), a fifteen-year-old female plaintiff sought a preliminary injunction, alleging that the school district violated her equal protection rights. Plaintiff was not allowed on the school's wrestling team. The court concluded that the school district's purposes in not allowing plaintiff on the wrestling team were either not "important governmental objectives" or "not substantially related" to its objectives. The court granted the preliminary injunction. (See note 3 in section 8.3.1.1., "Contact Sports," for a discussion of the Title IX claim in this case.)

2. In *Ridgefield Women's Political Caucus, Inc. v. Fossi*, 458 F.Supp. 117 (D. Conn. 1978), girls and taxpayer parents brought claims against town selectmen, seeking to prohibit the town from offering public property at a nominal price to a private organization that restricted membership to boys. The district court found for the girls' parents, ruling

that the town selectmen had no right to offer land at less than fair value to the private organization in question as long as this organization restricted membership and the town failed to offer girls recreational opportunities equivalent to those provided by the organization in question. Until such services were offered, any conveyance of the property at a nominal fee would constitute governmental support of gender discrimination in violation of the equal protection clause of the Fourteenth Amendment.

3. In *Richards v. United States Tennis Ass'n.*, 400 N.Y.S.2d 267 (N.Y. Sup. Ct. 1977), an action was brought by a professional tennis player, who had undergone a sex-change operation, against a professional tennis association that sought a preliminary injunction against the organization to prevent it from requiring the tennis player to undergo a sex-chromatin test to prove she was a female and eligible to participate in a women's tournament. The court granted the injunction and held that the test was grossly unfair, discriminatory, and inequitable, and violated the tennis player's rights under the New York Human Rights Law.

4. In *Frontiero v. Richardson*, 411 U.S. 677 (1973), the Supreme Court applied strict scrutiny to strike down a rule requiring female, but not male, service members to prove spousal dependency in order to receive increased military allowance. Although this is not a case that involves sports, it is nevertheless an important case because it shows that a court has the power to use the standard of strict scrutiny in evaluating claims of equal protection violations. Despite the fact that all of the judges did not agree on the classification of gender as a suspect class, the majority opinion stated, "(1) statutory classifications based upon sex were inherently suspect and thus must be subjected to close judicial scrutiny, and (2) under such standard of judicial scrutiny, the challenged statutes were unconstitutional as constituting an invidious discrimination against servicewomen in violation of the due process clause of the Fifth Amendment, the sole purpose advanced for the statutory discrimination being mere administrative convenience."

8.2. LEGAL CHALLENGES TO TITLE IX

8.2.1. Legality and Scope of Title IX

The Title IX regulations and accompanying policy interpretations were promulgated by the Department of Health, Education and Welfare (HEW) and were not finalized until July 1979, after the adoption of regulations and policy interpretations.

The NCAA brought the first legal challenge to Title IX. The NCAA sought declaratory and injunctive relief for the invalidation of the Title IX regulations promulgated by the HEW in *NCAA v. Califano*, 444 F.Supp. 425 (D. Kan. 1978), *rev'd.*, 622 F.2d 1382 (10th Cir. 1980). The NCAA specifically sought relief for the invalidation of the Title IX regulations promulgated by HEW with respect to gender discrimination in athletics. Summary judgment was granted to HEW, the district court holding that the NCAA did not have standing as an association representing its member schools to pursue the suit. The NCAA appealed the district court decision. The appeals court reversed the lower court ruling and held that while the NCAA does not have standing to sue in its own right, it does have standing to sue on behalf of its members (see Chapter 5, section 5.2.3., "Standing").

After the enactment of Title IX in 1972, a major point of contention had been whether the legislation applied only to the specific departments that received direct funding (commonly referred to as the "programmatic approach") or to the entire institution (referred to as the "institutional approach"). This dilemma had often been expressed in a debate as to whether Title IX was, or was not, program-specific.

An integral factor in the resultant litigation had been the determination of what constituted federal financial assistance. In some cases, it had been argued that federal student loan programs constitute federal aid to an institution, while other interpretations defined federal aid as only those funds specifically earmarked or directly given to a particular program. Therefore, in terms of the scope of Title IX, the questions became very complex: What constituted federal aid? Was indirect aid or direct aid required by the statute? Once federal assistance was found, was only the particular program that benefited from the aid or the entire institution subject to Title IX regulation?

Judgments in many of the cases shortly after the enactment of Title IX had been contradictory on the issue of what constituted federal financial assistance. In *Othen v. Ann Arbor School Board, Bennett v. West Texas State University*, and *Hillsdale College v. Department of Health, Education and Welfare* the courts took a programmatic approach (see notes 3, 4, and 7).

However, in the case of *Haffer v. Temple University*, the court took an institutional approach. The court found that the Temple athletic program should be subject to Title IX regulations even if it does not directly receive any federal funding for the athletic program. In the notes below, the settlement of this case is outlined in great detail. The wording of the settlement, and its recommendations, mirror the wording in the OCR interpretation of Title IX (see notes 5 and 6).

However, the most important case decided during this era was *Grove City College v. Bell* (see note 1). Finally, the issue of "programmatic" versus "institutional" was decided by the Supreme Court in favor of the "programmatic approach." The Supreme Court determined that the language of Title IX should apply only to specific programs that receive direct federal financial assistance. Until the passage of the Civil Rights Restoration Act of 1987, the *Grove City* case was the standard for judgment on Title IX. The next section will discuss how the Civil Rights Restoration Act of 1987 reversed the effect of *Grove City*.

NOTES _____

1. In *Grove City College v. Bell*, 465 U.S. 555 (1984), a private, liberal arts college refused to execute an "assurance of compliance" with Title IX. The Department of Education initiated proceedings to declare the college and its students ineligible to receive basic educational opportunity grants (BEOGs), and the college and four of its students filed suit after an administrative law judge ordered federal financial assistance terminated until Grove City met the requirements of Title IX. The U.S. Supreme Court ruled that the language of Title IX made it program-specific, that only those programs directly receiving federal funds were subject to the regulations of Title IX. This ruling applied to schools that participate in the BEOG program. Otherwise, one student receiving federal aid would trigger Title IX coverage of the entire institution, and this does not square with the program-specific language of the legislation.

2. In *Cannon v. University of Chicago*, 460 U.S. 1013 (1983), the Supreme Court held that Title IX granted an implied private right of action to individuals harmed by sex discrimination in federally funded educational institutions. Supporters of Title IX celebrated *Cannon* for providing victims of sex discrimination with the means to enforce their rights in the courtroom and for bolstering the efforts of overburdened administrative agencies.

Following the Court's recognition of a private right of action in *Cannon*, another debate regarding the scope of Title IX's protections arose in the federal courts. Due to the sparse legislative history of Title IX, a question had existed since its enactment regarding whether Title IX compliance was specifically levied against individual programs within the institution that received federal funds, or against the institution as a whole.

3. In *Othen v. Ann Arbor School Board*, 507 F.Supp. 1376 (E.D. Mich. 1981), *aff'd.*, 699 F.2d 309 (6th Cir. 1983), a complaint was filed on behalf of female student-athletes, charging the Ann Arbor school board and its golf coach with gender discrimination in violation of Title IX. The father of the girls sought a temporary restraining order immediately restoring his daughters to the 1979 golf team and prohibiting discrimination "against women who want to play on the Pioneer golf team." The district court denied the motion for an injunction and found the father/daughters had failed to demonstrate a likelihood of success on the merits.

The school board responded to the amended complaint with a motion for summary judgment, stating that none of the athletic programs at Pioneer received federal financial assistance and therefore were not covered by the provisions of Title IX. The district court found the athletic programs at Pioneer received no direct federal assistance, and the indirect federal assistance from "impact aid" was "de minimus." The court's finding that "the clear language of Title IX and the intent of Congress require that the Act [Title IX] be applied programmatically" had important ramifications in the case. Since it was determined that the athletic programs and activities under the jurisdiction of the Ann Arbor school board received no direct federal financial assistance, the school board was not obligated under the law to establish a golf team for girls. Therefore, the daughters were not excluded from participation, denied, or discriminated against in violation of Title IX.

4. In *Hillsdale College v. Department of Health, Education and Welfare*, 696 F.2d 418 (6th Cir. 1982), HEW issued an order disqualifying students from participation in federal aid programs in response to the refusal of Hillsdale's officials to sign an "assurance of compliance" with Title IX. Hillsdale appealed the HEW order. The court reversed and held for Hillsdale, reasoning that because Congress failed to adopt proposals that would have prohibited all discriminatory practices by an institution that receives federal funds, it was clear that, as enacted, Title IX adopts a "programmatic as opposed to institutional approach to discrimination on the basis of sex in education." Even though the court found that Hillsdale was subject to Title IX regulations in those programs receiving federal financial assistance, the court believed that while HEW had been given the authority to promulgate regulations for Title IX enforcement, in this case the order imposed was in excess of statutory authority, in that it would subject the entire college, rather than any one program, to the strictures of Title IX.

5. In *Haffer v. Temple University*, 524 F.Supp. 531 (E.D. Pa. 1981), *aff'd.*, 688 F.2d 14 (3d Cir. 1982), the defendant appealed the district court decision denying summary judgment to Temple University finding that Temple's athletic department was not exempt from Title IX regulation. Eight women undergraduates had filed a class action suit charging Temple University with gender discrimination in its intercollegiate athletic program in violation of Title IX. Temple had requested summary judgment, arguing that Title IX applied only to those educational programs or activities which received direct federal funding, and that the athletic department at Temple had received no such assistance.

Temple appealed, questioning whether the court's inclusion of the athletic program under Title IX jurisdiction was consistent with the wording of the statute, which required that the education program or activity receive "federal financial assistance" as a prerequisite for its inclusion in the realm of Title IX authority. The appeals court affirmed the lower court's opinion, and rejected the "program-specific" interpretation put forth by Temple, claiming that the entire institution should be considered the "program." In referring to *Grove City College* (appellate court decision), the court suggested, "The legislators [who enacted Title IX] did not contemplate that separate, discrete and distinct components or functions of an integrated educational institution would be regarded as the individual program to which section 901 . . . refer[s]." The court added that "if Temple University as a whole is to be considered the program or activity" for Title IX purposes, it follows that because the university as a whole receives federal monies, Title IX governs its intercollegiate athletic department. The court held that the district court's theory that federal monies received by the institution benefited the athletic program because it freed other university money for athletic program-related purposes was consistent with its finding that Title IX was applicable.

6. In *Haffer v. Temple University*, Consent Decree, Rollin Haffer et al. filed this lawsuit against Temple University, complaining that Temple violated the equal protection clause of the Fourteenth Amendment of the U.S. Constitution, the Pennsylvania Equal Rights Amendment, and Title IX of the Education Amendments of 1972 by discriminating against women student-athletes and potential student-athletes at Temple on the basis of gender in the provision of opportunities to participate in intercollegiate athletics, athletic financial aid, and athletic resources.

While denying allegations, Temple entered into a consent decree dated June 9, 1988, settling the case. The parties agreed to the following conditions:

i. An increase in opportunities for women to participate in intercollegiate athletics that are comparable to the opportunities provided its men students.

1. Temple will provide sufficient resources for its women's intercollegiate athletic crew team.
2. Temple will establish a women's intercollegiate athletic swimming team.
3. With respect to Temple's intercollegiate athletic teams which were in place during the 1986–87 academic year (that is, not including women's crew and swimming), certain other guidelines were established to deal with:

    a. Increases or decreases in participation.
    b. Discontinuance of teams.

4. Temple will maintain the overall percentage of women participating in intercollegiate athletics equal to the percentage of men participating if a men's team is added.
5. . . . [T]o determine the percentage of women and men participating in the overall intercollegiate athletic program, women and men student-athletes who participate on more than one team will be counted separately for each team on which they participate.

ii. Temple will provide to its women student-athletes a percentage of athletic financial aid that, in the aggregate and averaged over three years, will not be less than two percentage points below the participate rate of women student-athletes in the overall intercollegiate athletic program, also averaged over those same three years, with certain other provisions.

iii. The percentage of money that Temple will spend on its women's intercollegiate athletic teams each year, in the aggregate, will be within 10 percentage points of the participation rate of women student-athletes in the overall intercollegiate athletic program in that year, provided that expenditures on home game events, coaches' salaries and benefits, and post season competition will be excluded from the aggregate percentage requirement (these will be treated under specific guidelines agreed to by the two parties).

iv. Temple will hire an additional full-time weight-training coach by February 1, 1989. Temple will provide to its women student-athletes weight-training coaching, facilities, and equipment comparable to the weight-training coaching, facilities, and equipment that it provides to its men student-athletes, consistent with the needs of each sport.

v. Temple will hire a full-time employee to promote Temple's women's intercollegiate athletics by February 1, 1989.

vi. Temple continues to recognize that its women student-athletes are entitled to treatment that is comparable to the treatment provided to its men student-athletes in the remaining aspects of the intercollegiate athletic program beyond those addressed in paragraphs 1 through 5 of this Consent Decree.

1. Subject to the steps set forth in subparagraph B below, Temple will continue to provide

treatment to its women student-athletes that is comparable to the treatment it provides to its men student-athletes in the following areas:

    a. Athletic administration, including the assignment of support staff.
    b. Locker rooms and practice, competitive, and other facilities.
    c. Athletic medicine, including medical and training services and facilities.
    d. Uniform and equipment managers and other uniform and equipment-related support, including laundry.
    e. Academic advising, including the provision of tutors to accompany teams on trips when both the academic advisor and head coach determine that it is necessary.
    f. Awards and honors.
    g. Practice and competitive schedule.
    h. Sports information.
    i. Fund-raising.
    j. Cheerleaders, band(s), and mascot(s).

2. Temple will:

    a. By November 1, 1988, carpet the women's locker room at Temple Stadium.
    b. Rearrange the awards in the intercollegiate athletic award display cases so that the women's awards are exhibited in a manner comparable to that of men's awards.

By October 1, 1989, and by October 1 of each year thereafter, Temple will file with the Court and serve on plaintiff's counsel reports setting forth Temple's compliance with the terms of this Consent Decree for the immediately preceding academic year [these reports have extensive requirements which are outlined in detail in the Consent Decree].

7. In *Bennett v. West Texas State University*, 525 F.Supp. 77 (N.D. Tex. 1981), *rev'd*, 698 F. 2d 1215 (5th Cir. 1983), *cert. denied*, 466 U.S. 903 (1984) plaintiffs, six female athletes, filed a class action suit charging West Texas State University (WTSU) with gender discrimination, based on the denial of equal opportunity in the institution's intercollegiate athletic program. The athletes contended that WTSU had intentionally discriminated against female athletes in numerous areas, including the allocation of athletic scholarship money, the scheduling of games and practice times, and the provision of locker room, practice, and office facilities. The athletes stated that the effect of the university's policies was to exclude them from full participation and benefits, and to subject them to gender discrimination in violation of Title IX. The district court rejected the athletes' contentions, finding that the athletic department of WTSU was not subject to Title IX regulation. The court ruled that the language of Title IX showed "the clear intent of Congress" in that the terms "recipient" and "programs" limited Title IX application to specific programs or activities that received direct financial assistance. This decision was later reversed without opinion after the *Grove City College* decision (see 698 F.2d 1215 [5th Cir. 1983]).

8. In *Yellow Springs Exempted Village School District v. Ohio High School Athletic Ass'n.*, 443 F.Supp. 753 (S.D. Ohio 1978), *aff'd.*, 647 F.2d 651 (6th Cir. 1981), a suit was brought against the Ohio High School Athletic Association (OHSAA) and the Ohio Board of Education challenging the association's rule excluding girls from participation in contact sports. In 1974, two female students competed for and earned positions on the Morgan Middle School's interscholastic basketball team. The board excluded them from the team and then created a separate girls' basketball team. The district court held that the "Association's exclusionary rule deprives school girls of liberty without due process of law. Freedom of personal choice in matters of 'education and acquisition of knowledge' is a liberty interest protected by the due process clause of the Fourteenth Amendment." The appeals court upheld portions of the district court's decision and ruled that Title IX focuses on "recipients" of federal aid. Even though OHSAA was not itself a recipient of federal aid, it may not adopt a rule that limits the abilities of recipient schools to furnish equal athletic opportunities for girls and boys.

8.2.2. Post-Civil Rights Restoration Act Litigation

The passage of the Civil Rights Restoration Act in 1987 restored Title IX's applicability to athletic programs across the country. In March 1988, the U.S. Congress acted to clarify this issue when it voted to override President Ronald Reagan's veto of the Civil Rights Restoration Act of 1987 (see note 1). Enactment of this legislation served "to restore the broad scope of coverage and clarify the application of Title IX of the Education Amendments of 1972." Thus, Congress returned Title IX applicability to the "institutional approach"; accordingly, athletic departments within institutions benefiting from federal assistance are subject to the Title IX strictures. Passage of the Civil Rights Restoration Act counteracted the effects of the Supreme Court's decision in *Grove City College* (see note 1 in section 8.2.1., "Legality and Scope of Title IX"). Therefore most colleges, both public and private, were subject to Title IX.

The passage of the Civil Rights Restoration Act also restored strength to the administrative enforcement of Title IX. The ability of the Office of Civil Rights (OCR) to effectively investigate possible Title IX violations by institutions has always been contingent upon the prevailing judicial sentiments and legislative enactments regarding Title IX at a particular time. While Title IX does not require the creation of athletic programs or the same sport offerings for both genders—for example, a football program for women or a volleyball program for men—it does require equality of opportunity in accommodation of interests and abilities, in athletic scholarships, and in other benefits and opportunities.

Another reason for the increased strength of Title IX occurred in 1992, with the decision in *Franklin v. Gwinnett County Public Schools* (see note 8). The court's decision in *Gwinnett* stated that monetary damages were a valid remedy for violations of Title IX. Now, an added incentive was available for athletes and attorneys to bring claims of Title IX violations: money. A large increase of Title IX cases was seen because student-athletes were able to pay for private attorneys, without relying upon the Office for Civil Rights or worrying about burdensome legal bills. This trend has continued, with private attorneys undertaking Title IX cases and reducing the number of cases brought by OCR.

As mentioned above, there are three areas of Title IX compliance that institutions must meet: financial assistance, athletic benefits and opportunities, and effective accommodation of athletic interests and abilities. However, cases subsequent to the passage of the Civil Rights Restoration Act have focused most on the analysis of the accommodation of interests and abilities. This type of analysis is evident in *Cohen v. Brown University*, 101 F.3d 155 (1st Cir. 1993), *cert. denied*, 520 U.S. 1186 (1997); *Favia v. Indiana University of Pennsylvania*, 7 F.3d 332 (3d Cir. 1993) (see note 7); *Roberts v. Colorado State University*, 814 F.Supp. 1507 (D. Colo. 1993) (see note 6); and *Cook v. Colgate University*, 992 F.2d 17 (2d Cir. 1992) (see section 8.3.6., "Varsity Sport Versus Club Sport").

In the *Cohen v. Brown University* leading case, plaintiff female student-athletes brought a Title IX complaint against the university after women's gymnastics and women's volleyball, along with men's golf and men's water polo, were dropped to club status in the spring of 1991 because of financial difficulties the university was experiencing. The plaintiffs claimed that Brown violated the "equal opportunity" provision for participation under Title IX, and that the interests and abilities of the female student-athletes were not being effectively accommodated.

The district court, 809 F.Supp. 978 (D.R.I. 1992), granted a preliminary injunction against Brown University, ordering the immediate restoration of the women's gymnastics and women's volleyball teams to their former status as fully funded intercollegiate varsity teams. The First Circuit Court of Appeals upheld the district court's preliminary injunction, stating that the ordering of Brown University to return the two women's sport programs to varsity status was a fair and lawful solution. Both of these courts applied a three-part test in determining the accommodation of interests and abilities issue:

1. Whether intercollegiate level participation opportunities for male and female students are provided in numbers substantially proportionate to their respective enrollments.

2. Where the members of one gender have been, and are, underrepresented among intercollegiate athletes, whether the institution can show a history and continuing practice of program expansion that is demonstrably responsive to the developing interests and abilities of the members of that gender.

3. Where the members of one gender are underrepresented among intercollegiate athletes, and the institution cannot show a continuing practice of program expansion such as that cited, whether it can be demonstrated that the interests and abilities of the members of that gender have been fully and effectively accommodated by the present program.

The plaintiffs argued that Brown University did not meet any of these requirements because the female athlete proportion stood at 39%, compared to an undergraduate female enrollment of 48% to 49%, and no women's varsity sport had been added since 1982. The university failed to meet the third part of the three-part test because it had refused to elevate the women's fencing team to varsity status, showing that the underrepresented sex had not been fully accommodated.

Brown University argued that the plaintiffs were not interpreting Title IX legislation accurately. Brown asserted that Title IX provisions explicitly recognize that equal opportunity does not require proportionality, and that the interests and abilities of the students, not the relative proportion of the genders, determine what participation opportunities must be offered to each gender. Brown argued that the 60% male to 40% female athletic participation ratio was merely a reflection of the interests and abilities of the student body. Therefore, Brown was effectively accommodating the interests and abilities of the students through the participation opportunities it was providing. Brown University also argued that if Title IX required full and effective accommodation of the underrepresented gender, then this requirement would violate the Fifth Amendment's equal protection clause by putting male athletes at a disadvantage.

The district court and court of appeals, in addressing both the plaintiff's and the defendant's arguments, found that with the demotion of the four sports, two women's teams and two men's teams, from varsity to club status, the percentage of male and female athletes did not change. Thus, women athletes at Brown still constituted 39% of the total number of student-athletes. The courts went on to say that this was not an example of effectively accommodating the interests and abilities of the underrepresented gender because there were women interested in competing and participating in additional activities, as the interest and talent at Brown in women's gymnastics and volleyball teams demonstrated. This critical ruling by the court set a standard for women in that full accommodation of the interests and abilities of the underrepresented gender must be met, and that Brown's argument regarding its 60/40 participation proportion being appropriate will not hold when analyzing Title IX compliance. In addition, keeping the percentage of female athletes at 39% does not effectively accommodate the equitable proportion of athletic opportunities available to each gender as required by Title IX. Brown did not meet the full accommodation test, and therefore a violation of Title IX was occurring. The court of appeals discussed the Fifth Amendment argument and ruled that Brown supplied no evidence that showed men were more likely to engage in athletics than women. In addition, the court stated that in view of congressional and administrative urging that women, if given the opportunity, will naturally participate in athletics in numbers equal to those of men, the court did not find that the regulation offended the Fifth Amendment.

The court of appeals upheld the district court's granting of a preliminary injunction, which ordered Brown University to restore the women's gymnastics and women's volleyball teams to their previous varsity status. These rulings were based on an analysis of one part of the three areas that Title IX policy interpretations state should be used when investigating Title IX compliance—effectively accommodating the interests and abilities of the underrepresented gender. Other Title IX cases and court decisions have also used the analysis of the interests and abilities component to rule on Title IX compliance cases (see notes 2 and 3).

In the leading case of *Boucher v. Syracuse University* (see note 4), the university was able to find a safe harbor under Title IX by employing the defense that it had shown "a continuing practice of program expansion such as that cited, whether it can be demonstrated that the interests and abilities of the members of that gender have been fully and effectively accommodated by the present program." The university had plans to add three women's sports to varsity status in the near future, and therefore the court decided that although the women's needs were not being currently met, this plan would bring Syracuse under Title IX compliance. As of 2002, Syracuse is the only university that has been able to successfully defend against a Title IX claim in court by arguing that the program had shown a history of expansion for women.

In the case of *Pederson v. Louisiana State University* (see note 2), plaintiff female athletes at Louisiana State University (LSU) charged that they had not been offered equitable sports opportunities at the university. The Fifth Circuit court ruled against LSU, rejecting LSU's argument that women are less interested in participating in sports than men. The court went on to reprimand LSU for taking such a position, stating that "advancing this argument is remarkable, since of course fewer women participate in sports, given the voluminous evidence that LSU has discriminated against women in refusing to offer them comparable athletic opportunities to those it offers its male students." Courts have shown an unwillingness to accept the argument that women are less interested in sports than men are, and therefore do not merit equal opportunity and funding. The parties in *Pederson* settled for $1.2 million in 2001.

As was mentioned in the introduction to this chapter, Title IX is not without its detractors in interscholastic and intercollegiate athletics. Athletic departments, traditionally male dominated, have been compelled to add opportunities for women in athletics, usually without increased budgets. This has led to tough financial decisions in most intercollegiate athletic departments, and a real challenge to maintain scholarship levels for male athletes. In fact, many male athletes have felt that they have been discriminated against in the name of gender equity. Many athletic departments have been forced to cut the number of scholarships that they offer to male athletes, cap rosters, and/or the number of men's varsity sports that are offered to ensure compliance with the OCR and Title IX. For more information on cases and articles concerning male backlash against Title IX and reverse discrimination, see note 4 in the introduction to this chapter.

NOTES

1. The following is language from the Civil Rights Restoration Act of 1987, which restores the impact of Title IX on athletic departments:

PUBLIC LAW 100–259-Mar. 22, 1988

Public Law 100–259
100th Congress

An Act

To restore the broad scope of coverage and to clarify the application of title IX of the Education Amendments of 1972, section 504 of the Rehabilitation Act of 1973, the Age Discrimination Act of 1975, and title VI of the Civil Rights Act of 1964.

Be it enacted by the Senate and House of Representatives of the United States of America in Congress assembled,

SHORT TITLE

SECTION 1. This Act may be cited as the "Civil Rights Act of 1987."

SEC. 2. The Congress finds that—

(1) certain aspects of recent decisions and opinions of the Supreme Court have unduly narrowed or cast doubt upon the broad application of title IX of the Education Amendments of 1972, section 504 of the Rehabilitation Act of 1973, the Age Discrimination Act of 1975, and title VI of the Civil Rights Act of 1964; and

(2) legislative action is necessary to restore the prior consistent and long-standing executive branch interpretation and broad, institution-wide application of those laws as previously administered.

EDUCATION AMENDMENTS AMENDMENTS

SEC. 3. (a) Title IX of the Education Amendments of 1972 is amended by adding at the end the following new sections:

"INTERPRETATION OF 'PROGRAM OR ACTIVITY' "

"SEC. 908. For the purposes of this title, the term 'program or activity' and 'program' mean all of the operations of—

"(1)(A) a department, agency, special purpose district, or other instrumentality of a State or of a local government; or

"(B) the entity of such State or local government that distributes such assistance and each such department or agency (and each other State or local government entity) to which the assistance is extended, in the case of assistance to a State or local government;

"(2)(A) a college, university, or other post-secondary institution, or a public system of higher education; or

"(B) a local educational agency (as defined in section 198(a)(10)) of the Elementary and Secondary Education Act of 1965), system of vocational education, or other school system;

"(3)(A) an entire corporation, partnership, or other private organization, or an entire sole proprietorship—

"(i) if assistance is extended to such corporation, partnership, private organization, or sole proprietorship as a whole; or

"(ii) which is principally engaged in the business of providing education, health care, housing, social services, or parks and recreation; or

"(B) the entire plant or other comparable, geographically separate facility to which Federal financial assistance is extended, in the case of any other corporation, partnership, private organization, or sole proprietorship; or

"(4) any other entity which is established by two or more of the entities described in paragraph (1), (2), or (3);

any part of which is extended Federal financial assistance, except that such term does not include any operation of an entity which is controlled by a religious organization if the application of section 901 to such operation would not be consistent with the religious tenets of such organization."

2. In *Pederson v. Louisiana State University*, 213 F.3d 858 (5th Cir. 2000), female student-athletes sued Louisiana State University (LSU) for Title IX violations, alleging that LSU denied them equal opportunity to participate in intercollegiate athletics, LSU denied them the opportunity to compete for athletic scholarships, and LSU denied them equal access to benefits and services. Females made up only 29% of LSU's student-athletes but made up 49% of the student population. The court ruled that LSU did not have a history of expanding women's athletic programs and did not accommodate the interests and abilities of females. In addition, the court stated, "[i]f an institution makes a decision not to provide equal athletic opportunities for its female students because of paternalism and stereotypical assumptions about their interests and abilities, that institution intended to treat women differently because of their sex." Therefore, the discrimination was intentional. This determination that the discrimination was intentional opened the door for monetary damages. The parties settled for $1.2 million damages award in 2001.

3. In *Horner v. Kentucky High School Athletic Ass'n*, 206 F.3d 685 (6th Cir. 2000), a group of female student-athletes sued the Kentucky High School Athletic Association for its failure to sanction fast-pitch softball, claiming that it was a violation of Title IX. Plaintiff failed to establish an intentional violation as necessary to obtain monetary damages for Title IX violations. The case was dismissed in favor of the defendants.

4. In *Boucher v. Syracuse University*, 164 F.3d 113 (2d Cir. 1999), a group of female students interested in competing in softball and lacrosse at the varsity level sued Syracuse University on Title IX grounds. Plaintiffs argued that Syracuse did not effectively accommodate the interests and abilities of its female students. Importantly, the court indicated that Syracuse *would* be able to take refuge in a Title IX "safe harbor"—that is, it had showed a plan that demonstrated the university's attempts to increase athletic opportunities for women over a period of time. Although Syracuse had not added a new women's varsity sport in fourteen years at the time of the lawsuit, the university had installed a plan to add three new women's varsity sports in the near future. The court never reached the merits of the claim because Syracuse added women's lacrosse as a varsity sport after the commencement of the lawsuit and planned to introduce women's softball as a varsity sport. Therefore, the court ruled that the issue was moot.

5. In *Kelley v. Board of Trustees University*, 35 F.3d 265 (7th Cir. 1994), members of the men's swimming team sued the university on Title IX and equal protection grounds after it eliminated the team along with three other varsity sports. The court held that termination of the men's program "was a reasonable response to the requirements of [Title IX]." Also, the court ruled that the university did not violate equal protection because gender equity was an important objective and eliminating the men's swimming team was substantially related to that objective. "Title IX's stated objective is not to ensure that the athletic opportunities available to women increase. Rather its avowed purpose is to prohibit educational institutions from discriminating on the basis of sex."

6. In *Roberts v. Colorado State University*, 814 F.Supp. 1507 (D. Colo. 1993), plaintiffs contended that a violation of Title IX occurred and/or had been occurring at Colorado State University after the women's softball team was terminated on June 1, 1992. The court used the same three-part "effective accommodation" test used in the *Brown* and *Favia* cases. The court stated that the plaintiffs had the burden of proving the first prong, that participation opportunities for male and female students are not proportionate to their respective enrollments. Once the plaintiffs established this lack of proportionality, then the defendants had the burden of proving either the second prong, that the institution could show a history and continuing practice of program expansion, or the third prong,

that the institution can demonstrate that the interests and abilities of the underrepresented gender have been accommodated. After the termination of the women's softball team, women athletes made up approximately 38% of the athletes, while enrollment of women at Colorado State University was 48% of the undergraduate student population. The court found that the percentage of female athletes was not substantially proportionate to the undergraduate enrollment percentage of females, and that the defendant could not show evidence of program expansion so that the interests and abilities of the female students were being effectively accommodated. The court, therefore, found a violation of Title IX and ordered Colorado State University to reinstate the women's softball team.

7. In *Favia v. Indiana University of Pennsylvania*, 7 F.3d 332 (3d. Cir. 1993), Indiana University of Pennsylvania (IUP) announced in August 1991 that the women's gymnastics and field hockey teams, along with the men's soccer and tennis teams, would be eliminated as a result of a reduction in the athletic department's budget. IUP had an undergraduate enrollment of 44% men compared to 56% women, while the athletic department comprised 62% men and 38% women. After the elimination of these four teams, the percentage of male and female athletes would not change. Women students brought a lawsuit arguing violation of Title IX and sought the reinstatement of the two women's teams. In ruling in favor of the plaintiffs, the court applied the three-part test contained in the policy interpretation: comparison of athletic participation opportunities for each gender proportionate to their respective enrollments; whether the institution can show a history and continuing practice of program expansion; and whether the interests and abilities of the members are met by the present program. The court found that IUP had failed to override the proportionality requirement of the test by failing to show a history of expanding the number of athletic opportunities for women or demonstrating that it had fully and effectively accommodated the interests and abilities of women students. The court ordered the immediate restoration of the two women's teams to their former status, with university backing and funding equivalent to that furnished during their last year as a varsity team.

8. In *Franklin v. Gwinnett County Public Schools*, 503 U.S. 60 (1992), a female high school student sued her school district for the continued sexual harassment she suffered from a male teacher. Plaintiff claimed that the school district knew of the sexual harassment but did nothing, in violation of Title IX. The defendant claimed that Title IX does not authorize monetary damages as a remedy. The Supreme Court disagreed with the defendant, stating, "We conclude that a damages remedy is available for an action brought to enforce Title IX." The Supreme Court held, however, that damages are only available when the plaintiff in a Title IX claim can prove that the violation was intentional. There was no question in this case that the sexual harassment was an intentional violation.

8.3. GENDER DISCRIMINATION CASES INVOLVING INDIVIDUAL ATHLETES

The subsections and cases that follow are discussed in terms of the presence or absence of teams available to either gender. Within each category, the subsections and cases are further divided into those dealing with contact sports and those dealing with non-contact sports. This was done because the approach taken—and sometimes the results reached—by the courts differ due to more important factors.

The division of subsections and cases is not by legal theory, since very often the litigant makes use of one, two, or even three prominent theories—for example, equal protection, Title IX, and state Equal Rights Amendments (in certain states).

The courts view contact sports and non-contact sports differently. Thus, in cases involving gender discrimination in athletics, the arguments used will vary depending on whether or not the particular sport is designated a contact sport. Under Title IX, contact sports include boxing, wrestling, rugby, ice hockey, football, basketball, and other sports in which the purpose or major activity involves bodily contact. In some jurisdictions, baseball and soccer have also been labeled contact sports.

In a sport designated a "contact," sport, certain arguments are commonly propounded. The most frequent argument raised by defendants is that women, as a group, lack the physical qualifications necessary for safe and reasonable competition against men in a sport in which bodily contact is expected to occur. It is argued that women are more susceptible to injury because they have a higher percentage of adipose (fatty) tissues and a lighter bone structure. Because of these differences, the argument goes, contact sports are dangerous for all women. Physiological differences between the genders have generally been found to be a valid reason for the exclusion of one sex from a contact sport.

Plaintiffs counter this argument by insisting that determinations of physical capability should be made on a case-by-case basis. When there is no other opportunity for participation in a certain sport, a blanket prohibition is overinclusive, and violates equal protection by assuming that all women have identical physical structures and that all men are stronger and more athletically capable than women. Indeed, the health and safety rationale behind such total exclusion may fail a court challenge, as has been demonstrated in some cases. In one case, a woman who was five feet, nine inches tall and weighed over 200 pounds was denied a chance to play football because her supposedly lighter bone structure would render her more susceptible to injury. There were, however, no height or weight requirements for men, and the court thus found exclusion from participation to be unacceptable. (See *Clinton v. Nagy* in Section 8.3.1., "Men's Team, No Women's Team.")

Although the most important consideration used to substantiate separate teams for contact sports is the health and safety of the participants, this argument does not apply to non-contact sports. Since there is no legitimate and important state interest for allowing exclusion from non-contact sports, citing gender as the sole exclusionary factor would constitute a violation of the U.S. constitutional guarantees of the equal protection clause. Thus, the arguments made by defendants in non-contact sports gender discrimination cases are different.

One argument is that if men and women are allowed to compete together and/ or against each other, the psychological development of both would be impaired. This stance is generally based on a variation of the "tradition" argument, which says that allowing men and women to compete as equals will irreparably disturb the innate nature of relationships between the genders.

Another argument is that if men and women are allowed to compete together, men will dominate the coed teams. The underlying rationale here is that since men are inherently stronger and more physically capable than women, coed teams will actually limit opportunities for women. Plaintiffs argue that a justification of this sort does not take into account individual differences among participants. It also does not recognize the argument that if women are given opportunities to compete against men from the beginning of their athletic careers, their capabilities will improve and men may not be able to totally dominate the athletic field.

8.3.1. Men's Team, No Women's Team

The general rule in both contact and non-contact sports is that when only a men's team is available, both genders must be allowed to try out for and play on that team. In contact sports under Title IX, females do not have to be allowed to try out for male teams. However, if the institution does not allow a woman or girl to try out, it must then conduct the tryouts in a non-discriminatory manner (see note 1). In ERA and equal protection cases, courts are split on the issue of allowing females to participate on male teams in contact sports, when there are no teams in the same sport. Determination as to the student-athlete's capability and risk of injury should be made on an individual basis, with the recognition that the contact or non-contact sports designation makes a difference only if there is opportunity for athletes of both genders to compete. If there is ample opportunity for women to compete on their own, courts appear to be less apt to allow women to compete with men in contact sports.

8.3.1.1. Contact Sports

In cases where contact sports are involved and there is no women's team, there is a split in decisions as to whether to allow a female to play on the men's team. In some cases, as represented by *Lantz v. Ambach*, 620 F. Supp. 663 (S.D.N.Y. 1985) and *Saint v. U. Nebraska School Activities Ass'n*, 684 F. Supp. 626 (D. Neb. 1988) (see notes 5 and 6), the courts have upheld the plaintiff's gender discrimination claim and have allowed participation on the men's team. In other cases, the plaintiff female has been unsuccessful because she has not been able to prove that she has a right to participation (see note 2) or that her arguments fall under the auspices of Title IX (see note 4).

While most recent court cases have generally held that women do not possess a right to participate on all-male teams, in *Mercer v. Duke University*, 190 F.3d 643 (4th Cir. 1999), the federal appellate court ruled that Duke had the right to prevent a female from trying out for an all-male contact sport. However, once Duke allowed a female to try out for the team, she had to be afforded the same treatment as all other players (see note 1).

Due to various factors, including the evolution of women's sport opportunities, an increased use of co-ed sports teams, and the willingness to settle cases before litigation arises, the volume of these types of cases has decreased in recent years. Although recent cases have generally been decided against female plaintiffs, a split still remains.

NOTES ———————————————————————————

1. In *Mercer v. Duke University*, 190 F.3d 643 (4th Cir. 1999), female plaintiff sued Duke University for Title IX violations. Plaintiff was a kicker for her high school football team and tried out for Duke's football team. While she did not make the team, she did attend practices and participated in conditioning drills. Plaintiff was allowed to participate in an intrasquad game. After that game, the head football coach told the media that plaintiff was on the team. In addition, Duke's sports information director asked plaintiff to participate in several interviews. Plaintiff did not play in any games her second year; however, she was on the roster that was submitted to the NCAA and her picture appeared in Duke's football yearbook. At the beginning of plaintiff's third year, the coach informed her that she was being dropped from the team. At the trial court level, the plaintiff's claim was dismissed because the court reasoned that Title IX provided a blanket exemption for contact sports. However, the appeals court noted that while generally the school could

exclude plaintiff from the team because football is a contact sport, Duke violated Title IX once it let her on the team and then removed her because of her gender. The appeals court stated, "We hold that where a university has allowed a member of the opposite sex to try out for a single-sex team in a contact sport, the university is . . . subject to Title IX and therefore prohibited from discriminatory action against that individual on the basis of his or her sex." Although Duke had no obligation to allow Mercer to try out for the team, once it allowed her to try out, it could not discriminate against her based on her gender. Therefore, schools can avoid Title IX claims for equal participation in contact sports simply by refusing to allow members of the excluded sex to try out for the team. The decision of the trial court was overturned upon appeal by the plaintiff. In assessing damages, Mercer received $2 million in punitive damages, and $1 million in compensatory damages.

2. In *Barnett v. Texas Wrestling Ass'n*, 16 F.Supp. 2d 690 (N.D. Tex. 1998), two female high school athletes wanted to participate on the all-boys wrestling team, and there was no corresponding female wrestling team at the school. The court dismissed their Title IX claim against the association rule forbidding female wrestlers to compete against boys in the North Texas Open Wrestling Tournament. The court reasoned that because wrestling was a contact sport, the females did not have a right to participate on the team.

3. In *Adams v. Baker*, 919 F.Supp. 1496 (D. Kan. 1996), female plaintiff was not allowed to compete on her high school wrestling team. Plaintiff alleged Title IX violations in her action for a preliminary injunction. The court noted, "[b]ecause wrestling is a contact sport, Title IX does not require that Valley Center High School allow a female to try out for the boys' wrestling team." The court ruled that plaintiff was not likely to succeed on the merits of her Title IX claim and, therefore, an injunction was not warranted.

4. In *Libby v. South Inter-Conference Ass'n*, 728 F.Supp. 504 (N.D. Ill. 1990), a female high school student brought a civil rights action against a high school athletic association, challenging a rule prohibiting her from playing interscholastic soccer on the boys' team, where a girls' team did not exist. After a series of temporary restraining orders, which allowed her to compete in the state tournament, the case was dismissed as moot because the season had ended. Plaintiff was not awarded attorney's fees because she was not the prevailing party.

5. In *Saint v. Nebraska School Activities Ass'n.*, 684 F.Supp 626 (D. Neb. 1988), a female high school sophomore sought a temporary restraining order to restrain the Nebraska School Activities Association from refusing to permit her to wrestle on the high school boys' wrestling team while trial was pending. The high school did not have a girls' wrestling team. A U.S. District Court judge ruled in favor of plaintiff, granting a temporary restraining order. The judge reasoned that plaintiff showed a reasonable probability of success on the merits in the claim, and the plaintiff would suffer irreparable harm if the restraining order were denied.

6. In *Lantz v. Ambach*, 620 F.Supp. 663 (S.D.N.Y. 1985), the court prohibited enforcement of a New York public high school regulation that prohibited mixed gender competition in football, as a violation of the Fourteenth Amendment, and permitted a sixteen-year-old healthy female student to try out for junior varsity football. Although the court acknowledged an important governmental objective in protecting the health and safety of female high school students, it found the regulation was overbroad and lacked reasonable relation to the objective.

7. In *Leffel v. Wisconsin Interscholastic Athletic Ass'n.*, 444 F.Supp. 1117 (E.D. Wis. 1978), plaintiff brought a class action suit charging that an interscholastic athletic association's rule limiting co-educational athletics violated her civil rights as guaranteed under the equal protection clause. The court granted summary judgment for the plaintiff, finding that:

> exclusion of girls from all contact sports in order to protect female high school athletes from unreasonable risk of injury was not fairly or substantially related to a justifiable government objective in the context of the Fourteenth Amendment, where demand for relief by plaintiffs would be met by establishing separate girls' teams with comparable programs.

The plaintiffs were granted the right to participate in a varsity interscholastic program in any sport in which only a boys' team was provided.

8. In *Hoover v. Meiklejohn*, 430 F.Supp. 164 (D. Colo. 1977), an action was brought by plaintiff Hoover, who wanted to play on her high school soccer team. The Colorado High School Athletic Association limited interscholastic soccer team membership to boys. The district court held for Hoover, based on an equal protection analysis. The court held that the appropriate analysis required a triangular balancing of the importance of the opportunities being unequally burdened or denied against the strength of the state's interests and the character of the group being denied the opportunity. The court found that a complete denial, as in this case, violated Hoover's rights to equal protection. The court determined that the school had three options. It could allow coed teams, it could discontinue the sport for males, or it could field a second all-female team.

9. In *Muscare v. O'Malley*, Civil No. 76-C-3729 (N.D. Ill. 1977), an action was brought by a twelve-year-old girl who wanted to play tackle football in Chicago Park District football games. There was a touch football program available for girls. In ruling for the girl, the court reasoned that offering a sport for males, yet not to females, is a violation of equal opportunity rights under the Fourteenth Amendment.

10. In *Lavin v. Chicago Board of Education*, 73 F.R.D. 438 (N.D. Ill. 1975), *Lavin v. Illinois High School Ass'n.*, 527 F.2d 58 (7th Cir. 1977), a class action lawsuit for declaratory, injunctive, and monetary relief against the Chicago Board of Education was instituted because plaintiff Lavin was denied participation in interscholastic athletics based on her gender. Lavin and another classmate tried out for the varsity basketball team at their high school and were denied positions on the squad because of Illinois State High School Association rules. Lavin contended that the Fourteenth Amendment guarantee of equal protection had been violated. The appeals court reversed and remanded the trial court's summary judgment for the board of education and awarded monetary damages to the athletes. On remand, the trial court denied the class action claim; Lavin was no longer a member of the "class" because of graduation. In addition, the trial court reasoned that she did not present an argument that showed she was qualified enough to make the boys' squad, and therefore was not a member of that particular "class" of girls either. The trial court allowed Lavin's individual claim for damages.

11. In *Clinton v. Nagy*, 411 F.Supp. 1396 (N.D. Ohio 1974), a twelve-year-old girl alleged that recreation and city officials deprived her of equal recreational opportunities in refusing to allow her the opportunity to qualify to play recreational league football because of her gender. Pursuant to 42 U.S.C. §1983, the girl sought to prohibit the officials from denying her equal recreational opportunities on the basis of gender and to receive a declaratory judgment that "the policies, customs, and practices of the defendants are in violation of the Constitution." The court held that when a regulation is based on a gender-based classification, "the classification is subject to scrutiny under the Equal Protection Clause of the Fourteenth Amendment to ascertain whether there is a rational relationship to a valid state purpose." The court therefore decided the case for the girl. In so doing, the court stated that organized contact sports are considered an opportunity and means of developing strength of character, leadership qualities, etc., "yet, although these are presumably qualities to which we desire all of the young to aspire, the opportunity to qualify to engage in sports activities through which such qualities may be developed has been granted to one class of the young and summarily denied to the other."

12. See Chapter 5, section 5.2.4., "Injunctive Relief," for an explanation of the standards required for an injunction.

13. See Chapter 4, section 4.10., "Waiver and Release of Liability," for a discussion of waivers and releases of liability. The plaintiff in *Clinton v. Nagy* (see note 11) signed one before being allowed to participate.

14. For more information on the contact sports exemption, see the following law review articles:

(a) Abigail Crouse, "Comment: Equal Athletic Opportunity: An analysis of *Mercer v. Duke University* and a Proposal to Amend the Contact Sport Exception to Title IX," 84 *Minnesota Law Review* 1655 (2000).

(b) James Puszczewicz, "Chalk Talk: The Fourth Circuit Kicks a Hole through Contact Sport Exemption," 29 *Journal of Law and Education* 107 (2000).

(c) Suzanne Sangree, "Title IX and the Contact Sports Exception: Gender Stereotypes in a Civil Rights Statute," 32 *Connecticut Law Review* 381 (2000).

8.3.1.2. *Non-contact Sports*

In cases in which non-contact sports are involved and there is a men's team and no women's team, the majority of cases allow the women to participate on the men's team. Specifically, women have been allowed to participate on men's teams in cross-country (see notes 3, 4, and 9), baseball (see note 1), golf (see notes 7 and 8) and tennis (see notes 6 and 10) where there were no women's teams. Few courts have prevented females from participating on the men's teams. In cases where private organizations are involved, the plaintiff women must also prove state action (see note 11), which cannot always be demonstrated. One area of athletics where the separation between genders became controversial was in Little League Baseball. It was not until after a series of lawsuits in the mid-1970s that Little League Baseball began to allow girls to participate in official competition (see note 11).

Litigation in this area of gender discrimination has decreased due to increased opportunities for women's teams in interscholastic athletics, as well as an increased acceptance of females participating on traditionally all-male teams. Finally, it is increasingly rare to find interscholastic or intercollegiate athletic programs that do not field teams for both genders in non-contact sports such as tennis, cross-country, golf, and softball/baseball.

NOTES

1. In *Israel v. West Virginia Secondary Schools Activities Commission*, 388 S.E.2d 480 (W. Va. 1989), a female high school student brought a gender discrimination action against the School Activities Association after she was refused the opportunity to play on the boys' high school baseball team. In reversing the lower court's decision, the appeals court held that the regulation prohibiting girls' participation in baseball violated federal and state equal protection standards, and the games of baseball and softball were not substantially equivalent for purposes of determining whether equal athletic opportunities are provided to boys and girls in high school.

2. In August 1983, Mary Decker, Grete Waitz, and fifty other leading female runners filed a gender discrimination suit against the International Olympic Committee (IOC), the Los Angeles Olympic Organizing Committee, the International Amateur Athletic Federation, and The Athletics Congress, among others. (See *Martin v. International Olympic Committee*, 740 F.2d 670 (9th Cir. 1984.) The suit was filed in Los Angeles Superior Court and sought an order that would force the defendants to include 5,000- and 10,000-meter runs for women at the 1984 Olympic Games in Los Angeles. These events were part of the men's events and were historically excluded from the women's program because of the belief that women could not physically handle the distances. The court denied the request for injunctive relief. The IOC added these events to the women's program for the 1988 Olympic Games in Seoul, South Korea.

3. In *Bednar v. Nebraska School Activities Ass'n.*, 531 F.2d 922 (8th Cir. 1976), the mother of a high school student brought a civil rights action on behalf of her daughter, who had been denied the opportunity to participate on the boys' cross country team

because of her gender. There was no girls' team. The district court issued a preliminary injunction prohibiting the school from excluding Bednar from competition. The school association appealed the decision, but the court of appeals affirmed, finding that since Bednar was one of the top competitors in her event and her qualification for higher levels of competition was likely, she would be subject to irreparable harm if she were not allowed to compete.

4. In *Gilpin v. Kansas State High School Activities Ass'n.*, 377 F.Supp. 1233 (D. Kan. 1973), plaintiff, a junior at Southeast High School in Wichita, Kansas, brought a civil rights suit against the Kansas State High School Activities Association (KSHSAA). Gilpin claimed she was deprived of equal protection by a KSHSAA rule that prevented her from participating in interscholastic cross-country competition solely on the basis of her gender.

The court held that because Southeast High School offered no cross country program for girls, the KSHSAA rule effectively deprived Gilpin of an opportunity to compete at all. The court held that "although the Association's overall objective is commendable and legitimate, the method employed to accomplish that objective is simply overbroad in its reach. It is precisely this sort of overinclusiveness, which the Equal Protection Clause disdains." The district court determined that the KSHSAA rule prohibiting mixed competition was unconstitutional as applied to Gilpin and accordingly granted her the requested injunctive relief.

5. In *Brenden v. Independent School District*, 342 F.Supp. 1224 (D. Minn. 1972), *aff'd.*, 477 F.2d 1292 (8th Cir. 1973), plaintiff's high school student-athletes brought an action against Independent School District 742, alleging violation of their constitutional rights under the Fourteenth Amendment and Civil Rights Act (42 U.S.C. §1983). The plaintiffs contended that the Minnesota State High School League (MSHSL) rule prohibiting girls from participating in boys' interscholastic athletic competition was arbitrary and unreasonable as applied to their particular situations, and thus constituted a violation of their rights under the equal protection clause of the Fourteenth Amendment.

Because of the circumstances—the girls were capable of competing on the boys' team, that no girls' team existed at their respective schools in the sports in which they wished to participate, and that plaintiffs were kept from participation solely on the basis of gender—the court found the application of the rule to be arbitrary and unreasonable. Since the classification by gender had no fair or substantial relation to the objective of the interscholastic league rule, its application to plaintiffs was in violation of the equal protection clause of the Fourteenth Amendment. The district court granted the requested injunctive relief and prohibited the MSHSL from imposing sanctions on the schools or any of their opponents stemming from plaintiffs' participation on boys' interscholastic athletic teams.

6. In *Morris v. Michigan State Board of Education*, 472 F.2d 1207 (6th Cir. 1973), plaintiff Morris brought an action against a state high school athletic association rule barring mixed competition in interscholastic sports. Morris and a female friend wanted to play on the high school boys' tennis team. There was no girls' team. Morris contended a violation of equal protection under the Fourteenth Amendment. The lower court ruled for Morris. The appeals court affirmed the decision but remanded the suit to the lower court to have non-contact sports added to the wording of the order granting the injunction. As a result of the case, Michigan Laws Act 183 was enacted, which permitted women to participate with men on non-contact sports teams.

7. In *Reed v. Nebraska School Activities Ass'n.*, 341 F.Supp. 258 (D. Neb. 1972), plaintiff, a student-athlete at Norfolk High School, brought an action that challenged a state high school athletic association's practice of providing a public school golf program for boys while providing none for girls, and prohibiting girls from interscholastic participation with or against boys. Reed sought a preliminary injunction prohibiting the Nebraska School Activities Association and school officials from denying her membership on the boys' golf team. The court held for Reed, stating that Reed would lose the benefits of participation when the season expired and that the loss would be irretrievable.

8. In *Haas v. South Bend Community School Corp.*, 289 N.E.2d 495 (Ind. 1972), a female who was seeking injunctive relief from a state high school athletic association rule barring mixed competition on sports teams brought a suit. Plaintiff Haas had made the "B" golf team but was denied the opportunity to play with the "A" team because of the association's rule. The lower court held for the association. The decision was later reversed by the appellate court, which held that the rule was a violation of equal protection under the Fourteenth Amendment and the Civil Rights Act. The court found the association's arguments to be insufficient justification for barring girls from non-contact sports or from denying girls the chance to qualify.

9. In *Hollander v. Connecticut Interscholastic Athletic Conference, Inc.*, 164 Conn. 654 (Conn. Super. Ct.), *appeal dismissed*, 295 A.2d 671 (Conn. Ct. App. 1972), an action was brought by plaintiff Hollander, who wanted to run on the boys' cross country team at her high school. The Connecticut Intercollegiate Athletic Association barred mixed competition. The court worked out an agreement with the association to allow girls to compete on boys' teams in non-contact sports. Despite that, the court held for the defendant association based on Fourteenth Amendment equal protection arguments. The court expressed the opinion that allowing girls to compete on the same teams with boys would bring into question the physical safeguard for girls and the "removal of challenge and incentive for boys to win."

10. In *Gregoria v. Board of Education*, No. A-1277–70 (N.J. Super. Ct. App. Div. 1971), plaintiff Gregoria, who wanted to play on the high school boys' tennis team, brought an action. There was no girls' team. The board of education would not permit her to play. The trial court ruled in favor of the board of education. The appeals court affirmed the lower court's ruling that the "psychological well-being of girls is a rational reason for exclusion."

11. The following cases involve suits against Little League and non-interscholastic youth teams:

(a) In *Perkins v. Londonderry Basketball Club*, 196 F.3d 13 (1st Cir. 1999), a ten-year-old female basketball player on a mixed-gender team, brought suit against a voluntary tax-exempt organization formed by several community groups. The organization sponsored a tournament with separate brackets for boys and girls teams, but no bracket for mixed-gender teams. As a result, the organization told the plaintiff's town that she could not play with its All-Star team in the tournament. The plaintiff's town did not have an all-girls team. Due to the fact that the hosting organization was private, the U.S. First Circuit Court of Appeals affirmed the lower court's decision that the organization's conduct did not amount to state action, thereby dismissing the plaintiff's suit.

(b) In *Rappaport v. Little League Baseball, Inc.*, 65 F.R.D. 545 (D. Del. 1975), a group of parents and plaintiff girl filed suit against the Little League because of its policy of excluding girls from participation. The Little League changed its policy after the complaint was filed. The court ruled the case moot.

(c) In *McGill v. Avonworth Baseball Conference*, 516 F.2d 1328 (3d Cir. 1975), the court of appeals affirmed the trial court's decision for the conference because the girl had failed to show significant state involvement in the league's discrimination. The court reasoned that the waiver of a $25 fee for use of the public playing field was de minimus; that analysis of nature, value, and proportion of state aid to the conference did not end the court's inquiry; and that the nexus between the state's and the conference's allegedly offensive policy was not sufficiently close so that the conference's action could be fairly treated as state action in that the conference was granted nonexclusive scheduled use of four public playing fields, school buildings were used only for once-a-year registration purposes, and no government officials were involved in determining eligibility requirements.

(d) In *Fortin v. Darlington Little League, Inc.*, 376 F.Supp. 473 (D.R.I. 1974), *rev'd.*, 514 F.2d 344 (1st Cir. 1975), an action was brought by a ten-year-old girl who was denied the opportunity to try out for Little League baseball solely because of her gender. Plaintiff Fortin argued that the baseball park where the team played was public property, a fact that supplied sufficient proof to find the required state action. The appeals court ruled for the girl, reversing the lower court's decision. The appeals court found that the league's preferred dependency on city baseball diamonds introduced significant state involvement to find state action. The appeals court also rejected the league's argument that the discrimination was appropriate because females would injure more easily than males, because it was not supported by the facts.

(e) In *King v. Little League Baseball, Inc.*, 505 F.2d 264 (6th Cir. 1974), an action was brought by a twelve-year-old girl who wanted to play on a Little League team. The national Little League Baseball rules excluded girls from competing. However, the Little League Regional Board permitted plaintiff King to try out, and she made the team on the basis of her ability. The team was notified by the National Little League Association that if King continued to play or practice with the team, the team would lose its charter. King was dropped from the roster. The town revoked the team's privilege to use the municipal field for games. King was then put back on the roster, and the team lost its charter.

The case was dismissed and affirmed on appeal. The courts held that there was not sufficient state action involved in the defendant's enforcement of the "no girls" rule to bring it under the color of state law. The courts agreed that they did not have jurisdiction over the subject matter in the case.

(f) In *National Organization for Women, Essex County Chapter v. Little League Baseball, Inc.*, 318 A.2d 33 (N.J. Super. Ct. App. Div. 1974), the Essex County chapter of the National Organization for Women (NOW) filed suit on behalf of eight-to-twelve-year-old girls who wanted to play Little League Baseball. NOW contended this discrimination against girls was a violation of New Jersey's antidiscrimination laws. In affirming a lower court order for the girls, the superior court held that the evidence permitted the finding that girls of the particular age concerned were not subject to greater hazard of injury while playing baseball than boys of the same age group, and that the Little League did not fall within any statutory exemptions.

8.3.2. Women's Team, No Men's Team

In most cases where an athletic program sponsors women's teams but no corresponding men's teams, the sport is non-contact. Unlike the situations contained in the previous section, where a men's team but not a women's team was provided in a non-contact sport, men are generally not allowed to play on all-female teams. However, there have been exceptions.

One sport that has recently tested the above doctrine is interscholastic field hockey. A sport that is played by both genders on the international level, field hockey is considered in most areas of the United States to be a women's sport on the high school level. Courts are split over whether field hockey should be considered a contact sport or not. If field hockey is construed as a contact sport, exclusion of males would be permitted under Title IX without any inquiry into purposes or motives for the exclusion (see note 2). However, if field hockey is found to be a non-contact sport, the plaintiff could proceed on a Title IX claim.

In 2001, Massachusetts, California, and Maine were the only three states that allowed boys to play on high school field hockey teams. In Massachusetts, six of the state's high school field hockey teams had boys on their rosters, including the two Division I state champion teams from the two previous years (see note 4). While several parents and opposing coaches have called for a ban on male players, or a realigned league for males only, such action would violate the Massachusetts Interscholastic Athletic Association's (MIAA) rule 43, which states, "No student shall be denied in any implied or explicit manner the opportunity to participate in any interscholastic activity because of his or her gender." In the 1970s, the MIAA had a rule explicitly excluding boys from girls teams, but that rule was found invalid by the Supreme Judicial Court of Massachusetts based on equal protection laws and Massachusetts' ERA in *Attorney General v. Massachusetts Interscholastic Athletic Ass'n*, 393 N.E.2d 284 (Mass. 1979).

If field hockey gains popularity among high school age boys, it is likely that court cases over male inclusion in the sport will increase. A similar trend occurred with volleyball (see notes 4, 6, 8, 9, and 10), which began in the United States as a traditionally female sport, but saw a rise in male participation in the 1990s.

Male plaintiffs that bring claims of discrimination for exclusion from female teams generally use the same legal theories that females use in bringing claims of discrimination for not being allowed participation on men's teams. The two most common theories used by plaintiffs are Equal Protection and Title IX. Most courts will not uphold a Title IX claim unless the plaintiffs can show that opportunities for males have been limited (see notes 3, 7, and 8). Similarly, equal protection arguments have often been denied because courts have held that athletic associations have a rational reason for separating men's and women's athletic teams or allowing women to field single-sex squads (see notes 6 and 9).

In cases in which there is a women's team and no men's team for non-contact sports, the majority of decisions have not allowed the male to participate on the women's team. Only in *Gomes v. Rhode Island Interscholastic League* (see note 10) did the court uphold the male's gender discrimination claim and allow him to play on the women's volleyball team. The *Gomes* case, however, is not a very strong precedent. In this situation Gomes received a judgment for an injunction in the middle of the season. The appellate court was going to attempt immediate review of the issue, but the league persuaded the court to wait until the end of the team's schedule so that the season would not be disrupted. The merits of the case were never evaluated since the court deemed the case moot because Gomes had graduated.

The majority of the decisions in this area are similar to *Clark* v. *Arizona Interscholastic Ass'n.* (see note 6), with the court refusing to allow boys to compete on the girls' volleyball team. The plaintiff male has been successful for a variety of reasons, including lack of state action when a private organization is involved (see note 11), prohibition of males on women's teams to redress disparate treatment of females in scholastic athletic programs (see note 4), promotion of athletic opportunities for females (see note 9), and the fact that males already have more athletic opportunities than females (see note 7). In addition, there has been some litigation on what types of sports constitute "contact sports." For instance, the argument has now arisen over whether field hockey should be considered a contact sport (see notes 2 and 3). As with the previous sections concerning discrimination against individual athletes, the number of these types of cases has decreased in recent years due to increased opportunities and lack of willingness to enter into costly litigation.

NOTES

1. In *Maine Human Rights Commission v. Maine Principals Ass'n*, No. CV-97–599 1999 Me. Super. LEXIS 23 (Me. Super. Ct. Jan. 21, 1999), two male high school students in Maine brought a case alleging that they were being discriminated against under the Maine Human Rights Act. The court commented on the peculiarity of the fact that the students did not bring a Title IX or equal protection claim, but did not enter into analysis on those issues. The Maine Human Rights Act declares it "unlawful to deny any person equal

opportunity in athletic programs on the basis of sex." The court believed that the plaintiffs had to show that the defendant had deprived them of their right to overall athletic opportunities, and not just participation in field hockey. In its conclusion, the court summarized the general doctrine used by most courts stating, "there is a substantial relationship between excluding boys from playing field hockey and providing equal opportunities for girls in athletics. Conversely, the evidence also establishes that permitting boys to compete with girls in field hockey will likely result in an overall lessening of equal opportunities for girls in athletics." The court, therefore, found for the defendant school association.

2. In *Williams v. School District*, 998 F.2d 168 (3d Cir. 1993), male plaintiff tried out for the girls' field hockey team. Plaintiff made the team and was even given a uniform. School officials then said that plaintiff could not play on the team. The district court granted plaintiff's motion for summary judgment, stating that field hockey is not a contact sport and therefore plaintiff should be allowed to participate on the girls' field hockey team. However, the court of appeals reversed the district court's decision by concluding that field hockey is a contact sport. A contact sport is one in which "the purpose or major activity . . . involves bodily contact." Title IX provides that "exclusion is permitted if the sport involved is a contact sport."

3. In *Kleczek v. Rhode Island Interscholastic League, Inc.*, 768 F.Supp. 951 (D.R.I. 1991), male plaintiff sought to participate on his high school girls' field hockey team because there was no boys' field hockey team. The Rhode Island Interscholastic League (RIIL) refused to let the boy participate on the girl's team. RIIL was a private entity but it got funds from member schools. South Kingstown High School, the plaintiff's high school, did receive federal funds. However, these funds were "restrictive" in that they were specifically earmarked for particular programs (math, science, etc.). The court held that plaintiff had not shown that he was likely to succeed on the merits of his "Title IX claim for three reasons: (1) the programs and activities of the defendants in question do not receive federal funds; (2) the overall athletic opportunities for males at South Kingstown High School have not been limited; and (3) the evidence indicates that field hockey is not a 'noncontact sport.' "

4. For more information on boys playing Massachusetts field hockey cases, see Mike Wise, "In Field Hockey, a Twist on Title IX," *New York Times*, section 5; page 1, Oct. 18, 2001.

5. In *Clark v. Arizona Interscholastic Ass'n*, 886 F.2d 1191 (9th Cir. 1989), the brother of plaintiff in *Clark* v. *Arizona Interscholastic Ass'n* (see note 6), brought a civil rights action challenging a rule of the association prohibiting him from competing on the girls' high school volleyball team. The appeals court affirmed the lower court's decision in favor of the association. As in the earlier *Clark* case, the judge reasoned that the rule was substantially related to the goal of redressing past discrimination and promoting equality of athletic opportunity between the sexes.

6. In *Clark v. Arizona Interscholastic Ass'n*, 695 F.2d 1126 (9th Cir. 1982), *cert. denied*, 464 U.S. 818 (1983), plaintiffs were Arizona high school students who demonstrated their prowess in volleyball by participating on national championship teams sponsored by the Amateur Athletic Union. The student-athletes were not, however, able to participate on their high school volleyball teams. Their schools sponsored interscholastic volleyball teams only for girls, and a policy of the Arizona Interscholastic Association (AIA) had been interpreted to preclude boys from playing on girls' teams, even though girls were permitted to participate on boys' athletic teams.

The trial court found that the rules and regulations of the AIA do not violate the equal protection clause of the Fourteenth Amendment. It held that the maintenance of a girls-only volleyball team "is substantially related to and serves the achievement of the important governmental objective" of (1) promoting equal athletic opportunities for females in interscholastic sports, and (2) redressing the effects of past discrimination. On appeal, the trial court decision was affirmed, upholding the rule prohibiting boys from playing on the girls' volleyball team.

7. In *B.C. v Cumberland Regional School District*, 531 A.2d 1059 (N.J. Super. A.D. 1987), a male high school student challenged an athletic association rule prohibiting him from competing on the girls' field hockey team. In affirming the lower court's decision, the court held that a rule prohibiting boys from playing on the girls' field hockey team is permissible under both the state and the federal Constitution. The court reasoned that were plaintiff permitted to compete on the girls' team, his personal interest would be gained at the cost of denying females the right to have equality of athletic opportunities with their male counterparts.

8. In *Mularadelis v. Haldane Central School Board*, 427 N.Y.S.2d 458 (N.Y. App. Div. 1980), plaintiff Mularadelis, a member of his high school's girls' tennis team, who was told by the school board that he could no longer play on the team, brought a lawsuit. The appeals court reversed a lower court decision and held for the school board on the basis that Title IX allowed for the exclusion of boys from the girls' team when there were, overall, more athletic opportunities for boys in the community.

9. In *Forte v. Board of Education, North Babylon Union Free School District*, 431 N.Y.S.2d 321 (N.Y.Sup. Ct. 1980), an action was brought by plaintiff Forte on behalf of his son, a seventeen-year-old high school student who wanted to play on the North Babylon High School volleyball team, which was all-female. The court held for the school district. The court reasoned that the rule the school district had enacted was a discernible and permissible means of redressing disparate treatment of females in interscholastic athletic programs.

10. In *Petrie v. Illinois High School Ass'n.*, 394 N.E.2d 855 (Ill. 1979), an action was brought by plaintiff Petrie, who wanted to play on the girls' high school volleyball team since the school had no boys' team. The appeals court affirmed a lower court decision, which upheld the association's rule. The court found no violation of state law and reasoned that the association's rule "substantially related to and served the achievement of the governmental objective of maintaining, fostering, and promoting athletic opportunities for girls."

11. In *Gomes v. Rhode Island Interscholastic League*, 469 F.Supp. 659 (D.R.I. 1979), *vacated as moot*, 604 F.2d 733 (1st Cir. 1979), plaintiff Gomes, a senior at Rogers High School in Newport, Rhode Island, brought an action under the federal civil rights statute. He sought preliminary injunctive relief prohibiting school officials from preventing his participation on the girls' volleyball team since the school offered no separate male squad in this sport. Rogers High allowed Gomes to join the all-female team but did not use him in Rhode Island Interscholastic League competition for fear of league disqualification.

Consequently, Gomes brought suit against the league at the start of the volleyball season. He alleged that the rule against male participation in volleyball competition violated both the Fourteenth Amendment and Title IX. Without reaching the constitutional issues, the district court ruled in Gomes's favor. The district court found that the exception for separate-gender teams under Title IX was not applicable since defendants sponsored no men's volleyball teams and opportunities for boys to play the sport previously had been nonexistent. Since the district court decision was rendered in the middle of the volleyball season, the league persuaded the appeals court that implementation of the district court's order would disrupt the remainder of the season. The appeals court stopped the implementation of the order pending review. The merits of the case were never reached on appeal since the case was dismissed as moot because the season had ended and Gomes was graduating.

12. In *White v. Corpus Christi Little Misses Kickball Ass'n.*, 526 S.W.2d 766 (Tex. Civ. App. 1975), an action was brought by plaintiff White, a ten-year-old boy who was not allowed to register to play in the girls' kickball association because of his gender. The district court held for the association, and the boy appealed. On appeal, the boy argued that denial of right to play because of his gender was a denial of equal protection under

both federal and state constitutions. The appeals court denied his claim because he had failed to establish the requisite state action. His participation was denied by a private organization acting without any connection to government except that the games were played in a public park.

8.3.3. Women's Teams and Men's Teams

Four different types of legal arguments are raised in cases in which there are teams for both genders. The first type is in cases in which the plaintiff women argue that "separate but equal is not equal." In these situations the women sue to participate on the men's team because the competition may be better and the women are far superior to the participants on the women's teams. As *O'Connor v. Board of Education of School District No. 23* (see note 3 in section 8.3.3.2., "Contact Sports") illustrates, the court will generally approve "separate but equal" teams and rule against plaintiff females who want to play on boys' teams based on playing ability arguments.

The second type of argument is that the separate teams are not equal, especially with respect to the benefits and opportunities provided to the teams. In *Aiken v. Lieuallen* (see note 6 in section 8.3.3.2., "Contact Sports"), plaintiff female athletes contended that they were discriminated against in the areas of transportation, officiating, coaching, and the school's commitment to competitive programs. In a similar situation, *Blair v. Washington State University* (see note 1 in section 8.3.3.2., "Contact Sports"), the court awarded damages to plaintiff female athletes and ordered equivalent funding for men's and women's athletic programs.

The third type of case occurs when two teams exist, but the women compete under different rules than the men (see section 8.3.4., "Same Sport, Different Rules"). These situations, challenged on equal protection grounds, have produced mixed results. The trend recently does not allow different rules to exist when those rules are based purely on the gender of the athletes, especially when those rules place those who play under them at a disadvantage if they want to continue in the sport.

The fourth type of case involves different seasons for the same men's and women's sport (see section 8.3.5., "Same Sport, Different Seasons"). The courts have historically held that separate seasons of play are not a denial of equal protection of the law; however, the sentiment within the court system is changing, as evidenced by the decision in *Communities for Equity v. Michigan High School Athletic Ass'n* and in *Alston v. Virginia High School League, Inc.* (see notes 1 and 2 in section 8.3.5., "Same Sport, Different Seasons").

8.3.3.1. Separate but Equal

When there are both men's and women's teams in the same sport, challenges for participation on the other team have been unsuccessful. The doctrine of "separate but equal" remains applicable to gender distinctions, even though it has been rejected for distinctions based on race. Thus, if separate teams exist for men and women, there may be a prohibition against coed teams or against women competing against men. The doctrine of "separate but equal" raises the critical question of whether or not such separate teams are substantially equal. The fact that two teams exist does not necessarily satisfy the doctrine. "Separate but equal" is based on the concept that the exclusion of a group is not unconstitutional if the excluded group is provided with comparable opportunities. If women are excluded from the men's basketball team but are provided with an equal team of their own, the school district will not be in violation of the Title IX under the "separate but equal" theory. When the genders are segregated in athletics, there must be an overall equality of expenditures (see note 1), coaching, and access to facilities. Without this substantial equality, the existence of separate teams and the prohibition of women competing with men may be unconstitutional.

Apart from these circumstances, the segregation of the genders in athletics is generally upheld, although the court is careful to examine the specific circumstances in each case before making a determination. The court usually considers whether or not the particular sport in question is considered to be a contact or a non-contact sport. Physiological differences between the genders have been found to be a valid reason for the exclusion of one gender from a contact sport. Contact sports include boxing, wrestling, rugby, ice hockey, football, basketball, and other sports in which the major activity involves bodily contact. As the rights of female athletes have increasingly been served in recent years, the number of cases in this area has decreased. The quality of competition has increased in women's sports, making females less likely to demand an opportunity to play on men's teams. Furthermore, the treatment of female athletic teams has begun to equal the support that male teams receive on the interscholastic and intercollegiate levels, leading to a decrease in "separate but equal" cases.

NOTE

1. In 2002, the Hampton, Virginia City Council was scrutinized by press reports, such as one in *USA Today*, because it had spent $7,000 on rings for Phoebus High's 2001 state champion boys' football team, but gave no money to championship girls' teams. Because the school receives federal funds, this may have been a Title IX violation. The boys and girls track teams at another Hampton high school also won state titles. The city manager pointed out in his defense to the media that neither of these two other teams requested ring money. For more information, see Dan Cronin, "Kournikova Wins, Faces V. Williams," *USA Today*, Sports; pg. 11 C, February 13, 2002.

8.3.3.2. Contact Sports

In cases in which there are both women's and men's teams in contact sports, the courts have generally not allowed a female to participate on the men's team. In *O'Connor v. Board of Education of School District No. 23* (see note 3), the court denied the gender discrimination allegation of a female who wanted to participate in better competition by playing on the men's team. The other issue that may be raised is whether the separate men's and women's teams are in fact equal. For example, in *Aiken v. Lieuallen* (see note 6), members of the female basketball team at the University of Oregon argued that they did not receive the same treatment as the men's basketball team at the university. The school was found to be in violation because it discriminated against the female players in the areas of transportation, coaching, and officiating.

NOTES

1. In *Blair v. Washington State University*, 740 P.2d 1379 (Wash. 1987), female athletes and the coaches of female athletes brought a gender discrimination action under the state Equal Rights Amendment. The trial court ruled for plaintiffs and awarded damages, in-

junctive relief, attorney fees, and costs. On appeal, the Washington Supreme Court affirmed the lower court's conclusion of gender discrimination but modified the lower court's calculations on comparative scholarships between male and female athletes and attorney fees.

2. In *Michigan Department of Civil Rights, ex rel. Forton v. Waterford Township Department of Parks and Recreation*, 387 N.W.2d 281 (Mich. 1986), plaintiff brought a Civil Rights Act claim based on defendant's policy of maintaining a gender-based elementary-level basketball program. The appeals court reversed the district court's decision and ruled in favor of the plaintiff. The court reasoned that (1) separate leagues involved were not equal and could not withstand equal protection analysis, and consequently violated the Civil Rights Act, and (2) subsequent modification of policy to allow up to two girls to participate on each boys' basketball team and two boys on each girls' basketball team did not cure the statutory violation.

3. In *O'Connor v. Board of Education*, 645 F.2d 578 (7th Cir. 1981), *cert. denied*, 454 U.S. 1084 (1981), an appeal was instituted in response to a district court order granting a preliminary injunction to restrain defendant school board from refusing to permit female plaintiff from trying out for the boys' sixth grade basketball team. The plaintiff argued that the school board's policy of maximizing participation in sports by providing for separate but equal boys' and girls' interscholastic sports teams violated Title IX. The appellate court held that the trial court abused its discretion in granting a preliminary injunction restraining the school board because the plaintiff failed to show a reasonable likelihood of success on the merits.

4. In *Lafler v. Athletic Board of Control*, 536 F.Supp. 104 (W.D. Mich. 1982), the court upheld the denial of a woman's application to box in the flyweight division of the Golden Gloves boxing competition under the Fourteenth Amendment, the state public accommodation statute, and the state Equal Rights Amendment. The court cited Title IX regulations permitting establishment of separate male-female teams in contact sports and the Amateur Sports Act provisions providing for separate programs for females and males.

5. Two student-athletes filed a complaint with the Oregon Board of Education, alleging that Oregon State University (OSU) offered athletic programs of lesser quality to female student-athletes than were offered to their male counterparts. A settlement reached in July 1980, titled "OSU Conciliation Agreement for Sex Equality in Intercollegiate Athletics," implemented a five-year plan at OSU designed to put the men's and women's athletic programs on an equal competitive basis.

6. In *Aiken v. Lieuallen*, 593 P.2d 1243 (Or. Ct. App. 1978), an action was brought by plaintiff taxpayers and parents of student-athletes on the University of Oregon's women's varsity basketball team who appealed a determination by the chancellor of the State Board of Higher Education that the university was not violating state statute ORS 659.150, which prohibited discrimination on the basis of gender in state-financed education programs. The plaintiffs filed a complaint in March 1977, alleging that the following four areas of Oregon's athletic program were in violation of ORS 659.150: transportation, officiating, coaching, and commitment to competitive programs. A contested case hearing was held in October 1977, in which the hearing officer determined that the university was in violation of ORS 659.150.

The findings and recommendations were issued in March 1978, and were submitted to the Oregon chancellor of higher education for review and entry of an order. The chancellor reversed the hearing officer's decision and found that the university was not in violation of the statute. The appeals court reversed the chancellor's order and sent the case back for further proceedings. The court, after reviewing the plaintiffs' allegations of discrimination in the areas of transportation, officiating, coaching, and university commitment, stated that upon the second hearing, the chancellor should address these allegations to determine whether the university's actions have led to "unreasonable differentiation of treatment" under ORS 659.150. Determinations of the unreasonableness of actions should include evaluations of whether or not the action by the university had a disparate effect on the opportunity for women to participate in athletics.

7. In *Hutchins v. Board of Trustees of Michigan State University*, 705 F.2d. 454 (6th Cir. 1982), the women's basketball team from the East Lansing campus of Michigan State brought a Title IX complaint against Michigan State University and the board of trustees, alleging that the men's team was receiving better treatment. The alleged better treatment included more money for traveling and better facilities. The court held for the women's basketball team and issued a temporary restraining order disallowing the better treatment of the men's team.

8.3.3.3. *Non-contact Sports*

In cases in which there are both women's and men's teams in non-contact sports, the courts have generally not allowed the female to participate on the men's team. The rationale is that separate but equal is equal, since this enhances athletic opportunities for females. As mentioned previously, as the quality of female athletics has grown since the 1980s, the demand by women to participate on men's teams for increased competition has decreased sharply. This trend is evidenced in the notes, with few cases being heard since the inception of Title IX in 1972.

NOTES ————————————————————————

1. In *Ruman v. Eskew*, 343 N.E.2d 806 (Ind. Ct. App. 1975), an action was brought by plaintiff Ruman, who wanted to play on the high school boys' tennis team, even though there was a girl's team at her school. The Indiana High School Athletic Association prohibited girls from playing on boys' teams if girls' teams in the same sport existed. The court held for the defendant and upheld the rule, since it was reasonably related to the objective of providing athletic opportunities for both males and females. The court of appeals affirmed the judgment of the trial court.

2. In *Ritacco v. Norwin School District*, 361 F.Supp. 930 (W.D. Pa. 1973), a high school graduate and her mother filed a class action challenging a Pennsylvania Interscholastic Athletic Association (PIAA) rule that in effect required separate girls' and boys' teams for interscholastic non-contact sports. The district court ruled in favor of the defendant school district. It held that since the school district had not deprived Ritacco of her constitutional rights in violation of the Civil Rights Act, 42 U.S.C. §1983, she was entitled to neither declaratory judgment nor injunctive relief. The court held that "separate but equal" in the realm of athletic competition is justifiable and permissible when a rational basis for the rule exists, and that gender, unlike race, is not an inherently suspect classification for purposes of determining a denial of equal protection. The court concluded that the PIAA rule forbidding coeducational non-contact sports teams did not invalidly and unfairly discriminate against females.

3. In *Gregoria v. Board of Education*, No. A-1277–70 (N.J. Super. Ct. App. Div. 1971) (unreported), the trial court refused to prohibit enforcement of the New Jersey Athletic Association's rule prohibiting coed interscholastic sports, including non-contact sports such as tennis. Among the rational bases for the policy, the court cited the psychological impact on males, the need for additional female trainers, and the possibility of insufficient bathroom facilities. The appeals court affirmed the lower court's ruling that the "psychological well-being of girls is a rational reason for exclusion."

8.3.4. Same Sport, Different Rules

Cases and issues in this section have traditionally arisen in basketball because women's basketball is often played under different rules than men's basketball.

As evidenced by *Dodson v. Arkansas Activities Ass'n.* (see note 1), the cases have evolved from a generally disparate treatment of student-athletes rather than from different rules of a sport. However, the use of different rules for male and female teams in the same sport has declined.

8.3.4.1. Contact Sports

In cases in which there are different playing rules for women's and men's teams in contact sports, there is a split in decisions as to whether the women's rules should be changed to conform with the men's. The plaintiff women in these cases generally have alleged gender discrimination based on the rule differences with men's sports and also the reduced opportunity to compete against other women (who had the advantage of playing under men's rules) for college scholarships. In *Dodson v. Arkansas Activities Ass'n.* (note 1), the court ruled for the plaintiff, stating that no valid reason exists for women to have to use different rules than men in playing basketball. However, in *Jones v. Oklahoma Secondary School Activities Ass'n.* (note 2) and *Cape v. Tennessee Secondary School Athletic Ass'n.* (note 3), the courts ruled for the defendant athletic associations, mostly for administrative reasons. Due to the growth of women's sports on the national level, the use of different rules for men and women has become an antiquated practice. Therefore, since the 1980s, this type of litigation has not arisen frequently.

NOTES

1. In *Dodson v. Arkansas Activities Ass'n.*, 468 F.Supp. 394 (E.D. Ark. 1979), plaintiff Dodson, a female junior high school basketball player in the Arkadelphia, Arkansas, public school system, brought an action in January 1977 against three defendants: the school district, the superintendent, and the Arkansas Activities Association. Her suit challenged the constitutionality of rules for girls' junior and senior high school basketball, which in Arkansas differed from those under which boys played. The court held that "none of the reasons proffered [for the rule differentiation] are at all relevant to a gender-based classification." The defendant stated that "no physiological differences between males and females . . . prohibit females from playing five-on-five basketball." And the primary justification given for the gender-based distinction between rules was simply that of tradition. The court ordered that the defendants be permanently prohibited and restrained from enforcing different rules for girls and boys playing junior and senior high school basketball in Arkansas.

2. In *Jones v. Oklahoma Secondary School Activities Ass'n.*, 453 F.Supp. 150 (W.D. Okla. 1977), plaintiff Jones sought an injunction to suspend the association's split-court basketball rules, arguing that they created an arbitrary and unreasonable distinction between boys and girls that violated her right to equal protection. The court held for the athletic association. Jones's Title IX arguments were dismissed because she did not follow administrative procedures. Her Fourteenth Amendment argument was seen as faulty because her allegations concerning her reduced opportunity to compete in the future and a reduced likelihood for college scholarships did not rise to the level of an equal protection interest. Her claims that such rules interfered with her enjoyment of the game as well as her physical development also did not establish a cognizable equal protection claim.

3. In *Cape v. Tennessee Secondary School Athletic Ass'n.*, 424 F.Supp. 732 (E.D. Tenn. 1976), *rev'd. per curiam*, 563 F.2d 793 (6th Cir. 1977), plaintiff Cape, a high school student, challenged the "split-court" rules used in women's basketball. These rules, she claimed, denied her the full benefits of the game as well as an athletic scholarship to college. The

court held for the athletic association and dismissed Cape's arguments, which were based on a private right of action under Title IX and the Fourteenth Amendment. The court held that Cape, who sought to challenge the regulations, must first exhaust all administrative remedies with the Department of Health, Education and Welfare under Title IX before her suit could be addressed in federal court.

8.3.4.2. Non-contact Sports

The courts have allowed different rules for men and women's non-contact sports. The courts can apply a rational relationship test and find that the physical and psychological differences between male and female athletes justify different rules (see note 1). Cases of this type have not arisen recently, however, and if a court were to try a case involving similar facts, the decision might be different from the verdict in *Bucha* (note 1). Due to the increased uniformity of men's and women's rules in all sports, cases such as this have not arisen in recent years.

NOTE ───

1. In *Bucha* v. *Illinois High School Ass'n.*, 351 F.Supp. 69 (N.D. Ill. 1972), plaintiffs, two female students at Hinsdale Center Township High School, brought a class action challenging the Illinois High School Association (IHSA) bylaws placing limitations on girls' athletic contests that were not applicable to boys' athletics. The girls sought to have the court declare the IHSA rules in violation of the equal protection clause of the Fourteenth Amendment and to prohibit the enforcement of the bylaws. They also sought a judgment against all defendants in the amount of $25,000.

The defendants—IHSA, its directors, and the Board of Education of Hinsdale Township—based their motions to dismiss on three arguments: (1) the IHSA and the board of education were not persons within the meaning of 42 USC §1983 (1970); (2) the challenged discrimination was not an action under color of state statute, ordinance, regulation, custom, or usage; and (3) the challenged discrimination did not constitute a deprivation of a right guaranteed by the U.S. Constitution and laws.

Concerning the defendants' first argument, the court held that "all defendants may properly be prohibited as persons under §1983, but only the individual defendants can be liable for the damages sought." On the second argument, the court rejected defendants' contention that the acts of the IHSA did not amount to state action and therefore could not be reached under §1983.

On the third and final argument, the court reviewed the girls' complaint that the athletic association denied them equal protection, stating that the relevant inquiry was whether the challenged classification based on gender was rational. Because participation in interscholastic athletics is not a constitutionally guaranteed right and the Illinois courts do not interfere with the policies of a voluntary association such as the IHSA unless it acts "unreasonably, arbitrarily, or capriciously," the girls had asserted their claims based on an equal educational opportunity argument and not the right to interscholastic athletic participation.

The court found a factual basis for defendants' claim that the physical and psychological differences between male and female student-athletes would lead to male domination of coed interscholastic sports and result in decreased female athletic participation, should unrestricted competition between the genders be permitted. It held that "the uncontroverted existence of a bona fide athletic program for girls coupled with the physical and psychological differences . . . also support the rationality of the IHSA's decision to conduct girls' interscholastic sports programs different from boys'."

The district court entered summary judgment in favor of all defendants on the basis that the traditional equal protection standard "requires this court to defer to the judgment of the physical educators of the IHSA once a rational relationship has been shown to exist between their actions and the goals of interscholastic athletic competition."

8.3.5. Same Sport, Different Seasons

Until the decision of *Alston v. Virginia High School League, Inc.*, 108 F.Supp. 2d 543 (W.D. Va. 2000), the courts had allowed different seasons for men and women in the same sport as long as there was a rational basis for the difference. For example, in one case, an athletic association scheduled men's swimming in a different season (fall) than the women's season (winter), and was challenged on gender discrimination grounds. The athletic association's decisions were upheld. The court reasoned that there was a reasonable basis for the decision: the lack of available pool time for both women's and men's teams to practice during the same season. However, in *Alston*, the association scheduled girls' sports seasons depending on the level of competition, but did not use the same method for boys' sports. It is important to note that the plaintiffs in *Alston* were successful using the theory of Title IX in their case. However, the plaintiffs in *Ridgeway v. Montana High School Ass'n*, 633 F.Supp 1564 (D. Mont. 1986) (see note 3), employed Title IX in their arguments, and were unsuccessful in their claim. The increased likelihood that plaintiffs will prevail in this type of case is illustrated by these two cases.

NOTES ───────────────────────────────

1. In *Communities for Equity v. Michigan High School Athletic Association*, 178 F. Supp. 2d 805 (W.D. Mich. 2001), the plaintiffs alleged that they were discriminated against because female sports were scheduled at less advantageous times than male sports in Michigan. Six girls' sports were played in non-traditional seasons, causing recruiting disadvantages and requiring certain female teams to play outdoor sports in more frequently inclement weather. The association alleged that it needed to have some of the boys' and girls' teams play in different seasons for logistical reasons. The court responded by saying that if such logistical concerns are valid, the association should "split advantageous and disadvantageous sports equally" between the sexes. The court found that the associations' scheduling of the interscholastic athletic seasons of girls' sports was in violation of the Equal Protection Clause of the Fourteenth Amendment of the U.S. Constitution, Title IX, and Michigan's Elliott-Larsen Civil Rights Act. The court also ordered the association to bring its scheduling of the seasons into compliance with such laws by the 2003–2004 school year.

2. In *Alston v. Virginia High School League, Inc.*, 108 F.Supp. 2d 543 (W.D. Va. 2000), female high school students brought suit alleging violations of Title IX and equal protection. The Virginia High School League (VHSL) scheduled girls' sports for different seasons, depending on the level of competition for each individual school. Defendant motioned for a dismissal of the case. The court concluded that a Title IX claim does not subsume an equal protection claim and, therefore, the defendant's motion to dismiss was denied. After the motion for dismissal was denied, the plaintiff students were successful in their claim, overturning case precedent against females. VHSL was not found to have a legitimate, compelling reason to schedule the girls' seasons differently than the boys'.

3. In *Ridgeway v. Montana High School Ass'n.*, 633 F.Supp. 1564 (D. Mont. 1986), the court decided not to overturn the decision of the Montana High School Association (MHSA), which allowed the seasonal placement of girls' basketball (fall) and girls' volleyball (winter) to remain as is, contrary to the prevailing seasonal placement for the sports throughout the rest of the country. The court agreed with the reasoning advanced by the

MHSA, which determined that a change in seasonal placement would not facilitate "the goal of maximizing participation in athletics by the most students."

4. In *Striebel v. Minnesota State High School League*, 321 N.W.2d 400 (Minn. 1982), an action was brought by plaintiff female student-athlete against the Minnesota State High School League (MSHSL), challenging the constitutionality of a MSHSL rule that authorized "separate seasons of play for high school athletic teams separated or substantially separated according to gender." The MSHSL had established separate seasons for boys and girls in tennis and swimming. The district court held that the league's policy of establishing separate seasons for boys and girls was constitutional and in compliance with the statute. The court found that under the circumstances presented, separating teams by season was a "reasonable means of achieving maximum participation by both sexes in the high school athletic program." On appeal, the Minnesota Supreme Court held that "where limited athletic facilities make it necessary to schedule high school boys' and girls' athletic teams in separate seasons and neither was substantially better than the other, that scheduling decision was not a denial of equal protection of the law."

8.3.6. Varsity Sport Versus Club Sport

Another trend that has been occurring in recent Title IX litigation involves the argument that a sport that has been operating under "club" status should be raised to "varsity" status when the counterpart gender has a varsity team in that same sport. This argument has been used by women athletes who feel that denial of varsity status to their sport is a violation of Title IX, given that the male student-athletes have a varsity team in the same sport. This argument is based on the Title IX interpretation that calls for proportional ratios of sport participation opportunities offered to men and women student-athletes. The plaintiffs would have to prove initially that the school was out of compliance with Title IX and that adding this particular sport program as a varsity sport would constitute compliance with Title IX. If the school thought it was not in compliance with Title IX, it could raise the women's team to varsity status, thereby increasing participation opportunities.

The plaintiffs could also argue a Title IX complaint based on equal benefits and opportunities provided to the sport programs. The plaintiffs' argument could revolve around the fact that if a school offers a varsity team in a particular sport for men, then it must offer the same sport for women at the varsity level and provide it with the benefits and opportunities that the men's team receives. The plaintiffs would need to prove that student-athletes have the interest and ability to compete on the varsity level, and that there is ample competition to sustain a team. This type of argument was used in *Cook et al. v. Colgate University* (see note 2), in which the plaintiff female student-athletes argued that their club sport of women's ice hockey should be raised to varsity status and that failure to do so was a violation of Title IX. This approach to Title IX compliance is relatively new, and the courts have yet to rule on this type of complaint.

NOTES

1. In *Bryant v. Colgate University*, 996 F.Supp. 170 (N.D. N.Y. 1998), Colgate University was sued on Title IX grounds for the club status of its women's ice hockey team. The court determined that Colgate was not within the "substantially proportionate" safe harbor provided by the OCR policy interpretations and granted the plaintiffs summary judgment on this issue. However, the court ruled that there were factual disputes as to the other two safe harbors—accommodation of interests and abilities and a continuing practice

of increasing women's opportunities—and, therefore, denied the plaintiffs' motion for summary judgment on these two issues. Colgate subsequently settled the suit and granted women's ice hockey varsity status.

2. In *Cook v. Colgate University*, 802 F.Supp. 737 (N.D. N.Y. 1992), the plaintiff female student-athletes argued that refusal by Colgate University to raise their club ice hockey team to varsity status was a violation of Title IX because they were being denied the benefits and opportunities that were afforded to their male ice hockey-playing counterparts. Shortly after women students were admitted into the university in 1970, a women's ice hockey club team was formed. In 1979, 1983, 1986, and 1988, the women's ice hockey club team applied for varsity status and was denied by the university. Varsity status is important in that it provides the team with full-time coaches, designated schedules, rules and regulations, equipment, practice facilities, travel accommodations, and appropriate budgetary support. Colgate University argued that individual programs should not be looked at (a comparison in this instance involving the support received by the men's varsity ice hockey team versus the women's club ice hockey team) and that no evidence had been presented to show that Colgate's athletic program discriminates against women.

The district court ruled for the plaintiffs and ordered Colgate to grant the women's ice hockey team varsity status and to provide all the amenities that accompany such a designation. The court ruled that Title IX is designed to protect not only a particular class of persons (women as a whole within the athletic department), but individuals as well. Therefore, a separate team comparison is appropriate when analyzing Title IX compliance. The court stated that because Colgate sponsors separate ice hockey teams for each gender, the court has the authority to compare the two programs according to the Title IX equal opportunity and benefit areas.

Colgate University also set forth six reasons why rejection of varsity status for the women's team took place: women's ice hockey is rarely played on the secondary level; championships are not sponsored by the NCAA; the game is played by only approximately fifteen colleges in the East; hockey is expensive to fund; there is a lack of general student interest in women's ice hockey; and there is a lack of ability among the members of the women's club team. The court stated that the only real reason why the requests for varsity status were denied was that hockey is expensive to fund and elevating the team to varsity status would have a dramatic financial impact on the university. The court went on to state that financial problems and funding shortfalls are not legitimate excuses for Title IX violations.

Colgate University appealed this decision (*Cook v. Colgate University*, 992 F.2d 17 (2d Cir. 1993)). The U.S. Court of Appeals heard the case and vacated the lower-court decision by ruling that the case was moot because all five of the plaintiffs either had graduated or were scheduled to graduate in May 1993. In August 1993, a new class action suit was filed against Colgate, bringing the same complaint against the institution (see note 1).

Chapter 9

CONTRACT LAW

9.1. PRINCIPLES OF CONTRACT LAW

Contract law underlies the daily activities of all facets of every athletic organization. Contracts are formed in order to document formal agreements, and are referred to if the terms of such agreements come into dispute. A dispute may involve parties such as television networks, athletes, coaches, teachers, mascots, hot dog vendors, halftime show entertainers, secretaries, insurance companies, and season ticket holders.

Many non-lawyers misunderstand the meaning of the word "contract." A contract is *not* necessarily a piece of paper (or several pages of paper) with multiple parties' signatures at the bottom. With the exception of cases outlined in section 9.1.5., "Statute of Frauds," a "handshake deal" or a simple quid pro quo promise can be considered a legally binding contract. However, the existence of a written contract helps to prove that an agreement took place, and preserves the details of such an agreement in case a dispute and/or litigation occurs. Consequently, the chapter will deal primarily with *written* contracts rather than *oral* contracts.

This chapter begins with an introduction to contract law in general, and explores the way in which contracts are formed and enforced. The second part of the chapter focuses more directly on sports law, and examines contracts that professional, intercollegiate, and interscholastic sports organizations encounter. While the chapter will not discuss every type of athletic contract, it will emphasize the unique characteristics of many of the more common types. It will also emphasize the importance of proper contract drafting, and analyze precedent-setting cases. Many of these cases demonstrate the problems that can arise vis-à-vis disputed contracts in sports. Understanding the facts of these cases, and subsequent judicial decisions, will benefit those who will enter into similar agreements.

NOTES _____

1. There are three major sources of contract law:

(a) *Common Law*: Common law is based on previous court decisions regarding fact situations not specifically dealt with by statute. These previous court decisions provide guidelines in determining the legality of a contract.

(b) *Restatement of Contracts*: The American Law Institute (ALI) first published *Restatement of Contracts* in 1932; the most recent (2nd) edition was published in 1981. It has organized and summarized this country's common law concerning contracts. Attorneys and the judiciary rely on it for precedent.

(c) *Uniform Commercial Code* (U.C.C.): The U.C.C., a uniform statute that every state except Louisiana has enacted, involves commercial transactions (not land or services). Athletic administrators most often would deal with the U.C.C. when dealing with contracts that specifically cover the sale of goods—for example, sporting goods and game tickets. Several educational institutions have been given copyright permission to publish articles of the U.C.C. on the Internet (for limited purposes of study, teaching, and academic research). One such Web site is www.law.cornell.edu/ucc/ucc.table.html

2. There has been debate over whether an NCAA scholarship or letter of intent constitutes a legally binding contract. This issue is addressed in Chapter 6, section 6.2.2., "Participation Rules."

3. Television contracts are discussed in Chapter 14, section 14.2., "Broadcast Contracts."

4. An example of a Standard Player Contract can be found in section 9.2.1.9., "Example of a Standard Player Contract—NFL."

5. An example of a college coaches' contract can be found in section 9.2.5., "Coaches' Contracts: Professional and Collegiate Sports."

6. An example of a physician's contract can be found in section 9.2.7., "Physicians' Contracts."

7. An example of an official's contract can be found in section 9.2.8., "Officials' Contracts."

8. Athlete endorsement and international contracts are discussed in Chapter 12, section 12.1., "Agency Law."

9.1.1. Formation of a Contract

The major legal concepts involved in the formation of a contract are offer, acceptance, consideration, legality, and capacity.

9.1.1.1. Offer

For a contract to come into existence, the parties involved must agree on the terms of the deal. To reach the stage at which there is mutual assent, the parties must go through a process of offering and accepting the terms of the contract. To form a contract, the parties must come to an agreement on the major or essential terms of the contract. The terms of a contract are interpreted objectively, and if necessary, interpretations concerning the terms are answered by determining the intent of the parties forming the contract.

An offer is a conditional promise made by the *offeror* to the *offeree*. The offeror is the party who makes the offer; the offeree is the person(s) to whom an offer is made. The offer is conditional because the offeror will not be bound by the promise unless the offeree responds to the offer in the proper fashion. The *Second Restatement of Contracts* defines an offer as "the manifestation of willingness to enter into a bargain, so made as to justify another person in understanding that his assent to that bargain is invited."

An offer usually includes the following essential terms:

(a) The parties involved
(b) The subject matter
(c) The time (and place) for the subject matter to be performed
(d) The price to be paid.

For example, College A offers to play at College B in football on January 1, 2005, at 2 P.M. for the sum of $1,000 plus complimentary tickets. College B accepts the offer and signs a written contract with College A. In this example, an exchange of promises has been made and the essential terms of parties, time, place, performance, and price have been incorporated. Note, however, that the number of complimentary tickets has not been specified. By itself, this would not void a contract; rather, it would be expected that this number would be the number of tickets usually given to the opposing team as a standard practice for football games.

Most offers contain a pair of promises—a conditional promise made by one party that is premised on the second party's promising to do some act in return. This exchange of promises is categorized as a *bilateral contract*. When an offer is made by one party to a proposed contract to the second party to the contract, it creates a *power of acceptance*, because if the second party accepts the offer, a contract is formed. For example, A promises to pay B $100 if B promises to officiate a basketball game for A. This is an example of a bilateral contract.

A *unilateral contract* is a contract that does not involve an exchange of promises. It instead involves an exchange of a promise in return for an act by a second party. The second party is not bound to do anything, but if the second party chooses to do the requested act, the first party is bound to the terms of his or her promise. For example, a promoter promises Fighter A that if he will fight Fighter B, the promoter will pay A $100. A has not agreed to fight B, but if A does fight B, then the promoter is bound to pay A $100.

An *option contract* involves an offer by one party to keep an offer open exclusively to a second party, for a stated period of time, if the second party agrees to pay a fee (or some other consideration) to the first party for keeping the offer open. For example, a real estate broker offers a basketball team the opportunity to purchase 200 acres of land for $2 million in order to build a playing facility, and also offers that if the basketball team pays a $100,000 security deposit, the $2 million price will remain fixed for six months. This six-month interval can allow the team to obtain zoning approval, league approval, and financing. Although the terms of an option contract are negotiable, the following is a likely scenario. If the basketball team takes advantage of this provision in the specified time, the $100,000 will go toward the total asking price of $2 million. If the basketball team pays the $100,000 security deposit, but does not pay the additional $1.9 million within six months, the real seller keeps the $100,000 and the offer of the fixed price is off the table.

An offer made in jest is not a valid offer and creates no power of acceptance in the second party. Similarly, an offer is not made if it is just an expression of opinion. It is also important to distinguish preliminary negotiations from an offer that creates a power of acceptance. Consider the following example: the athletic director of College A calls the athletic director of College B and says College A would be interested in playing College B in men's basketball during the 2005 season. College B's athletic director then sends out a game contract to College A's athletic director that states, "I accept your offer and will play you on February 1, 2005 at 8 P.M. at the Slam-Dunk Center for $10,000." College A has not entered into the contract because its athletic director's call was only a solicitation of a contest and not an offer creating the power of acceptance in College B's athletic director. College A was only beginning preliminary negotiations. College A may still agree to the deal, but is under no obligation to do so.

Advertisements are generally not considered offers to sell, but rather are viewed as an invitation to the public to buy. For example, a minor league hockey team advertises an upcoming game in the local newspaper. The game is a sellout, but fans still want to buy tickets to the game. The team is under no obligation to sell more tickets to the game, because the advertisement was just an invitation for the public to buy tickets—not a specific offer to sell tickets to all fans. However, an advertisement that includes the phrase "First come, first served" is considered an offer. Thus, the first person to respond to the advertisement accepts the offer, creating a binding contract with the advertiser. A valid offer is created only with the first person to respond to the offer.

9.1.1.2. Acceptance

An *acceptance* can be made only by the party to whom the offer was made. For example, the women's Olympic lacrosse team offers to buy twenty helmets from Manufacturer A for $100 each. Unknown to the equipment manager of the lacrosse team, Manufacturer B has bought Manufacturer A's business. The equipment manager has dealt with Manufacturer B before, and does not like its warranty policy. Manufacturer B accepts the order from the equipment manager. However, the equipment manager refuses to accept delivery from Manufacturer B and does not have to do so, since the offer to purchase the helmets was made to Manufacturer A and therefore does not create a power of acceptance in Manufacturer B.

The party accepting the offer, the *offeree*, may be required to accept the offer from the party making it, the *offeror*, in a specified manner (e.g., by letter). In some instances, which may depend in part on past practice between the parties, an offer may be accepted in silence (offeree makes no response to offeror). To avoid confusion as to whether an official offer has been made, all contact should be in writing, and the responses should be recorded.

Mutual assent is a condition that occurs when the offeree clearly accepts the offeror's offer. A problem may result with mutual assent when an acceptance varies in its terms from the initial offer. According to common law, acceptance must be a mirror image of the offer (see note 1). However, the U.C.C. does allow for some exceptions (see note 3).

The offeree's power of acceptance can be terminated in four ways:

1. By rejection or counteroffer by the offeree
2. By a lapse of time
3. By revocation by the offeree
4. By death or incapacity of either party to the contract.

The following examples illustrate these reasons for termination:

- Rejection or counteroffer: Notre Dame offers to play Georgia Tech in field hockey on October 15, 2005. Georgia Tech rejects the October 15 date and instead offers to play on October 16. The offer made by Notre Dame was terminated by Georgia Tech's rejection, and the October 16 date is considered a counteroffer. The responsibility would then be placed on Notre Dame either to accept the new date or to reject it and counteroffer (see note 1).

- Lapse of time: The University of Massachusetts sends a letter of intent to a proposed scholarship student-athlete which states that if the letter of intent is not signed by a certain date, it is no longer valid. Student-athlete is considering a number of different scholarship offers and allows the letter of intent to lapse. After the deadline date, the student-athlete later reconsiders and requests a new letter to be sent. The University of Massachusetts has subsequently offered the scholarship to another individual, and notifies the initial offeree that its offer of a scholarship had lapsed.

- Revocation: A promoter in Stockholm, Sweden, contacts the Colorado Avalanche and offers to schedule an exhibition game in London on August 15, 2005, between the Colorado Avalanche and the New York Rangers to take advantage of Peter Forsberg's popularity in his native country. The Avalanche says it will think about the offer. Before the Avalanche can respond to the offer, Forsberg decides to retire. Upon hearing of the retirement, the promoter immediately informs the Avalanche that its offer is revoked.

- Death or incapacity: The New York Knicks, of the NBA, offer their first round draft pick a four-year deal worth $8 million. Before the draftee can respond, he is fatally injured in a car collision. Therefore, the offer cannot be accepted because the draftee's death makes the performance of a contract impossible.

NOTES

1. In *Los Angeles Rams v. Cannon*, 185 F.Supp. 717 (S.D. Ca. 1960), Billy Cannon signed a contract with the Los Angeles Rams of the NFL for the 1960, 1961, and 1962 seasons. Pursuant to Paragraph 13 of the NFL Constitution, which states that the NFL commissioner needs to sign any player contract before it can become officially recognized, the commissioner signed the 1960 contract. The Houston team from the rival American Football League (AFL) contacted Cannon prior to the 1960 season, and signed him to a more lucrative deal. Cannon subsequently revoked his contract with the Rams. The Rams attempted to get an injunction barring Cannon from playing for the Houston team, and the court was forced to determine whether a valid contract offer and acceptance had occurred. The court reasoned that Cannon had been offered three years (1960–1962) and that the submission of the signed 1960 contract should be viewed as a counteroffer because the original terms had changed. Thus, Cannon's contract with the Rams was void because the Rams had not accepted the three-year deal, and Cannon had not accepted the one-year deal.

2. In *Detroit Football v. Robinson*, 186 F.Supp. 933 (E.D. La. 1960), Robinson, a college football star, signed a contract with the Detroit Lions of the NFL while he was still in his last year of college. Pursuant to Paragraph 13 of the NFL Constitution, the contract was sent to the commissioner for his approval. Before the commissioner signed the contract, the Dallas Club from the AFL approached Robinson about securing his services, and did so shortly thereafter, signing him to a lucrative contract. Detroit attempted to get an injunction to stop Robinson from signing with Dallas because he had entered into a binding agreement with them. The court found that the contract Robinson signed with Detroit was really an offer, and that acceptance occurred only when the commissioner signed the contract. Thus, Robinson's contract with Detroit was revoked.

3. Under the U.C.C. provisions for the sale of goods, an acceptance that differs from the offer will be enforceable, as long as the acceptance is not expressly conditioned on the offeror's accepting the new terms. This is provided that one party to the contract is not a merchant. For example, an equipment manager for the Pittsburgh Steelers orders twenty football helmets with face guards and chinstraps for $100 each. The manufacturer accepts the order (offer) but notes on its order acknowledgment form that chin straps are not usually included, but they can be included in this sale for an additional $1 per helmet. This is considered "a proposal for addition to the contract" and will not become part of the contract until the equipment manager agrees to it. If the chinstraps are essential to the formation of the entire contract, then a contract may be deemed not to have come into existence at all.

9.1.1.3. *Consideration*

In addition to mutual assent (offer and acceptance), it is essential for the formation of most contracts that there be some form of consideration—that is, the value that each party to the contract is exchanging. For example, Bob offers Scott his tickets to a boxing match for $25. Scott accepts. This is a binding contract because Bob is giving up his tickets, and Scott is giving up $25. Each party has pledged to give up something to benefit the other. Another example would involve a coach who agrees to work for Team A, to the exclusion of other teams, for a period of two years, at an annual salary of $1 million per year. The coach is giving his services and experience to Team A, and in return Team A gives the coach a salary. Consideration is often at issue as the essential element needed in a contract to make it legally enforceable. Without consideration, there may be a promise to do an act, but it may not be legally enforceable as a contract. Consideration can be contrasted to the giving of a gift, which may involve a promise to do something of value but involves no promise to do anything in return for receiving it. For example, A offers to wash B's car as a birthday gift. However, since B is not obligated to do anything for A, there is no consideration.

Generally, past consideration cannot be a basis for enacting a legally binding current contract. Past consideration is an act that could have served as consideration if it had been bargained for at the time the contract was formed. Since consideration involves an exchange, parties cannot bargain (or exchange) for something that has already occurred.

There are three important concepts that can help establish or negate the existence of legal consideration:

1. Mutuality of obligation
2. Preexisting duty rule
3. Promissory estoppel.

The doctrine of *mutuality of obligation* states that the consideration given by all parties to the contract must be legally sufficient, and $1 is usually sufficient. However, it is important to note that the consideration given by the parties does *not* need to be equal.

For example, assume that a brand new hockey arena contracts to sell in-arena advertising space to a local insurance firm for $10,000. Later, the hockey team discovers that the market value of the advertising space is actually $100,000, and therefore it refuses to honor the contract. The insurance firm then sues the hockey team for breach of contract. During trial, the attorney for the hockey team claims that the contract lacks mutuality because it is unequal. The judge in such a trial is likely to reject the hockey team's defense, and will probably allow the transaction to go through. However, if the hockey team had contracted to sell the ad space to the insurance firm for an "amount to be negotiated later," the judge would likely rule the contract invalid. The consideration given by the parties lacks mutuality of obligation because it lacks definiteness.

In the professional sports context, the issue of mutuality was predominant in a series of cases in professional baseball in the late 19th century. In *Metropolitan Exhibition Co. v. Ewing*, 42 F. 198 (C.C.D. N.Y. 1890), the defendant had signed a contract with another team after playing the previous season with the plaintiff. The plaintiff claimed that due to the right of reservation, known as the "reserve system," the player was not free to sign with any other club. The court found that the terms of the reserve system were not adequately defined in the contract, so it was unclear what the consideration would be for the following season. Thus, Ewing was allowed to sign with another team. In a similar case, *Metropolitan Exhibition Co. v. Ward*, 9. N.Y.S. 779 (N.Y. Sup. Ct. 1890), the court found that the player contract between Ward and the plaintiff was invalid because of lack of mutuality. The court explained that the reserve system allowed the team to keep a player in perpetuity, while also granting the team the opportunity to terminate the contract on ten days' notice. Because the contract did not express what the teams were obligated to forfeit in exchange for the players' forfeiture of job security and leverage, the contract was revoked. These two cases will be discussed further in section 9.2.2., "Defenses to Standard Player Contract Breaches."

Professional baseball learned something from these cases and altered their player contracts to state that in exchange for a large salary the player agreed to the reserve system and the ten-day termination notice. Professional baseball was confident that the new language would satisfy the obligation of mutuality. In *Philadelphia Ball Club, Ltd. v. Lajoie*, 51 A. 973 (Pa. 1902), the court granted an injunction to the Philadelphia club barring Lajoie from playing for any other team. On the issue of mutuality, the court reasoned:

> The defendant has the possibility of enforcing all the rights for which he stipulated in the agreement, which is all that he can reasonably ask; furthermore, owing to the peculiar nature and circumstances of the business, the reservation upon the part of the plaintiff to terminate upon short notice, does not make the whole contract inequitable.

These early cases enforce the rule that contracts need not be equitable to be enforced, but within the contract itself, there does need to be a stipulation that clearly identifies the consideration, that is, what each party to the contract is giving and receiving (see notes 2 and 3).

The *preexisting duty rule* states that duties imposed by law or by a prior contract will not serve as adequate consideration. For example, a baseball team promises to give its bus driver medical benefits if the driver increases his hours. However, this would be considered inadequate consideration if the team had already promised medical benefits in the bus driver's original contract.

The doctrine of *promissory estoppel* allows the occasional enforcement of a contract that is not supported by consideration. Under this doctrine, a court will enforce a contract with inadequate consideration if a promise is made that the promisor should reasonably expect would, and which does, induce forbearance or reliance on the part of the promisee. For example, assume that an athletic director tells an employee that since she has been a dedicated and hard worker, when she retires, the athletic department will give her $500 per month for the rest of her life. Relying on this statement, the employee does not purchase an additional retirement plan. While there is no valid consideration given, the court may choose to enforce a contract here because the employee relied on the statement of the athletic director (see note 1).

NOTES

1. In 2001, Florida Marlins outfielder Cliff Floyd claimed that National League manager Bobby Valentine promised him a spot on the National League All-Star team. Based on this, Floyd claims that he bought $16,000 in non-refundable plane tickets so that his family could watch him play the All-Star Game in Seattle. Valentine did *not* name Floyd to the All-Star team, and denies that he ever made such a promise to Floyd. Hypothetically, if Floyd could have proven to a judge that Valentine promised him an All-Star spot, it is possible that the judge would have invoked the doctrine of promissory estoppel and forced Valentine to name Floyd to the All-Star team or make him whole (pay him $16,000). Floyd never threatened action over the matter, and the matter was rendered moot when another player's last-minute injury opened up a spot for Floyd on the All-Star team.

2. In the *Matter of Arbitration Between Phoenix Suns and Athletic Union of Constantinople* (1997), the Phoenix Suns sought the services of a basketball player, Iakovos "Jake" Tsakalidis, who was under contract to play for the Greek professional team, AEK, through the 2000 season. Phoenix argued that the contract was null and void for various reasons, including the lack of mutuality, and therefore Tsakalidis should be allowed to exit his

contract without penalty, to play in the NBA. In arbitration, the claimant Suns were successful. The arbitrator ruled that the contract was invalid under Greek law because the "penalty clause" within the contract was illegally severe, and was an excessive curtailment of Tsakalidis's freedom to pursue his basketball career. The Suns were therefore able to sign Tsakalidis because the Greek contract had been nullified. AEK subsequently challenged the arbitrator's decision in an English court, but the court upheld the arbitrator's decision to allow Tsakalidis out of his contract.

3. In the *Matter of Arbitration Between Toronto Raptors and Budocnost* (1997), the Toronto Raptors, in a case similar to the *Tsakalidis* case, sought to gain the services of Aleksandar Radojevic, who was under contract to play for Budocnost of the Yugoslavian Basketball League through the 2000–2001 season. The arbitrator decided that Radojevic's contract with Budocnost was not a valid contract because it did not specify the compensation that would be awarded Radojevic for the final three years of his contract with the team.

9.1.1.4. Legality

Another requirement for an enforceable contract is the *legality* of the underlying agreement. The general rule is that the courts will not enforce a contract that is illegal. The courts are concerned with two types of illegalities: statutory violations and violations of public policy not expressly declared illegal by statute.

Statutory violations include gambling contracts, contracts with unlicensed professionals (doctors, lawyers, accountants), and contracts that violate laws regulating consumer credit transactions (loan sharks).

Contracts that may violate public policy include contracts that waive tort liability and contracts that interfere with family relationships. With these contracts, no general rule for determining their legality can be given, except to say that the more egregious the provisions, the less likely that they will withstand judicial scrutiny. For example, courts would not be likely to uphold a contract of a bungee-jumping company that waives tort liability in the event that the company provides a bungee cord that is too long, and the customer dies (see Chapter 4, section 4.10., "Waiver and Release of Liability"). Another contract clause that might violate public policy is an egregious *covenant not to compete*. A covenant not to compete is a contractual agreement where an employee promises not to work in a similar job in the same industry for a certain period of time after his or her term of employment is completed. Covenants not to compete are frequently contained in coach's contracts (see note 2).

A court or arbitrator's decision to uphold a covenant not to compete also depends on the reasonableness of the geographic scope and length of time. For example, former Indiana University basketball coach Bobby Knight had a noncompete clause in his original 1982 contract saying that he would forfeit his deferred pay if he joined another Big Ten conference team, a state of Indiana team, or a state of Kentucky team after leaving his job at Indiana University. There was some debate about the legality of this clause when Knight was terminated in 2000. While the clause was clear about geographic scope (Big Ten, Indiana, Kentucky), a court or arbitrator might have found that region to be excessively large. Also, the non-compete pact did not dictate any time period, though many such pacts do. The Knight non-compete clause was rendered moot when he accepted a job at Texas Tech University in 2001, since the Big Ten and states of Indiana and Kentucky were not involved. In summary, covenants not to compete are contracts that must be reasonable in terms of scope of work, duration, and scope of geographic location. For more information on Bobby

Knight's contract at Indiana University, see section 9.2.5., "Coaches' Contracts: Professional and Collegiate Sports."

Although both types of illegal contracts (statutory and public policy) are generally unenforceable, the severity of this approach has led courts to seek ways to moderate the impact. The principle of restitution has been used to achieve this moderation. *Restitution* requires that no one who has conferred a benefit or suffered a loss should be unfairly denied compensation. In a case where the underlying bargain is illegal, the court may find it appropriate to reimburse or "make whole" the party who unfairly suffered a loss (see section 9.1.9., "Remedies for a Breach of Contract").

NOTES

1. Secret contracts that violate salary cap rules are illegal under league collective bargaining agreements. In 2000, an independent arbitrator found that the Minnesota Timberwolves had signed a secret contract with Joe Smith in an effort to circumvent the cap. This contract was ruled illegal, and therefore invalid. In addition, the arbitrator upheld Commissioner David Stern's penalty against the Timberwolves of a $3.5 million fine, a loss of five first round draft picks, and a loss of re-signing rights for Smith.

2. Disputes over coaches' "covenants not to compete clauses" can also occur at the professional level. After winning the Super Bowl as head coach of the St. Louis Rams in 2000, Dick Vermeil resigned in the middle of his multiyear deal with the team. The team accepted his resignation, and paid him $500,000 to work as its consultant and a $2 million "thank you" bonus for helping win the Super Bowl championship. Later in 2000, Vermeil accepted a three-year, $10 million contract to become head coach of the Kansas City Chiefs. The Rams protested, claiming that his resignation agreement implied that the sixty-four-year-old Vermeil was retiring from coaching for good. The matter was arbitrated by NFL Commissioner Paul Tagliabue in 2001. He agreed with the Rams, finding that while the agreement did not prohibit Vermeil from seeking a coaching position, "the clear purpose and effect of the agreement . . . was that Vermeil would remain retired from coaching through the 2001 season." Tagliabue transferred a second round and a third round draft pick and $500,000 from the Chiefs in order to "make the Rams whole."

3. Covenant not to compete laws vary from state to state. See Mark A. Kahn, "Non-Compete Agreements and California Law: *Application Group, Inc. v. Hunter Group, Inc,*" 14 *Berkeley Technology Law Journal*, 283 (1999).

4. In *Vanderbilt University* v. *DiNardo*, 174 F.3d 751 (6th Cir. 1999), the defendant football coach unsuccessfully argued that his termination clause was actually a non-compete clause, illegal under Tennessee law.

9.1.1.5. Capacity

In addition to the offer and acceptance, the capacity of a party to make or accept an offer is an important factor in the formation of a valid contract. *Capacity* is defined as the ability to understand the nature and effects of one's acts. If one lacks capacity, that person (and *only* that person) may void the contract. The person who has entered into the contract with a person who lacks capacity cannot void the contract. The general rule with regard to contracts is that anyone who has reached the age of majority (eighteen years of age in most states) and is mentally competent has the capacity to enter into a contract. A contract entered into by a minor, or one who has not yet reached the age of majority, is considered voidable, but only by the minor. A minor has the right to disaffirm a contract before reaching the age of majority and for a certain amount of time after reaching the age of majority. Although minors have the right to disaffirm a contract, they are liable for any tangible benefits they have received or still possess. Like minors, incompetents may be liable for the value of tangible benefits received. However, if one has been adjudicated mentally incompetent and a guardian has been appointed, the contract is void. Finally, one who is extremely intoxicated with drugs or alcohol, and has no awareness of his or her actions, may not have the capacity to enter into an agreement.

Capacity does not only apply to individuals, as members of organizations can have the capacity to bind a corporation to a contract. A corporate agent can be a natural person or another corporation that is authorized to act for the corporation—in signing off on contracts. An athletic director of a college is authorized to bind the school in certain areas; thus the athletic director has corporate capacity to act on behalf of the athletic department and/or school. Likewise, the president of a professional sports team is authorized to act on the team's behalf and therefore has corporate capacity. However, the same team's assistant general manager may not possess corporate capacity.

NOTE

1. For a case involving the capacity of a minor to sign a professional contract, see section 9.2.3., "Tortious Interference" for *Central Red Army Club v. Arena Associates*, 952 F. Supp. 181 (S.D.N.Y, 1997).

9.1.1.6. *Drafting a Contract*

Before reviewing the different contracts one may find in the sports industry, it is important to understand the makeup of a contract. The following explanation offers a brief description of each section in a typical contract.

1. *Opening*. Identifies the parties to the agreement, the date of the contract, and its effective date.
2. *Representations and warranties*. Contains information regarding the rights and qualifications of the parties to enter into an agreement, as well as any express or implied warranties regarding the subject matter of the contract.
3. *Operational language*. Contains the subject matter of the contract. The precise rights and duties of the parties under the contract are explained.
4. *Other clauses*. Certain other clauses may be included, depending on the nature of the contract. Compensation, rights to arbitration for any disagreements, and the right to assign the contract are typical examples.
5. *Termination*. Discusses the length of the contract and the means of ending the contract.
6. *Entire agreement and amendments*. Details the comprehensiveness of the contract and its relation to other agreements, as well as the methods by which the contract can be amended.
7. *Closing*. Contains the signatures of the parties to the contract, any acknowledgments, and the signatures of any witnesses.

9.1.2. Mistakes in Contracts

Mistakes frequently occur in the contracting process. The claim of a mistake is raised by one seeking to rescind the contract or is raised as a defense to avoid liability under the contract. Courts will act differently depending on whether a contractual mistake is unilateral or mutual. *Unilateral mistakes* are those made by one party at the time the contract was formed as to a basic assumption and have an adverse material effect on the agreed exchange. The contract may be voidable by the adversely affected party where the other party actually knew or had reason to know of the mistake at the time the contract was made, or where his fault caused the mistake. For example, if the Skydome in Toronto contracts with the NFL for an exhibition game, the Skydome will assume that the selected teams' starting players will play in the game. If the NFL purposely sends each team's practice squad, it has knowingly misrepresented itself. Another example would be if one professional team knowingly traded a player who was injured to another team, without disclosing the injuries. In this example, there is a possibility the trade could be voided, but there is also the possibility that the team receiving the injured player would have to follow the *caveat emptor* (buyer beware) rule. To protect themselves from this type of situation, teams should make the trades conditional upon the passing of a physical examination (see note 1).

On the other hand, a *mutual mistake* occurs when both parties make a mistake about a basic assumption of the contract. The contract is voidable by the party that is adversely affected. For example, Wahoo University entered into an agreement to purchase 125 football helmets made of a compound called "plastex" from Tribex Corporation. Unknown to both the buyer and the seller, two different compounds called "plastex" could be used to make football helmets. Wahoo University thought it was ordering one form of the compound while Tribex used the other form of "plastex." Courts would void the contract upon the discovery of the mutual mistake, since neither party was aware of the ambiguity.

NOTES

1. When trades occur in professional sports, it is difficult for one team to prove that another team misrepresented the health of a traded player. Teams must generally abide by the principle of *caveat emptor* (buyer beware). In 2001, the Toronto Blue Jays sought relief from MLB Commissioner Bud Selig after at least one of the players received in a six-player trade turned out to be seriously injured. The players had passed an initial physical, but pitcher Mike Sirotka (the key player in the trade from the Chicago White Sox) showed a season-ending shoulder injury in a subsequent physical. The Blue Jays hoped that Selig would rescind the trade, in which they had relinquished star pitcher David Wells. Selig refused to grant the Blue Jays relief, citing the *caveat emptor* rule: "Although there is a dispute about whether certain facts about Sirotka's condition were disclosed before the clubs agreed to the trade, the Toronto club . . . had the opportunity to make the trade conditional [on the passing of a second physical examination]."

2. For more information on how courts interpret mistakes in contracts, see Andrew Kull, "Mistake, Frustration, and the Windfall Principle of Contract Remedies," Vol. 43 *Hastings Law Journal* 1 (November 1991).

9.1.3. Parol Evidence Rule   "We negotiate a contract"

When a written contract is finalized and the parties agree that it represents the final expression of their agreement, the contract may be considered to be an *integration of agreement*. Often a contract will contain an integration clause that stipulates that the written document represents the total agreement between the parties. When this occurs, the contract is considered the *total expression of the agreement*.

The *parol evidence rule* prohibits the admission of oral statements, preliminary agreements, or writings made prior to or at the time of signing that would in any way alter, contradict, or change the written contract. However, this evidence may be used to show the intention of the parties whenever the objective of the contract cannot be ascertained from the language employed. In its strictest form, the parol evidence rule bars any evidence of preliminary agreements, writings, or oral understandings between the parties to an agreement from being introduced in court when the contract was considered integrated at its signing. For example, at some point in negotiations over a professional athlete's player contract, there may have been discussion between the agent and the team over a guaranteed contract for the player. Due to the evolving nature of negotiations, the agent drops the request for a guaranteed contract. Under the parol evidence rule, the player cannot later demand a guaranteed contract because the topic was discussed in negotiations. However, if the player and his agent believe that they did indeed negotiate a guaranteed contract, the player may have the option of using an internal resolution mechanism (grievance procedure) or an external mechanism (court).

9.1.4. Conditions of a Contract

For a contract to be binding, one or more conditions must be met by each of the parties in order for each party to be in compliance with the contract. The non-occurrence of a condition on the part of either party operates to void the contractual duty by the other party. Conditions may be expressed (stated directly in the agreement), implied (tacitly understood between the parties as part of the agreement), or constructive (not agreed upon at all by the parties but imposed by a court to ensure fairness).

Generally there are two types of conditions: a condition precedent and a condition subsequent. A *condition precedent* is one that must occur before a contract will be considered binding on the parties. For example, before a Major League Baseball player's contract is official, the commissioner of Major League Baseball must sign the contract. Without the commissioner's signature, the contract is void. Another example would be if two NCAA basketball schools entered into a regular season game contract for the 2003–2004 season, but with the condition precedent that the contract would only apply if the two teams make the NCAA basketball tournament in the 2002–2003 season. A *condition subsequent* occurs when the parties condition a contract on an event's non-occurrence. For example, assume that a college has decided to open a training facility on campus and has contracted with one company to provide exercise equipment. A condition subsequent would allow the school to break the contract with the supplier and to contract with another supplier in the event that the original supplier does not have the exercise equipment ready by one week prior to the facility's opening.

9.1.5. Statute of Frauds

Certain types of contracts are unenforceable under the *statute of frauds* unless they are in writing. The statute of frauds, which has its roots in English common law, is designed to prevent injustices resulting from fraudulent claims or promises that were never kept. The exact rules vary from state to state. However, most states require that the following contracts must be in writing:

- Contracts for goods over $500
- Any agreement made upon consideration of marriage
- Agreements for the sale of land or of interests in land; an interest in land includes the sale or mortgaging and leasing of real property and the creation of easements
- The contract cannot be performed within one year
- Suretyship agreements (when one party assumes responsibility for another party's debts)
- Promises of executors and administrators to answer out of their own will for the debts or damage caused by the estates that they administer

NOTE _____

1. For information pertaining to the connection between the Statute of Frauds and employment contracts, see Lucy Haroutunian, "Employee, You Have a Job for Life: But Is This Oral Promise Enforceable Under the Statute of Frauds?" 50 *Baylor Law Review* 493 (Spring 1998).

9.1.6. Assignment and Delegation of a Contract

Rights and obligations of a contract may be assigned and duties under a contract may be delegated without nullifying the contract. Generally all rights under a contract may be assigned to another party. When one assigns a contract to another party, he or she gives up all claims under the contract as well. For example, when a professional sports team trades a player to another team, they are assigning that player's contract to a team that did not originally enter into the contract. However, the new team must abide by the player's contract, unless both sides agree to begin negotiations on a new contract. Potential difficulties arising from assignment and delegation of a contract are averted if a player possesses a non-assignment clause or "no-trade" clause.

Delegation of duties under a contract does not create a transfer in the same sense as an assignment, because the original party is not relieved of all obligations under the contract. The delegating party may be held liable for any breaches of the contract even if the breach was caused by the party that was delegated the responsibility. For example, assume a university has a contract with Supplier A for the purchase of ten cases of tennis balls. If Supplier A will not be able to fulfill the agreement on time, it may delegate its duties for the supply of tennis balls to Supplier B. While this delegation is valid, Supplier A will still be liable for any breach in the original contract with the university if Supplier B does not properly fulfill the duties under the contract.

9.1.7. Breach of Contract

A *breach of contract* can be broadly defined as a failure to perform a duty imposed under a contract. A contract may be either *totally* or *partially* breached by any party that has entered into it. A *total* breach of contract occurs when one of the parties has not fully engaged in the specific performance that is outlined in the contract. If one of the parties has engaged in the specific performance outlined in the contract, but not to the exact extent as outlined, there may be a *partial* breach of contract.

Example 1: *Total* Breach of Contract

- Team A and Team B agree to play a total of two basketball games (the first game at Team A's home venue and the second at team B's home venue).
- The contract states that the home team must pay the visiting team $10,000 within one week after each event.
- A day *before* the first game, Team B informs Team A that it will not play the games as agreed upon in the contract.

Example 2: *Partial* Breach of Contract

- Team A and Team B agree to play a total of two basketball games (the first game at Team A's home venue and the second at Team B's home venue).
- The contract states that the home team must pay the visiting team $10,000 within one week after each event.
- A day *after* the first game is played, Team B informs Team A that it will not play the second game as agreed upon in the contract.

The distinction between *total* and *partial* breach of contract is important because of the burden placed on the aggrieved party. A total breach (example 1) discharges the aggrieved party of any duty to perform, and the aggrieved party may immediately file suit. Therefore, in example 1, Team A becomes released from its obligations in the contract. It may immediately sue Team B to recover damages for such things as advertising and lost concession revenues for the canceled event (see subsection 9.1.9., "Remedies for a Breach of Contract"), and it is not obligated to travel to Team B's arena for the second game. A partial breach (example 2) may not discharge the aggrieved party from a duty to perform, but the aggrieved party may file suit immediately to collect any damages that are due. In other words, Team A may still have to pay Team B its $10,000 guarantee for the first game, despite the breach of contract. However, it may file suit for damages suffered due to the partial breach by Team B (lost television revenue, etc). According to *Restatement of Contracts*, a party cannot simultaneously sue for total and partial breach.

Litigation for breach of contract often occurs relative to players' or coaches' contracts such as in *Alabama Football Inc. v. Stabler* (see note 4).

NOTES

1. Temple University and the University of Cincinnati's men's basketball teams scheduled a pair of basketball games, one to be played on Cincinnati's home court in 1999–2000 and one to be played on Temple's home court in 2000–2001. The two teams played the game in the 1999–2000 season, as scheduled. However, Cincinnati canceled the 2000–2001 game when it learned that it had mistakenly scheduled too many regular season games according to NCAA rules. Unfortunately for Temple, its athletic department did not have time to find another opponent for a makeup home game. Temple estimated that it lost $100,000 in expected revenue. The schools then entered into a handshake agreement whereby the schools would play two games on Temple's home court in future seasons and Cincinnati would reimburse Temple for reasonable expenses from the canceled game (e.g., reprinting schedule cards). While Cincinnati offered to make up the game in a future season, Temple still sent an $85,000 bill to Cincinnati, contending that a makeup game would not be sufficient to make it whole. Cincinnati found that amount to exceed reasonable reimbursement costs. Cincinnati grudgingly paid the $85,000 bill, but Athletic Director Bob Goin canceled the future games, vowing to never play Temple again during his tenure.

2. In *Rayle v. Bowling Green State University*, 739 N.E. 2d 1260 (Ct. Cl. Ohio 2000), a seat license/season ticket holder brought a breach of contract suit against a university after the university refunded his deposit when he refused to pay an increased annual service charge on his seats. The court held that the university did not breach contract by refunding the plaintiff's money, but instead that the plaintiff had breached contract by refusing to pay the annual service charge on his seats after he was notified that the fee would increase. The court also held that the university may reasonably increase the value of their seats, and reallocate seats when their customers refuse to pay the charges.

3. Season ticket holders of the Cincinnati Bengals, unhappy with their seating location in the newly constructed Paul Brown Stadium, filed a breach of contract suit against the team and Hamilton County in September 2000. The team had sold season tickets prior to a change in stadium design. The change in the stadium design reduced the number of seating zones from forty-nine to forty, thus pushing many season ticket holders farther from the most desirable middle-of-the-field seats. The team, county, and ticket holders settled the case in June 2001, prior to trial. In the settlement, ticket holders were given the option of either taking a partial cash refund and keeping their seats, or changing seats with no cash refund. Under the settlement, county taxpayers would be liable for a maximum of $2.5 million, which is the total of the refunds going to the 1,750 season ticket holders.

4. In *Alabama Football Inc. v Stabler*, 319 So.2d 678 (Ala. 1975), Ken Stabler, a successful quarterback with the Oakland Raiders, sought damages after his contract with the WFL's Alabama franchise was breached. In 1973, he signed a lucrative deal with Alabama that included a signing bonus of $100,000 to be distributed in $50,000 increments in 1973 and 1974. The team paid the first $50,000, and then paid the next $20,000, but failed to pay the remaining $30,000. Stabler filed suit claiming breach of contract, and was declared a free agent. The court held that financial condition was not an excuse for non-performance of a contract, therefore the Alabama franchise's inability to pay Stabler constituted a breach of contract.

5. For information pertaining to international breach of contract issues, see Elbi Janse van Vuuren, "Termination of International Commercial Contracts for Breach of Contract," 15 *Arizona Journal of International and Comparative Law* (Spring 1998): 583.

9.1.8. Defenses to a Breach of Contract

In a breach of contract case, the defense will usually attempt to *attack the elements* of the contract and prove that a contract did not exist. Concerning the element of offer, the defense in a breach of contract case may argue that the offer was a solicitation and should be considered preliminary negotiation rather than a legal contract offer. Concerning the element of acceptance, the defense may argue that the contract in question is not whole because the proper acceptance was not achieved. For example, in Major League Baseball, a new player contract is not considered official unless the commissioner has signed the contract.

If a party cannot successfully attack the validity of the contract, there are three defenses to a breach of contract suit: *impossibility of performance, frustration of purpose*, and *impracticability*. *Impossibility of performance* occurs when a party to the contract promises something that becomes impossible to perform through no fault of his or her own. This defense is used when the subject matter is destroyed, the action required under the contract becomes illegal, or there is death or incapacity of one of the parties to the contract. For example, if a facility has a contract to host a tennis tournament, but the facility is destroyed by a tornado, it is impossible for the facility to host the event. Even if the event has to be canceled due to rain, a court may accept the defense of impossibility of performance, although this issue is usually addressed in the contract.

The defense of *frustration of purpose* is used when the value of performance to be obtained becomes useless to a party because of an unforeseen change in the circumstances. For example, a college signs a contract with a landscaping company to landscape the college's golf course. However, if the state government decided to take possession of the land by eminent domain to build a highway, the purpose for which the university contracted would be frustrated.

The final defense for a breach of contract suit is *impracticability*. This defense can be used when the cost of performance is greatly increased due to an unforeseen occurrence. This is a narrowly interpreted defense and is rarely used. The courts will allow performance to be excused under this defense in cases of war, embargo, or crop failure. If the defense can prove any of these three defenses, the court may not grant relief to the complaining party.

9.1.9. Remedies for a Breach of Contract

There are three primary remedies for a breach of contract: monetary damages, specific performance, and negative injunction.

For reasons described later, courts normally prefer to implement the first of the three remedies for breach of contract, monetary damages. Monetary damages can be determined by three different methods:

- *expectation* interest
- *reliance* interest
- *restitution* interest.

Based on the facts of the case, a plaintiff will usually use one of these three methods when arguing for monetary damages. An *expectation* interest is the benefit that a party *expects* to get as the result of a contract; a *reliance* interest is the loss suffered by a party when it makes expenditure decisions after relying on another party's unfulfilled contractual promise; a *restitution* interest is that which restores a party to its condition prior to the formation of an unfulfilled contractual promise.

To illustrate the way in which the remedies may be distributed in a particular case, consider the following hypothetical example. The International Olympic Committee (IOC) chooses Toronto, Canada, to host the 2008 winter Olympics. In preparation for the event, $15 million is spent renovating existing buildings and constructing a needed short-track speed skating facility. In addition, $5 million is spent advertising the Olympics, and $2 million is spent luring advertisers to the project. Financial officers from the Toronto group anticipate that profits from the event will surpass $20 million. A year before the Olympics in Toronto, a scandal is discovered that links the Toronto delegation to fraud. In response, the IOC strips the Games from Toronto and awards them to Stockholm, Sweden. The Toronto group files suit against the IOC for breach of contract. Assume that the case is decided in favor of Toronto, with a finding that there was no fraudulent behavior by the Toronto delegation.

The court's monetary damage award would depend on whether it based its decision on an expectation, reliance, or restitution interest. Under *expectation* interest, the court could force the IOC to reimburse Toronto for any profit it might have expected to derive from the games, in this case $20 million. Under *reliance* theory, the court could hold the IOC responsible for all the costs Toronto incurred by relying on the contract to host the 2008 Games. In this case $15 million spent on construction, $5 million spent on advertising, and $2 million spent luring advertisers to the project. Under *restitution* interest, the court could require the IOC to reimburse to the Toronto party any payments made to the IOC in connection with securing the Olympic bid. Therefore, the reliance theory would be the argument Toronto would likely make, since it yields a possible damage award of $22 million.

One problem with monetary damages is that the aggrieved party must be able to translate the injury into a financial sum and be able to justify that amount to the court. Also, there are times when monetary damages would be inadequate compensation for the breach of contract. Thus, a second type of remedy for breach of contract is equitable relief. One type of equitable relief is *specific performance*. *Specific performance* requires the performance of a contract in the specific form in which it was made. For example, if a contract for the sale of land is breached, the court could require the defendant to give up the land as stipulated in the contract. A sport-related example might concern sports memorabilia. For example, a fan catches a historic home-run ball and decides to sell the ball to a collector for $2000. The next day, the fan hears that the ball could be worth up to a million dollars, so he decides not to follow through with the original contract with the collector, and instead seek other offers. The court could order specific performance and require the fan to sell the ball to the collector for $2000, because of the uniqueness of the item and the inability of the collector to go out and buy a replacement.

It is important to note that courts rarely require a contract for personal services, like a coach or player's contract, to be specifically performed. The courts usually reason that this would be a form of indentured servitude. Indentured servants are those who are obligated under a contractual obligation to another. The Thirteenth Amendment to the U.S. Constitution prohibits indentured servitude and slavery. Therefore, in cases where monetary damages would be insufficient, a common reaction on the part of the aggrieved party is to appeal to the courts for a *negative injunction* rather than specific performance. This second type of equitable relief forbids a party from providing services for parties other than the aggrieved party. For example, if a player leaves a team midway through a contract and signs with a team in another league, the team that held the original contract would attempt to get an injunction stopping the player from playing for the other team in the other league. Most sports leagues have systems of arbitration in place in their collective bargaining agreements to prevent such litigation. However, if one of the aggrieved parties is not covered by the arbitration agreement, or if a party believes that the arbitrators failed to follow proper procedure (see Chapter 11, section 11.3.13., "Arbitration"), the issue may end up in court. It may also wind up in court if two teams from different leagues are involved.

For example in *Boston Celtics Limited Partnership v. Shaw*, 908 F.2d 1041 (1st Cir. 1990), basketball player Brian Shaw signed a two-year contract with Il Messaggero Rona (Italian League team) in 1989, with the second year voidable if he decided to play in the NBA. If such a decision was made, he would have to inform Il Messaggero between June 20 and July 20, 1990, of his decision to leave. In January 1990, Shaw signed a five-year contract with the NBA's Boston Celtics, to begin after he had rescinded his contract with Il Messaggero during the designated period. On June 6, 1990, Shaw informed the Celtics that he would play out his contract with Il Messaggero and would join the Celtics one year later than the contract stated. The Celtics took the matter to arbitration, arguing that Shaw was not abiding by the terms of the contract because of his decision to stay with Il Messaggero for the 1990–1991 season. The arbitrator ruled in favor of the Celtics. Shaw then defied the arbitrator's rule and prepared to play in Italy. The Celtics requested relief from federal district court, requiring Shaw to rescind his contract in Italy and play for the Celtics. The Celtics received a negative injunction to keep Shaw from playing with Il Messaggero for the 1990–1991 season. Shaw appealed the decision, claiming that the arbitrator had failed to follow proper procedure; that he had signed the contract in a weak moment while he was homesick (lack of mental capacity); and that he was not represented by an agent during negotiations with the Celtics. The court found that the arbitrator did follow proper procedures, and that Shaw was a "college graduate" and veteran player of proper mental capacity to understand the standard player contract.

9.2. TYPES OF ATHLETIC CONTRACTS

The previous sections of this chapter showed how contract law, in general, applies to the business of sports. The remainder of this chapter deals with contract issues that are more specific to the sports world. In the sports industry, officials, administrators, players, and companies will be involved in a wide variety of contractual agreements: coaches' contracts, players' contracts, facility contracts, licensing contracts, physicians' contracts, officials' contracts, equipment contracts, and others. The following sections include examples of contracts at the inter-scholastic, collegiate, professional, and Olympic levels. While this section will by no means cover *every* type of athletic contract, it will provide various different contracts and precedent setting cases in various segments of the sports industry. (See exhibit 9.1.)

9.2.1. Standard Player Contract

A Standard Player Contract or Uniform Player Contract contains many unique provisions that separate it from other employment contracts, due to the unique nature of sport. Most professional sports leagues require that teams use standard player contracts exclusively when they employ a player. In other words, even prior to the advent of collective bargaining in sports (see Chapter 11, section 11.2., "Collective Bargaining"), teams were not allowed to hire players in a "handshake" deal, and written contracts had to conform to certain uniform criteria. Historically, certain items in uniform contracts benefited teams to the detriment of players (e.g., the reserve clause). However, some items in the standard contract are beneficial to players. For example, in most leagues the Collective Bargaining Agreement prevents teams from requiring a player to pay for his/her own lodging and travel expenses. It can be argued that some type of uniformity is advantageous to all parties involved—players, agents, teams, and the league. A lack of uniformity would force the parties to devote much more time to reviewing contracts, thereby hindering each group's ability to transact business efficiently.

While player contracts are "standard" or "uniform," that does not mean they are entirely inflexible. If allowed by existing agreements (league bylaws, Collec-

Exhibit 9.1
Typical Clauses in a Sports Contract

CONTRACT

Opening — This Agreement made and entered into this 1st day September 20 XX, by and between the athletic authorities of Powerhouse University and the athletic authorities of Anyschool University, stipulates:

Representations & Warranties — First: Whereas, Powerhouse University and Anyschool University are the owners to the rights for their individual basketball teams to compete in NCAA intercollegiate competition.

Second: That the basketball (men's) teams representing the above named institutions shall meet and play at_____ (site) _____ on_____ (date) , 20____, and at _____ on_____ ,20_____.

Operational Language — Third: That in consideration of playing this game,

(1) That the Host Team shall provide the Visiting Team one rights-free radio outlet for the broadcast of the game by its designated radio station and/or network.

(2) That television rights to the game remain property of the Big Time Conference and the Powerhouse University.

(3) That the Host Team shall provide the Visiting Team with forty (40) complimentary tickets.

(4) That a minimum of 200 tickets shall be made available for sale to the Visiting Team, but that unsold tickets be returned to the Home Team no later than 72 hours prior to the game.

Other Clauses — Fourth: That the officials for the game shall be provided by the conference.

Fifth: That the game shall be played under the eligibility rules of the respective institutions.

Sixth: Either party failing to comply with condition of Article One, either by cancellation or failure to appear, shall forfeit

Termination — money in the amount of Big $$ unless such cancellation shall be by mutual consent, in which case this agreement shall be null and void.

Entire Agreement and Amendments — Seventh: This agreement constitutes the entire agreement and understanding between Powerhouse University and Anyschool University and cancels, terminates and supersedes any prior agreement or understanding relating to the game contest. There are no representations, agreements, warranties, covenants or undertakings other than those contained herein. None of the provisions of this Agreement may be waived or modified except expressly in writing signed by both parties. However, failure of either party to require the performance of any term in this Agreement or the waiver by either party of any breach thereof shall not prevent subsequent enforcement of such term nor be deemed a waiver of any subsequent breach.

Closing — Witnessed by: Powerhouse University

_____   _____
Business Manager   Director of Athletics
of Athletics

Witnessed by: Anyschool University
                                 (Visiting Institution)

_____   _____
Business Manager   Director of Athletics
of Athletics

tive Bargaining Agreements), parties may negotiate player "bonuses" or perquisites (perks) for players, as well as restrictions on players. These perks may include the use of a private plane or a larger hotel room. Sometimes teams may attempt to negotiate a clause allowing a team to terminate the contract of a player with a history of drug abuse in the event that the player suffers a relapse (see Chapter 7, section 7.2.4.1., "National Football League").

The following examples illustrate some of the provisions found in player contracts in the major professional leagues.

9.2.1.1. Reserve or Option Clause

The Player Contract has changed significantly since it was introduced in professional baseball in the early 1880s. At that time, the contract was a one-page document which simply stated that the player would play for the designated club for a period of one year. At first, the contracts were interpreted to mean that after the player played the year, he had the choice of signing a new contract with another team. However, when competitive bidding for players caused their salaries to increase, owners initiated the "reserve system." This rule allowed each team to designate five players that no other team could sign. Soon after, the reserve system was expanded to include the entire team, and the standard player contract was modified to include a statement that gave the team an "option" on the players' services in the year following the expiration of the contract. Players signed a contract each year, effectively giving the team the right to that player in perpetuity until it no longer wanted the player.

Players fought this restriction in the courts, using contract law as the basis for their arguments. Initially, courts were sympathetic to the players, and ruled that the one-sided contracts were not enforceable. However, in the twelve years that elapsed between the *Ewing* and *Ward* decisions and the *Lajoie* decision, the owners modified the language in the player contract so that mutuality of obligation was explicitly stated (see section 9.1.1.3., "Consideration"). The players were, in effect, agreeing to abide by the restrictive reserve system in exchange for higher salaries.

Due to the success of the MLB Player Contract in curtailing players' salaries, other professional sport leagues, including the NHL, NBA, and NFL, employed the use of the Standard Player Contract. Each league's reserve clause withstood legal scrutiny until players began challenging their respective systems under *antitrust* theory instead of under *contract* law (see Chapter 10, section 10.2., "Application of Antitrust Law to Professional Sports"). In 1976, the "option" in Major League Baseball's Standard Player Contract was deemed by an arbitrator to be valid only for one year, and was not meant to bind a player to a team in perpetuity. In *Messersmith/McNally* (see note 1), an arbitration panel ruled that when a player plays out the option year of his contract, he is considered to be a free agent. Since the successful challenges of reserve systems, teams must negotiate with players' unions in order to install very limited versions of reserve clauses into a Player Contract and/or Collective Bargaining Agreement. Therefore, a Standard Player Contract may bind a player to a team for a period of years, but *not* in perpetuity.

NOTE

1. Messersmith/McNally is the shorthand name of the case for *In re Twelve Clubs Comprising National League of Professional Baseball Clubs and Twelve Clubs Comprising*

American League of Professional Baseball Clubs, Los Angeles and Montreal Clubs and Major League Baseball Players Association, Grievance Nos. 75-27 and 75-23, Seitz, Chairman of Arbitration Panel, December 23, 1975. It is the case that paved the way for free agency in baseball. (For more, see Chapter 11, "Labor Law.")

9.2.1.2. *Unique Skill Provisions*

Unique skill provisions are contained not only in the Standard Player Contracts of professional athletes, but also in the contracts of many coaches and entertainers. Understanding these provisions requires an understanding of *remedies for a breach of contract* (see section 9.1.9.). As previously discussed, the courts have three options when a party violates a contract: monetary damages, specific performance, and negative injunctions. As a general rule, the more unique the skill involved, the more difficult it is for a court to award monetary damages. For example, if a carpenter or telephone operator signs an employment contract, and then quits his/her job before completing the term of the contract, his/her skills can be replaced. It may cost the employer a significant amount of money to replace the employee (advertising the position, training the replacement employee), but courts can remedy such a breach with *monetary damages.* However, if Alex Rodriguez were to breach his contract with the Texas Rangers, in order to play for an upstart rival baseball league, it would be virtually impossible for the Rangers to replace him. Even if the courts forced Rodriguez and the "rival baseball league" to pay the Rangers $1 billion in monetary damages, the Rangers would not be able to use that money to replace Rodriguez (there are no comparable shortstops who are on the open market), and thus the Rangers could not be made whole.

In 1902, Napoleon Lajoie was analogous to Alex Rodriguez—a leading slugger at a middle infield position; baseball's most coveted and unique commodity at the time (see note 1). Consequently, when Lajoie jumped from the National League to the rival American League, it was relatively easy for his attorneys to convince the court that he possessed *unique skills.*

In the years since *Lajoie,* professional sport leagues have drafted the Standard Player Contract so that the unique skills provision applies to all players, not just the superstars. For example, the NHL player contract states:

> Section 6: The player represents and agrees that he has exceptional and unique knowledge, skill and ability as a hockey player, the loss of which cannot be estimated with certainty and cannot be fairly or adequately compensated by damages. The Player therefore agrees that the Club shall have the right, in addition to any other rights which the Club may possess, to enjoin him by appropriate injunctive proceedings without first exhausting any other remedy which may be available to the Club, from playing hockey for any other team and/or for any breach of any of the other provisions of this contract. (1995 NHL Collective Bargaining Agreement)

In other words, by signing the Standard Player Contract the player is allowing the league to seek a *negative injunction* rather than *monetary damages.* This provision has been put to the test in cases such as *Shaw* (see section 9.1.9., "Remedies for a Breach of Contract," and *Central New York Basketball, Inc. v. Barnett* (see note 2). Unlike Napoleon Lajoie, neither of the players at issue in these cases was a superstar of his respective era. Nevertheless, the holdings in both cases suggest that courts will consider all players, even "role" players, unique and indispensable to a club. Courts will issue negative injunctions to prevent such players from breaching their contracts and playing for teams in other leagues.

NOTES

1. In 1901, Lajoie won the American League triple crown and had the highest fielding average of any second baseman. He ranks third, trailing only Babe Ruth and Willie Mays, on the list of the top players in the history of baseball, according to John Thorn, Pete Palmer, and Michael Gershman, *Total Baseball*, 7th ed. (Kingston, N.Y.: Total Sports Publishing, 2001).

2. In *Central New York Basketball, Inc. v. Barnett*, 19 Ohio Op.2d 130, 181 N.E. 2d 506 (Ohio C.P. 1961), the Syracuse NBA franchise filed a breach of contract suit against player Richard Barnett, after Barnett signed a contract with the Cleveland franchise in the rival ABL. The Syracuse team contended that (1) Barnett had entered into a verbal contract to return to Syracuse and (2) even if Barnett did *not* enter into a verbal contract (as Barnett claimed), the Syracuse team held a legally binding renewal clause that allowed the club to retain his services. The court agreed, and enjoined Barnett from playing for Cleveland (negative injunction), adding that basketball players' unique skills make them more difficult to replace than employees in other industries. "Whether Barnett ranks with the top basketball players or not . . . he is of peculiar and particular value for plaintiff."

9.2.1.3. *Hierarchy of Contracts*

What separates a professional athlete's Employment Contract from other employment contracts is the fact that professional athletes are bound by several other agreements, including a Collective Bargaining Agreement. To address the fact that athletes in professional sports leagues play under an individual contract and a Collective Bargaining Agreement, the Standard Player Contract may include a provision that deals with this issue. Section 18 of the NHL Standard Player Contract reads:

> Section 18. The Club and the Player severally and mutually promise and agree to be legally bound by the Constitution and By-Laws of the League and by any Collective Bargaining Agreement that has been or may be entered into between the member clubs of the League and the NHLPA, and by all of the terms and provisions thereof, copies of which shall be open and available for inspection by the Club, its directors and officers, and the Player, at the main office of the League, the main office of the Club and the main office of the NHLPA. This Contract is entered into subject to the Collective Bargaining Agreement between the NHL and the NHLPA and any provisions of this Contract inconsistent with such Collective Bargaining Agreement are superseded by the provisions of the Collective Bargaining Agreement.

Therefore, the Player Contract cannot contain language that is contradictory to the Collective Bargaining Agreement between the players' union and the league, or to the league's Constitution and Bylaws. For example, a baseball player and MLB team could not draw up a contract for the player to play for $100 per game (even if the player was willing to do so) if the Collective Bargaining Agreement stipulates that teams must pay players a salary of at least $200,000 per season.

9.2.1.4. *Player Exclusivity*

Because owners pay millions of dollars to field a team, they want certain assurances that the players they sign to multimillion-dollar deals will not sustain injury in an activity that is not related to that athlete's primary sport. To address this issue, Uniform Player Contracts contain player exclusivity clauses, which allow teams to limit a player's physical activity during the off-season or his participating in activities that may cause injury, such as beach volleyball, in-line skating, or skydiving. For example, Section 7 of the NHL Standard Player Contract reads: (see note 3)

> The Player and the Club recognize and agree that the Players' participation in other sports may impair or destroy his ability and skill as a hockey player. Accordingly the Player agrees that he will not during the period of his contract or during any period when he is obligated under this Contract to enter into further contract with the Club engage or participate in football, baseball, softball, hockey, lacrosse, boxing, wrestling or other athletic sport without the written consent of the Club, which consent will not be unreasonably denied.

Occasionally, players get permission to play in two different professional sports leagues. Deion Sanders, Bo Jackson, and Brian Jordan all played simultaneously in the NFL and MLB. Multiple-sport players are the exception, but those who do play two sports professionally will have language written into their respective player contracts that address the situation.

NOTES

1. New England Patriots running back Robert Edwards was seriously injured during a beach football game during Pro Bowl weekend in 1999. The Patriots initially claimed Edwards had violated his Player Contract, and thus was not entitled to compensation. Edwards contended that the event was league-sponsored because it was part of Pro Bowl weekend, a league-sanctioned event. The situation was further complicated by the fact that participants in the beach football game had signed waivers absolving the NFL of any liability. However, the Patriots and the NFL did eventually agree to compensate Edwards for the $3 million that remained on his five-year $5.75 million contract.

2. Players have been terminated with cause due to injuries sustained in forbidden activities. In 1994, the Atlanta Braves terminated the guaranteed contract of outfielder Ron Gant after he broke his leg in an off-season motorcycle accident. Carney Lansford (1991) and Paul Quantrill (1999) were both injured in off-season snowmobiling accidents. The Oakland Athletics had the option of terminating Lansford's guaranteed contract but chose not to do so. The Blue Jays had the right to terminate Quantrill by paying him one-sixth of the amount remaining on his contract. The two sides instead restructured his contract with incentives based on the number of days spent on the active roster.

3. NHL Standard Player Contract was quoted from the Collective Bargaining Agreement, which was negotiated on August 11, 1995, and taking retroactive effect as of September 16, 1993. This agreement expires in September 2004.

9.2.1.5. Assignability

In professional sports, players are often traded during the course of their contract. The Standard Player Contract details what rights the player has if a trade occurs. Section 17 of the NFL Standard Player Contract clearly states that during the term of a contract, a player may be traded, and must report to his new team or risk suspension or fine:

> Section 17. Assignment. Unless this contract specifically provides otherwise, Club may assign this contract and Player's services under this contract to any successor to Club's franchise or to any other Club in the League. Player will report to the

assignee Club promptly upon being informed of the assignment of his contract and will faithfully perform his services under this contract. The assignee Club will pay Players necessary traveling expenses in reporting to it and will faithfully perform this contract with Player.

The Major League Baseball contract goes into more detail in outlining the method of payment. According to the MLB Standard Player Contract, the team that trades the player is known as the assignor, and the team that traded for the player is the assignee. MLB has the following language in the Standard Player Contract that outlines the obligations of the assignor and assignee in the case of a trade:

> After a trade, all rights and obligations of the assignor club transfer to the assignee club, provided that:
> 1. The assignor Club is liable to pay the Player for services rendered up to the date he is traded;
> 2. The assignee Major League Club is obligated to pay the player the amount stated in Paragraph 5 for the remainder of the term of the contract as such is stated in Paragraph 5;
> 3. Unless the assignor and assignee agree otherwise, if the assignee club is a National Association Club, the assignee Club is liable only to pay the Player at the rate usually paid by the assignee Club to other Players of similar skill and ability in its classification. Therefore, the assignor Club is liable to pay the difference of the remainder of the term of the contract between an amount agreed to in Paragraph 5 and the amount paid by the assignee Club.

If a player refuses to report to the new team he has been traded to, the team may go to arbitration to enforce the contract with the player. If the player continues to withhold his services, the team may seek damages, and will continue to hold the contract until its expiration.

9.2.1.6. Bonus Clauses

Bonus provisions are often used in player contracts, especially for players in the "skilled" positions, but bonus clauses are not a required feature of a Standard Player Contract. There have been many instances where bonus clauses have been written in an ambiguous manner, which has led to disputes over whether the bonus provision has been met or fulfilled. For example in *In the Matter of Arbitration Between Alan Page and the Minnesota Vikings, July 23, 1973*, Page, a member of the Minnesota Vikings, signed a contract in 1972 that read "shall receive a bonus in the amount of $2,500 if he is selected 'All-Pro' by any of the following: AP, UPI, PFW, or *The Sporting News*." Page was named to the second team All-NFL squad by the AP, and was chosen as a defensive tackle on the All-NFC team, as selected by *The Sporting News*. Page sought to claim his bonus, and the Vikings refused, claiming he had not made "All-Pro" status. The arbitrator found that because the player had received the highest award possible by the AP, he was entitled to his bonus.

Therefore, to alleviate the potential for litigation or arbitration, bonus provisions must be written in a specific and comprehensive manner. For example, the following example is not specific enough:

> Said player shall receive a bonus in the amount of $250,000 if he is one of the top three kickers in the National Football League.

This language does not indicate what type of kicker this provision is for (i.e., punter, field goal kicker, combined punter/field goal kicker) nor what statistical category would be used (i.e., total versus average yards). A more detailed provision might read:

> Said player, a punter, shall receive a bonus in the amount of $250,000 if he finishes in the top three punters for total yards (most yards punted) for the 1999–2000 regular season National Football League schedule.

This more detailed language will protect the interests of both the team and the player, and reduces the likelihood of litigation.

NOTES

1. In *Arbitration Between Patrick Ewing and the New York Knickerbockers (Collins, 1991)*, the issue revolved around a provision in Ewing's contract that stated he would be able to void the 1991 year from his contract if four other players earned more "salary compensation" than Ewing. Prior to the 1991 season, it was clear that three others would make more than Ewing, but there was a dispute concerning Larry Bird's contract. Bird had signed a one-year contract for $2,200,000 plus a $4,870,000 bonus. Ewing calculated Bird's salary compensation at $7,070,000 rather than $2,200,000, (as the Knicks contended). The arbitrator found in favor of the Knicks, reasoning that there was no definition of "salary compensation" in Ewing's contract. Therefore, Ewing was behind only three other players in terms of salary and was not entitled to terminate the final year of his contract.

2. In the *Matter of Arbitration Between Major League Baseball Players Association (Dennis Lamp) and The Toronto Blue Jays* (1987), the issue was whether or not Blue Jays relief pitcher Dennis Lamp was intentionally held out of games during the final weeks of the season in an effort to deter him from reaching the requisite number of appearances in his contract to guarantee a contract extension. Arbitrator George Nicolau ruled for the Blue Jays, stating that the decision on whether or not to pitch Lamp was one for the field manager, and that there was no evidence that the decision not to pitch Lamp was based on any directive from the Blue Jay front office in an effort to deny Lamp his contract extension.

9.2.1.7. Health Regulations

Because the threat of injury in professional sports is prevalent, both owners and players want to ensure that in the event of injury, each side is protected in one way or another. Collective Bargaining Agreements contain provisions that stipulate what remedies are available in the case of injury, either temporary or career-ending. The Standard Player Contract also may contain language that protects the clubs from paying large salaries to unhealthy players. Consequently, contracts often require a player to adhere to a team's medical advice, and allow the team to penalize him (or in some cases terminate him) if he refuses to do so (see note 1). However, unions have negotiated clauses into CBA's allowing a player to seek a second medical opinion if a team doctor makes a decision regarding surgery or other invasive procedure. The MLB Standard Player Contract contains the following language:

> Regulation 2. The Player, when requested by the Club, must submit to a complete physical examination at the expense of the Club, and if necessary to treatment by a regular physician or dentist in good standing. Upon refusal of the Player to submit

to a complete medical or dental examination, the Club may consider such refusal a violation of this regulation and may take such action as it deems advisable under regulation 5 [fine/suspension] of this contract. (1996 MLB Collective Bargaining Agreement)

There is a clause in the Major League Collective Bargaining Agreement which allows the player to seek a second medical opinion. The club shall pay the cost for the second evaluation if the physician is on the accepted list of medical specialists chosen by the clubs. Expenses for second evaluations by medical specialists who are not on the accepted listing will be authorized and paid only by prior mutual agreement between the Player and the Club (see 1996 MLB Collective Bargaining Agreement Article XIII D).

NOTES

1. Los Angeles Clippers player Rodney Rogers filed a grievance, claiming that the team had improperly fined him for being overweight. Rogers's contract contained a weight clause requiring his weight to be checked twice per month from July, and also allowing the club to fine him for being overweight. Rogers returned to training camp after the prolonged NBA lockout of 1998–1999 at thirty-three pounds over his promised weight. The team assumed that he was also overweight during the lockout, even though the twice-monthly weigh-ins never occurred. Arbitrator Roger Kaplan ruled in 2000 that the Clippers had no right to fine Rogers for being overweight during the lockout, and required the team to return to him $716,464 in improper fines. However, Kaplan ruled that Rogers *was* liable for the $197,560 in fines for the time it took for him to reach his contracted weight after the first weigh-in.

2. The NBA Uniform Player Contract has a provision that waives the player's right to sue an NBA team for the violent actions of one of its players. Paragraph 6(c) requires the player to waive any claims he may have as a result of violent conduct that occurs during an exhibition, practice, or game. It is important to note that this provision does not stop the player from filing suit against the player who acted in a violent way (see Chapter 3, section 3.3., "Intentional Torts"). The need for this provision arose out of a suit filed by Houston Rocket coach Rudy Tomjanovich against the Los Angeles Lakers. In *Tomjanovich v. California Sports Inc.*, No. H-78–243, 1979 U.S. Dist. LEXIS 9282 (S.D. Tex. Oct. 10, 1979), the plaintiff alleged that Laker forward Kermit Washington punched Tomjanovich in the face, causing fractures of the nose, jaw, and skull, facial lacerations, and a brain concussion. Instead of suing Washington for an intentional tort, Tomjanovich sued the Lakers under respondeat superior (vicarious liability). The jury in the case awarded Tomjanovich $3.6 million. Tomjanovich settled out of court with the Lakers after the decision was appealed. The Houston Rockets sued the Lakers for the loss of Tomjanovich's services, and settled out of court.

9.2.1.8. Full Performance

The matter of whether or not a contract "tolls" during player "holdouts" or retirements is addressed in certain standard player contracts. The absence of such a clause might result in litigation or arbitration, as occurred between the NHL's Ottawa Senators and Alexi Yashin.

The Senators of the NHL filed a breach of contract complaint against their star player Yashin, after he held out for increased salary during the entire 1999–2000 season. Since the season would have been the last of Yashin's multi-year contract, he demanded to be granted free agency after the 1999–2000 season. However, the Senators believed that Yashin owed the team another year, since he did not play for the Senators in the final contract year specified by the contract. This matter of whether or not a contract "tolls" during player holdouts had been addressed in the NFL and NBA Collective Bargaining Agreements (a Standard Player Contract does not expire until "full performance" is given). However, the matter was not addressed in any previous NHL collective bargaining document.

When the matter went to arbitration, arbitrator Lawrence Holden ruled that Yashin could not become a free agent until he honored the last year of his contract, even though the player's association (NHLPA) had explicitly rejected the NHL's attempts to insert a "full performance" clause in the previous Collective Bargaining Agreement (CBA). Holden was compelled by the NHL's argument that the league was merely attempting to codify the "full performance" provision, and that its absence from the CBA doesn't mean that it was not implied.

Yashin honored the arbitrator's decision and returned to the Senators for the 2000–2001 season (see note 1). The precedent in the Yashin case means that teams currently hold a player's "full performance" rights in the NHL, NBA, and NFL until the player finishes the contracted number of years. There is currently no precedent-setting case or explicit Standard Player Contract clause governing the issue in Major League Baseball (see note 3). Certain legal scholars may argue that the "full performance" rule is implied (see note 2). However, the *Yashin* arbitration decision is not a precedent for Major League Baseball.

NOTES _____

1. After Yashin returned to the Senators for the 2000–2001 season, Senators owner Rod Bryden wanted to sue Yashin for $930,000, for damages that resulted from Yashin's holdout. Bryden arrived at the $930,000 figure by arguing that if Yashin had not held out during the 1999–2000 season, the club would have reached the second round of the playoffs. Bryden agreed to drop the suit when Yashin agreed to make a charitable contribution of more than $100,000 (Canadian) to the Ottawa Hospital.

2. In Basil M. Loeb, "Deterring Player Holdouts: Who Should Do It, How to Do It, and Why It Has to Be Done," 11 *Marquette Sports Law Review* (Spring 2001): 275, Loeb discusses the Yashin decision and states: "The labor agreements in baseball, football and basketball all contain language that serves to prevent a player from getting around a contract by sitting out." However, the article does not cite the *specific* clauses, in Major League Baseball labor agreements, that do so.

3. For more information on the rationale behind Lawrence Holden's Yashin decision, see Jeffrey A. Rosenthal, "The Yashin Arbitration: Ending Hockey Holdouts?" *New York Law Journal* (July 14, 2000). The author also distinguishes the NFL and NBA as having explicit full performances clauses, as opposed to MLB.

9.2.1.9. *Example of a Standard Player Contract—NFL*

The Standard Player Contract has evolved over the last century and is now a complex and cohesive document that clearly spells out the obligations of the parties involved (see exhibit 9.2).

9.2.2. Defenses to Standard Player Contract Breaches

Since the inception of professional baseball in the 1880s, there has been a significant amount of litigation surrounding the validity of the Standard Player Contract. It is important to note that with the advent of collective bargaining in professional sports, very few contractual cases now go to court; contractual disputes are more likely to be handled by an independent arbitrator or are settled

Exhibit 9.2
NFL Player Contract

THIS CONTRACT is between_____
_____, hereinafter "Player," and_____
_____,
a _____
corporation (limited partnership) (partnership), hereinafter "Club," operating
under the name of the _____
_____ as a member of the National Football League,
hereinafter "League." In consideration of the promises made by each to the other,

Player and Club agree as follows:

    1.   TERM. This contract covers _____ football season(s), and will begin on the date of execution or March 1, _____, whichever is later, and end on February 28 or 29, _____, unless extended, terminated, or renewed as specified elsewhere in this contract.

    2.   EMPLOYMENT AND SERVICES. Club employs Player as a skilled football player. Player accepts such employment. He agrees to give his best efforts and loyalty to the Club, and to conduct himself on and off the field with appropriate recognition of the fact that the success of professional football depends largely on public respect for and approval of those associated with the game. Player will report promptly for and participate fully in Club's official mandatory mini-camp(s), official pre-season training camp, all Club meetings and practice sessions, and all pre-season, regular season and post-season football games scheduled for or by Club. If invited, Player will practice for and play in any all-star football game sponsored by the League. Player will not participate in any football game not sponsored by the League unless the game is first approved by the League.

3. OTHER ACTIVITIES. Without prior written consent of the Club, Player will not play football or engage in activities related to football otherwise than for Club or engage in any activity other than football which may involve a significant risk of personal injury. Player represents that he has special, exceptional and unique knowledge, skill, ability, and experience as a football player, the loss of which cannot be estimated with any certainty and cannot be fairly or adequately compensated by damages. Player therefore agrees that Club will have the right, in addition to any other right which Club may possess, to enjoin Player by appropriate proceedings from playing football or engaging in football-related activities other than for Club or from engaging in any activity other than football which may involve a significant risk of personal injury.

    4.   PUBLICITY AND NFLPA GROUP LICENSING PROGRAM.

    (a)   Player grants to Club and the League, separately and together, the authority to use his name and picture for publicity and the promotion of NFL Football, the League or any of its member clubs in newspapers, magazines, motion pictures, game programs and roster manuals, broadcasts and telecasts, and all other publicity and advertising media, provided such publicity and promotion does not constitute an endorsement by Player of a commercial product. Player will cooperate with the news media, and will participate upon request in reasonable activities to promote the Club and the League. Player and National Football League Players Association, hereinafter "NFLPA," will not contest the rights of the League and its member clubs to telecast, broadcast, or otherwise transmit NFL Football or the right of NFL Films to produce, sell, market, or distribute football game film footage, except insofar as such broadcast, telecast, or transmission of footage is used in any commercially marketable game or interactive use. The League and its member clubs, and Player and the NFLPA, reserve their respective rights as to the use of such broadcasts, telecasts or transmissions of footage in such games or interactive uses, which shall be unaffected by this subparagraph.

Exhibit 9.2 (continued)

(b)   Player hereby assigns to the NFLPA and its licensing affiliates, if any, the exclusive right to use and to grant to persons, firms, or corporations (collectively "licensees") the right to use his name, signature facsimile, voice, picture, photograph, likeness, and/or biographical information (collectively "image") in group licensing programs. Group licensing programs are defined as those licensing programs in which a licensee utilizes a total of six (6) or more NFL player images on products that are sold at retail or used as promotional or premium items. Player retains the right to grant permission to a licensee to utilize his image if that licensee is not concurrently utilizing the images of five (5) or more other NFL players on products that are sold at retail or are used as promotional or premium items. If Player's inclusion in a particular NFLPA program is precluded by an individual exclusive endorsement agreement, and Player provides the NFLPA with timely written notice of that preclusion, the NFLPA will exclude Player from that particular program. In consideration for this assignment of rights, the NFLPA will use the revenues it receives from group licensing programs to support the objectives as set forth in the By-laws of the NFLPA. The NFLPA will use its best efforts to promote the use of NFL player images in group licensing programs, to provide group licensing opportunities to all NFL players, and to ensure that no entity utilizes the group licensing rights granted to the NFLPA without first obtaining a license from the NFLPA. This paragraph shall be construed under New York law without reference to conflicts of law principles. The assignment in this paragraph shall expire on December 31 of the later of (a) the third year following the execution of this contract, or (b) the year in which this contract expires. Neither Club nor the League is a party to the terms of this paragraph, which is included herein solely for the administrative convenience and benefit of Player and the NFLPA. The terms of this subparagraph apply unless, at the time of execution of this contract, Player indicates by striking out this subparagraph (b) and marking his initials adjacent to the stricken language his intention to not participate in the NFLPA Group Licensing Program. Nothing in this subparagraph shall be construed to supersede or any way broaden, expand, detract from, or otherwise alter in any way whatsoever, the rights of NFL Properties, Inc. as permitted under Article V (Union Security), Section 4 of the 1993 Collective Bargaining Agreement ("CBA").

5.   COMPENSATION. For performance of Player's services and all other promises of Player, Club will pay Player a yearly salary as follows:

$_____for the 19_____season;

$_____for the 19_____season;

$_____for the 19_____season;

$_____for the 19_____season;

$_____for the 19_____season.

In addition, Club will pay Player such earned performance bonuses as may be called for in this contract; Player's necessary traveling expenses from his residence to training camp; Player's reasonable board and lodging expenses during pre-season training and in connection with playing pre-season, regular season, and post-season football games outside Club's home city; Player's necessary traveling expenses to and from pre-season, regular season, and post-season football games outside Club's home city; Player's necessary traveling expenses to his residence if this contract is terminated by Club; and such additional compensation, benefits and reimbursement of expenses as may be called for in any collective bargaining agreement in existence during the term of this contract. (For purposes of this contract, a collective bargaining agreement will be deemed to be "in existence" during its stated term or during any period for which the parties to that agreement agree to extend it.)

6.   PAYMENT. Unless this contract or any collective bargaining agreement in existence during the term of this contract specifically provides otherwise, Player will be paid 100% of his yearly salary under this contract in equal weekly or bi-weekly installments over the course of the applicable regular season period, commencing with the first regular season game played

Exhibit 9.2 (continued)

by Club in each season. Unless this contract specifically provides otherwise, if this contract is executed or Player is activated after the beginning of the regular season, the yearly salary payable to Player will be reduced proportionately and Player will be paid the weekly or bi-weekly portions of his yearly salary becoming due and payable after he is activated. Unless this contract specifically provides otherwise, if this contract is terminated after the beginning of the regular season, the yearly salary payable to Player will be reduced proportionately and Player will be paid the weekly or bi-weekly portions of his yearly salary having become due and payable up to the time of termination.

7. DEDUCTIONS. Any advance made to Player will be repaid to Club, and any properly levied Club fine or Commissioner fine against Player will be paid, in cash on demand or by means of deductions from payments coming due to the Player under this contract, the amount of such deductions to be determined by Club unless this contract or any collective bargaining agreement in existence during the term of this contract specifically provides otherwise.

8. PHYSICAL CONDITION. Player represents to Club that he is and will maintain himself in excellent physical condition. Player will undergo a complete physical examination by the Club physician upon Club request, during which physical examination Player agrees to make full and complete disclosure of any physical or mental condition known to him which might impair his performance under this contract and to respond fully and in good faith when questioned by the Club physician about such condition. If Player fails to establish or maintain his excellent physical condition to the satisfaction of the Club physician, or make the required full and complete disclosure and good faith responses to the Club physician, then Club may terminate this contract.

9. INJURY. Unless this contract specifically provides otherwise, if Player is injured in the performance of his services under this contract and promptly reports such injury to the Club physician or trainer, then Player will receive such medical and hospital care during the term of this contract as the Club physician may deem necessary, and will continue to receive his yearly salary for so long, during the season of injury only and for no subsequent period covered by this contract, as Player is physically unable to perform the services required of him by this contract because of such injury. If Player's injury in the performance of his services under this contract results in his death, the unpaid balance of his yearly salary for the season of injury will be paid to his stated beneficiary, or in the absence of a stated beneficiary, to his estate.

10. WORKERS' COMPENSATION. Any compensation paid to Player under this contract or under any collective bargaining agreement in existence during the term of this contract for a period during which he is entitled to workers' compensation benefits by reason of temporary total, permanent total, temporary partial, or permanent partial disability will be deemed an advance payment of workers' compensation benefits due Player, and Club will be entitled to be reimbursed the amount of such payment out of any award of workers' compensation.

11. SKILL, PERFORMANCE AND CONDUCT. Player understands that he is competing with other players for a position on Club's roster within the applicable player limits. If at any time, in the sole judgment of Club, Player's skill or performance has been unsatisfactory as compared with that of other players competing for positions on Club's roster, or if Player has engaged in personal conduct reasonably judged by Club to adversely affect or reflect on Club, then Club may terminate this contract. In addition, during the period any salary cap is legally in effect, this contract may be terminated if, in Club's opinion, Player is anticipated to make less of a contribution to Club's ability to compete on the playing field than another player or players whom Club intends to sign or attempts to sign, or another player or players who is or are already on Club's roster, and for whom Club needs room.

12. TERMINATION. The rights of termination set forth in this contract will be in addition to any other rights of termination allowed either party by law. Termination will be effective upon the giving of written notice, except that Player's death, other than as a result of injury incurred in the performance of his services under this contract, will automatically terminate this contract.

Exhibit 9.2 (continued)

If this contract is terminated by Club and either Player or Club so requests, Player will promptly undergo a complete physical examination by the Club physician.

13.   INJURY GRIEVANCE. Unless a collective bargaining agreement in existence at the time of termination of this contract by Club provides otherwise, the following injury grievance procedure will apply: If Player believes that at the time of termination of this contract by Club he was physically unable to perform the services required of him by this contract because of an injury incurred in the performance of his services under this contract, Player may, within 60 days after examination by the Club physician, submit at his own expense to examination by a physician of his choice. If the opinion of Player's physician with respect to his physical ability to perform the services required of him by this contract is contrary to that of the Club's physician, the dispute will be submitted within a reasonable time to final and binding arbitration by an arbitrator selected by Club and Player or, if they are unable to agree, one selected in accordance with the procedures of the American Arbitration Association on application by either party.

14.   RULES. Player will comply with and be bound by all reasonable Club rules and regulations in effect during the term of this contract which are not inconsistent with the provisions of this contract or of any collective bargaining agreement in existence during the term of this contract. Player's attention is also called to the fact that the League functions with certain rules and procedures expressive of its operation as a joint venture among its member clubs and that these rules and practices may affect Player's relationship to the League and its member clubs independently of the provisions of this contract.

15.   INTEGRITY OF GAME. Player recognizes the detriment to the League and professional football that would result from impairment of public confidence in the honest and orderly conduct of NFL games or the integrity and good character of NFL players. Player therefore acknowledges his awareness that if he accepts a bribe or agrees to throw or fix an NFL game; fails to promptly report a bribe offer or an attempt to throw or fix an NFL game; bets on an NFL game; knowingly associates with gamblers or gambling activity; uses or provides other players with stimulants or other drugs for the purpose of attempting to enhance on-field performance; or is guilty of any other form of conduct reasonably judged by the League Commissioner to be detrimental to the League or professional football, the Commissioner will have the right, but only after giving Player the opportunity for a hearing at which he may be represented by counsel of his choice, to fine Player in a reasonable amount; to suspend Player for a period certain or indefinitely; and/or to terminate this contract.

16.   EXTENSION. Unless this contract specifically provides otherwise, if Player becomes a member of the Armed Forces of the United States or any other country, or retires from professional football as an active player, or otherwise fails or refuses to perform his services under this contract, then this contract will be tolled between the date of Player's induction into the Armed Forces, or his retirement, or his failure or refusal to perform, and the later date of his return to professional football. During the period this contract is tolled, Player will not be entitled to any compensation or benefits. On Player's return to professional football, the term of this contract will be extended for a period of time equal to the number of seasons (to the nearest multiple of one) remaining at the time the contract was tolled. The right of renewal, if any, contained in this contract will remain in effect until the end of any such extended term.

17.   ASSIGNMENT. Unless this contract specifically provides otherwise, Club may assign this contract and Player's services under this contract to any successor to Club's franchise or to any other Club in the League. Player will report to the assignee Club promptly upon being informed of the assignment of his contract and will faithfully perform his services under this contract. The assignee club will pay Player's necessary traveling expenses in reporting to it and will faithfully perform this contract with Player.

18.   FILING. This contract will be valid and binding upon Player and Club immediately upon execution. A copy of this contract, including any attachment to it, will be filed by Club with the League Commissioner within 10 days after execution. The Commissioner will have the

Exhibit 9.2 (continued)

right to disapprove this contract on reasonable grounds, including but not limited to an attempt by the parties to abridge or impair the rights of any other club, uncertainty or incompleteness in expression of the parties' respective rights and obligations, or conflict between the terms of this contract and any collective bargaining agreement then in existence. Approval will be automatic unless, within 10 days after receipt of this contract in his office, the Commissioner notifies the parties either of disapproval or of extension of this 10-day period for purposes of investigation or clarification pending his decision. On the receipt of notice of disapproval and termination, both parties will be relieved of their respective rights and obligations under this contract.

19.   DISPUTES. During the term of any collective bargaining agreement, any dispute between Player and Club involving the interpretation or application of any provision of this contract will be submitted to final and binding arbitration in accordance with the procedure called for in any collective bargaining agreement in existence at the time the event giving rise to any such dispute occurs.

20.   NOTICE. Any notice, request, approval or consent under this contract will be sufficiently given if in writing and delivered in person or mailed (certified or first class) by one party to the other at the address set forth in this contract or to such other address as the recipient may subsequently have furnished in writing to the sender.

21.   OTHER AGREEMENTS. This contract, including any attachment to it, sets forth the entire agreement between Player and Club and cannot be modified or supplemented orally. Player and Club represent that no other agreement, oral or written, except as attached to or specifically incorporated in this contract, exists between them. The provisions of this contract will govern the relationship between Player and Club unless there are conflicting provisions in any collective bargaining agreement in existence during the term of this contract, in which case the provisions of the collective bargaining agreement will take precedence over conflicting provisions of this contract relating to the rights or obligations of either party.

22.   LAW. This contract is made under and shall be governed by the laws of the State of

_____.

23.   WAIVER AND RELEASE. Player waives and releases any claims that he may have arising out of, related to, or asserted in the lawsuit entitled White v. National Football League, including, but not limited to, any such claim regarding past NFL Rules, the College Draft, Plan B, the first refusal/compensation system, the NFL Player Contract, pre-season compensation, or any other term or condition of employment, except any claims asserted in Brown v. Pro Football, Inc. This waiver and release also extends to any conduct engaged in pursuant to the Stipulation and Settlement Agreement in White ("Settlement Agreement") during the express term of that Settlement Agreement or any portion thereof. This waiver and release shall not limit any rights Player may have to performance by the Club under this Contract or Player's rights as a member of the White class to object to the Settlement Agreement during its review by the court in Minnesota. This waiver and release is subject to Article XIV (NFL Player Contract), Section 3(c) of the CBA.

24.   OTHER PROVISIONS.

(a)   Each of the undersigned hereby confirms that (i) this contract, renegotiation, extension or amendment sets forth all components of the player's remuneration for playing professional football (whether such compensation is being furnished directly by the Club or by a related or affiliated entity); and (ii) there are not undisclosed agreements of any kind, whether express or implied, oral or written, and there are no promises, undertakings, representations, commitments, inducements, assurances of intent, or understandings of any kind that have not been disclosed to the NFL involving consideration of any kind to be paid, furnished or made available to Player or any entity or person owned or controlled by, affiliated with, or related to Player, either during the term of this contract or thereafter.

(b)   Each of the undersigned further confirms that, except insofar as any of the

Exhibit 9.2 (continued)

undersigned may describe in an addendum to this contract, to the best of their knowledge, no conduct in violation of the Anti-Collusion rules of the Settlement Agreement took place with respect to this contract. Each of the undersigned further confirms that nothing in this contract is designed or intended to defeat or circumvent any provisions of the Settlement Agreement, including but not limited to the Rookie Pool and Salary Cap provisions; however, any conduct permitted by the CBA and/or the Settlement Agreement shall not be considered a violation of this confirmation.

(c)   The Club further confirms that any information regarding the negotiation of this contract that it provided to the Neutral Verifier was, at the time the information was provided, true and correct in all material respects.

25.   SPECIAL PROVISIONS.

THIS CONTRACT is executed in six (6) copies. Player acknowledges that before signing this contract he was given the opportunity to seek advice from or be represented by persons of his own selection.

_____   _____

PLAYER   CLUB

_____   _____

Home Address   By

_____   _____

Telephone Number   Club Address

_____   _____

Date   Date

_____

PLAYER'S CERTIFIED AGENT

_____

Address

_____

Telephone Number

_____

Date

Copy Distribution: White-League Office   Yellow-Player

Green-Member Club   Blue-Management Council

Gold-NFLPA   Pink-Player Agent

before litigation. Players' unions have bargained over the basic structure of the Standard Player Contract and have ensured that if a dispute does arise, it is dealt with in the grievance procedure, as outlined in the Collective Bargaining Agreement. However, this process only refers to athletes participating in the same league. If a player jumps from one league to another, the grievance procedure in either league is inapplicable and the judicial system may be used.

Before collective bargaining agreements established required internal mechanisms for resolving contract disputes, conflicts were decided in the court system. The most common disputes arose when a player decided to join another team in the same league, or jump to another league, before his initial contract had expired. It is important to remember that prior to the 1970s, player contracts ran in perpetuity, so that a player did not have the option of free agency at some point in his career (see Chapter 10, section 10.3.1.1., "History of the Reserve System"). Due to the appearance of rival leagues in all sports, players in the traditional leagues were wooed away from their existing contracts to participate in the upstart leagues. If a player walked out on a contract, the original team with which the player had a contract, often claimed a breach of contract and used the courts to enforce the original contract.

One of the first cases to deal with this issue was the aforementioned *Metropolitan Exhibition Company v. Ewing*, 42 F. 198 (C.C.D. N.Y 1890). In this case, the defendant ballplayer attempted to sign a contract with the Players' League, a rival league established by disenchanted players, while he was still supposedly under contract to his team in the National League. The club attempted to get an injunction stopping Ewing from signing a contract with the new team. The court analyzed whether the plaintiff club had met the requirements to be granted an injunction. The requirements, as outlined by the court, were the following:

1. The breach must be one for which monetary damages would be inadequate compensation.

2. The party seeking the injunction must not have "unclean hands" (any underhanded or devious past behavior employed by a party that is seeking an injunction—courts do not wish to endorse this type of behavior, and will deny relief to such parties).

3. The injunction sought must not be unduly oppressive to the defendant.

4. The contract must have mutuality or be founded on adequate consideration.

5. The terms of the contract must be definite.

The court found that the contract between the club and Ewing did not satisfy the fifth requirement, that the terms of the contract must be definite. The court found that the right of reservation was not adequately defined in the contract, and therefore the other terms of the contract were ambiguous. This issue was raised again in the same year in *Metropolitan Exhibition Company v. Ward*, N.Y.S. 779 (N.Y. Sup. Ct. 1890). In this case, the plaintiff attempted to obtain an injunction stopping the defendant from playing for anyone but the plaintiff, in accordance with the reserve clause and the standard player contract. Similar to its ruling in *Ewing*, the court in *Ward* found for the defendant because the contract was lacking in mutuality or definiteness. The court stated that a written agreement containing a reserve clause is not really a contract, but instead "is merely a contract to make a contract if the parties can agree."

As mentioned in section 9.1.1.3., "Consideration," concerning the lack of mutuality, the court found that the club had an unfair advantage over the player because the club could reserve the player in perpetuity (conceivably for the rest of that player's career); in contrast, the player could be terminated on ten days' notice. But in *Philadelphia Ball Club, Ltd. v. Lajoie*, 51 A. 973 (Pa. 1902), a case decided twelve years after *Ewing* and *Ward*, the court found that the Standard Player Contract could be enforced when the club specifically stated in the contract that the right of reservation, in conjunction with the right to terminate with ten days' notice, was in exchange for the salary to be paid to the player. It is important to emphasize that mutuality is not synonymous with equality; the club may have the upper hand in the contractual relationship. But the consideration was explicitly stated and the contract was negotiated without coercion, and therefore the contract was upheld. The Philadelphia Ball Club was granted an injunction, preventing Lajoie from playing in the rival American League.

Over the course of the 20th century, players used five defenses against breach of contract claims:

1. Unclean hands: occurs when the party seeking equitable relief has acted improperly, so that the court does not wish to endorse its behavior. This behavior does not have to be illegal or coercive (see defense 3), but only questionable enough for an injunction not to be granted.

2. Lack of mutuality: occurs when one party to the contract does not receive adequate consideration. For example, a professional player contract must state the length of the contract, in addition to what the player receives (salary) for his services.

3. Illegality and Unfair Bargaining Position: occurs when one party to a contract uses illegal or coercive means to create the contract.

4. Lack of commissioner's approval: occurs when the commissioner has not officially signed a player contract, and such act is required under the terms of league bylaws or a Collective Bargaining Agreement.

5. Collusion: occurs when two or more employers (teams) engage in concerted activity whereby the result is detrimental to the employee (player). For example, in the mid-1980s, Major League Baseball owners engaged in collusion when they agreed, en masse, not to sign any free agents during the off-season (see Chapter 11, section 11.4.4., "Baseball Collusion Cases").

It is important to note that many claims of breach of contract have occurred when ballplayers moved from one team to a team in a rival league. During periods when there was no rival league, there are usually fewer breach of contract claims. After the *Lajoie* decision, players turned from contract law to antitrust law and arbitration in order to challenge their restrictive player contracts (see Chapter 10, section 10.3.1., "The Baseball Exemption").

NOTES ⎯⎯⎯⎯⎯⎯⎯⎯⎯⎯⎯⎯⎯⎯⎯⎯⎯⎯⎯⎯⎯⎯⎯⎯⎯⎯⎯⎯⎯⎯⎯

1. In 2001, the Major League Baseball Players Association (MLBPA) filed a grievance with the Commissioner's office against the New York Yankees, claiming that the Yankees refused to pay a portion of a prorated signing bonus to Cuban defector Andy Morales. Morales allegedly had lied about his age in order to increase the value of his contract (four years and $4.5 million), claiming to have been born in 1974 when he was allegedly born in 1971. However, the MLBPA contended that the Yankees could not terminate the contract. The Yankees, on the other hand, hoped to recoup their entire investment in Morales. This case is pending. See Ken Davidoff, "Yankees Notebook," *New York Newsday*, July 16, 2001, p. A41. Also see www.espn.go.com/mlb/news/2001/0717/1227355.html

2. For the use of the "unclean hands" defense, see *Boston Celtics Ltd. Partnership v. Shaw*, 908 F.2d 1041 (1st Cir. 1990); *Washington Capitols Basketball Club Inc. v. Barry*, 304 F.Supp. 1193 (N.D.Cal. 1969); and *Weegham v. Killefer*, 215 F.168 (W.D. Mich.) *aff'd.*, 215 F. 289 (6th Cir. 1914).

3. The "lack of mutuality" defense was used in *American League Baseball Club of Chicago v. Chase* (N.Y. Sup. Ct. 1914); *Philadelphia Ball Club, Limited v. Lajoie*, 202 Pa. 210, 51 A. 973 (Pa. 1902); and *Connecticut Professional Sports Corp. v. Heyman*, 276 F.Supp. 618 (S.D.N.Y. 1967).

4. The illegality defense was used by an owner, although unsuccessfully, to avoid adherence to a Standard Player Contract. Star pitcher James "Catfish" Hunter signed a two-year contract with the Oakland Athletics in 1974. Included in his contract was a special covenant that deferred half of his $100,000 salary to the designees of his choice, in this case, to a life insurance provider. Charles Finley, owner of the Oakland club, agreed to this provision. In July, Hunter contacted the Internal Revenue Service and submitted to it an agreement for a deferred payment compensation investment account. Under such a plan, Hunter would avoid tax liability on the $50,000. On August 1, Hunter delivered the IRS/life insurance agreement to Finley; his signing it would make the contract complete. Finley stalled in signing the papers when he discovered that the tax liability was shifted to himself, and soon after, refused outright to transfer the $50,000 to the life insurance provider. In October, the Players Association filed two grievances on Hunter's behalf: (a) to reimburse the $50,000 payment and (b) to make Hunter a free agent. The Player's Association argued that the failure to make the deferred payment constituted a breach of contract and allowed the pitcher to exercise his rights to terminate the contract and become a free agent. The arbitration panel found that Finley had breached the club's duty outlined in the contract, and therefore the pitcher had the right to terminate his agreement with the A's. Finley appealed the decision of the arbitrator in *American and National League of Professional Baseball Clubs v. Major League Baseball Players Ass'n*, 130 Cal. Rptr. 626 (Ct. App. 1976), claiming that his signature on the life insurance document would have been illegal (assisting Hunter in "tax evasion") and that the arbitrator exceeded the scope of his authority in making Hunter a free agent. Courts generally will not overturn arbitration decisions (see chapter 11, section 11.3.13., "Arbitration"), but Finley claimed that court should overturn the Hunter decision because "the 'reserve clause' is not subject to arbitration." The court rejected both of Finley's allegations, citing a recent court decision which stated that the reserve clause was subject to arbitration: *Kansas City Royals Baseball Corp. v. Major League Baseball Players Ass'n.*, 532 F.2d 615 (8th Cir. 1976). That court case stemmed from MLB's appeal of the *Messersmith/McNally* decisions that resulted in baseball players gaining free agency rights (see chapter 11, section 11.3.9., "Free Agency").

5. The "commissioner's approval" defense is still applicable in some professional leagues. In Major League Baseball, the commissioner must sign the contract before it is considered valid. However, in the National Football League, there is a clause in the Standard Player Contract that enforces the validity of the contract prior to the commissioner's signature.

9.2.3. Tortious Interference

Tortious interference occurs when a third party knowingly interferes in a contract already in place between two parties. Not only can this occur between players and agents, but also with coaches who are pursued by potential employers (see note 4), as well as with sponsors and sports organizations (see note 5). To prove a claim of tortious interference the plaintiff will have to show the following:

1. There existed a binding contract.

2. The wrongdoer had knowledge of the contract's existence

3. There existed a purposeful intent to interfere with the contract

4. Plaintiff suffered actual damages

5. Interference by the third party was the proximate cause of the damages.

One case involving the doctrine of tortious interference is *Central Red Army Club v. Arena Associates, Inc.*, 952 F.Supp. 181 (S.D.N.Y. 1997), in which a hockey player attempted to leave his contract with a team in Russia to play hockey in the United States. Sergei Samsonov had played with the Central Sports Army Club (CSKA) since 1986, and had developed into a dominant player by the mid-1990s. At the end of the 1995–1996 season, the CSKA signed Samsonov to a new one-year contract, but because of a power struggle in Russian hockey at the time, the terms of Samsonov's deal could not be met. Samsonov left Russia and signed a contract with the Detroit Vipers of the International Hockey League. Detroit officials believed Samsonov was free to contract with them because his Russian contract had been breached, and also because he had signed the contract when he was under the age of eighteen with no parent acting as guardian. The CSKA informed the Vipers management that Samsonov was still under contract in Russia, and included in its correspondence a copy of the contract. The CSKA filed a lawsuit against the Vipers, alleging tortious interference with the contractual relationship between Samsonov and the CSKA.

The court was first faced with the decision of whether to grant an injunction preventing Samsonov from playing hockey for the Vipers. The court considered the likelihood of success on the merits for CSKA, and concluded that it would not be successful on the merits. Concerning the claim of tortious interference, the court ruled that the contract was void because Samsonov had signed the contract while a minor. However, the court noted that even if a legitimate contract had existed, CSKA would still lose the case because it had not been able to prove (a) that there had been inducement by the defendant (b) that the defendant was aware of the contract between CSKA and Samsonov, and (c) that the defendant had an improper motive. Samsonov continued to play for the Vipers, and was subsequently drafted by the Boston Bruins of the NHL.

NOTES

1. A trading card company brought a tortious interference claim against a major professional league players union in *Cardtoons, L.C. v. Major League Baseball Players Ass'n*, 208 F.3d 885 (10th Cir. 2000), *cert. denied*, 531 U.S. 873 (2000). The plaintiff had contracted with a manufacturing company to produce humorous trading cards featuring satirical caricatures of active baseball players. When the MLPBA heard about this plan, it sent a "cease and desist" letter threatening to sue both Cardtoons and the manufacturing company for copyright infringement. As a result of this threat, the manufacturing company backed out of the deal to produce the cards. Cardtoons then sued the MLPBA for tortious interference. The MLBPA defended itself by claiming that "threatening to sue" does not constitute tortious interference. The U.S. Appeals Court disagreed, remanding the case to a federal trial judge after the U.S. Supreme Court denied certiorari. The trial judge must determine whether *state* law protection exists for the players union's threatening letter. The case of *Cardtoons, L.C. v. Major League Baseball Players Association*, 199 F.R.D. 677 (N.D. Okla. 2001) is pending.

2. In *Omnipoint Communications Inc. v. New York Yankee Partnership and Bell Atlantic Nynex Mobile*, Index No. 601910/97, Seq. Nos.: 001, 002 (N.Y. Sup. Ct. 1999) the plaintiff sued the Yankees for breach of contract and Bell Atlantic for tortious interference. Omnipoint entered into an agreement with Sports Advertising Network, Inc. (SANI), a Yankee

agent, to display advertisements in the bullpen at Yankee Stadium. Omnipoint was informed that the Yankees would not honor the contract because it had signed a contract with Bell to use the space for signage. Omnipoint filed suit. The Yankees contended that SANI did not possess the authority to enter into such an agreement on the team's behalf, and thus the claim was unwarranted. The court found that Bell had not tortiously interfered because the original contract between Omni and SANI was not valid due to the fact that neither actual nor apparent authority could be established. The court granted summary judgment to both the Yankees and Bell, and dismissed the charges.

3. In 1996, one month after winning the Stanley Cup as coach of the New York Rangers, Mike Keenan announced he was leaving New York to sign as coach of the St. Louis Blues even though he had completed only the first year of his five-year contract. Keenan claimed a material breach of his contract had occurred when he was not given his bonus by the Rangers in a timely fashion. The Rangers filed suit to get a declaratory judgment as to the validity of Keenan's contract. Before the matter was argued in court, the Blues and the Rangers came to an agreement to trade several players to the Rangers in exchange for the services of Keenan. After a hearing with Commissioner Gary Bettman, Keenan was suspended for sixty days and fined $100,000 for "conduct detrimental to the league." The Blues were fined $250,000 for negotiating with Keenan while he was still under contract to coach the Rangers.

4. For a tortious interference case involving a professional coach, see *New England Patriots Football Club, Inc. v. University of Colorado*, 592 F. 2d 1196 (1st Cir. 1979). This case is discussed further in section 9.2.5., "Coaches' Contracts: Professional and Collegiate Sports."

5. For tortious interference in sponsorship agreements, see *National Football League Properties v. Dallas Cowboys Inc., Texas Stadium Corporation and Jerral W. Jones*, F. 922 Supp. 849 (S.D.N.Y. 1996). It is described further in section 9.2.4.6., "Sponsorship Litigation Cases."

6. Footwear company Reebok sued its former track and field chief, Mark Bossardet, for $2 million in U.S. District Court in Boston in 1995, after Bossardet allegedly lured the popular marathon runner Uta Pippig to his new company, Nike. Reebok also sued Nike for interfering with its contract with Pippig. The case was settled prior to trial.

7. A case that closely resembles *Central Sports Army Club* is *Professional Hockey Club Central Sports v. Detroit Red Wings*, 787 F.Supp. 706 (E.D. Mich. 1992). In this case, Viacheslav Kozlov had entered into a contractual agreement with CSKA, but was subsequently injured and hospitalized for two months. Kozlov was released from military service and dismissed from the hockey team. The Red Wings asked CSKA about Kozlov, but were told he was still under contract. The Reds Wings then approached Kozlov independently and signed him to a contract. The Red Wings were subsequently charged with tortious interference and accused of "abducting" Kozlov. However, Circuit Court justice Sharon Tevis Finch held that "Kozlov had demonstrated a substantial likelihood of success on the merits of his claim that his alleged contract with the Hockey Club is void."

8. In *Bonelli v. Volkswagen of America*, 421 N.W.2d 213 (Mich. Ct. App. 1987), the plaintiff filed a tortious interference claim against Volkswagen and the Amateur Hockey Association of the United States (AHAUS) for their actions concerning a contract the plaintiff had with AHAUS regarding the print and poster rights to the 1980 U.S. Olympic Hockey Team. After signing the deal with Bonelli, the AHAUS signed a deal with Volkswagen that granted the automobile company the use of "team photos" in their advertising campaign. Bonelli argued that he was given rights to the team photos. The appellate court found that Volkswagen had prior knowledge of the contract between Bonelli and AHAUS but continued with its advertising campaign anyway. The court noted that "the defendants had performed an intentional interference inducing of causing a breach or termination of plaintiff's business relationship or expectancy." Bonelli was awarded a judgment of $1.6 million.

9. In *Cincinnati Bengals Inc. v. Bergey*, 453 F.Supp. 129 (S.D. Ohio 1974), an NFL

team attempted to obtain an injunction to prevent the defendant from playing in the new rival league, the World Football League (WFL). The case was unique because, although Bergey signed his WFL contract while he was under contract in the NFL, the WFL contract was not scheduled to commence until *after* he fulfilled his contract with the NFL. The court ruled in favor of the defendant, stating "It was not unlawful . . . during the time when Bergey was under a valid contract with the Bengals, to negotiate and enter into a contract for Bergey's personal services, the performance of which was not to commence until after the expiration of Bergey's contract with the Bengals . . . Plaintiff [did not establish] a likelihood of success in its claim that it suffered a tortious interference with its right to full performance under Bergey's contract."

9.2.4. Marketing, Endorsement, and Sponsorship Contracts

Marketing in professional sports has grown dramatically since the 1980s, and now constitutes a billion-dollar industry. Corporations pay large sums of money to sponsor tennis or golf tournaments, merchandising companies compete to get contracts with the major professional sport leagues, and companies pay athletes millions to endorse products ranging from deodorants to credit cards. Because these agreements often involve large sums of money and involve obligations that impact many different parties, the written contracts are usually complex and lengthy in nature. It is important that those who are drafting sponsorship contracts have a clear understanding of their client's desires and the applicable legal issues.

Marketing, endorsement, and sponsorship contracts are similar to employment contracts in that they identify the parties, set time limits, list the obligations of the parties, and set forth provisions in case one party cannot carry out its obligations as stipulated in the contract. The companies that sponsor a player, league, or event want to ensure that what they are putting money toward is going to be a good investment and offer a healthy return in the form of increased exposure and sales for a company's product. However, industry professionals are not always able to control the actions of their contracted partners. It is common for top talent not to show up for an event or for a league to breach terms of an agreement. In the contract that is signed between a sponsor and the hired talent/league/event, there are a few stipulations that promotion specialists should include to ensure their financial well-being in case of unexpected breach. Stipulations such as indemnification, force majeure, and liability insurance help protect sponsors when events occur that are out of their control.

A sponsorship contract, whether it is between a company and a player, or between a company and a sporting event, is a legally binding agreement that ensures each party will fulfill obligations in its part of the agreement. Situations like those described above often arise where there is controversy surrounding particular terms of the agreement and/or where one party does not feel the agreement is being carried out under the terms of the contract. In addition, the contract language will attempt to make clear what the obligations of each party are in the event of an unforeseen circumstance, such as a labor dispute, a natural disaster, player injury, or company (sponsor) bankruptcy. Several provisions that appear in sponsorship contracts which deal with issues that may be raised during the term of an agreement are discussed below.

To avoid unnecessary litigation, marketing contracts are written comprehensively in an attempt to cover all eventualities. Therefore, player endorsement contracts are very detailed when it comes to the obligations of the endorsing athlete. The following is an example of a typical section in a player endorsement contract that outlines the obligations of the player:

> Athlete agrees during the term of this Agreement, or any extension thereof, to: a) Permit Company to use his photograph in connection with the advertising and promotion of football merchandise whether or not bearing his name, facsimile signature, or nickname; b) Demonstrate, discuss, and emphasize the newest features of Company's football products at every opportunity; c) Lend himself to such press interviews, radio, and/or TV appearances arranged for him by Company as are compatible with his own practice and play requirements; d) Cooperate to the maximum extent possible, compatible with his practice and play requirements, in effective Company promotional and public relations activities by endeavoring to become acquainted with Company dealers and their sales personnel in each market area; e) Cooperate with Company in giving advice, suggestions, and recommendations concerning the acceptability and playability of current Company football lines, the development of new Company football lines, and information about significant football product and football market trends; f) Cooperate to the maximum extent possible in making publicized personal appearances in store promotion events significant to general speaking invitations; g) In connection with such promotion, it is agreed that Company shall pay to Athlete all basic traveling expenses such as transportation, hotel, meals, and the like, incurred by Athlete relative to such promotion, if specifically requested by Company.

In the event of a legal dispute, the contract clearly indicates what terms the athlete is forced to abide by. For example, if the promoted athlete refused to make public appearances on behalf of the sponsor, there would be a violation of (f) in the athlete's obligations as outlined above. However, the language is ambiguous enough to allow for some disagreement: Are four appearances enough to satisfy the contract language?

9.2.4.1. Impact of League Rules

When these contracts concern athletes from professional sports leagues, it is important to know whether the leagues have policies surrounding the marketing of its athletes. Whereas the NFL has very little language concerning this issue, the NHL has taken a much more specific approach:

25.1. No player shall be involved in any endorsement of alcoholic beverage and/or tobacco products.

25.2. When a player obtains an endorsement for himself, he shall receive the entire fee therefor and may mention the name of his Club for identification purposes only. A player shall not use the sweater or Club insignia without the consent of the Club, which shall not be unreasonably withheld, and if consent is granted, Section 25.4 shall be applicable.

25.3. In the case of a team endorsement, which includes the individual likeness or name of any player, the proceeds thereof shall be divided one-half to the players and one-half to the Club. The Club shall not use the individual personality, including his likeness, of any player in any endorsement without his consent, which shall not be unreasonably withheld.

25.4. In the case of a single player wearing the sweater or identified with the insignia of the Club in connection with an endorsement, two-thirds of the fee thereof shall be paid to the player, and one-third shall be paid to the Club. (1996 NHL Collective Bargaining Agreement, Article 25.)

Prior to any negotiation over a sponsorship contract, the sponsor must be aware of the applicable provisions in the relevant Collective Bargaining Agreement.

9.2.4.2. Sponsorship Rights

Professional sports leagues and other athletic associations usually have a small number of primary sponsors that give the league or association a set amount of money and/or product and services in exchange for sponsorship rights. That means the company sponsoring the league or association, has the right to use the leagues' or associations' logo(s) while promoting its product. For example, MasterCard has been the official sponsor of Major League Baseball, and as the official sponsor has certain rights as outlined in its contract. One of those rights is that MasterCard can use the following statements when promoting its credit cards:

a. "Official Card of Major League Baseball"
b. "Major League Baseball Prefers MasterCard"
c. "Preferred Card of Major League Baseball"
d. "Major League Baseball Preferred Card."

Sponsors of professional leagues also usually have the right to use league logos in programs, advertising campaigns, promotional events, and publications. The contract will clearly identify what logos the company is allowed to use when promoting the league. For example, Major League Baseball's agreement with MasterCard allows the credit card company to use the MLB logo, the logos of the American and National Leagues, and the logos for the All-Star Game and post-season series. However, some restrictions do apply. In the MLB-MasterCard agreement there is a provision that limits MasterCard's rights to use the likeness of players, because the Collective Bargaining Agreement between MLB and the MLBPA has assigned those rights to the Players Association.

When a sponsor decides to commit millions of dollars to sponsoring an event, the sponsor wants to be certain that its financial commitment will result in increased publicity for the company. In addition, the sponsor of the event wants to ensure that similar products are not sponsored throughout the event. For example, a credit card company sponsoring a golf tournament will want to make sure that rival credit card companies are not also publicized as sponsors. The following language has been used to clarify the sponsor's rights at the tournament:

Golf Tournament hereby grants to *Sponsor* the right for the 1999 through 2002 Tournaments, to be the exclusive sponsor of the Tournaments within the payment services product category (the "Product Category") defined as follows: (1) all card-based payment and/or account access devices (including without limitation, credit cards, charge cards, automated teller machine (ATM) cards, prepaid cards, smart cards, telephone calling cards, electronic benefits transfer cards, travel and entertainment cards, on-line and off-line point-of-sale debit cards, cheque guarantee cards, and cards that combine two or more of the foregoing functions; (2) travelers cheques and travel vouchers; (3) ATMs and ATM networks; and (4) money wire transfers.

When a company sponsors an athlete to market a product, the sponsor wants to be sure that said athlete will be a visible presence in his/her respective sport. For example, if a company is sponsoring a professional golfer, it may include the following language in the agreement to ensure that the golfer is playing in high profile tournaments and a specific number of tournaments.

> Provided *Spokesman* is physically capable of tournament play, *Spokesman* shall enter/participate in not less than 22 official PGA TOUR events per year, which shall include the Masters, US Open, British Open, PGA Championship and other PGA Tour events. As a part of such minimum appearance commitment, *Spokesman* shall, subject to qualification, appear in all 4 "major" golf tournaments, the Players Championship, the Ryder Cup, the Presidents Cup, and other prominent golf events as the parties may agree. In the event *Spokesman* cannot participate in at least four (4) such tournaments in any calendar year, the Term of this agreement shall be extended for an additional one-year period upon the terms and for the fees set forth for the year in which the *Spokesman* fails to play such minimum number of tournaments.

The sponsor of an event, league, association, or athlete must clearly state the obligations of the contracting party so as to avoid unnecessary litigation.

9.2.4.3. Indemnification

The indemnification clause is used to protect the investment the sponsoring company is making, whether it is in a league sponsorship agreement or in a player endorsement contract. This clause is especially important because it pertains to the endorsement contracts professional athletes enter into. In the wake of increased publicity surrounding athletes' arrests for violent behavior and for drug-related charges, many athlete endorsement contracts have an indemnification clause that protects the company from a player's actions. The following is an example of one.

> The Parties agree that *Spokesman* is not an employee of *Sponsor*, but is in an independent contractor relationship to *Sponsor*, at all times. Pursuant to such relationship, *Spokesman* agrees to indemnify, defend, and hold harmless *Sponsor*, its agents and employees, from and against any and all claims, damages, liabilities, losses, costs or expenses, including reasonable attorney fees, arising out of the breach of any obligation hereunder or any alleged act or omission of *Spokesman*, and *Sponsor* agrees to indemnify, defend and hold harmless *Spokesman* from and against any and all claims, damages, liabilities, losses, costs or expenses, including reasonable attorney fees, arising out of the breach of any obligation hereunder or an alleged act or omission of *Spokesman*. In the event of a claim of indemnification, the party being indemnified shall give the party providing the indemnification prompt notice of such event and shall cooperate in the provision of such indemnification.

9.2.4.4. Right to Terminate

A company makes the decision to sponsor an athlete because it feels that the athlete will represent its product well to the public. However, to protect itself from athletes that get into legal trouble or no longer represent the "values" of the sponsor, a sponsorship agreement will often include "right to terminate" language. Here is an example.

> *Sponsor* may terminate this agreement at any time with no further obligation to pay *Spokesman* any amount thereafter otherwise owing should *Spokesman*, at any time during the term of this agreement: (1) die or become unable to perform his obligations hereunder in a competent and professional manner; (2) become the subject of or cause adverse publicity, shame, scandal or embarrassment to himself or to *Sponsor* through any statement, action, association or otherwise; or (3) make any statement or take any action which *Sponsor* believes could or would disparage any *Sponsor* product, service trademark or service mark.

9.2.4.5. *Force Majeure and Work Stoppage*

A *force majeure*, or work stoppage, provision is normally associated with facility or event contracts, but recently it has become increasingly common in athletic sponsorship contracts, especially those between a manufacturer and a league or association. The term "force majeure" means "superior force," and in the context of a professional sports contract, the term refers to unforeseeable natural or human events that are beyond the control of the parties to the contract, and that render performance of the contract impossible. A work stoppage provision protects one, or both, parties in the event of a work stoppage, either a strike or a lockout. Only recently have licensing agreements begun to include a force majeure clause. This is due in part to the dramatic growth of work stoppages in professional sports.

To deal specifically with the issue of labor disputes, many sponsorship contracts now have a provision that specifically identifies protection against work stoppages. In the Major League Baseball agreement with a sponsor, there is a clause that identifies the remedy should a work stoppage occur:

> Notwithstanding anything contained in this agreement to the contrary, in the event that during the Term as a result of a labor dispute between the MAJOR LEAGUE BASEBALL owners and the Major League Baseball Players Association a MAJOR LEAGUE BASEBALL regular season or post-season is delayed or interrupted for fifteen (15) days or more, the rights fee and spending commitment payable by Sponsor in the year during which such delay or interruption occurs shall be reduced hereunder on a percentage basis, the numerator of which shall be the number of dates during the regular and post-season in that year on which at least one MAJOR LEAGUE BASEBALL game was scheduled to be played (collectively "Game Days") and because of such labor dispute was not played, and the denominator of which shall be the total number of Game Days in that year.

9.2.4.6. *Sponsorship Litigation Cases*

Most sponsorship contracts are carried out successfully, and no contractual disputes arise between the parties. In the event of a dispute, some contracts have mechanisms, such as binding arbitration, so that the judiciary does not need to get involved. However, in the absence of such mechanisms, the courts are called upon to render decisions.

An example of a conflict in the area of sponsorship is the case of *National Football League Properties v. Dallas Cowboys Football Club*, 922 F. Supp. 849 (S.D.N.Y. 1996). The NFL created the Properties Division in 1982, and the exclusive club marks (logo, name, insignia) of each team were transferred there. The Properties Division negotiates contracts with companies to act as sponsors of the NFL. The revenue generated from these leaguewide licensing contracts is evenly distributed among the teams in the league, consistent with the belief in the NFL that revenue sharing helps maintain competitive balance and a strong league. As a condition for these leaguewide exclusive agreements, individual teams are not permitted to enter into similar agreements on their own. At the time of this case, the NFL had Coca-Cola as the official soft drink of the NFL, and Visa as the league's official credit card. Dallas owner Jerry Jones entered into agreements with various competitors, including Dr. Pepper, Pepsi-Cola Company, Nike, and American Express, thus undermining the investment of the NFL's official sponsors.

The important facet of this case is that the claim made by Jones that it was not the Cowboys that had the sponsorship agreements with rival companies, but rather *Texas Stadium Corporation (TSC)*, which was independent of the NFL. Jones also argued that, as part of the agreements with TSC, the sponsors did not have the right to use marks of the Cowboys for commercial use; thus there was no conflict with the NFL Properties Division. The League argued that the defendants had breached the implied covenant of good faith dealing in contract; breached the Cowboy's obligations as the party to receive the NFL Trust; breached their fiduciary duty to the other member clubs of the NFL; and tortiously interfered with the property rights granted by NFL Properties to its licensees. The main issue in this case was whether the agreements between the TSC and the sponsors would "trick" the public into thinking those sponsors were the official sponsors of the NFL. The case was dropped and a settlement reached, although details of the settlement were not released to the public.

The *Cowboys* case clearly illustrates the conflicts that may arise in the arena of sponsorship. Several important legal issues raised by this case are dealt with in this chapter, as well as other chapters in the book: the legal theories of breach of contract, tortious interference, and the relationship between competing contracts.

NOTES

1. Toronto Raptor star Vince Carter was ordered to pay $13.5 million plus attorneys' fees in 2000, after an arbitrator ruled that he breached his contract with Puma. Carter had claimed that he stopped wearing Puma shoes because the shoes did not fit him properly, and because Puma had not fulfilled its promise to create a Vince Carter "signature shoe." In addition to the financial penalty, the arbitrator issued an injunction barring Carter from endorsing a competitor's shoe for three years. Carter subsequently paid additional money to Puma (a settlement), allowing him to endorse a competitor's shoe before the three-year injunction expired.

2. NBA player Shawn Kemp filed a $4.1 million breach of contract suit against Reebok International after Reebok terminated his endorsement contract in September 2000. Reebok did so after Kemp was quoted in a newspaper saying that his "all time favorite shoe" was made by Nike. His endorsement contract contained a clause forbidding him to make disparaging comments about Reebok. Kemp eventually agreed to drop the suit and also agreed to pay Reebok an undisclosed amount to settle a counter suit filed by the company. In its suit, Reebok claimed Kemp owed it a little over $1 million in advance royalties.

3. In *Adidas America Inc. v. NCAA*, 40 F.Supp.2d 1275 (D. Kan. 1999), the shoe manufacturer brought suit against the NCAA concerning the NCAA's Bylaw 12.5.5, which

limited the size of commercial logos that may appear on student-athletes' uniforms and apparel. This case arose out of the fact that the uniforms Adidas supplied to certain schools had three long stripes down the sleeve or pant leg, which were larger than the allowable logo according to Bylaw 12.5.5. The court reasoned that the NCAA and its member institutions did not realize any economic or competitive advantage because of the rule, that the rule was consistent with the NCAA's policy of limiting commercialization in intercollegiate athletics, and that Adidas failed to prove that a preliminary injunction was necessary. The court found in favor of the NCAA.

9.2.5. Coaches' Contracts: Professional and Collegiate Sports

A coach's contract is similar to most other employment contracts. Unlike a Standard Player Contract for athletes, the coaching contract is usually individually drafted for star coaches, with more items independently negotiated. It sets forth the nature and duration of the employment, the compensation to be paid to the employee, and other terms and conditions of employment. The employer-employee relationship between the team or institution and the coach is similar to the typical employer-employee relationship in the business world. A coach's contract can contain distinctive clauses, such as provisions for a percentage of gate receipts at certain events, unique provisions for termination, bonuses for high graduation rates, large bonuses for remaining with the institution for a number of years, and covenants not to compete.

Exhibit 9.3 contains excerpts from Bobby Knight's disputed contract at Indiana University, which was signed in 1982, extended in 1991, and terminated by the university in 2000. Knight's contract contains some fairly unusual clauses such as in Section 3, which gives Knight approval of all matters associated with the men's basketball program. Due to Knight's alleged physical abuse of players, assistant coaches, fans, members of the media, and members of the student body, University President Myles Brand claimed that Knight's termination in 2000 was "for cause." In Section 11 of the contract Brand could terminate Knight "for cause" if the coach has "engaged in conduct contrary to generally accepted standards in the coaching profession or has been guilty of personal conduct which would be grounds for punitive discharge of any employee of the University generally." Perhaps the most compelling physical evidence against Knight was a videotape showing Knight with his hand around former player Neil Reed's neck. Nevertheless, in June 2001, the Associated Press reported that Knight was considering a $7 million wrongful termination suit against the university (see note 1). In December 2001, it was reported that Knight would pursue the lawsuit in 2002.

The standard evaluative measure of a coach is his or her ability to produce a winning team. A coach who is not successful in producing a winning program is a possible candidate for termination. The termination of a coaching contract constitutes a breach of contract for which the team or institution can be held liable for damages. Sometimes, this liability has been avoided by either making a lump-sum payment based on the dollar value of the remaining years of the contract to the coach or continuing periodic payments to the coach for the remaining term of his or her contract, as if the coach were still employed (see note 2).

A 1983 decision, *Rodgers v. Georgia Tech Athletic Ass'n.*, 303 S.E. 2d 467 (Ga. Ct. App. 1983), suggests that a college institution or professional sports team may

Exhibit 9.3
Bobby Knight's Employment Contract

EMPLOYMENT AGREEMENT

THIS AGREEMENT is between THE TRUSTEES OF INDIANA UNIVERSITY, a statutory body corporate and politic of the State of Indiana, hereinafter called "University", and ROBERT M. KNIGHT, hereinafter called "Coach".

W I T N E S S E T H:

In consideration of the mutual promises hereinafter contained, the parties hereto promise and agree as follows:

WHEREAS, Coach has for some ten (10) years served University under an employment contract as Head Basketball Coach; and

WHEREAS, it is generally the case that both the contracts of coaches and career security are unstable; and

WHEREAS, it is the desire of the parties to enter into an Employment Contract which may provide opportunity for reasonable security in employment of Coach with University, consistent with the rendering of service, and by providing certain special features which shall compensate Coach in part for the career instabilities peculiar to his profession.

1. **EMPLOYMENT**. The University hereby employs and Coach hereby accepts employment as Head Basketball Coach of the Indiana University Men's Varsity Basketball team upon the terms and conditions set forth in this Agreement.

2. **TERM AND RENEWAL OPTION**. The term of this Agreement shall be from September 1 through June 30 of each year for a period of ten (10) years, ending on June 30, 1992, unless extended, terminated or renewed as specified elsewhere in this Agreement.

On or before May 30, 1992, if this Agreement is then in force, the Coach may tender to the University written notice advising the University that he is exercising his option to extend this Agreement for a period of One (1) year, upon the same terms and conditions as are in effect on June 30, 1992. The Coach may so renew this Agreement four (4) more times, for a total of five (5) one (1) year renewal terms.

3. **DUTIES**. The Coach promises and agrees to perform all of the duties of Head Basketball Coach to the best of his ability and experience, and within the policies, rules, regulations and decisions of the Intercollegiate Conference of Faculty Representatives (Big Ten) and the National Collegiate Athletic Association (NCAA) now in effect or as may be revised during the period of this Agreement.

Coach should devote his professional time to the faithful performance of his duties as required by this Contract; but he shall be permitted to accept employments from time to time so long as such other employments do not conflict or interfere with full performance in good faith of his duties as Coach.

Coach shall make four (4) speaking engagements per year at University functions. The selection of the specific University functions shall be at Coach's discretion but shall include at least two (2) Varsity Club functions. Should Coach agree in his sole discretion to make more than four (4) speaking engagements during a given year, such agreement shall not constitute a waiver of limitation herein provided.

During the period that Coach is Head Basketball Coach, he shall have approval of all matters associated with Men's Varsity Basketball at Indiana University, including, but not limited to the following:

(a) Facilities for practices, scheduling of games, exhibitions, tournaments, scrimmages, and related matters;
(b) Practice time for Men's Varsity Basketball Team;
(c) Recommended persons selected as radio and television announcers;
(d) Selection of staff to include trainer, coaches, secretaries, and sports publicist for Basketball;

Provided, however, that no provision in this Agreement concerning Coach's "approval" shall control or apply to situations in which University deems itself required by statutory, contractual or conference of NCAA constraints to act otherwise than as Coach desires (by way of illustration: Situations where a faculty athletics committee or an athletic director is given authority under Intercollegiate Conference or NCAA rules to which University

Exhibit 9.3 (continued)

is subject. Situations in which federal laws or regulations concerning employment or equal access to facilities or programs applies).

4. **COMPENSATION.** The University agrees to pay Coach for rendering services described herein the following compensation:

   A. Salary. The University agrees to pay Coach a salary of Sixty Three Thousand Six Hundred Dollars ($63,600.00) for the first year of this Agreement (less all amounts required to be withheld from salary by federal, state and local authorities). The salary shall be payable in ten (10) equal monthly installments in accordance with University's regular payroll procedures. In each of the subsequent years of the term of this Agreement, Coach's salary shall be increased by an amount equal to the average percentage salary change for continuing academic personnel of his rank at the Indiana University Bloomington Campus.

   B. Benefits. It is understood and agreed that during the term of this Agreement Coach shall be provided medical insurance and life insurance consistent with Standard University policies and procedures. Further, it is understood and agreed that Coach may elect to participate in the TIAA and CREF benefits available to University's employees in the same classification as Coach.

This section has been redacted.

5. **EDUCATION.** University shall provide to each of the Coach's children, namely Timothy Knight and Patrick Knight, four (4) years of undergraduate education. It is understood and agreed that each of Coach's children may attend the school of his choice, but that the University's obligation shall be limited to an amount equivalent to an in-state student's expense at Indiana University's Bloomington Campus for a comparable education program at the time of Coach's children's enrollment including room, board, tuition, fees and books. Death or disability of the Coach during the period covered by this contract will not alter provision of this section.

6. **WORKING FACILITIES.** The coach shall be furnished with a private office, stenographic help, and such other facilities and services, suitable to his position and adequate for the performance of his duties as Head Coach.

7. **AUTOMOBILE.** University shall provide Coach the use of an automobile, new each year, and University shall bear all expenses for insurance, repairs, tires, maintenance and gasoline.

8. **AIRPLANE.** Coach shall be permitted the use of a plane made available to University, in accordance with University policy, in consideration and support of his transportation requirements as Head Basketball Coach at Indiana University.

9. **CHANGE OF STATUS.** If the University at any time desires, Coach shall cease to serve as Head Basketball Coach when so advised in writing. In such event Coach shall receive no further compensation based upon this Agreement except as follows:

This section has been redacted.

He shall receive the salary, commencing at $63,600.00 and increased year by year as provided in paragraph 4A. until June 30, 1992:

This section has been redacted.

His own decision, of which he shall advise University in writing, then all obligations to Coach under this Agreement shall cease except the following:

Obligation to manage the fund shall continue as set forth in paragraph 4.C.

Exhibit 9.3 (continued)

10. **DEATH OR DISABILITY OF COACH**.

This section has been redacted

If the Coach is disabled so as to be unable to be Head Basketball Coach, Coach shall receive two-thirds of the amounts payable under 4.A.

11. The Head Basketball Coach will be expected to continue his best efforts in striving for an excellent basketball program and will comply with all Conference and NCAA rules as well as with Indiana University's intercollegiate athletic policies. He will be expected to notify the Athletic Director promptly about any charges of violation or events of such kind that may come to his attention and that he will take the necessary steps to insure that his coaching staff understands, accepts, and fulfills these same responsibilities.

Should the Athletic Director notify the President of the University that the Coach has failed in serious ways to comply with the expressed terms of this employment agreement, has engaged in conduct contrary to generally accepted standards in the coaching profession or has been guilty of personal conduct which would be grounds for punitive discharge of any employee of the University generally, and the Athletic Director recommends his discharge, then the University may terminate his employment for cause. Before any such action is taken he will be notified by the President of such a recommendation and shall be given the opportunity to have in writing the specific reasons on which that recommendation is based and to discuss and offer explanations to the President or his delegate. If after such opportunity the President's opinion is that the recommendation is proper, he will be notified in writing of the decision and the termination will take effect on the dates specified in the President's final notification...Coach of the original notice. The President's decision will be final.

12. Arrangements for operation of summer basketball teaching camp and facilities will be established through regular University contract and addendum.

13. **NOTICES**. Any notices required or permitted to be given under this agreement shall be sufficient if in writing, and if sent by registered or certified mail to his residence in the case of Coach, or to its principal office, in the case of the University.

IN WITNESS WHEREOF, the parties have executed this Agreement in duplicate, this ___ day of _____, 1982.

COACH:

UNIVERSITY:

_____

THE TRUSTEES OF INDIANA

UNIVERSITY
ROBERT M. KNIGHT

BY: _____

John W. Ryan, President
Indiana University

ATTEST:

John D. Mulholland,

_____

Treasurer

Exhibit 9.3 (continued)

ADDENDUM TO EMPLOYMENT AGREEMENT

This Addendum is made to modify a certain Employment Agreement (Agreement) executed on June 2, 1982 by Robert M. Knight (Coach in this Agreement) and The Trustees of Indiana University (University in this Agreement) and previously extended by Agreement through June 30, 1997.

For good and valuable consideration receipt of which is hereby acknowledged, it is hereby agreed that the Employment Agreement shall be modified by deleting paragraph 2 of the Agreement in its entirety and substituting:

2. **TERM**: The term of this Agreement shall extend through and including June 30, 2002.

All other provisions of the Agreement and its Addendum dated January 17, 1991, shall remain in full force and effect for the full term of the Agreement as extended.

Dated: March 18, 1991

COACH: INDIANA UNIVERSITY:

_____   _____
ROBERT M. KNIGHT   EDGAR G. WILLIAMS,
                                          Acting Director of
                                          Intercollegiate Athletics

Exhibit 9.3 (continued)

Pursuant to Coach Knight's employment agreement, contributions have been made to a deferred compensation fund during the term of the contract which commenced in 1982. The following is a list of the contributions that were made:

Contributions to Deferred Compensation Plan

Date	Amount	Amount
8/1/82	$ 46,559.00	$ 31,800.00
9/1/82	$ 42,400.00	$ 31,800.00
9/1/83	$ 44,846.00	$ 31,635.00
9/1/84	$ 44,777.00	$ 35,833.00
9/1/85	$ 52,841.00	$ 39,631.00
9/1/86		$ 43,198.00
9/1/87		$ 45,842.00
9/1/88		$ 48,978.00
9/1/89		$ 52,309.00
9/1/90		$ 56,060.00
9/1/91		$ 57,960.00
9/1/92		$ 60,018.00
9/1/93		$ 62,257.00
9/1/94		$ 64,131.00
9/1/95		$ 66,831.00
9/1/96		$ 69,304.00
9/1/97		$ 71,522.00
9/1/98		$ 73,990.00
9/1/99		$ 77,697.00
9/1/00		$ 80,533.00
Subtotals	$ 231,423.00	$ 1,103,329.00
Total Contributions	$1,334,752.00	

The deferred compensation will be forfeited if, within eight years after Coach Knight leaves the University, he directly or indirectly affiliates with any NCAA Division I level men's basketball program located within the states of Indiana or Kentucky, or at any member institution of the Big Ten Conference in the capacity of coach, assistant coach, scout, recruiter, or in any other capacity in which he was employed by Indiana University.

The deferred compensation is to be paid out over a ten-year period.

be liable to its former coach for more than the salary stated in the contract. Pepper Rodgers, the head coach of the Georgia Tech football program at the time he was fired, sued the school for damages relating to the perquisites (fringe benefits) he had lost as a result of his termination. The parties settled out of court prior to trial on the issue after the Georgia court ruled that the inclusion of the word "perquisite" in Rodgers' contract might permit a jury to award Rodgers some of the damages he was claiming. In light of the *Rodgers* case, institutions now sometimes construct a "Pepper Rodgers clause" in order to limit the amount of fringe benefits that the school must pay in the event that the coach is terminated (see note 5).

At the collegiate level, even if an institution is willing to pay for the damages associated with termination, the institution may encounter procedural problems in attempting to rid itself of its coach prior to the expiration of his or her contract. In *Yukica v. Leland*, No. 85-E-191 (N.H. Super. Ct. 1985), the New Hampshire Superior Court granted the Dartmouth College head football coach an order restraining the college's athletic director from terminating his coaching contract, which, as interpreted by the court, provided that notice of termination was to be given twelve months prior to actual termination.

Termination of a coaching contract may not necessarily occur due to the actions of an institution or team. A coach may wish to leave the institution before his or her contract expires, so as to move to a higher-profile job that may offer higher pay, increased exposure, and greater benefits. As these positions become available, a coach may leave his or her current position to assume similar responsibilities with another team or institution. This departure before the end of the contract term constitutes a breach for which a coach can be held liable (see note 4).

If a coach is performing well or has an excellent track record, teams and institutions can take proactive contractual steps to retain him or her. One such method is a loyalty bonus. For example, Rick Pitino signed a contract to become men's basketball coach at the University of Louisville in 2001. Pitino's contract calls for a $5 million bonus if he completes the six years of the deal. However, several options remain open to a team or institution if a coach departs before the expiration of the coaching contract. For one, the team or institution may attempt to block the move of the coach and force him or her to work out the present contract. In *New England Patriots Football Club. Inc. v. University of Colorado*, 592 F.2d 1196 (1st Cir. 1979), the U.S. Court of Appeals held that a clause in Chuck Fairbanks's coaching contract with the Patriots, which required him to refrain from contracting elsewhere for his coaching services, was a proper basis for a preliminary injunction to enjoin the University of Colorado from employing Fairbanks while he was under contract with the Patriots.

Another potential solution to either party's desire for an early termination of a coaching contract is to provide for a buyout clause at an agreed amount. Under a mutual buyout clause, either the institution or the coach may unilaterally and prematurely terminate the contract during its term and be responsible only for damages in the agreed amount. This is also referred to as *liquidated damages*. However, while it appears that such a provision in a contract would leave little room for controversy, sometimes problems do arise. For example, in *Vanderbilt University v. DiNardo*, 174 F.3d 751 (6th Cir. 1999), the defendant signed a five-year contract in 1990 to coach the Vanderbilt football team and was offered an extension of that contract in 1994, one year before the original contract was to expire. After negotiations, it appeared the two sides had reached an agreement on a two-year extension. Later that same year, DiNardo accepted the head coach position with Louisiana State University. Vanderbilt demanded three years in liquidated damages (for the final year of the five-year agreement, plus the two years from the recently negotiated extension) from DiNardo, pursuant to the original five-year contract signed in 1990.

Vanderbilt charged DiNardo with breach of contract after he did not reply to their liquidated damages request. The district court found in favor of Vanderbilt, and the matter was brought to the 6th Circuit Court of Appeals for review. DiNardo argued that the clause in his Vanderbilt contract was not a liquidated-damages clause but rather a "non-compete" clause, which is unenforceable under Tennessee law (see section 9.1.1.4., "Legality"). The court found that the clause was for liquidated damages, and therefore legal, since it was reasonable in relation to the anticipated damages for breach, measured prospectively at the time the contract was entered into, and not grossly disproportionate to the actual damages. The court reasoned:

> Vanderbilt hired DiNardo for a unique and specialized position, and the parties understood that the amount of damages could be easily ascertained should a breach occur. Contrary to DiNardo's suggestion, Vanderbilt did not need to undertake an analysis to determine actual damages . . . the fact that liquidated damages declined each year DiNardo remained under contract, is directly tied to the parties' express understanding of the importance of a long-term commitment from DiNardo. Furthermore, the liquidated damages provision was reciprocal.

The court determined that the liquidated damages provision was enforceable. The case was affirmed in part and sent back to the district court for further review.

NOTES _____

1. After the Neil Reed tape surfaced, Indiana did not fire Knight, but instituted a "zero tolerance" policy for improper behavior. Knight allegedly violated that policy, and was terminated when he grabbed a student by the arm and swore at him after the student referred to him as "Knight" instead of "Mr. Knight" or "Coach Knight." In addition to wrongful termination, Bobby Knight's legal claim against Indiana University includes slander, intentional infliction of emotional distress, tortious interference with potential contracts, and libel. In addition to the wrongful termination suit from Knight, Indiana is facing a separate lawsuit by Indiana basketball fans, claiming that Knight's firing violated the state's "open meeting law."

In a request for a jury trial against Bobby Knight, former Assistant Coach Ronald Felling listed several examples of Knight's alleged improper conduct. The alleged conduct included:

  a. Firing Felling for disloyalty, then summoning his other assistant coaches into an office to watch him assault Felling. The assault included a punch to Felling's chest, knocking him into a television set.

  b. Making racist remarks at a restaurant, then putting a restaurant patron in a "choke-hold" after the patron confronted him about the remarks.

  c. Threatening I.U. Athletic Department secretary Jeanette Hartgraves, to the point that Athletic Director Clarence Doninger was forced to physically restrain him. Hartgraves alleged previous assaults; such as having a potted plant hurled in her direction.

  d. Physically and verbally abusing player Neil Reed to the point where he left the team (a videotape did confirm that Knight had put his hand around Reed's neck in a practice).

  e. Assaulting a Puerto Rican policeman prior to the 1979 Pan Am Games. Knight was convicted in absentia for this offense, and sentenced to six months in jail. Puerto Rico subsequently dropped the extradition request and the charges.

  f. Pushing a student photographer into bushes.

  2. In 2001, Utah State University reached a settlement with football coach Dave Arslanian, after he contended that an administrator had secretly hired a new coach five weeks before he was fired. Arslanian was fired in the middle of a multiyear contract. The university had originally contended that Arslanian was entitled only to his salary. However, to avoid litigation, the university agreed to continue paying the coach's benefits.

  3. In 2000, Sanya Tyler, an associate athletic director and the women's basketball coach at Howard University, sued the university for $105 million for wrongful termination and breach of contract. Tyler had won a $250,000 discrimination suit against the school in 1995 (see Chapter 15, section 15.3.2.7., "State Discrimination Laws"), and claimed that her 2000 firing was a retaliation for winning that suit. The case is pending.

  4. In 1998, basketball coach Larry Shyatt agreed to pay $286,000 to the University of Wyoming in order to settle a lawsuit stemming from his breaching his contract in order to become head coach of Clemson University. Shyatt claimed that he had an unwritten agreement with Wyoming that allowed him to leave in the event of a head coaching vacancy at Clemson (Shyatt was once an assistant coach at Clemson). However, Wyoming denied this claim. According to Wyoming officials, the settlement amount was equal to what Shyatt would have made if he had continued to be Wyoming's head coach, plus $40,000 in legal costs. For more information, see http://sportsillustrated.cnn.com/basketball/college/news/1998/08/14/shyatt_wyoming/

  5. For further information about termination settlements and other issues regarding college coaches, see Martin J. Greenberg, "Representation of College Coaches in Contract Negotiations," *Marquette Sports Law Journal* (1992). Greenberg, who has been an attorney for several college coaches, addresses the issue of "reassignment" clauses. Sometimes a contract will not allow a university to fire a coach, but it can reassign him or her to a lesser position. He states: "[A reassignment clause] states that a coach can be assigned to a new position, such as head of the gym or head of the latrine committee." . . . This situation actually arose with Don Morton [former University of Wisconsin football coach]. Because he had no other job, Morton decided to take the latrine job. He thought, "I'll get my salary, my fringe benefits, my car and my country club membership. . . ." Morton essentially said, "I'll be happy to clean toilets for the remaining three years for the total package." What ultimately happens when a situation like this arises? There is some type of financial settlement, because [colleges will not usually] hang out their dirty laundry in public." Also see James T. Gray and Martin J. Greenberg, *Sports Law Practice* (Charlottesville, VA: Lexis Law Publications, 1998).

  6. Occasionally institutions hire coaches as "at-will" employees, where no contract exists. In these cases, the courts have given the institutions complete discretion to terminate contracts at will. *Frazier v. University of District of Columbia*, 742 F.Supp. 28 (D.D.C. 1990) is an example of an at-will employee who unsuccessfully challenged his dismissal. However, at-will coaches are protected by the doctrine of wrongful termination (see Chapter 15, section 15.3.1., "Employment-at-Will Contracts").

  7. In *Earl Bruce v. The Ohio State University*, No. 87-CV11–7430 (Franklin County, Ohio, 1987), a coach brought a $7.45 million breach of contract suit after his termination over alleged recruiting violations. Plaintiff also raised the issues of slander and wrongful discharge. The case was settled for $471,000.

  8. In *Parker v. Graves*, 340 F.Supp. 586 (D.C. Fla. 1972), a coach was dismissed for conduct that he claimed was protected under the First Amendment. The coach sued the University of Florida for wrongful discharge. In denying plaintiff's First Amendment

claim, the court balanced the coach's rights against his responsibility as a public school employee to provide orderly administration.

9.2.6. Coaches' Contracts: High School

High school coaches are generally teachers first and coaches second. High school coaches are given either a *divisible contract* or an *indivisible contract*. To have a divisible contract means that an individual will have separate coaching and teaching contracts. This can cause problems if one of the individual's contracts is terminated. A teacher in high school is usually eligible for tenure after a specified number of years of teaching. For a coach, however, this is not usually the case. A practical problem arises when a coach is dismissed from his or her job as coach but has tenure as a teacher, and decides to remain at the school in that capacity. If the teacher/coach has a divisible contract, a dispute is generally avoided. However, if the teacher/coach has an indivisible contract, this has led to litigation.

The same issue arises when a coach resigns from a coaching position, but chooses to keep his/her teaching position. The courts have taken different views on whether a contract is divisible or not, with the facts of the case, the language of the contract, and the Collective Bargaining Agreement being important factors for the court to consider. In *Brown v. Board of Education* the court ruled that the plaintiff was hired as a teacher and coach. Therefore, the plaintiff could not resign from one post without resigning from the other (see note 8). However, in *Swager v. Board of Education*, the court ruled that the plaintiff could resign from his coaching duties without affecting his position as a math teacher (see note 6). To address the problem of divisible teacher-coaching contracts, some school districts require the individual to sign an indivisible contract. Under this type of contract, the loss of either position results in the loss of both positions.

High school teachers and coaches are often unionized, and therefore, their contracts are governed by a Collective Bargaining Agreement. Consequently, coaches must follow the grievance arbitration procedure rather than go through the court system. Grievance arbitration is the submission of the parties' grievance to a private arbitrator(s) who listens to the disputed question and gives a binding decision regarding the dispute (see Chapter 11, "Labor Law"). It is important to note that some cases still go to court, because not all teachers are unionized, and a few decisions made by arbitrators are challenged.

In cases where the interpretation of an employment contract is questioned, the court or arbitrator must carefully scrutinize the wording of the contract to determine its precise meaning. Most disputes involving high school coaches revolve around the issue of dismissal. There are two types of dismissal cases: procedural and substantive.

In *procedural* dismissal cases, the reason for dismissal is not challenged, but the procedure followed by the employer to dismiss the employee is challenged. Cases are often brought by a coach who claims that he/she was dismissed without proper notice or hearing. In *Bell v. Vista Unified School District*, 92 Cal. Rptr.2d 263 (Cal. Ct. App. 2000), a high school football coach filed suit claiming that the school district violated the state's open-meeting law by firing him without giving him twenty-four hours' notice of the meeting. The appellate court agreed, ordering the district to reinstate the plaintiff as football coach. The California Supreme Court refused to hear the district's appeal. Plaintiff and the district also settled allegations of wrongful termination, with the district agreeing to pay Bell $125,000.

In *substantive* dismissal cases, the court must assess whether the reason for the dismissal is valid under the terms of the contract. For example, in *McLaughlin v. Machias School Committee*, 385 A. 2d 53 (Me. 1978), a teacher who struck a student in the face during a pickup basketball game was dismissed as "unfit to teach." The teacher challenged the dismissal, and the Maine Supreme Court ruled that the school committee was acting within its rights when it dismissed the teacher. In substantive dismissal cases, courts must determine whether there is just cause for termination.

NOTES

1. A school district can be sued for wrongful termination by a teacher/coach, even if the employee's contract does not mention coaching responsibilities. In the case of *Kingsford v. Salt Lake City School District*, 247 F.3d 1123 (10th Cir. 2001), a high school math teacher brought suit after his termination as football coach. He had been hired more than a decade earlier as a teacher only, but had subsequently taken on coaching responsibilities in several sports. The district court determined that the plaintiff had obtained a property interest in his position as head football coach (see Chapter 5, section 5.4., "Associations and Constitutional Issues"). The school district used an immunity defense in order to avoid having to demonstrate cause for the coach's termination. That defense was rejected, and the case was remanded.

2. In *Cruciotti v. McNeel*, 396 S.E.2d 191 (W. Va. 1990), an unsuccessful applicant for the position of physical education teacher brought action against the school district, alleging that the job posting, which described the opening as "physical education teacher and athletic trainer," constituted an improper joining of employment positions. In affirming the lower court's decision, the Supreme Court of Appeals held that the position of athletic trainer was "extra-curricular," and therefore required a separate contract for employment.

3. In *State ex. rel. Dennis v. Board of Education*, 529 N.E. 2d. 1248 (Ohio 1988), a substitute teacher, who was also a football, basketball, and track coach, was given written notice that his contracts to coach football and basketball would not be renewed. He was not, however, given notice that his substitute teaching and track coaching contracts would not be renewed (though they, too, were not). The coach brought action claiming a procedural violation against the board of education for not giving him notice of nonrenewal of his contracts as substitute teacher and track coach. The court of appeals ruled that the coach was to be reinstated as track coach and substitute teacher.

4. In *Matter of Hahn*, 386 N.W. 2d 789 (Minn. Ct. App. 1986), a girls' basketball coach challenged the hearing officers' conclusion that the school board properly refused to renew her coaching contract. The court of appeals held that the school board established adequate reasons for not renewing the coaching contract.

5. In *Smith v. Board of Education*, 341 S.E. 2d 685 (W.Va. 1985), a teacher and football coach was dismissed from his coaching duties without prior notice and without explanation. The issue before the court was whether a coach was entitled to the same procedural rights that a teacher has under the West Virginia code. The court concluded that a coach was entitled to the same procedural rights, and Smith was reinstated.

6. In *Swager v. Board of Education*, 688 P.2d 270 (Kan. Ct. App. 1984), a teacher brought an action against the board of education to reinstate him as a math teacher after the board had misinterpreted his resignation as basketball coach as a resignation from teaching *and* coaching. In ruling for the teacher, the appellate court reasoned that were his position as teacher not renewed, he would be entitled to certain due process requirements, including a hearing that the board never provided.

7. In *Board of Education v. Youel*, 282 N.W. 2d 677 (Iowa 1979), the court found that plaintiff's conduct as football coach amounted to just cause for termination despite the fact that most of his salary came from his position as mathematics teacher. The question of partial termination was not at issue in the case, and the court expressed "no opinion as to whether Youel, had he requested, was entitled to stay on as mathematics teacher."

8. In *Brown v. Board of Education*, 560 P.2d 1129 (Utah 1977), a teacher who was also a coach resigned from his coaching duties. The school district, claiming that he could not resign from his coaching duties without also resigning from his teaching duties because they were not separate contracts, treated the resignation as a resignation from both duties. The issue in this case was whether the contract to coach and teach was a divisible contract, thus permitting the teacher to resign from one of his duties without affecting the other. The court ruled that the contract was not divisible, and thus the plaintiff's resignation was a resignation from both duties.

9. In *Stang v. Independent School District*, 256 N.W. 2d 82 (Minn. 1977), a high school basketball coach brought action against a school district, alleging it had failed to give him proper written notice and a hearing prior to his dismissal as coach. In ruling for the school district, the court held that the coach was not a teacher within the meaning of the Teacher Tenure Act, and thus was not entitled to written notice and a hearing.

9.2.7. Physicians' Contracts

There is a need to have a physician available for athletic activities, on the professional, college, and high school level. Injuries are a possibility in all athletic contests, and immediate diagnosis and treatment of an injury by a qualified doctor are desirable and often critical. The presence of a physician at certain athletic contests may be a requirement of most teams' or schools' insurance policies. Some college and university team doctors are actual employees of the institution. However, this is the exception rather than the rule. Physicians are normally signed as independent contractors, and as a result, the hiring party avoids liability under the doctrine of vicarious liability. The following is an example of what might appear in a college physician's contract:

> It is understood and agreed that Physician is an independent contractor with regard to all consulting services to be rendered hereunder, and is not acting as College's agent, employee or servant. It is also understood that Physician is not an insurer of results in any medical treatment rendered under the terms of agreement.

The key difference between an employee and an independent contractor is the degree of control and direction exercised over the physician's work by the institution or team. An employee is subject to a much higher degree of control than an independent contractor. Most physicians at the collegiate and professional levels have their own practices or are employees of an HMO, and work with teams or schools on a part-time basis, thus classifying themselves as independent contractors. A physician's contract is a basic employment contract with terms and conditions of employment listed within the contract (see exhibit 9.4).

9.2.8. Officials' Contracts

Officials are generally hired by a league or conference, or in some intercollegiate or interscholastic situations, by the institution. Cases have been litigated

Exhibit 9.4
Physician's Contract

AGREEMENT

STATE_____

COUNTY_____

THIS AGREEMENT made and entered into the _____day of _____, 19xx, by and between _____, a college having its principal place of business in ____ _____ (hereinafter referred to as "College"), and DR. _____, a citizen and resident of _____, (hereinafter referred to as "Physician").

WITNESSETH:

WHEREAS, College is desirous of obtaining the services of Physician in connection with its intercollegiate sports program, and

WHEREAS, Physician is skilled in the practice of medicine and is willing to assist College with its medical programs in its intercollegiate sports program,

NOW THEREFORE, in consideration of the convenants and promises contained herein, the parties agree as follows:

1. College hereby retains and Physician agrees to be retained by College as College's consultant in College's intercollegiate sports program for the school year 1985–86.

2. Physician will act as a consultant with the College's coaches, trainers, athletes and other personnel with regard to medical problems incurred by athletes in the College's intercollegiate sports program. Physician's consulting services shall include attendance at home football games whenever possible. In Physician's absence, he will attempt to find qualified medical help to attend. Physician will be available for consultation one day per week.

3. Physician agrees to review participation medical records on a yearly basis.

4. Physician shall make recommendations to the coaching staff, trainers, and other personnel as to the handling of all medical matters with regards to the athletes in the College's intercollegiate sports program. Such recommendations shall include prescribing treatment for injuries and other medical problems, and recommendations for surgical and other hospital procedures when necessary. All physician charges for such surgery and other hospital procedures are not covered under the terms of this agreement.

5. Physician shall make decisions on athletes practicing, returning to practice or playing in athletic contests. In absence of Physician, he will delegate authority to another physician, head trainer or sports medicine coordinator.

6. Physician will supervise student trainers and graduate assistants through the head athletic trainer and sports medicine coordinator.

7. Physician will make the decision to send an athlete to another physician or delegate that decision to another individual.

8. If an athlete seeks a second opinion without consent of team physician, payment is not guaranteed.

9. As compensation for all consulting services rendered hereunder, College agrees to pay to Physician the sum of $_____ to be paid upon execution of this agreement.

10. It is understood and agreed that Physician is an independent contractor with regard to all consulting services to be rendered hereunder, and is not acting as College's agent, employee or servant. It is also understood that Physician is not an insurer of results in any medical treatment rendered under the terms of this agreement.

11. This agreement is to be construed under and governed by the laws of the State of ____.

IN WITNESS WHEREOF, the parties hereto have executed this agreement in duplicate originals on the day and year first above written.

_____COLLEGE   DR: _____

By: _____   By: _____

over the years as to whether officials are employees or independent contractors. This issue has come up in the area of torts (see Chapter 3, "Legal Principles in Tort Law") and workers compensation. Like a physician, actions by an official may make the hiring party liable for any damages if an employer-employee relationship is established. To ensure that they are not held liable under vicarious liability, many hiring parties will draft contracts that make officials independent contractors (see exhibit 9.5).

While the courts have generally agreed that decisions made by officials are not subject to court examination, officials may find themselves in court as the plaintiff in a case, due to breach of contract (see Chapter 4, section 4.7., "Liability of Officials, Referees, and Umpires"). For example, in *Clemons* v. *Big Ten Conference*, No. 96 (N.D. Ill. 1997), the plaintiff, a football official for the Big Ten, had his contract canceled prior to the 1994 season. Clemons challenged his termination by claiming that the termination was due to his weight, and he had thus been discriminated against under the Americans with Disabilities Act and Title VII. Clemons's work performance had come under review in 1993 when he placed poorly on the officials' rating system used by the Big Ten to monitor its officials. Clemons was placed on probation and told to lose weight, which the conference believed had affected his ratings in a negative way. When Clemons reported to the officials' clinic in August 1994, he had gained more weight, and was subsequently terminated. The court concluded that it was not unreasonable for the conference to demand that its officials maintain an acceptable weight insofar as that their weight may interfere with their officiating duties. The court also found that Clemons had been given sufficient notice after the 1993 season to deal with his weight problem, and since he had not, the conference was justified in taking the actions it did. The court granted summary judgment to the Big Ten Conference.

9.2.9. Facility Contracts

When an institution in amateur athletics, or a team in a professional sports league, does not own an arena or stadium, it is necessary to enter into an agreement for the use of such a facility. In addition to the use of the facility (games, practices, locker rooms, etc.), as well as control of parking, sponsorship, advertising and signage revenue, consideration should be given to the amount of rent charged, the method of payment, and the specific services provided for the facility owner. The responsibility for the promotion of the event, and the provision of personnel to run the arena (security personnel, concessions, ticket takers, work crews, etc.) need to be addressed in the contract. The time of the event(s) and the availability of the arena for warm-ups before the event should also be explicitly stated in the contract. In addition, any potential schedule conflicts between multiple parties leasing the facilities should be addressed in the drawing of an agreement.

Many facility-team contracts have explicit sections titled "Obligations of the (Team or League)" and "Obligations of the (Facility)" (see exhibit 9.6).

Third-party agreements, such as radio or television contracts between the institution and the media, also need to be considered in the drafting of a contract for the use of a facility in case certain accommodations are necessary. Insurance requirements must also be considered. Generally, a facility requires specific types

Exhibit 9.5
An Official's Contract

MODEL CONTRACT BETWEEN
SCHOOLS AND SPORTS OFFICIALS

Please note that this is a "Model" and may have to be modified to fit the particular circumstances of your local association and/or schools at which you officiate. Also, it is based upon general principles of law; therefore, you should review it with a local attorney prior to using it due to differences of state law.

The _____ (home school) [hereinafter "School"] of _____ (city and state) and _____ (official's name) of _____ (official's address) [hereinafter "Official"] enter into the following Agreement:

1. CONTEST. The Official agrees to officiate a _____ (level) _____ (sport) contest between _____ (home school) and _____ (visitor school) at _____ (place) _____ (city and state) on _____ (date) at _____ (time). The other official(s) is/are _____ _____.

2. PAYMENT. In consideration of such services, the _____ (home school) will pay the Official within _____ days of the game date a fee of _____ (amount), plus mileage at the rate of 20 cents/mile for _____ miles, in the amount of $_____.

3. OFFICIAL'S STATUS. The Official agrees to work this game as an independent contractor.

4. OFFICIAL'S REPRESENTATION. The Official represents that he/she is, or will be by the date of the contest, a duly licensed official in this state authorized to officiate this contest. If it is found to be otherwise, this Agreement shall become null and void.

5. INTERPRETATION. The Constitution, By-Laws and rules and regulations of the ____ (state association) and of the _____ (local association) are considered a part of this Agreement and shall govern, except as modified by this Agreement, any disputes arising out of this Agreement. Both parties to this Agreement agree to be so bound.

6. VOIDING OF CONTRACT. This contract shall become null and void upon probation or suspension of either the School or the Official by the _____ (state association).

7. CANCELLATION/POSTPONEMENT. This contract may be canceled at any time by the mutual written consent of both parties. This contract is voidable if either party cannot comply with its terms for any sufficient reason.

A. Sufficient Reason. If the contest is canceled by mutual written consent or for sufficient reason (including, but not limited to, unfavorable weather, illness, accident, or injury) and the Official is not notified in time to prevent travel to the game site, the Official shall be paid the round-trip mileage at the rate of 20 cents/mile. If the contest begins, but is then canceled due to unfavorable weather, the Official shall be paid the fee and mileage expenses set forth in Paragraph 2.

B. Insufficient Reason. If the game is canceled for any insufficient reason, or if either school participating in the contest no longer desires the Official to officiate, the Official shall be paid the fee.

C. Rescheduling. If the contest is postponed and rescheduled, the Official shall be paid the fee set forth in Paragraph 2. If the agreed time of the contest is changed, the Official will be given the first opportunity to officiate at the new time, but if the Official is unable to do so, the Official shall be paid the fee set forth in Paragraph 2.

D. Official's Failure To Officiate. If the Official fails to officiate the game for a reason other than a sufficient reason, then the Official shall pay the school an amount equal to the fee within _____ days of the game date.

E. Payment. Payment of the fee and/or mileage as a result of cancellation, rescheduling, or postponement shall be made by the School and received by the Official within _____ days after the original date set for the game.

Exhibit 9.6
Facility Contract

THIS AGREEMENT is made this 28th day of February 2001 between _(Conference)_ and _(Facility Operator)_.

WHEREAS, the _(conference)_ is a collegiate athletic conference comprised of institutions which have Division 1 men's and women's intercollegiate basketball programs; and

WHEREAS, _(Facility Operator)_ is the operator and/or manager of a multi-purpose sports and entertainment arena located in _(city, state)_, known as _(facility name)_; and

WHEREAS, the _(Conference)_ desires to hold its 2003 men's and women's basketball tournaments at the arena pursuant to the terms of this Agreement; and

WHEREAS _(Facility Operator)_ desires to make the Arena available to the _(Conference)_ for the holding of its 2003 men's and women's basketball tournaments pursuant to the terms of this Agreement;

NOW, THEREFORE, in consideration of the mutual promises exchanged below, the parties agree as follows:

1. **_(Conference)_ 2003 Tournaments**. The _(Conference)_ will hold its 2002 men's and women's basketball tournaments (Tournament) at the Arena pursuant to the terms of this Agreement. The term of this Agreement shall expire on June 30, 2003, except for those provisions that extend beyond the terms of this Agreement. _(Facility Operator)_ agrees that it shall not schedule any events of any type in the Arena during the Tournament, including the day and night prior to the first game.

2. **Tournament Dates**. The dates for the tournament are as follows:

    March _____, 2003

    Game times will be mutually agreed upon by the parties. This schedule may be changed upon mutual written agreement of the parties and is subject to change should the NCAA change its schedule.

3. **Lump Sum Payment to _(Conference)_**

4. **Net Revenue Payment to _(Facility Operator)_** _(Conference)_ agrees to pay the _(Facility Operator)_ 60% of all net revenue from the Tournament within 60 days following the end of the Tournament. "Gross Revenue" shall consist of all revenue derived from the sale of tickets in connection with the Tournament, revenue from sponsorships sold in connection with the Tournament (net of implementation costs and commissions) (except to the extent provided in paragraph 25 and not including title sponsorship revenue which shall be divided as provided in paragraph 14), Net Merchandise and Program Revenue (as defined in paragraph 23), and any other items mutually agreed upon in writing. "Net revenue" is defined as gross revenue less Tournament expenses approved in writing by the __(Conference)__ and ___(Facility Operator)___ which are incurred by ___(Conference)___ or _(Facility Operator)___ including the $_____ annual guaranteed payment identified in Paragraph 3 and less all applicable taxes. _(Conference)_ and the _(Facility Operator)_ agree to settle the finances relating to the Tournament within 60 days following the end of the Tournament.

5. **Ticket Promotion and Sales**. Ticket prices shall be mutually agreed upon by the parties. **They shall not be less than the prices set forth in Exhibit A.** _(Conference)_ and _(Facility Operator)_ will make reasonable efforts to produce promotional mailing materials and ticket order forms and have these materials mailed to all institutions' alumni as identified by the _(Conference)_ and to cause all-session brochures to be available for distribution by November 1 of the

Exhibit 9.6 (continued)

year proceeding the Tournament. These expenses shall be a Tournament expense. *(Facility Operator)* agrees to include the Tournament as part of the **usual** package purchased by its suite holders for events at the **Arena** and the income from **(1) the value of the tickets for each seat in each suite used, with the value to be $_____ per seat per session or $_____ for all sessions and (2) with the full regular ticket value four seats in each of the suites, which may be separately sold,** _____ to be included in Gross Revenue **for the Tournament.**

6.   **Tournament Expenses.** In addition to all other terms of this Agreement, *(Facility Operator)* shall be responsible for the following items and services related to the operation of the Tournament which shall be Tournament expenses: Jumbotron presentations, court set-up and tear down, building security, telephone line installation, police, EMT, utilities, post-event cleaning, public address announcers, ticket sellers and takers, house electricians, hospitality areas, mutually agreed upon marketing materials, press room meals and refreshments, computerized ticket printing, sound technicians, table rentals, pipe and drape rentals, office equipment rentals for *(Conference)* office, program printing and group sales expenses. The *(Conference)* shall be responsible for the following which shall be a Tournament expense: game officials, statisticians, scorekeepers. Tournament expenses shall included the foregoing as well as any other expenses designated as Tournament expenses in this Agreement and any other expenses mutually agreed upon in writing by the parties as Tournament expenses.

7.   **Tournament Suite/Parking.**

8.   **Tournament Title Sponsor Suite**. *(Facility Operator)* shall provide the Tournament's title sponsor with a suite for the duration of the Tournament. *(Facility Operator)* shall provide the usual and customary suite services to the title sponsor suite including food and beverage services at in-house catered rates. This suite is in addition, at the option of the title sponsor, to any other suite the Tournament title sponsor may generally have and use in the Arena.

9.   **(Conference) Office Space.** *(Facility Operator)* shall provide the *(Conference)* office space with out charge for the *(Conference)* exclusive use beginning at 8:00 a.m. on the Wednesday preceding the Tournament and continuing to 12:00 noon on the day following the day of the championship game of the Tournament. This office space will serve as the Tournament headquarters and the administrative office for all Tournament-related events. The office shall be located in a place to be mutually agreed upon at least 180 days prior to the start of the Tournament. The office shall be equipped with the following with out charge to the *(Conference)* for the equipment or lines: two fax machines with capability to send to 48 recipients and telephone lines, high speed photocopier with collator, stapler and four direct outside telephones and telephone lines. Telephone charges, including long distance calls, supplies and related items will be a Tournament expense or may be provided as a trade sponsorship.

10.   **Media Relations.**

11.   **Locker and Training Room Facilities.** *(Facility Operator)* shall provide four locker rooms for use by participating institutions in the Tournament. Each locker room shall include at least 15 separate lockers/stalls for the players, training table and chalkboard or marker board with chalk, markers, erasers and prepared to accommodate both men's and women's teams and readied and available in accordance with daily Tournament schedule. *(Facility Operator)* shall provide use of the _____ *(Facility)* _____ and other **team** training rooms **and equipment therein** for use

Exhibit 9.6 (continued)

throughout the Tournament without any charge to the _(Conference)_. _(Facility Operator)_ shall secure and have sufficient security personnel available to guard all locker rooms and officials' dressing rooms before, during and after game competition. All persons who use the locker rooms shall conduct themselves and treat the facilities in an appropriate manner for the use of such facilities.

12.　**Practice Schedule/Facilities.**　_____(Facility Operator)___, without charge to the _(Conference)_ and the _____ shall jointly develop a practice schedule and secure convenient practice sites and times in the Arena and/or off-site for all institutions participating in the Tournament. The practice schedule shall be mutually agreed upon in writing at least 30 days prior to the first game of the Tournament. The__(Facility Operator)____ shall cause the host institution, _____University, to make its on-campus practice facilities available for use during the Tournament and to coordinate such use with _(Conference's)_ operations personnel.

13.　**Title Sponsorship.** _(Conference)_ shall use its best efforts to secure a title sponsor for the Tournament and if _(Conference)_ so secures it shall provide 60% of the gross sponsorship fee to the _(Facility Operator)_, which amount shall be in addition to the $_____ payment in Paragraph 3. The other 40% shall belong solely to _(Conference)_. No commission shall be charged by _____(Facility Operator)____ relating to procurement of a title sponsor. The _(Conference)_ current Tournament title sponsor, _(Sponsor)_ shall have the right to sponsor this Tournament and _(Conference)_ agrees that this in no way violates any agreement it has with any other bank. If _(Sponsor)_, the current title sponsor of the _(Conference)_ Tournament, decides to sponsor this Tournament or the _(Conference)_ secures a new title sponsor, then that sponsorship fee shall be likewise split as set forth earlier in this paragraph.

14.　**Associate, Trade and Other Sponsorships.**

15.　**Banners and Signage.** _(Facility Operator)_ shall design and produce, subject to prior written approval of the designs and materials by the _(Conference)_, which shall not be unreasonably withheld, an inventory of banners and signage for use before and/or during the Tournament. Except as otherwise provided below, the costs of design, production, installation and removal shall be a Tournament expense. A schedule of required banners and signage is set forth below and shall be in place at all locations, not including the inside of the Arena, at least 3 days prior to the day of the Tip-Off Banquet and remain through the evening of the day after the Tournament championship game, unless otherwise mutually agreed to in writing. All in-Arena banners and signage shall be in place by the morning of the evening of the Tip-off Banquet.

　　　(1)　　two "Welcome _(Conference)_ Tournament" banners containing the _(Conference)_ color logo at each hotel hosting _(Conference)_ teams;

　　　(2)　　four "Welcome _(Conference)_ Tournament" banners containing the _(Conference)_ color logo at _____ Airport.

　　　(3)　　three 3' by 8' "_(Conference)_ Tournament" banners containing the _(Conference)_ color logo and dates of the Tournament on exterior of the Arena and regular announcement of the Tournament on the outside Arena electronic signboard at least 21 days prior to the start date of the Tournament up until and during the Tournament;

Exhibit 9.6 (continued)

(4)   two 4' by 25' "*(Conference)* Tournament" banners containing the *(Conference)* color logo and dates of the Tournament suspended across streets surrounding the Arena subject to local law permitting this to be done;

(5)   ten 8' by 15' *(Conference)* individual member institution banners to be hung from the rafters of the Arena during the Tournament.

(6)   vertical "Welcome Fans" banners containing the *(Conference)* color logo hung from light poles surrounding the Arena and headquarters hotel subject to local law permitting this to be done and with the number and placement of banners to be mutually agreed upon by the _____ and _____; the light poles in and around the Arena parking lots have banners that are in place pursuant to a contract between ___ *(Conference)* and the sponsor.

_____ acknowledges that the banners provided for in item (5) above may be re-used in connection with possible future tournaments, and shall be stores by _____until such time as mutually agreed to in writing.

16.   **Signage/Logos.**

17.   **Additional Signage/Logos.**

18.   **NCAA Floor Markings.**

19.   **Arena Marks.**

20.   **In-Arena Advertising.** *(Facility Operator)* shall advertise the *(Conference)* Tournament throughout the term of this Agreement on Arena inside and outside message boards, the Jumbotron and other marketing mediums within *(Facility Operator's)* control, including but not limited to, event schedules, public address announcements, media ads, *(Three Teams that Play in Facility)* and other commercial means in a manner and in such frequency as is mutually agreed upon in writing and in a manner to highly promote the Tournament. With regard to the aforementioned three teams, *(Facility Operator)* will use its best efforts and assist the *(Conference)* in so obtaining, but *(Facility Operator)* **may not be able to do so** since it does not own or manage these three teams. The *(Conference)* may, at its own option and expense, develop high quality supplemental graphics or in-arena television produced features for use by *(Facility Operator)* in the Arena if such are approved by *(Facility Operator)*, to advertise the *(Conference)* Tournament throughout the term of this Agreement without charge to the *(Facility Operator)* or such advertising and in a manner and in such frequency as mutually agreed upon in writing and in a manner to promote the Tournament.

21.   **Tournament Promotions.** *(Conference)* and *(Facility Operator)* shall develop a mutually agreed upon schedule of marketing promotions to be conducted during pre-game, half-time, and between game segments of Tournament games. These costs, if any, of these promotions above the amounts paid for by sponsorships, shall be a Tournament expense and shall be mutually agreed upon in writing in advance. The promotions shall include those conducted on behalf of Tournament and the *(Conference)* broadcast network sponsors. The *(Conference)* broadcast network Tournament promotions will be scheduled and supervised by representatives

Exhibit 9.6 (continued)

of the _(Marketing Company)_ marketing firm. A list of the _(Marketing Company)_ people and their addresses, telephone and fax numbers is attached as **Exhibit D.**

22. **Tournament Programs and Other Merchandise.**

23. **Official Ball.**

24. **Awards.**

25. **Tournament Staffing.**

26. **Medical Services.** _(Facility Operator)_ shall arrange for a certified EMT unit to be on-site with an ambulance during all Tournament games. This is a Tournament expense. _(Facility Operator)_ shall identify a local hospital that shall handle all emergencies involving the _(Conference)_ Tournament and provide the _(Conference)_ with its name, address, and telephone number 30 days prior to the Tournament.

27. **Security/Radio Units**

28. **Tip-Off banquet and Men's Championship Pre-Game Reception.**

29. **_(Conference)_ Administrators/VIP Reception.**

30. **Hotels.**

31. **Hotel Rooms.**

32. **Marketing Services.**

33. **NCAA Championships.**

34. **_(Conference)_ and Member Institutions' Names**

35. **Confidential Information.**

36. **_(Facility Operator)_ Insurance.** _(Facility Operator)_ agrees to obtain and maintain in effect policies of insurance with carriers licensed to do business in the State of_____ which shall include at least general liability, workers' compensation, property damage and products liability insurance. The general liability, products liability and property damage coverages shall contain coverage amounts of no less than $1,000,000 per occurrence with at least $2,000,000 annual aggregate limit. _(Facility Operator)_ shall provide _(Conference)_ with these Certificates of Insurance confirming the existence of these insurance policies and naming the _(Conference)_ and its member institutions as additional insureds on the general liability policy, but solely with respect to the operations of _(Facility)_. This Certificate of Insurance shall be provided to the _(Conference)_ at least 60 days prior to the start of the Tournament.

37. **_(Conference)_ Insurance.** _(Conference)_ agrees to obtain and maintain in effect policies of insurance with carriers licensed to do business in the state of _____ which shall include at least general liability, property damage and workers' compensation coverage. The general liability policy shall contain a coverage amount of no less than $1,000,000 per occurrence and shall, in addition, provide by endorsement or otherwise coverage with respect to athletic participants in the Tournament. The _(Conference)_ agrees to provide _(Facility Operator)_ with a Certificate of Insurance confirming the existence of the foregoing insurance and naming _(facility)_, County of _____ and the _____County _____ Authority, and their respective related

Exhibit 9.6 (continued)

and affiliated entities, as additional insureds on the general liability policy, and shall provide this to _(Facility Operator)_ at least 60 days prior to the start of the Tournament.

38. **Copyright and Trademark Notices and Registrations.** _(Facility Operator)_ agrees that the vendor(s) selected to sell _(Conference)_ Tournament licensed products shall be required to agree in writing that in any instance where the _(Conference)_ and/or member institutions' marks or logos are used, in conjunction with or related to the Tournament, the following general notice shall be prominently attached (i.e. on the product, on a label, on the packaging material or on a separate slip of paper attached to the product): "This is an officially licensed product of the _(Conference)_. The insignias and names depicted on this product are marks which are the exclusive property of the _(Conference)_ and/or its member institutions and shall not be reproduced or used in any manner without the _(Conference)_ prior written consent." _(Facility Operator)_ shall have any licensee agree in writing that it acknowledges and agrees that it shall not have nor acquire any right, title or interest in or to the name, marks or logos of the _(Conference)_ and/or its member institutions by virtue of this Agreement or any other agreement.

39. _**(Facility Operator)**_ **Indemnification.** The _(Conference)_ shall at all times defend (if _(Facility Operator)_ so requests in writing), indemnify and hold harmless _(Facility Operator)_ , its affiliates, employees, agents and licensees, from and against any and all claims, actions, liabilities, losses, damages, costs and expenses including, without limitation, reasonable attorney's fees and disbursements, arising out of or relating to: (1) any breach or alleged breach of any representation, warranty, covenant or agreement of the _(Conference)_ or (2) any injury sustained by any person or damage to property as a result of any claimed negligent, grossly negligent or reckless act or omission or intentional wrongdoing of the _(Conference)_, its agents or employees and its member institutions and their respective agents or employees. This paragraph shall survive the termination of this Agreement and shall be effective even after this Agreement ends for any reason, voluntary or involuntary.

40. **(Conference) Indemnification.** _(Facility Operator)_ shall at all times defend (if the _(Conference)_ so requests in writing), indemnify, and hold harmless the _(Conference)_, its employees, agents, independent contractors and member institutions, from and against any and all claims, actions, liabilities, losses, damages, costs and expenses including, without limitation, reasonable attorney's fees and disbursements, arising out of or relating to: (1) any breach or alleged breach of any representation, warranty, covenant or agreement of _(Facility Operator)_ or (2) any injury sustained by any person or to property as a result of any claimed negligent, grossly negligent or reckless act or omission or intentional wrongdoing of _(Facility Operator)_ its agents or employees. This Paragraph shall survive the termination of this Agreement and shall be effective even after this Agreement ends for any reason, voluntary or involuntary. With respect to the indemnification of this and the immediately preceding paragraph and upon the written request of any indemnitee to be requested as soon as practicable after learning of a claim demand or action, the indemnitor will assume the defense of any claim, demand or action against such indemnitee and will, upon request by the indemnitee, allow the indemnitee (to the extent permitted by the indemnitor's insurer in the case of insured claims) to participate in the defense thereof, such

Exhibit 9.6 (continued)

participation to be subject to the control of the indemnitor and at the expense of the indemnitee. Settlement by

the indemnitee without the indemnitor's prior written consent shall release the indemnitor from the indemnity as

to the claim, demand or action so settled. All provisions of this Paragraph shall apply to any claim of any nature

that may be made by any person or entity against *(Facility Operator)* related to *(Facility)*, the parking lots or

areas and their adjacent walkways under *(**Facility Operator's**)* **control or supervision** and used by persons

attending the Tournament and any related events. All provisions of this Paragraph shall also apply to any claim

of any nature that may be made by any person or entity against any person or entity that acts as a vendor,

concessionaire or otherwise provides any goods, services, equipment or anything else to the Arena related to

the Tournament and any related events.

41. **Defense/Settlement of Claim.**

42. **Status of _____**

43. **Waiver.**

44. *(Conference) Warranty/(Facility Operator) Warranty.*

45. **Non-Assignability.** This Agreement is not assignable without the written mutual agreement of the parties,

     except that _____ may assign this Agreement, or any part of this Agreement, to an affiliate or any

     entity that acquires all or the majority of the assets.

46. **Renewal.**

47. **Arbitration.** Any controversy or claim arising out of or relating to this Agreement or the breach thereof, shall be

     submitted to a single arbitrator, to be privately mutually agreed upon by the parties prior to the private arbitration

     in _____ but shall be conducted in accordance with the regular Commercial Arbitration Rules of the

     American Arbitration Association as if the arbitration were to be held under the auspices of the American

     Arbitration Association. A Final Judgement upon the Award rendered by the arbitrator, which may include,

     without limitation, interest, filing fees, costs and expenses, but not attorney's fees, may be entered in any court

     having jurisdiction over the party found responsible. Each party is responsible for its own attorney's fees. The

     parties consent to the jurisdiction of the State of _____ and the state and federal courts located in

     _____ for the purpose of any action of any type arising out of or relating to this arbitration or

     Agreement or any terms of this Agreement for any issue that may be outside the scope of arbitration, including

     but not limited to the vacation, modification or confirmation of the arbitrators Award. The parties agree that the

     law of the State of _____ shall govern any action that is filed in court arising out of or relating to this

     arbitration proceeding or Agreement.

48. **Entire Agreement.** This Agreement constitutes the full and complete understanding of the parties related to the

     Tournament and related events covered by this Agreement. This Agreement may not be modified except by a

     single writing signed by both parties.

49. **Signing Authority.**

Exhibit 9.6 (continued)

50. **Force Majure**. If either party is unable to perform due to national, regional or local disaster or emergency, labor dispute, fire, accident or other event beyond such party's reasonable control, then such party that is unable to perform as a consequence thereof shall not be deemed in breach of this Agreement.

51. **Compliance with Rules**.

52. **Compliance with Laws**.

53. **Control of Facility**.

54. **Defacement of Property**.

55. **Evacuation of the Arena**.

56. **Interruption or Termination of Event**. *(Facility Operator)* and the *(Conference)* jointly retain the right to cause an event not to take place or the interruption of any event in the interest of public safety and when *(Facility Operator)* and the *(Conference)* agree such act is necessary.

57. **Rules and Regulations.**

58. **Non-Discrimination.**

IN WITNESS WHEREOF, the parties have executed this Agreement as of the date set forth on the first page of this Agreement.

BY :_____

    (Conference)

    TITLE: PRESIDENT

BY: _____

    (Facility Operator)

    TITLE:

Date:_____

of insurance coverage to be carried by the institution before it will allow the institution to use the facility for a particular event.

Most facility or game contracts have a "force majeure" provision that strikes liability from both parties in the event of an unforeseen circumstance. For example:

> In the event that said exhibition game shall not be played on the said date or some postponed date mutually agreeable to both parties by reason of war, insurrection, strikes, riots, destruction of stadium, act of God, or other force majeure beyond the control of contracting parties, then an exhibition game will be played at said location at a time and date agreed upon by both parties within one year of canceled date.

When complex, million-dollar contracts are being brokered, there is the potential for conflict between the contracting parties. To deal with these problems or disagreements outside of the formal court system, many contracts will have arbitration clauses. This allows potential disagreements to be settled by an independent arbitrator. For example:

> Any dispute, controversy, or claim arising out of, or relating to this agreement, or breach, or termination, shall be settled by binding arbitration in accordance with the rules of the American Arbitration Association. The parties hereby expressly and knowingly agree that judgment upon award rendered in such arbitration shall be binding on the parties and may be entered in any court having jurisdiction thereof.

NOTES

1. In *Metropolitan Sports Facilities Commission v. Minnesota Twins Partnership*, No. C2-01-2010, 2002 Minn. LEXIS 73 (Minn. Feb. 4, 2002). In 2001, Major League Baseball planned to buy and then eliminate the Minnesota Twins (as well as the Montreal Expos) before the 2002 season began. In response, the Metropolitan Sports Facilities Commission (owners and operators of the Hubert H. Humphrey Metrodome) alleged a breach of contract claim against the Minnesota Twins and requested a temporary injunction to keep the Twins at the Metrodome. In addition, the group also sued Major League Baseball for interference with contractual relations and prospective advantage. The court ordered the Twins to play their entire 2002 major league home baseball schedule in the Hubert H. Humphrey Metrodome and ordered Major League Baseball not to interfere "in any way" with the Twins doing so. The court stated, "based on the irreparable harm that will result if the commission does not receive the benefit of its bargain—which will occur if the Twins breach their promise to play their 2002 home games at the Metrodome—as well as the interests in maintaining the status quo pending resolution on the merits, the possibility of success on the merits, the public policy concerns, and the minimal administrative burdens on the district court, we hold that appellants failed to show that the district court abused its discretion in issuing the temporary injunction."

2. In December 2000, the city of Pontiac, Michigan, filed a breach of contract suit against the Detroit Lions, charging that although the Lions were planning on playing in newly built Ford Field starting in 2002, the team was under contract to play at the Silverdome until their lease expired in 2006. Silverdome officials also claimed that the move would cause city residents and businesses significant economic harm. The city claimed it would lose between $50 million and $112 million in lost parking and concession revenue over the four years the Lions would have played at the Silverdome. The two sides reached an agreement in November 2001, one week before the matter was to go to trial. The Lions agreed to pay the city of Pontiac $26.25 million in damages to settle the breach of contract claim.

Chapter 10

ANTITRUST LAW

INTRODUCTION

Since the 1970s, antitrust litigation has played an important role in influencing the business of the major professional sports leagues in North America. For years, professional sports leagues in the United States and Canada believed that they were protected from antitrust challenges under the broad antitrust immunity afforded professional baseball. However, players and their unions have challenged restrictive player rules since the end of the 1960s—in particular, the draft, the reserve system, the commissioner's powers, and free agent compensation systems. In addition, new competing leagues have challenged established leagues' monopoly power, and owners have challenged league rules restricting expansion and relocation of franchises. To challenge restrictive league policies, players, owners, and competing leagues have relied on antitrust theory.

Antitrust litigation has also played an important role at the intercollegiate level. Member universities, coaches, athletes, and shoe companies have all brought suit against the NCAA in order to recover damages resulting from the NCAA's perceived monopoly power. With varying degrees of success, these plaintiffs have used antitrust theory against the NCAA for its restrictions regarding issues such as broadcasting, coach's earnings, athlete eligibility, and commercialism.

This chapter will briefly discuss the history of antitrust law in the United States, and then its history in sports industry. Finally, it will chronicle the most important sports antitrust cases and discuss their relevance to the industry. Understanding antitrust law is crucial before persons in the sports industry can ascertain the rationale behind many rules and structures of organizations such as the NCAA, MLB, and MLS.

10.1. OVERVIEW OF ANTITRUST LAW

Beginning in the late 1880s, the federal government, in conjunction with the states, developed legislation to promote competition and prevent monopolies that might lead to the suppression of competition. A monopoly is defined as exclusive control by one group of the means of producing or selling a product. To monopolize is to dominate by excluding others. In 1890, the Sherman Act was passed by Congress to put an end to unfair monopolization and to protect the American consumer by promoting free and open market competition. Since 1890, each state has also passed legislation that has mirrored the Sherman Act. With regard to the sports industry, it is usually the Sherman Act that is applicable, not the state antitrust acts, due to the interstate travel by teams and television and radio broadcasting across state lines. However, if a sport league operates solely within a particular state's borders, then the state antitrust laws will be applicable.

The antitrust provisions most relevant to professional sports are Sections 1 and 2 of the Sherman Act and Section 3 of the Clayton Act.

Exhibit 10.1
Sherman Act Section 1: Claims and Defenses

Plaintiff	Defense
1. Restraint of trade	1. Attack elements of claim
a) 3 Cs (combination, concert, conspiracy)	2. Restraint of trade defense:
	a) Single entity
b) Unreasonably restrains trade	b) Non-statutory labor exemption
c) Interstate commerce	c) Rule of reason

Courtesy of Lisa Pike Masteralexis.

10.1.1. Sherman Act, Section 1: Restraint of Trade

Section 1: This section proscribes contracts or agreements in restraint of trade:

> Every contract, combination in the form of trust or otherwise, or conspiracy, in restraint of trade or commerce among the several States, or with foreign nations, is declared to be illegal. Every person who shall make any contract or engage in any combination or conspiracy hereby declared to be illegal shall be deemed guilty of a felony, and, on conviction thereof, shall be punished by fine not exceeding $10,000,000 if a corporation, or if any other person, $350,000, or by imprisonment not exceeding three years or by both said punishments, in the discretion of the court.

A Section 1 violation requires proof of three elements:

1. The existence of an agreement among two or more distinct persons or entities
2. The activity unreasonably restrains trade
3. The activity affects interstate commerce.

To prove that an agreement is a restraint of trade, the plaintiff must show that the agreement is between two separate entities, rather than between different units in a single entity. To prove this, the plaintiff must show that there was a *combination* between parties, that the two parties acted in *concert*, and that they engaged in a *conspiracy*. The plaintiff must also demonstrate that the challenged agreement *unreasonably restrains trade*; that is, that the challenged conduct's anti-competitive results outweigh the conduct's pro-competitive results. Finally, the plaintiff must prove that *interstate commerce* has been affected. This last element is especially important to professional sport leagues, because judicial decisions concerning this issue early in the twentieth century concluded that interstate commerce did not exist in relation to professional sports. This issue will be explored in more detail later in the chapter.

Proof that the challenged agreement constitutes an unreasonable restraint on trade depends upon the nature of the challenged conduct. Therefore, two methods of analysis may apply: the *"per se rule"* and the *"rule of reason."* Practices that are deemed illegal "per se" are those that fall within a division of conduct that is inherently anti-competitive, like price-fixing, horizontal agreements, and group boycotts. If the conduct is found to be illegal "per se," the court will not inquire into the business purpose or the actual effect of the offending practice. For example, the Sherman Act has as one of its aims the promotion of price competition. Therefore, agreements that fix, control, raise, lower, maintain, or stabilize the prices charged for products or services have long been viewed to be so destructive to competition that they are automatically considered in violation of the act, without the need to prove the harm. Therefore, horizontal market agreements among competitors that restrict their competition at the same level of the market has traditionally been viewed as a per se violation of the Sherman Act. In addition, any agreement between two separate entities that allocates territories or divides customers is considered a violation. The Supreme Court stated in *Northern Pacific v. United States*, 356 U.S. 1 (1958):

> There are certain agreements or practices which because of their pernicious effect on competition and lack of any redeeming virtue are conclusively presumed to be unreasonable and therefore illegal without elaborate inquiry as to the precise harm they have caused or the business excuse for their use.

In cases where the per se analysis is used, the defense does not have an opportunity to defend the offending agreement; the defense's emphasis is on requesting that the rule of reason analysis be applied instead.

The "rule of reason" analysis applies to conduct that is not manifestly anti-competitive. The relevant inquiry is whether the challenged conduct unreasonably restrains competition. The principal purpose of the rule of reason standard is to determine whether the challenged conduct has pro-competitive results or anti-competitive results. To successfully prove an antitrust violation using the rule of reason standard, the plaintiff must prove three things:

1. There is an agreement between two separate entities.
2. The agreement adversely affects competition in a relevant market.
3. The anti-competitive effects of the agreement outweigh the pro-competitive effects.

The rule of reason doctrine allows the defendant to legitimize or argue its reasons for the agreement. To be considered lawful, the action taken must be found to be no more restrictive than necessary to achieve a legitimate business purpose. Therefore, a defendant using this standard will attempt to prove that there is a legitimate business reason for the restraint, and that the restraint in question is in its least restrictive form. The defense will argue that without such restrictions, the business will be adversely affected and there will be a negative impact on the welfare of the consumer.

In *Smith v. Pro Football Inc.*, 593 F.2d 1173 (D.C. Cir. 1978), the court was forced to determine whether the National Football League draft was a per se violation of the antitrust laws. Smith argued that the draft was comparable to a group boycott, which was considered a per se violation of the Sherman Act. A group boycott is a concerted refusal to do business with horizontal competitors. Smith argued that the draft did not allow football players to do business (i.e. sign player contracts) with horizontal competitors (teams other than the one that drafted the player). The court found that the draft was not a group boycott because the NFL clubs were not competitors in an economic sense, and the draft did have *some* pro-competitive effects. However, under the rule of reason standard, the court found that the draft was anti-competitive:

> The draft is anti-competitive in its effect on the market for players' services, because it virtually eliminates economic competition among buyers for the service of sellers. The draft is allegedly "pro-competitive" in its effect on the playing field; but the NFL teams are not economic competitors on the playing field, and the draft, while it may heighten athletic competition and thus improve the entertainment product offered to the public, does not increase competition in the economic sense of encouraging others to enter the market and to offer the product at a lower cost. . . . The draft's "anti-competitive evils," in other words, cannot be balanced against its "pro-competitive virtues" and the draft be upheld if the latter outweigh the former. In strict economic terms, the draft's demonstrated pro-competitive effects are nil.

10.1.2. Sherman Act, Section 2: Monopolization

Whereas Section 1 of the Sherman Act is aimed at multiple parties acting in concert, Section 2 prohibits *unilateral* monopolization and attempted monopolization.

> Section 2: This section proscribes monopolization or attempt to monopolize. Every person who shall monopolize, or attempt to monopolize, or combine or conspire with any other person or persons, to monopolize any part of the trade or commerce among the several states, or with foreign nations, shall be deemed guilty of a felony, and, on conviction thereof, shall be punished by fine not exceeding $10,000,000 if a corporation, or if any other person, $350,000, or by imprisonment not exceeding three years, or by both said punishments, in the discretion of the court.

To prove that a monopoly exists, two elements must be met: the possession of monopoly market power and the use of unacceptable means to acquire, entrench, or maintain that market power. It is important to note that monopoly market power is different from market share. A product may be superior to its competition and, for good reason, would hold a larger market share. As a hypothetical example, imagine that a product holds 80% of a relevant market share. A competitor might then challenge the way in which that product gained or maintained that market share. Assume that Product A holds 80% of the market share in New England, and Product B holds 20%. Product B may challenge Product A by claiming that Product A attempted to keep Product B from gaining increased market share through the use of predatory or exclusionary tactics (see notes 1 and 2). In its defense, Product A will claim a larger relevant market (i.e., the relevant market is the entire United States, not just New England), and claim natural monopoly (better product). Product A will also attempt to show that it does not have the power to control prices or exclude competition.

The objective of antitrust legislation, as it pertains to monopolization, is to ensure that companies which hold a natural monopoly in a given market do not actively discourage the rise of similar products in that market. For example, in *AFL v. NFL*, 323 F.2d 124 (4th Cir. 1963), the newly formed American Football League argued that the established National Football League possessed monopoly status in the area of professional football (the product) throughout the seventeen cities in which the NFL currently had teams (the relevant market), and attempted to use its monopoly power to keep the AFL from maintaining stability

Exhibit 10.2
Sherman Act Section 2: Claims and Defenses

Plaintiff	Defense
1. Monopoly	1. Not a monopoly
a) Interstate commerce	a) Larger relevant market
b) Monopolization	b) No power to control prices or exclude competition
	2. Natural Monopoly

Courtesy of Lisa Pike Masteralexis.

or success in those regions (see note 4). The appeals court found that the relevant market was not restricted to seventeen cities but, rather, was nationwide and encompassed over thirty viable sites for professional football. The court ruled against the AFL on the monopolization charge because the plaintiff was not able to show that the NFL was exercising monopoly power in the relevant market.

NOTES

1. It is important to reiterate that the example of Product A and Product B and the "80%" figure is merely a hypothetical example. In many cases, a much smaller market share would be considered anti-competitive by federal authorities. For example, the Federal Trade Commission considers any market with a Herfindahl-Hirschman Index (HHI) of more than 1800 to "have adverse competitive consequences [that] ordinarily require no further analysis." HHI is calculated by summing the squares of the top four firms. Mathematically, that means the top firm should always have less than 42.43% of market share in an *ordinary* relevant market—usually much less. For more information, consult the FTC's Web site, and specifically its *1992 Horizontal Merger Guidelines* (Revised in 1997), at http://www.ftc.gov/bc/docs/horizmer.htm

2. Examples of predatory or exclusionary tactics in a professional sport context are (1) an established league expands into the territory of a new rival league, thus pitting the established league team against the new team with respect to competing for the support of local fans, media, and marketing; (2) an established league increases its roster size when a rival league forms.

3. In *Tanaka v. University of Southern California*, No. 00-55046, 2001 U.S. App. LEXIS 11837 (9th Cir. June 7, 2001), the court rejected a student-athlete's Section 1 claim based on the failure to identify a proper relevant antitrust market. The college soccer player had brought suit against her former university after the university allegedly retaliated against her for transferring to a rival school within the same athletic conference. The former school "retaliated" by invoking a never-before-invoked conference rule that would require the student to relinquish a year of financial aid and athletic eligibility at the new institution. Though the student-athlete had been recruited by schools across the country (a national market), the schools involved in the complaint were both in the Los Angeles area. Hence, according to the court, the plaintiff "failed to allege that the transfer rule has had significant anticompetitive effects within a relevant market."

4. The American Football League was created in 1960 by Lamar Hunt, who had attempted to obtain an NFL team in Dallas, and included teams in Houston (Oilers), Denver

(Broncos), Oakland (Raiders), Dallas (Texans), Los Angeles (Chargers), Buffalo (Bills), Boston (Patriots) and New York (Titans). By 1968, the Miami (Dolphins) and Cincinnati (Bengals) had joined the new league. The AFL was able to secure a television contract with ABC, and pooled its television revenues to ensure equal shares to all teams. The NFL would later initiate a similar policy.

10.1.3. Clayton Act

10.1.3.1. Treble Damages

The Clayton Act (1914) determines that when a breach of the Sherman Act has been proven, the monetary damages awarded are to be trebled (tripled). The Clayton Act states:

> [A]ny person who shall be injured in his business or property by reason of anything forbidden in the antitrust laws may sue therefor in any district court in the United States in the district in which the defendant resides or is found or has an agent, without respect to the amount in controversy, and shall recover threefold the damages by him sustained, and the cost of suit, including a reasonable attorney's fee.

Therefore, if a company is found to have violated the antitrust laws, the damages stipulated by the court are trebled. This can result in very large damage awards, especially in the sports industry. For example, when Al Davis won his antitrust suit against the NFL in *Los Angeles Memorial Coliseum Commission v. NFL*, 726 F.2d 1381 (9th Cir. 1984), the trebled damages amounted to more than $30 million. The NFL settled with Davis by paying $18 million and allowing the Raiders to move from Oakland to Los Angeles. More recently, the successful antitrust suit against the National Collegiate Athletic Association by coaches whose maximum earnings had been limited by NCAA rules, *Law v. NCAA*, 134 F.3d 1010 (10th Cir. 1998), resulted in a $54.5 million damages settlement. With regard to the *Law* decision, each Division I institution was forced to pay a pro-rated share of the damages award. The threat of trebled damages, and the fact that winning an antitrust case is weighted in favor of the plaintiff, acts as a deterrent to companies, or leagues, from violating the antitrust laws.

10.1.3.2. Statutory Labor Exemption

Congress also passed the Clayton Act to offer protection to labor unions whose legitimacy was being challenged by employers. Between 1890 and 1914, with the support of the courts, employers had successfully challenged a union's right to organize collectively as a violation of the antitrust laws, specifically that unions acted in concert, combination, and conspiracy, and therefore restrained trade. Employers argued that workers were conspiring against both their employers and the consumers by organizing unions, and by participating in work stoppages.

Section 6 of the Clayton Act provides the first source of an exemption for labor-related activity:

> The labor of a human being is not a commodity or article of commerce. Nothing contained in the antitrust laws shall be construed to forbid the existence and operation of labor . . . organizations from lawfully carrying out the legitimate objects thereof; nor shall such organizations, or the members thereof, be held or construed to be illegal combinations or conspiracies in restraint of trade, under antitrust laws.

The statutory exemption declares that labor unions are not combinations or conspiracies in restraint of trade, and therefore insulates them from retribution for certain labor practices, such as striking or picketing. Professional sports leagues have not often raised the statutory exemption as a defense because the common interpretation of Section 6 of the Clayton Act is that the law was enacted solely for the benefit of labor unions.

10.2. APPLICATION OF ANTITRUST LAW TO PROFESSIONAL SPORTS

Antitrust law has impacted professional sports in a dramatic way, especially since the 1970s. The National Football League alone has been involved in over sixty antitrust cases in its history. Interpretation of the antitrust laws has defined the nature and structure of professional sports leagues, from player mobility restrictions to franchise relocation regulations. When antitrust challenges were first made against professional sports leagues, in the early 20th century, the courts determined that professional sports was not a business, and therefore could not be subject to antitrust legislation. That judicial viewpoint has changed dramatically since the 1970s, and with new interpretations of the antitrust laws in the professional sports context, the leagues therefore have been forced to change to comply with the law.

In this section, we will look at two types of antitrust cases: challenges against a league by its players, or owners, and challenges against an established league by a rival league. This examination is often organized sport-by-sport, rather than chronologically. However, the reader can refer to exhibit 10.3 in order to ascertain the context of certain litigation in relation to litigation in other sports.

10.2.1. Player Restraints and Antitrust Theory

In 1922, in the case of *Federal Baseball Club of Baltimore, Inc. v. National League of Professional Baseball Clubs*, 259 U.S. 200 (1922), the Supreme Court ruled that the professional sport of baseball was not a business involved in interstate commerce, and therefore was not in violation of the antitrust laws. After the *Federal Baseball* decision, other professional sports leagues may have assumed that they, too, were immune from antitrust challenges. However, beginning in the 1950s and peaking in the 1970s and 1980s, players began to use the antitrust laws again to challenge restrictive league rules that prevented players from earning market value, or even having the choice of where to play. After *Federal Baseball*, several decisions changed the way in which the judiciary examined antitrust cases involving professional sports. In *United States v. Shubert*, 348 U.S. 222 (1955), the Supreme Court found that the antitrust laws extended to both the production and the operation of theatrical productions across the United States. In that same year, in *United States v. International Boxing Club*, 348 U.S. 236 (1955), the Supreme Court determined that the defendant's promotion of boxing across state lines constituted trade or commerce among several states, as outlined in the Sherman Act. The Court ruled against the defendant and opened up the possibility that antitrust laws could indeed apply to the sports industry, contrary to the rulings involving professional baseball.

Why did the courts suddenly shift away from the belief that professional sports should not be considered a business? For one thing, professional sports leagues were run as a business: players signed employment contracts and were forced to abide by the labor laws of the time; owners of clubs entered into employment contracts with concession workers, security personnel, and medical personnel; the leagues entered into radio and television broadcasting contracts with national and local broadcasters; and, most important, owners ran their leagues with the goal of making a profit. In addition, it was very clear that professional sports leagues conducted business across state lines, with the significant addition of radio and then television broadcasts across state lines. For these reasons, the courts decided that professional sports leagues were in fact businesses, and therefore subject to the federal antitrust laws.

It is also important to understand why professional athletes were able to challenge the leagues' restrictive regulations using antitrust law. Each team in a league was viewed as a separate business entity, with separate ownership. Therefore, if two or more teams decided to enact and follow certain rules, such as a college draft, they would be acting in *concert, combination,* and *conspiracy,* the very things prohibited by Section 1 of the Sherman Act. It is also important to keep in mind that for an agreement between two business entities to be considered an antitrust violation, it must have *anti-competitive* consequences and be an *unreasonable* restraint on trade.

Players, represented by the "Players Associations," began to actively challenge particular rules that specifically limited a player's mobility (see sections "Football," "Hockey," and "Basketball"). Players argued that rules or regulations which restricted their ability to put their skills on the open market for bidding, violated Section 1 of the Sherman Act, in that the players' ability to demand market value were restrained by league rules.

From their inception, professional sports leagues have used various devices to bind players to specific teams, and limit player mobility. Some of these devices include the following:

1. The "reserve clause," in player contracts until the mid-1970s, gave teams the unilateral right to renew a player's contract in perpetuity. Some Standard Player Contracts still give teams the unilateral right to renew a player's contract, but *not* for a player's entire career.

2. The "draft," which allows only one professional team to draft an eligible player, allows the selected player to negotiate solely with the team that selected him.

3. The "compensation system," still in effect in several leagues, requires a team signing a free agent player to compensate the player's former team by giving up draft picks, players, and/or money.

4. The "right of first refusal" allows a player's prior team to match any competing offer and retain the player's services. This rule still exists in more moderate forms.

Each of these mechanisms allow(ed) the original team of a player to restrict or impede that player's ability to offer his services to the highest bidder. The reserve system, which was the most restrictive form because it had the potential to bind a player to a single team over that player's entire career, resulted in a loss of bargaining power on the part of the player, which in turn depressed his salary. More important, from a legal standpoint, the above-mentioned restrictions imposed upon professional athletes violated antitrust laws. A player's ability to earn a fair market salary was artificially stifled by league owners who illegally acted

Exhibit 10.3
Antitrust Litigation and Legislation Relevant to Big Four Sports

Year	Major League Baseball	National Football Lg.	Nat. Basketball Assoc.	National Hockey Lg.
1890	Sherman Act: Put an end to unfair monopolization and protected consumers by promoting free market competition			
1914	Clayton Act: All damages from Sherman Act violations are tripled; unions do not violate the Sherman Act			
1922	Federal Baseball: Baseball is exempt from antitrust laws			
1953	Toolson: affirms baseball's antitrust exemption			
1955	Shubert and United States Boxing: Antitrust laws may apply to sports besides baseball			
1957		Radovich: Antitrust laws do apply to sports besides baseball		
1961	Sports Broadcasting Act: Television contracts of Big Four Sports are exempt from antitrust scrutiny			
1963		AFL v. NFL: NFL is not yet a nationwide monopoly		
1970-2	Flood: reaffirms baseball's antitrust exemption		Haywood: League age rule is too restrictive	Philadelphia: reserve clause illegally keeps players away from WHA
1974		Kapp: Draft, Standard Player Contracts restrain trade		
1975			Robertson: Draft, reserve system restrain trade	
1976		Mackey: Leagues can't force teams to compensate other teams for signing free agents		

448

1978-9		*Smith v Pro Football*: Draft is more anticompetitive than competitive		
1982		*NASL*: NFL can't prevent owners from owning teams in other leagues		*McCourt*: League is protected from antitrust due to labor exemption
1984		*Raiders*: NFL can't prevent franchise relocations	*Wood*: College players can't sue league if unhappy with union's CBA	
1987		*USFL*: NFL did not use predatory tactics vs USFL; USFL awarded only $3	*Bridgeman*: Labor exemption remains in effect after CBA expires	
1989		*Powell*: Labor exemption remains in effect even after bargaining impasse		
1992-3	*Piazza*: Baseball's antitrust exemption applies only to reserve clause - not franchise relocation	*McNeil*: Labor exemption expires after decertification		
1996-8	*Curt Flood Act*: Antitrust exemption for baseball overturned by legislature. Ownership exemption still maintained	*Brown*: Labor exemption defense applies even if challenged matter was not negotiated during collective bargaining		

in concert, combination, and conspiracy by maintaining unreasonably restrictive league regulations.

In their defense, leagues and owners have asserted that restrictive policies such as the college draft, salary cap, and restrictions on free agency are essential to maintaining a competitive league, and thus are *reasonable* restraints on trade. By "reasonable," they mean that the pro-competitive effects of the rules outweigh the anti-competitive effects. For example, owners contend that the purpose of the college draft is to give struggling teams a chance to compete with the better teams in the league by giving them first choice from the pool of eligible players. Owners also maintain that league rules restricting the ability of players to move from team to team are necessary to build fan loyalty and to prohibit one team from signing all the quality players. Owners state that these rules are reasonable because the viability of the leagues depends on evenly balanced teams that are able to compete every time on the field, court, or ice. In addition, owners have maintained that such regulations allow teams to remain financially solvent, and that the abolition of these regulations would result in bankruptcy.

Players whose salaries had been kept artificially low due to the restrictive rules of the leagues, challenged those restrictive rules using antitrust theory. They focused their attention on two types of common player restraints: (1) those restricting a player's ability to sign with another team and (2) those requiring compensation to be given to the former team by the team acquiring the player. It is the first, a restriction on freedom of movement, that has caused the greatest amount of litigation in this area. The following is a brief explanation of the antitrust challenges in professional football, hockey, and basketball that relate specifically to player restraints.

10.2.1.1. Football

The first case to challenge a sports league following the *International Boxing* decision was *Radovich v. NFL*, 231 F.2d 620 (9th Cir. 1956). In this case a former Detroit Lion challenged a league decision to blacklist him after he had played two seasons in the rival All American Football Conference, following his Lions career. The challenge was under Sections 1 and 2 of the Sherman Act. The district court and the appeals court determined that football was similar to baseball in its operation, and therefore should be granted the immunity from the antitrust laws that professional baseball enjoyed. The Supreme Court, however, reversed the lower court decisions and found that the business of football was clearly engaged in interstate commerce, and was therefore subject to antitrust laws. In addition, the Court noted "that were we considering the question of baseball for the first time upon a clean slate we would have no doubts that baseball should be subject to antitrust laws." (See *Radovich v. NFL*, 352 U.S. 445 (1957)). The significance of this case is that it clearly illustrated that the antitrust immunity afforded baseball should not apply to other professional sports leagues, a view that would be echoed in *Flood v. Kuhn* (see section 10.3.1.4., "Baseball Anomaly Upheld: *Flood*").

In *Kapp v. NFL*, 390 F.Supp. 73 (N.D. Cal. 1974), the plaintiff was able to prove that NFL player restrictions, including the college draft, the Standard Player Contract "reserve clause," and the option clause, were restraints of trade. Using the rule of reason analysis, the court found the challenged restrictions "so patently unreasonable," and that they went "far beyond any possible need." The court decided in favor of Kapp. As a result, the NFL modified its draft so as to appear to be in a less restrictive form.

In *Mackey v. NFL*, 543 F.2d 606 (8th Cir. 1976), the plaintiff challenged the "Rozelle Rule," whereby a team signing a player from another team was required to pay compensation in the form of draft picks, players, or money. The court found for the plaintiff, using the rule of reason analysis. Following the decision, the NFL Players Association negotiated a new Collective Bargaining Agreement that eliminated the Rozelle Rule and in its place created the Right of First Refusal/Compensation System.

The college draft was challenged in *Smith v. Pro Football Inc.*, 593 F.2d 1173 (D.C. Cir. 1978). The district court applied the per se doctrine and ruled in favor of the plaintiff. The D.C. Court of Appeals also ruled in favor of the plaintiff, but rejected the per se rule, instead applying on the rule of reason.

The Right of First Refusal/Compensation System was challenged unsuccessfully in *Powell v. NFL*, and successfully in *McNeil v. NFL* and *Jackson v. NFL*, which are discussed in more detail in section 10.3.5., "Exemption After Decertification: *McNeil*."

10.2.1.2. Hockey

In *Philadelphia World Hockey Club, Inc. v. Philadelphia Hockey Club, Inc.*, 351 F.Supp. 462 (E.D. Pa. 1972), the plaintiff was a competing league which argued that the "reserve system" used by the NHL clubs, which bound a player to a team in perpetuity, was a violation of Section 1 of the Sherman Act. The plaintiff wanted the per se doctrine applied, but the court refused, citing the "relative paucity of litigation on this type of reserve clause." Using the rule of reason, the court found that some type of reserve system was necessary:

> For maximum customer receptivity and profit it is in the best interest of any club that its opponents not generally be viewed by the public as totally incompetent and utterly unable to compete effectively. . . . Thus, if it is not possible to keep the competitive challenge of all teams within some reasonable parameters, some type of intraleague reserve clause may be desirable and in fact necessary.

The case was settled out of court when several teams from the World Hockey Association were merged into the NHL.

The reserve system was again challenged in *McCourt v. California Sports Inc.*, 460 F.Supp. 904 (E.D. Mich. 1978). In this case a professional hockey player challenged the decision that he was to be compensation for his team's signing of a free agent. He challenged the decision using antitrust theory against the league's compensation system. He won a preliminary injunction because he was able to convince the court that he had a likelihood of success on the merits:

> Like the "Rozelle Rule," bylaw 9A applies to all players without regard to status or ability; it applies to the average player and to the superstar alike; it is unlimited in duration and acts as a perpetual restriction upon a player's ability to freely contract for his services. Bylaw 9A cannot be justified by any legitimate business purpose and is more restrictive than necessary to achieve the NHL's announced goal of maintaining competitive balance. It inhibits and deters teams from signing free agents, decreases a player's bargaining power in negotiations, denies players the right to sell their services in a free and open market, and it depresses salaries more than if competitive bidding were allowed.

The case was later decided on appeal, *Dale McCourt v. California Sports Inc.*, 600 F.2d 1193 (6th Cir. 1979), in favor of the NHL due to the non-statutory labor exemption (discussed in detail later in this chapter).

NOTES

1. The World Hockey Association (WHA) was formed in 1971 and signed a number of NHL stars, including Bobby Hull, Gerry Cheevers, and J. C. Tremblay. The WHA operated for a number of seasons before merging several teams with the NHL. For more information on the WHA, WFL, and ABA, see Gary Davidson, *Breaking the Game Wide Open* (New York: Atheneum). For historical information about the ABA specifically, see Terry Pluto, *Loose Balls* (New York: Simon and Schuster, 1990).

2. For information about the history of the USFL, see Jim Byrne, *The 1 Dollar League: The Rise and Fall of the USFL* (New York: Prentice-Hall, 1986).

10.2.1.3. Basketball

The first successful antitrust case against player restrictions in the National Basketball Association was *Denver Rockets v. All-Pro Management*, 325 F.Supp. 1049 (C.D. Cal. 1971). In this case, basketball star Spencer Haywood successfully challenged the NBA's age restrictions for entry into the league. At issue in this case were Sections 2.05 and 6.03 of the NBA Bylaws. Those sections stated that persons were ineligible to play in the NBA, under any circumstances, until four years after their original high school classes had graduated. After one year in junior college and one additional year at the University of Detroit, Haywood signed a professional contract with a team in the NBA's rival American Basketball Association (ABA). After a highly successful first season, in which Haywood garnered ABA "Rookie of the Year" honors, Haywood and his team became embroiled in a contract dispute. Consequently, Haywood signed a contract with the NBA's Seattle Supersonics. NBA Commissioner, Walter Kennedy, disapproved the contract, claiming that Haywood was not yet eligible to play under NBA Bylaws 2.05 and 6.03, and threatened sanctions if Haywood attempted to play.

Haywood was allowed to play under a preliminary injunction, while this case was being litigated. During the case, Haywood argued that the NBA's Bylaws constituted a group boycott, a Section I Sherman Antitrust violation, against persons less than four years out of high school. The court agreed, granting Haywood partial summary judgment and denying the NBA an opportunity to argue its "rule of reason" defense (it applied the per se standard). The court stated, "Sections 2.05 and 6.03 of the Bylaws of the National Basketball Association are declared to be illegal under Section 1 of the Sherman Act." This case effectively opened the doors for players to leave college early in order to play in the NBA.

During the same period as the *Kapp* and *Philadelphia* decisions, a class of plaintiffs brought a class action suit against the National Basketball Association challenging the college draft, the reserve system, and compensation practices. In *Robertson v. NBA*, 389 F.Supp. 867 (S.D.N.Y. 1975), as in the previous two cases, the plaintiff attempted to prove that the restrictive measures taken by the NBA were violations of antitrust law. The court agreed, and found the restrictions to be a per se violation of the Sherman Act:

> It is difficult for me to conceive of any theory or set of circumstances pursuant to which the college draft, blacklisting, boycotts, and refusals to deal could be saved from Sherman Act condemnation, even if defendants were able to prove at trial

their highly dubious contention that these restraints were adopted at the behest of the Players Association.

The next antitrust challenge to the NBA occurred in 1984, after the NBA and the NBA Players Association had come to an agreement on a new Collective Bargaining Agreement that contained a salary cap. In *Wood v. NBA*, 602 F.Supp. 525 (S.D.N.Y. 1984), a rookie challenged the salary cap as an unreasonable restraint on trade. The court found against the plaintiff because of the non-statutory labor exemption defense (see section 10.3.2., "The Non-Statutory Labor Exemption"). NBA players challenged the NBA's restrictive rules when the 1983 agreement expired in 1987, in *Bridgeman v. NBA*, 675 F.Supp. 960 (D.N.J. 1987), but were unsuccessful because the court found the labor exemption to remain in effect even when a Collective Bargaining Agreement had expired.

NOTE

1. In *Molinas v. NBA*, 190 F.Supp. 241 (S.D.N.Y. 1961), a player who had been suspended indefinitely for gambling sued the NBA for entering into a conspiracy with its member teams in restraint of trade. The appeals court found that Molinas was not able to prove a conspiracy and that the charges did not fall under the Sherman Act.

10.2.2. Ownership Restraints and Antitrust Theory

Similar to player restraints, professional sports leagues have rules and regulations that govern the actions of the particular league's owners. What is different about the rules that govern owners, compared to the rules that restrict players, is that ownership standards are predetermined by the league (see note 1), whereas player restrictions are promoted by the ownership and carried out by the league. Leagues have attempted to regulate the actions of owners and potential owners so as to maintain financial stability for the league, and to improve or maintain the league's image. Each league has rules that prohibit owners from criticizing game officials. This is to maintain the integrity of the officials. All professional sports leagues have rules that make it difficult for new franchises to be established in the same geographic area as an existing franchise. This rule is in place to allow the established team to maintain its fan base and not have it eroded by a new team a few miles away. Owners accepted these rules because they understood that they were in place for the best interests of the game and, more important, because these rules did not financially hurt them.

One rule that did financially hurt the owners was franchise relocation restrictions. Beginning in the late 1960s, owners of professional sports teams began to lobby their local governments for public money to be used for new stadium construction. Several teams received new stadiums. Among them were the Houston Astros, whose new stadium was the then state-of-the-art Astrodome. Owners realized that increased profits could be obtained by getting a publicly financed stadium with luxury seating and increased capacity. If the local government refused to publicly support arena/stadium construction, the owner would threaten to move to a city or region that was willing to support the franchise. However, league rules dictated that owners could not relocate a franchise to another city or region unless other owners unanimously—or in other leagues nearly unanimously—consented to the relocation (see note 1). Each professional sports league had rules pertaining to this issue, and although they varied slightly, each league's policies had the same effect: franchise relocation was kept to an absolute minimum.

From a legal standpoint these restrictions clearly impeded an owner's right to increase the profitability of his team by relocating to a city or region that was willing to publicly finance a stadium or arena. According to antitrust theory, to prove a Section 1 violation, there must be interstate commerce, a restraint of trade, and an agreement between at least two entities. Owners who were denied the right to relocate their franchise argued that their ability to increase profits was restrained by league rules, and that the league owners acted in concert, combination, and conspiracy with each other. The leagues argued that the rules were a reasonable restraint on trade because they had pro-competitive effects. It was in the league's best interest to have a strong and loyal fan base, because such loyalty resulted in league stability and easier marketability.

Leagues were able to maintain a high level of control over the franchises in this area until one owner challenged the right of the league to restrain an owner's ability to relocate a franchise.

NOTE

1. Depending on the league, team owners might have varying levels of influence on the decisions of the league office. For example, MLB owners can prevent the league from allowing the relocation of an American League team if 25% of AL owners and more than 50% of NL owners oppose the relocation. Furthermore, any MLB ownership group can prevent the league office from forcing its team to switch leagues.

10.2.2.1. Raiders v. NFL

By the mid-1970s the National Football League claimed to have developed the most extensive fan base and achieved the highest level of stability of all the professional sports leagues, based on the fact that the NFL had not had a franchise relocation since the Chicago Cardinals moved to St. Louis in 1960. One reason for this was the fact that a unanimous vote by the NFL's Board of Governors was needed to allow such a move. This rule was put under scrutiny when Carroll Rosenbloom moved the Los Angeles Rams from the Los Angeles Memorial Coliseum to Anaheim Stadium in Orange County. The Governors approved the move, and the Rams moved after the 1976 season. The Los Angeles Memorial Coliseum Commission, the body that administered the Coliseum, immediately began to seek a replacement for the Rams, either an expansion franchise or a current NFL team willing to relocate. Al Davis, owner of the Oakland Raiders, had reached an impasse with the Oakland Coliseum over a new lease, and decided to relocate the Raiders to Los Angeles and play out of the Memorial Coliseum in 1980. Rule 4.3 of the NFL Constitution stated that a unanimous vote was required to move a franchise into the home territory of another team. Since the Raiders would be within seventy-five miles of Orange County (Rams), unanimous consent was required by the owners. In March 1980, the NFL owners voted 22–0 against the proposed relocation.

The result was *Los Angeles Memorial Coliseum Commission v. NFL*, 726 F.2d 1381 (9th Cir.), *cert. denied*, 469 U.S. 990 (1984), commonly referred to as *Raiders*. The issue before the district court was whether the rule, which stated that unanimous approval of the relocation of a franchise was required by the ownership, was in violation of antitrust laws. The trial court found the antitrust laws had been violated and ruled against the NFL.

The 9th Circuit upheld the district court's decision. Using the *rule of reason* standard, the court found that the restriction on franchise movement was anticompetitive because it perpetuated local monopolies. The court argued that the move to Los Angeles would promote competition rather than stifle it. The court rejected this argument:

> [The] NFL made no showing that the transfer of the Raiders to Los Angeles would have any harmful effect on the League. Los Angeles is a market large enough for the successful operation of two teams, there would be no scheduling difficulties, facilities at the L.A. Coliseum are more than adequate, and no loss of future television revenue was foreseen. Also, the NFL offered no evidence that its interest in maintaining regional balance would be adversely affected by a move of a northern California team to southern California.

The court awarded damages of $4.6 million to the Coliseum, and $11.5 million to the Raiders, both of which were trebled. The NFL settled by paying out a total of $18 million and granting the franchise move.

The impact of this judicial decision on professional sports is important to consider. While the jurisdiction of the 9th Circuit does not encompass the entire United States, the *Raiders* decision suggested that professional sports leagues do not have the authority to dictate to their members whether or not they can relocate their franchise. Movement of franchises in the NFL, NBA, and NHL since the *Raiders* decision illustrates that these leagues must have reasonable franchise relocation policies (see note 3). It is also important to recall that Major League Baseball is protected under its antitrust exemption from challenges to league ownership issues. The Curt Flood Act of 1998, which will be discussed later in this chapter, altered the exemption only in that players are now allowed to sue using antitrust theory. Prior to the passage of the Curt Flood Act, prospective owners had tested whether MLB's antitrust exemption applied to franchise ownership (see note 1). But in light of the Curt Flood Act, owners, prospective owners, and competitor leagues are explicitly precluded from using antitrust theory against MLB.

NOTES

1. In *Piazza v. MLB*, 831 F.Supp. 420 (E.D. Pa. 1993), a potential ownership group, attempting to bring baseball to the Tampa area, brought a Sherman Act Section 1 antitrust claim against MLB and its teams for prohibiting their purchase of the San Francisco Giants. Plaintiffs also alleged that defendants had discriminated against them due to their Italian-American heritage and had unfairly associated them with "the Mafia." Despite offering $15 million more than any other ownership group, their offer was denied in favor of a group that would keep the team in San Francisco. The court rejected MLB's argument that its antitrust immunity applied in this case, favoring plaintiff's arguments that the antitrust exemption was limited to the reserve clause. The Federal Appellate Court agreed with this decision by rejecting MLB's appeal. This led to an estimated $6 million cash settlement for the plaintiffs. These types of suits are less likely to occur again in MLB due to the Curt Flood Act of 1998. For more information on *Piazza* and its relationship to the Curt Flood Act, see John Wolohan, "The Curt Flood Act of 1998 and Major League Baseball's Federal Antitrust Exemption," 9 *Marquette Sports Law Journal* 347 (Spring 1999).

2. In *NBA v. SDC Basketball Club Inc.*, 815 F.2d 562 (9th Cir), *cert. denied*, 484 U.S. 960 (1987), the San Diego Clippers attempted to move to Los Angeles but the NBA blocked the move. On summary judgment the district court said the NBA would lose according to the precedent set forth in *Raiders*. The 9th Circuit disagreed with the district court's ruling on summary judgment and stated that *Raiders* did not lay down a ban on any rule involving the issue of franchise relocation. Thus the case deserved a full trial, where its merits would be decided. The NBA subsequently altered its franchise relocation rules to include objective standards as outlined by the court in *Raiders*.

3. The following franchise relocations have occurred in "Big Four" sports since the *Raiders* decision. NHL: the Minnesota North Stars relocated to Dallas (Stars); the Quebec Nordiques to Colorado (Avalanche); the Hartford Whalers to North Carolina (Hurricanes); the Winnipeg Jets to Phoenix (Coyotes). NFL: Baltimore Colts to Indianapolis (Colts); St. Louis Cardinals to Phoenix (Cardinals); Los Angeles Raiders back to Oakland (Raiders); Los Angeles Rams to St. Louis (Rams); Cleveland Browns to Baltimore (Ravens); Houston Oilers to Tennessee (Titans). NBA: Kansas City Kings to Sacramento; San Diego Clippers to Los Angeles; Vancouver Grizzlies to Memphis; Charlotte Hornets to New Orleans. MLB: No franchise has relocated since fourteen years prior to the *Raiders* decision, Seattle Pilots to Milwaukee (Brewers).

4. Franchise applicants have also used the antitrust laws to challenge denied franchise applications. In *Levin v. NBA*, 385 F.Supp. 149 (S.D.N.Y. 1974), Levin, a prospective buyer of the Boston Celtics, was denied the franchise because of what some owners referred to as a "shady" background. Levin sued, using antitrust theory. The court found that the denial of Levin's application was not an antitrust violation because the rejection did not have an anti-competitive impact: Levin still had the opportunity to compete with the league, and was not excluded from that. A similar case is *Mid-South Grizzlies v. NFL*, 720 F.2d 772 (3rd Cir. 1983). The appeals court found that the challenge was unsubstantiated because the plaintiff still had the capacity to compete against the NFL, and was not being denied that right even though the team was denied entry into the League.

5. One of the first cases to deal with the issue of franchise relocation was *San Francisco Seals Ltd. v. National Hockey League*, 379 F.Supp. 966 (C.D. Cal. 1974), which concerned denial by the League of a proposed move for the NHL team from San Francisco to Vancouver. In granting summary judgment for the NHL the court found there was no restraint of trade or commerce in the relative market.

10.2.2.2. Raiders v. NFL *Revisited*

In a more recent and separate case, Al Davis again brought suit against the NFL for alleged interference in his attempt to relocate the franchise. Davis claimed that he tried to move the Raiders from the Los Angeles Coliseum to a proposed new site in Hollywood Park in 1994. He accused the NFL of sabotaging this deal by pushing for a second team to play in the Los Angeles market, and asked the jury for $1.2 million in damages. The league countered that Davis was never serious about moving to Hollywood Park, but was merely using the site as leverage in order to get a better stadium deal in Oakland. In fact, Davis did accept a deal to move the Raiders back to Oakland in 1995. The deal included $63 million in loans, payments, and benefits. A federal jury voted 9–3 in favor of the NFL after a six-week trial in 2001.

It is important to point out that Davis's legal theories in the 2001 case were not overtly based on antitrust, but instead on the theories of breach of contract, "unjust enrichment," and fraud. Ironic in light of the original *Raiders* case, Davis's 2001 lawsuit stemmed from the NFL's alleged decision *not* to enforce his monopoly power over the Los Angeles market. Nevertheless, because the 2001 case centered on a league's ability to dictate franchise movement, it is notable in the context of sports antitrust cases.

NOTE _____

1. The *Los Angeles Times* and its Web site (www.latimes.com) provided comprehensive coverage of the 2001 Raiders trial. Also see Ken Peters's Associated Press account, "Litigious Raiders Lose Latest Suits Against NFL," May 22, 2001. At the time of this decision, it was one of many suits involving Al Davis and the Raiders.

10.2.3. Interleague Antitrust Challenges

This section focuses on antitrust litigation that originated from the competition between rival leagues. Competition between competing leagues originates from the time baseball was gaining widespread popularity at the end of the 19th century. The first such litigation surrounding competing leagues was the 1922 *Federal Baseball* decision that created the "baseball exemption" from antitrust laws. The litigation from that case, as well as others that followed, centered on the theory that established leagues, like Major League Baseball or the National Football League, held a monopoly over that particular industry and used anti-competitive measures to maintain that monopoly.

It is important to remember that to prove that a Section 1 antitrust violation exists, the plaintiff must show that there is an agreement between two or more entities, that the agreement adversely affects competition in a relevant market, and that the anti-competitive effects outweigh the pro-competitive effects. The professional sports league that has had the most litigation in this area is the NFL.

In *American Football League v. NFL*, 323 F.2d 124 (4th Cir. 1963), the AFL sued the NFL under the Sherman Antitrust Act. While the plaintiffs filed Section 1, 2, and 3 claims, the case primarily focused on the section 2 claim that the NFL was using its monopoly status to put the AFL out of business. The court was forced to determine whether the NFL enjoyed monopoly power, and, if so, was it using its monopoly power to undermine the fledgling AFL. To determine this, the court was forced to judge what the "relevant market" was. The AFL argued that the relevant market was the seventeen cities where the NFL had franchises. The NFL argued that the relevant market was the entire country, and when put in that context, it was clear the NFL did not hold monopoly status, since many cities were available.

The court found that a relevant market for antitrust analysis was the national market for players, television rights, and spectators. The court determined that there were approximately thirty areas in the country that could maintain a professional football team. The appeals court affirmed the district court and noted:

> The District Court's finding that [the NFL] did not have the power to monopolize the relevant market appears plainly correct. In 1959, it occupied eleven of the thirty-one apparently desirable sites for team locations, but its occupancy of some of them, such as New York and San Francisco-Oakland was not exclusive, for those metropolitan areas were capable of supporting more than one team.

The court concluded that the NFL had a natural monopoly in the cities where franchises already existed, and was not using predatory tactics against the AFL. Soon after the appeals court decision, the American Football League and the National Football League merged into a single league for the purposes of maintaining player salaries and ending further legal skirmishes. The merger itself was anti-competitive and violated the antitrust laws, because the only two leagues in an industry were merging, thus taking away all competition in a single industry, the business of professional football. Congress allowed the merger to take place after the 1961 Sports Broadcast Act was amended. The amendments allowed "a joint agreement by which the members of two or more football leagues combine their operations in expanded single leagues . . . if such agreement increases rather than decreases the number of professional football clubs to operate." With congressional approval, the two leagues merged in 1970 and immediately began a series of expansions.

NOTES ⸻

1. Major League Baseball has not faced a competitor league since 1914, when the Federal League folded. The National Hockey League formed in 1917 and did not face a competitor professional hockey league until the emergence of the World Hockey Association (1973–1979). The National Basketball Association has faced two challenges to its stature as the predominant pro basketball league: the American Basketball League (1961–1962) and the American Basketball Association (1967–1976). The National Football League has had several competitor leagues: the All-American Football Conference (1946–1949), the American Football League (1960–1966), the World Football League (1974–1975), the United States Football League (1983–1985), and the XFL (2001). In women's sports, competition from the WNBA caused the ABL to fold in December 1998. In 1996–1997, the ABL was the best-attended women's professional team sports league in the United States.

2. The AFL began play in 1960 and consisted of teams in Boston, Buffalo, Houston, New York, Dallas, Denver, Los Angeles, and Oakland. The League had a broadcast contract with ABC until 1965, when NBC took over the contract. Dallas moved to Kansas City in 1963 and became the Chiefs. These eight franchises, plus two expansion teams (Miami and Cincinnati) joined the NFL in the merger of 1970.

10.2.3.1. USFL v. NFL

The National Football League was embroiled in antitrust challenges after a competitor league attempted to operate in several of the same markets as the NFL. In *United States Football League v. NFL*, 842 F.2d 1335 (2d. Cir. 1988), the upstart United States Football League sued the NFL for monopolizing professional football and using predatory tactics to limit the growth of the USFL. The USFL had decided to move its season schedule from the spring (when it did not compete with the NFL playing season) to the fall (in direct competition with the NFL) but was unable to secure a television deal that would broadcast its games. The USFL argued that the NFL had used predatory tactics against it by securing television deals with the three major networks at that time—CBS, ABC, and NBC. The fact that the NFL rotated the Super Bowl among the three networks gave the NFL the leverage it needed to ensure that none of the networks carried USFL games. Without a television contract, the USFL had no way of competing against the NFL. The USFL also argued that the NFL was clearly trying to put the rival league out of business by expanding into USFL geographic areas and increasing rosters.

For example, The USFL alleged that the NFL and the City of Oakland conspired to destroy the USFL's Oakland Invaders in exchange for the NFL's promise that Oakland would receive an NFL team. The city of Oakland had already lost the NFL Raiders to Los Angeles (see section 10.2.2.1., "*Raiders v. NFL*"), when Raiders' owner Al Davis moved the team over the objections of NFL owners and citizens of Oakland. In fact, the USFL used Davis's testimony in this case to supplement its argument that the NFL was using predatory tactics, as Davis had admitted under oath that he "sensed" the NFL wanted to "destroy" the Invaders. The USFL further alleged that the NFL attempted to "co-opt" its players with a supplemental draft of USFL players and with a roster increase.

The jury found in favor of the USFL insofar as it was able to prove that the NFL did indeed enjoy a monopoly, which was in clear violation of Section 2 of the Sherman Act. The jury did not find that the NFL used predatory tactics to sabotage the USFL. The jury awarded the USFL $1.00 in damages, which was trebled to $3.00, pursuant to the Clayton Act. There are two primary reasons why the USFL received such a small damage award. First of all, the jury "expressly rejected" the USFL's television claim, which had alleged that the NFL had used its monopoly power with the networks to keep the USFL from procuring lucrative contracts. While the USFL alleged various counts of anticompetitive behavior, the television accusation was the "heart of this case" by the USFL's own admission. Secondly, the jury believed that the USFL itself was largely responsible for its unappealing product:

> [T]here was evidence that the USFL abandoned its original strategy of patiently building up fan loyalty and public recognition by playing in the spring. The original plan to contain costs by adherence to team salary guidelines was discarded from the start. Faced with rising costs and some new team owners impatient for immediate parity with the NFL, the idea of spring play itself was abandoned even though network and cable contracts were available. Plans for a fall season were therefore announced, thereby making 1985 spring play a "lame-duck" season. These actions were taken in the hope of forcing a merger with the NFL through the threat of competition and this litigation. The merger strategy, however, required that USFL franchises move out of large television markets and into likely NFL expansion cities. Because these moves further eroded fan loyalty and reduced the value of USFL games to television, the USFL thereby ended by its own hand any chance of a network contract. . . . The Sherman Act does not outlaw an industry structure simply because it prevents competitors from achieving immediate parity. This is particularly so in the case of major-league professional football because Congress authorized a merger of the two leagues existing in 1966 and thus created the industry structure in question.

The USFL attempted to obtain injunctive relief against the NFL based on the jury's finding of monopolization. The USFL sought one of three possible reliefs: (1) USFL teams were to be merged into the NFL; (2) the NFL was to be split into two separate leagues; or (3) the NFL would be forced to give up one of its three television contracts. The injunctive relief was denied due to an unlikelihood of success on the merits, and the USFL subsequently folded.

10.2.3.2. NASL v. NFL

The main issue at stake in *North American Soccer League v. NFL*, 670 F.2d 1249 (2d Cir.) *cert. denied*, 459 U.S. 1074 (1982) was whether NFL rules that banned "cross-ownership"—that is, ownership of a team in another professional sports league—were in violation of antitrust laws. The North American Soccer League contended that the ban monopolized the pool of potential owners. Cross-ownership had long been a contentious issue between NFL owners, who had an informal policy in place prohibiting NFL owners from owning controlling interest in franchises in other professional sports leagues. In 1978 the cross-ownership policy was strengthened by imposing substantial fines on teams that did not divest their ownership holdings in other professional sports leagues. After the stricter guidelines were initiated, the NASL filed its suit.

At the district court level the court found in favor of the NFL, relying on the League's "single-entity" defense that the League was protected against the antitrust laws because a single corporation cannot act in concert with itself. The district court noted that the ban was indeed anti-competitive, but the single-entity defense protected the League against prosecution.

On appeal, the United States Court of Appeals, Second Circuit, denied the NFL's argument of the single-entity defense. The court relied on the *rule of reason* standard to weigh the pro-competitive effects against the anti-competitive effects of the cross-ownership ban. The NFL argued that the ban "assures it of the undivided loyalty of its teams' owners in competing effectively against the NASL in the sale of tickets, and broadcasting rights." Despite the League's contention, the court found that the NFL was unable to provide any evidence of pro-competitive effects of the ban. The court stated:

> [In] the undisputed circumstances here the enormous financial success of the NFL league despite long existing cross-ownership by some members of NASL teams demonstrates that there is no market necessity or threat of disloyalty by cross-owners that would justify the ban. Moreover, the NFL was required to come forward with proof that any legitimate purposes could not be achieved through less restrictive means. This it has failed to do.

The appellate court reversed the ruling of the lower court, entering a permanent injunction to prohibit the NFL's ban on cross-ownership. The U.S. Supreme Court subsequently denied the NFL's request for *certiorari*. Two years later, a jury reached a verdict on the remanded damages question, awarding the NASL one dollar in punitive damages. The league, already in financial distress and hoping for a multi-million dollar damage award, folded that same year.

NOTES

1. In the NBA case *Robertson v. NBA*, 389 F.Supp. 867 (S.D.N.Y. 1975) focused on the ABA-NBA merger and its anti-competitive nature. The players in the class action suit argued that the merger would depress salaries due to the lack of competition. In addition, the merger between two pro leagues was anti-competitive by nature. The court agreed that the merger would eliminate all competition and that Congress would have to grant the League an exemption. The merger was part of the *Robertson* settlement, which included a system of free agency beginning in 1976.

2. In *Philadelphia World Hockey Club, Inc. v. Philadelphia Hockey Club Inc.*, 351 F.Supp. 462 (E.D. Pa. 1972), the Philadelphia team in the World Hockey Association, a rival professional hockey league to the established National Hockey League, sued the NHL under Sections 1 and 2 of the Sherman Act, because of the reserve clause, the NHL's affiliations with minor leagues, and its monopoly power. On a motion for a preliminary injunction the court found it likely that the reserve clause violated Section 2 by preventing players from joining WHA teams, and that the NHL did indeed have monopoly power, and overwhelming control over the supply of players who could play pro hockey. The case was settled out of court when four WHA teams (Edmonton Oilers, New England Whalers, Quebec Nordiques, and Winnipeg Jets) were admitted into the NHL, while the Birmingham Bulls and Cincinnati Stingers were paid to fold.

10.2.4. Antitrust Litigation in Professional Tennis and Golf

Several decades after *United States* v. *Boxing Club of New York* (see section 10.2.1., "Player Restraints and Antitrust Theory"), individual sports continued to undergo antitrust scrutiny. While the majority of sports antitrust litigation has involved team sports, the concepts of antitrust law are still crucial to professionals in all areas of the sports industry. Governing bodies of individual sports such as the PGA or WTA unite the most outstanding performers in their respective fields. If an athlete, agent, or equipment manufacturer is excluded by such organizations, there are no alternatives within the sport's market that are financially equivalent. Trade is inherently restrained and markets are inherently monopolized. The question then becomes whether there is a legitimate business reason to restrain trade or to monopolize. In short, is the apparent illegal activity good for the sport and/or the sport's consumers?

In 1995, the Women's Tennis Association enacted rules that prohibited tournament participation by players younger than fourteen, and limited participation by players aged fourteen to eighteen (see note 2). This rule was adopted after certain high-profile women's tennis players suffered physical and emotional difficulties after achieving success at a young age. For instance, Jennifer Capriati was arrested on shoplifting and drug charges in years following her Olympic (1992) and French Open (1993) successes. Hence, the age eligibility rule was designed to phase-in younger players rather than overwhelm them with constant tournaments. Players such as Anna Kournikova and Serena Williams openly complained that the rule restrained their earning power.

The WTA's rule has not been successfully challenged in the courts. In 1998 Mirjana Lucic of Croatia unsuccessfully petitioned for an injunction in an Australia court in order to play in the Australian Open (see note 2). However, also in 1998, the parents of fourteen-year-old Monique Viele threatened to sue unless their child was allowed to participate in a WTA event. To avoid litigation, the WTA modified its rules to allow fourteen-year-olds to enter one WTA tournament that season.

It is unclear whether or not the tournament's age eligibility requirement would withstand antitrust scrutiny in the United States. But if it were tested, the WTA would likely invoke at least one rule-of-reason defense. As WTA Tour CEO Bart McGuire stated, "the [age eligibility] rule helps to foster a better game, better competition, and ultimately, that helps the players make more [money] and stay in the game longer" (see note 1).

There is a tennis precedent for successful application of rule-of-reason defense of eligibility rules against antitrust claims. In *Heldman v. United States Lawn Tennis Ass'n*, 354 F.Supp. 1241 (S.D.N.Y. 1973), the plaintiff claimed that the USLTA violated the Sherman Act by blacklisting players who participated in the plaintiff's tennis tour from entry into USLTA-sanctioned events. The court denied the plaintiff's motion, saying that the eligibility provisions could be permitted because they helped ensure the uniformity of rules for player rankings and the orderly scheduling of tournaments. The plaintiff appealed this decision, but the case was settled prior to the appeal being heard.

A racket manufacturer filed suit in *Gunter Harz Sports, Inc. v United States Tennis Ass'n*, 665 F.2d 222 (8th Cir. 1981), after the USTA prohibited the use of a tennis racket with double strings in tournaments. A double-strung racket manufacturer cited Section 1 of the Sherman Act, alleging that the USTA's prohibition amounted to a group boycott. The court ruled in favor of the USTA, determining that double-strung rackets harmed the essence of the game by excessively altering the spin on the ball.

The ability for agency firms to host tournaments was tested in *Volvo North American Corp v. Men's International Professional Tennis Council*, 857 F.2d 55 (2d Cir.), *cert. denied* 487 U.S. 1219 (1988). Prior to the suit, the defendant Men's International Professional Tennis Council (MIPTC) took issue with the fact that agency firms Pro Serv and IMG were allowed to represent tennis players and also run major tennis tournaments. The MIPTC felt that it was a conflict of interest, and therefore proposed the Conflicts of Interest Rule. The Conflicts of Interest Rule would require that any player-agent involved in producing an MIPTC-sanctioned event must obtain MIPTC approval before awarding any player a wild card position in the event. Wild card positions are those offered to players without regard to their rankings, and are usually awarded independently by the owners and producers of an event.

But agency firms, along with Volvo, alleged conspiracy against the MIPTC for proposing this and other restrictions. Specifically, plaintiffs accused the MIPTC of using its power over male tennis players "to impose restrictions . . . which hamper the ability of actual and potential competitors . . . to conduct competing tennis events." Although this case was settled, it is interesting to note that the court first rejected the MIPTC's single-entity defense, stating that it was indeed capable of conspiracy as a "joint venture."

As in tennis, golf associations have been forced to defend their restraints on trade as legitimate business practices essential to their sport. One type of restraint on trade claim occurred when an association imposed discipline on its members. In *Blalock v. Ladies Professional Golf Association*, 359 F.Supp. 1260 (N.D. Ga. 1973), a golfer was suspended for one year by the LPGA's executive board after discovering that she had illegally moved her ball during tournament play on several occasions. The court held that the exclusion of Blalock constituted a group boycott, and was thus a per se violation of Section 1 of the Sherman Act. Since the LPGA did not allow LPGA members, such as the plaintiff, to compete in other tournaments, the court determined that excluding the plaintiff from the LPGA tour had, in effect, excluded her from the entire market. Just as the court in *Volvo North American* treated the WIPTC as a "joint venture," so the court in *Blalock* treated the LPGA as a "collective action." This designation might have made the single-entity defense difficult, had rule-of-reason been allowed by the court.

While the Federal District Court in *Blalock* felt that the PGA unreasonably restrained trade, the Federal Appellate Court ruled differently in *Deesen v. Professional Golfers' Ass'n*, 358 F.2d 165 (9th Cir.), *cert. denied*, 385 U.S. 846 (1966). A professional golfer brought a Section 1 claim after being denied entrance to PGA events due to his repeated poor performance. The plaintiff alleged that the PGA's eligibility rule unreasonably restrained trade and had the effect of a group boycott. The court rejected the Section 1 claim using the rule of reason standard finding that the PGA's requirement for performance standards was indeed reasonable.

The inconsistency and unpredictability of court holdings in seemingly similar cases makes antitrust law in individual sports particularly complicated. Nevertheless, the above cases should provide some benchmarks for practitioners in these areas. Finally, it should be noted that individual sports are normally devoid of players unions in the usual sense. Because of this, collective bargaining does not occur between athletes and governing bodies. When the non-statutory labor exemption is discussed later in the chapter, readers should keep in mind that individual sports organizations (like the USTA and LPGA) cannot gain antitrust immunity by bargaining with their players.

NOTES ────────────────────────────────────

1. For a comprehensive article weighing Section 1 restraint of trade vs. rule-of-reason in favor of the good of a particular sport, see Ryan Rodenberg, "Age Eligibility Rules in Women's Professional Tennis," 7 *Sport Lawyer's Journal* 183 (Spring 2000).

2. The WTA age eligibility rule prohibits a player who has not reached her fourteenth birthday from participating in any professional tournament on the WTA tour. Players between the ages of fourteen and fifteen are allowed to participate in a maximum of seven "minor league" satellite or challenger events. Players age fifteen to sixteen are allowed to compete in a maximum of eight WTA tournaments. Eighteen-year-olds are allowed to enter an unlimited number of tournaments on the WTA tour.

10.3. DEFENSES TO ANTITRUST CHALLENGES

10.3.1. The Baseball Exemption

10.3.1.1. History of the Reserve System

The first antitrust challenges against professional sports leagues occurred in the early twentieth century. Professional baseball, the oldest professional team sport in the United States, was established in 1869 when Harry Wright created the first salaried team, the Cincinnati Red Stockings. In 1876 the National League was created, and was considered the principal professional baseball league. The National League clubs signed each player to a one-year contract, later referred to as the Standard Player Contract. An element of that contract was the "reserve clause," which prohibited any player from negotiating with any team other than the one with which the player had originally signed. In addition, the contract stipulated that each year the team could exercise an "option" on the player's services for the following season. Thus, a player was bound to a team in perpetuity, or until he was traded, released, or retired. Players initially used contract law to challenge the restrictive Standard Player Contracts, but quickly turned to antitrust law when professional baseball revised the contracts to protect themselves from challenges under contract law (see note 1).

Plaintiffs first used antitrust law to challenge the "reserve clause" in 1914, in *American League Baseball Club v. Chase*, 149 N.Y.S. 6 (N.Y. Sup. Ct. 1914). While antitrust theory was not the main legal theory being used to challenge the League, the Sherman Act was introduced as possibly applicable to a professional sports league. However, the Court found that the Sherman Act did not apply because baseball was not engaged in interstate commerce.

> Baseball is an amusement, a sport, a game that comes clearly within the civil and criminal law of the state, and it is not a commodity or an article of merchandise subject to the regulation of Congress on the theory that it is interstate commerce.

Therefore, the third element needed to prove a restraint of trade could not be satisfied.

NOTE _____

1. In *Metropolitan Exhibition Co. v. Ewing*, 42 F. 198 (S.D.N.Y. 1890), the court ruled that the plaintiff could not force the defendant to play for them because the terms of the Standard Player Contract were not definite, and therefore the right of reservation could not be enforced. In *Metropolitan Exhibition Co. v. Ward*, 9 N.Y.S. 779 (N.Y. Sup. Ct. 1890), the court denied an injunction to the plaintiff because the Standard Player Contract lacked both definiteness and mutuality, and the plaintiff was unlikely to win a case on the merits. In *Philadelphia Ball Club Limited v. Lajoie*, 51 A. 973 (Pa. 1902), the court found in favor of the plaintiff because mutuality and definiteness were found to exist in the contract. The court stated, "The mere difference in the rights stipulated for, does not destroy mutuality or remedy."

10.3.1.2. *Creation of the Baseball Exemption:* Federal Baseball

In 1915, many of the teams from the failed Federal League were compensated in a variety of ways by the other leagues. The owner of the Baltimore franchise rejected a monetary settlement and accused the National League and the American League of illegally conspiring to monopolize the business of baseball. The case was decided in favor of the plaintiff at the district court level, and treble damages were awarded. The court of appeals reversed the decision. The case ultimately went before the Supreme Court, which issued a decision in 1922 (see exhibit 10.4). The Court, presided over by Justice Oliver Wendell Holmes, determined that the Sherman Act could not be used successfully against Major League Baseball. The Court cited three relevant reasons:

1. That "the business is giving exhibitions of baseball which are purely state affairs," and therefore, no interstate commerce exists
2. That just because there was travel from state to state, "the travel is a mere incident, not the essential thing"
3. That players were not a commodity, and thus "not related to production."

This precedent-setting case held that baseball was not engaged in interstate commerce, meaning that Sections 1 and 2 of the Sherman Act had not been violated. The "baseball exemption," which was to last for over seventy-five years, and in some respects continues today, gave the professional sport of baseball blanket protection against antitrust challenges from players, maverick owners, and competitor leagues. The significance of this ruling is that it allowed the owners to authoritatively maintain the reserve clause, control franchise location, and maintain the subordinate structure of the minor leagues, without fear of a reprisal in the form of an antitrust challenge.

Exhibit 10.4

FEDERAL BASEBALL CLUB OF BALTIMORE, INC. v. NATIONAL LEAGUE OF PROFESSIONAL BASEBALL CLUBS, ET AL.
No. 204.
SUPREME COURT OF THE UNITED STATES
259 U.S. 200; 42 S. Ct. 465; 1922 U.S. LEXIS 2475; 66 L. Ed. 898; 26 A.L.R. 357

Argued April 19, 1922.
May 29, 1922, Decided

ERROR TO THE COURT OF APPEALS OF THE DISTRICT OF COLUMBIA.

ERROR to a judgment of the Court of Appeals of the District of Columbia reversing a judgment for triple damages under the Anti-Trust Acts recovered by the plaintiff in error in the Supreme Court of the District and directing that judgment be entered for the defendants.

SYLLABUS: 1. The business of providing public baseball games for profit between clubs of professional baseball players in a league and between clubs of rival leagues, although necessarily involving the constantly repeated traveling of the players from one State to another, provided for, controlled and disciplined by the organizations employing them, is not interstate commerce. P. 208.

2. Held that an action for triple damages under the Anti-Trust Acts could not be maintained by a baseball club against baseball leagues and their constituent clubs, joined with individuals, for an alleged conspiracy to monopolize the baseball business resulting injuriously to the plaintiff. P. 209.
269 Fed. 681; 50 App. D.C. 165, affirmed.

COUNSEL: Mr. Charles A. Douglas and Mr. William L. Marbury, with whom Mr. L. Edwin Goldman and Mr. William L. Rawls were on the briefs, for plaintiff in error.

Defendants are voluntary associations and corporations engaged upon a vast scale, involving the investment of millions of dollars, in the business of providing, by the transportation from State to State of baseball teams and their necessary attendants and equipment, exhibitions of professional baseball. The court is not concerned with whether the mere playing of baseball, that is the act of the individual player, upon a baseball field in a particular city, is by itself interstate commerce. That act, it is true, is related to the business of the defendants, but it can no more be said to be the business than can any other single act in any other business forming a part of interstate commerce.

The question with which the court is here concerned is whether the business in which the defendants were engaged when the wrongs complained of occurred, taken as an entirety, was interstate commerce, or more accurately, whether the monopoly which they had established or attempted to establish was a monopoly of any part of interstate commerce.

At the foundation of the business of one of these leagues -- in its primary conception -- is a circuit embracing seven different States. No single club in that circuit could operate without the other members of the circuit, and accordingly in the very beginning of its business the matter of interstate relationship is not only important but predominant and indispensable.

Exhibit 10.4 (continued)

Each game symbolizes a contest of skill between the two cities that have been brought together by means of interstate communication and travel. Each team of each club in the league carries with it, and it is essential to the profit of the enterprise that it should carry with it, its representative character; it symbolizes the great city that it represents to those assembled to witness the contest.

In addition to this representative city and state aspect, there is also the element of intersectional rivalry. Experience has shown that the game is most largely patronized when clubs are so located as to provide a contest for supremacy between the Eastern and Western sections of the country.

It is necessary to distinguish between baseball as a sport, that is, where it is played merely as a means of physical exercise and diversion, and this business of providing exhibitions of professional baseball. The business of Organized Baseball represents and has represented for many years, an investment of colossal wealth. Defendants who dominate Organized Baseball are not engaged in a sport. They are engaged in a money-making business enterprise in which all of the features of any large commercial undertaking are to be found. When the teams of the National or American Leagues or of any other league are sent around the circuit of the league, they go at the direction of employers whose business it is to send them, and whose profits are made as a result of that business operation.

When the profit-making aspect of the business is examined, it will be found that the interstate element is still further magnified. The vast investment of capital which has been made in it is required, among other things, in order to provide a place at which the teams in the league may play their contests. Each club has a ball park, with stands erected upon them, sometimes, as in the case of a major league club, costing several millions of dollars. Every club in the league earns its profit not only by the drawing capacity of its team at home, but also by that of the teams of the clubs which its team visits in the various cities in the league. The gate receipts in all of the cities in which the clubs are located are divided according to a definite proportion, fixed by agreement between the club of the city in which the game is played and the club employing the visiting team.

In no other business that can now be recalled is there such a close interrelationship and interdependence between persons in one State and persons in another. The personality, so to speak, of each club in a league is actually projected over state lines and becomes mingled with that of the clubs in all the other States. The continuous interstate activity of each is essential to all the others. The clubs of each league constitute a business unit embracing territorially a number of different States. While each club has, of course, a local legal habitat, yet from a practical business standpoint it is primarily an ambulatory organization.

It is difficult to perceive the relevancy of any discussion about an article of commerce in this case. Commerce may be carried on in one of its forms by traffic in articles of merchandise, but there are countless forms in which it may be carried on without traffic in such articles. *Gibbons v. Ogden*, 9 Wheat. 189.

It is also difficult to discern the relevancy of the contention that personal effort is not an article of commerce. Personal effort, while it may not be an article of commerce, is often commerce itself, but we are not concerned with any such question here. It may be passed by saying that it has been adjudicated by this court in the *Hoke* case, 227 U.S. 308, that interstate commerce may be created by the mere act of a person in allowing himself to be transported from one State to another, without any personal effort; and further that it is

Exhibit 10.4 (continued)

very difficult to see how International *Textbook Co. v. Pigg*, 217 U.S. 91, could have been decided as it was, except upon the principle that the mere exchange of instruction and information, which is about as purely a matter of personal effort as anything that can be imagined, may be a subject of interstate commerce.

If transactions in interstate commerce were to be judged by their isolated ultimate results, as the defendants seek to separate the act of a player in throwing a ball upon a ball field from all the steps which are taken to bring the ball player in the due course of business from other States, of course their interstate character could be plausibly argued away. By such a process of reasoning the American Tobacco Company, for instance, might have removed its gigantic monopoly from the operation of the Sherman Act. See *United States v. American Tobacco Co.*, 221 U.S. 106, 184; *Standard Oil Co. v. United States*, 221 U.S. 1, 68; *Swift & Co. v. United States*, 196 U.S. 375.

In the business now under consideration throughout the playing season the ball teams, their attendants and paraphernalia, are in constant revolution around a preestablished circuit. Their movement is only interrupted to the extent of permitting exhibitions of baseball to be given in the various cities. When exhibitions in one city are completed the clubs resume, according to the agreement made, and plan of business long established, their course of travel on to another city, and thus on and on until the schedule of exhibitions is completed. The interruption in interstate movement is nothing like as great as that in the *Swift Case*, supra. The constant movement of the teams from State to State during a period of over five months each year, is under a single direction and control and in pursuance of one object.

See *Champion v. Ames*, 188 U.S. 321; *Pensacola Telegraph Co. v. Western Union Telegraph Co.*, 96 U.S. 1; *United States v. Patten*, 226 U.S. 525; *Loewe v. Lawlor*, 208 U.S. 274; *Western Union Telegraph Co. v. Foster*, 247 U.S. 105. See particularly *Marienelli v. United Booking Offices*, 227 Fed. 165, where the question was presented as to whether a company engaged in booking vaudeville performers for a circuit embracing theatres in cities in different States was engaged in interstate commerce within the Sherman Act. Also, *Motion Picture Patents Co. v. Universal Film Mfg. Co.*, 235 Fed. 401.

It is common knowledge that baseball is the preeminent American sport. Millions of people follow the daily reports of the results of the games in the press, and in the large cities gather in the afternoons around the newspaper offices to see the bulletin reports of the scores. Not only so, but vast numbers of people travel from one city to another for the purpose of witnessing the games. Telegraph facilities are installed at all the ball parks in the Major Leagues, and in those of the more important Minor Leagues, where reports of the games are sent out and are received throughout the country.

Each league contracts for a uniform type of baseball, which is used in tremendous numbers and shipped by the manufacturer from time to time as they are needed by the various clubs.

These incidents, while in themselves not determinative of the question of whether or not the business is interstate in character, yet, when considered in connection with its main features, emphasize the truth of what has before been said, that there is scarcely any business which can be named in which the element of interstate commerce is as predominant as that in which defendants are engaged.

The agreement and combination entered into and maintained by defendants whereby the entire business in the United States of providing exhibitions of professional baseball was brought under the control of defendants and their confederates in Organized Baseball,

Exhibit 10.4 (continued)

amounted in law to a conspiracy in restraint of trade among the several States and a monopoly or an attempt to monopolize a part of commerce among the several States within the meaning of the Sherman Act.

There is no testimony in this case legally sufficient to show that the plaintiff has waived its right to recover damages under the Sherman Act.

Mr. George Wharton Pepper, with whom Mr. Benjamin S. Minor and Mr. Samuel M. Clement, Jr., were on the brief, for defendants in error.

Organized Baseball is not interstate commerce and does not constitute an attempt to monopolize within the Sherman Act.

Personal effort, not related to production, is not a subject of commerce; and the attempt to secure all the skilled service needed for professional baseball contests is not an attempt to monopolize commerce or any part of it. Clayton Act, § 6; *Paul v. Virginia*, 8 Wall. 168; *Hooper v. California*, 155 U.S. 648; *Metropolitan Opera Co. v. Hammerstein*, 147 N.Y.S. 532; *In re Duff*, 4 Fed. 519; *In re Oriental Society*, 104 Fed. 975; *People v. Klaw*, 106 N.Y.S. 341. The Department of Justice has ruled that the business conducted by Organized Baseball was not in violation of the Sherman Act; and also that the business of presenting theatrical entertainments is not commerce. Distinguishing: *International Textbook Co. v. Pigg*, 217 U.S. 91; and *Marienelli v. United Booking Offices*, 227 Fed. 165. The only case in which the question whether Organized Baseball is within the Sherman Act has been directly passed upon is that of *American Baseball Club of Chicago v. Chase*, 149 N.Y.S. 6; in which the court answered the question in the negative.

Congress has not imposed a penalty upon the transportation of players for baseball purposes, and therefore *Hoke v. United States*, 227 U.S. 308, is not point. While Congress may regulate the movement of persons in interstate commerce, when it has not regulated movement as such, the doing of an act essentially local is not converted into an interstate act merely because people came from another State to do it.

OPINION BY: HOLMES

OPINION: MR. JUSTICE HOLMES delivered the opinion of the court.

This is a suit for threefold damages brought by the plaintiff in error under the Anti-Trust Acts of July 2, 1890, c. 647, § 7, 26 Stat. 209, 210, and of October 15, 1914, c. 323, § 4, 38 Stat. 730, 731. The defendants are The National League of Professional Base Ball Clubs and The American League of Professional Base Ball Clubs, unincorporated associations, composed respectively of groups of eight incorporated base ball clubs, joined as defendants; the presidents of the two Leagues and a third person, constituting what is known as the National Commission, having considerable powers in carrying out an agreement between the two Leagues; and three other persons having powers in the Federal League of Professional Base Ball Clubs, the relation of which to this case will be explained. It is alleged that these defendants conspired to monopolize the base ball business, the means adopted being set forth with a detail which, in the view that we take, it is unnecessary to repeat.

The plaintiff is a base ball club incorporated in Maryland, and with seven other corporations was a member of the Federal League of Professional Base Ball Clubs, a corporation under the laws of Indiana, that attempted to compete with the combined defendants. It alleges that the defendants destroyed the Federal League by buying up some of the constituent clubs and in one way or another inducing all those clubs except

Exhibit 10.4 (continued)

the plaintiff to leave their League, and that the three persons connected with the Federal League and named as defendants, one of them being the President of the League, took part in the conspiracy. Great damage to the plaintiff is alleged. The plaintiff obtained a verdict for $80,000 in the Supreme Court and a judgment for treble the amount was entered, but the Court of Appeals, after an elaborate discussion, held that the defendants were not within the Sherman Act. The appellee, the plaintiff, elected to stand on the record in order to bring the case to this Court at once, and thereupon judgment was ordered for the defendants. 50 App. D.C. 165; 269 Fed. 681, 688. It is not argued that the plaintiff waived any rights by its course. *Thomsen v. Cayser*, 243 U.S. 66.

The decision of the Court of Appeals went to the root of the case and if correct makes it unnecessary to consider other serious difficulties in the way of the plaintiff's recovery. A summary statement of the nature of the business involved will be enough to present the point. The clubs composing the Leagues are in different cities and for the most part in different States. The end of the elaborate organizations and sub-organizations that are described in the pleadings and evidence is that these clubs shall play against one another in public exhibitions for money, one or the other club crossing a state line in order to make the meeting possible. When as the result of these contests one club has won the pennant of its League and another club has won the pennant of the other League, there is a final competition for the world's championship between these two. Of course the scheme requires constantly repeated travelling on the part of the clubs, which is provided for, controlled ant disciplined by the organizations, and this it is said means commerce among the States. But we are of opinion that the Court of Appeals was right.

The business is giving exhibitions of base ball, which are purely state affairs. It is true that, in order to attain for these exhibitions the great popularity that they have achieved, competitions must be arranged between clubs from different cities and States. But the fact that in order to give the exhibitions the Leagues must induce free persons to cross state lines and must arrange and pay for their doing so is not enough to change the character of the business. According to the distinction insisted upon in *Hooper v. California*, 155 U.S. 648, 655, the transport is a mere incident, not the essential thing. That to which it is incident, the exhibition, although made for money would not be called trade or commerce in the commonly accepted use of those words. As it is put by the defendants, personal effort, not related to production, is not a subject of commerce. That which in its consummation is not commerce does not become commerce among the States because the transportation that we have mentioned takes place. To repeat the illustrations given by the Court below, a firm of lawyers sending out a member to argue a case, or the Chautauqua lecture bureau sending out lecturers, does not engage in such commerce because the lawyer or lecturer goes to another State.

If we are right the plaintiff's business is to be described in the same way and the restrictions by contract that prevented the plaintiff from getting players to break their bargains and the other conduct charged against the defendants were not an interference with commerce among the States.

Judgment affirmed.

10.3.1.3. Baseball Exemption Reaffirmed: Toolson

Players continued to challenge the reserve clause using antitrust theory, and two such cases reached the Supreme Court. In *Toolson v. New York Yankees*, 346 U.S. 356 (1953), a professional baseball player challenged the reserve system. The Supreme Court affirmed the district court's determination that upheld the exemption because Congress had not attempted to change the decision created by *Federal Baseball*. The Court based its decision on four factors:

1. Congressional awareness for three decades of the Courts ruling in *Federal Baseball*, coupled with congressional inaction
2. The fact that baseball was left alone to develop for that period upon the understanding that the reserve system was not subject to federal antitrust laws
3. A reluctance to overrule *Federal Baseball* with consequent retroactive effect
4. A professed desire that any needed remedy be provided by legislation rather than by court decree.

Justices Burton and Reed dissented, claiming that the sport of baseball was clearly interstate commerce, and therefore the exemption should be lifted. Justice Burton wrote:

> Congress, however, has enacted no express exemption of organized baseball from the Sherman Act, and no court has demonstrated the existence of an implied exemption from the Act of any sport that is so highly organized as to amount to an interstate monopoly or which restrains interstate trade or commerce.

10.3.1.4. Baseball Anomaly Upheld: Flood

The Supreme Court was forced to make another determination over the validity of the professional baseball antitrust exemption in *Flood v. Kuhn*, 316 F. Supp. 271 (S.D.N.Y. 1970). Curt Flood, a player with the St. Louis Cardinals, was traded to the Philadelphia Phillies after playing with the Cardinals for twelve seasons. He appealed to Commissioner Bowie Kuhn to reject the trade, based on the fact the Philadelphia organization had a history of acute racism. The request was denied by the commissioner. Flood then brought suit against Kuhn and Major League Baseball for violating antitrust laws and sought a preliminary injunction against the trade. The district court cited *Federal Baseball* and *Toolson*, ruling against Flood. The appeals court affirmed.

The Supreme Court granted *certiorari* because of the apparent confusion in this area of the law. Much of the confusion arose out of the fact that other professional sports leagues did not enjoy an antitrust exemption even though the league structure in other sports and professional baseball was almost identical. The contradictions within the Supreme Court forced Justice Blackmun to outline an eight-point decision in *Flood v. Kuhn*, 407 U.S. 258 (1972):

1. Professional baseball is a business and is engaged in interstate commerce.
2. With its reserve system enjoying an exemption from the federal antitrust laws, baseball is an anomaly. *Federal Baseball* and *Toolson* are an aberration confined to baseball.
3. This anomaly has been affirmed in *Shubert*, *International Boxing*, *Radovich* and other cases.

4. Other professional sports operating interstate are not so exempt.

5. The advent of radio and television has not occasioned an overruling of *Federal Baseball* and *Toolson*.

6. Congress has remained inactive in overruling the exemption, or making the reserve system subject to antitrust laws. Thus, this has been deemed to be something other than mere congressional silence and passivity.

7. The Court has expressed concern about the retroactivity of a court decision as compared with a legislative decision that is only prospective in operation.

8. The court noted in *Radovich* that the slate is not clean and has not been for half a century.

Blackmun ended his decision with "the remedy, if any indicated, is for congressional, and not judicial, action." As a result of this decision, baseball's blanket antitrust exemption was affirmed. However, for the other professional sports leagues, there is no exemption. As discussed in section 10.2.1., "Player Restraints and Antitrust Theory," players and the players' associations in football, hockey, and basketball challenged their respective leagues' reserve system using antitrust theory.

10.3.1.5. *The Curt Flood Act*

The Curt Flood Act of 1998 is the culmination of three Supreme Court decisions, dozens of unsuccessful congressional acts, and hundreds of law review articles. Following the Court's recommendation that professional baseball's antitrust exemption be remedied by Congress, several members of the House of Representatives and the Senate lobbied successfully to pass the new act, which does not completely erase baseball's exemption, but does limit it significantly. The purpose of the act is stated thus:

> Sec. 2 Purpose. It is the purpose of this legislation to state that Major League Baseball players are covered under the antitrust laws (i.e. that major league baseball players will have the same rights under the antitrust laws as do other professional athletes, e.g. football and basketball players), along with a provision that makes it clear that the passage of this Act does not change the application of the antitrust laws in any other context or with respect to any other person or entity.

Specifically, the act gives Major League Baseball players the same antitrust rights that other professional athletes enjoy; namely, the right to sue their employers under the Sherman Act if an antitrust violation has occurred.

> Sec. 3. Application of the Antitrust Laws to Professional Major League Baseball. The Clayton Act (15 U.S.C. 12 et seq) is amended by adding at the end of the following new section: Sec. 27. (a) Subject to subsections (b) through (d), the conduct, acts, practices, or agreements of persons in the business of organized professional major league baseball directly relating to or affecting employment of major league baseball players to play baseball at the major league level are subject to the antitrust laws if engaged in by persons in any other professional sports business affecting interstate commerce.

However, the act does not completely remove baseball's exemption; the following section clearly states that baseball's antitrust exemption still applies to all non-player areas:

any conduct, acts, practices, or agreements of persons engaging in, conducting, or participating in the business of organized professional baseball relating to or affecting franchise expansion, location or relocation, franchise ownership issues, including ownership transfers, the relationship between the Office of the Commissioner and franchise owners, the marketing or sales of the entertainment product of organized professional baseball and the licensing of intellectual property rights owned or held by organized professional baseball teams individually or collectively.

Therefore, Major League Baseball players now have the ability to use the Sherman Act, whereas owners upset over a franchise relocation decision, as in *Piazza* (note 1 in section 10.2.2.1., "*Raiders v. NFL*"), do not enjoy that same right.

Both the Major League Baseball Players' Association and MLB management lobbied for this legislation. The rationale for the MLB players' support is clear— they gained the right to sue the league on antitrust grounds. The rationale for MLB management support is more elusive. Some experts contend that management was pressured into supporting the act during collective bargaining. However, there is another school of thought which says that MLB benefited from the act (see note 1). Since the language of the amendment explicitly states that *major league* baseball players may use the Sherman Act, MLB continues to be shielded from antitrust lawsuits filed by minor league and amateur players. Second, even if MLB players do sue on antitrust grounds, their likelihood of success is poor unless they first decertify their union. The concepts of decertification and the non-statutory labor exemption will become more clear to the reader after reading Sections 10.3.2. through 10.3.5., "The Non-statutory Labor Exemption," "Early Uses of the Non-statutory Labor Exemption," "Exemption After Expiration of Collective Bargaining Agreement," and "Exemption After Decertification," where the precedents in other sports are discussed. Moreover, as mentioned previously, the Curt Flood Act restores MLB autonomy over decisions regarding franchise relocations. Thus, MLB need not fear another legal battle and settlement as seen in *Piazza*.

NOTES ————————————————————————————

1. In John Wolohan's "The Curt Flood Act of 1998 and Major League Baseball's Federal Antitrust Exemption," 9 *Marquette Sports Law Journal* 347 (Spring 1999), the author sets out to determine "why baseball was willing to give up part of its cherished antitrust exemption." The author argues that by cooperating with the players' association and jointly lobbying Congress, MLB was actually able to *strengthen* the exemption—specifically in the areas of minor leagues, the draft, franchise relocation, intellectual property, and broadcasting. "With the passage of the Curt Flood Act, baseball can now argue that Congress has acted."

2. In *Minnesota Twins Partnership v. State of Minnesota*, 592 N.W.2d 847 (Minn. 1999), the Minnesota Supreme Court ruled that the state could not force the MLB team to turn over its financial records in an investigation of an alleged antitrust violation. In overturning the lower court's ruling, the Supreme Court stated, "The business of professional baseball is exempt from federal and state antitrust laws; therefore, Minnesota's Attorney General may not enforce compliance with civil investigative demands served on appellants pursuant to an investigation of potential violations of Minnesota's antitrust laws based on a proposed sale and relocation of the Minnesota Twins baseball team."

10.3.2. The Non-statutory Labor Exemption

Section 10.1.3., "Clayton Act," discussed the *statutory* labor exemption. This section and several subsequent sections refer to the *non-statutory* labor exemption. In order to avoid confusion, the non-lawyer should understand that it is accepted practice to refer to the *non-statutory* labor exemption as simply "the labor exemption." Likewise, when the reader sees "the labor exemption" mentioned anywhere in this text, he or she should assume that the author is referring to the *non-statutory* labor exemption.

The non-statutory labor exemption is the result of three Supreme Court decisions that relate to antitrust challenges against joint actions taken by employers acting in concert with unions. In *Allen Bradley Co. v. Local Union No. 3, International Brotherhood of Electrical Workers*, 325 U.S. 797 (1945), *Amalgamated Meat Cutters & Butcher Workmen of North America v. Jewel Tea Co.*, 381 U.S. 676 (1965), *United Mine Workers v. Pennington*, 381 U.S. 657 (1965), the courts found that unions have:

1. An implied labor exemption from antitrust laws to enter into contracts with multi-employer bargaining units
2. The right to advance legitimate employee goals that restrain trade no more than is necessary to achieve those goals.

Therefore, a collective bargaining agreement between a union and employers is exempt from antitrust challenges unless it violates certain criteria. For example, the court found in *Bradley* that a union and its employer could not combine to dominate a market to exclude outside competitors:

> We know that Congress feared the concentrated power of business organizations to dominate markets and prices. It intended to outlaw business monopolies. A business monopoly is no less such because a union participates, and such participation is a violation of the Act.

In *Jewel Tea*, the court found that the subject which allegedly violates antitrust legislation must be a mandatory subject of bargaining. The court stated, "Employers and unions are required to bargain about wages, hours and working conditions, and this fact weighs heavily in favor of antitrust exemption for agreements on these subjects." The court also maintained that the product of the Collective Bargaining Agreement needed to be made through arm's-length bargaining. Ten years later, in *Connell Construction Co. v. Plumbers and Steam Fitters Local Union*, 421 U.S. 616 (1974), the court interpreted the goals of the exemption:

> The Court has recognized . . . that a proper accommodation between the congressional policy favoring collective bargaining under the NLRA and the free competition in the business markets requires that some union-employer agreements be accorded a limited non-statutory exemption from antitrust sanctions.

These judicial decisions concluded that a union-employer Collective Bargaining Agreement does not constitute a conspiracy, combination, or concerted activity, and thus does not violate antitrust laws. In the sports industry, the non-statutory labor exemption would become the owners' chief defense against antitrust challenges brought by players or their unions.

10.3.3. Early Uses of the Non-statutory Labor Exemption: *Philadelphia*, *Mackey*, and *McCourt*

The issue of the labor exemption in the professional sports context was first addressed in *Philadelphia World Hockey Club, Inc. v. Philadelphia Hockey Club, Inc.*, 351 F.Supp. 462 (E.D. Pa. 1972). The World Hockey Association (WHA), a rival professional hockey league, challenged the NHL's "reserve system" using antitrust law, and argued that the League's monopoly over the available hockey player talent pool clearly handicapped the new league from getting top-quality players. The NHL used the labor exemption defense, claiming that the rule in question was part of the Collective Bargaining Agreement between the NHL and the National Hockey League Players Association (NHLPA), and therefore, had been agreed to by the union. The district court found that the reserve clause which was the subject of the challenge had predated the first Collective Bargaining Agreement, and therefore had not been the result of serious, intensive bargaining. The court stated:

> Here there is no evidence that the NHLPA was a joint conspirator with the NHL in creating and retaining the reserve clause. The evidence establishes the NHLPA's persistent opposition to the present reserve system. The reserve clause was more than a sturdy teenager when the NHLPA was born.

It is important to recall the precedents set forth by the non-sport cases concerning the labor exemption. In the preceding case, the plaintiff was able to prove that the rule was not the result of arm's-length bargaining, and therefore, the labor exemption should not apply. The case went to trial on the merits, and after several decisions for the plaintiff, the case was settled with the merger of several WHA teams into the NHL.

The most significant case concerning antitrust laws and the applicability of the non-statutory labor exemption in professional sports is *Mackey v. NFL*, 543 F.2d 606 (8th Cir. 1976). In this case, the plaintiff, a group of present and former professional football players, challenged the "Rozelle Rule," which required a team that signed a veteran free agent to compensate the player's former team with cash, a draft choice, or other players. The decision awarding the compensation was made by the commissioner. The plaintiff argued that the compensation system, if not agreed to by the teams, was a restraint on trade, because the threat of losing players, draft choices, and/or money deterred most teams from taking advantage of the system. Therefore, there existed a restriction on player movement, the "market" was restrained, and the result was lower player salaries. The NFL raised the labor exemption defense, claiming the system was a condition of the Collective Bargaining Agreement that had been negotiated collectively by the League and the NFL Players Association, and therefore the League was exempt from antitrust challenges.

The court ruled against the NFL and offered the following analysis:

> Under the general principles surrounding the labor exemption, the availability of the non-statutory exemption for a particular agreement turns upon whether the relevant federal labor policy is deserving of preeminence over federal antitrust policy under the circumstances of the particular case. Although the cases giving rise to the non-statutory exemption are factually dissimilar from the present case, certain

principles can be deduced from those decisions governing the proper accommodation of the competing labor and antitrust interests here.

The court in *Mackey* then looked at the three primary non-sport cases, *Jewel Tea*, *Bradley*, and *Pennington*, and proceeded to set up a three-pronged test to determine when a professional sports league could use the labor exemption against antitrust challenges.

1. The restraint on trade must primarily affect only the parties to the Collective Bargaining Agreement
2. The issue must concern a mandatory subject of bargaining
3. The issue must have been achieved through arm's-length bargaining.

In *Mackey*, the plaintiff was not able to prove all three elements. Concerning the third element, the court found that even though the compensation system had indeed been bargained over and included in the 1970 Collective Bargaining Agreement, it had not been accomplished through arm's-length bargaining. The court reasoned that the Players Association had had little bargaining power and was not in a position to negotiate it out of the agreement. The court determined that the League could not use the labor exemption. The court then looked at whether the Rozelle Rule did indeed have anti-competitive results, and whether it was in its least restrictive form. The court concluded:

> [We] agree with the district court's conclusion that the Rozelle Rule is significantly more restrictive than necessary to serve any legitimate purposes it might have in this regard. First, little concern was manifested at trial over the free movement of average or below average players. Only the movement of better players was urged as being detrimental to football. Yet, the Rozelle Rule applies to every NFL player regardless of his status or ability. Second, the Rozelle Rule is unlimited in duration. It operates as a perpetual restriction on a player's ability to sell his services in an open market throughout his career.

The appeals court affirmed the conclusions reached by the district court and remanded the case back to that court for further proceedings. The NFL avoided the trial by dismantling the "Rozelle Rule" and replacing it with the Right of First Refusal/Compensation system as outlined in a new Collective Bargaining Agreement with the NFL Players Association.

The "Mackey Test," as it came to be known, became the marker against which other antitrust cases in professional sports would be compared. There was now a discernible test that could accurately determine if the labor exemption could be used as a defense by professional sports leagues against antitrust challenges.

One of the first cases to apply the three-pronged test was *McCourt v. California Sports Inc.*, 600 F.2d 1193 (6th Cir. 1979). The plaintiff in this case challenged the reserve system used by the National Hockey League, which severely limited player mobility. It is important to recall that the WHA challenge against the NHL in 1972 had not been decided on the merits, so there had been no official court decision on whether the NHL's reserve system in fact violated Section 1 of the Sherman Act. In 1978, Dale McCourt, a member of the Los Angeles Kings, was awarded to the Detroit Red Wings as compensation for a Los Angeles signing of a free agent. McCourt immediately filed suit against the National Hockey

League, claiming the League's free agent compensation system was in violation of federal antitrust laws. The court applied the three-pronged test to determine if the defense was able to use the labor exemption. As in *Mackey*, the court found that the plaintiff met the first two requirements. However, the *McCourt* court differed in its interpretation of the final element: whether the issue had been a result of arm's-length bargaining. The court in *McCourt* found that the NHLPA's failed attempt to get the reserve system provision out of the agreement was not an indicator that arm's-length bargaining had in fact not occurred. The court reasoned that "what the trial court saw as a failure to negotiate was in fact simply the failure to succeed, after the most intensive negotiations, in keeping an un-wanted provision out of the contract." Therefore, the labor exemption defense was available for the League to use.

The significance of the *Mackey* decision and the subsequent rulings is that provisions in a Collective Bargaining Agreement that allow for player restraints (i.e., draft or free agent compensation) are protected by the non-statutory labor exemption, as long as they meet the required three-pronged test as outlined in *Mackey*.

NOTES

1. The "Mackey Test" was further tested in *Wood v. NBA*, 809 F.2d 954 (2nd Cir. 1987). In 1984, a rookie challenged the salary cap that had just been negotiated between the League and the NBA Players Association. The court ruled against the plaintiff because the salary cap had been negotiated in good faith between the two parties, and therefore the League was protected by the labor exemption, even though the plaintiff player and others similarly situated were not yet in the league or the union.

2. In *Zimmerman v. NFL*, 632 F.Supp. 398 (D.D.C. 1986), a potential NFL player brought suit against the League and challenged the supplemental draft system that had been instituted to allow NFL teams to draft former USFL players after the USFL had gone out of business. The plaintiff claimed the draft was in violation of federal antitrust laws because players were restricted from bargaining with more than one team and this restriction impeded their earning potential. The court applied the Mackey test and found that the draft had been a result of bona fide arm's-length negotiations between the NFL and the NFLPA. It further stated:

> It is not the Court's function in the context of the labor exemption to evaluate the relative bargaining process and strategy of the parties, to determine who secured the better deal or whether there was adequate consideration exchanged.

10.3.4. Exemption After Expiration of Collective Bargaining Agreement: *Bridgeman* and *Powell*

After *Mackey* the important question in this area of the law became: Does the non-statutory labor exemption continue beyond the expiration of a Collective Bargaining Agreement, and if so, for how long?

The first case that challenged the courts to make a decision on this matter was *Bridgeman v. NBA*, 675 F.Supp. 960 (D.N.J. 1987). This case was a class action suit filed by NBA players in 1983 which challenged the continued imposition by the NBA of the salary cap, college draft, and right of first refusal, after the Collective Bargaining Agreement between the NBA and the NBA Players Association had expired in 1982. The plaintiffs claimed that the labor exemption was void because the Collective Bargaining Agreement had expired, and therefore the restrictive measures that were protected before, were now in violation of antitrust laws as covered under the Sherman Act. The players wanted to go to trial on the merits.

The *Bridgeman* court was forced to decide if the NBA maintained its labor exemption after the Collective Bargaining Agreement between itself and the Players Association had expired. The court came to three conclusions:

1. It rejected the players' assertion that the labor exemption ended immediately after the agreement expired.
2. It stated that the labor exemption was not indefinite after a Collective Bargaining Agreement expired.
3. The labor exemption was still applicable even after impasse had been reached, but not indefinitely.

The *Bridgeman* court had not answered an important question: When, exactly, did the labor exemption end, if it could not be used indefinitely? The ambiguous nature of the *Bridgeman* decision, which allowed the NBA to continue using the labor exemption as a defense against antitrust challenges, ensured that the question would be raised again.

The question was raised again in *Powell v. NFL*, 678 F.Supp. 777 (D. Minn. 1988). After the aborted 1987 strike by the NFL Players Association, a group of NFL players filed a class action suit against the NFL that challenged the Right of First Refusal/Compensation system on the fact that the system was in violation of Section 1 of the Sherman Act because it restrained player movement. The NFL moved for summary judgment based on the labor exemption. The Players Association argued that the exemption was no longer applicable because the Collective Bargaining Agreement had expired and an impasse had been reached. The court agreed with the NFL's assertion that the labor exemption should be maintained for some period of time after the agreement had expired because the terms and conditions of that agreement would still be in effect. The court concluded that the impasse would mark the point at which the labor exemption ceased to exist, and therefore the trial could move forward based on the merits.

The appeals court reversed the district court's ruling in a 2–1 decision in *Powell v. NFL*, 930 F.2d 1293 (8th Cir. 1989). The court felt the exemption should continue even after impasse had been reached. Said the appeals court: "We believe, however, that the non-statutory labor exemption protects agreements conceived in an ongoing collective bargaining relationship from challenges under the anti-trust laws." In essence, the court stated that as long as the conditions imposed by the league resulted from good faith bargaining during the collective bargaining process, the exemption continued after expiration of the Collective Bargaining Agreement and after impasse. This decision is important because as long as the NFL and the NFLPA maintained a continuing bargaining relationship, and as long as the NFL maintained the status quo, the contract provisions in the agreement were exempt from antitrust litigation, regardless of the fact the Collective Bargaining Agreement had expired.

In dissenting, Judge Lay stated that the only alternative now available to unions would be decertification. He stated:

> The only labor policy of which I am aware that is accommodated by exempting the laws protective of free competition is bona fide collective bargaining. Yet this court's unprecedented decision leads to the ineluctable result of union decertification in

order to invoke rights to which the players are clearly entitled under the antitrust laws. The plain and simple truth of the matter is that the union should not be compelled, short of self-destruction, to accept illegal restraints it deems undesirable. Union decertification is hardly a worthy goal to pursue in balancing labor policy with the antitrust laws.

10.3.5. Exemption After Decertification: *McNeil*

As a result of the *Powell* decision, the NFLPA decided to decertify as the bargaining representative of the National Football League players in order to allow individual players to challenge the NFL's restrictive practices using antitrust theory. After decertification, there would be no bargaining relationship between the players and the NFL, which meant that the League would not be able to use the labor exemption as a defense. Without the labor exemption, the case could then go to trial on the merits.

A new lawsuit, brought forward by a group of players, challenged the NFL's "Plan B" free agency under the antitrust laws. The League had altered its Right of First Refusal/Compensation system prior to the lawsuit in hopes that it would be able to prove, under the rule of reason analysis, that the right of first refusal/compensation system was a necessity for the survival of the league, and was in its least restrictive form. Plan B free agency allowed unrestricted free agency status to any player who was not protected by his team. Each team was permitted to protect thirty-six players; those thirty-six players would be subject to the Right of First Refusal/Compensation system.

In *McNeil v. NFL*, 790 F.Supp. 871 (D. Minn. 1992), New York Jets running back Freeman McNeil and other NFL players argued that Plan B free agency restrained players' ability to offer their services on the open market because the compensation deterred other teams from pursuing restricted free agents. The players argued that this violated Section 1 of the Sherman Act. The court rejected the NFL's request for summary judgment based on the labor exemption, and allowed the case to go to trial on the merits. In the trial, the court reasoned that because the players were not represented by a union, no bargaining relationship existed between the players and the League, and thus the first prong of the Mackey Test could not be met. The players successfully argued that Plan B was an unreasonable restraint on trade, and was not in its least restrictive form.

Immediately after the *McNeil* decision, Keith Jackson and nine other NFL players filed a lawsuit against the NFL and sought an injunction from the court to make the ten players unrestricted free agents. In *Jackson v. NFL*, 802 F.Supp. 226 (D.Minn. 1992), the plaintiffs used the doctrine of collateral estoppel to demonstrate a likelihood of success on the merits. The doctrine of collateral estoppel is appropriate where

1. The issue is identical to one raised in a prior adjudication.
2. There is a final judgment on the merits.
3. The estopped party was a party or in privity with a party to the prior adjudication.
4. The estopped party was given a full and fair opportunity to be heard on the adjudicated issue.

The court determined that, based on the *McNeil* decision, the outcome was likely to be the same, and therefore the injunction should be granted. The court ordered:

All defendants are temporarily enjoined, for a period of five days from the date of this order, from enforcing the Right of First Refusal/Compensation Rules of Plan B against plaintiffs Keith Jackson, Webster Slaughter, D. J. Dozier, and Garin Veris.

Following the *McNeil* and *Jackson* decision, a class action suit was filed against the NFL on behalf of current or former NFL players (*White v. NFL*, 836 F. Supp. 1458 (D. Minn. 1993)).

All players who have been, and are now or will be under contract to play professional football for an NFL club at any time from August 31, 1987, to the date of final judgment in this action and the determination of any appeal therefrom, have been, are now, or will be eligible to play football as a rookie for an NFL team.

With these court victories, the players and the owners reached a tentative agreement on January 6, 1993, which came to be referred to as the *White* settlement. The players immediately recertified the NFLPA as their official bargaining representative, and incorporated the *White* settlement into a new Collective Bargaining Agreement (1993–2000, extended to 2007 in 2001) that gave NFL players free agency in exchange for a salary cap.

10.3.6. Non-statutory Labor Exemption Today: *Brown*

Even though it appeared clear that the labor exemption defense would be upheld in a court of law when a Collective Bargaining Agreement existed between the league and the players' association, individual players continued to challenge leagues using antitrust theory. In *Brown v. Pro Football, Inc.*, 782 F.Supp. 125 (D.D.C. 1991), plaintiffs, NFL developmental squad members, filed a class action suit against the NFL, challenging the league's restriction on their earnings. The players argued that during the period when the NFL Players Association had decertified, the League had instituted a new rule that placed a cap on the earnings of practice squad members. When NFL players recertified the Players Association after the *White* settlement, the new rule was made a part of the Collective Bargaining Agreement. The practice squad players argued that the rule had not been the result of negotiations, and thus it had not been reached through arms'-length bargaining, the third prong of the *Mackey* test. Thus, the players argued, the labor exemption should not apply and the case against the NFL should move forward on the merits.

The district court in *Brown* concluded:

1. The labor exemption should end immediately after the expiration of a Collective Bargaining Agreement.
2. The standard set in *Powell* hindered, rather than facilitated, the execution of a Collective Bargaining Agreement.
3. If an exemption were to apply after expiration, it should end at impasse.
4. If the challenged restraint had not been part of the expired agreement, the exemption could not apply.

The fourth conclusion of the court meant that the case could move forward on the merits because the new rule had not been part of the old Collective Bargaining Agreement. However, the district court's decision was overturned by the D.C. Circuit Court of Appeals in *Brown v. Pro Football Inc.*, 50 F.3d 1041

(D.D.C. 1995). In a 2–1 decision, the court found that unionized employees do not have the right to challenge their employer under antitrust laws. The court remarked that "injecting the Sherman Act into the collective bargaining process would disrupt the balance by giving unions a powerful new weapon, one not contemplated by the federal labor laws." Therefore, the appeals court concluded that the labor exemption was applicable regardless of whether a Collective Bargaining Agreement was in place, whether it had expired, or whether impasse had been reached, and passed.

The U.S. Supreme Court reviewed the decisions of the district and appeals courts in *Brown v. Pro Football Inc.*, 518 U.S. 231 (1996) and issued a definitive answer on the topic. The Court found that the labor exemption was applicable even though the restrictive actions were not included in the Collective Bargaining Agreement. The Supreme Court laid out a new four-pronged test for antitrust immunity, requiring that the challenged conduct:

1. Took place during and immediately after a collective bargaining negotiation
2. Grew out of, and was directly related to, the lawful operation of the bargaining process
3. Involved a matter that the parties were required to negotiate collectively
4. Concerned only the parties to the collective bargaining relationship.

The decision by the Supreme Court is vague enough to invite further legal challenges surrounding the labor exemption issue. However, the decertification route appears to be the most viable option for players' associations that want to challenge league rules or policies that restrict trade and violate the Sherman Act, after the expiration of a collective bargaining agreement. In the 1998–1999 NBA lockout, several players voiced the opinion that the players should decertify the National Basketball Players Association and challenge the league on antitrust grounds. This can be an effective strategy, because leagues are fearful of having a court decide that their draft, salary cap, or free agency is too restrictive and violates the Sherman Act. However, it can also have negative consequences for players, because without a union, the league can decide to unilaterally implement new rules without having to bargain over them. The NBPA ultimately decided not to decertify.

The NFLPA and the NFL went to the extraordinary step of including a provision in their agreement that deals specifically with the non-statutory labor exemption.

10.3.7. Single-Entity Defense

The "single-entity" defense is relevant in two areas in professional sports: traditional leagues using the defense against specific antitrust challenges, and new leagues structuring themselves as a single entity so as to avoid antitrust challenges. The single-entity defense, which was used as early as the 1970s, defends against Section 1 challenges because it attacks the first element needed to prove a violation: a plurality of actors. It strikes at the heart of this element: a single entity is incapable of contract, combination, or conspiracy. If there is no contract, combination, or conspiracy, then there can be no Section 1 violation.

Traditional leagues have used the defense in an attempt to block challenges against restrictive league rules, such as the college draft, salary cap, and restrictions on free agency. These leagues, specifically the NFL, NHL, and NBA, have all argued in different lawsuits that they are structured as single entities because they share broadcast revenue and licensing revenue, they advertise collectively, and all the teams in the leagues fall under a single administrative body (Commissioner's Office). Overall, this argument has not proven to be successful.

The NFL has used the single-entity defense more than any other professional sports league. It first used the single-entity defense against the North American Soccer League when the soccer league sued the NFL for violating Section 1 of the Sherman Act because of the NFL's rules concerning cross-ownership of a franchise. In *NASL v. NFL*, 670 F.2d 1249 (2nd Cir. 1982), the NASL argued that the rule was a group boycott, subject to per se analysis, and that the soccer league had been unjustly injured by the cross-ownership rule because it unreasonably restricted the pool of experienced capital investors.

In the Second Circuit the court rejected the NFL's use of the single-entity defense. The court concluded that the teams comprising the NFL were separate economic entities working together in a "joint venture," rather than as a single entity. The court explained:

> Although NFL members thus participate jointly in many of the operations conducted by it on their behalf, each member is a separately owned, discrete entity which does not share its expenses, capital expenditures or profits with other members. Each also derives separate revenues from certain lesser sources, which are not shared with other members, including revenues from local TV and radio, parking and concessions.

The court concluded that although cooperation existed, there was no evidence to suggest that the NFL was a single corporation.

The NFL raised the single-entity defense again in *Los Angeles Memorial Coliseum Commission v. NFL*, 726 F.2d 1381 (9th Cir.) *cert. denied*, 469 U.S. 990 (1984). Both the district court and the Second Circuit rejected the defense. The Second Circuit stated that what the NFL sought was blanket protection from the antitrust laws even though it had been found guilty of breaking antitrust laws on previous occasions: *Mackey, Kapp, NASL,* and *Smith*. The court also looked at the way in which profits and losses were distributed in the league, and found that each individual team was responsible for its own losses, and alone reaped the rewards of profit. In addition, the court noted that each team in the NFL had an individual identity. Concerning this issue, the court stated:

> These attributes operate to make each team an entity in large part distinct from the NFL. It is true that cooperation is necessary to produce a football game. However, as the district court concluded, this does not mean that "each club can produce football games only as an NFL member." This is especially evident in light of the emergence of the United States Football League.

As in *NASL*, the court found that the NFL was comprised of a plurality of actors instead of one single actor and, therefore, rejected the single entity defense. The NFL had initiated the single-entity defense on each occasion it was challenged with an antitrust lawsuit, and in each circumstance the defense had been denied by the courts. Based on the court determinations of the 1970s and 1980s, it did not appear that the single-entity defense would be a viable one for traditionally structured leagues like the NFL, NBA, and NHL (MLB was protected by the "baseball exemption," discussed earlier, and did not fear antitrust suits by opposing leagues). However, in the early 1990s, a case was decided that changed the way in which the single-entity defense could be applied.

In *Chicago Professional Sports Limited Partners v. NBA*, 754 F. Supp. 1336 (N.D. Ill. 1991), the Chicago Bulls sued the NBA, claiming the NBA's allocation of broadcasting rights violated the antitrust laws because it restrained trade: the NBA limited the number of games that "superstations" could televise. Prior to the 1990–1991 season, the NBA allowed each team to televise twenty-five games on a superstation. Superstations are distant signal television stations whose programming is carried via satellite to cable systems outside of the station's local broadcast range. Some examples are WTBS in Atlanta, WWOR in New Jersey, and WPIX in New York, and in this case, WGN in Chicago. The NBA's Board of Governors voted to change that rule for the 1990–1991 season by limiting the number to twenty. The Bulls contracted with WGN to show twenty-five games over the 1990–1991 season and successfully sought an injunction to move the limit from twenty to twenty-five. The injunction was upheld on appeal in *Chicago Professional Sports Limited Partnership v. NBA*, 961 F.2d 667 (7th Cir. 1992), and the injunction raised the number of games available to superstations to thirty.

In 1993, the NBA revised its broadcasting contracts to make them more compatible with the Sports Broadcast Act, and in the process limited the number of games available to superstations to fifteen per season. This prompted another round of litigation that was decided on appeal in *Chicago Professional Sports Limited Partnership v. NBA*, 95 F.3d 593 (7th Cir. 1996). As in the first case, the court ruled that the Sports Broadcast Act did not apply to the dispute, and therefore the Sherman Act could be used to challenge the NBA.

In its defense, the NBA argued it was a single entity, and was therefore immune to Section 1 challenges. It argued that it created a single product—NBA Basketball—that competed with other basketball leagues, other sports leagues, and other forms of entertainment. The NBA attempted the single entity defense even though precedent had already been established in aforementioned cases such as *NASL* and *Smith* that the NFL, which the NBA resembled in league structure, was not a single entity.

However, the 7th Circuit determined that none of the sports cases, or the nonsports cases, imposed a characterization on exactly how a single entity was structured. Therefore, the court concluded, such analysis should be done on a league-by-league basis, and within a particular league, analysis should occur "one facet at a time." The court left open the possibility that the NBA could be considered a single entity when dealing with licensing broadcast rights, but considered a joint venture when dealing with certain player mobility restrictions. The case was remanded back to the district court. The case was settled out of court in December 1996, when the Bulls agreed to accept the fifteen-game limit, with the understanding that WGN could televise an unlimited number of games in the Chicago area only. No actual precedent had been set because the trial was not decided on the merits, but the 7th Circuit decision, stating that the single-entity defense could be used by the NBA, suggests that the defense may be raised again in the future.

The most recent case to involve the single-entity defense was *Fraser v. Major League Soccer*, 97 F.Supp.2d 130 (D. Mass. 2000), *Aff'd by*, 284 F.3d 47 (1st Cir. 2002). MLS soccer players decided to bypass the unionization process so that they could challenge the League's restrictive player restraints using antitrust theory. Had the players unionized first, the League would have been protected by the labor exemption. The players argued that the system MLS employed to restrain player mobility violated the antitrust laws for several reasons:

1. Player salaries are unilaterally determined by a single person, Deputy Commissioner Sunil Gulati.
2. MLS enforces a salary cap, the rules of which are known only to MLS and kept secret from the players.
3. MLS, U.S. Soccer, and the world governing body, FIFA, inserted a system of "transfer fees" into the Standard Player Contract that can prevent MLS players from signing with teams in other countries, even *after* their MLS contracts have expired.
4. The MLS Standard Player Agreement denies players a fair share of group licensing rights.
5. The Standard Player Agreement contains a "reserve clause," struck down in other sports, giving teams unilateral rights to renew their players' contracts.

MLS argued that it was a single entity, and was therefore exempt from Section 1 challenges because it was not acting in combination, concert, or conspiracy with anyone. In contrast to previous cases such as *NASL* and *Smith*, MLS was able to cite more specific evidence that it was indeed a single entity. For example:

1. Profits and losses are shared in a manner similar to a corporation rather than like a traditional sports league.
2. All players are employees of MLS, rather than employees of the individual teams. Players receive paychecks from the league rather than from individual teams.
3. MLS has the right to assign marquee players to certain teams. While teams may make some transactions (e.g., trades), MLS must approve all such transactions.
4. Individual teams do not own the right to their logos.

The players argued that the MLS structure was merely a "sham," concocted by owners in order to avoid antitrust scrutiny. Nevertheless, the district court was compelled by MLS's argument, and ruled in 2000 that MLS is indeed a single entity incapable of conspiracy. This did not vindicate MLS on all counts. For example, the issue of "transfer fees" was later settled by a jury, although again in favor of MLS (see note 2). The plaintiffs quickly appealed the district court's decisions. In 2002, the 1st U.S. Circuit Court of Appeals affirmed the district court's verdict, agreeing that players failed to show that MLS is not a single entity, in that the league not only owns the teams themselves, but also all intellectual property related to the teams. The court also found that the players failed to prove that the United States was the relevant geographic market and that the relevant product market was limited to Division I professional players.

Even though the district court's single-entity opinion on *Fraser* was affirmed, the case represents somewhat of a panacea for start-up leagues. Even before the *Fraser* decision in 2002, three prominent leagues were created on the MLS model (see note 4). The *Fraser* decision is significant because it implies that leagues structured like MLS are exempt from Sherman Act Section 1 antitrust claims.

NOTES

1. For a more detailed analysis of the *Fraser* case, see Glenn Wong and John Shukie, "All for One: MLS Players Fail to Take Down the League's Single Entity Structure," vol. 28, no. 8 *Athletic Business* 18 (August, 2000); and Paul D. Abbott, "Antitrust and Sports— Why Major League Soccer Succeeds Where Other Sports Have Failed," 8 *The Sport Lawyer's Journal*, 1 (Spring 2001).

2. The district court in *Fraser* rejected the plaintiff's claim that transfer fees were illegal on a per se basis. A federal jury in Boston then rejected the claim that MLS and FIFA (Federal Internationale de Football Association) conspired to impose the fees. However, if MLS ever enforces transfer fees (it has never done so to date), those fees could be susceptible to rule of reason scrutiny. The topic of transfer fees is discussed further in section 10.4., "Antitrust Law and International Soccer: *Bosman*."

3. The district court in *Fraser* also rejected the plaintiff's Section 2 monopolization claim. At the time of MLS's inception in 1996, there was no "Division I" professional soccer in the United States. Therefore, the creation of MLS expanded earning opportunities for players rather than restricting them. Judge George A. O'Toole rejected notions that either consumers were harmed or MLS had behaved as a monopoly, stating: "There was no substantial basis in the evidence for concluding that MLS, if it was a monopsonist, behaved in the way monopsonists do when they abuse their market power" (see *Fraser*).

4. Leagues that have used the single-entity structure included NASL, American Professional Soccer League, Continental Indoor Soccer League, National Professional Soccer League, U.S. Interregional Soccer League, Major Indoor Lacrosse League, Roller Hockey International Hockey League, World League of American Football, American Basketball League, Major League Soccer, Women's National Basketball Association, Women's United Soccer Association, and the XFL.

5. The Supreme Court rejected the claim that joint ventures are protected against antitrust challenges in *United States v. General Motors Corp.*, 121 F.2d 376 (7th Cir.), *cert. denied*, 314 U.S. 618 (1941).

6. There has been much discussion among legal scholars as to whether each NFL team has a separate and individual identity. While the court points out that any team can decide to play elsewhere, analysts contend that this view is misguided. Do the New York Yankees really have the choice to leave MLB and play in the Northern League? Or the Detroit Red Wings to leave the NHL to play in the IHL?

7. The NFL attempted to use the single-entity defense in *McNeil* and *Sullivan*. In both cases, the defense was rejected.

8. Ordinarily, professional sports leagues are protected from antitrust challenges under the Sports Broadcast Act of 1961, which states:

> The antitrust laws . . . shall not apply to any joint agreement by or among persons engaged in conducting the organized professional team sports of football, baseball, basketball or hockey, by which any league of clubs participating in professional football, baseball, basketball or hockey contests sells or otherwise transfers all or any part of the rights of such league's member clubs in the sponsored telecasting of the games of football, baseball, basketball or hockey, as the case may be, engaged in or conducted by such clubs.

10.4. ANTITRUST LAW AND INTERNATIONAL SOCCER: *BOSMAN*

This chapter's discussion of *Fraser v. MLS* in the previous paragraphs mentioned "transfer fees." Transfer fees are monies that can be demanded by a player's former team *after* expiration of that player's contract, in the event that the player signs with a different team. The rationale behind transfer fees is that the new team should compensate the old team for his training and development.

However, as seen in the NFL during the "Rozelle Rule" and Right of First Refusal/Compensation System, threats of compensation can effectively deter new teams from courting free-agent players in the first place. However, the difference between transfer fees and systems such as the "Rozelle Rule" is that transfer fees affect players wishing to move from one country to another. In other words, a soccer player could fulfill his contract in Spain, and then be unable to play soccer in Brazil if the Brazilian team was unwilling to pay a transfer fee.

FIFA, the international governing association for soccer, created this rule. Moreover, FIFA rules are incorporated into the Standard Player Contracts or league documents of various soccer leagues worldwide—including MLS.

Jean-Marc Bosman was a Belgian national who played for RC Liège, a Belgian Division I soccer team. His five-year contract was due to expire at the end of June 1990. RC Liège made him an offer to extend his contract for one year, at one quarter of his current salary. Bosman refused those terms, and then negotiated a contract with a French team. The French team then negotiated a transfer fee with RC Liège "for a one year temporary transfer, and adjusted upward if the French club decided to make the transfer permanent" (see note 3). RC Liège, concerned about the French club's financial position, voided the deal, leaving Bosman unemployed at the start of the 1990–1991 season. Bosman sued RC Liège in a Belgian court, arguing that the transfer fee rule violated Article 48 of the Treaty of Rome, which governs the free movement of workers (see note 3).

This case, *Union Royale Belge des Sociétés de Football Association ASBL v. Bosman*, eventually reached the European Court of Justice (ECJ). In 1995, the ECJ ruling had two effects on European soccer (see notes 2 and 3). First of all, the ruling eliminated the "non-nationals" rule, which had limited the number of foreign players that could be employed in a UEFA (Union des Associations Européennes de Football) soccer match. More important, the ECJ held that the application of transfer fees was a violation of European law. Hence, if a player completes his contract with a team of one nation, he is free to sign with the team of another nation. European teams grudgingly accepted the *Bosman* decision after the European Commission threatened fines for non-compliance. The teams claimed that the non-nationals rule and transfer fees were both essential to maintain the integrity of soccer, very much as Major League Baseball claimed that the reserve clause was essential to baseball in *Flood* and other cases.

The *Bosman* ruling is significant to sports law in the United States because of the growth of soccer in the United States. While the court that ruled in *Bosman* has no jurisdiction in the United States, appellate court judges are likely to look at the reasoning presented by the European Court of Justice. So far, MLS has not imposed transfer fees, although it has sold players to other teams during the term of the players' contracts. Nevertheless, it is important to point out that the scope of the ECJ decision was limited to transfer fees involving two different teams in the European Union. Theoretically, if an MLS player became a star in the United States, the MLS could then sell him to a European Union team even *after* expiration of the player's contract (see note 1). This would be acceptable under both European law and the current holding in *Fraser*.

NOTES

1. For a more detailed analysis of the *Fraser* case and its relevance to the future of professional sports leagues, see Paul D. Abbott, "Antitrust and Sports—Why Major League

Soccer Succeeds Where Other Sports Have Failed," 8 *The Sport Lawyer's Journal* 1 (Spring 2001).

2. For more on the aftermath of *Bosman* in European soccer, see Patrick Closson, "Penalty Shot: The European Union's Application of Competition Law to the *Bosman* Ruling," 21 *Boston College International and Comparative Law Review* 167 (Winter 1998).

3. For more information on the implications of *Bosman* for the "non-nationals" rule, see Rachel B. Arnedt, "European Union Law and Football Nationality Restrictions," 12 *Emory International Law Review* 109 (Spring 1998).

4. In September 1998, the television network BSkyB purchased the British soccer team Manchester United for approximately $1 billion. However, in 1999 the British government's Monopolies and Mergers Commission voided the sale on antitrust grounds. Because BSkyB owned exclusive rights to televise Premiere League games live, the government contended that the media company would thwart competition and harm the quality of British soccer. BSkyB is a subsidiary of News Corporation, which owns the Fox Entertainment Group in the United States.

5. The *Bosman* ruling outlawed intra-Europe transfer fees *after* the expiration of a player's contract. However, it is important to emphasize that transfer fees may still be invoked *while* a player is under contract. In other words, player contracts can be sold from one team to another for cash. In July 2001, the Spanish soccer power Real Madrid purchased the contract of Zinedine Zidane from Juventus for a then-record $65 million.

10.5. ANTITRUST LAW AND THE NCAA

In the past, amateur athletic organizations have not been subject to the type of antitrust litigation faced by the professional sports industry. However, with the increased prominence of amateur athletics and the money now involved, organizations such as the NCAA are increasingly subject to antitrust litigation. While the NCAA is not the only amateur organization that has faced antitrust challenges, this section will focus mostly on it and its member conferences, institutions, coaches, and athletes.

Historically, defendant college athletic organizations had been successful in arguing that the antitrust laws were not applicable to them because college athletics are not "trade" or "commerce" as defined by the Sherman Act. College organizations have traditionally argued that since their athletic associations are nonprofit organizations, their primary purpose is educational and noncommercial in nature, and hence cannot be defined as trade or commerce. However, beginning in the early 1970s, successful suits were filed against college athletic organizations other than the NCAA, and it was found that these organizations were indeed involved in trade and commerce. By 1984, the Supreme Court would determine that even the NCAA was involved in trade and commerce.

10.5.1. Decisions Before *Board of Regents*

In 1972, the federal antitrust laws were first applied to amateur athletics in *Amateur Softball Ass'n. v. United States,* 467 F.2d 312 (10th Cir. 1972). In this case, the governing organization for softball in the United States was deemed not exempt from antitrust laws. The court reasoned that even though the primary purpose of the association was noncommercial, subsequent actions or operations of an amateur athletic association could trigger application of the Sherman Act. A similar result occurred in *Tondas v. Amateur Hockey Ass'n. of the United States,* 438 F. Supp. 310 (W.D.N.Y. 1977). The court held in this case that the amateur hockey association had significant market and economic power to trigger possible antitrust applications.

The NCAA faced several antitrust challenges in the late 1970s and the early 1980s. In *College Athletic Placement Services, Inc. v. NCAA*, No. 74-1144, 1974 U.S. Dist. LEXIS 7050 (D. N.J. Aug. 22, 1974), the court found no violations of the Sherman Act for an amendment by the NCAA to its constitution that would render students who obtained information from services such as the plaintiff's ineligible for intercollegiate competition. The court applied the rule of reason test and found that the NCAA amendment was neither anti-competitive nor intended to damage the plaintiff. Instead, the amendment was consistent with the NCAA objective of preserving amateurism in sports.

In *Hennessey v. NCAA*, 564 F.2d 1136 (5th Cir. 1977), the district court found that NCAA Bylaw 12–1, which put a limitation on a school coaching staff, had sufficient impact on interstate commerce (it curtailed the interstate flow of assistant coaching services) to fall within the Sherman Act. The court, however, ruled that the bylaw's fundamental objective was to preserve and foster competition in intercollegiate athletics, and that it was thus permissible under the rule of reason and was not a violation of the Sherman Act.

In *English v. NCAA*, 439 So. 2d 1218 (La. Ct. App. 1983), a college football player, after transferring twice from a four-year college to a two-year college, was declared ineligible for another season of competition because of an NCAA transfer rule. The plaintiff's challenge to the NCAA transfer rule was based on Louisiana antitrust laws. The court held that Louisiana antitrust laws were inapplicable to the NCAA, because the NCAA is engaged in interstate commerce and therefore subject only to federal antitrust law. The court also ruled, however, that if the Louisiana antitrust laws were applicable to the NCAA, the court would still rule for the defendant, because the NCAA rules were reasonable and not a violation of the state antitrust laws.

In *Association for Intercollegiate Athletics for Women v. NCAA*, 558 F.Supp. 487 (D.D.C. 1983), *Aff'd by*, 735 F.2d 577 (D.C. Cir. 1984), the courts held that the NCAA's dominance of the amateur sports television market does not by itself create a monopolistic practice against a rival association, since no illegal tying arrangement existed.

10.5.2. The NCAA's Reduced Power over Television: *Board of Regents*

While the NCAA was successful in defending antitrust cases between 1972 and 1984, it was successfully challenged in *NCAA v. Board of Regents*, 468 U.S. 85 (1984). The NCAA operated a college football television plan that limited the number of televised Division I college football games. The University of Oklahoma and the University of Georgia were members of the College Football Association (CFA), which negotiated an independent television contract allowing for a larger number of appearances on television. When the NCAA announced that it would take disciplinary action in response to this independent contract, the University of Oklahoma and the University of Georgia filed suit, claiming that (1) by fixing the price of broadcasts and threatening to boycott potential advertisers, the NCAA had violated Section 1 of the Sherman Act; and (2) by monopolizing the market of televised college football, the NCAA had violated Section 2 of the Sherman Act.

The district court ruled against the NCAA on both Section 1 and Section 2 counts, going so far as to call the NCAA a "classic cartel." The 10th Circuit Court of Appeals later rejected the plaintiff's Section 2 claim, but upheld the Section 1 claim on a per se basis. Finally, the Supreme Court affirmed the decision of the appellate court in a 7–2 decision, holding that the NCAA television plan violated antitrust laws through an unreasonable restraint on trade and also illegal price fixing. While dissenting Justice White argued that the NCAA's television policy was reasonable because it "foster[ed] the goal of amateurism by spreading revenues among various schools," the majority of justices felt that the harm to the consumer (fewer televised games) outweighed the benefits gained by the NCAA (see note 3 in next section).

This decision was important for three reasons: (1) it was the first successful challenge of the NCAA based on antitrust theory; (2) it had a significant impact on the NCAA and intercollegiate athletic departments by reducing television revenues for most institutions; and (3) the U.S. Supreme Court rendered the decision, and thus it has served as a precedent for future cases.

The precedent set by the Supreme Court has prompted other judges to consider the NCAA differently, depending on whether it acts as a regulator of amateur athletic competition (scholarship limits, grade eligibility) or as a regulator of commerce (televised game limits, limiting coaches' salaries). While the former behavior is generally allowed by the courts, the latter may be punishable under antitrust laws.

10.5.3. Decisions After *Board of Regents*

Following the *Board of Regents* decision, several athletes filed antitrust challenges against the association, but were unsuccessful. In *McCormack v. National Collegiate Athletic Ass'n*, 845 F.2d 1338 (5th Cir. 1988), the court decided that the NCAA's eligibility rules placing restrictions on student-athletes' compensation did not constitute illegal price-fixing and were not in violation of the Sherman Act. In *Banks v. NCAA*, 746 F. Supp. 850 (N.D. Ind. 1990) and *Gaines v. NCAA*, 746 F. Supp. 738 (M.D. Tenn. 1990), football players unsuccessfully challenged the NCAA on antitrust theory with regard to eligibility rules. The Indiana federal district court in *Banks* ruled that the NCAA eligibility rules in question were subject to scrutiny under the Sherman Act, but concluded that the rules were pro-competitive and, using the rule of reason test, were reasonable on the basis of their intentions. In *Gaines*, the Tennessee federal district court ruled that the NCAA eligibility rules were not subject to scrutiny under the Sherman Act. However, the court went on to state that, assuming the antitrust laws did apply to the NCAA eligibility rules, the rules were reasonable under the rule of reason test.

A crucial round of antitrust litigation against the NCAA occurred in the class action suit *Law v. NCAA*, 134 F.3d 1010 (10th Cir. 1998). Effective in August 1992, NCAA Bylaw 11.02.3 limited the earnings of certain Division I assistant coaches to $16,000. The plaintiffs, known as "restricted-earnings" coaches (REC), challenged the NCAA rule as a violation of Section 1 of the Sherman Act. The district court granted summary judgment in favor of the coaches and issued a permanent injunction restraining the NCAA from initiating any restrictions on coaches' earnings. The 10th Circuit affirmed the district court's decision and stated, "Because the REC Rule was successful in artificially lowering the price of coaching services, no further evidence or analysis is required to find market power to set prices." The NCAA argued that the pro-competitive effects of the rule outweighed the anti-competitive effects and offered three justifications: (a) retention of entry-level coaches; (b) reduction of costs; (c) maintenance of competitive equity. After considering the defendant's justifications, the court concluded:

> Thus, on its face, the REC Rule is not directed towards competitive balance nor is the nexus between the rule and a compelling need to maintain competitive balance sufficiently clear on this record to withstand a motion of summary judgment.

The damage issue was remanded to jury, which returned a verdict in favor of the plaintiffs for $22.3 million in April 1998. With trebling, this would have resulted in an award of $66.9 million—the largest judgment ever levied against the NCAA. Instead of appealing the damages verdict, the NCAA agreed to a $54.5 million settlement.

The holding of *Law* was consistent with *Board of Regents*, in the sense that the NCAA's antitrust immunity ceased to exist once the NCAA acted in a commercial capacity (restricting coaches' salaries; limiting the supply of televised games) rather than as a regulator of amateur athletic competition (enforcing academic eligibility standards, etc.). However, the *Board of Regents* precedent was tested in the case of *Adidas Am., Inc. v. NCAA*, 64 F. Supp. 2d 1097 (D. Kan. 1999). The plaintiffs alleged that NCAA limits on the size of advertising logos on player uniforms constituted an illegal restraint of trade. However, the court determined that the logo size rule was consistent with the NCAA's objective of limiting commercialization in intercollegiate athletics. The court granted the NCAA's motion to dismiss the complaint, and then rejected Adidas's motion to amend judgment (see note 2).

In late 2000 and early 2001, the NCAA became the target of multiple antitrust lawsuits regarding the decision to change the limits on the number of basketball games played by its member institutions. Prior rules allowed Division I men's teams to play in twenty-eight regular season games. However, certain "exempt" tournaments, such as the Maui Invitational, Great Alaska Shootout, and Preseason NIT, counted as only one game toward the twenty-eight-game limit, even if the schools played more than one game in these tournaments. Effective in 2001, teams would have been allowed twenty-nine regular season games, but would not be given exemptions for the aforementioned tournaments. Sponsors and promoters of such tournaments filed separate lawsuits in Ohio and New York, fearing that the proposed changes would put them out of business.

The NCAA and its members claim that the changes are necessary to reduce travel and reduce the number of classes missed by student-athletes. However, critics contend that the rule change is a ploy to allow schools to have extra home games and increase ticket revenue (see note 1). In 2001, fearing an expensive legal battle, the NCAA tabled its efforts to reduce or end tournament exemptions in either 2001 or 2002. However, the association has not ruled out abolishing the exemptions in subsequent years.

NOTES

1. For more information on this controversy, see Steve Wieberg, "NCAA proposes end to tourney exemptions; Preseason basketball events prepare to sue over change," *USA Today*, Sports, p. 10C, April 11, 2001.

2. Matthew Mitten argues that the *Adidas* decision does not comply with the Supreme Court precedent dictated in *Board of Regents*. See "Applying Antitrust Law to NCAA Regulation of 'Big Time' College Athletics," 11 *Marquette Sports Law Review* 1 (Fall 2000).

3. For further explanation of when the courts are likely to consider NCAA rules to be in violation of antitrust laws, see Richard Hunter and Ann Mayo, "Issues in Antitrust, the NCAA, and Sports Management," 10 *Marquette Sports Law Journal* 69 (Fall 1999).

4. In the case of *Baum Research & Development v. Hillerich & Bradsby Co.*, 31 F.Supp.2d 1016 (E.D. Mich. 1998), a baseball bat manufacturer brought a Section 1 complaint, alleging that the NCAA and several other bat manufacturers conspired to keep other bat manufacturers out of amateur baseball. The court concluded that the NCAA's rules and actions did not violate or deter competition. On the contrary, the court stated that the plaintiff's lack of success in the market stemmed from competition itself. In a separate case in 1998, Easton Sports Inc. sued the NCAA for $267 million in damages after the Rules Committee suggested changes in aluminum bats. The NCAA suggested the changes in order to reduce injuries caused by lively bats. However, Easton called the rule change an illegal restraint of trade that would render $140 million worth of bats obsolete. In effect, outlawing lively bats would constitute a group boycott by NCAA members. The case was settled in 1999 when the NCAA adopted bat standards that were not as restrictive as the ones that Easton protested.

5. In *Board of Regents v. NCAA*, 561 P.2d 499 (Okla. 1977), University of Oklahoma assistant football coaches asserted that an NCAA bylaw limiting the number of coaches a Division I school might employ was a violation of the Sherman Act by preventing coaches from practicing their lawful profession. The appellate court overruled the decision of the trial court, stating that the NCAA rule appeared to be a reasonable one, rationally related to its announced objective of curtailing costs of NCAA members. The court concluded that the restraint did not prevent coaches from exercising their lawful profession, but merely limited the number of coaches any given school could employ.

6. In *Jones v. NCAA*, 392 F.Supp. 295 (D. Mass. 1975), the plaintiff was an American ice hockey player who was compensated for five years while playing junior hockey in Canada prior to entering Northeastern University. Because he had received compensation for playing, Jones was declared ineligible to compete at Northeastern. Jones argued that the NCAA violated the antitrust laws by declaring him ineligible to compete. With respect to the antitrust allegations, the court held that the Sherman Act does not apply to the NCAA or its members in the setting of eligibility standards for intercollegiate athletics.

CONCLUSION

Antitrust law is particularly complicated in the sports industry because both amateur and professional sports leagues often claim a legitimate business purpose for engaging in activity that would be considered illegal in other industries. Professional leagues claim a legitimate business purpose because of the unique nature of sport and their atypical business models. The cases in this chapter were discussed in order to bridge this complexity, and to highlight the common themes of sports antitrust law. The holdings of these cases have especially impacted labor (see Chapter 11) and broadcasting (see Chapter 14). Consequently, the reader may elect to refer back to this chapter if aspects of such topics require clarification.

Chapter 11

LABOR LAW

INTRODUCTION

The difference between a college athlete and a professional athlete is that a professional athlete is considered by the courts to be an employee, whereas the courts have determined a college athlete to be primarily a student. Therefore, as employees, professional athletes are covered under state and federal labor laws. College athletes, on the other hand, do not have the protection of the labor laws; instead, they are protected by school, conference, and league rules, in addition to constitutional laws and applicable athletics-related legislation. Nevertheless, while administrators of intercollegiate and interscholastic athletics need not deal with *players* insofar as labor law, they often must deal with unionized employees such as clerical workers and groundskeepers. Furthermore, many high school coaches are members of teachers' unions. Consequently, it is beneficial for such individuals to understand the rights and expectations that labor law bestows upon employers and employees.

Labor law was designed to protect both employees and employers from the sometimes antagonistic relationship that may develop between the two parties. Labor law is a set of rules that govern the workplace, and affect both employees and employers. Labor law outlines what rights employees have and what rights their employers have. One of the cornerstones of modern American labor law is the right of employees to choose to join or assist a labor union. A union is a trade organization that represents employees in a particular work site, with its primary responsibility to negotiate and administer a Collective Bargaining Agreement for its employees (see note 2). A Collective Bargaining Agreement is a contract between an employer and a union that sets minimum standards in areas such as wages, benefits, health and safety, and vacation time, and usually contains a dispute resolution mechanism, commonly referred to as a grievance procedure.

Professional athletes were first organized into unions as far back as the 1950s, in an effort to wrest increased salary, job security, pensions, and player mobility from the leagues. Unionization in the National Hockey League (NHL), National Basketball Association (NBA), Major League Baseball (MLB), and the National Football League (NFL), along with more recent unionization efforts in the Women's National Basketball Association (WNBA) and Major League Soccer (MLS), has had a tremendous impact on professional athletes and professional sports leagues. As the business of professional sports grew tremendously in the 1980s and 1990s, so did the power of the professional sports players' association (see note 1).

What makes professional sports labor relations so complex and unique is the fact that players in professional sports leagues are covered under a Collective Bargaining Agreement between the union (or players' association) and the employer (league), in addition to being covered under an individually negotiated contract (see note 3). Players are also bound by the rules and regulations of the league, or league bylaws, which in some circumstances may contradict the interpretations of a Collective Bargaining Agreement or players' contract, and in that case, a court may be called in to settle the dispute. Therefore, in professional sports, there is a combination of labor law and contract law at work.

This chapter will offer an introductory look at the relevant labor laws that affect professional sports, including an examination of the National Labor Relations Act, the National Labor Relations Board, and case law surrounding unfair labor practices and collective bargaining. In addition, this chapter will analyze the development of unionization in professional sports and scrutinize several provisions in current Collective Bargaining Agreements from the NHL, NFL, MLB, and NBA. Finally, this chapter will briefly discuss the often stormy relationship that exists between the leagues and the various players' associations by examining work stoppages and other legal issues.

NOTES

1. For a description of how the business of professional sports has changed, refer to Chapter 1. For an overview of labor relations in professional sports see Paul Staudohar, *Playing for Dollars: Labor Relations and the Sports Business* (Ithaca, N.Y.: Cornell University Press, 1996).

2. While a union is sometimes confined to one particular work site, the National Labor Relations Board (NLRB) can approve or order multiple work site bargaining units. For example, NFL players work at multiple work sites (e.g., Soldier Field in Chicago, Raymond James Stadium in Tampa) on teams with different ownership. However, all NFL players are represented by the NFLPA. The NLRB is likely to order/approve multiple work site units if there is a centralization of management or significant interchange of employees among the work sites, or if all employers and employees agree on such an arrangement. While multiple work site and multiple employer units are the norm in pro sports, the case of *North American Soccer League v. National Labor Relations Board*, 613 F.2d 1379 (5th Cir. 1980), tested this concept. In this case, the NASL claimed that players should be required to bargain with each individual team, not the league as a whole. The court denied this claim, because the NASL, not individual teams, exercised "a significant degree of control over . . . selection, retention, and termination of the players, the terms of individual player contracts, dispute resolution, and player discipline."

3. In this chapter, "employer" refers to owners, leagues, and particular management groups, such as Major League Baseball's Labor Relations Department (formerly the Player Relations Committee) and the NFL Management Council. An "employee," in this chapter, is a professional athlete playing for a professional sports league. The unions that are referred to in this text are the National Hockey League Players Association, the National Basketball Players Association, the Major League Baseball Players Association, the National Football league Players Association, and the Women's National Basketball Players Association.

11.1. DEVELOPMENT OF LABOR LAW

Labor relations law is derived from statutory law, judicial decisions and interpretations, constitutional rights, and administrative decisions by agencies of the U.S. government. Statutory law can be created or amended by legislation at the federal, state, or local level of government. Examples of statutory labor laws include the Clayton Act, the Norris-LaGuardia Act, and the National Labor Relations Act. Judicial decisions and interpretations occur when a court issues a decision or interpretation that creates a change in existing legislation, or sets a precedent interpreting an existing law differently. For example, in *Federal Baseball Club v. National League of Professional Baseball Clubs*, 259 U.S. 200 (1922), the court ruled that the sport of baseball was not subject to antitrust laws because it was not engaged in interstate commerce. That decision set a precedent that was affirmed in two later judicial decisions involving professional baseball. Had the court in *Federal Baseball*, or subsequent decisions, interpreted the law differently and not given professional baseball an antitrust exemption, then a different precedent would have been established. It is important to note that if a legislature is dissatisfied with a court's interpretation of a statute, the legislature has the power to amend or override the court's interpretation. An example of this is the Curt Flood Act of 1998, which Congress passed to limit the antitrust exemption professional baseball had held since the *Federal Baseball* decision.

11.1.1. History of Labor Law

In the early 1800s, there was an absence of legislative direction as it pertained to labor law, and thus the judicial system not only controlled the relationships between labor unions and employers, but also played a key role in limiting the rights of unions until the 1930s. During this period, workers began to organize into guilds or unions in an attempt to "bargain" with their employers for a fair wage. Workers realized that employers were more likely to respond to groups than to individuals, and therefore began a process of bargaining for groups of employees rather than individuals. If the employer refused, workers would "strike" at their work site as a sign of protest, and not return to work until the particular issue had been resolved. Employers, who frequently did not know the trade themselves, found themselves losing money, and customers, during these labor battles. They turned to the courts for a remedy.

The earliest and most important case in early labor law history is the Philadelphia *Cordwainers'* decision in *Commonwealth v. Pullis* (Phila. Mayor's Ct. 1806), which declared that collective organizing was a "criminal conspiracy." The trial judge stated:

> Our position is that no man is at liberty to combine, conspire, confederate and unlawfully agree to regulate the whole body of workmen in the city. The defendants are not indicted for regulating their own individual wages but for undertaking by a combination, to regulate the price of labor of others as well as their own.

The court found that workers acting in concert with each other were acting in a conspiracy. Therefore, all actions by groups of employees—picketing, striking, holding union meetings—could be considered a conspiracy and were punishable by fine or imprisonment. This decision aroused much protest from workers and was finally overturned by the 1842 decision in *Commonwealth v. Hunt*, 4 Met. 111 (1842). This case established that if the collective action in question was beneficial to the worker, or group of workers, then conspiracy charges could not apply.

In the wake of *Commonwealth v. Hunt*, employers turned to the civil courts as a means to protect themselves from union organizing and work stoppages in their workplaces. More and more workers were protesting unsafe working conditions, squalid housing, and poverty wages. During the latter half of the 1800s and the beginning of the 1900s, labor battles were fought both in the courts and on the picket line. As union-employer violence escalated at the turn of the twentieth century, Congress was forced to rethink the labor laws that were governing workers throughout the country. Between 1914 and 1947, Congress passed and amended several pieces of legislation that would shape labor relations for the rest of the 20th century:

1. Clayton Act (1914). This act, signed in 1914, was seen as a victory for the labor movement because it stated that "the labor of a human being is not a commodity or article of commerce." This ensured that unions would not be subject to the Sherman Antitrust Act of 1890. In addition, the Clayton Act restricted the rights of employers to use injunctions against its employees: "no . . . injunction shall be granted in any case between an employer and employees . . . growing out of a dispute concerning terms or conditions of work." However, many employers were still able to receive injunctions by proving the threat of violence on the picket line.

2. Norris-LaGuardia Act (1932). This act, often referred to as the Federal Anti-Injunction Act, limited the power of the federal government to issue injunctions and limit union activity. The Norris-LaGuardia Act stated that when a labor dispute was found, federal courts were forbidden to issue any injunction that forbade either the refusal to work or peaceful picketing. However, this act could not limit or stop state courts from issuing injunctions.

3. The Wagner Act (1935). Officially referred to as the National Labor Relations Act (described further below), this piece of legislation gave workers the right to join or assist unions, without fear of employer retribution. This statute was the first piece of legislation that gave workers the right to freely pursue unionization. The Wagner Act covers all areas of labor law, including representation elections, unfair labor practice charges, and duties of representation.

4. Taft-Hartley Act (1947). Officially referred to as the Labor Management Relations Act, this legislation was an amendment to the Wagner Act, in the face of increased union unrest and employer pressure. The main change to the Wagner Act was the addition of unfair union practices, which prohibited unions from pressuring employees to join or assist a union or a unionization drive.

11.1.2. National Labor Relations Act (as Amended in 1947)

Most employees working in private firms are covered by the NLRA. It is important to note that not all employees are covered by the act, however. The following is a list of employees who are excluded from coverage by the NLRA:

1. Employees of federal, state, or local governments
2. Airline or-railroad employees
3. Spouses and children of employees
4. Independent contractors
5. Domestic servants
6. Agricultural workers
7. Supervisors and managers.

Some of the workers in these industries are protected under other pieces of legislation. For example, rail and air transportation workers are covered under the Railway Labor Act of 1926.

11.1.3. National Labor Relations Act, Section 7

One of the most important sections in the NLRA is Section 7:

> Employees shall have the right to self-organization, to form, join, assist, labor or-
> ganizations, to bargain collectively through representatives of their own choosing,
> and to engage in other concerted activities for the purpose of collective bargaining
> or other mutual aid or protection, and shall also have the right to refrain from any
> or all of such activities except to the extent that such right may be affected by this
> agreement requiring membership in a labor organization as a condition of employ-
> ment as authorized in section 8(a)(3).

Congress created this right because it recognized that workers have more power, or bargaining strength, as a group rather than as individuals. Section 7 assures workers of certain rights:

1. The right to form and organize labor organizations
2. The right to become members of labor unions or to refuse to join
3. The right to bargain collectively through representatives of their own choosing
4. The right to engage in other concerted activity for the purpose of collective bargaining, such as strikes, boycotts, and picketing.

11.1.4. National Labor Relations Act, Section 8

Section 8 of the NLRA protects the rights workers are entitled to under Section 7. If an employer violates a worker's right under Section 7, it is called an *unfair labor practice*. Section 8 outlines what constitutes an unfair labor practice:

1. 8(a)(1) An employer is forbidden from interfering, restraining, or coercing its employees from exercising their rights under Section 7.
2. 8(a)(2) Attempting to dominate, interfere with the formation of, and finance and support a labor union are all prohibited.
3. 8(a)(3) Employers are forbidden to discriminate against employees on account of their union relationship.
4. 8(a)(4) Employers are forbidden to fire, discipline, or lay off an employee because he or she has filed an unfair labor practice.
5. 8(a)(5) Employers must bargain in good faith over wages, hours, terms of employment.

If an employer is found to have breached any Section 8(a) articles, there are six possible remedies: (1) back pay; (2) reinstatement; (3) bargaining order; (4) rerun election; (5) cease and desist order; (6) injunctive relief. Back pay and reinstatement are two remedies that are commonly utilized if an employee wins a Section 8(a) unfair labor practice charge. This is because many employees are terminated for engaging in union organizing and other union activities. Rerun elections are initiated if it is found that the employer has interfered with the formation of a union, and such interference resulted in a negative certification vote.

Section 8 also identifies *unfair union activities*:

1. 8(b)(1) Unions are prohibited from coercing or restraining employees as stated under the rights of the Act.

2. 8(b)(2) Actions that cause an employer to discriminate against an employee for the purpose of encouraging or discouraging union membership are prohibited.

3. 8(b)(3) The union must bargain in good faith.

If a labor organization is found to have breached any of the articles in Section 8, there are five possible remedies: (1) injunctive relief; (2) bargaining order; (3) cease and desist order; (4) damages; (5) disestablishment of the union or withdrawal of recognition. In most cases, the employer will seek an injunction against the union if Section 8(b) violations occur, although the issuance of a bargaining order is also an effective means to ensure that a Collective Bargaining Agreement is negotiated in good faith.

NOTES

1. The constitutionality of the Wagner Act was tested in *National Labor Relations Board v. Jones and Laughlin Steel Corp.*, 301 U.S. 1 (1937). The NLRB found Jones and Laughlin Steel Corp. in violation of the National Labor Relations Act, Section 8(a), after the company was found to have coerced and intimidated employees in order to stop them from organizing a union. The NLRB then petitioned the Circuit Court of Appeals to enforce the order, which was subsequently denied, because the court believed the order lay beyond the range of federal power. The case was sent to the Supreme Court, which concluded that the act was valid, as applied in *Jones and Laughlin Steel Corp.* and reversed the circuit court's decision.

2. The NLRA gives employees the right to strike, but there are certain limitations on this right. If a Collective Bargaining Agreement exists in which the employer has agreed to binding arbitration in place of a no-strike clause, the employer may seek an injunction to stop a strike or walkout. Employees engaging in an economic strike may be permanently replaced, whereas in an unfair labor practice strike, they may not.

11.1.5. Unfair Labor Practice Procedures

When an employee's rights have been violated, as outlined in the National Labor Relations Act, that employee has the ability to file an unfair labor practice charge. The NLRA was created to protect the rights of employees, and the NLRB was created to administer and enforce the NLRA. The filing of an unfair labor practice charge illustrates how the NLRA and the NLRB are interconnected. The following is the process that the charging party needs to go through when filing an unfair labor practice charge:

1. *Filing the Charge.* An unfair labor practice charge must be filed within six (6) months of the conduct that gave rise to the allegations. Any person may file a charge with the NLRB, at the closest NLRB regional office.

2. *Investigation.* The NLRB regional director will conduct an investigation to determine whether the charge has merit and should advance through the process. This process is similar to "discovery." If the charge is found to have merit, the regional director will file a complaint. If the charge does not have merit, it is dismissed, but may be appealed through the Office of Appeals, a division of the NLRB.

3. *Hearing.* When a complaint is issued, the charging party is represented by the General Counsel's Office and the hearing is set before an administrative law judge. The hearing is similar to a formal trial, but without the jury.

4. *Decision.* The administrative law judge will render a decision, which may be appealed by either party to the NLRB or to the appropriate court of appeals.

11.1.5.1. Interference with Organizing or Bargaining Collectively

The goal of Section 8(a)(1) is to stop employers from interfering with employees' right to join a labor union. Examples of this interference include threats of bankruptcy, firing, or layoff; interrogations of union members or organizers; offering rewards to employees who go against the union; or spying on union meetings (see note 1).

NOTE _____

1. A clear violation of Section 8(a)(1) would occur if a high school athletic association transferred the contract of its football referees, after those referees formed a union. Other Section 8(a)(1) violations are not so clear-cut. For example, during the NBA lockout in 1998, Commissioner David Stern made comments that strongly encouraged the players to adopt the NBA's proposal and not to decertify their union. While no lawsuits were filed, these comments constituted coercion and a Section 8(a)(1) violation, according to John Croke in "An Examination of the Antitrust Issues Surrounding the NBA Decertification Crisis," 5 *Sports Lawyers Journal* 163 (Spring 1998).

11.1.5.2. Domination and Assistance

The goal of Section 8(a)(2) is to prohibit the use of company unions, favoritism of one union over another, or endangering the independence of a union. Employers are prohibited from exercising control over the operations of a union, including having undue influence in the decision-making process. Company unions are unions that purport to be independent organizations, but are not certified by the NLRB and are, in actuality, instruments of the employer. An example of this on the pro sport level would be the early years of the MLBPA, which had its executive director picked by MLB, and also was financed and controlled by the league. Section 8(a)(2) prohibits this type of arrangement, although no suit was ever filed by the MLBPA with the NLRB over this issue. In 2001, the NLRB accused Arena Football League owners of coercing players into joining a company union (AFLPOC) by using offers of financial assistance and threats of job loss. The league denied these claims, and its involvement with the AFLPOC, before settling this issue with the players in 2001.

NOTE _____

1. Players of the Philadelphia Eagles filed an unfair labor practice charge in 1993, charging that the Collective Bargaining Agreement reached by the NFL-NFLPA after the *White* settlement was invalid because the NFLPA had not yet recertified its union status. The players claimed that the agreement was therefore a violation of Section 8(a)(2) and possibly of 8(b)(1)(A). The charge was eventually dropped after an ownership change, but there remains a question as to whether the deal reached in 1993 between the NFL and NFLPA rests on solid legal ground.

11.1.5.3. Discrimination

The purpose of Section 8(a)(3) is to eliminate discriminatory behavior by employers against employees due to their relationship with a union. Some forms of discrimination include demotion, discharge, reduction in pay, change in job classification, and change in work site. In these circumstances, the union must prove that the employer acted with malice because of union affiliation (see note 1).

NOTE _____

1. A violation of 8(a)(3) in professional sports usually occurs when a player is traded, reassigned, or waived due to his or her union activities. See *In re: Nordstrom*, 292 NLRB 899 (1989). In this case, Seahawk player Sam McCullum was allegedly released from the team because of his union affiliation. For the subsequent case on the amount of back pay owed to McCullum, see *National Football League and the National Football League Player Association*, 309 NLRB 78 (1992).

11.1.5.4. Retaliation

The aim of Section 8(a)(4) is to protect employees who file unfair labor practice charges against their employer with the NLRB. Employees who either initiate charges or offer testimony during an NLRB unfair labor practice hearing are protected against employer retaliation (actions similar to those that are relevant to Section 8(a)(3)).

11.1.5.5. Duty to Bargain in Good Faith

When a union is recognized by the National Labor Relations Board, the employer of the unionized employees is required to bargain in good faith with the union representing those employees. Refusal to bargain is a violation of Section 8(a)(5). Case law surrounding Section 8(a)(5) has focused on what, beyond the mere willingness to sign an agreement, is necessary in order to establish good faith bargaining. Simply put, a party that makes no concessions and rejects the other side's proposals outright, has for all intents and purposes refused to bargain in good faith. For example, if the WNBA bargaining representatives went into negotiations offering a scant increase in salary to the players and refused to discuss any other issues, it could be argued that they were bargaining in bad faith. In addition, an employer that refuses to give the union information that is relevant to negotiations may be in violation of 8(a)(5) (see notes 1 and 2).

NOTES _____

1. An example of a violation of 8(a)(5) of the NLRA occurred when members of the U.S. Men's National Soccer Team, initially recognized by the U.S. Soccer Federation, were unable to bargain a contract because of the USSF's refusal to bargain. See *USSF, Inc. and the United States Men's National Soccer Team Players*, Case 5-CA-26593 (May 30, 1997). The NLRB issued a complaint against the USSF and ordered it to bargain with the player's union. See also *Morio v. North American Soccer League*, 501 F.Supp. 633 (S.D.N.Y. 1980), where the NASL unilaterally changed the conditions of employment without negotiating with the players. The players' union successfully won an injunction that rendered the changes voidable.

2. If impasse has not been reached, good faith bargaining must occur on all mandatory subjects of bargaining. In both *Silverman v. Major League Baseball Player Relations Committee, Inc.*, 516 F. Supp. 588 (S.D.N.Y. 1981), and *NFL Management Council and NFLPA*, NLRB case No. 2-CA-13379 (June 30, 1976), the players filed suit against management for failing to provide relevant information during bargaining. This constituted an NLRA Section (8)(a)(5) violation.

11.1.5.6. Protection from Unions

Section 8(b)(1) prohibits unions from forcing its members to engage in a concerted activity (e.g. strikes). This means that a union cannot discipline a member who does not agree to strike with the rest of the union. Section 8(b) of the NLRA also includes rules that prohibit a union from encouraging any individual employed by a person engaged in commerce or in an industry affecting commerce to engage in a strike. This section of the NLRA has not traditionally applied to the realm of sports. Section 8(b)(1) also prevents a union from restraining its members from engaging in concerted activity. Furthermore, a union cannot coerce management during its selection of representatives for collective bargaining. Some states have extended additional protection to workers from unions in the form of "right to work" laws (see note 1).

NOTE _____

1. In 1993, members of the Washington Redskins, unhappy with the Collective Bargaining Agreement that came out of *White v. NFL*, 41 F.3d 402 (8th Cir. 1994), withheld their union dues, $5000 for the season. The NFLPA sought to have the players suspended after an arbitrator ruled in favor of the union. However, at both the federal level, *NFLPA v. Pro-Football Inc.*, 857 F.Supp. 71 (D.D.C. 1994), and the state level, *Orr v. National Football League Players Ass'n*, 147 LRRM 2845 (Va. 1994), decisions were rendered in favor of the players. The players claimed that they worked in a right to work state, and therefore were not required to join the union or pay dues. The players were able to make this assertion because their practice facilities were located in Virginia, and they convinced the court that their time spent in Virginia outweighed their affiliation with the District of Columbia.

11.1.6. National Labor Relations Board

The National Labor Relations Board (NLRB) is a federal administrative agency that was established to administer and enforce the National Labor Relations Act. The first board took office on August 27, 1935, after Congress had passed the Wagner Act. The board has two primary responsibilities:

1. Supervising and conducting representation elections
2. Adjudicating employer and union unfair labor practices.

The NLRB is located in Washington and is made up of two separate branches: (1) the board itself, made up of five members, and (2) the general counsel, an independent officer who is responsible for prosecuting unfair labor practice cases. It has divided the country into several regions, with each region having an office, a director, staff, attorneys, and agents. Appeals of decisions made at the regional level go to the federal NLRB or the general counsel.

The general counsel has two primary functions:

1. To determine whether, when, and upon what basis unfair labor practice charges shall be prosecuted. The general counsel has the exclusive authority to prosecute a complaint; his determination not to issue a complaint is not subject to board or court review.
2. To supervise all employees in the regional offices and all attorneys (except those serving as administrative law judges or legal assistants to board members). But the appointment, transfer, demotion, or discharge of any regional director or of any officer in charge of a subregional office must have prior approval of the board.

The board has five main functions, as outlined in the NLRA:

1. To prevent and remedy unfair labor practices committed by employers or labor organizations

2. To determine representatives (i.e., to select a union) for purposes of collective bargaining

3. To determine the authority of representatives to have union shop provisions in their Collective Bargaining Agreement (see note 1)

4. To determine jurisdictional disputes that have led to the filing of unfair labor practice charges

5. To poll employees on their employer's last offer in "national emergency" situations.

NOTE

1. In a "union shop," a worker must join the union. In an "agency shop," a worker is not required to join the union but must pay initiation fees and union dues. For more information, see Michael Evan Gold, *An Introduction to Labor Law*, rev. ed. (Ithaca, N.Y.: Cornell University Press, 1998).

11.1.7. Certification of a Union

Before an employer and the union representing a unit of workers meet to negotiate a contract, the affected employees need to go through a process to be properly recognized as a union. There are three ways for a union to be certified:

1. NLRB election

2. Voluntary recognition

3. Board-ordered recognition without election.

Typically, an employer will voluntarily recognize a group of workers as a union only if the union has a particularly high level of bargaining power over the employer, or if the employer feels that most employees support unionization. The NHL, NBA, MLB, and NFL all voluntarily recognize the respective players associations (see note 2). If not voluntarily recognized by management, workers need to get 30% of the workers at a work site to sign a card declaring they would like to unionize. The NLRB will then hold an election at the work site and the employees will vote by secret ballot on whether to join the union. If more than 50% of the workers vote in favor of unionization, a union has been created and management will be required, under the NLRA, to negotiate a contract with that union. If an employer believes there was a problem with the certification election, it may refuse to bargain with that union, although the courts and the NLRB have not looked favorably upon this tactic, and it usually results in a violation of Section 8(a)(5).

NOTES

1. In *North American Soccer League v. NLRB*, 613 F.2d 1379 (5th Cir. 1980), the NLRB made a decision on representation in unionized sports. In *NASL*, the appeals court found that a leaguewide bargaining unit was the most practical unit structure, opposing the argument made by the league, which asserted a team-by-team unit structure. In the other professional leagues, their units are also structured on a leaguewide basis, rather than by team, or by position.

2. In the NFL, NBA, NHL, and MLB, players associations are "voluntarily" recognized in the sense that there was no NLRB election or board-ordered recognition. This does not necessarily mean that the leagues recognized the unions willingly. For example, the NBPA claims that the NBA refused to recognize the union at its inception in 1954, and did not do so until the players' threatened boycott of the 1964 All-Star Game. For more information, see www.nbpa.com/aboutus/history.html

11.2. COLLECTIVE BARGAINING

Collective bargaining is an activity whereby two groups, union and management representatives, attempt to resolve conflicting interests by exchanging commitments pertaining to the terms and conditions of employment. Normally, employees are looking to secure better wages, job protection, health benefits, health and safety regulations, and a say in the practices that affect their daily work lives. Employers, on the other hand, want to maintain control of the workplace and make decisions they feel are in the best interests of the company or business. The collective bargaining process is designed to come to a compromise between these stands and to reach a contract.

11.2.1. The Collective Bargaining Process

A typical Collective Bargaining Agreement is a complex document that deals with a broad range of diverse issues. A professional sport Collective Bargaining Agreement is no different. It may establish a detailed wage scheduling system while others have different levels of minimum pay according to seniority. It contains a job classification system, a pension plan, and a clause determining how seniority or service is calculated. It also contains management promises of safe working conditions, no discrimination, and union recognition. It may also include articles that are specific to professional sports, such as salary arbitration, free agency, the college draft, and salary cap. More recent agreements have included maternity leave, drug policies, and counseling programs. A typical agreement also contains disciplinary measures and a definition of "just cause." Thus Collective Bargaining Agreements cover a wide range of issues and may be lengthy documents that affect most aspects of an employee's job.

The negotiating process actually begins before each side sits down at a table to negotiate. Prior to this stage, each set of representatives must determine what the important issues are. For the union, a bargaining committee is appointed or elected by the membership to represent the union in negotiations with management. The bargaining committee will determine, through surveys, meetings, or one-on-one discussions, what issues the union members feel strongly about. The bargaining committee will rely on reports from its representatives on each team. If the union is in its infancy, or bargaining its first contract, its demands will, in all likelihood, revolve around benefits, a minimum salary, and a pension plan. If the union has been in existence for many years, its demands will be more complex and may include increased free agency, salary arbitration, and an injury grievance procedure.

There are three factors that impact what a union will ask for in negotiations:

1. Maturity of the union
2. Bargaining power and leverage
3. Company/league stability.

The *maturity of the union* may play an important role in determining what a union will ask for in negotiations. If a union is negotiating its first contract, the power is on the side of management because the union, in all likelihood, lacks bargaining power, and is content to set minimum standards for wages, benefits, and a pension plan. Many unions negotiating their first contract are content with those items, and pursue items like player mobility or salary arbitration in subsequent negotiations (see note 1).

On the other hand, an established union has experience, public awareness, and many years of negotiations under its belt. Established unions like the United Auto Workers (UAW) and the Major League Baseball Players Association (MLBPA) have comprehensive contracts that are the result of decades of negotiations and renegotiations. The MLBPA is viewed by many to be the most successful labor union in sports. In fact, it is considered by some to be the nation's strongest trade union of *any* kind.

Bargaining power is another important factor a union needs to address. Bargaining power is the power a union brings with it to the negotiating table. UAW workers have a high level of bargaining power because a strike could cost auto companies billions of dollars in lost revenue. In addition, many established unions have funds set aside in the event of a strike/lockout that can be distributed to members during a work stoppage. With respect to professional athletes, their bargaining power can be high because of the popularity of the respective sport or stars and the lack of public acceptance for replacement players, and also because of the importance of sporting events to television networks and advertisers. However, in recent years, public opinion is no longer guaranteed to be in favor of the athletes in the case of a strike. The baseball strike in 1994–1995, and the lockout in the NBA in 1998, are two examples of public support being split between the owners and the players. Therefore, unions need to find their source of bargaining power and determine how it can best be applied. If it is high, and the threat of a strike is great, it is more likely that the union's demands will be met. However, if management believes public opinion will be in its favor in the event of a strike, it will have this in their favor in negotiations.

Company stability is another factor that can seriously affect negotiations. If a company is suffering because of a recession or a downturn in the economy, its negotiating team may ask for concessions or a wage rollback. In professional sports, during the 1982 NBA negotiations, the league claimed that it could not afford to maintain operations unless a salary cap was instituted. The NBA Players Association audited the league's financial records and agreed that a cap was necessary. Much of the dissension between labor and management in the NBA in the 1990s has been due to the fact that the league has become extremely profitable and teams in the league are no longer in fear of insolvency. However, in the agreement that came out of the lockout during the 1998/1999 season, the NBA's salary cap provisions were in fact strengthened, a significant plus for the owners. The owners in Major League Baseball and the National Hockey League have argued for a salary cap, yet neither the NHLPA nor the MLBPA has acceded to these demands.

NOTE

1. The WNBA went into its first collective bargaining negotiations in 1998 seeking increased minimum salaries, job protection, and health benefits. Terms of the settled

Exhibit 11.1
Mandatory and Permissive Subjects of Bargaining

Mandatory	Permissive
Rate and method of pay	Change in the bargaining unit
Work rules, discipline, drug testing	Identity of the bargaining agent
Safety	Status of supervisors
Grievance and arbitration procedures	Settlement of unfair labor practice charges
Health insurance, pensions, and layoff compensation	Internal union or company affairs

agreement included $25,000 rookie minimum; $30,000 veteran minimum; a maximum of three ABL (then a competitor league) players on the roster for the 1999 season; year-round health insurance; 401K plan; maternity policy; and group licensing.

11.2.2. Mandatory and Permissive Subjects of Bargaining

When two parties sit down at the negotiating table, there are certain items they are forced to negotiate. Mandatory subjects, as outlined in the NLRA, are wages, hours, and terms and conditions of employment. Economic weapons, such as the strike or the lockout, may be used to force the other party to agree to a proposal on a mandatory subject. An economic weapon cannot be legally used to force the other party to an agreement on a permissive subject. Permissive subjects are topics that may be bargained at the table if both sides are willing to do so, but if one side does not want to discuss a permissive topic, it is not required to do so. Exhibit 11.1 illustrates some examples of each category.

For example, in the professional sports industry, mandatory subjects of bargaining would include the college draft, the salary cap, a limitation on roster size, and health and safety issues. An example of a permissive subject of bargaining would be regulation of tickets for players. Permissive subjects of bargaining are included in collective bargaining agreements based on the willingness of both parties to negotiate over the issue. If a union is strong, it will be able to negotiate permissive subjects. Conversely, if the union is weak, it will likely be unable to bargain these permissive subjects.

After the parties have come to an agreement on an item, they may "sign off" on it. That usually means that each chief negotiator initials the written language, and that item cannot be bargained over during that round of negotiations unless consented to by both sides. After each item has been agreed to or dropped, negotiations have finished. The length of Collective Bargaining Agreements varies considerably, depending on the power of the union, how long the union has been in existence, the type of work being done, and the size of the union. Some collective bargaining agreements are five pages. Others are over 200 pages. The

NBA-NBPA 1999–2004 agreement is over 300 pages, including approximately 100 pages of exhibits. It is important to remember that relevant issues will change depending on the industry and the different sports. For example, what may be important to steelworkers will be different in many respects from those working as bus drivers, secretaries, graduate student employees, or professional athletes. Similarly, the important issues for professional basketball players may be different from those of professional hockey players.

11.2.3. Ratification

Once an agreement has been reached on a tentative contract, the union must take it back to its membership for ratification. Ratification occurs when a vote is accepted by the membership. In most cases, the union needs 50% plus one of its membership to vote in favor of the contract for it to be ratified. Some unions have stipulations in their constitutions that dictate that 60% or 75% or more of the membership needs to vote in favor of the agreement for the ratification to be legitimate. If a union does not think the majority of its members support the agreement, it will return to the table for further negotiations. The negotiating team for management must present the contract to the owners and, depending upon the management structure, there also may need to be a vote. If the contract is ratified by both parties, the agreement will be implemented for the period that was agreed to in negotiations. The next round of bargaining will usually begin three to six months before the agreement expires.

11.2.4. Decertification

If a union member or group of members decide they are unhappy with the way their union is being run or maintained, they have several options with which to initiate changes. There are internal remedies in the union's bylaws or constitution that may include disciplinary measures and other such avenues. Another option that is available is decertification. To decertify a union is to break all formal ties with the union and give up the right to collectively bargain a Collective Bargaining Agreement. After a petition is sent to the NLRB calling for a *decertification election*, an NLRB representative will conduct the election and the employees will vote, by secret ballot, whether to stay in the union or to decertify. As in a certification election, 50 percent plus one need to vote in favor of decertification for it to pass. If it does pass, all the employees who had been represented by a union would no longer have any affiliation with the union and no Collective Bargaining Agreement would be in place. Players would no longer have a grievance procedure, a minimum salary, or health care/insurance. The league would also have the right to implement any new rules it deemed necessary (e.g., hard salary cap). When a union decertifies, its members lose all rights they had in the collective bargaining agreement. Union decertification has been uncommon to this point in professional sports due to the potential negative consequences it can have on a players union.

As discussed in section 11.3.3., "NFL Players Association," there has been only one example of a decertification in professional sports, and it was due not to player unrest but rather to union leadership strategy. In 1992, NFL players voted to decertify the NFLPA as their exclusive bargaining representative, so that they could sue the NFL on antitrust grounds, which they did. The NFL owners were protected from antitrust litigation when a collective bargaining agreement was in place, but without one, there was no legal way of legitimizing several of their restrictive policies, mainly the Right of First Refusal system, which limited player mobility. Following decertification, NFL players won a series of class action lawsuits against the league and finally settled in 1993, in what became known as the *White* settlement. The settlement became part of a new Collective Bargaining Agreement, and the NFLPA was again certified as the official bargaining representative of professional football players.

11.3. COLLECTIVE BARGAINING IN PROFESSIONAL SPORTS

Professional athletes began seeking union representation over a hundred years ago, but there was not an official players' union until the mid-1950s. Since that time, professional sports has been subject to continued labor conflict, especially since the 1970s. Each players' association has been involved in at least one work stoppage, and hundreds of games have been lost due to strikes and lockouts. Labor conflict in professional sports will be examined in greater detail in section 11.4., "Labor Disputes in Professional Sports." It is important to understand the history behind the unionization efforts of professional athletes, and to see what gains have been made since the 1970s.

Contracts in professional sports are different from *most* other forms of unionized employment, in that employees can negotiate their own contracts (see chapter 9, section 9.2.1.3., "Hierarchy of Contracts"). For example, it is typical that a union of butchers, teachers, or grocery workers will negotiate salaries into the collective bargaining agreement. Butchers with two years of seniority will get "x" dollars, butchers with five years of seniority will get "y" dollars, and so on. Therefore, such butchers will not be required (or allowed) to individually negotiate their salaries with their employer. In most professional sports leagues, the Collective Bargaining Agreement sets a minimum salary and perhaps a maximum salary (a cap), but players and their agents are free to negotiate within such parameters. One notable exception is the WNBA, which has a salary scale based on seniority and draft position.

11.3.1. The Players Association in Professional Sports

Most professional team sports athletes in the United States and Canada are represented by a labor union, more commonly referred to in the sports industry as a Players Association. These associations grew out of player frustrations with the way in which they were being treated by the league they played in and by the owners of their team. Many of these associations began as unofficial guilds started by players who had been adversely affected by a league or owner decision. By the 1960s, players in the NHL, NFL, MLB, and NBA had all been officially unionized and had begun collective bargaining negotiations with their respective leagues. Today, with the addition of the unionized athletes in the WNBA, players associations have become a powerful tool for the players, and may also be involved in licensing, marketing, representing players in disputes and certifying player agents.

11.3.2. NHL Players Association

National Hockey League players actively pursued unionization in the early 1950s, and by 1957, with Ted Lindsay as president, the NHL Players Association (NHLPA) was born. When the association was initially formed, it had not been legally recognized as a union by the league, but was still able to negotiate with the owners that a percentage of the money from a new television deal was to go directly into the players' pension fund. When the NHL expanded in 1967 from six to twelve teams, the players were officially certified as a union and made Alan Eagleson the NHLPA's first executive director (see note 1). Between 1967 and 1991, there were no work stoppages in the NHL. In 1991 Bob Goodenow became executive director after the players had become dissatisfied with Eagleson's leadership and concerned about allegations of embezzlement and fraud surrounding his tenure as executive director. Under Goodenow, the NHLPA has engaged in two work stoppages (1992 and 1994–95) and has managed to thwart all attempts by the owners to implement a salary cap. In addition, the NHLPA has expanded its marketing and licensing division, with over fifty staff people working in areas such as labor law, product licensing, and community relations.

NOTES ───

1. In 1995, former NHL players filed a class action lawsuit against Alan Eagleson and all individual NHL teams. Among the claims made by the players: Eagleson accepted the reserve system that limited player mobility, to the detriment of the players; he urged players to approve the NHL-WHA merger without demanding concessions; agreed to remove player representatives from the player pension fund, which gave control over the fund to the owners; and he cooperated with the NHL to maintain a union dominated by the interests of the NHL, to the detriment of the players. The conspiracy case was decided against the players in 1998 because they had waited too long to sue (statute of limitations). The U.S. Supreme Court upheld the decision in 2001 by refusing to hear the players' appeal. However, in 1997 Eagleson pled guilty to fraud and theft charges stemming from his actions as executive director of the NHLPA, spent six months in prison, and faced more than $1 million in fines.

2. For a description of the resistance to hockey player unionization in North America, see David Cruise, *Net Worth: Exploding the Myths of Pro Hockey* (Toronto: Penguin Books, 1992).

3. Further information on the NHLPA is available at their Web site: www.nhlpa.com/

11.3.3. NFL Players Association

The NFL Players Association was formed in 1956, although between 1956 and 1967 little progress was made for the players, except for a small increase in their pension fund. However, beginning in the early 1970s, NFL players fought for increased benefits and increased player mobility in the courts and on the picket line. The first work stoppage in professional sports occurred in 1968 when NFL players boycotted the league's pre-season games, and were subsequently locked out by the owners at the beginning of the regular season. Another short conflict occurred in 1970, during the merger of the AFL and the NFL, followed by a failed strike attempt in 1974, after the expiration of the agreement signed in 1970. Under the leadership of Executive Director Ed Garvey, a former attorney and player advocate, the NFLPA won two court decisions, *Smith v. Pro Football*

Inc. and *Mackey v. National Football League*. These victories provided the players with leverage to negotiate new agreements. The 1976 *Mackey* decision abolished the "Rozelle Rule," which severely limited player mobility. However, in the 1977 and 1982 negotiations, the NFLPA gave up its fight for less restriction of player mobility in favor of increased minimum salaries, increased benefits, and an increased contribution to the pension fund, with the 1982 agreement coming after a fifty-seven-day strike. After an aborted strike in 1987, the NFLPA challenged the league's restrictive rules and regulations, using antitrust theory, in the court system. The NFLPA was decertified after not finding success in *Powell v. the NFL*, which allowed the players to successfully sue the NFL on antitrust grounds. After the successful *McNeil* verdict, the NFLPA was re-recognized, and subsequently signed a long-term collective bargaining agreement with the NFL (see notes 2 and 3).

NOTES

1. In *Powell v. NFL*, 678 F.Supp. 777 (D. Minn. 1988), NFL players challenged the NFL's restrictions on free agency, specifically the Right of First Refusal/Compensation system under antitrust law. The case went to the Appeals court, *Powell v. National Football League*, 930 F.2d 1293 (8th Cir. 1989), where the court found that the NFL was protected against antitrust litigation due to the labor exemption. The Supreme Court denied *certiorari*.

2. *McNeil v. NFL*, 777 F. Supp. 1475 (D. Minn. 1991) occurred after the National Football League Players Association decertified so that players could sue the league, using antitrust theory. The labor exemption, which protects leagues from antitrust challenges when there is a Collective Bargaining Agreement in place, is no longer applicable when a union has decertified. In *McNeil*, the players challenged Plan B free agency (the owners' response to the challenge against Right of First Refusal), and were successful. Following *McNeil* another lawsuit was filed, *White v. NFL*, 41 F.3d 402 (8th Cir. 1994), which culminated in the "White settlement," the basis for a new Collective Bargaining Agreement between the players and the league.

3. In June 2001, the NFL and NFLPA extended their 1993 collective bargaining agreement through the 2007 season. The deal extends the salary cap through the 2006 season with an uncapped year in 2007 as an incentive for the sides to extend the agreement again. It also provides a new set of minimum salaries, based on experience in the league, with a ten-year veteran earning at least $750,000. In addition, a cash pool was established so that a ten-year player earning $750,000 will count only $450,000 against the salary cap that year. Prior to this extension, NFL teams were cutting long-time veteran players to save room under the cap. The players' association also negotiated a graduated increase in its percentage of designated gross revenues (this does not include *all* revenues—see section 11.3.10., "Salary Cap"), from 63 percent in 2002 to a high of 65.5 percent in 2005, then back to 64.5 percent in 2006.

4. For a description of how the business of professional football has changed, see Jon Morgan, *Glory For Sale: Fans, Dollars and the New NFL* (Baltimore, MD: Bancroft Press, 1997); David Harris, *The Rise and Decline of the NFL* (New York: Bantam Books, 1986); Gene Klein and David Fisher, *First Down and a Billion* (New York: William Morrow, 1987).

5. The NFL Collective Bargaining Agreement can be viewed at www.nflpa.org

11.3.4. National Basketball Players Association

The National Basketball Players Association came into existence in 1954, with Boston Celtics' superstar Bob Cousy as its first president, at a time when player unrest in professional basketball was reaching a very high level due to owner ambivalence toward player demands. However, it was not until 1964, after NBA players threatened to boycott the All-Star Game, that the NBA formally recognized the NBPA and agreed to a pension plan. The league then entered into the first Collective Bargaining Agreement in professional sports in 1967. The first executive director of the NBPA was Larry Fleischer, who maintained a low profile and allowed NBA players like Oscar Robertson, Paul Silas, and John Havlicek to help keep the players' union in operation during its formative years. In the early 1980s, the NBA and team owners asked the players to accept a hard salary cap due to the precarious financial position of the NBA and its teams. The NBPA accepted, but only after reviewing the financial records of the teams. With the sport achieving great levels of financial success and popular acceptance by the 1990s, the players, under the leadership of Executive Director Billy Hunter, demanded that the salary cap be dismantled. In 1998 the NBA encountered its first significant work stoppage when the owners locked out their players prior to the beginning of the 1998 season. In January 1999 the NBA season was salvaged when the players agreed to further limits on the salary cap and new minimums for rookies, in exchange for minor concessions. This Collective Bargaining Agreement expires in June 2004, with an NBA option to extend the contract through June 2005.

NOTE

1. The NBA Collective Bargaining Agreement can be viewed and downloaded on the NBPA Web site www.nbpa.com

11.3.5. MLB Players Association

The first players' association was the Brotherhood of Professional Baseball Players, formed in 1887, in response to the National League's initiation of the reserve clause in the player contract. The Brotherhood, led by its first president (and also a player), John Montgomery Ward, battled the reserve clause and other contractual issues through the court system. In 1891, the Brotherhood was dissolved due to financial reasons, then reemerged in 1900 for 2 years. The next attempt at organizing a players' union came in 1946, when members of the Pittsburgh Pirates formed the American Baseball Guild, and attempted to bargain with Pirates management (see note 1). This effort failed, but it motivated the players to stand up for their rights and benefits. In 1953, the Major League Baseball Players Association was formed after player representatives were barred from meetings with the owners. The MLBPA, under the leadership of Marvin Miller (1967–1993), enjoyed considerable success at the bargaining table and became the model for all other players' associations. However, this success came at a price: Major League Baseball experienced seven major work stoppages between 1972 and 1994, including the cancellation of the 1994 World Series. Under the leadership of Donald Fehr (1994–present), the MLBPA is one of the strongest unions in the United States.

NOTES

1. While there were no prominent efforts to form a players' union between 1900 and 1946, the Federal League of 1914–1915 was very much an outgrowth of player discontent

with the National and American Leagues. Some major stars jumped to the Federal League, including Joe Tinker, Three Finger Brown, and Hal Chase. This league had the impact of a players' association, because player salaries increased in the National and American Leagues due to the rival league's presence. The three leagues negotiated a settlement prior to the 1916 season, and the Federal League agreed to disband. The Baltimore franchise was unhappy with this settlement, and brought the *Federal Baseball* case, discussed at length in Chapter 10, particularly in section 10.3.1.2., "Creation of the Baseball Exemption: *Federal Baseball*." For a comprehensive online history of the Federal League, see www.toyou.com/fl/

2. For a more detailed introduction to unionization in professional baseball, see John Helyar, *Lords of the Realm* (New York: Ballantine Books, 1994); Marvin Miller, *A Whole Different Ballgame: The Sport and Business of Baseball* (New York: Birch Lane Press, 1991); and Roger Abrams, *Legal Bases: Baseball and the Law* (Philadelphia: Temple University Press, 1998).

11.3.6. Other Players Associations in North America

Following are discussions of three other players' associations: the WNBA, the Arena Football League, and the Canadian Football League. In addition, there is a brief discussion on potential player associations.

11.3.6.1. WNBA Unionization

In early November 1998, WNBA players chose the NBPA, which represents NBA players, as their representative in collective bargaining with the NBA owners of the women's professional league. The NBPA quickly made an immediate impact; the draft for the 1999 season was delayed in the wake of protracted negotiations with the owners. A final settlement was reached in time to start the season on schedule. In addition to the players' gaining a 401K plan, dental benefits, a restriction on ABL players (see note 1), and increased salaries, the deal also includes the following:

1. The union is allowed to use its logo, which the WNBA owns, for marketing and licensing, for two non-profit events.
2. ABL players are not required to sign contracts with an automatic league option for a second year, and therefore will be under the rookie pay scale for only one season. (This provision became moot after the ABL's bankruptcy in 1999.)
3. Players are required to make up to twenty-two promotional appearances: eight paid for commercial sponsors, four unpaid for their team, and up to ten unpaid promotional.
4. The group licensing agreement was extended to a fifth year, or a fourth if either side exercises its option to reopen negotiations after three years. In Year 5, as in Years 3 and 4, players will receive 50 percent of royalties from the sale of player-identified licensed products.

NOTE _____

1. The ABL was a women's professional basketball league that competed with the WNBA from 1996 to 1999. The 1998 WNBA collective bargaining agreement stipulated that during the 1999 season, WNBA teams could include on their rosters up to three players who last played in the American Basketball League (ABL)—except for the league's two new teams, the Orlando Miracle and the Minnesota Lynx, which could include up to five former ABL players. After the 1999 season, there were restrictions on the number of

former ABL players on WNBA rosters. The issue became moot in 1999, when the ABL folded.

11.3.6.2. Arena Football League Unionization

The circumstances surrounding the unionization of Arena Football League players illustrate the difference between labor relations in the sports industry and in other industries. They also illustrate the confluence of labor and antitrust law in professional sports.

At the end of 1999, AFL players began to re-evaluate their relationship with AFL owners. The players believed that AFL owners had joined together to eliminate competition for their services, prohibited injury and other contractual guarantees, and fixed the terms of employment for each player at uncompetitive levels. Then came a rather unique sequence of events:

1. The players voted to be represented by the Arena Football League Players' Organizing Committee (AFLPOC) in 2000.

2. Players then filed a complaint with the NLRB in February 2000, alleging the league's owners forced them to become part of the union.

3. The AFLPOC and Arena Football League negotiated a six-year collective bargaining agreement.

4. In August 2000, the Collective Bargaining Agreement was thrown out and the NLRB moved to have the AFLPOC decertified. This occurred after NLRB officials claimed that owners coerced players into joining the union through offers of financial assistance and threats of job loss—violations of Sections 8(a)(2) and 8(a)(3) of the National Labor Relations Act.

5. The players filed a Sherman Act Section 1 antitrust lawsuit in Federal District Court in New Jersey.

6. In May 2001, owners and players reached a tentative settlement. Players agreed to drop all of their pending NLRB and antitrust claims in exchange for a minimum salary increase from $900 per game to $1,400 per game, and salary guarantees for injured players. The deal also guarantees that the players receive a salary cap share of 63 percent of the designated gross revenue, which includes money from TV and radio contracts, as well as ticket sales, but not parking and concessions. *Important*: Under the settlement, if players don't form a union by the end of the 2001 season, owners can break the agreement.

7. In June 2001, players began new certification elections, deciding whether they would be represented by the AFLPOC or the Arena Football League Players' Association (AFLPA). The AFLPA received 77% of the votes and was later certified by the NLRB as the collective bargaining representative for AFL players. The AFLPA is supported by the United Food and Commercial Workers International Union.

In most industries, management would strongly prefer that their employees not unionize. Not so, in many professional team sports. Regardless of whether the AFL players' "company union" accusations are accurate, it is clear that AFL owners want the players to join some type of union. This is because of the antitrust immunity granted to sports leagues by the nonstatutory labor exemption (see Chapter 10, section 10.3.2., "The Non-statutory Labor Exemption").

11.3.6.3. Canadian Football League Players Association

The Canadian Football League Players Association (CFLPA), formed in 1965, initially requested a pension plan, revision of the Standard Player Contract, and increased salaries for Grey Cup (Canadian Super Bowl) participants. While the league did address all of these matters in the next few years, and even granted restricted free agency in 1971, relations became more contentious by early 1974. First of all, the CFLPA believed that the league had retaliated against prominent union members. Gary Schreider, the first president of the CFLPA, was traded to three different teams and then released (see note 1). Second, the CFLPA resented that players were not compensated for ten weeks of training camp and pre-season games. In June 1974, the players engaged in a "voluntary retirement" strike during training camp. CFL owners flew replacement players into training camp. The strike ended three weeks later, with the players receiving their requested pre-season pay.

Since the mid-1970s, the CFL and CFLPA have maintained relatively amicable relations. This is largely due to the league's precarious financial situation. The CFL nearly folded in the late 1990s, and the CFLPA has recognized all along that it cannot make the demands that are made by some of the other players' unions. Nevertheless, the current collective bargaining agreement expired after the 2001 season. While the old agreement guaranteed players at least 50% of gross revenue, the league's success will determine whether the CFLPA will ask for a larger share in the upcoming negotiations.

NOTE

1. CFLPA history is available on its Web site, www.cflpa.com

11.3.6.4. Potential Unionization of Minor League Baseball and College Athletics

Minor league baseball players and intercollegiate athletes have not formed players associations. Some of the reasons for this are logistical, but other reasons have a legal basis. In a logistical sense, most minor league and collegiate players are unwilling to make the sacrifices and take the risks necessary for unionization due to their short careers at such levels. In other words, assuming unionization attempts could be successful, the fruits of unionization would probably arrive after the initiators had graduated or moved on to other leagues. Thus, any effort to unionize would be purely altruistic.

In a legal sense, minor league baseball players would be inhibited from unionizing due to the Curt Flood Act of 1998 (see Chapter 10, section 10.3.1.5., "The Curt Flood Act"). While the act ended MLB's immunity against antitrust suits from *major* league players, it reaffirmed MLB's antitrust protection from minor league players, umpires, owners, and other groups. Other minor league players who have unionized, such as minor league hockey players, have used the per se Sherman Act violation inherent in their league's reserve clause in order to gain negotiating leverage (see note 1). Because MLB is exempt from Sherman Act scrutiny, minor league baseball players would not have that type of leverage if they unionized.

In revenue-producing intercollegiate sports such as men's Division IA football and Division I basketball, the athlete's market value often exceeds the economic value of his scholarship. Furthermore, men's basketball coaches can receive millions of dollars for having their players wear certain brands of shoes, while the players are compensated only with an athletic scholarship (see note 2). Periodically over the years, there have been attempts to unionize college athletes. However, the *Rensing* decision (see note 3) held that intercollegiate athletics are inherent to a student-athlete's educational experience, and therefore, the athletic scholarship does not establish an employment relationship (see Chapter 6, section 6.2.2., "Participation Rules"). Because the NLRA's jurisdiction is restricted to employer-employee relationships, unionization would be difficult unless this decision is overturned.

NOTES

1. Prior to the passage of the Curt Flood Act, David M. Szuchman argued for the unionization of minor league baseball players in "Step Up to the Bargaining Table: A Call for the Unionization of Minor League Baseball," 14 *Hofstra Labor Law Journal* 265 (Fall 1996).

2. For more information about the hurdles that college athletes would face prior to unionization, see Steven L. Ukeiley, "No Salary, No Union, No Collective Bargaining: Scholarship Athletes are an Employer's Dream Come True," 6 *Seton Hall Journal of Sports Law* 167 (1996).

3. In *Rensing v. Indiana State University Board of Trustees*, 444 N.E. 2d 1170 (Ind. 1983) the Indiana Supreme Court ruled that a college scholarship is not a contract of employment, and therefore an athlete who is injured during intercollegiate competition or practice, is not eligible for workers compensation benefits. The court held that there must be a mutual belief that an employer-employee relationship exists, and that it is clear in the NCAA constitution that intercollegiate sports are viewed as part of the educational system, and are therefore distinguishable from the professional sports business.

11.3.7. Collective Bargaining Agreements in Professional Sports

Notwithstanding unique provisos such as salary caps and salary arbitration, Collective Bargaining Agreements (CBAs) between professional leagues and their players' associations contain many of the same elements found in the CBAs of other industries. It is important to remember that unionized athletes are actually covered under two contracts: their own Standard Player Contract and the Collective Bargaining Agreement negotiated between the league and the players' association. Therefore, when a players' association negotiates with a league, they do not bargain over individual player's salaries, but over the "terms and conditions" of employment. For example, rather than negotiate over a player's salary, the NFLPA and the NFL will negotiate over a salary cap that may limit the amount a rookie may make in his first year. However, it will be up to that rookie and his agent to negotiate with the individual club over his contract, within the limits set by the Collective Bargaining Agreement. It is important to remember that an athlete may negotiate anything into the Standard Player Contract as long as it does not violate the Collective Bargaining Agreement in the league, or any other relevant labor laws.

11.3.8. Outline of a Professional Sports Collective Bargaining Agreement

The text below offers a brief introduction to some of the relevant issues that are addressed in Collective Bargaining Agreements in sports. It is important to remember that Collective Bargaining Agreements can be extremely long and complicated. The 1993–2007 agreement between the NFL and NFLPA is 210 pages in length, contains sixty articles, ten Appendixes, and six letters of agreement. The following is designed to give the reader an idea of some of the issues that are covered in a professional sports Collective Bargaining Agreement:

1. Union/Management Rights: This section includes a management rights article, which outlines what rights the league may retain in order to run its business. Also in this section is an article detailing union security rights, which includes dues deductions, licensing programs, and meetings.

2. Commissioner Discipline: The commissioner may have rights reserved under the Collective Bargaining Agreements, such as levying fines, being the final signatory on player contracts and trades, imposing disciplinary measures, and acting in the best interests of the game.

3. Standard Player Contract: A Standard or Uniform Player Contract is incorporated into the Collective Bargaining Agreement, so that the players association can negotiate any changes to the contract with the league.

4. Grievance Procedure: This gives players the right to challenge decisions that are made by the league or by the owners that may violate the Collective Bargaining Agreement. In addition, the procedure can be used to clarify language in the agreement or in individual contracts that may be vague or ambiguous. An impartial arbitrator is selected to issue decisions on disputes that arise.

5. College Draft: Most aspects of the college draft (also known as the "first year player" draft) are included in this section, including length of draft, number of rounds, assignment of draft rights, and undrafted rookie rights.

6. Salary Cap: This section deals with the implementation of a device to put a ceiling on what total player salaries may be for a club. This section outlines what type of salary cap is being used: a hard cap, which sets a tight limit on what a team may spend on player salaries, or a soft cap, which sets limits but allows for certain exceptions, like the Larry Bird Exception in the NBA (see section 11.3.12., "Hard Cap v. Soft Cap").

7. Free Agency: This article deals with player mobility, and the restrictions on that mobility. It outlines when players are eligible for free agency, whether it is restricted or unrestricted, and what type of compensation may be paid (usually for restricted players).

8. Related Player/Club Issues: This section of a Collective Bargaining Agreement deals with articles relating to squad size, off-season workouts, off-season training camps, pre-season training camps, and practice squads. Normally, time limits and roster limits are established for these areas, in addition to compensation to the players and fines clubs may impose.

9. Salaries/Economics: This section outlines the salaries, and limits thereon, for all players in the league. Formulas may be established to determine what percentage of league club revenue player salaries will comprise, if a salary cap is in place. In addition, this section details what maximum and minimum salaries exist for different player groups (such as rookie minimums).

10. Benefits: Professional athletes have negotiated for many benefits, including pensions; medical, dental and optical care; insurance packages; disability; and workers' compensation. These sections outline the benefits available to the players, in addition to restrictions, time limits, and possibly limits on use or availability.

11. Incidentals: These include expenses, per diem allocations, meal allowance, moving expenses, and others. The related articles outline when such incidentals are available and what limits there are on their use.

12. There are many other topics and areas that may be part of a Collective Bargaining

Agreement, such as anti-collusion, agent certification, duration, definitions, league expansion and others.

NOTE _____

1. For an example of Collective Bargaining Agreements see the NBPA's Web site www.nbpa.com or the NFLPA's Web site at www.nflpa.org

11.3.9. Free Agency

One of the most contentious issues between players and owners over the years has been player freedom. Before union representation, players fought for increased mobility and pay (free agency) in the courts, using contract law and, later, antitrust theory. The initial attempts by player associations in the late 1960s and early 1970s to bargain for free agency proved fruitless. However, two major events in the mid-1970s altered player mobility in professional sports, and since that time, free agency has developed differently in all the professional sports leagues.

When baseball was first organized into a league structure in the 1880s, players signed one-year contracts and were deemed free agents after that contract. After each contract, players found themselves on the open market, signing contracts with the team that offered the highest salary. As a result, salaries grew at a rapid pace, which in turn caused owners to claim they were losing money at an astounding rate. In 1886 the league imposed the "reserve system," whereby each team would reserve five players whom other teams in the league could not sign. Within ten years, the number of reserved players went from five to ten per team, and then to the entire team. The reserve system tied a player to his original team in "perpetuity," or until he was traded or retired. This system relied on the Standard Player Contract, which had a clause that stated the team that the player was signing to play for had an option on that player's services the following year. Each year the player signed the same contract, thus giving the team an "option" year after year after year. When professional football, hockey, and basketball leagues formed, they modeled their "reserve systems" after baseball's.

Free agency was first established in baseball in 1976 after an arbitrator ruled in the *Messersmith/McNally* arbitration decision (see note 1) that the option year in the MLB Standard Players Contract could be applied for only one year, and was not to be "optioned" year after year. Therefore, the option clause had a one-year life expectancy if a player decided to "play out his option." Arbitrator Peter Sietz ruled that if a player chose not to re-sign with his original club after the option year, he was a free agent. The owners challenged the decision of the arbitrator in *Kansas City Royals Baseball Corp. v. Major League Baseball Players Association*, 532 F.2d 615 (8th Cir. 1976), but the court ruled against the owners, stating that the arbitrator had jurisdiction over the case, and had made an appropriate award. In the wake of this decision, the MLBPA and MLB began negotiating a settlement. The owners were fearful that free agency after two years of service would result in major salary increases and significant player movement. After a series of negotiations, an agreement was eventually reached that allowed unrestricted free agency for professional baseball players after six years of major league service.

The *Messersmith/McNally* decision and the resulting Collective Bargaining Agreement both had a significant impact on the game of baseball. Immediately following the decision, twenty-four players became free agents and were free to negotiate with any team in the league. The result was that the average player salary rose by 50% in the following year, and several clubs began the practice of offering multi-year deals. Owners, fearful that their star players might "test the market" when they became eligible for free agency, signed these players to rich long-term contracts.

Around the time of the *Messersmith/McNally* ruling, the other professional sports leagues began negotiations with their respective players' associations to come to an agreement on the issue of free agency. The NFL was using the "Rozelle Rule," a rule which forced a team signing a free agent to compensate the player's original team. For all intents and purposes, this rule restricted any player movement, because the high price of signing a free agent player (draft pick, active player, cash) was too costly. The 1976 *Mackey* decision held that the Rozelle Rule was too restrictive under antitrust laws, and the NFL was forced to negotiate with the NFLPA over a new player mobility policy. The NFLPA, with the support of its members, agreed to a Right of First Refusal (ROFR)/Compensation system in exchange for increased benefits, increased minimum salaries, and increased funding of the pension plan. The ROFR/Compensation System was almost as restrictive as the Rozelle Rule, and it was not until the early 1990s that the players' association, after the favorable decisions in the *McNeil* and *White* cases, was able to negotiate a less restrictive free-agency system into the Collective Bargaining Agreement.

At present, the NHL, NBA, NFL, and MLB all have some form of free agency. All leagues have some form of "unrestricted," or nearly unrestricted, free agency. It is unrestricted in that once a player has reached a negotiated time limit (six years of service in the MLB), he can sign with any team that makes an offer (see note 2). "Restricted" free agents are players who have reached a certain service level and may entertain offers from other clubs; however, if a club signs a restricted free agent, they must compensate the player's original team. The "restricted" free agent status is different in each league. Below is an example of the NFL's free agency system for veterans from the 1993–2007 agreement (see exhibit 11.2).

Exhibit 11.2
Article 19 Veteran Free Agency

Section 1. Unrestricted Free Agents:

a) Subject to the provisions of Article 20 (Franchise and Transition Players) any player with five or more Accrued Seasons, or with four or more Accrued Season in any Capped Year, shall at the expiration of his Player Contract, become an unrestricted Free Agent. Such player shall be completely free to negotiate and sign a Player Contract with any Club, and any Club shall be completely free to negotiate and sign a Player Contract with such player, without penalty or restriction, including but not limited to, Draft Choice Compensation between Clubs, or First Refusal Rights of any kind, subject to the signing period set forth below.

Section 2. Restricted Free Agents:

a) Any Veteran player with three or more Accrued Season, but less than five Accrued Season (or less than four Accrued Season in any Capped Year) shall, at the expiration of his last Player Contract during such period, become a Restricted Free Agent. Any such player shall be completely free to negotiate and sign a Player Contract with any such player, subject to the restrictions set forth in this article.

b) In order to receive the following specified Rights of First Refusal and/or Draft Choice Compensation with respect to a Restricted Free Agent, the prior Club of a Restricted Free Agent must tender the player a Qualifying Offer on or before the date of the Restricted Free Agent Signing Period, as follows:

For Restricted Free Agents with three Accrued Seasons:

1. Right of First Refusal: one year Player Contract with Paragraph 5 salary of at least $275.000.
2. Right of First Refusal and Draft Selection at Players Original Draft round: one year Player Contract with a Paragraph 5 salary of at least a) $275,000, or b) 110% of the player's prior years Paragraph 5 salary, whichever is greater.
3. Right of First Refusal and One First Round Draft Selection: one year Player Contract with a Paragraph 5 salary of at least a) $600,000, or b) 110% of the player's prior year's Paragraph 5 salary, whichever is greater.
4. Right of First Refusal, One First Round Draft Selection and One Third Round Draft Selection: one year Player Contract with a Paragraph 5 salary of at least a) $800,000, or b) 110% of the player's prior year's Paragraph 5 salary, whichever is greater.

In the event a Prior Club withdraws its Qualifying Offer, the Restricted Free Agent shall immediately become an Unrestricted Free Agent and shall be completely free to negotiate and sign a Player Contract with any Club, and any Club shall be completely free to negotiate and sign a Player Contract with any such player, without being subject to First Refusal, Draft Choice Compensation, Signing Period, or any other limitation of any kind.

NOTES ───

1. In 1975, Andy Messersmith (Los Angeles Dodgers) and Dave McNally (Montreal Expos) challenged baseball's reserve clause by playing out the season without signing new contracts. Both contended that the reserve clause only allowed a team to renew a player's contract for one year, while the team owners contended that the clause could be invoked year after year. Messersmith and McNally did not sign their contracts in 1975 because

they wanted higher salaries than their owners were willing to give. After the season, they argued that they had played out their option year and were free agents capable of selling their services to the highest bidder. The dispute went to arbitration. In what was considered the biggest victory for the players in baseball history, arbitrator Peter Seitz found that the reserve clause merely gave the owners an additional option year, thus leaving Messersmith and McNally, free agents, free to sign with another team. After an unsuccessful appeal of Seitz's decision, Major League Baseball negotiated a Collective Bargaining Agreement with the players, giving them many new rights and freedoms. This decision began the modern era of free agency, which was reflected in the rapid increase in player salaries.

2. Under the agreement set to expire in 2002, MLB's free agency is not truly "unrestricted." Teams signing free agents are required to provide a draft pick to the team that loses the free agent. However, in contrast to the NFL, NBA, and NHL high draft picks are not likely to succeed in baseball. More than 35% of the players drafted in the *first* round between 1987 and 1996 failed to reach the major leagues (www.espn.go.com/gammons/s/2001/0602/1208718.html). Consequently, few see this compensation in baseball as a deterrent to free agent signings.

11.3.10. Salary Caps

The salary cap—a restriction or limit on the amount of money that may be made available by the league to pay player salaries—has been the center of considerable labor unrest since the 1980s. The first salary cap in professional sports was initiated by the NBA in 1982, and was included in that year's Collective Bargaining Agreement. The only other Big Four league to currently have a salary cap is the National Football League, which accepted one as part of the *White* settlement, in 1993, while exchanging increased free agency rights and increased salary minimums. Neither the National Hockey League nor Major League Baseball has a salary cap, although owners in both leagues claim one is necessary to stop the upward spiral of player salaries and the disparity between small and large market teams.

The salary cap does have a noticeable impact on player salaries. As part of the 1993–2001 NFL collective bargaining agreement, the salary cap was not to be initiated until the second year of the agreement (1994–1995). Therefore, the 1993–1994 season would be the first season in which players enjoyed free agency rights and were not restrained by a salary cap. During the 1993–1994 season, the average team salary was $42.9 million, an increase of 51% over 1992–1993, as players tested the free agency market and signed large contracts. For the 1994–1995 season, the salary cap was initiated, and according to the "defined gross revenue" formula (DGR is explained in section 11.3.11., "Calculation of Salary Cap"), the cap was set at $34.6 million, almost $9 million less than the average a year before. Thus teams were faced with having to drop almost $9 million from their payrolls. They accomplished this by waiving more expensive veteran players and signing rookies to less expensive contracts. Star players and first round draft picks continue to sign lucrative deals, but the salary cap has hurt the salaries of veteran players who are past their prime.

NOTES ───

1. Owners cite the rise in player salaries as the reason for salary cap restrictions. The average salary in the NFL rose from $198,000 in 1986 to $1.17 million in 2000; NBA average salaries rose from $390,000 in 1986 to nearly $4 million in 2001. The NBPA

boasts that its members now have "the highest salaries of any labor organization in the world."

2. Team attempts to circumvent the cap has led to various litigation: (a) In 2000, an independent arbitrator found that the Minnesota Timberwolves had signed a secret contract with Joe Smith in an effort to circumvent the cap. The arbitrator upheld Commissioner David Stern's penalty of a $3.5 million fine, a loss of five first round draft picks (one pick was later reinstated) and a denial of the Larry Bird exception for Smith. (b) Also in 2000, the San Francisco 49ers organization was cited for several cap violations by NFL Commissioner Paul Tagliabue. Former 49ers executive Carmen Policy and General Manager Dwight Clark were fined a total of $500,000. The 49ers did not lose any draft picks or have any contracts voided. c) In *Matter of NBA*, 630 F.Supp. 136 (S.D.N.Y. 1986), the New York Knicks attempted to circumvent the cap by paying Albert King a large signing bonus, which, according to the NBA salary cap provisions, was spread evenly over the contract. The NBA argued that the Knicks were attempting to circumvent the cap by offering the large bonus, in place of regular salary that would go against the cap. The district court found in favor of the league. See also *Bridgeman v. NBA In re: Chris Dudley*, 838 F.Supp. 172 (D.N.J. 1993) which focused on the "one year opt out" provision, which allowed players to terminate their deals after one year. The NBA accused Chris Dudley of signing a contract with the Portland Trail Blazers, which included the opt out provision, with the intention of opting out after one year, and then re-signing with them using the Larry Bird exemption (meaning his salary would not count against the team's salary cap). The special master and the district court found in favor of Dudley and the Blazers.

3. The NBA attempted to unilaterally implement a salary cap in 1982, which was successfully challenged in *Lanier v. NBA*, 82 Civ. 4935 (S.D.N.Y. 1982). A special master (the "judge" who oversees all litigation surrounding a particular dispute; in this case the *Robertson* settlement) ruled in favor of the players, on the grounds that the salary cap violated the provisions of the *Robertson* settlement. The players association and the league agreed to include a salary cap in the 1983 Collective Bargaining Agreement. The salary cap was later revised, after the *Bridgeman* settlement, in 1988.

11.3.11. Calculation of Salary Cap

Salary caps in professional sports have been designed as a percentage of certain league revenues. Therefore there must be agreement between the league and the player association as to what will constitute "defined gross revenue" (DGR). DGR usually consists of gate receipts, local and national television and radio broadcast revenue, and a percentage of income from luxury suites, licensing income, concessions, and merchandising. The 1993–2007 NFL-NFLPA agreement defines DGR as:

(1) regular season, pre-season and post-season gate receipts (net of admission taxes, and surcharges paid to stadium or municipal authorities which are deducted for purposes of calculating gate receipts subject to revenue sharing) including ticket revenue from luxury boxes, suites and premium seating subject to gate receipt sharing among NFL teams; and

(2) proceeds include Copyright Royalty Tribunal and extended market payments from the sale, license or other conveyance of the right to broadcast or exhibit NFL pre-season, regular season and play-off games on radio and television, including, without limitation, network, local, cable, pay television, satellite encryption, international broadcasts, delayed broadcasts (which shall not include any broadcast of an NFL pre-season, regular season, or play-off game occurring more than 72 hours after the live exhibition of the game, unless the broadcast is the first broadcast in the market), and all other means of

distribution, net of any reasonable and customary NFL expenses related to the project; and

(3) proceeds from the sale or conveyance of any right to receive any of the revenues described above. (Article 24)

The NBA definition is similar, although it is referred to as "basketball related income," and encompasses many of the same details.

NOTE ——————————

1. The NFL-NFLPA agreement also outlines what is not to be included in the calculation of DGR: proceeds from the assignment, sale, or trade of a player's contract, proceeds from the sale of an existing franchise, or the grant of an NFL expansion franchise, dues or capital contributions received by the NFL, fines, "revenue sharing" among NFL teams, interest income, insurance recoveries, sales of interests in real estate and other property. The following list refers to "excluded DGR": revenues derived from concessions, parking, local advertising and promotion, magazine advertising, sales of programs and novelties, stadium clubs, and signage (Article 24).

11.3.12. Hard Cap v. Soft Cap

The NFL salary cap is often referred to as a hard salary cap—a cap that cannot be exceeded. On the other hand, the NBA salary cap is often referred to as a soft cap, one that has exceptions and which may allow teams to sign players to contracts that put them over the cap limit. For example, if the salary cap in the NFL is $67 million (2001), then no team is able to spend more than $67 million on player salaries. In the NBA, by contrast, several exemptions allow teams to go over the cap. One of these is called the "Larry Bird" exemption, which was created so that teams would not lose established hometown players due to salary cap limits. In other words, a team can exceed its salary cap in order to sign one of its own free agent players, as long as he has played for the team for three years. The 1999–2004 Collective Bargaining Agreement between the National Basketball Association and the National Basketball Players Association produced several changes to the salary cap. Notable features of the new salary cap include the following:

1. There is no cap on the percentage of revenues to be used toward player salaries during the first three seasons. During years 4–6, there will be a cap of 55%. If the owners exercise their option for a seventh season, there is a cap of 57%.

2. Maximum salary for players with less than six years' experience is $9 million (or 25% of salary cap); for players with seven to nine years' experience, the maximum is $11 million (or 30% of the cap); and for players with over ten years' experience, there is a maximum of $14 million (or 35% of the cap).

3. Rookies will be subject to a three-year wage scale with the team holding an option for the fourth year and right of first refusal for the fifth year.

4. "Larry Bird" players cannot receive more than a 12% raise, and all other players cannot receive more than a 10% raise per year.

5. Certain exceptions to the salary cap: there is a "middle-class" exception that allows teams over the cap to sign a "middle-class" player to a $1.75 million contract during the first year of the deal ($2 million in year 2; $2.25 million in year 3; and the average salary in the NBA for years 4–6).

The NBA salary cap is considered a "soft cap" because it is clearly flexible. Although the salaries at the high end of the salary bracket have been capped with little room for exception, the Larry Bird Exception and the "middle class" exception give teams flexibility in signing one franchise and/or role player above the cap.

11.3.13. Arbitration

In professional sports, conflicts regularly arise over the rights of players as outlined in the terms of the Collective Bargaining Agreement, Standard Player Contract, and league/governing body documents. Before unionization in professional sports, the commissioner of each sport had the final say in handling disputes, grievances, or other conflicts. While the commissioner still enjoys considerable power, such as the ability to veto a trade, approve or disapprove a contract, or implement a fine, the commissioner's power in the grievance procedure has been greatly diminished (see note 2).

When unionization occurred on a wide scale in professional sports, one of the first demands that the players' associations made was for the implementation of a grievance procedure that was not controlled by the league. The intent of the grievance procedure is twofold: first, to keep litigation outside of the formal court system (the arbitration process is quicker, cheaper, and private); and second, to give players *due process* rights. A grievance is an alleged wrong that is contrary to the written language or the intent of the written language in a Collective Bargaining Agreement or, by implication, a league bylaw and/or Standard Player Contract. The NFL-NFLPA 1993–2007 agreement defines a grievance as:

> **Non-Injury Grievance. Section 1. Definition.** Any dispute (hereinafter referred to as a grievance) arising after the execution of this Agreement and involving the interpretation of, application of, or compliance with, any provision of this Agreement, the NFL Player Contract, or any other applicable provision of the NFL Constitution or Bylaws pertaining to terms and conditions of employment of NFL players, will be resolved exclusively in accordance with the procedure set forth in this Article, except wherever another method of dispute resolution is set forth elsewhere in this Agreement, and except wherever the Settlement Agreement provides that the Special Master, Impartial Arbitrator, the Federal District Court or the Accountants shall resolve a dispute.

Players associations argued for an independent arbitrator to preside over grievances because they identified a conflict of interest in the commissioner acting as arbitrator. First, players asserted the commissioner would not be able to remain impartial if the grievance was against a decision he himself had made. Second, the players claimed that the commissioner of a professional sports league is hired and fired by the owners of that league, and therefore is not an impartial entity but may have a bias for the owners. Players demanded a system whereby an independent party would act as final arbitrator. What eventually emerged was a grievance procedure for certain disputes that contained numerous steps, including a hearing with the commissioner, and ended with a final and binding decision made by an impartial arbitrator. As mentioned previously, the commissioner retained jurisdiction for some disputes.

It is important to note that the basic grievance procedure is used for violations of the Collective Bargaining Agreement, and also of any contracts and/or rules and regulations that are referred to in the contract. Therefore, a violation of the Standard Player Contract is handled through the grievance procedure. In addition to the basic grievance procedure, players have negotiated a salary arbitration process (NHL, MLB) and an injury grievance process (NFL). Below is a brief outline of the grievance procedures as found in the Collective Bargaining Agreements in the National Football League and Major League Baseball.

MLB Procedure (Article 10, Basic Agreement)

a) Grievant makes a verbal complaint to club or player representative, followed by discussion. If matter is not resolved, a written grievance is filed. A representative issues an opinion to player and MLBPA.

b) Grievant appeals decision to a representative of the Players Relations Committee, followed by discussion. Written opinion is issued.

c) Grievant appeals decision further to a tripartite arbitration panel, consisting of a representative of management, a representative of the MLBPA, and an impartial chairperson of the panel.

*Not included in this procedure; salary, benefits, commissioner matters (matters that deal with the integrity of baseball).

NFL Procedure (Article 7, Basic Agreement)

a) Non-Injury. This procedure pertains to the terms and conditions of employment and applies to all non-injury disputes that result from a violation of the Collective Bargaining Agreement, players' contract, and all other documents listed in the agreement. The grievance goes through a joint panel made up of NFLPA representatives and Management Council representatives. If appealed, the grievance goes to the Player Club Relations Committee, and if still not resolved, goes to a notice arbitrator who submits a list of arbitrators, one of which must be chosen. Decision by arbitrator is final and binding. It should be noted that if the grievance involves a suspension, the player or the NFLPA has the right to appeal directly to the notice arbitrator.

b) Injury. This type of grievance occurs when a player's contract is terminated due to an injury sustained while working for the team. The player must file a written grievance within twenty days, specifying injury, time of injury, and activity involved. The club may claim several defenses, including (a) player did not pass pre-season test, (b) player did not disclose injury, (c) injury occurred before pre-season and player signed a waiver, (d) injury was non-football-related. A neutral physician will examine the player and submit a report. If report is appealed, the procedure is the same as for a non-injury grievance.

NOTES

1. The courts will almost always respect the decision of binding arbitration unless they uncover an egregious procedural error or if the decision is inconsistent with the National Labor Relations Act. The sanctity of arbitration was affirmed by the U.S. Supreme Court in *Major League Baseball Players Ass'n v. Garvey*, 532 U.S. 504 (2001). When arbitrators penalized MLB teams $280 million for their collusion in the 1980s (see section 11.4.4., "Baseball Collusion Cases"), the arbitrators ruled that the MLBPA would have authority to divide the money. Former San Diego Padre Steve Garvey was unhappy with his share of the settlement, and sued the MLBPA. The district court awarded Garvey his requested $3 million. However, the Supreme Court overruled the lower court in an 8–1 decision, stating: "In discussing the courts' limited role in reviewing the merits of arbitration awards,

Exhibit 11.3
Player Grievance and Arbitration Rights in 2002

League	Grievance Procedure	Injury Grievance	Salary Arbitration
MLB	X		X
NHL	X		X
NBA	X		
WNBA			
NFL	X	X	

we have stated that 'courts . . . have no business weighing the merits of the grievance [or] considering whether there is equity in a particular claim.' When the judiciary does so, it usurps a function which . . . is entrusted to the arbitration tribunal."

2. The commissioner's power to veto a trade is seldom used. However, there are cases where the commissioner will veto a trade in the best interests of the game. After the 1998–1999 regular season, the New York Islanders attempted to trade star forward Ziggy Pallfy to the New York Rangers for players and cash. Commissioner Gary Bettman, afraid the small-market Islanders were "selling off" their high-priced talent, vetoed the deal and said that any trade the Islanders made could not involve cash. Pallfy was later traded to the Los Angeles Kings. In 1976, Oakland Athletics owner Charlie Finley sold players Rollie Fingers, Joe Rudi, and Vida Blue for a total of $3.5 million to the Boston Red Sox and New York Yankees. MLB Commissioner Bowie Kuhn voided the deals, citing his "best interests of baseball" powers.

11.3.14. Grievance Procedures in Professional Sports

Exhibit 11.3 outlines the types of grievance procedures that apply for each of the four major professional sports leagues.

Before grievance arbitration is initiated, a procedure exists to determine whether cases can be decided without going to arbitration. For example, if a provision in a Collective Bargaining Agreement has been accidentally violated, management will, in all likelihood, attempt to settle the dispute outside of the formal process. This could also be the case if a provision has been so obviously violated that going through the procedure would be sure to result in a loss. An impartial arbitrator is retained when both parties feel correct in their interpretation of the case and believe an impartial arbitrator would agree with their explanation.

Earlier, this chapter discussed the *Messersmith/McNally* arbitration decision that paved the way for free agency in professional baseball. This case is significant because it illustrates the importance that the grievance procedure can have. Baseball players had challenged the use of the reserve system, using antitrust theory in the court system, but had been unsuccessful in all those cases because of the antitrust immunity enjoyed by professional baseball. The players next turned to the grievance procedure as a mechanism to settle the dispute. The MLB Players Association believed that the option clause, which was part of the Standard Player

Contract was applicable for only one year after the initial contract expired. The league contended that the option clause gave it the right to renew a player's contract year after year, as had been done since the 1880s. The league attempted to argue that the arbitrator did not have jurisdiction over the case, but the arbitrator, Peter Seitz, dismissed this defense. Seitz found in favor of the players and granted them the right to unrestricted free agency. More important, the decision confirmed that the option on a contract was valid for one year only.

It is important to remember that the purpose of grievance arbitration is to limit the amount of litigation that enters the formal court system. The courts have increasingly yielded to the decisions made by arbitrators, and have also been reluctant to interpret grievance arbitration clauses. Only when there is a clear breach of the purpose of the procedure will the court system intervene.

A decision made by an arbitrator will usually serve as a precedent only *within* that particular sport. For example, an NBA arbitration hearing reduced the suspension of Latrell Sprewell for the 1997 assault on his coach P. J. Carlesimo (see Note 2b). However, if identical circumstances were to occur with an NHL player and his coach, the arbitrator would *not* be compelled to consider the facts of the Sprewell case. On the other hand, arbitrators must consider past decisions and practices of commissioners, clubs, and arbitrators *within* the same sport. For example, when an MLB arbitration panel reduced the suspension of John Rocker for his "sexist, racist, homophobic and xenophobic" remarks, it did so in part because of baseball's historical indifference and lack of clear policy regarding similar incidents (see note 2a).

NOTES

1. Three cases in 1960 illustrated that the Supreme Court was inclined to favor arbitration as a dispute mechanism: *Steelworkers v. American Mfg. Co.*, 363 U.S. 564 (1960); *Steelworkers v. Warrior & Gulf Navigation Co.* 363 U.S. 574 (1960); and *Steelworkers v. Enterprise Wheel and Car Corp.*, 363 U.S. 593 (1960). In these cases, the Supreme Court upheld the decisions of arbitrators, sending a clear message that if an arbitration procedure exists in a Collective Bargaining Agreement, and the arbitrator rules in a professional manner, then the arbitrator's decision will be upheld. These cases are often referred to as the Steelworker Trilogy.

2. According to Article 12, Section A, of the 1997–2001 MLB-MLBPA Collective Bargaining Agreement, an independent arbitrator has the ability to overturn discipline imposed on players by the commissioner if the arbitrator finds no "just cause" for the discipline given. Article XXXI, Section 8, of the 1999–2004 NBA-NBPA Collective Bargaining Agreement gives an independent arbitrator the ability to overturn discipline imposed on a player if the financial impact on that player exceeds $25,000.

(a) In *In the Matter of the Arbitration Between Major League Baseball Players Association and the Commissioner of Major League Baseball*, Grievance No. 00–3; John Rocker; Das, Chairman of Arbitration Panel, March 1, 2000, Atlanta Braves pitcher John Rocker saw his disciplinary sentence reduced by the arbitration panel. Commissioner Bud Selig had suspended Rocker with pay for all of spring training and nearly a month of the regular season, and also fined Rocker $20,000, after Rocker made disparaging remarks in a *Sports Illustrated* interview. In those remarks, Rocker denigrated "Japanese woman" drivers; referred to an African-American teammate as a "fat monkey"; bemoaned the presence of "queer[s] with AIDS" on New York City subways; and admitted that he was "not a very big fan of foreigners." The commissioner urged the panel to uphold the sentence, arguing that Rocker's comments insulted numerous members of MLB's fan base, damaged the business of the Braves and Major League Baseball, endangered the safety of those on the field, and increased security costs during Braves games. The MLBPA argued that Rocker should receive no punishment because (1) Rocker was not "under contract" at the time of his remarks (claiming the Uniform Contract runs only from spring training until the World Series); (2) the Collective Bargaining Agreement does not allow discipline for speech; (3) MLB and the Braves encouraged Rocker to cooperate with the media, and he was merely complying; and (4) previous incidents of "politically incorrect" speech had gone unpunished. Arbitrator Shyam Das rescinded Rocker's spring training suspension, reduced his regular season suspension by thirteen days, and reduced his fine to $500. Das cited an absence of specific rules about speech by players, noting that pitcher Bob Knepper had not been disciplined after he made sexist comments in the 1980s. Das also noted that Rocker's punishment for speech was more severe than that imposed on baseball's drug offenders. Das justified the reduction in Rocker's fine due to the limit specified by Article 1, Section 3 (a), of the Major League Agreement for fines imposed by the commissioner on a player for conduct not in the best interest of baseball. For more information on this case, see Roger Abrams, "Off His Rocker: Sports Discipline and Labor Arbitration," 11 *Marquette Sports Law Review* 167 (Spring 2001).

(b) In *Arbitrator's Decision and Award Involving Latrell Sprewell, the National Basketball Players Association, the Golden State Warriors, and the National Basketball Association,* John D. Feerick, Grievance Arbitrator, March 4, 1998, NBA player Latrell Sprewell saw his punishment reduced by the arbitrator. Sprewell had attacked his coach, P. J. Carlesimo, during practice on December 1, 1997. In that attack, "between seven and ten seconds elapsed during which the Grievant had his hands around the Coach's neck." Carlesimo was not injured. Sprewell then left the court for "between ten and 20 minutes," before returning for an apparent second attempted attack of Carlesimo. However, he was restrained before reaching the coach. The Warriors terminated Sprewell's contract and the nearly $25 million remaining on it, claiming they had "cause" to do so because of the assault. Commissioner David Stern suspended Sprewell from the NBA for one year, emphasizing the "premeditated nature" of the second incident. The NBPA appealed, calling the sanctions against Sprewell "arbitrary and capricious" and lacking "just cause." Arbitrator Feerick overruled the Warriors and the NBA, holding that the Warriors must honor the final two years of Sprewell's contract or trade him. Feerick did, however, uphold the suspension for the remainder of the season (not the full calendar year Stern had imposed) and the player's resulting loss of $6.5 million in salary. He reasoned that the team's and league's dual penalties violated the principle of double jeopardy, and that league sanctions against more harmful player violence had been less severe in the past. Specifically, assaults resulting in serious injuries had produced suspensions no longer than twenty-six games. Sprewell subsequently filed suit against the NBA and the Warriors in federal district court, seeking the $6.4 million in salary that he lost during his suspension. Sprewell was denied relief in *Sprewell v. Golden State Warriors,* 231 F.3d 520 (U.S. App. 2000). For more information, see Roger A. Javier, "You Cannot Choke Your Boss & Hold Your Job Unless You Play in the NBA: The Latrell Sprewell Incident Undermines Disciplinary Authority in the NBA," 7 *Villanova Sports and Entertainment Law Journal* 2 (2000).

(c) In *In the Matter of the Arbitration Between Major League Baseball Players Association and the Commissioner of Major League Baseball,* Grievance No. 92–7, Suspension of Steven Howe; Nicolau, Chairman of Arbitration Panel, November 12, 1992, Commissioner Fay Vincent banned New York Yankee pitcher Steve Howe from baseball for life, for violating the terms of his reinstatement in 1990 after being suspended during the 1988 and 1989 seasons. Between 1982 and 1988 Howe was hospitalized for drug-related treatment six times, and was reinstated in 1990 on the condition that he refrain from using or selling drugs. However, the arbitrator found that there was no "just cause" for the lifetime ban because Vincent did not do all that was contractually required for Howe (periodic drug tests) prior to the total ban. For more information, see Chapter 7, section 7.2.4.3., "Major League Baseball."

3. In *Kansas City Royals Baseball Corp. v. Major League Baseball Players Ass'n,* 532 F.2d 615 (8th Cir. 1976), Judge Heaney upheld the arbitration decision in the *Messersmith/ McNally* arbitration case (see Section 11.3.9., "Free Agency") and noted that "the arbitration panel did nothing more than to interpret certain provisions of the Uniform Player's Contract and the Major League Rules. Accordingly, the award must be sustained."

4. Fred Dryer, of the Los Angeles Rams of the NFL, attempted to bypass the usual

contract dispute resolution plan as outlined in the Collective Bargaining Agreement between the NFL and NFLPA, and have his matter decided by a California state court in *Dryer v. Los Angeles Rams*, 709 P.2d 826 (Cal. 1985). The Rams petitioned to have the court compel arbitration as outlined in the Collective Bargaining Agreement. The court denied the petition by the Rams because it felt that since all contract disputes could go before the commissioner, it failed to meet the "minimum levels of integrity" required. The California Supreme Court reversed the decision, and found that since an arbitration system that covered the dispute was in place, the court would not interfere.

11.3.14.1 Unlawful Discharge

One area in which grievances are commonly filed pertains to unlawful discharge or termination. While this issue is not as pervasive in professional sports as it is in other industries (due in part to the high number of guaranteed professional sports contracts), there have been several cases where players feel they have been unjustly terminated or discharged. The Collective Bargaining Agreements in the NBA, NFL, and MLB all have language that allows a team to lawfully discharge a player when he fails to exhibit sufficient skill.

NFL: Player understands that he is competing with other players for a position on Club's roster within the applicable player limits. If at any time, in the judgement of the Club, Player's skill or performance has been unsatisfactory as compared with that of other players competing for positions on Club, or if Player has engaged in personal conduct reasonably judged by Club to adversely affect or reflect on Club, then Club may terminate his contract (Article 2 of the NFL's Uniform Player Contract).

MLB: The Club may terminate this contract upon written notice to the Player (but only after requesting and obtaining waivers of this contract from all other Major League Clubs). If the Player at any time . . . fails, in the opinion of the Club's management, to exhibit sufficient skill or competitive ability to qualify or continue as a member of the Club's team . . . (MLB's Uniform Player Contract, Article 7(b)).

NBA: The Club may terminate this contract upon written notice to the Player (but only after complying with the waiver procedure) if the Player shall at any time: Fail in the sole opinion of management to exhibit sufficient skill or competitive ability to qualify to continue as a member of the Club's team (NBA Uniform Player Contract, Article 20 (b)(2)).

When players file grievances over what they feel is an unfair discharge, arbitrators must determine whether that player lacks the necessary "skill" to compete at the professional level, or whether that player acted in a way that violated his contract. If neither is found, the player wins the grievance. Arbitrators have insisted that objective criteria be used by clubs to determine whether a player no longer has the proper "skill" to play. It is important to note that guaranteed player contracts (contracts that cannot be bought out, or terminated for any reason) protect those players whose skill has decreased. The player may be terminated but will be paid.

NOTES ———————————————————————————

1. Cincinnati Bengals punter Lee Johnson was cut on December 7, 1998, one day after criticizing the team's ownership. The following day, he was fined one game check of more than $20,000 for conduct detrimental to the team. Johnson appealed the decision, stating that timing proved he was cut for his comments and not for his performance. The NFLPA also argued that a player cannot be fined after he is released. The Bengals cited a loyalty clause in Johnson's contract, which they argued allowed them to cut Johnson. The case

was settled a year later for $12,000, while Johnson was a member of the New England Patriots.

2. *In the Matter of Arbitration Between NBA (Atlanta Hawks) and NBPA (Ken Charles)*, Seitz, Arbitrator, June 22, 1978. In this case, Charles was released from his three-year contract with the Hawks after only fifteen months, and challenged that decision based on the fact that the Hawks did not adequately follow the termination guidelines set forth in the collective bargaining agreement. The Hawks failed to give Charles a written notice of the termination, as was required, and also failed to offer a compelling reason for the termination. The Hawks argued that Charles did not fit into their new style of play, and was therefore expendable. The record shows that Charles started in twenty-one of the team's first twenty-two games before his termination. Seitz ruled that the Hawks failed to provide sufficient evidence for the termination, and the club was required to pay Charles his entire salary for the remaining period of his contract.

3. *In the Matter of Arbitration Between Detroit Lions and Mitchell Hoopes*, Searce, Arbitrator, September 2, 1978. In this case, punter Mitchell Hoopes was placed on waivers and released after he had missed an important field goal, and had subsequently been publicly chastised over the miss by the head coach. The coach claimed Hoopes was placed on waivers because too much pressure was placed on him after the public criticism. Hoopes filed the arbitration claiming that he was released for a reason that was not identified in the Collective Bargaining Agreement. The arbitrator, Searce, acknowledged that a player could be released from his contract based on skill and performance, but concluded that the release was not solely motivated by the skill and performance levels of Hoopes. Searce ordered the Lions to pay the remaining portion of Hoopes' 1977 salary.

11.3.15. Salary Arbitration

Salary arbitration is a process used only in Major League Baseball and the National Hockey League. The basic premise behind the procedure is to give players who have played a certain number of years an opportunity to have their salary set by a neutral third party based on "market conditions." In both the baseball and hockey procedures, players present their cases before arbitrators who make decisions based on evidence given by both the team and the player. Players file for arbitration for two reasons: (1) the player believes he can win his case; (2) the player is using the threat of arbitration as a bargaining tool in his negotiations with his team.

John Gaherin, who acted as a labor negotiator for Major League Baseball *owners*, had suggested the idea of salary arbitration for baseball in the 1960s. Gaherin and his successor, Ed Fitzgerald, encouraged the owners and the commissioner to adopt salary arbitration for two reasons: (1) to end player holdouts; and, more important (2) to dissuade the players in their efforts to end baseball's antitrust exemption and the reserve clause (see chapter 10, section 10.3.1., "The Baseball Exemption"). Fitzgerald convinced the owners to adopt salary arbitration in 1973, three years before free agency. The measure passed the owners by a 22–2 vote, and had the approval of Commissioner Bowie Kuhn.

Major League Baseball uses what is known as final-offer or last-best offer arbitration. The system is set up so that representatives of the player and the team each submit a figure they believe the player is worth for one season of play. The arbitrators, as per the Collective Bargaining Agreement, will consider: (1) career contribution; (2) quality of previous seasons; (3) players' past compensation; (4) competitive salaries; (5) physical and mental defects; (6) recent performance record of the club. The arbitrators will then pick either the salary given by the player, or by the team. The arbitrators must choose one of the two salaries given, and may not select a compromise salary. It is important to remember that neither party knows what the other is going to offer. As an example, consider one of the first salary arbitration cases. In 1974, the Minnesota Twins offered pitcher Dick Woodson $23,000 for one year, and Woodson offered to pitch for $30,000. The arbitrator therefore was forced to decide whether Woodson was worth more or less than $26,500 (the midpoint). If the arbitrator felt that Woodson was worth less than $26,500, he would be given $23,000. If the arbitrator felt that Woodson was worth more than $26,500, he would be awarded $30,000. As it turned out, the arbitrator found in favor of Woodson, and he was granted $30,000.

While the Minnesota Twins were quite dismayed at the Club's loss in this early hearing, the salary arbitration awards have increased significantly since the mid-1970s. The combination of free agency and arbitration-mandated salaries has produced salary arbitration hearings with millions of dollars at stake, rather than the few thousand that were at stake in the Woodson case. For example, in 2001, Atlanta Braves outfielder Andruw Jones offered to play for $8.2 million. The Braves offered Jones $6.4 million, a $2.7 million raise over his previous year's salary of $3.7 million. Arbitrators Howard Block, Roger Kaplan, and Elisabeth Neumeier found in favor of Jones, and Jones received the $8.2 million salary. Again, this does not necessarily mean that arbitrators felt Jones was worth $8.2 million, but it does mean that the arbitrators felt that Jones was worth more than $7.3 million (the midpoint of $8.2 and $6.4 million).

The National Hockey League's system of salary arbitration is different from that of Major League Baseball. The NHL uses conventional interest arbitration, under which the arbitrator is not forced to pick "either/or," but estimates what the arbitrator believes the player is worth and offers that as the decision. Like the system employed in Major League Baseball, neither party in a salary arbitration dispute knows what the other is going to offer. For example, if the Mighty Ducks of Anaheim offered Paul Kariya an $8 million one-year contract and Kariya asked for $11 million, the arbitrator could decide Kariya is worth $9.5 million and award that salary.

The 1993 salary arbitration hearing between the Boston Bruins and Raymond Bourque offers a valuable look into the machinations of the salary arbitration process. Bourque asked for a contract that would pay him approximately $4.25 million per year, and the Bruins offered $1.8 million per year. The arbitrator, Richard Bloch, began his analysis by reviewing Bourque's achievements and contributions to the Bruins over his fourteen-year career. The arbitrator then compared Bourque's statistics with twenty-three other top defensive players; in these comparisons, he appeared near or at the top of almost all. Bloch noted in his decision:

> It is fully appropriate, in the course of fashioning the contract award, to place one's self in the parties' position, considering the "market" for a player or given category of player and attempting to discern, to whatever extent possible, the respective positions and the responses. In this context, even accepting a frame of reference that would accommodate non-defensive players, for comparison purposes, the long-term nature of those arrangements and the impact of salary may simply not be ignored.

The arbitration award was set at $2.25 million per year, based on comparisons with other notable impact players, including Steve Yzerman, Eric Lindros, and Joe Sakic.

If a team feels the player is likely to win a large award in arbitration, the team will do all it can to settle before the case goes to an arbitrator. Even when players lose their arbitration cases, they usually receive an increase in salary over the previous year.

NOTES

1. Salary arbitration has had a tremendous impact on salaries in Major League Baseball. In 1976, the average player salary was $51,501; in 1991, the average salary rose to $891,188; in 2001, the average salary of a baseball player was approximately $2.26 million.

2. For more information on salary arbitration in baseball, see Roger Abrams, *The Money Pitch: Baseball Free Agency and Salary Arbitration* (Philadelphia: Temple University Press, 2000). Also see John Helyar, *Lords of the Realm* (New York: Ballantine Books, 1994).

3. For more information on salary arbitration in hockey, see exhibit 11.4.

11.4. LABOR DISPUTES IN PROFESSIONAL SPORTS

Labor disputes in professional sports are now as much a part of the game as franchise relocations and coach firings. The last three decades have produced over a dozen work stoppages in the four major professional leagues, costing teams and players hundreds of millions of dollars, and angering thousands of fans. It is a reality that where there is collective bargaining, there exists the possibility of a strike by the players, or a lockout initiated by the owners. Below is an outline of the work stoppages each league has participated in, followed by some analysis and explanation on strikes, lockouts and other notable labor disputes that have arisen in professional sports.

NOTE

1. In November 2001, Major League Baseball voted to buy and then eliminate two of the league's lowest revenue producing teams. Although MLB admitted that it considered eighteen franchises for possible contraction, it was widely believed that the Minnesota Twins and Montreal Expos franchises were selected for contraction. This situation caused concern for the MLBPA, as the contraction would eliminate at least fifty jobs for MLB players. The MLBPA quickly filed a grievance, contending that the contraction plans were subject to collective bargaining and couldn't be carried out without the players' consent. The union also contended that the owners violated the labor contract and damaged the free-agent market as a result of the contraction issue. Faced with this grievance and the ongoing Collective Bargaining Agreement negotiations, in February 2002 Commissioner Bud Selig postponed the plan to eliminate teams in 2002, but vowed to push forward with contraction for 2003. The issue is still pending as of summer 2002, as the Montreal Expos were sold to Major League Baseball, which will run the franchise in 2002. In addition, a legal injunction was granted in the case of the Twins to keep them in Minneapolis (see Chapter 9, section 9.2.9., "Facility Contracts").

11.4.1. Strikes

A strike occurs when a group of employees refuse to work, and vow not to return to work until their demands have been met. The right to strike is regulated by legislation, namely the National Labor Relations Act (as amended in 1947). There are two kinds of strikes: a *primary strike* and a *secondary strike*. A primary strike occurs when employees of a company strike against their employer: Major League Baseball players strike against their employer, Major League Baseball (MLB). A secondary strike, which may be illegal under 8(b)(4)(b) of the National Labor Relations Act, occurs when a group of employees at one company strike their employer to protest a

Exhibit 11.4
NHL Salary Arbitration, 1995–2004 Collective Bargaining Agreement

12.1.   Eligibility.

A player is eligible to elect salary arbitration if the player meets the qualifications set forth in the following chart and in Section 12.1(b) below:

First Contract Signing Age	Minimum Level Professional Experience Required to Be Eligible for Salary Arbitration
18-20	5 years professional experience
21	4 years professional experience
22-23	3 years professional experience
24	2 years professional experience
25 and older	1 year professional experience

A player aged 18 or 19 earns a year of "professional experience" by playing ten or more NHL games (regular season and/or playoffs) in a given season. A player aged 20 or above (or who turns 20 between September 16 and December 31 of the year in which he signs his first Player Contract) earns a year of professional experience by playing ten or more professional games under NHL contract in a given season. (b) Only players who qualify as Restricted Free Agents as described in Section 10.2 and who have not signed an Offer Sheet may elect salary arbitration.

Evidence.

Subject to the limitations set forth in subsection (iii) below, the parties may present whatever witnesses, affidavits, documents and other relevant evidence they choose to present at the hearing. The Arbitrator, on behalf of any party, or on his own behalf, may call witnesses or request documents or other evidence, as he deems necessary to resolve the dispute. The Arbitrator in his discretion shall be the judge of the relevancy and materiality of the evidence offered and/or the weight, if any, to attach to any evidence and shall not be bound by any formal legal rules of evidence. All evidence shall be presented in the presence of all the parties, unless a party is in default, having failed to appear for the hearing, or has waived his right to be present. Statistical evidence asserted in a party's affirmative case must be included in such party's brief in order to be admissible.

The parties may offer evidence of the following:

a)   the overall performance, including official statistics prepared by the League (both offensive and defensive) of the Player in the previous season or seasons;
b)   the number of games played by the Player, his injuries or illnesses during the preceding seasons;
c)   the length of service of the Player in the League and/or with the Club;
d)   the overall contribution of the Player to the competitive success or failure of his Club in the preceding season;

Exhibit 11.4 (continued)

    e)   any special qualities of leadership or public appeal not inconsistent with the fulfillment of his responsibilities as a playing member of his team;

    f)   the overall performance in the previous season or seasons of any player(s) who is alleged to be comparable to the party Player whose salary is in dispute; and

    g)   The Compensation of any player(s) who is alleged to be comparable to the party Player, provided, however, that in applying this or any of the above subparagraphs, the Arbitrator shall not consider a player(s) to be comparable to the party Player unless a party to the arbitration has contended that the player(s) is comparable; nor shall the Arbitrator consider the Compensation or performance of a player(s) unless a party to the arbitration has contended that the player(s) is comparable.

Order of Proceedings.

Unless otherwise determined by the Arbitrator or mutually agreed to by all parties, the order of proceedings shall be as follows:

(A) Affirmative case of the Player and the NHLPA;
(B) Affirmative case of the Club and the League;
(C) Rebuttal and closing argument of the Player and the NHLPA;
(D) Rebuttal and closing argument of the Club and the
        League;
(E) Surrebuttal by the Player and/or the NHLPA, where permitted in accordance with subsection 12.5(c) hereof.

Reopening of Hearings.

At any time before a decision is issued, a hearing may be reopened by the Arbitrator on his own motion or on motion of any party for good cause shown.

---

strike happening at another company (see note 3). For example, if MLB players go on strike to support striking professional hockey players, that is a secondary strike. According to labor law, secondary strikes do so at their own risk (i.e., MLB teams could potentially terminate such players, with cause).

There are two kinds of primary strikes: *unfair labor practice strikes* and *economic strikes*. An unfair labor practice strike occurs when a group of employees strike because of an employer's unfair labor practice. For example, if a player in the NFL is discharged because of his union affiliation, NFL players may initiate a strike. Another example of an unfair labor practice strike occurs when employees strike because of their employer's failure to bargain in good faith (e.g., 1994 MLB strike). An economic strike occurs when employees strike over wages, hours, or working conditions, and usually takes place when employees are seeking a new Collective Bargaining Agreement. Debates regarding whether or not a strike is an unfair labor practice or an economic dispute are determined by the NLRB.

Employees who are engaged in a lawful strike may not be discharged from their jobs because of the strike. However, they may be replaced by replacement workers for the period of their strike, and may be replaced permanently, depending upon the type of strike. If the strike in question is an economic strike, strikers can be permanently replaced, but must be reinstated as vacancies occur. Employees who strike

Exhibit 11.5
National Basketball Association

Year	Stoppage	Dates	Significant Issue(s)
1995	Lockout	September	Salary cap/free agency–unresolved
1996	Lockout	July	Salary cap
1998	Lockout	July, 1998–January 1999	Cap on rookie salaries, limit on "Larry Bird" raises, increase in minimum salary

Exhibit 11.6
Major League Baseball

Year	Stoppage	Date	Resolution
1972	Strike	April 2–14	Salary arbitration established; increased pension fund
1976	Lockout	March 1–17	Owners accept free agency
1980	Strike	March 26–April 3	Salary arbitration preserved; increased pension fund
1981	Strike	June 12–July 31	Compensation rules for free agency severely limited
1985	Lockout	March	Minimum salary raised; salary arbitration experience raised from two to three years
1990	Lockout	March	Number of players eligible for salary arbitration expanded
1994-95	Strike	August 94–April 95	Agreed to begin season without a CBA; 1994 World Series cancelled

over an unfair labor practice may be temporarily replaced, but with the end of the strike, they have full reinstatement rights, including their seniority and benefits. In addition to players, umpires have also gone on strike (see note 1).

NOTES

1. With their Collective Bargaining Agreement set to expire on December 31, 1999, Major League Baseball umpires, under the guidance of union head Richie Phillips, staged

Exhibit 11.7
National Hockey League

Year	Stoppage	Dates	Resolution
1992	Strike	April	"Player compensation systems"– unresolved
1994–95	Lockout	August– January	Rookie salary cap; revised salary arbitration rules; veteran free agency changes

Exhibit 11.8
National Football League

Year	Stoppage	Dates	Resolution
1968	Walkout/Lockout	Fall	Increased pension fund
1970	Strike	July	Increased pension contributions
1974	Strike	Fall	Owners keep Rozelle Rule
1975	Strike	August	Owners break strike
1982	Strike	September– November	Increased minimum salaries; no percentage of revenue for players
1987	Strike	Fall	Players abort strike; sue owners on antitrust grounds

a group resignation. They did so because of a no-strike pledge in their Collective Bargaining Agreements. Phillips believed that all sixty-eight umpires were going to resign. However, only fifty-seven did so, and twenty-seven of those fifty-seven quickly rescinded. Major League Baseball accepted the resignation of twenty-two of the umpires, the majority of whom were shocked that their negotiating ploy had failed. Phillips filed an unfair labor practice charge, which was rejected by the NLRB. The umpires then voted to decertify in November 1999, and re-form without Phillips. The matter went to arbitration, and was eventually decided by arbitrator Alan Symonette in May 2001, *In the Matter of the Arbitration Between the Major League Umpires' Association and the National League of Professional Baseball Clubs & the American League of Professional Baseball Clubs*, Case No. 14 300 1395 99. MLB was ordered to rehire nine of the twenty-two umpires who had resigned. Among those not rehired were umpires shown to have deficient skills and those with less than five years of major league experience, who were not protected by "merit" and "skill" provisions. In February 2002, baseball owners agreed to rehire another five of the twenty-two umpires who lost their jobs in the failed mass resignation of 1999 and to allow four more of the umps to retire with back pay and benefits.

2. The Women's National Basketball Association's third season was at risk in 1998, after the WNBPA threatened to strike if a Collective Bargaining Agreement was not in place by the opening game of the season. An agreement was reached in time, although the annual college draft was delayed.

3. Sympathy strikes are different from secondary strikes in that sympathy strikers are not themselves striking against an employer because of a dispute; rather, they are honoring a picket line that may be in place *at their work site*, but manned by another work group. For example, if NBA referees went on strike—and replacement referees were being used—NBA players could decide not to cross the referees' picket line, and engage in a sympathy strike by not playing their games until the referee dispute was settled. It is important to note that sympathy strikers will be classified in the same category as the strikers they are supporting. Therefore, if the sympathy strike is over an economic issue, the sympathy strikers will be considered economic strikers.

11.4.2. Lockouts

A lockout which is used by an employer to preempt a strike occurs when an *employer* prohibits its employees from working. There are two types of lockouts: defensive lockouts and offensive lockouts. A defensive lockout occurs when an employer fears a strike by its employees at a time when it is most vulnerable (e.g., right before the play-offs in sports), and thus initiates a lockout at a time that is more conducive to the company (e.g., during the off-season). An offensive lockout occurs when an employer initiates a lockout in an effort to put economic pressure on its employees, a tactic normally used during negotiations of a new Collective Bargaining Agreement.

A recent offensive lockout in professional sports occurred when the National Basketball Association locked out its players during the summer of 1998 because of stalled negotiations over a new Collective Bargaining Agreement. The owners had initiated the negotiations after voting to reopen the Collective Bargaining Agreement signed in 1996. The lockout began on July 1, 1998, after the union and the league could not come to an agreement on a "hard salary cap."

Several important legal issues were addressed during this lockout. The players association filed a grievance with arbitrator John Feerick in an attempt to get players with guaranteed contracts paid during the lockout. On October 20, 1998, Feerick ruled in favor of the league, and announced that owners would not have to pay guaranteed contracts during the work stoppage. The lockout continued, and in early January 1999, Commissioner Stern spoke of the possible use of replacement players for the 1999–2000 season. On January 6, 1999, the NBA and the NBPA reached agreement on a new Collective Bargaining Agreement. It is important to note that had replacement players been used in the lockout, several new legal issues would have been raised. The NBA may not have been able to use replacement players in their Canadian franchises, as the provinces of British Columbia (Vancouver Grizzlies) and Ontario (Toronto Raptors) ban replacement workers. In addition, the question of whether or not locked out employees can be permanently replaced would have been raised. Both of these questions would have been important legal issues had the lockout continued and if replacement players been used, and these issues may have been litigated.

NOTES

1. The NBA had locked out its players twice in the 1990s prior to the lockout in 1998. In 1995 the league initiated a one-month lockout after the players refused to ratify a new

Collective Bargaining Agreement. No games were lost. The owners again locked the players out in July 1996 after there was disagreement between the league and the union over $50 million in television revenue redistribution. That lockout ended after several hours, after the sides were able to resolve this issue.

2. Unions have argued that an employer lockout is in violation of 8(a)(3) of the NLRA because it discourages an employee from participating in union activity. The courts have not agreed with this argument, and allow both defensive and offensive lockouts, equating the lockout with employees' right to strike. However, a lockout will be considered illegal if it is waged over a *permissible*, rather than a *mandatory*, subject of bargaining. A lockout will also be considered illegal if it is waged to coerce workers into voting against their union in an upcoming election. For more information, see Michael Evan Gold, *An Introduction to Labor Law*, rev. ed. (Ithaca, N.Y.: Cornell University Press, 1998).

11.4.3. Impasse

Both strikes and lockouts are usually the result of some form of "impasse" in negotiations over a particularly contentious issue, such as free agency or a salary cap. Impasse occurs when the two sides in negotiations have bargained in good faith but have reached a deadlock position on a particular issue or issues. A number of factors determine whether a good-faith impasse has occurred:

1. Bargaining history
2. The good faith of the parties
3. Length of negotiations
4. Importance of the issues that are in disagreement
5. The understanding of the parties as to the state of negotiations
6. Fluidity of positions
7. Demonstration of willingness by parties to consider a proposal.

At no time before good faith impasse can an employer unilaterally implement a change in wages, hours, or terms and conditions of employment. When a good faith impasse is reached, the employer has the right to implement its "last-best offer," or parts thereof. The employer cannot implement something that is worse than what was proposed to the union. When an impasse has been reached, the union has the choice to accept it, file an unfair labor practice charge arguing impasse had not been reached, or strike over the matter. To ensure that employers are not able to charge impasse after the first bargaining session, 8 (a)(5) of the NLRA protects unions against surface bargaining, which occurs when an employer is clearly bargaining in appearance only, with the intention of avoiding an agreement rather than reaching one (see note 3).

An example of a dispute in professional sports that dealt with the issue of impasse, the calling of a strike, and several unfair labor practice charges is the 1994–1995 labor dispute between Major League Baseball and the Major League Baseball Players Association. In March 1994, the league and the players' association began negotiations on a new Collective Bargaining Agreement, and agreed to continue to work under the terms of the expired agreement (1990–1993). In these negotiations, the owners wanted to negotiate a salary cap similar to the "hard cap" won by the NFL in its negotiations with the NFLPA in 1993. MLB argued that small market teams such as the Montreal Expos and the San Diego Padres could not afford to pay the high salaries demanded by their star players.

These teams and their fans watched as those stars, through free agency or trades, went to teams that could afford their services: the New York Yankees or the Atlanta Braves. The league proposed a salary cap of 50% of league revenues. During the previous season, the players had received 58% of revenue.

The players' association rejected the league's proposal, arguing that it was not up to the players to solve the revenue distribution problems of the league. The players went on strike on August 11, 1994. Despite a federal mediator, and a plea from U.S. President Bill Clinton, the strike forced the cancellation of the rest of the season and the World Series, and put the 1995 season in jeopardy.

On December 22, 1994, the league declared an impasse in negotiations, unilaterally implemented a salary cap, and abolished salary arbitration. In response, the players' association instructed its members not to sign any individual contracts, and then filed unfair labor practice charges against the league for unilaterally changing mandatory subjects of bargaining prior to impasse being reached. The league softened their stance concerning the salary cap, but argued that salary arbitration and free agency were permissive subjects of bargaining (not related to wages, hours, and terms and conditions of employment), and could therefore be changed unilaterally. The NLRB found that the changes made by the league dealt specifically with wages, hours, and terms of employment, and were therefore mandatory subjects of bargaining, not subject to unilateral change. On March 27, 1995, the NLRB filed a petition that sought a temporary injunction, which would return these items to the status quo. The injunction was granted in *Silverman v. Major League Baseball Player Relations Committee, Inc.*, 880 F.Supp. 246 (S.D.N.Y. 1995)—and Major League Baseball unsuccessfully appealed—*Silverman v. Major League Baseball Player Relations Committee, Inc.*, 67 F.3d 1054 (2nd Cir. 1995). Subsequently, the owners and players agreed to begin the 1995 season without a Collective Bargaining Agreement in place, and continued operating under the terms of the 1990–1993 Collective Bargaining Agreement. The league and the players' association finalized a new agreement on November 26, 1996, effective from January 1, 1997 until November 2001.

Another important legal issue that was raised during the 1994–1995 strike was the possible use of replacement players. As stated earlier, if the work stoppage is an economic strike, then the striking employees can be permanently replaced, whereas if it is an unfair labor practice strike, only temporary replacements can be used. The Major League Baseball Players Association strike was deemed economic, and the league announced it would use replacements to start the 1995 season. Two problems arose concerning replacement players. In Ontario, Canada, home of the Toronto Blue Jays, legislation banned the use of replacement workers during strikes, which meant that the Blue Jays would not be able to play any home games at the Skydome in Toronto. Second, the state of Maryland passed similar legislation that would effectively stop the Baltimore Orioles from playing in the state of Maryland using replacement players. Replacement players were indeed hired for spring training games, including exhibition games at some major league parks (e.g., the opening of Coors Field in Denver). However, the strike ended before the replacement player issue could be resolved, so the question surrounding the legality of replacement players in certain states and provinces is still open to question.

NOTES

1. Attendance at Major League Baseball games declined from a pre-strike average of 31,612 per game in 1994 to 26,889 per game in 1996.

2. For a comprehensive description of labor law in the United States, see Bruce Feldacker, *Labor Guide to Labor Law*, 4th ed. (Englewood Cliffs, N.J.: Prentice-Hall, 2000).

3. The NLRB has identified the following bargaining tactics as evidence of surface bargaining: (1) refusing to meet at reasonable times and places; (2) refusing to give basic information to the union needed for meaningful bargaining; (3) refusing to discuss certain issues with the union at all; (4) agreeing to minor issues but refusing to bargain over economic issues; (5) rejecting union proposals without making counterproposals; (6) stalling negotiations by reintroducing proposals that have previously been withdrawn. For more information, see www.nlrb.gov

11.4.4. Baseball Collusion Cases

In January 1986, the MLBPA filed a grievance against MLB for boycotting the free agent market after the 1985 season, and violating Article 18 of the Basic Agreement, which stated: "Players shall not act in concert with other Players [see note 1] and Clubs shall not act in concert with other Clubs." In accordance with the grievance arbitration system in baseball, a tripartite panel was assigned, with Thomas Roberts as the impartial chairperson.

The dispute arose out of the fact that during the off-season between the 1985 and 1986 seasons, only four of the thirty-three available free agents changed teams, and all four of them were marginal players. In *Major League Baseball Players Association v. Twenty-six Major League Baseball Clubs*, A-123, A-136 (1987) (Roberts), Arbitrator Roberts found that Article 18 had been violated and that clubs had a "common understanding that no club would bid on the services of a free agent until his former club no longer desired to sign him." Therefore, owners acted in concert to deprive players of their right to free agency. In January 1988, Roberts made seven players immediate free agents, and in August 1989, awarded those players $10.5 million in damages.

In 1988, a second collusion suit was filed by the MLBPA against the MLB, again for acting in concert against the players in regard to free agency. During the 1986–1987 off-season, the owners instituted a plan that would allow the free agent's original team to attempt to re-sign the player before any other team could sign him. The owners established an "information bank" that listed offers to players, amounts of those offers, and when those offers took place. Under this system, no player would receive an offer from a club, other than his original one, until his present team illustrated on the "information bank" that it was no longer interested in the player.

Arbitrator George Nicolau found that the owners had again violated Article 18, and had acted in concert with each other. In his decision Nicolau stated:

> Thus, participating clubs were acting together so that information to which only one was privy—offers it had made to particular players—could be shared, used, and acted upon by others for their own benefit to the possible detriment of the club supplying that intelligence.

In August 1988, Nicolau found in favor of the players and granted twelve players free agent status. In 1990, Nicolau presided over a third collusion case, *Major League Baseball Players Association v. Twenty-six Major League Clubs* 1 (1990) (Nicolau, Arb.), pertaining to the 1987–1988 off-season, where the owners again used an "information bank." Nicolau again found for the players, and a settlement of $280 million was reached.

To prevent collusion from happening in other sports, anti-collusion articles

Exhibit 11.9
Article 20. (E) Individual Nature of Rights (from 1997–2001 Collective Bargaining Agreement)

(1) The utilization or non-utilization of rights under XIX(A)(2) and Article XX is an individual matter to be determined solely by each Player and each Club for his or its own benefit. Players shall not act in concert with other Players and Clubs shall not act in concert with other Clubs.

(2) Upon any finding of a violation of Section (E)(1) of this Article XX by two or more Clubs, any injured Player (or Players) shall be entitled to recover in monetary damages three times the lost baseball income, he (or they) would have had but for the violation.

have been included in all Collective Bargaining Agreements. Article 20 of the MLB Collective Bargaining Agreement, which outlines a player's free agency rights, also includes an anti-collusion clause (see Exhibit 11.9). In addition, to ensure that collusion does not take place, the Collective Bargaining Agreement contains a letter of good faith from the owner's chief negotiator to the player's chief negotiator. The letter, in Attachment 15 of the agreement, promises that the owners will not operate an "information bank" during the term of the agreement.

NOTES

1. In 1966 Los Angeles Dodger pitchers Don Drysdale and Sandy Koufax both requested raises to bring their salaries to $100,000. When they were rebuffed, they staged a spring training holdout, claiming they would not re-sign with the Dodgers unless they were signed as a package. The Dodgers could not tolerate the idea of being without two of their best players. Thus, the holdout proved successful after the Dodgers awarded them a total of $240,000. This group holdout behavior is now prohibited by the Collective Bargaining Agreement in exchange for management's agreement not to collude.

2. The baseball collusion cases remained unsettled in 2001. In *Major League Baseball Players Ass'n v. Garvey*, 532 U.S. 504 (2001), the Supreme Court rejected Steve Garvey's claim for a larger share of the $280 million settlement, citing an unwillingness to overturn a decision from binding arbitration.

3. For more information on the baseball collusion cases, see James Gilbert Rappis, "The Use of Contract Interpretation by Professional Sports Arbitrators," 3 *Marquette Sports Law Journal* 215 (1993).

CONCLUSION

Understanding the development and application of labor law in sports is important for both employers and employees in the world of professional sports. Particularly in professional sports, labor law provides the guideline for the often complex and contentious relationship between players and owners. Issues regarding Collective Bargaining Agreements and labor disputes are among the most pressing and relevant issues in modern professional sports. It is clear that an understanding of these issues, as well as the history, laws and processes involved in professional sports labor relationships is important for anyone in sports law or in sports. For those not involved in sports where the athletes are unionized, sports managers and sports lawyers may face the possibility that the athletes might want to unionize. In addition, these sports managers and sports lawyers may deal with non-playing personnel who are unionized. This is particularly true in facilities, as well as colleges and universities.

Chapter 12

AGENCY LAW

INTRODUCTION

As professional, intercollegiate, and Olympic sports have blossomed into billion-dollar industries since the 1980s, the role of the player agent has grown significantly within the world of sports. The prominence of agents within sports has paralleled the booming economic growth of the sports industry. With millions of dollars on the line in many player contracts, the need for competent representation has increased considerably (see Chapter 1). Though historically many sports contracts were negotiated solely between the player and the organization, it is now rare to find a proven or entry-level professional athlete who does not employ the services of an agent. The need for knowledgeable and capable sports agents within the sports industry continues to be important for athletes.

Representing athletes is more than negotiating contracts. When an agent signs a contract with a client to represent him or her, the parties are entering into a legal relationship that usually encompasses many responsibilities. An agent, in addition to negotiating the contract with a professional team or organization, may also be responsible for marketing the athlete, financial management of the athlete's portfolio, counseling the athlete in times of trouble, dealing with any disputes that may arise involving the player, administering or drafting a player's will or trust, and handling any off-the-field legal issues. In order to negotiate effectively on behalf of his or her client, an agent must be well versed in a league's Collective Bargaining Agreement, Standard Player Contract, salary information, and rules and regulations of the league team and/or organization. Before entering into contract negotiations on behalf of a player, the agent must ensure that they are licensed or certified to negotiate with team representatives under either the players association's rules and regulations and/or state legislation governing agents. Agents are both non-lawyers and lawyers, and the use of the word "agent" can apply to both groups. Player associations, in order to protect the best interests of their member-players, require that agents be certified before they can conduct contract negotiations, in order to assure that agents will represent their clients effectively. In reality, a successful sports agent must be knowledgeable about not only contract law (see Chapter 9), but also about how antitrust law affects professional athletes (see Chapter 10), how labor law influences professional sports (see Chapter 11), eligibility issues affecting collegiate athletes (see Chapters 5 and 6), and the intellectual property rights of their client (see Chapter 13).

In addition to representing athletes, agents may handle representation for coaches, managers, and administrators. Individuals in these high-profile positions usually have the same need for representation as the athletes. Some associations do not allow agents to represent both athletes and coaches, citing a potential conflict of interest. With respect to representing coaches, agents do not have the benefit of a Collective Bargaining Agreement or Standard Player Contract to work from in the contract negotiations. The focus of this chapter is on player representation; for more information on coaches' contracts, refer to Chapter 9, Section 9.2.5.1, "Coaches' Contracts: Professional and Collegiate."

Although league players associations require certification of player agents, "anyone" can be a sports agent. The life of an agent, popularized in the movie *Jerry Maguire* and television series *Arliss*, appears to be exciting, fast-paced, and very attractive for a person who wants to work in the field of sports. Also, until the late 1980s and early 1990s it was an occupation that had managed to avoid significant litigation and legislative scrutiny. This lack of regulation and legislation led to a very competitive atmosphere. With the increased attractiveness of being a sports agent, and the potential money an agent can make, situations have arisen where agents have attempted to circumvent NCAA rules and/or state laws. Therefore, many states have passed legislation to deal with problems that may arise with athlete agents. With the approval and aid of the NCAA, the passage of the Uniform Athlete Agent Act in 2000 (see Section 12.7., "Government Regulation—Uniform Athlete Agent Act"), is gaining approval in many states by offering the promise of consistent, widespread regulation of agent activity.

One of the most important duties of a responsible sports agent is to provide sensible, realistic guidance to athletes who are dealing with possible professional career opportunities in sports. However, when dealing with intercollegiate athletes, an agent should be aware of the issues that may affect the eligibility of student-athletes, specifically the payment to or employment of an athlete. These areas are addressed in Chapter 6, in sections 6.2.2.8., "Pay and Expenses: NCAA" and 6.2.2.9., "Employment: NCAA." Due to the extensive regulations placed upon college athletes, it is important that an agent also be aware of NCAA regulations governing contact with agents in order to avoid compromising an athlete's eligibility.

An athlete faces many pressures when deciding whether or not to turn pro. The money an athlete can earn as a professional may make forfeiting college eligibility a very attractive proposition. The money may be viewed by the athlete as a way of becoming self-supporting and/or helping his or her family. A student-athlete may feel the pressure to secure these considerable financial awards before his or her amateur eligibility ends in order to avoid the risk that a career-threatening injury during his or her amateur career will limit the chances of ever earning the large salary. An agent must be careful not to jeopardize the eligibility status of the athlete by negotiating a contract or representing the athlete. However, the agent may serve as an adviser to the player and his or her family, and can advise on the draft, the industry, the sport, and likely contract offers. While it is true that an athlete may have a difficult time retaining eligibility in the face of attractive offers of a professional contract, some agents have unrealistically boosted the expectations of an athlete who may then be drafted lower than promised. The athlete has subsequently made a bad decision to leave college for a pro career, and in many situations this has not worked out for the athlete.

It is the athletes themselves who must ultimately make the critical decisions impacting their lives. They first must decide, with the knowledgeable input of others, if they are ready to compete at the professional level. They then must try to establish, with this same input, which round they will be drafted in, approximately how much they will be paid, and, if drafted, whether or not it will be the right team for them. Professional drafts are very difficult for athletes and agents to predict because the process of drafting is an inexact science, with athletes predicted to be chosen early in a draft sometimes falling a number of rounds. In professional basketball and football, the athletes usually do not have the luxury of picking a desired team. In all professional team sports, however, athletes in certain situations can discourage teams from drafting them. Prospective draftees can make it clear that they will not sign or play for a particular team, announce that they will decide to play a different sport if they are drafted by a particular team, or make it plain that they will play only if given a large signing bonus. Athletes must also decide whether they are physically and mentally prepared for the rigors of the game, both on and off the court or field.

Another consideration is what will happen if they wait to turn pro. By waiting, they may sacrifice a large contract. On the other hand, they may improve their draft status and make more money after another season of collegiate play.

Student-athletes who do not want to employ an agent need to know to whom they can turn for assistance. Will the league office give them some direction? Will the club that is interested in drafting them be helpful in giving some direction? And who from the club is best to talk to? Even before being drafted, the athletes will also want to talk with a representative of the players' union to obtain salary information and to find out about other resources the players association can offer.

This chapter will provide a basic foundation of the information and issues that need to be considered and understood before representing clients who are aspiring pros or current professional athletes.

The chapter first examines the basics of agency law in the United States. It then scrutinizes the varying definitions of a player agent. The following three sections deal with the relationship between the agent and the league's entry draft, the league's Standard Player Contract, and the league's players association. The next section discusses the varying functions of an agent. Section 12.7 discusses government and private regulations facing agents, including the Uniform Athlete Agent Act. This section also deals with state athlete-agent legislation and applicable NCAA rules and regulations that have been enacted to protect athletes from unscrupulous agents. The chapter concludes with brief sections on individual player sports, the opportunities available to U.S. athletes who want to play in foreign leagues, and endorsement contracts.

NOTES

1. See the following books for a discussion of the role and history of athlete agents:

   a. Ronald M. Shapiro, Mark A. Jankowski, James Dale, and Cal Ripken, *The Power of Nice: How to Negotiate So Everyone Wins—Especially You!* Rev. ed. (New York: John Wiley and Sons, 2001).

   b. David Allen Smith, *From the Prom to the Pros: The Athlete's, Parent's, and Coach's Guide* (Santa Ana, CA: Seven Locks Printing, 2000).

   c. Robert H. Mnookin, Lawrence Susskind, and Pacey C. Foster, eds., *Negotiating on Behalf of Others: Advice to Lawyers, Business Executives, Sports Agents, Diplomats, Politicians and Everybody Else* (Thousand Oaks, CA: Sage, 1999).

   d. Marc Roberts and Theresa Foy Digeronimo, *Roberts Rules: Success Secrets from America's Most Trusted Sports Agent* (Franklin Lakes, NJ: Career Press, 1998).

   e. Allen Steinberg and Michael Dorso, *Winning with Integrity* (New York: Random House, 1998).

   f. Robert H. Ruxin and Gary A. Uberstine, *Athlete's Guide to Agents*, 3rd ed. (Boston: Jones and Bartlett, 1993).

   g. Ron Simon, *The Game Behind the Game: Negotiating in the Big Leagues* (Stillwater, MN: Voyageur Press, 1993).

   h. Kenneth L. Shropshire, *Agents of Opportunity: Sports Agents and Corruption in Collegiate Sports*, 2nd ed. (Philadelphia: University of Pennsylvania Press, 1992).

   i. Robert Fisher and William L. Ury, *Getting to Yes: Negotiating Agreement Without Giving In* (London: Viking Penguin, 1991).

   j. Alexander Wolff and Armen Keteyian, *Raw Recruits* (New York: Pocket Books, 1991).

   k. Bob Woolf, *Friendly Persuasion: How to Negotiate and Win* (New York: Berkeley Publishing Group, 1991).

2. For a discussion of corruption and competition in sports agency, see Bryan Couch, "How Agent Competition and Corruption Affects Sports and the Athlete-Agent Relationship and What Can Be Done to Control It," 10 *Seton Hall Journal of Sports Law* 111 (2000).

12.1. AGENCY LAW

To gain a complete understanding of the role of a sports agent, it is necessary that the basics of agency law be discussed first. The agency relationship is a fiduciary relationship between one person—the agent—who agrees to act for, and under the direction or control of another—the principal. The principal is the one for whom an action is taken, and the agent is the one who acts. The agent acts on behalf of the principal (in our case, the athlete), is subject to the control of the principal, and can act on the principal's behalf only with his or her consent. A fiduciary relationship implies that an obligation of trust and confidence exists between the principal and agent.

Three elements of an agency relationship are especially important to comprehend: *consent, on behalf of,* and *subject to the control of. Consent*, in agency relationships, does not have to be given in written form. Instead, as long as the relationship is consensual, an agent does not need a contract to work for the principal. In fact, anyone, including children, can be agents even though they do not have the capacity to contract for themselves. Only the principal in the relationship must have capacity, consistent with the basics of contract law (see Chapter 9).

Acting *on behalf of* a principal signifies that an agent is not conducting negotiations for his or her own best interest; rather, they are for the profit of the principal in the relationship. When an agent is *subject to the control of* the principal, the agent must act under the direction of the principal. Also important to an agency relationship is an understanding of the duties owed by a principal to an agent. Under agency law, the principal owes three fiduciary duties to the agent: to compensate, to reimburse and to indemnify the agent. The principal is also liable on contracts negotiated by the agent where the agent possesses the authority to enter into the contract on the principal's behalf. A principal will not be liable under a contract where an agent has no authority to enter into it.

12.2. PLAYER AGENTS

A player agent, also called a player representative, is a person authorized by a player to act in his or her name. The promise of compensation is not required to establish the relationship, although such compensation is usually presumed. The definition of who and what constitutes an agent can differ from organization to organization and from state to state. For example, the definition of an agent by the National Football League may not be the same as the definition used by a particular state agent's legislation. Also, the definition used by the state of Georgia for an athlete agent is not the same as the definition used by the state of California, for example. Below are the two different definitions of an athlete agent, as provided by the agent-athlete legislation in the states of Georgia and California. Note how the California legislation exempts attorneys under certain circumstances.

Georgia Legislation

Athlete Agent—A person who, directly or indirectly, recruits or solicits an athlete to enter into an agent contract or professional sports services contract with that person or who for a fee procures, offers, promises, or attempts to obtain employment for an athlete with a professional sports team.

—Athlete agent definition does not include the owner, employee, or other representative of a professional sports team, provided that such owner, employee, or other representative does not recruit or solicit such athlete to enter into an agent contract or professional sports services contract or for a fee does not procure, offer, promise, or attempt to obtain employment for such athlete with a professional sports team. (See Ga. Code Ann. 43-4A-7.)

California Athlete Agent Law

Athlete Agent—A person who, directly or indirectly, recruits or solicits an athlete to enter into any agent contract, endorsement contract, financial services contract, or professional sports services contract, or for compensation procures, offers, promises, attempts, or negotiates to obtain employment for any person with a professional sports team or organization or as a professional athlete.

—Athlete agent does not include a person licensed as an attorney, dealer in securities, financial planner, insurance agent, real estate broker, sales agent, tax consultant or other professional person, when that professional person provides only the type of services customarily provided by that profession. Such exemption does not apply when a licensed professional engages in the conduct described under the athlete agent definition above.

—Athlete agent does not include any person acting solely on behalf of a professional sports team or organization.

—Athlete agent does not include a licensed talent agency unless the talent agency directly or indirectly recruits or solicits a student-athlete to enter into an agent contract, endorsement contract, financial services contract or professional sports services contract; or for compensation, procures, offers, promises, attempts or negotiates to obtain employment for any person to perform on-field play with a professional sports team or organization. (See Cal. Bus. and Prof. Code 1889b.6.)

The definition of agents on the intercollegiate level is discussed in section 12.7.3., "NCAA Regulations." Basically, an agent is any person who represents an athlete in exchange for a fee, whether the fee is paid in the present or the future.

NOTES

1. For a discussion of limits placed upon fees for sports agents, see Diane Sudia and Rob Remis, "Ethical and Statutory Limitations on Athlete-Agent Income: Fees, Referrals, and Ownership Interests," 27 *Florida State University Law Review* 787 (Summer 2002).

2. In the following cases the courts dealt with unethical practices of sports agents:

   a. In *Hillard v. Black*, 125 F.Supp.2d 1071 (2000), agent William Black was found to have illegally taken money from two of his clients, Ike Hilliard and Fred Taylor, both NFL players. Black sold shares in a company of which he was president to these clients at an inflated price, took the money, and deposited it into a sham company, with the money being funneled directly to him. At this level, Black was attempting to have the case dismissed, but his request for dismissal was denied. After Black was suspended for three years, he brought a case against the league, alleging that its conduct was racially motivated (*Black v. National Football League Players Ass'n*, 87 F.Supp.2d 1 (D.D.C. 2001)).

b. In *Total Economic Athletic Management of America v. Pickens*, 898 S.W.2d 98 (1995), TEAM America had signed a contract to represent Pickens in negotiations with National Football League teams. However, Pickens entered into a contract with another contract adviser prior to the negotiation, and used this adviser for the negotiation. Upon appeal of the district court, the appeals court upheld the ruling, ordering Pickens to pay $20,000 in damages to TEAM America.

3. In *Faigin v. Kelly*, 184 F.3d 67 (1st Cir. 1999), A. J. Faigin, the former agent for Buffalo Bills quarterback Jim Kelly, brought a defamation suit against Kelly because Kelly had made negative comments about Faigin in his autobiography. The appeals court upheld a summary judgment for Kelly on the trial court level. Although the statements from the autobiography were found to be defamatory, the jury at the trial court level decided "that Faigin had failed to prove actual malice and, pursuant to the court's instructions, returned a verdict for the defendant." Because Faigin could not prove that the statements were false, he was unsuccessful in his claim.

4. For a discussion of an agent's ability to sue for defamation of character, see Mark Gatto, "Defamation—An Athlete's Statements Regarding the Conduct of His Agent Can Be Actionable Under State Defamation Laws—*A. J. Faigin v. Kelly*, 978 F.Supp. 420 (D.N.H. 1997)," 9 *Seton Hall Journal of Sports Law* 263 (1999).

12.3. TEAM SPORTS PLAYER DRAFTS

With signing bonuses and first-year contracts reaching millions of dollars for rookies in the NBA, NFL, NHL, and MLB, it is obvious that reaching the professional ranks can be very lucrative for an athlete. The status of being a "professional" represents a very high level of achievement. It also represents a challenge, for the athlete must maintain this status and avoid an early end to his or her professional sports career. The average time span of a professional career is estimated at three to five years, depending upon the sport, and many athletes achieve their highest skill only to fall from the professional ranks within a short period. In order to successfully represent an athlete, an agent must become knowledgeable about the league entry draft, and how its rules and regulations can affect his or her client. Due to the uncertainty of success upon reaching the professional ranks, it is imperative that the athlete agent place his or her client in the most favorable draft position (see exhibit 12.6 for a description of the salaries for 2001 NBA first round draft picks).

Agents should be aware of the realistic chances that their clients have in the draft. For example, a player who is projected to be a top five pick in the NBA draft may not have to try out for as many teams as the player who is projected to be a late first round or early second round pick. The two most important legal documents for the agent are the Standard Player Contract and the Collective Bargaining Agreement (see Section 12.4., "The Standard Player Contract"). The end product of negotiations between an agent and the player's club will be the player's contract, which of course includes the player's compensation. Agents must have an in-depth understanding of the league's Standard Player Contract, applicable bonus clauses, salary comparisons, minimum salary requirements, and other language, such as guarantees, before entering into contract negotiations with the organization (see Chapter 3 and section 12.5.1., "Salary Information").

The draft is used by each professional team sport as a means of distributing new talent among the various teams in the league and helping the weaker teams in the league improve. Generally, each team will make a selection in reverse order of finish from the previous season and can trade to improve its draft position. Another important purpose of the draft is to reduce the number of teams with which an incoming player can negotiate. This, in theory, has the effect of minimizing players' negotiating leverage and thereby reducing player salaries but also equalizes talent among teams. However, this has not worked to the leagues' complete satisfaction. The NBA, NFL and NHL have put in other restrictions such as salary caps, salary maximums and luxury taxes.

Each of the four major professional leagues holds an annual draft. As will be discussed further in the following four sections, the eligibility, duration of eligibility, and signing rules for the drafts vary from one sport to another. For illustration purposes, greater detail will be given to the drafting procedures of the National Football League. A brief overview of the rules and regulations of entry drafts for Major League Baseball, the National Basketball Association, and the National Hockey League are also provided.

12.3.1. National Football League Draft

The NFL has perhaps the most restrictive draft eligibility rules of the four major professional leagues. Only college players who have completed their eligibility or have submitted a letter to the NFL forfeiting their remaining college eligibility may be drafted. All players who have been out of high school for three years and wish to be eligible for the NFL draft must submit a letter announcing their intentions to the NFL by the January 12 preceding the draft. In 2001 thirty-six players were granted this special eligibility in the NFL draft, including the first overall pick, Virginia Tech quarterback Michael Vick (a sophomore who had completed a redshirt year). In addition, a player who graduates before his eligibility expires must submit a letter stating his intention to be graduated before the fall semester prior to the draft if he wants to be drafted. In this case, the team that selects this player cannot offer the athlete a contract until it receives word from the NFL office that he has in fact graduated. If the player fails to graduate, the club loses the selection and the player forfeits his college eligibility. The NFL draft usually occurs in the last week of April and, per the league Collective Bargaining Agreement, lasts seven rounds.

The NFL also has a supplemental draft for players who become eligible after the draft but before the start of the NFL season. Former Cleveland Browns quarterback Bernie Kosar graduated early from college, and therefore became eligible for the supplemental draft. After choosing Kosar in the first round of the supplemental draft, Cleveland had to give up its first round selection in the next NFL draft as compensation in this situation.

Any NFL draftee must be offered a minimum contract by June 7, or he is free to negotiate with any team. Article XVI of the NFL Collective Bargaining Agreement outlines the regulations governing the NFL draft. Excerpts from this document are in exhibit 12.1. If a draftee chooses not to sign, he is eligible for the next NFL draft, but once again is limited to one club in negotiations. However, if a drafted player does not play professional football for two years, he may then sign with any team. A player who plays professionally in the Canadian Football League or any other professional football league, and whose rights are held by an NFL club, can negotiate with that club for only two years. After that point the player may negotiate with any NFL team, but the team that held his original

Exhibit 12.1
College Draft

Section 2. Number of Choices: With the exception of the 1993 Draft, the Draft shall consist of seven rounds, with each round consisting of the same number of selection choices as there will be Clubs in the NFL the following League Year, plus a maximum number of additional Compensatory Draft Selections equal to the number of Clubs then in the League, with such Compensatory Draft Selections reserved for Clubs losing certain Unrestricted Free Agents. For the 1993 League Year only, the Draft shall consist of eight rounds without any additional Compensatory Draft Selections, except any additional selections as provided in Article XX (Franchise and Transition Players), Section 13. To the extent that the Compensatory Draft Selections referred to in Article XX (Franchise and Transition Players), Section 13 are not all awarded for use in the 1993 League Year Draft, such remaining selections are reserved for the Drafts in subsequent League Years under this Agreement in addition to the maximum number of selections set forth in the first sentence of this Section 2. Each Draft to be held after the *1996 League Year shall be held between February 14 and May 2,* on a date which shall be determined by the Commissioner.

*Extension Agreement 6/6/96

Section 3. Required Tender: A Club that drafts a player shall be deemed to have automatically tendered the player a one year NFL Player Contract for the Minimum Active/Inactive List Salary then applicable to the player pursuant to the terms of this Agreement. The NFL or the Club shall provide the player with notice of such Required Tender before or immediately following the Draft.

. . .

Section 5. Other Professional Teams:

(a)   Notwithstanding Section 4(b) above, if a player is drafted by a Club and, during the period between the Draft and the next annual Draft, signs a contract with, plays for or is employed by a professional football team not in the NFL during all or any part of the 12 month period following the initial Draft, then the drafting Club (or any assignee Club) shall retain the exclusive NFL rights to negotiate for and sign a contract with the player until the day of the Draft three League Years after the initial Draft, and shall thereafter have a Right of First Refusal as described herein, and the player may receive offers from any Club at any time thereafter. The player shall notify the NFLPA and the NFL of his desire to sign a contract with an NFL Club, and of the date on which the player will be free of his other contractual obligations of employment, if any. Within thirty days of receipt of such notice by the NFL or the date of the availability of such player, whichever is later, the NFL Club that drafted the player must tender a one year written Player Contract to the player in order to retain its rights to that player, as detailed below.

(b)   For a player to whom the drafting Club retains the exclusive NFL rights to negotiate pursuant to Section 4(a) above, the Club must tender a one year Player Contract with salary of at least the Minimum Active/Inactive List Salary for players with less than one credited season, as defined in Article XVIII (Veterans

Exhibit 12.1 (continued)

With Less Than Three Accrued Seasons), Section 3, within the thirty day period specified in subsection (a) above. The amount of such tender and/or any Player Contract entered into with the player shall be subject to the Entering Player Pool as set forth in Article XVII (Entering Player Pool). If the player is released through waivers, the player immediately becomes a Free Agent, with the right to sign an NFL Player Contract with any Club, and any Club is then free to negotiate for and sign a Player Contract with such player, without any Draft Choice Compensation between Clubs or First Refusal Rights of any kind, or any signing period.

    (c)   For players with respect to whom the drafting Club retains a Right of First Refusal pursuant to this Section 5, during each League Year the player shall be treated as if he were a Restricted Free Agent not subject to Draft Choice Compensation, as described in Article XIX (Veteran Free Agency), Section 2, except as otherwise set forth in this Section 5. For such players subject to a Right of First Refusal, the Club must tender a one year Player Contract with at least the Minimum Active/Inactive List Salary for players with two or more Credited Seasons, as defined in Article XVIII (Veterans With Less Than Three Accrued Seasons), Section 3, within the thirty day period specified in subsection (a) above. The amount of such tender and/or any Player Contract entered into with the player shall not be subject to the Entering Player Pool. If the Club does not make or withdraws the Required Tender, the player immediately becomes a Rookie Free Agent, with the right to negotiate and sign a Player Contract with any Club, and any Club is then free to negotiate for and sign a Player Contract with such player, without any Draft Choice Compensation between Clubs or First Refusal Rights of any kind, or any signing period.

    (d)   This Section 5 shall apply to any player drafted in the 1990 League Year or thereafter, except that tenders to and Player Contracts entered into with players drafted in the 1990, 1991 and 1992 League Years shall not be subject to the Entering Player Pool. Any player drafted prior to the 1990 League Year shall be governed by rules identical to the provisions set forth in Article XIII of the 1982 Collective Bargaining Agreement.

Section 6. Return to College: If any college football player who becomes eligible for the Draft prior to exhausting his college football eligibility through participation is drafted by an NFL Club, and returns to college, the drafting Club's exclusive right to negotiate and sign a Player Contract with such player shall continue through the date of the Draft that follows the last season in which the player was eligible to participate in college football, and thereafter the player shall be treated and the Club shall have such exclusive rights as if he were drafted in such Draft by such Club (or assignee Club).

. . .

Section 8. Subsequent Draft: A Club that, in a subsequent Draft, drafts a player who (a) was selected in an initial Draft, and (b) did not sign a contract with the NFL Club that drafted him or with any assignee Club during the signing period set forth in Sections 4 through 6 above, shall, during the period from the date of the subsequent Draft to the date of the Draft held the subsequent League Year, be the only NFL Club that may negotiate with or sign a Player Contract with such player. If such player has not signed a Player Contract within the period beginning on the date of the subsequent Draft and ending on the thirtieth day prior to the beginning of the regular season, the Club loses all rights to trade its

Exhibit 12.1 (continued)

exclusive negotiating rights to such player or any Player Contract that it signs with such player for the player's initial League Year. After the Tuesday following the tenth week of the regular season, the player and the Club may only sign a Player Contract for future League Year(s), except as provided in Section 4(c) above. If the player has not signed a Player Contract by the day of the next annual College Draft following the subsequent Draft, the player immediately becomes a Rookie Free Agent, with the right to negotiate and sign a Player Contract with any Club, and any Club is then free to negotiate for and sign a Player Contract with such player, without any Draft Choice Compensation between Clubs or First Refusal Rights of any kind, or any signing period.

Section 9. No Subsequent Draft: If a player is drafted by a Club in an initial Draft and (a) does not sign a contract with a Club during the signing period set forth in Sections 4 through 6 above, and (b) is not drafted by any Club in the subsequent Draft, the player immediately becomes an Undrafted Rookie, with the right to negotiate and sign a Player Contract with any Club, and any Club is then free to negotiate for and sign a Player Contract with such player, without any Draft Choice Compensation between Clubs or First Refusal Rights of any kind, or any signing period.

Extension Agreement 6/6/96

rights can match the offer and thereby retain the player. As can be seen in exhibit 12.1, the rules and regulations regarding the NFL draft are complex. It is crucial that an agent for a prospective NFL football player be aware of all of the details of that league's draft. For example, section 5 of exhibit 12.1 outlines the rights of athletes who were originally drafted by NFL teams but have chosen to play professional football elsewhere. This clause is extremely important for an agent who represents a player who was originally drafted in the NFL, chose to play in the Canadian Football League, but then decides to enter the NFL.

If a college athlete enters the NFL draft, he cannot return to the NCAA in Division I regardless of whether or not he is drafted (see note 1). In Bylaw 12.2.4.2., the *2001–2002 NCAA Division I Manual* states:

> An individual loses amateur status in a particular sport when the individual asks to be placed on the draft list or supplemental draft list of a professional league in that sport, even though:
>   (a) The individual asks that his or her name be withdrawn from the draft list prior to the actual draft;
>   (b) The individual's name remains on the list but he or she is not drafted; or
>   (c) The individual is drafted but does not sign an agreement with any professional athletics team.

There is a different rule for aspiring NBA players. An intercollegiate basketball player can enter the NBA draft and retain eligibility as long as that player does not retain the services of an agent (see section 12.3.3., "National Basketball Association Draft").

NOTE

1. In the following cases the NCAA rules not allowing athletes to return to college after entering into the NFL draft were upheld:

   a. In *Banks v. NCAA*, 508 U.S. 908 (1993), Braxton Banks, a former Notre Dame football player, decided to enter into the 1990 NFL draft. Banks was not selected in the NFL draft and petitioned the NCAA to return to college to finish the one year of eligibility that he had remaining. Banks was denied, and he brought a claim stating that the NCAA rule violated antitrust statutes. Banks was unsuccessful on both the trial court and appeals court levels because he failed to allege any anti-competitive effect on the market by the employment of these rules.

   b. In *Gaines v. NCCA*, 746 F.Supp. 738 (M.D. Tenn. 1990), Bradford Gaines, a college football player for Vanderbilt University, declared himself eligible for the 1990 NFL draft. Gaines was not selected by any NFL team in the draft, and wished to complete his senior season of eligibility at Vanderbilt. Gaines sought a preliminary injunction allowing him to play, and claimed that because he had not signed a contract with an agent or a team, he had retained his amateur status. Gaines was unable to prove likelihood of success on the merits of his case, and the court denied his preliminary injunction request.

12.3.2. Major League Baseball Draft

Major League Baseball has the most complicated rules of any of the professional drafts. Each year Major League Baseball conducts a first-year player draft on or about June 10 (a January amateur free agent draft, as well as "secondary drafts," for previously selected players, was eliminated in 1986). The players eligible for the first-year player draft consist of high school graduating seniors (or those without remaining eligibility); certain four-year college players; junior college players; and all other amateur players not previously selected. It is important to note that Major League Baseball does not conduct a worldwide draft, unlike all other professional team sport leagues. The MLB draft is limited to players from the United States, Canada, and Puerto Rico. Furthermore, players signed outside of the United States, Canada, and Puerto Rico need be only sixteen years of age. However, in the 2002 labor negotiations for a new Collective Bargaining Agreement, the issue of a worldwide draft is a potential topic for negotiations (see note 1).

A high school player who is drafted may sign with the professional club if his eligibility has expired prior to his graduation from high school because of (1) the student's age, (2) his completion of the maximum number of semesters in attendance, or (3) the ending of the maximum number seasons in which he is eligible to participate in any major sport. A student who drops out of high school prior to expiration of his athletic eligibility, and remains out for at least one year, may thereafter be signed to a contract for immediate service. If, over the summer, a player does not sign with the club that drafted him, the player will automatically sever his draftee relationship with that particular club by attending his first class at a *four-year college*. The player then cannot be selected in future June first-year player drafts until:

1. The player reaches age 21

2. The player completes his junior year.

Consequently, it is not uncommon to see one team draft a player in the summer he graduates high school, another team draft him three years later (after his junior year of college), and then for another team (or the same team) to draft him following his senior year of college. It is common for agents to use the threat of his/her player's attending or returning to a *four-year college* as leverage in negotiating a signing bonus.

A *junior college* player is eligible for selection at any first-year player draft. However, upon reentering junior college, such a player cannot be signed until completion of the college baseball season.

Once a player is drafted, the onus is on the team to begin negotiations within fifteen days and offer the player a contract. Since initial minor league salaries have maximum ceilings of $850 per month at lower levels of the minor leagues, the signing bonus is one of the major items of negotiation for selected players, especially those chosen in the earlier rounds.

Other relevant considerations include the following:

1. Foreign players, defined as athletes from outside the United States, Canada and Puerto Rico, may sign with major league teams when they are sixteen, with the restriction that they must turn seventeen by the end of their first professional season.

2. Draft order is determined in alternating fashion between the American League (AL) and National League (NL) teams, with the NL team with the worst record picking first in even numbered years and the AL team selecting first in odd years.

3. College players (excluding junior college players) must turn twenty-one within forty-five days of the draft in order to be eligible for it. All junior college players are eligible for the draft.

4. Drafted players who enter (or return to) junior college remain eligible to sign with the team that drafted them until seven days before the next year's draft.

5. A drafted player cannot be traded until a year after he signs his first pro contract.

A player's NCAA eligibility is not affected when he is drafted by a club. This regulation does not apply to basketball and football, however. A high school athlete in these sports who enters a professional draft automatically forfeits intercollegiate eligibility.

NOTE _____

1. According to *The Report of the Independent Members of the Commissioner's Blue Ribbon Panel on Baseball Economics*, July 2000, Section IV.5.2., "Currently, forty percent of all players signing first-year contracts are excluded from the draft because they do not reside in the United States, Puerto Rico or Canada. With the recent dramatic escalation of signing bonuses to free agent first-year players from the Far East, the Dominican Republic, Venezuela, Cuba, and Australia, high revenue clubs now sign the majority of talented high-profile foreign players. *The implementation of a worldwide draft would ensure all clubs, regardless of revenue, relatively equal access to the crucial foreign player market*" (emphasis in original).

12.3.3. National Basketball Association Draft

The NBA holds its annual draft in June, after the completion of the playoffs. The draft consists of two rounds, with teams selecting in reverse order of finish in the previous year. The NBA developed a lottery system in response to critics who claimed some teams were purposely losing games in order to gain a higher draft pick. All thirteen teams that do not make the play-offs participate to determine their draft order. However, the team with the worst record in the league is guaranteed a pick no worse than the fourth overall, to try to ensure the availability of a quality player for the team that needs such a player most. Also, this lottery is weighted, meaning that teams that finish with a worse win-loss record will have a greater chance to attain high draft picks. All players whose college eligibility has expired are automatically included in the draft pool. Any other player who wants to enter the draft must notify the NBA.

The participation in the draft effectively renounce the athlete's remaining or future intercollegiate eligibility. If a college player changes his mind, he must rescind his notification before the deadline passes in order to maintain intercollegiate eligibility. Any college undergraduate may ask to be drafted by submitting his name to the NBA at least forty-five days prior to the draft. High school seniors can enter the draft by notifying the NBA (see Article X, "NBA Draft," NBA Collective Bargaining Agreement). Once the player sends notification to the NBA of his intention to enter the draft, he loses his NCAA eligibility, whether selected by a team or not, unless the player withdraws from the draft by a specific date, and has not signed with a player agent or received any compensation. Under NCAA rules, basketball players can be reinstated if they have not contracted with an agent. This rule does not apply to other sports.

Once a player is drafted, the NBA team must offer him at least a minimum contract by September 5. A rookie pay scale was adopted within the NBA Collective Bargaining Agreement that sets a rookie's salary depending on where the player is picked in the draft order (see exhibit 12.6 and see Article VIII, "Rookie Scale," NBA Collective Bargaining Agreement). If the player declines the offer, his rights are held by the team until the next draft. If a player signs a professional contract with another league (such as the Continental Basketball Association or a European league) after being drafted by an NBA team, the NBA team retains the rights to negotiate with the player within the period ending one year from the earlier of the two following dates: (1) the date the player notifies the NBA team that he is immediately ready to sign a contract or (2) the date of the college draft occurring in the twelve-period month from September 1 to August 30 in which the player notifies the NBA team of his availability and intention to play in the NBA during the season immediately following the stated twelve-month period (Article X, Section 4, NBA Collective Bargaining Agreement).

NOTES

1. See Bappa Mukherji, "The New NBA Collective Bargaining Agreement: The Changing Role of Agents in Professional Basketball," 2 *Vanderbilt Journal of Entertainment Law & Practice* 96 (Winter 2000).

2. The NBA Collective Bargaining Agreement can be found in its entirety at www.nbpa.com

12.3.4. National Hockey League Draft

The NHL holds its annual draft on the Saturday of the second full week in June. Any amateur or Junior Hockey player who will turn eighteen years of age by September 15 is eligible. Any player who has gone undrafted previously may be selected until he is twenty years of age as of the next September 15. If, after twenty years of age, he has not been drafted, he is a free agent able to negotiate with any team.

A drafted player must receive a bona fide offer by the next draft or he is eligible to be drafted again, or if he reaches twenty years of age, he becomes a free agent. There is no maximum age requirement for European players, who must be drafted before they can sign. Finally, any drafted player who remains in college remains the property of the drafting team until 180 days after he graduates or leaves school.

Unlike football and basketball, and similar to baseball, participation in the NHL draft is not detrimental to collegiate or high school eligibility. If a player is selected but decides not to sign, he can still participate on the amateur level (see note 2).

NOTES

1. In *Gandler* v. *Nazarov*, No. 94 Civ. 2272, 1995 U.S. Dist. LEXIS 8325 (S.D.N.Y June 15, 1995), Andrei Nazarov was a seventeen-year-old Russian hockey prospect who met with agent Alexander Berkovich in 1992. Nazarov did not have an attorney or speak English. Berkovich, representing International Sports Advisors Co. (ISAC), did not provide a Russian translation of the representation agreement with ISAC. ISAC contended that Nazarov breached the agreement the two parties had entered, because it claimed that it had not been paid for services it had performed for Nazarov, and that he had prematurely terminated the contract. The case concerned forum selection for the trial, Nazarov arguing that the trial should not be held in the United States. In December 2000, a decision was reserved pending an evidentiary hearing. The case was then settled.

2. For more information on NHL draft eligibility, refer to Article 8, "Entry Draft," of the National Hockey League Collective Bargaining Agreement (available at www.sabres history.com/nhlcba/cba.html).

12.4. THE STANDARD PLAYER CONTRACT

The Standard Player Contract is one of the cornerstones of the Collective Bargaining Agreement negotiated between the players association and league management, and provides the basic guidelines for an agent and the club in their negotiations for a player's contract (see Chapter 11, section 11.3.7., "Collective Bargaining Agreements in Professional Sports"). A Standard Player Contract is a form contract used by all players and teams in a league. It has several advantages for teams and agents alike. By employing a Standard Player Contract, agents and organizations avoid the negotiation of language and the potential problems associated with drafting unique contracts for each athlete. The use of a Standard Player Contract ensures that all athletes and teams within a league will work with the same basic rights and privileges, negotiating only salary, possibly a few changes in the Standard Player Contract, and additional bonus clauses. Negotiating individual issues such as "Pre-Season Compensation" and "Prohibited Substances" (see exhibit 12.2, Section 3(b) and Section 8), would prove to be a very problematic task for individual cases. Therefore, the language of the Standard Player Contract is decided during negotiations over the Collective Bargaining Agreement, and is uniformly applied to all players within the league. Another benefit of the Standard Player Contract is that much of the language has withstood the test of time, and has been interpreted, clarified, and revised through grievances raised by the players associations.

The Standard Player Contract is written in conjunction with the league's Collective Bargaining Agreement. Therefore, all athletes and teams are subject to the clauses and provisions within the Collective Bargaining Agreement (see Chapter 9, section 9.2.1.3., "Hierarchy of Contracts").

Although the Standard Player Contract is usually a lengthy document, each clause within it serves a distinct purpose. It is important for an agent to be aware of each clause, and especially some clauses that may be revised during some negotiations. For example, in exhibit 12.2, Sections 12 and 16 are two unique clauses in the NBA Uniform Player Contract. Section 12, for example, does not allow the player to participate in any other athletic sport that could endanger his health without the consent of his team. This clause is crucial for an agent to be aware of before the agent considers signing their client up to participate in a local charity football game (see Chapter 9, section 9.2.1.4., "Player Exclusivity"). Section 16 of the NBA Standard Player Contract is a vital clause because it outlines the acceptable reasons for termination of a player's contract. It is crucial that an agent be aware of these guidelines, especially in a situation where the client may have been wrongfully terminated.

While the Standard Player Contract provides a basis for negotiating contracts, it does not include all possible areas for negotiation. Performance and award bonus clauses are frequent issues for individual negotiations (see Chapter 9, section 9.2.1.6., "Bonus Section"). For example, a player in Major League Baseball may be awarded a salary bonus if he wins the Cy Young Award or receives a Gold Glove. It is often the desire of the player and his agent to include a bonus clause in the player's contract because it can provide for the contingency that the player will be worth more than the current accomplishments or prospects indicate. In some instances, the bonus clause may be used as an incentive to sign. This signing bonus can serve more than one purpose. It can also provide up-front money that may be the only guaranteed money for a player who does not sign a guaranteed contract. For example, a late round NFL draft pick may receive a $20,000 signing bonus, and still be cut from the team during training camp. If the player is released before the regular season begins because of a failure to make the team, he at least gets to keep the signing bonus, even though the rest of the contract becomes null and void. Note in the final paragraph of exhibit 12.3, a standard signing bonus form used by the NFL, that only actions of the player, such as refusing to report, practice, or play for his team will cause the default of the signing bonus.

Bonus clauses are also used to compensate a player who has exceeded expectations, usually based on performance. It is important to structure the bonus so that the proper salary escalation is allowed if the player fulfills or exceeds expectations. Different leagues attach different names to the same type of bonus clause. Generally, however, bonuses are based on draft position (the signing bonus), statistical performance (see exhibit 12.4), volume of play, awards and honors, and other contingencies such as "morals clauses." It is important to note that in Major League Baseball bonuses can be based only upon quantitative, and *not* qualitative, performances. In the National Football League, contracts can include bonuses that provide money for players who report to pre-season camp on time. The use of signing bonuses is also a way that NFL teams can "manage" the league's salary cap. Signing bonuses can be prorated over the length of the contract to make the salary more cap friendly (see Chapter 11, section 11.3.10., "Salary Cap"). Exhibit 12.4 provides insight on the basis of providing bonuses to athletes in professional sports. The NBA has taken the step of including language in the Collective Bargaining Agreement to cover certain issues that are commonly

Exhibit 12.2
National Basketball Association Uniform Player Contract

NATIONAL BASKETBALL ASSOCIATION
UNIFORM PLAYER CONTRACT

THIS AGREEMENT made this __ day of_____ is by and between
_____ (hereinafter called the "Team"), a member of the National
Basketball Association (hereinafter called the "NBA" or "League") and _____, an
individual whose address is shown below (hereinafter called the "Player"). In consideration of
the mutual promises hereinafter contained, the parties hereto promise and agree as follows:

1. TERM.

The Team hereby employs the Player as a skilled basketball player for a term of _____
year(s) from the 1st day of September _____.

2. SERVICES.

(a) The services to be rendered by the Player pursuant to this Contract shall include: (i)
training camp, (ii) practices, meetings, and conditioning sessions conducted by the Team
during the Season, (iii) games scheduled for the Team during any Regular Season, (iv)
Exhibition games scheduled by the Team or the League during and prior to any Regular
Season, (v) the NBA's All-Star Game (including the Rookie Game) and every event conducted
in association with such All-Star Game (including, but not limited to, a reasonable number of
media sessions and any event that is part of an All-Star Skills Competition if the Player had
previously agreed to participate in that Competition), if the Player is invited to participate
therein, (vi) Playoff games scheduled by the League subsequent to any Regular Season, and
(vii) promotional activities of the Team and the League as set forth in paragraph 13 herein.

(b) If the Player is a Veteran, the Player will not be required to attend training camp earlier than
2 p.m. (local time) on the twenty-ninth (29th) day prior to the first game of any Regular Season.

Notwithstanding the foregoing, if the Team is scheduled during a particular NBA Season to
participate outside of North America in an Exhibition game or a Regular Season game during
the first week of the Regular Season, such Veteran Player may be required to attend the
training camp conducted in advance of that Regular Season by 2 p.m. (local time) on the thirty-
second (32nd) day prior to the first game of the Regular Season. Rookies may be required to
attend training camp at an earlier date, but no earlier than ten (10) days prior to the date that
Veterans are required to attend.

(c) Exhibition games shall not be played on the three (3) days prior to the opening of the
Team's Regular Season schedule, nor on the day prior to a Regular Season game, nor on the
day prior to and the day following the All-Star Game. Exhibition games prior to any Regular
Season shall not exceed eight (including intra-squad games for which admission is charged),
and Exhibition games during any Regular Season shall not exceed three.

3. COMPENSATION.

(a) Subject to paragraph 3(b) below, the Team agrees to pay the Player for rendering the
services described herein the Compensation described in Exhibit 1 or Exhibit IA hereto (less all
amounts required to be withheld by federal, state, and local authorities, and exclusive of any

Exhibit 12.2 (continued)

amount(s) which the Player shall be entitled to receive from the Player Playoff Pool). Unless otherwise provided in Exhibit I, such Compensation shall be paid in twelve (12) equal semi-monthly payments beginning with the first of said payments on November 15th of each year covered by the Contract and continuing with such payments on the first and fifteenth of each month until said Compensation is paid in full.

(b) The Team agrees to pay the Player $1,500 per week, pro rata, less all amounts required to be withheld by federal, state, and local authorities, for each week (up to a maximum of four (4) weeks for Veterans and up to a maximum of five (5) weeks for Rookies) prior to the Team's first Regular Season game that the Player is in attendance at training camp or Exhibition games; provided, however, that no such payments shall be made if, prior to the date on which he is required to attend training camp, the Player has been paid $10,000 or more in compensation with respect to the NBA Season scheduled to commence immediately following such training camp. Any Compensation paid by the Team pursuant to this subparagraph shall be considered an advance against any Compensation owed to the Player pursuant to paragraph 3(a) above, and the first scheduled payment of such Compensation (or such subsequent payments, if the first scheduled payment is not sufficient) shall be reduced by the amount of such advance.

(c) The Team will not pay and the Player will not accept any bonus or anything of value on account of the Team's winning any particular NBA game or series of games or attaining a certain position in the standings of the League as of a certain date, other than the final standing of the Team.

4. EXPENSES.

The Team agrees to pay all proper and necessary expenses of the Player, including the reasonable lodging expenses of the Player while playing for the Team "on the road" and during the training camp period (defined for this paragraph only to mean the period from the first day of training camp through the day of the Team's first Exhibition game) for as long as the Player is not then living at home. The Player, while "on the road" (and during the training camp period only if the player is not then living at home and the Team does not pay for meals directly), shall be paid a meal expense allowance as set forth in the Collective Bargaining Agreement currently in effect between the NBA and the National Basketball Players Association (hereinafter "the NBA/NBPA Collective Bargaining Agreement"). No deductions from such meal expense allowance shall be made for meals served on an airplane. During the training camp period (and only if the player is not then living at home and the Team does not pay for meals directly), the meal expense allowance shall be paid in weekly installments commencing with the first week of training camp. For the purposes of this paragraph, the Player shall be considered to be "on the road" from the time the Team leaves its home city until the time the Team arrives back at its home city.

5. CONDUCT.

(a) The Player agrees to observe and comply with all Team rules, as maintained or promulgated in accordance with the NBA/NBPA Collective Bargaining Agreement, at all times whether on or off the playing floor. Subject to the provisions of the NBA/NBPA Collective Bargaining Agreement, such rules shall be part of this Contract as fully as if herein written and shall be binding upon the Player.

(b) The Player agrees (i) to give his best services, as well as his loyalty, to the Team, and to play basketball only for the Team and its assignees; (ii) to be neatly and fully attired in public; (iii) to conduct himself on and off the court according to the highest standards of honesty, citizenship, and sportsmanship; and (iv) not to do anything that is materially detrimental or materially prejudicial to the best interests of the Team or the League.

Exhibit 12.2 (continued)

(c) For any violation of Team rules, any breach of any provision of this Contract, or for any conduct impairing the faithful and thorough discharge of the duties incumbent upon the Player, the Team may reasonably impose fines and/or suspensions on the Player in accordance with the terms of the NBA/NBPA Collective Bargaining Agreement.

(d) The Player agrees to be bound by Article 35 of the NBA Constitution, a copy of which, as in effect on the date of this Contract, is attached hereto. The Player acknowledges that the Commissioner is empowered to impose fines upon and/or suspend the Player for causes and in the manner provided in such Article, provided that such fines and/or suspensions are consistent with the terms of the NBA/NBPA Collective Bargaining Agreement.

(e) The Player agrees that if the Commissioner, in his sole judgment, shall find that the Player has bet, or has offered or attempted to bet, money or anything of value on the outcome of any game participated in by any team which is a member of the NBA, the Commissioner shall have the power in his sole discretion to suspend the Player indefinitely or to expel him as a player for any member of the NBA, and the Commissioner's finding and decision shall be final, binding, conclusive, and unappealable.

(f) The Player agrees that he will not, during the term of this Contract, directly or indirectly, entice, induce, or persuade, or attempt to entice, induce, or persuade, any player or coach who is under contract to any NBA team to enter into negotiations for or relating to his services as a basketball player or coach, nor shall he negotiate for or contract for such services, except with the prior written consent of such team. Breach of this subparagraph, in addition to the remedies available to the Team, shall be punishable by fine and/or suspension to be imposed by the Commissioner.

(g) When the Player is fined and/or suspended by the Team or the NBA, he shall be given notice in writing (with a copy to the Players Association), stating the amount of the fine or the duration of the suspension and the reasons therefore.

6. WITHHOLDING.

(a) In the event the Player is fined and/or suspended by the Team or the NBA, the Team shall withhold the amount of the fine or, in the case of a suspension, the amount provided in Article VI of the NBA/NBPA Collective Bargaining Agreement from any Current Cash Compensation due or to become due to the Player with respect to the contract year in which the conduct resulting in the fine and/or the suspension occurred (or a subsequent contract year if the Player has received all Current Cash Compensation due to him for the then current contract year). If, at the time the Player is fined and/or suspended, the Current Cash Compensation remaining to be paid to the Player under this Contract is not sufficient to cover such fine and/or suspension, then the Player agrees promptly to pay the amount directly to the Team. In no case shall the Player permit any such fine and/or suspension to be paid on his behalf by anyone other than himself.

(b) Any Current Cash Compensation withheld from or paid by the Player pursuant to this paragraph 6 shall be retained by the Team or the League, as the case may be, unless the Player contests the fine and/or suspension by initiating a timely Grievance in accordance with the provisions (6)f the NBA/NBPA Collective Bargaining Agreement. If such Grievance is initiated and it satisfies Article XXXI, Section 13 of the NBA/NBPA Collective Bargaining Agreement, the amount withheld from the Player shall be placed in an interest-bearing account, pursuant to Article XXXI, Section 9 of such Agreement, pending the resolution of the Grievance.

Exhibit 12.2 (continued)

7. PHYSICAL CONDITION.

(a) The Player agrees to report at the time and place fixed by the Team in good physical condition and to keep himself throughout each NBA Season in good physical condition.

(b) If the Player, in the judgment of the Team's physician, is not in good physical condition at the date of his first scheduled game for the Team, or if, at the beginning of or during any Season, he fails to remain in good physical condition (unless such condition results directly from an injury sustained by the Player as a direct result of participating in any basketball practice or game played for the Team during such Season), so as to render the Player, in the judgment of the Team's physician, unfit to play skilled basketball, the Team shall have the right to suspend such Player until such time as, in the judgment of the Team's physician, the Player is in sufficiently good physical condition to play skilled basketball. In the event of such suspension, the Compensation (excluding any signing bonus or Incentive Compensation) payable to the Player for any Season during such suspension shall be reduced in the same proportion as the length of the period during which, in the judgment of the Team's physician, the Player is unfit to play skilled basketball, bears to the length of such Season.

(c) If, during the term of this Contract, the Player is injured as a direct result of participating in any basketball practice or game played for the Team, the Team will pay the Player's reasonable hospitalization and medical expenses (including doctor's bills), provided that the hospital and doctor are selected by the Team, and provided further that the Team shall be obligated to pay only those expenses incurred as a direct result of medical treatment caused solely by and relating directly to the injury sustained by the Player. Subject to the provisions set forth in Exhibit 3, if in the judgment of the Team's physician, the Player's injuries resulted directly from playing for the Team and render him unfit to play skilled basketball, then, so long as such unfitness continues, but in no event after the Player has received his full Compensation for the Season in which the injury was sustained, the Team shall pay to the Player the Compensation prescribed in Exhibit 1 to this Contract for such Season. The Team's obligations hereunder shall be reduced by (i) any workers' compensation benefits, which, to the extent permitted by law, the Player hereby assigns to the Team, and (ii) any insurance provided for by the Team whether paid or payable to the Player.

(d) The Player agrees to provide to the Team's coach, trainer, or physician prompt notice of any injury, illness, or medical condition suffered by him that is likely to affect adversely the Player's ability to render the services required under this Contract, including the time, place, cause, and nature of such injury, illness, or condition.

(e) Should the Player suffer an injury, illness, or medical condition as provided in this paragraph 7, he will submit himself to a medical examination and appropriate medical treatment by a physician designated by the Team. Such examination when made at the request of the Team shall be at its expense, unless made necessary by some act or conduct of the Player contrary to the terms of this Contract.

8. PROHIBITED SUBSTANCES.

The Player acknowledges that this Contract may be terminated in accordance with the express provisions of Article XXXIII (Anti-Drug Program) of the NBA/NBPA Collective Bargaining Agreement, and that any such termination will result in the Player's immediate dismissal and disqualification from any employment by the NBA and any of its teams. Notwithstanding any terms or provisions of this Contract (including any amendments hereto), in the event of such termination, all obligations of the Team, including obligations to pay Compensation, shall

Exhibit 12.2 (continued)

cease, except the obligation of the Team to pay the Player's earned Compensation (whether Current or Deferred) to the date of termination.

9. UNIQUE SKILLS.

The Player represents and agrees that he has extraordinary and unique skill and ability as a basketball player, that the services to be rendered by him hereunder cannot be replaced or the loss thereof adequately compensated for in money damages, and that any breach by the Player of this Contract will cause irreparable injury to the Team, and to its assignees. Therefore, it is agreed that in the event it is alleged by the Team that the Player is playing, attempting or threatening to play, or negotiating for the purpose of playing, during the term of this Contract, for any other person, firm, corporation, or organization, the Team and its assignees (in addition to any other remedies that may be available to them judicially or by way of arbitration) shall have the right to obtain from any court or arbitrator having jurisdiction such equitable relief as may be appropriate, including a decree enjoining the Player from any further such breach of this Contract, and enjoining the Player from playing basketball for any other person, firm, corporation, or organization during the term of this Contract. The Player agrees that the Team may at any time assign such right to the NBA for the enforcement thereof. In any suit, action, or arbitration proceeding brought to obtain such equitable relief, the Player does hereby waive his right, if any, to trial by jury, and does hereby waive his right, if any, to interpose any counterclaim or set-off for any cause whatever.

10. ASSIGNMENT.

(a) The Team shall have the right to assign this Contract to any other NBA team and the Player agrees to accept such assignment and to faithfully perform and carry out this Contract with the same force and effect as if it had been entered into by the Player with the assignee team instead of with the Team. The Player further agrees that, should the Team contemplate the assignment of this Contract to one or more NBA teams, the Team's physician may furnish to the physicians and officials of such other team or teams all relevant medical information relating to the Player.

(b) In the event that this Contract is assigned to any other NBA team, all reasonable expenses incurred by the Player in moving himself and his family to the home territory of the team to which such assignment is made, as a result thereof, shall be paid by the assignee team. Such assignee team hereby agrees that its acceptance of the assignment of this Contract constitutes agreement on its part to make such payment.

(c) In the event that this Contract is assigned to another NBA team, the Player shall forthwith be provided notice orally or in writing, delivered to the Player personally or delivered or mailed to his last known address, and the Player shall report to the assignee team within forty-eight (48) hours after said notice has been received (if the assignment is made during a Season), within one (1) week after said notice has been received (if the assignment is made between Seasons), or within such longer time for reporting as may be specified in said notice. The NBA shall also promptly notify the Players Association of any such assignment. The Player further agrees that, immediately upon reporting to the assignee team, he will submit upon request to a physical examination conducted by a physician designated by the assignee team.

(d) If the Player, without a reasonable excuse, does not report to the team to which this Contract has been assigned within the time provided in subsection (c) above, then, upon consummation of the assignment, the Player may be suspended by the assignee team or, if the assignment is not consummated or is voided as a result of the Player's failure to so report, by the assignor Team. In either case, the Player's Compensation may be reduced by the NBA by the imposition of a fine in an amount equal to the lesser of (i) ten (10) percent of the Player's full Compensation for the then-current Season, or (ii) $50,000.

Exhibit 12.2 (continued)

11. VALIDITY AND FILING.

(a) This Contract shall be valid and binding upon the Team and the Player immediately upon its execution.

(b) The Team agrees to file a copy of this Contract, and/or any amendment(s) thereto, with the Commissioner of the NBA as soon as practicable by facsimile and overnight mail, but in no event may such filing be made more than forty-eight (48) hours after the execution of this Contract and/or amendment(s).

(c) If pursuant to the NBA Constitution and By-Laws or the NBA/NBPA Collective Bargaining Agreement, the Commissioner disapproves this Contract (or amendment) within ten (10) days after the receipt thereof in his office by overnight mail, this Contract (or amendment) shall thereupon terminate and be of no further force or effect and the Team and the Player shall thereupon be relieved of their respective rights and liabilities there under. If the Commissioner's disapproval is subsequently overturned in any proceeding brought under the arbitration provisions of the NBA/NBPA Collective Bargaining Agreement (including any appeals), the Contract shall again be valid and binding upon the Team and the Player, and the Commissioner shall be afforded another ten-day period to disapprove the Contract (based on the Team's Room at the time the Commissioner's disapproval is overturned) as set forth in the foregoing sentence The NBA will promptly inform the Players Association if the Commissioner disapproves this Contract.

12. OTHER ATHLETIC ACTIVITIES.

The Player and the Team acknowledge and agree that (i) the Player's participation in other sports may impair or destroy his ability and skill as a basketball player, and (ii) the Player's participation in basketball out of season may result in injury to him. Accordingly, the Player agrees that he will not, without the written consent of the Team, engage in (x) sports endangering his health or safety (including, but not limited to, professional boxing or wrestling, motorcycling, moped-riding, auto racing, sky-diving, and hang gliding), or (y) any game or exhibition of basketball, football, baseball, hockey, lacrosse, or other athletic sport, under penalty of such fine and/or suspension as may be imposed by the Team and/or the Commissioner of the NBA. Nothing contained herein shall be intended to require the Player to obtain the written consent of the Team in order to enable the Player to participate in, as an amateur, the sport of golf, tennis, handball, swimming, hiking, softball, or volleyball.

13. PROMOTIONAL ACTIVITIES.

(a) The Player agrees to allow the Team or the League to take pictures of the Player, alone or together with others, for still photographs, motion pictures, or television, at such times as the Team or the League may designate. No matter by whom taken, such pictures may be used in any manner desired by either the Team or the League for publicity or promotional purposes. The rights in any such pictures taken by the Team or by the League shall belong to the Team or to the League, as their interests may appear.

(b) The Player agrees that, during any year of this Contract, he will not make public appearances, participate in radio or television programs, permit his picture to be taken, write or sponsor newspaper or magazine articles, or sponsor commercial products without the written consent of the Team, which shall not be withheld except in the reasonable interests of the Team or the NBA.

Exhibit 12.2 (continued)

(c) Upon request, the Player shall consent to and make himself available for interviews by representatives of the media conducted at reasonable times.

(d) In addition to the foregoing, and subject to the conditions and limitations set forth in Article II, Section 8 of the NBA/NBPA Collective Bargaining Agreement, the Player agrees to participate, upon request, in all other reasonable promotional activities of the Team and the NBA. For each such promotional appearance made on behalf of a commercial sponsor of the Team, the Team agrees to pay the Player $1,000 or, if the Team agrees, such higher amount that is consistent with the Team's past practice and not otherwise unreasonable.

14. GROUP LICENSE.

(a) The Player hereby grants to NBA Properties, Inc. the exclusive rights to use the Player's Player Attributes as such term is defined and for such group licensing purposes as are set forth in the Agreement between NBA Properties, Inc. and the National Basketball Players Association, made as of September 18, 1995 and amended January 20, 1999 (the "Group License"), a copy of which will, upon his request, be furnished the Player; and the Player agrees to make the appearances called for by such Agreement.

(b) Notwithstanding anything to the contrary contained in the Group License or this Contract, NBA Properties may use, in connection with League Promotions, the Player's (i) name or nickname and/or (ii) the Player's Player Attributes (as defined in the Group License) as such Player Attributes may be captured in game action footage or photographs. NBA Properties shall be entitled to use the Player's Player Attributes individually pursuant to the preceding sentence and shall not be required to use the Player's Player Attributes in a group or as one of multiple players. As used herein, League Promotion shall mean any advertising, marketing, or collateral materials or marketing programs conducted by the NBA, NBA Properties (or any subsidiary of NBA Properties) or any NBA team that is intended to promote (x) any game in which an NBA team participates or game telecast or broadcast (including Pre-Season, Exhibition, Regular Season, and Playoff games), (y) the NBA, its teams, or its players, or (z) the sport of basketball.

15. TEAM DEFAULT.

In the event of an alleged default by the Team in the payments to the Player provided for by this Contract, or in the event of an alleged failure by the Team to perform any other material obligation that it has agreed to perform hereunder, the Player shall notify both the Team and the League in writing of the facts constituting such alleged default or alleged failure. If neither the Team nor the League shall cause such alleged default or alleged failure to be remedied within five (5) days after receipt of such written notice, the National Basketball Players Association shall, on behalf of the Player, have the right to request that the dispute concerning such alleged default or alleged failure be referred immediately to the Grievance Arbitrator in accordance with the provisions of the NBA/NBPA Collective Bargaining Agreement. If, as a result of such arbitration, an award issues in favor of the Player, and if neither the Team nor the League complies with such award within ten (10) days after the service thereof, the Player shall have the right, by a further written notice to the Team and the League, to terminate this Contract.

16. TERMINATION.

(a) The Team may terminate this Contract upon written notice to the Player if the Player shall:

(i) at any time, fail, refuse, or neglect to conform his personal conduct to standards of good citizenship, good moral character (defined here to mean not engaging in acts of moral

Exhibit 12.2 (continued)

turpitude, whether or not such acts would constitute a crime), and good sportsmanship, to keep himself in first class physical condition, or to obey the Team's training rules; or

(ii) at any time commit a significant and inexcusable physical attack against any official or employee of the Team or the NBA (other than another player), or any person in attendance at any NBA game or event, considering the totality of the circumstances, including (but not limited to) the degree of provocation (if any) that may have led to the attack, the nature and scope of the attack, the player's state of mind at the time of the attack, and the extent of any injury resulting from the attack; or

(iii) at any time, fail, in the sole opinion of the Team's management, to exhibit sufficient skill or competitive ability to qualify to continue as a member of the Team; provided, however, (x) that if this Contract is terminated by the Team, in accordance with the provisions of this subparagraph, prior to January 10 of any Regular Season, and the Player, at the time of such termination, is unfit to play skilled basketball as the result of an injury resulting directly from his playing for the Team, the Player shall (subject to the provisions set forth in Exhibit 3) continue to receive his full Compensation, less all workers' compensation benefits (which, to the extent permitted by law, and if not deducted from the Player's Compensation by the Team, the Player hereby assigns to the Team) and any insurance provided for by the Team paid or payable to the Player by reason of said injury, until such time as the Player is fit to play skilled basketball, but not beyond the Season during which such termination occurred; and provided, further, (y) that if this Contract is terminated by the Team, in accordance with the provisions of this subparagraph, during the period from the January 10 of any Regular Season through the end of such Regular Season, the Player shall be entitled to receive his full Compensation for said Season; or

(iv) at any time, fail, refuse, or neglect to render his services hereunder or in any other manner materially breach this Contract.

(b) If this Contract is terminated by the Team by reason of the Player's failure to render his services hereunder due to disability caused by an injury to the Player resulting directly from his playing for the Team and rendering him unfit to play skilled basketball, and notice of such injury is given by the Player as provided herein, the Player shall (subject to the provisions set forth in Exhibit 3) be entitled to receive his full Compensation for the Season in which the injury was sustained, less all workers' compensation benefits (which, to the extent permitted by law, and if not deducted from the Player's Compensation by the Team, the Player hereby assigns to the Team) and any insurance provided for by the Team paid or payable to the Player by reason of said injury.

(c) Notwithstanding the provisions of subparagraph 16(b) above, if this Contract is terminated by the Team prior to the first game of a Regular Season by reason of the Player's failure to render his services hereunder due to an injury or condition sustained or suffered during a preceding Season, or after such Season but prior to the Player's participation in any basketball practice or game played for the Team, payment by the Team of any Compensation earned through the date of termination under paragraph 3(b) above, payment of the Player's board, lodging, and expense allowance during the training camp period, payment of the reasonable traveling expenses of the Player to his home city, and the expert training and coaching provided by the Team to the Player during the training sea son shall be full payment to the Player.

(d) If this Contract is terminated by the Team during the period designated by the Team for attendance at training camp, payment by the Team of any Compensation earned through the date of termination under paragraph 3(b) above, payment of the Player's board, lodging, and expense allowance during such period to the date of termination, payment of the reasonable traveling expenses of the Player to his home city, and the expert training and coaching

Exhibit 12.2 (continued)

provided by the Team to the Player during the training season shall be full payment to the Player.

(e) If this Contract is terminated by the Team after the first game of a Regular Season, except in the case provided for in subparagraphs (a)(iii) and (b) of this paragraph 16, the Player shall be entitled to receive as full payment hereunder a sum of money which, when added to the salary which he has already received during such Season, will represent the same proportionate amount of the annual sum set forth in Exhibit 1 hereto as the number of days of such Regular Season then past bears to the total number of days of such Regular Season, plus the reasonable traveling expenses of the Player to his home.

(f) If the Team proposes to terminate this Contract in accordance with subparagraph (a) of this paragraph 16, it must first comply with the following waiver procedure:

(i) The Team shall request the NBA Commissioner to request waivers from all other clubs. Such waiver request may not be withdrawn.

(ii) Upon receipt of the waiver request, any other team may claim assignment of this Contract at such waiver price as may be fixed by the League, the priority of claims to be determined in accordance with the NBA Constitution and By-Laws.

(iii) If this Contract is so claimed, the Team agrees that it shall, upon the assignment of this Contract to the claiming team, notify the Player of such assignment as provided in paragraph 10(c) hereof, and the Player agrees he shall report to the assignee team as provided in said paragraph 10(c).

(iv) If the Contract is not claimed, the Team shall promptly deliver written notice of termination to the Player at the expiration of the waiver period.

(v) The NBA shall promptly notify the Players Association of the disposition of any waiver request.

(vi) To the extent not inconsistent with the foregoing pro visions of this subparagraph (f), the waiver procedures set forth in the NBA Constitution and By-Laws, a copy of which, as in effect on the date of this Con tract, is attached hereto, shall govern.

(g) Upon any termination of this Contract by the Player, all obligations of the Team to pay Compensation shall cease on the date of termination, except the obligation of the Team to pay the Player's Compensation to said date.

17. DISPUTES.

In the event of any dispute arising between the Player and the Team relating to any matter arising under this Contract, or concerning the performance or interpretation thereof (except for a dispute arising under paragraph 9 hereof), such dispute shall be resolved in accordance with the Grievance and Arbitration Procedure set forth in the NBA/NBPA Collective Bargaining Agreement.

18. PLAYER NOT A MEMBER.

Nothing contained in this Contract or in any provision of the NBA Constitution and By-Laws shall be construed to constitute the Player a member of the NBA or to confer upon him any of the rights or privileges of a member thereof.

19. RELEASE.

Exhibit 12.2 (continued)

The Player hereby releases and waives every claim he may have against the NBA and its related entities and every member of the NBA, and against every director, officer, owner, stockholder, trustee, partner, and employee of the NBA and its related entities and/or any member of the NBA and their related entities (excluding persons employed as players by any such member), and against any person retained by the NBA and/or the Players Association in connection with the NBA/NBPA Anti-Drug Program, the Grievance Arbitrator, the System Arbitrator, and any other arbitrator or expert retained by the NBA and/or the Players Association under the terms of the NBA/NBPA Collective Bargaining Agreement, arising out of or in connection with (i) any injury that is subject to the provisions of paragraph 7, (ii) any fighting or other form of violent and/or unsportsmanlike conduct occurring during (he course of any practice and/or any Exhibition, Regular Season, and/or Playoff game (on or adjacent to the playing floor or in or adjacent to any facility used for practices or games), (iii) the testing procedures or the imposition of any penalties set forth in paragraph 8 hereof and in the NBA/NBPA Anti-Drug Program, or (iv) any injury suffered in the course of his employment as to which he has or would have a claim for workers compensation benefits. The foregoing shall not apply to any claim of medical malpractice against a Team-affiliated physician or other medical personnel.

20. ENTIRE AGREEMENT.

This Contract (including any Exhibits hereto) contains the entire agreement between the parties and sets forth all components of the Player's Compensation from the Team or any Team Affiliate, and there are no undisclosed agreements of any kind, express or implied, oral or written, promises, undertakings, representations, commitments, inducements, assurances of intent, or understandings of any kind that have not been disclosed to the NBA (a) involving consideration of any kind to be paid, furnished, or made available to the Player, or any person or entity controlled by or related to the Player, by the Team or any Team Affiliate, either during the term of this Contract or thereafter, or (b) concerning any future Renegotiation, Extension, or other amendment of this Contract or the entry into any new Player Contract.

EXAMINE THIS CONTRACT CAREFULLY BEFORE SIGNING IT.

THIS CONTRACT INCLUDES EXHIBITS _____, WHICH ARE ATTACHED HERETO AND MADE A PART HEREOF.

IN WITNESS WHEREOF the Player has hereunto signed his name and the Team has caused this Contract to be executed by its duly authorized officer.

Dated:_____   BY:_____

                     Title:_____

                     Team:_____

Dated: _____   Player:_____

                     Player's Address: _____

Exhibit 12.3
Signing Bonus Form Used by the NFL

SIGNING BONUS

Between _____ and _____
　　　　　　(Club)　　　　　　　　　　(Player)

　　As additional consideration for the execution of NFL Player Contract(s) for the year(s) _____, and for the Player's adherence to all provisions of said contract(s), Club agrees to pay Player the sum of $ _____ .

　　The above sum is payable as follows:

$ _____ upon execution of this rider (Player acknowledges receipt of said sum); and

$ _____ on _____ 19_____ ; and

$ _____ on _____ 19_____ ; and

$ _____ on _____ 19_____ .

　　It is expressly understood that no part of the bonus herein provided is part of any salary in the contract(s) specified above, that said bonus will not be deemed part of any salary in the contract(s) specified above if Club exercises an option for Player's services in a season subsequent to the final contract year, and that such obligations of Club are not terminable if such contract(s) is (are) terminated via the NFL waiver system.

　　In the event Player, in any of the years specified above or an option year, fails or refuses to report to Club, fails or refuses to practice or play with Club, or leaves Club without its consent, then, upon demand by Club, Player will return to Club the proportionate amount of the total bonus not having been earned at the time of Player's default.

Date: _____

Club: _____　　Player: _____

By: _____

---

addressed in the addendum of the contract. Serving the same purpose as the Standard Player Contract, this standardization avoids the potential problems associated with drafting separate, unique bonus clauses for each individual athlete.

Although there is a standard form for the Uniform Player Contract in professional leagues, agents and organizations may make changes to this document to suit their particular needs as long as the clauses do not violate the Collective Bargaining Agreement. The Collective Bargaining Agreement for the NBA includes a section on "allowable amendments" that discusses in what particular ways the agent and the organization can amend certain provisions of the Uniform Player Contract. This section is presented below.

Section 3. Allowable Amendments.

In their individual contract negotiations, a player and a Team may amend the provisions of a Uniform Player Contract, but only in the following respects:

(a) By agreeing upon provisions (to be set forth in Exhibit 1 to a Uniform Player Contract) setting forth the Cash Compensation to be paid or amounts to be loaned to the player for each Season of the Contract for rendering the services described in such Contract.

Exhibit 12.4
Statistical Bonus Provisions in Football, Basketball, and Hockey

FOOTBALL

Quarterback:	250 passing attempts	$
	150 completions	$
	Pass 1,000 yards	$
	Pass 1,500 yards	$
	Pass 2,000 yards	$
	Pass 5 touchdowns	$
	Pass 10 touchdowns	$
Running Back:	Rushes for 400 yards	$
	Catches over 40 passes	$
	Scores 6 touchdowns	$
	Scores 5 touchdowns rushing	$
	Scores 3 touchdowns rushing	$
	Leads NFC or AFC in scoring	$
Defense:	Leads team in total tackles	$
	Leads team in assists	$
	Leads NFL in tackles	$
	Leads NFC in tackles	$
	Leads or ties linebackers in interceptions	$
	Returns interception for touchdown (each)	$
	Leads or ties team in tackles for loss	$
	Fumble recoveries (each recovery)	$
	Ties or leads team in interceptions	$
	Leads NFL in interceptions	$
	Leads NFC in interceptions	$
	Leads or ties team linebackers for quarterback sacks	$
	Quarterback sacks (each sack)	$

BASKETBALL

In addition to other monies Player shall receive the following, if such are attained in any year under this contract:
For averaging over 20 points per game, the sum of $_____ .
For leading the team in scoring, the sum of $_____ .
For leading the NBA in assists or steals, the sum of $_____ .
For being in the top five in the NBA in scoring, the sum of $_____ .

HOCKEY

30 goals or	65 points	$_____ , and
35 goals or	75 points	$_____ , and
40 goals or	85 points	$_____ , and
45 goals or	95 points	$_____ , and
50 goals or	105 points	$_____ .

(b) By agreeing upon provisions (to be set forth in Exhibit 1 to a Uniform Player Contract) setting forth the Non-Cash Compensation to be paid or provided to the player for rendering the services described in such Contract.

(c) By agreeing upon provisions (to be set forth in Exhibit 1 to a Uniform Player Contract) setting forth lump sum bonuses, and the payment schedule therefor, to be paid as a result of: (i) the player's execution of a Uniform Player Contract or Extension (a "signing bonus"), (ii) the exercise or non-exercise of an option pursuant to Articles VII and XII, (iii) the player's achievement of agreed-upon benchmarks relating to his performance as a player or the Team's performance during a particular NBA Season, subject to the limitations imposed by paragraph 3(c) of the Uniform Player Contract, or (iv) the player's achievement of agreed-upon benchmarks relating to his physical condition or academic achievement, including the player's attendance at and partic- ipation in an off-season summer league and/or an off-season skill and conditioning program designated by the Team (subject to the limitations imposed by Section 11(h) below). Any amendment agreed upon pursuant to subsections (iii) or (iv) of this sub- section (c) must be structured so as to provide an incentive for positive achievement by the player and/or the Team; and any amendment agreed upon pursuant to sub- section (iii) must be based upon specific numerical benchmarks or generally recog- nized league honors. By way of example and not limitation, an amendment agreed upon pursuant to subsection (iii) may provide for the player to receive a bonus if his free-throw percentage exceeds 80%, but may not provide for the player to receive a bonus if his free-throw percentage improves over his previous season's percentage.

(d) By agreeing upon provisions (to be set forth in Exhibit 1 to a Uniform Player Contract) with respect to extra promotional appearances to be performed by the player (in addition to those required by paragraph 13 of such Contract) and the Compensation therefor.

(e) By agreeing upon a Compensation payment schedule (to be set forth in Exhibit 1 to a Uniform Player Contract) different from that provided for by paragraph 3(a) of the Uniform Player Contract; provided, however, such amendment shall comply with the provisions of Section 11(f) below and that no such amendment shall be permitted with respect to any Season in which the player's Compensation is not greater than the Minimum Player Salary called for with respect to that Season pursuant to Section 6 below.

(f) By agreeing upon provisions (to be set forth in Exhibit 2 to a Uniform Player Contract) stating that the Cash Compensation provided for by a Uniform Player Con- tract (as described in Exhibit 1 to such Contract) shall be, in whole or in part, and subject to any conditions or limitations, protected or insured (as provided for by, and in accordance with the definitions set forth in, Section 4 below) in the event that such Contract is terminated by the Team by reason of the player's:

    (i) lack of skill;
    (ii) death not covered by an insurance policy procured by a Team for the player's benefit ("non-insured death");
    (iii) death covered by an insurance policy procured by a Team for the player's benefit ("insured death");
    (iv) disability or unfitness to play skilled basketball resulting from a basketball- related injury not covered by an insurance policy procured by a Team for the player's benefit ("non-insured basketball-related injury");
    (v) disability or unfitness to play skilled basketball resulting from any injury or illness not covered by an insurance policy procured by a Team for the player's benefit ("non-insured injury or illness");
    (vi) disability or unfitness to play skilled basketball resulting from an injury or illness covered by an insurance policy procured by a Team for the player's ben- efit ("insured injury or illness");

(vii) mental disability not covered by an insurance policy procured by a Team for the player's benefit ("non-insured mental disability"); and/or

(viii) mental disability covered by an insurance policy procured by a Team for the player's benefit ("insured mental disability").

(g) By agreeing upon provisions (to be set forth in Exhibit 3 to a Uniform Player Contract) limiting or eliminating the player's right to receive his Cash Compensation (in accordance with paragraphs 7(c), 16(a)(iii), and 16(b) of the Uniform Player Contract) when the player's disability or unfitness to play skilled basketball is caused by the re-injury of an injury sustained prior to, or by the aggravation of a condition that existed prior to, the execution of the Uniform Player Contract providing for such Cash Compensation.

(h) By agreeing upon provisions (to be set forth in Exhibit 4 to a Uniform Player Contract) (i) entitling a player to earn Cash Compensation upon the assignment of such player's Uniform Player Contract, or (ii) prohibiting or limiting the Team's right to assign such player's Contract to another Team, subject, however, in either case (i) or (ii) to the provisions of Article XXIV.

(i) By agreeing upon provisions (to be set forth in Exhibit 5 to a Uniform Player Contract) permitting the player to participate or engage in some or all of the activities otherwise prohibited by paragraph 12 of the Uniform Player Contract; provided, however, that paragraph 12 of the Uniform Player Contract may not be amended to permit a player to participate in any public game or public exhibition of basketball not approved in accordance with Article XXIII of this Agreement.

(j) By agreeing upon provisions (to be set forth in Exhibit 6 to a Uniform Player Contract) establishing the date and time of a physical examination of the player to be performed by a physician designated by the Team within seventy-two (72) hours of the execution of the Contract, the passage of such examination by the player (in the sole discretion of the Team) to be a condition precedent to the validity of the player's Uniform Player Contract.

(k) By agreeing to delete clauses (b)(ii) and/or (b)(iii) of paragraph 5 of the Uniform Player Contract in their entirety.

(l) By agreeing to delete paragraph 7(b) of the Uniform Player Contract in its entirety and substituting therefor the provision set forth in Exhibit 7 to a Uniform Player Contract.

(m) By agreeing either (i) to delete paragraph 13(b) of the Uniform Player Contract in its entirety, or (ii) to delete the last sixteen words of paragraph 13(b) of such Contract.

(n) By agreeing upon provisions for the purpose of terminating an already-existing Uniform Player Contract prior to the expiration of its stated term, stating as follows: (i) that the Team will request waivers on the player in accordance with paragraph 16 of the Contract immediately following the Commisssioner's approval of such amendment; and (ii) should the player clear waivers and his Contract thereupon be terminated, that the amount of any Cash Compensation protection or insurance contained in the Contract will immediately be reduced or eliminated. In addition to the foregoing, the parties may also agree that (x) as a result of the termination of the Contract, the payment schedule for any Compensation remaining to be paid will be accelerated over a shorter period or stretched over a longer period (subject, however, to Section 11(f) below), and/or (y) that the Team's right of set-off under Article XXVII of this Agreement will be modified or eliminated.

(o) By agreeing upon provisions (to be set forth in Exhibit 8 to a Uniform Player Contract) stating that the Contract will be assigned to another team within forty-eight (48) hours of its execution, such assignment and the consummation of such assignment to be conditions precedent to the validity of the Contract; provided, however, that any such sign-and-trade transaction must comply with Article VII, Section 8(e).

Once an agent representing the player and management reach an agreement on a final contract proposal, it is usually up to the athlete to give his approval to the agent, at which point the contract is formed. After consummation of the contract, the player is legally bound to perform to the best of his abilities during the term of the contract, and management must perform its part by remunerating the athlete as expressed in the agreement.

Although both sides are committed to the agreement legally, a common issue in pro sports has been renegotiation of contracts. The athlete will often initiate renegotiation after a season in which he performed well beyond the expectations at the time of the original agreement, or the market for a player of this caliber has shifted upward. For example, a baseball player who signs a long-term contract early in his career may be well underpaid by the end of his contract due to the rapid salary escalation in Major League Baseball. From a management perspective, the club is not obligated to consider the athlete's request; however, teams are often compelled to do so in order to keep the player happy and motivated. Most clubs have established policies regarding renegotiation, which vary from firm non-renegotiation to frequent renegotiation. One of the most common alternatives used by many teams is to reward players by adding on years at the end of a contract at an increased salary, and possibly combining this with a signing bonus. Professional basketball contracts are not renegotiable.

A team will normally initiate renegotiation for one of two reasons. First, especially in baseball, a team will decide to "lock up" a player in order to avoid salary arbitration (see Chapter 11, section 11.3.15., "Salary Arbitration") or to delay free agency (see Chapter 11, section 11.3.9., "Free Agency"). In 1999, the Colorado Rockies were obligated to pay their star second-year first baseman, Todd Helton, only the minimum salary of $200,000. However, Helton's agent, Mike Moye, negotiated a four-year, $12 million contract with the Rockies prior to the season. Why would the Rockies agree to this? Because the Rockies were concerned that after 2000 (Helton's third full year), he would command much more than this amount in salary arbitration. Then, in 2001, the Rockies "tore up" Helton's 1999 contract and replaced it with an eleven-year, $151 million contract. Why would the Rockies agree to this? Because the Rockies felt that after 2003 (Helton's sixth full year), he would command much more than this amount on the free agent market.

The second reason that teams, especially NFL teams, initiate renegotiation is to fit veteran players under the salary cap or under a team's budgetary constraints. In the NFL, where contracts are not guaranteed, teams may convince a player that if he does not renegotiate his contract, he will be released. In Major League Baseball, where contracts *are* guaranteed, a team may convince certain players to defer money in order to improve the team's cash flow. For example, several Arizona Diamondback veteran players agreed to defer contractual payments prior to the 2001 season.

12.5. RELATIONSHIP OF PLAYERS ASSOCIATION AND AGENTS

The players association for a professional league is the organization that works on the athlete's behalf when negotiating the Collective Bargaining Agreement with league officials (see Chapter 11, section 11.3.7., "Collective Bargaining in Professional Sports"). These associations are recognized by the National Labor Relations Board (see Chapter 11, section 11.1.6., "National Labor Relations

Board"). However, the responsibilities of a players association go beyond simply negotiating and administering the Collective Bargaining Agreement. Players associations also designate the right to negotiate individual contracts to the agents, while continuing to oversee and monitor the process, and also holding the power to repeal this right. Since functions of players associations were discussed extensively in Chapter 11, this section will focus on the relationship between the players association and the agents who represent players within a league.

Although the players associations have many responsibilities, one of their primary functions is to negotiate the Collective Bargaining Agreement with the league, which sets forth the terms and conditions of employment for the players, including minimum salaries and other benefits (see Chapter 11, section 11.3.7., "Collective Bargaining Agreements in Professional Sports").

Beyond their primary responsibility of negotiating and administering the league Collective Bargaining Agreement, players associations also work with players who have filed for grievance arbitration, as per the Collective Bargaining Agreement, with the league. Players associations utilize a wide variety of resources including experienced labor attorneys to work with the agent. However, it is usually the players association attorney who has the primary responsibility during the grievance procedure.

Perhaps the most important aspect of the relationship between the agent and the players association is the association's involvement in negotiating individual contracts. The association actually has the right to negotiate contracts on an individual basis for each of its players, but it generally transfers this right to the agent while still overseeing the entire process. It is in the best interest of the players association to keep a close eye on contract negotiations because "bad" contracts can cause a "ripple effect" within the league. If a star player, who theoretically "deserves" to make $2 million, is underpaid due to the incompetence of his or her agent, and receives only $1 million, players with similar abilities and histories may have difficulty arguing that they should make any more than $1 million even if they are worth more. Furthermore, in NHL and MLB salary arbitration (see Chapter 11, section 11.3.15., "Salary Arbitration"), arbitrators may be compelled to award a salary arbitration eligible player a lesser amount of money after another player at his position signs for less than his "market value" salary. Both the Major League Baseball Players Association and National Hockey League Players Association are actively involved in the process of salary arbitration between teams and players.

Marketing is another area in which players associations are actively involved. Players associations are charged with providing licensing rights for trading cards and other products that bear the likenesses of players within the league (see Chapter 13, section 13.1.5., "Trademark Infringement"). Players associations also handle group licensing contracts that provide revenue to the association, which is divided equally among all players in the league.

Another important feature of the relationship between the agent and the players association is the registration and certification process that agents need to undergo to become licensed to represent athletes and negotiate contracts in various professional leagues. These players associations are moving to control the player-representative relationship in order to prevent unprincipled, unintelligent and unprepared agents from representing clients within their players association.

The National Football League, as a result of provisions inserted into the 1982 Collective Bargaining Agreement, set a precedent for all professional sports leagues. The NFL Players Association, pursuant to those provisions, imposed registration and other requirements, including maximum fee schedules, on all agents acting as contract advisers for NFL players. The following are the requirements for an agent to receive certification from the National Football League:

1. A completed application and a *non-refundable* application fee of $1,200 if representing less than 10 active players; $1,700 if representing 10 or more active players
2. A degree from an accredited four-year college/university
3. Mandatory attendance at a two-day seminar in Washington, DC
4. Successful completion of written, proctored examination

These regulations are in place in the NFL for any person who wishes to provide representation services to any player in the NFL, including rookies. Other professional sports players associations have followed the NFLPA's lead and established guidelines for the registration and regulation of agents. The National Basketball Associations's Collective Bargaining Agreement contains the following restrictions on player agents:

Article XXXVI: Player Agents

Section 1. Approval of Player Contracts. The NBA shall not approve any Player Contract between a player and a Team unless such player: (i) is represented in the negotiations with respect to such Player Contract by an agent or representative duly certified by the Players Association in accordance with the Players Association's Agent Regulation Program and authorized to represent him; or (ii) acts on his own behalf in negotiating such Player Contract.

Section 2. Fines. The NBA shall impose a fine of $20,000 upon any Team that negotiates a Player Contract with an agent or representative not certified by the Players Association in accordance with the Players Association's Agent Regulation Program if, at the time of such negotiations, such Team either (i) knows that such agent or representative has not been so certified or (ii) fails to make reasonable inquiry of the NBA as to whether such agent or representative has been so certified. Notwithstanding the preceding sentence, in no event shall any Team be subject to a fine if the Team negotiates a Player Contract with the agent designated as the player's authorized agent on the then-current agent list provided by the Players Association to the NBA in accordance with Section 4 below.

The final facet of the relationship between the player agent and players associations concerns the role of the players associations in resolving disputes between players and their agents. Players associations have taken the responsibility of settling any disputes that arise over fees or the interpretation of contracts through an arbitration process. The following excerpt is taken from the Major League Baseball Players Association Regulations Governing Player Agents:

Section 5

Introduction

In establishing this new system for regulating Player Agents it is the intention of the MLBPA that the impartial arbitration process shall be the exclusive method for resolving any and all disputes between Players and Player Agents that arise out of agreements or contracts between them. This will insure that all such disputes—which involve essentially internal matters concerning the relationship between individual Players, the MLBPA in its capacity as their exclusive bargaining representative, and Player Agents performing certain specified representative functions—will be handled and resolved expeditiously by the neutral decision-maker established herein, instead of through more costly and time-consuming formal court proceedings.

Specifically, the provisions of this section shall apply with respect to two types of disputes: (a) those between a Player and a Player Agent with respect to the existence, meaning, interpretation, or enforcement of any contract between them; and (b) those between a Player and the MLBPA concerning any action taken by the MLBPA in connection with certification.

(A) Procedure for Resolving Player-Player Agent Disputes

The following procedure shall apply to disputes between a Player and Player Agent with respect to the existence, meaning, interpretation, or enforcement of any contract or agreement between them.

1. *Filing*

A Player or Player Agent shall initiate the dispute resolution procedure by filing a written grievance setting forth in plain and understandable terms the facts and circumstances giving rise to the grievance, the provision(s) of the agreement(s) alleged to have been violated, and the relief sought. Any such grievance must be timely filed and served on the other party, with copy to the Association, within one hundred eighty (180) days from the later of (a) the date of the occurrence of the event upon which the grievance is based, (b) the date on which the facts became known or reasonably should have become known to the grievant, or (c) the effective date of these Regulations.

If a *Player* initiates any such grievance, he must serve the written grievance by mail or personal delivery to the Player Agent's official business address and must furnish a copy of the grievance to the Association, in an envelope marked "Attention: Agent Regulation," at the Association's offices located at 805 Third Avenue, New York, NY 10022.

If the *Player Agent* initiates any such grievance, he must serve the player by mail or personal delivery to the Player at either the Player's permanent or in-season residence and must furnish a copy of the grievance to the Association in the same manner as required in the case of a Player-filing.

2. *Answer*

The party against whom a grievance has been filed ("the respondent") shall answer the grievance in writing by mail or personal delivery within thirty (30) days of receipt of the grievance. The respondent must also provide a copy of his answer to the Association at the same time. The Answer shall admit or deny the facts alleged in the grievance and shall also set forth briefly the reasons why the respondent believes that the grievance should be denied.

3. *Arbitration*

The MLBPA shall then notify both parties in writing that their disputes will referred to arbitration.

4. *Arbitrator*

Promptly after the effective date of these Regulations, the MLBPA shall name one or more professional and skilled impartial arbitrators to serve as the Impartial Arbitrator of a dispute subject to this Section 5(A).

5. *Proceedings*

Promptly after the Impartial Arbitrator is notified by the MLBPA of a pending case, he shall schedule a hearing on the dispute in New York City, or in such city as the parties, with the concurrence of the Impartial Arbitrator, may agree upon, or in such city as the Impartial Arbitrator may on his own motion direct. At such hearing, the parties—the Player and the Player Agent—may appear in person or by legal counsel or other representative. The parties to the dispute and the MLBPA, as well, will have the right to present, by testimony or otherwise, any evidence deemed by the Impartial Arbitrator to be relevant to the grievance.

The rules of the procedure hearings shall be established by the Impartial Arbitrator and, to the extent deemed practicable to him, shall conform to the Voluntary Labor Arbitration Rules of the American Arbitration Association.

Upon close of the hearing, the Impartial Arbitrator will advise the parties and the MLBPA whether he desires Briefs to be filed or whether he desires the parties and MLBPA to present their arguments orally. The Impartial Arbitrator shall fix the time Briefs are to be filed or the time and place oral arguments are to be presented.

Within thirty (30) days after the receipt of Briefs or the presentation of oral arguments, the Impartial Arbitrator shall issue a written award, including an appropriate remedy if the grievance is sustained. That award shall constitute a full, final, and complete resolution of the grievance and will be binding on the Player and Player Agent involved.

6. *Costs*

Each party will bear the costs of its own witnesses and counsel. Costs of arbitration, including the fees and expenses of the Impartial Arbitrator, will be borne equally between the two parties to the grievance; provided, however, that if the Arbitrator concludes that a party's case is frivolous, he may assess that party with some or all of the opposing party's costs. If the Impartial Arbitrator grants a money award, it shall be paid within thirty (30) days, or such other period as he may direct.

Hearings ordinarily will be transcribed unless the parties and the MLBPA, with the concurrence of the Impartial Arbitrator, agree otherwise, or unless the Impartial Arbitrator so directs. Costs of the transcript, the making of which will be arranged by the Association, will be divided equally among the parties and MLBPA.

7. *Time Limits*

When a dispute has not yet been noticed to the Impartial Arbitrator, the time limits of this Section 5(A) may be extended by the Association, upon good cause shown by either party. Such requests for an extension of time shall be in writing, and served on the opposing party. When a dispute has been noticed to the Impartial Arbitrator, the time limits of this Section may be extended to the Impartial Arbitrator, upon good cause shown by either party or the MLBPA. Such requests for an extension of time shall be in writing, and, if filed by a party, served on the opposing party and MLBPA, or, if filed by the MLBPA, served on both parties.

NOTES

1. In the arbitration case of *Rona v. Major League Baseball Players Association*, the MLBPA was trying to prevent Barry Rona from becoming a certified agent for baseball players because he had been deeply involved in a collusion scandal (see Chapter 11, section 11.4.4., "Baseball Collusion Cases") against free agency by owners within the league. Rona was former executive director and general counsel of the Player Relations Committee, the owners' labor unit. The association was attempting to deny Rona certification because in their own rules and regulations it is stated that the association may bar any agent whose conduct "may adversely affect his credibility [or] integrity . . . to serve in a representative and/or fiduciary capacity on behalf of the players." The independent arbitrator, Collins, concluded that the MLBPA did not have any solid evidence of Rona's wrongdoing in the collusion cases, only that he was the legal counsel for some of the figures in the case. Because the MLBPA had denied Rona's certification on these grounds, Collins decided that the MLBPA's ruling was arbitrary and capricious, and ordered that Rona be certified as an agent by the MLBPA.

2. In the case of *Collins v. NBPA*, 850 F. Supp. 1468 (D. Colo. 1991), an agent who had his certification revoked by the National Basketball Players Association sought to regain his certification, claiming that the NBPA certification process broke antitrust laws

because it constituted a group boycott, and that the dismissal was unfair because it had been based on Collins's breach of fiduciary duties as a investment agent and money manager, but not as a sports agent. The court concluded that the NBPA was allowed under the labor exemption provided by the Sherman Act to have a certification process. Secondly, the court decided that, in acting in the best interests of their players, the NBPA could investigate the outside actions of players agents.

3. The registration guidelines for NFL player agents can be found at the NFLPA Web site, www.nflpa.org/agents/main.asp?subPage=Agent+Regulations

4. For more information on the registration guidelines for agent certification in major professional team sports, the players associations can be contacted at the following addresses:

a. Major League Baseball Players Association
12 East 49th Street
24th Floor
New York, NY 10017
212-826-0808
www.bigleaguers.yahoo.com

b. National Football League Players Association
2021 L Street, N.W.
Suite 600
Washington, DC 20036
800-372-2000
www.nflpa.org

c. National Basketball Players Association
1700 Broadway, Suite 1400
New York, NY 10019
(212) 655–0880
www.nbpa.com

d. National Hockey League Players Association
777 Bay Street
Suite 2400
Toronto, ON
M5G 2C8
www.nhlpa.com

12.5.1. Salary Information

Contracts negotiated by agents can include a variety of salary items, including a base salary, signing bonus, training camp reporting bonuses, and deferred compensation packages. Signing bonuses are popular with draft picks because they give the rookie a nice payout before the first year in the professional league. Signing bonuses are also available in Major League Baseball and the National Hockey League, where many players also have guaranteed contracts. The NFL does not have many guaranteed contracts, which makes signing bonuses very attractive for unproven players, since it is the only guaranteed compensation that they will receive. The National Basketball Association does not employ signing bonuses; however, most contracts in the league are guaranteed.

Comparing the four professional leagues—National Basketball Association, National Football League, National Hockey League, and Major League Baseball—the highest average salary is paid in the sport of basketball (NBA), with Major League Baseball not far behind. Exhibits 12.5 through 12.10 contain information on salaries or team payrolls for each of the "Big Four" professional sports leagues.

12.6. FUNCTIONS OF THE PLAYER AGENT

Agents who represent professional athletes are called on to render a wide variety of services for their clients. The diversity of services, in fact, is such that it is unreasonable to expect one individual to master all the knowledge and skills necessary to accomplish the tasks required. Among other realities, this has led to a separation of law and management functions, and player representatives are examining a number of options that would allow them to provide all the services required by today's professional athletes.

The traditional role of the player agent has been to negotiate the player's

Exhibit 12.5
2002 Major League Baseball Team and Player Salaries

Rank	Team	Opening Day Payroll	Average Salary
1	Yankees	$125,928,583	$4,342,365
2	Red Sox	$108,366,060	$3,612,202
3	Rangers	$105,302,124	$3,631,108
4	D-Backs	$102,820,000	$3,115,758
5	Dodgers	$94,850,952	$3,648,114
6	Mets	$94,633,593	$3,639,754
7	Braves	$93,470,367	$3,015,173
8	Mariners	$80,282,668	$3,211,307
9	Indians	$78,909,448	$2,630,315
10	Giants	$78,299,835	$2,899,994
11	Blue Jays	$76,864,333	$2,650,494
12	Cubs	$75,690,833	$2,703,244
13	Cardinals	$74,098,267	$2,849,933
14	Astros	$63,448,417	$2,349,941
15	Angels	$61,721,667	$2,204,345
16	Orioles	$60,493,487	$1,890,421
17	Phillies	$57,955,000	$2,069,821
18	White Sox	$57,052,833	$2,113,068
19	Rockies	$56,851,043	$2,105,594
20	Tigers	$55,048,000	$1,966,000
21	Brewers	$50,287,833	$1,734,063
22	Royals	$47,257,000	$1,629,552
23	Reds	$45,050,390	$1,501,680
24	Pirates	$42,323,598	$1,459,434
25	Marlins	$41,979,917	$1,499,283
26	Padres	$41,425,000	$1,428,448
27	Twins	$40,225,000	$1,547,115
28	Athletics	$39,679,746	$1,469,620
29	Expos	$38,670,500	$1,381,089
30	Devil Rays	$34,380,000	$1,227,857
	Total/Average	**$2,023,366,494**	**$2,384,236**

contract and represent the athlete on any other law-related issues with the club. Representation today may also include marketing of the player's name; arranging and negotiating personal appearances; offering financial and investment advice, tax planning and tax return preparation, and personal, legal, and financial counseling. An athlete must consider either retaining different advisers for legal, financial, and investment advice, or a small firm that subcontracts and/or coordinates the various services, or a multifaceted management group that can provide all of these services within one company. With demands for the full range of services coming to the fore, pressures are mounting to set up a business organization that will respond to a plethora of needs.

The move in the agency market toward agencies offering a "conglomerate" of services has truly changed the way agents approach signing an athlete. In the

Exhibit 12.6
2001 NBA First Round Picks and Contract Status

Pick # and Player Chosen	Drafting Team	Salary Maximum
1. Kwame Brown-Glynn Academy HS	Wizards	3 years, $11.9 millio
2. Tyson Chandler-Dominguez HS	Bulls	3 years, $8.741 milli
3. Pau Gasol-Spain	Grizzlies	3 years, $7.85 millio
4. Eddy Curry-Thornwood HS	Bulls	3 years, $7.077 milli
5. Jason Richardson-Michigan St. University	Warriors	3 years, $6.409 milli
6. Shane Battier-Duke University	Grizzlies	3 years, $5.821 milli
7. Eddie Griffin-Seton Hall University	Rockets	3 years, $5.314 milli
8. De Sagana Diop-Oak Hill Academy HS	Cavaliers	3 years, $4.868 milli
9. Rodney White-UNC-Charlotte	Pistons	3 years, $4.475 milli
10. Joe Johnson-University of Arkansas	Celtics	3 years, $4.251 milli
11. Kendrick Brown-Okaloosa-Walton CC	Celtics	3 years, $4.038 milli
12. Vladimir Radmanovic-Yugoslavia	Sonics	3 years, $3.836 milli
13. Richard Jefferson-University of Arizona	Nets	3 years, $3.644 milli
14. Troy Murphy-University of Notre Dame	Warriors	3 years, $3.462 milli
15. Steven Hunter-Depaul University	Magic	3 years, $3.289 milli
16. Kirk Haston-Indiana University	Hornets	3 years, $3.125 milli
17. Michael Bradley-Villanova University	Raptors	3 years, $2.968 milli
18. Jason Collins-Stanford University	Nets	3 years, $2.820 milli
19. Zach Randolph-Michigan State University	Blazers	3 years, $2.693 milli
20. Brendan Haywood-UNC-Chapel Hill	Wizards	3 years, $2.585 milli
21. Joseph Forte-UNC-Chapel Hill	Celtics	3 years, $2.482 milli
22. Jeryl Sasser-Southern Methodist University	Magic	3 years, $2.383 milli
23. Brandon Armstrong-Pepperdine University	Nets	3 years, $2.287 milli
24. Raul Lopez-Spain	Jazz	3 years, $2.196 milli
25. Gerald Wallace-University of Alabama	Kings	3 years, $2.108 milli
26. Samuel Dalembert-Seton Hall University	76ers	3 years, $2.038 milli
27. Jamaal Tinsley-Iowa State University	Grizzlies	3 years, $1.979 milli
28. Tony Parker-France	Spurs	3 years, $1.967 milli

Source: ESPN.com 7/23/01

National Football League, for example, an agent is allowed to receive a maximum of 3% of his client's total contract. Agents are free, however, to set a higher percentage of compensation on other contracts, such as endorsements. Agents may take anywhere from 10% to 25% of the total compensation for athlete endorsements. This high percentage on endorsement contracts explains why so many people are willing to get into the field of player representation when the maximum commission on a contract is only 3%.

While 3% is a maximum commission, in the competitive world of athlete representation, many agents will work for a lower percentage in an attempt to gain clients. Also, with the introduction of salary caps in the NBA and NFL, the amount of money that players are making is not increasing at the same pace it was in the mid-1990s. Also, with salary scales (NBA) or rookie salary maximums (NBA), some superstars have negotiated contracts without an agent. These ath-

Exhibit 12.7
Major League Baseball Average Player Salaries

1989	$497,254	1995	$1,110,766
1990	$597,537	1996	$1,119,981
1991	$851,492	1997	$1,336,609
1992	$1,028,667	1998	$1,398,831
1993	$1,076,089	1999	$1,606,770
1994	$1,168,263	2000	$1,988,034

Source: Major League Baseball Players Association

Exhibit 12.8
National Football League Average Player Salaries

1989	$389,000	1995	$752,000
1990	$430,000	1996	$807,000
1991	$488,000	1997	$725,000
1992	$551,000	1998	$1,000,000
1993	$729,000	1999	$1,043,000
1994	$674,000	2000	$1,200,000

Source: National Football League Players Association

Exhibit 12.9
National Basketball Association Average Player Salaries

1989-90	$653,000	1995-96	$1,636,000
1990-91	$823,000	1996-97	$1,979,000
1991-92	$1,003,000	1997-98	$2,297,000
1992-93	$1,113,000	1998-99	$2,640,000
1993-94	$1,296,000	1999-00	$3,180,000
1994-95	$1,441,000		

Source: National Basketball Player's Association

Exhibit 12.10
National Hockey League Average Player Salaries

1990-91	$271,000	1995-96	$892,000
1991-92	$368,000	1996-97	$984,500
1992-93	$467,000	1997-98	$1,167,713
1993-94	$572,161	1998-99	$1,297,649
1994-95	$733,000	1999-00	$1,355,201

Source: National Hockey League Players Association

letes hire an attorney to review the contract on an hourly basis, and therefore pay thousands, not millions, of dollars in fees. Players who have done this include Ray Allen and Chris Webber in the NBA. Agency conglomerates, which include marketing firms, player agents, and financial advisers, were formed in order to provide the athlete with "total representation," and also provide an agency more avenues to produce revenues. Companies such as IMG, SFX, Assante, and Octagon have been among the leaders in this consolidation of services under one umbrella organization. While some agents still work alone or in small partnerships (e.g., the Scott Boras Corporation in baseball), the trend in the sports agency business is toward companies that can provide individualized service to players by offering a wide range of functions under one organization.

Some players seek the services of an agent who has a unique specialization that makes him or her especially appealing. For example, Herbert Rudoy is an attorney based in Chicago who specializes in representing European basketball players who play in the NBA. His client list includes Tony Kukoc, Arvydis Sabonis, and Zydrunas Ilgauskas of the NBA. Players may sign with Rudoy because he has knowledge of the unique situations faced by European players in the NBA, and maintains contacts in Europe should the athlete return to Europe to play.

Agents use a variety of methods to charge their clients for services rendered. The most common is for an agent to take a percentage of the total value of the player contract—anywhere from 3% to 10%. Some agents will represent a player in contract negotiation for a predetermined fee, regardless of the time spent or the amount of the contract. Agents may also elect to charge an hourly rate—usually between $100 and $300. The other alternative is a combination of a stated percentage (usually less than 7%) and a predetermined or hourly fee, whichever is less.

One disadvantage for the athlete in agreeing to pay an hourly fee to the agent is that the athlete is obligated to that agent even if he or she doesn't make the team. However, if the athlete makes the team, the fee based on an hourly rate may be less than the contingency fee. If the athlete and agent have agreed to a contingency fee, however, there is no obligation to pay the agent if the athlete does not make the team. On the other hand, the athlete may find paying an hourly fee to the agent a disadvantage if the agent extends the contract negotiations are protracted. These fees can become enormous in view of the salaries paid to some of today's superstar athletes. The escalation of player salaries has made the percentage method very popular among agents. Because of the tremendous amount of money available, some agents are tempted to lure top athletes illegally, even while they are still in school.

The point to remember is that the player representative is in a business that demands a number of services. Before proceeding with other considerations, such as the legal and ethical constraints placed on player representatives, the functions themselves must be considered. In the following sections, the basic functions of a sports agent will be discussed briefly. As can be seen, negotiating contracts only constitutes one aspect of the sports agent's job.

NOTES ————————————————————————————

1. For more information on trends in agency, see Kenneth L. Shropshire, *Agents of Opportunity: Sports Agents and Corruption in Collegiate Sports*, 2nd ed. (Philadelphia: University of Pennsylvania Press, 2001).

2. The following excerpt is from an information pamphlet that was sent to prospective professional athletes by a sports consulting firm that was attempting to establish itself:

What We Do

Contract negotiation: We deal directly with management to obtain the maximum commitment regarding salary, benefits and contract provisions.

Endorsements and appearances: We will seek to supplement our clients' regular income by promoting product endorsements and personal appearances. We will both pursue appearance possibilities and negotiate on our clients' behalf for endorsement fees.

Investments: We will review investment recommendations and proposals with our investment consultants. In addition, we will draw upon investment research from several investment banking and brokerage firms to augment our investment consultants.

Financial planning, insurance, legal and tax matters: We will also:

1. Evaluate our clients' financial condition and establish a proper plan to insure maximum use of present and future earnings.

2. Have outside insurance consultants analyze our clients' insurance programs and make recommendations as to adequacy of individual and group life, health and accident and disability insurance programs. We will make recommendations to our clients according to their needs after reviewing our consultants' proposals.

3. Provide complete legal advice in all areas of general law as they may affect our clients' needs.

4. Prepare personal Federal, state and other necessary tax returns—and provide complete professional advice on foreign tax matters, tax-sheltered investments and other areas of tax specialization.

Our policy will be to care for the normal needs of the client and this effort will be incorporated into the negotiation fee.

Our clientele will be normally drawn from those who are not superstars and it is our feeling that we should not charge them excessively. We are sure that our fees are at least ½ to ⅓ of those fees charged by other people in the athletic representative field.

We want to establish a feeling of honesty and fairness with our clients. We are sure that from our clients will come superstars with whom we will become more involved. But, we will always maintain a policy of providing low cost and honest service to the average professional athlete.

In most cases, our advice to the athletes will be to let their money grow in savings or in AAA bonds. Then, when they have reached superstar status and/or have a large enough cash base, we will have them diversify their investments.

Outside Consultants

Investment advisers. We will receive investment advice from professional investment counselors and investment banking and brokerage firms. Our investment counselors include:

Investment Banking and Brokerage Houses.

We work closely with several brokerage houses including [names of firms].

Investment research and recommendations which are acted upon by us will realize brokerage commissions to those firms. Therefore, there will be no outside fee expense in conjunction with such investments.

Attorneys and tax specialists. We receive legal and tax advice from several major law firms.

Insurance, pensions, profit sharing, etc. Our insurance consultants include representatives and managers of several major insurance companies—to include: [names of firms].

Advertising consultants. Our advertising consultants are creative directors, artists and copywriters at several advertising agencies and provide leads of client firms seeking professional athletes as well as advice on public relations, fee schedules and promotions.

12.6.1. Negotiating

The player agent must be able to obtain the necessary background information, map the appropriate strategies, and have the flexibility to counter alternatives in order to represent the client effectively. When entering into contract negotiations for a client, the agent must be prepared, not only in terms of the issues to be brought up, but also in regard to refuting or responding to management's claims.

A good agent will know the market value of his client, based on salaries of comparable players (position, ability, service). The agent should also have detailed information about the team with respect to his client's likelihood of success, chances of starting, depth at client's position, and the negotiation history of the club. This type of preparation is of paramount importance if an optimal contract is to be negotiated.

One important point to remember in the sports context is that, in a sense, one rarely stops negotiating. The signed contract is usually only the first step. A number of occurrences during the term of the contract may call for even greater skill on the part of the negotiator, a point emphasized later in the chapter.

A second important point is the interconnections between the negotiating function and the functions described below. One cannot, and should not, attempt to completely isolate one from the others. As noted earlier, a single individual cannot effectively handle all functions, at least not in most situations. So knowing how to deal with the overlaps while dividing the functions efficiently calls for careful thought, planning, and organizational structure.

In the sports of baseball and hockey an agent may also have to deal with the process of salary arbitration. This process, unique to these sports, may necessitate the agent's employing outside assistance from a person(s) with expertise in this particular field.

NOTES

1. In *Detroit Lions, Inc. v. Argovitz*, 580 F.Supp. 542 (E.D. Mich. 1984), Detroit Lions free agent running back Billy Sims, under the guidance of his agent, Jerry Argovitz, signed a contract with the Houston Gamblers on July 1, 1983. On December 16, 1983, Sims signed a second contract with Detroit, and filed a complaint in Oakland County Circuit Court seeking a determination that the July 1, 1983, contract between Sims and the Houston Gamblers was invalid because the defendant, Jerry Argovitz, breached his fiduciary duty when negotiating the Gamblers contract. The court concluded that Argovitz breached his duty to Sims by having significant ownership interest in the Houston franchise, and not representing him properly in contract negotiations with Detroit. The contract between Sims and Houston was rescinded by the court.

2. In *Brown v. Woolf*, 554 F.Supp. 1206 (S.D. Ind. 1983), a professional athlete brought action for constructive fraud and breach of fiduciary duty against the defendant agent. The athlete claimed the agent negotiated a contract for him with a new team of the National Hockey League. After reaching an agreement for compensation, the new team began to have financial difficulties and eventually defaulted on their contractual obligations. Plaintiff claimed he was paid only $185,000 of the total $800,000 contract, but the defendant agent received his full $40,000 fee (5% of the contract). Plaintiff also contended the agent breached his fiduciary duty to the plaintiff by failing to conduct any investigation into the financial stability of the new team. The district court denied the defendant's motion for a summary judgment.

3. In *Zinn v. Parrish*, 644 F.2d 360 (7th Cir. 1981), an agent recovered damages after being terminated by a player. Leo Zinn, the agent for Cincinatti Bengals cornerback Lemar Parrish, was successful in recovering after Parrish terminated him in 1974, shortly after Zinn negotiated a four-year contract for Parrish. Zinn sought to recover his 10% commission on the 1974–1977 contracts, and did so. The court ruled that Zinn fulfilled the terms of the contract to use reasonable efforts to procure professional football employment, despite failing to obtain jobs or contracts in many cases, it was not a failure to perform.

4. In *Buse v. Vanguard Group of Investment Cos.*, No. 91-3560, 1996 U.S. Dist. LEXIS 19033 (E.D. Pa. Dec. 20, 1996), an athlete filed suit against an investment company, after his agent misrepresented his pension and retirement plan. The plaintiff (Buse) argued that

the Vanguard Group should be liable for complying with a request from the plaintiff's agent (Skinner) to liquidate one half of his pension plan and mail it to the agent on the behalf of Buse. The court held for the plaintiff, agreeing that these actions constituted a breach of fiduciary duty.

5. In *Pro Tect Management Corp. v. Worley*, No. 89 Civ. 3026, U.S. Dist. LEXIS 14574, at *1 (S.D.N.Y. Oct. 30, 1990), an agent whose contract with a player made prior to the NFL draft was terminated in favor for another, sued for breach of contract.

12.6.2. Counseling

Counseling is an often overlooked function of vital importance, both during negotiations and after the contract is signed. Making certain the client understands what is at stake in a professional sports contract may prevent later disillusionments.

For the non-superstar, the contract may be largely illusory, in that it exists only if the player makes the team. There are no guarantees. Such rudimentary facts are not always grasped by the client. Making the team and contract rights are not always paired in the client's mind. Such information must be conveyed.

After the contract is signed, other problems call for counseling. For example, the player makes the team but is sitting on the bench. Personal frustrations become predominant. Players may also have family problems that an agent can assuage, or damaging outside influences that an agent can steer his or her client away from. As will be discussed in the following section, agents must also direct their clients in business matters, because these are not generally areas where the athlete has any formal experience. In these and many other contexts, the counseling function is crucial.

12.6.3. Managing

Many athletes come out of college with little self-discipline and an almost total lack of knowledge about financial matters. The money soon disappears if the client is left unsupervised.

Not all player representatives get into money management, and those who do not, should advise the client as to where such assistance can be obtained. An ongoing relationship between the representative and a firm that deals in management and investments should be explored. Agents who are not experienced in financial matters should be careful when managing their client's money. As evidenced by the case of *People v. Sorkin* (see note 1), it is in the best interests of an agent who is not experienced in financial matters to hire the outside assistance of someone who is experienced.

NOTES

1. In *People v. Sorkin*, 407 N.Y.S.2d 772 (N.Y. App. Div 1978), Richard Sorkin, an agent for several New York Islanders of the NHL, was sentenced to jail for grand larceny. He pleaded guilty to stealing $360,000 from players he represented. He had lost almost $300,000 in the stock market due to poor investments, and also had lost $600,000 to bookmakers. Sorkin was representing over 300 players at the height of his representation career.

2. In *Jones v. Childers*, 18 F.3d 1899 (11th Cir. 1994), an NFL player (Gordon Jones) brought a successful suit against his agent and financial advisor for fraud, negligence, breach of contract and breach of fiduciary duty.

3. In January 2002, a federal jury found sports agent William "Tank" Black guilty of fraud, conspiracy and obstruction of justice in the theft of up to $14 million from professional football players he represented. The case centered on testimony from NFL players who claimed Black used his position as their agent to steal millions from them through bogus investments. Black was sentenced to five years in prison.

12.6.4. Marketing

There is a prevailing attitude, although a mistaken one, that most professional athletes do well because of lucrative endorsements and other types of outside income. In truth, such wealth is largely reserved for the top stars. Other athletes do what they can do to supplement their income with personal appearances at local clubs, dinners, commercial establishments, and other less-than-top-dollar affairs. Even so, the possibilities for some types of outside income does exist. How aggressively they are sought on behalf of the client varies with the representative, but some willingness of the representative to assist the client in seeking supplementary income is demanded. With that in mind, a few rules and regulations should be noted.

First, chances are that either the player's contract with the club or the league's Collective Bargaining Agreement will have some provisions regarding endorsements. These should be reviewed before any action is taken. Second, the other side of the marketing issue is being vigilant about protecting the player's name and image. These are property rights capable of protection under a variety of legal theories, including rights of publicity and privacy (see Chapter 13). Instances in which athletes have had to resort to the courts over alleged infringements are many, although in more than one case the player was held to have signed away his rights through the broad grant contained in an earlier contract. These cases should be fair warning to the player agent about the careless granting of rights.

Cases in this area continue to appear as athletes are more and more often viewed as celebrities whose names and images have commercial potential. Together with the ever-growing number of cases dealing with the rights of celebrities in other entertainment areas, these cases have brought about a substantial body of law revolving around rights of privacy and publicity.

12.6.5. Resolving Disputes

When things have gone awry under an existing contract, and the other side is believed to have done something that must be redressed legally, the player's representative basically has two possibilities for action: arbitration or litigation. Arbitration has preempted litigation in many situations in professional sports. A player agent must be aware of this because the time period in which arbitration complaints must be filed is often short. Rights are easily waived. The arbitration process, which is usually initiated through the player's association, is specified in the Collective Bargaining Agreement between the association and the league. This document has become indispensable to the player agent. Litigation is a feasible alternative in some situations. Alleged antitrust violations by a league or club, for example, are still the province of the courts, although the leagues have become increasingly insulated from attacks due to their protection under the Sherman Act, Clayton Act, and non-statutory labor exemption (see Chapter 10,

Section 10.3.2., "The Non-Statutory Labor Exemption"). Even so, the cases still occur (see Chapter 11, section 11.3.14., "Grievance Procedures in Professional Sports").

12.6.6. Planning

Most athletes' careers last only a short time. The average career for a professional athlete, assuming he/she makes the team in the first place, is four to five years, varying slightly by the sport played. Thus, for many, there is never anything beyond the first contract. For this reason, the player agent must prepare the client for what will occur in the not-too-distant future. Such a task is easy to describe, but difficult to carry out.

Athletes may claim that they realize theirs will not be a long career, but it is hard to grasp just how short a career can be. Most players are not really prepared for the end. Their attitude is invariably "next year, perhaps, but not now."

The player agent may be unable to cushion the psychological blow completely. The hope is that the client has had sufficient time to produce enough income so that at least some preparations can be made for the financial transition. Achieving this goal relates to the managing function, but it also requires the future ingredient of careful planning. The player agent may need to obtain professional assistance in order to assist the athlete in planning for a new career. A player agent in this business for any period of time will have to confront this problem.

12.7. GOVERNMENT REGULATION—UNIFORM ATHLETE AGENT ACT

In 2001, the National Conference of Commissioners on Uniform State Laws approved a draft of legislation entitled the Uniform Athlete Agent Act (see note 1). The power of a uniform act is that it creates legislation that is the same across each state in the country. The Uniform Athlete Agent Act will be proposed to each state government in the country, and it is then up to the individual states whether or not the act will be considered and adopted. While it is not known whether or not the act will be passed by each state legislature, states that adopt the legislation of the Uniform Athlete Agent Act will provide some degree of uniformity and consistency to athlete agent regulation. As will be discussed in Section 12.7.1., "State Regulations," many states have promulgated legislation which varies considerably from state to state.

Beginning in 1997, the NCAA, in conjunction with the National Conference of Commissioners on Uniform State Laws, sought to draft legislation that would make the athlete agent laws of every state consistent. In 2001, twenty-eight states had athlete agent laws; however, the regulations were often vastly different, complex and confusing due to their lack of uniformity. The NCAA supported the Uniform Athlete Agent Act in order to supply athletes and agents alike with one set of rules and regulations to follow when conducting business. The act would benefit agents, athletes, and colleges. Agents will not have to register in numerous states, which leads to massive amounts of paperwork and fees. The athlete will know his or her rights regardless of the state in which he or she attends school. Finally, colleges will be better able to police the actions of athlete agents under this new legislation.

In 2002, the Uniform Athlete Agent Act was gaining momentum in state legislatures across the country. It had been passed by 18 jurisdictions including 16 states (Alabama, Arizona, Arkansas, Delaware, Florida, Hawaii, Idaho, Indiana, Minnesota, Mississippi, Nevada, New York, Tennessee, Utah, Washington, West Virginia, the District of Columbia, and the U.S. Virgin Islands) and was pending in 12 other legislatures. Although it is difficult to predict how many states will adopt the Uniform Athlete Agent Act, it is obvious that, if passed, this legislation will have a tremendous impact upon player agents across the country, and will lead to a greater consistency in the application of agent laws and regulation of athlete agents.

NOTES

1. The following is the legislation approved by the NCAA and the National Conference of Commissioners for Uniform State Laws:

Uniform Athlete Agents Act (2000)*
Uniform Athlete Agents Act

SECTION 1. SHORT TITLE. This [Act] may be cited as the Uniform Athlete Agents Act.
SECTION 2. DEFINITIONS. In this [Act]:

(1) "Agency contract" means an agreement in which a student-athlete authorizes a person to negotiate or solicit on behalf of the student-athlete a professional-sports-services contract or an endorsement contract.

(2) "Athlete agent" means an individual who enters into an agency contract with a student-athlete or, directly or indirectly, recruits or solicits a student-athlete to enter into an agency contract. The term does not include a spouse, parent, sibling, [or] grandparent[, or guardian] of the student-athlete or an individual acting solely on behalf of a professional sports team or professional sports organization. The term includes an individual who represents to the public that the individual is an athlete agent.

(3) "Athlete director" means an individual responsible for administering the overall athletic program of an educational institution or, if an educational institution has separately administered athletic programs for male students and female students, the athletic program for males or the athletic program for females, as appropriate.

(4) "Contact" means a communication, direct or indirect, between an athlete agent and a student-athlete, to recruit or solicit the student-athlete to enter into an agency contract.

(5) "Endorsement contract" means an agreement under which a student-athlete is employed or receives consideration to use on behalf of the other party any value that the student-athlete may have because of publicity, reputation, following, or fame obtained because of athletic ability or performance.

(6) "Intercollegiate sport" means a sport played at the collegiate level for which eligibility requirements for participation by a student-athlete are established by a national association for the promotion or regulation of collegiate athletics.

(7) "Person" means an individual, corporation, business trust, estate, trust, partnership, limited liability company, association, joint venture, government; governmental subdivision, agency, or instrumentality; public corporation; or any other legal or commercial entity.

(8) "Professional-sports-services contract" means an agreement under which an individual is employed or agrees to render services as a player on a professional sports team, with a professional sports organization, or as a professional athlete.

(9) "Record" means information that is inscribed on a tangible medium or that is stored in an electronic or other medium and is retrievable in perceivable form.

(10) "Registration" means registration as an athlete agent pursuant to this [Act].

(11) "State" means a State of the United States, the District of Columbia, Puerto Rico, the United States Virgin Islands, or any territory or insular possession subject to the jurisdiction of the United States.

(12) "Student-athlete" means an individual who engages in, is eligible to engage in, or may be eligible in the future to engage in, any intercollegiate sport. If an individual is permanently ineligible to participate in a particular intercollegiate sport, the individual is not a student-athlete for purposes of that sport.

SECTION 3. ADMINISTRATION; SERVICE OF PROCESS; SUBPOENAS.

(a) The [Secretary of State] shall administer this [Act].

(b) By engaging in the business of an athlete agent in this State, a nonresident individual appoints the [Secretary of State] as the individual's agent to accept service of process in any civil action related to the individual's business as an athlete agent in this State.

[(c) The [Secretary of State] may issue subpoenas for any relevant material under this [Act].]

SECTION 4. ATHLETE AGENTS: REGISTRATION REQUIRED.

(a) Except as otherwise provided in subsection (b), an individual may not act as an athlete agent in this State before being issued a certificate of registration under Section 6 or 8.

(b) An individual may act as an athlete agent before being issued a certificate of registration for all purposes except signing an agency contract if:

(1) a student-athlete or another acting on behalf of the student-athlete initiates communication with the individual; and

(2) within seven days after an initial act as an athlete agent, the individual submits an application to register as an athlete agent in this State.

(c) An agency contract resulting from conduct in violation of this section is void. The athlete agent shall return any consideration received under the contract.

SECTION 5. REGISTRATION AS ATHLETE AGENT; FORM; REQUIREMENTS.

(a) An applicant for registration shall submit an application for registration to the [Secretary of State] in a form prescribed by the [Secretary of State]. [An application filed under this section is a public record.] Except as otherwise provided in subsection (b), the application must be in the name of an individual and signed by the applicant under penalty of perjury and must state or contain:

(1) the name of the applicant and the address of the applicant's principal place of business;

(2) the name of the applicant's business or employer, if applicable;

(3) any business or occupation engaged in by the applicant for the five years next preceding the date of submission of the application;

(4) a description of the applicant's:

(A) forming training as an athlete agent;

(B) practical experience as an athlete agent; and

(C) educational background relating to the applicant's activities as an athlete agent;

(5) the names and addresses of three individuals not related to the applicant who are willing to serve as references;

(6) the name, sport, and last known team for each individual for whom the applicant provided services as an athlete agent during the five years next preceding the date of submission of the application;

(7) the names and addresses of all persons who are:

(A) with respect to the athlete agent's business if it is not a corporation, the partners, officers, associates, or profit-sharers; and

(B) with respect to a corporation employing the athlete agent, the officers, directors, and any shareholder of the corporation with a 5% or greater interest;

(8) whether the applicant or any other person named pursuant to paragraph (7) has been convicted of a crime that, if committed in this State, would be a felony or other crime involving moral turpitude, and identify the crime;

(9) whether there has been any administrative or judicial determination that the applicant or any other person named pursuant to paragraph (7) has made a false, misleading, deceptive, or fraudulent representation;

(10) any instance in which the conduct of the applicant or any other person named pursuant to paragraph (7) resulted in the imposition of a sanction, suspension, or declaration of ineligibility to participate in an interscholastic or intercollegiate athletic event on a student-athlete or educational institution;

(11) any sanction, suspension, or disciplinary action taken against the applicant or any other person named pursuant to paragraph (7) arising out of occupational or professional conduct; and

(12) whether there has been any denial of an application for, suspension or revocation of, or refusal to renew, the registration or licensure of the applicant or any other person named pursuant to paragraph (7) as an athlete agent in any State.

(b) An individual who has submitted an application for, and received a certificate of, registration or licensure as an athlete agent in another State, may submit a copy of the application and a valid certificate of registration or licensure from the other State in lieu of submitting an application in the form prescribed pursuant to subsection (a). The [Secretary of State] shall accept the application and the certificate from the other State as an application for registration in this State if the application to the other State:

(1) was submitted in the other State within the six months next preceding the submission of the application in this State and the applicant certifies the information contained in the application is current;

(2) contains information substantially similar to or more comprehensive than that required in an application submitted in this State; and

(3) was signed by the applicant under penalty of perjury.

SECTION 6. CERTIFICATE OF REGISTRATION; ISSUANCE OR DENIAL; RENEWAL.

(a) Except as otherwise provided in subsection (c), the [Secretary of State] shall issue a certificate of registration to an individual who complies with Section 5(a).

(b) Except as otherwise provided in subsection (c), the [Secretary of State] shall issue a certificate of registration to an individual whose application has been accepted under Section 5(b).

(c) The [Secretary of State] may refuse to issue a certificate of registration if the [Secretary of State] determines that the applicant has engaged in conduct that has a significant adverse effect on the applicant's fitness to serve as an athlete agent. In making the determination, the [Secretary of State] may consider whether the applicant has:

(1) been convicted of a crime that, if committed in this State, would be a felony or other crime involving moral turpitude;

(2) made a materially false, misleading, deceptive, or fraudulent representation as an athlete agent or in the application;

(3) engaged in conduct that would disqualify the applicant from serving in a fiduciary capacity;

(4) engaged in conduct prohibited by Section 14;

(5) had a registration or licensure as an athlete agent suspended, revoked, or denied or been refused renewal of registration or licensure in any State;

(6) engaged in conduct or failed to engage in conduct the consequence of which was that a sanction, suspension, or declaration of ineligibility to participate in an interscholastic or intercollegiate athletic event was imposed on a student-athlete or educational institution; or

(7) engaged in conduct that significantly adversely reflects on the applicant's credibility, honesty, or integrity.

(d) In making a determination under subsection (c), the [Secretary of State] shall consider:

(1) how recently the conduct occurred;

(2) the nature of the conduct and the context in which it occurred; and

(3) any other relevant conduct of the applicant.

(e) An athlete agent may apply to renew a registration by submitting an application for renewal in a form prescribed by the [Secretary of State]. [An application filed under this section is a public record.] The application for renewal must be signed by the applicant under penalty of perjury and must contain current information on all matters required in an original registration.

(f) An individual who has submitted an application for renewal of registration or licensure in another State, in lieu of submitting an application for renewal in the form prescribed pursuant to subsection (e), may file a copy of the application for renewal and a valid certificate of registration from the other State. The [Secretary of State] shall accept the application for renewal from the other State as an application for renewal in this State if the application to the other State:

(1) was submitted in the other State within the last six months and the applicant certifies the information contained in the application for renewal is current;

(2) contains information substantially similar to or more comprehensive than that required in an application for renewal submitted in this State; and

(3) was signed by the applicant under penalty of perjury.

(g) A certificate of registration or a renewal of a registration is valid for [two] years.

SECTION 7. SUSPENSION, REVOCATION, OR REFUSAL TO RENEW REGISTRATION.

[(a)] The [Secretary of State] may suspend, revoke, or refuse to renew a registration for conduct that would have justified denial of registration under Section 6(c).

[(b)] The [Secreatry of State] may deny, suspend, revoke, or refuse to renew a registration only after proper notice and an opportunity for a hearing. The [Administrative Procedures Act] applies to this [Act].

SECTION 8. TEMPORARY REGISTRATION. The [Secretary of State] may issue a temporary certificate of registration while an application for registration or renewal is pending.

SECTION 9. REGISTRATION AND RENEWAL FEE. An application for registration or renewal of registration must be accompanied by a fee in the following amount:

(1) [$] for an initial application for registration;

(2) [$] for an application for registration based upon a certificate of registration or licensure issued by another State;

(3) [$] for an application for renewal of registration; or

(4) [$] for an application for renewal of registration based upon an application for renewal of registration or licensure submitted in another State.

SECTION 10. FORM OF CONTRACT.

(a) An agency contract must be in a record, signed by the parties.

(b) An agency contract must state or contain:

(1) the amount and method of calculating the consideration to be paid by the student-athlete for services to be provided by the athlete agent under the contract and any other consideration the athlete agent has received or will receive from any other source for entering into the contract or for providing the services;

(2) the name of any person not listed in the application for registration or renewal who will be compensated because the student-athlete signed the agency contract;

(3) a description of any expenses that the student-athlete agrees to reimburse;

(4) a description of the services to be provided to the student-athlete;

(5) the duration of the contract; and

(6) the date of execution.

(c) An agency contract must contain, in close proximity to the signature of the student-athlete, a conspicuous notice in boldface type in capital letters stating:

WARNING TO STUDENT-ATHLETE

IF YOU SIGN THIS CONTRACT:

(1) YOU MAY LOSE YOUR ELIGIBILITY TO COMPETE AS A STUDENT-ATHLETE IN YOUR SPORT;

(2) BOTH YOU AND YOUR ATHLETE AGENT ARE REQUIRED TO TELL YOUR ATHLETIC DIRECTOR, IF YOU HAVE AN ATHLETIC DIRECTOR, WITHIN 72 HOURS AFTER ENTERING INTO AN AGENCY CONTRACT; AND

(3) YOU MAY CANCEL THIS CONTRACT WITHIN 14 DAYS AFTER SIGNING IT. CANCELLATION OF THE CONTRACT MAY NOT REINSTATE YOUR ELIGIBILITY.

(d) An agency contract that does not conform to this section is voidable by the student-athlete.

(e) The athlete agent shall give a copy of the signed agency contract to the student-athlete at the time of signing.

SECTION 11. NOTICE TO EDUCATIONAL INSTITUTION.

(a) Within 72 hours after entering into an agency contract or before the next scheduled athletic event in which the student-athlete may participate, whichever occurs first, the athlete agent shall give notice in a record of the existence of the contract to the athletic director of the educational institution at which the student-athlete is enrolled or the athlete agent has reasonable grounds to believe the student-athlete intends to enroll.

(b) Within 72 hours after entering into an agency contract or before the next athletic event in which the student-athlete may participate, whichever occurs first, the student-athlete shall inform the athletic director of the educational institution at which the student-athlete is enrolled that he or she has entered into an agency contract.

SECTION 12. STUDENT-ATHLETE'S RIGHT TO CANCEL.

(a) A student-athlete may cancel an agency contract by giving notice in a record to the athlete agent of the cancellation within 14 days after the contract is signed.

(b) A student-athlete may not waive the right to cancel an agency contract.

(c) If a student-athlete cancels an agency contract, the student-athlete is not required to pay any consideration under the contract or to return any consideration received from the agent to induce the student-athlete to enter into the contract.

SECTION 13. REQUIRED RECORDS.

(a) An athlete agent shall retain the following records for a period of five years:

(1) the name and address of each individual represented by the athlete agent;

(2) any agency contract entered into by the athlete agent; and

(3) any direct costs incurred by the athlete agent in the recruitment or solicitation of a student-athlete.

(b) Records required by subsection (a) to be retained are open to inspection by the [Secretary of State] during normal business hours.

SECTION 14. PROHIBITED ACTS.

(a) An athlete agent may not do any of the following with the intent to induce a student-athlete to enter into an agency contract:

(1) give any materially false or misleading information or make a materially false promise or representation;

(2) furnish anything of value to a student-athlete before the student-athlete enters into the agency contract; or

(3) furnish anything of value to any individual other than the student-athlete or another registered athlete agent.

(b) An athlete agent may not intentionally:

(1) initiate contact with a student-athlete unless registered under this [Act];

(2) refuse or willfully fail to retain or permit inspection of the records required by Section 13;

(3) violate Section 4 by failing to register;

(4) provide materially false or misleading information in an application for registration or renewal of registration;

(5) predate or postdate an agency contract; or

(6) fail to notify a student-athlete prior to the student-athlete's signing an agency contract for a particular sport that the signing by the student-athlete may make the student-athlete ineligible to participate as a student-athlete in that sport.

SECTION 15. CRIMINAL PENALTIES. The commission of any act prohibited by Section 14 by an athlete agent is a [misdemeanor] [felony] punishable by [].

SECTION 16. CIVIL REMEDIES.

(a) An educational institution has a right of action against an athlete agent or a former student-athlete for damages caused by a violation of this [Act]. In an action under this section, the court may award to the prevailing party costs and reasonable attorney's fees.

(b) Damages of an educational institution under subsection (a) include losses and expenses incurred because, as a result of the activities of an athlete agent or former student-athlete, the educational institution was injured by a violation of this [Act] or was penalized, disqualified, or suspended from participation in athletics by a national association for the promotion and regulation of athletics, by an athletic conference, or by reasonable self-imposed disciplinary action taken to mitigate sanctions.

(c) A right of action under this section does not accrue until the educational institution discovers or by the exercise of reasonable diligence would have discovered the violation by the athlete agent or former student-athlete.

(d) Any liability of the athlete agent or the former student-athlete under this section is several and not joint.

(e) This [Act] does not restrict rights, remedies, or defenses of any person under law or equity.

SECTION 17. ADMINISTRATIVE PENALTY. The [Secretary of State] may assess a civil penalty against an athlete agent not to exceed [$25,000] for a violation of this [Act].

SECTION 18. APPLICATION AND CONSTRUCTION. In applying and construing this Uniform Act, consideration must be given to the need to promote uniformity of the law with respect to its subject matter of this [Act] among States that enact it.

SECTION 19. SEVERABILITY. If any provision of this [Act] or its application to any person or circumstance is held invalid, the invalidity does not affect other provisions or applications of this [Act] which can be given effect without the invalid provision or application, and to this end the provisions of this [Act] are severable.

SECTION 20. REPEALS. The following acts and parts of acts are hereby repealed:

SECTION 21. EFFECTIVE DATE. This [Act] takes effect————.

2. The following is a sample letter developed by the NCAA to be sent to state legislators by NCAA institutions:

Uniform Athlete Agent Act Sample Letter to Legislator

SAMPLE LETTER
[to be sent after legislation is introduced in your state]

Dear [**Senator**] or [**Representative**] [Last Name]:

After three years of work, The National Conference of Commissioners on Uniform State Laws (NCCUSL) recently approved the Uniform Athlete Agent Act (UAAA), a model state law governing the relationships between student-athletes, athlete agents and academic institutions. The National Collegiate Athletic Association (NCAA) and its member institutions are seeking its adoption in every state, and I am writing to urge your support and co-sponsorship of [S. _____ or H.R. _____], recently introduced in the [your state's] legislature.

The problems associated with illegal athlete agent conduct are far greater than the casual observer might believe. Far too often, the actions of athlete agents engaged in unsavory practices result in the loss of student-athlete eligibility, the imposition of financial penalties on the student-athlete's institution and the taint of a "scandal" on both the institution and the larger intercollegiate sports community. In an effort to address these problems, at least 28 states have enacted statutes regulating athlete agents. However, existing laws vary considerably from state-to-state and many statutes contain provisions that are vague and not enforced by the state. As a result, athlete agents largely ignore existing state registration requirements as well as other provisions contained in current athlete agent laws.

The purpose of the UAAA is to protect the interests of student-athletes and institutions by providing for a uniform regulation of athlete agents. The UAAA provides for:

• Uniformity of state laws. These laws are designed to provide a single set of regulations that will ensure greater compliance among athlete agents.

• A reciprocal registration provision and a reasonable fee schedule making agents more likely to register due to the efficiency of this process and the cost savings it provides for athlete agents.

• Consumer information, both professional and criminal in nature, to enable better evaluation of the athlete agents to provide competent representation.

• Notice to institutions when a student-athlete signs an agency contract.

• The Secretary of State or other appropriate agency to issue subpoenas enabling the state to obtain relevant material that will assist in the enforcement of the act.

• Criminal, civil and administrative penalties that will be enforced at the state level.

On behalf of [name of institution], I urge your support of [S._____ or H.R._____] and thank you in advance for your efforts to address this important issue.

3. The following is a fact sheet distributed by the NCAA regarding the positive features of the Uniform Athlete Agent Act:

Uniform Athlete Agent Act Fact Sheet

WHAT IS THE UNIFORM ATHLETE AGENT ACT?

After three years of work, the National Conference of Commissioners on Uniform State Laws recently approved the Uniform Athlete Agent Act (UAAA). The UAAA is designed to provide a single set of state regulations that will govern athlete agent conduct. The UAAA ensures greater protection for student-athletes and educational institutions while providing a more manageable and cost-efficient regulatory scheme for athlete agents and states.

WHY DO WE NEED TO ADOPT THE UNIFORM ATHLETE AGENT ACT?

• Protection for student-athletes: The primary purpose of the UAAA is to protect student-athletes and educational institutions from athlete agents who engage in unsavory and, oftentimes, illegal practices.

• Protection for colleges and universities: The UAAA acts as a strong deterrent against improper athlete agent conduct that often subjects institutions to negative publicity and harsh sanctions, including the forfeiture of games and substantial financial penalties.

• Uniformity of state laws: The UAAA is designed to provide a single set of regulations that will ensure greater compliance among athlete agents.

• Reciprocal agent registration and reasonable fees: Reciprocal registration and a reasonable fee schedule provide a system that allows states to honor the registration of athlete agents from states with similar laws. Agents are more likely to register with states due to the efficiency and cost effectiveness of the UAAA prescribed process.

- Strong penalties for violators: The UAAA provides for criminal, civil and/or administrative penalties to be imposed against violators.
- Additional tools for state law enforcement: The right to exercise subpoena power enables the state to obtain relevant information that assists in the enforcement of the act.
- Important consumer information: It is vital for student-athletes, parents and institutions to have access to information contained in the agent application, both professional and criminal in nature, to ensure that the most informed decisions are made regarding athlete agent representation.
- Widespread support: The UAAA is endorsed by the National Collegiate Athletic Association and its 1,000 member universities and colleges, the National Conference of Commissioners on Uniform State Laws and a number of other organizations.

4. For more information on the Uniform Athlete Agent Act's effect upon sports agents, see Robert N. Davis, "Exploring the Contours of Agent Regulation: The Uniform Athlete Agent Act," 8 *Villanova Sports & Entertainment Law Forum* 1 (2001).

12.7.1. State Regulations

While the NCAA is encouraging and supporting each state legislature in the country to pass the Uniform Athlete Agent Act, numerous states have, since the 1980s, enacted legislation to regulate the conduct and practice of sports agents. As of 2002, twenty-eight states had laws dealing with sports agents and three states had legislation pending. These state laws are very diverse, but the common legislation followed by most states requires sports agents to register with the state and pay a registration fee. In addition, some states require sports agents to post a surety bond, which may be utilized to satisfy any damages caused to an athlete by the acts of an agent. Specified acts upon which an athlete can receive monetary payment due to the agent's misconduct include intentional misrepresentation, fraud, deceit, or any unlawful or negligent act.

As was seen in section 12.2., "Player Agents," legislation varies from state to state. The definition of an athlete agent can differ from state to state, and the definition of a "gift" from an agent to a student-athlete can differ as well. With the passage of the Uniform Athlete Agent Act, the NCAA is hoping that all inconsistencies between state legislation will be eradicated, and replaced with a single model.

NOTES _____

1. The following are statutory citations for state athlete-agent legislation:

ALABAMA:
[Ala. Code 8-26-7, -22]

ARKANSAS:
[Ark. Code Ann. 17-16–205, -207]

CALIFORNIA:
[Cal. Bus. and Prof. Code 18896.6, 18897.63]

COLORADO:
[Col. Rev. Stat. Ann. 23-16-105, -106, -107]

CONNECTICUT:
[Conn. Gen. Stat. Ann. 20-554, -556]

FLORIDA:
[Fla. Stat. Ann. 468.456, .4564]

GEORGIA:
[Ga. Code Ann. 43-4A-7, -16]

INDIANA:
[Ind. Code Ann. 35-46-44]

IOWA:
[Iowa Code Ann. 9A.8, .9]

KANSAS:
[Kan. Stat. Ann. 44-1503, -1508, -1509]

KENTUCKY:
[Ken. Rev. Stat. Ann. 164.04]

LOUISIANA:
[La. Rev. Stat. Ann. 4:422, 422.1, 424, 425]

MARYLAND:
[Md. Code Ann. Bus. Reg. 4-403, -423]

MINNESOTA:
[Minn. Stat. 32JE.33]

MISSISSIPPI:
[Miss. Code Ann. 73-41-3, -7, -13]

NEVADA:
[Nev. Rev. Stat. Ann. 398.085]

NORTH CAROLINA:
[N.C. Gen. Stat. 78C-71]

NORTH DAKOTA:
[N.D. Cent. Code 9-15-04]

OHIO:
[Ohio Ann. 4771.01]

OKLAHOMA:
[Okla. Stat. Ann. tit. 70, 821.62, .64, .65]

OREGON:
[H.B. No. 3628, 70th Leg., Reg. Sess. 3, 6]

PENNSYLVANIA:
[18 Pa. C.S. @ 7107]

SOUTH CAROLINA:
[S.C. Code Ann. @ 59–102.10]

TENNESSEE:
[Tenn. Code Ann. 49-7-2112, -2114, -2118]

TEXAS:
[Tex. Occ. Code Ann. 2051.004, .251-.256, .301-304, .351]

WASHINGTON:
[Rev. Code Wash. 18.175.010]

2. For more information on government regulation of athlete agents, see the following:

a. Diane Sudia and Rob Remis. "The History Behind Athlete-Agent Regulation and the Slam-Dunking of Statutory Hurdles," 8 *Villanova Sport & Entertainment Law Forum* 67 (2001).

b. "Appendix A, Statutory Regulation of Agent Solicitation of Athletes," 10 *Seton Hall Journal of Sports Law* 234 (2000).

c. "Appendix A, Statutory Regulation of Agent Contracts with Athletes," 10 *Seton Hall Journal of Sports Law* 339 (2000).

d. "Appendix A, Statutory Regulation of Agent Gifts to Athletes," 10 *Seton Hall Journal of Sports Law* 302 (2000).

e. Diane Sudia and Rob Remis, "Statutory Regulation of Agent Gifts to Athletes," 10 *Seton Hall Journal of Sports Law* 265 (2000).

f. Diane Sudia and Rob Remis, "Athlete Agent Contracts: Legislative Regulation," 10 *Seton Hall Journal of Sports Law* 317 (2000).

g. Phillip Closius, "Hell Hath No Fury like a Fan Scorned: State Regulation of Sports Agents," 30 *University of Toledo Law Review* 511 (Summer 1999).

h. Rob Remis and Diane Sudia, "Escaping Athlete-Agent Statutory Regulation: Loopholes and Constitutional Defectiveness Based on Tri-Parte Classification of Athletes," 9 *Seton Hall Journal of Sports Law* 1 (1999).

12.7.2. Ethical Constraints

The player representative who is also an attorney faces the constraints imposed by the canon of ethics (see note 4). This can be particularly troublesome when competing with nonlawyers who do not face similar requirements (see note 1). Issues relating to solicitation are foremost among these concerns (see note 2).

Another ethical area is somewhat more subtle. This relates to dealing with athletes who have remaining college athletic eligibility. Under the NCAA rules, any number of activities involving the athlete with a prospective representative may cause forfeiture of the athlete's remaining eligibility. While these regulations do not impose restrictions directly on the player representative, they do raise ethical issues for that person. It is also possible that a court might view a representative's activities, whereby the representative causes an athlete to lose eligibility, as constituting "unclean hands." This could affect the representative's legal remedies in certain situations.

It should also be pointed out that attorneys who represent players often face ethical concerns with respect to renegotiation. Many of these agents may advise a client not to renegotiate a contract because they believe in the sanctity of contracts. One way to circumvent this is to include a "reopener clause" in the original contract, which would allow renegotiation to take place if certain stated situations come about.

NOTES _____

1. In the case of *Cuyahoga County Bar Association* v. *Glenn*, 72 Ohio St.3d 299, 649 N.E.2d 1213 (Ohio 1995), Glenn, the agent for a National Football League player, Richard Dent, was not allowed to practice law in the state of Ohio because he had misrepresented Dent by committing fraud, and undertaking conduct that led to a failure to properly represent his client, including seizing some of Dent's money without his consent ($20,000) and refusing to give it back.

2. For more information on the legal constraints placed upon sports agents who are also attorneys, see Stacey M. Nahrwold, "Are Professional Athletes Better Served by a Lawyer-Representative Than an Agent? Ask Grant Hill," 9 *Seton Hall Journal of Sports Law* 431 (1999).

3. For a discussion of the constraints upon athlete agents concerning solicitation, see Diane Sudia and Rob Remis, "Athlete-Agent Solicitation of Athlete Clients: Statutory Authorization and Prohibition," 10 *Seton Hall Journal of Sports Law* 205 (2000).

4. The American Bar Association's Ethical Code (EC) of Professional Responsibility states:

> [A] lawyer should maintain high standards of professional conduct and should encourage fellow lawyers to do likewise. He should be temperate and dignified, and he should refrain from all illegal and morally reprehensible conduct. . . .
>
> EC 2-3 Advice is proper only if motivated by a desire to protect one who does not recognize that he may have legal problems or who is ignorant of his legal rights or obligations. Hence

the advice is improper if motivated by a desire to obtain personal benefit, secure personal publicity, or cause litigation to be brought merely to harass or injure another.

EC 2-4 A lawyer who volunteers advice that one should obtain the services of a lawyer generally should not himself accept employment, compensation or other benefit in connection with that matter.

These considerations should be followed by all American Bar Association members. Nevertheless, the position of player representative allows for opportunities to violate some of these recommendations.

12.7.3. NCAA Regulations

The NCAA, in an attempt to maintain its status as an "amateur" organization, has taken a tough stance on agents and athlete eligibility. The *2001–02 NCAA Division I Manual* states clearly, "An individual shall be ineligible for participation in an intercollegiate sport if he or she has ever agreed (orally or in writing) to be represented by an agent for the purpose of marketing his or her athletics ability or reputation in that sport. Further, an agency contract not specifically limited in writing to a sport or particular sports shall be deemed applicable to all sports and the individual shall be ineligible to participate in any sport" (*2001–02 NCAA Division I Manual* Bylaw 12.3.1). However, "securing advice from a lawyer concerning a proposed professional sports contract shall not be considered contracting for representation by an agent under this rule, unless the lawyer represents the student-athlete in negotiations for such a contract" (*2001–02 NCAA Division I Manual*, Bylaw 12.3.2). This second bylaw has not always been enforced, however, especially in the case of baseball players who have been eligible for the professional draft directly out of high school.

In order to build or protect their personal interests, some agents will contact, offer inducements to, and attempt to sign student-athletes with remaining college eligibility. They may also entice athletes to leave college early to join professional teams. Inducements may take the form of cash, "loans," and/or the use of a car or other benefits. This transfer to, and acceptance of money or other benefits by, student-athletes are in direct conflict with the principles of amateurism and specifically violate rules related to receiving compensation or pay and limits on the amount and type of acceptable remuneration (*2001–02 NCAA Division I Manual*, Bylaw 12.1).

Because several player agents have represented student-athletes in contract negotiations under the guise of supplying legal advice, the NCAA Council issued a clarification concerning the use of legal counsel by student-athletes. The *2001-02 NCAA Division I Manual* states, "A lawyer may not be present during discussions of a proposed contract offer with a professional organization or have any direct contact (i.e., in person, by telephone, or by mail) with a professional sports organization on behalf of the student-athlete. A lawyer's presence during such discussions is considered representation by an agent" (*2001–02 NCAA Division I Manual*, Bylaw 12.3.2.1). The council asserted, however, that any student-athlete may retain counsel for the purpose of reviewing a contract offered by a professional team. Nevertheless, the student-athlete who decides to have legal counsel contact a professional team concerning a contract offer has effectively hired counsel as an agent and is no longer eligible. In addition, the NCAA specifies that a contract between an athlete and an agent that does not specifically refer to a particular sport (i.e., simply a general employment contract) will result in the loss of eligibility for the athlete in all sports. The NCAA also prohibits contracts for future service: "An individual shall be ineligible per Bylaw 12.3.1 if he or she enters into a verbal or written agreement with an agent for representation in future professional sports negotiations that are to take place after the individual has completed his or her eligibility in that sport" (*2001–02 NCAA Division I Manual*, Bylaw 12.3.1.1). This rule applies at all times, and therefore includes contracts made prior to matriculation at college.

It is crucial to understand, however, that the NCAA cannot pass any bylaws that punish the agents themselves, because they are not part of the NCAA. Therefore, the NCAA punishes the school or university where a student was found to be in violation of bylaws regarding agents. Several programs, including the University of Alabama, have been penalized because an athlete entered into a professional contract or agreed to be represented by an agent before the expiration of his collegiate eligibility. In the case of University of Alabama, Derrick McKey and Tony Coner, two star players on the university basketball team, were found to have received illegal payments from agent Norby Walters. (For more on Walters and fellow agent Lloyd Bloom, see note 1.) McKey lost his senior season of eligibility, and the university had to repay $253,447 in NCAA tournament revenue when the allegations were found to be true (see note 1 for a discussion of other similar cases). Other such cases have resulted in the forfeiture of victories, the disqualification of teams from NCAA tournaments, and teams being forced to return television and/or tournament participation monies.

The offer sheet is one method by which agents may attempt to circumvent NCAA rules. An offer sheet is presented by the player agent to the student-athlete, who often mistakes it for a contract. The student-athlete signs this form prior to the expiration of college eligibility, but the agent will not sign it until after the student-athlete's eligibility has expired. Since most student-athletes are not versed in the technicalities of the requirements for a binding contract, they often believe they have a contract with the agent, and will stop dealing with other agents. Agents who use this tactic to reserve players claim the offer sheet is not an agency contract until the representative executes the document at the close of student-athlete's playing season. Since no contract exists, there can be no violation of NCAA rules. The NCAA disagrees, however, believing that the substance of its rules clearly prohibits any agreements to provide future services, even if the agreement does not constitute an enforceable contract.

Currently, the NCAA has a career counseling program in individual institutions to assist student-athletes who are contemplating forgoing their remaining college eligibility to pursue a career in professional sports (*2001–02 NCAA Division I Manual*, Bylaw 12.3.4) (see note 3). The institution organizes the counseling panel, which consists of three people from the institution who will advise the student-athlete. The guidelines by which the panel is selected are left to the discretion of the university. For the most part, it is suggested that the panel consist of employees of the institution. The committee can consist of a member of the bar, a law professor, or a teacher of business law, someone who deals with financial matters, and a person chosen at random. The NCAA also allows one full-time member of the athletic department staff to serve as a panel member. During the actual advising and counseling sessions, no agent or prospective agent may be present.

The institution decides whether or not to organize such a panel; it is not required by the NCAA. In institutions that have set up counseling panels, the student-athletes are able to utilize the panel's services at any time. They do not have to wait for their eligibility to expire. Some of the responsibilities of the panel are to establish policies that indicate the manner by which an agent can contact a student-athlete, to provide support and guidance during interviews with prospective agents, and to coordinate presentations by speakers for the benefit of the student-athlete. Some state laws and/or universities have set up "career days" for their athletes in lieu of these career counseling panels. Some universities, including the University of Texas, have made these career days mandatory for their athletes to attend.

NOTES

1. The story of New York agent Norby Walters and his partner, Los Angeles agent Lloyd Bloom, provides a disturbing example of abuse, corruption and manipulation in the relationship between college athletes and agents. The relationship between Walters, Bloom and the players they represented led to numerous court cases (see notes a and b below) and ultimately, a federal indictment. In the early to mid-1980s, Walters and Bloom were able to sign many of the nation's top college football players on their way to the pros. Stories began to surface that Walters and Bloom had offered the athletes cash, loans, cars and introductions to celebrities in an effort to induce the athletes to sign with them, before they had completed their eligibility. Through investigation of this matter, the U.S. Attorney was able to prosecute Walters and Bloom under the RICO statutes. Details soon emerged that when the athletes began to ask to be released from their contracts, Walters and Bloom would threaten them with physical harm by organized crime associates. Walters was convicted, but subsequently saw his conviction overturned. A few years later, Lloyd Bloom was found murdered, "gangland style," in his apartment.

   a. In *Walters v. Fullwood*, 675 F.Supp. 155 (S.D.N.Y. 1987), two agents, Walters and Bloom, brought a breach of contract claim against Brent Fullwood, a star running back for Auburn University, who had signed a contract with the two agents before his college eligibility had run out. Subsequently, Fullwood signed a contract with Lickliter after he had run out of collegiate eligibility. The agents were also suing Lickliter for tortious interference with contractual relations, for interfering with their contract with Fullwood. The court ruled against the two agents on the breach of contract claim because they had brought a case to court with "dirty hands." This doctrine signifies that someone who has broken the law is prevented recovery for damages arising out of that action.

   b. In the case of *United States v. Walters and Bloom*, 913 F.2d 388 (7th Cir. 1990), a criminal case was brought against two agents who had signed contracts with college athletes before their college eligibility had expired, and then allegedly used illegal means to maintain these contracts, such as threatening harm to the players if they broke the contract. The case was dismissed upon appeal due to errors during their initial trial that did not allow them to receive a fair trial. While the case was dismissed, the body of the decision supplies an interesting look at some techniques used by agents to gain the services of collegiate athletes.

2. In 1970, Howard Porter, a star basketball player for NCAA runner-up Villanova, was found to have signed a contract with the American Basketball Association three months before his collegiate eligibility had been exhausted. Porter was stripped of his title as tournament MVP, and Villanova was forced to forfeit its tournament victories as well as its tournament winnings.

3. For a discussion of NCAA rules regarding payment of student-athletes by agents, see Thomas R. Hurst and J. Grier Pressly, "Payment of Student-Athletes: Legal and Practical Obstacles," 7 *Villanova Sports & Entertainment Law Forum* 55 (2000).

4. At its 1984 convention, the NCAA approved a plan, recommended by its Special Committee on Players Agents, under which athletes career counseling panels would be established in individual institutions to assist student-athletes who are contemplating forgoing their remaining college eligibility to pursue a career in professional sports (*2000–01 NCAA Division I Manual*, Bylaw 12.3.4). In addition, should the athlete opt for a

professional career, the panel would assist in the selection of a competent representative or agent.

The NCAA, during the 1980s and 1990s, became more concerned with the actions of player agents, particularly as they relate to on-campus solicitation of student-athletes. Accounts of former college athletes stating that they had received illegal payments from agents while still in school have caused the NCAA to crack down in this area (see Chapter 6, Section 6.2.2.8., "Pay and Expenses: NCAA").

In 1982, the NCAA prepared a manual called *A Career in Professional Sports: Guidelines That Make Dollars and Sense*. This booklet was designed to help students obtain competent representation. It provided a more general discussion of the NCAA's athlete representation regulations.

During the 1984–1985 academic year, the NCAA initiated two programs designed to increase the information available to student-athletes concerning player agents and the transition from collegiate to professional athletics. The first program permitted an institution to provide counseling on professional careers to student-athletes through a panel appointed by the institution's chief executive officer. The panel would consist of employees of the institution outside of the athletic department. Each institution's panel was allowed to obtain information and expertise from a variety of sources (e.g., lawyers, financial consultants, professional sports teams, player associations, and player agents) in an effort to provide objective information about professional career opportunities and evaluate the various services and proposals extended by player agents.

The second program instituted by the NCAA was a player agent registration program. This was a voluntary program in which the player agent registered with the NCAA by supplying requested educational and professional information. The list of registered player agents was provided to the institutional career counseling panel, which would recommend agents on the list to the student-athlete. By registering, the agent agreed to notify the director of athletics at the institution before the first contact with an enrolled student-athlete with remaining eligibility or with the student-athlete's coach. During 1985–1986 the NCAA had over 400 agents registered in this program. The program was discontinued in August 1989.

12.8. REPRESENTATIVE AGENT-ATHLETE AGREEMENTS

The relationships established between the player representative and the client has traditionally varied greatly in terms of the formality of any agreement effectuated between the parties. The agreement has ranged from a handshake, to a letter of understanding, to a detailed contract. Increasingly, interested parties within professional sports are urging that greater formality and detail be introduced into the relationship in order to safeguard the rights of both parties. Players associations now provide form contracts for agents and players in order to simplify the process, avoid misconduct, and make the process consistent throughout the league. While the players associations maintain jurisdiction over the contracts that are signed between players and agents regarding performance, the associations do not maintain control over the execution of contracts concerning marketing and financial management.

NOTES _____

1. For a discussion of issues concerning jurisdiction over agency contracts made on the Internet, see Margaret Danjhal, Daniel S. Strick, and Mark A. Conrad, "Contracting on the Web: Collegiate Athletes and Sports Agents Confront a New Hurdle in Closing the Deal," 8 *Villanova Sports & Entertainment Law Forum* 37 (2001).

2. In the case of *Speakers of Sport v. Pro Serv*, 178 F.3d 862 (7th Cir. 1999), the plaintiff,

Speakers of Sport, brought a case against Pro Serv for tortious interference with contractual relations, accusing Pro Serv of illegally taking their client, Ivan Rodriguez, a major league catcher. Pro Serv gave the impression to Rodriguez that he would be able to earn $2 to $4 million dollars in endorsements if he joined their agency. Speakers of Sport alleged that these statements to Rodriguez were false, and that they constituted tortious interference. On appeal of a summary judgment for Pro Serv on the trial court level, the court affirmed this judgment, stating, "There is in general nothing wrong with one sports agent trying to take a client from another if this can be done without precipitating a breach of contract. That is the process known as competition, which though painful, fierce, frequently ruthless, sometimes Darwinian in its pitilessness, is the cornerstone of our highly successful economic system."

3. For examples of a standard athlete-agent contract, see Martin J. Greenberg and James T. Gray, *Sports Law Practice*, 2d. ed., Vol. 2, 811, 815 (Milwaukee: LEXIS Law Publishing, 1998). Greenberg and Gray give examples of the standard National Basketball Players Association athlete-agent contract as well as an example of the National Football League Players Association's standard athlete-agent contract.

12.9. INDIVIDUAL PERFORMER SPORTS

Tennis, golf, boxing, track, horse and auto racing, and other sports in which the athlete largely competes as an individual rather than on a team or in a league present far different issues than those which have been considered to this point. A few of the important considerations will be raised here, but a comprehensive review is not provided.

The compensation method and the contracts are much different for individual sports. For example, athletes in individual performer sports do not enjoy the security of a Standard Player Contract or NLRB-recognized collective bargaining (see Chapters 9 and 11). Hence, individual sport organizations do not unilaterally implement a drug policy or code of conduct, or take other legal actions that affect wages, hours, and terms and conditions of employment. In tennis, golf, and cycling there are players associations or informal unions—perhaps not unions in the full sense, as in team sports, but important in terms of giving their blessings to certain activities, including the types of contracts tendered to players. Thus, when it comes to tournaments and races, the sponsor-athlete obligation assumes great uniformity as to many of the terms.

Endorsement contracts are staples in individual performer sports. These are not discussed here, except to note their prevalence and importance. But they are analogous with league player endorsements.

Finally, for many of the individual performer sports, there are clubs or resorts that wish to have a player's name associated with the facility. Any number of deals are possible, ranging from straight money payments to trade-outs and other enticements.

12.10. FOREIGN LEAGUES

As sports become more international, there are an increasing number, although still relatively small in total, of opportunities for U.S. athletes to play "professionally" in foreign countries. In football, there are the Canadian Football League and NFL Europe. For baseball players, Japan, Mexico, and the Far East offer opportunities, generally for marginal Major Leaguers. In basketball and hockey, leagues exist around the world, with the quality of play varying substantially from country to country, and usually below the quality of the United States. This discussion focuses on the Big Four professional team sports. However, one clear exception to this rule is the sport of soccer, where elite American players can make substantially more money by playing abroad against better competition.

Many foreign professional leagues limit the number of non-citizens who can play on any one team. This makes the scramble for spots by U.S. players an intense one, particularly in the better leagues. For example, the Italian basketball league is considered the strongest outside the United States, and top American players can be paid well, even though the league is classified as amateur under international rules. Each Italian team is severely limited as to how many foreign players can make the squad. It takes a top U.S. player, one just below the NBA level, to secure a contract, unless the player can claim Italian citizenship and not count against a team's foreign player quota. Exhibit 12.11 is a Standard Player Contract between basketball players and teams in Europe, Asia, and the Middle East.

In March 1997, the National Basketball Association and FIBA (Fédération Internacionale de Basketball), the international governing body for the sport, reached an agreement to use an independent arbitrator when disputes arise over the transfer of players to and from international teams and the National Basketball Association. The agreement also provides for arbitration for a number of other disputes that could arise in international basketball. The NBA did not wait long to test this new arbitration method, with the Toronto Raptors and Phoenix Suns seeking the services of European athletes who, they contended, were playing abroad under invalid contracts (see notes 1 and 2). The FIBA arbitration system has proven to be a very beneficial addition to handle these types of disputes.

NOTES ————————————————————————————

1. In the *Matter of Arbitration Between Phoenix Suns and Athletic Union of Constantinople* (1997), the Phoenix Suns sought the services of a basketball player, Iakovos "Jake" Tsakalidis, who was under contract to play for the Greek professional team AEK through the 2000 season. Phoenix argued that the contract was null and void for various reasons, and that Tsakalidis should be allowed to exit his contract without penalty to play in the NBA. In arbitration, the claimant Suns were successful. The arbitrator ruled that the contract was invalid under Greek law because the "penalty clause" within the contract was illegally severe, and was an excessive curtailment of Tsakalidis's freedom to pursue his basketball career. The Suns were therefore able to sign Tsakalidis because the Greek contract had been nullified. AEK subsequently challenged the arbitrator's decision in an English court, but the court upheld the arbitrator's decision to allow Tsakalidis out of his contract.

2. In the *Matter of Arbitration Between Toronto Raptors and Budocnost* (1997), the Toronto Raptors, in a case similar to the Tsakalidis case, sought to gain the services of Aleksandar Radojevic, who was under contract to play for Budocnost of the Yugoslavian Basketball League through the 2000–2001 season. The arbitrator decided that Radojevic's contract with Budocnost was not a valid contract because it did not specify the compensation that would be awarded Radojevic for the final three years with the team.

3. In *Behagen v. Amateur Basketball Association*, 884 F.2d 524 (10th Cir. 1989), Ronald Behagen, a former All-American at the University of Kentucky, was not granted a reinstatement of amateur status by the Amateur Basketball Association, the national governing body for amateur basketball in the United States at the time, because he had participated professionally and received compensation for his play in the United States. Due to this

Exhibit 12.11
Italian League Contract

THIS AGREEMENT made this _____ day of _____ , 2001, by and
between _____, (hereinafter referred to as "PLAYER") and
_____ CLUB _____ (hereinafter referred to as "CLUB").

WITNESSETH:

In consideration of the mutual promises hereinafter contained, the parties hereto
promise and agree as follows:

I.   The CLUB hereby employs the PLAYER as a skilled basketball player
for a term of two seasons which shall begin upon the execution of this contract
and will end after PLAYER'S last official Play-off or Italian Cup game. The
PLAYER'S employment during the term of this contract shall include attendance
and participation in regular season games and all exhibition, and play-off and
official games scheduled or entered by the CLUB. The PLAYER shall be free to
transfer to any other team in Italy or Europe at the conclusion of the second
season without the payment of any transfer fee. This agreement cannot be sold
or transferred to any other basketball club without the express written consent
and approval of the PLAYER.

II.   For the 2001-2002 season, the CLUB agrees to pay the PLAYER for
rendering services described herein as follows:

        A.   Twelve (12) equal monthly payments of $10,000 US Dollars,
commencing August 1, 2001, with the final payment on July 1, 2002, for a
total of $120,000.
        B.   Signing Bonus of $30,000 US Dollars is to be paid immediately
to the PLAYER.
        C.   A total of $25,000 US Dollars for living expenses which is to be
paid to the PLAYER in 12 monthly payments, payable the first of each month
commencing August 1, 2001, with the final payment on July 1, 2002. There
will be eleven equal payments of $2,000 per month and a final payment of
$3,000.
        D.   The salary is to be net, and free and clear of all foreign taxes.
Should the payment of taxes be required, it is the responsibility of the CLUB
to pay them and to provide the PLAYER with paid tax receipts evidencing
said payments. The tax receipts shall be given to the PLAYER within fifteen
(15) days following the last official tax payment day. All taxes are to be paid
by the CLUB and only the CLUB is responsible for said tax payments.

III.   For the 2002-2003 season, the CLUB agrees to pay the PLAYER for
rendering services described herein as follows:

        A.   Twelve (12) monthly payments in US Dollars as follows:
$16,000 payable on August 1, 2002, continuing with eleven equal monthly
payments of $14,000 each, payable on the first of each month beginning
September 1, 2002. The final payment will be paid on July 1, 2003.
        B.   Reporting Bonus of $30,000 US Dollars is to be paid
immediately to the PLAYER, payable within seven (7) days of PLAYER'S
arrival in ITALY.
        C.   A total of $25,000 US Dollars for living expenses which is to be
paid to the PLAYER in 12 monthly payments, payable the first of each month
commencing August 1, 2002, with the final payment on July 1, 2003. There
will be eleven equal payments of $2,000 per month and a final payment of
$3,000.
        D.   The salary is to be net, and free and clear of all foreign taxes.
Should the payment of taxes be required, it is the responsibility of the CLUB
to pay them and to provide the PLAYER with paid tax receipts evidencing
said payments. The tax receipts shall be given to the PLAYER within fifteen

Exhibit 12.11 (continued)

(15) days following the last official tax payment day. All taxes are to be paid by the CLUB and only the CLUB is responsible for said tax payments.

IV. BONUSES: The CLUB agrees to pay the PLAYER the following bonuses for both seasons covered by this Contract:

> A.   Bonuses for all home, away and play-off victories to be the same as those paid to all other players on the team.
> B.   All bonuses are to be net, and free and clear of all Italian taxes and subject to the same terms as stated in Paragraph IIB.

V.   The CLUB agrees to provide the following to the PLAYER for each season covered by this Contract:

> A.   Two (2) round-trip business class airplane tickets and Five (5) round-trip economy class. PLAYER is to be reimbursed by CLUB for any travel expenses including shipping of excess baggage to a limit of $500 for his trip to Italy.
> B.   CLUB will provide for the PLAYER a fully furnished apartment or house, to be approved by the PLAYER. Said furnishings shall include a king-size bed, a color television set, video recorder, cable television service, personal computer with Internet access, and a stereo system. All rent and utilities will be paid by the CLUB. The CLUB will provide insurance for all personal belongings in the house or apartment. CLUB will install a telephone at their expense but the PLAYER will be responsible for all calls made. PLAYER shall pay for his own Internet access.
> C.   CLUB will provide all medical, dental (not cosmetic), hospital and surgical costs which will cover all injuries and/or illnesses.
> D.   CLUB will provide PLAYER with the use of a Jaguar or similar class automobile for the duration of this contract. CLUB will pay all taxes, registration, license, any maintenance costs, gas and oil. The PLAYER will be responsible for any fines or tickets issued to the car or its driver.
> E.   CLUB will provide the PLAYER with an Italian language tutor.
> F.   CLUB will provide the PLAYER with 24-hour access to a gym and the use of a rebounding machine.
> G.   CLUB will provide PLAYER with ten (10) seats to all home games.
> H.   CLUB is to pay all proper and necessary expenses of the PLAYER while playing for the CLUB on the road and during training camp if the PLAYER is not living at his home at the time. The CLUB will pay the total cost of room and board in the above circumstances.

VI.   This is a fully guaranteed contract which includes injuries as well as skill, and all terms are valid and binding upon the CLUB and the PLAYER immediately upon its execution. By executing this contract the PLAYER has exhibited sufficient skill to qualify to continue as a member of the CLUB'S team for the seasons covered by this contract. However, if the CLUB transfers this agreement to any other team in the Italian Federation, the CLUB remains liable for any and all sums of money due to the PLAYER. If the CLUB determines that it no longer wishes to retain the playing services of the PLAYER due to its opinion as to his skill or injury, the CLUB must still make all payments due to the PLAYER on a timely basis for the 2001-2002 and 2002-2003 seasons.

VII.   A.   The PLAYER agrees to abide by the rules of the Italian Federation and of FIBA and to observe and comply with the requirements of the CLUB concerning his behavior whether on or off the playing floor. The CLUB may establish reasonable rules of behavior for the team and discipline for the players. The PLAYER agrees to obey his coach and be punctual for all games,

Exhibit 12.11 (continued)

practices and club meetings. Said rules shall be attached to this contract as an exhibit.

        B.   PLAYER and his attorney must be supplied with an English translation of all CLUB rules and fines before Paragraph VIIA hereinabove is accepted. If some of the rules seem too vague, PLAYER may ask for a clarification. If some of the fines seem too excessive, PLAYER will seek reductions, all before this Paragraph is made a part of this Agreement. PLAYER'S attorney must be notified in writing of each and every infraction before any disciplinary action may be taken by the CLUB.

VIII.   If PLAYER is forced to initiate legal action to ensure payment of this contract and its provisions, CLUB is to bear all legal costs and attorney's fees. The CLUB and PLAYER agree to submit to the laws of Italy to resolve any such dispute.

IX.   This Agreement may be executed in counterparts, each of which shall constitute an original but all together shall constitute one and the same Agreement. Facsimile copies of the signed Agreement may be transmitted between the parties hereto and a facsimile copy of a signed Agreement shall be deemed a counterpart hereof.

X.   The contract shall be interpreted and enforced in accordance with the laws of Italy.

XI.   This contract contains the entire Agreement between the parties and no other Agreement, oral or otherwise regarding the subject of this contract shall be deemed to exist or bind any of the parties hereto.

IN WITNESS WHEREOF, the parties have hereunto set their hands.

_____ :   PLAYER

_____ :   CLUB

lack of reinstatement, Behagen was not able to continue playing basketball in Europe in an "amateur league." Behagen settled with FIBA (the international governing body for basketball), but brought a claim of antitrust violations and due process violations against the Amateur Basketball Association. Upon appeal, the court overturned the previous decision and decided for the Association on both counts. It said that the actions of the Association were not antitrust violations, but that under the Amateur Sports Act, the Association had the power to take such actions because they are the sole governing body for a sport within the country. Behagen was not able to prove that the association was a state actor, and therefore was unsuccessful in his lack of due process constitutional claim.

    4. In *Ponce v. Basketball Federation*, 760 F.2d 375 (1st Cir. 1985), the Federation appealed a district court's decision to grant Ponce an injunction allowing him to continue playing in Puerto Rico despite not achieving the certification requirements of citizenship needed. On appeal, the court decided for the Federation, against which Ponce had brought an equal protection claim, claiming his rights had been violated because he was an American citizen, but not from Puerto Rico. The appeals court found that the actions of the federation did not constitute state action, and therefore they could not be held liable for violations of equal protection.

12.11. ENDORSEMENT CONTRACTS

Athletes, because of their talents and wide appeal to the public, can be of great interest to a company wanting to increase its exposure and promote their products. Endorsement contracts are entered into frequently in professional sports; the athlete allows the advertising agency or company to use his or her name and image in product promotional activities. In entering into these endorsement contracts, the player must be careful to understand exactly how his or her name and image will be used. In addition, the professional team and league may have certain restrictions on the use of this athlete in the company's promotional activities (e.g., the athlete could be prohibited from wearing the team's uniform unless an endorsement fee is also paid to the professional league) (see Chapter 9).

Exhibit 12.12 contains an endorsement contract between a professional athlete and a well-known sporting goods manufacturer.

Exhibit 12.12
Athlete Endorsement Contract

AGREEMENT

This Agreement, made an entered into this thirteenth day of September 2001, by and between
_____ having its principal place of business at _____,
(Company)   (Address)
_____(hereinafter referred to as "Company"), and _____ (hereinafter
Player's Company)
referred to as "Enterprises").

WITNESSETH

WHEREAS, Enterprises has the sole and exclusive right to provide the services of _____
                                                                                    (Player)
(hereinafter referred to as "Athlete") and to license the name _____ for the purposes of this
Agreement as hereinafter set forth; and

WHEREAS, Athlete is recognized and widely known throughout the world as an expert basketball player; and

WHEREAS, Athlete's name by virtue of his ability and extensive experience, has acquired secondary meaning in the
mind of the purchasing public important to the advertisement, promotion, and sale of Endorsed Product as defined in
Paragraph One (1)(d) below and

WHEREAS, Company is engaged in the manufacture, distribution, and sale of Endorsed Products and is desirous of
acquiring the exclusive right to utilize Athlete's Endorsement (as defined in paragraph One (1) (a) below) and services
in connection with the sale, advertisement, and promotion of Endorsed Products:

NOW THEREFORE, in consideration of the mutual covenants as set forth herein and for other good and valuable
consideration, it is agreed as follows:

1. Definitions. As used herein, the terms set forth below shall be defined as follows:
    a. "Athletes Endorsement" shall include only the right to use the name, nickname, likeness,
        photograph, signature, initials, statements, facsimile, and endorsement of Athlete;
    b. "Contract Territory" shall mean the world;
    c. "Contract Year" shall mean the twelve (12) month period commencing on each thirteenth day of
        September during the Term of the Agreement;
    d. "Endorsed Products" shall mean any athletic footwear, athletic apparel, caps, visors, and athletic
        bags as may now or hereinafter be manufactured, distributed, marketed, licensed, and/or sold by
        Company or on Company's behalf.

2. Term of Agreement. The Term of this Agreement shall commence September 13, 2001, and shall
    continue until September 12, 2005.

3. Commercial Materials. In connection with this Agreement. "Commercial Materials" shall mean those
    materials produced pursuant to Paragraphs Six (6) and Fifteen (15) hereof, including, without limitation,
    radio and television commercials, video tapes, audio tapes, still photographs (including those lifted from
    television commercials or video tapes), billboards, all forms of print advertising, point-of-purchase
    materials, posters, product packaging, hang tags, the name(s) of products(s), all collateral materials,
    Company's Annual Report, materials produced for promotional purposes, materials used for trade
    contests, trade publications, and all internal and/or external sales and marketing pieces.

4. Grant of Endorsement Rights. Subject to the terms and conditions hereinafter set forth. Enterprises
    hereby grants to Company the exclusive right and license, within the Contract Territory and during the
    Term, to utilize the Athlete's Endorsement in connection with the advertisement, promotion, and sale of
    Endorsed Products.

5. Retention of Endorsement Rights. Subject to the provisions of Paragraph Four (4) above, Company
    agrees that Enterprises shall retain all rights in and to Athlete's name and endorsement and, whether
    during the Term or any extension thereof, Enterprises shall not be prevented from using, or permitting
    and licensing other to use. Athlete's name or endorsement in connection with the advertisement,
    promotion, or sale of any product or service other than the type of products included in the definition of
    Endorsed Products within the Contract Territory. However, Enterprises agrees that Athlete will not
    endorse any non-athletic footwear or apparel products, which are sold under the trademark or trade name
    of a competitive manufacturer of performance athletic footwear. Enterprises agrees that it shall consult

Exhibit 12.12 (continued)

with Company prior to the grant of the Athlete's Endorsement to any other Company, showing due regard for Company's considerations. Company, however, shall have no specific right of approval over Enterprise's other endorsement opportunities.

Company further agrees that upon the expiration or other termination of this Agreement, for any cause whatsoever, it will immediately cease using the Athlete's Endorsement, the Athlete's name, or any facsimile thereof for advertising, promotional, or any other purpose whatsoever, except pursuant to the following paragraph.

However, Enterprises agrees that the Company shall have the right, for a period not to exceed ninety (90) days following the date of the expiration or earlier termination of this Agreement, to continue to sell and distribute all printed promotional materials and, in the event Enterprises has materially breached this Agreement and Company has purchased media time, broadcast materials featuring Athlete which have been produced by or for the Company and are in inventory prior to the date of such termination ("closing inventory").

6. **Use and Ownership of Commercial Materials**

    A.   Commercials. During the Term of this Agreement, company shall have the exclusive right to broadcast, use, and reuse the television and radio commercial(s) and video and audio materials produced hereunder in the Contract Territory and in any and all media.

    B.   Print Commercial Materials. During the Term of this Agreement, Company shall have the right to use the Athlete's Endorsement, the Commercial Materials, or any part thereof in print for publication and display in the Contract Territory as Company, subject to the reasonable approval by Enterprises and its business representative, may determine, including all forms of print advertising, cooperative advertising, retail tie-in promotions, point-of-purchase materials, product(s), name(s), billboards, posters, Company's Annual Report, materials produced for promotional purposes, internal and/or external sales and marketing pieces, trade contests, trade publications, hangtags and generally to Company's employees and shareholders.

7. **Protecting Athlete's Endorsement.** Company agrees that it will take all necessary reasonable steps during the Term and any extension thereof to protect Athlete's Endorsement, the Athlete's name or any facsimile thereof, in connection with the promotion, advertisement, and sale of Endorsed Products.

8. **Technical Features.** Company acknowledges that for Athlete to successfully compete on a championship level in professional basketball, his shoes may have to incorporate certain technical features that he requires. In this connection, company agrees to consult with Enterprises, its business representatives, Athlete and/or technical advisor of Enterprises' choice, to make any modifications to the particular model of Company product, which he will wear, in competitive play. Enterprises agrees that Athlete and his business representatives and/or technical advisor will cooperate with Company with respect to design and technical features in order to facilitate and maximize the working relationship between Company and Enterprises. Enterprises further acknowledges the possibility that such modifications may be accomplished through the use of custom designed orthodic insert devices. Company agrees to furnish Enterprises, its business representatives, and/or technical advisor, for their inspection and review, samples of the model of Company shoes Athlete selects to wear in competitive play. Enterprises, its business representatives, and/or technical advisor agree to promptly notify Company of their evaluation of such sample model Endorsed Product submitted to them for review and Company shall use its genuine best efforts to incorporate Enterprises' its business representatives, Athlete's and/or technical advisor's recommendations and suggestions into the final design of said shoes.

9. **Direction and Control.** Athlete's services, pursuant to the terms and conditions of this Agreement, may be on-camera or off-camera, as Company may select and shall be rendered under Company's direction and control at such times and locations as shall be designated by Company, subject to reasonable prior notice to Enterprises and subject to Athlete's then existing professional commitments. The commercials to be produced hereunder may be taped, filmed, or recorded in such a manner as Company may determine.

10. **Premier Spokesman.** The parties mutually agree that one of the major inducements for Enterprises to enter into this long-term contract is Company's assurance that Athlete will be advertised and promoted as one of its premier "flagships" in basketball, particularly professional basketball, for as long as he continues to be an All-Star Player. In this connection, Company agrees to utilize Athlete during the Term as one of its spokesmen and ambassadors in the advertising, promotion and sale of Company's basketball products and basketball related products, particularly the articles of Company product

Exhibit 12.12 (continued)

contained in the Endorsed Products. In achieving this goal and business purpose, Company agrees to consult with Enterprises and its business representatives, _____, regarding advertising and promotional campaigns and strategy featuring Athlete.

11. Marketing Commitment. The parties acknowledge that the successful introduction to the public and continued profitability of the Company's basketball products and the overall Company-Enterprises relationship mandates an aggressive marketing commitment by Company. It is the specific intent and understanding of the parties that Company will aggressively advertise and promote its relationship with Enterprises and the sale of the Endorsed Products in a manner consistent with Paragraph Six (6) of this Agreement in order to maximize the sales of endorsed products.

12. Use of Endorsed Products. Athlete warrants and represents that he is a user of the Endorsed Products and that, during the Term of this Agreement, he shall continue to use the Endorsed Products exclusively. Enterprises further warrants and represents that all personal endorsements or representations made by or attributed to Athlete with his consent in the Commercial Materials produced hereunder are true and accurate.

13. Athlete to Use Endorsed Products. Enterprises agrees that during the Term and within the Contract Territory Athlete will exclusively wear Company athletic shoes and Company athletic apparel whenever he is playing competitive basketball, posing for basketball photographs, conducting basketball-related promotional interviews, or is otherwise engaged in basketball and athletic-related promotional activities, and shall not wear the athletic shoes and, where appropriate, the athletic apparel of a company competitive with Company.

14. Endorsed Products for Athlete's Use. During the Term, Company shall supply Enterprises, at no charge, with such quantities of Endorsed Products as Athlete may reasonably request for his own personal use and for personal use of his immediate family. In addition, company agrees to supply Enterprises at no charge such quantities of Endorsed Products as Athlete may reasonably request for gifts to others, up to an aggregate wholesale value of Four Thousand U.S. Dollars ($4,000) during each Contract Year.

15. Athlete to Be Available to Company
    a.   If requested by Company, Enterprises agrees to make Athlete available for up to twenty (20) days in each Contract Year, at times and places as designated by the Company, subject to reasonable prior notice to Enterprises and subject to Athlete's then-existing professional commitments, to make personal appearances, pose for photographs, and otherwise assist Company in the preparation of advertising and promotional materials utilizing the Athlete Endorsement; provided, however, that such appearances shall include the production of radio and television commercials. Company and Enterprises agree that the Athlete's obligations for the aforementioned twenty (20) days shall be allocated as follows:

        (i)   Up to five (5) consecutive days may take place outside of the United States;

        (ii)   Up to nine (9) days may be spent producing television and radio commercials, posing for photographs, and making elite level corporate appearances; and

        (iii)   Up to six (6) days may be spent making personal appearances within the United States.

Each such "day" as used herein, shall be defined as consisting of no more than eight (8) hours per appearance, excluding travel time, for the production of radio and/or television commercials, and no more than four (4) hours excluding travel time, for photography sessions or personal appearances.

    b.   Company agrees to reimburse Enterprises for first class, round-trip travel as well as all other reasonable travel, hotel, meals, and expenses incurred by Athlete in connection with such appearances on behalf of the Company. On all appearances, Athlete shall be accompanied by a representative of either Company or Enterprise at Company's expense.

16. Optional Appearances. "Optional Appearance" shall mean any appearance by Athlete requested by Company in excess of the twenty (20) appearances per Contract Year, as set forth in Paragraph Fifteen (15) above. For each Optional Appearance, Enterprises shall receive a mutually agreeable fee, payable within ten (10) days following each Optional Appearance. No appearance by Athlete shall be deemed an Optional Appearance unless made upon the prior written request of the Company.

Exhibit 12.12 (continued)

17.   <u>Approval of Advertising and Promotional Materials.</u> Company agrees to submit to Enterprises and its business representatives _____ , for their approval, a copy of all advertising and/or promotional materials utilizing the Athlete's Endorsement at least five (5) working days prior to their release to the general public; and Company further agrees that the same shall not be released without prior written approval of Enterprises or its business representatives. Enterprises and its business representatives agree however, that they shall not unreasonably withhold or delay their approval of said materials and that in the absence of disapproval within five (5) working days of receipt thereof, said advertising and promotional materials shall be deemed approved. Enterprises further agrees that once said materials are deemed approved, Company shall have the right to make multiple uses of said materials without submitting to Enterprises and its business representatives for approval of every such use.

18.   <u>Annual Compensation.</u> In consideration for the rights and benefits granted to Company pursuant to the Agreement, Company agrees to pay Enterprises the following amounts as Annual Compensation in each Contract Year

	Contract Year	Annual Compensation
First	September 13, 2001 through September 12, 2002	$300,000 (Three Hundred Thousand US Dollars)
Second	September 13, 2002 through September 12, 2003	$300,000 (Three Hundred Thousand US Dollars)
Third	September 13, 2003 through September 12, 2004	$300,000 (Three Hundred Thousand US Dollars)
Fourth	September 13, 2004 through September 12, 2005	$300,000 (Three Hundred Thousand US Dollars)

The annual compensation due and owing Enterprises by Company in each Contract Year shall be paid quarterly on or before January 1, April 1, July 1, and October 1 of each Contract Year except that the initial quarterly payment hereunder shall be made on the first business day of January 2002 (i.e. Enterprises Compensation for the first quarter shall cover the period commencing September 13, 2001 and ending December 31, 2001) and except that the final payment due hereunder shall be made on September 12, 2005, in lieu of the first business day of October 2005 in the amount of a full quarterly payment.

If Company decides, in its sole discretion, to manufacture and market Endorsed Products which bear the name, nickname, likeness and/or initials of Athlete directly on the Product, or by means of decals or labels, or on packaging therefore (such as Endorsed Products to be known as "Signature Products") at any time during the Term, Company agrees to pay Enterprises Royalty Compensation on the net sales of all such Signature Products in an amount to be mutually agreed upon by Company and Enterprises. Such Royalty Compensation shall be deemed to be full consideration for the use by Company of all trademarks owned and registered by Enterprises.

19.   <u>Bonus Compensation.</u> In addition to all other Compensation provided for herein, Company agrees to pay Enterprises the following Bonus Compensation in the applicable Bonus Years (as defined below) the total amount of sales revenues, less returns, accrued by Company from the sale of (i) ____Company)____ brand men's basketball shoes (as designated in ____(Company's)____ product line catalogues, but not including children's basketball shoes); and (ii) fifty percent (50%) of the sales revenues, less returns, of _____ brand women's performance basketball shoes during the applicable Bonus Year equals or exceeds the amounts set for in the table below, within thirty (30) days of the end of each Bonus Year:

Exhibit 12.12 (continued)

Total Amount of Sales Revenues, Less Returns Accrued by Company from Sale of Products Defined in Paragraph Nineteen (19)	Amount of Bonus For Bonus For Bonus Years One and Two	Amount of Bonus For Bonus For Bonus Years Three and Four
$250,000,000 through $349,999,999	$100,000	$150,000
$350,000,000 through $499,999,999	$250,000	$250,000
$500,000,000 and above	$500,000	$500,000

For the purposes of this section only, the First Bonus Year shall begin on March 1, 2002 and continue through February 28, 2003; the Second Bonus Year shall begin on March 1, 2003 and continue through February 28, 2004; the Third Bonus Year shall begin on March 1, 2004 and continue through February 28, 2005; and the Fourth Bonus Year shall begin on March 1, 2005 and continue through February 28, 2006.

20. Reductions
   a. Company shall have the right to reduce the amount of the Annual Compensation payable to Enterprises in accordance with Paragraph Eighteen (18) hereof in the event Athlete plays in fewer than Seventy-six (76) official NBA regular season games during each Contract Year by an amount equal to Three Thousand Three Hundred Thirty-Three U.S. Dollars ($3,333) for each game missed below Seventy-six (76) games.
   b. Company shall have the right to reduce the amount of Bonus Compensation payable to Enterprises in accordance with Paragraph Nineteen (19) hereof, in the event Athlete plays in fewer than Fifty (50) official NBA regular season games during any Contract Year, by an amount equal to Fifty Percent (50%) of the Bonus Compensation otherwise payable to Enterprises in such Contract Year. In this connection, it is agreed that each Bonus Year, as described in Paragraph Nineteen (19) above, shall correspond to same ordinal Contract Year, as defined in paragraph 1c. above. For example, the First Bonus Year shall correspond to the First Contract Year.

21. Active Basketball Professional. During the Term of this Agreement, Athlete shall remain active as a National Basketball Association ("NBA") professional basketball player. Company shall have the right, by written notice to Enterprises, to terminate this Agreement and to be relieved of all its obligations hereunder, including without limitation, its obligation to pay any compensation to Enterprises, if for any reason during the Term of this Agreement, Athlete fails to be on either the active or injured reserve list of any NBA Team.

22. Payments to Enterprises. All payments to be made to Enterprises pursuant to this Agreement shall be made by check in U.S. Dollars and made payable to and mailed to it.

23. Time Is of the Essence.
   a. Company acknowledges that time is of the essence in the payment of all compensation due Enterprises and Enterprises acknowledges that time is of the essence in the performance of his obligations. Company hereby agrees that in the event any payment due Enterprises is not received by Enterprises or its business representatives within thirty (30) days of the date set forth in this Agreement for such payment that, in the event written notice has been proved to Company and Company has failed to cure such nonpayment in five (5) days, Enterprises shall be paid interest at the rate of two percent (2%) per month or the maximum interest rate permitted by U.S. law, whichever is less, on the total balance due and owing Enterprises, calculated from the actual payment date set forth herein. In addition, Enterprises shall also have the right and option to terminate this Agreement, effective upon the expiration of thirty (30) days following written notice to Company of his election to so terminate for failure of Company to perform in accordance with the provisions hereof, unless such payment has been received by Enterprises or its business

Exhibit 12.12 (continued)

representatives within such thirty (30) day period. The reservation of specific rights by Enterprises herein shall not preclude Athlete from exercising any other remedy it may have at law or in equity to enforce the terms of this Agreement.

b. Enterprises hereby agrees that if Athlete should fail to appear for the filming of a previously scheduled television commercial without providing Company at least one (1) day's prior notice of his inability to appear, and his failure to appear was not due to a strike, boycott, war, act of God, labor troubles, rift, delay of commercial carriers, restraint of public authority, or for any other reason, similar or dissimilar, he shall reimburse Company for an amount equal to twenty-five percent (25%) of Company's out-of-pocket production costs, for said commercial, not to exceed Seventy-five Thousand U.S. Dollars ($75,000).

24. Insurance. Company shall have the unrestricted right to obtain disability, life and any other types of insurance policies covering Athlete if Company, in its sole discretion, so chooses, and Enterprises agrees that Company or its designee shall be the beneficiaries of such policies. Promptly following Enterprise's execution of this Agreement, Enterprises agrees that Athlete shall submit to physical examinations, undertake any reasonable actions, and execute all documents required to assist Company in obtaining such insurance.

25. Special Right of Termination by Enterprises. Enterprises shall have the right to terminate this Agreement upon thirty (30) days prior written notice to Company in the event of the occurrence of any of the following:
a. If Company is adjudicated as insolvent, declares bankruptcy, or fails to continue its business of selling Endorsed Products; or
b. If Company fails to make payment to Enterprises of any sums pursuant to this Agreement within the thirty (30) days following the receipt by Company of written notice from Enterprises that such payment is past due.

26. Special Right of Termination by Company. Enterprises agrees that Company shall have the right to terminate this Agreement upon written notice to Enterprises:
a. In the event of Athlete's death during the Term; or
b. In the event Athlete is convicted of a felony or any other crime involving moral turpitude; or
c. In the event Athlete is permanently disabled; or
d. In the event the commercial value of Athlete is substantially impaired by reason of the commission by Athlete of any act or acts.

27. Breach
a. By Enterprises: If Enterprises or Athlete at any time commits a material breach of any provision of this Agreement or at any time Enterprises or Athlete fails or refuses to fulfill his obligations hereunder, and fails to remedy the same within thirty (30) days after having received such notice, then Company may, by written notice to Enterprises specifying the default or breach by Enterprises or Athlete, terminate this Agreement forwith. In the event this Agreement is terminated prior to the expiration of the Term of the Agreement, the Company's sole obligation shall be to pay to Enterprises the compensation that may be due to Enterprises as of the date of termination. Company shall have no further obligation or liability to Enterprises except as to any amount due as a result of the use or reuse of any commercial(s) broadcast pursuant to this Agreement.
b. By Company: In the Event Company fails to make any payment due pursuant to Paragraphs Eighteen (18) and Nineteen (19) hereof within thirty (30) days after having received written notice from Enterprises of Enterprises' representative and fails to remedy the same within thirty (30) days after having received such notice, or Company at any time commits a material breach of this Agreement, and fails to remedy the same within thirty (30) days after having received notice from Enterprises specifying the breach, then Enterprises may, in addition to all other remedies available to it in law or equity, terminate this Agreement by written notice to Company specifying the default or breach by Company.

28. Right of First Negotiation. During the Term of this Agreement and for a period of thirty (30) days following the expiration or earlier termination of this Agreement, Enterprises shall negotiate in good faith only with Company and not with any third party or entity concerning Athlete's endorsement of any products which are the same as or similar to or otherwise compete with the Athlete's Endorsed Products. If, at the end of such thirty (30) day period, Enterprises and Company are unable to reach an agreement concerning Athlete's endorsement of the Endorsed Products, Company shall submit to Enterprises, in writing, its last best offer for a new contract. Enterprises shall then be free to negotiate a new contract with any company of its choice. However, Enterprises agrees that Company shall have the right of first

Exhibit 12.12 (continued)

refusal to match any offer from a new company which is one hundred twenty-five percent (125%) or less the total guaranteed compensation set forth in Company's last best written offer.

29. <u>No Disparagement.</u> Enterprises agrees that at no time during and after the Term of this Agreement shall Athlete disparage his association with the Company, its product, employees, advertising agencies or other connected with the Company. The provisions of this paragraph shall survive any termination of this Agreement.

30. <u>Trademarks.</u> In the event that Enterprises should desire to obtain at any time during the Term a trademark or trademarks in any part of the Contract Territory which include any part or all of the Athlete's Endorsement, Company, if so requested by Enterprises, shall execute any and all documents which Enterprises reasonably believes to be necessary and/or desirable for successful registration and protection of such trademark or trademarks registered in the name of Enterprises. Upon use of such trademark, if requested by Company, Enterprises agrees to grant Company a license for the exclusive use of such trademark during the Term in connection with the manufacture, advertisement, promotion, distribution, and sale of Endorsed Products which licensee shall be coextensive and coterminous with the endorsement rights granted pursuant to this Agreement with respect tot he Athlete Endorsement. Said licensee shall not require any increase in the Compensation payable to Enterprises hereunder, but shall contain any additional provisions, not inconsistent herewith, which Enterprises reasonably believes are necessary for the protection of such trademark registered in the name of Enterprises. However, it is understood that Enterprises shall acquire no interest whatsoever in the Company trade name.

31. <u>Warranties.</u> Company and Enterprises warrant that they are free to enter into this Agreement and that the rights granted hereunder will not infringe upon the rights of any third party. Enterprises' execution, delivery, and performance of this Agreement shall not violate the rights of any third party or breach any agreement in which Enterprises is a party.

32. <u>Indemnity.</u>
    a.   Company agrees to protect, indemnify, and save harmless Enterprises and/or Athlete from and against any and all expenses', damages, claims, suits, actions, judgments, and costs whatsoever, including attorney's fees, arising out of, or in any way connected with, any claim or action including but not limited to personal injury or death resulting from the advertisement, manufacture, distribution, sale or use of any Endorsed Products. The provisions of this paragraph shall survive any termination of this Agreement or any act or omission of Company.
    b.   Enterprises and/or Athlete shall at all times indemnify and hold harmless Company and its officers and directors from and against any and all claims, damages, liabilities, costs and expenses, including reasonable attorney's fees, arising out of or related to any breach or alleged breach by Enterprises of any representation, warranty or agreement made by Enterprises herein or any act or omission of Enterprises.

33. <u>Force Majure.</u> If, for any reason, such as strike, boycott, war, act of God, labor troubles, riot, delay of commercial carriers, restraint of public authority or for any other reason, similar or dissimilar, beyond Company's control, Company shall be unable to use and/or reuse the Commercial Materials or the services of Athlete for any period of time during the Term of this Agreement, then Company shall have the right to extend the Term of this Agreement for an equivalent period thereof, without additional Compensation to Enterprises.

34. <u>Assignment.</u> Neither Enterprises nor Company shall have the right to grant sublicenses hereunder or to otherwise assign, alienate, transfer, encumber, or hypothecate any of its rights or obligations hereunder, except that Enterprises shall have the right to assign the financial benefits hereof and Company hereby consents to such assignment upon receipt by Company of written notice thereof from Enterprises or its business representative.

35. <u>Waiver.</u> The failure of Company and Enterprises at any time to demand strict performance by the other of any of the terms, covenants, or conditions set forth herein shall not be construed as a continuing waiver or relinquishment thereof, and either party may, at any time, demand strict and complete performance by the other of said terms, covenants, and conditions.

36. <u>Employer/Employee Relationship.</u> Enterprises' and/or Athlete's relationship with Company shall be that of an independent contractor, and nothing contained in this Agreement shall be construed as establishing and employer/employee relationship, partnership, or joint venture between Company and

Exhibit 12.12 (continued)

Enterprises and/or Athlete. Accordingly, there shall be no withholding for tax purposes from any payment by Company to Enterprises herein.

37.   Notices. All notices and/or submissions hereunder shall be sent via Certified Mail. Return Receipt Requested, to the parties at the following addresses, or such other addresses as may be designated in writing from time to time:
            Company

            Enterprises
Notices shall be deemed given upon deposit of same with the postal authority.

38.   Terms of Agreement Confidential. It is hereby agreed that the specific terms and conditions of this Agreement, including, but not limited to, the financial terms and the duration, are strictly confidential, and shall not be divulged to any third parties without the prior written consent of both Company and Enterprises, unless otherwise required by law.

39.   Significance of Paragraph Headings. Paragraph headings contained hereunder are solely for the purposes of aiding in speedy location of subject matter and are not in any sense to be given weight in the construction of this Agreement. Accordingly, in case of any question with respect to the construction of this Agreement, it is to be construed as though paragraph headings had been omitted.

40.   Governing Law. This Agreement shall be governed by and construed in accordance with the laws of the Commonwealth of Massachusetts regardless of the fact that any of the parties hereto may be or may become a resident of a different state or jurisdiction. Any suit or action arising shall be filed in a court of competent jurisdiction within the Commonwealth of Massachusetts.

The parties hereby consent to the personal jurisdiction of said court within the Commonwealth of Massachusetts.

41.   Severability. If any provision of this Agreement or the application thereof shall be invalid or unenforceable to any extent, the remainder of this Agreement or the application thereof shall not be affected, and each remaining provision of this Agreement shall be valid and enforceable to the fullest extent permitted by law.

42.   Service Unique. The parties hereto agree that the services to be performed by Athlete and the rights granted to Company hereunder are special, unique, extraordinary, and impossible to replace, which gives them a peculiar value, the loss of which could not reasonably or adequately compensated in damages in an action at law, and that Athlete's failure or refusal to perform obligations hereunder would cause irreparable loss and damage. Should Athlete fail or refuse to perform such obligations Company shall be entitled, in addition to any other legal remedies Company may have, to ex parte injunctive or other equitable relief against Enterprises to prevent the continuance of such failure or refusal or to prevent Athlete from performing services for, or granting rights to other in violation of this Agreement, and Company's exercise of such right shall not constitute a waiver or any other additional rights at law or pursuant to the terms of this Agreement, it being understood that all such remedies shall be cumulative.

43.   Union Membership. Enterprises warrants and represents that Athlete is, and will remain during the Term of this Agreement, a member in good standing of all unions, guilds, or other organizations having jurisdiction over Athlete's services as rendered under this Agreement. In the event Company is assessed or incurs any expense, including without limitation, any fine or penalty, as a result of Athlete's failure to remain a member in good standing or otherwise comply with the regulations governing members of such union, guild, or other organization, then Enterprise shall immediately pay to such union, guild or other organization any such expense, fine, or penalty assessed against Company as a result thereof, and if Company actually incurs and pays any such expenses, fine, or penalty, Enterprises will reimburse Company the full amount of any such expense, fine, or penalty, including attorneys' fees incurred or paid by Company.

44.   Entire Agreement. This Agreement constitutes the entire understanding between Company and Enterprises and cannot be altered or modified except by an agreement in writing signed by both Company and Enterprises. Upon its execution, this Agreement shall supercede all prior negotiations,

Exhibit 12.12 (continued)

understandings, and agreements, whether oral or written, and such prior agreements shall thereupon be null and void and without further legal effect.

IN WITNESS WHEREOF, the parties hereto have caused this Agreement to be executed as of the date first above written.

ACCEPTED AND AGREED:

_____	_____
(Company)	(Player)
_____	_____
(Date)	(Date)

ASSENT AND GUARANTEE

In order to induce _____ ("Company") to enter into the Agreement dated September 13, 2001 between Company and _____ ("Athlete"), by his signature below, hereby assents to the execution of the Agreement and agrees to be bound by the terms and conditions thereof relating to the Athlete. Athlete acknowledges, warrants and represents that he has read and understands the Agreement, that he is free to perform the provisions on his part to be performed pursuant thereto, that he shall comply with all of the provisions thereof which refer to him and that he shall not enter into commitments in conflict therewith. Athlete represents that all warranties and representations made by which concern him are true and that he will fully perform all of obligations under the Agreement. Further, Athlete personally guarantees that he will perform all of the terms and conditions of the Agreement on its part to be performed. Finally, Company shall be under no obligation to make any payments whatsoever to Athlete in connection with the services and materials to be provided and/or rendered by Athlete pursuant to the Agreement, except as may be specifically provided in said Agreement.

Date_____

(Athlete)

Chapter 13

INTELLECTUAL PROPERTY LAW

INTRODUCTION

To familiarize the reader with intellectual property law, and introduce the concept of intellectual property, this chapter begins with an example of how a typical sporting event intersects with intellectual property. First, the names of the competing teams, their respective uniforms, and other related items should be registered as trademarks. The owners of the teams have a property interest in all of the merchandise for sale to the general public. This interest ensures that the owners receive revenue when jerseys, hats, socks, T-shirts, or any other piece of apparel is sold to fans.

Once the games start, there is music played. The music is copyrighted and owned by other entities. The owners must get permission, or a license, to use this music. This music is generally licensed through one of the two leading agencies (ASCAP or BMI) that handle the license for a fee. These licensing agencies represent the musicians, and collect licensing fees for all public performances of their music, whether it is on radio, television, or the Internet. After these royalties are collected by the agencies, they are distributed to the writers and copyright holders of the songs. Songs are usually packaged together so that the purchaser gets more than one song for the fee. The fee varies according to such factors as the popularity of the song, the number of times the song is used, and the number of songs purchased at a time.

The home team usually sells a program detailing information about the game and its participants. Some of the information is normally obtainable by the general public, but when it is compiled in this certain way, it becomes copyrightable and a property interest. Additionally, the game will likely be videotaped and broadcast over the radio and/or television. This is significant because once it is broadcast on film, radio, or television, the actual game itself has created a copyrightable interest; use or broadcast of the game is now a property interest and can be bought and sold. (See Chapter 14.)

The players also have a property interest in their name and likeness. The players are recognized publicly because they compete in a national or local spotlight. In intercollegiate or Olympic situations, the players do not own their own pictures, but the university or governing body does. This is a significant difference between professional athletes and collegiate and Olympic athletes. The concept of the player's right to publicity has become a major topic of dispute. The right to publicity is the athlete's right to control and profit from the commercial use of his or her name or likeness. Although there has been a demand for a federal law concerning the right to publicity, many states have laws that protect the right to publicity for people who are considered to be "celebrities." Laws concerning the right to publicity currently vary from state to state. However, collegiate and Olympic athletes cannot capitalize on their own identity during the games/events. This has caused some conflicts because colleges, schools, and governing bodies can make enormous amounts of money from a player's likeness and affiliation for what is a relatively small investment (e.g., a college scholarship). One example is a university selling jerseys with a particular player's number. The university, not the player, earns money from this merchandise, even though it may be the player's popularity that is driving the sale. As demonstrated, many issues of property interest are raised when a sporting event occurs.

Whether it is the trademarked logo of a favorite sports team, the copyrighted broadcast of a sporting event, or the patent of the sporting equipment used during the game, intellectual property is an important and ever-increasing legal issue in the sports industry. The legal system provides certain rights and protections for owners of property. The kind of property that results from mental labor is called intellectual property. Rights and protections for owners of intellectual property are based on federal, patent, trademark, and copyright laws and state trade secret laws. In general, trademarks protect a name or symbol that identifies the source of goods or services; copyrights protect various forms of written and artistic expression; and patents protect inventions of tangible things.

Chapter 13 first presents the legal principles of intellectual property law, including relevant legislation, terms, and the basics of intellectual property law (subsections "The Lanham Act" through "Service Marks and Collective Marks"). The chapter then discusses the functions of trademarks, trademark infringement, and ambush marketing. Some of the recent cases that have defined the crucial issues involved in the use of sports trademarks are discussed within subsections ("Identification Function of a Trademark" through "Trademark Infringement"). The subsection "Licensing Program for Intercollegiate Licensing Programs" covers the relationship of intellectual property law to intercollegiate athletics. It discusses licensing programs, the increasing use of licensing agents by colleges and universities for the sale of products bearing school logos, and issues concerning nicknames and trademark laws. The final section of "Trademark Law" discusses trademark law and its application to the Olympic Games. The final two sections of Chapter 13 deal with copyright and patent law. The section on copyright law contains a discussion of the growing issues in copyright law and the Internet.

NOTE

1. For additional information on licensing and intellectual property in professional sports, see the following:

   (a) CNNSI.com, *Joining Forces: Yankees, Manchester United Announce Joint Marketing Deal,* February 6, 2001.

   (b) ESPN.com, *Court Curtails Gridiron.com's Activities,* July 12, 2000.

   (c) Todd Archer, "Is Baseball Back? Despite a Strike and Owners' Lockout, It Remains the National Pastime," *Cincinnati Post,* March 30, 1998, Sec. D, p. 1.

   (d) George Hostetter, "Super (Bowl) Sales Packers Favored by Fresno NFL Fans—Green Bay Apparel Outselling Denver," *Fresno Bee,* January 23, 1998, Sec. C, p. 1.

   (e) "Impact on League, No Jordan Means Dollar Will Shrink," *Orange County Register,* January 13, 1999, Sec. D. p. 4.

   (f) Brandon L. Grusd, "The Antitrust Implications of Professional Sports' League-Wide Licensing and Merchandising Agreements," 1 *Virginia Journal of Sports and the Law* 1, Spring 1999.

13.1. TRADEMARK LAW

The names, logos, and symbols associated with sports organizations have become very marketable items. Their primary purpose has historically been to create an identifiable image through which an athletic organization can promote the sale of its product or service. More recently, however, the sale of a name, logo, or symbol in association with caps, pennants, T-shirts, jerseys, and other souvenirs has become a significant revenue generator in and of itself for an athletic organization. As a result, these organizations have fought many legal battles to

Exhibit 13.1
Trademarked Logos

Reprinted with permission of Major League Baseball.

retain the exclusive right to dictate who will put their name, logo, or symbol on these profitable items. The pictures shown in exhibit 13.1 are trademarks owned by Major League Baseball teams.

The licensing of trademarks is big business in sports. In addition to gate receipts, television, and other sources of income, the consumer's appetite for sport-related items with a team affiliation has created a significant revenue stream for many sport organizations. Most professional sports leagues, for example, have developed licensing programs to capitalize on the public demand. College athletic departments, conferences, and the NCAA itself, as well as other organizations such as the U.S. Olympic Committee and the U.S. Tennis Association, have done likewise.

In professional sports leagues, the league has the rights and controls team marks. The leagues (such as Major League Baseball, the National Football League, the National Basketball Association, and the National Hockey League) formed separate entities, often known as a "properties" division, that primarily deal with the licensing of the league and club trademarks (including teams and league names and logos) to vendors who manufacture products featuring these marks and, in turn, sell these products to retailers and to the general public. The merchandising revenue is then divided among the teams, usually on an equal or pro rata basis. A pro rata distribution of licensing revenues helps smaller-market clubs compete with larger-market clubs in their leagues. For example, merchandise with the New York Yankees logo might comprise more than 10% of licensing revenues among clubs for Major League Baseball clubs, yet the Yankees are entitled to only 1/30 of the revenue generated from the licensing of Yankee marks.

Like the leagues, players associations have formed entities that handle licensing issues for athletes. For example, the NFL Players Association (NFLPA) formed Players, Inc., which is the licensing arm of the NFLPA. Players, Inc. provides marketing and licensing services to companies interested in using names and likenesses of current and past NFL players. Any program involving six or more NFL players requires a Players, Inc. license. The revenues received from this licensing is then distributed, pro rata, to the players and used for other association needs. These revenues can be quite significant; for example, it has been reported that the licensing revenues for each MLB Player are over $100,000 per year.

Not surprisingly, consumer demand for merchandise associated with professional and amateur athletic organizations has prompted a number of manufacturers to attempt to cash in on this lucrative opportunity by using names, logos, or symbols associated with a team or organization without authorization. Such attempts have, on a number of occasions, resulted in litigation in which the athletic organization sought to protect its exclusive right to its name, logo, or symbol, usually on the basis of trademark laws.

NOTE ───────────────────────────────────────

1. For more information, see Eric Fisher, "NBA, Reebok Reach 10-Year Merchandising Agreement," *Washington Times*, p. B7, August 2, 2001.

13.1.1. The Lanham Act of 1946

The Federal Trademark Act of 1946, 15 U.S.C. §§1051–1127, commonly known as the Lanham Act, governs the law of trademarks, the registration of trademarks, and remedies for the infringement of registered trademarks. Many common law principles governing this area have been incorporated into the Act. The Lanham Act was passed to "simplify trademark practice, secure trademark owners in their goodwill which they have built up, and to protect the public from imposition by the use of counterfeit and imitated marks and false descriptions." This act sets trademark guidelines for colleges, universities, corporations, organizations, and individuals. The general purpose of trademark legislation is to protect the owner of the mark, as well as prevent others from using distinctive marks that will confuse people into thinking they are dealing with the owner of the trademark when they are not.

The Lanham Act's definition of "trademark" was distilled from, and is consistent with, definitions appearing in court decisions both under prior trademark laws and the common law. *Trademark* is defined as "any word, name, symbol, or device or any combination thereof adopted and used by a manufacturer or merchant to identify his goods and distinguish them from those manufactured or sold by others." Trademarks refer to goods and are distinguished from service marks and collective marks.

13.1.2. Service Marks and Collective Marks

The Lanham Act also protects service marks and collective marks. A *service mark* is "a mark used in the sale or advertising of services to identify the services of one person and distinguish them from the services of others." While a trademark identifies and distinguishes the source and quality of a tangible product, a service mark identifies and distinguishes the source and quality of an intangible service. An example of a service mark is "NCAA." This stands for events or products related to the National Collegiate Athletic Association, as differentiated from other sporting bodies and associations. The term *collective mark*, as defined in the Lanham Act, means a trademark or service mark used by the "members of a cooperative, association, or other collective group or organization and includes marks used to indicate membership in a union, an association or other organization." An example of a collective mark in sports is Major League Baseball. A trademark serves the following functions:

Exhibit 13.2
Collective Marks

Reprinted with permission of Major League Baseball.

1. It designates the source of origin of a particular product or service, even though the source is unknown to the consumer.
2. It denotes a particular standard of quality, which is embodied in the product or service.
3. It identifies a product or service and distinguishes it from the products or services of others.
4. It symbolizes the goodwill of its owner and motivates consumers to purchase the trademarked product or service.
5. It represents a substantial advertising investment and is treated as a species of property.
6. It protects the public from confusion and deception, ensures that consumers are able to purchase the products and services they want, and enables the courts to fashion a standard of acceptable business conduct.

League and sports teams' names and logos, when used to identify the activities of leagues and teams, are service marks.

Normally, a mark for goods appears on the product or on its packaging; a service mark appears in advertising for the services. In sports, trademarks are used to promote team loyalty and the sale of licensed merchandise; service marks are used for promoting athletic events. The overall objective behind establishing a trademark is to set one brand apart from another. The registration of a trademark ensures the owner that competitors will not capitalize on the owner's efforts to establish brand loyalty and that no good will come by from confusing consumers through the use of the same mark or a similar mark.

An example of a trademark is "Boston College Eagles." The actual name of the school and its nickname identify the mark as representing that particular school. In addition, the colors of red and yellow in conjunction with the Boston College logo help consumers identify with that institution.

Common law protection is secured by the use of the trademark and extends only so far as is necessary to prevent consumer confusion. State registration is advantageous for local business that cannot qualify for federal registration is advantageous for local businesses that cannot qualify for federal registration because the mark is not used in interstate or foreign commerce, and it is quick and inexpensive in most states. State registration is also useful for local anti-infringement and anticounterfeiting efforts.

13.1.3. Identification Function of a Trademark

Although the trademark may not disclose the origin of the goods, it does provide the purchaser with a way of recognizing the goods of a particular seller or manufacturer. When the seller or manufacturer has conveyed origin and authenticity of the goods to the purchaser through the trademark, the seller or manufacturer has something of value. This identification function of the trademark also serves as a symbol of the goodwill established by a business. Trademarks therefore "are symbols by which goodwill is advertised and buying habits established." *Goodwill* is a business value that arises from the reputation of a business and its relations with its customers. It is unique to the particular business. Goodwill has also been defined as "buyer momentum" and "the lure to return." Goodwill is an intangible asset of a business. An *intangible asset* exists only in connection with something else. It is an idea or formula, not something that can be touched. A *tangible asset*, on the other hand, is something that can be touched. A pitching machine or hockey puck is a tangible asset.

Trademarks should be *distinctive*, and should not be either generic or merely descriptive of the goods or services to which they pertain. Words such as "cola," "table tennis," and "photocopier" are examples of non-distinctive or generic terms. Generic names of products and services do not qualify for trademark protection. They represent the actual product and are not associated with the source or manufacturer of the product. This is because the generic word defines only the product or service, not its source. The trademark laws, however, protect terms such as "Coca-Cola" and "Ping-Pong." They clearly are identified with the manufacturer and qualify as being distinctive terms. In many countries, trademarks that comprise only letters and/or numbers (the proposed trademark cannot be pronounced as a word or words or just has too few letters) or are surnames are considered indistinct. Nevertheless, these legal flaws in trademarks are not always fatal, and in a number of instances, a trademark registration can still be obtained for trademarks that are arguably (1) descriptive, (2) a surname, (3) geographic, or (4) indistinct. When non-distinctive words become distinctive and qualify for trademark protection, they are said to have acquired secondary meaning.

Trademarks are generally distinctive symbols, pictures, or words that sellers affix to distinguish and identify the origin of their products. Trademark status may also be granted to distinctive and unique packaging, color combinations, building designs, product styles, and overall presentations. Service marks receive the same legal protection as trademarks but are meant to distinguish services rather than products. In the United States, trademarks may be protected by both federal statutes, under the Lanham Act, and by state statute and/or common law. The United States Congress enacted the Lanham Act under its constitutional grant of authority to regulate interstate and foreign commerce. A trademark registered under the Lanham Act has nationwide protection. However, if a trademark is not registered under the Lanham Act, it still may be protected. Under state common laws, marks are protected as part of the common law of unfair competition, and registration of the mark is not required to prove ownership.

Trademark or service mark rights continue indefinitely, since these marks identify the source of goods or services. A mark can be registered for ten years and can be renewed for subsequent ten-year periods. This procedure is in contrast to other forms of intellectual property protection, such as patents or copyrights, which have finite terms. Between the fifth and sixth year after the date of initial trademark registration, the registrant must file an affidavit setting forth certain information to keep the registration active. If an affidavit is not filed, the registration is canceled. To maintain rights in the mark, it must be used, must not be abandoned, and must be protected so as not to become generic.

13.1.4. Secondary Meaning

Secondary meaning is a mental recognition in the buyer's mind associating symbols, words, colors, and designs with goods from a single source. Secondary meaning is a very important concept in trademark law. Secondary meaning "tests the connection in the buyer's mind between the product bearing the mark and its source." In a commercial sense, secondary meaning is buyer association, mental association, drawing power, or commercial magnetism. The purpose of the Lanham Act is to prevent consumer confusion as to the source of goods. If a good has acquired secondary meaning, the public associates the product with a certain source and the mark is then afforded greater protection under federal law. For example, the Cleveland Indians' trademarked logo is distinct, unique, and widely associated with the Major League Baseball Club, even though neither the word "Cleveland" nor "Indians" appears anywhere in the design (see Exhibit 13.3). Due to its widely recognized association with the baseball club, the Lanham Act would likely prevent the unauthorized use of similar images to promote other products. Secondary meaning is particularly important when the trademark is non-distinctive. Non-distinctive marks may not be registered and protected under the Lanham Act as trademarks until they have become distinctive of the goods in commerce. It is also possible to receive trademark status for identification that is not on its face distinct or unique, but developed a secondary meaning over time that identifies it with the product or seller. The owner of a trademark has exclusive right to use it on the product it was intended to identify, and often on related products (for an example of a case involving secondary marks, see note 2).

An example of a non-distinctive mark is a *descriptive mark*. A mark is descriptive if it describes the intended purpose, function, or use of the goods, the size of the goods, the class of users of the goods, a desirable characteristic of the goods, or the end effect upon the user. Some examples of descriptive marks are "Beer Nuts" for salted nuts, "Holiday Inn" for a motel, and "Raisin Bran" for cereal made with raisins and bran. Descriptive marks are considered weak marks and, at most, are given narrow trademark protection. Weak marks, as the name suggests, are marks that only describe the product, and are not necessarily a unique/creative name. Descriptive marks are not usually given trademark protection, as they do not adhere to the Lanham Act's distinctiveness requirement. Descriptive marks also lack secondary meaning, since the mark does not cause mental recognition of the product in the buyer's mind.

However, secondary meaning does not have to be demonstrated when the trademark is distinctive. Distinctive marks may be registered and protected under the Lanham Act as trademarks. Some examples of distinctive marks are arbitrary, fanciful, and suggestive marks, which are considered strong marks, and therefore are given strong trademark protection. *Arbitrary marks* are those "words, names, symbols, or devices" that are in common linguistic use but that, when used with the goods or services in issue, neither suggest nor describe any ingredient, quality, or characteristic of those goods or services. Some examples of arbitrary marks are "Cobra" golf clubs and "Puma" athletic wear. *Fanciful marks* are coined words that have been invented for the sole purpose

Exhibit 13.3
Cleveland Indians—Secondary Meaning

Reprinted with permission of Major League Baseball.

of functioning as a trademark. Such marks comprise words that are either totally unknown in the language or are completely out of common usage at the time, as with obsolete or scientific terms. Some examples of fanciful marks are "Clorox" bleach, "Kodak" photographic supplies, and "Polaroid" cameras. *Suggestive marks* are legally indistinguishable from arbitrary marks. An example of a suggestive mark would be "Greyhound" for a bus line, a name that suggests speed and sleekness. Suggestive marks generally imply a characteristic of the product they represent. For example, the name "Harlem Globetrotters" suggests that the team is a group that travels around the world playing basketball.

NOTES

1. In *GRIDIRON.Com, Inc. v. National Football Players Ass'n* 106 F.Supp.2d 1309 (S.D. Fla. 2000), plaintiffs sued for a declaration that it did not violate defendant's licensing agreement with NFL players. The defendant has a licensing agreement with 97% of NFL players. The defendant defines a group-licensing program as one that utilized six or more NFL players. The plaintiff operates a group of Web sites "devoted to professional football" that utilizes the images of over 150 players. The court held that "plaintiff's contractual agreements with the players violates defendant's proprietary rights in six or more NFL players' images." The court permanently enjoined the plaintiff from using the images of six or more NFL players.

2. In *Resorts of Pinehurst, Inc. v. Pinehurst National Corp.*, 148 F.3d 417 (4th Cir. 1998), plaintiff sued for trademark infringement of the mark "Pinehurst." Defendant used the mark in association with several golf courses in the same geographic area as plaintiff's famous Pinehurst golf courses. The court noted that the plaintiff had acquired secondary meaning in the mark so that it was associated with a source rather than a geographic area. Additionally, the court ruled that there was a likelihood of confusion in that both the plaintiff and defendant received mail, deliveries, and phone calls that were actually meant for the other. The court granted plaintiff's request for an injunction and directed the district court to immediately and permanently enjoin the defendant from using the mark "Pinehurst."

3. In *Jaguar Cars, Ltd. v. NFL*, 886 F.Supp. 335 (S.D.N.Y. 1995), a suit was brought by Jaguar Cars, Ltd. against the NFL when the NFL franchise in Jacksonville decided to use the name "Jaguars" and the image of a sleek jaguar that resembled the emblem serving as hood ornaments on Jaguar automobiles. The case was eventually settled out of court.

4. In *In re National Novice Hockey League, Inc.*, 222 U.S.P.Q. 638 (TTAB 1984), the Trademark Board refused to register the marks *National Novice Hockey League* and *NNHL* because of the likelihood of confusion with the National Hockey League.

13.1.5. Trademark Infringement

An inherent threat to trademark owners of highly visable sporting events, teams, schools and the Olympics is the pirating of their marks. Capitalizing on the fans' desire to identify with a favorite franchise or athletic organization, numerous businesses have exploited the goodwill and marketability of sports organizations by producing anything from hats to T-shirts to jerseys to pennants that carry a team name, nickname, team player name or number, logo, or symbol of the organization without authorization. This type of exploitation can have damaging consequences. First, the unauthorized use of a mark is injurious, because the market demand for any product or service is finite, and sales of unlicensed merchandise will reduce licensed sales, especially since it can be underpriced. Second, assuming consumer confusion, if the unlicensed merchandise is of a lesser quality, it will reflect negatively on the quality of the licensed merchandise and also on the organization. Thus the goodwill and the reputation that the trademark owner established would be damaged, resulting in a decreased value of the trademark. Therefore, it is very important for sports organizations to protect their marks. After being made aware of the infringement, the trademark owner can demand that the activity cease. If the demand is ignored, the owner is left with no other recourse but to pursue legal remedies provided under the Lanham Act and common law.

The Lanham Act defines *trademark infringement* as the reproduction, counterfeiting, copying or imitation, in commerce of a registered mark "in connection with the sale, offering for sale, distribution, or advertising of any goods or services on or in connection with which such use is likely to cause confusion or to cause mistake, or to deceive without consent of the registrant." In order to be successful in a trademark suit, the trademark owner must first establish a protectable property right in the name or mark it seeks to defend. Second, the owner must establish that the infringing party's use of a similar mark is likely to cause confusion, mistake, or deception in the market as to the source, origin, or sponsorship of the products on which the marks are used.

Trademark rights are established by (1) *actual use of the mark*, or (2) the *filing of a proper application to register a mark* in the United States Patent and Trademark Office (USPTO) stating that the applicant has a bona fide intention to use the mark in commerce regulated by the U.S. Congress. Federal registration is not required to establish rights in a mark, nor is it required to begin use of a mark. However, federal registration can secure benefits beyond those rights acquired by merely using a mark. For example, the owner of a federal registration is presumed to be the owner of the mark for the goods and services specified in the registration, and to be entitled to use the mark nationwide. In addition, under the Lanham Act, the registration of a mark with the U.S. Patent and Trademark Office (USPTO) (see exhibit 13.4 for an example of a state trademark registration form) constitutes prima facie evidence that the registrant owns the mark and has the exclusive right to use the mark, and that the registration itself is valid. The burden is then placed on the one challenging the mark to rebut the presumption of validity.

There are two related but distinct types of rights in a mark: the right to register and the right to use. Generally, the first party who either uses a mark in commerce or files an application in the USPTO has the ultimate right to register that mark. The USPTO's authority is limited to determining the right to register. The right to use a mark can be more complicated to determine. This is particularly true when two parties have begun use of the same or similar marks without knowledge of one another and neither has a federal registration. Only a court can render a decision about the right to use, such as issuing an injunction or awarding damages for infringement. When making its decision, the court will attempt to determine factually which party was the first to use the mark in commerce. Second, the court will weigh the positive and negative reasons for allowing each party to use the particular mark.

There are three ways that an organization or individual can lose rights in a mark. First, abandonment of a trademark is stopping the use of it with an intention not to resume its use. The second is by licensing the mark to others without controlling the nature and quality of the licensee's goods or services under the mark. Finally, rights to a mark may be lost when there is misuse of the mark by the organization—or a failure to police against the mark's misuse by others—so that it ceases to indicate source but becomes just another generic word in the language, such as "escalator," "aspirin," and "cellophane."

A defendant in a trademark infringement case, in addition to contending that the "word, name, symbol, or device" is indistinguishable from that of other owners or manufacturers, may contend that the mark is functional and, therefore, not worthy of trademark status. A functional mark can be defined as a mark that does not describe or distinguish the product, but is necessary for the product to exist. This was one of the key issues in *Dallas Cowboys Cheerleaders Inc. v. Pussycat Cinema, Ltd.*, 604 F.2d 200 (2d Cir. 1979), where the defendant alleged that cheerleading uniforms were a purely functional item necessary for the performance of cheerleading routines and, therefore, incapable of becoming the subject of a trademark.

The infringer may also contend that the owner of the mark, though once possessed of a property interest in the mark, had abandoned or relinquished its right. Here, however, rather than relying on the owner's failure to prosecute alleged infringers or allowing the uncontrolled use of the mark for a period of time as evidence of abandonment, the infringer must establish both the intent of the owner to abandon the mark and the loss of all indication as to the source of the mark's origin. Abandonment of a mark is not as simple as stopping the use of a trademark. In *Indianapolis Colts, Inc. v. Metropolitan Baltimore Football Club, L.P.*, 34 F.3d 410 (7th Cir. 1994), a case involving the former Baltimore Colts team that moved to Indianapolis, the Canadian Football League and one of its owners were sued for using the name Baltimore CFL Colts, even though the owner of the Baltimore Colts had moved his franchise to Indianapolis and there were no longer any Baltimore Colts. The court enjoined the CFL team from using the name because it was likely to confuse a substantial number of consumers.

Even though an alleged infringer may be unable to prove the validity of a mark, this does not settle the infringement issue under the Lanham Act. The owner of the mark still bears the burden of establishing that the infringement is likely to cause confusion, mistake, or deception in the market as to the source, origin, or sponsorship of the products on which the mark is used. One might expect that the similarity or duplication of a registered mark would be sufficient to establish confusion, but such has not been the case. Courts generally have required the production of evidence to establish that individuals make the critical distinction as to sponsorship or endorsement, or direct evidence of actual con-

Exhibit 13.4
Trademark Registration Form, State of Oklahoma

File in Duplicate

Print Clearly

TRADEMARK REGISTRATION

TO: **Oklahoma Secretary of State**
2300 N. Lincoln Blvd., State Capitol Building, Room 101
Oklahoma City, OK 73105-4897
(405) 522-3043

The undersigned, in order to register a trademark in the state of Oklahoma pursuant to the provisions of 78 O.S., Section 23, here submits the following:

1.   The trademark name or design: _____

AND one specimen or facsimile of such trademark is **ATTACHED HERETO**.

2.   A description of the goods or services used in connection with the trademark:_____
       (See the procedure sheet for a list of general classes of goods and services)

3.   The mode or manner in which the mark is used in connection with the goods or services:_____

4.   The statutory classification(s) of such goods or services:

       Class Number(s):_____

       Class Name(s):_____

5.   The date of first use of the trademark by the applicant or his/her predecessor in business:
       (a.) Anywhere: _____; and (b) in Oklahoma:_____

6.   Applicant's full and exact name:_____

       _____

7.   Applicant's business address:_____

       _____

Exhibit 13.4 (continued)

8.   Applicant is:

- an individual doing business as:_____
- incorporated in the state of:_____
- other legal entity:_____

The undersigned applicant is the owner of the trademark and no other person has the right to use such trademark in this state either in the identical form thereof or in such near resemblance thereto as might be calculated to deceive or to be mistaken therefor.

Signed this _____ day of _____, _____.

_____
signature

_____
Title, if applicable

(SOS Form 0045-6/99)

fusion between the authentic and counterfeit products. The "likely to cause confusion" issue has proven to be the key question in the majority of sports trademark cases. The Ninth Circuit interpreted it thus:

> In order to determine whether there is a likelihood of confusion in a trademark infringement case, the Court must consider numerous factors, including *inter alia*, the strength or weakness of the marks, similarity in appearance, sound, and meaning, the class of goods in question, the marketing channels, evidence of actual confusion, and evidence of the intention of defendant in selecting and using the alleged infringing [mark].

Of paramount concern is whether there is a likelihood of confusion such that the public believes that the goods are endorsed or authorized by someone other than the trademark owner. As can be seen through the Ninth Circuit interpretation of likelihood of confusion, the court must take numerous factors into account when judging whether or not two marks are likely to be confused (see notes 6, 8, and 14 for cases decided on likelihood of confusion arguments).

An important early case dealing with likelihood of confusion in sports is *National Football League Properties, Inc. v. Wichita Falls Sportswear, Inc.*, 532 F.Supp. 651 (W.D. Wash. 1982) (see note 14). In this case, the defendant company, Wichita Falls Sportswear, was manufacturing and selling NFL football jersey replicas that, due to their similarity to authentic NFL jerseys, created the likelihood of confusion in the minds of the consumer. Wichita Falls manufactured jerseys in the blue and green colors of the Seattle Seahawk uniforms. The court held that NFL Properties had the burden of proving (1) that the secondary meaning of the descriptive term (e.g., Seattle) related the jersey to the NFL team, and (2) that Wichita Falls' activities created a likelihood of confusion. The NFL was able to prove that placing Seattle on the jersey created a likelihood of confusion in the buyer's mind over whether or not these were authentic, licensed jerseys.

In addition, there are circumstances where products display a disclaimer proclaiming that the trademark owner does not endorse the articles. In *Boston Professional Hockey Ass'n. v. Dallas Cap & Emblem Mfg.*, 510 F.2d 1004 (5th Cir. 1975), the defendant manufactured products that contained registered and unregistered marks of various NHL teams. The defendant included a disclaimer on its products indicating that use of the marks was not authorized. The court concluded that the defendant's use of a disclaimer did not prevent liability under the Lanham Act. The court's conclusion was based on the belief that there would likely be a degree of consumer confusion. The confusion requirement was met since "the defendant duplicated the protected trademarks and sold them to the public knowing that the public would identify them as being the team's trademarks. The certain knowledge of the buyer that the source and origin of the trademark symbols were in [the] plaintiff's satisfies the requirement of the act." In addition, the court found that the team had an interest in its own individualized symbol and was entitled to legal protection against such unauthorized duplication.

In *Major League Baseball Players Ass'n v. Dad's Kid Corp.*, 806 F.Supp. 458 (S.D.N.Y. 1992), the defendant manufactured a baseball card, called the Tri-Card, by using three authentic licensed baseball cards originally made by MLBPA's licensees. Defendant corporation disclaimed any copyright or trademark rights with respect to the baseball cards used to manufacture the Tri-Card. The disclaimer provided that Dad's Kid Corp. disclaimed any proprietary rights to the name and logo of Major League Baseball and of the Major League Baseball Players Association. The district court held that (1) there was no likelihood of confusion as to origin as required for injunction, since genuine cards were used to produce the display item and the manufacturer put the disclaimer on the packaging of its products, and (2) manufacturer had not misappropriated the publicity rights of major league players. This decision was important as it held that baseball players had little, if any, publicity rights with respect to the use and reuse of their pictures on cards, after the original sale of the card by an official licensee, for which the players received a royalty payment.

Another issue dealing with licensing is the situation where the permission of two organizations is needed to produce goods or services. In professional sports, the athlete has a right to publicity and desires to have an influence over what products bear his likeness. By the same token, leagues stand to profit from licensing players' names and likenesses to many producers in order to benefit the entire league economically. For example, in *Major League Baseball Properties, Inc. v. Pacific Trading Cards, Inc.*, 150 F.3d 149 (2d Cir. 1998), the Major League Baseball Players Association gave permission to the defendant to produce trading cards; however, the league did not provide its permission. Major League Baseball Properties, Inc., the licensing arm for the Major League clubs, sued the defendant, seeking to block distribution of the company's cards. Major League Baseball Properties, Inc., alleged that the defendant violated the clubs' trademark rights. Specifically, the Major League Baseball Properties argued that the team logos and uniforms could not be used without their permission. Pacific had had a licensing agreement with the owners until the previous year. Pacific countered that it was not violating trademark rights because it was not using the owners' pictures of the players and was not marketing the cards as officially owner-endorsed. The district court did not issue a preliminary injunction prohibiting distribution of the baseball cards. However, on appeal, the district court's decision was vacated in order for the matter to be settled out of court.

NOTES ───

1. In *International Star Class Yacht Racing Ass'n v. Tommy Hilfiger U.S.A., Inc.*, 146 F.3d 66 (2d Cir. 1998), plaintiff, the International Star Class Yacht Racing Association, sued the defendant, a clothing design and marketing company, for trademark infringement of the mark "Star Class." The court held that defendant had infringed plaintiff's mark and enjoined defendant from using the mark. Plaintiff requested an accounting for profits based on the bad faith of the defendant. Plaintiff claimed that defendant conducted an improper trademark search. The district court denied injunctive relief as to ISCYRA's insignia and an accounting of Hilfiger's profits, actual damages, and attorney fees in finding that Hilfiger had not acted in bad faith. On appeal, the issue of whether or not Hilfiger acted in bad faith was remanded back to the district court, who later affirmed their decision, stating that "although there is some evidence that points toward the existence of bad faith, we cannot say, after review of the record, that we are left with [the] definite and firm conviction that a mistake has been committed."

2. In *Pebble Beach Company v. Tour 18 Ltd.*, 155 F.3d 526 (5th Cir. 1998), defendant owned and operated a public golf course in which several of the golf holes were copied from more famous golf courses, particularly Pinehurst No. 2, Pebble Beach, and Harbour Town owned by Sea Pines, the plaintiffs in this case. None of the courses had a copyright or trademark registration for the specific golf holes that were copied. Therefore, the

defendant was successful against the owners of Pinehurst No. 2 and Pebble Beach. However, the suit involving Harbour Town came down to a trade dress issue. Trade dress is defined as the distinctive packaging or design of a product that promotes the product and distinguishes it from other products in the marketplace. The trade dress issue in question was that the defendant copied Harbour Town's most famous golf hole, hole 18, which is better known as the "Lighthouse Hole." The court stated:

> For the plaintiffs to prevail on their service-mark and trade dress infringement claims, they must show (1) that the mark or trade dress, as the case may be, qualifies for protection and (2) that Tour 18's use of the mark or trade dress creates a likelihood of confusion in the minds of potential consumers. With trade dress, the question is whether the "combination of features creates a distinctive visual impression, identifying the source of the product."

The court ruled that the "Lighthouse Hole" had acquired secondary meaning for the plaintiff and; therefore, was worthy of protection. The court also held that consumers were likely to be confused as to the affiliation of the golf course. Therefore, the defendant violated plaintiff's rights and the court required the defendant to remove the lighthouse from its golf course.

3. In *Johnny Blastoff, Inc. v. Los Angeles Rams Football Company*, 48 U.S.P.Q. 2d (BNA) 1385 (W.D. Wis. 1998), both plaintiff and defendant claim exclusive rights for the use of the mark "St. Louis Rams." Plaintiff registered the mark in Wisconsin with the intent of using it in conjunction with a fictional cartoon storyline. The defendant registered the mark in Missouri after the announcement that the Los Angeles Rams were moving to St. Louis and would change their name to the St. Louis Rams. The court noted, "As between competing claimants to a trademark, the party who first appropriates the mark through use acquires superior rights." The court held that a substantial portion of the public associated the mark "St. Louis Rams" with the defendant at the time of plaintiff's registration. The court found that there was a likelihood of confusion by prospective purchasers of the goods and services of the parties. The court disagreed with plaintiff's argument that the "Rams" mark had become generic and that therefore the defendants lost their rights in the mark. Plaintiff argued that the use of "Rams" by several college football teams made "Rams" generic. The court held that this was irrelevant to a professional football team.

4. In *Dream Team Collectibles, Inc. v. NBA Properties, Inc.*, 958 F.Supp. 1401 (E.D. Missouri 1997), a lawsuit resulted over the rights to the mark "Dream Team." Plaintiff produced "unframed collages of sports trading cards and sports-related merchandise." The defendant held the rights to market and license merchandise associated with the 1992 men's basketball Olympic team, which became known as the "Dream Team" because the team consisted of NBA stars. The plaintiff claimed "reverse confusion," which occurs when a junior user (the second user of the mark) appears to have superior rights to the mark in the public's eye, so that the senior user (the first user of the mark) actually appears to be the infringe. The court concluded that there was a genuine issue of material fact as to whether defendant or the media associated the mark "Dream Team" with the basketball team. While both NBA Properties and Dream Team Collectibles made summary judgment motions on this issue, the court granted Dream Team Collectibles' motion. The court held that NBA Properties had cited no authority for the "proposition that cancellation of a mark is warranted when a party demonstrates some unlawful use of a mark by its owner who, for the most part, is using the mark lawfully."

5. In *Cardtoons, L.C. v. Major League Baseball Players Association*, 95 F.3d 959 (10th Cir. 1996), plaintiff "brought this action to obtain a declaratory judgment that its parody trading cards featuring active Major League Baseball players do not infringe on the publicity rights of members of the Major League Baseball Players Association." Plaintiff used the likenesses of Major League players to poke fun at the game of baseball and how much players were paid. The court held that there was no trademark infringement because there was not a likelihood of confusion on the part of the consumer. The court did hold that

plaintiff infringed on MLBPA's publicity rights under state law. "Publicity rights . . . are a form of property protection that allows people to profit from the full commercial value of their identities." However, the plaintiff's First Amendment rights outweigh MLBPA's publicity rights, and therefore the plaintiff may continue to produce the parody cards.

6. *Monster Communications, Inc. v. Turner Broadcasting System, Inc.*, 935 F.Supp. 490 (S.D.N.Y. 1996) deals with film footage of the Muhammad Ali-George Foreman heavyweight title fight that took place in Zaire. Plaintiff "made and owns an 84 minute motion picture called 'When We Were Kings.' " Defendant planned to air a movie on Turner Network Television called *The Whole Story*. Plaintiff claims that defendant's movie "contains between 41 seconds and 2 minutes" of footage to which plaintiff owned the rights. The court held that even if the plaintiff were able to prove protectible rights in the footage, the defendant would prevail because it would be able to prove fair use of the copyrighted material. Plaintiff's injunction request to prevent defendant's broadcasting of its movie was denied.

7. In *National Basketball Ass'n Properties, Inc. v. YMG, Inc.*, No. 93 C 1533, 1993 U.S. Dist. LEXIS 15864 (N.D. Ill. Nov. 5, 1993), the plaintiff, which holds the exclusive license from the NBA and its member teams to license others to manufacture and sell merchandise bearing NBA trademarks, brought an action for trademark infringement. An investigator employed by the plaintiff ordered merchandise from the defendant that had NBA logos on it. After a determination that the goods were counterfeit, NBA Properties executed a seizure of the goods. Although the merchandise bore NBA registered trademarks and purported to be "officially licensed" merchandise, YMG was not licensed to embroider, distribute, or sell merchandise bearing reproductions of NBA trademarks. Summary judgment was granted to the plaintiff.

8. In *Maryland Stadium Authority v. Becker*, 806 F.Supp. 1236 (D. Md. 1992), the owner of Camden Yards baseball park brought a trademark infringement action against a vendor that used the words "Camden Yards" on T-shirts and other clothing items. The district court held for the plaintiff and reasoned that evidence concerning the owner's promotional efforts and media coverage given to the park was sufficient to establish that the plaintiff had adopted and used the "Camden Yards" mark before the vendor started using the mark. Additionally, the court held that there was enough evidence to establish that the owner's "Camden Yards" mark had acquired secondary meaning and that vendor's action created a likelihood of confusion.

9. In *National Football League Properties, Inc. v. Playoff Corp.*, 808 F.Supp. 1288 (N.D. Tex 1992), NFL Properties, exclusive licensing representative for the NFL, asserted claims for trademark infringement and unfair competition under the Lanham Act and state statutes against a company that planned to market football trading cards. On plaintiff's motion for preliminary injunction, the district court held that although the plaintiff showed a substantial likelihood of success on the merits, plaintiff failed to show that irreparable harm would result from failure to issue an injunction. The motion was denied.

10. In *Harlem Globetrotters, Inc. v. Harlem Magicians, Inc.*, 872 F.2d 1025 (6th Cir. 1989), plaintiff filed suit alleging that the defendant violated plaintiff's registered trademarks "Harlem Globetrotters" and "Magicians of Basketball" by using the words "Harlem Magicians." In 1964, a consent agreement, which had been approved by the court system, permanently enjoined the defendant from using the terms "Harlem," "Globetrotters," or "Trotters" to promote its basketball team. The court of appeals held that the 1964 consent agreement was valid, and therefore the defendant violated the plaintiff's trademark rights.

11. In *Boston Athletic Association v. Sullivan*, 867 F.2d 22 (1st Cir. 1989), the defendant sold T-shirts with the logos "Boston Marathon" and "B.A.A. Marathon" printed on them. Plaintiff brought action against the defendant for infringement of plaintiff's trademark. In reversing the lower court's decision, the judge ruled that the shirts infringed on BAA's trademark, and enjoined the defendant from manufacturing and selling the shirts.

12. In *National Football League Properties, Inc. v. New Jersey Giants, Inc.*, 637 F.Supp.

507 (D.N.J. 1986), the defendant company exploited the fact that the New York Giants football team played their home games in New Jersey. The company manufactured and sold T-shirts and other merchandise displaying the name "New Jersey Giants." The New York Giants and NFL Properties, Inc., brought action against the company, alleging infringement of the New York Giants' trademark. In ruling for the plaintiffs, the judge permanently enjoined defendant from further use of the name New Jersey Giants on merchandise and as the company name. The court held that "Giants" and "New York Giants" are valid service marks worthy of protection, and that under the Lanham Act, owners of service marks and owners of trademarks are protected from other marks that are likely to cause consumer confusion. The Giants would only be afforded this protection if their marks possessed secondary meaning at the time defendant began using them. The court found that there was strong evidence showing that secondary meaning in the marks "Giants" and "New York Giants" had been proven.

13. In the important sports trademark case *National Football League Properties, Inc. v. Wichita Falls Sportswear, Inc.*, 532 F.Supp. 651 (W.D. Wash. 1982), it was the court's scrutiny of the consumer confusion issue that led to the plaintiff's success in preventing the defendant sportswear company from manufacturing and selling NFL football jersey replicas which created the likelihood of confusion. NFL Properties alleged that its trademark rights were violated when Wichita Falls manufactured jerseys in the blue and green colors of the Seattle Seahawk uniform. The court held that NFL Properties had the burden of proving (1) that the secondary meaning of the descriptive term (i.e., Seattle) related the jersey to the NFL team, and (2) that Wichita Falls' activities created a likelihood of confusion. The NFL was able to prove that placing Seattle on the jersey created a likelihood of confusion in the buyer's mind over whether or not these were authentic, licensed jerseys.

14. In *ETW Corp. v. Jireh Publishing Inc.*, 99 F.Supp. 2d 829 (N.D. Oh. 2000), the U.S. District Court for the Northern District of Ohio addressed the question of right of publicity. The Ohio district court granted summary judgment to the publisher of a print that depicts golfer Tiger Woods, despite the fact that 5,000 copies of the print had been issued. The court found that the use of Woods' likeness in the work, a "limited edition" art print titled "The Masters of Augusta," was not "for purpose of trade." Noting that a certificate of authenticity accompanied the work and that the print's packaging included a statement by the artist expressing his desire to create "serious art" about sports, the court found that the print was not a "mere poster" or item of "sports merchandise" but rather "an artistic creation seeking to express a message" entitled to broad constitutional protection. Accordingly, the Ohio district court held, the common law right of publicity could not prohibit its sale.

13.1.6. Ambush Marketing

Within the sports industry, a recent trend related to trademark law has been "ambush marketing." Ambush marketing is defined as the intentional efforts of a company to weaken or "ambush" a competitor's official association with a sports entity that was acquired through the payment of sponsorship fees. The company that is ambushing has not paid any money to the sports organization to affiliate its organization with the event. Companies have undertaken this marketing tactic through many different avenues including the purchase of advertising time on television before and during an "official" event. The purchase of commercial time allows the ambushing company to associate itself with a sporting event without having to pay the official sponsor fees.

Another form of ambush marketing is the sponsoring of a contest surrounding a sporting event without using the name of the event in its promotional materials.

Ambush marketing may be difficult to challenge legally (see note 2). This is because the ambushing company usually takes steps to avoid creating a "likelihood of confusion," which is prohibited by the Lanham Act. Disclaimers are often used to communicate information to the consumer that the company sponsoring the contest or featured in the commercial is not a sponsor of the sporting event, is not affiliated with any such sponsors, and claims no ownership rights to the sporting event.

Ambush marketing has been costly to sports organizations trying to sell rights to their sporting events to companies for sponsorship revenue. As more and more ambush marketing occurs, the value placed on "official sponsor" language can decrease and the sports organizations lose out financially. It is extremely difficult for the sports organizations to challenge ambush marketing techniques. First, companies have become increasingly sophisticated and creative in their methods of testing the gray area between legal marketing activity, which is covered by the commercial and free speech provisions of the First Amendment and the fair-use doctrine and illegal marketing activity that could constitute trademark infringement and unfair competition. Sports organizations need to show that a "likelihood of confusion" exists in the consumer's mind, a very difficult thing to prove. The following are examples of how ambush marketing can occur in the sports industry. One example of ambush marketing is the purchase of advertising signage around an event where a main competitor is also purchasing signage. This type of ambush marketing is prevalent around major events with multiple promotional and advertising opportunities such as the Olympics or the Super Bowl. Another example is if a competing office supply store sets up a gigantic billboard on the street leading to the Staples Center in Los Angeles. Finally, a company buys advertising on a television show that is sponsored by its main competitor. All of these forms of ambush marketing attempt to weaken the effect of an official sponsorship without spending the money for the sponsorship.

The second reason it is hard to challenge ambush marketing is that few decided cases address the legal parameters of ambush marketing, and fewer still specifically refer to the term *ambush marketing* (see notes 1 and 2). Third, most ambush marketing campaigns last only a brief period of time, making the time and cost of litigation prohibitive. Sports organizations are also fearful of the consequences of a negative ruling on ambush marketing, which could open the floodgates to future problems. However, sports organizations can defend themselves against ambush marketing by planning ahead and anticipating the actions of competitive marketers. One method of defense is to make sure that all potential issues are specifically and precisely addressed in the contract stage. An organization should use the contract to maintain tight reign over elements that are under their control (i.e., trademark registration, names, logos, mascots). Legislation, such as the Ted Stevens Amateur Sports Act (see section 13.1.8., "Trademark Law and the Olympics"), has also helped strengthen the rights of organizations who are battling ambush marketing.

NOTES ⎯⎯⎯⎯⎯⎯⎯⎯⎯⎯⎯⎯⎯⎯⎯⎯⎯⎯⎯⎯⎯⎯⎯⎯⎯⎯⎯⎯

1. In *Master Card International v. Sprint Communications Co.*, 23 F.3d 397 (2d. Cir. 1994), Master Card had signed an exclusive agreement with the 1994 World Cup organizers to be the sole credit-card sponsor for the event. Sprint signed on with the event and proceeded to manufacture cards that bore the World Cup symbol. These cards contained

a number that the user either entered into the phone upon hearing a prompt or read to the operator. The cards, however, lacked a magnetic stripe that would permit them to be scanned by a card reader and also lack any information relating to the cardholder that could be used for making a credit purchase from a vendor. However, because Master Card was the official credit-card sponsor, the court enjoined Sprint from manufacturing these calling cards that bore the name and logo of the World Cup.

2. The following case shows how creative companies can be in marketing, while not violating the law, as well as the difficulty the court has in drawing the line. In *National Hockey League, et al. v. Pepsi-Cola Canada Ltd.*, 42 C.P.R.3d 390 (B.C. 1992), the National Hockey League filed a lawsuit alleging that Pepsi-Cola Canada, a company without rights to NHL trademarks, had engaged in misappropriation and unfair competition by using marks "confusingly similar" to those owned by the NHL. In Spring 1990, Pepsi-Cola Canada conducted a consumer contest called the "Diet Pepsi $4,000,000 Pro Hockey Playoff Pool," whereby fans matching information under bottle caps with actual NHL Playoff results became eligible for prizes. In addition, Pepsi-Cola Canada sponsored the broadcasts of the NHL play-off games throughout Canada and used its commercial spots to advertise the promotion.

On all promotional materials connected with this contest and at the beginning of all commercials during the play-off games, Pepsi-Cola Canada displayed a disclaimer disassociating Pepsi-Cola Canada and its promotion from the NHL. The NHL claimed that not only was use of these disclaimers an admission by Pepsi-Cola Canada that it was aware of the misrepresentations contained in its advertising, but also that use of the words "National Hockey League" in the disclaimers was itself a trademark infringement.

The Supreme Court of British Columbia ruled against the NHL, holding that Pepsi-Cola Canada had used sufficient disclaimers in its promotional announcements and commercial advertising to make consumers aware that it was not officially associated with the NHL. The judge stated that Pepsi's product is soft drinks and the NHL's product is hockey, and therefore there can be no confusion in the consumer's minds as to which product belongs to which company. The judge refused to accept the arguments brought forth by the NHL about the disclaimers used by Pepsi-Cola Canada, stating that a company can use the trademark of another company in its disclaimers because this allows the company to convey its promotional offer to the consumers truthfully and accurately. The use of disclaimers by Pepsi-Cola Canada was found to be sufficient to alleviate any potential confusion among consumers.

13.1.7. Licensing Programs for Intercollegiate Athletics

In search of the economic benefits to be reaped from the sale of caps, pennants, T-shirts, jerseys, and souvenirs bearing a school's name or logo, many universities have instituted licensing programs in order to merchandise properties associated with their athletic teams. What is developing is a situation analogous to that in the major professional sport leagues, in that a licensing agent handles the licensing program for one or more university athletic departments. One such agent, the Collegiate Licensing Company, in 2001 represented over 180 colleges and universities, several post-season football bowl games, multiple college conferences, and the Downtown Athletic Club, the presentor of the Heisman Trophy.

There are several reasons why a university or bowl game might use a licensing agent. For example, a university may not have the expertise or time to register the marks, negotiate licensing agreements with manufacturers, police mark infringers, and litigate when necessary. Also, a licensing agent often packages marks to manufacturers on a state, regional, or conference basis. For example, a licensing agent will package all of the marks of the Atlantic Coast Conference to one manufacturer. Therefore, a manufacturer who desires to produce Duke University apparel will also acquire the rights to produce apparel for Wake Forest University, another member of the ACC. This may save on costs for the manufacturer, who does not have to negotiate separately with each school.

Along with the advantages of using a licensing agent there are several potential disadvantages. The university may prefer to control the selection of manufacturers and the quality of products, as well as to maintain flexibility in arranging licensing agreements. For example, universities that handle their own licensing programs may vary fees according to the type of product, the sales volume, whether the item is academically oriented, and other factors. A university that contracts with a licensing agent generally pays 40 to 50% of the royalty revenues generated to the agent, which reduces the university's net royalty revenues to 3 or 4% (instead of 6 to 8%). Also, the university may prefer to retain control of the decision-making authority with respect to enforcement of mark infringement cases (see exhibit 13.5 for an example of a licensing agent's contract).

Universities face a number of decisions and challenges in the area of trademarks and service marks. Initially, there is the decision of whether to begin a licensing program. If the answer is affirmative, the university should consider registering the existing marks on both the state and the federal level. The university may later be faced with the decision of whether to register a new mark, for instance the phrase "Phi Slamma Jamma" for the University of Houston basketball team in the 1980s. The university must weigh the advantages and disadvantages of handling the licensing program itself or contracting with a licensing agent. In either situation, the university must establish public association between the mark, as used on various products, and the university's sponsorship. The university must decide whether and what collateral marks and products will be sold. Finally, the university must be able to enforce the marks. If the university undertakes its own licensing program, it must police the mark wherever the products are sold. This may be only on a local basis in the state or region of the university, or it may be on a national basis if the school has a national reputation and sells its products nationwide.

Policing marks against infringers is one of the key determinants of long-term success for intercollegiate licensing programs. This is a costly and timely undertaking, and one that may well reduce the profitability of a licensing program for universities that do not realize significant royalty revenues. It remains to be seen whether universities will be able to establish the expertise, allocate the manpower, and spend the dollars necessary for effective enforcement of their marks. This issue alone may be a compelling reason for many universities to contract with a licensing agent, who, with tremendous economies of scale, can police and enforce marks.

Regardless of whether the university decides to handle the licensing program by itself or to contract with a licensing agent, it must make some decisions regarding the distribution of royalty revenues. Among the alternatives to be considered in distributing royalty revenues are appropriating money for athletic scholarships, for the general scholarship fund, for the general university fund, and/or returning the money to the campus bookstore. There is a wide range of ways in which colleges and universities have distributed royalty revenues on campus.

Exhibit 13.5

The following agreement was provided by Grimes & Battersby, attorneys specializing in intellectual property and licensing, with offices at Three Landmark Square, Ste. 405, Stamford, CT 06901.

THIS AGREEMENT is effective as of {Date} by and between {Owner Name}, a {Owner Inc.} corporation with offices at {Owner Address} ("**LICENSOR**") and {Licensee Name}, a {Licensee Inc.} corporation with offices at {Licensee Address} ("**LICENSEE**").

W I T N E S S E T H:

WHEREAS, **LICENSOR** is the sole and exclusive owner of the Property or Properties identified more fully in Schedule A attached hereto (the "Property");

WHEREAS, **LICENSOR** is the sole and exclusive owner of the Trademark identified more fully in Schedule A attached hereto (the "Trademark");

WHEREAS, **LICENSOR** has the power and authority to grant to **LICENSEE** the right, privilege and license to use, manufacture and sell those types of products that incorporate or are otherwise based on the Property as identified in Schedule A attached hereto (the "Licensed Products") and to use the Trademark on or in association with such Licensed Products;

WHEREAS, **LICENSEE** has represented that it has the ability to manufacture, market and distribute the Licensed Products in the countries identified in Schedule A attached hereto (the "Territory") and to use the Trademark on or in association with the Licensed Products;

WHEREAS, **LICENSEE** desires to obtain from **LICENSOR** an exclusive license to use, manufacture, have manufactured and sell Licensed Products in the Territory and to use the Trademark on or in association with the Licensed Products; and

WHEREAS, both **LICENSEE** and **LICENSOR** are in agreement with respect to the terms and conditions upon which **LICENSEE** shall use, manufacture, have manufactured and sell Licensed Products and use the Trademark;

NOW, THEREFORE, in consideration of the promises and agreements set forth herein, the parties, each intending to be legally bound hereby, do promise and agree as follows.

1. License Grant

A.   **LICENSOR** hereby grants to **LICENSEE**, for the Term of this Agreement as recited in Schedule A attached hereto, the exclusive right and license to use, manufacture,

Exhibit 13.5 (continued)

have manufactured, sell, distribute and advertise the Licensed Products in the Territory. The license includes, but is not limited to, a license under any and all patents and copyrights and any applications therefore which have been filed or may be filed in the future with respect to the Property. It is understood and agreed that this license shall pertain only to the Licensed Products and does not extend to any other product or service.

B.   **LICENSOR** hereby grants to **LICENSEE** for the Term of this Agreement as recited in Schedule A attached hereto, a royalty- free, exclusive license to use the Trademark on or in association with the Licensed Products in the Territory as well as on packaging, promotional and advertising material associated therewith.

C.   **LICENSEE** may not grant any sublicenses to any third party without the prior express written consent of the **LICENSOR**, which consent may be withheld for any reason.

D.   **LICENSEE** shall not make or authorize any use, direct or indirect, of the Licensed Products, like or similar, in any other country outside the Territory and will not knowingly sell the Licensed Products to persons who intend or are likely to resell them in any country outside the Territory.

2. Term of the Agreement

This Agreement and the provisions hereof, except as otherwise provided, shall be in full force and effect commencing on the date of execution by both parties and shall extend for a Term as recited in Schedule A attached hereto (the "Term").

3. Compensation

A.   In consideration for the licenses granted hereunder, **LICENSEE** agrees to pay to **LICENSOR**, during the Term of this Agreement, a royalty in the amount recited in Schedule A attached hereto (the "Royalty") based on **LICENSEE**'s Net Sales of Licensed Products.

B.   In the event that **LICENSEE** grants any previously approved sub-licenses for the use of the Property in countries outside of the United States, **LICENSEE** shall pay **LICENSOR** {Sub- Licensing Percentage} PERCENT of the gross income received by **LICENSEE** from such sub-licensees.

C.   The Royalty owed **LICENSOR** shall be calculated on a quarterly calendar basis (the "Royalty Period") and shall be payable no later than thirty (30) days after the termination of the preceding full calendar quarter, i.e., commencing on the first (1st) day of January, April, July and October with the exception of the first and last calendar quarters which may be "short" depending upon the effective date of this Agreement.

D.   With each Royalty Payment, **LICENSEE** shall provide **LICENSOR** with a written royalty statement in a form acceptable to **LICENSOR**. Such royalty statement shall be certified as accurate by a duly authorized officer of **LICENSEE**, reciting on a country- by-country basis, the stock number, item, units sold, description, quantity shipped, gross invoice, amount billed customers less discounts, allowances, returns and reportable sales for each Licensed Product. Such statements shall be furnished to **LICENSOR** whether or not any Licensed Products were sold during the Royalty Period.

Exhibit 13.5 (continued)

E.   **LICENSEE** agrees to pay to **LICENSOR** a Guaranteed Minimum Royalty in accordance with the terms of Schedule A attached hereto (the "Guaranteed Minimum Royalty"). As recited in Schedule A, a portion of the Guaranteed Minimum Royalty for the first year shall be payable as an Advance against royalties (the "Advance"). The actual royalty payments shall reflect the amount of all Guaranteed Minimum Royalty payments including any Advances made.

F.   "Net Sales" shall mean **LICENSEE**'s gross sales (the gross invoice amount billed customers) of Licensed Products, less discounts and allowances actually shown on the invoice (except cash discounts not deductible in the calculation of Royalty) and, further, less any bona fide returns (net of all returns actually made or allowed as supported by credit memoranda actually issued to the customers). No other costs incurred in the manufacturing, selling, advertising, and distribution of the Licensed Products shall be deducted nor shall any deduction be allowed for any uncollectible accounts or allowances.

G.   A Royalty obligation shall accrue upon the sale of the Licensed Products regardless of the time of collection by **LICENSEE**. For purposes of this Agreement, a Licensed Product shall be considered "sold" upon the date when such Licensed Product is billed, invoiced, shipped, or paid for, whichever event occurs first.

H.   If **LICENSEE** sells any Licensed Products to any party affiliated with **LICENSEE**, or in any way directly or indirectly related to or under the common control with **LICENSEE**, at a price less than the regular price charged to other parties, the Royalty payable **LICENSOR** shall be computed on the basis of the regular price charged to other parties.

I.   The receipt or acceptance by **LICENSOR** of any royalty statement, or the receipt or acceptance of any royalty payment made, shall not prevent **LICENSOR** from subsequently challenging the validity or accuracy of such statement or payment.

J.   Upon expiration or termination of this Agreement, all Royalty obligations, including any unpaid portions of the Guaranteed Minimum Royalty, shall be accelerated and shall immediately become due and payable.

K.   **LICENSEE**'s obligations for the payment of a Royalty and the Minimum Royalty shall survive expiration or termination of this Agreement and will continue for so long as **LICENSEE** continues to manufacture, sell or otherwise market the Licensed Products.

L.   All payments due hereunder shall be made in United States currency drawn on a United States bank, unless otherwise specified between the parties.

M.   Late payments shall incur interest at the rate of ONE PERCENT (1%) per month from the date such payments were originally due.

4. Audit

A.   **LICENSOR** shall have the right, upon at least five (5) days written notice and no more than once per calendar year, to inspect **LICENSEE**'s books and records and all other documents and material in the possession of or under the control of **LICENSEE** with respect to the subject matter of this Agreement at the place or places where such records are normally

Exhibit 13.5 (continued)

retained by **LICENSEE**. **LICENSOR** shall have free and full access thereto for such purposes and shall be permitted to be able to make copies thereof and extracts therefrom.

B.   In the event that such inspection reveals a discrepancy in the amount of Royalty owed **LICENSOR** from what was actually paid, **LICENSEE** shall pay such discrepancy, plus interest, calculated at the rate of ONE AND ONE-HALF PERCENT (1 1/2%) per month. In the event that such discrepancy is in excess of ONE THOUSAND UNITED STATES DOLLARS ($1,000.00) **LICENSEE** shall also reimburse **LICENSOR** for the cost of such inspection including any attorney's fees incurred in connection therewith.

C.   All books and records relative to **LICENSEE**'s obligations hereunder shall be maintained and kept accessible and available to **LICENSOR** for inspection for at least three (3) years after termination of this Agreement.

D.   In the event that an investigation of **LICENSEE**'s books and records is made, certain confidential and proprietary business information of **LICENSEE** may necessarily be made available to the person or persons conducting such investigation. It is agreed that such confidential and proprietary business information shall be retained in confidence by **LICENSOR** and shall not be used by **LICENSOR** or disclosed to any third party for a period of two (2) years from the date of disclosure, or without the prior express written permission of **LICENSEE** unless required by law. It is understood and agreed, however, that such information may be used in any proceeding based on **LICENSEE**'s failure to pay its actual Royalty obligation.

5. Warranties and Obligations

A.   **LICENSOR** represents and warrants that it has the right and power to grant the licenses granted herein and that there are no other agreements with any other party in conflict herewith.

B.   **LICENSOR** further represents and warrants that the Property and/or Trademark do not infringe any valid right of any third party.

C.   **LICENSEE** represents and warrants that it will use its best efforts to promote, market, sell and distribute the Licensed Products.

D.   **LICENSEE** shall be solely responsible for the manufacture, production, sale and distribution of the Licensed Products and will bear all related costs associated therewith.

E.   It is the intention of the parties that **LICENSEE** shall introduce the Licensed Products in all countries in the Territory on or before the Product Introduction Date recited in Schedule A and commence shipment of Licensed Products in all countries in the Territory on or before the Initial Shipment Date recited in Schedule A. Failure to meet either the Product Introduction Date or the Initial Shipment Date shall constitute grounds for immediate termination of this Agreement by **LICENSOR**.

6. Notices, Quality Control and Samples

Exhibit 13.5 (continued)

A.   The Licenses granted hereunder are conditioned upon **LICENSEE**'s full and complete compliance with the marking provisions of the Trademark, patent and copyright laws of the United States and other countries in the Territory.

B.   The Licensed Products, as well as all promotional, packaging and advertising material relative thereto, shall include all appropriate legal notices as required by **LICENSOR**.

C.   The Licensed Products shall be of a high quality which is at least equal to comparable products manufactured and marketed by **LICENSEE** and in conformity with a standard sample approved by **LICENSOR**.

D.   If the quality of a class of the Licensed Products falls below such a production-run quality, as previously approved by **LICENSOR**, **LICENSEE** shall use its best efforts to restore such quality. In the event that **LICENSEE** has not taken appropriate steps to restore such quality within thirty (30) days after notification by **LICENSOR**, **LICENSOR** shall have the right to terminate this Agreement.

E.   Prior to the commencement of manufacture and sale of the Licensed Products, **LICENSEE** shall submit to **LICENSOR**, at no cost to **LICENSOR** and for approval as to quality, six (6) sets of samples of all Licensed Products which **LICENSEE** intends to manufacture and sell and one (1) complete set of all promotional and advertising material associated therewith. Failure of **LICENSOR** to approve such samples within ten (10) working days after receipt hereof will be deemed approval. If **LICENSOR** should disapprove any sample, it shall provide specific reasons for such disapproval. Once such samples have been approved by **LICENSOR**, **LICENSEE** shall not materially depart therefrom without **LICENSOR**'s prior express written consent, which shall not be unreasonably withheld.

F.   At least once during each calendar year, **LICENSEE** shall submit to **LICENSOR**, for approval, an additional twelve (12) sets of samples.

G.   The **LICENSEE** agrees to permit **LICENSOR** or its representative to inspect the facilities where the Licensed Products are being manufactured and packaged.

7. Notice and Payment

A.   Any notice required to be given pursuant to this Agreement shall be in writing and delivered personally to the other designated party at the above-stated address or mailed by certified or registered mail, return receipt requested or delivered by a recognized national overnight courier service.

B.   Either party may change the address to which notice or payment is to be sent by written notice to the other in accordance with the provisions of this paragraph.

8. Intellectual Property Protection

A.   **LICENSOR** shall seek, obtain and, during the Term of this Agreement, maintain in its own name and at its own expense, appropriate intellectual property protection for the Property and Trademark.

Exhibit 13.5 (continued)

B.   In the event that **LICENSEE** requests that **LICENSOR** obtain intellectual property protection for a particular item or in a particular country where **LICENSOR** had not, heretofore, obtained such protection, **LICENSOR** agrees to take reasonable steps to obtain such protection, provided, however, that **LICENSEE** shall be obligated to reimburse **LICENSOR** for the cost of filing, prosecuting and maintaining same.

C.   It is understood and agreed that **LICENSOR** shall retain all right, title and interest in the original Property as well as in any modifications or improvements made to the Property by **LICENSEE**.

D.   The parties agree to execute any documents reasonably requested by the other party to effect any of the above provisions.

E.   **LICENSEE** acknowledges **LICENSOR**'s exclusive rights in the Property and, further, acknowledges that the Property and/or the Trademark are unique and original to **LICENSOR** and that **LICENSOR** is the owner thereof. **LICENSEE** shall not, at any time during or after the effective Term of the Agreement, dispute or contest, directly or indirectly, **LICENSOR**'s exclusive right and title to the Property and/or the Trademark or the validity thereof. **LICENSOR**, however, makes no representation or warranty with respect to the validity of any patent, trademark or copyright which may issue or be granted therefrom.

F.   **LICENSEE** acknowledges that the Property and/or the Trademark have acquired secondary meaning.

G.   **LICENSEE** agrees that its use of the Property and/or the Trademark inures to the benefit of **LICENSOR** and that the **LICENSEE** shall not acquire any rights in the Property and/or the Trademark.

9. Termination

The following termination rights are in addition to the termination rights provided elsewhere in the Agreement:

A.   Immediate Right of Termination. **LICENSOR** shall have the right to immediately terminate this Agreement by giving written notice to **LICENSEE** in the event that **LICENSEE** does any of the following:

(1) fails to meet the Product Introduction Date or the Initial Shipment Date as specified in Schedule A; or

(2) after having commenced sale of the Licensed Products, fails to continuously sell Licensed Products for three (3) consecutive Royalty Periods; or

(3) fails to obtain or maintain product liability insurance in the amount and of the type provided for herein; or

(4) files a petition in bankruptcy or is adjudicated a bankrupt or insolvent, or makes an assignment for the benefit of creditors, or an arrangement pursuant to any bankruptcy law, or if the **LICENSEE** discontinues its business or a receiver is appointed for the **LICENSEE** or for the **LICENSEE'S** business and such receiver is not discharged within thirty (30) days; or

Exhibit 13.5 (continued)

(5) breaches any of the provisions of this Agreement relating to the unauthorized assertion of rights in the Property and/or the Trademark; or

(6) fails, after receipt of written notice from **LICENSOR**, to immediately discontinue the distribution or sale of the Licensed Products or the use of any packaging or promotional material which does not contain the requisite legal legends; or

(7) fails to make timely payment of Royalties when due two or more times during any twelve-month period.

B.   Immediate Right to Terminate a Portion. **LICENSOR** shall have the right to immediately terminate the portion(s) of the Agreement relating to any Property and/or Licensed Product(s) and/or for any country in the Territory if **LICENSEE**, for any reason, fails to meet the Product Introduction Dates or the Initial Shipment Dates specified in Schedule A or, after the commencement of manufacture and sale of a particular Licensed Product in a particular country, ceases to sell commercial quantities of such Licensed Product in such country for three (3) consecutive Royalty Periods.

C.   Right to Terminate on Notice. This Agreement may be terminated by either party upon thirty (30) days written notice to the other party in the event of a breach of a material provision of this Agreement by the other party, provided that, during the thirty (30) days period, the breaching party fails to cure such breach.

D.   **LICENSEE** shall have the right to terminate this Agreement at any time on sixty (60) days written notice to **LICENSOR**. In such event, all moneys paid to **LICENSOR** shall be deemed non-refundable and **LICENSEE**'s obligation to pay any guaranteed moneys, including the Guaranteed Minimum Royalty, shall be accelerated and any yet unpaid guaranteed moneys shall become immediately due and payable.

10. Post Termination Rights

A.   Not less than thirty (30) days prior to the expiration of this Agreement or immediately upon termination thereof, **LICENSEE** shall provide **LICENSOR** with a complete schedule of all inventory of Licensed Products then on-hand (the "Inventory").

B.   Upon expiration or termination of this Agreement, except for reason of a breach of **LICENSEE**'s duty to comply with the quality control or legal notice Marking requirements, **LICENSEE** shall be entitled, for an additional period of three (3) months and on a non-exclusive basis, to continue to sell such Inventory. Such sales shall be made subject to all of the provisions of this Agreement and to an accounting for and the payment of a Royalty thereon. Such accounting and payment shall be due and paid within thirty (30) days after the close of the said three (3) month period.

C.   Upon the expiration or termination of this Agreement, all of the rights of **LICENSEE** under this Agreement shall forthwith terminate and immediately revert to **LICENSOR** and **LICENSEE** shall immediately discontinue all use of the Property and the like, at no cost whatsoever to **LICENSOR**.

Exhibit 13.5 (continued)

D.   Upon termination of this Agreement for any reason whatsoever, **LICENSEE** agrees to immediately return to **LICENSOR** all material relating to the Property including, but not limited to, all artwork, color separations, prototypes and the like, as well as any market studies or other tests or studies conducted by **LICENSEE** with respect to the Property, at no cost whatsoever to **LICENSOR**.

11. Good Will

LICENSEE recognizes the value of the good will associated with the Property and acknowledges that the Property and all rights therein including the good will pertaining thereto, belong exclusively to **LICENSOR**.

12. Infringements

A.   **LICENSEE** shall have the right, in its discretion, to institute and prosecute lawsuits against third persons for infringement of the rights licensed in this Agreement.

B.   If **LICENSEE** does not institute an infringement suit within ninety (90) days after **LICENSOR**'s written request that it do so, **LICENSOR** may institute and prosecute such lawsuit. Any lawsuit shall be prosecuted solely at the cost and expense of the party bringing suit and all sums recovered in any such lawsuits, whether by judgment, settlement or otherwise, in excess of the amount of reasonable attorneys' fees and other out of pocket expenses of such suit, shall be divided equally between the parties.

C.   Upon request of the party bringing the lawsuit, the other party shall execute all papers, testify on all matters, and otherwise cooperate in every way necessary and desirable for the prosecution of any such lawsuit. The party bringing suit shall reimburse the other party for the expenses incurred as a result of such cooperation.

13. Indemnity

A.   **LICENSEE** agrees to defend and indemnify **LICENSOR**, its officers, directors, agents and employees, against all costs, expenses and losses (including reasonable attorneys' fees and costs) incurred through claims of third parties against **LICENSOR** based on the manufacture or sale of the Licensed Products including, but not limited to, actions founded on product liability.

B.   **LICENSOR** agrees to defend and indemnify **LICENSEE**, its officers, directors, agents and employees, against all costs, expenses and losses (including reasonable attorneys' fees and costs) incurred through claims of third parties against **LICENSEE**, challenging the authenticity of the originally submitted Property; provided however, that such indemnity shall only be applicable in the event of a final decision by a court of competent jurisdiction from which no appeal of right exists and shall be limited up to the amount of the actual moneys received by **LICENSOR** under this Agreement. Further, this indemnity does not cover any modifications or changes made to the Property by **LICENSEE**.

14. Insurance

LICENSEE shall, throughout the Term of the Agreement, obtain and maintain at its own cost and expense from a qualified insurance company licensed to do business in {State}, standard

Exhibit 13.5 (continued)

Product Liability Insurance naming **LICENSOR** as an additional named insured. Such policy shall provide protection against any and all claims, demands and causes of action arising out of any defects or failure to perform, alleged or otherwise, of the Licensed Products or any material used in connection therewith or any use thereof. The amount of coverage shall be as specified in Schedule A attached hereto. The policy shall provide for ten (10) days notice to **LICENSOR** from the insurer by Registered or Certified Mail, return receipt requested, in the event of any modification, cancellation or termination thereof. **LICENSEE** agrees to furnish **LICENSOR** a certificate of insurance evidencing same within thirty (30) days after execution of this Agreement and, in no event, shall **LICENSEE** manufacture, distribute or sell the Licensed Products prior to receipt by **LICENSOR** of such evidence of insurance.

15. Force Majeure

It is understood and agreed that in the event of an act of the government, or war conditions, or fire, flood or labor trouble in the factory of **LICENSEE** or in the factory of those manufacturing parts necessary for the manufacture of the Licensed Products, which prevents the performance by **LICENSEE** of the provisions of this Agreement, then such nonperformance by **LICENSEE** shall not be considered as grounds for breach of this Agreement and such nonperformance shall be excused while the conditions herein prevail and for two (2) months thereafter. 16. Jurisdiction and Disputes A. This Agreement shall be governed in accordance with the laws of the State of {State}.

B.   All disputes under this Agreement shall be resolved by the courts of the State of {State} including the United States District Court for the {District} and the parties all consent to the jurisdiction of such courts, agree to accept service of process by mail, and hereby waive any jurisdictional or venue defenses otherwise available to it.

17. Agreement Binding on Successors

The provisions of the Agreement shall be binding upon and shall inure to the benefit of the parties hereto, their heirs, administrators, successors and assigns.

18. Waiver

No waiver by either party of any default shall be deemed as a waiver of prior or subsequent default of the same or other provisions of this Agreement.

19. Severability

If any term, clause or provision hereof is held invalid or unenforceable by a court of competent jurisdiction, such invalidity shall not affect the validity or operation of any other term, clause or provision and such invalid term, clause or provision shall be deemed to be severed from the Agreement.

20. No Joint Venture

Nothing contained herein shall constitute this arrangement to be employment, a joint venture or a partnership.

21. Assignability

Exhibit 13.5 (continued)

The license granted hereunder is personal to **LICENSEE** and shall not be assigned by any act of **LICENSEE** or by operation of law unless in connection with a transfer of substantially all of the assets of **LICENSEE** or with the consent of **LICENSOR**.

22. Integration

This Agreement constitutes the entire understanding of the parties, and revokes and supersedes all prior agreements between the parties, including any option agreements which may have been entered into between the parties, and is intended as a final expression of their Agreement. It shall not be modified or amended except in writing signed by the parties hereto and specifically referring to this Agreement. This Agreement shall take precedence over any other documents which may be in conflict with said Agreement.

IN WITNESS WHEREOF, the parties hereto, intending to be legally bound hereby, have each caused to be affixed hereto its or his/her hand and seal the day indicated.

{Owner Name}   {Licensee Name}

By: By:
Title: Title:
Date: Date:

SCHEDULE A

1. Licensed Properties

The following Licensed Properties form part of this Agreement: {Property}

2. Licensed Trademarks

The following Licensed Trademarks form part of this Agreement: {Trademarks}

3. Licensed Products

The following Licensed Products form part of this Agreement: {Licensed Products}

4. Territory

The following countries shall constitute the Territory: {Territory}

5. Term

This Agreement shall commence on the date executed by both parties and shall extend for an initial Term of:

{Initial Term} YEARS

Exhibit 13.5 (continued)

LICENSOR hereby grants **LICENSEE** {No. Options} separately exercisable options (the "Options") to renew this Agreement for additional {Option Term} year extended Terms on the same terms and conditions provided for herein, provided:

(a) **LICENSEE** provides written notice of its intention to exercise this Option within sixty (60) days prior to expiration of the then in-effect Term; and

(b) **LICENSEE** shall have paid **LICENSOR** total royalty income of at least {Option Minimum} during the then in-effect Term.

6. Royalty Rate

LICENSEE shall pay the following royalty rate: {Royalty Rate}.

7. Guaranteed Minimum Royalty and Advance

LICENSEE agrees to pay **LICENSOR** an Advance of {Advance} upon execution of this Agreement.

LICENSEE agrees to and will pay **LICENSOR** a Guaranteed Minimum Royalty of {Minimum Royalty} for each calendar year during the Term of this Agreement.

8. Product Liability Insurance

{PL Insurance} {$ } combined single limit, with a deductible amount not to exceed Two Thousand, Five Hundred Dollars ($2,500), for each single occurrence for bodily injury and/or for property damage.

9. Product Introduction/Initial Shipment

The Product Introduction Date for all Licensed Products in all countries in the Territory shall be {Intro Date}.

The Initial Shipment Date for all Licensed Products in all countries in the Territory shall be {Ship Date}.

13.1.7.1. *Litigation Involving Intercollegiate Licensing Programs*

The practice of licensing college trademarks is a multimillion-dollar industry. Revenues from the sale of licensed products bearing the logos of popular colleges and universities can bring in millions of dollars annually. Therefore, it is not surprising that litigation has arisen between universities, manufacturers, and retailers over who owns the rights to the marks of the school. Discussed below is an early case that arose when colleges and universities and manufacturers were first beginning to realize the potential revenue from trademarked items.

In *University of Pittsburgh v. Champion Products, Inc.*, 686 F.2d 1040 (3d Cir.), *cert. denied*, 459 U.S. 1087 (1982), the U.S. District Court declined to extend the *Wichita Falls* holding (see section 13.1.5., "Trademark Infringement," note 13) to intercollegiate athletics, thus reversing an appeals court decision that had applied the *Wichita Falls* rationale. The initial decision of the court of appeals had extended the *Wichita Falls* decision by holding that the University of Pittsburgh had a right of relief against a manufacturer that allegedly infringed the university's trademark. This was seen as an especially important development in sports trademark law, because manufacturers/sellers had enjoyed unrestricted use of educational institutions' symbols for years.

However, the district court, on remand from its original decision that dealt with an unrelated question, found that "there is no likelihood of confusion, whether of source, origin, sponsorship, endorsement, or any other nature, between the soft goods of . . . Pitt." Soft goods include such items as T-shirts, hats, and sweatshirts. The court declined to apply the *Wichita Falls* rationale, which the appeals court had suggested might govern. Therefore, Champion was allowed to produce goods bearing the Pittsburgh logo without fear of litigation.

Since the 1930s, the school had goods with its insignia manufactured and sold by one company, initially for the school's athletic department, somewhat later for retail sales in the local area, and eventually for national distribution. In the mid-1970s the school registered its marks under state and federal trademark laws in order to protect what it believed were valuable rights. This was due to the increasing popularity and national prominence of Pitt's football team. School officials sought to enter into a licensing agreement with Champion for continued use of the insignia. Champion was the premier manufacturer of "soft goods" imprinted with the insignia of educational institutions and reproduced emblems of more than 10,000 schools, colleges, and universities. At the time, the company reported annual sales in excess of $100 million. Champion had no such licensing agreement with any other schools, and Champion refused to enter into an agreement with Pitt.

Pitt went to court to stop Champion's unauthorized use of the school's insignia. The district court denied Pitt's request for a temporary injunction pending trial due to the doctrine of laches (neglect to take lawful action for an unreasonable time). The court of appeals, however, ruled that Pitt's delay in bringing an infringement action did not prevent its right to future injunctive relief. The case was remanded to the district court.

In the district court, the plaintiff in the case had to prove four elements to be successful in its case. These elements, considered essential for success in any trademark case based on unfair competition, were likelihood of confusion, nonfunctionality, secondary meaning, and priority of use. In the district court's ruling against Pitt, the court stated that Pitt *did not* "provide any real evidence of confusion." The court held that the university's presentation was very weak, and instead of showing a likelihood of confusion, the university showed little chance of any confusion whatsoever. The district court, in discussing the functionality aspect of the case, noted that "the insignia on these soft goods serves a real, albeit aesthetic function for the wearers." Similarly, the court found no likelihood that, in regard to secondary meaning, the university was being associated with the manufacture of the product.

Finally, as to priority of use, Pitt had to show that it had priority "of trademark use in commerce." The district court ruled that the Pitt insignia was an ornament and not eligible for trademark protection. The court noted that Pitt had failed to prove any of the elements necessary to make its case.

While this chapter has focused on the legal issues involved in trademarks, litigation may well be obviated by purely business considerations. On the intercollegiate level, despite its success on the merits in the *University of Pittsburgh* case, Champion Products settled the case and executed a licensing agreement with the university. There are several reasons for the move to licensing agreements and away from litigation. First, the manufacturer that challenges the university faces litigation expenses. Second, a manufacturer may have other business dealings with a university that may be adversely affected by litigation. For example, Champion Products supplied uniforms for intercollegiate athletic programs at many universities, and the loss of this business has been costly. When Champion settled the Pitt case by executing a licensing agreement, many other manufacturers decided to do the same.

NOTES

1. Other issues in the intercollegiate athletics area are raised in *Texas A&M University System v. University Book Store, Inc.*, 683 S.W.2d 140 (Tex. App. 1984). University Book Store, Inc. (UBC) and four other retail book stores filed suit against Texas A&M in August 1981. UBC operated stores near the university's campus in College Station and wanted to sell goods with the Texas A&M marks on them. Texas A&M refused to allow UBC to do so.

The case was tried without a jury, and a judgment was rendered for UBC; the trial court canceled Texas A&M's marks. The judgment was based on the trial court's finding that Texas A&M "is not the owner of the described marks" because it has not used the marks, and the conclusion that "the certificates of registration should be canceled pursuant to Art. 16.16(a)(4)(B), Tex. Bus. & C. Code."

Texas A&M appealed on two grounds, asserting that (1) the trial court erred in failing to dismiss this suit on their plea of sovereign immunity (see Chapter 4, Section 4.4.1., for a discussion on sovereign immunity), and (2) the trial court's finding that Texas A&M does not own the service marks because of lack of use is not supported by any evidence.

The court of appeals reversed the district court's decision. It based its decision on sovereign immunity and also held:

> We disagree with appellees' contentions that the University is not the owner of the service marks and that the registrations are unlawful or invalid acts. The service marks carried rebuttable presumptions of the validity of the registrations, of the University ownership of the service marks, and of the University's exclusive right to use the mark in connection with higher education services.
>
> The court of appeals reasoned, "There is no evidence rebutting the University's use of the marks in connection with its higher education services."

A number of different considerations were raised in the *Texas A&M University System* case, in contrast to the *University of Pittsburgh* case. First, a retailer was involved instead of a manufacturer. Second, the plaintiff in *Texas A&M University System*, challenged the marks and, as a plaintiff, could not successfully raise a laches argument, since laches is generally viewed as a defense. And third, *Texas A&M University System* involved state institutions, which consequently raised sovereign immunity arguments.

2. In *Board of Governors v. Helpingstine*, 714 F. Supp. 167 (M.D.N.C. 1989), the court held that the failure of the University of North Carolina at Chapel Hill to prosecute substantial uncontrolled use of its marks by third parties from its founding in 1795 until the inception of its licensing program in 1982 did not result in abandonment because the university's marks did not lose significance as indications of origin.

3. In *Illinois High School Ass'n. v. GTE Vantage, Inc.*, 99 F. 3d. 244 (7th Cir. 1996), plaintiff brought suit against defendant to protect its trademark, "March Madness." Defendant holds a license for "March Madness" from the NCAA. The plaintiff began using the term "March Madness" in the 1940s. An announcer first used "March Madness" to describe the NCAA basketball tournament in 1982. Beginning in 1993–94, the NCAA began licensing the use of the term to producers and suppliers. The court ruled that the IHSA

did not have trademark that the law would protect, so far as the use of the term "March Madness" in connection with the NCAA Tournament is concerned. This theory is based on the fact that the term "March Madness" in connection with the NCAA tournament was a term first appropriated to the NCAA by the media, and if the media call the NCAA tournament "March Madness," that is what the public will call it. Because of the free-speech clause of the First Amendment, the IHSA could not have stopped the media from calling the NCAA Tournament "March Madness," which is what the public now know it as. Therefore, the defendant was not the one responsible for "blotting out" the exclusive association of "March Madness" with the Illinois high school basketball tournament.

13.1.7.2. Trademark Law and Nicknames

Intellectual property law affects various aspects of intercollegiate athletics. Universities must be careful to protect their copyrights as well as trademark rights. For example, the Washington Redskins recently lost federal protection of its trademarks because the term "redskin" was considered disparaging to groups of Native Americans (see note 2). This does not foreclose the Washington Redskins from using their logos or names, but it does not allow them federal trademark protection. They can license merchandise with their name and logo and utilize state trademark common law for protection. However, as noted earlier, federal protection is more desirable.

This could affect collegiate and school sports in a similar way. Some colleges and universities have already altered their team nicknames or changed some of their practices. St. Johns University and the University of Massachusetts are two examples of schools that have already switched from the nickname Redman. In addition, the University of Oklahoma mascot, "Little Red," no longer does war dances on the sidelines. Miami University (Ohio) changed its name from the Miami Redskins to the Miami Red Hawks.

NOTES

1. In *White v. Board of Regents*, 614 N.W.2d 330 (Neb. 2000), the defendant began a line of merchandise called "Huskers Authentic." At about the same time, the plaintiff registered the mark "Husker Authentics" for use in his store where he sold Nebraska merchandise. The court noted that defendant began use of the mark before plaintiff. The court stated, "We conclude . . . that the University had prior common-law rights superior to those of [plaintiff] in the trade name 'Husker Authentics' and that therefore the district court properly canceled [plaintiff's] registration."

2. In *Harjo v. Pro-Football, Inc.*, 50 U.S.P.Q.2d 1705 (T.T.A.B. 1999), a group of Native American rights advocates petitioned the Trademark Trial and Appeal Board of the U.S. Patent and Trademark Office, against the Washington Redskins of the NFL. The Redskins had six different marks that contained Native American images or names that were offensive to the petitioners. In June 1999 the Patent and Trademark Office issued an order to cancel the registration of the marks held by the Redskins due to their offensive nature. The Redskins have appealed the cancellation of the marks.

3. A legal dispute arose between Ohio State University (OSU) and Ohio University (OU) over the use of the word "Ohio." OU registered the mark "Ohio" but OSU objected to the mark's registration in 1997 after it became concerned that names such as Ohio Stadium might be in jeopardy. The issue was ultimately settled out of court. The parties agreed that OU gets to keep the trademark but that OSU gets to use it, too. "In the proposed settlement, Ohio State would drop its challenge of Ohio University's trademark, giving the Athens school the unchallenged trademark. Ohio State would retain some rights to the word Ohio in future marketing and merchandising, when those uses are in keeping with traditional OSU uses. An example would be commemorative OSU track uniforms

featuring the Ohio logo, like those worn by track legend Jesse Owens in the 1930s." The Ohio attorney general will mediate any future disputes. "Old Pals Settle OU-OSU Battle over Four-Letter Word," *The Columbus Dispatch*, April 29, 1999, Sec. A, p. 1.

4. In the late 1980s Georgia Tech officials obtained trademarks for the national and international use of the word "Buzz," as it related to sporting events and clothing. In 1998, Georgia Tech filed a trademark suit against the Salt Lake City Buzz minor league baseball team. In its trademark suit, Georgia Tech alleged that the Salt Lake Buzz merchandise confused the buying public into being mistaken for Georgia Tech's. The case was settled and, as a result of the settlement, the Salt Lake City team can no longer use the word "buzz" in its team's name, Web site, or for merchandising purposes.

5. In *Univ. of Georgia Athletic Ass'n v. Laite*, 756 F.2d 1535 (11th Cir. 1985), the Laite Distributing Co., a wholesaler of novelty beers, began marketing "Battlin' Bulldog Beer." The beer was sold in red and black cans bearing the portrayal of an English bulldog wearing a red sweater emblazoned with a black "G." The bulldog had bloodshot eyes, a football tucked under its right "arm," and a frothy beer stein in its left "hand." The Eleventh Circuit held that the University of Georgia's "bulldog" mascot is not a descriptive mark and is therefore protectable without a showing of secondary meaning. The court reasoned that the selection of an English bulldog as a mascot for its athletic teams is "suggestive, if not downright arbitrary" and the University of Georgia obtained preliminary and permanent injunctive relief in federal district court based on the "likelihood of confusion" between the "Battlin' Bulldog" and the "University of Georgia Bulldog."

6. In *Board of Trustees v. Professional Therapy Services, Inc.*, 873 F. Supp. 1280 (W.D. Ark. 1995), the University of Arkansas sought to protect their trademarked "Razorback" mascot name from being used within the name of a local clinic. The school filed a federal trademarked infringement claim under Section 32 of the Lanham Act against the Razorback Sports and Physical Therapy Clinic in 1989, when two university-associated athletic trainers became clinic consultants and limited partners. For a design logo, the clinic used a red, running Razorback hog, and distributed promotional materials emphasizing its relationship with the university. The court granted summary judgment in favor of Arkansas. Chief Judge Waters, in considering the factors relevant to determining the existence of a likelihood of confusion, found in favor of the university, stating:

> The following factual and legal conclusions are undisputed. First, the visual impression created by the dominant elements of the RAZORBACK marks and the Clinic's marks is highly similar. Second, the RAZORBACK marks are strong ones that distinctively identify the University in the public mind. Third, the Clinic's services and the University's are competitive or so closely related as to suggest a common source. And no degree of care on the part of the Clinic customers can remedy any likelihood of confusion that may exist.

> These undisputed conclusions demonstrate a likelihood of confusion and a serious risk to the University that it will lose control over its public image as a provider of medical services, if the Clinic continues to use its marks. Also, there is no reasonable expectation that further evidence presented by the Clinic will change the court's mind in respect to the undisputed facts discussed above and the legal results that flow from them, especially since this case is before the court on cross-motions for summary judgment. Summary judgment is therefore granted for the University on the Lanham Act cause of action.

13.1.8. Trademark Law and the Olympics

The Olympic Games also present intellectual property issues. The International Olympic Committee owns the familiar "Olympic Rings," giving it the right to use the mark all over the world. In the United States, the U.S. Olympic Committee (USOC) has pursued violators who tried to use the protected marks and terminology of the USOC. In fact, protection has been provided not only through use of trademark law but also through the Ted Stevens Amateur Sports

Act (The goal of the Act is to promote and coordinate amateur athletic activity in the United States, to recognize certain rights for U.S. amateur athletes, to provide for the resolution of disputes involving national governing bodies, and for other purposes.), which contains a section devoted entirely to the protection of Olympic terminology and symbols (subchapter 1—Corporation):

Excerpts from Ted Stevens Olympic and Amateur Sports Act:

§220506. Exclusive right to name, seals, emblems, and badges

(a) EXCLUSIVE RIGHT OF CORPORATION.—Except as provided in subsection (d) of this section, the corporation has the exclusive right to use—

(1) the name "United States Olympic Committee";

(2) the symbol of the International Olympic Committee, consisting of 5 inter-locking rings, the symbol of the International Paralympic Committee, consisting of 3 TaiGeuks, or the symbol of the Pan-American Sports Organization, consisting of a torch surrounded by concentric rings;

(3) the emblem of the corporation consisting of an escutcheon having a blue chief and vertically extending red and white bars on the base with 5 interlocking rings displayed on the chief; and

(4) the words "Olympic", "Olympiad", "Citius Altius Fortius", "Paralympic", "Par-alympiad", "Pan-American", "America Espirito Sport Fraternite", or any combina-tion of those words.

(b) CONTRIBUTORS AND SUPPLIERS.—The corporation may authorize con-tributors and suppliers of goods or services to use the trade name of the corporation or any trademark, symbol, insignia, or emblem of the International Olympic Com-mittee, International Paralympic Committee, the Pan-American Sports Organiza-tion, or of the corporation to advertise that the contributions, goods, or services were donated or supplied to, or approved, selected, or used by, the corporation, the United States Olympic team, the Paralympic team, the Pan-American team, or team members.

(c) CIVIL ACTION FOR UNAUTHORIZED USE.—Except as provided in sub-section (d) of this section, the corporation may file a civil action against a person for the remedies provided in the Act of July 5, 1946 (15 U.S.C. 1051 et seq.) (popularly known as the Trademark Act of 1946) if the person, without the consent of the corporation, uses for the purpose of trade, to induce the sale of any goods or services, or to promote any theatrical exhibition, athletic performance, or com-petition—

(1) the symbol described in subsection (a)(2) of this section;

(2) the emblem described in subsection (a)(3) of this section;

(3) the words described in subsection (a)(4) of this section, or any combination or simulation of those words tending to cause confusion or mistake, to deceive, or to falsely suggest a connection with the corporation or any Olympic, Paralympic, or Pan-American Games activity; or

(4) any trademark, trade name, sign, symbol, or insignia falsely representing as-sociation with, or authorization by, the International Olympic Committee, the In-ternational Paralympic Committee, the Pan-American Sports Organization, or the corporation.

(d) PRE-EXISTING RIGHTS AND GEOGRAPHIC REFERENCE.—

(1) A person who actually uses the emblem described in subsection (a)(3) of this section, or the words or any combination of the words described in subsection (a)(4) of this section, for any lawful purpose before September 21, 1950, is not prohibited

by this section from continuing the lawful use for the same purpose and for the same goods or services.

(2) A person who actually used, or whose assignor actually used, the words or any combination of the words described in subsection (a)(4) of this section, or a trademark, trade name, sign, symbol, or insignia described in subsection (c)(4) of this section, for any lawful purpose before September 21, 1950, is not prohibited by this section from continuing the lawful use for the same purpose and for the same goods or services.

(3) Use of the word "Olympic" to identify a business or goods or services is permitted by this section where—

(A) such use is not combined with any of the intellectual properties referenced in subsections (a) or (c) of this section;

(B) it is evident from the circumstances that such use of the word "Olympic" refers to the naturally occurring mountains or geographical region of the same name that were named prior to February 6, 1998, and not to the corporation or any Olympic activity; and

(C) such business, goods, or services are operated, sold, and marketed in the State of Washington west of the Cascade Mountain range and operations, sales, and marketing outside of this area are not substantial.

The USOC has been involved in several lawsuits against different businesses that attempted to use the words and/or symbols of the Olympics. These cases have generally involved attempts by various companies to use variations on the word "Olympics" in association with their organization, product or event. Organizations frequently try to appropriate the notions of goodwill, purity, competition and ethics from the Olympic games. The USOC has been largely successful in these cases, as demonstrated by the following notes.

NOTES ───

1. In *United States Olympic Committee* v. *Toy Truck Lines*, 237 F.3d 1331 (Fed. Cir. 2001), the USOC was successful, upon appeal, against a manufacturer of toy trucks. The manufacturer had applied for a trademark for its trucks that bore the mark "Pan-American" on their side. Initially, the Patent and Trademark Office allowed this registration, even though the USOC had registered the marks "PAN AMERICAN GAMES, USA PAN AM TEAM, and PAN AM GAMES" for use with selling various goods. The appeals court reversed the decision of the Patent and Trademark Office, stating that the USOC had a legal right to the mark "Pan American." The court reasoned that the protection granted to the USOC's use of the Olympic words and symbols differs from the normal trademark protection in that the USOC did not need to prove that a contested use is likely to cause confusion, and that an unauthorized user of the word does not have available the normal statutory defenses.

2. In *O-M Bread* v. *United States Olympic Committee*, 65 F.3d 933 (Fed. Cir. 1995), the plaintiff, O-M Bread Company, attempted to register a bread product that would bear the name "Olympic Kids Bread." The USOC opposed the registration of this mark because it holds the rights to the word "Olympic" with the U.S. Patent and Trademark Office. Upon O-M Bread's appeal, the USOC was successful because it had clearly registered the mark in question. The court felt even though the marks "Olympic" and "Olympic Kids" were different, the two marks were still likely to cause confusion. "Further, as in determining likelihood of confusion, it is not relevant whether a portion of the mark is disclaimed or does not have strong trademark significance, such as the word 'kids.' No part of the mark can be ignored in comparing the marks as a whole."

3. In *San Francisco Arts & Athletics, Inc.* v. *United States Olympic Committee*, 483 U.S.

522 (1987), the United States Olympic Committee brought action against San Francisco Arts & Athletics, Inc. (SFAA), for using the word "Olympics" in its promotion of the "Gay Olympic Games." The USOC alleged a trademark violation under the Lanham Act. The court of appeals affirmed the lower court's summary judgment for the USOC and issued a permanent injunction against SFAA from further using the word "Olympics."

4. In *United States Olympic Committee v. Intelicense Corp.*, 469 U.S. 982 (1984), the defendant, a Swiss corporation, had a license from the International Olympic Committee to market pictograms bearing the Olympic rings. Because the defendant did not have the consent of the USOC, it was found to be in infringement of the trademark granted by the Amateur Sports Act and was enjoined from all further sales in the United States.

5. In *United States Olympic Committee v. Olymp-Herrenwasche-fabriken Bezner GmbH & Co.*, 224 U.S.P.Q. 497 (TTAB 1984), a German sportswear manufacturer applied to register the mark "Olymp" to be placed on shirts, blouses, and collars. The USOC objected to the registration of this mark because of the similarity with the word "Olympic," which was already protected. This application was denied by the Trademark Board because of the likelihood of confusion of these products with the athletic uniforms and equipment bearing the registered mark of the USOC.

6. In *United States Olympic Committee v. Union Sport Apparel*, 220 U.S.P.Q. 526 (E.D. Va. 1983), the Trademark Board enjoined the defendant sportswear manufacturer from marketing clothing bearing a logo of three interlocking rings and the letters "U.S.A." The court determined that the defendant was trying to take advantage of the goodwill created by the USOC and thus infringed the trademark established in the Amateur Sports Act. The court held that not only had the defendants violated the Amateur Sports Act of 1978 but also issued an order awarding the USOC treble damages, its costs and attorney's fees, and defendant's wrongful profits. The awarding of costs, attorney's fees, and wrongful profits represented a first in the USOC's legal battles against trademark exploitation. The court's rationale in the awarding of damages was based upon a finding of deliberate and willful infringement.

7. In *United States Olympic Committee v. International Federation of Bodybuilders*, 219 U.S.P.Q. 353 (D.D.C. 1982), the defendants were enjoined from using a seven-ring symbol, similar to the Olympic interlocking ring symbol, in their magazines or for purposes of advertising various products. This ruling was based on the trademark protection granted through the Amateur Sports Act. The term "Mr. Olympia," used to refer to the winner of a professional bodybuilding contest, was allowed.

8. In January 2002, the U.S. Olympic Committee, enforcing its trademark rights before the 2002 winter games, sued the Discount Tire Co. The complaint stated that the tire company advertised its product using the image of five interlocking tires on four different billboards in the Salt Lake City region. Olympic marks are granted special protected status in U.S. law under the Amateur Sports Act. The case is pending.

13.2. COPYRIGHT LAW

Copyright law issues are found in television, radio broadcasting, media guides, team or school publications, league or conference publications, music, and the Internet. Copyright law protects the expression of ideas, but not the ideas themselves. In the sports setting, some examples of copyrighted works include the music played at sporting events, the media guides or programs sold at sporting events, and even the sporting event itself after it has been recorded/broadcast for television or radio. More in-depth discussion of how copyright law impacts broadcasting and sports, can be found in Chapter 14.

Intangible items cannot be copyrighted because it is virtually impossible to protect an idea, something that exists in the mind only. It is much more practical to protect items that are identifiable on paper, videotape or audiotape, and so on. "Copyright protection subsists . . . in original works of authorship fixed in any tangible medium of expression, now known or later developed, from which they can be perceived, reproduced, or otherwise communicated, either directly or with the aid of a machine or device." Copyright law protects works such as books, pictorials, graphic and sculptural works, music, photographs, movies, and computer programs (see notes 3 and 5).

The owner of a registered copyright enjoys the ability to block the unauthorized copying or public performance of a work protected by copyright (see note 7). In the United States, the law that governs copyrights is Title 17 of the United States Code (§§101–810; 1001–1010). It incorporates the Berne Convention, which is an international treaty regarding copyrights that most countries have signed. Copyright law is often described as a bundle of rights. As established by 17 U.S.C. §106, "the owner of copyright under this title has the exclusive rights to do and to authorize any of the following:

(1) to reproduce the copyrighted work in copies or phonorecords;

(2) to prepare derivative works based upon the copyrighted work;

(3) to distribute copies or phonorecords of the copyrighted work to the public by sale or other transfer of ownership, or by rental, lease, or lending;

(4) in the case of literary, musical, dramatic, and choreographic works, pantomimes, and motion pictures and other audiovisual works, to perform the copyrighted work publicly;

(5) in the case of literary, musical, dramatic, and choreographic works, pantomimes, and pictorial, graphic, or sculptural works, including the individual images of a motion picture or other audiovisual work, to display the copyrighted work publicly; and

(6) in the case of sound recordings, to perform the copyrighted work publicly by means of a digital studio transmission.

Copyright law arises upon creation and, under current law, endures for the life of the author plus seventy years. Copyright law applies to both unpublished and published works. Registration of a copyrighted work with the Copyright Office in Washington, D.C., is not required for existence of the copyright; however, it is a prerequisite to a lawsuit for copyright infringement and to certain legal remedies (e.g., injunctive relief). The familiar copyright notice is no longer required on copies of works published after March 1, 1989. However, it is still in the copyright owner's interest to place a copyright notice on publicly distributed copies of published works. The notice should include the copyright symbol, ©, or the word "Copyright" or its abbreviation, followed by the year of first publication of the work and the name of the copyright owner.

Some copyrighted material can, however, be used without the owner's permission in the context that the work is for "fair use." Section 107 of the Copyright Act of 1976 provides that "the fair use of a copyrighted work, including such use by reproduction in copies or phonorecords or by any other means specified by that section, for purposes such as criticism, comment, news reporting, teaching (including multiple copies for classroom use), scholarship, or research, is not an infringement of copyright." Also, according to Section 107, there are several factors that must be considered in making a determination of fair use. Those factors are as follows:

1. The purpose and character of the use, including whether such use is of a commercial nature or is for nonprofit educational purposes

2. The nature of the copyrighted work

3. The amount and substantiality of the portion used in relation to the copyrighted work as a whole

4. The effect of the use upon the potential market for or value of the copyrighted work.

For example, in sports, in one particular case, ABC used a biography about the legendary wrestler Dan Gable without permission from the copyright owner, Iowa State University. ABC argued that it was not subject to copyright infringement because it used a portion of the biography as fair use and that the information was of a public interest; however, the court found that ABC was not exempt because of fair use. The network's use of the film had a profit-making character, and the network usurped an extremely significant market for the film. See *Iowa State University Research Foundation, Inc. v. American Broadcasting Company, Inc.*, 621 F.2d 57 (2d Cir. 1980).

One area where copyright law and sports have recently intersected concerns the providing of real-time scores of professional sporting events without the consent of the governing leagues (see notes 2 and 3). In *Morris Communications Corporation v. PGA Tour* (note 2) and *Motorola v. NBA* (note 3), the courts allowed companies to provide real-time scores through their Web sites and hand-held pagers, respectively. Although the leagues/organizations own the rights to broadcast the games, the companies have been allowed to provide real-time scores because they are not rebroadcasts of the game, and are solely providing information, not commentary or detailed information. With the expansion of Internet technology, this may be an area of copyright law that will see more litigation in the future.

NOTES

1. In January 2002 intellectual property dispute, former Baltimore Ravens player Billy Davis sued the team and coach Brian Billick for allegedly stealing his idea for a documentary about the trials and tribulations of a typical NFL training camp. According to Davis, Billick and the Ravens turned his idea for a documentary called "The Final Cut" into the HBO series "Hard Knocks: Training Camp with the Baltimore Ravens." He claims that he first brought up the idea to Billick in May 2000. The coach was allegedly excited by the idea and asked Davis for a written synopsis explaining the documentary in more detail. The lawsuit also names HBO Sports and NFL Films as defendants. Davis accused the defendants of copyright infringement, fraudulent inducement and conversion. The case is pending.

2. In *Morris Communications Corp. v. PGA Tour, Inc.* 117 F.Supp. 2d 1322 (M.D. Fla. 2000), the PGA was denied an injunction allowing it to stop Morris from providing "real-time scoring" for professional golf events. The process went as follows. The company employed "hole reporters" who follow each group of golfers on the golf course and tabulate the scores of each player at the end of each hole of golf played. The scores are then collected by volunteers located at each of the eighteen greens on the golf course, who, with the aid of handheld wireless radios, relay the scoring information to a remote production truck staffed by personnel employed by defendant. The scores of all participating golfers are then processed at the remote production truck and transmitted by the defendant to its Web site, pgatour.com. At the same time, real-time scores are also transmitted to an on-site media center where members of the media are able to access the scores.

The PGA was not successful with its injunction, unable to prove irreparable harm by allowing this practice to continue. The appeal of this decision is pending.

3. In *NBA v. Motorola, Inc.*, 105 F.3d 841 (2d Cir. 1997), the NBA filed suit against the manufacturer and promoter of handheld pagers that provided real-time information about professional basketball games, alleging copyright infringement. The league also sought to enjoin an online provider of the same information. The court of appeals held that the professional basketball games were not "original works of authorship," and therefore there was no copyright infringement.

4. In *Jacob Maxwell, Inc. v. Veeck*, 110 F.3d 749 (11th Cir. 1997), plaintiff composed a song, "Cheer! The Miracle Is Here," for the defendant minor league baseball team, the Miracle. Plaintiff sued for copyright infringement after defendant failed to pay for the song and allegedly used the song without permission. Defendant was supposed to acknowledge plaintiff as the writer and producer of the song but failed to do so. It seems that plaintiff gave defendant permission to use the song even though he had not yet been paid and, in fact, sent defendant a letter encouraging the use of the song. Plaintiff also attended many Miracle games and did not at that time revoke permission after failing to hear the requisite acknowledgment. The court held that plaintiff's conduct indicated a nonexclusive license to make use of the song and, therefore, there was no copyright infringement. The court granted the defendant summary judgment.

5. In *Hoopla Sports and Entertainment, Inc. v. Nike, Inc.*, 947 F.Supp. 347 (N.D. Ill. 1996), the organizer of an international high school age all-star basketball game brought action against the shoe manufacturer that sponsored a competing game and the television station that broadcast the game. The plaintiff alleged copyright infringement, among other legal theories. On the defendant's motion to dismiss, the district court held that the idea for the game was not copyrightable. Additionally, even if the basketball game was copyrightable, the organizer failed to comply with the necessary prerequisites to copyright the game.

6. *Monster Communications, Inc. v. Turner Broadcasting System, Inc.*, 935 F.Supp. 490 (S.D.N.Y. 1996) involves film footage of the Muhammad Ali-George Foreman heavyweight title fight that took place in Zaire. Plaintiff "made and owns an 84 minute motion picture called 'When We Were Kings.'" Defendant planned to air a movie on Turner Network Television called *The Whole Story*. Plaintiff claimed that defendant's movie "contains between 41 seconds and 2 minutes" of footage to which plaintiff owns the rights. The court held that even if the plaintiff were able to prove protectible rights in the footage, the defendant would prevail because it would be able to prove fair use of the copyrighted material. Plaintiff's injunction to prevent defendant's broadcasting of its movie was denied.

7. In *NFL v. Cousin Hugo's, Inc.*, 600 F.Supp. 84 (E.D. Missouri 1984), the NFL sued a restaurant for intercepting and broadcasting live telecasts of St. Louis Cardinals' football games. The district court held that the NFL was entitled to a temporary restraining order preventing the defendant's actions.

13.2.1. Copyright Law and the Internet

The Internet is becoming a troublesome area for intellectual property law without clear-cut answers. Internet problems cover several areas, including broadcast rights, the use of sports teams' names and logos, and the use of athletes' names.

Ever-growing technology presents a problem for sports organizations. Right now, fans can listen to games, just as they would the radio, over the Internet. Currently, teams own the rights to broadcast games over the Internet. In the future, we will likely see Internet broadcast rights negotiated the same way we see television and radio rights negotiated today. However, the advent of Internet broadcasting brings about some new potential problem areas and issues, including the "policing" and protecting the rights holder across an entity as broad and global as the Internet.

Two federal acts that have been passed to address the ever-changing legal problems of intellectual property and the Internet are the Digital Millennium Copyright Act (DMCA) and the No Electronic Theft Act (NET Act) (see note 1). The DMCA was implemented to ensure that a holder of a copyright cannot have its copyrighted material posted on the Internet without authorization. Among other things, the act allows for penalties for people who attempt to circumvent copyright protection systems, or sell equipment that allows people to avoid these protection systems. The NET Act makes it illegal for someone to willfully infringe a copyright (1) for purposes of commercial advantage or private financial gain, or (2) by the reproduction or distribution, including by electronic means, during any 180-day period of one or more copies of one or more copyrighted works that have a total retail value of more than $1,000. The basic premise behind the NET Act is to punish people who willfully infringe upon copyrighted material on the Internet for financial gain.

Another problem in this area is "cybersquatters." Cybersquatters are people who register sports teams' domain names before the team does. Many of these cybersquatters register the domain names in hopes of later selling the domain names to the named party. The Anticybersquatting Consumer Protection Act (15 U.S.C. §1125(d)) was enacted to prevent the deliberate and bad-faith registration of Internet domain names in violation of trademark rights. (For a review of the legislation, see note 2.) Cybersquatting is also a problem for athletes. Cybersquatters register the names of famous sports figures, or even potentially famous sports figures, in hopes of later selling the Internet addresses to the athletes at a profit.

The major sports leagues have begun to take a proactive approach to cybersquatters. The four major leagues and the Collegiate Licensing Company formed the Coalition to Advance the Protection of Sports Logos (CAPS). This group has brought action against two cybersquatters under the Anti-Cybersquatting Protection Act (ACPA) (see note 2). The group brought action in late 1999 against Jeff Burgar, a profile cybersquatter, who registered names such as *chargers1.com*, *redskins1.com*, and *goclippers.com* The action "resulted in the transfer of 175 domain names and a $16,000.00 penalty against Burgar." Although the leagues are attempting to be proactive in protecting their marks on the Internet, cybersquatters are becoming more creative. Cybersquatters are even registering the names of high school athletes who may make it big in the future (see notes 2 and 3 for a discussion of cases involving cybersquatters).

The Anti-Cybersquatting Consumer Protection Act also provides some protection to individual athletes.

> Any person who in good faith registers a domain name that consists of the name of another living person, or a name substantially similar thereto, without that person's consent, with the specific intent to profit from such name by selling the domain name for financial gain to that person or any third party, shall be liable in a civil action by such person.

This section of the act indicates that individual persons will have the ability to bring a civil suit if another uses his or her name. However, the cybersquatter must have the specific intent to profit from the sale of the domain name.

In addition to the ACPA, organizations and individuals can utilize the Uniform Domain Name Dispute Resolution Policy promulgated by the Internet Corporation for Assigned Names and Numbers (ICANN). This policy provides an arbitration process that offers an alternative to litigation for domain name disputes. The policy requires that the domain name be identical or confusingly similar to the trademark owner's mark. The owner must also demonstrate that the registered domain name was registered in bad faith and that the registrant has no legitimate interest in the domain name.

Even though these methods for domain name resolution have been developed, there is some question as to how successful they will be. The ACPA has not yet been challenged in court, and ICANN's dispute resolution policy is still relatively new. It remains to be seen whether or not either of these will be successful in preventing the problem of cyber squatting. Perhaps the best lesson is to register your domain name early, even before you become famous, and before anyone else does.

NOTES

1. More information on the DMCA and the NET Act can be found at www.Thomas. loc.gov.

2. The ACPA (www.Patents.com/acpa.htm) provides:

A person shall be liable in a civil action by the owner of a mark, including a personal name which is protected as a mark under [the Lanham Act], if, without regard to the goods or services of the parties, that person

a) has a bad faith intent to profit from that mark, including a personal name which is protected as a mark under [the Lanham Act]; and

b) registers, traffics in, or uses a domain name that

i. in the case of a mark that is distinctive at the time of registration of the domain name, is identical or confusingly similar to that mark;

ii. in the case of a famous mark that is famous at the time of registration of the domain name, is identical or confusingly similar to or dilutive of that mark; or

iii. is a trademark, word, or name protected by reason of section 706 of title 18, United States Code, or section 220506 of title 36, United States Code.

The section outlines nine factors that may be considered in determining whether or not the registration took place in bad-faith.

In determining whether a person has a bad faith intent described under [the section above], a court may consider factors such as, but not limited to

i. the trademark or other intellectual property rights of the person, if any, in the domain name;

ii. the extent to which the domain name consists of the legal name of the person or a name that is otherwise commonly used to identify that person;

iii. the person's prior use, if any, of the domain name in connection with the bona fide offering of any goods or services;

iv. the person's bona fide noncommercial or fair use of the mark in a site accessible under the domain name;

v. the person's intent to divert consumers from the market owner's online location to a site accessible under the domain name that could harm the goodwill represented by the mark, either for commercial gain or with the intent to tarnish or disparage the mark, by creating a likelihood of confusion as to the source, sponsorship, affiliation, or endorsement of the site;

vi. the person's offer to transfer, sell, or otherwise assign the domain name to the mark owner or any third party for financial gain without having used, or having an intent to use, the domain name in the bona fide offering of any goods or services, or the person's prior conduct indicating a pattern of such conduct;

vii. the person's provision of material and misleading false contact information when applying for the registration of the domain name, the person's intentional failure to maintain accurate contact information, or the person's prior conduct indicating a pattern of such conduct;

viii. the person's registration or acquisition of multiple domain names which the person knows are identical or confusingly similar to marks of others that are distinctive at the time of registration of such domain names, or dilutive of famous marks of others that are famous at the time of registration of such domain names, without regard to the goods or services of the parties; and

ix. the extent to which the mark incorporated in the person's domain name registration is or is not distinctive and famous within the meaning of subsection (c)(1) of section 43.

The Act also provides that bad faith shall not be found when the registrant had reasonable grounds to believe that the use of the domain name was fair and lawful.

3. In the case of *NBA Properties, Inc. v. Adirondack Software Corporation*, WIPO Arbitration and Mediation Center, Administrative Panel Decision, case no. D2000–1211 (2000), NBA Properties was attempting to claim the Web site *www.knicks.com* away from Adirondack Software Corporation, which had registered the domain name through Network Solutions, a Web domain name registration company, in 1995. The league attempted to contact Adirondack unsuccessfully over the course of four years, starting in 1996. At one point Adirondack allegedly sent a letter to Network Solutions transferring the site to the NBA, but Network Solutions deemed the letter insufficient, and no further attempts were made. Network Solutions put the site on "hold," pending a resolution between the two parties, but when none was had by March 30, 2000, Network Solutions informed the NBA that the site would be taken off hold. At that point, the Knicks brought their case to the WIPO Arbitration and Mediation Center. In deciding the case for Adirondack, the court outlined four reasons that Adirondack should maintain its rights over the site:

1. Madison Square Garden is the rightful owner of the Knicks trademark, and therefore NBA Properties does not have the rights to the mark, or standing to bring the case.

2. Adirondack did not register the domain name solely in order to sell the rights, as evidenced by its attempt to transfer the rights to the NBA at one point.

3. Adirondack does not have a pattern of registering domain names that are trademarked items.

4. The domain name was not registered to disrupt the business of the NBA.

5. The domain name was not used to attract users to a Web site other than the site of the owners.

4. In *ISL Marketing and Federation Internationale de Football Association v. Nutt*, Case No. D2000–0363, World Intellectual Property Organization Administrative Panel Decision, July 17, 2000, ISL and FIFA brought a complaint against the respondent who registered *fifa-world-cup.com*. FIFA has registrations for the following marks internationally and in certain European countries: FIFA World Cup, FIFA, and World Cup. The panel found that respondent's domain name was confusingly similar to FIFA's marks, that the respondent had no rights in those marks, and that he acted in bad faith in registering the domain name. The panel ordered the domain name to be transferred to the complainant.

5. In *Quokka Sports, Inc. v. Cup Int'l, Ltd.*, 99 F.Supp.2d 1105 (N.D. Cal. 1999), plaintiff, holder of the Internet rights to use certain America's Cup trademarks (licensed by America's Cup Properties, Inc.), filed suit requesting a temporary restraining order based on trademark infringement. Defendant had registered the domain name *americascup.com*. The court ruled "that the operation of the website at www.americascup.com is likely to cause consumer confusion." Additionally, the court stated that "[t]he website appears for all intents and purposes to be masquerading as an official site associated with the America's Cup event." The court further stated that plaintiff suffered irreparable harm in that traffic was being diverted from the official America's Cup Web site. The district court granted the temporary restraining order.

6. See Lauren Yamamoto, "20 Copyright Protection and Internet Fan Sites: Entertainment Industry Finds Solace in Traditional Copyright Law," *Loyola of Los Angeles Entertainment Review* (2000).

7. See Mark Brown, "A Tangled Web They Weave: Entrepreneurs Get Jump, Register Big Names," *Chicago Sun-Times*, July 28, 1999.

8. See James V. Grimaldi, "Olympics File Suit over Web Domains," *Washington Post*, July 14, 2000.

9. For examples of litigation regarding cybersquatting and the NCAA, see Scott A. Bearby, "Marketing, Protection and Enforcement of NCAA Marks," 12 *Marquette Sports Law Journal* 543 (Spring 2002).

13.3. PATENT LAW

A patent is a document, issued by the federal government, that grants its owner a legally enforceable right to exclude others from claiming ownership of the invention described and claimed in the document. The Patent Act governs patent protection. It allows an individual to acquire a patent for an invention or discovery of "any new useful process, machine, manufacture, or composition of matter, or any new and useful improvement thereof." There is a further specification that the invention or discovery be nonobvious. The Supreme Court has adopted the view that such patent protection is applicable to "anything under the sun that is made by man." Congress allows this right, through the Patent Act (35 U.S.C. §§1–376), for a term ending twenty years from the date of the filing of an application for patent, to encourage the public disclosure of technical advances and as an incentive for investing in their commercialization. Thus, the overall progress of technical innovation is favored, while at the same time inventors are rewarded for their specific contributions. Like other forms of property, the rights symbolized by a patent can be inherited, sold, rented, mortgaged, and even taxed. When a patent expires, or is held invalid, the right to exclude others from use of a patent ceases. The public is the ultimate beneficiary of the technical advance.

Examples of patents that are used in a sports setting include baseball "donuts" (warm-up weights that wrap around a baseball bat), golf swing machines, golf putting machines, and even athletic shoes. The "Nike Air" shoes and the "Reebok Pump" were both products used in the sports industry, and their technical innovation was patented to protect the inventor and the company that owned the rights.

Congress has specified that a patent will be granted if the inventor files a timely application at the U.S. Patent and Trademark Office that adequately describes a new, useful, and unobvious invention of proper subject matter. To be timely, an application must be filed within one year of certain acts (by the inventor or others) that place the invention in the hands of the public (e.g., patented or published anywhere in the world, on sale or in public use in this country). This one-year grace period, however, is not available in most foreign countries. A U.S. inventor who wants to obtain corresponding foreign patents must file an application in the United States before any written or oral public presentation of the invention complete enough to enable others to practice the invention. Moreover, the application must describe the best manner ("best mode") known to the inventor of carrying out the invention.

The proper subject matter of a patent is any product, process, apparatus, or composition, including living matter, such as genetically engineered bacteria or plants. Purely mental processes, newly discovered laws of nature, and methods of doing business are not proper subjects for a patent. Most inventors seek a patent to obtain the actual or potential commercial advantages that go along with the right to exclude others. Given the high cost of research and development, the opportunity to recoup these costs through commercial exploitation of the invention may be the primary justification for undertaking research in the first place.

The described invention must be new. This means that it must not have been invented first by another person or identically known, or used by others in this country, or patented or published anywhere in the world before the actual invention date (not the application filing date). The invention also must be useful. It must serve some disclosed or generally known purpose. Section 103 of the Patent Act has an additional requirement of unobviousness. Unobviousness means that the differences between the invention and the prior public knowledge in its technical field must be such that a person having ordinary skill in this field would not have found the invention obvious at the time it was made.

Patent rights can be commercially exploited in two basic ways: (1) directly, by the inventor's practice of the invention to obtain an exclusive marketplace advantage (as where the patent technology results in a better product or produces an old product less expensively) and/or (2) indirectly, by receiving income from the sale or licensing of the patent. It is important to note that a patent does not give the inventor the right to practice the invention. The inventor can practice his invention only if by so doing he does not also practice the invention of an earlier unexpired patent.

Licenses can be non-exclusive, allowing many parties, including the inventor, to practice the invention simultaneously. An example of a non-exclusive license is a baseball pitching machine. This device to help hitters during practice is used all over the country. A patent allows the inventor and many players to use the machine at the same time. A patent may also provide commercial advantages in addition to the potential for an exclusive market position or licensing income. A patent often lends business credibility to start-up ventures and can open doors to both markets. An improvement patent may also make it possible to cross-license any basic patents held by others that block the path to the market.

NOTES

1. In *Antonious v. Spalding & Evenflo Companies, Inc.*, 217 F.3d 849 (Fed. Cir. 1999), the plaintiff filed suit, alleging infringement of a design patent for iron golf clubs. The court, citing a U.S. Supreme Court case, provided that "[i]f, in the eye of an ordinary observer, giving such attention as a purchaser usually gives, two designs are substantially the same, if the resemblance is such as to deceive such an observer, inducing him to purchase one supposing it to be the other, the first one patented is infringed by the other." The court, in affirming the lower court's ruling, held that there was no patent infringement.

2. In the case of *Nike Inc. v. Wal-Mart Stores Inc.*, 138 F.3d 1437 (Fed. Cir. 1998), Wal-Mart was appealing a decision by the trial court to grant Nike $6 million because Wal-mart and the shoe manufacturer, Hawe Yue Inc., had allegedly infringed upon Nike's patent No. 348,765, which is a particular shoe design. The appeals court remanded the decision for a discussion of whether or not Nike had met the "marking statute." This marking statue deals with whether or not the patent holder affixes anything on the product which shows that the product is indeed patented.

3. For an idea of what type of sports-related materials can be patented, visit the Web site for the U.S. Patent and Trademark Office at www.uspto.gov/patft. For example, U.S. Patent # 5,419,561 is a method of miniature golf that is registered as follows:

> A method of playing traditional, championship golf using only a putter and a single golf ball, comprising the steps of: a) providing a reduced size golf course including a series of eighteen

holes each including a playing surface simulating grass and defining a teeing area and a putting green at opposite ends of a fairway, means for limiting the number of strokes to play said eighteen holes, using only a putter and a single golf ball, to a par 72, the said eighteen holes including four par-3 holes, four par-5 holes, and ten par-4 holes, b) Providing representations of natural hazards along said holes as bunkers and water hazards by selectively colored areas wherein a selected color is employed to represent a particular hazard and any penalty associated therewith, c) providing and indicating maximum distance boundaries across the fairways of said holes in selective manner past which the player must not stroke a ball with the putter without incurring a penalty, and d) said colored areas and boundaries being so arranged that the player may play the reduced area course with only a putter as if it were a full size championship golf course by virtue of the selective stroke distance boundaries and hazard indications and the player is prevented from reaching each of said greens in less strokes than it takes to reach the greens in said full size course using select clubs from a set of clubs.

Chapter 14

TELEVISION AND BROADCASTING

INTRODUCTION

All sports entities potentially have a valuable property right in the accounts and descriptions of their games and events, whether these activities are broadcast on radio, television, cable television, and/or the Internet. The importance of these contracts cannot be overstated, because they provide enormous amounts of revenue (see Chapter 1, Section 1.2.2., "Effects of Broadcast Contracts on Major League Baseball"), more than some organizations can make through all other sources of revenue combined. The value of this property right has led to numerous contentious lawsuits concerning who owns the rights to these broadcasts. These lawsuits have involved issues of copyright law (see Chapter 13), antitrust law (see Chapter 10), and contract law (see Chapter 9).

Copyright law and sports intersect whenever a sports organization broadcasts one of its games. The descriptions and accounts of these games are a copyrightable work, and the team may be entitled to royalty fees if the game is rebroadcast. Antitrust law and sports broadcasting meet when a sports organization attempts to negotiate broadcasting contracts on the behalf of its member teams. While this is allowed on the professional level as a result of the Sports Broadcast Act of 1961, the pooling of broadcast rights on the intercollegiate level has been the cause of litigation that has reached the Supreme Court. Finally, a holder of property rights will enter into contracts with many different organizations (networks, advertisers, cable companies) when broadcasting a sports contest. It is imperative for the rights holder to be aware of the different clauses and situations that exist in broadcast contracts. It is important for broadcast rights holders at all levels of sport to be aware of these legal considerations when entering into contract negotiations for the rights to their organizations' sporting event.

Chapter 14 begins with a section explaining why sports broadcasts are a protectable property right of the athletic organization owning the event. The history of legislation and evolution of case law is discussed to provide the reader with knowledge of the foundations of the law and sports broadcasting. Its subsections discuss how Congress and the Federal Communications Commission (FCC) further strengthened this legal right with the passage of the Copyright Act of 1976, as well as subsequent cable regulations. The second section of the chapter explores issues that are unique to different constituencies within the sports world, from professional to intercollegiate to Olympic organizations.

The third section discusses restrictions placed on the broadcasting organizations by a league or conference, as well as the restrictions placed upon sports television stations for the replaying of sports highlights. The fourth section concerns other issues in sports broadcasting that have recently emerged in litigation and may have a tremendous impact on the future of sports broadcasting.

In order to describe these legal considerations, some basic terminology relating to the broadcasting industry must be reviewed.

- *Standard Broadcast Television.* This is what most individuals consider "basic television." Local television stations broadcast programming that is received by local home television sets when the antenna picks up transmission signals. Standard broadcast television is broadcast on channels 2–69, with channels 2–13 known as very high frequency (VHF) and channels 14–69 known as ultra high frequency (UHF). UHF stations may include the local CBS, NBC, ABC, PBS, and FOX affiliates.

- *Cable Television* (formerly known as CATV [community antenna television]). This is a service provided to consumers by which traditional television programming and/or other broadcast signals (e.g., pay cable) are brought into the home of the subscriber via cable transmission (as opposed to over-the-air transmission), usually for an initial installation charge and a monthly subscription fee. Standard broadcast stations can also be brought into a subscriber's home through cable television, in order to receive a clearer picture. The stations that may fall into the cable television category include ESPN, CNN, TNT, FOX Sports Net, USA, and Lifetime.

- *Pay Cable*. This refers to a premium cable television service, which provides special channels to subscribers, for an additional cost, that carry unique programming such as sports. Examples of special channels are Showtime and HBO. These channels may televise sports, and historically have televised boxing matches.

- *Superstations*. These are local, independent, distant signal television stations whose programs, including sports, are carried via satellite to cable systems outside of the station's local broadcast range. Examples are TBS superstation in Atlanta, WGN in Chicago, WWOR in New Jersey, and WPIX in New York. These television stations often carry sports programming, such as the Atlanta Braves on WTBS and the Chicago Bulls on WGN.

- *Satellites*. Satellites provide a space-based distribution system of program services for standard broadcast and cable television. Satellites relay television signals across the world. The use of satellites to carry distant television signals is becoming more prevalent with the emergence of technology such as DSS, which can provide thousands of television stations from around the world to people who subscribe to this "home satellite" service.

- *Earth Station, Uplink, Downlink, and Transponder*. All of these are used in satellite transmissions of broadcast signals. The uplink is the ground-to-satellite transmission of a broadcast signal; a downlink is a satellite-to-earth transmission of a broadcast signal; and an earth station is a ground antenna designed to communicate with a satellite. A transponder is the part of the satellite that consists of a receiver to pick up the signals from the uplink, a processor to convert the signal's frequency and amplify its strength, and a transmitter to rebroadcast the signal on the downlink.

- *Fixation*. Fixation is recording all parts of a broadcast on film, videotape, or replay tape for purposes of protecting the copyright and the manner in which it was recorded.

- *Internet*. This is the worldwide interconnection of computer networks used by the government, academic institutions, businesses, and individuals. Each site on the Internet has its own "address," and users are able to access these sites. The Internet has had a profound impact on sports broadcasting because it has the capability to broadcast events worldwide, regardless of geographic location. Therefore, more people will have access to sports programming than ever before. However, who owns the rights to these Internet broadcasts will undoubtedly become a topic of litigation in the future.

- *Compulsory Licenses*. These are licenses issued by the government that give a broadcasting company the right to use a work or product that is owned by a separate copyright holder. The user of the work must pay a royalty fee for its use. The copyright holder is obligated to grant the license to any organization that agrees to pay the royalty fees.

- *Handheld Pagers/Cellular Phones*. These are small electronic devices manufactured by phone companies that, along with their regular uses, such as making phone calls, receiving text messages, and facilitating contact without grounded telephone lines, can provide real-time updates of sports scores.

- *Siphoning*. This is the shifting of programs from standard broadcast television to pay cable or subscription television. Siphoning has become an issue, with many pay-cable stations offering sports programming instead of standard broadcast television.

14.1. LEGAL FOUNDATION: ESTABLISHING THE PROPERTY RIGHT, HISTORY AND LAWS

In 1939, an intercollegiate baseball game between Columbia University and Princeton University became the first televised sporting event in the United States. While this was the first televised sporting event, issues concerning radio sports broadcasting had arisen for almost two decades prior to the airing of that game. Since 1921, athletic organizations have attempted to claim property rights over the broadcasts of their games and, in turn, charge money for the right to broadcast their sporting events to the public. While sport organizations do not charge money for the print media to write about the games, broadcasters have always been charged for their transmissions.

The courts and the government initially had difficulty deciding who owned the property rights to sports broadcasts: the team, the broadcasting station, the players, or the league. The ownership of this property right entitles an organization to fees, royalties, and therefore increased revenues. Generally, it has been decided, through the courts and legislation, that the home team is the owner of the property rights of a game, and therefore is entitled to any benefits, such as broadcasting fees and retransmission royalties. In the 1938 case of *Pittsburgh Athletic Co. v. KQV Broadcasting* (see note 3), the court decided that the home team holds the property rights of the game, and that they also control the right to disseminate these games, as well as the right to license these rights. The opposing clubs (i.e., the visiting team) do have a property right in that they own the rights to rebroadcast the games back to their own home region.

As mentioned above, the early cases in the area of sports broadcasting dealt with unauthorized radio broadcasts of professional sports contests (see notes 1–4). In cases of unauthorized use, the courts held that such use was a misappropriation of a club's property right to control "descriptions or accounts" of games, and to allow broadcast stations to do so would be an "unjust enrichment" for a station. For example, in *National Exhibition Co. v. Fass* (see note 2), the court ruled that a broadcaster could not immediately teletype the play-by-play of a baseball game without infringing upon the property rights of the original rights holder. *Property* is generally defined as "That which belongs exclusively to one . . . the unrestricted and exclusive right to a thing; the right to dispose of a thing in every legal way, to possess it, to use it, and to exclude everyone else from interfering with it" (*Black's Law Dictionary*).

This legal right to the sports broadcast, which was established by the earlier court decisions, was further strengthened when Congress enacted the Copyright Act of 1976. In enacting that law, Congress extended copyright protection to live sports broadcasts. This copyright protection had been established through court decisions, but now the protection was through legislation. Under this Act, copyright protection grants the owners of a copyrightable work the exclusive right to "perform the copyrighted work publicly." One of the important results of the Copyright Act was that it established a governmental agency known as the Copyright Royalty Tribunal. The tribunal was charged with deciding disputes over copyrights of broadcasts, collecting royalties for owners of copyrights, and disbursing these royalties to the proper owners.

Until the late 1970s it was widely believed by broadcast networks that the copyright of a sports broadcast belonged to them. However, in 1978 the Copyright Royalty Tribunal concluded that, based on the legislative history of the Copyright Act, the copyright of the game being broadcast belonged to the sports entity whose game or event was being telecast. It has been found that the broadcasting company, which pays money for the rights to broadcast an event, does not have this property right.

This holding by the tribunal was a very important one for the holder of broadcast rights. First, it signified that the sports organization or its parent had the ultimate right to decide whether it wants to have its sporting events (property) broadcast on one of the electronic media outlets. Second, it means that for any subsequent rebroadcast of the sports entity's game, the organization can expect to receive compensation.

As mentioned previously, another potential property issue raised in broadcasting revolves around who owns the rights to a game—the home team or the visiting team? Generally, this issue is resolved in the game contract, and such agreements usually give the property right to the home team or host sports entity. The visiting team usually receives a fee that could be from a TV or radio broadcast. An alternative option for the visiting team might be agreeing on no fee from TV and/or radio, but settling on a "home and home" series, where the visiting team hosts the game in the following season. However, one court has ruled that, based on common law, principles of misappropriation, and contractual interference, a visiting team controls the right to broadcast a game back to its home city and surrounding area (see *Wichita State University Intercollegiate Athletic Association v. Swanson Broadcasting Co.*, Case No. 81C130 (Kan. Dist. Ct. 1981).

NOTES

1. *In the Matter of A. E. Newton (WOCL)*, 2 FCC 281 (1936), was the first legal case (but not an official court case) that dealt with sports broadcasting. A. E. Newton was applying to the FCC, a government entity, to renew his radio license, a procedure undergone every five to seven years. It was made apparent that Newton, whose radio station, WOCL, originated from his home, had placed a radio in his house that was broadcasting a game of the 1934 World Series on the station WGR. Newton attached earphones to the radio and listened to the account of the game on WGR. After listening to the account of the game, Newton would relate, nearly simultaneously, the account of the game to his listeners. The FCC ruled that "when a station engages in practice here, its conduct is inconsistent with fair dealing, is dishonest in nature, and amounts to unfair utilization of . . . another's labor." However, despite its negative view of Newton's conduct, the FCC ruled that, from a strict point of view, Newton's rebroadcasting of the game did not constitute a retransmission of the game, and therefore was not in violation of statutes. No court ruling was ever made, and Newton's license was renewed.

2. In *National Exhibition v. Teleflash*, 24 F.Supp. 488 (S.D.N.Y. 1936), the producers of a baseball radio broadcast were seeking to stop defendants from providing a play-by-play radio broadcast through telephones used inside the stadium. Although the defendants did convey to the listeners what they were seeing in the game, the court did not find that the defendants were violating any rights of the broadcast organization. In his decision, the judge stated, "Even if ticket holders were the source of news about the plays, the tickets themselves are not shown to have contained any notice or statement of objection to the doing of what was done. A ticket was a complete license to see the game. What is there to prevent a man from telling in his own way, what he saw and telling it when and in the form he chose?" The court also said that the failure of the admission ticket to the game to state that the fans could not practice such conduct was another reason that the plaintiff was not successful.

3. In *Pittsburgh Athletic Co. v. KQV Broadcasting*, 24 F.Supp. 490 (W.D. Pa. 1938), the Pittsburgh Pirates brought a request for an injunction against KQV Broadcasting from broadcasting Pirates' home games without the team's consent. The defendants would place "reporters" outside of the stadium, where they still would see the baseball field. The

reporters would then provide a play-by-play broadcast of the game to listeners. The court ruled in favor of the Pirates' organization, stating, "The right, title and interest in and to the baseball games played within the parks of members of the National League, including Pittsburgh, including the property right in, and the sole right of, disseminating or publishing or selling, or licensing the right to disseminate, news, reports, descriptions, or accounts of games played in such parks, during the playing thereof, is vested exclusively in such members." It is interesting to note how closely this decision is followed in the message that is broadcast by a broadcast station during every professional sporting event.

4. In *National Exhibition Co. v. Fass*, 143 N.Y.S.2d 767 (N.Y. Sup. Ct. 1955), defendant, Martin Fass, was an independent sports reporter who would listen to radio broadcasts of the 1953 New York Giants baseball games, and then teletype the details of the games to other radio stations, which would immediately rebroadcast the news. Fass argued that the news was "in the public domain," and that he was not rebroadcasting the information, simply teletyping the information. Similar to the decision in *Pittsburgh Athletic Co. v. KQV Broadcasting*, the court found for the owner of the property right to the game, stating, "The aforesaid actions . . . have deprived plaintiff of the just benefits of its labors and expenditures in respect of the creation and production of baseball games and public dissemination of descriptions and accounts thereof and will continue so to do and will cause great and irreparable loss, injury and damage to plaintiff unless enjoined."

5. In *Zacchini v. Scripps-Howard Broadcasting Co.*, 433 U.S. 562 (1977), the plaintiff, Hugo Zacchini, conducted an act under the moniker "The Human Cannonball," and toured around the country, stopping at fairs and circuses. Zacchini did not charge an admission fee to see his exhibitions. However, without his permission, a reporter from a television station owned by Scripps-Howard taped an entire performance of Zacchini's and aired it on the station's evening newscast. Zacchini sued, stating that he was in the entertainment business, and that the broadcast of his performance on television was an "unlawful appropriation of plaintiff's professional property." In a split decision, the Supreme Court decided in favor of Zacchini, deciding that his right to publicity had been infringed upon.

6. In *Post-Newsweek Stations-Connecticut Inc. v. Travelers Insurance Co.*, 510 F.Supp. 81 (D. Conn. 1981), the plaintiff television station was attempting to obtain a preliminary injunction to allow it to cover the events, as news, of the International Figure Skating Championships being held in the Hartford Civic Center. The defendants had not allowed the plaintiffs to cover the event at all because ABC had been granted the exclusive broadcasting rights for the event. The contract had stated that ABC had "exclusivity against television news broadcasts of any length which would include video film or videotape coverage of any of the Championships prior to our telecasts." In deciding in favor of the defendants, and not granting the injunction, the court stated, "The plaintiff has no special right of access to this event, and . . . the contractual restrictions imposed do not violate the plaintiff's First and Fourteenth Amendment rights." This decision, although involving only a preliminary injunction and restraining order, was an influential decision in strengthening the property and copyright clauses in broadcasting contracts.

7. For more information on sports broadcasting and its effects upon professional and intercollegiate sports, see the following:

a. Gerald Scully, *The Market Structure of Sports* (Chicago: University of Chicago Press, 1995).

b. James Quirk and Rodney D. Fort, *Pay Dirt* (Princeton, N.J.: Princeton University Press, 1997).

c. Jerry Gorman, Kirk Calhoun, and Skip Rozin, *The Name of the Game: The Business of Sports* (New York: John Wiley and Sons, 1994).

14.1.1. Copyright Laws and Regulations

As noted previously, the Copyright Act of 1976 gave sports organizations a right to copyright the broadcast of their games or contests, ensuring a statutory property right. Organizations are most often impacted by the copyright laws in regard to *retransmission* of a broadcast of the organization's games or contests. This rebroadcasting most frequently occurs with cable television—for instance, when a local cable system broadcasts a game by picking up a distant signal television station. Under the 1976 law, cable television companies were granted a compulsory license that exempts them from having to seek permission to retransmit any programming that a standard broadcast television station is originating. A compulsory license is an agreement that gives a user the unlimited right to use a work or product, and accordingly the user will pay a set fee or royalty at a later time. The holder of the copyright must abide by compulsory licenses, which are issued by the government, and the copyright holder cannot refuse permission to rebroadcast if someone pays the mandatory royalty fees. This means that if a local television station is broadcasting a school's basketball game, and a cable system has the capability to pick up that transmission, the cable company can broadcast it over its cable system without the permission of the school, as long as it pays a fee. This system of compulsory licenses diminishes the value of a copyright holder's property because the license allows a wider distribution of the broadcast, which weakens contracts that the copyright holder might have with network television stations.

The Copyright Royalty Tribunal, as established by the Copyright Act of 1976, initially determined the fee that a user of a broadcast had to pay to the copyright holder. (See note 3 for more information on the Copyright Royalty Tribunal.) Sports organizations were not content with the amount of money that they were receiving from the Copyright Royalty Tribunal, and believed that they would be able to negotiate better arrangements if they could negotiate individually with the cable companies. In 1982, the "Big Four" (MLB, NBA, NFL, and NHL), other sports entities, and organizations such as the Motion Picture Association of America brought a case against the Copyright Royalty Tribunal, challenging the amount they received from the rebroadcasts of their games and performances (see note 2). However, in a judgment for the tribunal, the court upheld the distribution methods of the organization, stating that "it was impossible to satisfy all the claimants. . . . The Tribunal's decision has achieved an initial allocation of the Fund that is well within the metes prescribed by Congress."

The tribunal, constantly under scrutiny from sports organizations and non-sports copyright holders, was replaced in 1993 by the Copyright Royalty Tribunal Reform Act (see note 4). This Act replaced the Tribunal with the Copyright Royalty Arbitration Panel, which is directed by the Librarian of Congress. Under this system, the Arbitration Panel is charged with the same duties as the previous tribunal, deciding who is entitled to royalties and how much they are entitled to. The librarian, however, must approve the determination of these allocations before they are made official.

Cable is the only communications medium that has been permitted to present the accounts and descriptions of a club's games without individually negotiating for the right to do so. Obviously, this has resulted in a special privilege for cable broadcasters. However, Congress has not shown any willingness to abolish cable's compulsory license. Under existing FCC rules, cable systems may import literally hundreds of sports events (see section 14.2.2., "Broadcast Rights of a Professional League," for a discussion of siphoning). Sports teams have been concerned that such lack of restraint adversely affects gate receipts and broadcast revenues. Sports organizations have attempted through litigation and legislation to curb the ability of cable companies to rebroadcast games on a widespread scale (see note 1).

To combat the nearly free rein that cable companies benefit from, the FCC has enacted two rules that are still in effect and provide sports teams with some limited—but nevertheless important—control over cable importation of distant sports events. The first is known as the Sports or Same Game Rule (47 CFR 76.67). Under this rule, a team may require cable systems within thirty-five miles to delete the distant signal telecast of that team's home game—provided that the home game is not televised locally. For example, assume that the Boston Celtics and the New York Knicks are playing a game in Boston. If the Celtics are not televising the game in Boston, they may request affected cable systems in the Boston area to delete the telecast of the game by the Knicks. A cable system that fails to comply with such a request would be subject to a fine by the FCC, as well as a copyright infringement action, because its compulsory license extends only to programming that is authorized to be carried under FCC rules. The primary effect of the rule is to protect the club's home gate; however, the rule is also important in protecting the club's pay cable or subscription television contracts.

One other set of FCC rules that affords some limited control over the distribution of sports telecasts involves network non-duplication. Professional sports teams, either on their own or through their television flagship station, often establish a network of stations to televise their games. Under the FCC's network non-duplication rules (47 CFR 76.92), the stations in these communities are able to prevent local cable systems from carrying a duplicating telecast. This preserves the local station as the exclusive outlet for the event, and is especially applicable to prevent superstations from broadcasting a duplicating telecast.

In professional sports, the major piece of legislation dealing with broadcasting is the Sports Broadcast Act of 1961. This act immunizes from antitrust liability the pooled sale of telecasting rights by the four major professional sports leagues (MLB, NHL, NFL, and NBA). (See Chapter 10 for a discussion of antitrust law.) Thus, it allows the leagues to negotiate television packages, but it also restricts the ability of the leagues to define the geographical areas into which the pooled telecasts may be broadcast. It also protects college and high school football for Friday and Saturday telecasts within seventy-five miles.

Professional leagues were eager for Congress to adopt this legislation on behalf of the sports leagues because it allowed a league to pool the television rights of all teams together, giving them added power on their side of the bargaining table. If each team negotiated national contracts separately, it would create less revenue, since competition and nonexclusivity would prevail. This type of situation would also create an atmosphere where more popular teams, or teams in larger markets, would be able to negotiate more lucrative broadcasting contracts, thereby creating a financial gap between the teams within the league (see Chapter 1, section 1.2.2., "Effects of Broadcast Contracts on Major League Baseball," for a discussion of broadcast revenues). It should be noted that the act does not sanction pooling of rights for intercollegiate athletics. The act's exclusion of intercollegiate athletics led to the landmark case *University of Oklahoma v. NCAA* (see section 14.2.5.1., "Antitrust Issues in Broadcasting for Colleges," for a discussion of this case).

NOTES

1. In *Eastern Microwave Inc. v. Doubleday Sports Inc.*, 691 F.2d 125 (2d Cir. 1982), Doubleday Sports, the owner of the New York Mets baseball team, sued Eastern Microwave (EMI), a common carrier licensed by the FCC, whose services include the retransmission of the television signals of broadcast stations to markets outside the service areas of the broadcast stations. EMI retransmitted the signals of WOR-TV, including baseball games, without altering any of the programs, and had been doing so since 1965 without any complaints from WOR. The Mets sued EMI, charging that the rebroadcast of its games was a copyright infringement even though EMI was simply a passive carrier of the broadcasts, not altering the transmissions. The court decided for EMI, noting that EMI's conduct fell under the auspices of the Copyright Act of 1976, and that by making its royalty payments, as outlined by the act, EMI was not in violation of Doubleday's copyright. The court also held that it would be impossible for each carrier to negotiate with each copyright owner on an individual basis, and would create a situation that was not intended by Congress in the Copyright Act of 1976. However, this decision led to a petition by pro sports leagues and other copyright holders to the Copyright Royalty Tribunal to increase the royalties paid to the rights holders. Subsequently, the CRT imposed restrictions that made it nearly financially impossible for a carrier to import more than two superstations.

2. In *National Ass'n of Broadcasters v. Copyright Royalty Tribunal*, 675 F.2d 367 (D.C. Cir. 1982), the four major pro sports leagues, along with a number of other copyright holders, including the Motion Picture Association of America, brought action against the Copyright Royalty Tribunal, challenging the first distribution of the cable royalties by the tribunal. The judge stated, "Specific awards [to the plaintiff parties] are reversible only if the agency's [tribunal's] decision is not supported by 'substantial evidence' or is 'arbitrary, capricious, an abuse of discretion or otherwise not in accordance with law' as defined by the Administrative Procedure Act." The judge decided for the defendant tribunal, stating, "The Tribunal faced a difficult task in conducting the initial distribution of cable royalties because of the number of claimants and the inescapably qualitative problem of evaluating their competing claims. It was impossible to satisfy all the claimants, whose combined requests totaled roughly three times more than the finite amount of the Fund. We are satisfied that the Tribunal's resolution of the problem confronting it was reasonable, that its decisional criteria comported with congressional intent, and that its distribution of royalty shares finds rational support in the administrative record."

3. Under the original Copyright Royalty Tribunal, cable systems had to pay a royalty commission for telecasting the contest to a central fund. The tribunal was established to distribute these royalty payments to deserving sports entities (and non-sports copyright holders). The tribunal was also established so that each cable network and each rights holder would not have to negotiate for the rights to each game. With sports, the tribunal devised a distribution formula that weighed relative marketplace values of the programming retransmitted against the value to the cable system for using the broadcast and the harm inflicted by its broadcast to the copyright holder. The cable companies paid a royalty fee that was based on a sliding scale relative to their overall revenues. When the first royalty fees were divided for the year 1978, it was determined that sports would receive 12 percent of the total pool, which amounted to $15 million. In 1979 and 1980 the split was 15 percent of the pool to sports. From 1983 to 1990 the split was 16.35 percent of the pool.

4. The official legislative citation for the Copyright Royalty Tribunal Reform Act is HR 2840, the Copyright Royalty Tribunal Reform Act of 1993.

14.2. BROADCAST CONTRACTS

Copyright laws are just one area of contract language that must be scrutinized by athletic administrators in order to ensure that all the broadcast rights of an athletic organization are protected. A rights holder should be aware of all of the entities that could own rights to a game, and what regulations apply to the contest.

For example, a rights holder must be aware that an NFL team cannot negotiate for a Friday night football game due to the provisions in the Sports Broadcast Act, which provide for the protection of high school football games on Friday nights. Rights holders must adhere to rules of their association, conference, or league. For example, a college athletic department cannot negotiate to telecast an NCAA basketball tournament game or a conference championship game because it does not own the rights to these contests. In fact, universities may not be able to negotiate broadcast contracts for individual regular season games because the rights may have been assigned to the conference. After making sure that no other entity has rights to the contest, the university may then negotiate its contract. Therefore, the basics of contract law, which were covered in Chapter 9, are important. The following sections will focus on contract issues and clauses that are unique to the broadcast business. Whether a rights holder is a member of the NCAA, the NFL, or the United States Olympic Committee, it is imperative that he or she is aware of the unique clauses of the particular broadcast contracts, and how affiliation with certain organization may affect negotiations and the ability to contract with certain television networks. Aside from this knowledge, it is also crucial that a rights holder understand the basic clauses that should be covered in a standard broadcast contract.

14.2.1. Rights Granted

In a broadcast contract, the sports organization grants the rights to broadcast the game in exchange for some specified benefit, generally a rights fee from the broadcast organization. The broadcast organization may be only one station, or it may consist of a number of stations that form a network. Usually, a broadcast organization seeks exclusive rights to telecast a game. *Exclusive rights* are defined as rights granted by the sports organization to one broadcaster for the purpose of setting up a single-station broadcast or an exclusive network, and such rights do not permit any other broadcast organization to broadcast the event. Exclusive rights are the opposite of multi-originations—that is, when many broadcast organizations are given the right to telecast the same event.

Exclusive rights may be granted for different technologies. Therefore, an organization might negotiate exclusive rights contracts for live standard broadcast television, delayed standard broadcast television, cable television, radio, and/or Internet. Often, in intercollegiate athletic broadcast contracts, exceptions are included, even in exclusive arrangements, to allow for an origination by a student radio or television station of a sports broadcast so that the students can gain experience in sports broadcasting. A contract clause with a broadcasting organization might specify as follows: "The parties acknowledge that notwithstanding this agreement, [name] University may grant to University's student-run radio station the right to broadcast any game."

In general, any broadcast contract would include at a minimum the following clauses:

1. Term and scope of the contract, including event(s) to be broadcast
   a. Number of years

    b. Number of games

    c. Which type of contests being broadcast

2. Definitions-will elaborate on the important terms within the contract to avoid confusion. For example, terms such as "rights holder," "broadcast," and "termination," may be included in the definitions section.

3. Access and admission to events-outlines what type of access the broadcaster will have to the facilities, including how many people, and what cameras will be allowed.

4. Facilities furnished-the amount and type of facilities that the broadcasting company will have to work in. Can include the booth for broadcasters.

5. Stipulations, requirements and reservations-any other areas that are not covered in the general contract, or special needs on the part of either party.

6. Rights fee and schedule of payments-outlines the amount of money paid to the rights holder, and how that money will be distributed.

    Exhibit 14.1 is an example of a radio contract, and exhibit 14.2 is an example of a television or cable television contract.

14.2.2. Broadcast Rights of a Professional League

    As mentioned earlier, the Sports Broadcast Act of 1961 (Public Law 87–331, 15 U.S.C. 1292) greatly benefits the four major sports leagues. Each of these leagues is able to negotiate collectively with the television networks without being found in violation of antitrust statutes. One major advantage of this legislative benefit is that if the league divides national broadcasting revenues equally among all of the teams, teams that play in smaller markets receive the same as the largest markets. Another benefit is that it balances out national exposure. However, if teams were negotiating separate local contracts, this would most likely not be the case. For example, in the NFL (where no local television contracts for regular season games exist), the Green Bay Packers' share of the national broadcast revenue is the same as the New York Giants even though the difference in their media markets is millions of people.

    Unlike the situation in intercollegiate athletics, most professional leagues have a very organized system of determining who owns the rights to their broadcasts. In a professional league, when no network broadcast is involved, leagues formulate rules that provide for each team to broadcast both its home and away games. Teams in professional leagues do not usually interfere with each other's rights, since each desires to retain exclusivity in its own territory. Also, unlike other sports organizations, the four major sports league are able to pool their broadcast rights. For a brief description of local and national revenue for sports broadcasts in the four major professional sport leagues, see exhibit 14.3. As this exhibit shows, Major League Baseball depends the most on local television broadcast contracts for revenue, while the National Football League relies almost exclusively on its national television contract for income.

    A holder of broadcast rights must be aware of the rules that govern the league in which it competes before making any broadcasting decisions. In the four major sports leagues, the national rights fees that are acquired by the league are distributed equally among all of the teams. For example, in the NBA, the large national contracts with ABC/ESPN and TNT produce more revenue for the

Exhibit 14.1
Radio License Agreement

AGREEMENT made as of this _____ day of (month), 19_____ by and between CORPORATION on behalf of Radio Station WXXX-AM, (address) (Station) and _____ (Sports Organization).
The parties hereby agree as follows:

1. (a) Except as otherwise specified, (Sports Organization) grants (Station) the sole and exclusive right to broadcast and rebroadcast over the facilities of (Station), and to authorize the radio broadcast of, all (Sports Organization)'s games, including regular season and any post-season games to which (Sports Organization) has broadcast rights, (hereinafter the "Games") during the (name years) seasons. The parties acknowledge that notwithstanding this Agreement, (Sports Organization) may grant (i) to (Sports Organization's) student-run radio station in the right to broadcast any Game and (ii) to any opponent of (Sports Organization) in any Game the right to broadcast or grant broadcast rights with respect to that Game to another radio station or cable radio station.
(b) Broadcasting may commence hereunder from the point of origin of a Game up to thirty (30) minutes prior to the scheduled commencement of a Game and continue up to thirty (30) minutes simultaneously with its playing. (Station) may in its discretion broadcast a pre-Game and post-Game show in connection with the broadcast of the Games. (Unless otherwise indicated, reference to the "Game(s)" herein shall have the sole and exclusive right to sell or otherwise use all of the commercial time in the adjacencies prior to the pre-Game and subsequent to the post-Game Shows, together with all commercial time during the broadcast of each Game, and to retain all revenue derived therefrom.
(c) (Station) may terminate this Agreement effective (date) of any year while this Agreement is in effect upon prior written notice to (Sports Organization).
(d) (Station) and (Sports Organization) shall negotiate in good faith during the period beginning on (date) and ending on (date) (the "Negotiating Period") with respect to possible renewal of this Agreement.

2. For all rights granted by (Sports Organization) herein and for the performance of all the terms and provisions of this Agreement on the part of (Sports Organization) to e performed, (Station) agrees to pay and agrees to accept the annual license fee as follows:
(Station) shall pay (Sports Organization) fifty percent (50%) of the "adjusted net profits" made by (Station) in selling commercial availabilities in and adjacent to broadcasts of the Games. As used herein, "net profits" shall mean the (Station)'s revenues (net of agency commissions) derived from said commercial availabilities for each Game less all of (Station)'s reasonable and necessary costs attendant to producing and promoting the availabilities for each Game less all of (Station)'s reasonable and necessary costs attendant to producing and promoting the broadcast of the Games and selling the said availabilities , including, without limiting the generality of the foregoing, out-of-pocket advertising and promotion costs, talent and announcer fees, production and technical costs, transmission costs to (Station)'s facilities, travel costs for talent, production and technical personnel, rights fees, merchandising costs, coaches' show production cost including coaches' talent fee, Game statistical costs, and account executive commissions. (Station) shall retain the first five thousand dollars ($5,000) of net profits, for each Game, and the balance remaining shall be determined to be "adjusted net profits."
(Station) shall pay (Sports Organization) each year's license fee in one payment on or before the date following thirty (30) days after the last Game played by (Sports Organization) team during that year's season. (Station) shall provide

Exhibit 14.1 (continued)

(Sports Organization) with a statement of revenues and costs at that time. At (Sports Organization's) request, (Station) shall produce supporting documentation for the figures set forth in the statement of revenues and costs provided to (Sports Organization).

3. The rights granted (Station) in subparagraph 1(a) are confined to radio and do not include motion picture or television broadcasting rights, all of which are reserved to (Sports Organization) for its sole use and benefit at any time. In the event (Station) is unable to obtain facilities to broadcast a Game through circumstances beyond its control, it may produce and broadcast transcriptions, recordings and recreations of any such Game.

4. (a) (Station) shall have complete control over the production (including pre-and post-production) and format of its broadcasts hereunder, including, without limitation, length of coverage. (Station) shall select and employ the "play-by-play" and "color analyst" announcers; provided, however, that (Sports Organization) shall have the right to require the selection of different announcers if (Station's) selection is unacceptable to (Sports Organization).

(b) (Sports Organization) shall make available to (Station) without charge at all home Games held at (sites) and shall take all reasonable steps at all away Games played at the Byrne Meadowlands Arena or Madison Square Garden, to make available to (Station) suitable space for (Station's) equipment and broadcasting and technical personnel, including access, provision for electrical power lines, cable lines and such other equipment and facilities as (Station) deems necessary or desirable. (Sports Organization) shall use its best efforts to obtain such away Game facilities without charge to (Station). (Station) shall have the right to display the initials "WXXX-AM", and its frequency and trademark, on all equipment used in connection with broadcast of the Games; provided, however, (Sports Organization) cannot guarantee the foregoing with respect to the broadcast of away Games, as defined above.

(c) (Sports Organization) will and will cause its employees, and its head coach to cooperate with (Station) in all reasonable respects in all phases of the preparation, and post-Game shows and at no additional charge; provided, however, that the head coach shall be paid reasonable compensation of $_____ per game by (Station) for appearances of any coach's show.

(d) So far as it is authorized to do so, (Sports Organization) hereby grants to (Station), and (Station) may grant to others, the right to disseminate, reproduce, print and publish the names "(Sports Organization) Name" and the names, likenesses, voices and biographical material of (Sports Organization's) players and coaches, and of all personas connected with the attendant activities, as news or informative matter for publicity and/or advertising purposes in connection with any Game, but not for any direct endorsement or commercial product or service without (Sports Organization's) and any such person's written consent.

5. (Sports Organization) shall provide the following, at its own expense:
   (a) A (Station) dinner, at a (Sports Organization) or other suitable facility; prior to commencement of each season listed in paragraph 1(a) above, arranged in consultation with (Station)
   (b) A full page in each Game program which (Sports Organization) is responsible for producing to promote (Station)'s broadcast. (Station) shall provide (Sports Organization) printed copy for such ad.
   (c) Four (4) public address announcements promoting (Station)'s broadcast and acknowledging (Station)'s sponsors at every home Game held at Arena. (Sports Organization) shall use its best efforts to have such public address announcements promoting (Station's) broadcast and acknowledging sponsors at each home game of (Sports Organization) held at Byrne Meadowlands Arena or Madison Square Garden.

Exhibit 14.1 (continued)

    (d) Fifty (50) tickets to each (Sports Organization) home Game held at Arena. (Sports Organization) shall use its best efforts to provide such tickets at each home Game of (Sports Organization) held at Byrne Meadowlands Arena and Madison Square Garden.

6.   (a) (Station) has the right to preempt any Game, in whole or in part, and (Station) shall have fully discharged its obligations to (Sports Organization) with respect to the Games by payment of the applicable compensation set forth in paragraph 2 hereunder. If (Station) preempts any Game(s), (Station) shall either: (l) broadcast said Game(s) on another radio station at its expense; (ii) tape delay broadcast the Game(s) or (iii) broadcast a "split-feed" (as that term is commonly understood in the broadcast industry) of the Game(s)

    (b) In the event that the broadcasting of any Game is prevented or omitted because of: suspension or disruption or termination of a Game for any reason, Act of God; inevitable accident; fire, lockout, strike or other labor dispute; riot or civil commotion; act of public enemy; enactment, rule, order or act of any government or governmental instrumentality (whether federal, state, local or foreign); failure of technical facilities; failure or delay of transportation facilities; or any other cause of a similar or different nature; the revenues derived from the sale of availabilities for the broadcast of said Game shall not be included in computing the net profits, and the total number of Games shall be reduced.

7.   (Sports Organization) warrants that, to the best of its knowledge and ability:

    (a) It has the full right and power to grant (Station) the rights hereby granted and to enter into and fully perform this Agreement; and that the exercise by (Station) of the rights herein granted as contemplated by this Agreement will not violate any rights of any person, firm or corporation.

    (b) The Games are sanctioned by the National Governing Body and that the Games will be conducted in accordance with applicable National Governing Body rules. The Games shall be subject to and conducted in accordance with applicable National Governing Body rules. The Games shall be subject to and conducted in accordance with all applicable federal, state and local laws.

    (c) All representations to (Station) by (Sports Organization) and all representations made by (Sports Organization) to third parties about any and all elements of the Games shall be accurate and true and in all material respects. (Sports Organization) further warrants that it has made and will make full disclosure to (Station) with respect to all such elements of the Games as soon as practicable after (Sports Organization) has knowledge thereof.

    (d) All publicity which it issues or disseminates or otherwise makes available concerning all elements of the Games will be accurate and true in all material respects.

    (e) All rights herein granted to (Station) in and to the Games are and will be free and clear of liens and encumbrances of every kind and character which are the result of actions by (Sports Organizations).

    (f) None of the Games will contain any defamatory, scandalous, or obscene material contrary to law or to the generally accepted standards if the radio broadcast standards or the Federal Communications Commission.

    (g) There is no outstanding contract, commitment or arrangement, and no pending or threatened claim or litigation which is or may be in conflict with this agreement or which may in any way limit, restrict, impair or interfere with either party's rights hereunder.

    (h) No part or any of the Games will violate or infringe the copyright, trademark, performing patent, literary, intellectual, artistic or dramatic right, the right of privacy, or any other right or privilege or any third person or party.

Exhibit 14.1 (continued)

8. (a)   (Sports Organization) shall indemnify and hold harmless (Station) and any person, firm or corporation deriving rights from (Station) from all claims, damages, liabilities, costs and expenses (including reasonable counsel fees) arising out of or by, (I) any breach by (Sports Organization) of any warranty or agreement made by (Sports Organization) herein, (ii) any act or omission by (Sports Organization) or persons whose services are furnished by (Sports Organization) with regard to any use of any materials, personas or services furnished by (Sports Organization) in connection with (Station)'s production or broadcast of the Games.

(b) Station shall indemnify and hold harmless (Sports Organization) from and against any and all suits, claims, damages, liabilities, costs and expenses, including reasonable counsel fees, arising out of any breach by (Station) of any agreement made by it herein or our of the use of any materials or services furnished by (Station) or by any advertiser, if any, for and in connection with the broadcast of the Games.

(c) The indemnittee hereunder shall promptly notify the indemnitor of any claim, demand or litigation, and the indemnitor shall be solely responsible for the defense, settlement or payment thereof; provided that the indemnitee may, if it so desires, at its own cost and expense and by its own counsel, participate in any such defense, and in such event its counsel will cooperate with counsel for the indemnitor. Any settlement by an indemnitor under this Agreement which derogates from the rights of the indemnitee hereunder may be concluded only with the express approval of the indemnitee, which will not be reasonably withheld. Indemnitor's liability hereunder shall be limited to any judgement or settlement approved by the indemnitor. The foregoing indemnities shall survive this Agreement.

9. (a)   (Sports Organization) will comply with the requirements of Section 507 of the Federal Communications Act of 1934, as amended, concerning broadcast matter and disclosures required thereunder, insofar as that Section applies to persons furnishing program material for radio broadcasting. (Sports Organization) warrants and represents that none of the Games or related activities include or shall include any matter for which any money, service or other valuable consideration is directly or indirectly paid, promised to, or charged or accepted by (Sports Organization). (Sports Organization) shall exercise reasonable diligence to inform its employees, players and other persons with whom (Sports Organization) deals directly in connection with the Games and related activities, of the requirements of the said Section 507; provided, however, that no act of any such employee, player or any independent contractor connected with any of the Games or related activities hall constitute a breach of the provisions of this paragraph unless (Sports Organization) has actual notice thereof. As used in this paragraph, the term "service or other valuable consideration" shall not include any service or property furnished without charge or at a nominal charge for use in or in connection with the Games or related activities unless it is so furnished in consideration for an identification in such broadcast.....of any person, product, service, trademark or brand name beyond and identification which is reasonably related to the use of such "service or property in such broadcast," as such terms are used in the said Section 507.

(b) (Station's) Program Practices Department policies and standards shall apply to the Games and to the sites of the Games; (Station) agrees to provide (Sports Organization) with a copy of its program policies and standards. (Sports Organization) shall comply with and shall use its best efforts to cause those persons controlling each site to comply with all such policies and standards.

10. Each party acknowledges that the rights and privileges granted to the other pursuant to this Agreement are special, unique, extraordinary and unusual in character, and that the breach by either party of any of the provisions contained

Exhibit 14.1 (continued)

in this Agreement will cause the other party irreparable injury. In the event of any such breach by either party, the non-breaching party will be entitled to injunctive relief or other equitable relief to enjoin and restrain such violation for a period ending not less than one (1) year after the expiration or any termination of this Agreement.

11. (a) Except as otherwise specifically provided herein, all notices hereunder shall be in writing and shall be given by personal delivery, registered or certified mail or telegraph (prepaid) at the respective addresses hereinabove set forth, or such other address or addresses as may be designated by either party. Such notices shall be deemed given when mailed or delivered into a telegraph office, except that notice of change of address shall be effective only from the date of its receipt.

(b) Nothing herein shall create any association, partnership or joint venture or the relation of principal and agent between the parties hereto, it being understood that neither party shall have the authority to bind the other or the other's representatives in any way.

(c) This Agreement shall be construed in accordance with the laws of the State of _____ applicable to contracts made and fully performed therein.

(d) Neither party may assign, license or sublicense this Agreement or any of its rights hereunder to any person, firm or corporation, or any parent, subsidiary or affiliated corporation without the prior written consent of the other party. Any permitted assignment shall not relieve the assigning party of any of its obligations hereunder.

(e) If any provision of this Agreement, as applied to either party or to any circumstance, shall be adjudged to be void or unenforceable, the same shall in no way affect any other provision of this Agreement, the application of such provision in any other circumstance, or the validity or enforceability of this Agreement.

(f) No waiver by either party of the breach of any term or provision of this Agreement shall be construed to be a waiver of any prior or subsequent breach of the same or any other term or provision.

(g) This Agreement contains the entire understanding of the parties hereto relating to the subject matter herein contained, and this Agreement cannot be changed, rescinded or terminated orally.

IN WITNESS WHEREOF, the parties hereto have executed this Agreement as of the day and year first above written.

SPORT ORGANIZATION   STATION

By_____   By_____

Exhibit 14.2
Cable TV Agreement

AGREEMENT

THIS AGREEMENT, dated as of _____, is between
_____, a _____ corporation/partnership/etc. located at
_____ ("Licensor"), and _____, a
_____ corporation with offices at _____
("Licensee").

Licensor hereby grants to Licensee the exclusive rights to coverage, including but not limited to the production and distribution of one or more television programs, of the "Event(s)" described below, pursuant to the terms and conditions of this "Agreement."

1. EVENT(S)

    1.1 Name:

    1.2 Date(s):

    1.3 Starting Time(s):

    1.4 Site(s):

    1.5 Participants:

    1.6 Other Terms:

    1.7 Related Activities: For purposes of this Agreement, the term "Event(s)" includes all events and activities taking place at the Site(s) on the Date(s) of the Event(s).

2. FINANCIAL TERMS

    2.1 In consideration of all rights granted to Licensee and the performance of all Licensor's obligations hereunder, Licensee will make the following payment(s) to Licensor:

    2.2 Tickets. Licensor must provide to Licensee not fewer than 25 complimentary tickets to the/each Event in premium locations.

3. DISTRIBUTION

    3.1 Exclusive Rights. Licensee has the exclusive, perpetual right to distribute, transmit, exhibit, license, advertise, duplicate, promote, perform, telecast and otherwise exploit (collectively, "distribute") the Program(s) and its/their constituent elements and any other material pertaining to the Event(s) in Licensee's possession and control throughout the universe, by all means and media now known or subsequently developed, on a live and/or delayed basis, without limitation as to the number of uses. Licensee also has the right to make reproductions of the Program(s) and its/their constituent elements and to use, exhibit and deal with those reproductions in any manner or media whatsoever, including but not limited to the right to incorporate the Programs(s) and/or its/their constituent elements into other works for commercial profit.

Exhibit 14.2 (continued)

    3.2 Ownership of Program(s). Licensee will be the sole owner of the Program(s) and all of its/their constituent elements, including exclusive ownership of all copyrights in and to the Program(s).

    3.3 Obligation to Distribute. Licensee is not required to actually produce or distribute any Program, and Licensee fully discharges its obligations in this Agreement by paying to Licensor the compensation stated in section 2.1.

4.   FIRST NEGOTIATION AND FIRST REFUSAL

    4.1 Negotiating Period. Licensor will negotiate exclusively with Licensee for sixty days (the "Negotiating Period"), regarding the acquisition by Licensee for one or more years of rights to the next-occurring future Event(s). The Negotiating Period will begin on _____, or on an earlier date selected by Licensee with notice to Licensor. For this purpose, the term "Event(s)" will include any event that is a successor or substitute for or otherwise is equivalent to the Events to which this Agreement pertains.

    4.2 Offer/Reoffer Procedure. If Licensee and Licensor do not reach a new agreement during the Negotiating Period, then within three days thereafter Licensor must make a written offer to Licensee of the monetary consideration on which Licensor is willing to license such rights to Licensee (the "Offer"). With the exception of monetary consideration, this Offer cannot contain any terms or conditions that differ from those contained in this Agreement ("Nonconforming Terms"), other than as permitted by subsection 4.3, below. If Licensee does not accept the Offer within fourteen days after receiving it, Licensor may then enter into an agreement with a third party for those rights but not without first re-offering to Licensee the same terms contained in any such third-party offer (the "Reoffer"). Licensee must accept or reject a reoffer no later than seven days after receiving it.

    4.3 Other Requirements. The following additional requirements also apply to Licensee's and Licensor's negotiations of future rights:

        4.3.1   Licensor will not have any discussions or negotiations with any third party regarding the rights contemplated under this section 4 prior to the conclusion of the Negotiating Period;

        4.3.2   Licensee will not be required to negotiate with Licensor concerning, or to consider, any Offer conditioned upon, Licensee's acquisition of rights to any event or property other than television coverage rights to the Events;

        4.3.3   The parties will act at all times in complete good faith, consistent with the intent and spirit of this entire Agreement;

        4.3.4   Neither an Offer nor any Reoffer can be for rights pertaining to a period of less than one year;

        4.3.5   If Licensee and Licensor reach a new agreement pursuant this Section 4, then negotiations of any subsequent agreement between the parties for rights to future Events may include Nonconforming Terms; and

        4.3.6   In accepting an Offer or Reoffer, Licensee will not be required to comply with any term or condition that would be impossible for Licensee to perform or would conflict with any of Licensee's prior contractual commitments. Licensee will notify Licensor of any such terms or conditions as promptly as possible.

    4.4 Future Expectations. Licensor acknowledges that this Agreement's scope is limited to its specific subject matter and it does not entitle either Licensor or Licensee to any future rights or expectations with respect to each other except as explicitly provided herein.

5.   EVENT ARRANGEMENTS

    5.1 General Arrangements. Licensor is solely responsible for all arrangements (including any compensation) with the owner of the Site(s) for the staging of the Event(s) and

Exhibit 14.2 (continued)

with all participants and any officials involved in the Event(s). Those arrangements must afford to Licensee all rights and consents required or contemplated with respect to Licensee's rights hereunder. [For Event(s) as to which Licensee intends to distribute one or more Program(s) on a live or same-day, recorded basis, Licensor must: (i) consult and coordinate with Licensee's producer prior to the Event to integrate the Event format with Licensee's commercial format, and (ii) appoint a liaison officer to be responsible for and cooperate in calling time-outs and other structured interruptions so that Licensee's commercial format is satisfied and commercial and promotional announcements are properly spaced.] Licensor will use its best efforts to make available to Licensee such participants, officials and other persons connected with the Event(s) as Licensee may request for purposes of interviews and discussion.

5.2 Access. Licensor must assure that Licensee is provided, at no charge, with suitable space and locations at the Site(s), as Licensee determines from time to time (including at any advance technical survey conducted by Licensee), for its announcers and for the installation and operation of all microphones, television cameras and other equipment to be used by Licensee in connection with its production and transmission (including satellite uplink) of the Program(s). Licensor also must assure the availability of such electrical power as is necessary to operate such equipment and all necessary lighting for a first-quality television production, all at no charge to Licensee. Licensee will have the right to install, maintain and remove from the Site(s) and the surrounding premises such wires, cables and equipment as may be necessary for its coverage of the Event(s); but such facilities will not substantially interfere with the use of the Site(s) or with any of the means of ingress or egress. Licensee will have the right to bring into or adjacent to the Site(s) mobile units for the transportation of equipment and personnel. Licensor will provide or cause to be provided to all of Licensee's production personnel at no charge credentials allowing their admission to and access throughout the Site(s) for all purposes necessary to accomplish the production of the Program(s). Licensor will not grant access to the Event(s) to any third party for the purpose of operating audio-video equipment without Licensee's prior written consent, except as permitted by section 5.5.

5.3 Signage. Licensor represents and warrants that, without Licensee's prior written consent:

5.3.1   No sign, billboard or other display or announcement for any product or service will be visible or heard at the Site(s) during Licensee's coverage of the Event(s) except for permanent billboards affixed at the Site for display at all events conducted there (i.e., advertising intended for spectators at the Event and not for the television audience);

5.3.2   No sign or banner of any Event sponsor that has not purchased national commercial time within the applicable Program will be placed anywhere at the Site(s) that could be depicted on any Licensee camera during its production or distribution of any Program; and

5.3.3   Notwithstanding any other provision of this section 5.3, no sign, billboard or other display or public announcement for any television network, distribution service or station, Internet service or portal or any other entity engaged in the business of distributing sports-related audio-video content will be present at the Site(s) during the Event(s).

5.4 Music. The only music appearing in the Event(s) will be that music usually appearing in such Event(s), e.g., music played over a public address system. No music of the type normally included in entertainment programming will be played at the Event(s).

5.5 News Coverage. As the only exception to Licensee's exclusive audio-video coverage rights of the Event(s), Licensor may allow bona fide news organizations access to the Site for purposes of covering the Event(s) as (a) news story(ies). Such access will be

Exhibit 14.2 (continued)

governed by credentials issued by or on behalf of Licensor and will prohibit the live distribution or recording by any means or media of any portion of the Event(s). Licensee authorizes the use of a maximum of two minutes of excerpts from the Program(s) for use in bona fide news reports about the Event only during the 48 hours immediately subsequent to Licensee's initial distribution of its fully-produced television Program of the applicable Event.

6. PROGRAM PRODUCTION

6.1 Program(s). Licensee will have the exclusive right (except only as specifically provided to the contrary elsewhere in this Agreement) to produce audio, video and other material based on the Event(s), which Licensee may incorporate into one or more fully-produced television program(s) and otherwise utilize according to the term of this Agreement (collectively, all such material is referred to in this Agreement as the "Program(s)"). Licensee has complete control over the production and format of the Program(s), including (without limitation) the right to determine the length of the Program(s), to insert commercial and promotional announcements as it so chooses, to title or retitle each Program and to change or designate the name of any Event to the extent it is used in connection with a Program.

6.2 Production Personnel. Licensee has complete authority over the selection of announcers, commentators, technical and other personnel utilized in connection with the Program(s).

6.3 Banners. Licensee will have the right to display its name and other trademarks on banners, its equipment, and any platform or broadcasting booth used at the Site(s) in such a manner and at such locations as are readily visible to both the spectators at the Site(s) and the viewers watching the Program(s).

7. FORCE MAJEURE

If the staging or the coverage of any Event is prevented or cancelled due to any act of God, accident, labor dispute, fire, civil commotion, government action, inclement weather, failure of technical, production or television equipment, or for any other reason beyond the control of Licensor or Licensee, then neither Licensor nor Licensee will be obligated in any manner to the other with respect to the Event (including payment of any rights fee pertaining to the Event), but all other rights Licensee may have in this Agreement will remain in full force and effect. If, however, the Event should be postponed or delayed, then Licensee will have the right to elect to cover the Event on its rescheduled date according to all the terms of this Agreement or to not cover the rescheduled Event, in which case Licensee will not be obligated in any manner to Licensor therefor (including payment of any rights fee pertaining to the Event), but all of Licensee's other rights in this Agreement will survive.

8. PROMOTION AND PUBLICITY

Licensee has the right (and may grant others the right) to reproduce or disseminate in any medium, the name, likeness and voice of each person appearing in or connected with the Program(s) as well as names, trademarks, and other identities of Licensor and any other entities associated with the Event(s) and the Site(s) for all purposes connected with Licensee's exploitation of the Program(s) and Licensee's programming services, but not as a direct endorsement of any product or other services.

9. REPRESENTATIONS & WARRANTIES

9.1 By Licensor. Licensor represents and warrants to Licensee that:

9.1.1 (A) It has the full power and authority to make and perform this Agreement; (B) it has all rights necessary to its grant of rights to Licensee in this Agreement; (C) the making and/or performance of this Agreement does not violate any agreement with any third party; (D) the rights Licensee has acquired and its exploitation of those rights pursuant to this Agreement does

Exhibit 14.2 (continued)

not and will not infringe on or violate the rights of any third party; (E) it will do nothing to interfere with or impair any of Licensee's rights in this Agreement; (F) the Event(s) is/are sanctioned by all sports organization(s) and/or authority(ies) having jurisdiction over it/them, and the Event(s) will be conducted according to all applicable rules and regulations of such organization(s) and/or authority(ies); (G) a representative field of the top athletes in the applicable sport will participate in the Event(s); and (H) the Event(s) will be staged and conducted on the Date(s) and at the Starting Time(s) and Site(s) indicated above;

9.1.2 Licensor will not: (A) authorize or permit any other exhibition or distribution of the Event(s) by any medium in any manner or by any means whatsoever; (B) grant any rights inconsistent with the rights granted to Licensee by this Agreement; or (C) stage any event or competition materially similar to the Event(s) for production, distribution or recording.

9.2 By Licensee. Licensee represents and warrants to Licensor that it has the right to enter into this Agreement and perform all of its obligations pursuant to this Agreement.

10. INDEMNIFICATION

10.1 Mutual Indemnity. Licensee and Licensor each will indemnify, defend and hold the other harmless from any and all claims, costs, liabilities, judgments, expenses or damages (including reasonable attorneys' fees and other costs of suit) arising out of any breach or alleged breach of this Agreement or any representation made by it herein (including but not limited to any claim by a third party that the exercise of the rights of a party to this Agreement in accordance with its conditions and limitations infringes that third party's rights).

10.2 Procedure & Defense. In any case in which indemnification is sought hereunder:

(i) A party seeking indemnification ("Indemnitee") shall give the indemnifying party ("Indemnitor") prompt notice of any claim or litigation to which its indemnity applies; and

(ii) The Indemnitor shall have the right to assume the defense of any claim or litigation to which its indemnity applies and the Indemnitee will cooperate fully with the Indemnitor in such defense and in the settlement of such claim or litigation. Without limiting the generality of the foregoing, if the Indemnitor fails or refuses to assume the defense of any claim, action or cause of action to which its indemnity applies (whether or not suit has formally been brought), it shall be responsible for payment of any settlement of such claim, action or cause of action reached by the Indemnitee, as well as the costs and expenses (including reasonable attorneys' fees) incurred by the Indemnitee in defending such claim, action or cause of action and/or in reaching such settlement. In no case shall any such compromise or limitation implicate rights, obligations or property beyond the subject matter of this Agreement.

11. MISCELLANEOUS

11.1 Financial Disclosure. In conformity with § 508 of the Communications Act of 1934, as amended, concerning broadcasting matters and disclosure required thereunder, Licensor warrants and represents that it has not accepted or agreed to accept, and will not permit its employees, agents, representatives, contractors, or affiliate entities to accept any monies, services, or other consideration for the inclusion of any commercial material or matter in or as part of the Program(s).

11.2 Notices. All notices from one party to the other required by this Agreement will be given in writing and delivered to the respective addresses of Licensor and Licensee

Exhibit 14.2 (continued)

stated above (unless a party has notified the other of a change to its address). All notices will be sent via private courier, facsimile transmission or the United States Mail. All notices will be deemed given when delivered, as documented by courier receipt, facsimile transmission report confirmation or five days after being postmark via regular mail (postage prepaid) by the United States Postal Service.

11.3 Relationship of Parties. Licensor and Licensee are independent contractors with respect to each other, and nothing in this Agreement creates any partnership, joint venture or agency relationship between them.

11.4 Entire Agreement. This Agreement contains the complete understanding of the parties, supersedes all prior agreements whether written or oral pertaining to the subject-matter of this Agreement, and cannot be modified except by a written instrument signed by each party hereto. The descriptive headings of the several sections and paragraphs of this Agreement are inserted for convenience only and d not constitute a part of this Agreement.

11.5 Legal Disputes. This Agreement is to be governed by and construed according to th laws of the State of New York applicable to contracts performed entirely in that stat Each party consents to jurisdiction and venue in New York, New York for resolving any dispute arising under this Agreement. In any legal proceeding brought by one party against the other, the prevailing party will be entitled to recover from the other party its reasonable attorneys' fees and other costs of suit.

11.6 No Assignment. Licensor will not assign any of its rights or obligations hereunder without the prior written consent of Licensee, and any purported assignment withou such prior written consent is void.

11.7 Severability. Any provisions hereof found by a court to be void or unenforceable wi not affect the validity or enforceability of any other provisions.

AGREED   AGREED
LICENSOR   LICENSEE

By _____   By _____

Name _____
Name_____

Title _____
Title_____

Exhibit 14.3
Shared Television Revenue in "Big Four" Professional Sports

League	National Contracts	Local Contracts	Comment
NFL	Yes-All reg.season games	Yes-only pre-season games	90-95% of revenue is shared equally.
NBA	Yes-ABC, ESPN & TNT	Yes-for 70-82 games/year	For some, league contract constitutes more revenue. Some teams make more in local contracts.
NHL	Yes-game of the week	Yes	Most money comes from local contracts.
MLB	Yes-game of the week	Yes-most games	Most money comes from local contracts. Main reason for great revenue disparity in MLB.

teams than the smaller local contracts. However, in Major League Baseball, rights from local television contracts tend to produce more revenue for teams than the national contracts. Therefore, there is a larger disparity in broadcasting revenues between teams in large and small markets.

With the combination of local and national television contracts in the major professional sports, there have been conflicts over who owns the rights to certain games. Due to the large price tag for acquiring national television rights, networks increasingly want exclusivity when they are broadcasting contests. The most recent court decision that deals with this problem involves the Chicago Bulls, the superstation WGN, and the NBA.

The Bulls and WGN sued the NBA, claiming that the agreement between the league and NBC was an impermissible restraint on trade. The Bulls had negotiated a contract with WGN to broadcast twenty-five Bulls games during the 1991 season, yet NBC claimed this was in violation of their exclusive contract with the league, and WGN should not be allowed to broadcast so many games. The district court sided with the Bulls and WGN, and granted an injunction for the 1991 season; ultimately it made a permanent allowance of the number of games that could be televised by WGN, and declared the NBA's fee for broadcasting these games to be excessive.

However, the court of appeals disagreed with this decision and vacated the judgment. In *Chicago Professional Sports Limited Partnership v. NBA*, 95 F.3d 593 (7th Cir. 1996), Circuit Judge Easterbrook held that: (1) the Sports Broadcasting Act's exemption to antitrust laws was inapplicable to the league's contract to broadcast its teams' games; (2) teams need not have complete unity of interest for the league itself to be treated as a single firm for antitrust purposes; and (3) when acting in the broadcast market, the league was closer to a single firm than to a group of independent firms.

This decision is applicable only, however, to conflicts between superstations and network television contracts. NBC thought that twenty-five games being broadcast by WGN on a national scale would be an infringement on the exclusive rights to broadcast nationally granted to them in their contract. The Bulls, as a member of the NBA, had been part of the negotiations with the network, and therefore were held accountable for upholding the details of the deal.

NOTE _____

1. For more information on the broadcast rights of professional sports leagues, see the following:

    a. Franklin M. Fisher, Christopher Maxwell, and Evan Sue Schouten, "The Economics of Sports Leagues: The Bulls Case." 10 *Marquette Sports Law Journal* 1 (1999).

    b. Ivy Ross Rivello, "Sports Broadcasting in an Era of Technology: Superstations, Pay-Per-View and Antitrust Implications," 47 *Drake Law Review* 177 (1998).

    c. Timothy Deckert, "Casenotes: Multiple Characterizations for the Single Entity Argument? The Seventh Circuit Throws an Airball in *Chicago Professional Sports Limited Partnership v. National Basketball Association,*" 5 *Villanova Sports & Entertainment Law Journal* 73 (1998).

    d. Fredrick B. Weber, "*Chicago Professional Sports Limited Partnership v. National Basketball Association:* A Fan-Friendly Decision?" 6 *DePaul Journal of Art & Entertainment Law* 247 (1996).

    e. Alter S. Fogel, "The 'Superstation,' the NBA, and Antitrust: An Analysis of *Chicago Professional Sports Limited Partnership v. National Basketball Association,*" 47 *Rutgers Law Review* 1195 (1995).

14.2.3. Broadcast Rights of the NCAA and Conferences

Beyond contractual matters with broadcasters, a broadcast rights holder in intercollegiate athletics must also be concerned about the property rights to a broadcast of competing clubs and institutions, and within a league or conference arrangement. The NCAA exerts a large amount of power over broadcasting when administering its championships. For instance, with any championship sponsored by the NCAA, the association "owns all rights to each and all of its championships . . . these rights include . . . rights to television (live and delayed), radio broadcasting, filming, and commercial photography" (*2001–02 NCAA Division I Manual,* Bylaw 31.6.4). The NCAA grants rights to telecast its championships on a sliding scale that in part represents the attractiveness and marketability of the event. The NCAA, in awarding media rights, states that "television, radio and film rights shall be awarded in such a manner as to advance most fully the following interests:

(a) gate attendance,

(b) promotion of interest in the sport,

(c) promotion of intercollegiate athletics as a part of collegiate education, and

(d) promotion of the Association and its purposes and fundamental policy." (*2001–02 NCAA Division I Manual,* Bylaw 31.6.4.1)

The governing bodies of the NCAA for each championship make the decisions regarding the broadcast policy for the individual championships. For example, the *2001–02 NCAA Division I Manual* states, "Negotiations with respect to the awarding of any such rights shall be conducted by the president, who shall have authority to determine the specific terms and conditions and to execute contracts for the award of such rights in behalf of the Association. Inquiries concerning all such rights should be directed to the president at the national office" (Bylaw 31.6.4.1.1).

The NCAA also maintains the rights over the use of rebroadcasts of NCAA events:

> The Association reserves all rights to the use of still photographs, films and videotapes of its championships. . . . The filming or videotaping of NCAA championships by parties other than NCAA Productions (i.e., participating institutions or commercial film production companies) for any purpose other than news purposes may be permitted only with the advance written consent of the president. (*2001–02 NCAA Division I Manual*, Bylaw 31.6.4.2)

A conference within the NCAA may also have its own policies for broadcasting. In part, this will reflect how much power the individual conference member institutions have granted the conference to act as an agent for them in seeking broadcast possibilities. An athletic administrator must always be aware of what rights have been granted to a conference and what rights an institution retains. At a minimum, most conferences have the rights to conference championship event broadcasts.

An example of a conference's television policy for NCAA Division I-A football and Division I basketball would be that called for by the Southeastern Conference (SEC) in 2001–2002, a portion of which is reprinted here:

> 30.21 Television
>
> 30.21.1. Basketball. All television shall conform to the current SEC basketball television contracts.
> 30.21.2. Football. Football television and recording are governed by the following: (a) All telecasts of SEC football games are to be conducted in accordance with the current regulations of the Conference and in keeping with provisions of other entities to whom member institutions assign TV rights, except that no member institution may televise a game selected for a national or Conference syndicated package, on an alternative television medium (including pay-per-view) without the approval of the Commissioner.

Southeastern Conference Manual & Commissioner's Regulations, 2001–2002)

A typical conference agreement for delayed football broadcast rights within the conference is that used by the Pac-10 Conference in 2001–2002. It noted the following:

Delayed Football Television Rights

The Conference encourages the use of delayed television of all football games where possible as a means of promoting Pacific-10 football. An institution may telecast any game in which it participates or portion thereof on a delayed basis at the game's conclusion, providing that such delayed telecast does not conflict in time of release with any exclusive telecasting period provided ABC Sports or Fox Sports Net by the Conference. If the game in question is telecast by ABC, the institution cannot air a delayed telecast prior to 10:30 p.m., local time. An institution planning a delayed telecast should review the applicable provisions of each of these contracts and the times of scheduled releases on the date of its delayed release. (*Pacific-10 Conference, 2001–2002 Handbook*)

To ensure that the above policy was followed, the Pac-10 Conference included the following clauses in its conference television policies:

(a) Host Pac-10 Institution

The host institution shall have the following rights of release for a telecast:

(i) A live domestic release without restriction on the area of release, except that written permission is required from the visiting team's director of athletics to release the telecast into the home area of the visiting team; for a traditional rival game where both teams share a home area, the host team will have first right to televise a game in the home area.

(ii) Home area live release,

(iii) Domestic delayed release without restriction on the area, and

(iv) International live and delayed release.

(b) Visiting Pac-10 Institution

The visiting institution shall have the following rights of release for a telecast:

(i) A live domestic release without restriction on the area of release, except that written permission is required from the home team's director of athletics to release the telecast into the home area of the home team.

(ii) Home-area live release, except for a traditional rival game,

(iii) Domestic delayed release without restriction on the area, and

(iv) International live and delayed release, without the approval of the host institution.

(Pacific-10 Conference, 2001–2002 Handbook)

Allied conferences also need a policy for distribution of revenues, including broadcast revenue, among member institutions. In 2001–2002, the Southeastern Conference used the following system for distributing television revenue from football:

31.21 Revenue Distribution—Football

31.21.1 Distribution of Bowl Game Receipts. Distribution of revenue (after allowable deductions) generated from member institutions participating in bowl games shall be as follows: (SEC 6/1/95)

(a) For bowl games providing receipts which result in a balance of less than $2,000,000 (two million), the participating institution shall retain the first $600,000 plus 20% of the balance. The remainder shall be remitted to the Commissioner and will be divided into 12 equal shares with one share to the Conference one share to each of the other 11 institutions. (Participating institution does not share in the distribution shares.)

(b) For bowl games providing receipts which result in a balance between $2,000,000 and $5,999,999, the participating institution shall retain the first $800,000 plus 20% of the balance. The remainder shall be remitted to the Commissioner and will be divided into 12 equal shares, with one share to the Conference and one share to each of the other 11 institutions. (Participating institution does not share in the distribution of shares.) (Revised: 5/29/98 effective 6/1/98)

(c) For bowl games providing receipts which result in a balance $6,000,000 or more, the participating institution shall receive $2,500,000 ($2,600,000 if the SEC team is a participant in the Bowl Champions Series game which determines the National Championship). The remainder shall be divided into 12 equal shares, with one share to the Conference and one share to each of the other 11 institutions. (Participating institution does not share in the distribution of shares.) Should two teams from the SEC be selected to play in the Bowl Championship Series, each participating team shall receive $2,500,000 ($2,600,000 if the SEC team is a participant in the BCS game which determines the National Championship). The remainder shall be divided into 12 equal shares, with one share to the Conference and one share to each of the other 11 institutions. The two participating institutions' share from the respective BCS bowls shall be combined divided evenly between the two participating teams. (Revised 6/5/99)

(d) Institutions which participate in an Alliance Bowl shall receive an additional $150 per mile, one way.

31.21.2 Distribution of Football Television Receipts. Distribution of revenue generated from football television shall be as follows: (SEC 6/1/96)

(a) Network and National Cable Telecast (Effective June 1, 1996)

   (1) A member institution appearing in a non-conference game shall receive an appearance fee of $120,000.

   (2) A member institution appearing in a conference game shall receive an appearance fee of $40,000.

   (3) A member institution appearing in a conference game played on a non-traditional playing date shall receive an appearance fee of $150,000 as the home team and $100,000 as the visiting team.

   (4) All remaining revenue shall be divided into 13 equal shares with one share being distributed to each member institution and one share being distributed to the Conference.

(b) Conference Syndicated Program. Revenue from a conference football program shall be divided into 13 equal shares with one share to each member institution and one share to the conference office after home appearance fees and cross-over fees have been paid. (SEC 6/3/93)

   (1) Home appearance fees shall be paid as follows:
   First Home Appearance—No fee to host institution.
   Second Home Appearance—$20,000 to host institution.
   Three or more Home Appearances—$40,000 to host institution for each appearance after second home appearance.

   (2) Any cross-over fees shall be set by the SEC Executive Committee.

31.21.3 Football Championship Game Revenue. All revenue remaining from the championship game after expenses of planning and conducting the event have been deducted shall be divided as follows: (SEC 6/3/93)

(a) Each participating institution shall be reimbursed for the actual cost of transporting an official party of 150 (including student-athletes, coaches, administrators, cheerleaders, etc.) to the site (air or bus travel from campus to the site; local transportation is not included). (SEC 6/1/96) This amount shall be approved in advance by the conference office and must be supported by actual invoices. In addition, each participating institution shall receive $150,000 to cover all costs associated with institutional lodging, meals and local transportation. (SEC 6/1/96) Each participating institution will be financially responsible for payment for 150 rooms for two nights at the designated team headquarters hotel. (SEC 6/1/95)

(b) Each participating institution shall receive a band travel allowance of $40 per mile, one-way from its campus to the site (according to Rand-McNally Mileage Chart). (SEC 6/1/96) Each institution shall be financially responsible for 100 rooms for two nights at its designated band hotel. (SEC 6/1/95)

(c) All remaining revenue shall be divided into 13 equal shares, with one share distributed to each member institution and one share to the Conference office;

(d) Institutions may petition to the Executive Committee prior to the game for an increase in the travel allowance only in the event actual expenses exceed the designated amount.

In representing the members of an athletic conference, the conference administration must grant many of the same rights to a broadcast company that an individual institution would usually grant The Pac-10 Conference has a section with information on men's basketball television contracts in its 2001–2002 handbook.

3. Men's Basketball Television Policies.

The Pac-10's men's basketball television program(s) is defined in the contract(s) executed with the Conference's television partner(s) and may be found in that document(s). (6/99)

   a. Live Basketball Television Rights.

   (1) Institutional Telecast.

   When not selected for presentation on a Conference television program, each Conference basketball game, or non-Conference game hosted by a Conference member, will be available for live telecasting by the host institution and visiting Conference institution, as set forth in (2) below, provided such release would be permissible under terms of applicable Conference media contracts and policies, as such policies are set forth herein, and as otherwise provided below. (1/89, 6/95, 6/99)

   (2) Rights of Release.

   If the game is not televised as part of a Conference television program, the following are the bases on which the respective participating institutions may release a telecast of a game on a free, pay, or pay-per-view basis. (6/95, 6/99)

(a) Host Pac-10 Institution.

The host institution shall have the following rights of release for a telecast: (6/99)

   (i) A live domestic release without restriction on the area of release, except that written permission is required from the visiting team's director of athletics to release the telecast into the home area of the visiting team; for a traditional rival game where both teams share a home area, the host team will have first right to televise the game in the home area, (6/95, 5/97)

   (ii) Home-area live release, (6/95)

   (iii) Domestic delayed release without restriction on the area, (6/95) and

   (iv) International live and delayed release. (1/89, 6/95)

(b) Visiting Pac-10 Institution.

The visiting institution shall have the following rights of release for a telecast: (6/95, 6/99)

   (i) A live domestic release without restriction on the area of release, except that written permission is required from the home team's director of athletics to release the telecast into the home area of the home team, (6/95)

   (ii) Home-area live release, except for a traditional rival game, (6/95, 5/97)

   (iii) Domestic delayed release without restriction on the area, (6/95) and

   (iv) International live and delayed release, without the approval of the host institution. (1/89, 4/90, 6/91, 6/95)

(c) Visiting Non-Conference Institution.

The visiting non-Conference institution shall have rights to telecast a Pac-10 home game as provided in its game contract. It must observe the exclusive time periods and other terms provided the television companies in the applicable Conference media contracts. (6/95) (*Pacific-10 Conference 2001–2002 Handbook*)

14.2.4. Broadcast Rights for the Olympics

Broadcast rights for the Olympic Games are similar to those for the NCAA and professional leagues. They bargain for the licensing fee for their television broadcast rights for all of their events. In the end, they sell those rights to broadcast the games to one television network. Broadcast rights for the Olympic Games have become one of the most lucrative sources for revenue of any sporting event in the world. Prices for these rights have escalated over the past two decades, as NBC Sports paid $2.3 billion for the rights to the 2004 Summer Games, 2006 Winter Games, and 2008 Summer Games.

One area of broadcasting that has increasingly affected the broadcast rights and revenues of the Olympic Games is the attempts of broadcasters to illegally broadcast the Games over the Internet. With expanding technology, this practice has become much easier to accomplish without spending exorbitant amounts of money. The International Olympic Committee (IOC) has taken a proactive approach to apprehending these renegade broadcasters. The IOC can intercept illegal satellite transmissions, and trace the signals to the illegal broadcaster. Although it is difficult to discover all violators, the IOC is attempting to maintain its relationship with the networks, which have invested millions of dollars for exclusive rights.

NOTE _____

1. For more information on Olympic Games and broadcasting, see the following:

a. The IOC Web site at www.olympic.org. Within the section "Olympic Marketing," under the IOC Facts and Figures, the IOC provides a description of Olympic broadcast revenues and coverage.

b. Michiyo Nakamoto, "Skates on for Viewing Bonanza," *Financial Times* (London) February 5, 1998, p. 3.

14.2.5. Broadcast Rights of a Professional Team and Colleges

As mentioned earlier, professional sports teams, depending on their league affiliation, generally have the ability to negotiate contracts with local broadcast stations on top of the leaguewide contract, providing that the contract does not violate the leaguewide agreement. With the exception of the National Football League, all teams in the Big Four leagues are able to negotiate local television contracts for regular season games. Most colleges and universities relinquish their right to negotiate individual game broadcast contracts to their league or conference.

With the decision in *NCAA v. Board of Regents*, the trend in intercollegiate sports broadcasting took a major turn (see section 14.2.5.1., "Antitrust Issues in Broadcasting for Colleges," for an in-depth discussion). The current prevalent practice for colleges and universities is to have the conference office negotiate broadcasting contracts on behalf of all conference members. One notable exception to this rule is the negotiation of television contracts by schools with no conference affiliation, such as the University of Notre Dame in football, which negotiated a separate contract with NBC to broadcast its football games. Radio broadcasts are generally left up to the discretion of the participating universities.

In a non-conference game, an institution must also protect its broadcast rights. A typical contract clause would be similar to the one the University of Kentucky used: "Broadcasting rights to UK games are assigned exclusively to Host Creative Communications, Inc., of Lexington. One reciprocal rights fee waiver is guaranteed opponent schools visiting Lexington."

14.2.5.1. Antitrust Issues in Broadcasting for Colleges

As mentioned in the introduction to this chapter, antitrust law can have a major impact upon the broadcasting of sports events. Although basic antitrust law principles are discussed in Chapter 10, this section discusses the basic application of antitrust law to sports broadcasting where there is not an antitrust exemption. For holders of broadcast rights, on all levels of sport, that means being careful not to try to control the overall flow of their sports broadcasts, in a concerted action, such that a monopoly or other antitrust violations develop. It is always important to remember that the antitrust laws were designed to encourage the easy flow of any business activity into the general stream of commerce. In drafting such laws, legislators reasoned that it was important to have open and free market competition.

The best illustration of how antitrust law can affect athletics broadcasting is the case of *NCAA v. Board of Regents of University of Oklahoma*, 468 U.S. 85 (1984). (For more see Chapter 10, section 10.5.2., "The NCAA's Reduced Power over Television: *Board of Regents*"). On June 27, 1984, the Supreme Court of the United States, in a 7–2 decision, struck down the NCAA's 1982–1985 football television plan because it violated federal antitrust law. This section will detail the specifics of the case, and also its effect upon intercollegiate sports.

The ruling in this case immediately impacted networks, producers, syndicators, advertisers, and NCAA member institutions, all of which had to scramble to implement broadcast schedules for the 1984 season. This decision and its ramifications continue to be major factors in the broadcast industry for intercollegiate athletics.

At the time that the lawsuit was brought, an important group in the area of television and intercollegiate athletics was the College Football Association of America (see note 2). Beginning in 1979, the CFA started to believe that its voice in the formulation of football television policy was diluted in the 800-plus institutions of the NCAA membership, and did not reflect its own members' importance in obtaining a national television contract.

The CFA negotiated a contract of its own with the National Broadcasting Company (NBC) for the 1982 and 1983 football seasons. The NBC contract was more attractive to CFA members in terms of rights, fees, and appearances than the 1982–1985 agreements that the NCAA had with ABC and CBS. While CFA member institutions were considering whether to accept the NBC pact, the NCAA indicated that doing so would be in violation of NCAA rules and that disciplinary sanctions would result. This caused many CFA members that originally had approved the CFA-NBC contract to vote against accepting it. As a result of the CFA's failure to contract with NBC and continued dissatisfaction with the NCAA's television policy, the University of Georgia Athletic Association and the University of Oklahoma brought suit in November 1981. They challenged the NCAA's exclusive control over televised football games and contended that the NCAA was violating the Sherman Antitrust Act by its exclusive television contracts with two major networks—ABC and CBS (see note 3 for a brief history of NCAA football policies).

The NCAA argued that the television package was beneficial to its membership as a whole and accomplished two important purposes. First, it protected the live gate of college and high school football games, which resulted in a higher attendance at games. In support of this argument, the NCAA pointed to an increase in total attendance for NCAA football games in all but one year during the period 1953–1983.

Second, the NCAA contended that its plan had the positive effect of spreading television revenues and exposure to a greater number of member institutions. The NCAA also contended that limitations on the number of television appearances a member institution could make allowed a greater number of institutions to appear on television, which resulted in the schools' receiving substantially higher rights fees. In addition to these revenues, these institutions received invaluable television exposure and extensive media attention. As a result, the recruitment efforts of these institutions were enhanced.

The NCAA maintained that uncontrolled televising of football games would result in the creation of a football *super* power group, since a limited number of institutions would be attractive to television broadcasters. With increased revenues and media attention to the super power group, the NCAA predicted that the disparity among the member institutions would be increased. This would be contrary to the policies and purposes of the NCAA, since it would place irresistible temptations for the development of winning teams, thereby threatening the future of the sport.

Judge Burciaga, a federal district court judge, ruled in favor of the University of Oklahoma and the Georgia Athletic Association on September 15, 1982, reasoning that the television contracts between the NCAA and ABC, CBS, and Turner Broadcast System were in violation of the Sherman Antitrust Act, and therefore void. The court held that "[t]he right to telecast college football games is the property of the institutions participating in the games, and that right may be sold or assigned by those institutions to any entity at their discretion." Judge Burciaga found that the NCAA's television football controls constituted price-fixing, output restriction, a group boycott, and an exercise of monopoly power over the market of college football television. The court found that the membership of the NCAA agreed to limit production to a level far below what which occur in a free market situation. In addition, Judge Burciaga was not persuaded that the televising of college football games would have any negative impact on game attendance at non-televised games.

Judge Burciaga disagreed with the NCAA that the television controls helped maintain competitive balance among the football programs of various schools. In his reasoning, he compared the telecasting policies of NCAA football to those of NCAA basketball. The NCAA did not control the televising of regular season basketball games. The arrangements were left to the individual member institutions and conferences that contracted with various national and local television and cable companies. Judge Burciaga rejected the NCAA's contention that televising football was distinguishable from televising basketball; in fact, he held "the market in television basketball to be persuasive evidence of how a free market in television football would operate." Judge Burciaga's decision rendered illegal the NCAA's television contracts with ABC and CBS for $131.75 million each and with Turner Broadcasting System for $18 million. His decision voided a total of $281.5 million in television contracts.

The NCAA appealed the decision to the Court of Appeals for the Tenth Circuit, arguing that Judge Burciaga incorrectly concluded that there was price-fixing in the awarding of television contracts, since there was vigorous competition among the networks in bidding for the television contracts. The NCAA further argued that the court erred in its conclusion that the NCAA was not a voluntary association. In May 1983, the court of appeals upheld the district court's ruling.

As noted previously, in *NCAA v. Board of Regents*, the U.S. Supreme Court upheld the decisions of the district court and court of appeals. The Supreme Court summarized its decision by noting:

> The NCAA plays a critical role in the maintenance of a revered tradition of amateurism in college sports. There can be no question but that it needs ample latitude to play that role, or that the preservation of the student-athlete in higher education adds richness and diversity to intercollegiate athletics and is entirely consistent with the goals of the Sherman Act. But consistent with the Sherman Act, the role of the NCAA must be to *preserve* a tradition that might otherwise die; rules that restrict output are hardly consistent with this role. Today we hold only that the record supports the District Court's conclusion that by curtailing output and blunting the ability of member institutions to respond to consumer preference, the NCAA has restricted rather than enhanced the place of intercollegiate athletics in the Nation's life.

In wake of the Court's ruling in this case, a number of lawsuits related to the decision were filed. Unsatisfied with the CFA agreement, which forbade national appearances by member association teams on networks other than ABC or the Entertainment and Sports Programming Network (ESPN), the University of Southern California (USC), the University of California at Los Angeles (UCLA), along with the Pacific-10 Conference and the Big-Ten Conference, brought suit against the ABC-CFA agreement that prevented two games—UCLA against Nebraska and USC against Notre Dame—from being telecast (see *Regents of University of California v. ABC*, 747 F.2d 511 [9th Cir. 1984]). The suit sought preliminary and permanent injunctions against the defendants because the ABC-CFA exclusive agreement, it was charged, prevented *crossover* games, which are games between CFA member schools and non-CFA member schools. In granting the injunction for UCLA and USC, a federal district court sitting in Los Angeles noted that if the exclusion was allowed to stand, the schools would be harmed by loss of revenue. "By issuance of this order, ABC and ESPN are not measurably harmed, other than by some perceived diminution of their ability quickly to dispatch CBS from the market for nationwide football telecasts." Soon afterward, the parties to the suit settled their differences and dropped any further litigation. In general, such questions of property rights to broadcast ownership are now determined in the game contracts, as was discussed in section 14.2.1., "Rights Granted."

Soon after the decision, the Association of Independent Television Stations (INTV) filed two suits in federal district court aimed at opening the college telecast market further to local broadcast stations (see *Association of Independent Television Stations, Inc. v. College Football Ass'n*, 637 F.Supp. 1289 (1986)). INTV was a coalition of stations not affiliated with the major networks (ABC, CBS, and NBC). The suits sought on antitrust grounds to open *protected* time frames that the major networks have arranged with the different football governing bodies, such as the CFA. INTV's first suit was filed in Los Angeles against CBS and the Big-Ten and Pacific-10 Conferences. The second suit was filed in Oklahoma City against ABC, ESPN, the CFA, and the Big Eight Conference.

In March 1986, Judge Burciaga rejected the arguments of INTV and ruled that the CFA's plan granting some networks exclusively in two time periods was allowable under the antitrust laws. Judge Burciaga noted, "The CFA is a powerful entity. . . . Nonetheless, it remains to be demonstrated beyond a reasonable factual dispute that the CFA can both control price and restrict entry to the college football television market. The market is a different one than the court analyzed in 1982. Unlike the NCAA, the CFA . . . have their rivals."

Next, the U.S. government, through the Federal Trade Commission (FTC), scrutinized the CFA television contracts. The FTC has jurisdiction over enforcement of antitrust laws. In September 1990 the FTC filed an administrative complaint against the CFA and Capital Cities-ABC, claiming that their national television contracts were anti-competitive. The complaint alleged that consumers had been deprived of the selection of college football games because of the limitation on teams and games selected to be televised by the CFA-Capital Cities contract. The CFA withstood this challenge when Judge James P. Timony, an administrative law judge, ruled that the FTC has no jurisdiction over the television agreement because colleges and universities are not considered profit-making institutions over which the agency has legal responsibility. The FTC had argued that major college football programs are operated for commercial rather than educational objectives, and therefore are subject to antitrust laws despite the CFA's non-profit status. Judge Timony ruled, though, that the proceeds from the CFA's television rights to college football games go to the schools and have a non-profit educational purpose.

The CFA withstood this FTC challenge to its television contract but received a setback when the University of Notre Dame seceded from the CFA television contract with ABC and in January 1990 entered into its own agreement with NBC for $38 million. The original CFA contract was for $210 million, but had to be scaled down by about $25 million when Notre Dame defected and entered into its own agreement. Notre Dame's athletic director, Dick Rosenthal, said the NBC contract was a result of Notre Dame's non-approval of the ABC contract, which called for regional coverage. Rosenthal believed this would have demoralized the Fighting Irish, hurting their broad appeal. With the NBC contract, Notre Dame's home games are televised nationally. This contract was also more financially lucrative for the Fighting Irish, bringing in $1.2 million per game, which was divided equally between Notre Dame and its opponent. Under the CFA-ABC agreement, Notre Dame was paid $1.53 million during the 1988–1989 season. The CFA had no legal recourse against the University of Notre Dame because of the precedent of free and open competition in the television marketplace that the courts have found since the *NCAA v. Board of Regents* decision.

In comparison to collegiate football television contracts, in which the NCAA is no longer a party, collegiate basketball is another story. The NCAA has an eleven-year contract with CBS to broadcast the NCAA basketball championships. This contract will bring the NCAA up to $764 million by the year 2012–2013, which will account for nearly 90% of NCAA revenue (see Chapter 1, section 1.3.2.1., "Revenues"). This contract has not been subject to litigation by the schools or conferences because the NCAA owns the rights to their championship events, but does not control the rights to regular season games and conference playoffs.

The effects of *NCAA v. Board of Regents of University of Oklahoma* are still being felt in intercollegiate football. Now that all universities are able to negotiate contracts on their own, or with their conferences, the differences in revenues between small Division I universities and large Division I universities has increased. Notre Dame broke from the CFA to sign a contract with NBC for five years and $40 million. Realizing the power that colleges can have in negotiations, conferences began to realign to bring in traditionally strong football programs. Penn State joined the Big Ten and Florida State joined the Atlantic Coast Conference in order to strengthen the bargaining power of the conferences. With the power of these big-name universities behind them, conferences were able to negotiate lucrative conferencewide contracts. For example, in 2001 the SEC signed a six-year contract with CBS starting in 2002. It is important to remember, however, while many universities have profited from the greater number of games on national television, many other colleges in smaller conferences have lost revenue, and don't have the ability to obtain contracts that provide great amounts of revenue for the institution.

NOTES

1. The reactions to the decision in the *Oklahoma Board of Regents* case were predictably and decidedly mixed: "It's the worst possible thing that could have happened," said former University of Michigan athletic director Don Canham. Pennsylvania State University athletic director Jim Tarman reacted to the decision with concern, stating: "The worst scenario is that everyone is on their own. We don't feel that scenario is in Penn State's best interest or in the best interest of college football." Other parties were delighted by the Supreme Court's decision: "The position of the universities has been vindicated. The property right theory has been upheld," said Chuck Neinas, executive director of the College Football Association (CFA).

2. The CFA was composed of sixty-three NCAA Division I-A member institutions and included five of the major football-playing conferences—the Big 12, Southeast, Southwest, Atlantic Coast, and Western Athletic Conference—and major independents such as Notre Dame. The only major football-playing schools that were not CFA members were the Pacific-10 and Big Ten Conferences. The CFA was formed to promote the interests of Division I-A member schools within the National Collegiate Athletic Association structure.

3. The NCAA, since it was given authority by a vote of its membership at its annual convention in January 1952, had administered the live telecasting of games for its member institutions. The details of the television plan varied through the years. The plans, however, consistently limited the number of live television appearances an NCAA member institution could make in a year; prevented individual member institutions from contracting on an individual basis with national, local, and cable television companies; fixed revenue amounts for rights fees allocated by the NCAA to member institutions whose teams appeared as part of the network television contract; and allocated a percentage of the total television contract for the NCAA's operating budget.

14.2.6. Broadcast Rights of an Individual Player

In some instances, players who participate in an event have argued that they have a right to share in the rights fees for the broadcast. In *Baltimore Orioles, Inc. v. Major League Baseball Players Ass'n*, 805 F.2d 663 (7th Cir. 1986), players for the Baltimore Orioles argued that they owned a copyright to the telecasts of their games because they were the ones who were playing the game on the field. However, this argument did not succeed because the court found that the clubs, as employers of the players, owned a copyright to the telecasts of baseball games under the "work made for hire" doctrine, and this preempted any publicity right the players had under state law. Basically, this means that because the team, which owns the copyright to the broadcast, employs the players, they are not entitled to share in any of the broadcast fees.

NOTE

1. Initially, the district court in *Baltimore Orioles, Inc. v. Major League Baseball Players Ass'n*, Nos. 82 C 3710, 82 C 6377, 1985 U.S. Dist. LEXIS 15518 (N.D. Ill. Sept. 27, 1985) granted the Club summary judgment on the counts of the their copyright and "master-servant" claims. Under principles of master-servant law, the employer (Orioles) own all rights in and to Major League Baseball games created at their expense, and pursuant to their direction, supervision and control, including the right to telecast these games.

14.3. RESTRICTIONS IN SPORTS BROADCASTING

In many cases, sports organizations, on both the professional and the inter-collegiate level, will restrict certain parts of a sports broadcast. The following two sections will focus upon the restriction of advertising in broadcasts on the inter-collegiate level, and the restriction on the use of replays on the professional level. Each area of analysis has been marked by a singular, leading case.

14.3.1. Restrictions on the Use of Advertising

In addition to restricting the types of advertisements that can be shown on television during intercollegiate athletic contests (including no alcohol or tobacco ads), the NCAA restricts the amount of advertising that is allowed on player uniforms. In the case of *Adidas, Inc. v. NCAA*, 40 F.Supp.2d. 1275 (D. Kan. 1999), sporting goods manufacturer, Adidas, brought action against the NCAA alleging that the association's bylaw governing use of commercial logos on student-athlete's uniforms was a restraint of free trade (see note 1), and a violation of the Sherman Act. Adidas was unsuccessful in its claim, the court deciding that the purpose of the bylaw (*2001–02 NCAA Division I Manual*, Bylaw 12.5.4) was to preserve the integrity of college athletics and to avoid the commercial exploi-tation of student-athletes. Furthermore, the bylaw is designed to avoid excessive advertising that could potentially interfere with the basic function of the student-athletes' uniforms, which is to provide immediate identification of the athlete's number and team to his or her teammates and to the referee or umpire officiating the contest. There is no commercial purpose behind the creation and enforce-ment of Bylaw 12.5.5. Neither the NCAA nor its member institutions realize an economic or competitive advantage through the enforcement of Bylaw 12.5.5 against Adidas or other apparel manufacturers.

NOTE

1. The applicable NCAA bylaw, currently Bylaw 12.5.4(b), states the following: "The student athlete's institution's official uniform (including numbered racing bibs and warm-ups) and all other items of apparel (e.g., socks, headbands, T-shirts, wristbands, visors or

hats, swim caps, and towels) shall bear only a single manufacturer's or distributor's normal label or trademark (regardless of the visibility of the label or trademark), not to exceed 2¼ square inches in area (i.e., rectangle, square, parallelogram) including any additional material (e.g., patch) surrounding the normal trademark or logo. The student-athlete's institution's official uniform and all other items of apparel shall not bear a design element similar to the manufacturer's trademark/logo or that is in addition to another trademark/logo that is contrary to the size restriction" (*2001–02 NCAA Division I Manual*, Bylaw 12.5.4).

14.3.2. Restrictions on the Use of Replays

Cable television networks such as ESPN and FOX Sports devote much of their programming lineup to shows that provide highlights of the top games in sports. However, these networks do not own a copyright to the games that are being broadcast. The question, then, is how these networks can broadcast highlights without infringing upon copyrights.

In 1981, when ESPN was in its infancy, the Boston Red Sox, Boston Bruins, and WSBK-TV (a local Boston station) brought legal action against ESPN for showing game highlights without their permission. In *New Boston Television v. Entertainment Sports Programming Network, Inc.*, No. 81-1010-Z, 1981 U.S. Dist. LEXIS 15032 (D. Mass. Aug. 3, 1981), the court held that the copyright owner of the telecast has the right to charge a fee and place appropriate restrictions on the showing of highlights. However, the two sides in this case reached an agreement over the use of highlights, because it was advantageous for both. A club may welcome the promotional exposure that results from the showing of highlights in its home territory and may have little interest in deterring this practice by charging a fee.

14.4. OTHER IMPORTANT ISSUES IN BROADCASTING

Several other topics that deal with sports broadcasting will now be covered briefly. An athletic administrator should be aware of each of these issues, which include: (1) Internet rights for sports broadcasts; (2) siphoning of sport events from network television to pay television; (3) home taping of copyrighted events; (4) domestic and international piracy of satellite transmissions; (5) blackouts of scheduled programs; (6) handheld pagers; and (7) satellite distribution of sports games.

14.4.1. Internet Rights for Sports Broadcasts

The topic of who owns Internet rights for sports broadcasts is an area of litigation that so far has not been fully explored. The Internet is rapidly changing the way television and sports are marketed and utilized. First, the Internet is used by the sports entities (NFL, NBA, MLB, NHL, Olympics, and NCAA) to help promote their product by establishing Web sites to provide information and recent news related to the respective leagues and sports. In addition there are individual sites that are utilized by or are about some of the individual players. This is a great marketing tool that the sports leagues do not have to pay for, yet reaches millions of people. In addition to individual sites, the Internet is now used as a means to broadcast certain events. ABC and the NFL recently introduced a concept whereby one can watch certain professional football games on the Internet, if one has the proper equipment and software. Thus, one may be able to see a game that one normally would not, or a game one would have to pay for. However, the device still needs improvement in quality because there are different speed modems and other external circumstances that prevent the event from being seen at normal, "real time" speed.

NOTES ————————————————————————————

1. For more information on the Internet and broadcasting, see *Twentieth Century Fox Film, Corp. v. ICRAVETV*, Nos. 00-121, 00-120, 2000 U.S. Dist. LEXIS 1013 (W.D. Pa. Jan. 28, 2000). Although not a sports broadcasting case, this case is important because it deals with the ability of Web sites to provide real-time rebroadcasts of copyrighted events. The defendant provided users of his site the opportunity to watch television directly on their personal computers from his site.

2. For more information on Internet broadcasting, see Michael A. Geist, "ICRAVETV and the New Rules of Internet Broadcasting," 23 *University of Arkansas-Little Rock Law Review* 223 (2000).

14.4.2. Siphoning of Sports Events

Siphoning is the shifting of programs from standard broadcast television to pay cable or subscription television. With the expansion of pay television options offered on cable systems in the United States, this has become a more heated topic. Originally, the FCC (Federal Communications Commission) passed regulations that prohibited pay television from televising "specific" events that had been on standard broadcast television in the past five years. However, these regulations were struck down by the U.S. Court of Appeals for the District of Columbia in *Home Box Office, Inc. v. FCC*, 567 F.2d 9 (D.C. Cir.), *cert. denied*, 434 U.S. 829 (1977) (see note 1). The court ruled that the FCC was violating the First Amendment by making it too hard for pay cable networks to obtain and air sports programming. This court decision allows professional sports teams to put together pay cable packages for their games, which would not have been possible under the FCC rules.

NOTE ————————————————————————————

1. In *Home Box Office v. FCC*, 567 F.2d 9 (1977), Home Box Office (HBO) was bringing action against the FCC for anti-siphoning rules it had passed in reaction to the growing presence of HBO in the motion picture and sports industry. The regulations that FCC passed were as follows:

Acting under its rulemaking authority, the commission in 1975 issued rules that prohibited pay exhibition of (1) feature films more than three, but less than ten, years old; (2) specific sports events (e.g., the World Series) shown on broadcast television within the previous five years; (3) more than the minimum number of non-specific (i.e., regular season) sports events that had not been broadcast in any of the five preceding years, and in some cases only half that number; and (4) all series programs (i.e., programs with interconnected plot or substantially the same cast of principal characters). In addition, the Commission prohibited commercial advertising in conjunction with pay exhibition [**2] of programming and limited the overall number of hours of pay operation that could be devoted to sports and feature films to 90% of total pay operations.

The court ruled that the FCC had exceeded its jurisdiction in implementing such restrictions upon cable television, and that the rules had also infringed upon the plaintiff's

First Amendment rights. This decision was a very important one because it allowed sports television to be available on pay-cable television stations such as HBO, which have made large amounts of revenue on sporting events, including boxing matches.

14.4.3. Home Taping of Copyrighted Events

As sports events are being broadcast over the airwaves, viewers are able to tape them from their television sets. Although there has not been a case that deals specifically with sports games being taped from television, a landmark case was decided by the Supreme Court concerning copyright infringement by people who use their VCRs to tape copyrighted programs. In *Sony Corporation of America v. Universal City Studios, Inc.,* 104 U.S. 774 (1984), *rehearing denied,* 104 S.Ct. 1619 (1984), the Supreme Court overturned the Ninth Circuit's decision and held that home taping does not constitute copyright infringement. For sports teams this means that they will probably not be able to gain any royalty fees for the taping of their games from television (see note 1).

NOTE _____

1. In *Sony Corp. of America v. Universal City Studios, Inc.,* 464 U.S. 417 (1984), the Supreme Court reversed the ruling of the Ninth Circuit court, and ruled in a 5–4 split decision that home taping of television broadcasts does not constitute copyright infringement. The Ninth Circuit also held that the manufacturers of the video recorders were responsible for these copyright violations. On overturning the decision of the appellate court, the Supreme Court stated, "The sale of home videotape recorders to the general public did not constitute contributory infringement of copyrights on television programs."

14.4.4. Domestic and International Piracy of Satellite Transmissions

Domestic piracy is an increasingly important area of concern for athletic administrators. With the expansion of the availability of satellite technology, anyone with an "earth station" (see definitions in the introduction to this chapter) is able to intercept, or "pirate," sports broadcasts. Some of the most common offenders are bars trying to attract a clientele who otherwise might not be able to view the game. Section 705 of the Communications Act of 1934 prohibits the "unauthorized interception and retransmission of any radio communications that are not broadcast for the use of the general public." For example, the NFL and its clubs have sued bars/restaurants/hotels for broadcasting home games, via satellite, that are locally blacked out for certain reasons. The courts have consistently found that these establishments are violating copyright infringement law. In *NFL v. The Alley, Inc.,* 624 F.Supp. 6 (S.D. Fla. 1983), the court found that the local games could not be broadcast in this establishment because it used apparatus that is not commonly used in private homes. Even though the law is very clear on this issue, it is hard to enforce due to the large number of such establishments. Therefore, the act authorizes substantial monetary damages and criminal penalties to help deter violations from occurring.

The laws which govern international satellite piracy are much more lenient than the laws that regulate the United States. In fact, in some situations, some foreign governments have been known to sanction satellite piracy. Sports teams do not have very many alternatives in these situations, because the circumstances are out of their jurisdiction.

NOTE _____

1. In *NFL v. McBee*, 792 F.2d 726 (8th Cir. 1986), a bar owned by the defendant would intercept live broadcasts of blacked-out football games with a satellite dish, and then provide the game on the television at the bar, while fans would not be able to watch the game at home. The bar, however, did not qualify under any compulsory licenses and was found in violation of copyright infringement by broadcasting the game without the consent of the National Football League. Other similar cases have been decided in favor of the sports organization, unless the defendant can prove that it qualifies under a compulsory license to broadcast the game.

14.4.5. Blackouts of Scheduled Programming

Since the major expansion of television sports broadcasting in the 1950s, blackouts have become common in professional sports. Owners of sports organizations, concerned about protecting their home attendance, have ordered that within a certain radius of the home stadium, games be blacked out to encourage people to watch the game at the stadium instead of staying at home and watching the game on television.

The increase in popularity of football, however, led to the passing of anti-blackout legislation by the FCC in 1973. Even though waiting lists for tickets had reached as long as five years, NFL teams still insisted on maintaining blackouts in their home areas, arguing that there was no right to see sporting events for free on television. Perturbed by these actions, the FCC passed legislation which held that pro teams in the Big Four leagues must lift any blackouts of games if the contest has been sold out seventy-two hours prior to the start of the game. This legislation effectively got rid of many of the blackouts in the National Football League, and allowed more fans to watch the league's games.

NOTES _____

1. In *Blaich v. NFL*, 212 F.Supp. 319 (S.D.N.Y. 1962), fans of the New York Giants football team brought action against the NFL's policy of blacking out home playoff games within a seventy-five mile radius of the stadium. The plaintiffs contended that the NFL bylaw concerning blackouts involved only regular season games, and not playoff contests. The NFL bylaw used the generic term "games." The plaintiffs were seeking a preliminary injunction so that they would be able to watch the NFL championship game, which was to air later that week, in their homes. Although the court noted that the policy may not be a good one for public relations, the NFL's rule concerning blackouts of playoff games was, and the bylaw that used the generic term "game" applied to all games, including playoff contests.

2. In *United States v. NFL*, 116 F.Supp. 319 (E.D.Pa. 1953), the U.S. Dept. of Justice brought a case attempting to curtail the television "blackout" policies of the NFL, using antitrust theory. The bylaw for the NFL stated, "No club shall cause or permit a game in which it is engaged to be telecast or broadcast by a station within 75 miles of another League City on the day that the home club of the other city is either playing a game in its home city or is playing away from home and broadcasting or televising its game by use of a station within 75 miles of its home city, unless permission for such broadcast or telecast is obtained from the home club." Such permission was not generally granted by the home club, rendering the game "blacked out" in certain areas.

The court ruled that some of the blackout rules were legal, while others were not. The rules concerning blackouts of home games to protect the gate attendance were seen as reasonable, and were permitted. However, the rule concerning the blackout of all games was considered to be an unreasonable restraint of trade, and the league was ordered to repeal this regulation.

14.4.6. Handheld Pagers

In *NBA v. Motorola, Inc.*, 105 F.3d 841 (2d. Cir. 1997), the NBA brought an action against Motorola, which was manufacturing pagers that provided real-time scoring of NBA basketball games. They argued that Motorola was infringing on their copyright, among other allegations. The circuit judge, on appeal from a lower court, ruled for Motorola, holding that real-time updates of NBA scores were not an infringement upon the copyrights owned by the NBA. This decision has had an enormous effect upon the broadcasting of sports on the Internet. With this case as precedent, Internet sports sites are able to provide real-time sports scores for their visitors without fear of infringing upon copyrights.

14.4.7. Satellite Distribution

With the emergence of new methods of satellite distribution of television signals, holders of initial broadcast rights have had a difficult time maintaining exclusive control over the dissemination of their broadcasts. Specifically, the emergence of DirecTV, a satellite provider of nationwide sports and entertainment programming, has caused issues to arise among owners of broadcast rights. DirecTV, a digital satellite service, is a subscription service that can provide its viewers with the opportunity to receive up to 225 channels of movies, sports, and entertainment. Subscribers must purchase a small satellite that receives the signal from DirecTV's satellite. Viewers are able to purchase packages based on their preferences: sports, movies, or entertainment. For example, in 2001, viewers were able to subscribe to NFL Sunday Ticket™, a service that provides the subscriber with up to thirteen NFL games per weekend for $169. These packages are especially attractive for fans of NFL teams that do not live near their favorite team. Due to the NFL's television package, viewers will see their local team's games on television every week. However, with this technology, fans are able to choose which games they want to watch. While it seems like a blessing for the avid fan, this subscription service has met with some opposition from rights holders. Because of this method of distribution, its impact upon the television market has taken full effect, and cases involving DirecTV have been limited. However, one case, decided by the FCC, could prove to be a foreshadowing of litigation in the future.

In the Matter of DirecTV, Inc. v. Comcast Corporation, CSR 5112-P (1997), Federal Communications Commission, DirecTV claimed that Comcast, an owner of broadcast rights to professional sports teams in the Philadelphia area, was illegally disallowing it from transmitting their signals under Section 628(b) of the Cable Television Consumer Protection and Competition Act of 1992, which states:

> [I]t shall be unlawful for a cable operator, a satellite cable programming vendor in which a cable operator has an attributable interest, or a satellite broadcast pro-

gramming vendor to engage in unfair methods of competition or unfair or deceptive acts or practices, the purpose or effect of which is to hinder significantly or to prevent any multichannel video programming distributor from providing satellite cable programming or satellite broadcast programming to subscribers or consumers.

Comcast had bought the rights from the defunct Sports Channel, which had previously negotiated with DirecTV. Comcast created its own unique sports channel, SportsNet, and refused to negotiate with DirecTV for the rights to broadcast its games on DirecTV's system due to what Comcast said were "legitimate business purposes." Comcast delivers its programming only through terrestrial (land-based) distribution, and not satellite distribution, which Sports Channel had employed. Therefore, Comcast argued, it was not susceptible to laws regarding satellite transmissions, and was not obligated to enter into an agreement with DirecTV. The FCC arbitrator decided that Comcast was *not* obligated to negotiate with DirecTV for two reasons. First, its programming was not satellite programming, and therefore not subject to Section 628(b) of the Cable Television Consumer Protection and Competition Act of 1992. Second, it did not find that Comcast had engaged in unfair methods of competition or clearly evaded the rules of the FCC in order to block DirecTV from broadcasting its programming. Due to this decision, fans of the Flyers, Sixers, and Phillies must receive their games over the Comcast cable network, SportsNet, because DirecTV was not able to provide these games.

14.5. A BROADCASTING CHECKLIST

In addition to achieving a basic understanding of sports broadcasting rights within contracts, how sports broadcasts are copyrighted, and how antitrust laws affects sports broadcasting, athletic administrators can minimize legal problems that often accompany television and media broadcasts of athletic events by referring to the following broadcast checklist:

1. Establish who has the property right in a broadcast.
2. Make sure the requirements of the 1976 Copyright Act are being followed, especially in regard to "fixing" the broadcast and in filing for any royalty fees due with the Copyright Royalty Arbitration Panel.
3. Include proper broadcast rights clauses in any game or contest contract, including rights of opponents regarding broadcasts into their "home" territory.
4. Review conference or league rights to broadcast applicable championships or individual games or contests.
5. Review all facility lease or rental contracts and facility third-party contracts for possible broadcast rights problems.
6. Review all contracts with television, cable, radio broadcast stations, or the Internet to ensure proper clauses are included to protect the sports entity's property right in a broadcast.
7. Review all conference or league broadcast contracts for possible antitrust monopoly problems.

Chapter 15

BUSINESS LAW: BUSINESS STRUCTURES, TAX LAWS, AND EMPLOYMENT LAW

INTRODUCTION

Running any type of business, whether it is sports related or not, requires understanding a number of important legal issues. These issues are both varied and complicated. This chapter offers a general examination of some of the legal issues and basic principles related to the business side of sports. In addition, the chapter tries to identify some other legal issues possibly facing industry professionals who are unclear about tax (section 15.2), discrimination (section 15.3.2.) and sexual harassment (section 15.3.3.) laws.

The chapter begins by examining some of the most common business structures used by sport organizations. This section examines not only the traditional structures, such as partnerships and corporations, but also less traditional ones, such as limited liability corporations. The section will discuss some of the advantages of certain types of business structures for different sport businesses.

Next, the chapter examines the impact of federal, state, and local taxes on the owners of sports organizations. The federal tax laws are an important factor in determining which structure the business should use. The tax law section also examines the tax implications of unrelated business income, luxury box rentals, and stadium construction for both non-profit organizations, such as universities and colleges, as well as for-profit organizations, such as professional sports teams.

The final section looks at the legal issues governing the employer/employee relationship. Employment litigation is one of the fastest growing areas of litigation in the federal court system. The employment law section examines such diverse areas as equal pay, employment discrimination, age discrimination, and sexual harassment litigation. The employment law section also examines the Equal Employment Opportunity Commission (EEOC) guidelines titled "Enforcement Guidance on Sex Discrimination in the Compensation of Sports Coaches in Educational Institutions." The intent of the EEOC guidelines is to illustrate the proper legal analysis of pay disparity cases under both Title VII of the Civil Rights Act of 1964 and the Equal Pay Act. Finally, the chapter examines sexual harassment court decisions that provide guidance for organizations wishing to adopt policies to prevent problems.

15.1. BUSINESS STRUCTURES

Three of the most common business structures in sport are sole proprietorships, partnerships, and corporations. In selecting the appropriate business structure, there are a number of factors to be considered. These factors include limited legal liability, federal tax laws, formality, flexibility, access to capital, cost and ease of formation, and transferability of ownership in the business. The following sections describe various types of business structures and outline some of the advantages and disadvantages of each.

NOTE _____

1. For more specific information on the business structure of individual teams in "Big Four" professional leagues, see the following reports, published by Paul Kagan Associates, Inc. Information regarding the purchase of these reports is available at www.kagan.com

15.1.1. Sole Proprietorships

The simplest form of business organization to start and maintain, the sole proprietorship, is an unincorporated business that is owned by one individual. When starting a business, if an individual does not incorporate, the business will be a sole proprietorship by default. A well-known example in the sports industry was the Los Angles Dodgers when they where owned by Walter O'Malley and his family. As the sole proprietor, O'Malley was able to run the Dodgers without any interference from shareholders or partners. Under a sole proprietorship, the business has no existence apart from the owner.

The advantages of the sole proprietorship include lower costs, ease of formation, and single taxation. The cost of formation is low because there are no legal papers to file. Therefore no attorneys are needed, making it less expensive. Also, since an owner must include the income and expenses of the business on his/her own tax return, that owner pays no business tax. The disadvantages of the sole proprietorship include the unlimited personal liability for all the financial and legal risks of the business. The business has no existence apart from the owner. Its liabilities (debts) become the owner's personal liabilities. Two other disadvantages are that the life of the business is limited to the owner and the business' access to capital is limited to the owner's assets or borrowing power (see exhibit 15.1 for advantages and disadvantages). Borrowing power is particularly important for professional team sports due to increasing costs of owning a franchise. Even a recognized billionaire like Daniel Snyder needed to secure loans in order to purchase the Washington Redskins and Fed Ex stadium for approximately $800 million.

15.1.2. Partnerships

The most common form of business in Big Four professional leagues is the partnership. This is especially true since the National Football League does not allow corporate ownership of teams. A partnership is the relationship existing between two or more persons who carry on a trade or business for profit. Each person contributes money, property, labor, or skill and expects to share in the profits and losses of the business. The rights and obligations of the partners are equal, unless otherwise stated in a partnership agreement. While a written agreement is not required to form a legal partnership, one is recommended, to provide protection in the event of disputes, bankruptcy, or termination of the business. A partnership agreement should consist of a written accord outlining the rights and obligations of the partners and how profits and losses should be shared.

The advantages of a partnership include the low cost and ease of formation. As stated above, a partnership does not need a formal or legal agreement to be formed. Also, since the partners do not need to see a lawyer to develop the partnership agreement, the costs can be minimal. (In some cases these agreements are more complex, and partners *will* consult legal counsel.) Another ad-

Exhibit 15.1
Advantages and Disadvantages of Business Structures

Business Structure	Legal Liability	Taxation	Formality	Life of Organiz.	Access to Capital	Cost of Formation	Transfer-ability
SOLE PROPRIETORSHIP	Total	Single taxation	Very Informal	Limited	Limited	None	None
PARTNERSHIP	Total	Pass-through taxation	Informal	Limited	Limited	Minimal	None
LIMITED PARTNERSHIP	Total /Limited	Pass-through taxation	Formal	Limited	Limited	Minimal	None
C CORPORATION	Limited	Dual Taxation	Very formal	Unlimited	Unlimited	High	Unlimited
S CORPORATION	Limited	Pass-through taxation	Very formal	Unlimited	Unlimited	High	Unlimited
LLC	Limited	Pass-through taxation	Very formal	Limited	Unlimited	High	Limited
NONPROFIT CORPORATION	Limited	None	Very formal	Unlimited	Unlimited	High	Limited

vantage of the partnership is conduit or pass-through taxation. The partnership files an informational tax return only. The partners must then include the income or loss of the partnership in their own personal income tax returns. The informational return shows the results of the operation, allocating the profit or loss among the partners.

Some of the disadvantages include unlimited joint and several liability for the acts of general partners. In a partnership, each partner has a fiduciary duty toward the other partners, through which they share in the profits and losses and are legally bound by each other's actions, regardless of whether the partner consented or had notice of the wrongful action. Because of this unlimited joint and several liability for the acts of the other partners, individuals in a partnership need to trust their partners and be aware of their activities. Another disadvantage of the partnership is that since it is created by a contract, a partner cannot sell or transfer his or her share in the partnership. Also, if a partner dies or wants to dissolve the partnership, the partnership ends. Therefore, the life of the business is limited. Finally, the access to capital is limited to the partners' assets. (See exhibit 15.1.)

15.1.3. Limited Partnerships

"There is nothing quite so limited as being a limited partner of George Steinbrenner's," said New York Yankee limited partner John McMullen in 1979. The limited partnership is a cross between a corporation and a partnership. A limited partnership consists of one or more general partners who retain control over the business operation and one or more limited partners who invest money into the partnership. The limited partners receive profit or loss from the partnership but lack any control over the business. Prior to the formation of YankeeNets LLC in 1999, New York Yankees were probably the most publicized limited partnership in American sports. The general partner, George Steinbrenner, ran the day-to-day operations of the business, and the limited partners had no involvement in the business. When Steinbrenner and his partners bought the Yankees from CBS for $10 million in 1973, they borrowed $6 million. Of the $4 million in equity, only $168,000 was Steinbrenner's (see note 1).

Limited partnerships have the same advantages and disadvantages as a general partnership. These advantages include low cost and ease of formation, no formal or legal agreement to be formed is required, and conduit or pass-through taxation. The disadvantages include unlimited personal liability, unlimited joint and several liability for the acts of the other partners, and the inability to sell or transfer partnership interests.

The major difference between a general partnership and a limited partnership is that the limited partner(s) enjoys limited liability for the debts of the partnership. Since the limited partner has no involvement in the day-to-day operations of the business, his or her liability exposure is limited to the investment. As a result of the limited liability, limited partnerships are able to generate more investments. One disadvantage of the limited partnership is the lack of managerial input that the limited partner has in running the business. Once a limited partner is appointed to the management of the business, he or she becomes a general partner and has unlimited joint and several liability for the acts of the partnership. (See exhibit 15.1.)

NOTE _____

1. For information regarding George Steinbrenner's managing of the Yankees' limited partnership, see Anthony Bianco, "The Yankees: Steinbrenner's Money Machine," *Business Week* (September 28, 1998).

15.1.4. Corporations

The last business structure this section examines is the corporation. Corporations are different from partnerships and sole proprietorships in that they are generally treated as entities separate from the owners or shareholders. There are a number of different types of corporations, however. The following sections look at three types of corporations, and the benefits and disadvantages of each.

15.1.4.1. C Corporations

C corporations, or regular corporations, are separate legal entities created under and governed by the laws of the state of incorporation. As a separate legal entity, a corporation has many of the legal rights of an individual. A corporation can sue or be sued, carry on business activities, hire employees and own tangible and intangible assets. Unlike proprietorships or partnerships, however, a corporation must pay a separate tax on the business income, rather than it passing through to the owner's personal income tax.

A corporation may have an unlimited number of stockholders who, due to the separate legal nature of the corporation, are protected from the creditors of the business. The shareholders elect directors who have overall responsibility for the management of the corporation. The directors elect officers who carry out the wishes of the directors. Thus, a corporation is more complex than either a sole proprietorship or a partnership.

One of the biggest advantages to forming a corporation is limited liability. Unlike sole proprietorships or partnerships, where creditors of the business can hold the owner personally liable for all debts, the only personal liability to which a shareholder of a corporation is subject is the money they invested into the company. Another advantage of a corporation is that it has unlimited life extending beyond the illness or death of the owners, individual officers, managers, or shareholders. Since a corporation is a separate legal entity, ownership of the business may be transferred through the sale of stock, which makes changes in ownership simple. Finally, it is easier for a corporation to raise capital. This may be accomplished through the sale of stock or bonds. With sole proprietorships and partnerships, investors are much harder to attract because of the personal liability issue.

Some of the disadvantages of incorporating include the cost, the formal legal requirements, state and federal rules and regulations, and double taxation. To form a corporation, articles of incorporation must be filed with the secretary of state in the state of incorporation. Each state has its own legal procedures and regulations for forming and maintaining a corporation in good standing. Therefore, a corporation requires more paperwork and record keeping than a sole proprietorship. Also, unlike other forms of business entities, a corporation must pay taxes on the business income, rather than passing it through to the owner's personal income tax. In addition to the corporation paying tax, individual shareholders must pay taxes on dividends the corporation distributes. As a result, the corporation's profits are taxed doubly once at the corporate rate and once at the individual shareholder's rate. So, unlike a proprietorship or a partnership, where the owners of the business are able to deduct any losses in the business from their personal income taxes, the profits and losses of the corporation are attributed to the corporation, not the owners/shareholders. (See exhibit 15.1.)

While it might appear that the advantages of limited liability are so great that all businesses would want to be incorporated, the decision to incorporate solely for liability purposes should be weighed against the increased cost and complication of the corporate structure, plus taxation disadvantages. As shown in the next section, *every* business in the United States has to pay taxes or file an informational return. However, only businesses that fail can take advantage of unlimited liability protection.

15.1.4.2. S Corporations

The difference between an S corporation and a regular corporation is the special tax designation granted by the IRS to corporations that have already been formed. S corporations are most often used by service-oriented businesses that want the limited liability feature of the corporation but do not want the tax consequences of a C corporation. As stated above, when a general corporation makes a profit, it is required to pay a federal corporate income tax on the profit. If the company declares a dividend, the shareholders must report the dividend as personal income and pay more taxes. To avoid this "double taxation," subchapter S of the Internal Revenue Code allows S corporations to report all income or loss only once, on the personal tax returns of the shareholders.

Therefore, S corporations have the same basic advantages and disadvantages as C corporations, with the added benefit of special tax provisions. There are certain restrictions to forming an S corporation. First, the maximum number of shareholders is seventy-five. Second, stock ownership is limited to individuals, estates, and certain trusts, including small business trusts. Third, all the shareholders must be citizens or residents of the United States. Fourth, S corporations may issue only one class of stock (see exhibit 15.1 for advantages and disadvantages).

15.1.4.3. Limited Liability Corporations (LLCs)

LLCs were first introduced in the United States in 1977 and authorized for pass-through taxation (similar to partnerships and S corporations) by the IRS in 1988. Viewed by many business planners as the business form of the future, LLCs combine many of the advantages of corporations and partnerships. Under the LLC, investors receive limited liability protection from business debt, as well as the tax advantages of partnerships or S corporations. Also, while similar to S corporations, LLC do not have as many IRS restrictions. The LLC is so attractive that a number of new professional sports leagues have established themselves as LLCs. These new leagues include: Major League Soccer (MLS), the Women's National Basketball Association (WNBA), Women's United Soccer Association (WUSA), and NFL Europe. As an LLC, the league owns all the teams. Individuals only "invest" in the league, and there are technically no team owners (see note 1). For example, while Robert Kraft and Lamar Hunt own the NFL's New

England Patriots and Kansas City Chiefs, respectively, they do not own MLS's New England Revolution or the Kansas City Wizards. They are simply the investor/operators in MLS who run the Revolution and the Wizards, respectively. Some existing leagues have also reorganized as LLCs. For example, in 1999, after Isiah Thomas purchased the entire Continental Basketball League (CBL) for $10 million, one of the first things he did was to reorganize the CBL into an LLC.

LLCs have the same basic advantages as C corporations, such as limited liability, ease of transfer, and the ability to raise capital. The added advantages of the LLC include pass-through taxation, greater flexibility in management of the business, and less restrictive ownership requirements. For example, unlike the S corporation, LLCs can have an unlimited number of shareholders, and the shareholders do not have to be citizens or residents of the United States. Probably the most important difference, however, is that stock ownership is not limited to individuals, estates, and certain trusts; it is open to partnerships and other corporations. Another important advantage for professional sports leagues is that as a single entity structure, LLCs are exempt from federal antitrust law (see Chapter 10, section 10.3.7., "Single Entity Defense").

A major disadvantage of the LLC is the legal uncertainty surrounding the business structure. Due to the newness of the LLC, there is limited case precedent. However, a positive development occurred for proponents of LLCs in sport leagues in *Fraser v. Major League Soccer*, 97 F.Supp.2d 130 (D. Mass. 2000), *aff'd* 284 F.3d 47 (1st Cir. 2002). Major League Soccer claimed that the league was using the LLC as a way to circumvent federal antitrust laws. However, the appellate court disagreed by ruling in favor of the league (see exhibit 15.1).

NOTES

1. The idea of the league owning all of the teams is not new. In 1901, John Brush, owner of the National League Cincinnati baseball team, proposed that all eight National League teams should merge into a new holding company called the National Baseball Trust. Each team would then receive common stock in the new company. The stock was going to be divided based on each club's value: New York would receive 30%; Cincinnati, 12%; St. Louis, 12%; Boston, 12%; Philadelphia, 10%; Chicago, 10%; Pittsburgh, 8%; and Brooklyn, 6%. A board of directors, who would appoint managers (at a set salary) for each team and license and assign players wherever the board wanted them, would run the league. Although the idea was criticized by the press, it just barely failed to pass at the 1901 owners' meeting. See Harold Seymour, *Baseball: The Early Years* (New York: Oxford University Press, 1989).

2. For more information on LLCs, see Robert W. Hamilton, *Cases and Materials on Corporations: Including Partnerships and Limited Liability Companies* (St. Paul, Minn.: West Publishing, 1998).

15.1.4.4. Publicly Traded Corporations

With the cost of running a professional sports team increasing, a number of owners have contemplated "going public." In 1998, the Cleveland Indians took advantage of a change in Major League Baseball's rules allowing teams to offer stock to the public, and became the third professional sports team in the United States to move into the stock market. The two earlier teams were the Boston Celtics of the National Basketball Association and the Orlando Predators of the Arena Football League.

Like the other business structures, there are a number of advantages and disadvantages in taking a team public. The first and most important advantage is financial. In 1998, the Cleveland Indians raised $55 million by selling 4 million shares of stock in the team. However, since 1998, the Indians have again become a private company (see note 2). A secondary reason for going public is to increase the visibility of a team, and to foster fan loyalty through ownership in the team. Initial public offerings generate a lot of publicity. Also, if a fan is able to purchase a share of the team through stock ownership, he or she may perceive a financial interest in being loyal to the team.

There are a number of disadvantages to going public, however. First, the organization must comply with all Securities and Exchange Commission (SEC) rules and regulations. Second, the team must make a full financial disclosure concerning its profits and losses. Third, the team and owner(s) must be accountable to shareholders. As investors in the team, shareholders have certain rights, such as voting on the makeup of the board of directors and attending annual meetings. Finally, there are the added costs to the organization. The team must have annual board of directors' meetings, create and mail annual financial reports, assign staff for investor relations, and pay added legal costs.

Currently, there are three publicly traded sports franchises in the United States—the Boston Celtics (NBA), the Orlando Predators (Arena Football League), and the San Diego Flash (semi-pro "A" league soccer). Several major professional teams are owned, at least in part, by larger publicly traded companies. For example, twelve NHL, NBA, and MLB teams are owned by media companies: AOL/Time Warner (Atlanta Braves, Atlanta Hawks, Atlanta Thrashers); Cablevision (New York Knicks, New York Rangers); Comcast (Philadelphia Flyers, Philadelphia 76ers); Fox Entertainment Group (Los Angeles Dodgers); Gaylord Entertainment (Nashville Predators); Tribune Company (Chicago Cubs); and Walt Disney Co. (Anaheim Angels, Mighty Ducks of Anaheim).

The National Football League does not allow public or corporate ownership of its teams, notwithstanding the unusual "grandfather" exemption it grants to the Green Bay Packers. It is important to point out, however, that while the Packers raised nearly $24 million in a 1997 stock offering, it is not a public company in the traditional sense. While one can own stock in the Green Bay Packers, the team is not publicly traded. In publicly traded companies, the stock is available on officially recognized exchanges. The Orlando Predators are traded on the NASDAQ, and the Boston Celtics are traded on the New York Stock Exchange. Also, investors in publicly traded companies are able to transfer or sell their shares. Finally, the revenue and profits generated by the team are the primary income sources of the company, and the company is run in order to earn profits for its shareholders. In essence, the stockholders or investors own the company. The Green Bay Packers, unlike the Predators or Celtics, are a community-owned enterprise and operate on a non-profit basis. Investors are unable to buy shares in the Packers on an organized exchange, and they receive no dividends, no profits, no discounts, not even a financial report. Investors are able to transfer ownership of their stock only to family members, as gifts.

While it is still relatively uncommon to find publicly traded sports *teams*, it is fairly common for other types of sports businesses to go public. For example, most footwear and apparel companies (Nike, Reebok) are publicly traded and a handful of athletic venues are publicly traded (e.g., Churchill Downs), as are many sporting goods companies (e.g., Callaway, Rawlings, Russell). Even World

Wrestling Federation Entertainment became a publicly traded company in 1999 (see note 3).

NOTES _____

1. For more information on publicly traded sports companies see Brian R. Cheffins, "Playing the Stock Market: 'Going Public' and Professional Team Sports," 24 *Journal of Corporate Law* 641 (Spring 1999).

2. In November 1999, Richard Jacobs, the owner of the Cleveland Indians, announced the sale of the team to an investment group headed by an Ohio attorney, Larry Dolan, for $320 million. That $320 million figure included the buying back of stock, at a price more than 48% higher than its issued price in the previous year. This sort of return on investment is unusual for a sport franchise stock. Many investors purchase stock in a sport franchise in order to show fan loyalty rather than because of the stock's prospect for growth.

3. World Wrestling Federation Entertainment, Inc., sold 10 million shares of stock at $17 each in one of the most highly publicized initial public offerings of 1999. The media company later purchased World Championship Wrestling and created the short-lived XFL. The company is traded on the New York Stock Exchange (NYSE).

4. The Boston Celtics, a limited partnership, began selling stock in 40% of the team on the New York Stock Exchange (NYSE) in 1986. The team's owners used a limited partnership, primarily to take advantage of tax breaks. In 1998, when the tax advantages were no longer available to the limited partnership, the Celtics reorganized into two entities: a public limited partnership, taxable as a corporation, and a private limited partnership. The public limited partnership is the stock listed on the NYSE.

15.2. TAX ISSUES

Several of the tax issues facing athletic administrators revolve around the tax-exempt status of non-profit or not-for-profit organizations. Section 501(a) of the Internal Revenue Code governs organizations that seek to obtain an exemption from federal income tax. To qualify for the exemption, the athletic endeavor must be organized for one or more of the purposes set forth in section 501. Section 501(c)(3) of the code designates those organizations, which include religious, charitable, educational, scientific, literary, testing for public safety, fostering national or international amateur sports competition, or the prevention of cruelty to children or animals. State or municipal instrumentalities also fall under 501(c)(3), and these may include high schools and state universities. Therefore, activities such as the Olympics, national sports festivals, and state games may fall in the "national or international amateur sports competition" area. Athletic departments may be classified as "educational institutions" or "municipal instrumentalities." Booster clubs, Little Leagues, and Pop Warner Football may be classified as "charitable organizations."

15.2.1. Non-profit Organizations

An organization seeking non-profit status must file an application with the Internal Revenue Service (IRS). The purposes and proposed activities of the organization must be set forth in the corporate papers. In addition, a classified statement of receipts and expenditures, and a balance sheet for the current year and the three immediate prior years are needed for existing organizations. If a new organization is applying, a proposed budget for two full accounting periods and a current statement of assets and liabilities must be filed. After receipt of the necessary application materials, the IRS will issue a decision in a determination letter.

In making its decision, the IRS examines whether the petitioner has met the three requirements set forth in I.R.C. §501(c)(3). The three requirements for an organization to be exempt are (1) the corporation must be organized and operated exclusively for exempt purposes; (2) no part of the net earnings of the corporation may inure to the benefit of any shareholder or individual; and (3) the corporation must not engage in political campaigns or, to a substantial extent, in lobbying activities.

The only issue in dispute in most cases is the first requirement: that the corporation must be organized and operated exclusively for exempt purposes. The operational test requires the activities of an organization to be primarily those which accomplish an exempt purpose as described in Section 501(c)(3). A single substantial non-exempt purpose will disqualify an organization despite the importance of its exempt purpose. If an organization serves private rather than public interests, it also will not meet the operational test.

There are three main advantages to an organization that attains non-profit status. The first and major advantage is the exemption from federal income tax liability. The organization is not subject to any tax on the income it generates as long as it is related to the organization's exempt purpose. The second advantage is that services performed in the employ of a non-profit organization may be exempted from liability for the Social Security (FICA) taxes. This exemption could lower the operating costs of the organization. The third advantage is that contributions by an individual taxpayer or business to a non-profit organization qualify as charitable contributions and are deductible by the donor for income tax purposes. This is an obvious incentive for individuals and businesses to contribute to a particular organization.

However, non-profit status also has its disadvantages. The first is the amount of paperwork that must be filed. The second is that the application for exemption and the supporting documentation are available for public scrutiny. However, there are procedures for withholding the information from the public if the IRS determines that the disclosure would adversely affect the organization.

A variety of other restrictions placed on non-profit organizations should be considered before applying for the favorable tax treatment. For example, the assets of an organization must be permanently dedicated to the exempt purpose. This means that if the organization is dissolved, the assets must be distributed to another exempt purpose, or to the federal, state, or local government for a public purpose. Therefore, one cannot build profits through a non-profit organization, then dissolve the business and take the profits. In addition, although employees of a non-profit organization may be paid a salary, the salary cannot be tied to the profitability of the organization.

A non-profit organization is often incorrectly interpreted as a business that cannot make money in any tax year. This is untrue; the bottom line for a non-profit organization may be in the black. However, the profits may not be used to benefit the organizers or employees.

NOTES

1. In *Wayne Baseball, Inc. v. Commissioner*, 78 T.C.M. (CCH) 437 (1999), the court held that Wayne Baseball, a non-profit Delaware corporation whose principal activity is

the sponsorship of a highly competitive amateur baseball team, did not qualify as a I.R.C. §501(c)(3) charitable organization. In distinguishing the case from *Hutchinson* (see note 2), the court concluded that the only activity sponsored by Wayne Baseball was the operation of an adult amateur baseball team, whereas in *Hutchinson* the organization's primary activity was to promote baseball in the surrounding community by maintaining a baseball field for the public and providing coaches for Little League teams and a baseball camp.

2. In *Hutchinson Baseball Enterprises, Inc. v. Commissioner*, 696 F.2d 757 (10th Cir. 1982), the court found that the promotion, advancement, and sponsoring of amateur athletes qualified as an exempt purpose.

3. In *Mobile Arts & Sports Association v. United States*, 148 F.Supp. 311 (S.D. Ala. 1957), the U.S. District Court held that an organization whose purpose was to present an annual senior college bowl football game made substantial civic, educational, and cultural contributions to the community, and therefore qualified for exemption under Section 501 (c)(3).

4. For further details on non-profit organizations, see "How to Apply for and Retain Exempt Status for Your Organization," Internal Revenue Service Publication 557.

15.2.2. Unrelated Business Income

The tax on unrelated business income has become a major issue for tax-exempt athletic organizations, such as colleges and universities. A tax-exempt organization may be held liable for taxes on unrelated business income, which is income from a trade or business, regularly carried on, that is not substantially related to the charitable, educational, or other purpose constituting the basis for its exemption (see I.R.C. §511–513).

It is important for the college athletics administrator to understand how the structure and function of a college athletics department or program relates to the IRS rules and regulations pertaining to unrelated business income and subsequent taxation. The unrelated business income tax was enacted to accomplish two objectives: (1) to eliminate unfair competition between charitable organizations and the taxed private sector and (2) to increase federal tax revenues.

Intercollegiate athletics today have many schools with multimillion-dollar athletic budgets, the desire to win and produce revenue to perpetuate those budgets, and an increasing gap between the goals of the educational institution and the goals of the athletic department. Because of the current climate in intercollegiate athletics, there is an increasing need for athletic administrators to deal intelligently with conflicts that arise from activities that, while within an educational and tax-exempt institution, take on the characteristics and function of an "unrelated business."

Before looking closely at what constitutes unrelated business income according to the IRS definition, here is a general overview of the topic. In 1977, the IRS shocked the college athletics ranks when it issued a tax bill on the broadcast receipts of the Cotton Bowl. The tremendous backlash caused by this action pressured the IRS to reverse its position in 1978, thus creating a de facto exemption for college/university athletic programs. In 1997, Congress affirmed the IRS's allowing non-profit organizations, including colleges and universities, to deduct most forms of corporate sponsorship revenues. Decisions such as these raise eyebrows of those who perceive university athletic programs largely as profit-motivated entertainment industries that should be subject to taxation. These critics contend that, by and large, intercollegiate athletic programs are, both financially and philosophically, too far removed from the educational function of the institution to justify charitable, tax-exempt status.

The critical question in determining whether income is related or unrelated is whether the operation that produces the money—be it a big-time college football game, an on-campus health club, or a summer sports camp—meets the three characteristics of unrelated business income within a charitable institution. An institution's "unrelated business taxable income" is defined by the IRS as the net income of any

1. trade or business that is
2. "regularly carried on" *and* is
3. "not substantially related (aside from the need of such organization for income of funds or the use it makes of the profits derived) to the exercise or performance" of the college's educational function.

Generally, an unrelated business is not taxable when it (1) fails to meet all three criteria outlined above, (2) is operated entirely by volunteers, or (3) is carried on "primarily for the convenience of the college's members, students, patients, officers, or employees." One also must consider whether the business is "in serious competition" with the private sector. For instance, if a university athletic department conducted a money-making tennis facility that competed with a local, privately operated tennis facility, the income from the university tennis facility may be taxable according to IRS rules.

Any activity having these three characteristics is an "unrelated business," the income from which, after customary business deductions are taken, is taxed at the regular corporate rates, without regard to whether the entity actually carrying on the business is a charitable corporation. In short, the test of whether an unrelated business is taxable looks to the *source* of the income, irrespective of its use. Proof of the funds' proper use is now irrelevant to the questions of their taxability; instead, the critical question is whether the operation that produces those funds is an "unrelated business." In addition, any organization whose "unrelated" activities become predominant in the overall charitable function and goals of the institution risks losing its basic tax exemption. An organization's activities must still be primarily charitable in nature for it to qualify as a tax-exempt organization in the first place.

Of the three characteristics listed above, the most difficult to analyze, because of the broad definition of education, is whether or not an activity is "substantially related." Hence, the issue of substantial relatedness usually focuses on a more restrictive question: What is the activity's relationship to the exempt purpose? More specifically, does the activity *contribute importantly* to the accomplishment of the exempt purpose of the institution? These judgments are made on a case-by-case basis. For example, a college that uses its tennis facilities in the summer for a public tennis camp may receive unrelated trade or business income (Rev. Rul. 80-297, 1980-2 C.B. 196). Similarly, a university that leases its stadium to a professional football team and provides utilities, grounds maintenance, and security services is engaged in unrelated trade or business, and the income is not excludable as rent from real property (Rev. Rul. 80-298, 1980-2 C.B. 197). On the other hand, operation of a ski facility by an exempt school for its physical education program and also for recreational purposes by students attending the school is substantially related to the school's exempt purpose. Income from the use of the facility by the public, however, is unrelated business income (Rev. Rul. 78-98, 1978-1 C.B. 167).

The question of whether intercollegiate athletics, in general, contributes importantly to the institution's educational mission is a potential area for interpretation. However, until the courts decide otherwise, intercollegiate athletics will remain exempt from taxation as an unrelated business, despite the commercial aspects of these activities. This is because of legislative sympathy toward the educational institution and a hesitancy to tax college sports.

NOTES _____

1. For more guidance as to what constitutes "unrelated business income" at the university level, see www.universitytax.com/Faq_ubi.htm#ubil

2. In March 2000, the IRS proposed further regulation of the treatment of unrelated business income related to "exclusive provider" corporate sponsorship payments. For example, if a university granted "exclusive pour rights" to a soft drink company, such income would be taxable. The IRS and NCAA are currently lobbying Congress for and against this policy, respectively. NCAA President Cedric Dempsey wrote an editorial about this issue for the *NCAA News* in July 2000. See www.ncaa.org/news/2000/20000731/comment.html

3. The IRS in 1999 challenged Rod French's donation to the Iowa State University Foundation as a charitable contribution. French deducted 80% of the gift under Section 170, even though he received the use of a luxury box in the college's football stadium and basketball arena in return. In total, French claimed a deduction of $143,584. The IRS claimed that the deduction should be restricted under Section 274(1)(2), which limits such deductions to the sum of the face value of non-luxury box seat tickets for the seats in such box covered by the lease. The IRS later reversed itself and allowed the deduction under Section 170(1). See "Stadium Sky Boxes Can Be Deducted," *New York Times*, July 16, 1999, p. D7.

4. In *NCAA v. Commissioner*, 914 F.2d 1417 (10th Cir. 1990), the NCAA challenged the IRS determination that the income derived from the sale of advertising space in the programs of the 1982 NCAA men's basketball tournament was taxable as unrelated business income. In reversing the lower court's decision, the court of appeals ruled that the sale of advertising space was not a regularly carried on business, and therefore was not taxable as unrelated business income.

15.2.2.1. *Facility Rentals*

The use of facilities on campus for university-related activities such as intercollegiate, intramural, and physical education programs clearly qualifies as tax-exempt activity. When the university leases a facility to an outside group, however, the income derived may be classified as unrelated business income. For example, a university's rental income from professional sports teams is not tax-exempt simply because the university uses the same facility itself at other times. Even when a university leases a facility for an unrelated business, issues may arise with respect to determining the amount of tax. In *RPI v. Commissioner* (see note 2), the method of allocating fixed costs between the unrelated business use of a collegiate facility and the tax-exempt use of the facility is discussed.

NOTES _____

1. Private athletic facilities may deduct the proportional value of property that is used exclusively for tax-exempt functions. In *Atlanta Athletic Club v. Commissioner*, 980 F.2d

1409 (11th Cir. 1993), a private athletic club successfully argued that a piece of property should be designated as "recreational," and therefore exempt, because it was the site of a number of member activities such as Easter egg hunts, fishing tournaments, kite-flying contests, hot air balloon rides, and organized foot races. Members also jogged on the property, and used it for archery practice and flying model airplanes. The court required the club to prove that these non-commercial activities were taking place. Therefore, it behooves an athletic facility to keep detailed records of activities that occur on properties designated "tax-exempt."

2. In *Rensselaer Polytechnic Institute v. Commissioner*, 732 F.2d 1058 (2d Cir. 1983), a college used its field house for both tax-exempt purposes and unrelated business purposes; therefore, income from the unrelated business use was taxable. However, in this case, a dispute regarding how to allocate the deductible expenses, such as depreciation, between the taxable and tax-exempt uses of the facility arose. The plaintiff argued that the expenses should be divided in accordance with the relative amount of time the facility was used for each activity. For example, if the facility was used for tax-exempt purposes for five hours and for taxable purposes for five hours, half of the expenses could be used as a deduction for the taxable income. The commissioner, however, argued that the expenses should be allocated proportionally between the amount of time the facility was used for taxable purposes and the amount of time available for use, whether it was actually used or not. Therefore, even if it was used half for tax-exempt purposes and half for taxable purposes, they could not allocate half of the expenses to the taxable purposes because the time that the facility was dormant had to be factored into the equation. The judge ruled for the plaintiff college, holding that their method was "reasonable."

15.2.2.2. *Broadcast Receipts*

Broadcast receipts of tax-exempt organizations have long been an issue relative to taxes. The simple nature of broadcast receipts seems to imply a profit-making motive. However, this issue was directly addressed by the IRS in 1980 in Revenue Rulings 80-295 and 80-296. In these two rulings, the IRS concluded that revenue received by a tax-exempt athletic organization from the sale of broadcast rights to a radio or television network or to an independent producer does not constitute unrelated business income. This issue came to the forefront when the IRS tried to tax the broadcast receipts of the Cotton Bowl in 1977. The IRS later reversed its decision and subsequently issued the two revenue rulings addressing this issue. It should be noted that while revenue rulings are given some weight by the courts, they are not law.

15.2.2.3. *Sponsorship Revenue*

The IRS developed regulations (see Internal Revenue Code §513(i)) regarding the circumstances under which payments received by exempt organizations from sponsorship arrangements might result in income from unrelated trade or business. Section 513 (i)(2)(a) states that payments to an exempt organization are nontaxable contributions if there "is no arrangement or expectation that such person will receive any substantial return benefit other than the use or acknowledgment of the name or logo (or product lines) of such person's trade or business in connection with the activities of the organization that receives such payments." That is, the mere acknowledgment or recognition of a sponsor as a benefactor normally is incidental to the receipt of a contribution and is not in itself of sufficient benefit to the sponsor to give rise to unrelated trade or business income.

Where an exempt organization performs valuable advertising, marketing, and similar services on a quid pro quo basis for the sponsor, however, the payments are not contributions and questions of unrelated trade or business arise. For example, the payments would be taxable if they were tied to advertising a product or service or if the amount of "payment is contingent upon the level of attendance at one or more events, broadcast ratings, or other factors indicating the degree of public exposure" (I.R.C. §513(i)(B)(i)). For the purposes of this section, advertising includes any "messages containing qualitative or comparative language, price information, or other indications of savings or value, an endorsement, or an inducement to purchase, sell or use products or services."

The rules regarding sponsorship apply to broadcast as well as non-broadcast activities. Thus, the guidelines apply uniformly to all sponsorship activities without regard to the local nature of the organization or activities or the amount of the sponsorship payment. For example, an I.R.C. §501(c)(3) organization conducts an annual college football bowl game. The organization sells to commercial broadcasters the right to broadcast the bowl game on television and radio for $3 million. A major corporation agrees to be the exclusive sponsor of the bowl game and pays the organization $2 million. The organization acknowledges the sponsorship payment by adding the corporation's name to the title of the event. This does not constitute advertising within the meaning of I.R.C. §1.513-4 because it does not promote the sponsor's service, facility, or product.

In March 2000, the IRS proposed a regulation that "exclusive provider" agreements would be included under this regulation. An exclusive provider agreement is one that "limits the sale, distribution, availability, or use of competing products, services, or facilities in connection with an exempt organization's activity." For example, a university might extend "exclusive pour" rights to a soft drink company. The NCAA is currently monitoring IRS actions on this issue, and its members will likely push for congressional action if this IRS proposal is codified.

15.2.3. Scholarships

As a general rule, as long as the amount is used for qualified tuition and related expenses, any scholarship received by an individual who is a candidate for a degree at an educational organization is not included in the recipient's gross taxable income. The tax law defines "qualified tuition and related expenses" as tuition and fees required for enrollment, fees, books, supplies, and equipment required for courses of instruction.

The amount for room and board is considered taxable income. Also, any portion of the scholarship or grant representing payment for teaching, research, or other services required as a condition for receiving the scholarship is included in the recipient's gross taxable income. In addition, IRS notice 87-31 urges the grantor to supply the recipient with a calculation of the appropriate amount to be included in his or her gross income.

15.2.4. Charitable Contributions, Luxury Box Rentals, and Entertainment Expenses

Most amateur athletic organizations are set up as non-profit businesses and do not pay income taxes. However, the tax laws still affect the way they operate. A significant source of funds for many non-profit athletic organizations is the contributions of individuals and businesses. The attractiveness of these contributions for the contributor directly depends on the tax laws regarding itemized deductions. Since many athletic programs rely heavily on contributions, athletic administrators have kept a close eye on Congress's treatment of certain charitable contributions.

If the luxury box seats are at professional, or for-profit, sports stadiums, the IRS limits the amount of money businesses can deduct from their taxes as a business entertainment expense. I.R.C. §274(1)(2) of the Internal Revenue Code limits the amount of money an individual or business is able to deduct for a luxury box leased for more than one event to "the sum of the face value of non-luxury box seat tickets for the seats in such box covered by the lease."

The issue of whether I.R.C. §274 (1)(2) applies to intercollegiate athletics was not decided until 1999. The IRS has ruled that donors can deduct 80% of their gifts to universities under I.R.C. §170, which outlines the allowance of deductions even if the donor receives the use of a luxury box in the college's football stadium and basketball arena in return. The ruling was in response to a tax return filed by Iowa State University booster Rod French. French deducted $143,584 of the $200,000 donation he gave the university foundation as a charitable contribution. The IRS, which challenged the deduction because the booster received a ten-year lease on a luxury box and other stadium amenities, claimed that the donation should be covered under I.R.C. §274(1)(2).

The IRS appeals office reversed the decision, concluding that, based on the law's legislative history, Congress did not intend Section 274(1) to preclude an I.R.C. §170(1) deduction. I.R.C. §170(1) permits a deduction for amounts paid to an "institution of higher education" in return for the "right to purchase tickets for seating at an athletic event," but limits the deduction to 80%. Since a Section 170 deduction is allowed without regard to a trade or business, the Internal Revenue Service reasoned, I.R.C. §274 limitations did not apply.

15.2.5. Professional Sport Franchise Tax Issues

It is no secret that professional sports teams are valuable properties. Since the 1980s franchise prices have skyrocketed worldwide. Given the 2001 sale of baseball's Boston Red Sox for over $700 million, Daniel Snyder and others' $800 million purchase of the NFL's Washington Redskins in 1999, and BSkyB's overturned 1998 purchase of soccer's Manchester United, a top franchise in the 21st century, may be sold for more than $1 billion.

With the price of franchises so high, team owners have looked, and continue to look, to state and federal taxpayers for subsidies. The state and local subsidy is typically provided through below-market rents, guarantees, bonds funded by sales taxes, lottery proceeds, and taxes on hotels, parking, and car rentals. A federal subsidy is provided when tax-exempt state or local bonds are used to finance the facility. For example, the Baltimore Ravens stadium was financed with $86 million of tax-exempt bonds. Principal and interest on those bonds are repaid through state lottery funds, and the public share of stadium-generated revenue, which could not exceed 10% of the debt service on $86 million. In other situations, taxes on tourism, restaurant sales, car rentals, and other items are also potential sources for funding the municipality's debt obligations.

In 1996, the city of Cincinnati agreed to build Paul Brown Stadium after the Bengals' revised their lease in 1994 to state that if a stadium was not built by

2000, they were free to leave town. The county is paying for the stadium by a sales tax, which it raised by half a cent. The tax was voted on by residents and received 61% of the votes. In total, after calculating of construction, land purchases, and other costs, the cost to taxpayers exceeded $400 million. The Bengals' contribution to the stadium was $50 million.

States and cities are willing to build these stadiums for team owners because they believe that having a team is good for the local economy. In Cleveland, for example, the cost of the 1999 Cleveland Browns' stadium to taxpayers was over $250 million, but the city predicted that the Browns would generate over $80 million per year for the area's economy.

Some taxpayers, however, have challenged the tax breaks that state and local governments are providing team owners for stadium financing. One such challenge was in the case of *Giordano v. Ridge,* 737 A.2d 350 (Pa. Commw. Ct. 1999), in which a taxpayer challenged the constitutionality of the Capital Facilities Debt Enabling Act (CFDEA). The CFDEA authorized the undertaking of debt by the Commonwealth of Pennsylvania for the purpose of making grants to local authorities for the construction, repair, renovation, improvement, or equipment of qualifying capital projects. The taxpayer, Giordano, claimed that CFDEA violated Article VIII, Section 8 of the Pennsylvania State Constitution. Article VIII, Section 8, which states that "The credit of the Commonwealth shall not be pledged or loaned to any individual, company, corporation or association nor shall the Commonwealth become a joint owner or stockholder in any company, corporation or associations."

In rejecting the taxpayer's claim, the court found that acts of the General Assembly have a strong presumption of constitutionality, and that an act of the General Assembly may be declared unconstitutional only when it clearly and plainly violates the state constitution. Citing a Pennsylvania State Supreme Court case, the court held that the language in Article VIII, Section 8, does not prohibit loans from the Commonwealth to a municipal authority, even though the ultimate beneficiary of such a loan may be a private entity. Under the CFDEA, the money flows from the Commonwealth to a municipality or municipal authority, and not directly to the private entity. Therefore, even assuming that the credit of the Commonwealth was being pledged or loaned within the meaning of Article VIII, Section 8, it is to a municipality or authority, and not to any "individual, company, corporation or association."

NOTE

1. For more information on public financing of sport facilities, see Anoop K. Bhasin, "Tax-Exempt Bond Financing of Sports Stadiums: Is the Price Right?" 7 *Villanova Sports and Entertainment Law Journal* 181 (2000).

15.2.6. Depreciation Issues

A significant tax advantage for ownership of professional sports franchises is the reduction of personal taxes through the depreciation of player contracts. This concept was introduced in the 1950s by Cleveland Indians' owner Bill Veeck. Veeck convinced the IRS that he should be able to treat the player contracts as a "wasting asset," depreciating their contracts over a period of several years as a business would copy machines or personal computers. James Quirk and Rodney Fort's book *Hard Ball* (see note 1) illustrates the power of this tax shelter.

Suppose someone buys an NFL team for $200 million. The new owner assigns 50 percent of the purchase price to player contracts (the maximum allowed under the law) . . . and then depreciates the contracts over 5 years. . . . Suppose that revenue is $100 million per year and that costs, exclusive of player contract depreciation, are $90 million. Then, for the first five years of operation of the team, the books of the team will look like this:

Revenue	$100 million
Less Costs	$ 90 million
Less Depreciation	$ 20 million
Pretax profits	−$ 10 million

Critics such as Quirk and Fort contend that not only would the team owners receive a tax break, but the owners also might declare to fans and politicians that the team had suffered a "loss." Various litigation has resulted over the years relative to this tax shelter.

For example, in *Selig v. United States*, 740 F.2d 572 (7th Cir. 1984), Allan "Bud" Selig entered into a contract to purchase the Seattle Pilots baseball team for $10.8 million. The contract between the Pilots and Selig allocated $100,000 of the purchase price to equipment and supplies, $500,000 to the value of the franchise including league membership, and $10.2 million to the player contracts. Selig then attempted to amortize the $10.2 million over the players' five-year useful lives under Section 167(a) of the Internal Revenue Code. The Internal Revenue Service disallowed any allocation of the purchase price to player contracts.

The Seventh Circuit Court of Appeals, in upholding the district court, held that Selig properly allocated $10.2 million of the $10.8 million purchase price of the Seattle Pilots to the value of the 149 players he bought. In rejecting the government's claim, the Seventh Circuit held that allocation of $10.2 million to player contracts and $500,000 to the franchise was a reasonable determination of the fair market value of those assets at the time of acquisition. The taxpayer was therefore entitled to depreciation of player contracts on basis of that figure.

Another case involving the depreciation of player salaries is *Laird v. United States*, 556 F.2d 1224 (5th Cir. 1977). Laird bought the Atlanta Falcons of the National Football League for $8.5 million. Laird allocated $7.7 million of the purchase price to the value of the forty-two player contracts he acquired. The district court rejected that valuation and allocated only $3.03 million to the player contracts.

The Court of Appeals held that under the purchase agreement the taxpayer also received the television rights of the club, which were to last as long as the club remained a member of football league, and thus had an unlimited useful life and could not be amortized. The district court concluded that those rights had a present value of $4.3 million, and thus the court calculated that only $3.5 million remained for allocation to the franchise and the player contracts. The court allocated 88% of that amount to the players and only 12% to the franchise, noting that it was clear that the players are the primary assets of a professional football club. Without them, there could be no game.

NOTES ———————————————————————————————

1. For information on professional sport team tax shelters, see James Quirk and Rodney Fort, *Hard Ball: The Abuse of Power in Pro Team Sports* (Princeton, N.J.: Princeton University Press, 1999).

2. Also see the following: Stephen A. Zorn, "Couldna Done It Without the Players," 4 *Seton Hall Journal of Sports Law* 337 (1994), John R. Dorocak, "Tax Advantages of Sports Franchises. Part I: The Stadium," 1 *Law Review of Michigan State University Detroit College of Law* 579 (Fall 1999).

3. In *First Northwest Industries of America, Inc. v. Commissioner*, 649 F.2d 707 (9th Cir. 1981) the issue of tax depreciation of player salaries was brought to the courts by the group involved the 1967 purchase of the Seattle Supersonics expansion franchise in the NBA. The groups' strategy involved using the testimony of sports insiders to establish a valuation of the player contracts. These insiders presented detailed estimates of the value of each of the players acquired by the expansion franchise in the expansion draft. The government argued its mass asset theory and took the position that depreciation could not be allowed on player contracts because they were so intertwined with the other assets, which were acquired, that no amount logically could be allocated to the contracts. They argued that the contracts should account for only $450,000 of the purchase price, rather than the $1.6 million proposed by the owners. The court held that the value of the veteran player contracts was $500,000, or 28.6% of the total acquisition price. The court largely ignored the mass asset arguments as a method of depreciating player contracts.

4. In *Pittsburgh Athletic Co. v. Commissioner*, 27 B.T.A. 1074 (1933), *aff'd.*, 72 F.2d 883 (3d Cir. 1934), one of the first cases to deal with depreciation of player salaries, in which the IRS challenged the Pittsburgh Pirates' practice of taking a deduction each year for the cost of player contracts acquired and including in gross income any amounts the Pirates received for the sale of their contract players. In *Pittsburgh Athletic*, the court reinstated the practice of permitting current deductions for the cost of acquiring player contracts

5. In *United States v. Cleveland Indians Baseball Co.*, 532 U.S. 200 (2001), a case involving the taxation of back wages awarded to players as a result of baseball's collusion cases, the issue was whether or not those back wages should be taxed at the tax rates of the 1980s (when the players were wrongly denied wages) or in the 90s (when the arbitrators ruled in favor of the players and awarded damages to them). The court decided that the taxes should be paid at the tax rate when they were actually paid, and not the year when the wages should have been paid.

15.2.7. Player Salaries

Due to their high salaries, professional athletes need to be aware of the state and federal tax laws. For example, in *Hornung v. Commissioner*, 47 T.C. 428 (1967), the court was asked to determine whether the value of prizes that were won by NFL star Paul Hornung should be included in his gross income. During the 1961 National Football League championship game, Hornung won a Corvette from *Sport Magazine* as the outstanding player in the game. The fair market value of the Corvette automobile received was $3,331.04.

Hornung failed to include the fair market value of the car in his taxable income in 1962, claiming that the car was a gift. In holding that the value of the Corvette should be included in Hornung's gross income, the court found that had Congress intended to exempt prizes or awards for recognition of athletic prowess or achievement, it could readily and easily have done so. Since it had failed to do so, the value of the Corvette constituted gross income under Section 74, I.R.C. 1954. (See note 3.)

Professional athletes must also consider the income tax laws of various U.S.

states and Canadian provinces, especially if entering free agency. For example, a $5 million contract offer from a team in a state *without* income tax will be more valuable than a $5.1 million contract offer from a team in a state *with* a 5% state income tax. To complicate matters, many big league cities have begun taxing *visiting* athletes on a pro-rata basis. Cities such as New York and Philadelphia claim that they are entitled to tax income earned for work performed in their jurisdiction even if a player is based elsewhere. For example, if an NBA player for the Seattle Supersonics plays one of his eighty-two games in New York City, then 1/82 of the player's annual salary is taxable by New York City.

NOTES

1. For issues relating to state tax laws and the taxing of visiting teams, see John Lombardo, "Visiting Athletes Hit by Tax Welcome Mat," *East Bay Business Times*, June 22, 2001—also viewable online at www.eastbay.bcentral.com/eastbay/stories/2001/06/25/focus3.html

2. In 1996, MLB pitcher Scott Radinsky brought suit against the state of Illinois regarding its visiting player salary tax policy. The case, which has proceeded slowly, is pending and is considered the "test case" on this matter. See Mark Brown, "Squeeze Play," www.lib.niu.edu/ipo/ii000631.html

3. Section 74 of the Internal Revenue Code—PRIZES AND AWARDS.

(a) General Rule.—Except as provided in subsection (b) and in section 117 (relating to scholarships and fellowship grants), gross income includes amounts received as prizes and awards.

(b) Exception.—Gross income does not include amounts received as prizes and awards made primarily in recognition of religious, charitable, scientific, educational, artistic, literary, or civic achievement, but only if—

(1) the recipient was selected without any action on his part to enter the contest or proceedings; and

(2) the recipient is not required to render substantial future services as a condition to receiving the prize or award.

15.3. EMPLOYMENT LAW

In recent years the courts have begun to pay close attention to employment law issues, particularly in such areas as workplace discrimination, sexual harassment, and equal pay. With all the attention in the courts relative to employment law issues, it is not surprising that some of the practices of athletic departments are starting to come under the review of the courts. This section highlights some of the main legal issues governing the relationship between employers and employees. It begins by examining the theory of employment-at-will contracts and their impact on the employment relationship. Next is a review of some of the more important federal employment statutes and how the courts have applied these laws. The statutes include the Equal Pay Act, Title VII of the Civil Rights Act, and the Age Discrimination in Employment Act. There is also a review of the Equal Employment Opportunity Commission (EEOC) guidelines on the compensation of sports coaches in educational institutions. The EEOC guidelines are intended to provide guidance for colleges and the courts in addressing pay equity issues among college and university coaches. Title IX issues have also led to retaliation law suits in which the dismissed plaintiffs have claimed they were terminated after questioning their institutions' Title IX policies. Although this retaliation theory has been raised in the courts, it has not yet been successful (see section 15.3.2.1., "Equal Pay Act," notes 9 and 10).

15.3.1. Employment-at-Will Contracts

Many employment agreements are considered "at-will." The basic principle of an employment-at-will contract is that an employee who has been hired for an indefinite duration and may be terminated without cause at any time, without the employer incurring liability for breach of contract. Such indefinite employment contracts are deemed terminable-at-will. The classic statement of the at-will rule was that an employer may discharge an employee for "good cause or for no cause."

However, the terminable-at-will doctrine is not absolute. There are some situations when a discharged employee may have some recourse, but as a general rule these arrangements benefit the employer. To balance some of the unfairness of the employment-at-will contract, Congress and some state legislatures, relying on *Restatement (Second) of Contracts* (§205) have enacted statutory exceptions to limit the doctrine by imposing an implied covenant of good faith and fair dealing into the employment contract. The *Restatement (Second) of Contracts* (§205) states that every contract imposes upon each party a duty of good faith and fair dealing in its performance and enforcement. There is also a trend in some jurisdictions to restrict the employment-at-will doctrine for public policy reasons when, in a narrow class of cases, the discharge is contrary to a clear mandate of public policy as articulated by constitutional, statutory, or case law.

Not every employee is an employment-at-will employee. In athletics, it is common practice for athletic directors and coaches to be under contract for a specific length of time. (For more information, see Chapter 9, section 9.2., "Types of Athletic Contracts.")

15.3.2. Employment Discrimination Statutes

In an effort to eliminate discrimination in the workplace, the U.S. Congress has passed a series of laws that prohibit unlawful compensation discrimination and other discriminatory practices. The applicable federal statutes are the Equal Pay Act of 1963, Title VII of the Civil Rights Act of 1964, and the Age Discrimination in Employment Act of 1967, which are all enforced by the Equal Employment Opportunity Commission (EEOC). Another statute that prohibits discrimination based on gender, which is only briefly discussed in this section, because it deals mainly with participation issues and not employment issues, is Title IX of the Education Amendments of 1972. (For more information see Chapter 8, section 8.1.1., "Title IX.")

15.3.2.1. *Equal Pay Act*

The Equal Pay Act of 1963 (EPA) forbids an employer from paying different salaries to members of the two sexes "for equal work on jobs the performance of which requires equal skill, effort, and responsibility, and which are performed under similar working conditions" (29 U.S.C. §206(d)(1)).

The first step under an EPA analysis is to identify male and female comparators so that their jobs can be analyzed to determine whether they are substantially equal. In selecting comparators, a plaintiff cannot compare herself or himself to a hypothetical male or female; rather, a plaintiff must show that a specific employee of the opposite sex earned higher wages for a substantially equal job. As in all EPA cases, the skills, efforts, and responsibility required by the positions, as well as the conditions under which the jobs are performed, must be evaluated and compared on a case-by-case basis.

Once the comparators have been identified, the second step outlined under the EEOC guidelines is to determine whether the jobs are substantially equal. The EPA does not require that the jobs in question be identical, only that they are substantially equal. In determining whether two jobs are substantially equal, the courts have developed a two-step analysis. The first step requires the court to determine whether the jobs to be compared have a "common core" of tasks (i.e., a significant portion of the two jobs is identical). For example, the courts have found substantial equality in cases involving female coaches of girls' basketball and male coaches of boys' basketball (*Burkey v. Marshall County Board of Education*, 513 F.Supp. 1084, 1091 [N.D. W. Va. 1981]).

Once an individual has demonstrated that the coaching jobs are substantially equal, the second step of the analysis requires that the employer show that the reason for the unequal pay falls within one of the EPA's four affirmative defenses. These defenses include a seniority system, a merit system, a system that measures earnings by quality or quantity of production, or any other factor based on something other than sex.

A good example of how the courts have interpreted the EPA is *Stanley v. University of Southern California* (see note 2). In this case, Marianne Stanley, the former head coach of the University of Southern California (USC) women's basketball team, sued the university and its athletic director, alleging violations of the Equal Pay Act and the California Fair Employment and Housing Act. Stanley was fired by USC in 1993 after her contract expired and she was unable to renegotiate a new contract. Stanley sought a contract that would have paid her a salary equivalent to that of George Raveling, the USC men's basketball coach.

Although finding that the men's and women's coaching jobs share a common core of tasks, the Ninth Circuit Court of Appeals found that Stanley and Raveling had such different levels of experience and qualifications that the university was clearly justified in paying him more, based on his greater experience. Therefore, the court held that since the pay differential between Raveling and Stanley was based on the EPA's affirmative defense of seniority and experience, there was no violation of the EPA.

In reaching the decision, the Ninth Circuit also relied on the EEOC's guidelines on the compensation of sports coaches in educational institutions. (These guidelines are addressed later in this chapter.) The EEOC's guidelines recognize as an affirmative defense that "[s]uperior experience, education, and ability may justify pay disparities if distinctions based on these criteria are not gender based." Stanley appealed her case to the U.S. Supreme Court, but the court denied her petition for a *writ of certiorari* and ended her legal challenge.

NOTES

1. Equal Pay Act guidelines are viewable online at www.eeoc.gov/epa/

2. In *Stanley v. University of Southern California,* 178 F.3d 1069 (9th Cir. 1999), *cert. denied,* 120 S.Ct. 533 (1999), a female Division I women's basketball coach filed suit due to the discrepancy between her salary and that of the men's coach. On April 20, 1993, two months prior to the expiration of Stanley's contract, Stanley and Michael Garrett, the athletic director at USC, met to negotiate a new contract. At the meeting, Stanley asked for a salary equivalent to that of head men's basketball coach George Raveling. Garrett expressly stated that USC could not pay her that salary, but that he would make her a

formal offer in writing shortly after that meeting. On April 27, 1993, Garrett offered, in writing, a three-year contract providing $80,000 in year one, $90,000 in year two, and $100,000 in year three, with a $6,000 per year housing allowance for each of the three years. The parties met again on May 27, 1993, but were still unable to reach an agreement. On June 7, 1993, Stanley proposed a three-year contract providing $96,000 per year for the first eighteen months, and a salary equivalent to that of Raveling for the remainder of the term. Garrett rejected this offer. Stanley then retained an attorney, who on June 18, 1993, proposed to Garrett a three-year contract with an automatic two-year renewal provision, and total compensation of $88,000 for year one, $97,000 for year two, and $112,000 for year three, plus additional incentives. Garrett rejected this offer and withdrew the April 27 offer.

On June 21, 1993, Garrett sent to Stanley's attorney a written offer for a one-year contract for $96,000. Stanley's existing contract expired on June 30, 1993, but Stanley continued to perform her duties. On July 13, while on a recruiting trip, Stanley asked Garrett if he would still offer her a multi-year contract. He indicated that his June 21 one-year contract offer was USC's final offer. On July 15, Garrett revoked the offer, informed Stanley that he was seeking a new coach for the team, and requested that Stanley perform no further services for USC. On August 5, 1993, Stanley initiated this action in Los Angeles County Superior Court, making claims of sex discrimination and retaliatory discharge. On August 6, 1993, the Superior Court granted Stanley's request for a temporary restraining order reinstating her as head coach of the women's team at $96,000 per year, pending the hearing on a preliminary injunction. On that same day, defendants removed the action to federal court on the ground that the complaint stated claims arising under federal law. On August 30, 1993, the district court denied the motion for a preliminary injunction, and Stanley appealed. The Ninth Circuit Court affirmed the denial of the preliminary injunction. On November 29, 1999, the U.S. Supreme Court denied Stanley's petition for a *writ of certiorari*, thus ending her legal challenge.

3. In *Perdue v. City University of New York*, 13 F.Supp. 2d 326 (E.D.N.Y. 1998), the former women's basketball coach sued the university, alleging gender discrimination. Following a trial, a jury returned a verdict in favor of Perdue on her intentional discrimination claim and EPA claim, and awarded damages in excess of $800,000. The district court in approving the award found that the plaintiff's work was equal to that of the men's basketball coach and men's sports administrator, as required to support employee's EPA claim. The court also found evidence to support the determination that the EPA violation was willful, such as to entitle the employee to liquidated damages under the act. Finally, the court concluded that the evidence also supported Perdue's intentional discrimination claim under Title VII. The evidence, with regard to Perdue's claim of intentional discrimination, showed that Perdue had to do the laundry for the women's team, a task that the male coach of the men's team refused to do. She was also required to clean the gym before and after games played by her team; she had a smaller office, smaller budget, fewer assistant coaches who worked only part-time and no locker room for her team; and she was subjected to sexual slurs and improprieties. The evidence also showed that the university had a defiant attitude toward gender-equity compliance.

4. In *Dugan v. Oregon State University*, No. 95-6250-HO (D. Or. 1998), a former interim softball coach at Oregon State University sued the university when she was fired as coach and excluded from consideration as softball coach. In suing the university, Dugan argued that she was discriminated against and that her team's dismal showing had as much to do with the school's apathy as it did with her coaching abilities. Dugan, who was hired part-time to fill in for the full-time softball coach, only made $9,750 a year. She claimed that she was paid less than male coaches in similar jobs at the school and that the school did not put enough money into the program. The university argued that Dugan's performance was not adequate, and pointed out that the two committees that let her go were made up mostly of women. Dugan's record as a coach at Oregon State University was 64–201. The year she was replaced, the team went 0–24. In November 1997, an all-female jury awarded Dugan $1.275 million—$1.09 million to come from the school and $185,000 to come from Athletic Director Dutch Baughman. The school appealed. The appellate

court upheld the jury's verdict, but lowered the damages to $623,000. The state of Oregon also agreed to pay Dugan's legal bills of more than $460,000.

5. In *Harker v. Utica College of Syracuse University*, 885 F.Supp. 378 (N.D.N.Y. 1995), a former college women's basketball and softball coach claimed that the men's basketball coach was making more money in violation of the EPA; in 1992–1993, he earned $34,814 compared to her $29,916. On defendant's motion for summary judgment, the district court found that under the EPA, the jobs were substantially equal. While rejecting the defendant's claim that the male coach had more education (master's degree over a B.A.), the court did find the male coach's length of service to be a legitimate reason for the wage differential. The male coach had nine years of experience at the college level at the time the plaintiff was hired. As stated by the court, defendant was entitled to use individualized qualifications as legitimate grounds for wage differences, provided that such qualifications were not gender-based.

6. In *Bartges v. University of North Carolina-Charlotte*, 908 F.Supp. 1312 (W.D.N.C. 1995), *aff'd*, 94 F.3d 641 (4th Cir. 1996), the court found that the plaintiff, a part-time head softball coach and part-time assistant women's basketball coach, failed to prove that her combined responsibilities were substantially equal to those of several male comparators. The comparators had full-time positions, were responsible for substantially more athletes, and had greater supervisory and other coaching responsibilities.

7. In *Deli v. University of Minnesota*, 863 F.Supp. 958 (D. Minn. 1994), the former head coach of the university's women's gymnastics team brought action against the university, alleging that it improperly paid her less than the head coaches of the men's football, hockey, and basketball teams. The district court held that Title VII and the Equal Pay Act did not prohibit salary discrimination based on the gender of athletes being coached, and that the coach failed to demonstrate that her position was substantially equal to positions of coaches of men's teams. Deli had less responsibility compared to male comparators, who coached larger teams, supervised more employees, had greater responsibility for public and media relations, and coached teams that generated substantially more spectator interest and revenue.

8. In *EEOC v. Madison Community Unit School District*, 818 F.2d 577 (7th Cir. 1987), the court found equality between the coaches of several like sports (boys' and girls' tennis, boys' and girls' track, and boys' baseball and girls' fast-pitch softball), but set aside the district court's findings of equality between different girls' and boys' sports. The court explained that "there is no objection in principle to comparing different coaching jobs," but concluded that the record before it did not support a finding of cross-sport equality. In particular, the court noted that the male coaches of different boys' sports received different salaries, and one of the female plaintiffs was paid the same wage as one of the male coaches of a boys' team. So long as the evidence does not demonstrate that the differences in salaries are based on discriminatory factors, the situation will not be found in violation of the EPA.

9. In *Bowers v. Baylor University*, 862 F.Supp. 142 (W.D. Tex. 1994), a court ruled in one of the first athletic cases resulting from Title IX. This case was also a significant employment law case. Baylor University women's basketball coach Pam Bowers was fired in 1993, allegedly for NCAA violations. Immediately after her termination, Bowers filed a complaint with both the Office of Civil Rights and the Equal Employment Opportunity Commission. Baylor notified Bowers that she would be reinstated under her employment terms that had existed since 1979. Bowers continued her employment complaints with the federal agencies after being reinstated. In 1994, Bowers was terminated because of her unsuccessful win-loss record during her tenure at Baylor. Bowers filed suit, claiming that Baylor retaliated against her for challenging Baylor's allegedly discriminatory conduct. The court denied Baylor's motion to dismiss, stating that Bowers possessed a private cause of action against the school for damages under Title IX. The court granted the individual defendant's motion to dismiss, the administrators and employees of the school, "in and of themselves," were not educational institutions subject to the statute. This case was later settled out of court.

10. In *Atkinson v. Lafayette College*, No. 01-CV-2141, 2002 U.S. Dist. LEXIS 1432 (E.D. Pa. Jan. 29, 2002), the plaintiff alleged that she was terminated from her position as Director of Athletics at Lafayette College as a result of her raising issues of gender equality in the context of submitting various budgetary plans to comply with Title IX. Her suit alleged unlawful employment discrimination and retaliation in violation of Title VII, Title IX, and the Pennsylvania Human Rights Act. The U.S. district judge in this case ruled that the plaintiff could not sue the college for retaliation under Title IX, because individuals do not have standing to sue for enforcement of the anti-retaliation regulations. However, the plaintiff was allowed to continue with her discrimination suit, which is still pending as of summer 2002.

15.3.2.2. EEOC Coaching Pay Guidelines

On October 29, 1997, the EEOC approved and issued Notice No. 915.002, "Enforcement Guidance on Sex Discrimination in the Compensation of Sports Coaches in Educational Institutions." The purpose of the EEOC guidelines is to illustrate the proper legal analysis of pay disparity cases under both Title VII of the Civil Rights Act of 1964 and the Equal Pay Act. Citing studies that show substantial differences in salaries paid to coaches of women's and men's teams in educational institutions, the guidelines indicate that while compensation of men's and women's coaches does not have to be the same, any disparity cannot be based on a coach's gender (see notes).

Although the EEOC guidelines address both the EPA and Title VII, the majority of the guidelines examine which factors to use to determine whether certain jobs are substantially equal. The first factor is equal skills. In considering whether two individuals have equal skills, the guidelines look at such factors as experience, training, education, and ability. The second factor is equal effort. To determine whether the coaching jobs require equal effort, the guidelines look at the actual requirements of the jobs being compared, and do not limit analysis to coaches of like sports. Coaches, regardless of the sport, typically are required to perform the following duties at both the high school and the college level: (1) teaching/training; (2) counseling/advising of student-athletes; (3) general program management; (4) budget management; (5) fund-raising; (6) public relations; and (7) at the college level, recruiting.

The third factor is equal responsibility. The guidelines require the EEOC to look closely at the actual duties performed by the coaches to assess whether differences in responsibility justify unequal pay. It is important to keep in mind that the jobs need not be identical. In *Brock v. Georgia Southwestern College*, 765 F.2d 1026 (11th Cir. 1985), the employer tried to justify paying the female intramural sports coach less than the male coach of the men's basketball team by arguing that she had less responsibility because she had a smaller budget and did not have to arrange off-campus games. The court, however, recognized that the female coach instead had scheduling and budgetary responsibilities, and found that the two positions were substantially equal.

The fourth element in determining whether the jobs are substantially equal is similar working conditions. The EEOC guidelines note that most coaches work under similar conditions for purposes of the EPA.

After reviewing the factors necessary to determine whether certain jobs are substantially equal, the guidelines review the available affirmative defenses as mentioned in the previous section. The burden of demonstrating that one of the four exceptions to the act applies to the positions in question is on the employer.

While the first three defenses can be applied with little or no confusion, the EEOC guideline pays particular attention to the "factor other than sex" defense because of the particular questions it presents with regard to coaching cases. As a general matter, an employer who uses this defense must show that sex is not an element underlying the wage differential either expressly or by implication. The employer must also show that the wage differential is based on factors related to the performance of the business, in this case the educational institution. Some of the factors other than sex that have been advanced to justify pay differentials in coaching include revenue production; marketplace; reliance on the employee's prior salary; gender of athletes; experience, education, ability; and other duties.

NOTES

1. EEOC's guidelines for equal pay of coaches are available at www.eeoc.gov/docs.coaches.html

2. The *1997–98 NCAA Gender Equity Study* showed that even in small and less competitive Division III institutions, 58% of dollars spent on head coaches' salaries go to men's teams and 72% of assistant coaches' salaries are spent on men's teams. This report can be viewed online at www.ncaa.org/library/research/gender_equity_study/1997-98/

3. "A Confidential Report Details Salaries of Athletics Officials," a study published March 28, 1997, in the *Chronicle of Higher Education*, found that in 1996–1997, the median personnel expenditure for men's athletics was more than $1.9 million, while the median personnel expenditure for women's sports was $431,282.

15.3.2.3. Title VII of the Civil Rights Act of 1964

In addition to the EPA, unequal pay claims can also be brought under Title VII. Title VII of the Civil Rights Act of 1964 states that it is unlawful for an employer:

> (1) to fail or refuse to hire or to discharge any individual, or otherwise to discriminate against any individual with respect to his compensation, terms, conditions, or privileges of employment, because of such individual's race, color, religion, sex, or national origin; or
>
> (2) to limit, segregate, or classify his employees or applicants for employment in any way which would deprive or tend to deprive any individual of employment opportunities or otherwise adversely affect his status as an employee, because of such individual's race, color, religion, sex, or national origin. (42 U.S.C. §2000e-2002)

The burden of proof in a claim of unequal pay is the same in both EPA and Title VII cases. However, if the discrimination is based on more than unequal pay, the employee must satisfy the following four-part test. First, he or she must be a member of a protected class; second, he or she must have qualified for and occupied a particular position; third, despite his or her qualifications, he or she was treated less favorably than a coworker or fellow applicant; and fourth, the circumstances gave rise to an inference of discrimination. Once the plaintiff is able to show that he or she has been discriminated against in violation of Title VII, the employer must demonstrate a legitimate nondiscriminatory reason for the disparate treatment. Title VII allows the same four affirmative defenses as the EPA—seniority system, merit system, system based on quality or quantity of production, or any other factor other than sex.

Although there are some similarities between Title VII and the EPA, they are different in their scope of coverage. Title VII is much broader, covering all aspects of the employment relationship, not just wages (as the EPA does). Title VII also caps the maximum amount of money that can be awarded in damages at $300,000 in compensatory damages plus punitive damages and counsel fees.

15.3.2.4. *Gender Discrimination Cases Under Title VII*

An example of how the courts have applied Title VII to sex discrimination cases is *Ortiz-Del Valle v. NBA,* 42 F.Supp. 2d 334 (S.D.N.Y. 1999). Sandra Ortiz-Del Valle, a female basketball referee, sued the NBA, claiming that the league improperly failed to hire her as a NBA referee in violation of Title VII and the state of New York Human Rights Law. At the conclusion of a six-day jury trial, the NBA was found to have intentionally discriminated against Ms. Oritz-Del Valle due to her gender. The jury awarded Ortiz-Del Valle $100,000 in damages for lost wages, $750,000 for emotional distress, and $7 million in punitive damages.

After the verdict, the NBA moved for a new trial or, in the alternative, a reduction of damages. The NBA argued that Ortiz-Del Valle did not meet the qualifications. In rejecting the NBA's argument, the district court found that the NBA's requirements for referees were discriminatory. For example, Ortiz-Del Valle was told to upgrade her referee schedule and get an NCAA Division I men's schedule, but she was unable to obtain an NCAA Division I schedule because she is a woman. The NBA also invited various male referees into the NBA training program with less experience than she had and without an NCAA Division I men's schedule. The district court also held that there was enough circumstantial and direct evidence for a reasonable jury to have found a continuous policy barring women from employment as NBA referees. The evidence included the fact that no women were ever hired as NBA referees or invited to the NBA referee training camp until sometime in 1995. Statements were made to the plaintiff that she was "more qualified than some of the men" working for the NBA or the CBA, but that Darrell Garretson, chief of staff of officials, "had a problem with her being female." In addition, the employment form that potential NBA referees filled out had a space to indicate the name of the applicant's wife, but not the name of the applicant's husband.

The appeals court did, however, find that the damages awarded were grossly excessive. The court held that *remittitur,* the process by which a court compels a plaintiff to choose between reduction of an excessive verdict and a new trial, was appropriate in this case. Therefore, although the court found that the NBA violated Title VII and was liable, the damages were reduced to $250,000 in punitive damages, $76,926.20 in lost wages, and $20,000 for emotional distress.

The EEOC has also found that reverse discrimination is a violation of Title VII. For example, in *Medcalf v. University of Pennsylvania,* No. 00-07101, 2001 U.S. Dist. LEXIS 10155 (E.D. Pa. June 19, 2001), an EEOC investigation found that Penn officials discriminated against male applicants when hiring the new women's crew coach. The EEOC found that Penn took extraordinary measures to recruit only female candidates and that the university failed to interview Andrew Medcalf, the assistant men's rowing coach at Penn. Medcalf was overlooked even though he was highly recommended by both his immediate supervisor, who said he was highly qualified, and several current male and female rowers at Penn. The case went to federal court, where a jury awarded Medcalf over $115,000 in damages.

NOTES _____

1. In *Kemether v. Pennsylvania Interscholastic Athletic Ass'n,* 15 F.Supp.2d 740 (E.D. Pa. 1998), *aff'd,* No. 96-6986 1999 U.S. Dist. LEXIS 17326 (E.D. Pa. Nov. 8, 1999), a female basketball referee sued the Pennsylvania Interscholastic Athletic Association

(PIAA), alleging gender-based discrimination in her assignments to officiate high school interscholastic games. The district court, in rejecting PIAA's summary judgment argument, held that although the PIAA was not Kemether's employer during the regular season, for purposes of Title VII, the issue of whether PIAA was as an employment agency under Title VII precluded summary judgment.

2. In *Coble v. Hot Springs School District No. 6*, 682 F.2d 721 (8th Cir. 1982), the school district claimed that male coaches were entitled to higher salaries because of longer-term contracts and higher extra duty stipends than female coaches. The court rejected this argument by pointing out that "the assignment of extended term contracts and extra-duty stipends to particular coaching assignments is itself subject to employer discrimination on the basis of sex."

3. In *Lowrey v. Texas A&M*, 11 F.Supp.2d 895 (S.D. Tex. 1998), Jan Lowrey, the former women's basketball coach at Tarleton State University (part of the Texas A&M University System), charged that she was illegally discriminated against based upon gender. Specifically, Lowrey alleged that Tarleton demoted her from her position as Women's Athletic Coordinator and refused to promote her to the position of Athletic Director in retaliation for her role on a Gender Equity Task Force that had identified violations of both Title VII and Title IX at Tarleton. In denying summary judgment for the defendant the court found there was a valid claim for retaliation under Title VII and Title IX, as well as a pay discrimination claim under Title VII and the Equal Pay Act. A decision in the case is pending.

4. In *Pitts v. State*, No. CIV-93-1341-A (W.D. Okla. 1994), the coach of the women's Oklahoma State University golf team brought suit under Title IX, Title VII, and the Equal Pay Act. The men's golf coach received $63,000 in salary while the plaintiff received only approximately $35,712. Although the jury found no violation of the Equal Pay Act, the plaintiff was able to collect $30,000, with $6,000 for emotional distress, on the Title IX and Title VII claims.

5. In *Sobba v. Pratt Community College & Area Vocational School*, 117 F.Supp.2d 1043 (D. Kan. 2000), the plaintiff tennis coach/dormitory supervisor alleged that Pratt C.C. violated the Equal Pay Act by paying her less than male coaches in similar positions, and also engaged in unlawful gender discrimination in violation of Title VII by discriminating in wages. The plaintiff failed to convince the court that her work was "substantially equal" to that of certain male coaches who were paid more by the school to coach other sports. The plaintiff also alleged that the school gave "fluff" jobs to male coaches, while giving more difficult assignments to female coaches, such as assigning female coaches to the most difficult dormitories. This case was unique because Sobba coached both the men's and women's tennis teams. However, the court agreed with the defense's arguments that certain other sports required more skill and/or time to coach effectively. For example, the track coach was responsible for training athletes in multiple events and the softball coach was responsible for supervising more athletes. The softball coach was also responsible for managing a larger budget. The U.S. District Court granted partial summary judgment to the defendant.

6. In *Babyak v. Smith College*, No. 99-204 (Hamden Co., Mass. Dist. Ct. 2001), a jury awarded former Smith College basketball and soccer head coach James Babyak $1.65 million in an age and gender discrimination suit. The court agreed that the all-women's college discriminated against Babyak during his tenure at Smith. Babyak claimed that in the late 1980s Smith officials had demoted him from his position as Associate Athletic Director, as the administration allegedly preferred a female for the position. Babyak, who compiled a 188–216 record in sixteen seasons at Smith, claimed he was fired in 1997 because the college wanted a woman and someone younger for his position. Babyak's firing came after his basketball team had established a school record for wins, and his soccer team had won its sixth conference championship. The plaintiff also alleged that the school's athletic administration had become increasingly critical of his coaching style, despite having never attended a practice or a game. The $1.65 million award to Babyak included $600,000 in lost income, $550,000 for age discrimination, $250,000 for gender discrimination and $250,000 for retaliation. An appeal is pending.

15.3.2.5. Race Discrimination Cases Under Title VII

An example of how the courts have applied Title VII to race discrimination cases is *Wallace v. Texas Tech University,* 80 F.3d 1042 (5th Cir. 1996). Phillip Wallace was hired as an assistant basketball coach at Texas Tech University with a one-year contract. Wallace, an African American, had no prior coaching experience, but he had played on the Texas Tech basketball team during his college years. James Dickey, the head coach, also hired another assistant coach for the same period. The other assistant, a white male who had seven years of college coaching experience, was paid $57.83 per month more than Wallace. When Wallace's contract expired, it was not renewed and another African American replaced him.

Wallace sued Texas Tech and Dickey, alleging that they discriminated against him on the basis of his race in violation of Title VII. To succeed on a claim of race discrimination under Title VII, a plaintiff must first prove a prima facie case of discrimination. A plaintiff can prove a prima facie case through a four-element test that allows an inference of discrimination or through direct evidence of discriminatory motive. The four-element test requires that the plaintiff show (1) he or she is a member of a protected class; (2) he or she is qualified for the position; (3) he or she was discharged; and (4) after being discharged, he or she was replaced with a person who is not a member of the protected class.

In upholding the district court's judgment in favor of the university and head coach, the court of appeals held that Wallace failed to establish either that his contract was not renewed based on race or that his receiving a lower salary than a white coach was based on race. Wallace's contract was not renewed, the court concluded, because of poor job performance. Evidence showed that Wallace was unwilling to follow instructions, and that he repeatedly questioned Dickey's coaching judgment. As for the disparity in pay, the white coach had significantly greater college coaching experience. Title VII and the EEOC coaching guidelines state that differences in work experience are a valid nondiscriminatory rationale to justify different salaries for employees performing the same job. Since Texas Tech was able to establish a nondiscriminatory motive for the pay differential, the burden fell to Wallace to show that the articulated reason was only a pretext. Wallace was unable to prove this.

NOTE _____

1. In *Cobb v. University of Southern California*, 45 Cal. App. 4th 1140 (Cal. Ct. App. 1996), Marvin Cobb, assistant athletic director for the University of Southern California, filed racial discrimination and breach of contract claims against USC. He charged that he was denied promotions and harassed because of his complaints regarding the academic abilities and preparation of African American student-athletes. Specifically, Cobb alleged that the University failed to afford many of its African American student-athletes an educational opportunity. He also alleged that USC's recruitment of academically underprepared student-athletes, with only a minimal likelihood of succeeding academically, constituted exploitation. The jury awarded Cobb $2.1 million on the breach of contract claim (later reduced to $1.1 million). Cobb's discrimination claims were later dismissed.

15.3.2.6. Age Discrimination in Employment Act of 1967

Section 623 of the Age Discrimination in Employment Act of 1967 (ADEA) states that:

(a) it shall be unlawful for an employer

   (1) to fail or refuse to hire or to discharge any individual or otherwise discriminate against any individual with respect to his compensation, terms, conditions, or privileges of employment, because of such individual's age; or

   (2) to limit, segregate, or classify his employees in any way which would deprive or tend to deprive any individual of employment opportunities or otherwise adversely affect his status as an employee, because of such individual's age. (29 U.S.C. §623)

The burden of proof under the ADEA is similar to those for Title VII. To establish a prima facie case of age discrimination under the ADEA, the plaintiff must satisfy four elements: (1) he or she is a member of a protected class; (2) he or she was qualified for the position; (3) he or she was discharged; and (4) he or she was either (a) replaced by someone outside the protected class, (b) replaced by someone younger, or (c) otherwise discharged because of his or her age. The third alternative of the fourth element applies in circumstances where the plaintiff is not replaced.

The ADEA authorizes relief in the form of reinstatement, back pay, injunctive relief, declaratory judgment, and attorney's fees (29 U.S.C. §626(b)). In addition, in the case of a willful violation of the act, the ADEA authorizes an award of liquidated damages equal to the back pay award (29 U.S.C. §626(b)).

An example of how the courts have applied the ADEA to age discrimination cases is *Moore v. University of Notre Dame*, 22 F.Supp. 2d 896 (N.D. Ind. 1998). The plaintiff, Joseph Moore, was the offensive line coach for Notre Dame from 1988 until he was fired in 1996. Moore, who claimed that he was fired because he was "too old" and would not be able to continue to coach for another full five-year period, sued the university, alleging age discrimination under ADEA. Notre Dame claimed that Moore was dismissed because he did not measure up to the standards of Notre Dame. The university also claimed that Moore had intimidated, abused, and made offensive remarks to players.

In ruling against Notre Dame, a jury found that the school did in fact fire Moore because of his age, in violation of the ADEA. The district court, however, refused to grant Moore's request for reinstatement to his former coaching position. The court held that although reinstatement is the preferred remedy in a discrimination case, it is not always an appropriate remedy. Before reinstatement is ordered, the court must consider the hostility in the past employment relationship and the absence of an available position for the plaintiff. In this case, the court found that Moore's reinstatement would cause significant friction as well as disruption of the current football program. Even if Moore's return would not create hostility and undue friction, there was someone else currently occupying Moore's former position. Therefore, there was no available position for Moore.

In lieu of reinstatement, the court granted Moore's request for front pay. Front pay is a lump sum payment representing the difference between the earnings an employee would have received in his old employment and the earnings he can be expected to receive in his present and future (and, by hypothesis, inferior) employment. Although such an award remains discretionary with the court, front pay is an available remedy under ADEA. Its purpose is to ensure that a person who has been discriminated against on the basis of age is made whole, not to guarantee every claimant who cannot mitigate damages by finding comparable work, an annuity to age seventy. The court in *Moore* defined front pay as "a lump sum . . . representing the discounted present value of the difference between the earnings [an employee] would have received in his old employment and the earnings he can be expected to receive in his present and future, and by hypothesis, inferior, employment."

In determining the amount of front pay to award, the court should consider whether the plaintiff has a reasonable prospect of obtaining comparable employment; whether the time period for the award is relatively short; whether the plaintiff intends to work or is physically capable of working; and whether liquidated damages have been awarded. The final judgment against Notre Dame was $75,577.68 in front pay, $9,672.45 in costs, $394,865.74 in attorney fees and expenses, $42,935.28 in back pay, and an additional $42,935.28 in liquidated damages.

NOTES

1. In *Austin v. Cornell University,* 891 F.Supp. 740 (N.D.N.Y. 1995), two former seasonal employees of the university golf course sued Cornell University for age discrimination after they were not rehired. In rejecting Cornell's motion for summary judgment, the district court held that the plaintiffs raised genuine issues of material fact regarding Cornell's refusal to rehire them. In addition, the court held that the head golf professional and associate director of athletics could be individually liable.

2. Also see *Babyak*, section 15.3.2.4., note 6.

15.3.2.7. *State Discrimination Laws*

Besides federal statutes, discrimination claims may be brought under state laws, which may actually offer greater protection than the federal statutes. For example, under New Jersey's Law Against Discrimination (LAD), an individual is not only entitled to compensatory damages but may also be entitled to punitive damages and attorney's fees. Unlike Title VII, however, the LAD does not contain a damages cap. It is important to note that discrimination laws have different names in each state. For example, Marianne Stanley filed a state discrimination claim under the California Fair Employment and Housing Act. Most often, the state statutes can be found under the state's Human Rights Act.

NOTE

1. In 1995, a District of Columbia Superior Court jury awarded Sanya Tyler, an associate athletic director and the women's basketball coach at Howard University, was awarded $2.39 million in a sexual discrimination case against the university. The damages were later reduced to $250,000. The jury found that the university violated the D.C. Human Rights Act as well as Title IX and the Equal Pay Act by discriminating and retaliating against Tyler. While Tyler and her male counterpart had identical job descriptions, Tyler was paid $44,000 and the men's coach was paid $78,000. See, *The NCAA News*, October 2, 1995, p. 6. In 2000, Tyler sued the university for $105 million for wrongful termination, claiming that she was fired in retaliation for her earlier lawsuit. The case is pending.

15.3.3. Sexual Harassment

Sexual harassment, which is a violation of both Title VII and Title IX of the Education Amendments Act of 1972, is an important issue for athletic administrators. It is essential that athletic administrators have a basic knowledge of the legal aspects of sexual harassment, to ensure that their organization policies, procedures and practices can work towards its prevention. Sexual harassment is a serious offense, and coaches and administrators need to be aware that behavior once seen as merely rude or offensive may now result in legal action. Sexual harassment can be loosely defined as any unwelcome, unsolicited, non-reciprocal or uninvited behavior of a sexual nature that interferes with a person's work or education. This can include any conduct, including profane language, off-color jokes, leering, or ogling, that refers to sex. Any unwanted touching, patting, hugging, pinching or request for sexual favors in return for benefits also constitutes sexual harassment.

There are two types of sexual harassment: *quid pro quo* and *hostile environment*. *Quid pro quo* sexual harassment occurs when an employer or coach grants or withholds benefits, such as pay or scholarship, as a result of an employee's or athlete's willingness or refusal to submit to the employer or coach's sexual demands. The critical point is not whether the victim submits voluntarily, but whether the conduct he/she submits to is unwanted. *Hostile environment* sexual harassment exists when an employer's or coach's conduct is so severe that it creates an intimidating, hostile, or offensive environment that interferes with the employee's or athlete's ability to perform his or her work. Hostile environment sexual harassment is not necessarily sexual harassment because it involves sexual gestures, language, or activities, but because it is motivated by the victim's sex. The Supreme Court has also determined that the sex of the victim does not have to be different from that of the harasser for there to be sexual harassment.

Athletic administrators need to develop comprehensive policies and conduct training sessions in order for their staff and student-athletes to be knowledgeable about sexual harassment issues. The objective should be to ensure a safe environment while also demanding that sexual harassment of any kind will not be tolerated.

An example of how the courts have dealt with sexual harassment in the workplace under Title VII is *Faragher v. Boca Raton*, 524 U.S. 775 (1998). In *Faragher*, a former lifeguard for the city of Boca Raton sued the city under Title VII for sexual harassment, based on the conduct of her two supervisors. Faragher alleged that her supervisors had created a sexually hostile atmosphere at work by repeatedly subjecting her and other female lifeguards to uninvited and offensive touching, lewd remarks, and offensive references to women. Faragher claimed that this conduct, which went on for five years, constituted discrimination in the terms, conditions, and privileges of her employment, in violation of Title VII.

After concluding that the supervisors' conduct was sufficiently serious to alter the conditions of Faragher's employment and constitute an abusive working environment, the U.S. Supreme Court held that the city (employer) could be subject to vicarious liability (see Chapter 3, Section 3.6., "Vicarious Liability") under Title VII for discrimination caused by a supervisor. The employer, however, may raise an affirmative defense in such a case that looks to the reasonableness of employer's conduct in preventing and correcting harassing conduct and to the reasonableness of employee's conduct in seeking to avoid harm. In *Faragher*, the Supreme Court concluded that the city was vicariously liable because of its failure to exercise reasonable care to prevent harassing behavior.

The Supreme Court further specified the meaning of "reasonable care" in *Burlington Industries Inc. v. Ellerth*, 524 U.S. 742 (1998). In this hostile environment case, the defendant company argued that it should not be held vicariously liable because it possessed a well-advertised sexual harassment complaint procedure, which the plaintiff had failed to utilize. In offering decision for the court, Justice Kennedy explained that a clear and fair complaint procedure will normally absolve an organization from vicarious liability for hostile environment complaints.

> An employer is subject to vicarious liability to a victimized employee for an actionable hostile environment created by a supervisor with immediate (or successively higher) authority over the employee. When no tangible employment action is taken, a defending employer may raise an affirmative defense to liability or damages, subject to proof by a preponderance of the evidence. . . . The defense comprises two necessary elements: (a) that the employer exercised reasonable care to prevent and correct promptly any sexually harassing behavior, and (b) that the plaintiff employee unreasonably failed to take advantage of any preventive or corrective opportunities provided by the employer or to avoid harm otherwise. While proof that an employer had promulgated an anti-harassment policy with a complaint procedure is not necessary in every instance as a matter of law, the need for a stated policy suitable to the employment circumstances may appropriately be addressed in any case when litigating the first element of the defense. And while proof that an employee failed to fulfill the corresponding obligation of reasonable care to avoid harm is not limited to showing any unreasonable failure to use any complaint procedure provided by the employer, *a demonstration of such failure will normally suffice to satisfy the employer's burden under the second element of the defense* [italics added]. No affirmative defense is available, however, when the supervisor's harassment culminates in a tangible employment action.

Based on the above decision, it behooves all athletic organizations to (1) establish a grievance procedure for sexual harassment complaints and (2) publicize the organization's grievance procedure and its sexual harassment policy. It is important to point out that Justice Kennedy's opinion states that an organization *can* be vicariously liable for quid pro quo harassment, even if it possesses a grievance system. Therefore, an athletic organization should make every effort to eliminate an employee's harassing behavior before the behavior escalates to the withholding of benefits or a promotion.

The Department of Education Office of Civil Rights defines sexual harassment under Title IX thus:

> unwelcome sexual advances, requests for sexual favors, or other verbal or physical conduct of a sexual nature, imposed on the basis of sex, that could (a) deny, limit, or provide different aids, benefits, services or opportunities, (b) condition the provision of aids, benefits, services or opportunities, or (c) otherwise limit a student's enjoyment of any right, privilege, advantage, or opportunity protected by Title IX.

An example of how the courts have dealt with sexual harassment in federally funded institutions under Title IX is *Franklin v. Gwinnett County Public Schools*, 503 U.S. 60 (1992). The plaintiff, a female high school student, filed suit against the defendant, alleging that she was subjected to continual sexual harassment from Andrew Hill, a coach and teacher at the high school, and that school officials failed to stop Hill's continued harassment. According to the complaint, Hill initiated sexual discussions with Franklin in which Hill asked Franklin about her sexual experiences with her boyfriend and whether she would consider having sexual intercourse with an older man, that Hill forcibly kissed Franklin on the school grounds, and that on two or three occasions, Hill interrupted a class, requested that Franklin be excused, and took her to a private office where he subjected Franklin to coercive intercourse.

Franklin further alleged that even though school officials investigated and knew of Hill's sexual harassment of Franklin and other female students, school administrators took no action to halt Hill's sexual harassment of Franklin and even tried to discourage Franklin from pressing charges against Hill. The principal of the high school closed his investigation into Franklin's allegations when Hill resigned at the end of the school year, on the condition that all matters pending against him would be dropped.

In August 1988, Franklin filed a complaint with the Department of Education's Office of Civil Rights (OCR), alleging that she had been subject to sexual harassment in violation of Title IX. Following a six-month investigation, the OCR found the Gwinnett County School District in violation of Title IX. In particular, the OCR found that Gwinnett County School District had violated Franklin's rights by subjecting her to physical and verbal sexual harassment and by interfering with her right to complain about such conduct. The OCR, however, failed to act, and closed its investigation after being assured that the school district would implement a grievance procedure to prevent future violations. Unhappy with the outcome of the OCR's investigation, Franklin filed a Title IX lawsuit seeking damages against the Gwinnett County School District.

The U.S. Supreme Court, in reversing the lower courts, held that "Title IX placed on the Gwinnett County Schools the duty not to discriminate on the basis of sex, and when a supervisor sexually harasses a subordinate because of the subordinate's sex, that supervisor discriminates on the basis of sex." The same rule, the Court held, applies when a teacher or coach "sexually harasses and abuses a student."

NOTES

1. For more information on the prevention of sexual harassment in the workplace, see the Web site for the Educational Resource Information Center: www.ed.gov/databases/ERIC_Digests/ed429188.html. Also see Jim McKay, *Managing Gender* (Albany: State University of New York Press, 1997). For more information specific to the sports industry, see Lisa Pike Masteralexis, "Sexual Harassment and Athletics," 6 *Marquette Sports Law Review* 2 (April/May 1995).

2. In 1999, the University of Alabama at Tuscaloosa paid a university athletic department employee $350,000 to settle a sexual harassment case involving her and the head football coach, Mike DuBose. Alabama fired the athletic director, Bob Bockrath, in the wake of the sexual harassment allegations.

3. In *Davis v. Monroe County Board of Education*, 526 U.S. 629 (1999), a parent, on behalf of a fifth-grade student, sued school board and officials, alleging that the defendants violated Title IX, and 42 U.S.C. §1983, by failing to remedy a classmate's sexual harassment of the student. The Supreme Court held that a private action for damages may lie against a school board under Title IX in cases of student-on-student harassment, but only where the school acts with deliberate indifference and the harassment is so severe that it effectively bars the victim's access to an educational opportunity or benefit.

4. In *Gebser v. Lago Vista Independent School District*, 524 U.S. 274 (1998), a student who has been the victim of sexual harassment by an employee of an institution subject to Title IX may not bring a private damages claim against the institution "unless an official of the [institution] who at a minimum has authority to institute corrective measures on the [institution's] behalf has actual notice of, and is deliberately indifferent to, the [employee's] misconduct." This was a 5–4 U.S. Supreme Court decision.

5. In *Klemencic v. Ohio State University*, 10 F.Supp. 2d 911 (S.D. Ohio 1998), a student athlete at Ohio State sued the university and Thomas Ed Crawford, assistant coach of the women's track team, claiming sexual harassment. Klemencic alleged that she was subjected to quid pro quo sexual harassment by Crawford, and as a result of her refusal, was denied access to the team. The district court rejected Klemencic's argument, and found that the coach did not create a hostile educational environment when he asked the student to go out with him or by sending her a sexually suggestive magazine article.

6. In *Rosa H. v. San Elizario Independent School District*, 106 F.3d 648 (5th Cir. 1997), a high school student brought Title IX action against the school district, alleging the district's negligent failure to prevent a teacher of an after-school karate class from committing sexual abuse. The Fifth Circuit Court held that the student who has been sexually abused by her teacher could not recover from the school district under Title IX unless the school district actually knew there was substantial risk that sexual abuse would occur.

7. In *Doe v. Taylor Independent School District*, 15 F.3d 443 (5th Cir. 1994), a high school student brought civil rights action against the school district, superintendent, and principal, alleging sexual molestation by a teacher and coach. The court of appeals held that the student was deprived of her liberty interest recognized under the substantive due process component of the Fourteenth Amendment when her teacher sexually abused her. The court of appeals also held that school officials could be found liable for the actions of school employees when the student can show that the officials, by action or inaction, demonstrate deliberate indifference to the sexual harassment.

8. In *Alexander v. Yale*, 631 F.2d 178 (2d Cir. 1980), the first case to examine whether the scope of Title IX covered sexual harassment, five students sued Yale University, alleging that they were sexually harassed by Yale faculty members and administrators. The plaintiffs further alleged that Yale was in violation of Title IX by refusing to seriously consider the students' complaints of sexual harassment. The court held that a party seeking relief under Title IX must demonstrate a personal "distinct and palpable injury," and the relief requested must "redound to that party's personal benefit." Former students lacked standing to get any relief from sexual harassment charges.

ADDITIONAL LEGAL CONCERNS

INTRODUCTION

Athletic administrators and sports lawyers should be aware of and concerned about three additional legal areas: criminal law, illegal gambling, and federal disability legislation. The three areas covered briefly in Chapter 16 provide an overview and some background information on potential legal problems in these areas.

16.1. ATHLETE VIOLENCE AND CRIMINAL CONDUCT

Every year there are a number of incidents, either during an athletic event or off the field, that raise the public's interest and concern about athletes who are charged with criminal law offenses. Violence within the context of sports is a familiar subject to nearly every sports fan. Many of the incidents of violent conduct in sport go beyond the reasonable scope of risks associated with sport. For example, acts that are clearly criminal in the non-sport context seem to be licensed if they take place on the playing field. Many people consider the punishment of fines and suspensions for violent action on the field to be minor when compared with the nature of the conduct. For example, in 2000, Marty McSorley of the NHL's Boston Bruins took a two-handed swing with his hockey stick to the right temple of Vancouver Canuck Donald Brashear, causing him to fall and hit his head on the ice. Brashear was carried off on a stretcher, blood flowing from his nose, and taken a hospital, where he was diagnosed as having a concussion. Another example occurred in 1997, when Latrell Sprewell of the NBA's Golden State Warriors attacked his coach, P. J. Carlesimo, during practice and threatened to kill him (see note 3).

Such examples of violent conduct might have resulted in prison sentences had they taken place outside the sporting arena. Yet, McSorley's criminal trial resulted only in probation, while no criminal charges were filed in the case of Sprewell. With violent conduct in athletic competition on the rise, the ability of leagues to control violence through league-imposed fines and penalties has been questioned. Many people argue that legislative action is needed to curb the violence (see section 16.1.6., "Solutions to the Problem of Sports Violence") and others believe that criminal law should be more readily invoked.

Athlete violence and crime occurring "off the field" has also become a heated issue with sports organizations and fans, especially since the O. J. Simpson murder trial in the mid-1990s and the Thomas Junta "rink rage" case in 2001 (see note 4). However, most of this section will deal with athlete violence occurring *during* a game or practice, or perhaps right before or after the game or practice. Section 16.1.5., "Off-the-Field Conduct," briefly addresses the legal issues that arise when crimes are committed outside the scope of athletic competition.

Criminal law is based on society's need to be free from harmful conduct. Criminal law defines criminal conduct and prescribes the punishment to be imposed on a person convicted of engaging in such conduct. In addition to its broad aim of preventing injury to the health, safety, morals, and welfare of the public, criminal law is designed to uphold society's broader notions of morality.

Understanding the basis of criminal law makes it easier to understand why violent and possibly criminal behavior is looked on differently when the violence occurs in a sporting event. All the harm and violence are confined to the participants, who know and assume the risks of the game. The public, while sitting in the stands or watching on television, is not subjected to any risk of physical harm. This may be an underlying reason why society treats sports violence differently from violence in the streets. Yet, what about when the violent actions are upon fans or officials? (See sections 16.1.3., "Player Versus Fan Violence," and 16.1.4., "Player Versus Official Violence.")

Opponents of sports violence argue that this approach overlooks the interests of society as a whole in protecting society's notions of morality. Opponents contend that the incidents just cited evoke a sense of moral outrage and a feeling that some kind of punishment should be exacted. The existence in sporting events of socially unacceptable conduct that is treated with impunity conflicts with society's overall concept of good and bad conduct that has long been espoused by educational and religious institutions. However, violent conduct in sports continues to be punishable only by league sanctions that arguably are much less severe than punishment that would be ordered in criminal courts.

In order to determine whether or not criminal law sanctions should be imposed for incidents of sports violence, it is useful to examine the rationale behind criminal punishment. Prison terms are imposed for a purpose, and an examination of sports violence situations relative to criminal law may be helpful. A primary rationale for criminal sanctions is the prevention theory—that is, punishment will keep a criminal from becoming a repeat offender. The theory's aim is to rehabilitate the offender in the criminal justice system. In sports, rehabilitation would be a desirable goal if treating the offending athlete as a criminal would actually prevent the repetition of dangerous conduct.

A second theory behind punishment for criminal conduct is the deterrence theory, that exacting punishment for bad conduct deters others from committing crimes, lest they suffer the same fate. This, too, could perhaps have valuable applications in the area of sports violence. Athletes would, in theory, be less likely to engage in violent conduct that is outside the scope of the risks of the sport if they feared criminal punishment.

One final theory that is relevant to sports violence is the education theory of punishment, which states that the publicity surrounding a criminal trial and the subsequent punishment of criminals serves to educate the public as to the nature of right and wrong. This theory may be the strongest one for treating sports violence as a criminal act. By failing to treat violent acts as crimes simply because they take place in the limited area of sports, society is sending out a contradictory message and perhaps teaching the public, especially the younger public, that violent acts are permissible under certain circumstances.

NOTES —————————————————————————————

1. For more information on sports violence and criminal law, see:

(a) Jon Leizman, *Let's Kill 'Em: Understanding and Controlling Violence in Sports* (Lanham, MD: University Press of America, 1999).

(b) Jeff Benedict and Don Yaeger, *Pros and Cons: The Criminals Who Play in the NFL* (New York: Warner Books, 1998).

(c) Also see the following: Paul M. Anderson, "When Violence Is Not Part of the Game: Regulating Sports Violence in Professional Team Sports," 3 *Contemporary Issues in Law* 240 (1998).

2. Golden State Warrior Latrell Sprewell attacked his coach, P. J. Carlesimo, during a practice on December 1, 1997. In that attack, "between seven and ten seconds elapsed during which Sprewell had his hands around the Coach's neck." Carlesimo was not

injured. Sprewell then left the court for "between ten and 20 minutes," before returning for an apparent attempted second attack on Carlesimo. However, he was restrained before reaching the coach. The Warriors terminated Sprewell's contract and the nearly $25 million remaining on it, claiming they had "cause" to do so because of the assault. Commissioner David Stern suspended Sprewell from the NBA for one year, emphasizing the "premeditated nature" of the second incident. The Players Association appealed, calling the sanctions against Sprewell "arbitrary and capricious" and lacking "just cause." In *In Arbitrator's Decision and Award Involving Latrell Sprewell, The National Basketball Players Association, The Golden State Warriors, and The National Basketball Association* (John D. Feerick Grievance Arbitrator, March 4, 1998), Arbitrator Feerick overruled the Warriors and the NBA, holding that the Warriors must honor the final two years of Sprewell's contract or trade him. Feerick did, however, uphold the suspension for the remainder of the season (not the full calendar year Stern had imposed) and the player's resulting loss of $6.5 million in salary. He reasoned that the team and league's dual penalties violated the principle of double jeopardy, and that league sanctions against more serious player violence had been less severe in the past. Specifically, assaults resulting in serious injuries had produced suspensions no longer than twenty-six games. Sprewell subsequently filed suit against the NBA and the Warriors in federal district court, seeking the $6.4 million in salary that he lost during his suspension. Sprewell was denied relief in *Sprewell v. Golden State Warriors*, 231 F.3d 520 (9th Cir. 2000). For more information, see Roger A. Javier, "You Cannot Choke Your Boss & Hold Your Job Unless You Play in the NBA: The Latrell Sprewell Incident Undermines Disciplinary Authority in the NBA," 7 *Villanova Sports and Entertainment Law Journal* 209 (2000). Also see Chapter 11, section 11.3.14., "Grievance Procedures in Professional Sports."

3. In *Massachusetts v. Junta* (Middlesex [MA] Superior Court, 2002), a case involving violence between parents of athletes, in January 2002, a Massachusetts jury convicted Thomas Junta of involuntary manslaughter in the death of Michael Costin. In July 2000, the two fathers engaged in an argument during a youth hockey practice involving their 12 year old sons. Junta alleged that Costin, the boys' coach, was allowing too much rough play. Junta and Costin scuffled on the ice before the fight was broken up and Junta was removed from the arena. However, Junta soon returned to the arena and attacked Costin outside the boys' locker room. In the ensuing brawl, Junta repeatedly punched Costin and slammed his head into the floor. The resulting injuries lead to Costin's death. Junta was sentenced to six to ten years in prison.

16.1.1. Defining a Crime

In order to apply criminal law sanctions for undesirable conduct, the act that will incur penalties must first be defined in a way that ensures predictability. This issue is especially difficult in the area of sports violence. Certain sports involve a great deal of physical contact and intimidation. Therefore, a certain amount of physical but legal contact may be considered part of the game. The problem is in drawing a neat and predictable line as to when an act goes beyond the scope of the game and becomes criminal in nature.

The crime of battery is the offense that most often applies to sports violence. Battery can be defined as an unlawful application of force to the person of another, resulting in bodily injury. The requirement that the battery be "unlawful" is the key to the exemption of sports-related batteries. Although the issue is often couched in such legal terms as "consent" or "assumption of risk," the crux of the problem in distinguishing sports violence from criminal acts is unlawfulness. Society has often exempted sports violence from criminal law by treating it as lawful.

For conduct to be criminal, most offenses require that there be an *actus reus* and a *mens rea*, a guilty act accompanied by a guilty mind. The elements of a criminal battery are (1) a guilty state of mind (*mens rea*), (2) an act (*actus reus*), (3) a physical touching or harming the victim, and (4) causation—that is, the act must cause the touching or harm. The state of mind for criminal battery does not require actual intent. An extreme conscious disregard of known serious risks, called criminal negligence, will suffice. The criminal statutes in most states define some acts as aggravated battery and punish them as felonies. For example, the use of a deadly weapon or the causing of serious bodily injury is an example of aggravated battery. Interestingly, ordinary objects can qualify as deadly objects if they are used in a way that can cause death. Hockey sticks, baseballs, bats, and football helmets may qualify as deadly objects.

The violence that occurs in sports today clearly meets certain elements of battery in some cases. The unique factor is that the acts occur within the confines of athletics, which underscores the difficult issue of determining when an act within the confines of sports becomes a crime. The problem is that certain sports are extremely physical, and certain violent physical contact is condoned under the rules. Therefore, acts that are crimes on the streets become legal in the arena because it is difficult to meet the legal definition of criminal battery.

A defendant in a criminal prosecution involving sports violence has two defenses available: consent and self-defense. Consent is not normally a defense to a criminal act. The general rule is that one cannot consent to be the victim of a crime, and this rule is true except for certain specific cases; those exceptions are crimes in which a lack of consent forms one of the elements of the crime.

Sports violence, especially the crime of battery, falls in a more difficult area to define compared with non-sports-related violence. Battery is not a crime that has lack of consent of the victim as an element, but in certain battery cases, the unlawful-application-of-force element is not present because of consent. A consents-to application of force is not unlawful. The Model Penal Code (see note 1), Section 2.11, provides:

> When conduct is charged to constitute an offense because it causes or threatens bodily harm, consent to such conduct or to the infliction of such harm is a defense if: (a) the bodily harm consented to is not serious; or (b) the conduct and the harm are *reasonably foreseeable hazards* of joint participation in the *lawful* athletic contest or competitive sport [emphasis added].

The most difficult issue concerning the consent defense is drawing a line between reasonably foreseeable hazards that may be consented to and unreasonably foreseeable hazards that are not consented to. One of several different approaches on how to draw the line concerns looking at the normal violence associated with the sport. This means defining the scope of consented-to physical contact in a particular sport so that a participant in that sport would not be deemed to consent to acts that go beyond the scope.

The rules-of-the-game test is an alternative approach to the consent issue. A participant-victim is not deemed to have consented to acts that are illegal under the rules of the sport. This is a much weaker standard that would reduce the types of violence subject to a successful consent defense. The rules-of-the-game approach is an easier test to apply.

Some courts apply a test that looks toward the seriousness of the injury for a solution. This is a simplistic approach which reasons that the victim cannot be said to have consented to a grave injury. Another approach is the "reasonable foreseeability test," which is commonly used in the area of torts. Under this test, a participant would be held to have consented only to those acts of violence which were considered a reasonably foreseeable part of the sport.

Finally, it should be noted that in addition to the above tests, the *assumption-of-risk doctrine* of tort law is often discussed in the area of consent to criminal acts. Assumption of risk is very similar to the consent defense. A participant in a contact sport assumes the risk of violent contact and consents to the contact. But any injury that is serious enough to raise the specter of criminal prosecution should exceed the risk assumed by the participant. Therefore, the assumption-of-risk doctrine does not really add any useful analysis to the problem of the consent defense of battery.

The second major defense to a charge of battery is *self-defense*. The non-aggressor in a violent incident may use a reasonable amount of force against the aggressor when there is reason to believe that immediate danger of harm is imminent and that the use of force is required to avoid this danger. In the area of sports violence, such a defense brings about several considerations.

A successful showing of self-defense must prove that the force used by the non-aggressor was no greater than that used against him. Usually, for example, a case will involve escalating violence, such as when a hockey player punches an opponent and the opponent strikes back with his stick. This may cause some difficulty in determining when "reasonable force" has been used. Another problem is the requirement that the defendant have the honest belief that danger of immediate, serious, bodily injury is imminent. In many cases, the possibility of an honest belief is discredited because often the defendant provokes the attack, and this negates a self-defense argument. Finally, some jurisdictions would further limit the defense to those cases in which the defendant had no reasonable means of retreat. Therefore, a player who could have avoided seriously injuring another by breaking off the confrontation would not be able to plead self-defense.

Other factors can relieve a defendant of responsibility for a crime, even though they are not true defenses. Therefore, even though the prosecution proves each and every element of the crime charged, the defendant can escape punishment by showing that he acted in the heat of passion or was intoxicated. A person who acts as the result of an involuntary action may not have the mental element (*mens rea*) that is required under the definition of the crime.

The diminished responsibility theory has been used by the defense in criminal cases involving sports violence. Defense counsels in *Regina v. Maki*, *Regina v. Green*, and *State v. Forbes* raised the defense of involuntary action (see section 16.1.2., "Player Against Player Violence," and notes). Each defendant argued that players received training in the skills and the mental attitude necessary for a successful hockey player. Because of this training, the defendant's actions were not voluntary but merely instinctual responses or reflex actions. The question in these cases was whether or not the action causing the injury was a normal or regular part of the game, or whether it was an unreasonable response, considering the training each player had received.

NOTE _____

1. The common law system of dividing crimes into felonies and misdemeanors is gradually being replaced with newer systems based on statutes enacted by legislatures. Many of these newer systems are based on a model law called the Model Penal Code. The

Model Penal Code recognizes criminal conduct that is considered less serious than crimes that are generally classified as offenses and violations. Although the Model Penal Code has not been widely accepted by all states, it is still the closest thing to a uniform American criminal code. Approximately twenty-two states have adopted a variant of the Model Penal Code.

16.1.2. Player Against Player Violence

One of the first incidents of professional sports violence to result in litigation occurred on August 22, 1965, in Candlestick Park, San Francisco. In the third inning Juan Marichal, a pitcher for the San Francisco Giants, had thrown a pitch at Dodger Maury Wills's head, which caught the attention of the Dodgers dugout, but nothing had ensued. In the bottom of the third inning, Marichal was at bat against Sandy Koufax of the Dodgers. After the second pitch to Marichal, John Roseboro, the Dodgers catcher, threw the ball back to the pitcher and either nicked Marichal's ear or came close to it. Marichal turned to Roseboro and asked him why he did that. Roseboro came out of his crouch with his fist clenched. Marichal raised his bat and quickly struck Roseboro at least twice on the top and side of the head, opening a two-inch gash. After the incident, National League President Warren Giles fined Marichal $1,750, a record at that time, and suspended him for nine days or eight playing dates. No criminal charges were filed. However, Roseboro filed a $110,000 damage suit against Marichal a week after the incident. After numerous legal delays, the suit finally settled out of court for $7,500 in 1970.

The comparable cases of player against player violence that have occurred since *Marichal* have often resulted in larger cash awards, multiple parties being sued, and criminal charges. However, the punishments for such violence, and resulting awards, have varied drastically, depending on the legal jurisdiction and the league in which the violence occurred.

For example, in 1999 Wichita State University pitcher Ben Christensen noticed that the "on-deck" batter of the opposing team was "timing" his warm-up pitches, a breach of baseball etiquette. Bothered by this, Christensen threw a ball at the on-deck batter, University of Evansville's Anthony Molina, who was standing thirty feet from home plate in the on-deck circle. The ball fractured Molina's skull, broke three bones in his eye socket, and resulted in "lingering vision problems." Molina underwent three operations before playing again for Evansville in 2000. The DA's office investigated; however, no criminal charges were filed in the *Christensen* case. However, the pitcher's actions resulted in his being suspended for the remainder of the season; his pitching coach being suspended for the remainder of the season; and a $75,000 lawsuit against Christensen, the three umpires who worked the game, and Wichita State University (see Chapter 3, section 3.6., "Vicarious Liability").

The most frequent and brutal acts have occurred in hockey. Perhaps the most infamous of these attacks led to the case of *State v. Forbes*. The incident occurred in 1975 during a game between the Minnesota North Stars and the Boston Bruins (see note 7). In a case similar to *Forbes* in its brutality, nineteen-year-old winger Jesse Boulerice, a fifth-round pick of the Philadelphia Flyers in the 1996 draft, was charged with felony assault by the Wayne County, Michigan, prosecutors after striking another player in the face with his stick. The offense occurred during a first-period incident during game 4 of the Guelph Storm's sweep of the Whalers in the Ontario Hockey League's semifinals in 1999.

The Storm's forward, Andrew Long, checked Boulerice into the boards. After a shoving match, Long skated off to rejoin the play; Boulerice caught up and, with a baseball-style swing of his stick, clubbed Long across the bridge of the nose. Long was knocked unconscious and went into convulsions on the ice. He suffered a broken nose and cheekbone, a twenty-stitch gash, and a blood clot on his brain. Boulerice was ejected from the game and given a one-year suspension from the Ontario Hockey League. He eventually pleaded no contest to a reduced charge of aggravated assault and was sentenced to ninety days' probation.

Several other hockey players have faced criminal charges for their conduct on the ice (see notes 1, 2, 4, 8, and 9), but it's believed that only one, Dino Ciccarelli in 1988, was convicted and served time in jail for assaulting another player. Ciccarelli was sentenced to one day in jail and fined $1,000.

While it is difficult to convict an athlete for conduct during a game, it is not impossible. Another case that shows athletes, including amateur athletes, are not immune from criminal sanctions is *State of Washington v. Shelley*, Wash. Ct. App. 929 P.2d 489 (1997). During an intramural basketball game, Jason Shelley intentionally punched another player and broke his jaw. Shelley argued that the other player, who had a reputation as a rough player, was being physical and rough throughout the game. In upholding Shelley's conviction for assault in the second degree, the court of appeals held that while consent may be a defense to assault in athletic competitions, Shelley had failed to establish a factual basis for that defense. Consent is defined as contact that is contemplated within rules of the game. In this case, Shelley was unable to prove that the victim could consent to an intentional punch to the face, and that the action was, in some way, a natural part and within the rules of the game of basketball. If consent cannot be a defense to assault, then most athletic contests would need to be banned because many involve "invasions of one's physical integrity." However, since society has chosen to foster sports competitions, players necessarily must be able to consent to physical contact and other players must be able to rely on that consent when playing the game. This is the view adopted by the drafters of the Model Penal Code, which states: "[T]here are, however, situations in which consent to bodily injury should be recognized as a defense to crime. . . . There is . . . the obvious case of participation in an athletic contest or competitive sport, where the nature of the enterprise often involves risk of serious injury. Here, the social judgment that permits the contest to flourish necessarily involves the companion judgment that reasonably foreseeable hazards can be consented to by virtue of participation" (Model Penal Code, supra, §2.11 cmt. 2, at 396).

The court in *Shelley* further held that while the consent defense is not limited to conduct within the rules of the games, it is limited to conduct and harm that are a reasonably foreseeable hazard of joint participation in an athletic contest. Shelley's punch, the court of appeals concluded, was not a reasonably foreseeable hazard in the game of basketball, or even rugby or hockey. Therefore, Shelley's action was indefensible and constituted assault in the second degree.

NOTES

1. In 2000, a Vancouver, B.C., provincial judge found Boston Bruin Marty McSorley guilty of assault with a weapon. Though McSorley avoided prison, he was sentenced to eighteen months of probation. Earlier that year, McSorley had taken a two-handed swing with his hockey stick to the right temple of Vancouver Canuck Donald Brashear, causing him to drop and hit his head on the ice. While McSorley and Brashear had fought earlier

in the game, this hit occurred from behind and with less than ten seconds to go in regulation time. Brashear was carried off on a stretcher, blood flowing from his nose, and taken a hospital, where he was diagnosed with a concussion. McSorley claimed the hit was accidental. Judge William Kitchen rejected that defense, but justified the lack of a prison sentence by pointing out that McSorley had not earned any income since the incident due to his twenty-three-game suspension and $72,000 fine imposed by the NHL. Kitchen also noted that McSorley had sizable attorney's fees.

2. In 1999 Neal Goss, a fifteen-year-old Illinois high school hockey player, was sent crashing into the boards at a skating rink by a cross-check from a player at a rival high school. Goss suffered permanent paralysis as a result of the contact. The Lake County state's attorney charged the perpetrator (whose identity was protected due to his age), also fifteen, with two counts of aggravated battery (both felonies), alleging that the perpetrator caused great bodily harm and that his hockey stick was a deadly weapon. The state's attorney claimed the incident occurred *after* the buzzer sounded to end the game, indicating an intent to harm. In 2000, the defendant entered an Alford plea (similar to a no-contest plea) to a lesser misdemeanor charge, and was sentenced to two years' probation and 120 hours of community service. In justifying the reduced sentence, Associate Judge John Radosevich stated, "11 million people [the population of Illinois] are in part responsible because we promote competitiveness and, frankly, aggressiveness. . . . Everyone loves a winner, unless of course something goes haywire with the winning." Goss also filed a civil complaint—*Goss v. Illinois Hockey Officials Ass'n*, No. 99L-01386 (Ill. Cir. Ct.-Cook County, filed Dec. 8, 1999) against the referees and the league. Goss stated that the officials had ignored his complaints about illegal hits and abusive language from the defendant's team, and that these circumstances had led to the defendant's violent behavior. That civil case is pending.

3. In a 1997 heavyweight title fight in Las Vegas, boxer Mike Tyson, who was clearly trailing in the fight, made two attempts to bite the ear of his opponent, Evander Holyfield. Tyson was warned after his first attempt, then disqualified after his second attempt, during which he successfully bit off part of Holyfield's ear. Reconstructive surgery was required following the match. Holyfield declined to file charges against Tyson. However, Tyson was fined $3 million plus legal costs by the Nevada State Athletic Commission, and had his boxing license revoked for one year.

4. In Italy during a hockey game, the defendant, Jimmy Boni, and another player, Miran Schrott, were scuffling in front of the net when Schrott punched Boni. Boni retaliated by slashing Schrott across the chest with his stick. Schrott fell to the ice and died of cardiac arrest. The Italian government charged Boni with manslaughter, which, if he was convicted would carry a ten-to-eighteen-year prison term. The charges were filed even though the slash did not look very serious and did not even merit a minor penalty during the game. Boni pled guilty to a reduced manslaughter charge and was fined $1,600. *New York Times*, February 17, 1994, p. B16.

5. In *State v. Floyd*, 466 N.W.2d 919 (Iowa Ct. App. 1990), a fight broke out during a basketball game and the defendant, who was on the sidelines, punched and severely injured several opposing team members. Because neither defendant nor his victims were voluntarily participating in the game, the consent defense did not apply because the statute "contemplated a person who commits acts during the course of play, and the exception seeks to protect those whose acts otherwise subject to prosecution are committed in furtherance of the object of the sport." The court in Floyd noted that there is a "continuum, or sliding scale, grounded in the circumstances under which voluntary participants engage in sport . . . which governs the type of incidents in which an individual volunteers (i.e., consents) to participate."

6. In *People v. Freer*, 381 N.Y.S.2d 976 (N.Y. Dist. Ct. 1976), the victim was punched in the eye during a football game. The incident occurred after the victim had tackled the defendant and the play was over. The court held that while initially it may be assumed that the very first punch thrown by the complainant in the course of the tackle

was consented to by defendant, the act of tackling an opponent in the course of a football game may often involve contact that could easily be interpreted as a punch. The defendant's response cannot be mistaken or accepted. Clearly, defendant intended to punch complainant and there was no consent.

7. In *State v. Forbes*, No. 63280 (Minn. Dist. Ct. 1975), in December 1974, an NHL hockey game was played in Minnesota between the Boston Bruins and the Minnesota North Stars. Early in the first period, Henry Boucha, closely followed by David Forbes, chased a loose puck against the boards. Forbes proceeded to check Boucha, using his elbows as offensive weapons, as is commonly done by hockey players. After being elbowed, Boucha turned and knocked Forbes down. The referee penalized both players for a total of seven minutes. Once in their respective penalty boxes, they exchanged threats. Upon their return to the ice, Boucha had started to skate toward the North Stars' bench when Forbes said, "Okay, let's go now," and took a swing at Boucha. Forbes missed him with his hand but connected with his stick, just above Boucha's right eye. Boucha dropped to the ice, covering his injured face. Forbes then discarded his stick and gloves, jumped on top of Boucha, and proceeded to bang Boucha's head on the ice until he was forcibly removed.

Boucha was taken from the ice to the hospital, where twenty-five stitches were required to close the cut beside his right eye. When the patch was removed five days later, Boucha complained of double vision in the injured eye and underwent remedial surgery to repair a small fracture in the floor of the right eye socket.

After hearing evidence about the incident, NHL Commissioner Clarence Campbell suspended Forbes for ten games. Then, on January 15, 1975, Forbes was indicted by a Minnesota grand jury and charged with violating Minnesota statute, section 609.25, aggravated assault, which stated:

> Subdivision 1. Whoever assaults another and inflicts great bodily harm may be sentenced to imprisonment for not more than ten years or to payment of a fine of not more than $10,000 or both.
> Subdivision 2. Whoever assaults another with a dangerous weapon but without intent to inflict great bodily harm may be sentenced to imprisonment for not more than five years or to payment of a fine of not more than $5,000 or both.

At trial, the prosecution argued that Forbes had committed an aggravated assault on Boucha. The argument made was that criminal assault was a crime whether it was done in public or under game conditions. The defense argued a variation on the temporary insanity defense, basing its argument on the theory that from the age of four years, hockey players are taught not to let other players intimidate them. Coaches emphasize the need for physical violence against other players, and crowds cheer the sight of fighting and blood. The defense argued that given these circumstances, hockey, and not David Forbes, should be on trial. The trial ended in a nine to three hung jury in favor of the assault conviction. The prosecutor decided not to retry the case because he felt that the deep split in public opinion would make a required unanimous verdict virtually impossible.

8. In *Regina v. Maki*, 14 D.L.R.3d 164 (Ont P.C. 1970), Wayne Maki was charged with assault causing bodily harm after hitting Ted Green of the Boston Bruins with his stick during a game. The incident occurred when Maki and Green both went into the corner of the rink, chasing the puck. After some pushing and punching, Maki and Green started swinging their sticks. Green first struck Maki with his stick on the neck and shoulder Maki then struck Green about the side of the head, causing serious injury. The court dismissed the charges, stating that it could not say beyond any doubt that Maki intended to injure Green, that Maki was not under reasonable apprehension of bodily harm, or that Maki used excessive force under the circumstances. Though it did not enter into the court's decision, the defense of consent was addressed by the court because it had been raised. The court said that no sports league, no matter how well organized or self-policed, could render its players immune from criminal prosecution. The court ad-

mitted that all players who step onto a playing field or an ice surface assume certain risks and hazards of the sport, and in most cases the defense of consent (assumption of the risks) would be applicable. However, no athlete should be presumed to accept malicious, unprovoked, or overtly violent attacks as part of playing sport.

9. In *Regina v. Green*, 16 D.L.R.3d 137 (Ont P.C. 1970), a case arose from the same incident as *Regina v. Maki* and involved criminal charges of common assault against Ted Green, who hit Maki with both his gloved hand and his stick. In dismissing the charges, the court found that in the course of a hockey game, a player does not examine each potential action to determine if it is an assault. The roughness of the game has to permit certain actions that would be considered assault outside the confines of a NHL contest.

10. For additional instances of player v. player violence, see Chapter 3, "Legal Principles in Tort Law"—in particular Section 3.3., "Intentional Torts" and Section 3.2., "The Tort of Reckless Misconduct (Gross Negligence)."

16.1.3. Player Versus Fan Violence

Another area of concern for professional sport leagues is assaults involving players and fans. Players assaulting fans or fans assaulting players is nothing new. Hall of Fame baseball player Ty Cobb was suspended indefinitely after going into the stands to fight a heckler (who had lost both hands in an industrial accident) in 1912. More recently, at a game at Wrigley Field in Chicago in 2000, a Cubs fan grabbed the hat of Los Angeles catcher Chad Kreuter in the Dodgers' bullpen, instigating a wild brawl that spilled into the crowd. While no criminal charges were filed against the players, the incident led to Major League Baseball's suspension of nineteen Dodger players, coaches, and officials for a total of eighty-four games.

The players are not the only ones doing the assaulting. On September 24, 1999, in Milwaukee, a fan came onto the field and attacked Bill Spiers, the right fielder for the Houston Astros, by jumping Spiers from behind and knocking him to the ground. Spiers was removed from the game after suffering a welt under his left eye, a bloody nose, and whiplash. The fan was charged with two counts of battery, one for attacking Spiers and one for slugging a ground crew member who was defending the player, and one count of disorderly conduct.

A rare occurrence of players facing criminal charges in such circumstances occurred in 1980, when criminal and civil charges were filed against the Boston Bruins when all but two of the Bruins players entered the stands to engage in a general melee with some New York Rangers fans. All criminal and civil charges against the players and the Boston Bruins—*Guttenplan v. Boston Professional Hockey Ass'n., Inc.*, No. 80-415 (1981 U.S. Dist. LEXIS 10434 (S.D.N.Y. Jan. 19, 1981))—were later dropped after an investigation disclosed that the fans had instigated the fight by punching a Bruins player and throwing a stick at him.

In an attempt to reduce fan violence toward players and other fans, in 1996 the city of Philadelphia put a municipal court, "Eagles Court," inside the Philadelphia Eagles' football stadium. The court gathers fans who have violated the law and have been arrested during the game, and has them tried and convicted in Veterans Stadium, all on the same day. In supporting the court, Philadelphia Police Commissioner John Timoney stated that it helps deter serious offenses, such as carrying open containers and fighting, and has helped dampen rowdyism at games. The court also cuts down on the number of unruly Philadelphia football fans and makes going to a game safer for individuals and families.

NOTES ────────────────────────

1. In November 1999, during a NFL game in Denver, a group of fans began pelting the Oakland Raiders players with snowballs. Some of the snowballs were spiked with batteries. Charles Woodson, angry at being attacked, allegedly hurled a snowball that struck a female fan in the face. Another Raiders player, Lincoln Kennedy, went after a fan who had hit him in the face with a snowball. Woodson was charged with misdemeanor assault and Kennedy filed charges against the fan, whom he confronted after the game. In all, eight people were arrested, thirteen others were cited for misdemeanor assault and throwing objects, and two people had their season tickets revoked. *New York Times*, December 2, 1999, p. D6.

2. On February 6, 1995, during a time-out, Vernon Maxwell of the Houston Rocket went up into the stands and punched a fan. Maxwell claimed that the fan used racial slurs and made derogatory remarks about his family, which the fan denied. This misconduct earned Maxwell a ten-game suspension, with a loss of $228,000 in salary plus a $20,000 fine by the NBA. No criminal charges were filed. If they had been, Maxwell could have been charged with simple assault, a misdemeanor punishable by a year in jail and a $2,500 fine.

16.1.4. Player Versus Official Violence

While athletes, coaches, and fans have always disputed calls by officials, there have been a growing number of cases where athletes, coaches, and fans are assaulting officials because of the calls they make on the field. For example, in 2000, Carl Everett of MLB was suspended ten games for head-butting umpire Ron Culpa. Everett had accused Culpa of "showing him up" after Culpa demonstratively told him to keep his feet inside the batter's box. In 2001, in Hamilton, Ontario, Vincent Hill was charged with uttering threats, after allegedly threatening to "kill" the seventeen-year-old referee who had called a two-minute penalty on one of his eleven-year-old players.

The first athlete to be arrested and charged with battery for striking an official during a professional sporting event in the United States was Allan Leavell, a guard for the Tulsa Fast Breakers of the Continental Basketball Association. According to the police report, the incident occurred on March 30, 1990, after the ball went out of bounds in front of the Tulsa bench. Referee Peter Quinn called the ball out on Tulsa. Leavell, who was in the game, came up to Quinn and began arguing with him. Leavell then struck Quinn on the neck with his left hand, knocking him down. Besides the criminal charges, Leavell was fined $5,000 and suspended by the CBA for two years.

In 1996, a high school wrestler head-butted a wrestling official during a match in Washington. The official was knocked unconscious for about thirty seconds. The wrestler was charged with fourth-degree assault and faced a maximum penalty of two years' probation and thirty days in jail. Also in 1996, a hockey referee was repeatedly punched in the head and body, and speared in the groin with a stick, after allowing a controversial goal that ended the hockey game between the University of Moncton and the University of Prince Edward Island.

Even when the offending players face criminal charges, as above, the charges are usually minimal or dropped. While the lack of punishment received by the defendants in the above cases might be due to their lack of criminal records, some argue that there is a lack of comprehensive and effective laws to take care of these types of situations. In fact, only fifteen states have enacted statutes making it a criminal violation to assault a sports official (see note 1). On the professional sports level, leagues and players associations will usually encourage parties to resolve such conduct through their established grievance procedures, rather than allowing a case to proceed to trial (see Chapter 11, section 11.3.14., "Grievance Procedures in Professional Sports").

NOTES

1. In April 2001, New Mexico became the 15th state to enact protective legislation for sports officials. See www.naso.org/PressReleases/st77.htm

The following is an example of a statute protecting sports officials:

> Delaware Code Ann. Tit. 11, Section 614 provides: (a) Any person who intentionally causes physical injury to a sports official who is acting in the lawful performance of his duty shall be guilty of a Class A misdemeanor. Upon conviction of a second or subsequent offense under this section, such person shall be guilty of a Class G felony. (b) For the purposes of this section, the words "sports official" shall mean any person who serves as a referee, umpire, linesman, or in any similar capacity in supervising or administering a sports event, and who is registered as a member of a local, state, regional or national organization which provides training or educational opportunities for sports officials.

Other states that have enacted protective legislation for sports officials include: Arkansas [Ann. Section 5-13-209], California [Section 243.8], Georgia [Statute 16-5-23], Kentucky [1.KRS 508.025], Louisiana [Ann. Section 14-34-4], Minnesota [Charter 128C.08 Subdivision 2], Montana [Ann. Section 45-5-211], New Jersey [Ann. 2C: 44-1], New Mexico, North Carolina [Section 14-33(b)(9)], Oklahoma [Ann. 21, Section 650.1], Oregon, Pennsylvania [Ann. Section 2712] and West Virginia [Section 61-2-159].

2. In 1999, during a soccer game in South Africa, a referee shot and killed a player, in front of six hundred spectators, after the player, angry over a disputed goal, lunged at him with a knife. The shooting happened after some fans ran onto the field to protest the goal, which had cut the home team's lead to 2–1. The manager of the home team attributed the violence that occurs during many games, especially among heavy-drinking spectators, to the gambling on the township teams.

3. In the NFL, the minimum fine for physical contact with an official is $10,000, according to the 1993–2007 collective bargaining agreement. A prominent case occurred in 1999 when Cleveland Browns' lineman Orlando Brown shoved referee Jeff Triplette to the ground after Triplette accidentally threw a flag into Brown's eye. Brown was suspended from December 1999 until March 2000 for the offense. Subsequently, Brown sued the NFL for $200 million in damages, for negligence in failing "to properly supervise and enforce rules that flags be properly weighted and thrown in a proper fashion." Brown claimed that "he still feels pain in the eye and sees white flashes when he exerts himself." While Brown was one of the highest-paid NFL linemen at the time of the injury, he was unable to find employment or acquire endorsements after the incident. For more information, see www.sportslawnews.com/archive/Articles%202001/BrownNFLsuit.htm.

4. For more information concerning assaults on sports officials, see the National Association of Sports Officials' Web site, www.naso.org/naso.htm. In particular, see the link specifically related to the subject, www.ieway.com/naso/pro.html

5. For more information on legal concerns of sports officials, see Jerry Grunska, ed., *Successful Sports Officiating* (Human Kinetics, 1999). Also see Chapter 4, section 4.7., "Liability of Officials, Referees, and Umpires."

16.1.5. Off-the-Field Conduct

While athletes may be no more likely to commit a crime than other members of society (see note 1), the arrest of an athlete, whether at the high school or the professional level, is always a newsworthy event. For example, in 2000 when Rae Carruth of the NFL's Carolina Panthers was convicted of conspiracy to commit murder—ordering the 1999 drive-by shooting of his pregnant girlfriend—the story was front-page news all over the country just prior to the 2001 Super Bowl.

When athletes are arrested for off-the-field conduct, a number of problems arise. For example, can or should an organization punish an athlete before he is convicted of the crime? If it does not punish the athlete, the organization is seen as condoning criminal conduct and just interested in winning games. However, if the athlete is punished and forced to miss games, what does that do to the notion that everyone is innocent until proven guilty? Another problem that arises is that to protect their image, a number of organizations have tried to keep information from the media. In other words, the organization tries to control any information that is released to the public. This sometimes tends to make the organization look like it is hiding information and protecting criminals. Finally, collective bargaining agreements sometimes limit the amount of punishment that a league or team can impose on a player for off-the-field conduct. For example, the maximum penalty that the NFL may impose on a player for his first substance-related guilty or no-contest plea is a four-game suspension without pay.

Some believe that the league with the biggest problem with off-the-field conduct is the NFL. A 1998 study estimated that 21% of NFL players have adult criminal records (see note 2). While the NFL disputes that statistic, it nonetheless contends with negative perceptions due to the publicity of high-profile murder trials such as Rae Carruth's, not to mention numerous sexual assault and drunk driving arrests. To deter player misconduct, the NFL in March 1997 introduced a new violent crime policy as part of a larger plan to prevent criminal behavior. Any athlete charged with a violent crime is required to undergo counseling. If convicted, the player is subject to a fine or suspension without pay. A second conviction mandates a longer suspension and possibly banishment. The amount of the fine and length of suspension are up to the commissioner.

Initially, the fines issued by the league also tended to be small, compared to players' salaries. For example, in November 1998, Keith Poole of the New Orleans Saints attacked a man with a golf club. Under the league's policy, Poole was fined $4,500. However, in 2000, Baltimore Ravens' linebacker Ray Lewis was fined $250,000 for failing to cooperate with Atlanta police following a double homicide, in which he was at one time implicated but eventually exonerated. The league did not suspend Lewis, who went on to be named Defensive Player of the Year and Super Bowl MVP that season.

NOTES

1. In 2001, NFL Commissioner Paul Tagliabue claimed, "We track 3,000 to 4,000 players every year in terms of criminal misconduct. . . . And this year . . . we had 26 investigations—not offenses, investigations—and we've had 11 convictions." Tagliabue implied, as some sociologists have, that the NFL's numbers for criminal activity are in line with the rest of the population of American men in the same age group. However, Rick Morrissey of the *Chicago Sun Times* claims that Tagliabue's statistics are misleading: "Most of the men in the same age group don't make $1 million a year, most don't live in nice neighborhoods, most don't have their lives so structured and most don't have every need taken care of by fawning sports franchises." For more information, see www.chicagosports.com/content/column/0,2007,131190,00.html

2. The 21% statistic is from Jeff Benedict and Don Yaeger, *Pros and Cons: The Criminals Who Play in the NFL* (New York: Warner Books, 1998).

16.1.6. Solutions to the Problem of Sports Violence

There are two general methods for reducing the amount of athlete violence, particularly at the professional sports level—league control and government regulation. The following subsections will examine the advantages and disadvantages of each method.

16.1.6.1. League Control

While a few courts have prosecuted criminal activity that occurs within the scope of an athletic event, many other violent acts have gone unpunished. Many courts are overburdened, and will defer to a league's willingness to handle a matter internally. Likewise, the leagues and players associations will *always* prefer that matters of player violence be handled internally. For example, after the aforementioned McSorley incident, the NHL implored Vancouver authorities to allow the league to handle the matter through its grievance procedure. Nevertheless, Vancouver authorities saw the assault against Brashear as a matter that clearly belonged in the courts. As the following cases demonstrate, there are both advantages and disadvantages when the league or athletic organization acts to control violent behavior internally.

The first advantage of league or athletic sanctions are that the league and its officials are familiar with the rules and customs of their sport. Because of this familiarity, the leagues are better able to determine what types of aggressive behavior or acts are reasonably foreseeable hazards or acceptable conduct and which acts are unreasonable. Another benefit of internal league controls is the speed and certainty with which players are punished. In punishing violent behavior, internal controls are faster, usually within a few days, and more uniform and predictable. The final benefit of internal sanctions is that since the players are punished financially, through fines and suspensions, the penalties may be effective. For example, the $6.4 million in salary that Latrell Sprewell lost in 1998 because of league sanctions sends a much stronger message to players.

While there may be some advantages to internal league controls, some people argue that the league controls are ineffective in policing violence. One reason why people believe this is the league's conflict of interest. The leagues have a vested interest in keeping their players in the game. If the league suspends a player, it runs the risk of financial losses due to decreased fan support. This is especially true when the athlete is a superstar.

Another reason why people believe league controls are ineffective is that league punishments are deemed too lenient. The penalties are monetary—fines and suspensions—and are usually so small as to have little or no impact. This is especially true with modern professional athletes who earn millions of dollars a year. For example, in 1996, Dennis Rodman head-butted a referee after the referee had ejected Rodman from a game against the New Jersey Nets. The NBA fined Rodman, who earned $2.5 million per season, $20,000, and he received a six-game suspension for the incident. Although Rodman lost another $182,926 in salary during the suspension, critics argue the league's fine was not enough. In fact, a little over three weeks later, the NBA fined Nick Van Exel $25,000 and imposed a seven-game suspension, which resulted in a loss of $161,000 in salary, for assaulting another referee. Critics would argue that to be effective, fines and/ or suspensions should be increased substantially.

One of the reasons that fines and penalties for excessive violence are considered by some to be inadequate is the strength of certain players' unions, and the resultant limitation of the league's and the commissioners' powers. Players' associations, through the collective bargaining process, have been able to curtail the penalties the leagues can impose. (See Chapter 11, section 11.3.1., "The Players Association in Professional Sports.") For example, even though the NHL has worked hard to stop excessive violence, Article 18 of the league's collective bargaining agreement restricts the maximum fine the league can impose on a player to $1,000.

NOTE

1. For more information, see Jeffrey M. Schalley, "Eliminate Violence from Sports Through Arbitration, Not the Civil Courts," 8 *The Sports Lawyers Journal* 181 (Spring 2001).

16.1.6.2. Government Regulation

Critics of sports violence argue that there is too much violence in sports, and because of the ineffectiveness of both league disciplinary rules and criminal sanctions in preventing needless violence, the best and remaining solution would be to promulgate legislation. In the United States, these proposals have had little success, except in the area of violence against officials (see section 16.1.4., "Player Versus Official Violence"). However, federal and state bills to police sport violence have failed at both the federal and state levels (see notes).

NOTES

1. In 1991 the state of Massachusetts unsuccessfully tried to establish a law to provide penalties for assault and battery committed by athletes during professional sporting events.

2. The Sports Violence Arbitration Act of 1983 was introduced in the 98th Congress by Congressman Thomas A. Daschle of South Dakota. The bill would have established an arbitration board as an independent disciplinary body to handle sports violence incidents. However, the bill died from lack of support. The bill was intended to allow the professional leagues to control incidents of excessive violence more effectively without direct intervention by the federal government. Instead of a federal criminal statute, such as the proposed Sports Violence Act (see note 3), the Sports Violence Arbitration Act required each professional league to establish an arbitration panel that would have had the power to punish teams and players for conduct found to be inconsistent with the competitive goals of the sports. Proposed sanctions against the guilty player's team included payment of the injured player's salary and medical expenses, payment of compensatory damages if the player's career had ended, and/or payment of damages or relinquishment of a draft choice to the injured player's club for loss of the player's services—as well as fines. The guilty player would have been subjected to a severe fine and lengthy suspension at the discretion of the arbitration board. The act provided for a full evidentiary hearing process. The sponsor of the bill believed that its positive impact on the level of violence in professional sports would have great influence on play at the amateur level.

3. One major proposal in this area was the Sports Violence Act, introduced by Congressman Ronald M. Mottl before the House of Representatives in both 1980 (H.R. 7903)

and 1981 (H.R. 2263). The bill never made it to the floor of the house, and Congressman Mottl was not reelected in 1982. The act would have made it a criminal offense for a professional athlete to engage in excessive violence. Under the act, a player who "knowingly uses excessive physical force and thereby causes a risk of significant bodily injury to another person involved in that event" could be punished. Excessive physical force was defined as that which was unreasonably violent, had no reasonable relationship to the game, and could not have been reasonably foreseen or consented to. A federal criminal statute covering sports violence was seen as necessary because of the interstate nature of modern professional sports leagues and the lack of enforcement of criminal statutes by the states where professional athletes were involved in behavior that could be classified as a crime. Local assault and battery prosecutions, based on common-law notions of crime, had no relevance to the issues of sports violence because of the special problems of assumption of risk, consent, and self-defense that are present in sports cases.

16.2. ILLEGAL GAMBLING

The problems associated with illegal gambling and the influence it may exert on sporting events are of special concern for athletic administrators and others, because gambling affects the integrity of the games, the games themselves, and the public confidence in athletes and sports. Some argue that betting on games is encouraged by the press, which prints the "spread" (expected margin of victory for the favored team) of games and the "odds" in its sports pages, as well as advertisements for weekly tip sheets and betting aids. Although some contend that betting on athletics is enjoyable and is a form of entertainment, others contend that gambling has a negative impact on society and sports. For example, a 1998 study conducted by the University of Michigan surveyed 3,000 NCAA male and female student-athletes concerning gambling. The research revealed that 35% of student-athletes gambled on sports while attending college. Over 5% of male student-athletes wagered on a game in which they participated, provided inside information for gambling purposes, or accepted money for performing poorly in a contest. According to a 2000 University of Michigan study of 640 NCAA referees and officials, 40% admitted to gambling on sports, and 2% knew of officials who had called a game inaccurately due to gambling interests (see note 1).

The following sections examine the dangers of illegal gambling on athletics and the steps athletic administrators and organizations have taken to preserve the integrity of their sports. Although illegal gambling is a major problem for both intercollegiate and professional sports, they will be treated separately due to the unique legal problems each area presents.

NOTE _____

1. Also, according to the 2000 University of Michigan study of 640 NCAA referees and officials, 0.8% were rated as "pathological gamblers" and 2.2% had used a bookie. See Geralda Miller/Associated Press, "Study: NCAA Gambling Officials Admit to Gambling, Using Bookies," *Detroit News*, March 30, 2000. Viewable online at *http://detnews.com/2000/college/0003/31/20000330-26836.htm*

16.2.1. Intercollegiate Athletics and Gambling

Over the years gambling on intercollegiate athletics has steadily increased, most notably with the significant amount of money that is currently being wagered on the NCAA men's Division I basketball tournament. However, very little of that is *legal* betting, and for every dollar bet legally in the United States, approximately $150 is bet illegally (see note 1). Problems associated with and arising from wagering have continually plagued college athletics. The problem of greatest concern to the NCAA and legal authorities is the practice of "point shaving." Point shaving occurs when athletes are paid to score fewer points than they otherwise would, so that the point differential is less than the predicted "spread." Less frequently, players are paid to lose a game outright. In 1945, five Brooklyn College basketball players were expelled from school after they admitted to accepting bribes to lose a game. In 1951, thirty-two players at seven schools were caught shaving points in eighty-six games. A gambling scandal at Boston College during the 1978–1979 season led to the conviction of the basketball player Rick Kuhn, who was sentenced to ten years in prison on federal gambling charges (see note 6). In 1985, a gambling and drug scandal was uncovered at Tulane University. That incident, which involved a number of basketball players, led to Tulane President Eamon Kelly's decision to drop the Division I men's basketball program "forever." However, just four years later, in 1989, the program was revived for competition in the Metro Conference. In the 1990s, prominent point-shaving scandals occurred at Arizona State University and Northwestern University (see exhibit 16.1).

Consequently, the 21st century began with a call for governmental regulation of gambling on intercollegiate athletics. For example, in 2000, U.S. Representatives Lindsey Graham (South Carolina) and Tim Roemer (Indiana) introduced a bill to ban gambling on college and amateur sporting events. The bill was largely denounced due to legal gambling's (small) share of the total gambling problem. However, the 2001 Knight Commission report also called for federal legislation to ban amateur sport gambling in Nevada (see Chapter 5, section 5.3.2.1., "The Knight Commission"). Furthermore, a revised bill to outlaw college gambling was approved by the U.S. Senate Commerce Committee in May 2001. Senator John McCain of Arizona is pushing for the bill's passage into law.

The NCAA prohibits the participation in any form of legal or illegal sports gambling because of its potential to undermine the integrity of sports contests and jeopardize the welfare of the student-athlete and the intercollegiate athletics community. The NCAA's disapproval of illegal gambling on intercollegiate athletics is clearly spelled out in the following bylaw:

10.3 Gambling Activities
Staff members of the athletics department of a member institution and student-athletes shall not knowingly:
(a) Provide information to individuals involved in organized gambling activities concerning intercollegiate athletics competition;

(b) Solicit a bet on any intercollegiate team;

(c) Accept a bet on any team representing the institution; or

(d) Participate in any gambling activity that involves intercollegiate athletics through a bookmaker, a parlay card, or any other method employed by organized gambling. (*2001–02 NCAA Division I Manual*, Bylaw 10.3)

Exhibit 16.1
NCAA Gambling Chronology

1951 - Thirty-two players from seven institutions were implicated in a gambling scheme
designed to fix 86 games. Co-captains of the Manhattan College basketball team
were arrested for attempting to fix a game against DePaul. Three members of the
CCNY basketball team that won the NCAA and NIT Championships, along with
several other individuals, were arrested in a game-fixing scandal that involved a
number of teams. In this same year, basketball players from Long Island and Bradley
Universities were caught taking bribes·from gamblers.

1961 - The NCAA forced St. Joseph's (PA) to relinquish its third place finish in the NCAA
basketball tournament because of alleged student-athlete involvement with a
gambler.

1962 - Thirty-seven players from 22 institutions, including legendary New York playground
hero Connie Hawkins, then at Iowa, were implicated in a major gambling scandal
that resulted in the arrest and conviction of three gamblers charged with fixing
college basketball games. Former Columbia University athlete Jack Molinas served
five years in prison for his role in the scandal.

1981 - Boston College basketball players Rick Kuhn, Ernie Cobb, Jim Sweeney, and two
others were found guilty of shaving points during the 1978-79 basketball season. The
players, along with organized crime figure Henry Hill and New York gambler
Richard (the Fixer) Perry, fixed nine Boston College games. Kuhn, the only player
convicted, served 2 1/2 years in prison for his part in the conspiracy.

1985 - Four members of the Tulane basketball team, including John (Hot Rod) Williams, who
went on to play in the NBA, were accused of shaving points in exchange for cash
and cocaine. In the aftermath of this incident, the University suspended the program
for five years.

1989 - Four football players from the University of Florida were suspended for betting on
football games. That same year, nine athletes from four different sports at the
University of Arkansas were suspended for betting on college football games.

1990 - It is alleged that four players on the North Carolina State basketball team had
conspired with bookmakers to shave points in at least four games. Although the
players denied the charges and no charges were filed, the controversy and other
allegations of academic improprieties led to the dismissal of head basketball coach
Jim Valvano.

1992 - Nineteen University of Maine athletes from the football and basketball teams were
suspended for their participation in a gambling operation reported to be worth
$10,000 a week. That same year, a gambling operation involving student- athletes
from the University of Rhode Island and Bryant College was uncovered.

1994 - A starting running back from Northwestern University was suspended for gambling; he
denied that he intentionally fumbled the ball on the goal line in a game against Iowa.

1995 - Football and basketball players from the University of Maryland, including the starting
quarterback, were suspended for betting on college sports.

1996 - Thirteen members of the Boston College football team were suspended for betting on
college football as well as professional football and baseball games. Three of those
suspended were alleged to have bet against their own team.

1997 - A point-shaving scandal was uncovered at Arizona State University when two former
members of the basketball team admitted to shaving points on four home games in
the 1993-94 season. Two students from Arizona State were reported to have bet
$250,000 on a game against Washington State. According to federal law
enforcement officials, more money was wagered in the Arizona State case than in
any point-shaving scam in the history of intercollegiate athletics. Star player Steven
"Hedake" Smith was sentenced to a year in prison for his role, and declared
bankruptcy. Prosecutors claimed that Smith fixed the games in order to recoup a
$10,000 gambling debt to the scheme's mastermind, Benny Silman. Silman was
sentenced to 46 months.

Exhibit 16.1 (continued)

1998 - Former Northwestern University basketball players were indicted on charges of
   shaving points, conspiring to fix games, and accepting bets during the 1994-95
   season. Attention from this case expanded to include former football players from
   the Universities of Colorado and Notre Dame. The scheme was masterminded by
   Notre Dame place kicker Kevin Pendergast, who spent two months in prison. Two
   Northwestern players each spent one month in prison.

2000 – U.S. Representatives Lindsey Graham (South Carolina) and Tim Roemer (Indiana)
   introduced a bill to ban gambling on college and amateur sporting events. The bill
   was largely denounced due to legal gambling's small share of the total gambling
   problem.

The NCAA has continued to add to its investigative staff to keep up with the gambling problem. Many NCAA investigators are former FBI agents who attempt to maintain contacts with bookmakers, both in Nevada, where sports gambling is legal, and in states where it is not. This unorthodox relationship between bookmakers and NCAA investigators is based on mutual concern that sporting events not be rigged to reach a predetermined outcome. The bookmakers cannot afford a rigged game for economic reasons, because their winning percentages and profit margins are based on a "point spread," which they formulate on the theory that the game is not rigged. The NCAA and the individual schools' concerns are based on the integrity of the game and on their reputations.

The bookmakers usually alert investigators if there is a sizable change in the point spread on a particular game. Such a change is suspicious, and may indicate that bettors have placed large wagers on a team. Of course, heavy betting may occur for other reasons, such as a coach's announcement of an injury to a key player. If no legitimate reasons are found, however, it increases the possibility that gamblers have "fixed" the game by bribing a coach, player, or official. Remember, bribes are not necessarily made to ensure that a team loses—just that it wins by fewer points than the predicted point spread. Once suspicions are aroused, college officials, such as the president and athletic director, are informed by the NCAA. They may also be notified if investigators hear "street talk" about "something funny" going on in the institution's athletic program.

NOTES

1. "In 1996, Congress created a National Gambling Impact Study Commission and asked it to report on the effect of betting on the nation. In November 1998, commissioners were told that illegal sports betting takes in as much as $380 billion annually, dwarfing the $2.4 billion bet legally on sports in Nevada." See Geralda Miller/Associated Press "Study: NCAA Gambling Officials Admit to Gambling, Using Bookies," *Detroit News*, March 30, 2000. Viewable online at www.detnews.com/2000/college/0003/31/20000330-26836.htm

2. For more information on gambling in intercollegiate athletics, see Charley Rosen, *Scandals of '51: How the Gamblers Almost Killed College Basketball* (New York: Seven Stories Press, 1999).

3. Pursuant to the passage of the 1992 Professional and Amateur Sports Protection Act (PASPA), 28 USC Sec 3701, Nevada is the only place in the country where sports betting is legal. The PASPA did allow for the continuation of a sports lottery in Oregon and a hybrid form of sports betting in Wyoming and South Dakota.

4. Athletic conferences will address the gambling issue in different ways, some in a manner to disclaim responsibility and others in a matter that strengthens NCAA Bylaw 10.3. For example, in 1998 the Pac-10 adopted proposal 97-020, which specified that the provisions of NCAA Bylaw 10.3 are applicable to conference employees.

5. Nevada, the only state in the nation to allow legal sports gambling, does not permit betting on college games involving public or private institutions located in the state. The regulation was enacted in 1972 by the Nevada Gaming Control Board.

6. In *United States v. Burke*, 700 F.2d 70 (2d Cir.), *aff'd.*, 464 U.S. 816 (1983), Rick Kuhn, a former Boston College basketball player, was charged (along with four code-fendants) and convicted of racketeering by conspiring to fix at least six games, of sports bribery, and of violation of the Interstate Travel and Aid to Racketeering statutes. In sentencing Kuhn to a ten-year sentence, the court noted:

> The crimes in this case are especially significant in view of the ramifications which they have had on the world of sports, college basketball in particular. A group of gamblers and career criminals were able to band together and successfully bribe and influence college athletes. Their motivation was simple and clear—financial gain. The crime, however, reminds millions of sports fans that athletics can be compromised and are not always merely honest competition among dedicated athletes.
>
> While it is true that only one or possibly two athletes were compromised, the effect remains basically the same. Every college athlete may now come under suspicion by fans and coaches. This suspicion has existed previously due to earlier scandals dating back several years, and it is now renewed as a result of this offense.
>
> This 26-year-old defendant undoubtedly assumed one of the more essential roles in this offense. While it may be true that his performance during games was not particularly pivotal, his actions away from the basketball court are of significant importance. He was a member of the 1978–79 Boston College team who initially agreed to participate and thereafter recruited other players, maintained contact with the gamblers and accepted their payments.
>
> It is interesting to note that there was not testimony introduced at the trial which indicated a reluctance on the part of the defendant to participate (in point shaving) or a desire to terminate his involvement. Rather, he emerges as somewhat of a greedy individual who was more interested in collecting money from his criminal associates than he was in winning basketball games.
>
> The defendant is a product of a stable and supporting working-class family. From a young age, he developed natural abilities in athletics and was essentially successful in signing a professional baseball contract in 1973 and in attending college on a basketball scholarship three years later. Various individuals who have been [associated] with the defendant in his hometown of Swissville, Pennsylvania, have described him in very positive terms. The reasons therefore as to why he became involved in this offense remain unclear.
>
> On final analysis, deterrence emerges as the most important sentencing objective. A strong argument can be offered that the substantial term of incarceration imposed on this defendant will be recalled in the future by another college athlete who may be tempted to compromise his performance.

16.2.2. Professional Sports and Gambling

The success of the professional sports industry hinges on maintaining a high level of integrity, so that the viewing public has no doubt about the outcome of the event. If people were to believe that there was a connection between the teams and the players and organized gambling, the integrity of the game could be damaged. Therefore any connection to gambling raises serious concerns. For example, when Major League Baseball was in the process of approving the Walt Disney Company as the controlling owner of the Anaheim Angels, the league sought and received assurances from Disney that it would not have gambling on its cruise ships.

The connection between gambling and professional sports is not a recent occurrence in America. The decision to appoint the first commissioner of baseball,

Kennesaw Mountain Landis, was a direct result of the Chicago "Black Sox" fix of the 1919 World Series. *The Imperfect Diamond*, by Lowenfish and Lupien, recalls how Landis was appointed because of the public uproar over the Chicago "Black Sox" scandal:

> The tale of the "Black Sox" scandal has been memorably told by Eliot Asinof in *Eight Men Out*. Asinof observed how the closing of the racetracks during World War I had led the professional gamblers to flock to the ball parks. The owners did little to watch out for irregularities. Key contacts between gamblers and players were made easily. . . .
>
> In late June 1921, seven of the accused fixers of the 1919 World Series went on trial in a Chicago courtroom. Public sympathy was rising for the players—victims of Charles Comiskey's stinginess. "The magnates led the public to believe that the ballplayers got about $10,000 a year . . . when they got as little as $2,600," defense attorney Ben Short declared to the jury. "At the end of the season, they have nothing left but a chew of tobacco, a glove, and a few pairs of worn-out socks."
>
> It was a strange trial. The owners recognized that airing the game's dirty linen was not in their best interests. Therefore, they decided to provide good attorneys to aid in the players' defense. Later, baseball would punish its sinners by extralegal weapons in its arsenal.
>
> Powerful New York gambler Arnold Rothstein, deeply implicated in the scandal as the man who gave the go-ahead, greatly helped the owners' strategy by arranging for the theft of the players' confessions from the Chicago district attorney's office. Unable to use its most damning evidence in the trial, the prosecution was doomed. On August 2, 1921, the jury acquitted all the players.
>
> Some of the Black Sox dreamed of reinstatement for the duration of the 1921 season. Commissioner Landis, in office since March, quickly crushed that hope. He pronounced, "Regardless of the verdict of juries, no player that entertains proposals or promises to throw a game; no player that sits in a conference with a bunch of crooked players and gamblers where the ways and means of throwing games are discussed, and does not promptly tell his club about it, will ever play professional baseball." (Lowenfish and Lupien, *The Imperfect Diamond* [New York: Stein & Day, 1980], pp. 96, 103–104)

Ever since the "Black Sox" scandal, baseball has been extremely sensitive to the issue of gambling. In baseball, the general policy is that baseball owners, officers, directors, and employees cannot own or work for any legalized gambling entities, including casinos and racetracks. However, while the leagues have taken very firm stands against players and their involvement in gambling (see note 2), that has not always been the case with owners. For example, at the same time Bowie Kuhn was banning Willie Mays and Mickey Mantle from baseball (see note 2(c)), George Steinbrenner, owner of the Yankees, was able to keep his interest in the Tampa Downs racetrack in Florida. Baseball has since changed its rules to prohibit its owners from owning any interests in gambling operations, and did suspend Steinbrenner in 1990 for his involvement with former gambler Howard Spira during the 1980s.

The NBA, the NFL, and the NHL all allow their owners to own legal gambling operations, as long as they are not involved in any activity that includes taking bets on league games. The leagues have no prohibition on their owning racetracks or casinos as long as all league games are removed from the betting boards. For example, the NFL allowed Edward DeBartolo, Jr., then owner of the five-time

Super Bowl champion San Francisco 49ers, to pursue gambling licenses even though it bans coaches, players, and other personnel from making promotional appearances involving casinos and gambling cruises. However, in 1997 DeBartolo was forced to give up control of the team after it was discovered that he was the target of an investigation into gambling fraud and extortion. DeBartolo, who paid a $1 million fine for his involvement in the affair, has since given up his stake in the team and his estranged sister, Denise DeBartolo York, and her husband, John York, have assumed full ownership and control.

While the leagues may have no clear policy concerning the gambling interests of their owners, they have worked hard to keep people from gambling on their games through state lotteries and offshore sports books. The leagues lobbied for the passage of the Professional and Amateur Sports Protection Act of 1992 and for the Internet Gambling Prohibition Act of 1999 (see section 16.2.3., "Internet Gambling"). The Professional and Amateur Sports Protection Act of 1992 (28 U.S.C. §3701) prohibits state lotteries based on sports events, except in those states where such lotteries already existed.

Besides their lobbying efforts, the leagues have filed lawsuits to prohibit the use of their games in government lotteries. For example, in *NFL v. Governor of Delaware*, 435 F.Supp. 1372 (D. Del. 1977), the league sued the governor and the director of the state lottery to bar the state from using a lottery based on the outcome of NFL games. The league argued that such a lottery would harm the image of the league by forcing it into association with gambling. The NFL also claimed trademark violation and misappropriation. The court, in upholding the right of the state to conduct such a lottery, held that the use of NFL schedules, scores, and public popularity in the Delaware lottery did not constitute a misappropriation of the league's property. The court did, however, grant the NFL limited injunctive relief, which required the lottery to employ a disclaimer of association with the NFL on all tickets, advertising, and other materials prepared for public distribution.

Another state exempt form the Professional and Amateur Sports Protection Act of 1992 is Oregon. The Oregon Sports Action lottery took in $8.8 million in revenue in 1997 and paid out nearly $5 million in winnings. Profits go to intercollegiate athletics and scholarships at Oregon schools. Oregon also formerly used NBA games in state lotteries. It stopped, however, after being sued by the NBA in the mid-1990s. Although the case was settled, the state never resumed using NBA games, claiming that due to the number of games played every day, it was too difficult for the lottery to put out the programs and set the point spread on an ongoing basis.

NOTES _____

1. For more information on gambling in professional sports, see the following:

a. "Gambling and Sports Scandals," *USA Today*, November 25, 1999. www.usatoday.com/2000/century/sports/008.htm

b. Murray Chass, "The Line on Gambling in Sports a Bit Uneven," *New York Times*, January 18, 1998, sec. 8, p. 1.

c. "Touting the NFL," *USA Today*, October 20, 1998, p. C3.

2. Examples of league sanctions against athletes for gambling or associating with gamblers include the following:

a. In 1998, Australian cricket players Shane Warne and Mark Waugh admitted to taking money from Indian bookies in 1994. The players were fined, but not suspended. In 1999, the Australian Cricket Board admitted that the players should have been suspended in 1994, when the board discovered the offense, but they instead decided to deal with the matter quietly.

b. In 1989, Pete Rose, the all-time hits leader in Major League Baseball history, was banned from the game for his involvement with illegal gambling. The "Dowd Report," the investigation into Rose's wrongdoing, is viewable online and includes a scan of a betting stub and thumbprint that Dowd claims incriminate Rose. (See www.dowdreport.com/)

c. Former players and Hall of Famers Willie Mays and Mickey Mantle were both banned from organized baseball in 1983 after accepting jobs with Atlantic City gambling casinos. The players were reinstated in 1985 by the new baseball commissioner, Peter Ueberroth.

d. In 1963, NFL commissioner Pete Rozelle suspended Hall of Famer and Heisman Trophy winner Paul Hornung (Green Bay Packers) and Alex Karras (Detroit Lions) for an entire season for gambling activity, some of which involved their own teams. Five other players were fined $2,000 each for betting on games in which they did not play.

e. In 1921, eight members of the "Black Sox" (the 1919 Chicago White Sox) were banned from baseball for life by Commissioner Kennesaw Mountain Landis for throwing the 1919 World Series.

16.2.3. Internet Gambling

A growing problem involving sports gambling is the Internet, which provides gamblers with the opportunity to place wagers on professional and college sporting events from the privacy of their homes in virtual anonymity. The Internet also makes betting on sports easier. Instead of going through a bookie, all a gambler needs to place a bet are a computer, Internet access, and a credit card. Many of these bets are placed with casinos in "off-shore" locations in other countries where betting is legal.

In an attempt to police Internet gambling operations, which are illegal in the United States, the government has relied upon Section 1084 of Title 18 of the U.S. Code, "Transmission of wagering information; penalties." Section 1084 states that anyone engaged in the business of betting or wagering who knowingly uses wire communication facilities for the transmission in interstate or foreign commerce of a sports bet or wager is committing a federal crime. Section 1084, however, was enacted in 1961 and was targeted at sports betting over telephone lines. In an effort to update the law to address the Internet, which is quickly moving to a wireless environment and will soon move beyond section 1084 coverage, Senator Jon Kyl of Arizona proposed the Internet Gambling Prohibition Act in 1999. The Act would have made it a violation of federal law to accept bets from the United States over the Internet. In addition, the criminal penalties in Senator Kyl's bill would have served as a deterrent (see note 2). The bill was narrowly defeated in the House of Representatives in 2000, opposed by interests in the NFL and Las Vegas casinos.

In 2001, the U.S. Justice Department was dealt a further blow to its reliance on Section 1084 to combat Internet gambling. In June 2001, Nevada Governor Kenny Guinn signed into law AB466, the "The Nevada Internet Gambling Bill." The state law allows Internet gambling and establishes a licensing procedure and oversight of online gaming. The Justice Department claims the law is both illegal and defiant of federal law. However, Nevada officials contend that the law merely exists to "ensure a lawful and productive transition" to the inevitable day when Internet gambling is legalized. Under the bill, casinos and equipment manufacturers would pay between $50,000 and $500,000 for licensing, and would be taxed 6% on the value of every gambling transaction.

NOTES

1. For more information on the Nevada Internet Gambling Bill, see www.sportslawnews.com/archive/Articles%202001/Nevadainternetgambling.htm

2. The failed Senate Bill S.692, titled The Internet Gambling Prohibition Act of 1999, was introduced on March 23, 1999, and revised June 17, 1999. The act was intended to amend the federal criminal code to make it unlawful for any person engaged in a gambling business to knowingly use the Internet or any other interactive computer service (service) to (1) place, receive, or otherwise make a bet or wager; or (2) send, receive, or invite information assisting in the placing of a bet or wager. For more information, see www.sportslawnews.com/archive/Articles%202000/Internetgambling.htm

3. For more information on Internet gambling, see Steven Crist, "Cyber Gambling: Should It Be Stopped? Can It Be Stopped?," *Sports Illustrated*, January 26, 1998, pp. 82–92.

16.2.4. Fantasy Sports and "Office Pools"

Much like the issue of gambling over the Internet, gambling in fantasy leagues and "office pools" (see note 3 for definitions) presents a predicament for legal authorities. From a *de jure* (valid in law) perspective, such activity is clearly illegal and should be prosecuted in order to uphold respect for existing laws. From a *de facto* (a situation which is accepted for all practical purposes, but is not strictly legal or correct) perspective, there is far too much activity for authorities to police effectively, and the harm created by such activities is usually minimal or non-existent. Most fantasy leagues require an entry fee totaling less than $10 per week, and most "office pools," such as for the NCAA tournament or Kentucky Derby, require entry fees of $20 or less. While these activities seem to constitute gambling, in the legal sense of the word, they do not appear to be much of a threat to either the society at large or the integrity of sports. A criticism of gambling from a legal perspective is speculation that compulsive gamblers will commit illegal activity and mistreat their families because of their gambling debts. A criticism of gambling from a sports perspective is the speculation that gambling will lead to the fixing of games. Neither of these concerns appears to be valid in the context of fantasy sports and office pools, due to the small per-person amounts that are wagered.

Furthermore, certain states—such as Indiana, Wisconsin, New Jersey, and New York—have laws which stipulate that gambling is *legal* if it involves a game of "skill" rather than of "chance" (see note 1). For example, it would be legal to create a prize money pool for a chess tournament in such states, but not legal to create a prize money pool for a bingo tournament. One could argue, in these states, that one's ability to evaluate talent (players in fantasy leagues, teams or horses in office pools) is the "material factor" in the game, rather than luck. There is little case precedent in this area. In *Boardwalk Regency Corp. v. Attorney General of New Jersey*, 457 A.2d 847 (N.J. Super. Ct. Law Div. 1982), the court found that the material factor in the game of backgammon was a dice roll, not skill, and therefore gambling on backgammon was found to be illegal.

Professional sports leagues, players associations, the NCAA, and television networks have all benefited from the enthusiasm over fantasy leagues and office pools (see note 3 for participation data). The Major League Baseball Players Association (MLBPA) made this clear during debates over the Internet Gambling Prohibition Act of 1999 (see section 16.2.3., "Internet Gambling"). The language of the act suggested that individuals running fantasy leagues with an entry fee would be subject to a fine of up to $20,000, four years in prison, or both (see note 1). Consequently, the MLBPA sent its representative, Marianne McGettigan, to testify against the passage of the act, which was eventually defeated in 2000. In particular, McGettigan pointed out that sports leagues are impervious to the corruption of fantasy leagues due to the rules and structure of such leagues. In other words, participants have multiple players on different teams that may oppose one another during the season. Hence, there is no incentive to influence competition.

Because the Internet has spawned a boom in fantasy leagues, their legal future probably hinges on developments in Internet gambling law. Such laws will have less effect on office pools. While three million people participated worldwide in online office pools for the 2001 NCAA Division I-A men's basketball tournament, according to *Time.com*, the vast majority of office pools are cash enterprises kept within one locale. Consequently, office pools are prosecuted only sporadically by police (see note 2).

NOTES ————————————————————————————————

1. For more information on the legal implications of this issue, see Michael J. Thompson, "Give Me $25 on Red and Derek Jeter for $26: Do Fantasy Sports Leagues Constitute Gambling?" 8 *The Sports Lawyers Journal* 21 (Spring 2001).

2. In 2001, police in the town of Hartland, Wisconsin, broke up an "office pool" in which about twenty eighth grade students paid $5 each to gamble on the outcome of the annual men's college basketball championship tournament.

3. Description of fantasy leagues and office pools:

  a. In fantasy leagues, participants usually pay an entry fee (occasionally leagues are free) to draft a set number of players prior to a season. Over the course of a season, participants are awarded a certain number of points based on the statistics generated by their players. The participant with the greatest number of points at the season's end usually wins a cash prize. Between 14 and 30 million consumers participated in fantasy sports games in 2001, up from an estimated 1 million in 1989, according to Greg Johnson, "Fantasy Sports, Tangible Profits: Online Game Sites Are on Their Way to Turning Loyal Fans into Paying Customers," *Los Angeles Times*, April 3, 2001, p. C-1.

  b. Typically, participants contribute $5–20 to an "office pool." Each participant fills out a list of winners (a "bracket") in the case of a tournament or a predicted score in the case of an individual game (such as the Super Bowl). The person whose prediction is most accurate wins the entire pot, or in some cases there are second prizes, third prizes, etc., or the pot is divided accordingly. According to a 1999 Society for Human Resource Management study of 504 human resources managers, 30 percent knew of NCAA tournament pools in their workplace and 55 percent knew of Super Bowl pools in their workplace. Thirteen percent of respondents said the pools had a positive effect on productivity. However, most experts estimate hundreds of millions of dollars are lost on time spent filling out brackets and calling up sport Web sites on company time. For more information, see Tommy Cummings, "Productivity Sinks in Office Pools," *San Francisco Chronicle*, March 14, 2001, www.websense.com/company/news/features/01/031401.cfm

16.3. DISABILITIES

The line between a lawful refusal to extend affirmative action and illegal discrimination against handicapped persons will not always be clear. It is possible to envision situations where an insistence on continuing past requirements and practices might arbitrarily deprive genuinely qualified handicapped persons of the opportunity to participate in a covered program. (*Southeastern Community College v. Davis*, 442 U.S. 397 [1979])

In athletics, the line between lawful refusal to modify existing requirements and illegally discriminating against disabled persons is likely to be interpreted in the future. This is especially true in light of the U.S. Supreme Court's 2001 decision requiring the PGA to permit Casey Martin, a disabled golfer, to use a golf cart in competition. Since 1990, when the Americans with Disabilities Act (ADA) was signed into law, disabled athletes have used the ADA and other federal disability legislation to force high schools, colleges, the NCAA, and professional sports to change their rules to accommodate the individual's disability.

Yet, even with the enactment of the ADA, disabled athletes still face a number of obstacles in their struggle to participate in athletics. In an attempt to protect or shield themselves from liability, as well as to protect the athlete, a number of athletic organizations have developed policies prohibiting athletes with certain medical conditions or disabilities from participating in athletics or other extracurricular activities. This section examines the evolution of disability legislation and the impact the laws have had on athletes with disabilities.

16.3.1. Federal Laws Affecting Persons with Disabilities

As recently as the 1970s, children with learning disabilities were regularly denied access to a number of state public school systems because it was thought that their presence would interfere with the learning environment. In 1973, Congress began enacting legislation designed to increase the educational and social opportunities available to individuals with disabilities. The first law passed by Congress was the Rehabilitation Act of 1973, 29 U.S.C. Section 701 et seq. This was followed by the Education for all Handicapped Children Act of 1975, later renamed the Individuals with Disabilities Education Act (IDEA) in 1990. Congress has also passed the Amateur Sports Act, and most recently the Americans with Disabilities Act (ADA).

16.3.1.1. The Rehabilitation Act

One of the stated intents of the Rehabilitation Act is to provide individuals with disabilities the opportunity to participate in physical education and athletic programs or activities without being discriminated against due to their disability. Section 504 of the Rehabilitation Act states:

No otherwise qualified handicapped individual in the United States . . . shall solely by reason of his handicap, be excluded from participation in, be denied the benefits of, or be subjected to discrimination under any program or activity receiving Federal financial assistance.

In order for an individual to establish a claim under Section 504, he or she must successfully meet four requirements. First, the individual must show that he or she is a "handicapped individual." The definitions used in the Rehabilitation Act and the ADA are very similar in that they define an individual as having a "disability" if he or she has:

1. A physical or mental impairment that substantially limits one or more of the major life activities of such individual
2. A record of such an impairment or
3. being regarded as having such an impairment.

Second, the individual must show that he or she is "otherwise qualified" for the athletic activity. A person is otherwise qualified if he or she can meet all of a program's requirements in spite of his or her disability. Third, the individual must show that he or she is being excluded from athletic participation "solely by reason of" the disability. The fourth and final requirement is that the school or institution is receiving federal financial assistance.

The majority of challenges under Section 504 in athletics hinge on the judicial interpretation of the "otherwise qualified" element or the "solely by reason of" element. Therefore, an examination of the meaning of these two elements is important. The U.S. Supreme Court has interpreted the phrase "otherwise qualified person" to mean someone who is able to meet all of a program's requirements in spite of his or her disability. Therefore, the Rehabilitation Act does not compel an organization to disregard a disabled person's individual impairment. Nor does the act require the organization to make substantial modifications in its programs to accommodate the disabled individual.

However, even though there are no affirmative obligations on recipients of federal funds, there are situations where refusal to modify an existing program might become unreasonable and discriminatory. For example, in *Dennin v. Connecticut Interscholastic Athletic Conference (CIAC)*, 94 F.3d 96 (2nd Cir. 1996), the court was asked to decide whether a nineteen-year-old high school student suffering from Downs Syndrome could participate on his high school swim team. The plaintiff, due to his age, was prohibited from participating on his high school swimming team by the Connecticut Interscholastic Athletic Conference (CIAC). The court held that Dennin was "otherwise qualified" to participate on the swim team, and that it would be reasonable for the CIAC to accommodate him by waiving the age requirement. Waiving the rule, the court concluded, would not fundamentally or substantially alter the nature of the program in any way or undermine any of the stated purposes of the rule. Therefore, while an organization is not required to make fundamental or substantial modifications to accommodate the disabled, it may be required to make reasonable ones as long as the accommodations do not impose an undue hardship on the operation of its program. In determining whether an accommodation would impose an undue hardship, the court can considered the nature and cost of the accommodation.

The "excluded solely by reason of the disability" requirement is met if the disabled individual is being excluded due to his or her disability. For example, in *Poole v. South Plainfield Board of Education*, 490 F.Supp. 948 (D.N.J. 1980), the South Plainfield Board of Education refused to let Richard Poole wrestle for his high school because he had only one kidney. Poole, who was born with this condition, sued the school board, claiming that they were violating his rights under Section 504. In allowing Poole to compete, the court held that he was otherwise qualified to participate in high school sports and that he was being exclude from participation "solely by reason of" the fact that he had one kidney. The court also found that whatever duty the board may have had toward Poole was satisfied once it became clear that Poole and his parents knew of the dangers involved in Poole's participation on the team.

The issue of whether someone is being excluded "solely by reason of" their disability is more difficult when an individual, due to an illness or learning disability, is over the athletic association's maximum age requirement by the time he or she reaches the senior year of high school. For example, in *University Interscholastic League (UIL) v. Buchanan*, 848 S.W.2d 298 (Tex. Ct. App. 1993), two nineteen-year-old students, who were diagnosed with learning disabilities, sought a permanent injunction against the enforcement of UIL's rule requiring all athletes to be under nineteen years old. The UIL argued that the age requirement was necessary to ensure the safety of the participating student-athletes and to ensure the equality of competitors. The UIL also argued that the age rule did not discriminate against the plaintiffs because of their disabilities, but was applied equally against both disabled and non-disabled students. Therefore, the plaintiffs were ineligible due to their ages, not their disabilities. In allowing the athletes to compete, the court of appeals found that except for their disabilities the students would have been age-eligible to participate in interscholastic athletics. It was due to their learning disabilities that they were still in school. Therefore, the court of appeals held, the waiver of the age rule would have been a reasonable accommodation by UIL to ensure that disabled athletes achieve meaningful access.

16.3.1.2. Individuals with Disabilities Education Act (IDEA)

Enacted as the Education for all Handicapped Children Act of 1975, and amended and renamed the Individuals with Disabilities Education Act (IDEA), 20 U.S.C. Section 1400 et seq., in 1990, IDEA was designed to increase the educational opportunity available to disabled children and to secure the right of all disabled children to a free and appropriate public education that emphasizes special education and related services designed to meet their unique needs.

In order to satisfy the goal of Congress, IDEA requires that local educational agencies, together with the disabled student's teacher and parents, develop a written statement or an individualized education program (IEP) outlining achievable educational objectives for the student. Although the regulations adopted under the IDEA are less specific with regard to athletics than those pursuant to Section 504, IDEA does require each public agency to ensure that a variety of educational programs and services, including physical education, available to non-disabled children are available to those covered under the act. Besides providing educational programs and services, each public agency is required to provide non-academic and extracurricular activities and services, including interscholastic athletics, in such manner as is necessary to afford children with disabilities an equal opportunity for participation in those services and activities (34 C.F.R. Section 300.306(a)). For example, in *Lambert v. West Virginia State Board of Education*, 447 S.E.2d 901 (W.Va. 1994), a high school basketball player, who has been deaf since birth, won the right to require her school to provide her with a sign language interpreter so that she could compete on the girl's basketball team. The student was provided with a signer for her basic courses, but the West Virginia Board of Education refused to provide a signer for her vocational classes or her extracurricular activities. In holding that the board of education was required to provide a signer for the plaintiff, the court found that the assistance of a signer was a reasonable accommodation that provided the plaintiff with equal access to extracurricular activities.

Another example of a student-athlete's successfully using the IDEA to gain participation rights is *Crocker v. Tennessee Secondary School Athletic Ass'n*, 980 F.2d 382 (6th Cir. 1992). In *Crocker* the plaintiff transferred from a private school into his local public high school so that he could receive the special education he needed, which was not available in the private school. When the plaintiff attempted to participate in interscholastic athletics at his new school, the TSSAA ruled that he was ineligible. According to TSSAA rule, any student who transfers from one TSSAA member school to another is ineligible to participate in interscholastic sports for twelve months. The plaintiff argued that the TSSAA, by enforcing its transfer rule, was depriving him of his rights guaranteed under the IDEA. In ruling for Crocker, the court held that since the plaintiff's transfer was motivated by his disability, TSSAA's refusal to waive its transfer rule violated the IDEA.

In *Crocker*, however, the court failed to address the issue of whether the plaintiff's participation in interscholastic athletics was a related service that should have been incorporated into his individualized education program (IEP). The importance of including participation in interscholastic athletics in a student's IEP can be seen in *T.H. v. Montana High School Ass'n*, No. CV 92-150-BLG-JFB, 1992 WL 672982 (D. Mont. Sept. 24, 1992). The plaintiff, after being diagnosed as having a learning disability, was provided with an IEP in accordance with the IDEA. One component of T.H.'s IEP was that he participate in interscholastic athletics as a motivational tool.

Before his senior year, the Montana High School Association ruled T.H. ineligible to compete in interscholastic athletics due to his age. In finding for the plaintiff, the court held that while students have no constitutional right to participate in interscholastic sports—it is a privilege that may be withdrawn by the school or a voluntary association—when participation in interscholastic sports is included as a component of the IEP as a related service, the privilege of competing in interscholastic sports is transformed into a federally protected right.

16.3.1.3. The Amateur Sports Act

Another piece of legislation affecting the rights of disabled athletes is the Amateur Sports Act, 36 U.S.C. Section 371–396. The Amateur Sports Act names the U.S. Olympic Committee (USOC) as the coordinator of amateur athletics in the United States. As the coordinator of amateur athletics, one of the goals of the USOC is to "encourage and provide assistance to amateur athletic programs and competition for handicapped individuals, including, where feasible, the expansion of opportunities for meaningful participation by handicapped individuals in programs of athletic competition for able-bodied individuals." In order to accomplish its goal, the USOC established the Committee on Sports for the Disabled. The committee helps disabled athletes by removing unnecessary barriers to competition and supporting organizations that provide sports experiences for disabled individuals.

Under the Amateur Sports Act, updated in 1998, it has become the "first priority" of the USOC to merge Paralympic sports with existing able-bodied National Governing Bodies (NGBs). Responding to this mandate, the executive committee of the USOC met in December 1999 and promised to find additional funding for disabled athletes. The USOC, which supports about 20,000 elite disabled athletes, increased the funds it provided for games for the disabled from $1.7 million in the 1993–1996 quadrennial to $2,964,031 in 1997–2000. The executive committee also considered whether to transfer elite disabled athletes from the organizations that now govern them, disabled sports organizations, to the NGBs that oversee able-bodied athletes in those sports. The executive committee, however, stopped short of requiring NGBs to embrace disabled programs, and took no official stance on how the forty-five NGBs should handle programs for the disabled.

NOTES _____

talker a good game but does it fulfill

1. In 2001, five sports organizations for the disabled sent a formal letter of complaint to USOC President Sandra Baldwin, alleging "separate and unequal treatment" under the Amateur Sports Act Amendments of 1998. Although the act was intended to improve opportunities for the disabled, the protesting sports organizations (including Wheelchair Sports USA) claimed that, due to a segregated governance structure, "athletes with disabilities have been denied effective representation on USOC committees, including the important Athlete's Advisory Committee; cannot obtain services provided to Olympic athletes, such as medical insurance, equal access to training facilities and sports medicine clinics, and participation in the Athletes-in-Residence program." For more information, see www.sportslawnews.com/archive/Articles%202001/USOCDisabled.htm

2. Mark Shepherd, manager of the USOC's Disabled Sports Services, filed an $11 million disability discrimination lawsuit against the USOC in October 1999. In a twenty-three-count complaint, Shepherd said he did not receive the same staff, budget, or pay as other senior Olympic officials with similar responsibilities, and he said programs for disabled athletes receive less funding.

16.3.1.4. Americans with Disabilities Act (ADA)

While many people predicted that the Americans with Disabilities Act (ADA), 42 U.S.C. Section 12101 et seq., would have a large impact on athletic facilities and how they accommodated spectators with disabilities, the biggest impact the law has had is on athletic participation and coaching opportunities. Signed into law July 26, 1990, the ADA has as its purpose "to provide a clear and comprehensive national mandate for the elimination of discrimination against individuals with disabilities." The ADA focuses on eradicating barriers, by requiring public entities to consider whether reasonable accommodations can be made to remove any barrier created by a person's disability.

The three sections that athletic managers and attorneys should be aware of are Title I, which covers employment; Title II, which covers public services; and Title III, which covers public accommodations and services operated by private entities.

16.3.1.5. Title I—Employment (ADA)

Title I (42 U.S.C. Section 12112) provides that "no covered entity shall discriminate against a qualified individual with a disability because of the disability of such individual in regard to job application procedures, the hiring, advancement, or discharge of employees, employee compensation, job training, and other terms, conditions, and privileges of employment." In *Clemons v. Big Ten Conference*, No. 96C0124 1997 U.S. Dist. LEXIS 1939 (N.D. Ill. Feb. 19, 1997), a former employee, who had been terminated from his position as a college football official after he failed to comply with his employer's instructions to lose weight, brought action against the Big Ten Conference under ADA. The district court, in dismissing the case, held that the reason the employee was fired was because he failed to perform his job satisfactorily. The court also noted that the Big Ten Conference did not regard the employee as being disabled under ADA.

16.3.1.6. Title II—Public Services (ADA)

Title II (42 U.S.C. Section 12132), which is based on Section 504 of the Rehabilitation Act, provides that "no qualified individual with a disability shall, by reason of such disability, be excluded from participation in or be denied the benefits of the services, programs, or activities of a public entity, or be subjected to discrimination by any such entity."

In order for an individual to successfully state a claim under the ADA, he or she must establish the following elements. First, an individual must show that he or she is a "qualified individual with a disability." The ADA defines a "qualified individual with a disability" as any physically or mentally disabled individual "who, with or without reasonable modifications . . . meets the essential eligibility requirements for the receipt of services or the participation in programs or activities provided by a public entity." Second, the individual must show that he or she is "otherwise qualified" for the athletic activity. Third, an individual must show that he or she is being excluded from athletic participation "solely by reason of" his or her disability. The fourth element that an individual must show is that he or she is being discriminated against by a public entity.

Even if the plaintiff is able to meet all four elements necessary under Title II, the courts will still uphold as valid any rule, policy, or procedure if waiving it would constitute a fundamental alteration in the nature of the association or impose an undue hardship on the organization or poses a direct threat to the health or safety of others.

An example of how the courts have interpreted Title II of the ADA is *Johnson v. Florida High School Activities Ass'n*, 899 F.Supp. 579 (M.D. Fla. 1995). Dennis Johnson, a nineteen-year-old student, sought a preliminary injunction allowing him to play high school football and wrestle. At the age of nine months, the plaintiff suffered from meningitis and lost all hearing in one ear and most of his hearing in the other ear. Due to his hearing impairment, Johnson was held out of kindergarten for one year (his parent's decision) and forced to repeat the first grade (the school's decision). Before entering his senior year of high school, Johnson sought a waiver of FHSAA's age eligibility requirement. The FHSAA refused to waive the age requirement, stating that it was an essential eligibility requirement, and Johnson filed a lawsuit seeking an injunction.

The FHSAA, citing the Eighth Circuit Court's decision in *Pottgen v. Missouri State High School Activities Ass'n*, 40 F.3d 926 (8th Cir. 1994), argued that the plaintiff was not "otherwise qualified" to participate and that "no reasonable accommodation" could be made so as to make the plaintiff "otherwise qualified." The FHSAA also argued that Title II did not apply to it because it was not a "public entity" as defined by the ADA.

In rejecting the FHSAA's argument, the court held that the FHSAA had already been found to be a state actor. It followed, therefore, that the FHSAA was an instrument of the state and a public entity. As for the issue of whether the plaintiff was "otherwise qualified" to participate in interscholastic athletics—and if not, whether reasonable accommodations could be made to make him "otherwise qualified"—the court held that the age requirement serves as a simple threshold standard by which the FHSAA can achieve the desired goals of safety and fairness. Absent of these purposes, the age requirement has no purpose. Thus, to assert that the age requirement is an absolute, unwaivable rule is to place form over substance. The court also held that waiving the age-eligibility requirement did not fundamentally alter the nature or purpose of the program. The court reasoned that allowing the athlete to participate in interscholastic athletics did not "undermine the purposes of the age requirement." Furthermore, Johnson was not a "star athlete," nor was he more experienced than the other players. Because safety and fairness would not be compromised, the court concluded that waiving the age requirement constituted a "reasonable accommodation" and had to be undertaken.

16.3.1.7. Title III—Public Accommodations Operated by Private Entities (ADA)

Title III provides that "no individual shall be discriminated against on the basis of disability in the full and equal enjoyment of the goods, services, facilities, privileges, advantages, or accommodations of any place of public accommodation by any person who owns, leases, or operates a place of public accommodation" (42 U.S.C. Section 12182).

Under Title III of the ADA, the following private entities are considered public accommodations: motion picture houses, theaters, concert halls, stadiums, other places of exhibition or entertainment, camps, gymnasiums, health spas, bowling alleys, golf courses, or other places of exercise or recreation (42 U.S.C. 12181).

A key element in Title III cases is control. In *Cortez v. NBA*, 960 F.Supp. 113 (W.D. Tex. 1997), the court rejected a claim under Title III of the ADA against the NBA by a group of hearing-impaired spectators who had attended professional basketball games at the Alamodome. The plaintiffs were seeking interpretative and captioning services, as a reasonable accommodation, for deaf and hard-of-hearing individuals who attend NBA games at the Alamodome and other arenas. In dismissing the claim against the league, the court held that the league did not own, lease, or operate a place of public accommodation.

16.3.2. Application to Athletic Organizations

Most of the remainder of this chapter will chronicle the ways that various courts have interpreted laws which affect persons with disabilities. Though the text is broken down by industry sector, persons in *all* sectors of the sports industry should pay particular attention to the discussion of *PGA Tour v. Casey Martin* in section 16.3.2.4., "Professional Sports." First of all, as a U.S. Supreme Court decision, the judgment is binding throughout the land. Second, the Court's opinion provides a standard for "reasonable accommodation" and guidance as to how other courts should interpret what does or does not "fundamentally alter" a sport or sports organization.

16.3.2.1. *Youth Sports*

In *Anderson v. Little League Baseball, Inc.*, 794 F.Supp. 342 (D. Ariz. 1992), a youth baseball coach, who was confined to a wheelchair and had coached Little League Baseball for the previous three years as an on-field coach, sued the Little League after it adopted a policy prohibiting coaches in wheelchairs from on-field coaching. In support of the policy, the Little League pointed out that the ADA specifically "does not require a public accommodation to permit an individual to participate . . . when that individual poses a direct threat to the health or safety of others" (28 C.F.R. Section 36.208). The stated intent of the policy was to protect the players from collisions with the wheelchair during the game.

Whether a person poses a direct threat to the health or safety of others, the court held, may not be based on generalizations or stereotypes about the effects of a particular disability; but must be based on an individual assessment. There was no evidence, the court held, to indicate that the plaintiff posed a direct threat to the health or safety of others. The Little League's policy amounted to an absolute ban on coaches in wheelchairs in the coach's box, regardless of the coach's disability or the field or game conditions involved. Such a policy, the court held, falls markedly short of the requirements of the ADA.

Another case involving the ADA and youth sports was the 1999 conflict between Ryan Taylor and the Lawton Evening Optimist Soccer Association in Lawton, Oklahoma. Taylor, who has cerebral palsy, used a walker to help him get around and play. Fearing another player would trip over the walker and hurt Taylor or other children, the soccer association banned him from playing. The ban was lifted after U.S. District Judge David Russell found "it very remote that there could be some injury [from the walker]." The judge did, however, order that the walker be well padded.

16.3.2.2. *High School*

The area that has seen the most litigation is high school athletic association eligibility rules. The two eligibility rules that have come under attack the most are the age limit, which prohibits a high school athlete from participation in high school sports after reaching the state athletic association's maximum age requirement, and the eight-semester rule, which prohibits a high school athlete from participating in high school sports if he or she has been enrolled in grades nine to twelve, inclusive, for more than eight semesters.

The courts are almost equally divided on whether state high school athletic associations are required under federal disability law to waive an eligibility requirement. In West Virginia, New York, the Eighth Circuit, and the Sixth Circuit, the courts have held that waiving a state high school athletic association's age requirement was not required under the ADA because it would constitute a fundamental alteration in the nature of the state's interscholastic programs (see note 1). Other jurisdictions, including Connecticut, Oregon, Florida, and the Seventh Circuit, have concluded that the ADA does require high school athletic associations to waive their eligibility requirements (see note 2).

It is important to note, however, that while these rules may seem reasonable, it often takes a student with a disability extra time to finish high school. Therefore, when applied to older disabled students, especially in non-contact sports and in sports like wrestling, where competitors are matched by weight, some courts have found them to be unreasonable.

NOTES _____

1. The principal function of a state high school athletic association is to promulgate rules and regulations for its member schools that will promote fair athletic competition. When an athletic association's rule or regulation is challenged in a court of law, the court will generally defer to the judgment of the athletic association on eligibility matters unless there is evidence of fraud, collusion, or lack of jurisdiction, or when the school's actions were arbitrary or capricious. The courts, however, have also recognized the rights of disabled student-athletes to challenge an association's eligibility rules under the Rehabilitation Act and the ADA.

The following cases examine student challenges to state high school athletic association eligibility restriction.

   a. In *McPherson v. Michigan High School Athletic Ass'n*, 119 F.3d 453 (6th Cir. 1997), Dion McPherson challenged the validity of the Michigan High School Athletic Association's eight-semester eligibility rule, contending that the rule violates the Americans with Disabilities Act and Section 504 of the Rehabilitation Act. The Sixth Circuit, in overturning the district court's decision, held that the eight-semester rule was a necessary eligibility requirement, and that waiving it would impose an immense financial and administrative burden on the MSHAA. Therefore, accommodating McPherson would be unreasonable.

   b. In *Sandison v. Michigan High School Athletic Ass'n*, 64 F.3d 1026 (6th Cir. 1995). Ronald Sandison and Craig Stanley sought an injunction preventing the MSHAA from enforcing its nineteen-year age limit against them. The Sixth Circuit found that the plaintiffs had failed to meet two of the four elements necessary to bring a claim under Section 504 and the ADA. First, the court of appeals found that the plaintiffs were not "otherwise qualified" for participation on their high school track teams. A person is "otherwise qualified" to participate if, with reasonable accommodations, the individual can meet all the "necessary" requirements of the program. Waiving the eligibility rule and allowing older and more physically mature students to compete with younger students, the Sixth Circuit held, would be a fundamental alteration of the MSHAA. The Sixth Circuit also held that the plaintiffs failed to show that they were being excluded from participation "solely by reason of" their disabilities. The reason the plaintiffs were being denied the opportunity to participate in high school athletics, the court of appeals held, was due to their date of birth, not their disabilities.

2. Other cases that have upheld state eligibility requirements include *Hoot v. Milan School District*, 853 F.Supp. 243 (E.D. Mich. 1994); *Landers v. West Virginia Secondary School Activities Commission*, 447 S.E.2d 901 (W.Va. 1994); *Pottgen v. Missouri State High School Athletic Ass'n*, 40 F.3d 926 (8th Cir. 1994); *Reaves v. Mills*, 904 F.Supp. 120 (W.D.N.Y. 1995); *Sadler v. University Interscholastic League*, 1991 WL 633967 (W.D. Tex. 1991).

3. The following cases have concluded that the Rehabilitation Act and the ADA do require high school athletic associations to waive their eligibility requirement.

   a. In *Dennin v. Connecticut Interscholastic Athletic Conference*, 94 F.3d 96 (2nd Cir. Conn. 1996), the court was asked to decide whether a nineteen-year-old high school student suffering from Downs Syndrome could participate on his high school swim team. The plaintiff, due to his age, was prohibited from participating on his high school swimming team by the Connecticut Interscholastic Athletic Conference (CIAC). In determining that Dennin was "otherwise qualified" to participate on the swim team, and that it would be reasonable for the CIAC to accommodate Dennin by waiving the age requirement, the court concluded that waiving the rule would not alter the nature of the program in any way or undermine any of the stated purposes of the rule.

   b. In *Washington v. Indiana High School Athletic Ass'n*, 181 F.3d 840 (7th Cir. 1999), Eric Washington, a learning-disabled student at Central Catholic High School, obtained a preliminary injunction in the district court enjoining the IHSAA from denying him athletic eligibility. The IHSAA ruled that Washington was ineligible under the eight-semester rule. Washington challenged the IHSSA's policy on the ground that failure to grant a waiver of the eight-semester rule violates Title II of the ADA. The Seventh Circuit Court upheld the injunction, finding such a waiver reasonable. The court rejected IHSAA's claim that granting a waiver would impose an undue hardship because it would be flooded with other cases.

4. Other cases include *Bingham v. Oregon School Activities Ass'n.*, 37 F.Supp. 2d 1189 (D. Or. 1999); *Rhodes v. Ohio High School Athletic Ass'n.*, 939 F.Supp. 584 (N.D. Ohio 1996); *Johnson v. Florida High School Activities Association*, 899 F.Supp. 579 (M.D. Fla. 1995); *Booth v. El Paso Independent School District*, No. A-90-CA-764 (Tex. Dist. Ct. 1990).

16.3.2.3. Colleges, Universities, and the NCAA

The federal courts have faced many different issues on how to apply the ADA to intercollegiate athletes. For example, in *Ganden v. NCAA* the court ruled that waiving the NCAA's core academic requirements would fundamentally alter the nature of college athletics (see note 3). On the other hand, the court in *Butler v. NCAA* found that Title III of the ADA was applicable to the NCAA and ruled that waiving the NCAA's core requirements would not fundamentally alter college athletics (see note 4).

Future issues regarding college athletes with learning disabilities, however, may be reduced. In May 1998, the U.S. Justice Department and the NCAA entered into a consent decree that will allow hundreds of individuals with learning disabilities who do not meet the initial eligibility requirements to keep their fourth year of athletic eligibility. The decree also states that the NCAA will no longer disqualify a course simply because it includes the designations "special needs," "remedial," or "special education."

That decree resulted from the lawsuit filed by Michael Bowers (see note 1), who claimed he had been denied an athletic scholarship in 1997 (prior to the decree) due to his learning disability. Bowers's case for damages is pending, but even if he is unable to obtain relief, District Court Judge Stephen Orlafsky has already ruled that the NCAA is subject to the Americans with Disabilities Act because it is a "place of public accommodation." Consequently, the NCAA may be susceptible to increased disability claims.

NOTES

1. In *Bowers v. NCAA*, 130 F.Supp. 2d 610 (D. N.J. 2001), a learning-disabled football player was denied participation in athletics by NCAA rules as a college freshman due to a poor standardized test score. Bowers also claimed that colleges refused to recruit him because they knew he'd be a non-qualifier under NCAA rules. He therefore brought suit in 1997 under the ADA, the Rehabilitation Act, and the New Jersey Law Against Discrimination. As of 2002, the case was still awaiting trial after four judges' decisions. However, the court has established that (1) Bowers may recover monetary damages under the Rehabilitation Act if he can prove he was discriminated against intentionally, and (2) the NCAA is a place of public accommodation, and therefore subject to the ADA.

2. In *Tatum v. NCAA*, 992 F.Supp. 1114 (E.D. Mo. 1998), a basketball player with generalized anxiety disorder and a specific phobia related to testing brought suit against the NCAA when the NCAA failed to recognized his "untimed" test scores. According to NCAA Bylaw 14.3.1.4.3, untimed tests are recognized only for persons who are "learning disabled" or "handicapped." The NCAA contended that the plaintiff was neither. The court ruled in favor of the NCAA, refusing to grant injunctive relief due to an unlikelihood of success on the merits of the case.

3. In *Ganden v. NCAA*, No. 96 C 6953, 1996 U.S. Dist. LEXIS 17368 (N.D. Ill. Nov. 19, 1996), a college swimmer who had a learning disability sued the NCAA to permit him

to participate in swimming competitions until resolution of his claims against NCAA under the Americans with Disabilities Act. The district court, in finding for the NCAA, held that swimmer did not demonstrate reasonable likelihood of success at trial so as to be entitled to a preliminary injunction.

4. In *Butler v. NCAA*, No. C 96-1656 D, 1996 WL 1058233 (W.D. Wash. Nov. 8, 1996) a court found in favor of the student plaintiff Butler, who was offered a full scholarship to attend the University of Washington and play for its football team. However, the NCAA declared plaintiff academically ineligible to participate in Division I college athletics when he failed meet the NCAA core course requirements. As a result, Butler was removed from the football team and his scholarship was revoked. Butler sued the NCAA, claiming that the academic eligibility requirements discriminated against persons with learning disabilities in violation of Title III of the ADA. In rejecting the NCAA's motion to dismiss, the court found that even though Butler's likelihood of success on the merits might not be strong, the harm he would suffer if the court refused to issue a preliminary injunction far outweighed that of the NCAA.

5. In *Pahulu v. University of Kansas*, 897 F.Supp. 1387 (D. Kan. 1995), a college student, who was disqualified by the team physician from participation in intercollegiate football, brought suit against the university, alleging violation of the Rehabilitation Act. The district court held that Pahulu, who had been barred from playing football following the discovery that he had a congenitally narrow cervical canal, was not "disabled" within the meaning of the Act, even though intercollegiate football might be part of the major life activity of learning. The court also concluded that even if Pahulu was disabled, he was not otherwise qualified, given the university physician's conclusion that he was at extremely high risk for subsequent, and potentially permanent, severe neurological injury.

6. In *Knapp v. Northwestern University*, 101 F.3d 473 (7th Cir. 1996), a student who had been barred from participation in intercollegiate basketball because of a heart defect filed action against the university, seeking declaratory relief, preliminary and permanent injunctive relief, and compensatory damages under the Rehabilitation Act. In rejecting the student's claim, the court of appeals held that Knapp was not "disabled" within the meaning of the Rehabilitation Act because his condition did not affect the major life activity of learning. The court also held that playing intercollegiate basketball was not in and of itself a major life activity, because it was not a basic function of life on the same level as walking, breathing, and speaking. Finally, the court concluded that the existence of substantial risk of future harm and severity of injury risked made Knapp not "otherwise qualified" within the meaning of the Rehabilitation Act. As a matter of law, the court held Northwestern must be allowed to make its own determinations of substantial risk and severity of injury if they are based on reliable evidence.

7. In *Maddox v. University of Tennessee*, 62 F.3d 843 (6th Cir. 1995), a former assistant university football coach sued the university, its board of trustees, and its athletic director for disability discrimination, alleging that he was discharged on the basis of a disability, alcoholism. In granting the university's motion for summary judgment, the court of appeals held that the university did not discharge the coach solely because of a disability.

16.3.2.4. Professional Sports

The sport of golf has served as the primary proving ground for professional athletes to use disability laws in order to challenge organizational rules—in particular the cases of *Martin v. PGA Tour* and *Olinger v. U.S. Golf Association*.

The case of *Martin v. PGA* began when Casey Martin, a disabled professional golfer, brought action against the PGA Tour alleging that, by failing to make golf cart available to him, the PGA failed to make its golf tournaments accessible to disabled individuals in violation of Title III of the ADA. Title III pertains to public accommodations operated by private organizations, and the PGA is a private organization. Martin suffers from Klippel-Trenaunay-Weber syndrome, a degenerative circulatory disorder that prevents him from walking golf courses, and his disorder constitutes a disability under the ADA. In defense, the PGA Tour argued that its walking-only rule was an essential element of professional golf on the PGA and Nike tours, and that waiving the rule would fundamentally alter the nature of the sport. In addition, the PGA disputed that membership on the PGA Tour was "public accommodation," a requirement of Title III. The district court in *Martin v. PGA Tour, Inc.*, 994 F.Supp. 1242 (D. Or. 1998), held that use of golf cart, as reasonable modification to accommodate disabled professional golfer, would not frustrate the purpose of the association's walking-rule and would not alter the fundamental nature of professional golf tournament competition. In other words, the fatigue that Martin suffers, even with the aid of a golf cart, is greater than the fatigue his able-bodied competitors face when walking the course. Furthermore, the district court concluded that golf courses *are* places of public accommodation during tournaments.

The judgment of the Oregon District Court was affirmed by the Ninth Circuit Court of Appeals in *Martin v. PGA Tour*, 204 F.3d 994 (9th Cir. 2000). One of the arguments raised by the PGA Tour in the *Martin* case was that the court's decision would impose an undue hardship on the organization by forcing it to review numerous appeals by other golfers. As if to validate the PGA concerns, Ford Olinger, another professional golfer whose physical condition (bilateral avascular necrosis) prevented him from playing a full round of golf on foot, sought a court order allowing him to use a golf cart to qualify for and compete in the U.S. Open golf tournament. However, unlike Martin, the court in *Olinger v. U.S. Golf Ass'n.*, 55 F.Supp. 2d 926 (N.D. Ind. 1999), refused to apply the ADA. The district court held that while the USGA was subject to ADA with regard to golf tournaments, the use of golf cart at tournaments would fundamentally change the nature of the activity, and thus was not mandated by ADA. Athletic competition, the court held, presents ADA concerns different from those presented by the workplace. In the workplace, the pertinent inquiry is whether a particular otherwise qualified individual can perform the job if a reasonable accommodation is made to allow for the person's disability. The point of an athletic competition, in contrast, is to decide who, under conditions that are about the same for everyone, can perform an assigned set of tasks better than (not as well as) any other competitor. The set of tasks assigned to the competitor in the U.S. Open includes not merely striking a golf ball with precision, but doing so under greater than usual mental and physical stress. The accommodation Olinger sought, while reasonable in a general sense, would alter the fundamental nature of that competition. The lower court verdict was later affirmed by the Seventh U.S. Circuit Court of Appeals in *Olinger v. United States Golf Association*, 205 F.3d 1001 (7th Cir. 2000).

The conflicting Ninth and Seventh Circuit rulings on *Martin* and *Olinger* compelled the U.S. Supreme Court to grant *certiorari* of the *Martin* case in 2000. In *PGA Tour Inc. v. Casey Martin*, 532 U.S. 661 (2001), the Court affirmed the lower court ruling in favor of Martin in a 7–2 decision. The Court ordered the PGA Tour to allow Martin to use a cart, rejecting its argument that PGA golfers are not a protected class under Title III. The PGA Tour's argument was particularly invalid, the Court argued, because PGA golfers must pay a $3,000 fee to attend "Qualifying school" before qualifying for the Tour. Consequently, PGA golfers are not different from customers of any other private business.

Within days of the ruling in *Martin*, the U.S. Supreme Court ordered the Seventh U.S. Circuit Court of Appeals to reconsider its ruling in *Olinger*.

It remains to be seen how the *Martin* decision will affect other sports, and how broadly the ruling will be interpreted. Dissenting Justice Antonin Scalia expressed concern that judges would force Little League baseball umpires to grant children with attention deficit disorder four strikes instead of three. Justice Stevens, presenting the majority opinion, stated that "the waiver of an essential rule of competition for anyone would fundamentally alter the nature of [a] petitioner's tournaments." Consequently, future petitioners in other sports must prove that the rule that they wish to "waive" is not fundamental.

NOTES

1. In 2001, the PGA Tour dropped its ban that prevented caddie Lee Penterman from using a cart during competition. Penterman, who has cerebral palsy, was physically unable to walk the course on successive days. In agreeing to Penterman's use of the cart, the PGA ordered him to drive no faster than the other competitors walk, and to refrain from placing promotional messages on his cart. For more information, see www.sports.espn.go.com/golf/story?id=1234177

2. In January 2002, New England Patriots wide receiver Terry Glenn sued the NFL in U.S. District Court claiming that the league discriminated against him for a disability that prevented him from following the league's substance abuse program. Glenn claimed that he suffered from chronic depression, a disability recognized by the Americans with Disabilities Act. Glenn was suspended at the beginning of the 2001 season for failure to comply with the NFL's substance abuse policy. The case is pending.

16.3.2.5. Sports Facilities

In *Paralyzed Veterans of America v. D.C. Arena L.P.*, 117 F.3d 579 (D.C. Cir. 1997), the Paralyzed Veterans of America brought an ADA suit against the owners and operators of an athletic arena under construction (MCI Center) to require that wheelchair seating in the arena provide lines of sight over standing spectators. The district court ruled that most, but not all, wheelchair seating had to have sight lines over standing spectators. The court of appeals, in affirming the decision, held that the guidelines requiring that wheelchair areas in public accommodations covered by ADA provide their users with lines of sight comparable to those of members of the general public was entitled to deference.

One of these guidelines, issued by the Public Access Section of the Department of Justice (Standard 4.33.3), states that wheelchair areas shall be an integral part of any fixed seating plan and shall be located so as to provide people with physical disabilities a choice of admission prices and lines of sight comparable with those for members of the general public.

In December 1999, the New York Yankees settled a lawsuit by four disabled fans that alleged the Yankees were in violation of the Americans with Disabilities Act. Under the settlement, which effectively ended a bias lawsuit against the team and the city, the Yankees will offer wheelchair users and their companions about 300 pairs of seats in various areas of Yankee Stadium, including box seats. Disabled people also were given improved access to the stadium's concession stands, restaurants, and suites. The team also paid $25,000 to the federal government and contributed $10,000 to charities chosen by the four fans.

16.3.2.6. Athletes with AIDS

Another concern for athletic administrators is whether individuals testing HIV-positive or with the AIDS virus should be allowed to participate in athletic competitions. The U.S. Supreme Court, in *School Board of Nassau County v. Arline*, 480 U.S. 273 (1987), held that individuals with contagious diseases could be defined as handicapped persons under the meaning of Section 504 of the Rehabilitation Act.

While the plaintiff in *Arline* had tuberculosis, not HIV or AIDS, and the Supreme Court refused to address whether Section 504 would cover individuals with HIV or AIDS, the issue was addressed in *Doe v. Dolton Elementary School District*, 694 F.Supp. 440 (N.D. Ill. 1988). In that case, a twelve-year-old student who was infected with AIDS was excluded from attending school. In ruling for the student, the court, relying on *Nassau County v. Arline*, held that an individual with AIDS was likely to qualify as a handicapped individual under Section 504. Although the court did allow Doe to attend classes, it also placed certain limits on the activities the plaintiff could engage in, one of those activities being contact sports.

With increased public awareness about the transmission of HIV and the AIDS virus, however, administrators may have to address questions involving the participation by individuals testing HIV-positive or with the AIDS virus. For example, should athletes who test HIV-positive be excluded from participation in contact sports, such as football? The issue has yet to be tested in the courts, yet, as illustrated by the situations of Magic Johnson and Tommy Morrison (see Section 16.4., "AIDS Testing"), administrators may need to address the issue.

16.4. AIDS TESTING

Another issue that has come up is whether or not athletes should be tested for HIV. Although no league requires mandatory or random testing for HIV, the issue came to the forefront in November 1991 when Magic Johnson of the Los Angeles Lakers announced that he had the HIV virus and was retiring from basketball. When Johnson attempted to return to the NBA in 1992, a number of players and owners voiced concern over his playing in the league, and Johnson was compelled to retire again. Due to the reaction of the players and owners, the NBA began an AIDS education program, and in 1996 Johnson returned to the NBA as an active player.

One sport that does conduct HIV/AIDS testing is boxing. In 1996, heavyweight boxer Tommy Morrison announced that he had tested positive for HIV in a pre-fight physical. The states that require professional boxers to undergo mandatory HIV testing before they are licensed are Arizona, California, Colorado, Georgia, Indiana, Maryland, Massachusetts, New Mexico, Nevada, New York, Oregon, Pennsylvania, Utah, Washington, and the Commonwealth of Puerto Rico. Several other states have considered making pre-fight HIV testing mandatory.

GLOSSARY OF LEGAL AND SPORTS TERMS

Note: Exhibit 2.6 lists specific legal and sports-related abbreviations.

Acceptance: The offeree's notification to the offeror that he agrees to be bound by the terms and conditions of the offer.

Accommodation: Adjustment or settlement.

Accrue: Increase, add to, become due.

ACT: An assessment examination for college admission that consists of English, mathematics, reading, and science reasoning sections.

Addendum: Addition and/or change.

Adjudicate: Have a court make a decision or decide a dispute.

Administrative law: Law that affects private parties and is promulgated by governmental agencies other than courts or legislative bodies. The administrative agencies derive their power from legislative enactments and are subject to judicial review.

Advance: To give or grant funds.

Aff'd. (affirmed): To affirm a judgment, decree, or order is to declare that it is valid and right, and must stand as rendered by the lower court.

Affidavit: A written statement or declaration of facts sworn to by the maker, taken before a person officially permitted by law to administer oaths.

Age Discrimination in Employment Act (ADEA): Federal law passed in 1967 which states that an employer may not fail to hire, refuse to hire, discharge, demote, or discriminate against an employee based on his or her age.

Agent: One who is authorized by the principal to make contracts with third parties on behalf of the principal.

Amateur Athletic Union (AAU): An amateur athletic association dedicated to the development of amateur sports and physical fitness for amateur athletes of all ages.

Amateur Sports Act: Passed by the U.S. Congress in 1978 to reorganize and coordinate amateur athletics in the United States and to encourage and strengthen participation of U.S. amateurs in international competition. The act creates a governing structure for the USOC by empowering it to select one governing body (NGB) for each Olympic or Pan-American sport. Amendments, also known as the Ted Stevens Olympic and Amateur Sports Act, were made in 1998. Changes include the incorporation of athletes with disabilities into the governance structure by requiring the USOC to serve as the national Paralympic representative to the International Paralympic Committee, and requiring that athletic representatives, elected by fellow athletes, make up at least 20 percent of the membership and voting power of all USOC legislative bodies.

Ambush marketing: A company's intentional efforts to associate its product with an event, without paying the event sponsor, in an effort to give the consumer the impression that it is actually a sponsor of, or in some way affiliated with, the event. Ambush marketing can provide some, if not most, of the benefits of a legitimate, paid-for sponsorship at a fraction of the cost.

American Bar Association: National association of lawyers in the United States.

American Basketball Association (ABA): Professional basketball league that existed from 1967 to 1976.

American Basketball League (ABL): Defunct women's professional basketball league that existed from 1996 to 1999.

American Football League (AFL): Defunct corporation that operated a professional football league in the United States from 1960 to 1970, when it became the American Football Conference and merged with the National Football League. Note: Arena Football League is also abbreviated AFL.

Americans with Disabilities Act (ADA): A 1990 law created in order to eliminate discrimination against individuals with disabilities, and to mandate reasonable accommodations in order to remove barriers created by persons' disabilities.

Amicus curiae: Friend of the court; a third party who presents a brief to a court on behalf of one of the parties in a case.

Annotations: (1) Statutory: brief summaries of the law and facts of cases interpreting statutes passed by Congress or state legislatures that are included in codes; or (2) textual: expository essays of varying length on significant legal topics chosen from selected cases published with the essays.

Answer: The defendant's initial pleading on the alleged violation of criminal or civil law.

Anti-competitive: That which discourages competition among businesses.

Antitrust law: Legislation designed to promote competition in the business sector through regulation that will control the exercise of private economic power.

Appeal: A request from the losing party in a case that a higher court review the decision. Acceptance of the request and issuance by a writ of appeal is mandatory for the higher court.

Appeal denied: A refusal by the higher (or appellate) level court to review a lower court decision for error.

Appeal filed: A request by the higher (or appellate) level court to review a lower court decision for error.

Appellant: The party who appeals a decision from a lower court to a higher court.

Appellate court: Court of appellate jurisdiction.

Appellate jurisdiction: Covers cases tried or reviewed by the individual state's highest court involving federal questions, including those bearing on the U.S. Constitution, congressional acts, or foreign treaties. It also covers cases tried or reviewed by the U.S. courts of appeals or the U.S. district courts.

Appellee: The party against whom an appeal is taken.

Arbitrary marks: Words, names, symbols, or devices used to distinguish one product or service from another. The common definition of such words, names, symbols, or devices neither suggests nor describes any ingredient, quality, or characteristic of those goods or services. Such marks receive a broad scope of protection, such as the Lanham Act of 1946.

Arbitration: The hearing and settlement of a dispute between opposing parties by a neutral third party. This decision is often binding by prior agreement of the parties.

Arena Football League (AFL): Fifty-yard indoor football league, generally considered to be the second most elite professional football league in the United States. Note: American Football League is also abbreviated AFL.

Arraignment: The appearance of a defendant to a criminal charge before a judge for the purpose of pleading guilty or not guilty to the indictment.

Assault: An unlawful, intentional show of force or an attempt to do physical harm to another person. Assault can constitute the basis of a civil or a criminal action. *See also* **Battery**.

Assignee: A person to whom a right has been transferred.

Assignor: A person who assigns a right, whether or not he is the original owner thereof.

Association of Intercollegiate Athletics for Women: Defunct amateur athletic association that governed women's intercollegiate athletics before the National Collegiate Athletic Association assumed those duties in the mid-1980s.

Assumption of the risk: Knowledge by one of the parties to an agreement of the risks to be encountered, and that party's consent to take the chance of injury therefrom.

Athlete-agent laws: State legislatures have passed statutes that regulate the conduct of sports agents within the boundaries of that state. One such law is the Uniform Athlete Agents Act, which is designed to protect student-athletes and universities from unscrupulous agent behavior.

Attorney general opinions: Opinions issued by the government's chief counsel, at the request of a governmental body, that interpret the law for the requesting agency in the same manner as a private attorney would for his client. The opinions are not binding on the courts, but are usually accorded some degree of persuasive authority.

Authority: Refers to the precedential value to be accorded an opinion of a judicial or administrative body. A court's opinion is binding authority on other courts directly below it in the judicial hierarchy. Opinions of lower courts or of courts outside the hierarchy are governed by the degree to which they adhere to the doctrine of stare decisis. Authority may be either primary or secondary. Statute law, administrative regulations issued pursuant to enabling legislation, and case law are primary authority and, if applicable, will usually determine the outcome of a case. Other statements of or about law are considered secondary authority, and thus are not binding.

Battery: An unlawful use of force against another person resulting in physical contact (a tort); it is commonly used in the phrase "assault and battery," assault being the threat of force, and battery the actual use of force. *See also* **Assault**.

Bern Convention of 1886: Modified and amended since 1886 to suit the changing needs of international intellectual property regulation, the convention established a union for the protection of industrial property, and guarantees moral and economic rights. It provides that copies which infringe these rights can be seized, and the law of the country in which protection is claimed, governs the legal remedies for infringement.

Big Four Leagues: Unofficial, colloquial term for the four preeminent North American professional sports league (MLB, NBA, NFL, NHL).

Bill: Refers to a proposed law introduced in the legislature. The term distinguishes unfinished legislation from directly enacted law.

Blackout: A policy which states that if a sporting event is not sold out prior to a particular time and date, it may not be televised within a certain radius of a home stadium. This policy is intended to encourage people to buy tickets and attend the event instead of staying at home and watching the game on television.

Bona fide: Real, true, and actual.

Book value: The value at which a security is carried on the bank's balance sheet. Book value is often acquisition cost, plus or minus accretion or amortization, which can differ significantly from market value.

Branch banking: The right of banks headquartered in some states to take deposits, cash checks, and make loans at more than one location (branch) in the state. Where branch banking is not allowed, "unit banking" prevails.

Breach of contract: The failure to perform any of the terms of an agreement.

Brief: In American law practice, a written statement prepared by the counsel arguing a case in court. It contains a summary of the facts of the case, the pertinent laws, and argument of how the law applies to the facts supporting counsel's position.

Buckley Amendment: Federal legislation that regulates the release and review of student-athletes' records concerning academic and financial aid information.

Burden of proof: The necessity or duty of positively proving a fact or facts in a dispute on an issue raised between parties.

Business unit: A part of a bank managed and accounted for as a self-contained, independent business serving customers outside the bank and/or other business units in the bank. These units are encouraged to innovate and contribute to corporate profits, consistent with corporate policies and objectives.

Cable television: A service provided to consumers by which traditional television programming and/or other broadcast signals (e.g., pay cable) are brought into the home of the subscriber by way of cable transmission (as opposed to over-the-air transmission), usually for an initial installation charge and a monthly subscription fee. Standard broadcast stations can also be brought into a subscriber's home through cable television, in order to receive a clearer picture.

Canadian Football League (CFL): 110-yard outdoor professional football league. Currently, all franchises are based in Canada, although the league experimented with expansion into the United States in 1993.

Casebook: A textbook used to instruct law students in a particular area of substantive law. The text consists of a collection of court opinions, usually from appellate courts, and notes by the author(s).

Case law: The law of reported appellate judicial opinions, as distinguished from statutes or administrative law.

Cause of action: A claim in law and in fact sufficient to bring the case to court; the grounds of an action (e.g., breach of contract).

Cert. (certiorari) denied: A decision by an appellate court to refuse to review a lower court decision.

Cert. (certiorari) granted: A decision by an appellate court to grant a hearing to review a lower court decision.

Certification: Process whereby a union becomes officially recognized by the National Labor Relations Board as the exclusive bargaining agent for a particular set of workers.

Certiorari: A writ issued by a superior court to an inferior court that requires the latter to produce the records of a particular case tried therein. It is most commonly used to refer to the U.S. Supreme Court, which uses the writ of certiorari as a discretionary device to choose the cases it wishes to hear. The term's origin is the Latin meaning "to be informed of."

Charitable immunity: Similar to sovereign immunity in that it limits the liabilities of charitable organizations.

Citation: The reference to authority necessary to substantiate the validity of one's argument or position. Citation to authority and supporting reference is both important and extensive in any form of legal writing. Citation form is also given emphasis in legal writing, and the information is found in *A Uniform System of Citation*, 17th ed., published by the Harvard Law Review Association, Cambridge, MA.

Cited case: A case that is referred to in a court decision.

Civil law: (1) Type of law that is based on the writings of Justinian and his successors in the Roman empire; (2) the law concerning non-criminal matters in a common law jurisdiction; (3) one form of legal action for enforcement or protection of private rights and prevention or redress of private wrongs.

Civil Rights Restoration Act: Legislation enacted by Congress in 1988 that returned Title IX applicability to the "institutional approach"; therefore, in a collegiate setting, athletic departments or any program within an institution that receives federal funding is subject to Title IX legislation.

Claim: (1) The assertion of a right, as to money or property; (2) the accumulation of facts that give rise to a right enforceable in court.

Class action: A lawsuit brought by a representative party on behalf of a group, all of whose members have the same or a similar grievance against the defendant.

Clayton Act: A federal law passed in 1914 which stated that the "labor of a human being is not a commodity or article of commerce." The act also affirmed that no court shall grant an injunction in any case between an employer and employees which resulted from a dispute concerning the terms and conditions of employment." Also, nothing in antitrust law shall forbid the existence or legitimate activities of non-profit labor organizations created for self-help (*see* **Statutory labor exemption**).

Code: In popular usage, a compilation or a revised statute. Technically, the laws in force are rewritten and arranged in classified order, with the addition of material having the force of law taken from judicial decrees. The repealed and temporary acts are eliminated and the revision is reenacted.

Collective bargaining: The process by which the terms and conditions of employment are agreed upon through negotiations between the bargaining representative of the employees (union) and the employer (management).

Collective Bargaining Agreement (CBA): An agreement between a union and management that governs various aspects of the employment relationship. It may or may not cover items such as pension, insurance, minimum salary, drug testing, or anything related to wages, hours, and terms and conditions of employment.

Collective mark: A trademark or service mark used by the members of a cooperative association, or other collective group or organization; includes marks used to indicate membership in a union, an association, or other organization.

College Football Association (CFA): An amateur athletic association composed of NCAA Division I-A members who compete in football.

Collusion: A secret agreement between two or more persons for a fraudulent, unlawful, or deceitful purpose. This occurs in professional sports when teams secretly agree not to hire one another's players, secretly agree not to spend more than a certain amount of money on players, and/or secretly share information that they are forbidden to share under the terms of a collective bargaining agreement.

Common law: The origin of the Anglo-American legal systems. English common law was largely customary law, and unwritten, until discovered, applied, and reported by the courts of law. In theory, the common law courts did not create law, but discovered it in the customs and habits of the English people. The strength of the judicial system in pre-parliamentary days is one reason for the continued emphasis on case law in common law systems. In a narrow sense, common law is the phrase still used to distinguish case law from statutory law.

Comparative negligence: Doctrine in the law of negligence by which the negligence of the parties is compared, and a recovery is permitted when the negligence of the plaintiff was less than the negligence of the defendant.

Compensatory damages: A money award equivalent to the actual injury or loss sustained by the plaintiff.

Complaint: The plaintiff's initial pleading and, according to the Federal Rules of Civil Procedure, no longer full of technicalities demanded by the common law. A complaint need only contain a short and plain statement of the claim upon which relief is sought, an indication of the type of relief requested, and an indication that the court has jurisdiction to hear the case.

Compromise: An agreement reached by each party's giving up part of its claim(s), right(s), or property.

Compulsory license: A license issued by the government that gives a broadcasting company the right to use a work or product that is owned by a copyright holder. The user of the work or product must pay a royalty fee for its use. The copyright holder is obligated to grant the license to any organization that agrees to pay the royalty fee.

Condition precedent: A condition that must occur before a contract will be considered binding on the parties.

Condition subsequent: When parties condition a contract on an event's nonoccurrence.

Conferences: Subset of larger amateur sports associations, usually consisting of a number of schools that have similar institutional goals and interests. These schools compete against each other in a number of sports and often compete for conference championships in each of the sports.

Congressional documents: Important sources for legislative histories, which are often necessary for proper interpretation of statute law. Congressional documents are most accessible through specialized indexes, and include hearings before congressional committees, reports by or to House or Senate committees, and special studies conducted under congressional authority.

Consideration: Something to be done or abstained from, by one party to a contract, in order to induce another party to enter into a contract.

Constitution: Contains the fundamental law of any organization possessing one. Most national constitutions are written; the English and Israeli constitutions are unwritten.

Continental Basketball Association: A professional second-tier basketball league in the United States from 1978 until 2001.

Contract: An agreement between two or more parties. A preliminary step in making a contract is an offer by one party and acceptance by the other, in which the minds of the parties meet and concur in the understanding of terms. The elements of an enforceable contract are competent parties, a proper subject matter, consideration, and mutuality of agreement and obligation.

Contributory negligence: The negligence of a plaintiff that contributes to or enhances the complaining party's injuries. Contributory negligence is a bar to recovery at common law in some jurisdictions.

Copyright: A protection that covers published and unpublished literary, scientific, and artistic works, in every form of expression, provided that such works are fixed in a tangible or material form. Copyright laws give the creator the exclusive right to reproduce, prepare derivative works, distribute, display, and perform the work publicly. This protection is for a limited period of time.

Copyright Act of 1976: Legislation that extended copyright protection to live sports broadcasts, and granted the owners of a copyrightable work the exclusive right to "perform the copyrighted work publicly." One of the most important results of the Copyright Act was that it established a governmental agency known as the Copyright Royalty Tribunal.

Copyright Royalty Arbitration Panel: The organization that replaced the Copyright Royalty Tribunal. Under this system, the panel is charged with the same duties as the tribunal: deciding who is entitled to royalties, and how much they are entitled to. The Librarian of Congress must approve the determination of these allocations before they are made official.

Copyright Royalty Tribunal: A governmental agency that was charged with deciding disputes over copyrights of broadcasts, collecting royalties for owners of copyrights, and disbursing these royalties to the proper owners.

Corporation: A business that is its own legal entity, separate from its owners. For example, owners, also known as stockholders, cannot be held personally liable for a corporation's debts.

Counterclaim: A claim made by the defendant against the plaintiff in a civil lawsuit; it constitutes a separate cause of action.

Counteroffer: The offeree's response to an offer, in which the offeree proposes different or additional terms than were contained in the original offer. A counteroffer is construed as a rejection of the original offer, and a new offer by the original offeree.

Court of Arbitration for Sport (CAS): International court that deals exclusively with international sports-related disputes; created by former IOC President Juan Antonio Samaranch.

Covenant: An agreement or promise involving two or more parties.

Covenant not to compete: Also called a noncompete pact, it is a contractual agreement in which an employee promises not to work for certain rival companies for a certain period of time after his or her term of employment is completed.

Criminal law: One form (division) of legal action by which the government treats crimes and their punishments, usually by imprisonment, fine, or both.

Cross-Examination: The examination of a witness in a trial or hearing, or in taking a deposition, by the party opposed to the one who produced the witness.

Curt Flood Act: 1998 law that gave Major League Baseball players the right to sue under antitrust laws, but reaffirmed Major League Baseball's immunity from antitrust law in other cases, such as the sale of franchises.

Cybersquatters: People who register sports teams' domain names before the team does. Many of these people register the domain names in hopes of later selling them to the named party. This term also applies to people who register domain names of other famous persons or organizations.

Damages: Monetary compensation awarded by a court for an injury caused by the act of another. Damages may be *actual* or *compensatory* (equal to the amount of loss shown), *exemplary* or *punitive* (in excess of the actual loss and awarded to punish the person for the malicious conduct that caused the injury), or *nominal* (less than the actual loss—often a trivial amount; awarded because the injury is slight or because the exact amount of the injury has not been determined satisfactorily).

Database: The accumulation of textual or other material available to the user of an online computerized information service.

Decertification: Process whereby a union is no longer officially recognized by the National Labor Relations Board as the exclusive bargaining agent for a particular set of workers. Normally, this occurs after a majority of workers vote to dissolve, or decertify, the union.

Defamation: Anything published (libel) or publicly spoken (slander) that injuries a person's character, fame, or reputation by false and malicious statements.

Defendant: The party against whom legal action is taken; particularly, a person accused or convicted of a criminal offense.

Demurrer: A formal objection attacking the legal sufficiency of an opponent's pleadings. It is an assertion, made without disputing the facts, that the pleading does not state a cause of action, and that the demurring party is entitled to judgment.

Deposition: The testimony of a witness, taken out of court before a court reporter and under oath.

Descriptive marks: These marks describe the intended purpose, function, use, or size of the goods. They also describe the class of users of the goods, a desirable characteristic of the goods, or the end effect upon the user.

Digital Millennium Copyright Act (DMCA): Law implemented to ensure that copyrighted material can't be posted on the Internet without authorization. The act allows for the imposition of penalties upon persons who attempt to circumvent copyright protection systems, or sell equipment that allows people to avoid these protective systems.

Direct examination: The first interrogation or examination of a witness, on the merits, by the party on whose behalf the witness is called.

Direct Payment License: Program administered by USA Track and Field in which licensed athletes can receive endorsement fees, sponsorship monies, etc. directly and still maintain amateur eligibility.

Discharge: To release, usually from an obligation.

Disclosure: An argument that certain information possessed by associations, or meetings held by organizations, should be a matter of public record and, therefore, open to the public. The general meaning of disclosure is "to reveal facts."

Discovery: A method by which opposing parties may obtain information from each other, to prepare for trial and to narrow the issues to be presented at trial.

Distinctive marks: Marks that clearly are identified with the manufacturer of the product, and cannot be considered generic.

Diversity jurisdiction: That aspect of the jurisdiction of the federal courts which applies to suits between residents of different states.

Docket number: A number sequentially assigned by the clerk at the beginning of a lawsuit brought to a court for adjudication.

Doping: An athlete's use of drugs that enhance his or her performance, thereby providing advantage over competitors. The term typically refers to intentional users; however, the penalty for unintentional users is the same.

Draft: System commonly used in professional sports whereby a first-year player is selected by a particular team, and that team is granted exclusive bargaining rights with that player for a period of time.

Due care: The legal duty one owes to another according to the circumstances of a particular case.

Due process of law: A term found in the Fifth and Fourteenth Amendments of the U.S. Constitution and also in many states' constitutions. Its exact meaning varies from one situation to another and from one era to the next, but basically it is concerned with the guarantee of every person's enjoyment of his or her rights (e.g., the right to a fair hearing in any legal dispute).

Employment-at-will contract: An explicit or implicit agreement that allows an employer to fire an employee at any time, without cause. The employer cannot fire an employee for an illegal cause (e.g., retaliation, discrimination).

Endorse: (1) To sign; (2) to give testimony for, or associate one's self with, a particular product or service (e.g., an athlete "endorses" a restaurant).

Equal Pay Act: This law, passed in 1963, stipulates that an employer must pay equal salaries to men and women holding jobs that require equal skill, effort, and responsibility, and are performed under similar working conditions.

Equal protection: The constitutional guarantee that no person shall be unreasonably discriminated against.

Equal Rights Amendment: A proposed amendment to the U.S. Constitution to guarantee equal rights to women that was not ratified in the early 1980s but that certain states have adopted.

Equitable: Just; fair; reasonable.

Equity: Legal rules, remedies, customs, practices, and principles devised by courts of law to supplement those of the common law.

Et al.: And another; and others.

Evidence: Any form of proof presented at trial through the use of eyewitness testimony, records, documents, and concrete objects, and used to assist the trier of fact in making his determination of the case.

Ex parte: A hearing or examination in the presence of only one of the parties to a case.

Ex rel.: On behalf of, in the name of; a legal proceeding instituted by a state on behalf of an individual who has a private interest in the matter.

Exclusive rights: Rights granted by a sports organization to one broadcaster for the purpose of setting up a single-station broadcast or an exclusive network. Such rights do not permit any other broadcast organization to broadcast the event.

Fair Use Doctrine: Section 107 of the Copyright Act of 1976 provides that "the fair use of a copyrighted work, including such use by reproduction in copies or phonorecords or by any other means specified by that section, for purposes such as criticism, comment, news reporting, teaching (including multiple copies for classroom use), scholarship, or research, is not an infringement of copyright."

Fanciful marks: Coined words that have been invented for the sole purpose of functioning as a trademark. Such marks comprise words that are either totally unknown in the language or are completely out of common usage, such as obsolete or scientific terms.

Federal question: A case that contains a major issue involving the U.S. Constitution or a provision of an act of Congress or a U.S. treaty. The jurisdiction of the federal courts is governed, in part, by the existence of a federal question.

Felony: A serious criminal offense, as distinct from a misdemeanor. Typically, crimes for which the punishment may exceed on year in jail.

Fixation: Recording all parts of a broadcast on film, videotape, or replay tape for purposes of protecting the copyright and the manner in which it was recorded.

Forbearance: Refraining from doing something that one has a legal right to do.

Force majeure: A legal provision that protects a person or organization from the inability to fulfill a contractual obligation as the result of causes outside the control of the parties to a contract that could not be avoided by the exercise of due care—in sports, force majeure usually protects against a strike or lockout.

General partner(s): Individual(s) with unlimited responsibility for the operations and debts of a partnership.

Goodwill: A business value that arises from the reputation of a business and its relations with its customers, and is unique to the particular business. It has also been defined as "buyer momentum" and "the lure to return." It is an intangible asset of a business.

Governmental activity: An activity that can be performed only by the state.

Grievance arbitration: The submission of the parties' grievance to a private, unofficial person(s) who listens to the disputed question and contentions, then gives a decision regarding the dispute.

Health, Education and Welfare Department: A former cabinet department in the federal government that oversaw Title IX compliance.

Hearings: Extensively employed by both legislative and administrative agencies; they can be adjudicative or investigatory. Adjudicative hearing can be appealed in a court of law. Congressional committees often hold hearings prior to the enactment of legislation; these hearing are then important sources of legislative history.

Hearsay evidence: Evidence not based on the personal knowledge of the witness but on repeating what he or she has heard another say.

Holding: The declaration of the conclusion of law reached by the court regarding the legal effect of the facts of the case.

Holdout: A professional athlete who has contracted or has been compelled to play for a team, but refuses to play until the terms of his or her contract are renegotiated. It can also be used as a verb—to hold out form one's contract.

Hostile environment sexual harassment: Unwelcome sexual advances, requests for sexual favors, and other verbal or physical conduct of a sexual nature constitute "hostile environment" sexual harassment when such conduct has the purpose or effect of unreasonably interfering with an individual's work performance or creating an intimidating, hostile, or offensive working environment.

Immunity: A condition that protects against liability (tort) or prosecution (criminal law).

Impasse: A condition that exists when the parties to collective bargaining negotiations have bargained in good faith but have reached a deadlock position on a particular issue or issues.

In loco parentis: Placed in the position of the parents of the child, such as a coach or teacher given this status within a relationship with the student-athlete.

In personam: Against a person. A legal proceeding instituted to obtain decrees or judgments against a person.

In re: In the matter of, concerning; usual method of titling a judicial proceeding in which there are no adversary parties.

Incur: To take on or accept.

Indemnification: A legal provision that protects and/or reimburses, in whole or in part, a person or organization in the event of a loss, damage, or penalty.

Independent contractor: One who contracts to perform work according to his own methods and without being subject to the control of the employer except for the result of the contractor's work.

Indictment: A formal accusation of a crime made by a grand jury at the request of a prosecuting attorney.

Individuals with Disabilities Education Act (IDEA): A 1990 amendment to the Education for All Handicapped Children Act of 1975, designed to secure the right of disabled children to appropriate and cost-free education-related services.

Induce: To urge on or to lead into.

Initial eligibility requirements: Regulations formulated by college athletic associations to ensure that entering student-athletes are qualified for college.

Injunction: A judge's order that a person do or, more commonly, refrain from doing a certain act. An injunction may be preliminary or temporary, pending trial of the issue presented, or it may be final if the issue has already been decided in court.

Instructions to the jury: A judge's statement to a jury of the applicable law.

Instrument: Usually a document, such as a contract.

Intangible asset: An asset that exists only in connection with something else. It is an idea or formula, not something that can be touched. Goodwill is an example of an intangible asset of a business.

Interlocutory relief: Relief, usually an injunction, that lasts only during the course of a trial.

International Federations (IF): An IOC-recognized body for each sport; it sets its own rules and regulations governing eligibility of athletes for international competitions.

International Olympic Committee (IOC): World sanctioning body for the Olympic Games; it is located in Switzerland.

Internet: Worldwide interconnection of computer networks used by the government, academic institutions, businesses, and individuals. Each site on the Internet has its own "address," and users are able to access these sites for various reasons.

Interrogatories: Return questions directed to a party or witness, who must serve return answers to the questions under oath.

Jurisdiction: The power of a court to hear and determine a given class of cases; the power to act or a particular action.

Jurisprudence: (1) The science or philosophy of law; (2) a collective term for case law as opposed to legislation.

Knight Commission: Created in 1989 by the John and James L. Knight Foundation (a charitable organization) in order to reform college sports. The 2000–2001 commission consisted of NCAA representatives, university presidents, a trustee board chair, faculty, conference commissioners, athletic directors, coaches, athletes, authors, professional sports executives, television officials, a sports apparel representative, a gambling lobbyist, leaders of national higher education associations, and a U.S. senator.

Labor exemption: Created under the Clayton Act of 1914 to shield unions from antitrust liability. There are two types of labor exemptions: statutory and non-statutory. The modern use of the term describes "non-statutory" labor exemption. *See also* **Non-statutory labor exemption** and **Statutory Labor Exemption**.

Laches: Wrongful or unwarranted delay.

Ladies Professional Golf Association (LPGA): Organization dedicated to the promotion of golf worldwide, and claiming to be the largest women's sport organization in the world. The association is best known for a professional tour of elite women golfers. Affiliated with the PGA.

Lanham Act of 1946: Governs the law of trademarks, the registration of trademarks, and remedies for the infringement of registered trademarks.

Legislative history: Provides the meanings and interpretations (intent) of a statute as embodied in legislative documents. Also, citations and dates to legislative enactments, amendments and repeals of statutes are sometimes imprecisely identified as legislative histories. More accurate designations of the citations of legislative changes, as included in codes, are historical notes or amendatory histories.

Lexis-Nexis®: The pioneering computerized full text legal research system, which is a division of Reed Elsevier, Inc. The database organizes documents into "libraries" and "files." Documents include court decisions, law reviews, and statutory or administrative provisions.

Liability: The condition of being responsible either for damages resulting from an injurious act or for discharging an obligation or debt.

Libel: Written defamation of a person's character.

Licensing: The sale of an organization's logo or symbol to another organization that will use the logo or symbol for profit on "licensed" materials, such as apparel or trading cards.

Licensing agent: Person who oversees the licensing of the marks of an organization or a group of organizations. Often an agent will package the marks of several organizations to sell to manufacturers. Generally the agent receives a percentage of the profits from such licensing agreements.

Likelihood of confusion: A measure used by courts to determine whether or not the use of an organization's marks has reached a level such that the public believes that the goods are endorsed or authorized by someone other than the trademark owner.

Limited judicial review: Derives from a theory that courts should not review every legislative judgment of an organization, but rather defer to the organization's decisions. As a general rule, the legal system intervenes through judicial review only when legislative actions violate rights guaranteed by the Constitution, rights granted by the institution concerned, or basic notions of fairness.

Limited liability: An investment in which a partner cannot legally lose more than he or she invested.

Limited Liability Corporation (LLC): A business structure, legal in some states, in which owners receive the limited liability of a corporation (an S corporation) without having to adhere to S corporation restrictions. For example, an LLC can have more than seventy-five owner/investors, but an S corporation cannot.

Limited Partnership: An unincorporated business owned by two or more individuals, in which one or more partners retain control over the business and assume legal debts (general partners), and one or more other partners simply invest money in the business but relinquish both control of the business and responsibility for debts (limited partners).

Longevity rules: Regulations of an amateur athletic association that govern the maximum age or number of semesters for which athletes can participate in athletics in that particular athletic association.

Luxury suites: Also referred to as luxury boxes. Premiere seating with amenities sold by sports franchises, athletic departments, or arena owners—often to corporate clientele. Normally, corporations lease a particular suite for a season.

Major Indoor Soccer League: Defunct corporation that operated professional indoor soccer in the United States from 1978 to 1992.

Major League Baseball (MLB): Corporation that operates professional baseball in the United States and Canada; it is located in New York City.

Major League Baseball Players Association (MLBPA): A union that represents professional players in Major League Baseball.

Major League Soccer (MLS): Currently, the only "premiere" soccer league in the United States. It is structured in the single entity/limited liability corporation model.

Majority opinion: An appellate court decision in which the holding of the court is not unanimous.

Malfeasance: The doing of an act that is wrong and unlawful.

Malpractice: Professional misconduct or unreasonable lack of skill. This term is usually applied to such conduct by doctors and lawyers.

Misdemeanor: Offense lower than felony and generally punishable by fine or imprisonment of up to one year.

Misfeasance: Performance of a legal act in an illegal manner.

Mitigation of damages: A requirement in contract law that a plaintiff alleviate the damages of the one who has breached a contract.

Modified: Changed; a decision altered by the introduction of new elements or the cancellation of existing elements.

Moot question: A case that, because of changed circumstance or conditions after the litigation was begun, no longer contains a justiciable question.

Motion: A formal request made to a judge pertaining to any issue arising while a lawsuit is pending.

Naming rights fee: A fee that a company pays to place its name on a facility or, in the case of certain international sports, on a team.

National Association for Intercollegiate Athletics (NAIA): An amateur intercollegiate athletic association for small four-year colleges; it is located in Olathe, Kansas.

National Basketball Association (NBA): Corporation that operates professional basketball in the United States; it is located in New York City.

National Basketball Players Association (NBPA): A union that represents professional players in the NBA and WNBA.

National Collegiate Athletic Association (NCAA): The major intercollegiate athletic association for men and women in the United States; it is located in Indianapolis, Indiana.

National Federation of State High School Associations (NFSHSA): Amateur athletic association for interscholastic athletics in the United States; its headquarters are located in Indianapolis, Indiana.

National Football League (NFL): Corporation that operates professional football in the United States; it is located in New York City.

National Football League Players Association (NFLPA): A union that represents professional players in the NFL.

National Governing Bodies (NGBs): Governing bodies for individual sports sanctioned by the U.S. Olympic Committee. *See also* **USA Track and Field**.

National Hockey League (NHL): Corporation that operates professional hockey in the United States and Canada; it is located in New York City.

National Hockey League Players Association (NHLPA): A union that represents professional players in the NHL.

National Junior College Athletic Association (NJCAA): Amateur intercollegiate athletic association for two-year colleges in the United States; it is located in Colorado Springs, Colorado.

National Labor Relations Act (NLRA): A federal law which mandates that private employers bargain with certified unions and prohibits discrimination against workers who join a union. It also protects both workers and management from unfair labor practices.

National Labor Relations Board (NLRB): Federal administrative agency that was established to administer and enforce the National Labor Relations Act. The Board has to two primary responsibilities: supervising and conducting representation elections, and adjudicating employer and union unfair labor practices.

National reporter system: The network of reporters published by West Publishing Company; these reporters attempt to publish all cases of precedential value from all state and federal courts.

National Small College Athletic Association (NSCAA): An amateur intercollegiate athletic association for small four-year institutions; it is located in Warners, New York.

Negative covenant: An understanding in a deed or contract whereby a party obliges himself or herself to refrain from doing or performing some act.

Negligence: The failure to exercise due care.

Negotiation: The deliberation, settling, or arranging of the terms and conditions of a possible transaction.

No Electronic Theft Act (NET Act): A law that makes it illegal for someone to willfully infringe upon a copyright (1) for purposes of commercial advantage or private financial gain or (2) via reproduction or distribution, including electronic means. The basic purpose of the act is to punish people who willfully infringe upon copyrighted material on the Internet for financial gain.

Noncompete pact: *See* **Covenant not to compete.**

Nonfeasance: In tort law this term applies to nonperformance of some act that ought to be performed, omission to perform a required duty at all, or total neglect of duty.

Non-statutory labor exemption: A judicially derived expansion of the labor exemption that is based on the policy which favors collective bargaining and gives it preference over the antitrust laws. Therefore, union-management collective bargaining agreements that are the result of a good faith negotiation will be protected from antitrust laws. The provisions of the agreement usually cannot be successfully attacked as collusive or anti-competitive. The modern use of the term "labor exemption" is applied to the "non-statutory" labor exemption.

North American Soccer League: Defunct corporation that operated professional soccer in the United States from 1968 to 1985.

Obligation: Debt or duty.

Offer: An act by one person giving another person the legal power to create the obligation called a contract.

Offeree: One to whom a contract offer is made.

Offeror: One who makes a contract offer.

Office for Civil Rights (OCR): A governmental agency that is charged with providing an interpretation of Title IX and how it should be applied to programs that receive federal funding.

Opinion: An expression of the reasons why a certain decision (the judgment) was reached in a case. A *majority opinion* is usually written by one judge and represents the principles of law that a majority of the judge's colleagues on the court deem operative in a given decision; it has more precedential value than any of the following. A *separate opinion* may be written by one or more judges who concur in or dissent from the majority opinion. A *concurring opinion* agrees with the result reached by the majority, but disagrees with the precise reasoning leading to that result. A *dissenting opinion* disagrees with the result reached by the majority and thus disagrees with the reason and/or principles of law used by the majority in deciding the case. A *plurality opinion* (called a "judgment" by the Supreme Court) is agreed to by less than a majority as to the reasoning, but is agreed to by a majority as the result. A *per curiam opinion* is an opinion "by the court" that expresses its decision in a case but does not identify the author, A *memorandum opinion* is a holding of the whole court in which the opinion is very concise.

Option clause: In sports law, the club's right to renew a contract for a one-year period under the same terms and conditions as the previous year of the contract, including another option year, except that the option year of the contract will not contain an option clause. The only term that may differ in the option year is the salary, which varies from league to league, according to the provisions set forth in the contract and/ or Collective Bargaining Agreement.

Option contract: A contract that binds the offeror to hold the offer open for a specified period of time during which the offeree must give consideration to the option.

Ordinance: The equivalent of a municipal statute, passed by the city council and governing matters not already covered by a federal or state law.

Original jurisdiction: Jurisdiction to take cognizance of a cause at its inception, try it, and pass judgment upon the law and fact. It covers two types of cases: those involving ambassadors, ministers, and consuls, and those involving a state as one of the parties to a lawsuit.

Parallel citation: A citation reference to the same case printed in two or more different reports.

Parol evidence rule: Prohibits the admission of oral statements, preliminary agreements, or writings made prior to or at the time of signing that would in any way alter, contradict, or change the written contract.

Partnership: An unincorporated business owned by two or more individuals.

Patent: A document, issued by the federal government, that grants its owner a legally enforceable right to exclude others from making, using, or selling the invention described and claimed in the document for a limited period of time, without the permission of the inventor. Patents are property that can be bought, sold, hired, or rented. In addition, there are territorial rights (the holder of the patent has rights as it pertains to the product within the United States).

Pay cable: Refers to a premium cable television service, by which special channels are provided to subscribers for an additional cost. It is usually used for unique programming, such as movies or sporting events, unavailable on standard broadcast television or more basic cable television channels.

Per annum: Per year.

Per curiam: By the court. An opinion of the Supreme Court that is authored by the justices collectively.

Per diem: Per day.

Per se: By itself; inherently; in isolation.

Permanent injunction: An injunction intended to remain in force until the termination of the particular suit.

Personal seat license (PSL): A license sold by a facility that gives a patron exclusive right to purchase tickets for a particular seat for all or most of the facility's events. Terms of a PSL can be one year, several years, or the life of the facility. PSLs are commonly used to finance new arenas and stadiums of professional and intercollegiate athletic teams.

Petitioner: The party who brings an action, the party who seeks a *writ of certiorari*.

Piracy: The interception of broadcasts (including sports broadcasts) by satellite technology without consent of the rights holder.

Plaintiff: The party who brings an action; the complainant.

Precedent: A case that furnishes an example or authority for deciding subsequent cases in which identical or similar facts are present.

Preliminary injunction: An injunction granted at the institution of a suit to restrain the defendant from doing or continuing some act; it may be discharged or made perpetual as soon as the rights of the parties are determined.

Presidents Commission of the NCAA: An advisory body comprised of university presidents within the NCAA's governing structure; it can propose legislation to be voted upon by the NCAA membership.

Prima facie: At first sight; on the face of it; presumability; a fact presumed to be true unless disproved by some evidence to the contrary.

Pro-competitive: That which encourages competition among businesses.

Professional Golf Association (PGA): A 26,000-member organization dedicated to the promotion of golf worldwide. The association is best known for having a professional tour of elite men golfers. Affiliated with the LPGA.

Property: Tangible or intangible item or items that a person, group, or corporation has exclusive right to possess. That person, group, or corporation is called the "owner," and may legally exclude others from using or possessing its "property."

Proprietary activity: An activity that is done by the state but could be undertaken by the private sector.

Proximate cause: The act that is the natural and reasonably foreseeable cause of the harm or agent that injures the plaintiff.

Publicly traded: Denotes that a company's stock is available for purchase in a market that is widely accessible to all investors or consumers (such as the New York Stock Exchange or NASDAQ).

Punitive damages: Compensation in excess of actual or consequential damages. They are awarded to punish the wrongdoer, but only in cases involving willful or malicious misconduct.

Quid pro quo: This for that. Something given in exchange for something else.

Quid pro quo sexual harassment: Unwelcome sexual advances, requests for sexual favors, and other verbal or physical conduct of a sexual nature constitute "quid pro quo" sexual harassment when (1) submission to such conduct is made either explicitly or implicitly a term or condition of an individual's employment, or (2) submission to or rejection of such conduct by an individual is used as the basis for employment decisions affecting such individual.

Racketeer Influenced Corrupt Organization (RICO) Statute: A federal law that makes it a crime for organized criminal conspiracies to operate legitimate businesses.

Ratification: The adopting or confirming of an act that was previously executed without authority or of an act that was voidable.

Reckless misconduct: An action that falls between the unintentional tort of negligence and the intentional torts of assault and battery. Behavior characterized by intent on the part of the defendant to commit the act but no intent to harm the plaintiff by the act.

Redshirting: Means to extend the playing career of a student-athlete, by postponing or passing over a year of intercollegiate athletic participation, while not affecting the student-athlete's maximum allowable time for participating. The term is used in both college and high school athletics.

Regional reporter: A unit of the National Reporter System that reports state court decisions within a defined geographical area.

Regulations: Orders issued by various governmental departments to carry out the intent of the law. Agencies issue regulations to guide the activity of their employees and to ensure uniform application of the law. Regulations are not the work of the legislature and in theory do not have the effect of law. In practice, however, because of the intricacies of judicial review of administrative action, regulations can have an important effect in determining the outcome of cases involving regulatory activity. U.S. government regulations appear first in the *Federal Register*, published five days a week, and are subsequently arranged by subject in the *Code of Federal Regulations*.

Relinquish: To give up, surrender, or turn over.

Reports: (1) *Court reports* are published judicial cases arranged according to some grouping, such as jurisdiction, court, period of time, subject matter, or case significance; (2) *administrative reports or decisions* are published decisions of an administrative agency; (3) *annual statements of progress, activities or policy* are reports issued by an administrative agency or an association.

Res ipsa loquitur: A method of rebuttal to the presumption that defendant was negligent. It arises upon proof that the instrumentality causing the injury was not under defendant's exclusive control, and that the extent of injury was one that ordinarily does not happen in the absence of negligence.

Res judicata: An adjudicated matter; a legal issue that has been decided by a court.

Rescission: Canceling, annulling, voiding.

Reserve clause: In sports law, the club's right to renew a contract for a one-year period under the same terms and conditions as the previous year of the contract; the only term that may differ in the option year is the salary, which varies from league to league according to provisions set forth in the contract and/or Collective Bargaining Agreement.

Respondent: The party against whom legal action is taken; the party against whom a *writ of certiorari* is sought.

Rev'd. (reversed): A decision by an appellate court that voids a lower court decision based on some error made in the lower court. Often the case is remanded (sent back) to the lower court with instruction.

Right: That which a person is entitled to keep and enjoy, and to be protected by law in its enjoyment. A right constitutes a claim when it is not in one's possession. The word "right" also signifies an interest when used in regard to property. "Right" in this sense entitles a person to hold or convey his property at pleasure.

Rozelle rule: The rule, in effect from 1963 to 1976, generally required a team signing a contract with a player formerly employed by another team to pay compensation to that team. If the two teams could not agree, the Commissioner would determine compensation.

S Corporation: A corporation with seventy-five or fewer shareholders, enjoying the benefits of a corporation (limited liability) and the tax advantages of a partnership.

Salary cap: A league's limit on a particular player's and/or team's total salary expenditure.

SAT: A scholastic achievement test that measures intellectual ability in the mediums of math and English.

Satellites: Serve as a space-based distribution system of program services for standard broadcast and cable television. Satellites relay television signals across the world.

Secondary meaning: A mental recognition in the buyer's mind, associating symbols, words, colors, and designs with goods from a single source. It tests the connection in the buyer's mind between the product bearing the mark and its source. In a commercial sense, secondary meaning is buyer association, mental association, drawing power, or commercial magnetism.

Service mark: A mark used in the sale or advertising of services to identify the services of one person and distinguish them from the services of others. Identifies and distinguishes the source and quality of an intangible service.

Sexual harassment: A form of sex discrimination that violates Title VII of the Civil Rights Act of 1964. Sexual harassment is behavior of a sexual nature which is unwanted or unreciprocated by the recipient. It can take many forms, including but not limited to (1) physical sexual harassment, which includes staring, leering, gestures, and unnecessary touching; (2) verbal harassment, including propositions, demands or requests for sexual favors, suggestive remarks, innuendo, offensive comments about dress or appearance, and jokes of a sexual nature; and (3) visual harassment, including the display of pornographic pictures or other sexually suggestive materials.

Shepardizing: To look up a case citation in *Shepard's Citations*, especially in order to check the status of the case, parallel citations, or the use of the case in other jurisdictions.

Sherman Act: Federal law passed in 1890 to protect the American consumer by controlling unfair monopolization. It serves to promote free and open market competition. Sometimes called the Sherman Antitrust Act.

Single entity league: A type of sports league governance that evolved in the late 1990s so that the organization is not subject to antitrust law attack. It is a business structure in which one is not allowed to own an individual franchise. Instead, franchises (teams) are owned by the league and controlled by operator/investors.

Siphoning: The shifting of programs from standard broadcast television to pay cable or basic cable television.

Slander: Oral defamation of a person's character.

Sole proprietorship: An unincorporated business owned by one individual.

Sovereign immunity: Certain protections afforded to the state against tort liability, regardless of the circumstances, when the state is engaged in governmental function.

Specific performance: An equitable remedy whereby the court orders one of the parties to a contract to perform his or her duties under the contract. Usually granted when money damages would be an inadequate remedy.

Sports Broadcast Act of 1961: A statutory exemption from antitrust laws that allows the teams in each of the four major professional sports leagues in the United States to negotiate collectively with the television networks.

Standard broadcast television: What most individuals consider "basic television." Local television stations broadcast programming that is received by local home television sets when the antenna picks up air transmission signals. Standard broadcast television is broadcast on channels 2–69, with channels 2–13 known as very high frequency (VHF) and channels 14–69 known as ultra high frequency (UHF).

Standard of care: The level of caution that one should exercise.

Standard Player Contract: Also called a Uniform Player Contract. A "form" contract that must be signed by all players in a typical professional sports league, as stipulated by a league's bylaws or Collective Bargaining Agreement. Normally, Standard Player Contracts will be virtually identical from one player to another; with the exception of salary consideration, bonus clauses, and additional clauses.

Standing: The qualifications needed to bring legal action. The qualifications relate to the existence of a controversy in which the plaintiff has suffered or is about to suffer an injury or infringement upon a legally protected right that a court is competent to redress.

Stare decisis: To stand on what has been decided; to adhere to the decision of previous cases. It is a rule, sometimes departed from, that a point settled in a previous case becomes a precedent that should be followed in subsequent cases decided by the same court.

State action: Legal principle that the university, association, or governing body is shown to be part of the federal government, state government, or an arm or agency of a state government. State action must be proven to bring a constitutional law challenge.

State Equal Rights Amendments: Legislation passed by certain states that protect women from discrimination on the basis of their gender.

Statute of frauds: Has its roots in English common law and is designed to prevent injustices resulting from fraudulent claims or promises that were never kept. The exact rules vary from state to state.

Statutes: Acts of legislature. Depending upon its context in usage, a statue may mean a single act of a legislature or a body of acts that are collected and arranged according to a scheme or for a session of a legislature or parliament.

Statutes of limitations: Laws setting time periods during which disputes may be taken to court.

Statutory labor exemption: The "statutory" labor exemption created under the Clayton Act of 1914 allows unions to enter into agreements with management regarding the working conditions of the employees they represent, and stipulates that union activity does not constitute a restraint of trade under the Sherman Act.

Strict liability: Liability regardless of fault. Under tort law, strict liability is imposed on any person who introduces into commerce any good that is unreasonably dangerous when in a defective condition.

Subpoena: A court order compelling a witness to appear and testify in a certain proceeding.

Summary proceeding: A judicial action, usually a judgment or decision, that is taken without benefit of a formal hearing. Summary decisions of the Supreme Court are those made without the Court having heard an oral argument.

Summons: A notice to a person that an action has been commenced against him or her, and that he or she is required to appear in court and answer the complaint in such action.

Superstation: A local, independent, distant signal television station whose programs, including sports, are carried via satellite to cable systems outside of the station's local broadcast range.

Supreme Court: (1) The court of last resort in the federal judicial system. (It also has original jurisdiction in some cases.) (2) In most states, the highest appellate court or court of last resort (but not in New York).

Tangible asset: Something that can be touched. Examples of tangible assets are sports equipment and team apparel.

Tax shelter: A financial arrangement, such as the use of special depletion allowances, that reduces taxes on current earnings.

Ted Stevens Olympic and Amateur Sports Act: *See* **Amateur Sports Act.**

Temporary restraining order: An order, of limited duration, restring the defendant from doing a threatened act until the propriety of granting an injunction can be determined.

Terminate: To end or bring to an end.

Third party beneficiary: Party who is not privy to a contract, but for whom the contract is made and will benefit from it.

Title VII: Part of the Civil Rights Act of 1964 focusing on discrimination, on the basis of race, color, religion, sex, or national origin, in hiring/firing practices and advancement policies within companies.

Title IX: Part of the Educational Amendments of 1972. This law specifically and clearly recognizes the problems of sex discrimination and forbids such discrimination in any program, organization, or agency that receives federal funds.

Tolls: To delay, suspend, or hold off the effect of a statute.

Tort: A civil wrong that does not involve a contractual relationship. The elements of a tort are a duty owed, breach of that duty, and the resultant harm to the one to whom the duty is owed.

Trademark: A name, device, or symbol that has become sufficiently associated with a good or has been registered with a governmental agency; once it is established, the manufacturer has a right to bring legal action against those who infringe upon the protection given the trademark.

Trademark infringement: The reproduction, counterfeiting, copying, or imitation, in commerce, of a registered mark in connection with the sale, offering for sale, distribution, or advertising of any goods or services on or in connection with which such use is likely to cause confusion or to cause mistake, or to deceive, without consent of the registrant.

Trial court: The court before which issues of fact and law are tried and first determined as distinguished from an appellate court.

Unfair labor practice: Activity by management or union, under the National Labor Relations Act, that the National Labor Relations Board determines to be in violation of the act.

Uniform Athlete Agent Act: Legislation supported by the NCAA and passed by the National Conference of Commissioners on Uniform State Laws in 2000. It is designed to provide a single set of state regulations that will govern athlete agent conduct.

Uniform Commercial Code (U.C.C.): Code that governs numerous areas of commercial law and has been adopted as statutory law in nearly every state.

Uniform Player Contract: *See* **Standard Player Contract.**

United States Football League (USFL): Defunct professional football league that played games in the spring and summer months from 1983 to 1985.

United States Olympic Committee: Amateur athletic association that governs Olympic competition and eligibility in the United States. It is located in Colorado Springs, Colorado.

USA Track and Field (USATF): The National Governing Body (NGB) for track and field in the United States.

U.S.C.: United States Code. A compilation of congressional statutes and their amendments, organized into fifty subject titles.

U.S.C.A.: United States Code Annotated. A commercially published edition of the United States Code.

Vacated: Annulled, set aside, canceled, or rescinded; the canceling or rescinding of an entry or record or of a judgment.

Vacated case: When a judge sets aside or annuls an order or judgment that he/she finds improper.

Venue: The geographical area where a court with jurisdiction may try a case.

Vicarious liability: Imposes liability for a tortious act upon a person who in not personally negligent, but is held liable because of the relationship between the parties (i.e., a school may be held liable for a coach's tortious act because the school is the employer of the coach).

Void: Having no legal effect and not binding on anyone.

Voidable: That which may be legally annulled at the option of one of the parties.

Voluntary organizations: Associations consisting of members who wish to participate in association events, agree to abide by the rules of the association, and meet membership requirements.

Waiver: The voluntary relinquishment of a known right.

Westlaw: A computerized database and legal research system available through West Publishing Company. The database contains statutory material and cases from components of the National Reporter System.

Women's Basketball Association: Defunct corporation that operated a professional women's basketball league in the United States from 1978 to 1982.

Women's National Basketball Association (WNBA): The preeminent women's professional basketball league in the United States. It is structured in the single entity model and managed by the NBA. The league began play in 1997.

Women's United Soccer Association (WUSA): The leading women's professional soccer league in the United States. It is structured in the single entity model and began play in 2001.

Worker's compensation: Name commonly used to designate the methods and means created by statues for giving greater protection and security to the workers and their dependents against injury or death occurring in the course of employment.

World Football League: Defunct corporation that operated a professional football league in the United States in the 1970s.

World Intellectual Property Organization (WIPO): An international organization that regulates intellectual property. WIPO handles disputes among member countries through mediation, arbitration, and the administration of treaties.

World League of American Football (WLAF): Original name for "NFL Europe," an eight-team league playing American football in Europe.

Writ: A written order, of which there are many types, issued by a court and directed to an official or party, commanding the performance of some act.

Writ of appeal: A suit or action brought before the court that holds a federal act to be unconstitutional or a state action to be constitutional, or that involves a lower federal court deciding against the United States in a criminal case; a suit brought by the United States under the Interstate Commerce Act; or a federal district court hearing a suit involving a restraint on enforcement of a state or federal statue on the grounds that it is unconstitutional.

Writ of certiorari: An appellate court reviewing an action of an inferior court.

XFL: A 100-yard outdoor football league that existed for only one season (2001). It was structured in the single entity model and managed by World Wrestling Federation Entertainment, Inc.

INDEX

About the Author

GLENN M. WONG is Professor of Sport Management, University of Massachusetts, Amherst. Wong has authored or co-authored four books on sports and the law, including *The Essentials of Amateur Sports Law* and *Law and Business of the Sports Industries*.